The Back
Channel

For Jane,

Warmest wishes,

Bill Burns

'Bill Burns is a treasure of American diplomacy who I had the honour of watching in action and working closely with . . . In The Back Channel, Burns provides another great act of public service by giving us a smart, plain-spoken account of America's changing role in the world and the power and purpose of American diplomacy at its best.'
—Hillary Clinton, former U.S. Secretary of State

'From one of America's consummate diplomats, an incisive and sorely needed case for the revitalisation of our diplomacy—what Burns wisely describes as our "tool of first resort."'—Henry Kissinger, former U.S. Secretary of State

'Bill Burns' penchant for record-keeping paired with his colourful writing style combine to produce a compelling, fast-paced, and witty narrative ... This book is soon to become necessary reading for America's next generation of diplomats.'—Condoleezza Rice, former U.S. Secretary of State

'A reflective and candid story of a professional diplomat par excellence who deployed insight and inquisitiveness, skill and strength to advance Americas interests. Told with humour and humility, The Back Channel brings all the behind the scenes efforts into the light, and brings readers into the room to share the journey of a talented, tough minded diplomat who served as conduit and catalyst in making America stronger.'
—John Kerry, former U.S. Secretary of State

'The Back Channel is a masterfully written memoir from one of America's most accomplished and respected diplomats. Ambassador Burns not only offers a vivid account of how American diplomacy works, he also puts forward a compelling vision for its future that will surely inspire new generations to follow his incredible example.'
—Madeleine K. Albright, former U.S. Secretary of State

'Bill Burns is a stellar exemplar of the grand tradition of Wise Americans who made our country the indispensable nation in this world. The Back Channel shows how diplomacy works, why it matters, and why its recent demise is so tragic.'—Walter Isaacson, author of Leonardo Da Vinci

'The Back Channel deserves to be widely read – a great book filled with fascinating stories and the kind of wisdom that is sorely needed these days.'
—George P. Shultz, former U.S. Secretary of State

'The Back Channel demonstrates [Burn's] rare and precious combination of strategic insight and policy action. It is full of riveting historical detail but, more importantly, of shrewd insights.'
—James A. Baker III, former U.S. Secretary of State

'Bill Burns, one of the most respected diplomats of the post-Cold War years, has now written what I regard as the best diplomatic memoir of that period.'
—John Lewis Gaddis, Yale University

The Back
Channel

A MEMOIR OF AMERICAN
DIPLOMACY AND
THE CASE FOR ITS RENEWAL

William J. Burns

HURST & COMPANY, LONDON

First published in the United Kingdom in 2019 by

C. Hurst & Co. (Publishers) Ltd.,
41 Great Russell Street, London, WC1B 3PL

Printed in the United Kingdom by Bell and Bain Ltd, Glasgow

A Cataloguing-in-Publication data record for this book
is available from the British Library.

ISBN 978-1-78738-123-0

This book is printed using paper from registered sustainable
and managed sources.

www.hurstpublishers.com

For Lisa,
who has enriched my life
beyond measure, and made
everything possible

Contents

Prologue   3

1. Apprenticeship: The Education of a Diplomat   15

2. The Baker Years: Shaping Order   43

3. Yeltsin's Russia: The Limits of Agency   82

4. Jordan's Moment of Transition:
   The Power of Partnership   112

5. Age of Terror: The Inversion of Force and Diplomacy   147

6. Putin's Disruptions: Managing Great
   Power Trainwrecks   200

7. Obama's Long Game: Bets, Pivots, and Resets
   in a Post-Primacy World   243

8. The Arab Spring: When the Short Game Intercedes   293

9. Iran and the Bomb: The Secret Talks   337

10. Pivotal Power: Restoring America's Tool of
    First Resort   388

Acknowledgments   425

Appendix   429

Bibliography   471

Notes   477

Index   485

The Back Channel

Prologue

I REMEMBER CLEARLY the moment when I saw American diplomacy and power at their peak. I was seated behind Secretary of State James Baker at the opening of the Madrid Peace Conference in the autumn of 1991, feeling numb from exhaustion and excitement. Around a huge T-shaped table in the Spanish royal palace sat a collection of international leaders and—breaking a decades-long taboo—representatives of Israel, the Palestinians, and key Arab states. At the head of the table, alongside President George H. W. Bush, was Soviet president Mikhail Gorbachev. He was visibly tired and distracted, the leader of a faded superpower two months away from collapse. They were all united less by shared conviction about Arab-Israeli peace than by shared respect for American influence—fresh off the spectacular defeat of Saddam Hussein, the bloodless triumph of the Cold War, the reunification of Germany, and the reordering of Europe.

For a young American diplomat, Madrid was a heady moment. It was a dramatic illustration of how diplomacy could achieve what had seemed unthinkable. For the first time, Arabs and Israelis gathered in the same room, and agreed to the same terms for negotiations. With that, the door for the resolution of a conflict that had roiled the region and the world for more than four decades cracked open. They sat down together, against their instincts, because we asked, at a moment when well-framed U.S. requests were not easily ignored. It marked a time of uncontested American primacy in a world no longer bound by Cold War rivalry—when history seemed to flow inexorably in America's direction, the power of its ideas driving the rest of the world in a slow but irresistible surge toward democracy and free markets.

On that day in Madrid, global currents all seemed to run toward a period of prolonged American dominance. The liberal order that the United States had built and led after World War II would soon draw into its embrace the former Soviet empire, as well as the post-colonial world for which we had competed. Great power rivalry had rarely seemed so quiescent. Russia was flat on its back, China was still turned inward, and the United States and its key European and Asian allies faced few regional threats and even fewer economic rivals.

Globalization was gathering pace, with the American economy propelling greater openness in trade and investment. With only a single website and eleven million cellphones in use around the world, the promise of the information revolution was tantalizing, as was that of remarkable medical and scientific breakthroughs. The reality that a profoundly important era of human progress was unfolding only reinforced a sense of permanence for the nascent Pax Americana.

The question at the time was not whether America should seize the unipolar moment, but how and to what end. Should the United States use its unmatched strength to extend American global dominance? Or, rather than unilaterally draw and dominate the contours of a new world order, should it instead lead with diplomacy to shape an order in which old rivals had a place, and emerging powers had a stake?

* * *

ONE YEAR LATER, after President Bush had lost his bid for reelection, I was tasked with writing a transition memo to the incoming

Clinton administration and Secretary of State Warren Christopher. In it, I tried to capture the paradox for American statecraft. The memo began by welcoming the new administration to "a world in the midst of revolutionary transition, in which you will have both an historic opportunity to shape a new international order and a sobering collection of problems to contend with."

While "for the first time in fifty years we do not face a global military adversary," I wrote, "it is certainly conceivable that a return to authoritarianism in Russia or an aggressively hostile China could revive such a global threat." I argued that "alongside the globalization of the world economy, the international political system is tilting schizophrenically toward greater fragmentation." Ideological competition was not over—it was simply reshaped:

> The collapse of Communism represents an historic triumph for democracy and free markets, but it has not ended history or brought us to the brink of ideological uniformity. A great wave of democratic institution-building is taking place, driven by a surging post-Communist interest in the political and economic empowerment of individuals. But democratic societies that fail to produce the fruits of economic reform quickly, or fail to accommodate pressures for ethnic self-expression, may slide back into other "isms," including nationalism or religious extremism or some combination of the two. In much of the world, including parts of it that are very important strategically for us, Islamic conservatism remains a potent alternative to democracy as an organizing principle.[1]

The memo highlighted a number of other growing problems, from climate change to the AIDS epidemic and continued fragility in the Balkans. There were as many challenges as there were holes in my analysis. I couldn't yet grasp the pace and significance of China's rise, the intensity of Russia's resurgence, or the anger and frustration seething beneath so many authoritarian Arab societies. What was easier to see was the potential for diplomacy to harness unprecedented military, political, and economic advantage to promote American interests and help make the world more peaceful and prosperous.

The potential for American diplomacy seems far less evident today. The global order that emerged at the end of the Cold War has shifted dramatically. Great power rivalry is back: China is systematically modernizing its military and is poised to overtake the United States as the world's biggest economy, slowly extending its reach in Asia and across the Eurasian supercontinent; Russia is providing graphic evidence that declining powers can be at least as disruptive as rising ones, increasingly convinced that the pathway to revival of its great power status runs through the erosion of an American-led order.

Regional orders that seemed stable shortly after the end of the Cold War are now collapsing, none more so than in the region for which the Madrid Conference once held so much hope. The implosion of the Arab state system is the sharpest illustration of the risks of emerging vacuums and the dissipation of American influence. With tactical agility and a willingness to play rough, Vladimir Putin has reasserted a Russian role in the region that seemed unimaginable in that palace in Madrid, where Gorbachev's beleaguered presence was more a political convenience for the United States than a mark of Moscow's clout. A half-century-long American moment in the Middle East—inherited from the British, boosted by Desert Storm and Madrid, and badly damaged by the Iraq War in 2003—is now disappearing.

Meanwhile, a quarter century of convergence toward a Western model is giving way to a new form of globalization, featuring a new diversity of actors and the fragmentation of global power, capital, and concepts of governance. There is much that is positive in all of these trends. Hundreds of millions of people have risen out of poverty and into the middle class; unprecedented progress has been made in health and life expectancy; human society is more connected than ever before, with half the population of the globe now enjoying access to the Internet, and more than nine billion digital wireless devices in use.

In the United States and much of Europe, however, the backlash against globalization has been building. Donald Trump's election and Britain's decision to exit the European Union both reflected a deep popular unease, a growing anxiety that the dislocations of a globalized economy are not worth the benefits, that globalization not only doesn't lift all boats, but homogenizes political culture and obscures national identity. Those impulses, harnessed with demagogic flair by President Trump and European nationalists, have aggravated political polarization and incapacitated governance. Fewer than 20 percent of Americans now express confidence in government, half the figure in 1991. Gridlock is the default position in Washington and bipartisan compromise a distant memory.

The value of American leadership is no longer a given—at home or abroad. Fatigue with international intervention after nearly two decades at war has fed a desire to free the United States from the constraints of old alliances and partnerships and reduce commitments overseas that seem to carry unfair security burdens and economic disadvantage. The disconnect has grown between a disillusioned American public and the conceits of a Washington establishment often undisciplined in its policy choices and inattentive to the need to explain plainly the practical value of American leadership in the world.

Donald Trump didn't invent all of these trends and troubles, but he has fed them and made them worse. His erratic leadership has left America and its diplomats dangerously adrift, at a moment of profound transformation in the international order.

My own story helps shed light on how this came to pass, and how America's role has evolved. I hope it helps illuminate the back channels of my profession, and drags the argument for diplomacy into the light of public debate. I hope it also shows why the sidelining of diplomacy is so tragic, and why its restoration is so important. My goal is not to offer an elegy for American diplomacy but a reminder of its

significance, and of the wider value of public service, amid the mistrust and disparagement so willfully sown by so many.

Long before Trump's election, my diplomatic apprenticeship exposed me to the best—and worst—of American statecraft and its
practitioners, from the early rituals of my first overseas tour to a junior role in a Reagan White House recovering from the self-inflicted
wound of the Iran-Contra affair. I saw adept American diplomacy
under Bush and Baker and marveled at the skill with which they harnessed America's extraordinary leverage to shape a post–Cold War
order. In Boris Yeltsin's Russia, I learned the limits of American
agency when it is arrayed against the powerful forces of history. As
ambassador in Jordan, I was reminded that American leadership
could make a profound difference, especially to a partner undergoing
a precarious and consequential leadership transition.

During the post–9/11 years, I led an embattled Bureau of Near
Eastern Affairs in Washington as the inversion of the roles of force
and diplomacy intensified. The casting aside of the Bush 41 administration's unique mix of caution and daring, in favor of a disastrous
mix of militancy and hubris, fumbled an historic chance to reset
America's role in the world. Rather than successfully shaping a new
order, we compounded regional dysfunctions and undercut our influence.

The underlying challenge for the rest of my diplomatic career—
including as ambassador in Putin's Russia and the most senior career American diplomat from the end of the Bush 43 administration
through most of Obama's presidency—was how to adjust to a world
in which American dominance was fading, in part due to structural
forces, and in part due to our own grievous missteps. From reimag-
ining and realigning relationships with emerging global rivals like
Russia and China and partners like India, to navigating the turbulent waters of the Arab Spring and direct diplomacy with adversaries
like Iran, those years made clear to me that the tests awaiting the
next generation of diplomats will be even more formidable.

In the age of Trump, America is diminished, the president's world-view smaller and meaner, the world full of difficult currents. The enlightened self-interest at the heart of seventy years of American foreign policy is disdained, and the zero-sum joys of mercantilism and unilateralism are ascendant. Seen from the Trump White House, the United States has become hostage to the international order it created, and liberation is overdue.

Trump's worldview is the antithesis of Baker and Bush 41, who combined humility, an affirmative sense of the possibilities of American leadership, and diplomatic skill at a moment of unparalleled influence. The clock can't be turned back to that moment, of course; today's world is more complicated, crowded, and competitive. We are no longer the dominant power, but we can be the pivotal power for many years to come—best positioned among our friends and rivals to assemble and drive the coalitions and initiatives we need to answer the tests of our time.

The task will be to use what remains of the historic window of American preeminence to shape a new international order, one that accommodates new players and their ambitions while promoting our own interests. Neither unthinking retrenchment nor the muscular reassertion of old convictions will be effective prescriptions in the years ahead. The United States will have neither the singular unifying purpose of competition with the Soviet Union nor the singular unrivaled position of strength we enjoyed for nearly two decades after the end of the Cold War.

We will not be able to safeguard our values and interests on our own, or by big sticks alone. It will require persuading our partners as well as our adversaries of their stake in such an order. Only diplomacy can deliver on that.

* * *

SHORT OF WAR, diplomacy is the main instrument we employ to manage foreign relations, reduce external risks, and exploit opportunities to advance our security and prosperity. It is among the oldest of professions, but it is also among the most misunderstood, and the most unsatisfying to describe. It is by nature an unheroic, quiet endeavor, less swaggering than unrelenting, often unfolding in back channels out of sight and out of mind. Its successes are rarely celebrated, its failures almost always scrutinized. Even as visible and accomplished a practitioner as Henry Kissinger has called diplomacy "the patient accumulation of partial successes"—hardly the stuff of bumper stickers.[2]

A diplomat serves many roles: a translator of the world to Washington and Washington to the world; an early-warning radar for troubles and opportunities; a builder—and fixer—of relations; a maker, driver, and executor of policy; a protector of citizens abroad and promoter of their economic interests; an integrator of military, intelligence, and economic tools of statecraft; an organizer, convener, negotiator, communicator, and strategist.

Diplomatic engagement is not a favor to an adversary, but a means of reconnaissance and communication. It is a way to better understand trends, assess motivations, convey determination, and avoid inadvertent collisions. It is a method of maneuvering for future gain, a means of gaining wider support by demonstrating our willingness to engage and exposing the intransigence of rivals or foes.

The central function of diplomats is to try to manage the world's inevitable disorders and crises. Our embassy in Pakistan worked tirelessly in 2005–6 to organize the largest relief operation since the Berlin Airlift, in the wake of an earthquake that killed more than eighty thousand Pakistanis. In 2008–9, American diplomacy was at the heart of an international effort to stop an epidemic of piracy off the coast of East Africa. Senior American diplomats brought together the U.S. military, international relief organizations, and African governments to cope with the Ebola crisis in 2014. All of those efforts required substantial international cooperation. None could have been

accomplished by the United States alone—but none could have succeeded without American diplomatic leadership.

Diplomacy is also essential to the promotion of a level playing
field for American businesses abroad, to help open doors to the 95
percent of the world's consumers who live outside our borders, create
more jobs at home, and attract more foreign investment. Diplomats
manage visas for more than a million foreign students in the United
States, who generate about $40 billion every year for the American
economy, and for the tourists whose visits produce another $200 bil-
lion annually. Diplomats help American citizens in difficulty overseas, whose predicaments run the gamut from lost passports to
long-term imprisonment. They connect America to foreign societies,
run educational exchange programs, engage with people outside of
government, and try to cut through misunderstanding, mistrust, and
misrepresentation of American realities.

Diplomacy is a human enterprise, rooted in interactions between
people. Americans are often tempted to believe that the world re-
volves around us, our problems, and our analysis. As I learned the
hard way, other people and other societies have their own realities,
which are not always hospitable to ours. That does not mean that we
have to accept or indulge those perspectives, but understanding them
is the starting point for sensible diplomacy.

The process by which American diplomacy is implemented is also
all too human, full of the moments of clarity and courage, as well as
shortsightedness and clumsiness, that characterize any other human
endeavor. Policymakers and diplomats are often compelled to make
decisions under unforgiving time pressures, with inevitably incomplete information. That is hard to grasp from outside the arena, where
those realities can seem simpler and clearer than they do inside.

Diplomacy and the world it seeks to navigate have certainly
evolved in the nearly four decades since I joined the Foreign Service.
Nonstate actors—from the benign, like the Gates Foundation, to the

malign, like al-Qaeda—have steadily eroded what was once the near monopoly on power enjoyed by states and governments. The addition of cyberspace to the global commons, and advances in artificial intelligence, synthetic biology, and other technological domains, have added a new dimension to international competition, outpacing the capacity of governments to devise rules of the road. Global challenges like climate change and resource scarcity are no longer vague "emerging threats" but present-day crises. In American policymaking, there has been a growing tendency to centralize control and even execution in the White House, and to overrely on military force while allowing diplomatic muscles to atrophy, with dramatic military interventions squeezing diplomats to the margins.

* * *

AMERICAN DIPLOMACY IS adrift at a moment in history in which it means more than ever to our role as the pivotal power in world affairs. It will take a generation to reverse the underinvestment, overreach, and strategic and operational flailing of recent decades, not to mention the active sabotage of recent years under President Trump. The reconstruction of American diplomacy will require renewed investment in the fundamentals of the craft—the core qualities and roles that have always been the essence of what is required of effective diplomats: smart policy judgment, language skills, and a sure feel for the foreign landscapes in which they serve and the domestic priorities they represent. It will also require a more strategic adaptation than we've mustered during the course of my career, one that ensures we are positioned to tackle the consequential tests of tomorrow and not just the policy fads of today. Most important, it will require a new compact with the American people—leveling with them about the purpose and limits of American engagement abroad, and demonstrating that domestic renewal is at the heart of our strategy and priorities. Effective diplomacy begins at home, but it ends there, too—in better jobs, more prosperity, a healthier climate, and greater security.

What I learned all those years ago in that splendid hall in Madrid, and time and again throughout my long career, is that diplomacy is one of our nation's biggest assets and best-kept secrets. However battered and belittled in the age of Trump, it has never been a more necessary tool of first resort for American influence. Its rebirth is crucial to a new strategy for a new century, one that is full of great peril and even greater promise for America.

1

Apprenticeship:
The Education of a Diplomat

MY FIRST DIPLOMATIC mission was an utter failure. The most junior officer in our embassy in Jordan in 1983, I eagerly volunteered for what at the time seemed like a straightforward assignment: to drive a supply truck from Amman to Baghdad. It all seemed to me like an excellent adventure, a chance to see the thinly populated, rock-strewn desert of eastern Jordan, and visit Iraq, then in the midst of a brutal war with Iran.

The senior administrative officer at Embassy Amman was a grizzled veteran renowned for his ability to get things done, if not for his willingness to explain exactly how he accomplished them. He assured me the skids had been greased at the Iraqi border: Getting across would be no problem. The seven-hour drive to the border went uneventfully. Then, at the little Iraqi town of Rutba, adventure met Saddam Hussein–era reality. The skids, it turned out, had not been greased. An unamused security official rejected my paperwork and ordered me to remain in the truck while he consulted with his superiors in Baghdad.

I spent a cold, sleepless night in the cab of the truck, incapable (in that pre-cellphone age) of communicating my predicament to my colleagues in Amman or Baghdad, and increasingly worried that my diplomatic career would not survive its first year. At first light, an Iraqi officer informed me that I'd be proceeding to Baghdad under police escort. He allowed me one brief phone call from the local post office to the on-duty Marine security guard at Embassy Amman. I explained what had happened, and he was able to convey to my colleagues in Baghdad the circumstances of my delay.

With a dour policeman who introduced himself as Abu Ahmed beside me, I began the long drive through many of the dusty towns of Anbar Province that America's Iraq wars would make all too well known—Ramadi, Fallujah, Abu Ghraib. My travel partner had an unnerving habit of idly spinning the chamber on his revolver as we drove along the rutted highway. At one point he pulled out a popular regional tabloid with the cast of *Charlie's Angels* on the cover. "Do all American women look like this?" he asked.

As the late afternoon sun was beginning to fade, we stopped for gas and tea at a ramshackle rest stop run by two of his brothers, just outside Fallujah, his hometown. As we sipped our tea, sitting on wobbly plastic chairs, Abu Ahmed's nieces and nephews appeared to see the exotic American. I've always wondered what happened to them over the tumultuous decades that followed.

Abu Ahmed and I, weary and running out of things to talk about, finally arrived at a large police compound on the northwestern outskirts of Baghdad in early evening. I was relieved to see an American colleague waiting for me; I was less relieved to learn that the Iraqis refused to accept our customs documents and insisted on confiscating the truck and its cargo. There was nothing particularly sensitive in the truck, but losing a dozen computers, portable phones, and other office and communication equipment was an expensive proposition for a State Department always strapped for resources. We protested, but got nowhere.

My colleague made clear that he'd take this up with the Foreign

Ministry, which elicited barely a shrug from the police. Now separated from the truck and released by the police, I went back to our modest diplomatic facility and told my story over a few beers. The next day, I flew back to Amman. As far as I know, neither our truck nor our equipment was ever returned.

* * *

A LIFE IN diplomacy seems more natural in retrospect than it did when I was stumbling along from Amman to Baghdad all those years ago, learning my first lesson in professional humility. But public service was already in my blood. I grew up as an Army brat, the product of an itinerant military childhood that took my family from one end of the United States to the other, with a dozen moves and three high schools by the time I was seventeen.

My father and namesake, William F. Burns, fought in Vietnam in the 1960s and eventually became a two-star general and the director of the U.S. Arms Control and Disarmament Agency. He was an exemplary leader, thoughtful and exacting, someone whose high standards and model of public service I always wanted to approach. "Nothing can make you prouder," he once wrote to me, "than serving your country with honor." His was a generation accustomed to taking American leadership in the world seriously; he knew firsthand the dangers of ill-considered military conflicts, and what diplomacy could achieve in high-stakes negotiations. My mother, Peggy, was the devoted heart of our family. Her love and selflessness made all those cross-country moves manageable, and held us all together. Like my dad, she grew up in Philadelphia. They met in the chaste confines of a Catholic high school dance—with nuns wielding rulers to enforce "six inches for the Holy Spirit" between them—and built a happy life shaped by faith, family, and hard work.

Making our close-knit Irish Catholic family whole were my three brothers: Jack, Bob, and Mark. As in many Army families, constantly bouncing from post to post, we became one another's best friends. We shared a love of sports across seasons and places, and looked out for one another on all those first days in new schools.

My upbringing bore little resemblance to the caricature of the cosmopolitan, blue-blooded foreign service officer. Through the years, however, a few useful diplomatic qualities began to emerge in faint outline. Because we moved so often, I became adaptable, constantly (and sometimes painfully) adjusting to new environments. I grew curious about new places and people, increasingly accustomed to trying to put myself in their shoes and understand their perspectives and predispositions. I developed a detachment about people and events, an ability to stand back and observe and empathize, but also a reluctance—born of many departures—to get too close or too invested. I also came to know my own country well, with a feel for its physical expanse and beauty, as well as its diversity and bustling possibility. I grew up with not only an abiding respect for the American military and the rhythms of Army life, but a vaguely formed interest of my own in public service.

In 1973, I went to La Salle College on an academic scholarship, my dreams of a basketball scholarship long since surrendered to the hard realities of limited talent. A small liberal arts school run by the Christian Brothers in a rough neighborhood in North Philadelphia, La Salle offered a valuable education inside and outside the classroom. It was then a school with lots of first-generation college students, mostly commuters, who worked hard to earn their tuition, took nothing for granted, and prided themselves on puncturing pretension. La Salle, like Philadelphia in the 1970s, was not for the faint of heart.

The summer after my freshman year, I spent three months in Egypt with one of my best high school friends, Conrad Eilts, and his family. Conrad's father, Hermann F. Eilts, had become the American ambassador to Egypt when the United States restored diplomatic relations after the October 1973 war. An astute diplomat of the old school, Eilts was full of initiative and had a sure grasp of the region.

For a raw and untutored eighteen year-old, that summer in Egypt was a revelation. It was my first time outside the United States since I was a preschooler at an Army post in Germany. It was also my first time in the Arab world, and I was entranced by the scents and sounds, the commotion of the souk, and the rich intonations of Arabic. Conrad and I roamed across Cairo, then mostly barren of tourists and bursting with street life and the endless cacophony of its traffic. One night after midnight, we eluded narcoleptic Ministry of Antiquities security guards and a pack of wild dogs and scrambled in pitch darkness partway up the Great Pyramid of Cheops in Giza, looking out across Cairo's skyline until dawn began to break. We traveled to Luxor and Abu Simbel in Upper Egypt, and to the Siwa Oasis in the Western Desert, not far from the great World War II battlefield at El Alamein. It was the kind of adventure I could only dream about during previous summers bagging groceries in the Army commissary.

Later that summer, we went with Ambassador Eilts to visit President Anwar Sadat at his retreat in Mersa Matruh, on the Mediterranean coast west of Alexandria. While the ambassador met in private with Sadat, we swam in the warm blue sea, surrounded by the president's massive bodyguards. We then had a casual lunch on the veranda of Sadat's modest seaside home, with the president and his family all still in their swimsuits. Sadat was the picture of relaxation, puffing on his pipe and describing in his deep baritone his hopes for further steps toward peace with Israel. It was my first taste of the Middle East, and of American diplomacy, and I was already getting hooked.

During my senior year at La Salle, I won a Marshall Scholarship to study for three years at Oxford University. No one from La Salle had ever won a Marshall before, and I had applied with no expectations and minimal effort. Established by the British government in the early 1950s to commemorate the generosity of the Marshall Plan, the program gave thirty Americans each year a chance to study in the United Kingdom. The Marshall opened my eyes to a new, and initially intimidating, world of possibility. I felt out of my depth, surrounded by what seemed to me to be more worldly Ivy Leaguers, and out of place on Oxford's storied quadrangles.

From my base at St. John's College, I pursued a master's degree, and eventually a doctorate, in international relations. My supervisor in the master's program was an Australian academic named Hedley Bull. With a dry, self-deprecating wit and considerable patience for unformed young minds like mine, Bull was a superb intellectual guide. History was the key to understanding international relations, he insisted, and leaders most often erred when they thought they were immune to its lessons. His book *The Anarchical Society* remains as clear and compelling a framework for thinking about international order as I have ever read. Bull's thesis was straightforward: Even in a Hobbesian world, sovereign states have a self-interest in developing rules and institutions to help shape their interactions and enhance their chances for security and prosperity.

"You Americans," Bull told me at one of our weekly tutorials, "tend to be impatient about the world's imperfections, and convinced that every problem has a solution."

I asked what was so wrong with that.

"Nothing, really," he said. "I admire American ingenuity. But diplomacy is more often about managing problems than solving them."

I wrote my doctoral dissertation on the use of economic aid as an instrument of American policy toward Egypt in the Nasser era. The core argument was that economic assistance could reinforce areas of shared purpose, but it rarely had much effectiveness as a "stick" to alter fundamentally policies where no such common ground existed. Withdrawing aid for the Aswan Dam project, or American food aid, would not compel Egypt to abandon ties with the Soviets; it would more likely harden Egyptian defiance. Hardly a groundbreaking insight, but one that successive U.S. administrations would have to learn and relearn.

Beyond academics, Oxford was rarely dull. Grittier than its dreaming college spires might suggest, it was caught up in all the early turmoil of Margaret Thatcher's Britain, with angry labor unrest at the Cowley motor works on the eastern edge of town, and protests in support of Provisional Irish Republican Army hunger strikers on a square across from St. John's. I played on the university basketball team, and traveled widely around Europe and the Middle East during long vacation periods. Those years were a chance to see my own country through the eyes of others, and I soon discovered a genuine sense of pride and satisfaction in trying to explain America to them. That was not easy in the late 1970s, with Vietnam and Watergate still weighing heavily on American society and our image abroad.

Shortly after Iranian militants took American diplomats hostage in Tehran in November 1979, I took the train down to London to sit for the written portion of the Foreign Service exam at the old U.S. embassy on Grosvenor Square. A fellow American graduate student at Oxford had mentioned casually that fall that he planned to take the test, and encouraged me to come along. I wasn't yet convinced that diplomacy was the profession for me, nor was I sure that the State Department would think I had much to offer as a diplomat. But my experience in Cairo several years before, my admiration for my father's public service, and my curiosity about other societies and life abroad all made me want to give it a try. To my relief, the exam was straightforward—a combination of general knowledge questions, American civics, and geography 101.

I was thrilled to pass and later to navigate successfully the more nerve-racking oral exam with a trio of grim-faced officials. "What's the biggest challenge in American foreign policy today?" one asked. "I think it's us," I replied. Then, channeling my inner Hedley Bull, I explained, "After Vietnam, we have to do a better job of understanding which problems we can solve, and which we can manage." I cited Jimmy Carter's success in the Panama Canal Treaty and in the Camp David negotiations with Egypt and Israel as examples of the former, and grinding Cold War competition with the Soviets as an illustration of the latter. The examiners looked a little bored, and more than a little skeptical, but a few weeks later I got a formal letter of acceptance.

* * *

IN EARLY JANUARY 1982, I showed up to Foreign Service orientation in a dreary office building across the Potomac River from the State Department. I was seated alphabetically next to Lisa Carty—a tall, lovely New Yorker whose easygoing charm, kindness, and good humor soon captivated me. Lisa and I fell in love at a pace wholly out of character with our two relatively careful personalities, and would be married two years later.

The Foreign Service of the early 1980s was still a relatively small, somewhat insular institution, with about 5,500 officers staffing some 230 embassies and consulates overseas and a variety of Washington positions. Its "pale, male, Yale" reputation was well earned. At the time, nine out of ten foreign service officers were white, and fewer than one in four were women. It had only been a decade since married women and women with children were allowed into the service and since annual performance reviews stopped evaluating the "hostess skills" of wives. Homosexuality was no longer a basis for denial of employment, but it wasn't until 1995 that President Clinton banned the government from denying security clearances on grounds of sexual orientation.

Alexander Haig was secretary of state, the first of ten secretaries under whom I would serve. President Reagan had launched a massive military modernization program, part of an effort to reassert American purpose and influence in the wake of the Soviet invasion of Afghanistan in 1979 and the Iranian Revolution that same year. Conflicts in Central America transfixed official Washington, part of a wider contest with a Soviet Union that no one imagined was already in the last decade of its existence. Meanwhile, China's economic transformation was quietly gathering momentum, with Deng Xiaoping's reforms producing double-digit growth. It was a moment of turbulence and uncertainty across the globe—and a genuinely exciting time for a twenty-five-year-old just embarking on a diplomatic life.

The training course for new FSOs, known in bureaucratic jargon as "A-100," was about seven weeks long, though at times it felt interminable. It featured a procession of enervating speakers describing their islands in the great American policymaking archipelago, and offering primers on how embassies functioned and the foreign policy process worked.

By the end of the training period, I had learned more about administrative rules and regulations than I had about the nuances of diplomatic tradecraft. I was struck, however, by the expansive mandate of the profession. On any given day in any given country, diplomats were keeping a watchful eye on American citizens living and working in the country, encouraging local citizens to come visit and study in the United States, and building a wide range of contacts inside and outside government to explain and inform American policy.

Our class of entering officers was a wonderful, eclectic mix. Lisa and I were among the youngest in the group. The average age was thirty-two, with a former Jesuit priest in his mid-fifties at the far end of the actuarial scale. There were former Peace Corps volunteers and military veterans, a couple of high school teachers, and at least one failed rock musician.

With a princely annual salary of $21,000, an intriguing professional future, and a budding romance, I couldn't have been more content. In the last week of the A-100 course, we were given our first assignments. Mine was Amman, Jordan. I was delighted, given my exciting foray into the Arab world several years before, and the inevitable policy swirl of the region. Lisa had volunteered to go to Burkina Faso, which reflected her lifelong passion for development issues and made her very popular in the class, since no one else was too enthusiastic about the lifestyle awaiting them in Ouagadougou. In the perverse wisdom of the State Department, Lisa was assigned instead to Singapore. We dreaded our impending separation but knew it would be a fact of life in the Foreign Service. We got engaged before Lisa departed for Asia in late spring, leaving me to fend for myself for six months as an Arabic-language student in Washington.

Before I left for the Middle East, I wrote to Albert Hourani, the chief examiner for my Oxford doctorate and a brilliant scholar of the Arab world, to tell him where I had been posted. He replied warmly, noting that he had always found Jordan "a little quiet and unremarkable culturally, but interesting politically." He added that he had just agreed to provide academic supervision to King Hussein's oldest son, Prince Abdullah, who would be at Oxford in the coming year. While Hourani's note didn't make much of an impression on me at the time, Jordan and Abdullah would play a large part in the career I was just beginning.

* * *

AMMAN WAS DUSTY and nondescript in the early 1980s, a city of about a million people sprawled across a series of rocky hills and valleys on the central Jordanian plateau. When I arrived, King Hussein had been on the throne for thirty years, and had survived numerous assassination attempts. Jordan occupied a precarious perch in the region, surrounded by conflicts and sitting atop simmering tensions between the stubborn, clannish East Bank minority that dominated Jordanian politics and a Palestinian-origin majority harboring no shortage of resentments. Starved of natural resources, Jordan was heavily dependent on outside financial help and remittances from the Gulf.

As an introduction to Middle East politics and diplomacy, Jordan was especially well situated, at the crossroads of most of the major problems in the region—from the Lebanese civil war in the north, to the Iran-Iraq conflict in the east, and the Israeli-Palestinian dispute in the west. The American embassy itself was just the right size for a new FSO, big and central enough to provide exposure to a whole range of issues and professional challenges, but not so big that a junior officer would easily get lost in the machinery.

Dick Viets was the ambassador, a skilled and sophisticated diplomat, straight out of central casting with his white mane and ever-present pipe. Unlike most U.S. ambassadors in the Arab world, Viets had served in Israel, and had wide experience outside the Middle East, including in South Asia and as an aide to Henry Kissinger. He had a close and effective relationship with King Hussein, and a willingness to speak his mind to Washington. Viets's deputy, Ed Djerejian, and political counselor, Jim Collins, became lifelong mentors.

I spent my first year in Amman in the consular section, as was customary for new officers, no matter what their later specialties might be. My first boss was Lincoln Benedicto, who had spent time before the Foreign Service as a youth counselor in some of Philadelphia's toughest neighborhoods. He was a good manager with a razor-sharp sense for people who were trying to game the system, whether visa applicants or Americans down on their luck overseas. The Jordanian employees who staffed the consular section were a huge asset, an early demonstration for me of the critical role that foreign service nationals play at American diplomatic posts around the world. They were our trusted eyes and ears, patient guides, and the one thread of continuity of knowledge, expertise, and contacts as officers came and went.

I was not a stellar visa officer. I spent too much time practicing my Arabic in interviews with Bedouin sheikhs, and not enough time processing the endless stream of paperwork and visa applications that came with the job. I never particularly enjoyed my quarterly visits to the few young Americans imprisoned for drug offenses; Jordanian prisons were hard places, and there wasn't much I could do other than talk and try to offer a little bit of hope. My consular responsibilities gave me chances to travel outside Amman, however, and I eagerly sought out tasks that would get me on the road.

I persuaded Lincoln to let me spend two weeks with the Howeitat tribe in southern Jordan, ostensibly to improve my Arabic. By the early 1980s, the Bedouin spent more time in small pickup trucks than on camelback, although camels were still the ornery heart of their daily existence. Smuggling everything from cigarettes to televisions back and forth across the Saudi border was a primary, if not publicly advertised, income stream. I was kept at a polite remove from those activities, and spent most of my time testing the patience of local tribesmen with my grammatically challenged Arabic. Nearly every member of the Howeitat I encountered claimed to have played a prominent role in the filming of David Lean's *Lawrence of Arabia* two decades before. Set in the stark beauty of Wadi Rum and the Jordanian desert beyond the tiny port of Aqaba, the movie starred Peter O'Toole as Lawrence and Anthony Quinn as the great Howeitat tribal leader Auda Abu Tayi. The Howeitat were not quite as cinematic in person as the Anthony Quinn version, but my brief experience in their midst opened my eyes to the ways in which tradition and modernity were colliding across the Arab world, setting off disruptions that continue to reverberate.

In the summer of 1983, I moved to the political section, the part of the embassy charged with analyzing Jordan's domestic situation and foreign policy, and building contacts with key officials and political players. We were busy but happy, dealing with a steady stream of Washington visitors, keeping up with an active ambassador, and grappling with lots of interesting regional and domestic issues. Donald Rumsfeld, briefly the Reagan administration's Middle East envoy, swept through Amman a couple times that year, supremely confident but unfettered by much knowledge of the region. The wider regional landscape remained perilous, with the bombing of our embassy in Beirut in the spring of 1983 a terrible reminder of the increasing risks that American diplomats faced. The horrific attack on the U.S. Marine barracks in Beirut that October, in which 241 Marines were killed, reinforced the challenge.

Amman was hardly immune from those threats. In addition to periodic assassinations and attacks against Jordanian targets, our embassy warehouse was bombed, and a small car bomb was set off one weekday afternoon in the parking lot of the InterContinental Hotel across the street from the embassy. When I walked over afterward with one of our security officers to talk to the Jordanian police and intelligence officials who were investigating, a second car bomb was discovered, and fortunately defused. It had been set to go off some time after the first one, precisely to hit the crowd of officials and onlookers who would naturally gather. It was the first, but not the last, time that I was luckier than I was smart.

That set of events produced understandable alarm. The embassy was an old, cramped stone building, on one of Amman's main streets. With no obvious alternative locations in the short term, the decision was made to put up a sandbag wall in front of the building, two stories tall and six feet thick. The barrier was reassuring, if unphotogenic—until it collapsed after one of Jordan's rare rainstorms, transforming the entrance into a man-made beach.

My responsibilities in the political section were mainly to cover domestic politics, and to try to expand the embassy's relationships beyond our traditional palace and political elite sources. I worked methodically at that task, talking discreetly to Islamist politicians and Palestinian activists in Jordan's refugee camps. I wrote profiles of next-generation leaders and explored the politics of some of the major towns and cities, including Zarqa, the sprawling urban area just east of Amman, in which disenfranchised Palestinians and disgruntled East Bankers mixed uneasily (and from which Abu Musab al-Zarqawi, the founder of al-Qaeda in Iraq, would later emerge). In the spring of 1984, I covered the first parliamentary elections in nearly two decades—a cautious effort by King Hussein to let off some of the political steam that was building as economic conditions stagnated.

Toward the end of my tenure in the political section, I wrote a cable in which I tried to distill what I had learned and what worried me about the future of Jordan and the wider Arab world. Entitled "The Changing Face of Jordanian Politics," the cable began by noting that "the traditional system of power relationships which has underpinned the Hashemite regime for decades is beginning to buckle under increasing demographic, social, economic and political pressures."[1] By the end of the 1980s, 75 percent of Jordan's population would be under the age of thirty. Well over half would be living in the urban stew of Amman and Zarqa, largely cut off from their social and political roots in Palestine and elsewhere on the East Bank. The educational system had its flaws, but remained one of the best in the Arab world; when combined with decreasing economic opportunities, the resultant expectations gap could prove combustible.

"As material gains become more difficult for a growing number of Jordanians to obtain," I observed, "and as traditional social and political ties begin to fray, disaffected citizens are likely to turn increasingly to the political system for redress of their grievances. What they will probably find is a generally anachronistic and unresponsive structure, riddled with corruption, the preserve of a powerful but steadily diminishing proportion of the population intent upon shielding its power and wealth from interlopers. It is a system based on the fading realities of a bygone era, a time when East Bank tribal balance was the stuff of which political stability was made."

King Hussein's intuitive skill and personal grip on the imaginations of most Jordanians were significant brakes on serious instability. But the broad challenge, not just for Jordan but for the rest of the Arab world, was that meeting the demands for dignity and opportunity of the next generation, and the one beyond that, would eventually require greater agility and commitment to modernize creaky economic and political systems. Jordan under King Hussein and later King Abdullah would be better placed than most to cope, but it was not hard to anticipate many of the pressures that would eventually bubble over.

* * *

LATE IN THE summer of 1984, I returned to Washington for my next assignment. Lisa and I had been married earlier that year, and it was far easier for us both to find jobs in Washington than at a single overseas post. In what is a rite of passage for new officers learning the byzantine ways of the State Department bureaucracy, I took on a position as a staff assistant in the Bureau of Near East and South Asian Affairs. Lisa took a similar position in the Bureau of International Organization Affairs.

The Near East Bureau, or NEA, was in that era a proud, intense, and slightly inbred place. As one senior colleague put it to me on my first day on the job, it was a place where "three simultaneous wars are considered average." It was known as the "Mother Bureau" for its reputation for skillfully shepherding Arabists along their career paths, and for setting the standard among State's other regional bureaus for professionalism under pressure. Led by Assistant Secretary of State Dick Murphy, the bureau worked at a frantic pace, coping with constant crises in the region and congressional scrutiny at home. Murphy was a consummate gentleman and a wise professional, steeped in the perils and personalities of the Arab world.

My partner in the staff assistants' office during most of that year was David Satterfield. I always felt a little inadequate around David, who had immense facility in the arcane policy issues that bedeviled the bureau, bottomless energy, and a capacity to speak in crisp, precise talking points about any issue at any time. Our role in those low-tech days was basically to serve as the organizational hub for the bureau's policy work. We conveyed taskings from the secretary's office, reviewed and filtered the cables coming in from overseas posts, and made sure that Murphy was well prepared for his relentless schedule of meetings and trips. One of us would come in every morning at six to prepare a one- or two-page summary of overnight developments for Murphy's use in Secretary of State George Shultz's daily staff meeting. Given NEA's pace, we'd rarely get out of the office before nine or ten at night.

One of us would also accompany Murphy on his frequent overseas trips—shuttling between capitals, cultivating relationships, managing crises, and pushing large policy rocks up steep hills. The Middle East had its share of Sisyphean tasks. The bitter aftermath of the Israeli invasion of Lebanon a couple years earlier still consumed much of NEA's attention. Meanwhile, the grueling conflict between Iran and Iraq dragged on, with Washington quietly putting its thumb on the scale to support Saddam's Iraq. The familiar struggle to revive Arab-Israeli peace talks remained a priority, although as was so often the case it was a function more of aspiration than on-the-ground realities.

George Shultz's reliance on professionals like Dick Murphy, along with his own impressive integrity and intellect, won him many admirers in the department. Shultz was a firm believer in the importance of "tending the garden" in diplomacy, and expected Murphy to spend considerable time on the road, even when particular policy goals were so obviously elusive. One evening in the fall of 1984, I was walking with Murphy along the long wood-paneled corridor that runs down the middle of the seventh floor of the State Department, where the office of the secretary is located. Shultz appeared in the hallway outside his office as we walked past, and asked Murphy when he was heading back to the Middle East. Murphy replied that he had a number of commitments in Washington, including upcoming congressional testimony, and wasn't sure when he'd travel next. Shultz smiled and said, "I hope you can get back out there soon. It's important to keep stirring the pot."

The result of that conversation was a marathon trip, which stretched from North Africa to South Asia, and kept us on the road for nearly five weeks. My role was a mix of logistician and policy aide. Much of the trip involved shuttling between Israel, Lebanon, and Syria, as Murphy tried to broker a deal that would allow Israeli forces to withdraw from Lebanon, with Syrian forces not advancing southward beyond their positions in the Beqaa Valley. It was fascinating to watch him try to move the immovable Syrian president, Hafez al-Assad, who loved to filibuster with long soliloquies on Syrian history since the Crusades. Lebanese politicians, with deep-rooted survival instincts and an endless capacity for backbiting, were maddeningly entertaining. Israel's national unity government was frequently paralytic, with its two leaders and rotating prime ministers, Shimon Peres and Yitzhak Shamir, almost as suspicious of each other as they were of their Arab neighbors.

Nevertheless, Murphy somehow managed to maneuver the parties toward a slightly more stable disposition of forces, with the Israelis pulling back by the early summer of 1985 to a several-mile-wide "security zone" along Lebanon's southern border. Murphy's formula was equal parts persistence and ingenuity, steadily pressing for small practical steps, using American leverage carefully, and always conscious that this was another problem to be managed before it could ever be solved. As I was learning, diplomatic triumphs are almost always at the margins.

On that trip and several subsequent efforts over the next few months, Murphy worked hard to restart Arab-Israeli talks. Negotiations never materialized. Yasser Arafat was as hard to pin down as ever; King Hussein lost whatever patience he had for Palestinian machinations; and the Israeli side was immobile, with Shamir uninterested in negotiations over territory with anyone, and Peres interested only in negotiations with Hussein, without the headaches of Palestinian representatives and their desire for an independent state.

Iraq, then five years into its horrific war with Iran, was a particularly memorable stop. Tariq Aziz, Saddam's urbane and faintly menacing foreign minister, hosted Murphy for a long lunch of masgouf, the famous Iraqi fish dish. Aziz's security detail cleared a well-known restaurant on the Tigris of its patrons for the afternoon. Seated at an outdoor table overlooking the river, we could see Iraqi guards fanning out around the building, pistols drawn. The restaurant staff affected an air of normalcy, exchanging whispers about who these evidently

important foreigners were. Puffing on a big Cuban cigar, Aziz professed great optimism about Iraq's prospects on the battlefield, and
waxed poetic about the future of U.S.-Iraqi relations. Murphy was
unimpressed. As down-to-earth as Aziz was full of mobster charm,
Murphy smiled as we walked out of the restaurant and said, "He kind
of reminds you of Al Capone, doesn't he?" I learned a lot about diplomacy from Dick Murphy, although I had no idea then that fifteen
years later I'd wind up sitting in his office, not just emptying his out-
box.

Near the end of my assignment, I was asked by Deputy Secretary
John Whitehead's chief of staff if I'd be interested in becoming one of
Whitehead's two special assistants. He thought my experience in
NEA would serve me well in the stressful world of the seventh floor,
where the department's senior leadership wrestled with the problems
that couldn't be solved at lower levels. I spent the next year trying not
to prove him wrong.

Whitehead had just become George Shultz's deputy, after a remarkable career that had taken him from the U.S. Navy and the
D-Day invasion to the top of Goldman Sachs. Self-assured and
thoroughly decent, Whitehead shared Shultz's faith in the State Department, although he was always a bit bemused by the difficulty of
getting things done quickly, or at least as quickly as he had become
accustomed to at Goldman.

My first day on Whitehead's staff was very nearly my last. He was
an avid art collector, and had placed an original Degas ballerina min-
iature on the edge of his large desk. On my first morning, I walked in
quietly and put a folder in the inbox, only to accidentally knock the
Degas off the desk and onto the floor. Fortunately, the oriental carpet
was thick, the ballerina bounced undamaged, and the deputy secretary resumed his reading with only a mild grimace in my direction.

The rest of my tour went more smoothly. My new position gave
me a wide perspective on how the department worked, across the
whole range of policy issues and bureaus. Whitehead took a special

interest in economic issues, and played an important role in helping to open up East European economies as the Cold War was ending and the Soviet bloc was crumbling. I accompanied him on a variety of trips, from Europe to the Middle East and Africa. He helped manage the difficult aftermath of the *Achille Lauro* attack in the fall of 1985, when Palestinian terrorists murdered a wheelchair-bound American on a hijacked Italian cruise ship. He also took the lead in mobilizing European support for sanctions against Libya in the spring of 1986, after Muammar al-Qaddafi's agents struck a disco in West Berlin and killed several U.S. servicemen. Although himself a skeptic about the efficacy of economic sanctions, Whitehead was a skillful advocate, and his efforts in the mid-1980s laid the groundwork for a sanctions regime that two decades later helped persuade Qaddafi to abandon terrorism.

* * *

MY RUN OF professional good fortune continued in the summer of 1986, when I was assigned to the National Security Council's Near East and South Asia directorate, a four-person office covering Morocco to Bangladesh.

My new office was in room 361½ in the Old Executive Office Building, the elaborate structure next to the White House, which until World War II had housed the entire staffs of the State, War, and Navy departments. Whenever I got a little too full of myself, walking with my White House badge along the long, high-ceilinged corridors of the building or across West Executive Avenue for meetings in the White House, my ego would come right down to earth when I returned to my office. Room 361½ was a converted women's bathroom, the size of a walk-in closet, with exposed plumbing along the walls and a scent that served as a persistent reminder of the room's previous function.

My boss was Dennis Ross, a smart, even-tempered thirty-eight-year-old Californian with an academic background in Soviet and Middle East studies. The Reagan administration was still scarred by

its grim experience in Lebanon a few years before, groping unsuccessfully with various formulas for restarting Arab-Israeli negotiations,
and anxious about revolutionary Iran. We were all stretched thin in
the summer and fall of 1986, on an NSC staff whose core dysfunction
was quickly apparent even to a young and inexperienced diplomat
like me.

The modern NSC had grown out of the experience of the Kennedy
administration, when McGeorge Bundy led twenty or so political appointees and career professionals from State, Defense, and the intelligence community, organized in small regional and functional offices.
The main tasks of the NSC staff, then as now, involved staffing the
president for his foreign policy engagements; coordinating the preparation of options for presidential decision with the key cabinet agencies and ensuring that their views were clear, timely, and unfiltered;
and carefully monitoring implementation. The role of the national
security advisor and the NSC staff grew substantially under Richard
Nixon, who drew on the brilliance and ruthless bureaucratic agility of
Henry Kissinger to remake relations with China and the Soviet
Union, with the White House staff serving not only as coordinator
but also chief policy operator.

Ronald Reagan entered office in January 1981 committed to diminishing the role and reach of the NSC staff and reducing the tension between the NSC staff and cabinet principals that had continued
during the Carter administration. Reagan went through national security advisors at a rapid clip. John Poindexter, a Navy admiral, became Reagan's fourth NSC chief in four years at the end of 1985. A
decent man with a nuclear engineer's exacting intellect, Poindexter
was badly miscast in the role. Uncomfortable dealing with Congress
and the media, without personal or political connections to the president, not held in high regard by the leaderships of State, Defense, or
the CIA, he inherited a staff with some bad habits and explosive
secrets—which his own uncertain instincts and detached style proceeded to make worse.

The most dangerous of those secrets was a bizarre scheme that had begun earlier in 1985 as a clandestine effort by the NSC staff, working through a motley collection of Iranian and Israeli middlemen, to trade U.S. arms to Iran in exchange for the release of Americans held hostage in Lebanon. Poindexter's predecessor, Bud McFarlane, had championed the initiative, despite the long-standing U.S. policy against making concessions to terrorists. Beyond his interest in the return of American hostages, McFarlane saw the potential for a strategic opening to Iran, and contacts with "moderates" in Tehran. In May 1986, still engaged in the enterprise despite having handed over his post as national security advisor to Poindexter, McFarlane made a secret trip to Tehran with a small NSC staff team, in an unmarked Boeing 707 full of arms. The whole episode was the stuff of dark comedy, with McFarlane and his colleagues bearing a cake in the shape of a key to highlight their interest in an opening to Iran. No senior Iranians, let alone "moderates," emerged to meet McFarlane. Tehran did, however, buy the arms. It also eventually engineered the release of several American hostages by their Hezbollah captors in Lebanon.

What turned this strange story into a full-blown scandal that nearly brought down the Reagan presidency was a further twist. Led by Oliver North, a Marine lieutenant colonel in the NSC staff's political-military office, the White House had secretly diverted the proceeds of the arms sales to support the anti-Communist Contra forces in Nicaragua. Since Congress had formally forbidden the administration from funding the Contras, this was an illegal—and stunningly reckless—maneuver. Predictably, news of the arms-for-hostages effort leaked out in a Lebanese newspaper story in November 1986, and the Contra connection was soon exposed. Poindexter and North were gone by the end of the month.

As the Iran-Contra scandal unfolded, the NSC staff and the entire White House were in deep disarray. The president seemed stunned and adrift. Seeking a way out, he tasked a commission headed by

Senator John Tower of Texas to investigate the role the NSC staff had played in the scandal and recommend reforms. The Tower Commission Report, issued in February 1987, was sharply critical of the president's hands-off leadership style and the failings of the NSC, and advocated a long list of remedies. Frank Carlucci, a former career diplomat who had served as deputy director of the CIA and deputy secretary of defense, returned to government as Poindexter's successor. He brought as his deputy Colin Powell, a charismatic forty-nine-year-old Army general. Powell and Carlucci employed the Tower Commission Report as their "owner's manual," and quickly set about overhauling the staff and its structure.

Two-thirds of my colleagues on the NSC staff were soon transferred or fired. An experienced senior diplomat, Bob Oakley, was appointed head of the Near East–South Asia office, with Dennis staying on as his deputy and me remaining at the bottom of the organizational chart. Carlucci and Powell streamlined the overall NSC staff, installed a general counsel to ensure rigorous legal and ethical compliance, and insisted on strict accountability. They worked hard to rebuild trust with Secretary Shultz and Secretary of Defense Caspar Weinberger, restored the NSC staff to its nonoperational, coordinating role, and set up a disciplined system of interagency meetings, built around a Senior Review Group of cabinet principals, which Carlucci chaired, and a Policy Review Group of their deputies, led by Powell. Together with White House chiefs of staff Howard Baker and Ken Duberstein, Carlucci and Powell helped save the Reagan presidency, rebuild public and congressional trust in the White House, and support a renewed diplomatic push by Shultz that produced some significant late Cold War gains.

Powell made a particularly strong impression on me, as effective and natural a leader as I had ever encountered. Having grown up in the world of the military, I knew the significance of "command presence," and Powell personified the concept. Straightforward, demanding, and well organized, he was also warm and good-humored, with a ready smile and easy charm. His Policy Review Group meetings were precise and collegial. The departmental deputies never lacked for opportunities to lay out their views, but Powell made sure each session had a clear beginning, middle, and end—with a crisp statement of objectives, orderly discussion of options, and a concise summation of conclusions or recommendations to principals. For many meetings on Middle East issues, I'd write the talking points that Powell could draw on to guide the conversation. He always made them much more compelling.

Much of my work in 1987–88 revolved around the Persian Gulf, where the Iran-Iraq War ground on, and where our Gulf Arab allies remained deeply unsettled by the revelation of secret American overtures to a regime in Tehran that they despised and feared. The Gulf Arabs had still not recovered from the shock of the Iranian Revolution and all the uncertainties about American reliability that flowed from it. Every Iranian tactical advance in the war with Iraq sparked new worries.

Desperate to ward off the Iranians, the Iraqis had begun to attack Iranian oil tankers in the Gulf, trying to chip away at the resources that fueled the war effort. Since most Iraqi oil was exported by pipeline, and since it was hardly in Iran's interest to try to close the Strait of Hormuz on which its own oil exports depended, Tehran retaliated by striking the tankers of Saddam's Gulf Arab allies, especially Kuwait and Saudi Arabia. The resultant "tanker war" added a new theater to the conflict, and Iran's acquisition of Chinese-origin Silkworm antiship missiles threatened a rapid escalation. Late in 1986, the Kuwaitis approached both the United States and the Soviets for help in protecting their tankers, explicitly requesting that the United States "reflag" Kuwaiti-owned tankers—putting them under U.S. flag so that they would fall under the protection of the American Navy.

That touched off a series of complicated deliberations within the Reagan administration about how to respond. I joined Bob Oakley in weeks of Policy Review Group meetings, now chaired by John Negro-

ponte. An accomplished diplomat, Negroponte succeeded Powell as
deputy national security advisor in late 1987, when Powell took Carlucci's place and Carlucci moved to the Pentagon to replace Weinberger as secretary of defense. There were obvious downsides to
agreeing to reflagging, not least the danger of getting sucked into the
tanker war. Neither State nor the Navy were wildly enthusiastic about
the prospect. As Weinberger was departing, however, he had registered with Reagan his strong concern that ceding the opportunity to
the Soviets would be a major setback for American interests. Moreover, the White House was anxious to rebuild credibility and trust
with the Gulf Arabs, and to send a post-Iran-Contra signal of American resolve. The president formally announced U.S. willingness to
reflag in May 1987, just after the Iraqis had "inadvertently" fired a
missile at the USS *Stark,* killing thirty-seven Navy personnel. While
the intelligence was murky, I've never been convinced that the attack
on the *Stark* was entirely an accident, given Saddam's interest in
drawing the United States in and breaking the murderous stalemate
with Iran.

The reflagging operation was conceived as a relatively low-key exercise, but that quickly proved wishful thinking. The Navy had only a
handful of ships in the Gulf at the time, and had to make some major
adjustments. It was short on minesweepers, and we had to drum up
support from a number of European allies. The reflagging itself required endless legal gymnastics and interagency coordination. By late
July, however, the United States was able to begin protecting eleven
Kuwaiti tankers, now under U.S. flag, in convoys moving in and out
of the Gulf. It didn't take long, however, for other crises to emerge. In
September, a U.S. helicopter fired on an Iranian vessel caught laying
mines. The following month, the Iranians fired missiles at a U.S.-
flagged tanker in Kuwaiti waters, and U.S. Navy destroyers shelled an
Iranian offshore platform in response.

There was no letup in the first half of 1988, and I remember many
late nights and early mornings in the White House Situation Room

monitoring the latest collision. In April, the USS *Samuel B. Roberts* struck an Iranian mine, and ten sailors were injured. Two Iranian oil platforms and a number of Iranian naval vessels were destroyed in retaliation. Finally, in July, the USS *Vincennes* mistakenly shot down an Iranian civilian plane, killing 290 passengers and crew. It was a terrible tragedy, but reflected the mounting risks of conflict in the crowded waters and skies of the Gulf. In August, the Iranians finally agreed to a UN-brokered cease-fire with Iraq.

As tensions in the Gulf began to ease, my own role at NSC shifted unexpectedly. Dennis Ross left to serve as Vice President Bush's chief foreign policy advisor in his 1988 presidential election campaign. Bob Oakley became our ambassador to Pakistan after the tragic death of his predecessor, Arnie Raphel. I assumed that Colin Powell would bring in a senior official to run the Near East office for the last six months of the administration, and was genuinely surprised when he asked me to take on the role of senior director and chief of the office. At thirty-two, and barely into the middle ranks of the Foreign Service, I was very junior for such a promotion. I went over to see Powell in his West Wing office and explained that I was appreciative of his confidence but thought he should find someone more experienced. I had even brought a few names to suggest. "I wouldn't have asked you to do this if I wasn't convinced that you could," Powell replied evenly. I understood immediately that there was only one right answer, swallowed my self-doubt, and replied that I'd do my best to honor his trust. I walked back to the Old Executive Office Building unsure of how I'd handle the responsibility, but buoyed by his vote of confidence.

The remaining months of the Reagan administration were a blur. More crises inevitably erupted. In December 1988, a terrorist bomb brought down Pan Am Flight 103 over Lockerbie, Scotland. All 259 passengers and crew were killed, along with 11 people in Lockerbie who were struck by debris. Initial suspicions focused on the Iranians, seeking revenge for the *Vincennes* shoot-down, or a Syrian-based Palestinian terror group. But the investigation eventually pointed toward Libyan responsibility, setting off another tortured chapter in relations with Qaddafi, and eventually in my own professional life.

A final episode in the Reagan administration's efforts to promote Arab-Israeli peace occupied much of my last months at the NSC staff. Throughout the first half of 1988, against the unsettling backdrop of mounting violence in the West Bank, Secretary Shultz and Dick Murphy had labored doggedly to launch negotiations. The idea was that Jordan could represent Palestinian interests, and that there would be an "interlock" in the process whereby talks on the final status of the West Bank and Gaza would proceed even as discussions of transitional arrangements unfolded. The Shamir government in Israel was resistant—unwilling to concede much in the face of Palestinian violence. King Hussein was wary of exposing Jordan to more regional criticism and distrustful that Arafat would ever cede negotiating responsibility to Jordan. In July 1988, his frustration complete, the king publicly relinquished Jordanian legal and administrative ties to the West Bank, stating bluntly that the PLO now bore sole responsibility for negotiating Palestinian interests.

Since the mid-1970s, the United States had insisted that it would deal directly with the PLO only if it met three conditions: acceptance of UN Security Council Resolution 242 and the land-for-peace formula for resolution of the conflict; an end to violence; and recognition of Israel's right to exist. As King Hussein cut his ties to the West Bank, and nervous that new leaders might emerge that he could not control, Arafat began to probe the possibility of opening a dialogue with the United States. One private diplomatic track was opened by a Palestinian American activist close to the PLO chairman, and another initiative was championed by the Swedish foreign minister. A complicated dance ensued, with Arafat taking a series of steps that came close to the three American conditions, but didn't quite meet them. The White House largely deferred to Shultz, who was adamant that the criteria could not be compromised. I stayed in close touch with Dick Murphy and his deputy, Dan Kurtzer, as they tried to nudge the intermediaries toward the finish line, and kept Powell carefully informed.

Not long after Vice President Bush's sweeping victory in the presidential election in November, a significant complication developed. Arafat applied for a visa to come to the United Nations in New York at the end of the month. I thought there were powerful arguments to grant the visa, given U.S. obligations as host of the UN. But Secretary Shultz remained deeply concerned about PLO involvement in terrorism, and was determined to show Arafat that he would not bend until the three conditions for U.S. dialogue were met. The president and Powell deferred to Shultz, and Arafat was denied a visa. As Shultz anticipated, the denial did not slow PLO interest in opening a direct dialogue, and may have convinced Arafat that he couldn't cut any corners.

By early December, Arafat was edging close to the mark. I joined Powell and Shultz and a few other aides for a meeting with President Reagan in the Oval Office to discuss next steps. Shultz argued persuasively that it was important to take yes for an answer if Arafat met the terms. This would be a service to President Bush, who would inherit a dialogue with the Palestinians, and not have to sacrifice any early political capital to bring it about. President Reagan readily agreed. "Let's just make sure they stick to their end of the bargain," he said.

On December 14, Arafat made a public statement in Geneva that matched the American criteria, and our ambassador in Tunis was authorized to begin a direct dialogue with PLO representatives. While we were still a long way from serious peace negotiations, it was a useful step forward. Both President Reagan's foreign policy legacy and his place in history looked immeasurably better in December 1988 than they had two years before.

As the inauguration of President Bush approached in January 1989 and I prepared to return to the State Department after two and a half intense years at the White House, I realized how fortunate I had been, and how much I had learned. I wrote in my last personnel evaluation at the NSC staff that I now understood "how the policy process should work, and how it shouldn't." I had also begun to learn that the profession of a diplomat was only partially that of diplomacy; you had to know how to navigate politics and policymaking as well. My apprenticeship as a diplomat had been unusually rich and varied over less than seven years, with experience in an exceptional embassy and tours with two strong public servants at senior levels of the department, followed by a roller-coaster ride at the NSC staff that took me from the bizarre lows of Iran-Contra to heady responsibilities under Colin Powell. Now I was about to launch into a new and even more fascinating chapter, returning to the State Department as the Cold War ended and the world was transformed.

2

The Baker Years: Shaping Order

THE OLD CAUCASUS spa town of Kislovodsk was in terminal decline, much like the Soviet Union itself. It was late April 1991, and Secretary Baker and the rest of us in his bone-tired delegation had just arrived from Damascus. With Baker scheduled to meet with Soviet foreign minister Aleksandr Bessmertnykh the next morning, we stumbled around in the evening gloom to find our rooms in the official guesthouse, long past its glory days as a haven for the party elite. My room was lit by a single overhead bulb. The handle on the toilet came off when I tried to flush it, and what trickled out of the faucet had the same sulfurous smell and reddish tint as the mineral waters for which the town was famous. It wasn't a particularly alluring setting, but I hadn't slept in twenty-four hours and longed to collapse in the bed, rusty springs and all.

First I had to deliver a set of briefing points to the secretary. I walked down to his suite, which was bigger and better lit than the other rooms, although with similarly understated décor. The State Department security agent stationed outside the door knocked and let me in. Baker was sitting at a desk reading press clips, still in his crisp white dress shirt and characteristic green tie. He smiled wearily and motioned me to sit down. The secretary's stamina and focus on preparation were legendary, but he was exhausted. A day before, he had spent nine hours in a diplomatic cage fight with Syrian president Assad. Nearly motionless as he sat in his overstuffed armchair, Assad had relished the endurance contest with Baker, spinning out long monologues about Syria's history and regional intrigues, and ordering enough tea to overwhelm even the hardiest bladders. Unintimidated and undefeated in Damascus, Baker was nevertheless worn out.

He glanced at the paper I handed him. The range of issues that he was going to discuss with Bessmertnykh would have been hard to imagine at the outset of Baker's tenure two years before. There were points on Germany's peaceful reunification in the fall of 1990, and background notes on the Soviet Union's increasingly uncertain future, with hardliners battling reformers, Gorbachev beset by independence-minded republics, and the economy in free fall. Historic negotiations were under way to lock in conventional and nuclear arms reductions. And in the Middle East, Baker was seeking to capitalize on the military triumph over Saddam Hussein and produce an Arab-Israeli peace conference, ideally with Soviet co-sponsorship.

Looking up from the memo and across the tattered furnishings of his suite, Baker asked, "Have you ever seen anything like this?" I assured him I hadn't, and started to tell him all about my new handleless toilet. "That's not what I meant," he said, unable to restrain his laughter. "I'm talking about the *world*. Have you ever seen so many things changing so damn fast?" Embarrassed, I acknowledged that I hadn't. "This sure is quite a time," he said. "I bet you won't see anything like it for as long as you stay in the Foreign Service."

He was right. For all the exceptional people and complicated challenges I have since encountered, the intersection of skilled public servants and transformative events that I witnessed in the Baker years at the State Department remains special. The end of the Cold War, the peaceful disintegration of the Soviet Union, and the successful reversal of Iraqi aggression marked a new era in international order.

President George H. W. Bush was well suited for the unprecedented changes unfolding around him, drawing on his eight years in the White House as vice president, his tenure as CIA director, and his life in the diplomatic arena, first as ambassador to the United Nations and then as envoy to China. Jim Baker was his closest friend, a wily political player, a former White House chief of staff and secretary of the treasury. Brent Scowcroft became the model for future national security advisors, forging a close bond with President Bush, managing the policy process with fairness and efficiency, and displaying consistently sound judgment and personal integrity. Dick Cheney was a strong leader at the Pentagon, well versed in national security issues as well as the dark arts of Washington politics. Colin Powell had become chairman of the Joint Chiefs of Staff, bringing with him not only a stellar record of military service but also his successful tenure as Reagan's national security advisor.

Their combination of policy skill and political acumen served our country well when the tectonic plates of geopolitics began moving in dramatic and unexpected ways. This was a team that had its inevitable imperfections and blind spots, and its share of misjudgments and disagreements, but as a group they were as steady and sound as any I ever saw. At one of those rare hinge points in history, they were realistic about the potency as well as the limits of American influence. They realized that American dominance could lead to hubris and overreach, but they had a largely affirmative view of how American leadership could shape and manage international currents, if not control them. Theirs was an example that I never forgot, and that every successive administration tried to reach.

* * *

I OWED MY entry onto the fringes of Baker's circle to my old boss, Dennis Ross. After the campaign, in which he served as Bush's foreign policy advisor, Dennis chose to go with Baker to the State Department. He judged, correctly, that the secretary's tight relationship with the president would make him the key player in American diplomacy. As director of the Policy Planning Staff, Dennis was given responsibility for two critical issues, the Soviet Union and the Middle East. Sitting on the steps of the Old Executive Office Building one sunny late November afternoon, he asked if I'd join him as his principal deputy. I accepted—uncertain about another professional leap for which I felt unprepared.

Jim Baker ran the State Department through a tight, close-knit group, working out of a string of offices along the seventh floor's "mahogany row." At one end of the wood-paneled hallway sat Deputy Secretary Larry Eagleburger, a rumpled, blunt-spoken, chain-smoking Foreign Service veteran, sometimes bursting at the seams of his aspirationally sized pinstriped suits. Baker relied on Eagleburger to manage the building and help ensure harmonious coordination with Brent Scowcroft, Eagleburger's longtime friend and colleague under Henry Kissinger. At the other end sat Bob Zoellick, who served as counselor, and later undersecretary for economic affairs. Still only in his mid-thirties, Bob was brilliant, creative, and incredibly disciplined. He was precisely the kind of talent Baker needed by his side at a moment when the shelf life of conventional wisdom often seemed to be measured in days, not years.

Sitting in an office with a connecting door to the secretary's suite was Margaret Tutwiler. Though she was nominally assistant secretary for public affairs and department spokesperson, Margaret's actual role was far more expansive. She had served under Baker in the Reagan White House and at Treasury, and was fiercely protective of his image and political flanks. Beneath her Southern graciousness, Margaret was tough as nails, with exceptional instincts about people. Just beyond her office was Bob Kimmitt's set of offices as undersecretary for political affairs, the number three job in the department. Kimmitt's roots with Baker also went back to the Reagan White House. A

West Point graduate and Vietnam veteran, Kimmitt had a quick mind and immense organizational ability. He oversaw the department's regional bureaus, and played a crucial role in managing the day-to-day policy process. Between Kimmitt and Zoellick sat Dennis and me, a few corridors removed from the rest of the Policy Planning Staff.

Baker had mastered the politics of foreign policymaking. He knew how to maneuver people and bureaucracies, and his feel for the international landscape was intuitive and pragmatic. He was a superb problem-solver, and made no pretense of being a national security intellectual or grand strategist. He was cautious by nature, and always attuned to the risks of unforeseen second- and third-order consequences. He was unchained by ideology and open to alternative views and challenges to convention. He was as good a negotiator as I ever saw, always thoroughly prepared, conscious of his leverage, sensitive to the needs and limits of those on the other side of the table, and with a lethal sense of when to close the deal.

Baker deftly used his closest advisors to run the institution and supply the innovation and imagination he sought, with just the right touch on the reins to draw on the strengths of each of them. He could rely on Zoellick and Ross for ideas and strategy; Eagleburger and Kimmitt to get things done and steer the bureaucracy; and Tutwiler to watch his back and avoid political landmines. While Baker's early, closed style produced predictable grumbling at State, it evolved considerably over time. The accelerating pace of events and his own growing appreciation of the skills of career personnel encouraged him to rely on a wider circle. Career professionals were drawn in and exhilarated by Baker's clout and success, which put State at the center of American diplomacy at a time of massive global change.

I had always been intrigued by the Policy Planning Staff, which had been launched in 1947 by Secretary George Marshall, and whose first director was George Kennan, the Foreign Service legend and architect of the Cold War strategy of containment. Marshall's charge to Kennan and the five staff members he assembled was to "develop

long-term programs for the achievement of U.S. foreign policy objectives." He added one laconic bit of advice: "Avoid trivia."[1] Kennan and
his colleagues played a pivotal role in devising the Marshall Plan, and
in laying the early foundations for American policy during the Cold
War. After Marshall left State in 1949, Kennan grew disenchanted
with both what he saw to be the militarization of his original concept
of containment and Dean Acheson's less sympathetic view of Policy
Planning's bureaucratic prerogatives. His influence waning, he soon
left the department for a sabbatical at Princeton.

The role of Policy Planning varied widely in significance after
Kennan. Subsequent directors often struggled to sustain the attention of secretaries of state, and to find an effective balance between
long-term strategy and the operational challenges that preoccupy the
secretary and the rest of the department on any given day. Successful
Planning Staffs, such as Kissinger's, did both.

Baker's Policy Planning Staff was as consequential as Kissinger's
or Marshall's. Baker treated it as his own mini–National Security
Council staff, relying on us for ambitious initiatives as the Cold War
was ending, speechwriting, tactical support on his travels, and the
briefing papers and talking points and press statements that fueled
the diplomatic machine. His relatively insular style, as well as the
drama and scope of world events, gave Policy Planning a huge (and
daunting) opportunity to shape strategies and decisions.

We eventually grew to thirty-one staff members, drawn from career ranks at State, the Pentagon, and CIA, as well as an eclectic group
from outside government. I served as Dennis's principal deputy and
alter ego, doing my best to help lead and manage the staff, and frequently traveling with Baker. The staff was full of stars—scholars like
John Ikenberry and Frank Fukuyama, whose article on "The End of
History" was about to catapult him to fame; FSOs like Russia hand
Tom Graham, the always irreverent Bill Brownfield, and my good
friend Dan Kurtzer; and civil servants like Aaron Miller, another close
friend and Middle East specialist, and Bob Einhorn, one of the gov-

ernment's premier arms control experts. We had gifted political appointees, like Andrew Carpendale, Walter Kansteiner, and John Hannah; talented if overworked speechwriters; and young interns like Derek Chollet, one of the most promising foreign policy minds of his generation.

It was a remarkable group, and a heady time. Our connection to Baker and privileged status in the department did not endear us much to the rest of the institution, so I spent a fair amount of energy trying to build a collegial reputation for our team. Still, it was no surprise when Tom Friedman, then the *New York Times* correspondent at the State Department, wrote in the fall of 1989 that we were viewed by many in the department as "a group of still-wet-behind-the-ears whippersnappers with too much authority for their tender years."[2]

* * *

WET BEHIND THE ears or not, nothing would have prepared us for the events of 1989.

Having served as central players throughout the Reagan administration, President Bush and Secretary Baker were intimately familiar with their inheritance. They knew that Central America would remain a major source of partisan strife and a potential drain on the Bush administration's foreign policy capital on the Hill. They were more optimistic about Asia, and at least initially encouraged by the trajectory of relations with China. Japan's economic boom was real, but its threat to our own economy was grossly exaggerated. The vast expanse from Afghanistan to Morocco seemed more settled than it had been in some time: The last Soviet troops departed Afghanistan on the eve of President Bush's inauguration in January 1989, the Iran-Iraq War was over, and threats to shipping and access to Gulf oil had receded. The beginning of dialogue with the PLO seemed to offer a modest new opening on the Arab-Israeli peace front, even as violence continued between Palestinians and Israelis in the West Bank and Gaza.

The central drama, however, was unfolding in the Soviet Union.

Mikhail Gorbachev was still trying to reform Soviet rule, aiming to reverse a perilous economic decline while preserving Communist Party rule at home and Soviet influence abroad. He faced mounting problems: economic decay; food shortages; a hostile old guard in the party; growing ethnic unrest and separatist sentiment in non-Russian republics; restive allies in Eastern Europe; and an increasingly disillusioned public. And yet few expected the imminent demise of the Soviet bloc, let alone the Soviet Union itself.

Reagan, the old Cold Warrior, had seemed in his later years in office to understand the desperation in Gorbachev's maneuvers and the terminal rot in the Soviet system. But Bush, Baker, Scowcroft, and their colleagues remained skeptical. They entered office determined not to be hoodwinked by Gorbachev. If he failed, it was not apparent that the Soviet Union would fail; it seemed more likely that hardliners would supplant him and restore the hard edge of the Cold War.

Bush and Baker took a careful approach to managing relations with Gorbachev during the first half of 1989. At the president's direction, Brent Scowcroft and his deputy, Bob Gates, launched a long interagency review of our policy toward the Soviet Union. As the review proceeded, Gates called for a "conscious pause" in U.S.-Soviet diplomacy. "A lot has happened in the relationship in an ad hoc way," Gates wrote. "We've been making policy—or trying to—in response to what the Soviets are doing, rather than with a sense of strategy about what we should be doing."[3] Baker was careful in his first meeting with his Soviet counterpart, Eduard Shevardnadze, that March in Vienna, and in conversations with Shevardnadze and Gorbachev in Moscow in May. He made clear to both that the Bush administration appreciated the sweep and potential of the changes they were attempting, but also emphasized that neither he nor the president appreciated being cornered by bold public proposals or acts of "one-upmanship" designed to portray Washington as the recalcitrant party. For Scowcroft and Gates, as well as for Cheney, the jury was still out on Gorbachev. As Scowcroft later put it, "Were we once again mistaking a tactical shift in the Soviet Union for a fundamental transformation of the relationship?"[4]

My colleagues and I in Policy Planning played an active role in the internal review process, but grew restive with its methodical pace, especially as events in the former Soviet bloc gathered speed in the spring of 1989. Free elections took place in the Soviet Union for the Congress of People's Deputies, giving fiery new figures like Boris Yeltsin a nationally televised platform to press for faster changes. Elections in June in Poland swept Solidarity into power, forming the first non-Communist government in postwar Eastern Europe. Later that month, Hungary removed the barbed wire along its border with Austria, and two hundred thousand Hungarians attended the reburial of Imre Nagy, the officially rehabilitated leader of the 1956 revolution. True to his "Sinatra Doctrine" of nonintervention in the political evolution of Eastern Europe, Gorbachev let the Poles and Hungarians do things their way.

By the fall of 1989, the pace of change convinced Baker that the United States could no longer afford to take the wary, risk-averse approach favored by the Pentagon and NSC staff. Their argument was essentially that the administration should hold out for Gorbachev to make more concessions as his position weakened. Baker, however, advocated a more activist policy—a systematic effort to shape a rapidly changing European landscape and lock in strategic advantages in partnership with Gorbachev and Shevardnadze. Beginning in early September, we sent Baker a series of papers that outlined alternative scenarios for the USSR if Gorbachev's reform efforts collapsed. They ranged from the gradual crumbling of the Soviet system to a military coup and authoritarian modernization, but they all underscored the urgency of the moment and the value of doing all we could to support constructive change. In a conversation in his office that autumn, Baker told us that "history won't forgive us if we miss this opportunity because we were too passive or not creative enough." With Baker's careful prodding, President Bush was coming around to this view too.

In late September, Baker hosted Shevardnadze and a large Soviet delegation for several days of talks near his modest ranch in Jackson Hole, Wyoming. The setting was spectacular, with the Tetons looming above the lodge where the talks took place, and the Snake River running nearby. Shevardnadze clearly appreciated Baker's informal hospitality and their budding friendship.

Eduard Shevardnadze was a fascinating figure, a product of the Soviet system who saw its flaws in cold relief and had the courage to try to do something about them. A proud native of Georgia, he understood the forces of nationalism bubbling within the Soviet Union better than most senior leaders. He was also unflinching in his diagnosis of the paralytic Soviet economy, and far more realistic in his assessment of the dangers of a conservative reaction against reform than Gorbachev, the ebullient optimist. On the wider international stage, Shevardnadze understood that rapidly declining Soviet leverage required an effort to build a new relationship with the United States, as a way of both stabilizing the situation at home and preserving as much of the Soviet Union's global role as possible. In Baker, Shevardnadze found a similarly pragmatic partner.

There was tangible progress on a number of issues at Jackson Hole. Shevardnadze made clear that the Soviets would no longer link significant reductions in nuclear arms to the future of missile defense, a major breakthrough that would lead eventually to the Strategic Arms Reduction Treaty in 1991, the largest and most significant arms control treaty ever negotiated. Logjams were broken on bilateral agreements on nuclear testing and chemical weapons. And the Soviet foreign minister said flatly that arms shipments to Nicaragua would cease, and that Moscow would press the Cubans to stop their shipments too.

Shevardnadze also impressed Baker with his candor on the domestic challenges that Gorbachev faced. Rather than give formulaic responses when Baker raised American concerns about possible Soviet use of force against protestors in the Baltic states or striking coal miners in Russia, Shevardnadze was blunt about the unreconstructed views of some in the Soviet leadership, and the risks of violence. He resisted Baker's suggestion that Gorbachev begin to "cut loose" the Baltic states, explaining his worries about the chain reaction that might cause in other parts of the USSR. The overall directness and depth of their conversations solidified Baker's activist inclination, and helped prepare the ground for Bush's summit meeting with Gorbachev in Malta that December.

Baker went on to lay out the administration's evolving approach in a series of speeches and public statements in October. He argued that perestroika's success would be determined by the Soviets themselves, but that it created an historic opportunity for a new relationship with the United States based on greater "points of mutual advantage." Advances in arms control and resolution of regional conflicts were obvious examples; Baker also offered technical assistance in support of Soviet economic reforms, and painted a wider picture of "a Europe whole and free."

Meanwhile, it was hard to keep track of events in Eastern Europe. On November 9, a bungled attempt to relax restrictions on travel to the West resulted in the fall of the Berlin Wall. As Dennis Ross and I sat in his office that Thursday afternoon watching the riveting CNN footage of Berliners hammering chunks out of the wall, we could see that the world we had known was changing—we just could have never predicted how much, how far, or how fast. Within weeks, popular movements toppled autocrats in Bulgaria, Czechoslovakia, and Romania. We tried to think ahead, and in a subsequent Policy Planning paper laid out a series of initiatives aimed at "consolidating the revolutions of 1989 in Eastern Europe."[5] Noting that "the postcommunist reconstruction of Eastern Europe is no less challenging than the post-Nazi reconstruction of Western Europe," we pressed for concrete programs of technical and economic support, in cooperation with our European allies, and without provoking the Soviets.

By the time Gorbachev and Bush had their shipboard summit in

stormy Mediterranean seas off Malta a month after the fall of the
wall, the Soviet empire was no more. Gorbachev was matter-of-fact,
telling Bush that they were "simply doomed to dialogue, coordination
and cooperation. There is no other choice."[6] Building on the Jackson
Hole discussions, they agreed to major nuclear and conventional
forces cuts. Most interestingly, they signaled the possibility of a reunited, democratic Germany—a reality that had seemed unimaginable for the better part of four decades.

Nowhere was Baker's diplomatic agility and foresight more evident than in the rapid sequence of events that led, in less than a year,
from the tearing down of the Berlin Wall to Germany's formal reunification, within NATO, in October 1990. In discussions in Policy
Planning in mid-November 1989, Frank Fukuyama proposed that
Baker take the initiative and frame a series of principles on German
reunification. In a subsequent memo to the secretary, Frank stressed
several basic points: Germans—not outside powers—should determine their own future; reunification should occur in the context of
Germany's continued commitment to NATO, taking into account the
legal role and responsibility of the four Allied powers (France, the
United Kingdom, the United States, and the Soviet Union); the process should be gradual, peaceful, and step-by-step; and the Helsinki
Act provisions on the inviolability of borders should apply. These
early American principles helped set the tone and shape of the subsequent diplomatic process. They also helped Baker address Germany's
determination to make its own choices about its future; the early
skepticism of the French and British about any rapid move to reunification; and the obvious worries of the Soviets about the strategic
consequences of a united Germany. Shaping the principles of policy
debate, I learned, is often the first step toward winning it.

Baker also had to overcome more cautious sentiments within the
White House and other parts of the administration. One paper from
the European Affairs Bureau at State counseled Baker to avoid being

"stampeded" into premature diplomatic initiatives. Zoellick and Ross strongly disagreed. For several years, Zoellick kept the memo on his desk and used it to remind me, only partly in jest, of the overly cautious mindset of the Foreign Service. Baker hardly needed to be persuaded. Given the breathtaking pace of change in 1989, he had no interest in sitting on the sidelines.

We spent much of the Christmas holiday working to devise a framework that would translate Fukuyama's principles into a practical process. The memo that resulted outlined a "Two Plus Four" process, in which West Germany and East Germany would shape internal arrangements, and the four Allied powers would help guide external arrangements. Dennis sent it to Baker in late January 1990, and the secretary quickly realized the utility of the concept—the first part addressed the needs of the Germans (and the concerns of some in the administration), and the second addressed those of the Soviets, French, and British. With President Bush's support, Baker sold the concept to German chancellor Helmut Kohl and foreign minister Hans-Dietrich Genscher in early February, agreeing to use Two Plus Four negotiations to press for rapid German unification and full NATO membership, while reassuring the Soviets that NATO would not be extended any farther to the east, and would be transformed to reflect the end of the Cold War and potential partnership with the Soviet Union.

In meetings a few days later with Shevardnadze and Gorbachev in Moscow, Baker won their initial support, and began the effort to ease their resistance to membership of a unified Germany in NATO. Baker maintained that Soviet interests would be more secure with a united Germany wrapped up in NATO, rather than a Germany untied to NATO and perhaps eventually with its own nuclear weapons. He also said that there would be no extension of NATO's jurisdiction or forces "one inch to the east" of the borders of a reunified Germany. The Russians took him at his word and would feel betrayed by NATO enlargement in the years that followed, even though the pledge was never formalized and was made before the breakup of the Soviet Union. It was an episode that would be relitigated for many years to come.

The Two Plus Four approach was broadly blessed at a meeting of foreign ministers in Ottawa in mid-February and announced by Baker and Genscher. In May, Gorbachev conceded to Bush that Germany should be able to choose its own alliance arrangements. Increasingly beleaguered by unrest and economic stagnation at home, with violence and mounting separatist movements in the Baltics and the South Caucasus, Gorbachev had dwindling leverage. Bush provided him with a series of informal assurances about the nonthreatening evolution of NATO, reinforcing Baker's earlier commitments. In July, Kohl and Gorbachev announced a sweeping agreement on German reunification, within NATO. On October 3, 1990, the new, united Germany formally emerged.

*   *   *

GIVEN THE HISTORIC drama unfolding in Europe, it was not surprising that Middle East policy had taken a backseat during Bush's first eighteen months in office. That all changed at the beginning of August 1990, when Saddam Hussein invaded Kuwait.

All of us in the administration underestimated Saddam's sense of both risk and opportunity. He had ruined Iraq's economy during eight years of war with Iran, which left the urban infrastructure in a shambles, produced a war debt of more than $100 billion, and cost half a million Iraqi lives. Neither Kuwait nor Saudi Arabia had any interest in writing off his debt or in conspiring to raise oil prices. Despite his brutally repressive grip, Saddam worried that a bleak economic outlook would make Iraqis restive. At the same time, he saw opportunity in popular trends in the region. It wasn't hard to cloak himself as a militant Arab nationalist, first the defender of the Arab world against Persian theocrats, and now the champion of Arabs oppressed by corrupt rulers beholden to the Americans and soft on Israel. Moreover, he assumed the end of the Cold War meant Washington would have less incentive to intervene in the Middle East, and could be warned off with a sufficient display of strength.

America's Arab partners were not much more astute about Saddam. President Hosni Mubarak, King Hussein, and King Fahd all had encouraged Bush to reach out to the Iraqi dictator. With the end of the Iran-Iraq War, their view was that Saddam would naturally turn his attention to domestic recovery and modernization. Iraq would remain a bulwark against revolutionary Iran, and a complicated neighbor, but not a short-term threat. During his first year in office, Bush cautiously probed the possibilities with Baghdad. The United States extended credit guarantees for Iraqi grain purchases, and Baker met with his Iraqi counterpart, the wily Tariq Aziz. But by the spring of 1990, the secretary had begun to take a harder view, especially after Saddam made a vituperative speech threatening to "burn Israel." Ross told Baker that it was an "illusion" to think that Saddam could be a reliable partner.

Meanwhile, Saddam resurrected a long-standing border dispute with the Kuwaitis, and accused them of waging "economic warfare." By midsummer, he had begun to mass troops on the Kuwaiti border. The allure of Kuwait for Saddam was obvious. Its annual GDP was nearly half the size of Iraq's; with its oil fields, Saddam could control more than 10 percent of global oil supply and quickly be in a position to write off his war debt. The risks seemed modest—the Kuwaiti military would be no match for his combat-hardened forces.

Mubarak and other Arab leaders continued to assure Bush that Saddam was just bluffing and seeking to improve his hand in negotiations with the Kuwaitis over their border dispute. When Saddam unexpectedly summoned U.S. ambassador April Glaspie for a meeting on July 25, she reiterated formal American policy: The United States did not take a position on the merits of Iraqi-Kuwaiti territorial differences, but did certainly take the position that they had to be resolved peacefully. Afterward, in her cable to Washington, Glaspie

concluded that the United States had "fully caught Saddam's attention" and that he had committed to opening negotiations with Kuwait soon.[7] She was widely criticized later for not being emphatic
enough with Saddam about the consequences of the use of force, but
that was unfair. No one expected Saddam to launch a full-scale invasion, and President Bush sent a letter to Saddam on July 28 that was
not much tougher in tone or substance than Glaspie's exchange.

Undeterred, Saddam sent his military across the border into Kuwait on August 2, occupied the entire country within two days, and
immediately declared Kuwait to be Iraq's "nineteenth province."
Baker had been in Siberia the day before, meeting Shevardnadze. He
shared with Shevardnadze intelligence reports of the Iraqi military
buildup, as well as his mounting concern, but Shevardnadze was as
dismissive of the chances of an actual invasion as Arab leaders were.
Baker then flew on to Mongolia for a previously scheduled visit, and
was there when the Iraqi attack began. Ross advised him to travel
directly to Moscow and issue a joint statement with Shevardnadze
condemning Saddam's aggression. Nothing would carry more diplomatic impact, or symbolize more vividly how much U.S.-Soviet relations had changed. On August 3, barely twenty-four hours after the
invasion began, Shevardnadze and Baker stood together at Vnukovo
Airport outside the Soviet capital and denounced the attack. As Baker
later wrote, that moment really did mark the end of the Cold War.

On August 4, Policy Planning made a first attempt to try to frame
what was at stake. Entitled "The First Post–Cold War Crisis," our note
read, "Saddam believes that the end of the Cold War has fundamentally changed the basic strategic calculations of both superpowers.
Their main purpose for competition in Southwest Asia has been reduced and with it the priority they will place on preserving their cold
war alliances. Part of the reason for the shift in Soviet and American
policy, Saddam figures, is the dramatically increased cost of power
projection and active involvement in regional conflicts. Saddam, like
Khomeini ten years ago, is convinced that the myth of American

power is far greater in the Middle East than its practical bite, and that if confronted with real costs, Washington will not stay the course."[8]

Our paper continued, "Saddam is also banking on what he believes is a fundamental trend in Arab attitudes and politics. The process of change in Eastern Europe has excited many Arab intellectuals and the economic frustrations of boom and bust oil revenues along with urbanization has provided Islamist and nationalist demagogues with a ready mass base. Saddam is appealing to nationalist radical symbols, partly to outflank the Islamist radicals, and is playing to a widespread mass inclination to blame the U.S. for their political and economic troubles. His calculation is that any Arab regime that has to depend on the U.S. for protection is vulnerable to internal insurrection."

Our prescription was straightforward. We needed to defend Saudi Arabia, and then reverse Saddam's aggression. In a second, more detailed memo two weeks later, we underscored the argument: "With all that is now at stake in the Gulf, we cannot afford to settle for an outcome less than complete Iraqi withdrawal from Kuwait and restoration of Kuwait's legitimate government."[9] The paper laid out a two-step approach: First, bring maximum multilateral political and economic pressure to bear on Saddam; then follow up with a sustained program of containment to deny him any escape from the domestic consequences of having failed in Kuwait and capitulated to the Iranians.

If Saddam did not back down, the second purpose of our diplomacy would be to serve as a foundation for international support for military action against Iraq. Being perceived to have exhausted all reasonable nonmilitary options would be critical to building and maintaining such support. Inability to pressure Saddam to withdraw by means short of force would not be a "failure" of diplomacy—it would rather be the shrewdest kind of diplomacy, creating the basis for an international coalition that could achieve Iraqi withdrawal from Kuwait and manage the aftermath.

The dilemma we faced, however, was that we did not have much time, since Saddam was cleverly exploiting potential fissures in the international consensus. President Bush had succinctly laid out the American bottom line in a statement to the press soon after Saddam's invasion: The occupation of Kuwait, he said, "will not stand." He and his team then moved to accomplish that goal, with a skill and drive as fine as any example I saw in government. Dick Cheney flew to Saudi Arabia, where he announced a military operation to defend the Saudis, dubbed Operation Desert Shield. Colin Powell and his commander in the field, General Norman Schwarzkopf, began mobilizing U.S. forces for deployment in the region. Brent Scowcroft and Bob Gates managed an impressive interagency process and pushed the strategy forward. Secretary Baker coordinated with Scowcroft, Cheney, and Powell on building a massive international coalition, attracting military and financial contributions, marshaling economic pressure on Saddam, and creating a powerful diplomatic foundation for action. At the United Nations, Ambassador Tom Pickering expertly set in motion a series of Security Council resolutions, first condemning the Iraqi attack, then putting in place economic sanctions unprecedented in their scope, which would eventually cut off nearly all of Iraq's exports and external sources of revenue.

I joined Baker on his September "tin cup" mission, covering nine countries in eleven days. He ultimately secured more than $50 billion in contributions, essentially defraying the entire cost of the U.S. military operation. Baker's style was no-nonsense. He had a checklist of what he needed, and a rapidly growing U.S. military deployment in the Gulf to underline his credibility. In Jeddah, King Fahd dispensed with typical Arab indirection and told Baker the Saudis would provide whatever he wanted. The Kuwaiti amir, huddled with his family and government in Saudi exile, was just as receptive. The Turks immediately shut down the pipeline through which much of Iraqi oil exports flowed, and Baker arranged a substantial World Bank loan to help cushion the effects on Ankara. In Egypt, President Mubarak pledged to send Egyptian troops to join the coalition. While their military value was negligible, the symbolic power of Arab contingents alongside U.S. forces was considerable.

Baker also visited Damascus on that trip, beginning a series of encounters with the cunning and ruthless Hafez al-Assad, Syria's president since 1971. Unsentimental about Saddam, a rival of many years from the same rough school of Arab leadership, Assad was impressed by the display of raw American power unfolding in the Gulf. Assad indicated a receptiveness to joining the coalition, and was clearly intrigued by Baker. He was even more intrigued by the prospect of sticking it to Saddam.

In Bonn, Kohl and Genscher, already in political debt to Bush and Baker for their support for German reunification, promised financial support. Baker joined Bush in Helsinki for another summit with Gorbachev. The Soviet leader, struggling increasingly with the challenge of holding the USSR together, saw the value of using his relationship with Bush to preserve a central diplomatic role despite the Soviet Union's waning international prestige.

In November, I accompanied Baker on an even longer trip. This one covered twelve countries on three continents over eighteen days. Its principal aim was to shore up support for a decisive Security Council resolution to authorize the use of force if Saddam did not withdraw fully and unconditionally from Kuwait. Traveling on Baker's aircraft, which had been Lyndon Johnson's Air Force One, was always an intense experience.

Baker had a small private cabin up front, with a tiny desk and a couch on which he could barely stretch out. The rest of his senior staff sat in the adjacent cabin, which featured a horseshoe of couches around a large table, and the oversized chair that Johnson had often used when meeting with his aides. The pace was frenetic, with short sessions with Baker to review what had just transpired in the last stop and plan for the next one, and the rest of the flight spent making calls to Washington, preparing talking points for upcoming meetings, and drafting short reports for Baker to send to the president. Sleep was rare.

In the next cabin sat an overworked administrative team and diplomatic security detail, juggling all the constantly shifting logistics. At the back of the plane sat the State Department press corps—a particularly accomplished group, including Pulitzer Prize winners like Tom Friedman and *The Washington Post*'s David Hoffman. Baker and Margaret Tutwiler were masters at managing the press, respectful of their role and expertise. They knew that the relationship was a two-way street, and often tested ideas and formulas in off-the-record sessions on the plane. The department press corps, in turn, knew that Baker was a formidable figure at the heart of history in the making, and treated him with the same respect he showed them.

By the end of that grueling trip, Baker had secured substantial support for what became UN Security Council Resolution 678, passed on November 29, authorizing the use of "all necessary means" to force Saddam out of Kuwait if he did not withdraw by January 15, 1991. The Soviets joined the United States and ten other countries voting in favor of the resolution. The Chinese abstained, uneasy about the use of force and miffed that Baker had not visited Beijing. Cuba and Yemen voted against. Baker, who had spent several hours in Sanaa trying to woo Yemeni president Ali Abdullah Saleh, warned that this would be "the most expensive vote the Yemenis ever cast." He wasn't kidding. When Saleh declined to support the resolution, the State Department moved quickly to slash assistance to Yemen by 90 percent.

Saddam immediately rejected the UNSC ultimatum, but agreed to a meeting in early January in Geneva between Tariq Aziz and Baker, a last chance to end the crisis peacefully. I had never seen so much drama and anxiety surrounding a single meeting, and haven't since. War was imminent, with more than half a million coalition troops now assembled near the Kuwaiti border, the most impressive and powerful international coalition since World War II.

There were worries about significant casualties, especially given the potential for use of chemical weapons by Saddam, who had deployed them in the past against the Iranians and his own Kurdish population. There were also fears that Saddam would choose the moment in Geneva to have Aziz offer a partial withdrawal while retaining control of the disputed oil fields along the border. That would be unacceptable under the terms of the Security Council resolutions, but it could undermine congressional support and throw a wrench into the coalition, likely causing the Soviets and others to press for a further pause on military action. The coalition we had worked so hard to build could easily unravel.

Baker's preparations for the meeting were characteristically exhaustive. His talking points were the product of extensive consultation in Washington. I spent nearly the entire plane ride to Geneva working with Dennis on the final version. Baker never read such points verbatim, but given the gravity of the moment, he planned to stick closely to the script. He had virtually memorized his terse introductory remarks, which ended with him warning that he hoped Aziz understood that this was the "last, best chance for peace." Even his handshake with Aziz across the table at the start of the meeting had been well thought through; he was determined not to offer the conventional diplomatic smile, and kept a grim expression for the cameras. Aziz, usually full of bravado, looked tense.

Baker was carrying a long letter from Bush to Saddam, which among other things made clear that the United States would reserve the right to use any weapons in its arsenal if the Iraqis resorted to chemical weapons or any other weapons of mass destruction. Baker summarized the contents of the letter, but Aziz refused to take it or read it, perhaps unsure of how Saddam would react if he brought such an ultimatum home. After the meeting ended, with no sign of flexibility from the Iraqis, Baker addressed the biggest assemblage of international media I had ever seen. "Regrettably," he began, "in over six hours of talks, I heard nothing today that suggested to me any

Iraqi flexibility whatsoever on complying with the UN Security Council resolutions." War was coming.

On January 12, Congress voted to authorize the use of force. Thanks in large part to the international support that Bush and Baker had mobilized, Saddam's stubborn brutality and intransigence, and polling showing the support of two out of three Americans, skeptical American legislators had come around. On January 16, just after the deadline set by the UN Security Council had expired, the United States launched a massive air attack on Baghdad. I watched it on television at home that evening with Lisa, still uncertain about where this would all lead, but confident in the U.S. military, and proud of all that Bush and Baker had achieved in a classic model of diplomatic coalition-building.

While an overwhelming display of U.S. technological superiority, the air campaign still had its anxious moments. Coalition forces made a high priority of eliminating Iraq's Scud missile capability, amid fears that Saddam would launch warheads loaded with chemical weapons. Inevitably, some Iraqi missiles struck Israel, which Saddam wanted desperately to bait into retaliation, thus expanding the conflict into an Arab-Israeli war and threatening Arab support for the coalition. Bush and Baker had worked closely with Israeli prime minister Yitzhak Shamir to defend against Scud attacks, and to avoid walking into the trap that Saddam was trying to set. Larry Eagleburger made several trips to Israel to urge restraint. I accompanied him on one of those missions and admired the gruff ease with which he connected with Shamir and other senior Israelis—and watched with amusement when he removed his gas mask during missile raid alarms to take alternating puffs from his cigarette and asthma inhaler.

Showing political courage, Shamir did not respond to the missile attacks, trusting that the Americans would quickly crush the Iraqi military. The subsequent ground operation in late February lasted barely one hundred hours. Saddam's forces were routed, expelled from Kuwait, and fleeing headlong back into Iraq when President Bush ended hostilities. Bush's decision, unanimously supported by his chief advisors, reflected remarkable discipline. It was certainly tempting to continue to pummel the Iraqi military, chase them all the way to Baghdad, and perhaps bring down Saddam's regime. Bush and Baker knew, however, that the coalition mandate, codified by the UN Security Council, was to push the Iraqis out of Kuwait and restore the legitimate government there. Reaching beyond that goal ran the risk of disintegrating the coalition, with all the collateral damage that might do to shaping post–Cold War order. As Baker put it to a few of us in a conversation in his office after he returned from the White House on February 27, the last day of the ground operation, "Sometimes the most important test of leadership is *not* to do something, even when it looks really damn easy. Overreaching is what gets people in trouble."

Despite the focus on the immediate military and diplomatic priorities, we had tried to help Baker think ahead about the long-term opportunities and risks that would undoubtedly emerge after Saddam was forced to withdraw from Kuwait. On the Gulf itself, we argued in a November 1990 paper that a freestanding balance of power among Iraq, Iran, and the Gulf Cooperation Council states was implausible after the crisis.[10] We'd have to contain Saddam, and continue to provide support to the Saudis and their Gulf Arab partners. A little too hopefully, we suggested that "this crisis may increase the opportunity to improve U.S.-Iranian relations." In another piece, we highlighted the wider U.S. regional stake "in quietly encouraging our friends to recognize that broader political participation and greater economic openness are important if the Arab world is to share in the progress sweeping other parts of the world." We proposed an Arab regional development bank as one way to stimulate change. And we laid special emphasis on the potential for renewing Arab-Israeli negotiations, with Saddam's brand of radical Arab nationalism discredited and our own regional and global influence virtually un-challenged. Though wary of all the pitfalls, Baker was intrigued by what might be possible on that front.

* * *

ON THE WALL outside his office in Houston, former secretary Baker keeps several rows of framed newspaper cartoons. They depict, with varying degrees of cynicism, his relentless pursuit of a breakthrough on Middle East peace following the Gulf War, over nine trips to the region from March to October 1991—a reminder of how many people doubted that he could succeed, and of how improbable the whole ef-fort seemed.

Faced with the monumental demands of dealing with the Soviet Union and Europe at the end of the Cold War, Baker avoided getting drawn into Arab-Israeli issues. In the Middle East, he saw few op-portunities and lots of headaches. He had little patience for the end-less arguments about peace process theology. His early experience with Prime Minister Shamir, a stubborn Israeli nationalist deeply suspicious of anything that might weaken Israel's grip on the West Bank and Gaza, had been unhappy. In May 1989, Baker had told the annual American Israel Public Affairs Committee (AIPAC) confer-ence in Washington that "now is the time to lay aside, once and for all, the unrealistic vision of a greater Israel." Shamir was not amused. When Shamir's protégé, then–deputy foreign minister Bibi Netan-yahu, accused the administration of "lies and distortions," it was Ba-ker's turn to be unamused. He banned Netanyahu from the State Department for the next eighteen months.

The Arabs did not do much to endear themselves to Baker, either. The U.S. dialogue with the PLO opened at the end of the Reagan administration had been stilted and unproductive. When a radical Palestinian faction staged an unsuccessful attack along the Israeli coast near Tel Aviv in May 1990, Baker was irate at Arafat's refusal to condemn the raid, or even distance himself from the Palestinian group that was responsible. Shortly thereafter, Bush and Baker suspended the dialogue indefinitely. Baker told my colleague Aaron Miller, "If I had another life, I'd want to be a Middle East specialist just like you, because it would mean guaranteed permanent employment." Beneath the sarcasm, Baker's lack of interest in getting dragged into interminable problems was unambiguous. He hated being "diddled," and the Middle East seemed overrun with diddlers.

After the Gulf War in the spring of 1991, however, Baker saw an opening. The defeat of Saddam Hussein boosted Arab moderates. Mubarak felt more secure. The Saudis and the Gulf Arabs owed the Bush administration their survival. Assad was sobered by the steep decline of his Soviet patrons, and impressed by American military and diplomatic prowess. A connoisseur of power, he understood that the ground was shifting in the region. King Hussein of Jordan was anxious to get back in good graces with Bush and Baker after staying aloof from the Desert Storm coalition. Arafat's sympathy for Saddam left him in similarly difficult circumstances, cut off from Arab financial support and worried that he was losing touch with Palestinians in the West Bank and Gaza who were engaged in a fitful uprising against Israeli occupation. His leverage was decreasing too.

Yitzhak Shamir was uneasy about the outcome of the war. On the one hand, Saddam's ability to threaten Israel had been dealt a massive blow. On the other, however, Shamir was anxious about where newfound ties with key Arab states might take the U.S. administration. Gorbachev was increasingly consumed with the collapsing Soviet Union, and had little alternative to cooperating with Washington on the Middle East, so long as Soviet pride of place was preserved. All of this added up to a moment of diplomatic opportunity that was exceedingly rare in the Middle East. As Dennis Ross argued to Baker, "We've just seen an earthquake. We have to move before the earth resettles, because it will, and it never takes long."

There was also an element of pride and competitiveness in Baker's thinking. Crucial as his role had been in constructing the Desert

Storm coalition, the war was naturally a moment for presidential leadership. President Bush was center stage, the full might of the American military beside him. Now Baker had before him a chance to win the peace, to show what American diplomacy could accomplish in the wake of sweeping military successes. For the consummate problem-solver, what bigger challenge was there than Arab-Israeli peace?

Baker was not especially interested in the arcane details of Arab-Israeli issues, or the history and culture of the region. He had an enormously retentive mind for what he needed to know to navigate a negotiation and bridge differences, and a gift for managing complicated personalities. He lowballed public expectations, always convinced that it was better to underpromise and overdeliver. His refrain to those of us immersed in his peacemaking effort was that we had to "crawl before we walk, and walk before we run." Baker's near-term goal was not to secure a comprehensive peace agreement, but rather to use the leverage that the United States had, before it evaporated, and set in motion a process that would for the first time bring the Israelis and all the Arab parties into direct negotiations with one another, within a framework that might sustain the process and perhaps even eventually produce substantive accords.

He had in mind a two-track approach, tilted more to the Israeli insistence on separate bilateral talks with each of their Arab adversaries than the historic Arab argument for an international conference that could impose binding outcomes on the parties. In a nod to Arab and international opinion, the process would start with a meeting of all the parties, which would simply launch talks rather than prescribe their end states. Then there would be a set of individual negotiations: Syrian-Israeli, Lebanese-Israeli, and talks between Israel and a delegation of Jordanians and Palestinians not formally connected to the PLO. The conference would launch a second track, engaging all the parties as well as key global players on wider regional challenges like water, environment, and economic development. Consistent with discussions with Gorbachev in the run-up to the war, the Soviets would nominally co-sponsor the initial conference and the ensuing process.

Given his earlier frustrations with Shamir, Baker realized that the key was to create a structure so attuned to Israeli concerns that the prime minister couldn't back out. Baker had to persuade the Syrians to temper their animosity toward Israel, and cajole the Palestinians into swallowing hard and accepting conditions for their participation that they resented deeply.

Baker set out on the first of his post–Gulf War trips just after President Bush's triumphal address to a joint session of Congress on the evening of March 6. His broad aim was to outline his concept for reviving Arab-Israeli negotiations, and his tactical goal was to harvest the debt owed the United States for the defeat of Saddam, especially by the Gulf Arabs, and show Shamir that the Arabs were prepared to engage him directly.

The scene when we landed in Kuwait City on the early afternoon of March 9 was unforgettable. The airport's main terminal was pockmarked by shellfire, with broken glass and rubble everywhere. When we helicoptered north to see some of the damage done by the Iraqis in their scorched-earth withdrawal, the sky turned black. Saddam's forces had set fire to five hundred Kuwaiti oil wells, and billowing dark smoke was everywhere, the air thick with soot and flames shooting upward across the apocalyptic horizon.

The rest of the trip was modestly encouraging. In Cairo, Hosni Mubarak was exuberant about the way in which Bush and the coalition had humbled Saddam. "Jim," he boomed across his spacious office, "I don't think Shamir will change, but this is your best chance." Shamir himself was cautious, especially about the proposed opening conference, and insistent that Palestinian representatives had to be part of a joint delegation with Jordan and unconnected to the PLO. The secretary had a useful introductory discussion with a group of ten Palestinians from the West Bank and Gaza, led by Feisal Husseini, a well-respected member of a prominent East Jerusalem family, and Hanan Ashrawi, a Ramallah academic whose emergence as a secular, nonviolent female leader fluent in the language of the street as well as diplomacy made a strong impression. Baker stopped in Damascus to see Assad again, and found him wary but ready to engage. In Moscow, the Soviets told the secretary that they were quite interested in co-sponsorship of the process; Baker made clear in return that Moscow would need to first restore full diplomatic relations with Israel.

That first trip demonstrated Baker's skill in managing both regional personalities and his own personnel. On the latter, he relied on a tight Middle East team who accompanied him throughout his 1991 shuttle diplomacy. Dennis Ross was Baker's senior advisor, and then there were three more junior aides: Dan Kurtzer, Aaron Miller, and me. We churned out massive quantities of talking points for Baker's meetings, strategy papers for his shuttles, public statements, and cables. It was Margaret Tutwiler who coined the term "food processors" to describe our endless churn. It probably didn't do much for our street credibility as hard-nosed diplomats when the phrase made it into a *Washington Post* profile of our work later that fall, but it certainly captured the grinding rhythm of serious diplomatic enterprises.

Baker understood from the outset that building personal trust with a complicated and often intractable set of regional players would be critical. The three most crucial to the effort were Shamir, Assad, and the Palestinians. In constructing a process largely to the Israeli prime minister's specifications, Baker worked assiduously to win the confidence of the ever-suspicious Shamir. They were an unlikely pair—the smooth, artful Texas patrician whittling away methodically at the reservations of the hardline Israeli political veteran, whose soft-spoken demeanor belied a steely resistance to compromise and an abiding mistrust of anyone who might try to lure him down that path. But they developed a genuine, if sometimes grudging, mutual respect, without which the Madrid Peace Conference would never have happened.

Delivering Hafez al-Assad and Palestinian representatives to the negotiating table, on terms that Shamir could stomach, was the key to cutting off his diplomatic routes of escape. Baker spent dozens of hours with Assad in 1991. Their meetings were tests of stamina, will, and ingenuity, with Assad filibustering and probing constantly for weaknesses in Baker's arguments or assurances. Alternately tough and empathetic, sometimes raising his voice in exasperation or threatening to abandon his peacemaking effort, Baker clearly established himself in Assad's eyes as a formidable and worthy negotiating partner. Assad regularly stretched Baker's patience to the breaking point, but came to trust the secretary's commitment and pragmatic disposition.

The same proved true of the Palestinians with whom Baker wrestled over those eight roller-coaster months. Husseini, Ashrawi, and their colleagues were caught in a vise. Their options tightly limited by Israeli occupation, they were further constrained by their political subordination to the PLO leadership in Tunisia, popular suspicions in the West Bank and Gaza, and the difficult parameters that Baker insisted upon for Palestinian representation in negotiations. They had no easy choices, but they came to trust Baker enough to take the chance that once engaged in direct negotiations, even if nominally part of a joint delegation with the Jordanians, they could translate their weak hand into tangible progress toward self-determination.

With Shamir, Assad, and the Palestinians, Baker was ecumenical in his candor. In one of the many pungent Texas expressions that he introduced into the Middle East political lexicon, he threatened to "leave a dead cat on the doorstep" of any party that balked at the diplomatic possibility he was offering. As the months wore on, their worries about being blamed by Baker for failure grew, even as their suspicions about one another remained intense. None of them were eager to call his bluff.

Baker made two more trips to the region in April. The first included a stop along the Turkish border with Iraq, where hundreds of thousands of Kurdish refugees were camped, fleeing Saddam's post-war repression and sorely in need of assistance and protection. That sea of humanity made a powerful impression on all of us, and Baker reinforced the inclination of President Bush to do more to help. The scenes from his April talks with the Arabs and Israelis on that trip were less spectacular, but similarly worrisome. Shamir still took issue with any form of United Nations participation in the peace conference that Baker was proposing, and questioned whether UN Security Council Resolution 242, which had shortly after the 1967 war set out the basic formula of land for peace, should be the basis for negotiations. Assad, on the other hand, insisted on a clear UN role to provide "international legitimacy," a continuing role for the conference as the two tracks of negotiations unfolded, and a provision that the U.S. and Soviet co-sponsors would be expected to "guarantee" outcomes.

The Palestinians still maintained that they should be able to determine their own representatives, balking at Baker's position that they had to be part of a joint Jordanian-Palestinian delegation, and not include members either formally affiliated with the PLO or resident in East Jerusalem. Although King Hussein, anxious to get back in American good graces, pledged full Jordanian support for the process, and Mubarak remained a stalwart backer, the Saudis had begun to slide back into their familiar risk-averse, pre–Desert Storm position, and dragged their feet on whether they'd participate in the conference and the follow-on multilateral track negotiations. Baker left his last set of discussions, which included both the nine-hour "bladder diplomacy" episode with Assad and an equally frustrating stop in Jerusalem, increasingly concerned about whether the process would ever get off the ground.

In several more trips in late spring and summer, Baker steadily chipped away at the remaining resistance. There were predictable fits and starts in trying to persuade the Gulf Arabs to deliver on their commitments. When the Saudis pulled up short of making an expected announcement of their participation at one point, Baker pounded his hand on his desk and said in exasperation, "Those guys could fuck up a two-car funeral."

Slowly but surely, the parties were coming around. In May, the Saudis agreed to attend the conference, an historic first. We found a recipe for the conference structure that Shamir and Assad both reluctantly accepted, with a UN observer role. Assad was impressed by Baker's offer of a U.S. security guarantee of whatever Israeli-Syrian border was negotiated, complete with the possibility of American forces on the Golan Heights. Assad indicated formally in a letter to Bush in July that he would participate. Finally, the Palestinians agreed to attend under the terms that Baker had outlined.

Baker returned to the region for an eighth time in October. He had scheduled a meeting in Jerusalem on the afternoon of October 18 with the new Soviet foreign minister, Boris Pankin, after which we planned to issue the invitations to the peace conference. The parties were still nervous and important details still unresolved. The Palestinians, in particular, were having difficulty producing the list of fourteen names for their part of the joint delegation that they had promised, so that Baker could make sure they met the agreed criteria.

Baker met with Husseini, Ashrawi, and several of their colleagues at the very un–Middle Eastern hour of 7:45 that morning at the old U.S. Consulate General facility on Nablus Road in East Jerusalem. He was unhappy about the last-minute snag, and tired of the wrangling. Baker understood how hard it was for the Palestinians to navigate their own leadership in Tunis, and he put on a masterful performance that morning. He implored Husseini and Ashrawi to pull themselves together for one final push across the goal line. He was direct about the choice the Palestinians faced. The only way they could regain control over the West Bank and Gaza was through negotiations with the Israelis, and if the deck was stacked against them in procedural terms, that was still the best they could hope for. Arafat had made a major mistake taking sides with Saddam, and this was the price. The United States was not going to deliver an outcome for the Palestinians; they'd have to work hard through negotiations, but the Bush administration would ensure a fair process. As he gathered the Palestinian delegation around him at the end of the meeting, he gave them one final pep talk. "Lots of people like to say that you never miss an opportunity to miss an opportunity," Baker said. "Show them that they're wrong."

By midafternoon, however, the Palestinians were still struggling. It was clear that they weren't going to give Baker any more than seven names that day, and it was uncertain that they could agree on the remaining seven. The dead cat was not far from their doorstep.

The mood in Baker's suite at the King David Hotel was tense. Foreign Minister Pankin sat forlornly at one end of the living room, with little to say or do but wait for Baker to make his next move. Tired and disappointed, Baker said he was inclined to postpone the conference. Margaret Tutwiler started preparing a short statement to inform the horde of reporters gathered on the first floor of the hotel.

Baker had always encouraged Dan, Aaron, and me to speak up, especially when we had dissenting views. The three of us quickly huddled in Baker's cramped walk-in closet, and decided to make a case to move ahead with the invitation. With Pankin and his aides looking on passively, every bit the disoriented representatives of a fallen superpower, Dan laid out our concerns to Baker. It was true that there was no guarantee that the Palestinians would produce the required names, and there was a real risk if a premature invitation led to embarrassment. On the other hand, there was at least as big a risk that the momentum Baker had built in recent months would stall. The other parties were perfectly capable of throwing more wrenches into the works, and the whole effort could collapse. Aaron and I seconded Dan's recommendation that we take the plunge. Baker listened carefully, and said he wanted to think about it for a few minutes. He consulted with Pankin, as much for the sake of form as anything else, and then opted to issue the invitation. The Palestinians soon got their act together and came up with the remaining names.

The Madrid Peace Conference opened less than two weeks later, on the morning of October 30. There was no shortage of drama in the air; I still recall how angry Baker looked when Syrian foreign minister Farouk al-Sharaa, in a move that was gratuitously nasty even by the standards of the Assad regime, paused in a rebuttal to hold up a 1947 British Mandate wanted poster of Shamir, who had fought for Israel's independence as a member of the notorious Stern Gang. Usually the picture of self-control, Baker looked at that moment as if he wanted to throw his gavel across the room at Sharaa.

There were a number of other fits and starts over the next few days, but eventually each of the bilateral negotiations got under way, and the multilateral talks with a wider group of regional and international players started not long thereafter. Through all the ups and downs, we never lost sight of just how extraordinary it was to gather all these players and personalities and get them to agree to what each had for so long insisted was nonnegotiable.

The election of Yitzhak Rabin and a Labor government in Israel the following June led to the secret Oslo talks between the Israelis and Palestinians, a direct outgrowth of what Baker had launched in Madrid. I suspect Baker could have brokered a Syrian-Israeli agreement, had there been a second Bush 41 term, and perhaps a permanent-status Israeli-Palestinian deal. His skills, weight within the administration, relationships with all the key players in the region, and proven ability to deliver could not be easily replicated. He seemed like the right peacemaker at the right time.

* * *

THE REST OF the world was hardly quiescent while the Middle East absorbed so much American diplomatic energy. With the Cold War over, and the old bipolar international order crumbling, all sorts of new centrifugal forces were at work. As we put it in a Policy Planning Staff memo to Baker in the summer of 1991, the Soviet Union's "external empire" had disintegrated in 1989, and now its "internal empire" was beginning to as well.

The Soviet Union proved far more brittle than many of us had assumed. On August 19, 1991, a motley group of Soviet conservatives staged a putsch against Gorbachev, putting him under house arrest in Crimea. The Soviet vice president, Gennady Yanayev, appeared on state television and with hands trembling and voice unsteady declared that a new committee of which he was the deeply unconvincing head had taken charge of the country. Boris Yeltsin, the recently elected president of the Russian Federation, courageously faced down the coup plotters in Moscow, with the backing of significant elements of the Soviet military. As the coup attempt unfolded, Baker was on vacation in Wyoming, and Dennis and his family were in New Hampshire. Back in Washington, my colleagues and I tried to understand what had happened, and where it might lead. Andrew Carpendale and John Hannah drafted two papers for Baker, the first analyzing the coup and its implications, and the second laying out a framework for dealing with the likely fragmentation of the Soviet Union.

It was clear that Gorbachev, despite surviving the coup, was a desperately weakened leader. Yeltsin was the man of the hour. The failed putsch had stripped bare the fecklessness of the conservative opposition, opening the way for radical democratic and market reform and a range of independence movements. Our memo suggested that the only way Gorbachev could stay afloat politically was to become the champion of truly ambitious structural reform, and the only way the Soviet center could hold the union together was as the driver of meaningful political and economic change, in a much more loosely federated system. Both, we predicted, were quite unlikely.

The more prescriptive paper laid out a set of principles to help govern American policy toward the issue of a potential breakup of the Soviet Union, similar to what we had provided Baker on German reunification in 1990. On their face, the five principles we suggested were not controversial: peaceful self-determination; respect for existing borders without unilateral modifications; respect for democracy and rule of law; respect for human rights, especially minority rights; and adherence to international law and obligations. Nevertheless, as we had found on German reunification, clear policy guidelines were critical to shape our approach and the tactical choices before us.

Baker outlined the five principles at a White House press briefing in early September, and then traveled to Moscow to get a firsthand sense of the situation. The makeshift barricades around the Russian White House were still in place. Baker saw both Gorbachev and Yeltsin, who each professed to be optimistic about their political futures. The secretary came away skeptical that Gorbachev could survive politically, and persuaded that the challenge for the Bush administration was to help make the crash of the Soviet Union as bloodless as possible.

By late December, the Soviet Union had ceased to exist. After a poignant visit with Baker in Moscow and a last telephone call as leader of the Soviet Union with President Bush, Gorbachev resigned on December 25 and his country was no more. I went again with Baker to Moscow in January for the opening of the Middle East multilateral talks. That was a surreal experience, with the Russian tricolor now flying over the Kremlin, and Yeltsin's new, independent Russian government effectively inheriting the role of co-sponsor.

In February, I joined Baker's trip to a number of the other newly independent former Soviet states. We landed in a Yerevan that was almost totally dark as night fell, the Armenian power system failing and electricity shortages the norm. Baku was nearly as dismal, with rusting gas and oil pipes littering the roadside on the way in from the bedraggled airport. The Central Asian states were brighter, but just as poor. President Islam Karimov in Uzbekistan whipped out a small laminated card containing Baker's "five principles" for dealing with the process of post-Soviet independence, which he said he always kept in his coat pocket. Baker enjoyed Karimov's hospitality in Tashkent and especially in exotic Samarkand. On the plane afterward, however, he expressed his lack of faith in Karimov's democratic conversion, noting that "that guy pays about as much attention to those principles as I do to Uzbek music."

At Baker's urging, the Bush administration tried to be systematic about supporting the new independent states. The United States rapidly established embassies in each capital and set up substantial programs of humanitarian assistance, market economic advice, and defense conversion. It also launched the Nunn-Lugar program, to help ensure the safety and security of Soviet nuclear weapons, which were now spread at least temporarily across four sovereign states.

Other troubles were always bubbling up. In the latter part of the Bush administration, Yugoslavia began to splinter. Serbian forces laid siege to Sarajevo, Bosnia's capital, in the spring of 1992, and concerns mounted in European capitals as well as in Washington. In June, based on a strategy memo that Dennis and Andrew Carpendale had helped put together, the secretary recommended to the White House a robust plan to build diplomatic and economic pressure on the Serbs, and potentially even to deploy a multilateral force to break the siege and ensure that relief supplies got through. Brent Scowcroft supported Baker. Cheney and Powell were less enthusiastic. The Serbs momentarily backed down before the U.S. initiative got off the ground, and humanitarian supplies flowed into Sarajevo. The worst, however, was yet to come. The Bush administration, with a presidential reelection campaign in full swing and poll numbers dropping from their post–Desert Storm peak, was not eager to take risks in the Balkans, and content to let the Europeans take the lead. Its failure to act more forcefully only made the choices of the next administration more complicated.

In late summer, Baker moved to the White House to lead the president's floundering campaign and serve as chief of staff. Dennis went with Baker. Larry Eagleburger became acting secretary of state, and asked me to serve as acting director of Policy Planning. Sitting in George Kennan's old seat and still only thirty-six, I felt an uneasy pride,

One of our main preoccupations over the next six months was trying to think through the contours of an American strategy for managing post–Cold War order. We had begun this effort with a paper for Baker in late April 1992, entitled a little too expectantly, "Foreign Policy in the Second Bush Administration: An Overview."[11] In it, we cited the accomplishments of Bush's team, noting, "You and the President have much to be proud of in foreign policy. The end of the Cold War, a united Germany in NATO, peace in Central America, Desert Storm, and the first negotiations between Israel and all its Arab neighbors in forty-three years are singular achievements. But they amount to an unfinished agenda. Historians will ultimately judge you by how well you use the second term to translate those first-term successes into a coherent and enduring legacy. Above all, you will be judged by how well you have handled the two main consequences of the Cold War: the transformation of the former Soviet empire, and the victorious though fraying alliance of the U.S., Europe and Japan."

The memo emphasized that the starting point for a successful strategy had to include an updated set of assumptions about the international landscape beyond the Cold War. With no global security rival to counterbalance, we were left with an increasingly regional security agenda. "We have a long-term stake in stability in at least three key regions—Europe, East Asia and the Persian Gulf," I argued. "The end of the Cold War and the defeat of Iraq remove the immediate threat of a hostile power dominating one of those regions. What we face instead is the challenge of providing reassurance in a period of uncertainty, marked particularly by geopolitical upheaval and ethnic rivalry in Eastern Europe and the former Soviet Union, ambiguity about the post–Cold War military roles of Germany and Japan, and the unclear path of post-revolutionary Iran." I stressed the crucial significance of strengthening our international economic competitiveness as the foundation of our foreign policy.

Another assumption was that "the system of nation-states that developed during the Cold War, and the elites who governed those states, are caught in a swirl of both centralizing and decentralizing forces. The result is not the obsolescence of the nation-state, which still remains the central actor in international relations, but rather the transformation of the particular system of nation-states that we've grown accustomed to over the last half-century." I continued that "from the disintegrated Soviet empire to the Balkans, to much of Africa and the Middle East, what is happening is that traditional elites who have either excluded significant national or ethnic groups from power or failed to deliver political or economic goods are under attack. . . . The consequences of this political proliferation, and the crisis of legitimacy at its core, are uncertain ones for the U.S. On the one hand, there are enormous possibilities for nurturing democratic values and institutions, creating an international environment that could become more benign than ever for Americans. On the other hand, however, the search for legitimacy and national self-expression will often be a violent process—and it may lead to answers that meet local tests of legitimacy that aren't very democratic, like conservative Islamic regimes or nationalist authoritarian ones."

Defining our new leadership role would not be easy. America's powerful position, I wrote, did not "imply American dominance of a unipolar world. Power, especially economic power, is too diffuse for so simple a construct. We need to be mindful of the dangers of hubris and the deep suspicions of many governments . . . about American unilateralism." At the same time, I pointed out that "the reality remains that the United States, at least for the transitional period in history following the Cold War, occupies a unique position at the intersection of a diverse international system, remaining both a critical balancer in security sub-systems from Europe to Asia, and the only major player with a foot in each of three key economic sub-systems (the Americas, Europe and Asia). In short, while multilateralism may be one of the hallmarks of a post–Cold War order, it will have to be shaped largely by American leadership."

In November, Bill Clinton defeated Bush, whose foreign policy achievements were overshadowed by mounting popular appetite for change and a thirst for post–Cold War domestic renewal. As part of the transition process, we crystallized our views in a paper Eagleburger shared with incoming secretary of state Warren Christopher in January 1993. It was entitled "Parting Thoughts: U.S. Foreign Policy in the Years Ahead."[12] We had refined our thinking quite a bit from the earlier drafts—and the notion of describing an agenda for a second Bush term was obviously long buried. Much of the analysis of the international environment was similar to what we had laid out before, but we highlighted both the advent of new transnational threats and the challenge of building domestic support for active American leadership. "A variety of new transnational threats has appeared," I wrote, "particularly environmental degradation, drugs and the spread of deadly diseases like AIDS. Such dangers demand collective action rather than purely national responses. They also require an aggressive, new international scientific agenda, in which American leadership will be critical."

The thrust of our paper was careful and realistic. We tried to take into account likely domestic constraints. We were mindful of traditional security risks and the danger of regional hegemons emerging. We also saw a shifting global landscape, where security had to be defined in broader terms and new threats had to be considered. We stressed the importance of leading by example and building coalitions of countries around our central role. We were not persuaded that the demise of the Soviet Union and the end of the Cold War meant that the United States could take a detached view of the world, but we were also careful in our recognition of the perils of overreach and failing to connect ends to means. Ours was a strategy that accepted limits, but also reflected confidence in the capacity of the United States to at least manage problems, if not solve them. It was very much the worldview of Jim Baker, and many of the lessons we tried to articulate haven't lost their relevance today, more than a quarter century later.

3

Yeltsin's Russia: The Limits of Agency

IT WAS BARELY forty miles from Sleptsovskaya, a tiny Ingush border town overflowing with refugees, to the Chechen capital of Grozny. But in the late spring of 1995, it felt as if you were crossing from civilization, albeit in its tattered post-Soviet form, to a grim, darkened world in which civilization had lost its place. The main road ran alongside the Sunzha River east into Chechnya, full of ruts and potholes, with heavily mined fields on either side. I was riding with an embassy colleague in an old Soviet ambulance in search of a missing American humanitarian assistance expert named Fred Cuny. This was our first foray into Grozny, soon after the Chechen rebel leader, Dzhokhar Dudayev, and his forces had retreated south into the hills.

Our route was a kaleidoscope of reemerging normalcy and wartime brutality. Civilian traffic had returned, and roadside stands peddled everything from soft drinks and vodka to small arms and ammunition. Russian military vehicles rolled down the middle of the two-lane highway, scattering everything in their path, ridden by Russian troops who looked more like gang members than professional soldiers. Wearing bandannas, reflector sunglasses, and sleeveless T-shirts, and equipped with bandoliers and big knives in their belts, they tried hard to look intimidating. Some checkpoints along the way were manned by teenage conscripts notorious for shooting first and asking questions later, especially after darkness settled. Others were the preserve of *kontraktniki*, contract soldiers hardened by fighting in Afghanistan or more recent conflicts on Russia's former Soviet periphery. And then there were the OMON, the Ministry of Interior troops, cold-eyed and clad in black.

As we drove past the burned-out remains of houses and shops in Samashki, it was not hard to imagine the horrors of the night a few weeks before, when OMON soldiers swept into town and massacred more than two hundred Chechens, mostly women, children, and elderly men. Reportedly drunk and eager for revenge after their own losses in the Chechen campaign, OMON troops burned down homes with flamethrowers and threw grenades into crowded basements.

When we drove into Grozny itself, the scale of the devastation only grew. Forty square blocks in the center of the city had been leveled by Russian bombing in January and February—a campaign that left thousands dead. It was a scene that resembled a smaller version of Dresden 1945, or Stalingrad 1943.

Our brief trip gave us a glimpse of the terrible realities of that first Chechen war of the 1990s, which was in many ways a continuation of struggles between Russians and Chechens that went back nearly three centuries. It was also a glimpse of how far Russia had fallen since the collapse of the Soviet Union; here were the ill-fed and ill-trained remnants of the Red Army, once reputed to be capable of reaching the English Channel in forty-eight hours, now unable to suppress a local rebellion in an isolated part of Russia. And here was Boris Yeltsin, who had so courageously defied hardliners in August 1991 and buried the Communist system for good, exposed as an infirm and isolated leader unable to restore order and rebuild the Russian state. This was post-Soviet Russia at its low point, deeply humiliated and thrashing about, the promise of its post-Communist transition still not extinguished, but beginning to flicker.

It was no coincidence that Vladimir Putin would ride a ruthlessly successful prosecution of the second Chechen war several years later to become Yeltsin's unlikely successor. If you wanted to understand the grievances, mistrust, and smoldering aggressiveness of Putin's Russia, you first had to appreciate the sense of humiliation, wounded pride, and disorder that was often inescapable in Yeltsin's.

* * *

AS THE GEORGE H. W. BUSH administration wound down, I had been in Washington for eight years, and was well aware of how fortunate I had been. While it typically took at least two decades to rise to the ranks of the Senior Foreign Service, I had been promoted across that threshold in less than a decade. I was not interested in skipping more rungs on the career ladder. I wanted to refine my craft and get back overseas.

What I really wanted to do was work in what seemed to me to be the most interesting place an American diplomat could serve in the early 1990s: Russia. When the job of minister-counselor for political affairs in Moscow opened up, I leapt at the chance. Lisa was less than enthusiastic; she loved adventures, but this one would involve more professional sacrifices for her, and cold and dark was not the atmosphere she had aspired to as an Asia specialist. Ultimately, she came around to the idea. Part of the allure for both of us was the opportunity to spend a year at the old U.S. Army Russian Institute in Garmisch, at the foot of the Alps in Bavaria, where I would complete advanced Russian-language training. Now with two wonderful young daughters, Lizzy and Sarah, we also wanted a chance to decompress as a family. We arrived in Germany in the summer of 1993, and proceeded to spend as close to an idyllic year as we had in the Foreign Service.

I was the only diplomat among the group of U.S. Army officers studying Russian in Garmisch. Our instructors were all Russian émigrés. Some had been at the institute since the 1950s; others had come in the wave of Soviet Jewish emigration in the 1970s; a few younger teachers had arrived since the breakup of the Soviet Union. I loved the richness of the Russian language, and learned quickly. Lisa took introductory Russian with a class of special forces soldiers, and to this day has an alarmingly strong grasp of arcane military terminology in Russian. We took weekend trips around Europe, and went hiking and skiing whenever we could. In the late spring of 1994, I spent a couple weeks living with a working-class Russian family in St. Petersburg. It improved my vocabulary considerably—and opened up whole new vistas in Russian profanity, thanks to the family's ne'er-do-well eighteen-year-old son, an aspiring but not overly talented rock musician.

We arrived in Moscow in mid-July. I had read voraciously about the embassy's colorful history, enthralled by the stories of George Kennan and Chip Bohlen reporting from a Moscow transfixed by fear of Stalin's purges. A ramshackle mustard-colored building on the Garden Ring, the embassy was not far from the Moscow River and the Foreign Ministry. It had served as the U.S. chancery since the early 1950s, increasingly a firetrap and the target of massive bugging attempts. An electrical fire in 1991 had done considerable damage to the building. The spectacle of Russian intelligence agents rushing to the scene, thinly disguised as firefighters, had left an even more lasting impression.

A new embassy building, later discovered to have been bugged by the Russian construction crew, lay vacant and partially completed down the block from the old chancery. Directly in front of the main entrance stood an Orthodox church, so jammed with listening and monitoring equipment that it was known in the embassy community as "Our Lady of Telemetry," or alternatively, "Our Lady of Immaculate Reception." Across a busy street to the west was the Russian White

House, which still bore scars from the failed coup attempt against Yeltsin nine months before.

The American embassy was led by Ambassador Tom Pickering, a veteran of six previous ambassadorial posts, and the most capable professional diplomat for whom I ever worked. He was insatiably curious about every aspect of diplomatic work. He knew more about the widgets in the embassy boiler room than most of our technicians, and was an adroit problem-solver across the whole range of issues, from the plight of American citizens who had run afoul of Russian law to the delicate high policy work of managing relations with Yeltsin. Pickering's lack of Russian-language skills always frustrated him, but he was so quick (and his interpreter so good) that it never seemed too much of an impediment.

Pickering never met an instruction from Washington that he didn't want to first shape himself. He never wanted to be a diplomatic postman, simply waiting for orders from headquarters. His view was that he was the president's representative on the ground, paid not just to report on events but also to offer his best policy ideas and solutions, and sometimes to act first and ask for forgiveness later. Pickering's one weakness, as far as I could tell, was a need for speed on Russia's often menacing roads. Riding in the backseat of his armored limousine, impatient to get places and do things, he would offer running advice to his long-suffering driver about how to race in the wrong direction down one-way streets or maneuver through the reckless world of Moscow traffic.

There is no playbook or operating manual in the Foreign Service, and the absence of diplomatic doctrine, or even systematic case studies, has been a long-standing weakness of the State Department. Throughout my own formative years, good mentors mattered most of all—accomplished diplomats from whom I could draw essential lessons about negotiating and leadership. Experience was passed from generation to generation, and I never had a better role model than Tom Pickering.

In Russia, Pickering ran what was then one of the biggest American diplomatic missions in the world, including the embassy in Moscow and consulates in St. Petersburg, Yekaterinburg, and Vladivostok. Unlike almost all our other diplomatic posts, we had only a handful of locals working in our embassy and consulates in the summer of 1994, with roles from drivers and mechanics to consular clerks and assistants played by Americans. The Soviet government had refused to allow Russians to work for the U.S. mission after the spying and bugging crises of the mid-1980s, and Pickering was just beginning the process of rehiring them.

Pickering led a "country team," comprising the senior representatives of some twenty different U.S. agencies working at the embassy. State composed less than half of the total staff, with the remaining positions filled by Defense, Treasury, Commerce, Agriculture, and the intelligence community, among many others. I've always thought that the country team is the most effective example of interagency coordination in the U.S. government, at least from the point of view of the State Department. A strong ambassador, like Pickering, could not only ensure efficient implementation of policy through careful coordination among agencies in the field, but also shape policy formulation in Washington by working with the senior agency representatives at post.

As the president's representative, he had authority over other agencies in Russia, and more interagency clout than more senior officials in the State Department. Pickering used this wisely. He never had to wave around his presidential appointment letter to command the respect of other agency officials on his country team. His experience and attentiveness to their agendas won their loyalty, and he repeatedly demonstrated that he could help them advance their departmental goals through his own energy and access to senior Russian officials. In return, they gave him transparency and followed his lead. It's a credit to Pickering's leadership, and a mark of the strength of his country team, that I don't ever recall him being surprised by an action of intelligence or law enforcement representatives at the embassy, or anyone else. He didn't micromanage their affairs, but he set a clear policy direction and exercised his broad authority skillfully.

Ambassador Pickering's deputy chief of mission was Dick Miles, a wise, deeply experienced Russia hand. Down-to-earth, with excellent Russian-language skills, Dick had common sense and a talent for connecting with people across Russian society that proved to be huge assets for the embassy, and a strong example for the rest of us. As head of the political section, I was nominally the number three officer in the mission. Largely because of the frequency of Pickering's travels, I would spend half my nearly two years in Moscow as acting deputy chief of mission, and several weeks as chargé, when both Pickering and Miles were away.

We had twenty-seven officers in the political section, by far the biggest of any in the Foreign Service, as well as four administrative assistants, and two Russian nationals, who arranged appointments and translated documents in an office separated from the parts of the embassy where classified work was done. Our job was to provide ground truths, a granular sense of political and economic realities in Russia, so that policymakers in Washington could weigh them against all the other considerations overflowing their inboxes. We roamed widely across Russia's eleven time zones, trying to convey to Washington as clear an understanding as we could of the unfolding drama of a Russia struggling to absorb simultaneously three immense historical transformations: the collapse of Communism and the tumultuous transition to market economics and democracy; the collapse of the Soviet bloc and the security it had provided to historically insecure Russians; and the collapse of the Soviet Union itself, and with it a Russian empire built gradually over several centuries. Any one of those would have been difficult to manage; all three together were profoundly disorienting.

Travel in Russia in that chaotic time was always memorable. I spent one frigid afternoon talking to coal miners a thousand feet underground in Kemerovo, a fast-fading city in Siberia. In Vladivostok, then the murky heart of Russia's "wild east," I talked to a couple of local mafia pretenders, expansive in their description of new "business possibilities," none of which sounded much like the new market models that Western advisors were earnestly promoting in Moscow and St. Petersburg. Departing on one wintry trip to the North Caucasus, I watched in amazement as a technician for Air Dagestan, one of Aeroflot's countless dodgy post-Soviet spin-offs, went to work de-icing the wings of the battered old Ilyushin aircraft with a blowtorch. It wasn't much more reassuring to climb into the plane and walk past the cockpit, where the rheumy-eyed pilot was putting away a half-empty bottle of vodka.

Moscow had its own unique charms in the mid-1990s. I remember heading off one morning for an appointment in the Moscow mayor's office. As I walked toward the entrance, I noticed a number of Russians in suits lying spread-eagled in the snow, with a group of armed, uniformed men wearing black ski masks standing over them. It turned out that the men in ski masks were members of President Yeltsin's presidential guards, led by Yeltsin's increasingly powerful former bodyguard, Aleksandr Korzhakov. They were paying a courtesy call on executives of the Most Group, run by one of Russia's wealthiest oligarchs, Vladimir Gusinsky, whose offices were a few floors below the mayor's. Gusinsky had run afoul of Korzhakov, and this was how gentle reminders were conveyed in Moscow in 1994.

Moscow's lawlessness produced plenty of scary moments. One weekday afternoon in the early fall of 1995, someone fired a rocket-propelled grenade into the sixth floor of the chancery in broad daylight. The round pierced the wall and detonated in a copying machine, sending metal fragments and glass in all directions. Miraculously, no one was in the copying room at the time, and no one was injured or killed. The authorities rounded up a number of the usual suspects, but the culprit was never identified. It was symptomatic of life in Moscow in that era that it didn't seem wildly out of the ordinary for someone to have an RPG in the center of the city in the middle of the day.

* * *

BY THE SUMMER of 1994, Boris Yeltsin was a wounded figure, his limitations as a leader growing more and more apparent. Despite the sustained efforts of Bill Clinton and his administration to cultivate relations with the new Russia and accommodate the post-traumatic stress of the post-Soviet world, the limitations of U.S.-Russian partnership were also laid bare.

In his rivalry with Mikhail Gorbachev, Yeltsin had been the heroic destroyer of the old, calcified Soviet system. But he faltered in the next phase, the construction of an open political and economic system out of the rubble of Communism. At first, he gave full rein to a group of young reformers led by his first prime minister, Yegor Gaidar. Self-styled "kamikaze pilots," they rushed to reform, acutely conscious of the gravitational forces of impossibly high popular expectations, the hard realities of economic change, and the inevitable counterreaction of conservative factions. Hardship was the dominant feature on their landscape. Industrial production in Russia had fallen by half since 1989. Agricultural production was dropping too. At least 30 percent of the population lived below the poverty line, and massive inflation had wiped out the meager savings of a pensioner generation that had endured the trials of the Great Patriotic War (World War II) and postwar recovery. The public health system had collapsed, and contagious diseases like tuberculosis and diphtheria were reemerging. Nevertheless, Yeltsin and his small band of reformers pushed ahead. A massive and unwieldy "voucher program," theoretically offering shares in state-owned companies to individual citizens, resulted in the privatization of some 70 percent of the economy by the end of 1994. Somewhat predictably, the process was monopolized by a tiny minority, a new class of oligarchs who were as ruthless as they were entrepreneurial.

As reform spawned political resistance, Yeltsin seemed adrift. When the Duma's reactionary leadership challenged the constitutional basis of his rule in the fall of 1993, Yeltsin resorted to the use of force, relying on loyal military units to rout his opponents. While he believed he had no choice, the cost was high, politically and personally. New parliamentary elections at the end of the year boosted the rabid nationalist party of Vladimir Zhirinovsky, as well as a reemergent Communist Party. Lonely and overwhelmed, Yeltsin retreated steadily from day-to-day government business, drinking heavily to ease physical and political pain.

In December 1994, on the eve of a visit by Vice President Al Gore to Moscow, I tried to capture Russia's domestic predicament in a cable to Washington.[1] "Winter in Russia is not a time for optimists, and in some respects the popular mood here mirrors the descending gloom." Yeltsin's foreign policy sought to mask national weakness and reassert Russian prerogatives. "Born of a mood of national regret over the loss of superpower status and an equally acute sense that the West is taking advantage of Russia's weakness," I wrote, assertive policies abroad had become one of the few themes that united Russians amid continued bickering over domestic issues. Yeltsin was determined to reaffirm Russia's great power status and independent interests in Russia's so-called Near Abroad, the neighboring post-Soviet republics of Eurasia.

Stressing the attachment of Yeltsin and the country's political elite to Russia's sphere of influence in the former Soviet space, I emphasized mounting Russian concern about expansion of NATO. I noted that Yeltsin's tough public statements in the fall of 1994 about NATO expansion "were an unsubtle reminder of Russian angst about neglect of its interests in the process of restructuring European security institutions."

The cable concluded that "the honeymoon in American relations with the new Russia that blossomed in the immediate aftermath of the breakup of the Soviet Union is now long past." Russia had embarked on a long journey of redefinition, which would inevitably prove frustrating and perplexing as personalities shifted and policies collided, but that continued to hold potential for effective post–Cold War relations between us. It was critical, in my view, to "prioritize better among the many concerns on our agenda with the Russians. Two years ago, we could pretty much have it our way on a whole range of issues, so long as we paid some minimal deference to Russian sensibilities. That is no longer the case."

I visited a retired Soviet diplomat late one afternoon that winter in his modest apartment in central Moscow. He was a widower, alone with his memories and photographs of foreign postings across the Cold War. As we slowly drained a bottle of vodka, the snow falling silently outside his sitting room window, he reminisced about his career. He was not especially nostalgic about the Soviet system, and acknowledged its many weaknesses and cruelties. "We brought this upon ourselves," he said. "We've lost our way." It might take another generation for Russia to recover its confidence and purpose, but he had no doubt that it would. It would be a mistake to leave the impression with Russians that we had taken advantage of them when they were down on their luck. "Remember Churchill," he said. "In victory, magnanimity. You won't regret it."

The embassy urged caution on NATO enlargement. Before thinking seriously about extending offers of formal NATO membership to Poland and other Central European states, we recommended considering other forms of cooperation with former Warsaw Pact members, and perhaps a new "treaty relationship" between NATO and Russia. We underscored the utility of including Russia in the new "Contact Group" on Bosnia, which gathered together key European and American diplomats to resolve a conflict spinning out of control in the former Yugoslavia. Russia had limited weight on Balkan diplomacy, but engaging it systematically reduced its temptation to be a spoiler, and was a smart investment for the day when it would add more muscle to its assertiveness. Another good example was the inclusion of Russia in meetings of the "G-7"—the principal players in the post–Cold War West. The emergence of the "G-8" helped anchor a weak and floundering Russia in the respect and status that came with regular dealings with the G-7 countries.

President Clinton was quick to appreciate what was at stake. In a speech in April 1993, he noted, "The danger is clear if Russia's reforms turn sour—if it reverts to authoritarianism or disintegrates into chaos. The world cannot afford the strife of the former Yugoslavia replicated in a nation as big as Russia."[2] Clinton and Yeltsin developed a surprisingly close personal relationship, despite their differences in age and political culture, and despite all the storms in U.S.-Russian relations in the 1990s. Both big, hearty men blessed with natural political gifts if not born into political privilege, they helped navigate a complicated and uncertain era. Strobe Talbott, an accomplished Russian specialist and Clinton's former Oxford roommate, dubbed the president "the U.S. government's principal Russia hand."[3] Clinton made a high priority of managing Russia and its erratic president. As the head of a new bureau in the State Department overseeing policy toward Russia and the other former Soviet states, Talbott became the day-to-day manager of the relationship.

Talbott and his Russian counterpart, Deputy Foreign Minister Georgiy Mamedov, understood how to steer through their own bureaucracies and politics, and had a solid appreciation of each other's political limitations. Together, they constructed an elaborate architecture of cooperative U.S.-Russian mechanisms aimed at cementing an image of partnership between at least nominal equals. At the core was the Gore-Chernomyrdin Commission, led by Vice President Gore and Prime Minister Viktor Chernomyrdin, which was set up to organize relations between the two governments more systematically. Following its inaugural session in Washington in September 1993, the commission met twice yearly, home and away. Eventually growing to include eight different subcommittees, each co-led by an American cabinet officer or agency head along with his Russian counterpart, the commission fostered cooperation across a wide range of areas, from the environment to outer space. Gore and Chernomyrdin also developed an effective relationship. They were an unlikely duo, the ambitious young Tennessee politician with a penchant for technical detail, and the gray, sometimes inarticulate apparatchik. Nevertheless, their informal conversations on the margins of the commission meetings were often productive, and Chernomyrdin developed a reputation in the West for efficiency, at least by the low-bar standards of the old Soviet system.

For all the mechanisms and the high-level attention and visits, Russia's post-Soviet transition was proving a long and painful slog. As his health deteriorated and his political clout and attention span grew more attenuated, Yeltsin was anxious for an opportunity to show people that he was still capable of decisive and effective action, a political step around which Russians could unite. Reasserting Moscow's authority over Russia's increasingly disconnected regions was one obvious possibility, and the most obstreperous and defiant region of all, Chechnya, was a tempting target. With a rebellious history and an especially dark and forbidding presence in the Russian psyche, Chechnya seemed to Yeltsin to be overdue for the application of a strong hand. As tensions built in 1994, the embassy highlighted the danger signs on the horizon: "Yeltsin is by no means out of the woods on political arrangements with the regions—a serious misstep on Chechnya, to cite the most obvious trouble spot, could cause the unraveling of much of what has been achieved."[4] The serious misstep was not long in coming.

* * *

THROUGHOUT THE YEARS I served in Russia, I was always fascinated by the North Caucasus. At one time or another, I traveled to each of its five autonomous republics, which had been gradually swallowed up in the advance of Russian imperial power in the nineteenth century. With the snowcapped peaks of the Caucasus Mountains looming off in the south, there was a wildness and beauty to the terrain unlike anything else I saw across Russia's huge expanse. Mostly Muslim and mostly poor, the North Caucasus was one of the few parts of the Russian Federation in which populations were still growing. And like mountain peoples everywhere, they had a defiant streak.

Most defiant of all, at least in the eyes of suspicious Russians, were the Chechens. For nearly fifty years in the nineteenth century they had waged a guerrilla war against imperial Russia. During World War II, wary that the Chechens might side with the invading Nazis, Stalin brutally deported nearly the entire population—some four hundred thousand men, women, and children—to Kazakhstan. They returned more than a decade after the war, with a whole new set of historical grievances. When the Soviet Union collapsed, with Moscow distracted and struggling with reform, Chechnya grew increasingly restive and isolated—ripe for the reckless ambition of its first elected president, Dzhokhar Dudayev, a recently retired Soviet air force general. Erratic and self-important, Dudayev alternated between declarations of Chechnya's quasi-independence and protestations that he remained a "Russian patriot"; more mob boss than revolutionary, he manipulated Chechen clan politics and set up a variety of criminal rackets.

The truth, however, was that Chechnya's lawlessness differed only in degree from what was going on across much of Russia in the early 1990s. In many tangible respects, Chechnya remained a part of the Russian Federation, its borders open and its oil and gas flowing freely out of the republic, its meager pensions paid out of the Russian budget. Dudayev himself gradually lost popularity in Chechnya. While his thugs enriched themselves, local government services atrophied. Dudayev's openly rebellious behavior grated on Yeltsin, a deeply irritating reminder of his inability to assert his grip. Similarly proud, impulsive, and disinclined to compromise, they were heading for a tragic collision.[5] Demonizing rhetoric came easily to both, with Dudayev playing on decades of Chechen mistreatment at the hands of Russians, and Yeltsin exploiting the peculiarly hard view that most Russians had of Chechens.

Tired and isolated, Yeltsin relied more and more on an inner circle of conservative power ministers and drinking companions, whose capacity for court politics exceeded their professional competence. Their argument to Yeltsin was that subduing Dudayev gave him a perfect opportunity to assert his control, outflank nationalist opponents, and show his wider international audience that Russia was beginning to reemerge after its moment of weakness. In the summer of 1994, with their encouragement, Yeltsin set in motion a series of escalating efforts to bring Dudayev to heel.

Serial humiliations were the result, first a failed coup d'état using Chechen oppositionists, and then a botched intervention in late November backed by Russian troops. The Chechens paid and recruited to undertake the operation fled at the last minute, and a number of Russian soldiers were captured and paraded before television cameras. There still may have been a chance to pressure Dudayev, whose position at home had been steadily weakening, and eventually negotiate an acceptable arrangement for Chechnya within the Russian Federation. Yeltsin, whose sense of embarrassment was now overflowing, instead doubled down and authorized a full-scale military invasion in early December. His defense minister, Pavel Grachev, assured him that the Russian army would easily overwhelm Chechen resistance. He could not have been more wrong.

Disregarding the advice of a number of senior army officers, Grachev sent three armored columns, poorly prepared and poorly led, into Grozny. Dudayev's forces, led by a former Soviet colonel, Aslan Maskhadov, slaughtered hundreds of Russian troops in fierce urban combat, and routed the rest. Beaten back, a furious Grachev began an intense aerial and artillery bombardment, determined to, as he said, "make the rubble bounce." Over the next few weeks, bombs and shells rained down on the city. Much of the bombing came from high altitude, and winter fog obscured targets. The result was devastating;

many of the civilian victims were elderly ethnic Russians living in the center of the city, who had been unable to flee.

On New Year's Eve, the Russians resumed their ground offensive, pushing most Chechen fighters out of the city by the end of February 1995. Grozny was left in ruins, with thousands of civilians dead. The violence and brutality of the conflict was heavily and openly covered by a still largely independent Russian media.

Back in the embassy, Ambassador Pickering asked me to take stock of the debacle for Washington. In a January 11, 1995, cable entitled "Sifting Through the Wreckage: Chechnya and Russia's Future," I laid out our preliminary thoughts.[6] "The Chechen crisis . . . has already laid bare the weakness of the Russian state and the tragic flaws of its first democratically-elected President." We worried about what all this meant for the future of reform in Russia, and whether this might trigger more separatism in other republics. The ineptitude of the Russian military left a powerful impression. "Probably even more than the loss of civilian lives which has so exercised Moscow's liberal intelligentsia," the blundering performance in the initial assault "has led Russians, and especially elites, to question Boris Yeltsin's competence to govern."

The cable argued that step-by-step over recent months, Yeltsin and his advisors had blundered further into a quagmire, with bad policy choices begetting worse ones. "The tragic irony is that the same mulish stubbornness that produced Yeltsin's greatest triumphs may now prove to be his undoing." While it was now too late for Yeltsin to recover the heroic democratic mantle he once wore, it was still not too late (assuming no catastrophic deterioration of his health) for him to maintain enough of his authority to limp along. He still appeared to retain support among political elites in Russia's regions, where the Chechen crisis so far did not have the resonance that it had in the capital. Blunders in Chechnya had severely tested military discipline, but it did not yet appear to be at the breaking point.

In Russian foreign policy terms, however, Chechnya had become a growing, self-inflicted disaster. The consequences for Russia were varied but uniformly bad—"isolating it internationally, exposing its weakness to other former Soviet states over which it seeks influence as well as to attentive regional powers like Iran, China, and Turkey, and playing into the hands of former Warsaw Pact states who will seek to accelerate the process of NATO expansion." In Moscow, it was hardening attitudes about the United States and its allies. "Russians across the political spectrum already feel an acute sense that the West is taking advantage of Russia's weakness, and that is likely to become more rather than less pronounced as a result of the deeply embarrassing experience in Chechnya."

The mood was hardening in Washington too. President Clinton had suffered a resounding defeat in the November 1994 midterm elections, with newly ascendant Republicans questioning many of his foreign policy assumptions, including about Russia. The administration itself was initially sympathetic to Yeltsin's predicament in Chechnya, with Vice President Gore comparing it at one point to the American Civil War, and Secretary of State Christopher calling it "an internal Russian affair."[7] Pickering was persistent in trying to explain how flawed that line of thinking was, but later noted with some frustration that "there was very little interest in the notion of whether the Russians actually provoked some of this or not."[8]

As fighting in Chechnya continued through the spring of 1995, the administration's attitude finally sharpened. Christopher warned Foreign Minister Andrey Kozyrev in Geneva in late March that the Chechen war was "foolhardy" and "tragically wrong." Meanwhile, pressure in Congress mounted to cut off or reduce aid to Russia, which then amounted to nearly a billion dollars annually. While the White House managed to forestall those efforts, we made clear from Moscow that we should not "overestimate the leverage that assistance gives us. Many Russian politicians, reformers included, would not mind an opportunity now to tell us to take our aid and shove it."[9]

Events in Chechnya continued to chip away at Yeltsin's waning authority. In June 1995, a daring Chechen commander, Shamil Basayev, led a group of rebels north, out of Chechnya and into the neighboring Russian region of Stavropol. Bribing their way through Russian military checkpoints until they ran out of cash, Basayev and his fighters seized some sixteen hundred Russian hostages in a hospital in Budennovsk. Yeltsin was en route to a G-7 summit in Halifax, Canada, as the attack unfolded. Rather than return immediately to Moscow, he left Prime Minister Chernomyrdin to handle the crisis. Negotiating directly with Basayev in a series of dramatic telephone calls, Chernomyrdin agreed to allow Basayev and his men to drive back to Chechnya with some one hundred hostages, freeing the remainder in Budennovsk. Once safely back in the mountains south of Grozny, Basayev released all those he had forced to accompany him. We reported from Moscow that "some in the Russian government thought at first that Budennovsk would be a plus at Halifax—an opportunity to show critics in the West that the Yeltsin regime had been right all along about what it was dealing with in Chechnya. The hostage crisis turned out instead to be a mortal embarrassment, painfully demonstrating Yeltsin's detached and erratic leadership and once again exposing Russia's weakness."[10]

The Chechen conflict continued in bloody fits and starts until the summer of 1996, when a more enduring cessation of hostilities was agreed upon. It reignited a few years later, providing Vladimir Putin with his chance to put a much different mark on Russian leadership, but the impact of that first brutal war would be felt in Russian politics and Russian attitudes toward the wider world for many years to come.

* * *

NOTHING BROUGHT THE brutality and chaos of the Chechen conflict into sharper relief for us in the embassy than the tragic case of Fred Cuny. I met Cuny only once, when he came to see Ambassador Pickering in Moscow in late February 1995. Six foot three, wearing cowboy boots and speaking in a quiet Texas drawl that oozed self-confidence, Cuny was a magnetic presence. He had already built an international reputation as a humanitarian relief expert, the "master of disaster" who had worked his way through acute danger from Biafra to Iraq. Most recently, he had braved the bombardment of Sarajevo to help restore the water supply for trapped civilians.

Cuny explained to Pickering that he had just returned from two weeks in Chechnya, and had traveled widely in Grozny and to besieged towns and villages in its vicinity, on behalf of George Soros and his foundation. He painted a sobering picture. He was particularly concerned about the plight of thirty thousand mostly elderly, mostly ethnic Russian civilians surrounded by fighting in southern Grozny. Living in burned-out buildings and bomb shelters, many suffering from pneumonia, most people there were not cooking for fear of drawing Russian shelling, and most food was eaten raw. The fighting was still intense, and humanitarian convoys couldn't reach Grozny's southern neighborhoods. Cuny said those trapped there "could soon be dropping like flies."[11] He described his contacts with local Chechen commanders as well as Russian forces, and indicated that he planned to return to Chechnya in about a month. Pickering thanked him for his insights and Cuny agreed to stay in touch.

Cuny went back into Chechnya on March 31. His goal was to broker an agreement for humanitarian access, so that trapped civilians could be extracted safely and supplies could be delivered. Cuny was accompanied by two Russian Red Cross doctors, a translator, and a Chechen driver. They headed first toward the Chechen-held town of Bamut, southwest of Grozny, where Dudayev was believed to be headquartered. When Cuny and his team reached Bamut, Dudayev wasn't there. They tried to drive east, but on April 4 were apparently detained at gunpoint by Chechen intelligence forces on the outskirts of the village of Stary Achkoi. Later that day, Cuny's Chechen driver reappeared in Ingushetia, with a brief message from Cuny noting that he had been taken into custody but was "ok" and expected to be back shortly. That was the last message from him, and neither he nor the Russian doctors or translator were ever heard from again.

Fred Cuny's disappearance set off a four-month search that occupied much of the embassy's energy and attention, and eventually drew the personal engagement of President Clinton. Our efforts on his behalf reflected an important dimension of what American diplomats do overseas. Few such efforts, however, were as dramatic or intense as the search for Cuny.

As the weeks and months passed, there were tantalizing rumors that Cuny and his colleagues were still alive, somewhere in the murky world of wartime Chechnya. Pickering tasked me with managing the day-to-day embassy effort to find him. We pressed senior Russian officials repeatedly for more information and help conducting a serious search. They promised a lot, and delivered very little. Our contacts on the Chechen side were limited, but we worked hard to use intermediaries in the government of Ingushetia to find out more. Cuny's son and brother, along with some of his staff and representatives of Soros's foundation, spent considerable time in Ingushetia that spring and summer and made a number of courageous trips inside Chechnya in pursuit of leads.

We set up our own informal outpost in Ingushetia, manned on a rotating basis by several of my colleagues. President Clinton raised the Cuny case with Yeltsin in May, as did Vice President Gore during his visit in June. I traveled to the region twice, and met at length with President Ruslan Aushev of Ingushetia both times. He insisted that he and his government were "working overtime" in the search.[12] "We have scoured the republic of Chechnya and even gone into Georgia to investigate a rumor that Cuny had been taken across the frontier," he told me. "Unfortunately, it did not check out."[13]

At one point, a report emerged of a corpse that resembled Cuny at a hospital in the rebel-held town of Shatoy, well south of Grozny in the foothills of the Caucasus Mountain range. Philip Remler, an

American diplomat serving in the Organization for Security and Co-operation in Europe (OSCE) peace mission in Grozny, volunteered to drive down to Shatoy and try to verify the report. A white flag flutter-ing on the front of his OSCE vehicle did not prevent a Russian tank from firing several rounds at him.

At the tiny hospital in Shatoy, Philip huddled with a local doctor as the badly decomposed body was brought out to be examined. Dusk was falling, and the lights in the makeshift examination room were flickering. Philip used his satellite phone to get me on the line in Moscow. Relying upon a medical record that his family had shared with us, I described Cuny's distinguishing physical characteristics, in-cluding a metal surgical pin in one of his thighs. Philip confirmed that the body was that of a tall man. In a calm voice, with the sound of Russian shelling audible in the background, he said decomposition had rendered most other features indistinct, but it was clear that there were no pins in either leg. It wasn't Cuny.

In August, after exhausting every possible lead, the Cuny team concluded that it was most likely that Fred had been killed early in April by Chechen forces in western Chechnya, soon after his initial detention in Stary Achkoi. The family gave a press conference in Moscow and ended their search. The embassy shared the family's judgment about Fred Cuny's fate. Based on what we had heard from a variety of Ingush and Chechen sources during the course of our four-month search, we noted in a cable to Washington that "we sus-pect (but cannot prove) that there were rumors spread prior to Fred Cuny's last entry into Chechnya that would have fed Chechen suspi-cions."[14]

We suggested that such stories "were originated or fanned" by the FSB, the Russian successor organization to the Soviet Union's KGB. We added that "the FSB was well aware of Cuny's earlier travels in Chechnya" and his previous meetings with Chechen military com-mander Maskhadov. There were also reports circulating in March in western Chechnya that the two Russian Red Cross doctors accompanying Cuny were FSB agents. The FSB had ample incentive for a disinformation campaign, given the tensions swirling across Chechnya in those months, and their interest in discrediting the Chechen fighters. Such a disinformation effort, we wrote, "would not necessarily have been coordinated in Moscow (if the FSB had been well-coordinated, it might not have gotten into such a colossal mess in Chechnya in the first place)."

After months of painstaking effort, we came to a straightforward conclusion: Cuny was likely caught in between two intelligence services—the Chechens who pulled the trigger and the Russians responsible for setting the trap.

The whole tragic episode was wrapped in layer after layer of murkiness and deception. "It may well be that the double-dealing and disingenuousness of virtually all the parties with which we and the Cuny family have been dealing reflect some measure of shared culpability," we wrote. The hard reality was that "none of this should come as a surprise in the chaotic and often brutal world of the North Caucasus. But Fred Cuny, while no stranger to risk-taking in dangerous situations, still deserved better." So did the poor Chechen civilians and underfed, undertrained Russian conscripts who were both, in different ways, victimized by a war that wasn't foreordained in that awful winter of 1994–95. It was another blow to a post-Soviet transition in which problems were already overtaking possibilities. The Chechen debacle was emblematic of a Russia still trapped in its complicated past, struggling to find its way and regain its pride and purpose. And it reinforced the limits of American agency in influencing a future that only Russians could ultimately shape.

* * *

YELTSIN WAS BADLY wounded by the Chechen mess. After a heart attack in the summer of 1995, he looked increasingly incapable, politically or physically, of avoiding a fatal blow in Duma elections in December 1995, let alone running for reelection the following June.

The outlook for continued reform at home and the kind of partnership abroad to which both Yeltsin and Clinton still aspired was increasingly uncertain.

Despite the headwinds, Clinton continued to invest in their relationship, recognizing how central it was to any hope of keeping U.S.-
Russian relations on a stable footing. In the face of domestic criticism
and unease over Chechnya, Clinton went ahead with a long-planned
visit to Moscow in May 1995 to join several other leaders from the
victorious World War II alliance to celebrate the fifty-year anniversary
of Hitler's defeat. Clinton knew how much this meant to Yeltsin, and
to Russians more broadly. Even a half century later, the wartime sacrifices of the Soviet people, not least the loss of more than twenty
million of their fellow citizens, and the pride that came with their
indispensable role in crushing the Nazis, were powerful forces.

Any presidential visit is complicated, but this one was trickier
than most, given the fragile policy backdrop. As the "control officer," I
was responsible for coordinating negotiations with the Russians over
the schedule and agenda for the visit and supporting Ambassador
Pickering and the White House advance team. American presidents
don't travel light. Clinton came with more than two hundred staff
and security personnel, and a similar number of journalists. My team
tried but failed to persuade the Russians not to have a unit fresh from
combat in Chechnya join in the celebratory parade in Red Square.
When an enterprising White House press official foolishly tried to
forge a few extra credentials for American journalists, Kremlin security reacted with a predictable lack of amusement, but we avoided
anything more than a mild scuffle and a few sharp words.

This was my first extended encounter with President Clinton, and
I was impressed. He had a sure touch with Yeltsin, and an equally
sure command of substance. Clinton understood Yeltsin's political
constraints—both those imposed on him by Russia's turbulent weakness and those stemming from his own flawed decisions. "This guy is
in a tough spot," Clinton said to us before heading to see Yeltsin. "We

have to give him as much space as we can, because we're not going to find a better Russian partner."

President Clinton delivered a firm message on Chechnya, both privately in the Kremlin meetings and then publicly in a speech at Moscow State University. "Continued fighting in that region," he said in his televised remarks, "can only spill more blood and further erode support for Russia." Clinton was gracious with the overworked embassy staff and their families. The genuine appreciation that he conveyed in a brief conversation with Lisa and our two daughters, then six and three, helped make up for the long hours I had put in over the preceding weeks.

In broad foreign policy terms, Yeltsin had two principal concerns during Clinton's visit. Both would dominate much of the last year of my tour in Moscow—and much of the U.S.-Russian debate for many years to come. The first was maintaining a paramount Russian role among the states of the former Soviet Union. The second was preventing further erosion of Russia's position in post–Cold War Europe. As we reported in a cable a month after Clinton's visit, "nowhere are Russian sensitivities about being excluded or taken advantage of more acute than on the broad issue of European security. There is a solid consensus within the Russian elite that NATO expansion is a bad idea, period." The cable concluded that "it is very clear that the Russian elite sees NATO expansion . . . and Bosnia as parts of a whole—with concerns about NATO's role in Bosnia deepening Russian suspicions about NATO and its enlargement."[15]

Preoccupied with domestic issues early in his presidency, Clinton was reluctant to risk much American diplomatic capital in the Balkans, as the disintegration of Yugoslavia in the early 1990s spawned mounting ethnic bloodshed in Bosnia between the Muslim majority and a Bosnian Serb minority armed and supported by the new Serbian government in Belgrade. By 1994–95, the conflict consumed more attention and energy at the highest levels of the Clinton administration than any other foreign policy problem. NATO air forces

gradually stepped up their involvement to help protect Muslim civilians, especially after the massacre of some eight thousand Muslims in
Srebrenica in July 1995, and a brutal mortar attack on the central
marketplace in Sarajevo the following month that killed more than
three dozen innocent civilians. A renewed peacemaking effort was led
by Richard Holbrooke, then the assistant secretary of state for European affairs. Holbrooke was a brilliant diplomat, whose talents and
drive were matched only by his showmanship and sense of self—
memorably reflected in an otherwise routine State Department cable
noting his arrival in a Balkan capital, puckishly titled "The Ego Has
Landed."

For the Russians, the war in Bosnia served as another painful reminder of their weakness. While often frustrated by the brutality and
venality of the Serbian leadership, Yeltsin couldn't ignore the natural
affinity of Russians for Slavic kinsmen in Belgrade and among the
Bosnian Serbs. As NATO stepped up its air campaign, and as Holbrooke accelerated American diplomacy, the Russians resented their
secondary role. Holbrooke was not especially sympathetic, but took a
practical view of managing Russian sensibilities. "We felt that, despite
occasional mischief-making, Moscow would be easier to deal with,"
he later wrote, "if we gave it a place as a co-equal with the EU and the
United States" in the Contact Group.[16]

Holbrooke came to Moscow in October for a meeting of the Contact Group, the first hosted by the Russians. I met him at Vnukovo
Airport, and on the hourlong ride into Moscow was treated to a "full
Holbrooke," as he juggled calls to Secretary Christopher and Senator
Bill Bradley, unleashed a running commentary about Washington
politics, peppered me with questions about the already snowy landscape around us, made acerbic asides about the Russians, and complained bitterly about having to waste his time in Moscow when there
was more urgent work to be done in the Balkans. In the end, however,
Holbrooke's visit and Talbott's continuing, meticulous outreach to

counterparts in Moscow helped ease the Russian sense of grievance, and persuaded them to provide grudging support for the landmark 1995 Dayton Agreement and its implementation.

The issue of expanding NATO's membership to include Russia's former Warsaw Pact allies was a deeper challenge. Yeltsin and the Russian elite assumed, with considerable justification, that Jim Baker's assurances during the negotiation of German reunification in 1990—that NATO would not extend its reach "one inch" farther east—would continue to apply after the breakup of the Soviet Union. That commitment, however, had never been precisely defined or codified, and the Clinton administration saw its inheritance as fairly ambiguous. While Clinton himself was in no rush at the outset of his administration to force the question of enlarging NATO, his first national security advisor, Tony Lake, was an early proponent of expansion. Lake argued that the United States and its European allies had a rare historical opportunity to anchor former Communist countries like Poland, Hungary, and the Czech Republic in a successful democratic and market economic transition. A path to NATO membership would offer stability and reassurance, a compelling answer to historical fears of vulnerability to a revanchist Russia, as well as a newly reunified Germany. Amid the chaos of the former Yugoslavia, this argument struck a chord with Clinton.

Others in the new administration were less convinced. Talbott, and later Secretary of Defense Bill Perry, worried that starting down the road to formal enlargement of NATO would undermine hopes for a more enduring partnership with Russia, undercutting reformers who would see it as a vote of no confidence in their efforts, a hedge against the likely failure of reform. We shared similar concerns at Embassy Moscow. In a fall 1995 cable, we laid out the quandary: "The challenge for us is to look past the [government of Russia's] often irritating rhetoric and erratic and reactive diplomacy to our own long-term self-interest. That demands, in particular, that we continue to seek to build a security order in Europe sufficiently in Russia's interests so that a revived Russia will have no compelling reason to revise it—and so that in the meantime the 'stab in the back' theorists will have only limited room for maneuver in Russian politics."[17]

In an attempt to buy time and test Russian attitudes, the Pentagon developed the "Partnership for Peace," a kind of NATO halfway house that would build trust by offering all former Warsaw Pact states—including Russia—a formal relationship with NATO. Clinton indicated at the outset that PfP membership "can also lead to eventual membership in NATO," but there was no explicit signal of any decision to expand at that stage. Yeltsin and Foreign Minister Andrey Kozyrev indicated their interest in participating in PfP, dragging out talks in hopes of slowing down any movement toward NATO expansion. Nevertheless, momentum gathered over the course of 1994 toward enlargement, with Clinton declaring publicly in Warsaw in July that the question was not if but when. At an OSCE summit in Budapest in December, Yeltsin lashed back. He declared publicly that the end of the Cold War was in danger of becoming a "cold peace," and accused Clinton and the NATO allies of "giving up on democracy in Russia." In a later private conversation with Clinton, Yeltsin was equally direct about his concerns. "For me to agree to the borders of NATO expanding toward those of Russia," he said, "would constitute a betrayal on my part of the Russian people."[18]

"Hostility to early NATO expansion," we reported just after the Budapest outburst, "is almost universally felt across the domestic political spectrum here."[19] We tried to counter the characteristically American tendency to think that the right process could solve almost any substantive problem. "The Russian elite is much more focused on outcomes now," we wrote in a subsequent cable. "When consultations on Bosnia or NATO expansion or other neuralgic issues don't—in Russian eyes—affect Western behavior, resentment and disillusionment are bound to follow. In those circumstances, the process serves mainly to remind Russians of their own weakness."[20]

Clinton mollified Yeltsin by privately assuring him that no decisions on expansion would be made until after the Russian presidential elections in June 1996. Apart from the NATO issue, Yeltsin's health and political fortunes were both in poor shape as he maneuvered to win reelection. His heart ailments slowed him down, and heavy drinking didn't help. On one occasion in late 1995, when I was serving as chargé, Lisa and I joined a small party of senior Russian officials at Vnukovo Airport to welcome Yeltsin back from an overseas trip. He had clearly done a lot of unwinding on the flight home, and lumbered past us to his waiting limousine—a bodyguard steering the well-lubricated president by the elbow, while another aide mumbled the Russian equivalent of "nothing to see here folks, just move along."

With most of Russia's oligarchs banding together behind him, Yeltsin stumbled ahead to victory, defeating a gray, uncharismatic Communist candidate. His candidacy was also bolstered not so subtly by American advice and support, prompting a 1996 cover of *Time* that read "Yanks to the Rescue: The Secret Story of How American Advisers Helped Yeltsin Win." Vladimir Putin would later hold up that episode as evidence of American hypocrisy and political meddling, part of a bill of particulars that he would use to justify his own efforts to manipulate American politics.

After his reelection in November 1996, Clinton followed through on NATO expansion, with formal invitations extended to Poland, Hungary, and the Czech Republic in the summer of 1997. An elaborate NATO-Russia agreement was later reached, which helped address some of Yeltsin's concerns. Nevertheless, as Russians stewed in their grievance and sense of disadvantage, a gathering storm of "stab in the back" theories slowly swirled, leaving a mark on Russia's relations with the West that would linger for decades. No less a statesman than George Kennan, the architect of containment, called the expansion decision "the most fateful error of American policy in the entire post–Cold War era."

* * *

I FINISHED MY assignment in Moscow in early 1996, called back to Washington to become the executive secretary of the State Department, a senior career position that oversaw all the immediate staff support for the secretary of state. While it was a significant promotion, I missed Russia and the excitement of serving in a place in the midst of such consequential change.

In the years that followed, as debates about "who lost Russia" picked up steam, I thought often of what we had gotten right and what we had gotten wrong. The truth was that Russia was never ours to lose. Domestically, Russians had lost trust and confidence in themselves, and they would eventually have to remake their state and their economy. As the twentieth century wound to a close, Russians had been through generations of privation and tragedy. None of that could be fixed in a single generation, let alone a few years. None of it could be fixed by outsiders, even a United States at the peak of its post–Cold War dominance.

As Talbott later put it, "more therapy and less shock" would have been a better formula for easing Russia's transition to a market economy. But that was more a question of our sometimes flawed assumptions and advice than some grand missing economic initiative, a "Marshall Plan" that would have neatly transformed a broken post-Soviet economy. Russians would not have tolerated massive foreign intrusion reordering their economic life; they could only navigate that difficult landscape themselves.

When it came to international security arrangements, we were less Churchillian in our magnanimity. Sitting at the embassy in Moscow in the mid-1990s, it seemed to me that NATO expansion was premature at best, and needlessly provocative at worst. I understood and sympathized with the arguments for reassuring newly liberated Central European states, whose history created powerful reasons for anxiety about a revanchist Russia. I could plainly see the case for anchoring them quickly in Western institutions but thought a longer investment in the Partnership for Peace, prior to any move to formal NATO membership, made sense. It was wishful thinking, however, to believe that we could open the door to NATO membership without incurring some lasting cost with a Russia coping with its own historic insecurities.

Applied to this first wave of NATO expansion in Central Europe, Kennan's comments struck me as a little hyperbolic. It damaged prospects for future relations with Russia, but not fatally. Where we made a serious strategic mistake—and where Kennan was prescient—was in later letting inertia drive us to push for NATO membership for Ukraine and Georgia, despite Russia's deep historical attachments to both states and even stronger protestations. That did indelible damage, and fed the appetite of a future Russian leadership for getting even.

In the end, there proved to be no avoiding the sense of loss and humiliation that came with defeat in the Cold War and the collapse of the Soviet Union, no matter how many times we and the Russians told each other that the outcome had no losers, only winners. The forces of history would continue to reverberate, and Russia—as it had done throughout its tumultuous history—would eventually bounce back from catastrophe. There was bound to come a moment when Russia would have the capacity to toss off the junior-partner role that made it so uncomfortable, even as its long-term great power decline continued. That moment just came sooner than any of us anticipated.

4

Jordan's Moment of Transition: The Power of Partnership

KING HUSSEIN LOOKED awful. His face was drawn and pale, his eyes as cloudy as the sky on that piercingly cold January day in Amman. The king was near the end of a long battle with cancer, desperately ill and about to return to the Mayo Clinic in Minnesota for one last bone marrow transplant. Lisa and I joined the royal family and a handful of senior Jordanian officials at the airport to bid him farewell. The mood was heavy with anxiety and anticipation. After nearly a half century under Hussein's leadership, Jordanians were coming to grips with the prospect of losing the only ruler they had ever known.

A small receiving line formed on the way to the king's plane. He walked slowly, propping himself up with a cane in acute discomfort. His voice was uncharacteristically weak, but he was still as gracious as ever. I told him that our thoughts and prayers were with him, and that he—and Jordan—could count on our support. He squeezed my hand, smiled, and leaned in to whisper a few words of appreciation.

Queen Noor was in tears beside him, looking tired and sad, but trying hard to smile. Crown Prince Abdullah and Princess Rania, standing alongside Hussein and Noor, looked a little stunned, having learned within the last few days that they would become crown prince and princess—and before long, king and queen of Jordan.

After the king's plane had taken off, several of the royal guards—stalwart East Bank tribesmen—began to sob quietly. One elderly royal court official stopped me as I left, took me by the arm, and asked, "Do you ever think we'll see him again?"[1]

* * *

MY RETURN TO Jordan as ambassador, a little more than a decade after the end of my first diplomatic posting, was fortunate on several levels: It was unusual to have an opportunity to serve as ambassador so early in my career; it turned out to be an unusually interesting time to be in Amman, with the transition from Hussein to Abdullah emblematic of wider dramatic change in Jordan and the region; and it was as enjoyable a tour as our family ever had overseas. Lisa's work as the State Department's regional refugee coordinator often took her outside Jordan, driving her armored Suburban to visit Palestinian refugee camps from the outskirts of Damascus to the crowded center of Gaza. And my own job was a significant professional test, trying to steady and reassure a small but crucial partner at an historic inflection point.

I came to the assignment with the benefit of another demanding tour on the seventh floor behind me. Sitting between the offices of the secretary and the deputy secretary, I had spent more than two years leading the Executive Secretariat, a 160-person bureau that handled the relentless flow of information to the department's senior leadership; tasked material to prepare the secretary for meetings in Washington and abroad; organized the secretarial travel schedule; monitored implementation of secretarial decisions; and ran the Operations Center, the twenty-four-hour nerve center of the department, responsible for managing crises and connecting the secretary and senior officials to our embassies and their foreign counterparts.

It was a prestigious if mostly thankless job, with a punishing pace and recognition that usually came only when problems emerged or mistakes were made. The Operations Center typically juggled calls to foreign ministers and other senior foreign officials with remarkable dexterity, even in the most acute crises. On one memorable occasion early in my tenure, however, I got a late-night call from an irate senior department official, who had been accidentally connected to the wrong foreign minister. It hadn't helped that the minister on the line was a rival of the neighboring minister he had sought to speak to— and it really hadn't helped that my senior colleague had plowed through about five minutes of his talking points before realizing that he was speaking to the wrong person. Fortunately, the minister on the other end of the line had more of a sense of humor than my colleague, and calamity was averted.

Leading the Executive Secretariat was in a way the managerial and logistical complement on the seventh floor to the substantive work of the Policy Planning Staff. If Policy Planning was, especially in Baker's time, like a ship's navigation team, the Executive Secretariat was more like the engine room, where all the gears connected. The experience of leading both bureaus helped me understand how to marry policy ideas with policy action.

Warren Christopher was entering his last year as secretary when I began my new role as executive secretary in early 1996. Gentlemanly and deeply experienced, Christopher had served as deputy secretary under Secretary Cyrus Vance in the Carter years, and as deputy attorney general in the Johnson administration. Always well prepared, Christopher was as precise in his conversations with foreign counterparts or public statements as he was in his attire. In his bespoke suits, he could make even the most fastidious around him feel disheveled. I admired his quiet dignity and professionalism in a town that often prized self-promotion and chicanery. He was shy in public, but employed a dry wit, and took great pleasure in puncturing inflated egos. After one assistant secretary droned on at a morning staff meeting,

Christopher leaned toward me and deadpanned, "Remind me to bring my ejection button next time."

His successor, Madeleine Albright, thrived in her public role, and had a particular flair for putting foreign policy in practical terms. She could do diplomatic convolutions when she had to, but was much more in her element questioning the "cojones" of the Cuban regime after it shot down a defenseless civilian aircraft, or bluntly challenging Balkan despots. Proud to be the first woman to serve as secretary of state, Albright was a formidable presence on the international stage, extremely hardworking, and adept at managing hard issues and complicated personalities.

Along with Pat Kennedy, the acting undersecretary for management legendary for his bureaucratic wizardry, I led the department's transition effort from Christopher to Albright. This traditionally involved the preparation of dozens of voluminous briefing books on every conceivable issue that a new secretary might encounter, either in her confirmation hearing or in her early months in office. Given that Secretary Albright had already served as the U.S. ambassador to the United Nations for four years and was intimately familiar with most major policy questions, we tried to curb the department's enthusiasm for deforestation. Instead, we insisted that senior officials and chiefs of mission overseas craft their own personal notes to her. We knew that nothing would be more helpful to the incoming secretary than unvarnished first-person assessments of what had gone right and what had gone wrong during their tenures, what issues loomed on the horizon, and what strategies they would recommend going forward.

The results were mixed. Some of the first-person cables were exceptional—honest, insightful, and grounded in thoughtful policy prescriptions. Others were long-winded, whiny, self-absorbed, and deep in the weeds on issues that no secretary should have to address. For a new secretary, it was a useful introduction to the department she would now lead, with all its strengths, weaknesses, and idiosyncrasies.

"Friendly takeovers" in administrations of the same party, like the transition from Christopher to Albright, are supposed to be easy. Transitions from one party to another are assumed to be much more difficult. The reality is more complicated. New secretaries, no matter their party, want to put their own mark on personnel and policy. Much as Baker respected Shultz, he wanted to mold the department in his own way, and both he and President George H. W. Bush made clear that they were shaping the first Bush administration, not the third Reagan administration. Madeleine Albright was equally intent on putting her own stamp on the department, but I survived the reshuffle.

The administration was under heavy pressure to cut costs and streamline the foreign policy machinery from Senator Jesse Helms, the chairman of the Senate Foreign Relations Committee, a caricature of a neo-isolationist and a longtime critic of the Department of State and foreign assistance. With Helms leading the charge, Congress made clear its intention to cash in on the post–Cold War peace dividend, eventually shrinking the size of the foreign affairs budget by nearly half over the 1990s. Reading the tea leaves, the Clinton administration tried to get ahead of the cuts by laying out an affirmative vision for the most substantial restructuring of Washington national security institutions in a half century.

The secretary asked Pat and me to take the lead in managing one significant aspect of this effort—the complicated task of absorbing the Arms Control and Disarmament Agency (ACDA) and the U.S. Information Agency (USIA) into the State Department. ACDA, which my father led in the late 1980s, was much smaller than State, with about two hundred staff and a mission that remained essential but had shifted from its Cold War origins. Its consolidation into State was relatively straightforward. We created a new undersecretary position to absorb its key elements and transferred its professional cadre directly into the department.

USIA was a more difficult proposition. Its public diplomacy

mission—to expose other societies to American culture, ideas, and perspectives and make the case for American policy—was in many ways even more valuable in the post–Cold War world. It took years to fully merge the two personnel systems and bureaucratic cultures, and we lost much of USIA's public diplomacy expertise and program management skills along the way. That became painfully apparent in the aftermath of 9/11, especially in a roiling Islamic world. It became even more apparent when Putin's Russia mounted substantial disinformation campaigns a decade later.

The costs of the Helms-generated cuts and consolidation were long-lasting. At State, intake of new foreign service officers was virtually suspended for four years. This created substantial gaps at mid-level ranks a decade down the road, significantly hindering post–9/11 diplomacy as we struggled to find enough seasoned officers to fill key positions. History didn't end in the 1990s; we couldn't afford to rest on our laurels and await the inexorable march of globalization and American influence, and we paid a price for our shortsightedness.[2]

I learned more than I ever wanted to know about budgets, personnel, regulations, and congressional affairs during my two years as executive secretary. I knew, at least conceptually, that it was an investment that would pay off. But I missed doing diplomacy and was eager to return overseas.

Secretary Albright and Strobe Talbott, by now deputy secretary of state, could sense my impatience, and offered to support my candidacy to become ambassador to Jordan—if I agreed to extend for another year through the summer of 1998. It was a hard offer to refuse, not only because it would fulfill every young diplomat's dream to become an ambassador, but also because it would allow me to return to Jordan—and this time to experience it with Lisa and our daughters. I had a blessedly uneventful confirmation hearing before the Senate Foreign Relations Committee, and was sworn in by Madeleine Albright in late July. Sixteen years into the Foreign Service, I had come full circle.

* * *

IN A CABLE to President Clinton on the eve of King Hussein's funeral in Amman in February 1999, I reminded him of a comment
attributed to John Foster Dulles in the early 1950s. "King Hussein is
an impressive young fellow," Dulles said. "It's a shame that neither he
nor his country will last very long."[3] Nearly five decades later, Jordan
was still intact, and the king himself had become the region's longest-
serving head of state. He had survived a coup attempt in 1957, the
disaster of the Six-Day War in 1967, the events of Black September a
few years later, and a series of assassination attempts along the way.
He had not only kept Jordan afloat amid the unending turbulence of
the Middle East, but created a sense of national identity and an oper-
able, if still fragile, economy.

The practical dilemmas facing Jordan in the summer of 1998 were
nevertheless daunting. Water scarcity was an urgent problem; per
capita consumption was one-fortieth that of Americans. Unemployment ran at more than 20 percent, with underemployment an equally
flammable problem. The population of roughly five million was
growing rapidly, GDP growth was flat, and external debt was rising.
Jordan had few natural resources. It ran a growing trade deficit, importing most of its food and heavily dependent on outside assistance.
Hussein periodically had to employ austerity measures and tighten
budgets, but cuts in subsidies brought popular unrest, and the king
was generally unable to sustain serious economic reform programs.

As he neared his forty-seventh year on the throne, Hussein was
the embodiment of Jordan, the singular guarantor of national unity.
Down below, society was still riven by fault lines, some old and some
new. Over half the population was of Palestinian origin. East Bankers,
the townspeople and descendants of the Bedouin tribes who had
populated the hard hills and deserts east of the Jordan River before
the waves of Palestinian arrivals after the 1948 and 1967 wars, were
fiercely protective of their political control and prerogatives. Several

hundred thousand Iraqis had fled to Jordan after Desert Storm. Meanwhile, another newer fault line was widening, between the struggling poor of east Amman and other Jordanian cities and the conspicuously consuming residents of Abdoun and other neighborhoods in west Amman.

Political opposition was closely monitored by the General Intelligence Department (GID). Hussein sometimes let off steam through carefully managed political liberalization; in 1989, for example, he had allowed fairly open elections and the formation of a government that included Islamists. His rule was absolute, but wrapped in a tolerance and relative generosity of spirit that set Jordan apart from other regimes in the region.

If Hussein had a tough hand to play at home, his neighborhood was even rougher. While the king's longevity, shrewdness, and friends outside the region (in particular the United States) brought him some respect, it came mostly grudgingly. To the north, Hafez al-Assad's Syria looked down its nose at Jordan—which was a part of Greater Syria during Ottoman times, and was now a country most Syrians thought of as an historical anomaly. To the east lay Saddam Hussein's Iraq, isolated after Desert Storm but still menacing, a source of concessional oil and a market for Jordan's goods. To the south, Saudi Arabia often took a dim view of Hashemite Jordan, always mindful that the House of Saud had expelled Hussein's great-grandfather from the Hejaz in the 1920s. Across the Red Sea and Gulf of Aqaba was Egypt, self-consciously the center of the Arab world and usually disinclined to pay much attention to an inconsequential smaller Arab power like Jordan. And to the west was Israel, which had a strategic interest in a stable, moderate Jordan. Since the 1950s, Hussein had kept up secret contacts with the Israelis. After the Oslo Accords between the Israelis and the Palestinians, Hussein seized the opportunity to negotiate a peace treaty with Israel, solidifying his regional position and repairing the damage with the United States that lingered after the Gulf War.

By 1998, U.S.-Jordanian relations were quite healthy. President Clinton and Secretary Albright reintroduced me to King Hussein as their nominee for ambassador when the king visited Washington in June. I had been a background fixture in Hussein's meetings with senior Americans over the years, and his courtly mannerisms and deep, easy laugh were familiar. Clinton and the king had an excellent relationship. The president had obvious respect for Hussein's judgment and experience, and the king had an equally obvious, almost avuncular affection for Clinton's intellect and commitment to Arab-Israeli peace.

In that initial June conversation, Hussein was upbeat and looking ahead. "We'll do a lot together," he said. "You already know Jordan and our challenges. There is so much we can accomplish during this administration." Sadly, the king would return to the Mayo Clinic in July, before I arrived in Amman, with a recurrence of an even more deadly form of cancer. He would spend only a couple more weeks of his life in Jordan.

The embassy that I took over at the beginning of August 1998 was a much different place from the one I left in 1984. It occupied a new and much larger complex west of the old center of Amman, built in the early 1990s to fit the new security specifications for American embassies around the world. It contained 130 American employees and 270 Jordanians, roughly twice the staff of the embassy I had left. The compound was about the size of six or seven football fields, and was surrounded by a nine-foot wall. Inside were a sizable circular chancery building, a service annex and motor pool, a social club and swimming pool, and the ambassador's residence. Lisa and the girls and I enjoyed our new home; what it lacked in privacy it made up for in convenience, with my office a two-minute walk away.

Security was a persistent concern throughout our three years in Amman. On our third night in our new home, Lisa and I were awakened by a 2 A.M. phone call from the Operations Center, and a contingent of Marines in full combat gear barreling upstairs to help secure the residence. An urgent threat report warned that there would be an RPG attack on the embassy compound that night. Fortunately, the plotters were caught in time. A few days later, al-Qaeda struck two American embassies in East Africa, with massive loss of life.

Threats reemerged throughout our tour, and were particularly worrisome at the end of 1999, when a major al-Qaeda attack on Jordanian hotel and tourist sites was thwarted. We had entered a new era in diplomatic insecurity, in which risks—for many years a painful feature of embassy life—were increasing, and Washington's appetite for risk-taking was diminishing.

* * *

SITTING IN HIS hospital room in Minnesota in July 1998, King Hussein gave a television interview that jarred his Jordanian audience. "The doctors' diagnosis is lymphoma," he said with a weary smile. "My cancer is a new fight which I hope to win." There was reason for the king to be optimistic. He was only sixty-two, he'd already won a bout with bladder cancer earlier that decade, and he had one of the world's best teams of doctors treating him at Mayo.[4]

Jordanians, however, were uneasy. They had become utterly dependent on one man, and were not used to having him out of the country for months at a time. Through force of personality and political dexterity, Hussein had camouflaged societal divisions in Jordan and created a role for his country on the regional stage out of all proportion to its strategic weight and resources. Most Jordanians had grown unaccustomed to taking political responsibility, let alone thinking about what might follow after Hussein. There was no escaping that now.

Hussein's younger brother, Hassan, had served as crown prince since 1965, when the king had decided amid a particularly intense spate of assassination threats that it would be irresponsible to keep his oldest son, Abdullah, then only three years old, as his successor. Hussein and Hassan were eleven years apart in age, but the difference in their personalities seemed even wider. Intuitive and full of restless energy, the king had an easy rapport with Jordanians, at home with Bedouin sheikhs in the desert or military units in the field. Hassan was at heart an intellectual. It was hard to imagine him clambering atop a tank to speak to his troops, as Hussein had done so many times over the years. Oxford-educated and widely read, Hassan could come across as a bit detached from the world of most Jordanians—a disconnect reinforced by his official 1998 birthday portrait, in which he posed in full polo regalia, complete with helmet, mallet, and jodhpurs, seated on his favorite pony.

And yet beyond traits that were easy to caricature, Hassan was as devoted to Jordan as Hussein. He worked hard, was deeply knowledgeable about his country, and loyal to his brother. He also had more of a common touch than he was given credit for. When Secretary of Commerce Bill Daley visited Jordan in the fall of 1998, Hassan insisted on driving us back to Daley's hotel after dinner at his lovely old stone house on a hill overlooking downtown Amman. He got behind the wheel of his Land Rover, with a bemused commerce secretary riding shotgun and me in the backseat, and another vehicle full of royal guards in the rear. Pulling out of the palace gate, Hassan asked if we wanted to stop for tea in the Wehdat refugee camp, which was more or less on the way. Daley was haggard after a long day of meetings, but he knew it would be impolite to say no. And so the three of us wound up sitting at a tiny shop on one of the camp's densely packed streets at midnight, drinking tea surrounded by curious Palestinian teenagers and an increasingly nervous group of royal guards. Hassan was breezy and nonchalant, asking the shopkeeper about his family, engaging in small talk with other patrons, and basking in the moment.

King Hussein's long hospitalization in the second half of 1998 became, in effect, Hassan's dress rehearsal for the throne, after thirty-three years as crown prince. It didn't end well. There were all the hallmarks of Shakespearean drama—a dying king coming to terms with his own mortality; a beleaguered crown prince trying to show he was ready for a job that was fast receding from him; a royal family struggling with loss and dysfunction; sons coming of age in the midst of so much scrutiny and uncertainty; and courtiers angling for advantage. There were no real villains, just a chain of difficult circumstances and complicated personalities. The king had been drifting for some time toward a change in the line of succession. His illness merely accelerated that decision. His unease about Hassan was not about loyalty or intellect or commitment, but about whether he was the best person to lead Jordan through what the king knew would be a tough transition. And his sense of confidence in his sons had grown as they matured. Prince Abdullah, now in his late thirties, had become an accomplished and well-respected military officer. Prince Hamzeh, now eighteen and Hussein's eldest son by the last of his wives, Queen Noor, was a cadet at Sandhurst, with a manner and bearing much like his father's.

As uncertainties about the king's health and succession unfolded that fall and winter, my main task as ambassador was to place America's hand on Jordan's shoulder and do whatever I could to help steady a country on which the United States depended heavily. A stable Jordanian partner was essential to Israel's security and hopes for Palestinian-Israeli peace, and Jordan's geopolitical value as a moderate, reliable friend in a tough neighborhood was out of all proportion to its demographic and economic weight. This was a classic opportunity for American diplomacy, as the organizer and mobilizer of support from other countries and international institutions—and for an ambassador as conductor, orchestrating the varied instruments of the American bureaucratic symphony.

Crown Prince Hassan was gracious and welcoming from the start. Barely ten days into my new role, I had to call him a little after midnight to seek an urgent meeting and preview the cruise missile strikes that the United States was about to launch against al-Qaeda targets in Afghanistan in retaliation for the embassy attacks in East Africa.

Without hesitation, he agreed to see me, and we spent an hour or two drinking his favorite single malt scotch and discussing a variety of challenges beyond those lighting up the sky over Afghanistan. Hassan seemed a bit lonely, with few confidants outside his immediate family. That was partly a function of personality, but also partly because the king moved people in and out of his brother's inner circle and never allowed him to develop an independent political base. Hassan was understandably thin-skinned about stories drawing unflattering contrasts with his brother. He was too proud to look for sympathy but anxious for signs that people respected him in his own right. I went out of my way to make clear that I did.

Prince Abdullah and I were only a few years apart in age. He spent a year at Oxford soon after I finished there, and we had shared an academic mentor in Albert Hourani. At the time, Hourani described Abdullah to me in a letter as "smart and personable" but someone who seemed "destined more for a life of action than of books."[5]

In late August 1998, Prince Abdullah and his wife, Princess Rania, invited Lisa and me to an informal dinner at their home. A fan of Japanese cuisine, Abdullah was an accomplished cook, and prepared Kobe beef on the grill. The setting was relaxed and unpretentious, just like our hosts. The only other guests were from the royal family— Abdullah's brothers and sisters; his mother, Princess Muna, a lovely, down-to-earth person and King Hussein's second, British wife; and her father, Colonel Gardiner, a veteran of the Italian campaign in World War II. It was the first of a number of evenings that we would spend with Abdullah and Rania over the next few years, including each of the Thanksgivings we celebrated in Amman, when we supplied the turkey and they brought the pies. They were funny and unaffected, with Princess Rania a particularly good judge of people, and Prince Abdullah proud of his family and his growing responsibilities in the military.

With uncertainty about King Hussein's health hanging over everything, I tried hard to build as broad a set of relationships as I could, inside the royal family and across Jordanian society. I worked easily with the prime minister, Fayez Tarawneh, an affable East Bank technocrat, instinctively cautious but increasingly concerned about Jordan's economic predicament. The foreign minister, Abdul-Ilah al-Khatib, was a capable professional and good friend. Rima Khalaf, the minister of planning and one of the most senior women officials in the Arab world, was impressive and reform-minded. Samieh Battikhi was then the head of the General Intelligence Department, a shrewd and ambitious operator with a lifestyle obviously not purely a function of his government salary. The GID was already a crucial intelligence partner for the United States; it was also slowly becoming the power behind the throne.

Meanwhile, Crown Prince Hassan was trying to demonstrate that he could manage affairs in Hussein's absence, without appearing to usurp the king's authority. It was an extremely difficult balancing act. In September, Hassan stepped on the sensibilities of the Jordanian military leadership, questioning their budget submission and raising the issue of whether it would make sense to accelerate senior military retirements and make way for the next generation. Neither was an unreasonable thought—but military affairs were exclusively the king's preserve, and Hussein was upset when word filtered back to him at Mayo, undoubtedly flavored by the wounded sensitivities of his generals.

I had easy access to senior Jordanians throughout my time in Amman, and there were times when it seemed a little too easy, especially in this early period. On one occasion, Hassan invited me to sit in on an internal briefing from his military leadership in preparation for a forthcoming meeting of the U.S.-Jordanian Joint Military Commission. I did my best to be unobtrusive, but it was an awkward experience. The crown prince was pointed in his commentary, peremptory and a little patronizing in manner, interrupting the briefers repeatedly to question their arguments. His intent was straightforward. He wanted to ensure a tight presentation, and also to demonstrate his understanding of military realities. But it didn't go down well with the officers in the room. You could see them gritting their teeth—and thinking to themselves that King Hussein would never have treated them that way.

The crown prince stayed in regular contact with the king during his treatment, but chose not to visit him at Mayo. He thought his role was to mind the store in Jordan, and Hussein seemed to agree. But that put Hassan at a considerable tactical disadvantage, as other senior family members and officials, many of whom were not admirers of the crown prince, flew back and forth to see the king in the United States. The army chief, Field Marshal Abdul Hafez Marei Kaabneh, complained directly to the king on one visit that fall about Hassan, alleging that he was telling senior military officers that Hussein's condition was "irreversible," and that they would need to prepare for the possibility of a transition. Hassan later denied to me that he had ever said that. But the damage was done, and the king's irritation grew. Rumors reached Mayo that Princess Sarvath, Hassan's intelligent but occasionally sharp-elbowed wife, was agitating privately for Hassan to move immediately if he became king to make their son, Rashid, the new crown prince. Queen Noor, not a big fan of either Hassan or Sarvath, was with the king throughout his treatment, and fed his mounting discontent.

At President Clinton's request, Hussein flew from Mayo to Washington in late October to help prod the Israelis and Palestinians toward compromise at talks taking place at the Wye Plantation, on the Eastern Shore of Maryland. The king had a magnetic effect, and played a valuable role in producing the Wye River Memorandum, in which the Palestinians and Israelis finally settled on implementation of the redeployments and other interim arrangements in the West Bank that had been agreed to several years before. On the day of the White House signing ceremony, Hussein received a number of senior Jordanian visitors in Washington, among them former prime minister Abdul Karim Kabariti. They reinforced the king's concerns about the crown prince. Hussein told Kabariti that he was considering "major changes" when he returned to Jordan.

I heard versions of all of this from each of the protagonists as they returned to Amman. It was clear that the king's illness was sharpening his focus on the future, and that changes of some sort were looming. Their pace and scope obviously depended to some extent on his health. While the king was upbeat to Jordanians about his prognosis, the reports we were hearing were much more guarded and uncertain.

Hassan was concerned about his brother's health, and increasingly anxious about the reports of royal displeasure with his performance. He invited me and my exceptional CIA station chief, Rob Richer, to a private dinner soon after the Wye agreement, and fished politely for information on the king's health and disposition.[6] I was careful; there was no percentage in getting in the middle of what was a thorny royal decision. There had already been erroneous stories in the British press in the fall that the U.S. administration lacked confidence in Hassan. We had quickly knocked them down, and Madeleine Albright had even called Hassan to reassure him. Moreover, I was still not yet entirely convinced that the king would push Hassan aside. It seemed to me that our role in this delicate moment was to make clear our strong and enduring commitment to king and country, steer clear of political infighting, and keep our lines open.[7]

I had ample support from Washington. In November and December alone, we had visits to Amman from Secretary Albright, Secretary Daley, Secretary of Defense Bill Cohen, and CIA director George Tenet. I pressed the administration to do all we could to invest in our relationship with Jordan now; if Hussein's health worsened, more tangible backing at this point for Jordan's economy and security would put us in a stronger position to support the transition than if we had to scramble later to catch up with events.[8] The White House began to consider a supplemental assistance package and other contingency steps we might take to shore up the dinar and avoid financial panic.

By early January 1999, the king had completed his treatment at Mayo. It would take a couple weeks to determine whether his bone marrow transplant had cured his cancer, but popular expectations for a full recovery were high. I flew over to see him before he left the United States, just after New Year's. We met at the house the king had owned for some years in suburban Maryland, on a high wooded bluff overlooking the Potomac. It was a gloomy winter afternoon, with a clear view of the river through the leafless trees. He was weak, shivering beneath his heavy sweater. "I am eager to get home," he said. "It has been so long, and there is so much to do."

I congratulated him again on Wye. He smiled wanly, underscoring his skepticism about both Netanyahu and Arafat, but emphasized how much faith he had in President Clinton. "It will be good to work with you once I'm home," he continued. "I've had a lot of time to think about the future. I don't know how much time I have left in this world, and there are some things I need to do." Hussein left it at that, and made it clear that he didn't want to be drawn out. I returned to Amman convinced that a change in succession was coming.

Hundreds of thousands of Jordanians lined the streets to welcome the king back home on January 19. The next day, Hussein gave an interview to CNN's Christiane Amanpour, in which he hinted—for the first time in public—of changes to come. The king kept putting off a meeting with Hassan, and the crown prince knew what that meant. I saw him on the afternoon of January 21, and he told me that Princess Basma, the only sister of Hussein and Hassan, had just come over to tell him that he was on his way out. Hassan was in deep distress. "I truly can't understand why the king is so upset with me," he said. Nevertheless, he would handle the decision with dignity.

Finally, on the night of January 22, the king told Hassan he had decided to change succession. Earlier that day, he had informed Prince Abdullah that he would become crown prince. The king made his choice public on January 25, publishing an uncharacteristically mean-spirited letter detailing his disappointment in Hassan. His treatment had failed, and he would have to return to Mayo the next day for a last-ditch effort to save his life and a second bone marrow transplant.

At thirty-seven, Abdullah was nearly two decades older than his father had been when he took the throne. Jordan was a far more stable place than it had been then, but there was no shortage of challenges on the horizon, or regional predators. Abdullah knew how much he had to learn, but did not seem intimidated. Secretary Albright made a brief but timely visit to Amman on January 28, reassuring the new crown prince and pledging American support for Jordan. I saw Hassan again a few days later. There were no visitors waiting to see him, and he commented wryly that he didn't expect many to seek him out. He was clearly hurt by a turn of events that he still didn't fully comprehend, but he had no interest in seeking sympathy. I told him I admired the grace with which he was handling all this, and I meant it. For all his years of service as crown prince, Hassan's biggest contribution to the future of Jordan may have been the way in which he managed his biggest disappointment.

The king's second bone marrow transplant failed, and he headed home again one last time. He had lost consciousness by the time his plane landed in Amman on February 4, and his vital organs were beginning to shut down. In one final display of the stubborn courage that had taken him and Jordan so far, Hussein outlived his doctors' predictions of death for three more days. As I put it in a cable to Washington, "It was almost as if, conscious or unconscious, the King was determined to show that only he—not CNN or anxious foreign audiences or medical experts, or anyone else—would decide when he would make his exit. He lived a life that ran against the odds. John Foster Dulles was just the first in a long line of people to underestimate him, and Jordan. It is worth remembering that as all of us contemplate a future without King Hussein."[9]

February 7, the day King Hussein died, was another in the series of cold rainy days that seemed to reflect the Jordanian mood that winter. I made a point of walking around the embassy to talk to all of our Jordanian employees, individually or in groups. This was as wrenching a national moment as they had ever faced. Many had tears streaming down their faces. I wanted them to know that they could count on American friendship. Later that day, I talked again to King Abdullah. He was sad but unflustered as he prepared for what some would later call "the funeral of the century," which by Islamic tradition had to take place within twenty-four hours of his father's death.

It was an unforgettable tableau. Seventy-five countries sent representatives. President Clinton flew overnight to attend, along with the First Lady and three former presidents—George H. W. Bush, Jimmy Carter, and Gerald Ford. I couldn't imagine a more powerful gesture of American respect. The other leaders who came sent a similarly impressive signal. They made an unusual scene at Raghadan Palace, as strange a collection of bedfellows as I had ever witnessed, their tangled and occasionally lethal rivalries on full display.

There in one corner was the Israeli delegation, led by Prime Minister Netanyahu, looking warily across the room at Hafez al-Assad, whose own health was fading but who wanted to come in a curious show of admiration for the Hashemite ruler he had tried so hard to undermine over the years. Standing not far from the Israelis was Khaled Meshal, the Hamas leader whose assassination the Mossad had bungled in downtown Amman a year before. Arafat chatted amiably with Mubarak. Iraqi vice president Taha Mohieddin Maruf scowled from a distance, representing Saddam Hussein, who had only a month before employed his usual tact in referring publicly to King Hussein as a "throne dwarf." One of Muammar al-Qaddafi's sons talked with Crown Prince Abdullah of Saudi Arabia, whom his father would shortly plot to murder. Prime Minister Tony Blair and Prince Charles came from London, and President Jacques Chirac from Paris.

Even Boris Yeltsin came, ill and disoriented, and propped up in a corner of the room by two aides—intent upon honoring King Hus-

sein, and upon not missing such a remarkable gathering of his con-
temporaries. Bill Clinton worked the room as only he could, gripping
the arms of his counterparts and consoling Jordanian royal family
members. By early evening, the simple burial ceremony completed,
Air Force One had departed, and the other delegations had left for
home. Jordanians were left to consider the complicated world before
them, without the only leader most of them had ever known.

* * *

PRESIDENT CLINTON TOOK me aside at one point on the dreary
day of King Hussein's funeral, as we were walking across the tarmac
to Air Force One and his return flight to Washington. "The next few
months are going to be all about reassurance," he said. "I'm counting
on you to help support these people. Just let us know what you need."
The president was as good as his word, and over the next two years
the United States paid careful attention to Jordan's well-being. I drew
on everything I had learned over the years and every connection I had
in the executive branch and Congress to drum up and sustain interest
in supporting the Jordanians at this crucial moment. I was careful
not to oversell the risks King Abdullah faced, but determined to ex-
haust every possibility to show American reliability.

I believed it was profoundly in our interest to do so. As I wrote in
a cable soon after King Abdullah's accession, "We have a strong and
continuing stake in a stable Jordanian partner at the geographic and
political center of the Middle East. If we didn't have such a partner,
we'd have to invent one."[10]

The day before the funeral, President Clinton issued a public
statement stressing his confidence in the Jordanian economy, and
confirming that he would ask Congress for $300 million in supple-
mental military and economic aid. He pledged to work with G-7 and
Gulf Arab partners to mobilize more support, including steps to ease
Jordan's $7 billion external debt burden. He said he would work with
the World Bank and the International Monetary Fund to marshal ad-

ditional help. The president's vote of confidence helped stave off the run on the Jordanian dinar that officials in Amman had feared, and give the new king a little economic breathing space.

In succeeding months, the administration increased concessional wheat shipments to Jordan. It also expanded the Qualifying Industrial Zones (QIZ) program, which allowed duty-free access into the American market for goods produced in Jordan, so long as they had 8 percent Israeli content (one example was a luggage line manufactured at a QIZ in northern Jordan, in which Israeli-produced plastic handles accounted for the required percentage). By 2000, some forty thousand new jobs were created in Jordanian QIZs. More ambitiously, we provided enthusiastic support for Jordan's bid to join the World Trade Organization, which was accomplished in the spring of 2000. That was the essential first step in negotiating a bilateral free trade agreement, the first with an Arab country and only the fourth such U.S. agreement anywhere in the world.

When President Clinton and King Abdullah finally signed the free trade agreement in October 2000, it sent a signal of confidence in Jordan that was as much political as it was economic. Other than the precedential effect of the terms of the agreement, and making sure that American businesses could compete on a fair playing field in Jordan, there was relatively little consequence for the infinitely larger American economy. By contrast, it was an enormous psychological and practical boost for Jordan. Thanks to both the FTA and the QIZs, Jordan's exports to the United States shot up from barely $9 million in 1998 to over $1 billion by 2004. Annual U.S. assistance levels rose dramatically as well, from $7 million in 1996 to $950 million in 2003, as Jordan became the third-largest recipient of American aid in the world.

Meanwhile, King Abdullah plunged into his new role with considerable energy and drive. He quickly overcame doubts about his inexperience, and showed a flair for leadership at home and selling Jordan's case abroad. He understood that the outpouring of international and regional goodwill that followed his father's death would not last long. Without the baggage of the Gulf War and his father's refusal to join the Desert Storm coalition, Abdullah rebuilt bridges to the Saudis and Kuwaitis, and connected easily with next-generation leaders in Bahrain and the United Arab Emirates. Without the competitive tensions that had shaped his father's relationships with leaders like Hafez al-Assad, he solidified ties with Syria and other Arab neighbors. In his first year on the throne, he visited all of the G-7 capitals, including two productive trips to Washington, where he demonstrated even greater finesse than Hussein in cultivating Congress, and even less hesitation in asking for assistance.

At home, Abdullah built an appealing persona, exhibiting common sense and natural strengths as a unifier. Personable and practical, he got off to a good start with most of the sometimes cranky leaders of the East Bank establishment, and impressed many of the rising figures in Jordan's tiny and often inert and risk-averse private sector with his modernizing instincts. Abdullah could count on the loyalty of the military in which he had served for more than two decades. He tried to project a populist air, dressing in disguise as an elderly local and observing the bureaucracy at its plodding pace in Zarqa and other poorer parts of the country.

Prince Hassan kept his disappointment largely to himself, and his dignity intact. Samieh Battikhi remained at GID, watching the king's back but more and more prone to self-aggrandizement. A sturdy East Bank warhorse, Abdul Raouf Rawabdeh, a former mayor of Amman, became prime minister. Not exactly a poster child for reform, but good at soothing establishment sensibilities, the conservative Rawabdeh was balanced by the more risk-taking Abdul Karim Kabariti, now chief of the royal court. Kabariti reinforced the king's reformist impulses, and together they drove a fair amount of change: privatization of the telecommunications sector and several significant companies; legislation to protect intellectual property rights; a new economic consultative council; and a major initiative to attract investment in the information technology sector. The king himself didn't hesitate in that early era to roll up his sleeves and hold his ministers to timetables and action plans—a novel experience for most of them.

The king was easy to talk to, and we usually saw each other several times a week, whether at his office at the palace, at home in Amman or Aqaba, or at events around Jordan. I was always careful not to waste his time or abuse my access. I was equally careful to balance my relationships with the royal family and senior government officials with a range of other Jordanians, and to keep a sharp-eyed perspective on what was going right in this complicated transition and what challenges loomed.

"Clientitis" is a common affliction among diplomats, the tendency to gradually conflate the interests of the country you represent with those of the country in which you serve. One symptom is a selective blindness to the country's flaws, exacerbated by the seductive power of access and apparent influence. I tried hard to avoid that during my time in Jordan, but didn't always succeed. I kept my lines open to critics of the Jordanian elite and my attention fixed on obvious problems of economic stagnation; corruption that was small-bore by regional standards, but nonetheless pervasive; political repression that was modest compared to the practice of most of Jordan's neighbors, but nonetheless persistent; and institutional dominance by a Jordanian intelligence establishment that was a valuable regional partner for the United States and less thuggish than in most of the region, but nonetheless troublesome. I'm sure I occasionally sanded the edges of my judgments. A lot was at stake for the United States in the transition from Hussein to Abdullah, and in a region where imperfections were relative and successes rare, I had no doubt of the value of our support.

In one cable at the beginning of 2000, I wrote, "If you had asked most Jordanians a year ago, as King Hussein lay dying, how their country would fare without him, few would have predicted the impressive achievements in economic reform and regional diplomacy of

King Abdullah, whom they barely knew." I added, without hyperbole, that Abdullah "has done more to reform the structure of the Jordanian economy in the last six months than Jordan did in the entire previous decade." I was also quick to point out that the hard part was coming. I stressed that "if he is going to turn the promise and the glitter of his first year into enduring success in Jordan, the King will have to begin to show tangible results for structural economic reforms, start a process of opening up a sclerotic political system, and lay the basis for long-term protection of Jordanian interests in a region on the verge of some profound changes."[11]

The wider region remained a snakepit, despite the king's skill in navigating it. More than a decade before the Arab Spring, the social and economic forces building beneath the surface of the region were intensifying. In an April 2000 cable, I argued that "globalization, technological change and the expanding reach of independent media will only increase the pressures on the anachronistic, authoritarian regimes who dominate the Arab world—even ones as relatively tolerant and civil as the Hashemites."[12] On the immediate horizon were adversaries in the neighborhood, and troubles waiting to erupt. Two of the most obvious were Saddam Hussein's Iraq, badly wounded in the Gulf War but still a deeply complicated problem for Jordan, and the fragile relationship between Israelis and Palestinians on the other side of the Jordan River.

* * *

EVER SINCE THE end of the Gulf War in the spring of 1991, the United States had been engaged in a frustrating effort to contain Saddam Hussein, protect the Kurds, and prevent Iraq from menacing its neighbors. The UN Security Council had authorized no-fly zones in northern and southern Iraq, which the United States policed at considerable expense. A UN inspection regime (UNSCOM) had been established to work with the International Atomic Energy Agency to ensure that Saddam met his UNSC-mandated obligations to destroy any remaining infrastructure and stocks of weapons of mass destruction, as well as ballistic missiles with a range of more than ninety miles. Stringent economic sanctions remained in place to keep pressure on Saddam to comply.

Inevitably, this whole structure became increasingly difficult to manage. Early in President Clinton's tenure, Saddam mounted an unsuccessful plot to assassinate former president Bush in Kuwait. Clinton retaliated with missile strikes against Iraq. As the years went by, Saddam episodically challenged U.S. aircraft enforcing the no-fly zones, and the United States responded. The Iraqis angered the Americans with their practice of "cheat and retreat" in dealing with UNSCOM—refusing access to sites for long periods, eventually offering limited concessions under pressure, and then repeating the whole maddening process. Saddam declared eight large compounds, containing more than a thousand buildings, to be presidential palaces, exempt from inspection. In December 1998, the United States launched Operation Desert Fox, a series of air and missile strikes against Iraqi targets, to punish Saddam for his intransigence.

Jordan was exposed on several fronts, leaving Abdullah with a nettlesome set of competing demands. It was heavily dependent on a concessional oil arrangement with Iraq, tacitly permitted by the United States and the UN Security Council, and increasingly squeezed as oil prices rose in the late 1990s. Iraq remained an important and irreplaceable market for cheap Jordanian goods, especially pharmaceuticals. Jordanian popular sympathies also remained strongly with the Iraqis, amplified by the human impact of sanctions and aggravated by broader antipathy toward American policy in the region.

King Abdullah had no illusions about Saddam. He continued the quiet practice of exchanging information about Iraq with the United States and supported our forces involved in the no-fly zones. But he couldn't afford the economic or domestic political consequences of outright opposition to Saddam. The Gulf Arabs might have eased his calculus by substituting concessional oil for the Iraqi arrangement, but whether for reasons of lingering animus toward Jordan's position in the Gulf War or inertia never followed through. Abdullah was in a bind.

His own encounters over the years with the Iraqi leadership had been dispiriting, and often bizarre. King Abdullah once told me about an especially strange encounter. Some years before, in the late 1980s, King Hussein sent Abdullah and his younger brother, Prince Faisal, to Baghdad to get acquainted with Saddam's sons, Uday and Qusay Hussein. Uday, then still in his twenties, had not yet achieved the notoriety of his later years, when he regularly showed off the pet lions in his Baghdad palace, beat the members of the Iraqi national soccer team when they lost matches, and kidnapped and raped female Iraqi university students who caught his eye. Qusay was less visibly thuggish, but already developing a reputation as his father's son when it came to cunning brutality.

On the second day of the visit, their hosts took Abdullah and Faisal for a boat ride on a large man-made lake outside Baghdad. Expecting a quiet afternoon, both were more than a little shocked when Uday—always the thrill seeker—pulled out an RPG and fired it just ahead of his own security patrol a few dozen yards away. No one was hurt, but Uday didn't seem at all bothered by the prospect, acting as if this were just another way to spend an afternoon. Abdullah and Faisal were horrified. As Abdullah put it, "There are many people in my generation of leaders in the region with whom I already have a good rapport—but Uday is not one of them."[13]

After Abdullah became king, he grew increasingly anxious about the direction of American policy toward Iraq. He was skeptical that the Iraq Liberation Act (ILA), passed by Congress and signed into law by President Clinton late in the autumn of 1998, represented anything more than wishful thinking. The ILA stated explicitly that it was the goal of the United States to change the regime in Baghdad, but Abdullah saw no compelling strategy behind the rhetoric—and a lot of risk for Jordan along the way. He thought many of those most prominent in the exiled Iraqi opposition movement were frauds, or at best naïve. He was particularly caustic about Ahmed Chalabi, who had been run out of Jordan a decade before as head of a prominent local bank, following allegations of embezzlement.

As he emphasized to me with mounting concern in 1999 and 2000, the king saw Western sanctions policy as self-defeating. Saddam had successfully manipulated the UN's Oil for Food Program, aimed at easing the plight of ordinary Iraqis, to tighten his own grip on power. By late 2000, Abdullah told me that "it's more likely that Saddam will be killed by a meteor than that sanctions will undermine him."[14]

By the end of the Clinton administration, the king was arguing consistently that the United States was helping, not hurting, Saddam, allowing him to play the victim and exploit an increasingly tense regional situation. He maintained that Washington should abandon economic or civilian sanctions, and instead intensify measures prohibiting the import of military or dual-use items. These so-called smart sanctions had obvious drawbacks, since Saddam could exploit the revenue from unrestricted oil sales to solidify his regime, but Abdullah's argument was that he was more or less doing this anyway, and the United States needed to regain the initiative. It was certainly a self-serving position for Jordan, but that didn't make it wrong.

*   *   *

AS JORDAN'S CHALLENGE to the east became more worrisome, its dilemma to the west grew larger too. In that same conversation in Aqaba in late 2000 about Iraqi sanctions, the king expressed mounting concern about the Second Intifada, the Palestinian uprising that had been triggered by Ariel Sharon's provocative visit to the Temple Mount several weeks earlier. As he pointed out, Saddam was using the ugly spectacle in the West Bank to divert attention and pressure, and to fan regional animus toward American policy. Jordan was stuck in the middle, politically and physically. I cabled Washington later that day, restating the glaringly obvious: "It is important to take a step back and look soberly at the collateral damage that the unfolding tragedy across the river could do to relatively moderate countries like Jordan, which are not exactly a growth industry in this region these days."[15]

When King Abdullah took the throne, things had looked more positive across the river. The Wye agreement, which his father had so heroically inspired, was the latest incremental step toward the two-state solution envisioned by the Oslo Accords of 1993. Progress had been painful and halting, but by the beginning of 1999 the Palestinian Authority, led by Yasser Arafat, exerted some degree of control over 40 percent of the West Bank, and most of Gaza. In May of that year, Labor's Ehud Barak won the Israeli elections and ousted Likud's Bibi Netanyahu, a leader in whom neither Abdullah nor his father had had much faith.

Early in Barak's tenure, a new target of September 2000 was set for completion of negotiations about the permanent status of the West Bank and Gaza, the latest in a series of moving goalposts since Oslo. Barak decided, however, to concentrate first on negotiations with Syria. He disliked the incrementalism of the Oslo process, which he thought maximized domestic political cost in Israel for minimal strategic gains. The Syria track offered a chance to produce a big strategic reward, removing the more serious security threat posed by the Assad regime, as well as building leverage on Arafat in subsequent negotiations. With Hafez al-Assad's health a growing question mark, Barak felt a sense of urgency to test the possibility of an agreement with Syria.

Not surprisingly, the Palestinians were upset by Barak's sense of priorities. They had been negotiating for years, and had made clear their commitment to reaching an agreement. Assad, who had not budged an inch, was being rewarded with Israeli attention. King Abdullah was nervous too. While he was supportive of an Israeli-Syrian deal, it was a two-state solution that mattered most to Jordan's future. Establishment of a sovereign Palestine in the West Bank and Gaza would cement a sense of Jordanian national identity on the other side of the Jordan River, solidifying the unity of both East Bank Jordanians and Jordanians of Palestinian origin that Abdullah's father had worked for nearly half a century to accomplish. It also promised economic opportunities for Jordan beyond the thus far meager results of the Israeli-Jordanian peace treaty of 1994. Nevertheless, Abdullah did what he could to support Syrian-Israeli negotiations, in hopes that a breakthrough there would accelerate Israeli-Palestinian progress.

Abdullah traveled to Damascus in April 1999, two months after Assad's unexpected appearance at King Hussein's funeral. Assad was relatively upbeat about improving relations with Jordan, including on the thorny issue of water resources, where Syria held the high cards through its control of the headwaters of the Jordan and Yarmouk rivers. Abdullah also spent substantial time on that trip with Assad's son and heir apparent, Bashar. On the surface, Abdullah and Bashar seemed to share a few traits. Both were in their thirties, part of a new generation of Arab leaders. Both had the experience of unexpected elevations, Bashar when his elder brother Basil died in a car crash, and Abdullah when his father changed the line of succession on his deathbed. And both thought of themselves as modernizers, although Bashar's self-image was thinly drawn, the product of a year in London studying ophthalmology and his role as head of the Syrian Computer Society, as close to a hotbed of innovation as the deeply repressive Assad regime permitted.

Bashar took the king to the Alawite stronghold of Latakia on the Mediterranean, and drove him around the city for several hours while they talked about the region and the world. The king was a little bemused by Bashar's apparent naïveté; he asked Abdullah at one point what jet lag felt like, explaining that the longest flights he had ever taken were to London and back. The king said, however, that he thought Bashar might be capable of breaking out of some of his father's knuckle-dragging habits, and following through on any progress that might be made with the Israelis. Years later, the king ruefully acknowledged to me, "So much for first impressions."

In January 2000, the United States hosted Israeli and Syrian delegations at Shepherdstown, West Virginia. Barak led the Israeli team. The Syrian delegation was headed by Foreign Minister Farouk al-Sharaa, whose demeanor hadn't grown much more flexible or conciliatory in the decade since he had strained Jim Baker's patience at Madrid. The talks sputtered over nearly ten days with no breakthrough. In a final, high-stakes effort to reach a deal, Clinton met in Geneva in late March with a fast-failing Hafez al-Assad. Unconvinced that Barak would ever deliver the full return of Syrian territory occupied since the 1967 war, Assad refused to authorize the resumption of negotiations with the Israelis. The Syria track had run its course.

Barak and Clinton then turned to the Palestinian talks with renewed focus. Prodded by Barak, and hoping to cap his presidency with a Palestinian-Israeli peace agreement, Clinton decided to invite Arafat and Barak to Camp David, the scene of Jimmy Carter's dramatic success with Sadat and Begin more than twenty years earlier. It was a significant gamble. The Israelis and Palestinians were far apart on how much of the West Bank would be returned, and even further apart on the questions of Jerusalem and the right of Palestinian refugees to return. Arafat feared that he would be blamed for a breakdown in talks, and knew how deep disillusionment already ran among Palestinians after all the unmet expectations of the Oslo years. Never a diplomatic risk-taker, Arafat came to Camp David with great reluctance, drawn largely by the investment he had made in Clinton and American leadership, and always confident that he could wriggle out of any tight political situation if he had to.

For King Abdullah, this was a difficult juncture. In barely two years on the throne, he knew that he couldn't replicate the influence or prestige of his father, but he understood instinctively the importance of Jordan's unique position, enjoying healthy relations with all three key players—Palestinians, Israelis, and Americans. He found the Camp David experience frustrating. For reasons that were partly understandable but also partly mistaken, the U.S. team at Camp David kept a tight lid over the more than two weeks of intense negotiations at the secluded presidential retreat. Key Arab players who might have helped encourage Arafat became an afterthought, and when they were consulted it was often with only the skimpiest of background.

On one occasion late in the talks, for example, a senior American official at Camp David placed a call to the king to ask for his help in persuading the Palestinians to show more flexibility on Jerusalem, but never provided any context on what exactly we were hoping to achieve, or what had transpired so far. Much to my embarrassment, I wasn't any more successful in eliciting better information for the king. My concerns, however, were insignificant compared to the central dilemma: Despite herculean efforts by President Clinton, and unprecedented progress on the question of territory and the even more complex question of Jerusalem, the two sides were at an impasse. Camp David had come further than any previous effort but ultimately ended with no agreement and plenty of resentments.

Despite earlier promises to the Palestinians, the United States—attuned more to Barak's worsening domestic political predicament—appeared in the wake of Camp David to blame Arafat for the summit's failure. With popular Palestinian anger rising, Sharon's visit to the Temple Mount in late September set off a political firestorm, and in the ensuing violence a new Palestinian uprising was born. I accompanied King Abdullah to a meeting at Sharm el-Sheikh, where President Mubarak invited Barak, Arafat, and Clinton to try to find a way to ease the violence. It proved fruitless. The Israelis were intent upon driving home to the Palestinians that violence wouldn't produce any positive political results, and often responded with disproportionate force; Arafat, always sensitive to the popular mood and never shy about indulging in violence if it helped keep his position as political ringmaster intact, often played a double game.

Our ambassador to Egypt, Dan Kurtzer, and I were deeply concerned about where all of this was headed. Over the next few months, we took the unusual step of sending joint messages to Washington. We felt a responsibility to inject our perspective into the negotiating process from the outside, if we could not provide our views from the inside. In December, we sent the third and final message:

> As seen from Cairo and Amman, U.S. policy in the peace process and our overall posture in the region are still heading in exactly the wrong direction. With our interests under increasing scrutiny and attack, we are acting passively, reactively and defensively. There is no guarantee that a bolder, more activist American approach will stop the hemorrhaging—but it seems clear to us that things could get a lot worse unless we regain the initiative.
>
> Our stake in reversing the drift toward more violence, rebuilding American credibility, refocusing attention on the possibilities of a political process, and getting as far as we can over the next seven weeks toward a framework agreement is self-evident. What is less obvious is how to get from here to there. One option is to follow Barak's lead. That may serve what he sees to be his tactical interests at this point. But it's hard to see how it serves ours. A second option is to see if we can extract from the Palestinians a clearer sense of how far they're prepared to go right now, and then use that to craft an approach to Barak. But it's unlikely that Arafat will level with us at this point; and while recent Egyptian and Jordanian efforts with the Palestinians have been helpful, it's not at all clear that they will produce a workable starting point.
>
> That leaves it to us to lay out the hard truths—for all parties—that must underpin any enduring political solution. As we have tried to emphasize in our two previous telegrams, that will require the po-

litical will to stand up for what we have fought so hard for over the past eight years, and a readiness to declare the independence of our policy.[16]

The central recommendation we made was to "articulate a 'Clinton Vision' for the peace process." We argued that "we have a unique but wasting opportunity to take advantage of a remarkable asset: the personal reputation and demonstrated commitment of President Clinton. He has built up substantial personal credit with the parties over the years, and now is the time to use it. He can sketch a vision of what he believes a comprehensive peace will require of all parties—Palestinians, Israelis, and Arab states alike. He will have to be willing to say things to each party that they will not want to hear, but that is the definition of a balanced and credible approach."

Neither the White House nor the State Department probably needed our cable to convince them to produce what became the "Clinton Parameters"—a groundbreaking American proposal for a comprehensive two-state solution that was presented to the parties in late December and made public the following month, shortly before President Clinton left office. It was too late, however, with Clinton's term ending and the parties drifting further apart. Violence quickly consumed nearly a decade of political progress.

* * *

KING ABDULLAH, LIKE the rest of us, was worried about the stalemate in diplomacy and the worsening of Palestinian-Israeli violence. In a long conversation one afternoon in January 2001, he told me, "I'm generally an optimistic person, but now I'm worried. This region is drifting in a scary direction. People are getting angrier, and I don't have any good answers."[17] I didn't have much reassurance to offer. In a cable a couple months later, I reported more troubling indicators: "The mood amongst Jordanians is increasingly angry and disaffected—a mixture of intense frustration over rising violence across the Jordan River, fury at American policies that are seen to be not just unbalanced but aggressively anti-Arab, and discontent with the meager practical results of economic reform."[18]

After nearly three years as ambassador, I was worried too—not about Abdullah's leadership, but about the pressures that Jordan faced, and the inevitable uncertainties about the new administration's policies. These uncertainties took on particular significance for me when President Bush's new secretary of state, Colin Powell, called me a week or so after he was named to ask if I would serve as assistant secretary for near eastern affairs.

I had never worked for anyone I respected more than Powell, and I was thrilled by what his leadership would bring to American foreign policy. I had similar respect for Rich Armitage, who had been nominated as deputy secretary of state. I was confident in my knowledge of the region, and familiar with the main policy issues; I was far less confident in my ability to rise to the leadership and management challenge of heading one of the department's largest bureaus. I was just as unsure about the new administration's Middle East policy and feared we were sailing into even more treacherous waters in that troubled part of the world.

It was hard to say no to Colin Powell, however, or to a request to serve in such a critical post at such a critical time. I quickly accepted, asking only that we stay in Jordan until as close to the end of the school year as possible (which, given the vagaries of the Senate confirmation process, was a probability anyway), and that I be able to choose my deputies in the NEA front office.

I had learned over the years that the key to success in any demanding job is to surround yourself with people who are smarter and more experienced than you are. That's exactly what I did in NEA, working the phones hard from Amman in early 2001 to enlist three of the most capable Arabists I knew, all of whom were serving, like me, as ambassadors in the field. Jim Larocco, ambassador in Kuwait, agreed to come back to Washington as principal deputy assistant secretary. David Satterfield, our ambassador in Beirut, with whom I had worked many years before as lowly staff assistants for Dick Murphy, also readily agreed. Ryan Crocker, leading our embassy in Damascus, was the toughest sell. One of the best officers I had ever known, Ryan far preferred the dangers and challenges of the Middle East to the petty intrigues and bureaucratic machinations of Washington. He eventually relented, calling me from Damascus one afternoon, after I had nearly given up. "I'll join you at the Alamo," he said in his usual laconic way.

I was confirmed by the Senate in April, and began my new job immediately. The king and queen invited Lisa and me to Aqaba for the weekend, just before we left. It had been a remarkable three years, and I told the king how glad I was to have had the chance to work with him, and how much Jordan would always mean to me and my family.

"Neither of us expected all the things that have been thrown at us," he said. "I'm proud of what we've done together. You should be too."

5

Age of Terror: The Inversion of Force and Diplomacy

IT WAS JUST after midnight on a cold February morning in 2005, at a tent encampment in the Libyan desert. My route had been as circuitous and eccentric as the man I was coming to see. I flew into Tripoli on a U.S. military aircraft, landing at Mitiga airfield, formerly Wheelus Air Base, the largest overseas U.S. Air Force installation in the 1960s. An officious protocol officer drove us across the tarmac where one of Muammar al-Qaddafi's jets was parked. We quickly boarded the Libyan aircraft. Its décor was a bedraggled version of 1970s chic, with worn lime-green shag carpeting and swivel chairs that had long since ceased swiveling. For security reasons, the Libyans refused to specify our destination. We flew east along the Mediterranean coast to another military airfield, near Qaddafi's hometown of Sirte. There, we were hustled into a convoy of Land Rovers and driven south at breakneck speed for two hours through desert scrub and successive rings of Libyan security.

We finally slowed at the entrance to a small wadi, where Qaddafi sat in spartan splendor. His cavernous camouflage tent was unadorned save for a few white plastic lawn chairs, a sleeping mat, a small television, and a single light bulb hanging from the top of the tent. I was ushered in, and Qaddafi rose to greet me, wrapped against the nighttime chill in robes and a headscarf that covered most of his face. His attire was less flamboyant than in a previous encounter, when he wore a pajama-like outfit with a shirt featuring pictures of fellow African strongmen. Whenever he engaged in his disconcerting habit of pausing for two or three minutes in conversational midstream to stare at the ceiling, presumably to collect his thoughts, I would mentally try to name all the dictators so proudly displayed on his pajama top.

On this occasion, Qaddafi's mood and message meandered. We were nearing the end of a long and tortuous path to normalized relations, the product of many years of diplomacy—some covert, some overt—across administrations of both parties. Qaddafi complained mildly about the pace of change, but made clear that there would be no turning back from Libya's commitments to compensate victims of the Lockerbie bombing, renounce terrorism, and abandon its nuclear and chemical weapons programs. He bristled when I raised human rights concerns, and had not the slightest inclination to open up his profoundly weird and repressive system of "popular rule." He was unapologetic about his brutality, convinced that there could be no political order in his fractious society without it. In all the hours I spent with him and his lieutenants over four years, I never once forgot the blood on their hands. One of the 259 innocent victims on the Pan Am 103 flight bombed by Libyan operatives was my friend Matthew Gannon, a CIA officer with whom I had served in Amman in the early 1980s.[1] He had been on his way from Beirut to the States to spend Christmas with his wife and two young daughters. His loss had left me shaken.

Qaddafi rambled across the region in that early-morning discussion, offering views on people and problems that were, as I reported back to Washington, "a combination of the eerily insightful and the just plain eerie." Rarely making eye contact, speaking in a monotone, he limited his gestures to an occasional wave to a bodyguard stationed just outside the tent to refill our tea glasses. As in our previous conversations, Qaddafi went on at length about the Israel-Palestine issue, convinced that a two-state solution was receding, and a one-state "Isratine" inevitable. He predicted the fragmentation of Saudi Arabia into four separate states, reflecting his dim view of the House of Saud, and worried aloud that Iraq, already in the throes of sectarian conflict after the 2003 American invasion, was becoming "a breeding ground and magnet for extremists from around the Islamic world."[2] He got that out without a trace of irony—momentarily oblivious to Libya's long history as a terrorist haven.

I nevertheless came away hopeful. For thirty-five years, Qaddafi had tried to seize center stage with despicable acts and surreal performance art. Now he was starved to be taken seriously by the United States and others in the West. Neither the weirdness nor the ugliness and intractability of his own political system was going away, but maybe his attention seeking would evolve in less destabilizing ways.

At that moment in early 2005, the Libyan experience proved that diplomacy could accomplish significant changes in the behavior of difficult regimes. Of course it had to be backed up by other forms of leverage—many years of U.S. and multilateral sanctions; a solid international consensus, codified in UN Security Council resolutions; and the credible threat of force. It also mattered that we set consistent and achievable benchmarks for the negotiations on Lockerbie, terrorism, and weapons of mass destruction (WMD), delivered on our end of the deal, and over a period of years built up a fair amount of trust. Regime change was never the goal, and the Libyan leadership gradually developed a self-interest in changing behavior. It saw little benefit in winding up on the wrong side of the post–9/11 divide, and we provided a difficult but navigable pathway to a form of practical redemption.

Sitting there in that drafty desert tent, I was acutely aware that diplomacy with Libya was a model that paled in significance with the other model we had created during those same years—the shoot-first, dabble-in-diplomacy-later approach we took in Iraq. Shaped by post–9/11 apprehension and assertiveness, determination to preempt threats, and hubris and overreliance on force, we blundered our way into a war and its ugly aftermath. That inversion of force and diplomacy left scars that would long endure—for the region and for America's role in the world.

* * *

AS I PREPARED to leave Amman and return to Washington in the spring of 2001, a colleague warned that we'd be trying to grope our way through a wider Middle East that "really is the land of bad policy options." It was hard to argue with him.

I had watched with mounting concern as the violence of the Second Intifada worsened. Ariel Sharon's election victory over Ehud Barak in February 2001 signaled unmistakably that Israel's consuming focus would be on restoring order and security through force, not negotiations. Yasser Arafat remained risk-averse and duplicitous, maneuvering to stay atop an angry sea of Palestinians under occupation. Sharon and Arafat seemed locked in a stubborn war of attrition, each convinced that he could outlast the other, mutual enablers in a contest with no end in sight. In my Senate confirmation hearing in April, I tried to paint an honest picture: "Too many Israelis and Palestinians now feel less secure, less hopeful, and less certain that peace is possible. The result is an angry and disillusioned mood, much of it directed, fairly or unfairly, against the United States. Many Arabs think we don't care about their concerns; worse, many think we're actively hostile to them."[3]

Across the region, the deeper dysfunction of Arab societies and the autocrats who sat atop them was impossible to ignore. As the landmark Arab Human Development Reports would soon make clear, Arabs were falling further behind many other regions of the world. The combined GDP of all Arab countries, comprising a population of some three hundred million, was less than that of Spain, which had roughly one-tenth the number of people. Half of all Arabs were under the age of twenty, creating huge pressures that neither educational systems nor job markets could absorb, and only 2 percent had access to the Internet.

Amid this regional tumult, a new generation of leaders was emerging. Like King Abdullah of Jordan, new monarchs in Morocco and Bahrain were experimenting with economic and political openness. Even Bashar al-Assad briefly opened the window to a "Damascus Spring," with younger technocrats forming short-lived discussion groups to explore reform. The older generation was instinctively much more cautious. In the Gulf, there were abundant anxieties about risks from both Iraq and Iran, despite the reelection in June 2001 of Mohammad Khatami, the reformist president in Tehran. Hosni Mubarak, moored deeply in the status quo in Egypt, saw little reason for optimism in a region with so many unnerving changes afoot.

The view from Washington, as George W. Bush assembled his administration, was similarly cautious in the first half of 2001. President Bush's national security team was familiar, experienced, and tested. It seemed at the outset nearly as impressive as his father's, with Dick Cheney as vice president, Colin Powell as secretary of state, and Don Rumsfeld as secretary of defense. George Tenet stayed on as director of the CIA, and Condoleezza Rice became the national security advisor. Rice had captured succinctly the self-consciously realistic approach of the new administration in a *Foreign Affairs* article during the 2000 election campaign: In a Bush administration, there would be no more nation-building, no more overuse of the U.S. military as an instrument of humanitarian intervention, no more soft-headed multilateralism. The perceived fixation of the Clinton administration on the Middle East peace process would be a thing of the past. Rice was blunt about the use of force in general. The American military, she wrote, "is a special instrument. It is not a civilian police force. It is not a political referee. And it is most certainly not designed to build a civilian society." On Saddam, she was equally clear: "The first line of defense should be deterrence—if he does acquire WMD, his weapons will be unusable because any attempt to use them will bring national obliteration." Restraint and realism seemed to be the dominant guideposts, just as they were for Bush 41.

Colin Powell brought strong leadership to the State Department, and for all my misgivings about the Middle East at that moment and the challenges of my new role, I was genuinely excited to be working for him again. He and Rich Armitage were a formidable team, close friends and keenly attuned to the importance of building morale in the Department, modernizing its 1980s-era technology, and dragging American diplomacy into the twenty-first century. Powell enjoyed walking around the building, poking his head into offices, and offering passing employees a ride up in his private elevator. When President Bush visited the State Department for the first time to get a briefing for an early meeting with his Mexican counterpart, Powell had two junior desk officers sit across from the president and handle the presentation. That kind of empowerment set the tone throughout the department. Armitage worked hard to de-layer the institution and push responsibility downward wherever he could. He was always accessible, with a no-nonsense style leavened by an irreverent sense of humor. If you were summoned to his office after six in the evening, Motown tunes would be blaring down the august seventh floor corridor, and scotch would be served to ease the tensions of the day.

Powell and Armitage helped make it a good time to lead a regional bureau. They expected initiative, creativity, and loyalty, and didn't mind thoughtful disagreement. They emphasized the importance of leaders taking care of their people, and had little patience for martinets or senior officers who admired the problem rather than trying to solve it. I tried as best I could to help create that same atmosphere in NEA.

NEA was arguably the most challenging, if not the biggest, of the regional bureaus. With about forty-five hundred staff spread over

Washington and some two dozen embassies and consulates in the region, I was constantly preoccupied with security threats, policy dilemmas, or management problems of one stripe or another.

Sworn in to my new post at the beginning of May 2001, I set out to visit each of the sixteen countries in which we then had embassies. Over the next four years, I spent about half my time on the road. In a region as idiosyncratic and autocratic as the Middle East, modern communications technology was still no substitute for building personal relationships and face-to-face interactions.

My first trip was to Israel and the West Bank. Our aim was to orchestrate a cease-fire and stop the violence that had erupted nearly a year earlier. I joined George Tenet on a couple of those efforts, as he worked to persuade Palestinian and Israeli security officials to cooperate. "The situation we confront is bleak," I wrote at the time. "Arafat and Sharon are locked into a death dance in which each is looking to best or get rid of the other."[4] Prime Minister Sharon was courteous but unyielding in his determination to hit back hard against Palestinian violence, and to isolate and undermine Arafat, whom he was convinced was not only turning a blind eye to terrorist attacks but tacitly encouraging them. Arafat was just as dug in, manipulating violence for his own purposes and determined not to yield in the face of disproportionate Israeli force. On one visit, I arrived in Tel Aviv a few hours after a vicious suicide attack on a beachfront nightclub, in which twenty-one Israelis had been killed, most of them teenagers. I stopped by the site to lay flowers that morning, as Israeli emergency personnel were still searching for body parts and identifying the victims.

The savagery of Israeli-Palestinian violence was high on the agendas of most of the other Arab leaders I visited that summer. Hosni Mubarak was worried about the mood on the Egyptian street, and the impact on Egypt's treaty relationship with Israel. He had a grudging respect for Sharon's toughness, but worried that he was relying so much on force and so little on offering any kind of political future for

Palestinians that he would ultimately just dig the hole deeper. Mubarak was well acquainted with Arafat's slippery disposition, and knew that the weakness of his hand made him even less likely to concede much under Israeli pressure. Waving his arms in the air dismissively near the end of one conversation, he said, "Those two deserve each other, but we can't let them drag us all down." King Abdullah was even more exposed in Jordan, and shared Mubarak's frustration.

Distance insulated leaders in the Maghreb to some extent from the passions of the Levant. Morocco's King Mohammed VI was more concerned with establishing himself on the throne and the apparently inexhaustible conflict with the Algerians over the Western Sahara than the ugliness farther east. In Algiers, President Abdelaziz Bouteflika's comb-over remained one of the country's true architectural marvels. He dominated our three-hour conversation with his impressions of other leaders and their conflicts, without any hint of introspection. President Zine El Abidine Ben Ali in Tunisia professed to want to fight corruption and open up his political system, with an enthusiasm that seemed heavily contrived.

In Beirut, the political cast of characters eyed one another nervously, as they had for decades. Prime Minister Rafik Hariri took a wary view of Sharon, who had helped drive the Israeli invasion of Lebanon in 1982, and of Arafat, the proximate target of that invasion. Hariri was then still somewhat optimistic about Bashar al-Assad in Syria, who seemed to lack his father's guile and experience, but might give Lebanon more room to maneuver.

My first meeting with Bashar in Damascus offered a glimpse at the banality of an evil that would emerge in its full and horrific form ten years later. He asked me to see him at home, which was still the relatively modest house in which he had lived before becoming president. He greeted me at the door with his wife, Asma, alongside, a few of his children's toys visible in a corner of the living room. Asma had been raised in London and spoke fluent English. Bashar's was more halting, and we switched back and forth to Arabic.

Bashar was pleasant but cocksure, betraying none of the tentative-ness that you might expect from someone who had been in power for little more than a year. He pronounced himself with conviction on regional events and American policy (about which he had nothing good to say). He dismissed Arafat as vain and indecisive, and said air-ily that the only thing Sharon and Israel understood was force. He was patronizing about King Abdullah in Jordan, and displayed little deference toward Mubarak or the senior Gulf leaders. Bashar's fasci-nation with modernity seemed more about gadgets and technology than political or economic progress. As I later told Powell, the most generous conclusion you could draw was that Bashar was a work in progress, but we should have no illusions about any dramatic shift in Syrian behavior. His regime's capacity for mendacity and brutality would remain the cold heart of its survival strategy.

On the Arabian Peninsula, leaders were preoccupied with leader-ship transitions and domestic challenges, along with the emotions aroused in their own societies by nightly television images of violence in Palestine. I saw Ali Abdullah Saleh, Yemen's mercurial president, in Sanaa. He punctuated his comments with expansive waves of the camel riding crop he kept in his hand, which his aides ducked with a practiced air. Sultan Qaboos of Oman, with whom I would deal fre-quently years later when he hosted secret talks with the Iranians, was full of wise insights and quiet dignity. Amir Hamad in Doha engaged in the favorite Qatari sport, poking fun at the Saudis and asserting his own independence. Bahrain and Kuwait were eager to sustain strong relations with the United States, and not to get caught in any of the various regional crossfires.

I met Crown Prince Abdullah of Saudi Arabia, de facto ruler of his country given King Fahd's infirmity, at his horse farm outside Riyadh. In that conversation and a number of others over the succeeding years, I found him to be refreshingly direct and candid. He found American officials to be energetic but slow-witted students, naïve about the Middle East and often oblivious to the consequences of their actions (or inaction). In the summer of 2001, Abdullah's anxieties were mostly about the unfolding mess in Palestine. He urged greater White House interest and activism. Despite his frustrations, he was hospitable and warm. That evening, he challenged me to join him in a Bedouin form of bocce. With a twinkle in his eye, he asked if I knew how to play. When I said no, he smiled broadly and said, "Good." Although he had eased himself out of his chair with some apparent difficulty, he managed to bend his knees when he tossed, and had some well-honed flair in his wrist motion. His agility and experience more than compensated for our thirty-year age difference—and I knew when I was being played. The crown prince beat me handily.

I also stopped in Abu Dhabi to meet Sheikh Zayed, the aging but thoroughly engaging leader of the United Arab Emirates. Zayed made clear how pained he was by American policy on the Arab-Israeli issue. "Ten years ago," he said, "I had such hopes for the region and America. Now I don't have much hope left. I know that George Bush and Colin Powell are good men. Please help open their eyes to the consequences of what's happening." American political stock in the Middle East faced a bear market, and in the summer of 2001 the most pressing priority was to stop the hemorrhaging of capital caused by Israeli-Palestinian violence.[5]

Iraq and Saddam featured in all of these conversations, but didn't overwhelm them. Nor did they overwhelm debate in Washington. While the vice president and the Pentagon quietly agitated for a tougher line on Saddam and more active support for the exiled Iraqi opposition, there was not much sense of urgency. The immediate task was to try to put the sanctions regime on a more sustainable path and strengthen containment of Saddam. Powell took the lead in fashioning a new "smart sanctions" approach—lifting most of the ineffectual or even counterproductive sanctions on Iraqi civilians and substituting a more narrowly focused arms control regime to deny military and dual-use technology. The administration, like its predecessor, remained committed to the long-term goal of regime change in Baghdad, but also remained concerned about overreaching. In a closed briefing for some key senators after I returned from my travels in July 2001, I repeated that we had no doubt that Iraq and the region would be better off without Saddam, but added that that outcome obviously couldn't be imposed from the outside. I had no idea how quickly the mood in the administration could change.

* * *

I WAS AT my desk in the State Department on the morning of Tuesday, September 11, 2001, reading my daily intelligence briefs, when the first images of the attack on the World Trade Center in New York flashed across my television screen. I watched in horror as the second tower was struck, and as the full magnitude of the assault began to sink in. The department was evacuated amid reports of possible further attacks; thousands of employees, many with tears in their eyes, filed quietly out of the building. I walked hurriedly among the crowds, found Lisa, and hugged her tightly. I went back to my office an hour or so later, along with a small number of colleagues, uncertain of what to expect—beyond a vastly transformed world.

By that point, another hijacked aircraft had crashed into the Pentagon. Looking out my window on the sixth floor of the department, I could see the plumes of smoke across the Potomac. My thoughts turned quickly to ensuring that NEA personnel overseas were safe. Jim Larocco took the lead in calling each of our posts, and the bureau responded with its usual discipline and professionalism. On the seventh floor, Rich Armitage stayed in touch with the White House and with Secretary Powell, who was in Peru for a meeting of the Organization of American States. Powell began the eight-hour flight home as soon as he learned of the attacks, but wouldn't arrive until early evening.

That afternoon, sitting in a virtually deserted building, I tried to collect my thoughts and think ahead. It was already clear that al-Qaeda was responsible for the attacks. The first step would obviously be a sharp strike against them and their Taliban protectors in Afghanistan. Three thousand innocent people had just been slaughtered in the worst assault on American soil since Pearl Harbor. We had to respond decisively. But we also had to look for opportunities amid crisis. In the first few hours after the attacks, there was a huge outpouring of international sympathy and support. Vladimir Putin was one of the first leaders to call the president and offer Russia's solidarity, and the Iranian leadership was quick to denounce the attack. Was there a chance to mobilize regional and international action around a shared sense of revulsion? At this grim and painful moment, could the United States take advantage of almost unprecedented global support and retake the initiative in the Middle East? Could we shape a strategy that would not only hit back hard against terrorists and any states who continued to harbor them, but also lay out an affirmative agenda that might eventually help reduce the hopelessness and anger on which extremists preyed?

Our computer systems were down most of that day, so I sat at my desk and wrote a note to the secretary in longhand, as legibly as I could. It was a hurried effort, covering four pages of yellow legal paper.

My thinking was straightforward. The use of force and American military and intelligence leverage would be crucial in Afghanistan, but there were also considerable opportunities for imaginative and hard-nosed diplomacy. Adversaries like Iran had a stake in the removal of the Taliban, and a solid grasp of Afghan politics. Exploring cooperation with them might prove useful and create long-term openings.

The demonstration effect of success against the Taliban and al-Qaeda could also help focus the minds of other states dabbling (or immersed) in terrorism, like Libya and Syria. Tough diplomacy and the weight of post–9/11 international opinion could have a decisive effect on Qaddafi and Assad, and we should exploit the moment. I doubted that Saddam was capable of any such epiphanies, but argued that this was the best opportunity we had had in years to strengthen

containment of Iraq and build international support for "smart sanctions." We could use the terrible events of 9/11 as the antidote to containment fatigue, and shore up constraints that were bent but not yet
broken.

I added that we might also have opportunities to create the cooperative security arrangements among the Gulf Arab states that we
had discussed after Desert Storm a decade before but never made
systematic. Amid all the awful violence of the Second Intifada, we
might have an opening to reassert American leadership, press hard
against violence, and re-create a sense of political horizon for Israelis
and Palestinians. Finally, I encouraged a renewed focus from the new
administration on the longer-term drivers of instability across the
Middle East, on the value of carefully promoting greater economic
and political openness. A regional economic development bank was
one possibility; a new regional assistance initiative was another, with
incentives linked to measurable progress on reforms and cooperation
against terrorism.

The trauma of 9/11 confronted us with the reality that the Islamist
movement spawned in 1979—the year in which the Iranian Revolution, the Grand Mosque attack in Mecca, and the Soviet invasion of
Afghanistan unleashed lethal regional and ideological rivalries—had
become more extreme, more violent, and more global. There could be
no wishing it away. What was unfolding was less a clash of civiliza-
tions than a clash within a civilization, a deeply battered Islamic
world in the midst of a desperate ideological struggle. There were
limits to what we could do directly to shape that debate. What we
could do, however, was to help create a sense of geopolitical order that
would deprive extremists of the oxygen they needed to fan the flames
of chaos, and give moderate forces the sustained support they needed
to demonstrate that they could deliver for their people.

I handed the note to the secretary after he returned. He was tired
and understandably preoccupied, but appreciative. One of the things
I had admired most about Powell was the way he exuded confidence,

even in the worst of circumstances. I could feel that now, unspoken but unmistakable. As I walked out, I said he could count on NEA. He smiled wearily and said, "I know I can."

We followed up over the next few days with more specific memos on Iran, Libya, and the Israeli-Palestinian issue, along the same lines as my hastily handwritten note. At a senior staff meeting on September 13, the first after 9/11, Powell echoed some of these themes, stressing alongside a message of American firmness and resolve that we had to be attentive to opportunities for diplomacy in even the worst national tragedies.

As the U.S. military and the CIA moved swiftly in the fall of 2001 to support the Afghan opposition and overthrow the Taliban government in Kabul, we pedaled ahead slowly on a number of the Middle East initiatives we had suggested. In late September, Ryan Crocker began a direct dialogue with the Iranians about Afghanistan that helped produce a new Afghan government. In early October, I met quietly in London with a Libyan delegation led by Musa Kusa, Qaddafi's intelligence chief, resuscitating talks about Lockerbie and terrorism that had begun in the Clinton administration. I returned to Damascus that same month and met Bashar, who soon thereafter began a modestly useful information exchange, which in one instance provided advance warning of a terrorist plot against U.S. facilities in Bahrain.

In November, using the diplomatic momentum of the immediate post–9/11 period, Powell won Russian acceptance and UN Security Council passage of a "smart sanctions" framework for Iraq, which tightened controls on military and dual-use items, and loosened restrictions on civilian goods. That same month, he gave a speech in Louisville, Kentucky, emphasizing the importance of renewing a peace process between Israelis and Palestinians. He talked movingly about ending the daily humiliations of Palestinians under Israeli occupation, and with equal passion about Israel's right to security. He appointed retired General Tony Zinni, the former commander of U.S.

Central Command (CENTCOM), as a senior advisor to help negotiate a cease-fire and reopen the way to negotiations. All this was at least a start on the agenda I had tried to sketch, alone in my office, on that grim afternoon of September 11.

That agenda was soon eclipsed by an alternative view. The new administration had been shaken badly and felt a call to action—the more decisive the better. "Containment" didn't have much of a ring to it in the months after the al-Qaeda attacks on the homeland. It was not the season for nuance, caution, and compromise. It was the season for the risk-tolerant and the ideologically ambitious, bent on inserting ourselves aggressively into the regional contest of ideas, militarizing our policy, and unbuckling our rhetoric.

After the pain and surprise of 9/11, it was time for the muscular reassertion of American might, time to remind adversaries of the consequences of challenging the United States. For many in the White House and the Pentagon, that was a message best served unilaterally, unencumbered and undiluted by elaborate coalition-building. Lost in the moment was the reality that the approach we advocated at State was no less hard-nosed, just more sustainable and more mindful of risks.

Regime change in Iraq became the acid test of the administration's post–9/11 approach. The overthrow of the Taliban had come almost too quickly and too easily. For "paleoconservatives" like Dick Cheney and Don Rumsfeld, the message sent in Afghanistan was necessary but insufficient. Another, bigger blow had to be struck to deter enemies in a region in which force was the only language people understood. For "neoconservatives," like Deputy Secretary Paul Wolfowitz and Undersecretary Doug Feith at the Pentagon, Saddam's forcible ouster was not just a message, it was an opportunity to create a democratic model in Iraq, begin the transformation of the whole region, and reassert American hegemony after a post–Cold War decade of naïve attachment to the promise of a peace dividend.

For President George W. Bush, the world had changed after Sep-

tember 11, and the humble realist lens that he had used in the months
before no longer seemed to illuminate. Impatient and proud of his
decisiveness, the president found containment of Saddam to be too
passive, inadequate to the challenges of this moment in history. After
9/11, the policy terrain tilted rapidly away from the wider agenda for
which we argued, and toward a single-minded focus on toppling Saddam. So did the bureaucratic playing field, with Powell increasingly
isolated and considered by antagonists at the White House and the
Pentagon to be too independent, too popular, and too moderate—and
NEA considered a den of defeatists and Cassandras. In a Washington
that rarely lacked for infighting and policy combat, the road to war in
Iraq was distinctive for its intensity and indiscipline.

* * *

FOLLOWING 9/11, MY colleagues and I continued to believe we
could contain Iraq and avoid war. We worried that an ill-considered,
unilateral war to topple Saddam would prove to be a massive foreign
policy blunder. We did not, however, argue frontally against the bipartisan policy of eventual regime change, nor did we argue against
the possible use of force much further down the road to achieve it.
Instead, sensing the ideological zeal with which war drums were
beating, we tried to slow the tempo and direct debate in a less self-
injurious manner. None of us had any illusions about Saddam or the
long-term risk that his regime posed for the region. His brutality deserved every bit of international condemnation and ostracism it had
received. We did not, however, see a serious, imminent threat that
would justify a war. While most of us suspected that Saddam was
concealing some residual WMD capacity, the evidence was hard to
establish, and he always deliberately obscured his intentions in order
to deceive and intimidate regional and domestic enemies. His conventional military capabilities had been shattered in Desert Storm,
and his economy was in tatters after a decade of sanctions, and decades more of mismanagement.

As a result, there was little sense of urgency in the region about Saddam, and even less interest in supporting a military effort against him. "At age 74, Mubarak remains proud, cautious, and deeply preoccupied with stability at home and in the region," I wrote in one cable after a conversation with the Egyptian leader. Mubarak repeatedly warned me about the complexities of Iraqi society, the unpredictability of a post-Saddam world, and the negative regional consequences of any eventual use of force.[6] "Burns," the Egyptian president would say, "you must not underestimate how much trouble those Iraqis can be. They spend their whole lives plotting against each other." Most other Arab leaders were far more worried about the images of Palestinians being killed in the West Bank and stories of Iraqi civilian hardships under sanctions than they were about a near-term threat from Saddam. Broader international opinion was similarly unfocused on any immediate Iraqi threat. Even in London, where Prime Minister Tony Blair was determined to stay close to President Bush after 9/11, there was a strong sense that it would take time and considerable effort to build a legitimate case for Saddam's removal.

At the State Department, we were at first lulled into thinking that our arguments were getting traction. Before 9/11, the new administration's episodic interagency discussions about Iraq were long and painful, the kind of bureaucratic purgatory that exists when issues are being sharply debated but everyone knows there is neither the political will nor urgency to resolve them. Civilian officials from the Pentagon, often allied with the vice president's growing and increasingly independent national security staff, would press for more radical steps against Saddam. A particular favorite was to create a safe zone in southern Iraq, similar to the zone protecting the Kurds in the north, that could provide a launching pad for Iraqi oppositionists to undermine Saddam. Most of these ideas foundered on the obvious concerns—lack of internationally legitimate grounds for acting; lack of enthusiasm in the region; the potential military consequences; and the opportunity costs for other priorities on the early Bush 43 agenda.

The wiliest, most active, and least trustworthy of the Iraqi oppositionists agitating for American intervention to overthrow Saddam
was Ahmed Chalabi. I had first met him in Amman in the early
1980s. An Iraqi national from a well-connected Baghdad family, he
had fled the country after Saddam took power. In Amman, he ran the
Petra Bank and was a large fish in the relatively small pond of Jordanian high society. Smooth and smart, Chalabi established himself as
a leading figure among exiled Iraqi oppositionists during the 1990s,
based mostly in London, but spending increasing amounts of time
working the halls of Congress. He became head of the main umbrella
opposition group, the Iraqi National Congress, in 1992, and was one
of the principal architects of the Iraq Liberation Act.

Always a fertile source of ideas and information, much of it contrived but all of it delivered with conspiratorial enthusiasm, Chalabi
cultivated particularly close contacts at senior levels of the Pentagon
and the White House. He kept a disdainful distance from the Powell
State Department, an attitude we reciprocated. "That guy is a weasel,"
Rich Armitage said, in the least earthy description he could manage.
"And he will only lead us into trouble."

9/11 provided the opening for regime change proponents. Powell
mentioned to me on September 12 that Rumsfeld had raised the
threat posed by Saddam at the previous evening's NSC meeting, and
Wolfowitz pressed the issue again at a principals meeting at Camp
David a few days later. President Bush was intrigued enough to ask
the NSC staff for a quick investigation of whether Saddam had a role
in the 9/11 attacks. The answer was an unambiguous no. The president made clear that the immediate priority would be action against
the Taliban and al-Qaeda in Afghanistan. Nevertheless, the idea of a
preemptive strike to topple Saddam was slowly gathering steam. In
November, with the president's blessing, Rumsfeld instructed CENT-
COM to update contingency planning for Iraq, with the aim of "de-
capitating" the Iraqi leadership and installing a new provisional
government.

Before a White House meeting that same month, I sent a note to Armitage emphasizing that it was the "wrong time to shift our focus from Afghanistan." I explained that we needed "to show that we will finish the job [and] restore order, not just move on to the next Moslem state."[7] I added that the case for war was extremely weak. There was "no evidence of an Iraqi role" in 9/11, "no [regional or international] support for military action," and "no triggering event." There was a "relatively weak internal opposition [in Iraq]," and little clarity on what might happen on the day after. Other than that, it made perfect sense.

But the drumbeat only grew louder after the president's State of the Union speech at the end of January, when he took aim at the "axis of evil"—Iraq, North Korea, and Iran. That killed the diplomatic channel that Ryan Crocker had so skillfully developed with the Iranians. The headline role for Iraq was hardly a surprise, and a preview of the case for preemption that was building. Frustrated by the inconclusive evidence offered up by the intelligence community of Iraqi complicity in 9/11 and continuing WMD activities, senior civilians in the Pentagon and the vice president's staff probed even harder for any shred of information or analysis that would fit their predispositions. An "independent" intelligence unit was set up at the Pentagon under Doug Feith, charged with ferreting out the real story. As Armitage later put it, the war party within the administration was "trying to connect dots which were unconnectable."[8]

Despite efforts of Pentagon civilians and the vice president's office to lead the witnesses, many in the intelligence community continued to offer honest analysis, however unsatisfying it was to administration hawks. At State, the Bureau of Intelligence and Research reported repeatedly to Powell that it saw no firm evidence of reconstitution of Iraqi WMD. In the spring of 2002, the Defense Intelligence Agency forcefully and convincingly labeled one of the main sources for information on continuing Iraqi WMD activities to be a fabricator. In early 2002, a former State Department colleague, Joe Wilson, went to Niger on the CIA's behalf to track down a story that Saddam was trying to obtain yellowcake for an alleged covert uranium enrichment program, but found no corroboration.

After yet another trip to the Middle East in February, I told Powell that there was still no regional enthusiasm for any near-term military effort against Saddam. I was particularly struck by my conversations with Crown Prince Mohammed bin Zayed (MbZ) and other Emirati leaders. They warned that if the images on Al Jazeera showed American tanks occupying Iraq alongside Israeli tanks sitting atop the Palestinians, "it won't take long for anger to boil." MbZ concluded our meeting by putting the stakes in sharp relief: "You have an opportunity to do a very good thing for the region by overthrowing Saddam— or a very bad thing if the outcome is messy, Iraq breaks apart, or other regional problems are left untouched afterwards. You and we will either benefit or suffer from the consequences for many years to come."[9] He made no secret of which outcome he thought was the most likely.

And he wasn't alone. Mubarak, King Abdullah, and other Arab leaders worried "that [the United States] will come in, create a mess, and then leave them to deal with the consequences." Their anxiety reflected "a cold calculation that the risks posed by the uncertainties of regime change outweigh the current threat from Saddam." I noted that "the current Iraqi opposition is fractured, feeble, and incapable of organizing itself, much less bringing security, stability and civil society to a post-Saddam Iraq." I emphasized again my conviction, which I knew Powell shared, that "getting into Iraq would be a lot easier than getting out"—that the post-conflict situation would be a far bigger problem than the initial military operation.[10] In the face of such risks, I told a meeting of NEA ambassadors that February, "That's exactly why we would never go at this alone."

Unpersuaded by what we were reporting about attitudes in the region, and keen to underscore the gravity of the administration's concerns about Saddam, Vice President Cheney decided to travel to the Middle East himself in March. I joined his delegation as the senior State Department representative. The vice president, who combined a quiet, even-tempered exterior with a sharp intellect and rigid views, was gracious toward me throughout the ten-day trip. He included me in most meetings and welcomed my participation, if not always my perspective. I had a faint hope before the trip that first-hand exposure to the reluctance of regional leaders, and their preoccupation with quieting Israeli-Palestinian violence, would help convince the vice president that thoughts of war should wait until we had a better case and a better regional environment. Armitage was skeptical, and proved to be right. If anything, the trip seemed to solidify Cheney's view that early, forcible regime change would be the key to transforming the regional environment, not the other way around.

It didn't help that several of the Arab leaders appeared more restrained in their comments about Iraq than they had been with me. Arab political culture is full of winks and nods, and the message conveyed to Cheney in a number of capitals was essentially "Do this if you must, but do it right, and wake us when it's over." In London, Cheney said bluntly that the president was determined to overthrow Saddam, leaving the British unsettled about his willingness to go it alone if necessary. "A coalition would be nice," the vice president said, "but not essential."

For the rest of the spring and early summer, interagency debate continued. The NSC staff ran a process that tended to paper over sharp differences, mainly between Powell on one side and Cheney and Rumsfeld on the other, and at least from our point of view indulge the vice president's staff and the Pentagon civilians. Rumsfeld made no real attempt to conceal his contempt for the process, often claiming that he hadn't had time to read papers for major meetings and obfuscating or retreating into Socratic questions when he didn't want to show his hand.

We still thought we could "slow the train down," as Powell used to put it, but the truth was that it was gathering speed. I used a different, and equally mistaken, metaphor in a note to the secretary before an April 2002 meeting with the president. I urged him to "play 'judo' with the crazier assertions from OSD [Office of the Secretary of Defense]" and hope that by exposing the risks of war and its aftermath we could gain leverage.[11] That tactic had only marginal effect, especially in that post–9/11 moment when there was a bias for action, and prudence looked like weakness. In early June, the president gave a speech at West Point that underscored his growing impatience and sense of purpose. In the post–9/11 world, offense was the key to security, not defense. On Iraq, that meant that preventive action would be the default position. It was a deeply misguided prescription, but one that was far easier to sell within the administration and to the American public.

We took one last run later that summer at the argument for avoiding war—summarizing, all in one place, the profound risks of an ill-prepared and ill-considered conflict. David Pearce, a Foreign Service classmate then serving as head of the Iraq/Iran office in NEA, produced an initial draft outlining everything that could go wrong if we went to war. Ryan and I joined him in what quickly became the most depressing brainstorming session of our careers. The resultant memo, revised by David, was more a hurried list of horribles than a coherent analysis, a hastily assembled antidote to the recklessly rosy assumptions of our bureaucratic antagonists.

Many of the arguments in the memo, which we entitled "The Perfect Storm," look obvious in hindsight.[12] We highlighted the deep sectarian fault lines in Iraq, on which Saddam had kept such a brutal lid. We emphasized the dangers of civil unrest and looting if the Iraqi military and security institutions collapsed or were eliminated in the wake of Saddam's overthrow, and the risk that already badly degraded civilian infrastructure would crumble. We noted the likelihood that regional players would be tempted to meddle and take advantage of

Iraqi weakness. Iran could wind up as a major beneficiary. With no tradition of democratic governance and market economics, Iraq would be a hard place to test the upbeat assertions offered by Paul Wolfowitz and other advocates of regime change. If the United States embarked on this conflict, and especially if we embarked on it more or less on our own, and without a compelling justification, we'd bear the primary responsibility for post-conflict security, order, and recovery. That would suck the oxygen out of every other priority on the administration's national security agenda.

Looking back, we understated some risks, like the speed with which Sunni-Shia bloodletting in post-Saddam Iraq would fuel wider sectarian conflict in the region. We exaggerated others, like the risk that Saddam would use chemical weapons. Yet it was an honest effort to lay out our concerns, and it reflected our collective experiences and those of our generation of State Department Arabists, seared by the memory of stumbling into the middle of bloody sectarian conflict in Lebanon in the 1980s.

What we did not do in "The Perfect Storm," however, was take a hard stand against war altogether, or make a passionate case for containment as a long-term alternative to conflict. In the end, we pulled some punches, persuading ourselves that we'd never get a hearing for our concerns beyond the secretary if we simply threw ourselves on the track. Years later, that remains my biggest professional regret.

I gave the memo to the secretary late one day in mid-July. I don't think he ever forwarded the paper to the White House, but he later told me he used it in the dinner conversation that he had with the president and Condi Rice on August 5, when he laid out his reservations bluntly. As he later recounted to journalist Bob Woodward, Powell warned the president that if he decided to go to war, he'd wind up as "the proud owner of twenty-five million people. . . . This will become your first term." He stressed the risks of regional destabilization, the difficulty of encouraging democracy in Iraq, the unpredictability of postwar politics in such a deeply repressed society, and the potential for damage to the global energy market. In light of all those dangers, he repeated his case for building pressure on Saddam deliberately through the United Nations, first attempting to get weapons inspectors back in, and then obtaining an authorization to use force if necessary.

At least for a while, the president took Powell's concerns to heart and approved an effort to obtain a new UN Security Council resolution to test Saddam. The reality, however, was that we had shifted from trying to avoid war to trying to shape it. In a note to Powell later in August, I acknowledged that we were past the point of arguing with others in the administration about "whether the goal of regime change makes sense; now it's about choosing between a smart way and a dumb way of bringing it about."[13]

We had only marginally greater success in this next phase than we had in the first. Having lost the argument to avoid war, we had two main goals in shaping it and managing the inevitable risks. First, we sought to internationalize as much as possible the road to war. That was less about the military necessity of a coalition and more about the need for international support and involvement in postwar Iraq. If this meant delay and difficult diplomacy, it was worth it. In a read-ahead memo prior to a Principals Committee meeting in January 2003, I highlighted to Powell the gulf between State and the Pentagon: "DOD's plan calls for a military government with a civilian face, run out of OSD, lasting months or years, then turning control from U.S. to Iraqis. Our plan calls for U.S. handover ASAP to an interim international authority which monitors development of Iraqi institutions."[14]

To complement a push for international legitimacy and buy-in, the second concern was about domestic legitimacy in post-Saddam Iraq. Skeptical of Chalabi and some of the other external oppositionists, we argued vociferously with staffers in the Pentagon and the vice president's office against their preference, which was essentially to "have the U.S. government install a member of the external opposition as a Karzai-like figure in post-Saddam Iraq." I argued that "some oppositionists favored by Washington are largely despised by the Iraqi public." I emphasized that Iraqis "would resent not having a significant voice in choosing new leadership" and that "ensuring the cooperation and support of Iraqis inside the country will be critical." Armitage noted in the margin, "Exactly right."[15]

We began as early as March 2002 to try to organize a number of Iraqi exiles and technocrats around an effort to consider all the challenges of post-Saddam Iraq, and how best to cope with them. It was born in large part of Ryan Crocker's experience in post-Taliban Afghanistan, when he saw the urgent need to mobilize exiled oppositionists and technocrats to help build effective governance in Kabul. Dubbed the "Future of Iraq" project, this effort resulted over the following months in a seventeen-volume set of planning documents. They ranged from the future of Iraq's agricultural sector, to dealing with immediate security challenges, to a framework for a national consultative process for putting together a provisional government.

Chalabi saw the Future of Iraq project as a threat to his interest in monopolizing post-Saddam planning, and worked with his advocates in Washington to sideline it. The Pentagon mounted its own planning operation and ignored the work we had done. When Saddam was toppled, those seventeen volumes continued to gather dust.

As the domestic legitimacy debate wound on inconclusively, there were some tactical successes on the international legitimacy front. But they didn't come without considerable grumbling from hardliners in the administration, who saw the whole UN effort at best as a waste of time and at worst as a sign of weakness. Vice President Cheney squabbled with Powell in several principals meetings in August and September, and gave two speeches late in the summer pressing the case for regime change and downplaying any need for wider international backing. One Saturday that September, I was sent to represent State at a last-minute principals meeting on Iraq. Sitting across from the vice president, with Condi Rice chairing the meeting, I dutifully made the case for working through the UN to build international legitimacy and to enhance the leverage of coercive diplomacy. After listening politely but impatiently, the vice president replied, "The only legitimacy we really need comes on the back of an M1A1 tank."

Pressed also by the British, the president stuck with his commitment to Powell and joined in a high-level push for a new Security Council resolution. In October, a new U.S. National Intelligence Estimate made the sweeping assertion that Iraq "is reconstituting its nuclear program" and "has now established large-scale, redundant and concealed biological weapons agent production capabilities." That same month, by substantial majorities in both the Senate and House, Congress gave the president authorization to use force against Iraq. The margins for the congressional vote authorizing the use of force more than a decade before were far narrower, despite the more compelling reality of Saddam's invasion of Kuwait. It was yet another reminder of how much 9/11 had changed the political atmosphere. In early November, the UN Security Council passed Resolution 1441. It declared Saddam in "material breach" of his obligations, gave Iraq a "final opportunity" to comply, and warned of "serious consequences" if it did not.

At the end of November, with his attention focused by the new resolution and the congressional vote, Saddam suddenly took steps to comply, providing a first tranche of documents and allowing UN inspectors to return to Iraq for the first time in nearly four years. In December and again in January 2003, suspicious UN inspectors reported that Saddam remained in violation of his obligations and had not yet provided complete information or access. A number of us in the department made the case to Powell that we should give the inspectors more time and let 1441 play out a little longer, in the slim hope that Saddam would come clean. By that point, however, the secretary had run out the string with the White House.

On February 5, Powell made his famous presentation to the UN

Security Council about Saddam's noncompliance and continuing WMD activities. He said that the evidence of Iraq's breach of its obligations was "irrefutable and undeniable," and that Saddam was "determined to keep his WMD and determined to make more." The secretary had worked hard to peel away unsubstantiated material pressed on him by the vice president's staff and others, but most of what remained was eventually discredited. In the moment, it felt like the most persuasive—and honest—case that the administration could muster, from its most credible spokesperson. Over time, the damage done became more obvious, to both Powell's reputation and our country's. Powell would later call his speech "painful" and a permanent "blot" on his record. It was a hard lesson for all of us in the complexities of duty.

Late on the evening of March 19, the president announced in a nationally televised speech that we were at war again with Saddam. A dozen years before, I had sat with Lisa and watched the president's father make a similar, equally sobering speech. I had much deeper trepidation this time. This was not a war that we needed to fight.

* * *

THE MILITARY OPERATION proceeded with predictable efficiency. Iraqi forces crumbled, Baghdad fell in early April, and Saddam fled into hiding. The mood in much of the administration was triumphant, and the president declared "mission accomplished" in early May. It didn't take long, however, for many of the troubles we had foreseen to surface. After a visit to Baghdad at the beginning of July, I reported bluntly to Powell that "we're in a pretty deep hole in Iraq."

Looting and lawlessness had already taken a huge toll. Rumsfeld's determination to display the new lean, mobile, technologically innovative American way of war had made short work of conventional Iraqi military resistance, but was inadequate to the task of ensuring postwar order. Less than one-third the size of the Desert Storm coalition force, the U.S. military was badly overstretched on the ground in Iraq, especially as the Iraqi army and police melted away and insecurity mushroomed. The problem was compounded by two tragically misguided American decisions in May, first to ban Baath Party members from public-sector roles, and second to disband the Iraqi army. In that same July message to Powell, I relayed an anecdote from a friend in the CIA who had recently returned from Baghdad. Interrogated after an RPG attack on U.S. troops, an ex–Iraqi army captain admitted that he had taken fifty dollars from insurgent leaders to conduct the operation. "They took away my job and my honor," he explained. "I can't feed my family. There are many more like me."[16]

In the aftermath of the toppling of Saddam, the decision-making process in Washington was even worse than the prewar experience. In NEA, we continued to push for internationalizing the civilian administration of Iraq, with an immediate emphasis on security and order, preserving the Iraqi army and police, and engaging both Sunni and Shia leaders. We also continued to make the argument for careful cultivation of a new Iraqi governance structure, whose legitimacy would come largely from people inside the country, with exiled oppositionists playing a significant but supporting role.

Our colleagues in the Pentagon had a different view, far more suspicious of ceding oversight to international partners or the United Nations, and still far more attached to central roles for Chalabi and returning exiles. Setting them atop a provisional government would be a much quicker and less complicated way to establish new Iraqi leadership. Just three days after the launch of the war, on March 22, I stressed to Powell that it was already clear we were "being pushed in a dangerous direction on some critical postwar planning issues. . . . OSD and OVP have been working steadily to . . . [hand over] postwar Iraq to 'our' Iraqis (Chalabi and company), while keeping at bay other Iraqis, the rest of the U.S. Administration, and the UN and other potential international partners."[17]

Events in Iraq and incoherence in Washington soon overwhelmed the fledgling steps we managed to take toward a more inclusive political process. Jay Garner, the retired Army general leading the early transition effort, was well-intentioned but badly miscast. The atmosphere within his group was tangled, to put it mildly. One British colleague described Garner's team as "a bag of ferrets."[18]

Garner was quickly replaced by a retired diplomat, Jerry Bremer. Smart, disciplined, and supremely self-confident, Bremer seemed like a solid choice. He reported to the Pentagon, but had enormous room to maneuver. Rumsfeld was already experiencing periodic bouts of amnesia about his hard prewar press to manage the aftermath, and the White House was all too willing at the outset to defer to a strong-willed proconsul on the ground. Described to Secretary Powell by Henry Kissinger as a "control freak," Bremer was intent upon swiftly establishing his leadership and convincing Iraqis that there would be no return to the old political order.

Just before Bremer left for Baghdad, I joined Powell and Armitage for a quiet conversation with him at Powell's home in Virginia. The secretary made clear that he wanted to do all he could to help, and that Bremer could count on State to provide whatever support we could. Powell was candid about his frustrations with the interagency process and emphasized the importance of building an international structure in Baghdad to shepherd the transition and to keep focused on a legitimate, inclusive Iraqi political process. Bremer seemed appreciative.

He didn't mention anything in that discussion about his intention to issue sweeping orders shortly after his arrival in Iraq on de-Baathification and formal dissolution of the Iraqi army. Ahmed Chalabi was put in charge of implementing the broad injunction against Baath Party members, which he applied to its illogical extreme, tossing aside not only senior officials with blood on their hands, but schoolteachers and lower-level technocrats for whom party membership was an essential basis for employment. In different hands, implementation of the de-Baathification decision might have been far less catastrophic, but Chalabi ensured that it would have ruinous effect.

The disbanding of the regular military was similarly shortsighted, casting thousands of Sunnis with lethal training and an equally lethal sense of grievance into the hands of the insurgency. It was true that most of the Iraqi armed forces had not been physically defeated in battle; when the Turks blocked the movement of U.S. ground forces into northern Iraq, and the Americans quickly took Baghdad, most of the Iraqi military beyond the capital simply melted away. It would have been hard to reassemble them, and any such effort would likely have alienated the Shia majority. The cardinal sin, however, was to cut them off entirely, and not immediately ensure some form of payment or support to disbanded soldiers. In August, UN special envoy Sérgio Vieira de Mello was killed in an insurgent truck bombing of UN headquarters in Baghdad, and prospects for international administration of the Iraqi transition as well as for a provisional government that could bridge sectarian differences rapidly receded.

The Bremer-led Coalition Provisional Authority was a curious amalgam of American hubris, ingenuity, courage, and wishful thinking. It didn't take long for the CPA to mirror the wider dysfunction of the society Bremer was seeking to mold. Its reporting to Washington was constrained by Bremer's disinclination to be second-guessed and the fact that what little reporting there was had to come through the Pentagon. I told Powell at one point that "we learn more from *The Washington Post* than we do from CPA."

Partly for that reason, but mostly because of the sheer significance of our unfolding predicament, I visited Iraq a half dozen times during the CPA's yearlong existence. Each trip had an element of the surreal. After one of my visits to the Green Zone, I described CPA headquarters in Saddam's old Republican Palace to Secretary Powell as "reminiscent of the bar scene in *Star Wars*." In the faded and still creepy grandeur of Saddam's corridors, American and other coalition personnel swarmed busily at all hours of the day and night—military and civilian, armed and unarmed, veterans of post-conflict situations and young Republican neophytes, the hardworking and committed and the certifiably clueless. Ambitious young ideologues talked earnestly about remaking ministries and educational systems, or building a securities and exchange system whether the Iraqis knew they needed one or not. On one trip, I stopped in to see Bernie Kerik, the former New York Police Department commissioner who had come to advise the Ministry of Interior. He seemed perplexed by Iraq, and perked up only when an aide informed him of another urban explosion. He rushed out, eager to get to the scene and give a television interview, reassuring Iraqi viewers in Arabic translation that order was being restored and the perpetrators would be caught, much as he might have done in the more familiar boroughs of New York City.

I traveled widely outside Baghdad that year, from Erbil and the Kurdish north to Basra and the Shia-dominated south. The two principal Kurdish leaders, Jalal Talabani and Masoud Barzani, circled each other warily but made a united front in defending the autonomy that they had spent much of the previous decade building. In my visits to Mosul, Tikrit, and Baquba in late 2003, evidence of a mounting Sunni Arab insurgency was all too obvious. By the end of the year, Shia militia groups had begun to spring up too, with Muqtada al-Sadr emerging as a particularly difficult and incendiary voice. Iran and its Revolutionary Guards deepened their meddling, feeding off the sectarian strife. Turkey kept a careful eye on the north, and opened up channels of communication to the Iraqi Kurds. Across much of the country, security was fragile and infrastructure painfully inadequate. By the spring of 2004, the early self-assurance that had fueled the CPA was fading fast.

Violence in Anbar Province, where Sunnis were an aggrieved and well-armed majority, boiled over. The towns I had driven through on my misbegotten trip from Amman to Baghdad twenty years earlier filled American television screens with awful images. First were the scenes of the burned corpses of four Blackwater security contractors

being dragged through the streets and hung from a bridge in Fallujah, then it was images of detained insurgents being brutalized and
humiliated by their American captors at Abu Ghraib. That was only
more tinder for Abu Musab al-Zarqawi, the Jordanian extremist who
was already fanning the flames in Iraq and organizing the particularly vicious group that would later be known as al-Qaeda in Iraq. It
was an ugly spring, with reverberations that would stretch across the
next few bloody years.

Meanwhile, the White House finally agreed to replace the procon-
sular CPA with a more normal embassy structure, as the Iraqis moved
toward national elections and establishment of a new government.
Jerry Bremer left Baghdad in late spring, and John Negroponte took
over as ambassador. We set up a sizable mini-bureau inside NEA in
Washington to provide support for Embassy Baghdad, which remained a huge and exceptionally complicated diplomatic mission.
Much as Powell had predicted to President Bush in August 2002,
war in Iraq sucked the oxygen out of the administration's foreign policy agenda, and left lasting scars on America's influence and an already complicated region.

* * *

AS IRAQ BECAME the main event, the Israeli-Palestinian conflict
became a painful and distracting sideshow. It was hardly the most
promising diplomatic possibility that the administration had inherited. The White House thought the Clinton administration had
wasted political capital on a problem neither central to American interests nor ripe for solution. Like so much else in foreign policy, that
attitude hardened after the September 11 attacks, with Palestinian
violence looking increasingly like a part of the wider terrorist problem, Yasser Arafat its enabler, and Ariel Sharon a partner whose hard,
uncompromising reputation fit the mood in Washington. Nevertheless, the grinding violence of the Second Intifada was impossible to
ignore, and America's Arab friends were agitated about the impact on

their own populations, if not so much about the plight or aspirations of Palestinians themselves.

The net result was a policy of relative detachment, with the administration trying to do just enough to placate the Arabs without leaning too hard on Sharon or diverting from the emerging post–9/11 goals of regime change in Iraq and regional transformation. Middle East policy in the first term of the administration was a world of two parallel bureaucratic and conceptual universes. In one corner stood the vice president and his activist staff, the civilian leadership of the Defense Department, and most NSC staffers. Their view, shared increasingly by the president after 9/11, was not only that the road to a better future for the region lay through toppling Saddam, but also that the road to Israeli-Palestinian peace lay through toppling Arafat and thorough democratic reform of the Palestinian Authority. Too much talk about what such a future might hold for Palestinians, or about the corrosive impact of Israeli settlement activity in the meantime, was seen as a reward for bad Palestinian behavior and a distraction from the main challenge. They sought to park the peace process—and decades of bipartisan diplomatic convention—until the broader regional goal was accomplished.

In the other corner stood Powell and his team at the State Department, often supported analytically by CIA. Deeply skeptical about the rush to take on Iraq and its likely consequences in the region, we argued for more focus on the immediate fires that were burning, to create better long-term conditions for considering what to do about Saddam. We largely shared the view that Arafat had become an obstacle to progress. We also realized that the Clinton administration had underplayed the importance of Palestinian reform in its zeal for a political settlement, and that we had to put a higher priority on better Palestinian governance.

The inconvenient reality, however, was that the more Arafat posed as the victim, the more popular he became among Palestinians. There was considerable frustration with the Palestinian Authority's corruption in the West Bank and Gaza, but far more anger about Israeli use of force, the ritual humiliations of life under occupation, and the absence of hope for a two-state solution. In a note to Secretary Powell, I argued that the more we focused on those issues, the more pressure we could bring to bear on Arafat. "If we are prepared to lay out for all our partners some plain truths about what a two state solution will look like, and a clear roadmap for getting there . . . a great deal is possible. If we're not prepared, however, to speak those plain truths, we will get nowhere on Palestinian reform, achieve no real security for Israel, and our Arab friends will head in other directions." I continued, "This will require us to piss everybody off to some extent, and address our message to the peoples involved, not just to the stubborn old men who lead them."[19]

Against the backdrop of continuing Israeli-Palestinian violence, American policy moved fitfully and ineffectually down its two parallel tracks. Powell's Louisville speech in November 2001 launched an effort by Tony Zinni, the former CENTCOM commander, to achieve a cease-fire and the resumption of security cooperation between Israel and the Palestinian Authority. There couldn't have been a better person to lead such an effort, or a worse set of circumstances in which to try. Zinni was supported by Aaron Miller, my longtime friend and colleague at State, with his encyclopedic knowledge of the peace process and passion for promoting it. They were an unlikely but capable duo—the brawny and cerebral former Marine general, an Italian Catholic from Philadelphia, and the lanky Jewish peace process lifer from the suburbs of Cleveland—but their mission was nearly impossible. Then came the Israeli seizure of an Iranian-origin ship loaded with arms for Palestinian fighters. The failed voyage of the *Karine-A* was a damning indictment of Arafat, and effectively buried the chances that Zinni and Miller would get anywhere.

Trips to the region by Cheney and Powell followed in March and April, respectively. They offered a graphic illustration of the administration's parallel policy universes. Cheney's purpose was largely to test the waters on Iraq. He came away convinced that there was enough regional support for decisive action against Saddam, and that there was no point in investing much in the Palestinian issue in the meantime. Powell's purpose, by contrast, was to create some sense of possibility on the Israeli-Palestinian front, calm the situation on the ground as well as regional anger, and harness the energies of other international players before they set off on their own high-profile peace initiatives.

Powell's conversations in Arab capitals, and with Sharon and Arafat in particular, were a slog. As he put it to me late one evening over the rum and Cokes that he occasionally enjoyed, "This is the closest thing to a diplomatic root canal I've ever experienced." Saudi crown prince Abdullah had helped produce a promising initiative at the Arab League summit in Beirut at the end of March, which offered a vision of peace and normalization with the wider Arab world if Israel and the Palestinians reached a two-state solution. A terrorist attack in Netanya the week before the Beirut summit, in which thirty Israeli civilians were murdered at a Passover dinner, cast a huge cloud over Powell's efforts. Nevertheless, he managed to get the key players to agree to the possibility of a regional conference to discuss ways of ending the violence and getting back to a political process. We had kept the White House carefully informed about this effort during the trip, which only amplified Powell's ire when he was overruled, and informed in a series of calls with Washington late one night in Jerusalem at the end of his trip that he could not announce this publicly the next day, as we had planned. In the minds of many in the administration, the time to launch such an effort would be after the presumed transformative impact of Saddam's fall, not before.

I had rarely seen Powell so angry. I was sitting with him in his hotel suite, long past midnight, as he finished a White House call. He slammed the phone down, his jaw clenched and eyes flashing, and said, "Goddamn it. They never stop undercutting me. Don't they understand that we're just trying to prevent a bad situation from getting worse?" At his last stop in Cairo the next day, he asked me to stay in the region and keep trying to dampen tensions. "I've burned up my heat shield," he said. "Do the best you can."

I kept at it for most of the rest of April, with each depressing meeting or event flowing seamlessly into the next. After a string of bloody terrorist attacks, the mood in Israel was edgy. Israel had begun Operation Defensive Shield in late March, after the Netanya massacre, and was reasserting direct Israeli security control in areas ceded to the Palestinians under the Oslo Accords. Arafat himself was under a form of house arrest, bottled up in the presidential compound in Ramallah.

Prime Minister Sharon was invariably courteous in our discussions, but immovable. He had little appetite for what he often saw to be American naïveté, and operated on the conviction that the best diplomacy came when your adversary was pinned firmly to the floor. (He would always greet me by saying, "You're mostly welcome"—which my U.S. embassy colleagues would ascribe to his imperfect English, but that I always suspected reflected his ambivalence about my arrival.) Much as he used an intricate network of chutes to corral and direct the cattle at his beloved ranch in the Negev, Sharon was a master at keeping people focused on security and away from longer-term political issues. Arafat made it easy for him.

The Palestinian leader seemed strangely at home under siege in Ramallah—secure in his victimhood and eerily self-assured about his ability to wriggle out of yet another predicament. The scene around his sandbagged office building in the small presidential compound, the Muqatta, was stark, with vehicles in the surrounding area turned into rusting metal pancakes by Israeli tanks, and Israel Defense Forces snipers visible in the windows of nearby structures. Inside, corridors were lit by candles, black-clad security guards grasped their weapons, and twenty-something volunteer "human shields" from Europe and America crowded the hallway, a few surreptitiously handing me notes asking for help to return home. "Please call my mother and tell her I'm ok," one read, with a name and number neatly printed below. Arafat would sit beaming when you entered his makeshift meeting room, his machine pistol prominently displayed on the table in front of him for all—especially the cameras—to see. His aides and bodyguards would smile nervously, not quite as relaxed as Arafat about where all this was headed.

Salam Fayyad, the immensely decent Palestinian minister of finance, was trapped in the Muqatta for days at a time. He later told me a story that captured perfectly Arafat's hyperpersonalized approach to governing the Palestinian Authority. There was only one functioning air conditioner in the presidential office building in those months, in a room in which Arafat and several other senior PA officials worked and slept. Ever the micromanager, the Palestinian president would turn the air conditioner off at night, despite the heat and increasingly gamey smell of too many men with too little opportunity to wash. He slept while clutching the AC's remote control, one of the few remaining totems of his authority. One night, egged on by his colleagues, Fayyad pried the remote out of the sleeping grip of Arafat and turned the air-conditioning back on. With tongue in cheek, he concluded the story by drawing a larger lesson: "You really can devolve power if you assert yourself."

As Arafat and Sharon continued their zero-sum contest, the costs for people on both sides continued to rise. From the Dolphinarium Club in Tel Aviv to the Park Hotel in Netanya to the terrible bus bombing in Hadera, Palestinian suicide attacks took an awful human toll. The human tragedy on the other side was equally painful to watch. During that late April trip, I went with United Nations Relief and Works Agency for Palestine Refugees (UNRWA) officials to visit the Palestinian refugee camp in Jenin. It was one of the grimmest scenes I ever witnessed.

Ambushed by Palestinian extremists in the narrow alleyways of the camp, IDF units had laid waste to most of it, leaving 40 percent of the camp, an area roughly the size of five football fields, flattened into rubble. The IDF had withdrawn the day before, and the stench of decomposing bodies was overpowering. Survivors were digging with shovels, picks, and their bare hands, looking for bodies of relatives. The vacant expressions on the faces of the camp's children went straight through me. There was unexploded ordnance all around, and during our visit a local Palestinian physician trying to tend to the wounded was badly injured by an accidental detonation. The UNRWA medical clinic, the only such facility in the camp, was vandalized. The refrigerator containing vaccines was shot up, spoiling the medicine inside. Miraculously, a fifteen-year-old Palestinian boy was pulled alive from the rubble that afternoon, after being trapped for nearly two days.

It was the images of Palestinian suffering that animated Saudi crown prince Abdullah when he visited President Bush at his ranch in Crawford, Texas, on April 25. The crown prince showed Bush a binder of photos of Palestinian victims, and at one point threatened to leave Crawford early if the United States wasn't prepared to act more vigorously. Taken aback by Abdullah's vehemence, the president made clear that we'd weigh in with the Israelis to prevent them from expelling or killing Arafat, and would look for ways to make our broader concerns clear. Even the staunchest proponents of giving priority to taking down Saddam and "parking" the Palestinian issue began to realize that winning the acquiescence of key Arab partners for action against Iraq would require some semblance of diplomatic commitment on the Israeli-Palestinian front. Two months later, the result was the president's June 24 speech in the Rose Garden.

In American foreign policy, there are two kinds of major speeches: frameworks for action, and substitutes for action. The June 24 address was mostly the latter, an effort to deflect Arab and European pressures for active American diplomacy and buy time for the near-term priority of action against Saddam. Reflecting the untreated schizophrenia in the policy process, it was really two speeches, with only a thin connection between them. In the first part, the president laid out the transformative notion that the path to Palestinian statehood could only come through the removal of Arafat, serious democratic reform of the Palestinian Authority, and a cessation of violence. The second part laid out, in much more general terms, what might be possible for Palestinians at the end of the rainbow: a Palestinian state living side by side in peace and security with Israel. The clear implication was sequential, putting the onus squarely on the Palestinians to carry out unilateral regime change before there could be any progress toward a two-state solution.

The bureaucratic infighting over the drafting of the speech was ugly. While Condi Rice was a prime proponent of a presidential address, Vice President Cheney and Secretary Rumsfeld opposed the idea, which they saw as both an unnecessary diversion from the Iraq campaign and an undeserved reward for Palestinians. Powell and I made the argument that the second half of the speech had to be strengthened, spelling out in more detail what a state might look like and what responsibilities the Israelis would have along the way, especially regarding the cessation of settlement construction. That, we maintained, would be essential to get a serious hearing from Palestinians who understood the need for reform. The early White House drafts, however, were heavily weighted toward the front end of the speech. I didn't mince words with Powell. "Mr. Secretary," I wrote in a note in early June, "I have to be honest with you: this draft is junk. It contains no real sense of endgame. It vastly overestimates the attractiveness of a 'provisional state' for Palestinians. . . . Its tone is patronizing and preachy. No one—not even you—could sell this in the region."[20]

The Sharon government played an active role in the editing process, emphasizing Palestinian obligations as the precondition for eventual final status negotiations, and resisting anything more than an extremely light touch in sketching the possible contours of the outcome. Dov Weisglass, a senior advisor to Sharon, led a delegation to the White House in mid-June and suggested in one meeting that "the Palestinians are fed up with Arafat and just waiting for the Americans to give a signal that he's finished." I countered that "the one thing Palestinians are more fed up with than Arafat is the occupation. . . . If you want to marginalize and manipulate Arafat, give the Palestinians a real political horizon. The Prime Minister has not given Palestinians a whiff of hope for ending occupation, nor any kind of compelling political plan. If he had done so, we might be having a different conversation."[21] The reaction not only from Weisglass but also from most of the Americans in the room was polite but utterly dismissive.

By about the twentieth draft, we began to make a little headway, but it was a hard and unsatisfying debate. In one memorable conference call to review yet another draft, two of my senior colleagues from the Pentagon and the vice president's office tried to argue that there had to be parity in any reference to cessation of settlement activity in the West Bank, and that we should call on both Israelis and Palestinians to stop construction activity during negotiations. I didn't know whether to laugh or cry. In the end, the two halves of the speech hung uneasily together, with just enough in the latter part to give some slight credibility to the first. The reaction from the Sharon government was effusive. As one noted Israeli columnist wrote the next day, "The Likud Central Committee could not have written a speech like that." Arab reaction was swift and negative. Rice called me to ask what I was hearing from regional leaders, and I tested my capacity for understatement by replying that "it's pretty rough."

While the White House had hoped that the speech would tamp down international clamor for American diplomatic action, it predictably invited the question of how the administration intended to operationalize the president's vision. On June 25, I told Powell that "our most immediate challenge is the absence of a practical roadmap in the speech to end violence, transform Palestinian leadership, and restore hope."[22] In July, the Jordanian, Egyptian, and Saudi foreign ministers came to Washington to make a similar argument. Powell engineered a meeting for them with the president in hopes that they could help reinforce the case we were trying to make. Bush acknowledged the need for follow-up, but remained wary of investing much American capital. His view was that the speech had put the ball squarely in the court of the Palestinians and Arabs, and now they needed to act. Marwan Muasher, the gifted and energetic Jordanian foreign minister, pressed the president gently in this meeting and then during an August visit by King Abdullah to put together a plan to implement the June 24 vision. He pushed for a "roadmap" that would include benchmarks, timelines, mutual obligations, and a monitoring group to measure performance. The president eventually accepted the argument. In the Oval Office with King Abdullah in August, Bush motioned to me and told the king that "Bill can work with Marwan on this." That was the beginning of the Roadmap initiative, which became a classic illustration of how motion can imitate movement in diplomacy.

The Roadmap never suffered for lack of effort at State or among our Quartet partners: the UN, EU, and Russia. Its fatal flaw was lack of commitment and political will—in Jerusalem and Ramallah, as well as in Washington. The White House's priorities were elsewhere, and outside State there was no interest in the exercise. Doug Feith later called it "just a halftime show," occupying the space between the June 24 speech and the invasion of Iraq and "whatever serious diplomacy was going to be after the Iraq action."[23] To those of us in the halftime marching band crisscrossing the region in late 2002 and early 2003, that was not a very edifying image, but Feith certainly captured our irrelevance.

The Roadmap laid out three phases, with parallel Palestinian and Israeli actions in each, aimed ultimately at a two-state solution. We floated early drafts with the Israelis and Palestinians in the fall of 2002. Weisglass objected vehemently to the lack of strict sequencing in the Roadmap, insistent on postponing Israeli steps until the Palestinians had acted decisively on reform and ending violence. The Palestinians pushed for both sides to take steps in parallel. Meanwhile, reform began to gain some momentum, with the Palestinians producing a provisional constitution and Salam Fayyad accomplishing near miracles on budget transparency.

In the spring of 2003, Mahmoud Abbas was appointed prime minister, a first step toward devolving power away from Arafat. Long an advocate of negotiations but generally risk-averse and without any independent political base, Abbas at least offered the possibility of easing Arafat off center stage and opening up diplomatic opportunities with the Israelis. Taking advantage of this step, and the early if short-lived success of the invasion of Iraq, the White House finally assented to public release of the Roadmap at the end of April. The Palestinians grudgingly went along. The Israelis offered highly conditioned acceptance, with fourteen reservations aimed at ensuring strict sequencing within each phase of the Roadmap and the deferral of significant Israeli concessions or responsibilities. It was not an auspicious start, but there was nevertheless finally a small opening, which would require real American diplomatic muscle and willpower to explore, and a readiness to press both sides persistently on some uncomfortable issues. The White House's limited appetite for peacemaking soon became clear, especially as the debacle in Iraq unfolded.

I accompanied Powell on a trip to the region in early May, and returned later in the month with Elliott Abrams, the senior Middle East advisor on the NSC staff. Our main goal was to prepare the way for two summits. The first was hosted by President Mubarak in Sharm el-Sheikh at the beginning of June, and brought together a number of international and regional leaders to highlight a common front against terrorism. The second was hosted by King Abdullah in Aqaba immediately afterward, and included Sharon and Abbas. Its focus was launching the Roadmap process. Both events were long on ceremony and short on practical follow-through, although the president did have an admirably direct conversation with Sharon in Aqaba about curbing settlement activity and stepping up to Israel's responsibilities under the Roadmap. Bush was equally blunt with Abbas. A U.S. monitoring mission was set up, but by late summer a tenuous cease-fire in the West Bank and Gaza collapsed. Abbas resigned shortly thereafter, disillusioned both by American detachment and Arafat's refusal to empower him.

Late in the fall, Sharon told Abrams privately that he was considering a unilateral withdrawal from Gaza. It was a step that appealed to Sharon. Demographically, it removed from Israeli control and responsibility a large Palestinian population. Strategically, it offered a way for Israel to regain the initiative, keep the Roadmap in the glove compartment, divest itself of the troublesome Gazans, tighten its hold on the West Bank, and deflect any pressure for wider territorial concessions. As Weisglass put it in an interview in 2004, "The disengagement is actually formaldehyde. . . . It is the bottle of formaldehyde within which you place the President's formula so that it will be preserved for a very lengthy period."[24] Bush announced formal U.S. support for Gaza disengagement during an April 2004 visit by Sharon, adding public statements essentially endorsing Israel's positions on Palestinian refugees and on the permanent retention by Israel of the large settlement blocs along the 1948 Green Line. Both positions were generally consistent with the parameters that Bill Clinton had offered the Israelis and Palestinians in 2000, but Bush's reaffirmation directly to the Israelis, in the absence of any active negotiation, was notable, unnecessary, and poorly received by the Arabs.

With the already severely stricken Roadmap overdosed on Weisglass's formaldehyde, and the White House content to follow Sharon's lead on Gaza disengagement, there was little inclination to seize the last opportunity that arose in the administration's first term—the sudden death of Yasser Arafat in November, just a few days after President Bush's reelection. I was dispatched as the senior American representative to Arafat's official funeral in Cairo, a gesture of respect from the White House for Palestinians, if not for the Palestinian leader himself. It was a chaotic scene. At one point, I found myself in a receiving line just behind the leader of Hamas, Khaled Meshal, who looked only marginally more worried about being seen near me than I was about being seen near him.

In hindsight, it's hard to see how we could have gotten much traction on the Israeli-Palestinian issue once the White House had set Saddam's overthrow as its overriding regional objective. Arafat's default position had become inertia, riding the wave of Intifada violence rather than trying to tame it, content to drift in hopes that outside events might once again change his luck. Sharon had no interest in serious territorial compromise, and happily took advantage of Arafat's evasiveness. When a few modest openings emerged, such as Abbas's selection as prime minister in 2003 and then Arafat's death in 2004, the United States was too preoccupied with Iraq and too uninterested in the kind of hands-on role that Bush thought Clinton had fallen into. Purely as a diplomatic device, the Roadmap helped create the appearance of seriousness, preserved some sense of political possibility, and avoided stray international peace initiatives. In the end, however, it reflected a general post–9/11 habit of viewing diplomacy as an afterthought—as the halftime show, not the main event.

* * *

THERE WERE EXCEPTIONS, however, to the general pattern of dismissiveness toward diplomacy. Libya was one of them. Dealing with Qaddafi in this period was complicated, but certainly more heartening than the bitter failure of Iraq and the endless frustrations of dealing with Palestinians and Israelis. Diplomacy worked in Libya with painstaking effort over several administrations, producing a resolution of the Lockerbie terrorist attack, and Libya's abandonment of terrorism and weapons of mass destruction. It worked because we applied American and international leverage methodically to change Qaddafi's calculus and sharpen his self-interest in changing his be havior so he could preserve his regime. And it worked because we had far more running room for diplomacy in the Bush administration on this issue than we did on Iraq or the peace process.

The stage had been set over the previous decade, by the Bush 41 and Clinton administrations. In 1991, the United States and the United Kingdom formally indicted two Libyan intelligence agents in connection with the Lockerbie bombing, and made a set of five demands, which remained consistent over the next dozen years: The Libyans had to surrender the suspects for trial; accept responsibility for the actions of Libyan officials involved in the bombing; disclose all it knew of the bombing and allow full access to witnesses and evidence; pay appropriate compensation; and commit itself to cease all forms of terrorist action and assistance to terrorist groups. Fulfillment of all five demands would result in the lifting of the multilateral sanctions that had been imposed by the UN Security Council after Lockerbie.

When Qaddafi met the first demand and turned over the two suspects for trial in 1999, the Clinton administration opened direct, secret talks with the Libyans, led by Assistant Secretary of State Martin Indyk, in cooperation with the British. Indyk made clear that the lifting of U.S. national sanctions, built up since the Reagan-era conflicts with Qaddafi, would depend upon Libya giving up its nuclear and chemical weapons programs, which U.S. intelligence had been following closely since the 1970s.

When I resumed the secret channel in London in October 2001, I was careful to reiterate the main lines of the positions conveyed earlier by Indyk, including on WMD. Over the course of the next two years, in roughly a dozen meetings in London, Rome, and other locations, we made considerable progress. There were several reasons for this. First, Qaddafi was feeling the pressure of concerted U.S. and international sanctions. The energy sector was starved for investment, and the country's infrastructure was in shambles. Unemployment ran at 30 percent, and inflation at nearly 50 percent. Qaddafi worried

about his restive population, and in 1998 had sent troops to Benghazi
to put down an Islamist rebellion.

Second, we established a reliable diplomatic channel with serious
Libyan counterparts, well connected to Qaddafi. As had been the case
in the talks with Indyk, Musa Kusa, one of Qaddafi's closest aides, led
the Libyan delegation. Tall, thin, and poker-faced, Kusa had studied
sociology at Michigan State in the late 1970s, before returning to
Libya and a series of senior intelligence jobs—a line of work far removed from his academic stint in America. Kusa was accompanied
by two senior Libyan diplomats, Abdelati Obeidi and Abdel Rahman
Shalgham. From that first meeting in the fall of 2001, I found Kusa
and his colleagues to be cautious but capable, committed to making
progress, if always nervous about hidden agendas from us and the
whims of their mercurial boss. We offered him a "script" in that initial
discussion, which laid out exactly what we expected from the Libyans, and what we were prepared to do in return. We spent hours and
hours in tangled debate over subsequent months, in bilateral sessions
as well as trilateral discussions with the British. Slowly we began to
reach understandings on language and how to verify commitments—
and we also began to build up trust and personal rapport.

Third, we could rely on excellent intelligence coordination with
our CIA and MI6 colleagues. We tracked systematically Libya's gradual disengagement from the business of terrorism, from the high-
profile expulsion of the notorious Palestinian terrorist Abu Nidal to
the lower-key severing of financial and training links to other groups.
We also tracked the much less promising evidence of persistent Libyan efforts to expand their chemical and nuclear weapons programs,
which featured contacts with former Soviet scientists as well as the
A. Q. Khan network in Pakistan. U.S. intelligence helped interdict a
shipment of uranium enrichment technology from A. Q. Khan to
Tripoli in the fall of 2003. That played a crucial role in persuading
Qaddafi to finally give up his WMD programs and realize he could no
longer deceive us. Finally, we could rely on the credible threat of force

in the event that diplomacy failed, reinforced by the examples of Afghanistan in 2001 and Iraq in 2003.

By the early spring of 2003, Kusa was ready to confirm Libyan acceptance of the terms we had laid out on Lockerbie a decade earlier. Meanwhile, lawyers for the families of the victims were negotiating with the Libyans about compensation. In several wrenching meetings with the families that spring, I briefed them on the progress we had made, and stressed that we would not conclude any settlement until the compensation question was resolved. Those were among the most painful conversations I ever had in government. The dull, antiseptic State Department conference room in which we met only put in sharper relief the anguish of the family members around the table. No form of words, and no amount of compensation, could erase their loss or atone for the murders of so many innocent people, dozens of whom were American college students on their way home for the holidays after a semester abroad. The grief and anger in that room could not be bridged by empathy or rational diplomatic explanation, and I understood that. One furious mother told me to "go to hell with your Libyan friends" in a session that spring, but most of the families were appreciative of what we were trying to do and the limits of what we could produce. I wish we could have done more. In August, the lawyers reached a compensation agreement providing $2.7 billion to the families, $10 million for each of the victims.

Meanwhile, we began to move ahead on the WMD issue. In each of our private conversations over the previous year and a half, I had reminded Kusa that this question would have to be solved before any normalization of relations. He made no effort to deny that Libya had active nuclear and chemical weapons programs, and I made clear that we had solid evidence that it did. Libya would have to take fast, dramatic, concrete steps up front to rid itself of WMD and advanced missile programs, which we would verify before normalization. I always emphasized that there was no ulterior motive in this—we had no interest in regime change, but a powerful interest in Libya making the strategic choice to abandon WMD. We were demonstrating in the Lockerbie negotiations that we would follow through on our end of commitments if the Libyans acted on theirs. This was a moment when Qaddafi, ever the contrarian, could gain in stature by renouncing weapons that would only buy him trouble, especially in the new and more perilous post–9/11 world. Kusa indicated to me that he thought Qaddafi was increasingly drawn to that logic, especially as he learned to trust America's word in the Lockerbie talks. On the margins of our March 11, 2003, meeting in London, after he had finally confirmed acceptance of the Lockerbie terms, he told me quietly that Qaddafi "is ready to move decisively" on the issue of WMD.[25]

That same month, Saif al-Islam, Qaddafi's son and an erstwhile postgraduate student in London, conveyed much the same message to MI6. His father, he said, wanted to "clear the air." Strongly encouraged by Prime Minister Blair, President Bush agreed to send Steve Kappes, a senior CIA officer, to join British intelligence counterparts for follow-on conversations with Saif and Kusa. The WMD interdiction in the Mediterranean in the fall finally convinced Qaddafi that it was time to move. After a last round of talks in December, Qaddafi agreed, and announced on December 19 that he was giving up WMD. It was a significant achievement for Bush and Blair, at a time when the Iraq fiasco was becoming more and more difficult to manage.

I made three trips to Libya in the following year to ensure strict implementation. The Libyans stressed repeatedly their commitment to follow through. Their sensitivities were predictable, and focused mainly on the need to be careful to characterize our WMD efforts in Libya as "assistance" rather than "inspection," and the importance of showing the Libyan public concrete benefits of Qaddafi's decision to get out of the terrorism and WMD business.[26]

For all of our progress, we continued to have plenty of difficulties with the Libyan leader—we caught him plotting against Crown Prince Abdullah of Saudi Arabia in the fall of 2003; he detained a group of Bulgarian medical personnel on trumped-up charges in

2004; and his human rights practices continued to attract, rightly and regularly, our criticism. But his abandonment of terrorism and WMD was a substantial accomplishment, and a reminder of the value of diplomacy.

There was a lively debate within the Bush administration about why Qaddafi had acted, with Vice President Cheney and other hawks drawing a direct connection to Iraq and the demonstration effect of Saddam's removal. I always thought that was part of the answer, but only part, and not necessarily the decisive part. Afghanistan was evidence enough of our determination and capabilities after 9/11. Moreover, the track record we built up with the Libyans, on the foundation of what the previous administration had pursued, underscored that we were focused on changing behavior, not the Qaddafi regime, and that however difficult the choices and the pathway for the Libyans, our word could be trusted. Sanctions had taken a long-term toll. Qaddafi's political isolation in the international community was tightly sealed. He needed a way out, and we gave him a tough but defensible one. That's ultimately what diplomacy is all about—not perfect solutions, but outcomes that cost far less than war and leave everyone better off than they would otherwise have been.

* * *

BY THE END of the first term of Bush 43, and four years in NEA, I was exhausted. I had been proud to serve under Powell and Armitage and proud of the dedication, skill, and courage of my colleagues in the Near Eastern Affairs bureau. I was also deeply worried about the mess we had made in the Middle East, and disappointed in my own failure to do more to avoid it.

In January 2005, Condi Rice succeeded Powell as secretary. In the note I sent to her before our two-hour transition conversation, I wrote, "The Near East is a region dangerously adrift. . . . Across the Arab world a sense of humiliation and weakness is becoming more and more corrosive. Most regimes are perceived by their people to be corrupt and self-absorbed." Blunt about the depths to which America's standing in the region had fallen, with more than four out of every five Arabs expressing strong disapproval of the United States, I warned of further strategic setbacks in the second Bush term unless we shifted our approach. There could be "terminal chaos and warlordism in Iraq, the death of the two state solution for Israelis and Palestinians, the birth of a nuclear-armed, hegemonic Iran, and mounting popular pressures against Arab governments . . . unless we make common cause with regional partners in a coherent strategy for constructive change. . . . We have to be seen as part of the solution, not as part of the problem. That is not the case today."[27]

Arafat's death in November and the election of Mahmoud Abbas as the new Palestinian president in January 2005 offered an opening to reorient our approach. So did the tragic assassination of Lebanese prime minister Rafik Hariri in February, orchestrated by the overreaching Syrians, who now faced a huge popular backlash in Lebanon. We managed to take advantage of the moment to build international pressure and push Syrian forces out of Lebanon, for the first time since the Lebanese civil war began in the mid-1970s. The wreckage of the administration's first-term efforts, however, overwhelmed. The policy sins of commission were glaringly apparent, the sins of omission harder to measure but no less significant.

The Iraq invasion was the original sin. It was born of hubris, as well as failures of imagination and process. For neoconservative proponents, it was the key tool in the disruption of the Middle East—the heady, irresponsible, and historically unmoored notion that shaking things up violently would produce better outcomes. In a region where unintended consequences were rarely uplifting, the toppling of Saddam set off a chain reaction of troubles. It laid bare the fragilities and dysfunctions of Iraq as well as the wider Arab state system—proving that Americans could be just as arrogant and haphazard in their impact on Middle East maps as the original British and French mapmakers.

The chaos that spread across Iraq after 2003 created opportunities for Iranian mischief and influence, and helped reawaken broader competition between Sunni and Shia for supremacy in the Middle East. By 2004, King Abdullah in Jordan was already talking about fears of a "Shia crescent," arcing from Iran across Iraq and sympathetic Alawite allies in Syria to Lebanon. Afflicted by sectarian violence and Sunni Arab alienation, Iraq became a magnet for jihadists and regional terrorism. While we made halting attempts to promote greater political and economic openness throughout the Middle East, the debacle in Iraq, including the miserable images from Abu Ghraib, poisoned America's image and credibility. If this was how Americans promoted democracy, few Arabs wanted any part of it.

Poverty of imagination was another problem. Although we had tried in NEA to emphasize—repeatedly—all the things that could go wrong, all the reasons to avoid an ill-conceived war, and all the plausible alternative policy paths, none of us asked enough basic questions. None of us thought seriously enough about the possibility that Saddam had no WMD anymore and was obfuscating not to conceal his stockpiles but rather to hide their absence in the face of domestic and regional predators.

There was also a failure of process. Military interventions, especially in the dysfunctional circumstances of the modern Middle East, are always fraught with peril. Our capacity for underestimating that has become habitual. The polarization of views in the administration in the run-up to war in 2003 was stark and crippling, and never really resolved. Sometimes that was simply a function of wishful thinking, such as the neocon fantasy that Iraqis would quickly rise above a history devoid of consensual national governance and replete with sectarian rivalries, or the Rumsfeld notion that we could do regime change on the cheap. Prewar planning was erratic and stovepiped, with too little attention to the most fundamental questions about consequences and how best to anticipate and manage them. Immediate postwar policy suffered badly from seat-of-the-pants judgments, such as the momentous CPA decisions to disband the Iraqi army and cut its members loose financially, and to put Ahmed Chalabi in charge of a recklessly sweeping implementation of the ban on Baath Party members.

There was a continuous fixation on policy capillaries—hours and hours of discussion in the White House Situation Room about the ins and outs of restoring electricity across Iraq, or reconstruction of local health or education systems—without enough focus on the arterial issues of security and national governance, of how to keep the Kurds in, the Sunni Arabs engaged, and the Shia tempered in their new-found political advantage. There was all too often a massive disconnect between bold pronouncements in the cloistered Situation Room and the messy challenge of connecting them to the realities of the Middle East.

And then there were the more elusive sins of omission. Some were deeply personal. Having tried to highlight all the things that could go wrong, all the unanswered strategic and practical questions, and all the flaws in going it alone, why didn't I go to the mat in my opposition or quit? These are hard decisions, filled with professional, moral, and family considerations. I still find my own answer garbled and unsatisfying, even with the benefit of a decade and a half of hindsight. Part of it was about loyalty to my friends and colleagues, and to Secretary Powell; part of it was the discipline of the Foreign Service, and the conceit that we could still help avoid even worse policy blunders from within the system than from outside it; part of it was selfish and career-centric, the unease about forgoing a profession I genuinely loved and in which I had invested twenty years; and part of it, I suppose, was the nagging sense that Saddam was a tyrant who deserved to go, and maybe we could navigate his demise more adeptly than I feared.

In the end, I stayed, and my efforts to limit the damage had little effect. I wasn't alone in my uncertainty in those years. "There's honor in continuing to serve," said one longtime colleague, "so long as you're honest about your dissent. But you never entirely escape the feeling that you're also an enabler."

The wider sins of omission are really about opportunity costs, about the road not taken. How might things have been different for America's role in the world and for the Middle East if we had not invaded Iraq in the spring of 2003? What if we had tried to harness the massive outpouring of international goodwill and shared concern after the terrible attacks of September 11 in a different—more constructive —direction?

The eighteen months between 9/11 and the invasion of Iraq were one of those hinge points in history, whose contours are easier to see today than they were at that uncertain and emotional time. If we had avoided the debacle in Iraq, and instead projected American power and purpose more wisely, it seems obvious today that American interests and values would have been better served. That would have required a real attempt at coercive diplomacy in Iraq—not the one we employed, which was long on coercion and short on diplomacy. That would also have required patience in our diplomacy and a readiness to share in its design and execution. Instead, we opted for the more immediate satisfactions of unilateral impulses and blunt force, and kept the sharing part to a minimum. It was beyond our power and imagination to remake the Middle East, with or without the overthrow of Saddam, but we could certainly make an already disordered region worse and further erode our leadership and influence. And we did.

6

Putin's Disruptions: Managing Great Power Trainwrecks

VLADIMIR PUTIN HAS never been at a loss for tactical surprises, and he didn't disappoint this time. Sitting in a hotel near Red Square, we waited for the Kremlin to summon us. Well acquainted with Putin's penchant for one-upmanship, Secretary of State Condi Rice was relaxed and a little bemused as the first hour of delay stretched into a second. Her staff circled nervously, staring at their watches. The secretary was a pro, watching a Russian sports channel on television as she waited for Putin's inevitable trick play. It finally came as we approached the third hour. We got the call, but Putin was no longer at the Kremlin. We'd have to travel forty minutes to his compound at Barvikha, on the outskirts of the city. Diplomatic Security didn't like these kinds of surprises, but they had no choice. Rice shrugged. "Shall we?"

When we arrived, a presidential assistant escorted us to a lavishly appointed dining room. Arrayed around the long rectangular table, with Putin at its center, was nearly the entirety of Russia's Security Council. With a sardonic half-smile, Putin said he thought Rice, as a student of Russian history, would appreciate the setting. This was the modern Politburo, the court of the new Russian tsar. The point was as subtle as Putin himself: Russia was back.

Putin greeted the secretary and explained that the occasion for the celebration was the birthdays of Igor Ivanov, the sixty-one-year-old Security Council secretary and former foreign minister, and Dmitry Medvedev, the forty-one-year-old first deputy prime minister. It was a jovial meal, punctuated by frequent vodka toasts and liberal resort to Ivanov's supply of special reserve Georgian wine. Russia had recently embargoed a variety of Georgian products, but Ivanov, whose mother still lived in Tbilisi, evidently had a dispensation from the tsar.

Sitting across from Putin, Rice held her own. Putin played the instigator, poking and prodding about the war in Iraq, the prisoners in Guantanamo, and other unpleasant topics. Sergey Ivanov, the urbane defense minister, piled on at one point with a few acerbic comments about Ukraine, where the afterglow of the Orange Revolution in 2004 was quickly fading. "How's your beacon of democracy looking now?" he asked.

After dinner, Putin invited Secretary Rice to a separate sitting room. Foreign Minister Sergey Lavrov and I joined them in front of a roaring fire. Putin and Rice got straight to business. Rice raised a couple of concerns about the ongoing negotiations over Russia's entry into the World Trade Organization. Putin showed off his mastery of the dreary details of poultry imports and food safety standards, but seemed bored by it all. His mood changed abruptly when the secretary raised Georgia, cautioning the Russians to avoid escalation of frictions with President Mikheil Saakashvili over the breakaway republics of Abkhazia and South Ossetia. Standing up in front of the fireplace, Putin wagged his index finger and grew testy. "If Saakashvili uses force in South Ossetia, which we are convinced he is preparing to do, that would be a grave mistake, and the Georgian people would suffer the most. If he wants war, he will get it."

Rice stood at this point too, giving no ground to Putin and looming several inches taller than him in her heels. She repeated the risks for U.S.-Russian relations if there was conflict in Georgia. Having to look up at Rice hardly improved Putin's attitude. "Saakashvili is nothing more than a puppet of the United States," he said. "You need to pull back the strings before there's trouble." Gesturing toward the dining room next door, he added, "I'm going to tell you something that no one in there knows yet. If Georgia causes bloodshed in Ossetia, I will have no alternative to recognizing South Ossetia and Abkhazia, and responding with force." The conversation gradually deescalated, and Putin and Rice sat back down. Putin was exasperated, but concluded calmly, "We could talk for ages about this, but that's the point I want you to understand. If Saakashvili starts something, we will finish it."[1]

Having made his point, Putin excused himself to say good night to the birthday celebrants. He passed the baton to Sergey Ivanov, who reinforced Putin's message on Georgia. It hardly needed reinforcing. Putin's pugnacity left an impression. This was not the Russia I had left a decade earlier, flat on its back and in strategic retreat. Surfing on historically high oil prices and nursing fifteen years of grievances, convinced that the United States had taken advantage of Russia's moment of historical weakness and was bent on keeping it down, Putin was determined to show that he was making Russia great again and we better get used to it.

* * *

SERVING AS U.S. ambassador in Moscow was my dream job. Russia can be a hard place, especially for American diplomats, but the relationship between Russia and the United States mattered as few others did. Still struggling with its post-Soviet identity crisis, and a considerably less potent player on the international stage than the Soviet Union had been, Russia remained a force to be reckoned with. Its nuclear capacity was formidable. Its hydrocarbons were a significant factor in the global economy. Its geographic sprawl and history gave it influence across a range of international issues. Its diplomatic skill and permanent membership on the UN Security Council meant that it would have a say.

Having lived through Russia's complicated post-Soviet transition, I was fascinated by the great historical canvas on which Russians were now trying to paint their future. Often as preoccupied with their sense of exceptionalism as Americans were, they sought a distinctive political and economic system, which would safeguard the individual freedoms and economic possibilities denied them under Communism, and ensure them a place among the handful of world powers. I liked Russians, respected their culture, enjoyed their language, and was endlessly fascinated by the tangled history of U.S.-Russian diplomacy.

Following in the footsteps of Kennan and Bohlen, and the remarkable ambassadors who succeeded them, was a daunting challenge. It almost didn't happen. Late in my tenure as assistant secretary for near eastern affairs, Colin Powell had asked what I hoped to do next. I told him that I'd love to go back to Moscow, and he said he'd do everything he could to make that happen. He and Rich Armitage recommended me to the White House as the career Foreign Service candidate. There was precedent for noncareer appointees to Moscow, but they were the exception, and there didn't appear to be any such contenders as the transition to President Bush's second term unfolded in the winter of 2004–5. Nevertheless, several months passed without any decision, and I began to wonder about my chances, especially given all the reservations that my colleagues and I had expressed in the lead-up to the Iraq War.

In January, shortly after succeeding Powell as secretary of state, Rice approached me about serving as ambassador to Israel instead, making a strong case that she intended to make a priority of the Arab-Israeli peace process during her tenure. I was intrigued, but burned out on Middle East issues after four long years in NEA, and not enthusiastic about relitigating many of the same policy disagreements with many of the same personalities. I decided to push hard for Moscow, and Rice agreed to back Powell's recommendation. Eventually, the White House approved my nomination in the spring of 2005. I was confirmed by the Senate in July, and Lisa and the girls and I arrived in Moscow in early August.

Spaso House, named after the quiet little square on which it sits in central Moscow, was the immense neoclassical residence of the American ambassador and our new home. We often reminded our daughters not to get too used to its proportions or grandeur. The house we owned in Washington could easily fit into Spaso's Great Hall. The massive chandelier hanging from the two-story-high ceiling, with its dozens of crystals weighing twenty-five pounds apiece, left us in chronic fear that a guest would be impaled and U.S.-Russian relations imperiled. Beyond the Great Hall was the State Dining Room, with a table that seemed as long as a bowling lane, and, past that, a huge ballroom. A long gallery ran around the second floor of the house overlooking the Great Hall, with a series of bedrooms with twenty-foot ceilings, and a small family kitchen and dining room. In the basement, there was a much bigger kitchen and a labyrinth of storerooms, staff quarters, and mysterious passageways.

I never tired of legendary Spaso stories. One party in 1935, on the eve of the great purge trials, attracted most of the Soviet leadership save for Stalin. Few of the senior officials on the guest list that evening survived. Featuring a variety of acts from the Moscow circus, the party became the model for the famous ball scene in Mikhail Bulgakov's *The Master and Margarita*. The best act was accidental—when a trainer put a rubber nipple on a champagne bottle and fed a baby bear liberally, with predictably chaotic consequences. In the early 1950s, Kennan amused himself during his brief and lonely tenure as ambassador by reading Russian poetry aloud late at night in the darkened Great Hall. He assumed that his habit would only confuse his Soviet minders, who were of course recording virtually everything that was said in Spaso. Little had changed on the surveillance front by the time we arrived, and Lisa and I always assumed that the only way to have a private conversation in Spaso was to either go for a walk in the garden or turn on the radio to mask our voices.

We had a busy residence during those three years, welcoming tens of thousands of guests. Foreign Minister Sergey Lavrov and other cabinet officers came to private lunches. We hosted three thousand Russians for the Fourth of July. During the two hundredth anniversary of U.S.-Russian diplomatic relations in 2007, we held a series of events, including jazz concerts, films, lectures, and even a fashion show with Ralph Lauren. We celebrated space cooperation with astronauts and cosmonauts. I especially enjoyed sports diplomacy—bringing the NBA's Los Angeles Clippers, the Davis Cup tennis team, and the U.S. men's junior hockey team to Spaso and Russia. We even hosted Lizzy's senior prom, which conveniently allowed me—and my security detail—to keep her date within our sights for the duration of the evening. Lisa and I worked hard to include people from across generations and Russian society, from prominent Kremlin officials to political oppositionists and human rights activists. Barely a day went by without some event or reception. Spaso House was a huge asset, and we put it to full use.

The embassy itself was now operating out of the new chancery building, which had stood empty and forlorn during our previous tour, and whose top floors were now secure enough for classified work. The staff was still one of the largest in the world, with nearly 1,800 employees, including about 450 Americans, divided across Moscow and our consulates in St. Petersburg, Yekaterinburg, and Vladivostok.

With an exceptional team behind me and a fair amount of leeway from Washington, I threw myself into my new role. Real progress would be hard to come by. The Russia policy knot mostly just seemed to get tighter, with Washington increasingly preoccupied with troubles in the Middle East, and Moscow consumed by its grievances and captivated by its newfound ability to do something about them.

* * *

WHEN I LEFT Moscow after my first tour in 1996, I was worried about the resurgence of a Russia at once cocky, cranky, aggrieved, and insecure. I had no idea it would happen so quickly, or that Vladimir Putin would emerge over the next decade as the extreme embodiment of that peculiarly Russian combination of qualities.

Neither process moved in a straight line. Boris Yeltsin had stumbled repeatedly in his second term, lurching from a desperate financial crisis in 1998 to another war in Chechnya and diplomatic embarrassment in Kosovo. Late in his term, with his health failing, and anxious to protect his family and legacy, he anointed his successor, a man who had in the span of a few years vaulted from gray anonymity in the St. Petersburg mayor's office to a senior position in the Kremlin, leadership of the FSB, and finally the prime ministry. Putin had an unremarkable career in the KGB, but a string of St. Petersburg patrons helped him up the ladder, and he eventually earned Yeltsin's trust. He seemed in many ways the anti-Yeltsin—half a generation younger, sober, ruthlessly competent, hardworking, and hard-faced, he offered promise for Russians tired of Yeltsin-era chaos and disorder.

Putin's most striking characteristic was his passion for control—founded on an abiding distrust of most of those around him, whether in the Russian elite or among foreign leaders. Some of that had to do with his professional training; some had to do with his tough upbringing in postwar Leningrad. The only surviving child of parents scarred by the brutalities of World War II—his father badly wounded in the defense of Leningrad, his mother nearly dying of starvation during the siege—Putin shaped his worldview in urban schoolyards, where, as he put it, "the weak get beat." He learned to fend for himself, mastering judo and its techniques for gaining leverage against stronger opponents. However indifferent his record had been in university and the KGB, he didn't lack self-confidence. Nor did he doubt his capacity for reading his opponents and exploiting their vulnerabilities. He could charm as well as bully, and he was always coldly calculating.

The Russia that he inherited was full of troubles. In addition to the apparent political challenges that came with a crumbling state, the economy had descended into turmoil. After the August 1998 economic crisis, in which the stock market crashed, the government defaulted, and the ruble collapsed, unemployment and inflation soared, GDP contracted by nearly 5 percent, and oil production dropped to half its Soviet-era high. A rapid rise in hydrocarbon prices and aggressive economic reforms helped turn the Russian economy around during Putin's first term as president. By the summer of 2005, early in his second term, Russia's annual growth rate was averaging 7 percent, and unemployment had dropped by nearly half. Economic progress fueled Putin's popularity and gave him space to impose his brand of political order. He tamed the oligarchs by brokering an implicit deal—if they stayed out of his business, he'd stay out of theirs. If they waded into politics, he'd wade into their pockets. He made a brutal object lesson of the billionaire Mikhail Khodorkovsky in 2003, seizing his oil and gas company, Yukos, and sending him to prison. Others, like Boris Berezovsky, his former patron, were hounded into exile.

Putin's obsession with order and control, and restoring the power of the Russian state, was abundantly clear and widely popular. His formula was straightforward: Revive the state and its authority over politics, media, and civil society; regain control over Russia's natural resources to fuel economic growth; and reverse nearly two decades of strategic retreat, rebuild Russian prerogatives as a great power, and reassert Russia's entitlement to a sphere of influence in its own neighborhood. As I put it in a cable to Secretary Rice early in my tenure, "Uncomfortable personally with political competition and openness, [Putin] has never been a democratizer."[2]

Putin's view of relations with the United States was infused with suspicion, but early on he tested with President Bush a form of part-nership suited to his view of Russia's interests. He was the first for-eign leader to call Bush after 9/11, and saw an opening through which Russia could become a partner in the Global War on Terrorism. He thought the war on terror would give Russia a better frame in which to operate than the "new world order" that had dominated U.S. policy since the end of the Cold War. The implicit terms of the deal Putin sought included a common front against terrorism, with Russia back-ing the United States against al-Qaeda and the Taliban in Afghani-stan, and Washington backing Moscow's tough tactics against Chechen rebels. Moreover, the United States would grant Russia spe-cial influence in the former Soviet Union, with no encroachment by NATO beyond the Baltics, and no interference in Russia's domestic politics. Putin quickly set out to show that he could deliver on his end of the presumed bargain. In the face of considerable misgivings from his own military and security services, he facilitated U.S. military ac-cess and transit to Afghanistan through the Central Asian states.

As Putin quickly learned, however, this kind of transaction was never in the cards. He fundamentally misread American interests and politics. From Washington's view, there was no desire—and no reason—to trade anything for Russian partnership against al-Qaeda. We didn't have to purchase Russian acquiescence in something that was so much in its own interest, and we certainly didn't need to dis-card long-standing bipartisan priorities and partnerships in Europe to buy Putin's favor. He also misread American behavior, tending to see contrary American actions as part of some careful, duplicitous conspiracy to undermine him, not as the product of an administra-tion that was desperately consumed with its response to 9/11, indif-ferent to Putin's calculus, and generally disinclined to concede or pay much attention to a power in strategic decline.

Putin gave us more credit than we deserved for careful plotting against Russian interests. For Putin, the September 2004 Beslan school siege was a turning point. The whole world saw live the massacre of more than three hundred teachers, staff, and students. Putin saw Bush's response, which included warnings against overreaction and a dalliance with "moderate" Chechen elements to try to defuse tensions, as nothing short of a betrayal. The Orange Revolution in Ukraine that same year, and the Rose Revolution in Georgia before that, led Putin to conclude that the Americans were not only undercutting Russia's interest in its sphere of influence, but might eventually aim the same kind of color revolution at his regime. These disappointments were piled on top of his anger over the Iraq War, a symbol of America's predilection for unilateral action in a unipolar world, and President Bush's second inaugural address and its "freedom agenda"—which Putin believed included Russia near the top of the administration's "to-do" list. Democracy promotion, in his eyes, was a Trojan horse designed to further American geopolitical interests at Russia's expense, and ultimately to erode his grip on power in Russia itself.

By the summer of 2005, mutual disillusionment weighed heavily on attitudes in Moscow and Washington. The Bush administration saw a Russia uninterested in democratic values, unlikely to evolve anytime soon into a deferential member of an American-led international club or become a reliable junior partner in fighting terrorism. Putin had already begun to tilt in a more adversarial direction, increasingly persuaded that an American-led international order was constraining Russia's legitimate interests, and that chipping away at that order was the key to preserving and enlarging space for Russian influence. He also believed that he had a reasonably strong hand to play, with unprecedented domestic approval and support. "Outside Russia's borders," I argued in a cable, "Putin sees considerable room for maneuver in a world of multiple power centers, with the U.S. bogged down with difficulties, China and India on the rise in ways which pose no immediate threat to Russia, and the EU consumed with internal concerns. After years of being the potted plant of Great Power diplomacy, Putin, and many in the Russian elite, find it very satisfying to play a distinctive and assertive role."[3]

The diplomatic challenge was foreboding, and the stakes enormous. From the outset of my tenure as ambassador, I urged realism about the unlikely prospects for broad partnership with Putin's Russia, and pragmatism in our strategy. Realism demanded that we come to terms with the fact that relations were going to be uneasy, at best, for some time to come. We should shed the illusions that had lingered since the end of the Cold War, recognize that we were bound to have significant differences with a resurgent Russia, and seek a durable mix of competition and cooperation in our relationship. Pragmatism required that we draw clear lines around our vital interests, pick our fights on other issues carefully, manage inevitable problems with a cool head, and not lose sight of those issues on which we could still find common ground.

Putin understood as well as anyone that Russia had more than its share of vulnerabilities and blind spots, from demographic decline, to worsening corruption, to seething troubles in the North Caucasus. He was not inclined, however, to use Russia's moment of oil-driven prosperity to diversify and innovate, and unleash Russia's human capital. The risk to political order and control was too great. I was pessimistic that his outlook would change. As I wrote in an early cable to Washington:

> Over the next few years, at least, it's hard to see any fundamental rethinking of priorities on the part of Putin or his likely successors. . . . Some might argue that this suggests a "paradigm lost," a sense that a partnership that once was firmly rooted is now gone. The truth is that the roots for a genuine strategic partnership have always been pretty shallow—whether in the era of euphoric expectations after the end of the Cold War, or in the immediate aftermath of September 11. Russia is too big, too proud, and too self-conscious of its own history to fit neatly into "a Europe whole and free." Neither we nor the Europeans have ever really viewed Russia as "one of us"—and when Rus-

sians talk about "nashi" ("ours") these days, they're not talking about a grand Euro-Atlantic community.

So where does that leave us? Basically, we're facing a Russia that's too big a player on too many important issues to ignore. It's a Russia whose backsliding on political modernization is likely to get worse before it gets better, and whose leadership is neither overly concerned about its image nor much inclined to explain itself to the outside world. It's a Russia whose assertiveness in its neighborhood and interest in playing a distinctive Great Power role beyond it will sometimes cause significant problems.[4]

Pessimistic analysis, of course, did not constitute a strategy. My argument was that if the strategic partnership that had fitfully and loosely framed aspirations in Washington and Moscow for much of the 1990s was out of reach, it was worth testing whether a partnership on a few key strategic issues was possible. That might put the relationship on a steadier track, with limited cooperation balancing inevitable differences.

* * *

I REALIZED THAT stabilizing the relationship, after all the ups and downs of the previous decade and a half, would be a long shot. In our last conversation before I left for Moscow, Secretary Rice made clear that she shared my skepticism, although she encouraged the effort. A student of Russia, Rice was hard-nosed about Putin's repressive behavior at home and his determination to expand Russian influence in its neighborhood, but sympathetic to the notion that we ought to be able to work more effectively together on certain issues. She highlighted in particular nuclear cooperation, where Russia and the United States shared unique capabilities and unique responsibilities. We had a common interest in promoting the security of nuclear materials in our two countries and around the world. We had a similar interest in nonproliferation, especially the challenges posed by Iran and North Korea. And we had a stake in the stable management and further reduction of our existing arsenals.

We also discussed our shared interest in creating more economic ballast in our relationship. U.S. investment in Russia was minuscule, and bilateral trade insignificant, but possibilities were growing in sectors like energy and aerospace. Moreover, Putin had revived Russia's campaign to join the World Trade Organization. That would require a bilateral agreement with the United States, and the lifting of the Jackson-Vanik Amendment of 1974, which had denied the Soviet Union a normal trading relationship because of its restriction of Soviet Jewish emigration. That purpose had long since been achieved, but congressional reservations about other aspects of Russian behavior remained, and there were also continuing concerns about Russian barriers against agricultural products and piracy of intellectual property. Rice agreed that it made sense to make another push, as part of a long-term investment in a more open and competitive Russian economy. WTO accession would help reinforce the rule of law, and create a model of progress in the economic system that might someday spill over into the political system. The expansion of trade and investment would give both countries something positive to safeguard in the relationship, and more to lose if differences got out of hand.

I highlighted a third priority, encouraging the gradual increase of exchange programs, mainly aimed at bringing young Russian students and entrepreneurs to the United States and developing the network of some sixty thousand exchange alumni around Russia. With a mostly bleak outlook for any rapid improvement of relations, it made sense to continue to invest in the next generation of Russians and in their deepening stake in individual freedoms and interaction with the rest of the world.

I knew that each of these initiatives could easily be swallowed up by mounting friction over Ukraine and Georgia, as well as the Krem lin's tightening political squeeze at home. The next couple of years would be critical. Putin was term-limited, and at least according to the Russian constitution would step down as president in 2008. The Russian elite's obsession with succession would mount as that date grew closer, and it would be important to do all we could to anchor our relationship well before then.

In my first few months in Moscow, I was persistent in engaging senior Russians. One of the most important challenges for any ambassador is to develop wide-ranging contacts, to gain as solid a grasp as possible of the views of different players and their interactions. Russia in those years was particularly difficult terrain, with many senior officials suspicious of American diplomats, and oppositionists under intense scrutiny and pressure.

After I presented my credentials in an elaborate ceremony at the Kremlin, Putin took me aside and stressed his personal respect for President Bush, along with his disappointment in American policy. "You Americans need to listen more," he said. "You can't have everything your way anymore. We can have effective relations, but not just on your terms."

Sergey Ivanov, the minister of defense, was a longtime friend and former KGB colleague of Putin. A fluent English speaker, able to charm or bludgeon as circumstances required, Ivanov had aspirations to succeed Putin. Not shy about projecting strength, he had limited popular appeal, and not much of a political base beyond his personal bond with Putin. His steely personality and ambition unsettled others in Putin's orbit, and the fact that he had been a far more accomplished KGB officer than his friend may have unsettled Putin a little too. Alone in his office at the Defense Ministry, Ivanov was matter-of-fact about relations with the United States in our first meeting, sharply critical of American naïveté and hubris in underestimating the complexities of Iraq, as well as of Russia's neighbors. He said forthrightly that it was important to have stable relations between Russia and the United States, but a few "course corrections" were necessary.

Dmitry Medvedev, then the chief of presidential administration at the Kremlin, was another friend of Putin's with ambitions to succeed him. Medvedev was younger than Ivanov and softer around the edges. Unlike Putin and Ivanov, Medvedev was never a Communist Party member; his whole professional life had unfolded after the collapse of the Soviet Union. Like Putin, he came from St. Petersburg, but from the better side of the tracks. He grew up in a stable, well-educated suburban family that had escaped the purges and rejected atheism when it became politically possible. Diminutive, polite, lawyerly in manner, and utterly loyal to Putin, Medvedev nevertheless had a spine, and no shortage of drive. As I put it in a cable to Washington after our first meeting, "He would not have survived as long as he has in the dark and unforgiving corridors of the Kremlin if he did not."[5]

After an initial meeting in his office, Foreign Minister Sergey Lavrov came to a one-on-one lunch at Spaso House. Lavrov was a world-class diplomat and adept negotiator, with a keen eye for detail and an endlessly creative mind. He could also be prickly and obnoxious, especially if he had a dim regard for his counterpart or had to defend positions he knew were indefensible. A veteran of the peculiar form of multilateral torture that comes with long service at the United Nations, where he was Russia's permanent representative for nearly a decade, Lavrov had survived deadening hours of UN debate by becoming a gifted sketch artist and cartoonist. (I still have one of his doodles, a wolf's head whose detail betrays a particularly boring session with a visiting American delegation.) At lunch, after a large glass of his favorite Johnnie Walker Black, Lavrov dissected the mistakes he perceived in American foreign policy in the Bush administration. He took some pleasure in underscoring the ways in which he thought they opened up scope for Russian diplomacy, and warned of trouble ahead over Ukraine and Georgia. He was too smart and too skilled to ignore the potential for cooperation, especially on the economic and nuclear fronts.

One of my most interesting early encounters was with Vladislav

Surkov. Surkov was a young Kremlin political advisor—undoubtedly the only Kremlin official with a photo of the rapper Tupac Shakur on his wall. He was also the architect of Putin's then-fashionable concept of "sovereign democracy," which put a lot more emphasis on the first part of the term than the second.

Surkov and I later appeared together on a program at MGIMO, Russia's elite international affairs university for aspiring diplomats and entrepreneurs, focused unusually on the 125th anniversary of Franklin Delano Roosevelt's birth. With speculation running high about Putin's intentions in 2008, Surkov cleverly spun FDR's legacy to highlight his four terms in office, and their significance for the United States at a moment of crisis and transformation. I replied that the main lesson was not FDR's four terms, which were permitted at the time under our constitution, but rather his historic accomplishments in establishing the political and economic institutions that propelled America out of the Great Depression, through to victory with the Soviet Union in World War II, and into postwar prosperity. Personalities mattered, but democratic institutions endured. Surkov wasn't convinced.

Nor was he convinced by my pitch to think hard about the consequences of continued democratic rollback for the success of the upcoming G-8 summit in St. Petersburg. Like it or not, I stressed, the summit would bring eight thousand of his closest friends in the international media to Russia. They would have only a passing interest in the main summit theme—energy security. The stories on the domestic front would be far more captivating, and not very uplifting. Surkov just shrugged, reflecting his patron's utter disregard for international opinion.

I worked just as hard to cast a wide net for contacts and conversations beyond current government officials. Since traffic had become horrendous, I'd sometimes take advantage of the Moscow Metro, to the consternation of my security detail. The Metro retained its Soviet efficiency, with all its jostling and familiar wet wool smells in winter.

I met regularly with Putin's most outspoken opponents, including Garry Kasparov, the legendary former chess champion. Boris Nemtsov, a onetime presidential hopeful turned Putin critic, was always accessible and full of energy and opinions. (He would be murdered a few hundred meters from the walls of the Kremlin in February 2015.) I met frequently with a stalwart group of human rights activists, from the indomitable Lyudmila Alexeyeva, unbowed in her eighties, to younger advocates passionate about concerns that ran the gamut from brutality in Chechnya to environmental degradation and the rights of the disabled.

Moscow had no shortage of larger-than-life personalities. Reviled by many as the breaker of the Soviet empire, Mikhail Gorbachev kept a low profile, sitting in a spacious office in central Moscow, lonely after the death of his wife and concerned about Putin's increasingly authoritarian instincts. He seemed wistful about what might have been, and a bit lost in the new, gleaming, frantically acquisitive Moscow. Aleksandr Solzhenitsyn continued to write relentlessly at a small dacha complex outside Moscow, secure behind a tall green fence. When I went out to see him one late autumn afternoon, he spent a couple hours, as the light was dimming outside, talking about his life, the privations of the war and Communist rule, and the hope he had for Putin and for Russia. He distrusted the materialism of a Russia intoxicated by oil and excess, and emphasized his belief in the spiritual underpinnings of Russian exceptionalism. He saw nothing out of the ordinary about a Russia with predominant influence in the former Soviet space, "including our brothers in Ukraine." Although he had spent almost two decades in Vermont after his exile from the Soviet Union, he was not a convert to liberal internationalism, and especially not its hawkish neoconservative variant on full display in Iraq.

I made the best use I could of Russian television and newspaper interviews to convey American policy concerns and my commitment to healthier U.S.-Russian relations. I also took the somewhat unusual initiative of offering to appear before the Duma foreign affairs committee to answer questions about American policy. However imperfect my Russian-language skills, the nearly three hours I spent with Duma members that day were a good investment in our relationship. Several apologized afterward for being too harsh in their comments and questions. I assured them that congressional hearings in Washington could be at least as contentious.

I was convinced by my previous experience that no one could hope to understand Russia without exposure to the country beyond Moscow and St. Petersburg, nor could Russians understand America if all they had to draw upon was the caricature fed them by the Russian media, most of which was by now a wholly owned subsidiary of the Kremlin. I made some fifty extended trips outside Moscow during my three years as ambassador, from Kaliningrad in the west to Vladivostok in the east, and from the frigid Arctic north to Sochi on the Black Sea. Lisa and I traveled a good chunk of the Trans-Siberian Railway, still the best way to grasp Russia's sheer size. I spent a fascinating couple of days in Chukotka, just across the Bering Strait from Alaska, where Roman Abramovich, one of Russia's wealthiest men, served as governor by long distance, investing heavily in local infrastructure as part of what had become in Putin's Russia a kind of community service for oligarchs. I had poignant conversations with aging Soviet war veterans in Volgograd, the former Stalingrad.

There were plenty of vodka-filled evenings in Siberia and the Urals, where local governors and their aides tried to drink the visiting American ambassador under the table. Like my predecessors, I practiced all the tricks of the trade—surreptitiously draining my shot glass in the houseplants, slipping water into my glass, sipping instead of chugging—but I was badly outmatched. I continued to indulge my fascination with the North Caucasus, but never managed to return to Chechnya, now ruled harshly by Putin's rent-a-thug, Ramzan Kadyrov.

* * *

WE WORKED HARD to add more economic weight to the relationship and finally overcome trade disputes. Our aim initially was to
reach a bilateral trade agreement by the time of the G-8 summit in St.
Petersburg in July 2006, which seemed to fit Putin's agenda and give
us some negotiating leverage. The pace of negotiations was painfully
slow. Rapid progress in parallel U.S. negotiations with Ukraine, which
resulted in a bilateral accord and a normalization of trade relations in
the spring of 2006, only rubbed more salt in the wound for Putin. In
a classified email to Rice in April, I painted a gloomy picture. "We
have hit the point of diminishing returns in the negotiations. Absent
a bold move by the President to close the deal, the Russians are going
to slide backwards very quickly, as only they can do, into a swamp of
real and imagined grievances. Unfortunately, Putin is taking an increasingly sour attitude toward us on WTO. . . . He's now at the stage
where he's quite capable of shooting himself (and Russia) in the foot
by declaring that Russia doesn't need the WTO, and the U.S. can
shove it."[6]

U.S.-Russian negotiations lurched along, and a bilateral deal was
finally signed in November 2006—more than a dozen years after negotiations had begun. WTO accession and repeal of Jackson-Vanik
would drag on for another several years, and Russia grew to resent the
regulatory colonoscopy to which it was subjected—including revisions of hundreds of domestic laws and more than a thousand international agreements. This was nevertheless the single biggest step in
our economic relationship in more than a decade.

Meanwhile, we continued to work hard to enlarge two-way trade
and investment. I spent considerable time with American business
representatives, from the biggest energy companies to medium-sized
enterprises trying to get a foothold in the elusive Russian market.
Doing business in Russia was not for the fainthearted; one senior
American energy executive wound up in his company's version of the
witness protection program, shielded from rapacious Russian part-

ners taking apart a major joint venture. Despite the risk, there were profits to be made and markets to be opened, and I lobbied everyone from the most senior Kremlin officials to regional governors and local administrators on behalf of a level playing field for American companies. American direct investment in Russia increased by 50 percent in 2005–6, and business picked up in both directions.

The most ambitious commercial deal was a nearly $4 billion purchase of Boeing aircraft, including the new 787 Dreamliners. Boeing had a savvy local head of sales and operations, and had made Russian titanium an important component of the new, lighter-weight 787. It had also set up a research and design operation in Moscow that employed some fourteen hundred Russian engineers. It was a smart investment in Russian interest in acquisitions, and a powerful advertisement for what Russia had to offer at the high end of the technology industry. Formally signed in mid-2007, it was the largest nonenergy U.S. venture in post–Cold War Russia, and it encouraged other businesses in other sectors to give the Russian economy a try.

Our progress on nuclear cooperation was equally positive, and equally incremental. Bush and Putin had made broadly similar proposals for global civilian energy cooperation, aimed at boosting nuclear energy as a cleaner alternative to hydrocarbons, and reducing the risks of nuclear weapons proliferation. Among their common ideas was creation of multilateral enrichment facilities to eliminate the need for countries to enrich nuclear material or store and reprocess spent fuel—all of which posed serious proliferation risks. There was also shared interest in a variety of initiatives to ensure the safety and security of nuclear materials. Chafing at remaining the object of U.S. and international concerns about nuclear safety, Putin was eager to widen the lens and show cooperation in dealing with third-party challenges. We saw value in that too. When Qaddafi turned over enriched materials after we negotiated the end of his nuclear program, we arranged for the Russians to take custody. It was striking, and strangely satisfying, to see containers of enriched uranium that had been the object of so many of our efforts in Libya a couple years before sitting in a facility outside Moscow.

To codify our work in this field, we negotiated a bilateral civilian nuclear cooperation agreement in early 2007. Progress on civilian nuclear cooperation helped improve the atmosphere for collaboration on critical nonproliferation issues, especially Iran and North Korea. Although never an easy negotiating partner on UN Security Council resolutions, Russia joined in two significant sanctions measures against both countries in late 2006.

In addition to our efforts on the economic and nuclear fronts, I made a high priority of sustaining and expanding our exchange programs. Secretary of Education Margaret Spellings visited to discuss new bilateral education initiatives with her Russian counterpart, including university partnerships and exchanges of secondary school teachers in math and science. We looked for ways to expand English-language training programs in Russia, and Russian-language programs in the United States.

As we pushed forward on these initiatives, we relied on a high tempo of senior-level visits and meetings throughout 2005–6. President Bush met with Putin four times, and Secretary Rice led a steady stream of other cabinet visitors in 2006. Steve Hadley, Rice's successor as national security advisor, visited too, and was a sensible voice in the sometimes fractious Russia policy debates in Washington. High-level attention helped significantly, but didn't insulate the relationship from the troubling currents that were gathering momentum.

* * *

DESPITE ALL THESE efforts, the steadier track we were looking for in relations with Moscow seemed no closer at the end of 2006 than when I arrived eighteen months before—and in some ways even more remote. For understandable reasons, the patience of pragmatists like Rice and Bob Gates, who succeeded Don Rumsfeld at Defense late in

2006, and President Bush himself, wore thin, and neoconservatives saw an opening to push for a tougher approach. As he became more assertive about Russia's sense of entitlement in the former Soviet space, the dark side of Putin's rule at home clouded any remaining glimmers of political openness.

As Putin's fireplace exchange with Rice in the fall of 2006 made clear, he was growing impatient with Georgia and its president. Mikheil Saakashvili made no secret of his interest in NATO membership and closer ties to the West, and flaunted his relationships in Washington, where he had been lionized by many for his political dexterity during the Rose Revolution and his impressive economic success since then. Although he professed to seek a good relationship with Putin, his glee in poking the Russian bear was unbearable in the Kremlin. Russian policy was based on the presumption that it was entitled to expect—and if not forthcoming voluntarily, to enforce— a substantial degree of deference to its interests on the part of a small and poor neighboring country like Georgia. To Putin's growing annoyance, Saakashvili was defiantly nondeferential. Not unreasonably, he made clear his determination to recover Abkhazia and South Ossetia, parts of Georgia that had been under de facto Russian occupation for years. He was eager to make tangible progress toward NATO membership, and relished the leverage that any steps forward might give him with Moscow.

There was a growing danger that Saakashvili would overreach and the Kremlin would overreact. Reporting to Washington after a meeting between Putin and Saakashvili in June 2006, I noted, "No one evokes greater neuralgia in Moscow these days than Saakashvili." Putin's not-so-subtle message to the Georgian leader was: "You can have your territorial integrity, or you can have NATO membership, but you can't have both."[7]

Earlier that year, I had stressed in another cable that "nowhere is Putin's determination to stop the erosion of Russia's influence greater than in his own neighborhood."[8] Georgia was the proximate concern, but Ukraine remained the reddest of red lines for Putin. The Orange Revolution in 2004 was a massive blow for the Kremlin, a warning shot that Ukrainians might drift away from historic dependence on Moscow and toward formal association with the West. The next couple years brought some relief in the Russian leadership, as the victors in Kyiv indulged in the traditional Ukrainian habit of squabbling among themselves and bogging down the economy in corruption and bureaucratism. Putin was acutely sensitive to any signs that the Ukrainian government might encourage Washington to lay out a clearer path to NATO membership, and he was paranoid about American conspiracies.

Russia's domestic landscape was hardening too. As Putin looked ahead at the likely 2008 succession, he sought to eliminate any potential wild cards and to cow his opponents. Late in 2005, with his encouragement, the Duma introduced a draft law to severely restrict nongovernmental organizations, especially those receiving foreign funding. At the embassy we made strenuous efforts to push back, consulting with Russian NGOs as well as U.S.-based organizations still operating in Russia, and meeting with a variety of Duma leaders and Kremlin officials. I also enlisted my European counterparts in the effort, conscious that the Russian government was more likely to pay attention if we were part of a chorus of concerns, not a solo act. We made a little headway, and the legislation approved by the Duma in the spring of 2006 was slightly less onerous. Nevertheless, the trend line was clear. In case I had missed the message, Surkov drove the point home in a conversation that spring. "NGOs won't be able to act in Russia as they did in the color revolutions in Ukraine and Georgia. Period. In the '90s we were too weak and distracted to act. Now Russia will defend its sovereignty."

Ahead of the uncertain 2008 transition, many in the Russian elite were scrambling for wealth and power. Meanwhile, structural problems—corruption, the absence of institutionalized checks and balances, pressure on the media and civil society—were getting worse

"The real danger," I cabled Washington at one point, "is that the excesses of Putin's Russia are eating up its successes."[9] Murders of dissidents and prominent journalists were, sadly, not uncommon in Russia in this era. Paul Klebnikov, a courageous American journalist working for *Forbes*, had been killed in Moscow the year before I arrived. In the fall of 2006, the pace accelerated. Aleksandr Litvinenko, a former Russian security officer turned outspoken critic of the Kremlin, was poisoned in London and died a horrible, protracted death. Responsibility for his killing was traced directly to the Kremlin. Anna Politkovskaya, a fearless journalist for the liberal newspaper *Novaya Gazeta*, who had covered the wars in Chechnya and a variety of abuses in Russian society, was gunned down outside her Moscow apartment. Some suspected that it was no coincidence the murder fell on Putin's birthday.

As a mark of respect, I went to Politkovskaya's funeral. I had only met her once, but her reputation and life deserved to be honored, and it was also important for me to make a point about where the United States stood. I recall the day vividly—a cold late-autumn afternoon, dusk settling, a few snowflakes beginning to fall, long lines of mourners, about three thousand altogether, shuffling slowly toward the hall where Politkovskaya's casket lay. I was asked to speak, along with one of my European colleagues and a couple of editors at *Novaya Gazeta*. Speaking for a few minutes in Russian, I said that Politkovskaya embodied the best of Russia, and that the best way for all of us to honor her memory was to continue to support the ideals she cherished and the kind of Russia she sought. Not one representative of the Russian government showed up.[10]

* * *

AGAINST THAT DARKENING backdrop, 2007 began with another jolt. In early February, Putin became the first Russian leader to attend the Munich Security Conference, an annual gathering of transatlantic security experts and officials. He didn't waste the opportunity to unburden himself. He bitterly criticized American unilateralism, which had "overstepped its national borders in every way."[11] Warning his audience sardonically that his comments might be "unduly polemical," Putin plowed ahead, assembling in one edgy speech the criticisms he had been making for years. The audience was taken aback, but the senior American official there, Secretary of Defense Gates, responded with aplomb. He noted drily that he shared Putin's background in intelligence, but thought that "one Cold War was quite enough."

In an email to Rice shortly afterward, I tried again to explain the mindset in the Kremlin. "The Munich speech," I wrote, "was the self-absorbed product of fifteen years of accumulated Russian frustrations and grievances, amplified by Putin's own sense that Russia's concerns are still often taken for granted or ignored." Understanding the Kremlin was as much about psychology as about geopolitics. "It's immensely satisfying psychologically," I continued, "to be able to take a whack at people after so many years of being down on their luck, and for Russians nothing is more satisfying than poking at Americans, with whom they have tried to compare themselves for so long." This was a moment that had particular appeal for Russia's president. "A large element was pure Putin—the attraction of swaggering into a den of transatlantic security wonks, sticking out his chin, and letting them have it with both barrels."[12]

There was an element of political convenience for Putin too. Certainly trumpeting about enemies at the gate and overbearing American behavior was a way to divert attention from domestic insecurities. It was also a matter of deep conviction—his sense that Russia had been taken advantage of in the 1990s by oligarchs at home and hypocritical Western friends abroad, and that Putinism was at its core all about fixing the playing field for the Russian state. Putin was giving voice to the pent-up frustrations of many Russians, not just striking an expedient pose. His view of his legacy at that point, and the source of his popularity, was that he had restored order, prosperity, and pride to a Russia sorely lacking in all three when Yeltsin left office.

I had attempted a more detailed stocktaking a couple of weeks earlier in another personal note for the secretary. I reported that Putin's Russia remained a paradox. On the one hand, Putin and those around him had contracted a case of *golovokruzhenie ot uspekhov,* "dizziness from success," an old, Stalin-era slogan appropriate for a new post-Soviet elite awash in petrodollars. The international landscape looked more promising than it had in years, which fed their hubris:

> For most of the Russian elite, still intoxicated by an unexpectedly rapid revival of Great Power status, the world around them is full of tactical opportunities. America is distracted and bogged down in Iraq; China and India are unthreatening and thirsty for energy; Europe is consumed with leadership transitions and ultimately pliable; and the Middle East is a mess in which vestigial connections to troublemakers like Syria offer openings for diplomatic station identification. From the Kremlin's perspective, Russia's own neighborhood looks a lot better than it did a year ago, with NATO expansion less imminent, Ukraine's color revolution fading, Georgia at least temporarily sobered, and Central Asia more attentive to Russian interests.[13]

The picture at home, at least on the surface, looked similarly promising. Putin was now running at 80 percent approval in the polls. The annual economic growth rate was 7 percent, and Russia had put away $300 billion in hard currency reserves. A middle class was emerging, focused on rising standards of living and individual choices that their parents could only have dreamed of, and mostly oblivious to politics. The oligarchs were quiescent, and Putin and his circle, never content to live off their government salaries, were steadily monopolizing major sources of wealth.

"Behind the curtain, however," I continued, "stands an emperor who is not fully clothed." As elites became more convinced that Putin was leaving the presidency in 2008, he was finding it harder than he thought to manage a neat succession. The only real checks and balances in Russia revolved not around institutions, but around a single personality. It therefore fell to Putin to convince the motley crew in and around the Kremlin—from the hard men of the security services to the remaining economic modernizers—that his successor would not threaten the current order.[14]

Beneath all the impressive macroeconomic indicators and apparent stability, troubles lurked. Demographic decline was not an abstract problem if you were one of the lonely thirty million Russians east of the Urals—distributed sparsely over a vast swath of the earth, sitting on vast natural resources, and staring across a long border at nearly a billion and a half Chinese. Corruption was worsening rapidly, as was Russia's overdependence on unsustainably high-priced hydrocarbons and an equally unsustainable energy infrastructure showing its age and decay from serial underinvestment. The North Caucasus was deceptively quiet, with a security lid on its dysfunctions but no real solutions in sight. And even though it was hard to see a rational prospect for color revolutions bubbling up in Russia, the Kremlin was paranoid about external meddling and insecure about its own grip.

So where did that leave American strategy? I warned that the Russians would likely become even more difficult to deal with, noting that it was a safe prediction they would often "exhibit all the subtlety and grace of the 'New Russian' businessmen of the 1990's—with lots of bling, and a kind of 'I'm going to drive my Hummer down the sidewalk just because it feels good' bluster."[15] The Russians' thirst for respect was insatiable, their sensitivity to being taken for granted always turned on high.

For all its irritations, we couldn't afford not to engage Putin's Russia, tempting as that might sometimes be. We'd have to build on common ground where we could, and limit the damage where we couldn't. I urged that we keep the Europeans close, and be careful about pushing too hard on issues where our key allies might start to back away from us. I stressed in particular that we ought to be "careful about our

tactical priorities; if we want to have every issue our way, simultaneously, we'll make it harder to get what we want on the most important
questions."[16] That became a broken-record theme in my messages
and conversations over the remainder of my tenure. I knew how hard
it was to break the post–Cold War habit of assuming that we could
eventually maneuver over or around Moscow when it suited us, and I
knew that was especially difficult as an administration looked to cement its legacy on issues like European security and missile defense.
I also knew that we were running out of room for maneuver with
Putin, and risked bigger collisions on critical issues like Iran if we
weren't careful.

As 2007 unfolded, the question of who would succeed Putin when
his second term ended in 2008 weighed increasingly on the Russian
elite and clogged up much of the bilateral bandwidth. It was always a
mistake to assume anything about Putin, except that he would always
do all he could to keep people guessing. There was certainly the possibility that he would engineer a constitutional change to permit a
third consecutive term; Duma votes were not exactly a prohibitive
challenge for him. But most indications I had from him, as well as
from Sergey Ivanov, Surkov, and others, were that Putin at least cared
enough about appearances that he would step down. Surkov hinted
broadly on several occasions that Putin might well return for a third,
nonconsecutive term in 2012, which the constitution permitted. It
was also likely that no matter who became president in 2008, Putin
would remain the power behind the throne, in whatever role he chose.
Nevertheless, it would not be a small thing for a relatively young,
healthy, politically unchallenged leader to leave office voluntarily for
the first time in a thousand years of Russian history.

Putin was not, however, in any rush to show his hand, and hardly
ready to start crating his papers for the presidential library. Medvedev
and Sergey Ivanov were clearly the early front-runners. Medvedev,
then forty-two, seemed the more modern candidate, but he was also
seen as a little soft, an uneasy fit in the rough-and-tumble world of

Russian elite politics and international affairs. Ivanov, then fifty-four, was the more traditional model, like Putin a veteran of the KGB, with years of experience as minister of defense; but he was also seen as a little hard, his ambition and self-confidence an uneasy fit for the other hard men in Putin's circle, and perhaps for Putin himself.

Medvedev had been given a boost at the end of 2005, when Putin moved him from the Kremlin to become first deputy prime minister. He had a chance to mold a more independent political image, and was given charge of the "national priority projects," which targeted significant chunks of the federal budget toward improvement of housing, healthcare, and education. In January 2007, he led Russia's delegation to Davos and gave a well-received speech. But Putin was not content to become a lame duck so early. In February 2007, he moved Sergey Ivanov from Defense to become another deputy prime minister. His portfolio focused on reorganizing the aviation, shipping, and high-tech industries, and also included the increasingly profitable arms trade. It also freed him from the endless controversies of the Ministry of Defense, where hazing deaths of recruits and other scandals were political deadweights. Both Ivanov and Medvedev seemed well positioned.

Putin's concern that outside influence might undermine his orchestration of events bordered on the paranoid. The sharpest exchange I ever had with him came in a private conversation at the St. Petersburg Economic Forum in early June 2007. He accused the embassy and American NGOs of funneling money and support to critics of the Kremlin. "Outside interference in our elections," he said, "will not be tolerated. We know you have diplomats and people who pretend to be diplomats traveling all over Russia encouraging oppositionists." With the most even tone I could manage, I replied that the outcome of Russia's elections was obviously for Russians alone to decide. The United States had no business supporting particular candidates or parties, and simply would not do so. We would, however, continue to express support for a fair process, just as we did any place in the world. Putin listened, offered a tight-lipped smile, and said, "Don't think we won't react to outside interference."[17]

He was convinced we were bent on tilting the political playing field in Russia, and drew a straight line from the color revolutions in Georgia and Ukraine in 2003–4, which he genuinely believed were the product of American conspiracies, to his own 2008 succession drama. The rich irony of Putin's threat is not lost on me more than a decade later, after Russia's brazen interference in the 2016 American presidential election.

As 2007 drew to a close, Putin finally tipped his hand and declared that he would support Medvedev as his successor in the March 2008 presidential election. The logic of that choice became clearer in the next couple months, as rumors swirled that Putin would remain in government as prime minister—perfectly acceptable under the Russian constitution. It made sense to have the more malleable and less experienced Medvedev as his partner in this new "tandem" arrangement; it was hard to see Sergey Ivanov being comfortable in that role, or Putin comfortable with him. Russia's political landscape appeared to be stabilizing. U.S.-Russian relations, on the other hand, were heading in the opposite direction.

* * *

THE LIST OF irritants between us continued to grow, but several stood out. One was Kosovo, where the United States had championed a UN-led process to organize Kosovar independence from Serbia. The effort made practical and moral sense. The Kosovars overwhelmingly wanted independence, the status quo was unsustainable, and long delay invited another eruption of violence in the Balkans. For Putin, Kosovo's independence brought back bad memories of Russian impotence, and loomed as a test of how different his Russia was from Yeltsin's.

He also had worries, not entirely unfounded, that Kosovo's independence would set off a chain reaction of pressures, with some in the

Russian elite urging him to recognize the independence of Abkhazia, South Ossetia, and other disputed territories in the former Soviet Union. Putin was not at all shy about using those conflicts as levers, especially with Saakashvili, but his preference was to keep them frozen. He also knew that separatist tendencies in the North Caucasus, inside the Russian Federation itself, had not been fully extinguished, and he did not want to see them rekindled. "The notion that Russia can't be pushed around again as it was in 1999, and that the issue of North Caucasus separatism has been settled," I wrote in the summer of 2007, "are two of the cardinal elements of Putin's own sense of legacy, and he will fiercely resist revisiting either of them."[18] Nevertheless, the UN plan authored by former Finnish president Martti Ahtisaari was moving down the track, with Kosovo's independence within sight by the end of 2007.

A second problem was the question of NATO expansion, this time to Ukraine and Georgia. There had been two waves of NATO expansion since the end of the Cold War: Poland, the Czech Republic, and Hungary were offered membership in the second half of the 1990s, and then the Baltic states and four more Central European states a few years later. Yeltsin had gnashed his teeth over the first wave, but couldn't do much about it. Putin offered little resistance to Baltic membership, amid all the other preoccupations of his first term. Georgia, and especially Ukraine, were different animals altogether. There could be no doubt that Putin would fight back hard against any steps in the direction of NATO membership for either state. In Washington, however, there was a kind of geopolitical and ideological inertia at work, with strong interest from Vice President Cheney and large parts of the interagency bureaucracy in a "Membership Action Plan" (MAP) for Ukraine and Georgia. Key European allies, in particular Germany and France, were dead set against offering it. They were disinclined to add to mounting friction between Moscow and the West—and unprepared to commit themselves formally and militarily to the defense of Tbilisi or Kyiv against the Russians. The Bush administration understood the objections, but still felt it could finesse the issue.

Completing the trifecta of troubles was the vexing issue of missile defense. Anxious about American superiority in missile defense technology since the Soviet era, the Russians were always nervous that U.S. advances in the field, whatever their stated purposes, would put Moscow at a serious strategic disadvantage. Putin had swallowed the U.S. abrogation of the Anti-Ballistic Missile (ABM) Treaty early in the Bush administration, but resented it deeply as another example, in his eyes, of the United States throwing its weight around at Russia's expense. By 2007, the United States had begun fielding missile defense capabilities in Alaska and California, aimed at the emerging North Korean threat. More worrying for Putin were American plans to build new radar and interceptor sites in the Czech Republic and Poland to counter a potential Iranian missile threat. Putin didn't buy the argument that an Iranian threat was imminent; and even if it was, his specialists told him (not unreasonably) that it would be technically smarter to deploy new missile defense systems in the southeast Mediterranean, or Italy, and that Aegis shipborne systems could be an effective ingredient. No amount of argument about the technological limitations of systems based in the Czech Republic and Poland against theoretical Russian targets, however soundly based, swayed Putin and his innately suspicious military. Their longer-term concern was not so much about the particular technologies that might be deployed in new NATO states in Central Europe as it was about what those technologies might mean as part of a future, globalized American missile defense system. At the core of their opposition was also the weight of history. For many in Russia, especially in Putin's orbit of security and intelligence hardliners, you could build a Disney theme park in Poland and they would find it faintly threatening.

I had done my best over the previous two and a half years to signal the brewing problems in the relationship and what might be done to head them off. I knew I was straining the patience of some in Washington, who chafed at my warnings of troubles to come when they were consumed with the challenges that had already arrived. I decided, however, that I owed Secretary Rice and the White House one more attempt to collect my concerns and recommendations in one place.

On a typically dreary Friday afternoon in early February 2008, with snow falling steadily against the gray Moscow sky outside my office window, I sat down and composed a long personal email to Secretary Rice, which she later shared with Steve Hadley and Bob Gates. While more formal diplomatic cables still had their uses, classified emails were faster, more direct, and more discreet—in this case a better way to convey the urgency and scope of my concerns.

"The next couple months will be among the most consequential in recent U.S.-Russian relations," I wrote. "We face three potential trainwrecks: Kosovo, MAP for Ukraine/Georgia, and missile defense. We've got a high-priority problem with Iran that will be extremely hard . . . to address without the Russians. We've got a chance to do something enduring with the Russians on nuclear cooperation . . . and we've got an opportunity to get off on a better foot with a reconfigured Russian leadership after Medvedev's likely election, and to help the Russians get across the finish line into WTO this year, which is among the most practical things we can do to promote the long-term prospects for political and economic modernization in this proud, prickly and complicated society." I tried to be clear about what should be done:

> My view is that we can only manage one of those three trainwrecks without doing real damage to a relationship we don't have the luxury of ignoring. From my admittedly parochial perspective here, it's hard to see how we could get the key Europeans to support us on all three at the same time. I'd opt for plowing ahead resolutely on Kosovo; deferring MAP for Ukraine or Georgia until a stronger foundation is laid; and going to Putin directly while he's still in the Presi-

dency to try and cut a deal on missile defense, as part of a broader security framework.

I fully understand how difficult a decision to hold off on MAP will be. But it's equally hard to overstate the strategic consequences of a premature MAP offer, especially to Ukraine. Ukrainian entry into NATO is the brightest of all redlines for the Russian elite (not just Putin). In more than two and a half years of conversations with key Russian players, from knuckle-draggers in the dark recesses of the Kremlin to Putin's sharpest liberal critics, I have yet to find anyone who views Ukraine in NATO as anything other than a direct challenge to Russian interests. At this stage, a MAP offer would be seen not as a technical step along a long road toward membership, but as throwing down the strategic gauntlet. Today's Russia will respond. Russian-Ukrainian relations will go into a deep freeze. . . . It will create fertile soil for Russian meddling in Crimea and eastern Ukraine. On Georgia, the combination of Kosovo independence and a MAP offer would likely lead to recognition of Abkhazia, however counterproductive that might be to Russia's own long-term interests in the Caucasus. The prospects of subsequent Russian-Georgian armed conflict would be high.

I pushed my luck a little in the next passage. If, in the end, we decided to push MAP offers for Ukraine and Georgia, I wrote, "you can probably stop reading here. I can conceive of no grand package that would allow the Russians to swallow this pill quietly." On missile defense, I urged that we not be in a rush on the Polish and Czech deployment plans, continue to seek ways in which we might find a basis for cooperation with Russia, and work harder to link this issue to Russian collaboration in countering the Iranian missile and nuclear threats—which were, after all, the proximate reasons for our initiative. If we could get the Russians to work more closely with us and slow or block Iranian advances, that would serve the main strategic purpose that animated our plans in Central Europe.

I repeated my arguments for pressing ahead on economic and nuclear cooperation as Putin prepared to launch the "tandem" arrangement with Medvedev. We ought to engage the Russians on the possibility of a new strategic arms reduction accord, beyond the START agreement that would soon expire. We should continue to work hard on nonproliferation challenges. Iran was one important example. North Korea was another. The Russians had far less direct influence in Pyongyang than did the Chinese, but wanted to play a role.

My case for economic cooperation was still built around WTO accession and supporting American trade and investment. I always thought that over the longer term, that was one of the best of the limited bets available to us to advance the president's freedom agenda in Russia, helping slowly to deepen the self-interest of Russians in the rule of law. "That wouldn't change the reality," I noted, "that Russia is a deeply authoritarian and overcentralized state today, whose dismal record on human rights and political freedoms deserves our criticism." But over time it might reinforce the instincts for protecting private property and market-driven opportunity that were slowly building a middle class, and open up a massively undertapped market for American companies.[19]

Rice was appreciative and encouraged me to keep pressing my views. Both she and Gates shared at least some of my concerns on MAP, but I sensed that the debate in Washington was still tilting toward a strong, legacy-building effort to engineer a MAP offer for Ukraine and Georgia at the April 2008 NATO summit in Bucharest. There was similar fin-de-administration momentum behind the missile defense project in Poland and the Czech Republic, now that Kosovo's independence was a done deal.

Both Rice and Gates, and President Bush himself, had spent a lot of time in 2007 trying to engage the Russians on all these issues. Gates visited in April, not long after his encounter with Putin at Munich, and displayed a sure feel for the Russians, the product of decades of experience during the Cold War and his own savvy, pragmatic judgment and good humor. The latter was especially useful in his formal conversations with the new defense minister, Anatoliy Serdyukov, a former furniture trader from St. Petersburg who had endeared himself to Putin as chief of the federal tax collection service, and implementer of the brutal demolition of Mikhail Khodorkovsky several years before. Serdyukov was entirely unschooled in defense matters or diplomacy, and mostly read his talking points from a stack of index cards. Gates parried his points respectfully, occasionally passing me notes with his unvarnished thoughts about our host, who he concluded should have stuck to furniture sales.

Rice, determined to do what she could to ease tensions, came to Moscow in May. President Bush saw Putin on the margins of the G-8 summit in Germany in June, where Putin suggested the use of a Russian-operated radar facility in Azerbaijan, which he intended as an alternative, not a complement, to a Central European site. When Putin came to Kennebunkport, Maine, in July, the Russian leader added the possibility of using an existing early-warning facility at Armavir, in southern Russia. The two leaders agreed that their experts should study the ideas, in hopes of developing a joint approach. Extensive working-level discussions ensued. The limited technical capacity of the two Russian-proposed sites was one concern; the bigger issue was that the Russians saw their offers as a substitute for U.S. plans in Central Europe, while Washington was willing to consider them (at most) as add-ons.

The Kennebunkport meeting showed both the cordiality of the Bush-Putin relationship and its limitations. Relaxed and gracious at their summer home, the Bush family wrapped Putin and his delegation in warmth and hospitality. I told President Bush afterward that I thought Putin had been genuinely touched by the invitation, and he was not someone easily touched by gestures of any kind. But I left feeling that Russians and Americans were still talking past one another and hurtling down the track toward a wreck of one kind or another.

In March 2008, just before Medvedev was elected as president, I had an unusual conversation with Putin, which only reinforced my worries. President Bush had asked me to deliver a message to Putin. Its contents were straightforward: outlining again our position on Kosovo; emphasizing our hope that we could still work out some acceptable formula on missile defense; indicating that any move forward at the Bucharest summit toward NATO membership for Ukraine and Georgia should not be seen as threatening; and underscoring our continued commitment to Russia's accession to the WTO. President Bush also confirmed that he'd accept Putin's invitation to visit Sochi and hope they'd take advantage of their last meeting as presidents to discuss a "strategic framework" to guide the U.S.-Russian relationship.

Putin didn't often agree to separate meetings with me, and almost never saw other ambassadors. Most of our encounters during my tenure were on the margins of other events, or with visiting senior U.S. officials. This time I was invited to come to the presidential dacha at Novo Ogaryovo, just outside Moscow. I was asked to come alone. Arriving at the appointed time, I was ushered into a reception room, with the usual assortment of bottled Russian mineral water and snacks. Putin was just finishing a meeting with the Security Council, a protocol assistant told me. I half expected a replay of the experience Rice and I had had, and wondered if I was going to have to navigate that not especially receptive audience before my session with Putin. I was also thinking through how best to convey my fairly lengthy message, well aware that Putin had little patience for long-winded presentations.

Almost as if to spare me from my mounting anxiety, I was ushered into Putin's conference room. It was bright and airy, with light pine walls and furniture. Adding to the brightness, I quickly realized, were a dozen press cameras. Having been in Russia long enough to cultivate a bit of paranoia, I immediately thought this was a trap, an opportunity for Putin to lace into U.S. policy and its quavering representative.

I was wrong. With the cameras running, Putin made some general comments about the potential of the Russian-American relationship, despite our differences. Noting that my tour as ambassador was nearing its end, he thanked me for being an honest and professional envoy for my country. I stumbled around a little in Russian in my reply, emphasizing how much I enjoyed serving in Russia. We would inevitably have disagreements, sometimes sharp ones, but stable relations were in the interests of both our countries, and of the wider world. Putin nodded, the camera lights went off, and the press left.

With Sergey Lavrov sitting beside him and the rest of the room cleared, Putin looked at me with his customary expressionless demeanor and invited me to deliver the message I was bearing. I condensed my points as best I could, without losing any of their meaning or precision. It took me about ten minutes. Somewhat to my surprise, Putin didn't interrupt at all, and didn't roll his eyes or make side comments to Lavrov. When I finished, he thanked me politely and said he would look forward to seeing President Bush, and would offer a few preliminary comments—none of which, he added, would surprise me.

Putin's intimidating aura is often belied by his controlled mannerisms, modulated tone, and steady gaze. He'll slouch a bit and look bored by it all if not engaged by the subject or the person across from him, and be snarky and bullying if he's feeling pressed. But he can get quite animated if he wants to drive home a point, his eyes flashing and his voice rising in pitch. In this exchange, Putin displayed his full range.

As I took careful notes, he said, "Your government has made a big mistake on Kosovo. Don't you see how that encourages conflict and monoethnic states all over the world?" Shaking his head ruefully, he observed, "I'm glad you didn't try to tell me that Kosovo is not a precedent. That's a ridiculous argument." I smiled a little to myself, grateful that that was one point I had persuaded my colleagues in Washington to delete in the drafting process. Then Putin moved on to MAP. "No Russian leader could stand idly by in the face of steps toward NATO membership for Ukraine. That would be a hostile act toward Russia. Even President Chubais or President Kasyanov [two of Russia's better-known liberals] would have to fight back on this issue. We would do all in our power to prevent it." Growing angry, Putin continued, "If people want to limit and weaken Russia, why do they have to do it through NATO enlargement? Doesn't your government know that Ukraine is unstable and immature politically, and NATO is a very divisive issue there? Don't you know that Ukraine is not even a real country? Part of it is really East European, and part is really Russian. This would be another mistake in American diplomacy, and I know Germany and France are not ready anyway."

On other issues, Putin was mostly dismissive. Looking perturbed and waving his arm, he said the United States wasn't listening on missile defense. "Unfortunately, the U.S. just wants to go off on its own again." He was scathing on Jackson-Vanik. "You've been teasing us on this for years." It was "indecent" to keep prolonging the process, or leveraging Jackson-Vanik to settle agricultural trade issues. Even Soviet-era refuseniks, he said, were insulted by the continuation of the policy. They complained to him, "We didn't go to jail for the sake of poultry."

We went back and forth over some of these issues for over an hour. Putin's patience was wearing thin, and Lavrov was doodling intently, which I took as a signal to wrap things up. I thanked Putin for his time and said I would convey all his comments to Washington. I congratulated him on winning the Winter Olympics for Sochi in 2014, an effort in which he had invested significant personal energy, working hard on his English for the presentation to the International Olympic Committee, and even harder to grease the palms of its commissioners. Putin finally brightened, smiled, and said the Winter Olympics would be a great moment for Russia. He shook my hand, and I went back out to my car for the ride back to Moscow.

* * *

THE BUCHAREST NATO summit had moments of high drama, with President Bush and Secretary Rice still hoping to find a way to produce MAP offers. Chancellor Angela Merkel and President Nicolas Sarkozy were dug in firmly in opposition. In the end, the curious outcome was a public statement, issued on behalf of the alliance by Merkel and Rice, that "we agreed today that Ukraine and Georgia will become members of NATO."[20] There was no mention of MAP, which disappointed Kyiv and Tbilisi, but what the statement lacked in practical import it seemed to more than make up for in clarity of direction. Putin came the next day for a charged NATO–Russia Council meeting, and vented his concerns forcefully. In many ways, Bucharest left us with the worst of both worlds—indulging the Ukrainians and Georgians in hopes of NATO membership on which we were unlikely to deliver, while reinforcing Putin's sense that we were determined to pursue a course he saw as an existential threat.

President Bush arrived in Sochi two days later. Sochi was Putin's pride and joy, an old Soviet spa town on the Black Sea, with a temperate climate, pebbly beaches, and a few forlorn-looking palm trees set against snowcapped mountains an hour's drive away. Putin had built an expansive retreat just outside town, where he spent increasing amounts of time and received foreign visitors. The basic infrastructure, like so much of the rest of Russia outside the emerald cities of Moscow and St. Petersburg, was extremely run-down. The few hotels had all the beat-up charm that I remembered from the late Soviet era, and the Olympic skating, ice hockey, and skiing venues were still on the drawing board. A new airport was planned but construction had not yet begun; Air Force One looked out of place on the bedraggled runway, with weeds popping up through the concrete and the terminal building a ramshackle affair.

In a cable to the president and Secretary Rice before the visit, I had predicted that "while cocky and combative as ever, still without a mellow bone in his body, Putin will likely soften his roughest edges in Sochi."[21] To my relief, that had proven mostly true. Putin was certainly mad about NATO opening the door to Ukrainian and Georgian membership, and was already thinking of ways to tighten the screws on both to make his displeasure even clearer. Yet he also liked Bush and didn't want to embarrass him on his valedictory visit. Moreover, he was anxious to get the "tandem" experiment off to a good start and show both his international and domestic audiences that he could make it work. The Russian elite was still a little uncertain about the whole idea. In my message to the president, I had recounted an experience at an event in Moscow the previous week, during which I listened to longtime mayor Yuri Luzhkov pontificate at some length to a group about the merits of the tandem arrangement. When I asked him afterward if he really believed that, he laughed uproariously and said, "Of course not. It's the craziest thing I've ever heard."[22]

Relaxed by the setting, Putin and Bush covered the familiar range of issues thoroughly and civilly. Putin was pointed on Ukraine and Georgia in a smaller session with the president, repeating his view that we didn't understand what an unwieldy place Ukraine was, and how close Saakashvili was to provoking him. He didn't belabor his concern, however, and the overall atmosphere was remarkably cordial. At a concluding dinner, Putin and Medvedev sat with the president, talking and joking, and generally conveying a sense that our relationship was solid enough to endure whatever troubles lay ahead. The after-dinner entertainment featured Russian folk music and a group of local dancers who invited members of the delegations to join them on the small stage. Several Russian officials, their alcohol consumption outpacing their abstemious president, climbed up and danced energetically. I wasn't brave enough, clinging to what remained of my ambassadorial dignity. A few of my less inhibited colleagues made up in enthusiasm what they lacked in rhythm. Chuckling, President Bush said as we were walking out, "I didn't see you up there, but maybe that was smart. Our folks looked like mice on a hot plate."

* * *

I WOULD LEAVE Moscow a month later. Earlier that spring, Secretary Rice had asked me to return to the State Department as undersecretary for political affairs, the third-ranking position in the department and traditionally the highest post to which a career officer could aspire. I departed with a sense of foreboding. For all our efforts to steady the relationship, some kind of crash seemed more and more likely.

Putin was determined to take Saakashvili down a peg, and perhaps also to show, in the wake of the Bucharest statement, that the Germans and French were right to see Georgia's not-so-frozen conflicts as a long-term obstacle to NATO membership. He was clearly baiting the impulsive Georgian president, who may have wanted for his own reasons after Bucharest to act in South Ossetia and force a resolution of the disputes there and in Abkhazia. Rice visited Tbilisi in July and pushed Saakashvili hard not to take the bait. He heard other, more encouraging voices in Washington, including in the vice president's office, and couldn't resist the temptation to move, as the Russians continued to prod and provoke, their trap carefully laid. On the night of August 7, the Georgians launched an artillery barrage on Tskhinvali, the tiny South Ossetian capital, killing a number of Ossetes and Russian peacekeepers. Already poised, the Russians sent a large force through the Roki Tunnel between North and South Ossetia, routed the Georgians, and within a few days were on the verge of seizing Tbilisi and overthrowing Saakashvili. European diplomatic intervention led by French president Sarkozy, in close coordination with the United States, produced a cease-fire. The damage was done, however, leaving U.S.-Russian relations in their worst shape since the end of the Cold War.

The slow-motion trainwreck in U.S.-Russian relations that had its flaming culmination in Georgia in August 2008 had more than one cause. Certainly, the complexes of Putin's Russia were on vivid display—pent-up grievance, wounded pride, suspicion of American motives and color revolutions, a sense of entitlement about Russia's great power prerogatives and sphere of influence, and Putin's particular autocratic zeal for translating all those passions into calculated aggression. Saakashvili's impulsiveness didn't help. Neither did our own post–Cold War complexes, born of the self-confidence of the unipolar moment after the collapse of the Soviet Union and the searing experience of 9/11. Restraint and compromise seemed unappealing and unnecessary, given our strength and sense of mission. They seemed especially unappealing with Putin's Russia, a declining power with a nasty repressive streak.

Whether a crash could have been avoided, and a difficult but more stable relationship constructed, is a hard question. The next administration would take its own run at answering it, with a sustained effort to "reset" relations with Russia that produced early dividends. It ended, however, with an even bigger trainwreck, and not much to show for my quarter century of episodic involvement in relations between Russia and America. It was another lesson in the complexities of diplomacy, and the risks of wishful thinking—both about the disruptive Mr. Putin and our own capacity to maneuver over or around him.

Over the next decade, Putin's confidence and risk tolerance would deepen further. Increasingly convinced of his ability to "play strongly with weak cards," increasingly disdainful of "poor players" of stronger hands like the irresolute and divided Americans and Europeans, Putin gradually shifted from testing the West in places where Russia had a greater stake and more appetite for risk, like Ukraine and Georgia, to places where the West had a far greater stake, like the integrity of its democracies.

7

Obama's Long Game: Bets, Pivots, and Resets in a Post-Primacy World

IN THE SUMMER of 2005, Barack Obama, a newly elected Democratic senator from Illinois, was one of my first guests in Moscow. I had arrived with my family earlier that week, and Spaso House was still littered with unpacked boxes. I had yet to meet with all the members of my team, let alone complete my first round of courtesy calls with Russian officials. Obama, sensing my professional and domestic disorder, could not have been more gracious. With two young daughters of his own, he instantly connected with Lizzy and Sarah. He could sense that they were just getting their bearings in yet another new home and new school. He knew precisely what that felt like and went out of his way to relate, reassure, and comfort them.

Obama's travel partner was Republican senator Dick Lugar from Indiana—one of the most respected voices in the Senate, with enormous foreign policy expertise and credibility across the aisle and around the world. For more than a decade, he had been a regular visitor to Russia with Senator Sam Nunn of Georgia—his Democratic friend and co-sponsor of legislation that secured loose nuclear material and weapons left behind in the dissolution of the Soviet Union.

With Nunn now retired, Lugar hoped Obama would step into his shoes. Obama had a long interest in nuclear policy, and Lugar a keen eye for talent.

Obama and Lugar joined Lisa and me for an informal dinner at Spaso House one evening, together with Senator Chuck Hagel of Nebraska, a decorated Vietnam veteran and a leading Republican voice on foreign policy, who was on a separate visit to Russia. We talked until nearly midnight. Obama wanted to know about my experiences in Russia in the 1990s, and what I thought about Putin. He was curious about the run-up to the Iraq War in 2003 and where things were headed as the Sunni insurgency picked up steam. He seemed particularly interested in what it was like to work for Secretary Baker and how the Bush 41 administration coped with such an avalanche of transformative international events. "That was an impressive bunch," he said.

Lugar and Obama spent a couple days in Moscow. We had lots more time to talk, bouncing around in embassy minivans to and from meetings. At a former biological weapons lab outside Moscow, Obama watched warily as Lugar handled dusty old jars of toxins perched precariously on the shelves. As we sat down for lunch, Obama was equally wary of the green Jell-O mold on our plates. He looked to me, pointed at my untouched plate, and said, "You first, Mr. Ambassador. This is what diplomats get paid the big bucks to do."

The following day, Lisa and I were busily unpacking our boxes when my cellphone rang. The embassy duty officer had some inconvenient news: Officials at Perm airport were demanding payment of an exorbitant landing fee (from which official delegations were supposed to be exempt) before clearing the congressional delegation and its U.S. military plane to take off. Over the next three hours, I hunted frantically for a senior Russian official to spring Obama and Lugar. Sunday afternoons in August are not the most accessible moment for senior Russians, but I managed to track down the groggy first deputy foreign minister at his dacha near Moscow. He pulled the necessary strings, and Lugar and Obama made it to Ukraine later that day. I was lucky that my first (and only) senatorial detainees in Russia were two of the least affected members of Congress. Nevertheless, Obama would occasionally tease me about the incident in later years. "You're not going to pull another Perm on me, are you?" he'd ask, semi-kidding.

Perm-gate was a reminder that no matter how thoughtful the effort, no matter how carefully laid the plan, other forces and players had a vote too. It was a lesson I learned time and time again during the course of my diplomatic career, and it would rear its head regularly during President Obama's tenure in the White House. He inherited a world in which America's post–Cold War dominance—thanks to the forces of history and our unforced errors—was coming to an end. Although America's relative power and influence were diminishing, its myriad strengths seemed to ensure its preeminence for decades to come. The question for Obama was how to make best use of that preeminence to secure American interests and values in a more competitive world.

That required playing a long game—molding an emerging international order, realigning relationships with major powers like China, India, and Russia, and revitalizing diplomacy to achieve goals like preventing Iran from acquiring nuclear weapons. It also required a relentlessly adaptable short game, navigating through a landscape in which terrorism was still a threat, the weight of the military-intelligence complex was still far greater than diplomatic tools, and the pull of old dysfunctions in the Middle East would threaten to swallow the foreign policy agenda. It was a world of unsynchronized passions, full of collisions between the ambitions of the long game and the vexations of the short game.

* * *

IN QUESTIONS OF temperament, instinct, and worldview, President Obama and his secretaries of state, Hillary Clinton and John

Kerry, diverged in a number of ways, but they all saw the importance of getting America off of its war footing and reclaiming its diplomatic leadership. During the campaign, Obama's diagnosis of U.S. foreign policy was harsh: The United States had failed to prioritize interests and investments; had inverted the roles of force and diplomacy; had been stubbornly reluctant to engage adversaries directly; and had been too attuned to the siren song of unilateralism and often deaf to the hard task of coalition-building in a world in which both power and problems were more diffuse.

Obama's suspicions about the foreign policy establishment in Washington ran deeper than his predecessor's mistakes. He was skeptical, and eventually publicly dismissive, of its tendency to homogenize analyses and reduce complicated problems to simple tests of American credibility. For Obama, the "blob" was not a term of endearment, but a self-absorbed bipartisan elite whose insular judgments had led the United States into troubles, from Vietnam to Iraq.

Obama took office determined to break the chains of U.S. foreign policy pathologies and shift the terms of America's engagement in the Middle East. He sought to position the United States for long-term success by pivoting more attention and resources to Asia, where China's rise was rapidly unfolding; making bets on emerging geostrategic players like India; and resetting relations with critical if declining rivals like Russia.

Obama saw the Bush 41 model—the instinctive modesty of George H. W. Bush and the dexterity and restraint of Baker and Scowcroft—as one to emulate. The world he inherited, however, was far less propitious than theirs. Nor did he enter office with their experience and a Rolodex full of world leaders. For all the impossibly inflated expectations that greeted his inauguration, Obama would discover that the world was full of events that would make pushing the reset button on America's role infinitely difficult. After the recklessness of his predecessor, Obama's mantra of "not doing stupid shit" was a sensible guideline. But there were other scatological realities in foreign policy:

Shit happened too, and reacting to events outside neat policy boxes would be a persistent challenge.

If Obama was innately suspicious of the Washington establishment, Clinton and Kerry had come to embody it. Both had been on the national stage for decades. Both had voted for the 2003 Iraq War in the Senate. Both reveled in the personal relationships with world leaders that were the daily stuff of diplomacy, and prized their long connections with friends in high places. Their convictions about American leadership were traditional and assertive.

Clinton was most self-confidently an American exceptionalist, and least self-flagellating in her assessment of U.S. foreign policy and its blind spots. She was comfortable with the muscularity of America's role, and attuned to the benefit of being the hawk in the room. She was unfailingly sober and well prepared in her approach, unflappable when hard decisions had to be made but generally risk-conscious, and sometimes risk-averse, about big diplomatic bets.

I first met Hillary Clinton when she accompanied President Clinton to King Hussein's funeral in February 1999. In November of that year, she returned to Jordan to visit King Abdullah and Queen Rania. The backdrop was complicated. The day before in Ramallah, she had had to sit through a particularly nasty rant by Yasser Arafat's wife, Suha. In the midst of a public ceremony, and with the First Lady by her side, Suha accused the Israeli government of using poison gas against Palestinians. The simultaneous interpretation had apparently broken down or was garbled and Clinton—already bone-tired—missed much of what Mrs. Arafat was saying. When she embraced Suha at the end of the event, a mini-scandal erupted. Criticism in Israel and the United States quickly mounted, an unhelpful storm on the eve of her campaign for a Senate seat in New York.

Arriving in Petra in southern Jordan to tour the fabled Nabatean city before heading to Amman, Clinton seemed unfazed. There was very little angst or finger-pointing. Clinton decided to make a short statement to the press before leaving Petra, explaining what had happened and rejecting Mrs. Arafat's vile rhetoric. When that was done, we flew on to Amman, and Clinton was focused and even-keeled over the rest of a busy schedule. The following night, she invited Lisa and me to join her and her immediate staff for an after-dinner drink in her hotel suite. The First Lady was funny and relaxed, full of good questions about how the king and queen were coping with their first year on the throne, and how Jordan was faring. As we talked on the way home, Lisa and I were both struck not only by how smart and genuinely devoted to her staff Clinton was, but also by how quickly she picked herself up after setbacks and moved on.

John Kerry shared Clinton's tireless energy and perseverance. Kerry never met a diplomatic problem that he didn't want to take on, or that he thought would prove immune to his powers of persuasion. He was far more prone to improvising, always willing to be caught trying, and unintimidated by long odds or historical patterns. His was in some respects a more classical approach to diplomacy, focused on ending big conflicts and negotiating big international agreements, with a readiness to take big risks and even bigger falls.

I had met Senator Kerry off and on over the years, in Senate hearings and briefings. It was not until May 2012, when we wound up as roommates at a small retreat of Arab and international political leaders hosted by King Abdullah in Aqaba, that I got the chance to get to know him better. Abdullah kept these weekend gatherings informal and exclusive, with no staff or media allowed.

The king ensured that there was plenty of time for Hashemite hospitality and bonding. He organized a cookout in Wadi Rum, the spectacular desert setting not far from Aqaba where T. E. Lawrence had orchestrated the Arab Revolt against the Turks a century before. There was a shooting range, and dune buggies to race. Kerry and Senator John McCain, political opposites but longtime friends, roared off into the desert sunset, huge grins on their faces. That was John Kerry. He loved a challenge, loved competition, and loved being in constant motion.

With Lisa during A-100 training in early 1982 *(Courtesy of the author)*

With President Reagan, Secretary of State George Shultz, National Security Advisor Colin
Powell, and other senior advisors in the Oval Office in December 1988
(Courtesy Ronald Reagan Presidential Library)

Listening (back row, second from left) as President George H. W. Bush addresses the Madrid Peace Conference on October 30, 1991 (*Courtesy of the author*)

Secretary of State Madeleine Albright greeting Lisa, Sarah, and Lizzy during a 1998 ceremony marking the end of my term as executive secretary (*Courtesy of the author*)

Visiting the Palestinian refugee camp in Jenin on April 20, 2002 (*Courtesy of the author*)

With President George W. Bush and other senior foreign policy advisors in the
Oval Office in February 2003 *(Official White House Photo)*

With King Abdullah II in
Amman in November 2003
*(Yusef Allan/Jordanian Royal
Palace/Getty Images)*

With Egyptian president
Hosni Mubarak in Cairo in
September 2004
*(Amro Maraghi/AFP/
Getty Images)*

Celebrating a birthday on the road with
Secretary of State Colin Powell
(Courtesy of the author)

With Muammar al-Qaddafi in
2004 (Courtesy of the author)

During a December 2006 visit
to a school in Beslan, Russia,
where more than three
hundred died in a 2004
Chechen terrorist attack
(Kazbek Basayev/AFP/
Getty Images)

Meeting with Russian president Vladimir Putin at Novo Ogaryovo, the presidential dacha outside Moscow, in the spring of 2008 *(Alexander Zemlianichenko/ AFP/Getty Images)*

At a meeting between President Obama and Prime Minister Vladimir Putin held at Putin's dacha on July 7, 2009 *(Official White House Photo by Pete Souza)*

Meeting with President Obama and Secretary of State Hillary Clinton in the White House Situation Room on September 29, 2009, in advance of P5+1 negotiations with Iran *(Official White House Photo by Pete Souza)*

Leading the U.S. delegation (third from left, far side of table) in P5+1 talks with Iran in Geneva, Switzerland, on October 1, 2009 *(Dominic Favre/AFP/Getty Images)*

With Syrian president Bashar al-Assad prior to a meeting in Damascus in February 2010 *(Louai Beshara/AFP/ Getty Images)*

In the Oval Office (fourth from left) during a call between President Obama and Egyptian president Hosni Mubarak on February 1, 2011 *(Official White House Photo by Pete Souza)*

With President Obama on Marine One during
a trip to the Korean DMZ in March 2012
(*Official White House Photo by Pete Souza*)

Speaking with President Obama
in the Oval Office in June 2013
(*Official White House Photo by Pete Souza*)

With Secretary of State John Kerry
during negotiations with Iran in
Geneva in November 2013
(*Courtesy of the author*)

With Chinese vice president Li Yuanchao in Beijing in January 2014 *(Photo by Jason Lee—Pool/Getty Images)*

At the makeshift memorial honoring slain Maidan protesters in Kyiv, Ukraine, on February 25, 2014 *(State Department Photo)*

Greeting Indian prime minister Narendra Modi at Andrews Air Force Base during his first visit to the United States on September 29, 2014 *(Courtesy Government of India Press Information Bureau)*

Kerry and I shared a bungalow on the Aqaba compound, modest by most royal standards. Late at night, we had a couple beers and talked at length about American foreign policy. I found him incisive and well informed, with a conviction that it was far riskier to miss diplomatic opportunities than to throw yourself into them. He bore little resemblance to the stiff and self-important portrayal favored by critics. He was, as he so often liked to say about others, "the real deal."

For all their differences, however, Obama and his secretaries of state shared a broad view of the world they faced and the challenge for American diplomacy. While neither could be as close in personal and policy terms as Baker was with Bush 41, Clinton and Kerry were just as loyal to Obama and both became effective partners. Like the Bush 41 administration, they would confront a world undergoing seismic change with all its turbulence, uncertainty, and impossible balancing acts.

* * *

WHEN OBAMA WAS elected in 2008, and soon thereafter chose Hillary Clinton to be his secretary of state, I doubted that I would be asked to continue as undersecretary for political affairs. New administrations and new secretaries almost invariably made new appointments to the most senior jobs at State. So I was delighted when Clinton asked me to stay on soon after her nomination was announced, and even more enthused after we met on her first day in the transition office on the department's first floor. I realized that we had already inundated Clinton with massive briefing books, in the best State Department tradition that anything worth doing is worth overdoing. Figuring that a canned presentation was the last thing the incoming secretary needed or wanted, I put down a few notes on a single index card, focused on the main trend lines, the most significant troubles and opportunities ahead. I'd be the first senior career officer she'd be meeting as she got ready for her new role, and I didn't want to screw it up.

Our scheduled forty-five-minute session ran nearly two hours. We covered the waterfront of policy issues. Clinton had lots of questions— about substance, foreign personalities, and how best to work with the Pentagon and the NSC staff. I was impressed both by the depth of her knowledge and her easygoing style.

I introduced Secretary Clinton on her first day in office to an un-characteristically raucous crowd of employees at the main C Street entrance. The next day, President Obama made a visit, a visible early sign of his support for her, the department, and, as he said, "the importance of diplomacy and renewing American leadership." He backed those words with actions. He and Clinton moved quickly to win an increase in the international affairs budget, and issued a pres-idential directive emphasizing development as a core element of American foreign policy.

There was no question about the importance of strengthening di-plomacy and development alongside defense. But there were signifi-cant questions about what kind of investments we should make now and to what ends. The military was struggling with how to adapt it-self to an uncertain era defined by both potential great power colli-sions and small wars in far-off places. The State Department similarly struggled to settle on a theory of the case for what loomed over the horizon and the most realistic way to adapt given growing risks and scarce resources. There were plenty of slogans bandied about but less hard-nosed priority setting, and even less success in translating Obama's electoral mandate into a domestic political coalition to sup-port serious reforms and his long-term foreign policy ambitions.

Organizing the national security bureaucracy for this new era was an ongoing challenge. Having lived through the bureaucratic blood feuds of the Reagan and Bush 43 eras, I found the interagency atmo-sphere of the Obama administration to be congenial and disciplined. The president set the tone. He brooked no backbiting or game-playing, and expected that issues would be considered thoroughly and deliberately. He had limited patience for verbosity, and even less for melodrama. Obama's focus was on a "tight" process—rigorous review of the facts and problem at hand; patient examination of the various options; careful attention to second- and third-order consequences; and "buttoned down" execution of decisions. He understood right from the outset that a disciplined decision-making process would help ensure disciplined implementation. His national security advisors were sticklers for "regular order" and avoiding analytical or procedural shortcuts.

Obama's national security advisors, Jim Jones, Tom Donilon, and Susan Rice, chaired the Principals Committee (PC). This was the group of cabinet agency heads—with State, Defense, the Joint Chiefs, CIA, the director of national intelligence, and Treasury at its core, and other agency counterparts sometimes joining, depending on the subject. Vice President Biden always came to NSC meetings chaired by the president, and frequently to PC meetings. His experience in national security went back to the Vietnam era, and his was a significant and thoughtful voice at the table. Clinton and Bob Gates were almost always of like mind on key issues, a formidable pairing that carried on the informal alliance that Condi Rice and Gates had built late in the previous administration. That was a huge asset for State, and for the quality of decision-making, and a sharp contrast to the pitched battles we endured during Powell's tenure. It also filtered down to the next level, the Deputies Committee.

As undersecretary, and then later as deputy secretary, I probably spent more time with my colleagues in the claustrophobic, windowless confines of the White House Situation Room than I did with anyone else, including my own family. The meetings of the Deputies Committee, which comprised sub-cabinet officials led by the deputy national security advisor, were serious affairs. Our job was to propose, test, argue, and, when possible, settle policy debates and options, or tee them up for the decision of cabinet officials and the president. None of the president's deputy national security advisors, however, lost sight of the human element of the process. Denis

McDonough, who later became the president's chief of staff for the entire second term, was adept at poking holes in policy arguments and keeping people honest. His good humor and humanity also helped keep us sane and focused—his scribbled thank-you notes or expressions of sympathy for family emergencies were legendary.

We were, after all, a collection of human beings, not an abstraction—always coping with intense time pressures, in the era of instantaneous news cycles; always operating with incomplete information, despite the unceasing waves of open-source and classified intelligence washing over us; often trying to choose between bad and worse options. After a quarter century of sitting in the back benches in that room, it finally dawned on me that I had crept up distressingly close to the top of the policy food chain. In a lull between meetings one day during Obama's first term, I leaned over and said to Denis, "You know, I've finally realized that we're the adults now. We're it."

"Yup," he replied with a smile. "Scares the crap out of me sometimes. But we better make the most of it."

For all the quality and camaraderie of the interagency process in the Obama administration, it had its imperfections. The increasing complexity of issues, the increasing number of agencies engaged, and the need for White House oversight of the use of force in an age of frequent drone strikes and limited military operations bred overcentralization. Too many problems got pushed up too high in the interagency process, with the most senior officials sometimes consumed by tactical questions and the details of implementation.

That was compounded by the steady mushrooming of the NSC staff with each administration. At its Obama-era peak, it grew to a policy staff of three hundred, compared to just sixty in the Colin Powell NSC staff I had served on more than twenty years before. The deliberative, patient style of decision-making that was usually one of the strengths of the Obama administration could also sometimes become a weakness—a substitute for action, or a dodge. On challenges where there were no good choices, like Syria, tasking the ninety-seventh paper from the intelligence community on what Assad might do next was sometimes a convenient way to kick the can to the next meeting.

Despite the emphasis on diplomacy, the arm of American military might was extending, not diminishing. During the course of the Obama administration, reliance on drones and special operations grew exponentially. No one in the administration had to be lectured about the blowback risks, but no one managed to slow the addiction, either. It was too inconvenient to challenge the conventional wisdom about the seemingly low-risk, high-reward nature of drone strikes. Yet the conventional wisdom had some painful limits, not just for the impact of occasional botched strikes and the extrajudicial nature of our operations on our standing with Muslim societies around the world, but the ways it would warp our diplomatic relations and skew—and sometimes upend—our diplomatic agenda.

* * *

ONE OF THE best examples of both the quality of Obama's decision-making process and his capacity to navigate the often treacherous short-game choices posed by terrorist threats was the raid that killed Osama bin Laden. In early March 2011, CIA director Leon Panetta briefed Secretary Clinton privately about intelligence that had recently emerged on bin Laden, the best lead on his whereabouts since soon after 9/11. It indicated that he might be holed up in a walled compound near Abbottabad, Pakistan, north of Islamabad and not far from the Pakistani military academy. For obvious reasons, the information was being tightly held. Secretary Clinton was authorized to bring one other person at State into the circle, and she asked me to help her think through the options and the consequences of action. I joined her in a series of close-hold discussions in the Situation Room throughout the rest of the spring.

The intelligence on the compound continued to suggest that bin Laden might well be there, along with a number of family members. But it was never a sure thing. Obama and his cabinet principals care-

fully weighed the options. The first was a joint raid with the Pakistanis, which was quickly dismissed. There was simply too high a
chance that the Pakistanis were already complicit or would tip off bin
Laden. Other alternatives included aerial bombing of the compound
or a targeted drone strike. The former carried a substantial risk of collateral civilian casualties; neither would allow for confirmation that
bin Laden had been killed, or for collection of other intelligence at the
site.

The final option was the riskiest—a special operations raid. This
would mean a nighttime helicopter movement from a U.S. base in
Afghanistan, a dangerous operation on the ground by a team of Navy
SEALs, and then their extraction by helicopter back across Pakistan
to Afghanistan. A lot could go wrong, as it had in the Desert One
debacle in 1980 when the United States lost eight servicemen in an
aborted attempt to rescue the embassy hostages in Tehran. But by
2011, American special forces had carried out hundreds of similar
raids in Iraq and Afghanistan; when Admiral Bill McRaven, head of
Joint Special Operations Command, laid out this option for the president in the Situation Room, it was impossible not to feel his confidence.

The president convened his senior advisors for a final discussion
on Thursday afternoon, April 28. I rode over with Secretary Clinton,
and we agreed on the way that this was too important an opportunity
to miss, even if the odds were no better than fifty-fifty that bin Laden
was there, and that the special operations raid was the best of the options. It was hard to know how the Pakistanis would react, and a
failed raid could be a disaster for the president. But not attempting it
carried substantial risks too.

The intelligence update presented to the president that afternoon
was still inconclusive. When the president went around the room
asking for views, Vice President Biden recommended waiting for
more definitive intelligence. Bob Gates, who had lived through the
Desert One ordeal as an aide to the CIA director, agreed. Clinton, in a

rare break with Gates, laid out a calm, well-reasoned case for action, which Panetta reinforced. Most of the rest of the participants also favored action, and I joined them when the president polled the deputies in the room too. Obama concluded the meeting by saying that he would think about things overnight. The next morning, he told Donilon that he'd decided to launch, and McRaven began to set the operation in motion for Sunday.

On Sunday morning, I drove into the State Department on my own, parked my car, and walked the five blocks to the White House. I joined Clinton and the rest of Obama's team in the Situation Room for the long wait. At 2:30 P.M., we watched on a small video map as two Black Hawk helicopters took off for Abbottabad from Jalalabad in eastern Afghanistan. The next couple hours seemed like an eternity, and the raid itself began with gut-wrenching drama, when one of the two helicopters made a hard landing in the courtyard of the compound. The SEALs were unhurt, but they had to destroy the helicopter and adapt quickly. McRaven narrated the whole operation with incredible calm from a command post in Afghanistan. As the president and his senior aides sat in rapt attention, there wasn't a hint of second-guessing or backseat commentary. Then McRaven's voice came on the line to confirm "E-KIA"—the enemy had been killed in action. Bin Laden was dead. Never had I been prouder of the U.S. military, or of a president who had so coolly taken such a big risk. For a diplomat accustomed to long slogs and victories at the margins, this was an incredible moment.

The president announced the successful operation to the nation and the world at around 11 P.M. that night. Secretary Clinton and I divided a series of phone calls to notify key allies and leaders around the world. Late that night, my calls completed, I walked out the White House gate, heading back to my car. In front of the White House, all across Lafayette Square, was a large and boisterous crowd, waving flags and shouting "USA, USA, USA." I couldn't help but think, as I walked back to the State Department, of a much different moment nearly a decade before, standing in front of State with Lisa as the full import of the 9/11 attacks began to sink in. It had taken a long time, but a measure of justice had been done.

Amid the deliberations about the bin Laden raid that spring, Clinton called late one afternoon and asked me to come down to her office. The issue on her mind was not bin Laden, but finding a successor to Jim Steinberg, who had just decided to step down as deputy secretary. Smiling broadly, she got right to the point. "I'd like you to take Jim's place," the secretary said. "I trust you, the president trusts you, and everyone in this building trusts you. It would mean a lot to me personally if you'd agree." I smiled back, surprised but flattered, and mentioned that it was a little unusual to have a career person in that role.[1] "I know," she replied. "But you're the right choice, and I like the message it sends." I quickly accepted. This was a vote of confidence in the professional diplomatic service, not just me.

My work as undersecretary and deputy secretary stretched me across the whole range of issues in American foreign policy. On many days, it was a little like taking ten exams on ten different subjects, some of which I knew well, and some of which I didn't. I filled in for the secretary at meetings of foreign ministers, going to a G-8 ministerial in Italy on short notice, after Clinton fell and broke her elbow in the State Department parking garage, and later accompanying the president to the G-8 summit and Moscow. I spent considerable time testifying and consulting on Capitol Hill, and my travels took me to every part of the globe, from Africa and Latin America to the Balkans and Southeast Asia. Inevitably, I spent more time on some issues than others. And the issue that was at the core of the long game, and the heart of our revitalized diplomacy, was the effort to manage changing relations with the major powers, especially India, China, and Russia.

* * *

OBAMA INHERITED FROM Bush an emerging partnership with India. The world's biggest democracy, and soon to be the world's most populous country, India had begun an economic transformation in the early 1990s and was growing at a rapid clip. It remained, however, a nation of vast contradictions. Hundreds of millions of people had been lifted out of poverty and into a new middle class, but hundreds of millions more still lived on less than two dollars a day, without toilets or regular access to electricity. The tech sector was beginning to boom, but infrastructure was crumbling and pollution and urban overcrowding were worsening. Expansive national ambitions were slowed by a constipated, corrupt, and overbureaucratized political system. India was sometimes schizophrenic in its international ambitions, caught between a future that argued for a more assertive and agile role and a past that bogged down Indian diplomacy in the pedantic quarrels of a nonaligned world left behind by the end of the Cold War. As a matter of policy, India had been "looking east" to its future in a wider Asia for two decades. When Obama took office, it was still doing more looking than acting.

What had accelerated dramatically in the George W. Bush administration was the improvement in U.S.-Indian ties that had begun at the end of the Clinton administration. Sensing the historic opportunity that a rising India provided, Bush made a big strategic bet at the beginning of his second term. He decided to cut through the most difficult knot in our relationship with India—its nuclear program. India's decision to remain outside the Treaty on the Non-Proliferation of Nuclear Weapons (NPT), alongside Pakistan, Israel, and North Korea (which withdrew in 2003), and its refusal to put its nuclear facilities under international safeguards, proved for decades an immovable practical and symbolic roadblock to closer relations.

The president believed that bringing India in out of the nuclear cold would be a net plus for American strategy. The result, in the summer of 2005, was a crucial understanding announced by President Bush and Indian prime minister Manmohan Singh. India would seek to separate its military and civilian nuclear facilities and put the latter under the most advanced international safeguards, called the

Additional Protocol; it would put in place effective export control systems consistent with the Nuclear Suppliers Group (NSG), and would not transfer enrichment and reprocessing technologies to states that did not already have them; and it would continue its "unilateral moratorium" on nuclear testing. In return, the United States would bend domestic and international rules to accommodate the reality of India's nuclear program and its commitment to act responsibly.

It was not an easy call. Questions remained on just how aligned India would be with us, how significant the costs of the India exception would be to nuclear diplomacy and the broader nuclear nonproliferation regime, and whether the economic benefits for the American nuclear industry would ever live up to the hype. Proponents of the deal tended to overstate the promise and understate the risk; critics did the opposite, lambasted by Indian officials as "nuclear ayatollahs" whose nonproliferation zeal blinded them to wider possibilities. As a long-term strategic investment, however, Bush's decision was bold and smart. It was the essential prerequisite to unlocking the possibility of a strategic partnership that would be a huge asset in shaping the unfolding Pacific Century. The downsides were real but manageable, the returns promising, if delayed. There are no guarantees in diplomacy, but this was a bet worth making.

Producing that initial accord proved difficult, but Secretary Rice, National Security Advisor Hadley, and my predecessor as undersecretary for political affairs, Nick Burns, led a formidable diplomatic campaign. Congress passed the Hyde Act, laying out its expectations for implementation and amending U.S. law to permit civilian nuclear cooperation with India, but there continued to be resistance from members primarily concerned with nuclear proliferation. It was tough going in the Indian Parliament too, with opposition members complaining about infringements on Indian sovereignty. By the time I returned to Washington in the late spring of 2008, the process had stalled, and it looked as if this would be yet another challenge for the next administration to pick up.

Then Prime Minister Singh, in a burst of unforeseen political risk-taking, decided to press ahead in Parliament. With India's next national elections looming in the spring of 2009, time running out for his allies in the Bush administration, and uncertainty about the attitudes of their successors, Singh pushed for and won a confidence vote, clearing a major hurdle on the Indian side. The president and Secretary Rice made clear that they wanted to make a hard push to complete the agreement before the end of their term. Rice called me into her office in mid-June and said, "I know the odds on this are long. But Singh has taken a real risk, and we need to pull out all the stops." I dove in—the beginning of a three-month sprint to finish the civil nuclear agreement, and of another six years of active personal involvement in deepening and normalizing the U.S.-Indian partnership.

We had three more forbidding obstacles to clear: approval of India's nuclear safeguards program by the International Atomic Energy Agency (IAEA); agreement by the NSG to allow a so-called clean exemption for India, permitting it to engage in civil nuclear cooperation with other countries; and finally, passage by both houses of Congress of the civilian nuclear agreement. Of these, the NSG hurdle looked the highest, with six or seven member states in vocal opposition, and consensus a requirement. Passage by Congress would be tough on such a short timetable, but we had to move in sequence and hope that there'd be a small window left for hearings and a vote in September.

We had a skillful team, and Indian counterparts who had received similarly urgent marching orders from Manmohan Singh. President Bush, Secretary Rice, and Steve Hadley were indefatigable in making phone calls and leaning on other leaders, and our ambassador in New Delhi, David Mulford, was not shy about pushing the Indians to show maximum flexibility. John Rood and Dick Stratford, senior arms control officials at State, were excellent partners.

On August 1, the Indians won IAEA approval, clearing the first and lowest hurdle. The NSG was another matter. At an initial meeting of the NSG board in late August, consensus proved elusive. A number of the four dozen member states balked, with Austria, Ireland, and New Zealand among the most outspoken about the concern that India's nonproliferation commitments weren't strong enough. I was candid with Rice. "We really are at a crunch point," I wrote to her in a memo on August 27, "and the Indians are extremely nervous about their domestic politics, and not giving us much to work with at the NSG. . . . The obstacles on both sides are pretty steep."[2]

Both the secretary and the president urged Singh to sharpen the Indian text, and worked the phones with reluctant NSG members. Armed with a somewhat tighter draft, we set off with the Indians for the follow-on NSG board meeting in early September in Vienna. Rice asked me to lead the American delegation, a higher level than we would normally have used, to signal our determination.

This was an exercise in diplomatic blunt force as much as persuasion. I had to wake up senior Swiss and Irish officials in their capitals at four in the morning to push for a final yes. I argued our case but didn't belabor it. The point was simply that we needed this vote and were calling in a chit. There was no point in going back and forth on the merits; we were not looking to do any convincing. This was not elegant diplomacy. This was about power, and we were exercising it.

The votes eventually began to fall into place, and on September 6 the NSG finally approved India's exemption, following a formal pledge by New Delhi that it would not share sensitive nuclear technology or materials with others, and would uphold its moratorium on testing. There was still a lot of uneasiness within the NSG over the purely declaratory nature of the Indian commitments, but in the end it was enough. It was a few years before I was welcome again in Bern or Dublin, but we had cleared the second hurdle.

Although legislative days were limited with the November elections approaching, the congressional leadership agreed to give us a shot at passage in the fall of 2008. Rood and I testified before the

Senate Foreign Relations Committee on September 18 and made our
pitch—looking to take seriously the nonproliferation concerns but
overwhelm them with the strategic argument. By the end of the
month, both the Senate and the House voted to approve the deal.
Prime Minister Singh made a last visit to have dinner with President
Bush at the White House, a moment of genuine mutual satisfaction,
and a moment in which the promise of U.S.-Indian partnership
seemed tangible. The ever-polite Singh looked more bemused than
offended when his plate was whipped away with his fork still poised
in midair. It was his introduction to President Bush's penchant for
culinary speed dating, where business was the first and only course.
However abbreviated their dinner, their sense of pride was enduring,
and so was their achievement.

* * *

THE ADVENT OF the Obama administration initially unnerved the
Indian leadership. Fresh from their successful partnership with Bush,
Singh and his chief advisors were worried that Obama was less enthusiastic. In the near term, they feared the new president's campaign
focus on the "right war" in Afghanistan would "re-hyphenate" the relationship, seeing it through a wider lens that balanced American priorities with Pakistan and Afghanistan against strategic investment
with India. In the longer term, they were anxious that he would subordinate partnership with India to a "G-2" worldview, in which the
U.S.-China relationship was paramount. Obama's ambitious agenda
on nuclear issues was another source of concern—for all the unbur-
dening of the nuclear deal, India was still a square peg in the round
hole of the nonproliferation regime. As the most senior U.S. representative of continuity in relations with India, I worked hard to overcome misimpressions and sustain momentum.

It didn't take long to reassure the Singh government, and making
the case for India's significance was pushing on an open door with
Clinton and Obama. In an early memo, I reminded Clinton of the

heavy lift required to finalize the civil nuclear agreement the summer before, and added that "despite the difficulties—the reversals, recriminations, and negotiating brinksmanship—I was taken by the potential of our relationship. India is as remarkable as it is complicated, a democracy of many and competing voices, and without doubt an emerging Great Power with a growing role in Asia and beyond. I don't believe it will be an easy or quick task, but building a true American alliance with India is a mission worthy of our patience and investment."[3]

Obama and Clinton fully appreciated the importance of partnership with India, both on its own merits and as a key element in the "rebalance" toward Asia that they were beginning to shape. Step-by-step, we expanded the bilateral agenda, strengthening counterterrorism cooperation; looking for opportunities to work together in education and science; deepening two-way trade and investment; starting a systematic discussion on climate change; and significantly increasing defense cooperation. By the end of Obama's first term, India was conducting more military exercises with the United States than with any other country, and its acquisitions of American defense equipment had risen from a little over $200 million to $2 billion.

The president and Prime Minister Singh had a cordial first encounter in London on the margins of the G-20 summit in April, and Obama invited him to make a state visit—the first of his administration—in November 2009. The symbolism of that went a long way to assuage Indian anxieties, and Obama and Singh hit it off. The next year, Obama made a reciprocal state visit to India. He and Singh pressed ahead in a number of areas, as both the economic and defense dimensions of the relationship continued to grow. There were headaches, of course; nothing came easily in U.S.-Indian relations, and the Singh government lost political altitude and clout steadily after its reelection in the spring of 2009.

Pakistan remained a neuralgic topic; despite the president's best efforts with Singh, and my own quiet conversations with Shivshankar

Menon, the prime minister's national security advisor, the Indians had no interest in opening up much with us about their relations with the Pakistanis. Active back-channel talks between them had nearly brought about a breakthrough over Kashmir and other disputes in the spring of 2007, but the collapsing political position of Pakistani president Pervez Musharraf had brought them to an abrupt halt, and they had made no more than fitful progress since then. We were increasingly worried about the risks of nuclear confrontation, but the Indians were not much interested in talking about their perceptions or how to avoid escalation, let alone any American mediation role.[4]

The president took advantage of his 2010 visit to take another dramatic step to highlight his commitment to U.S.-Indian partnership. Speaking to India's Parliament, Obama repeated that the U.S.-India relationship was "one of the defining partnerships of the twenty-first century," and indicated for the first time his support for Indian permanent membership in a reformed UN Security Council. The announcement fit the moment and the setting, but it was not an easy decision. The United States had made only one other similar statement, some years before, in support of Japan's candidacy. The whole issue of expanding permanent membership was fraught with difficulty—in terms of procedures; preserving the efficacy of the institution; navigating the reservations of other permanent members; and managing the sensitivities of a number of players, including close allies and Security Council aspirants like Germany.

Susan Rice, our ambassador to the UN, was understandably concerned about taking this step, not least because the Indians hadn't exactly been reliable partners in New York over the years. On the morning of his speech to Parliament, I sat with the president and Tom Donilon, newly elevated as national security advisor, for one last secure conference call with Susan, who repeated her reservations and argued for more conditional language. I fully acknowledged the risks, but said I thought it would be a mistake to miss this opportunity.

Tom agreed. The president ultimately decided to go ahead—but made a point of stressing to Singh privately the difficulties involved in expanding permanent membership, and the importance of India doing its part to earn the seat in New York.

Over the next few years, U.S.-Indian relations continued to deepen. John Kerry followed in Clinton's footsteps and worked with Secretary of Commerce Penny Pritzker in the second Obama term to deepen the promise of economic ties. Implementation of the civil nuclear agreement was a slog. Menon and I finished a required nuclear reprocessing agreement in 2010, but that same year the Indian Parliament passed nuclear liability legislation that discouraged domestic, American, and other foreign firms from taking advantage of the commercial opportunities that were one of the attractions of the civilian nuclear deal. It took several years to develop a workable compromise. It was a deeply frustrating exercise, one that tested the patience and goodwill of Congress and much of the U.S. bureaucracy—and served as a gnawing reminder that whatever the long-term gains might be from the agreement, the near-term pains would not be inconsequential.

Narendra Modi succeeded Singh as prime minister after a landslide victory for his Bharatiya Janata Party (BJP) in the spring of 2014. Modi embraced a more confident role for India on the world stage, committed to making it a great power and its partnership with the United States far more strategic. He had bold ideas to propel India's economy and bureaucracy into the twenty-first century. The BJP, however, had harbored for years some worrying sectarian, Hindu nationalist tendencies. During Modi's tenure as chief minister of Gujarat, anti-Muslim violence had claimed more than a thousand lives, denting his image and complicating his relationship with the United States, which denied him a visa for more than a decade. The Indian electorate, however, was thirsty for a strong man to deal with domestic drift, and Modi's energy and vision offered a sense of possibility, both for India and for our partnership.

I was the first senior U.S. official to visit Modi in New Delhi, a week after his inauguration. I found him full of ambition, with a dry sense of humor and no evident hard feelings about the visa issue. He made clear his determination to invest in U.S.-Indian relations, and emphasized that he saw our partnership as one of the keys to his own domestic and regional ambitions. Modi was curious about American politics and how the next presidential contest was shaping up, and what could be done in the meantime to cement cooperation between Washington and New Delhi. He immediately accepted the invitation I conveyed from President Obama to visit Washington in September.

Obama and Modi developed a close rapport, and the September visit went well. Obama was the honored foreign guest on India's Republic Day in January 2015, a further sign of the strength of the relationship. While it was always going to be impossible to duplicate the drama of the civilian nuclear breakthrough, and while we would continue to have our differences on important questions of geopolitics and trade, the Obama administration deepened the roots of a partnership whose consequence for international order was growing, and whose utility in the administration's rebalance toward Asia was increasingly apparent.

* * *

A LITTLE BEFORE 10 P.M. on a Wednesday evening in April 2012, I got a call at home from the State Department Operations Center asking me to join a secure call with Secretary Clinton. I climbed up the stairs to my tiny attic office, ducking to avoid hitting my head on the beams. I had had my secure phone installed up there to avoid bothering Lisa and our daughters with the late-night calls that they had so often endured over the years. Chief of Staff Cheryl Mills, Policy Planning Director Jake Sullivan, and Assistant Secretary for East Asian and Pacific Affairs Kurt Campbell were already on the line.

When the secretary joined, with her usual even-keeled "now what?" tone, Campbell explained the dilemma before us: A blind, self-taught, forty-year-old Chinese human rights activist named

Chen Guangcheng had escaped house arrest in Shandong Province. Despite having broken his ankle, he had made his way to the Beijing suburbs, with the assistance of friends along the way. On the run from the state security services, he had telephoned a U.S. embassy contact, who drove out along with another embassy officer to meet with him a few hours later. Chen asked for refuge inside the U.S. embassy. The officers relayed this to the chargé, Bob Wang, who immediately sought guidance from Kurt. Wang said he thought the chances were slim that Chen could get into the embassy on his own, given his condition and the layers of Chinese security, but judged that the odds were high that American diplomats could drive him in if they went out and brought him back in their embassy vehicle. Wang added one more thing: His guess was that Chen had less than an hour before state security caught up with him.

It was not your average late-night phone call, but it was all too typical of the imperfect choices that secretaries of state often faced. The moral argument for bringing Chen in was powerful; this was yet another test of how much the United States was prepared to risk in defense of its values. On the other side was the obvious political problem: The Chinese government would be outraged. There was no clear pathway to negotiating an acceptable way out for Chen once he came in. To make matters even more complicated, Secretary Clinton was scheduled to fly to Beijing five days later for the next round of the Strategic and Economic Dialogue (S&ED)—the Obama administration's flagship cabinet-level meeting with the Chinese. The timing could not have been worse.

Clinton was matter of fact: no hand-wringing, no lamentation about lousy choices, no second-guessing of the embassy. She asked a few more questions about Chen and his background, and asked each of us what we thought. We all acknowledged the downsides, but recommended bringing Chen in. Clinton didn't hesitate. She knew there'd be a political storm with the Chinese, but suspected it was navigable, and she couldn't in any case justify saying no. She didn't try to pass the buck to the White House, recognizing the time pressures. She simply asked Jake to inform the NSC staff, in case they wanted to object, and authorized Kurt to give the green light to Bob Wang. I joined Jake for a secure call to Tom Donilon, who was not thrilled by the news and channeled Baker in reminding us that the dead cat would be on our doorstep if we messed this up.

At about 3 A.M. Washington time, Wang confirmed that Chen had made it into the embassy. Then we strapped ourselves in for the roller coaster. Kurt flew out to Beijing to begin discussions with an extremely unhappy Cui Tiankai, the vice foreign minister responsible for relations with the United States. Cui emphasized that the only solution was to turn Chen over to the Chinese authorities immediately, and left hanging the risk of blowing up the S&ED. I arrived a day later, on the evening of April 30, to lead another round of the Strategic Security Dialogue, a semiannual meeting aimed at some of the trickiest problems on the bilateral agenda—including cybersecurity, maritime security, and the future of nuclear arms and missile defense. Kurt and I had a long, hard two-hour conversation with Cui that night. I made the case as calmly as I could that the least messy of the options before us was to let Chen go to a Beijing hospital for treatment, let his family come from Shandong to join him there, and then let him do what he wanted—which was study law at a Chinese university. Cui initially balked. But as the night wore on, the political temperature lowered and he began to seem more amenable. It was obvious that neither he nor his superiors were eager to see the upcoming ministerial meeting sunk by the Chen affair. By the next morning, the Chinese had agreed to the approach we outlined.

But that didn't stop the roller coaster. In the hospital, Chen suddenly changed his mind. He now wanted to go to the United States immediately with his wife, and signaled the same thing in cellphone interviews with Western journalists. Cui was livid. "You can't do this," he said. "You have no idea how badly this will affect our relations." Eventually, with Clinton's direct intervention with her Chinese counterpart, Chen was allowed to go directly to New York as he had hoped. We breathed a huge sigh of relief—and so did the White House.[5]

This affair was far from the most significant crisis with the Chinese during the Obama administration, but it left a few lasting impressions. One was about Clinton's equanimity and leadership style in the face of the inevitable trade-offs and smothering time pressures of many policy choices. Another was about China's increasingly assertive direction. And still another was about the growing maturity of U.S.-China relations, whose resilience in the face of unavoidable difficulties required constant attention and investment. As I neared the end of a long diplomatic career, it was clearer than ever that nothing mattered more in American foreign policy than management of that relationship.

By now, China was no longer a great power on the rise, but one whose moment had come. The Iraq War and the financial crisis five years later had exposed American vulnerabilities. An increasingly feisty Chinese leadership saw an opening and began to question the wisdom of Deng Xiaoping's "hide your strengths and bide your time" philosophy, and it accelerated its ambitions not only to establish itself as a global economic peer of the United States, but to supplant it as the leading power in Asia. That did not mean that conflict was foreordained; the mutually beneficial entangling of the American and Chinese economies was a powerful incentive to avoid it. It did mean that the most critical test of American statecraft for President Obama and Secretary Clinton was managing competition with China, and cushioning it with bilateral cooperation and regional alliances and institutions. This was surely not a novel challenge—ever since Nixon and Kissinger, U.S. strategy had paid careful attention to China's emergence, and the Bush 43 administration had put considerable effort into encouraging China to be a "responsible stakeholder" in a changing international system. 9/11 and the Middle East sucked up high-level attention and resources, however, and Obama and Clinton were determined to rebalance American strategy back to Asia.

Clinton became the first secretary since Dean Rusk a half century earlier to take her first overseas trip to Asia, and returned often during her tenure. Obama surpassed every American president by making more than a dozen visits during his two terms. Beyond just showing up, they invested heavily in relationships across the region, with India as a western bookend, expanding ties to the fast-growing economies of Southeast Asia, and reaffirming crucial alliances with Australia, South Korea, and Japan. They began to expand the U.S. military and diplomatic presence in the region, explore a new trading arrangement that eventually emerged as the Trans-Pacific Partnership, and cultivate new, region-wide institutions like the East Asia Summit. Assistant Secretary Kurt Campbell was the leading subcabinet architect of the rebalance and its tireless champion. Once Tom Donilon became national security advisor partway through Obama's first term, he immersed himself in relations with China, traveling regularly to Beijing and building strong personal ties. So did Susan Rice after she succeeded Donilon.

Roaming across other issues and places, however, I was struck by the quality and increasing self-confidence of Chinese diplomacy. Leading the American delegation to the African Union summit in Addis Ababa one year, I found the Chinese presence nearly overwhelming, with President Hu Jintao at the head of a delegation many times the size of ours, and a gleaming new Chinese-constructed and -financed African Union headquarters building as the backdrop. I traveled to Beijing often to consult on Iran, Afghanistan, and Russia, among many other issues. I enjoyed long discussions with Dai Bingguo, Hu's principal foreign affairs advisor. Trained as a Soviet specialist, Dai had a clever, orderly mind, and a sure feel for how other leaderships operated. When I described to him at one point the progress that Obama and Medvedev were making in repairing relations, Dai smiled blandly and interjected, "You realize, of course, that nothing happens in Moscow without Putin's assent." His tone was polite, his expression amused, and his implication unmistakable—he really wasn't sure that we knew how things worked.

I spent a fair amount of time during the Obama years traveling in both Southeast and Northeast Asia. China had begun to throw its weight around in the South China Sea, intent upon—quite literally— shoring up its territorial claims through the creation of artificial islands, and staking out its commercial and resource interests. Irritated by Secretary Clinton's forthright statement at a meeting of the Association of Southeast Asian Nations (ASEAN) in Hanoi in the summer of 2010 that the United States had national interests in the South China Sea too, Foreign Minister Yang Jiechi basically warned the assembled ministers that China was the biggest player in the neighborhood, and they had better get used to it. Clinton astutely took advantage of Chinese overreach to strengthen our own ties in Southeast Asia. I tried to help with several visits to Vietnam and Indonesia, and stops in Australia and each of the other ASEAN capitals over the course of the next few years.

My father had fought in Vietnam in 1966–67, but there were few traces of war or resentment decades later in the boomtown cacophony of Ho Chi Minh City. In Cambodia, a survivor of Pol Pot's genocide guided me through the moving Tuol Seng Genocide Museum in central Phnom Penh, formerly the prison where he had once suffered. "Cambodia," I wrote Secretary Clinton afterward, "offers hope in the fundamental resilience of human beings, even after a whole society self-destructs amidst unspeakable horrors." Meeting Cambodia's current leader helped keep my expectations in check. "Having spent most of his adult life waking up every morning wondering who was going to try to kill him that day, Hun Sen remains a cunning, tough survivor, for whom political openness is not necessarily a natural condition." I went to Burma too, supporting the opening that Obama and Clinton had worked hard to create. After a lengthy conversation with the formidable Aung San Suu Kyi in 2012, I reported back to the secretary that it was already clear that "the mix within her of global human rights icon and steely Burmese politician is bound to be uneasy."[6]

After becoming deputy secretary in the summer of 2011, I became a more regular visitor to Tokyo and Seoul, and joined in trilateral meetings with both crucial allies, whose historical differences sometimes got in the way of common concerns about North Korea's nuclear ambitions and China's rise. I wasn't directly engaged in our fitful diplomacy on North Korea, but I shared my colleagues' frustration over the fruitlessness of the Six Party Talks, our inability to get a serious back channel with the North Koreans going, and our similar lack of success in beginning a quiet strategic conversation with the Chinese about the future of the Korean Peninsula. "Strategic patience" had a deceptively reassuring ring to it, but only seemed to narrow our strategic choices and fuel long-term impatience on all sides—especially after Kim Jong-un succeeded his father in 2012.

My involvement in U.S.-China relations became much more active and direct after 2011. Succeeding Steinberg, I led the American side in the semiannual Strategic Security Dialogue with the Chinese. These meetings brought together diplomats and senior military and intelligence officials. That sometimes made for an uneasy combination on the Chinese side, where my Foreign Ministry counterpart, Zhang Yesui, took the lead, with a number of People's Liberation Army (PLA) generals and senior security services representatives sitting alongside, most looking as if they'd like nothing better than to beam themselves out of the room.

The exchanges were rarely fun. We spent seven hours in one stretch laying out and debating specific information that we had about cyber-enabled commercial espionage by Chinese state organs, including the PLA. The Chinese summarily rejected our evidence. But there was a broader kind of cognitive dissonance at work too—for the Chinese, at least at that stage, the distinction we were drawing between espionage for national security purposes and cyber-spying for commercial advantage seemed artificial. In their view, governments used whatever means they could to build advantage, whether political or economic. We emphasized that we were determined to uphold that distinction, and we showed some teeth too. When our long presentation of concrete evidence got nowhere, and when the president's concerns were rebuffed or ignored, we announced indictments against several Chinese security officials. While the chances that they'd ever be offered up to the American judicial system were nil, our point was made, and the Chinese eventually reached a general understanding with us, significantly reducing cyber-enabled commercial thefts.

John Kerry's tireless efforts on climate change, and the Chinese leadership's belated realization that poisoning their population was a recipe for inconvenient domestic disturbances, led to the diplomatic breakthrough of the 2015 Paris climate agreement. Unfortunately, there were few other breakthroughs to celebrate. The gulf between us was growing, as were the risks of collision. Diplomacy played a critical role in keeping the temperature down and finding ways to get business done where there was obvious benefit to both of us. Obama believed that the Pacific Century could accommodate a risen China and a resilient and adaptable United States, and he worked hard to demonstrate American commitment to that idea. But as Chinese self-confidence grew and their sense of American drift deepened, it was inevitable that we'd test one another on whose version of regional order was ascendant. Nothing would matter more in American foreign policy than how that new great game played out.

* * *

AS PRESIDENT OBAMA attempted to rebalance American foreign policy for the long term, with new emphasis on Asia, he knew we needed to continue to invest in our closest allies in Europe. Obama and Clinton sought to strengthen transatlantic ties, especially with Germany, France, and the United Kingdom. The president built a particularly effective relationship over time with German chancellor Angela Merkel, whose cool intellect and no-nonsense style he greatly valued. While our core European allies would occasionally suffer from "pivot envy" as the Obama administration focused more and more visible attention on Asia, nothing remained more critical to our global interests than the transatlantic alliance. Strong ties to our European partners were essential to another long-game priority, a renewed effort at managing relations with Russia.

Obama's approach to Russia began cautiously. He told a television interviewer during the transition that he thought it made sense to explore a "reset" in relations. Differences over Russian aggression in Georgia remained serious, and there were plenty of other problems, but there was also common ground that could be plowed more effectively. Obama had talked during the 2008 campaign about his determination to reduce the dangers of nuclear war, his willingness to directly engage the Iranian regime, and his interest in a more successful approach to the war in Afghanistan. All of those priorities would benefit from a healthier U.S.-Russian relationship.

The Georgia conflict had further sobered my expectations, and my view continued to be that we'd be operating within a fairly narrow band of possibilities in relations with a Russia that was still far more Putin's than Medvedev's. We still could, however, seek a better balance between areas of cooperation and inevitable differences. I found a kindred spirit in Mike McFaul, the new senior Russia expert on the NSC staff. Mike and I had first met on the basketball court at the embassy in Moscow in the 1990s, during my first tour and his stint at the Carnegie Endowment's Moscow Center. He was as energetic in government as he had been on the court, driving the reset with similar determination and creativity.

McFaul was not, however, wildly enthusiastic about my first suggestion. I thought it would help reinforce the seriousness of the administration's approach to lay out our thinking comprehensively in a presidential letter, and then have the two of us deliver it in Moscow.

To Mike, this seemed very nineteenth-century; all that was missing was the quill pen. But I argued that the Russians tended to be traditionalists in their estimation of diplomatic seriousness, and that this would help. I eventually wore him down. We produced a long, systematic draft for the president, which Obama approved, and flew to Moscow in early February 2009. I also took along a handwritten note from Secretary Clinton to Foreign Minister Lavrov. Clinton was skeptical about how much could be accomplished in the reset, but believed it was worth a shot.

McFaul and I spent two days in intensive discussions with Lavrov and other senior officials. It went better than we expected. I told the secretary on February 13, "I left Moscow convinced that we have a significant opportunity before us, but realistic about how hard it is going to be to shift gears with a Russian leadership deeply distracted by a worsening economic predicament, and still conflicted about whether their interests are better served by a thaw in relations." I was struck by high-level anxiety in Moscow about the global financial crisis, which had quickly undercut Russia's boom. "The construction cranes that dominated the city skyline during my years as ambassador now sit idle," I wrote. "The bankers and senior officials gathered in the Finance Minister's anteroom while we were waiting to meet him ... had none of the swagger I remember before, and their gloom was palpable." The authoritarian modernization model of Putin and Medvedev was under considerable strain, and that strengthened the case in the Kremlin for testing a relaxation of tensions with us.[7]

On specific issues that the president raised in his letter to Medvedev, the Russians seemed cautiously receptive. Obama had made clear our areas of difference, particularly our disagreement over the status of Abkhazia and South Ossetia. He was equally straight about our human rights concerns. The Russians didn't belabor the Georgia conflict or beat their chests over U.S. policy in the former Soviet Union. Lavrov signaled immediate interest in talks about a new arms reduction agreement, with START due to expire at the end of 2009.

"No passage in the President's letter caught the Russians' attention more," I told Clinton, "than the paragraph on Iran and missile defense." Choosing his words carefully, the president had emphasized that he was in the process of reviewing U.S. missile defense strategy, including the plans for sites in Poland and the Czech Republic that had so exercised the Russians, and that—logically—progress in reducing the risks posed by Iran's missile and nuclear programs would have a direct impact on our review, since those were the threats against which our European plans were primarily targeted. The Russians couldn't miss the implication.[8]

In early March, Clinton had an introductory meeting with Lavrov in Geneva. It was marred only by a minor embarrassment, when Clinton sought to break the ice during a press availability at the outset by handing Lavrov a red button that was supposed to say "reset" in Russian, but instead was mistranslated as "overload." Gimmicks and Lavrov rarely mixed well. Lavrov didn't rub it in (at least not too much), and the secretary took it in stride. The media, however, had a field day.

The president had his first meeting with Medvedev in London at the beginning of April, on the margins of a G-20 meeting focused mostly on the continuing economic tidal wave caused by the 2008 financial crisis. They met at Winfield House, the elegant residence of the U.S. ambassador, in a tranquil corner of Regent's Park. As we waited in the dining room for Medvedev and his delegation to arrive, I must admit that I was thinking less of the nuts and bolts of the reset agenda and more of the first time I walked into that room, a shy twenty-two-year-old in a bad suit trying to fade into the elegant woodwork at a welcome reception for Marshall Scholars. The woodwork still beckoned, and my sartorial standards were only marginally improved, but I was feeling a little more at ease this time.

It was clear from the start that Medvedev was eager to build rapport with Obama and try to make some version of the reset an advertisement for his effectiveness as a president and world leader. That didn't mean that he was going to be a pushover; he was a tough defender of Russian interests, without his mentor's snark but operating within the bounds of Putin's hard-nosed views. He underscored his commitment to finalizing a successor to the START treaty by the end of the year, at substantially reduced levels of strategic nuclear weapons. He offered to allow the United States to fly troops and material through Russian airspace to Afghanistan—a big advantage for a U.S. administration eager to lessen dependence on supply lines through Pakistan. Most surprisingly, he admitted to Obama that Russia had underestimated the pace and threat of the Iranian nuclear and ballistic missile programs—probing to see how far a tougher line on Iran might get him on the missile defense issue. Despite Medvedev's sharp criticisms on missile defense and Georgia, the overall tenor of the conversation was surprisingly positive, with Medvedev at pains to show how comfortably he was settling into his presidential role.

It was not at all clear, however, that there was space in a one-man political system for a second player—and also not at all clear that that one man shared Medvedev's apparent enthusiasm for the reset. President Obama agreed to an early visit to Moscow to test both propositions. Caution might have dictated a slower pace, especially since Obama wouldn't visit Beijing for the first time until November, and had a massive domestic agenda to contend with and a steep recession still consuming much of his time and attention. Yet the president was in a hurry, on a number of fronts, and he wanted to see if the reset with Russia could get traction. He flew to Moscow during the first week in July, and I went along as the senior State Department representative.

The Medvedev meeting went smoothly. Most of it—three hours out of a little less than four altogether—took place in a small group. Both presidents were on top of their briefs, and had an easy rapport as they went back and forth over the issues. Obama put particular emphasis on the need to accelerate the New START negotiations, and on his concerns about Iran. Medvedev continued to hammer away at

Russian reservations about missile defense, stressing their general interest in some form of constraints on missile defense alongside strategic arms reductions, and specifically their opposition to the two Central European sites, which he argued would do little to address the modest medium-term Iranian threat. The practical accomplishments of their first six months working together, however, were already substantial, and hinted at even greater potential.

The following morning, Obama drove out to meet Putin at his Novo Ogaryovo dacha just outside Moscow. Jim Jones, McFaul, and I rode along with him in the "Beast," the heavily armored limousine that is flown out in advance to transport and protect the president on his overseas trips. Mike and I sat facing the president, and we talked generally about the meeting and how best to approach Putin. I described a few of my own interactions with him over the years, and suggested that he usually didn't react well to a long presentation, especially since he would see himself as the more senior and experienced leader. Why not ask him at the start for his candid assessment of what he thought had gone right and what he thought had gone wrong in Russian-American relations over the past decade? Putin liked being asked his opinion, and he certainly wasn't shy. Maybe it would set a good tone to let him get some things off his chest up front. The president nodded.

After President Obama's initial question produced an unbroken fifty-minute Putin monologue filled with grievances, raw asides, and acerbic commentary, I began to wonder about the wisdom of my advice, and my future in the Obama administration. The meeting was supposed to last one hour, and Putin had already eaten up most of the clock. He had arranged an impressive setting, sitting under a canopy on an elaborate patio, with waiters in eighteenth-century costumes bringing out an endless variety of dishes. I just drank coffee and listened to Putin's familiar litany—how he liked George W. Bush, but saw his efforts to build solid relations after 9/11 go unrequited; how the Bush administration had bungled Iraq and orchestrated color revolutions in Ukraine and Georgia. He was less concerned than Medvedev about the Iranian threat, and more caustic about missile defense and what he perceived to be the unwillingness of the Bush administration to listen to him. His manner was blunt, his language sometimes crude, and his overall demeanor self-servingly dismissive of the value of working with Americans. He had tried with Bush. It hadn't panned out. Why get burned again?

Obama listened patiently, and then delivered his own firm message on the reset. He was matter-of-fact about our differences, and made no effort to gloss over the profound problems that Russia's actions in Georgia had caused. He said it was in neither of our interests to let our disagreements obscure those areas where we could each benefit by working together, and where U.S.-Russian leadership could contribute to international order. We should test that, he explained, without inflating expectations. After all, we already had a lot of experience testing the alternative approaches—either getting our hopes up too high or retreating into more familiar adversarial stances—and they hadn't worked out so well. Putin didn't look persuaded, but he conceded that it made sense to try. "These issues are Dmitry's responsibility now," he said airily. "He has my support."

The discussion between Putin and Obama went two hours longer than planned, but it was well worth the anxiety it caused schedulers on both sides. As we rode back to Moscow, the president said Putin's capacity for venting didn't surprise him. The challenge, Obama recognized, was to "stay connected to this guy, without undercutting Medvedev." That was to prove much harder than we thought at the outset. When we suggested that Putin co-chair the new Bilateral Presidential Commission with Vice President Biden, he didn't bite; Putin didn't view vice presidents as his peers. We came up with other ideas—like Putin leading a Russian business delegation to the United States, which would give him occasion to visit Washington—but none stuck. Rank and structure, and Putin's own wariness, combined to make him elusive throughout the reset effort, leaving a vulnerability that we were never able to patch. By the time Putin and Obama met again, three years later, the reset had collapsed.

Despite my doubts about whether we could stay connected to Putin, there was no question that we were making progress on the reset. The transit arrangements that we had negotiated for moving materiel and troops to Afghanistan through Russian and Central Asian airspace proved invaluable. To help solidify our ties, McFaul and I set off on a trip to all five Central Asian states just after Obama's Moscow summit in the summer of 2009. Woody Allen famously observed that 90 percent of life is showing up; that certainly applies to American diplomacy in places like Central Asia, whose leaders were habitually autocratic, sensitive to American inattention, and squeezed between their big, ambitious Russian and Chinese neighbors.

In Kazakhstan, President Nursultan Nazarbayev appreciated the timely briefing on the Moscow talks, supported our pragmatic approach, and emphasized shrewdly that one of the keys to sustaining it would be finding a way to work with Putin as well as Medvedev, about whom he was politely dismissive. In Uzbekistan, President Islam Karimov wondered why Americans always stopped in Astana first and failed to grasp that Tashkent was the center of gravity in the small Central Asian solar system. His two-hour opening monologue was impressive for its sheer stamina, as well as for his dismal opinions of other regional leaders, whom he clearly regarded as venal lightweights (presumably in contrast to his weightier venality). Karimov was frosty about our human rights concerns, and pessimistic on Afghanistan, but willing to help. So was Kyrgyzstan's leadership. In Turkmenistan, President Garbanguly Berdimuhamedov was a distinct improvement on his clinically unbalanced predecessor. I survived our stop in Tajikistan, where my major accomplishment was to consume the deer's ear I was served as the guest of honor at a presidential banquet, a digestive exercise for which no amount of vodka seemed sufficient.

Back in Washington, the administration was focused on an intensive interagency review of the missile defense strategy that it had inherited. Obama made clear that he wasn't interested in catering to the Russians. He wanted to make sure that we were moving in the most effective way possible for dealing with the emerging Iranian missile threat.

The result of the review was a strong recommendation, supported by both Bob Gates and Hillary Clinton, to pursue an alternative, relying at least initially on systems based on Aegis cruisers in the Mediterranean and in southern Europe. The review concluded that this "phased adaptive approach" would be a technically superior defense against a potential Iranian threat over the near and medium term, and more sustainable politically in Europe. It left open the possibility of revisiting the original Polish and Czech plans further down the road. I pointed out in a note to Clinton in early September an obvious corollary benefit: "A fresh start on missile defense, entirely defensible on the technical merits, gives you and the President a stronger hand to play" with the Russians. "Far from letting the Russians off the hook, this approach is our best bet to corner them on Iran, and to press ahead on post-START and wider European security issues."[9]

We moved quickly to take advantage of the improving atmosphere with Russia to advance one of the president's central priorities— preventing Iran from developing a nuclear weapon. Cooperation with Moscow was at the heart of that effort; if we could prevent the Iranians from driving a wedge between us and the Russians, the chances for mobilizing the Europeans, Chinese, and other players in a united front improved substantially. Medvedev was persuaded by our willingness to work with Russia in good faith, negotiate directly with the Iranians, and offer reasonable compromises before pivoting to an effort to build more economic pressure against Iran. The result was UN Security Council Resolution 1929 in June 2010, the platform on which we were able to build unprecedented pressure against the Iranians, and ultimately bring them back to the negotiating table.

We made similar headway on the New START agreement. A determined US negotiating team, after lots of ups and downs along the way, worked out a solid accord in late 2009, just before the expiration of the original START treaty. It further reduced strategic nuclear arms, bringing them to their lowest levels since the dawn of the nuclear age. The president himself played a critical role in this, hammering out key compromises with Medvedev by phone and in meetings on the margins of international conferences. Hillary Clinton was instrumental in selling the deal on the Hill. The Senate voted in favor before the Christmas recess, with Republican opposition mollified by an agreement to invest billions in nuclear weapons modernization, some of which had questionable utility. It was another reminder of the costs of getting diplomatic business done in an increasingly polarized political system.

I accompanied Clinton to Moscow in March 2010, a moment when it felt like the reset might be taking hold. She had useful discussions with Medvedev and Lavrov, and we then went out to see Putin at his dacha. He was mildly combative at the outset of their meeting, while the press was still in the room, poking at continuing difficulties in the American economy and his skepticism about Washington's seriousness about deepening economic ties to Russia. Slouching a little in his chair, his legs spread wide in front of him, Putin looked every bit the kid in the back of the classroom with an attitude problem (an image that Obama once, undiplomatically, cited in public). Clinton took it all in stride, laughed off his barbs, and engaged in a crisp back-and-forth with Putin once the media were gone and the meeting unfolded. Accustomed to pushing people around and finding their weak spots, Putin seemed a bit frustrated by Clinton's measured reaction.

The secretary and I had talked earlier that day about Putin's love of the outdoors and fascination with both big animals and his own bare-chested persona. Shifting gears in the conversation, she asked him to talk a little about his well-publicized efforts to preserve Siberian tigers. A light seemed to go off, and Putin described with uncharacteristic excitement some of his recent trips to the Russian Far East. With what for him was borderline exuberance, he stood up and asked

Clinton to come with him to his private office. I trailed them down several hallways, past startled guards and assistants, as Putin led the way. Arriving at his office, he proceeded to show the secretary on a large map of Russia covering most of one wall the areas he had visited on his Siberian tiger trips, and those in the north where he planned to go that summer to tranquilize and tag polar bears. With genuine enthusiasm, he asked if former president Clinton might like to come along, or maybe even the secretary herself?

I had never seen Putin so animated. The secretary applauded his commitment to wildlife conservation, and said this might be another area where Russia and America could work more together. She politely deflected the invitation to the Russian Far North, although she promised to mention it to her husband. Riding back to her hotel in Moscow afterward, Clinton smiled and said that neither she nor the former president would be spending their summer vacation with Putin near the Arctic Circle.

The high point of the reset, in many ways, was Medvedev's visit to the United States in June 2010. New START had been ratified and signed. A strong new Security Council resolution signaled U.S.-Russian cooperation on Iran. Russian logistical support had enabled the president's Afghan surge. Medvedev's political stock was still dwarfed by Putin's in Russia, but he clearly saw an opportunity to show that he could promote Russian interests on the world stage—with his cordial relationship with Obama as exhibit A. That might be his ticket to a second term as president, amid rumors already beginning to swirl that Putin would return to the Kremlin instead.

Medvedev began his trip to the United States in Silicon Valley. He was intent upon developing Russia's technology sector, and had already launched a kind of tech hothouse just outside Moscow, aimed at incubating innovative new companies and technologies. Supported by the Russian state and a handful of oligarchs, it was a top-down model far removed from the West Coast garages in which Bill Gates and Steve Jobs had started their ascent, with little of the freewheeling entrepreneurial spirit that energized Silicon Valley. McFaul arranged for Medvedev to speak at Stanford, which he did with distinctly un-Kremlin-like flair, wearing blue jeans and reading his remarks from an iPad. He interacted with tech pioneers from Apple, Google, and Cisco, as well as with young Russian émigrés working in the Valley. For someone like me, who had long argued that Russia needed urgently to diversify its economy beyond what came out of the ground, it seemed like a hopeful moment.

Obama's conversations in Washington with Medvedev were similarly encouraging, focused on creating economic ballast that might support the relationship beyond the reset. They agreed to work together to complete Russia's entry into the World Trade Organization.

Even a spy scandal, which became public soon after Medvedev returned home, did not derail the reset. U.S. investigators had been piecing together for some months information about a network of Russian "sleeper" agents—Russian nationals who had taken on false American identities and burrowed into American society, preparing to eventually take on active espionage tasks. It was a story that later became the basis for a popular television series, *The Americans*—whose protagonists were a good deal more accomplished than the actual Russian sleepers. Nevertheless, the long-term risk they posed was real. After long sessions in the Situation Room in which we debated the options, the president decided to pursue a swap shortly after the Medvedev visit. The eleven sleeper agents were arrested, and then traded for four individuals imprisoned by the Russians on espionage charges. It was in some respects a classic Cold War tale—and a reminder that, for all the apparent promise of the reset, ours was still a fraught relationship.

* * *

IN 2011, THINGS began to get a lot more fraught and the reset began to lose altitude. Ever since the color revolutions in Georgia and Ukraine, Moscow had grown increasingly apprehensive about popular uprisings that might soon wash up on the walls of the Kremlin. The Arab Spring—the revolutions that erupted in Tunisia, Egypt, and across the region in early 2011—sent much of the Russian leadership into a cold sweat, as did Washington's evident sympathy for popular movements in the Arab world.

The case of Qaddafi's Libya was particularly challenging. As a revolt spread across Libya, Qaddafi threatened to slaughter rebels in Benghazi and other cities where the uprising was strongest. Key European states called for outside intervention to prevent massive bloodletting. In a break from past practice, the Arab League also was outspoken in its call for the United Nations to act and authorize intervention to protect civilians. The Russians supported a first Security Council resolution in February. And then in mid-March, after a direct request delivered persuasively by Vice President Biden to Medvedev in Moscow, Russia abstained and allowed passage of a second resolution authorizing "all necessary means" to safeguard Libyan civilians.

I accompanied the vice president on that trip, and the contrast between his conversations with Medvedev and those with Putin was striking. Medvedev acknowledged the humanitarian risks, and hinted that he was inclined to acquiesce in a limited military mission. He was also invested in Obama by this point, and that seemed to be a factor in his thinking. Putin was neither invested in Obama nor overly concerned about humanitarian risks. His main concern was the chaos that might result from outside intervention, and the precedent that would be set if another autocrat was toppled. Putin was dyspeptic about American policy in the Middle East, and sharply critical of our "abandonment" of Mubarak a month earlier.

While Putin clearly had serious doubts about the wisdom of catering to American preferences amid the Arab Spring, he deferred to Medvedev on the decision to abstain. If it didn't end well, he made clear he would add yet another black mark in his estimation of Medvedev's judgment and capacity to protect Russian interests in a rough and cold-blooded world—and another in his long list of grievances about American duplicity. In the fall of 2011, after Western military strikes that soon drifted beyond the original intent of the Security Council resolutions, Qaddafi was overthrown. In gruesome footage that Putin reportedly viewed repeatedly, rebels caught the Libyan dictator hiding in a drainage pipe and beat him to death.

Putin worried that Russia's vulnerabilities had grown, not diminished, since he had left the presidency, and concluded it was time to take back full control of the reins. The 2008 global financial crisis had hit Russia hard, sending hydrocarbon prices plummeting and curbing the high growth rates that Putin had enjoyed during his first two terms in the Kremlin. Although from Putin's perspective the war in Georgia and the sympathetic government of Viktor Yanukovich in Ukraine had put the brakes on the erosion of Russian influence in the former Soviet Union, the wider world looked more uncertain, with authoritarian leaderships falling across the Middle East and the United States throwing its weight behind regime changes. His self-assurance reinforced by years of sycophancy from the Russian elite and enviable public approval ratings, Putin concluded with the hubris that autocracy breeds that his was the only strong hand that could right Russia's course and steer it ahead. He announced in September his decision to run for president again in the March 2012 elections, and that Medvedev would replace him as prime minister.

Putin misjudged the reaction among the rising urban middle class in Moscow, St. Petersburg, and other major Russian cities. Resentful of his fait accompli, and restive for economic modernization and a more serious effort to combat corruption, they helped deliver a blow to his ruling party in the December 2011 Duma elections, which won only 49 percent of the vote, far less than its 64 percent total in 2007. When allegations of vote rigging and manipulation to produce even that unimpressive result began to build immediately after the elections, tens of thousands of demonstrators marched in the streets of Moscow and St. Petersburg in protest. Putin was surprised, angry, and more than a little unnerved.[10] By instinct and professional training a control freak, he was discovering that the growing middle class that he had helped create over the last decade wanted more than just consumerism. It also wanted a political voice.

I warned Clinton that there was more combustibility ahead. Putin and the tough guys around him were likely to invent or exaggerate American involvement in Russian affairs, partly to deflect attention from the unexpected domestic storm he had barreled into. It didn't take long for that to materialize. When Clinton made public comments critical of the conduct of the Duma elections—consistent in tone and substance with what we would have said in similar circumstances anyplace in the world—Putin lashed out, accusing her of sending the "signal" that drew demonstrators into the streets, and the State Department of quietly supporting opposition parties. Putin had a remarkable capacity for storing up grievances and slights and assembling them to fit his narrative of the West trying to keep Russia down. Clinton's criticism would rank high in his litany—and generate a personal animus that led directly to his meddling against her candidacy in the 2016 U.S. presidential election. Putin was an apostle of payback.

In early January 2012, Mike McFaul walked into this nasty set of circumstances as our new ambassador to Russia. He was well prepared for the job—an excellent Russian speaker with long years of experience in Russian affairs, and the White House architect of the reset. By the time of his arrival in Moscow, however, the Kremlin was in an increasingly edgy and vindictive mood, and Mike's hopes to start slowly and tread carefully proved elusive. I wanted him to get off on a good footing, and I intended to use a long-planned visit to help. The inadvertent result, however, was to help make his life even more complicated.

I arrived in Moscow during McFaul's first week as ambassador. We made the rounds of senior officials in the Kremlin and the Foreign Ministry, and encountered nothing unusual in our conversations. On my second morning, just before my departure, we met first with a group of political opposition leaders and then with a number of civil society activists. These kinds of sessions were a regular part of any such visit, and I had taken part in them throughout many years of service at the embassy and as a visitor from Washington. I don't recall much that was unusual about those conversations either, nor did we go out of our way to call attention to them. We mostly listened.

The Kremlin was poised to seize on any such contacts, however routine, as evidence of American plotting. State television ran a long, vituperative piece that same night, alleging that Russian opposition-ists had come to see Mike and me to "get their instructions" for the further disruption of Russian politics. This began a carefully choreo-graphed campaign against McFaul, whose proud history prior to gov-ernment service of study and support for democracy movements made him a convenient target for the Kremlin. As Medvedev and Surkov later acknowledged, McFaul's arrival was a perfect opportu-nity to manufacture a narrative about American meddling and rouse Putin's nationalistic political base in the run-up to the March presi-dential elections.[11] The nastiness never stopped, continuing long after Putin's election. It was a campaign clearly planned before McFaul's arrival or my visit, and would have been triggered at some early point. I just wish I hadn't provided such an immediate and visible trigger.

Relations relapsed quickly in 2012. Putin returned as president after winning 63 percent of the vote in March, but pointedly declined to come to the G-8 summit in Washington in May, sending Medve-dev instead. We were increasingly at loggerheads over how to manage the reverberations of the Arab Spring as the Kremlin clung to its cli-ent in Damascus and resisted outside pressure for a political transi-tion. With American support, Russia finally joined the World Trade Organization in August. That forced the issue of repeal of the Jackson-Vanik Amendment, without which the United States couldn't benefit from Russia's WTO accession. Repeal also reinforced a push in Con-gress to hit back at the Russian leadership in other ways—especially through the passage of the Magnitsky Act in December, which sanctioned Russian officials implicated in the terrible prison death of a young lawyer who had uncovered evidence of high-level corruption.

Just before stepping down as secretary of state in February 2013, Clinton sent a memo to President Obama cautioning that relations with Russia would get worse before they got better, and that Putin's return to the Kremlin had brought the curtain down on the reset. We would still manage to work with the Russians on the Iran nuclear negotiations, and Clinton's successor, John Kerry, would labor mightily to reach an understanding with Moscow on Syria. But the overall downward drift was hard to brake. In August 2013, the Russians granted temporary asylum to Edward Snowden, the former U.S. intelligence contractor who had leaked massive amounts of highly classified material, infuriating Washington. In response, Obama canceled a planned bilateral summit with Putin on the margins of a G-20 meeting in St. Petersburg in September. It seemed like we had hit bottom in the relationship.

Then Putin's pugnacity in Ukraine took us much deeper. Throughout 2013, the plodding, corrupt Yanukovich government in Kyiv was the object of a tug-of-war between the European Union and Russia. The EU sought to engage Ukraine in an association agreement, the first step on a long and uncertain road to membership. Putin's main geopolitical aspiration was the formation of the Eurasian Economic Union, a collection of former Soviet states that Russia could control— and that would be hollow without Ukraine. For Putin, Ukraine would never be just another country and tethering it to the West was an existential issue for him. He was determined to play hardball, convinced that Russia's future as a great power depended upon predominant influence in Ukraine. Yanukovich, whom Putin viewed as weak-willed, predictably vacillated, torn between his Russian patrons and a population solidly in favor of association with the EU and the long-term economic benefits that would flow from it. Finally, he backed away from a scheduled signing event with the EU in late November and accepted a $15 billion subsidy from Putin to opt for the Eurasian Economic Union.

Disgruntled Ukrainians poured into the Maidan, the historic main square in Kyiv, setting up camp and venting their frustration with Yanukovich. A full-fledged political crisis ensued. Violence broke out in February 2014, with government snipers killing several protestors and hard-right oppositionists responsible for the deaths of a number of police officers. An EU mediation effort produced a last-minute agreement to deescalate, but Yanukovich—by now fearful for his own life—fled to eastern Ukraine and then across the border to Russia. The protestors celebrated, the Rada impeached Yanukovich and elected an interim president, and this all seemed to be yet another historic chance for Ukrainians to shape a more promising future.

At that moment, I was in Sochi, leading the U.S. delegation to the closing ceremony of the 2014 Winter Olympics. Mike McFaul was there with me, only a couple days from the end of his tour in Moscow. We quickly agreed that Putin wasn't going to accept quietly the demise of Yanukovich and all his hopes for a deferential Ukraine. We tried to arrange a meeting with Putin in Sochi, but he was in no mood to talk. The White House asked me to stop in Kyiv, which I did two days later. The mood was exuberant but apprehensive, with senior officials worried about what Putin might do next. I went down to the Maidan one cold evening and visited the makeshift medical clinic that had been set up by protesters at St. Michael's Monastery near the square. You could feel the pride among the volunteer doctors and nurses, and the wounded demonstrators who were still there. I told Secretary Kerry that I thought this might be the moment when Ukraine got it right. It seemed that hope might finally triumph over experience in a country whose landscape was littered with two decades of political failure, squabbling leaders, endemic corruption, Russian meddling, and unfulfilled expectations.

Soon after I left Kyiv, Russia's "little green men" began to appear

in Crimea, the first of a wave of Russian military and security personnel in unmarked uniforms who would occupy Ukraine's Crimean
Peninsula. Putin formally announced the annexation of Crimea in
mid-March, and stepped up Russian military and separatist activity
in the Donbass, the heavily industrialized swath of southeastern
Ukraine long home to many ethnic Russians. Putin's message was
typically unsubtle: If Russia couldn't have a deferential government
in Kyiv, plan B was a dysfunctional Ukraine, in which the Kremlin
used an annexed Crimea and a violent and unstable Donbass to exert
leverage over Kyiv. The Western response was a series of sanctions
against Russia, demonstrating a solidarity between the United States
and key European allies that Putin didn't expect. It helped blunt his
push into the Donbass and relieve the pressure on Kyiv, even if it
could do little in the short term to reverse the annexation of Crimea.

In the early summer of 2014, after a difficult phone call between
Obama and Putin, I was sent along with Jake Sullivan, then the national security advisor to Vice President Biden, to meet quietly with
two senior Russian representatives—one from the Foreign Ministry
and the other from the Kremlin—and see if back-channel conversations might lead anywhere useful, particularly on the Ukraine crisis.
Over a long day in Geneva, at a hotel overlooking the lake, we went
round and round. The senior Russian diplomat was an old friend, but
had little to offer. The Kremlin official specialized in Borscht Belt
humor and meandering, politically incorrect stories about Russia and
its neighbors. Echoing Vladimir Putin to George W. Bush in 2008, he
insisted that "you Americans don't understand that Ukraine is not a
real country. Some parts are really Central Europe, and some are
really Russian, and very little is actually Ukrainian. Don't kid yourselves." His smarmy, patronizing air wasn't very endearing. "And you
shouldn't kid yourselves," I replied. "You've managed to create an even
stronger sense of Ukrainian nationalism than existed before. You've
swallowed up two million Crimeans, but made the other forty-two

million people a lot more Ukrainian, and a lot more determined to keep out from under your influence."

Jake and I took turns losing our patience as the day wore on and the conversation went nowhere. We left discouraged about the near-term prospects for implementation of the Minsk agreement that the Germans and French had been hammering out with the Russians and Ukrainians. Our bigger concern was that the Russians might up the ante and increase military pressure in the Donbass rather than deescalate. We sent a note back to the president that night outlining the Russian failure to take seriously this back channel and our own failure to convince them of the wisdom of taking the diplomatic off-ramp we tried to telegraph.

The reset was long dead.

* * *

THE ARC OF relations with Russia in the Obama era was achingly familiar. Inheriting the mutual acrimony of the war in Georgia, Obama made some tangible early progress in the relationship. We took significant strides together on Iran, Afghanistan, and strategic arms reductions. We helped the Russians finally overcome the last barriers to formal WTO accession, but never succeeded in putting much economic weight in the relationship, certainly not compared to China, nor even to the halting promise of economic ties with India. Early cooperation between us in response to the Arab Spring collapsed in recrimination, especially over Libya. For all the potential of the president's rapport with Dmitry Medvedev, we were never able to sustain an effective connection to Putin. There was also a certain hubris in the notion that we could somehow enhance Medvedev's political position by investing in the relationship between Obama and someone so utterly dependent on Putin for his role and influence.

While he was intrigued by Obama initially, it remained for Putin a matter of both conviction and convenience to paint the United States as a hostile force, maneuvering to undermine Russia's influence in its neighborhood and his own grip at home. Putin had created a trap for himself and for Russia; willful failure to diversify the economy and adopt the rule of law led to slow stagnation, from which foreign adventure offered only a temporary diversion. Like the experience of George W. Bush, early potential in U.S.-Russian relations was eclipsed by a relapse, and a new post–Cold War low. It was a pattern that hinted sometimes at historical immutability. It was also, however, the product of the personalities, preconceptions, disconnects, and choices of leaders on both sides. Like the rest of post–Cold War relations between Russia and the United States, it was a fascinating—and often depressing—story.

Obama's effort to keep pace with a changing international landscape and invest energy and political capital in shaping relations with that landscape's most significant players was admirable. Unlike George H. W. Bush, he was not moving from a world of bipolarity to rising unipolarity, but from a world of diminishing unipolarity to something far messier. It was a time for big bets, like the rebalance to Asia and the strategic partnership with India, both wise and well executed, if less ambitious and complete than initially hoped. It was a time for steadiness in dealing with China, and patient effort to avoid unnecessary collisions. It was also a time to test the proposition of more stable relations with Russia and hard-nosed cooperation on issues of shared interest.

For all the agility and imagination of the time, we didn't have the freedom to play our diplomatic cards like Bush 41. Diplomacy could open doors, or prevent them from slamming shut, but ultimately others had to decide whether to walk through them. Obama hoped that this new era of U.S. leadership would unleash faster and more dramatic adjustments. History had other ideas.

8

The Arab Spring: When the
Short Game Intercedes

ON THE AFTERNOON of February 1, 2011, President Obama joined his senior advisors in the Situation Room to review the unfolding drama of Egypt's revolution. He was pensive and steady, seized by the sense of possibility for Egypt and the region but sober about all the ways in which things could go wrong—for them and for us. "I'm worried that Mubarak is falling farther and farther behind events," he said. "I don't want us to."

A week into the revolution, the crowd in Tahrir Square had swelled to nearly one hundred thousand defiant and determined people. Now in his early eighties, President Mubarak was weary after three decades in power but stubbornly convinced that he knew what was best for Egypt. A lot was at stake. Since the 1979 peace treaty with Israel, Egypt had been a centerpiece of American strategy in the Middle East. It was a reliable security partner in the region, despite continuing political and economic corrosion at home. The compact between rulers and ruled had become more brittle, with the benefits of economic growth limited to a privileged few, a leadership growing more remote, and a young population increasingly consumed by a sense of indignity—fueled by their mounting awareness in a digital world of what others had that they did not.

Over the previous few days, Obama and Hillary Clinton had pressed Mubarak to address the legitimate demands of the protestors, indicate that he would step down soon, disavow any inclination to install his son as successor, and begin a shift to a new, democratically elected government. His fate was sealed. The scale and persistence of the protests made that clear. The hope was that Mubarak would come to grips with reality and set in motion an orderly transition. But he was not ready to go nearly that far. Hoping to stunt the momentum of the protests, he took the modest step of filling the long-vacant vice presidency with his intelligence chief, Omar Suleiman. Mubarak was reluctant to concede more, even as the ground continued to shift rapidly beneath him.

The Situation Room meeting began with an update from our embassy in Cairo, an intelligence assessment, and a review of the diplomatic state of play. An hour in, word was passed to the president that Mubarak was about to make a hastily arranged televised address. Hopeful that the Egyptian leader was finally ready to move, Obama interrupted the meeting to turn on CNN's live coverage, and we all sat there, watching expectantly. Secretary Clinton stood next to the president, clutching a cup of coffee from the White House Mess. Those around the table contorted their heads every which way to catch a glimpse of the television. Tom Donilon, seated to the left of the president, didn't even bother. He knew what was coming.

Predictably, Mubarak offered half a loaf. He promised not to run again in the fall elections, but had nothing to say about not grooming his son as successor or beginning to transfer some of his powers in the meantime. "That won't cut it," Obama concluded. The television screen faded to black, and the room fell quiet. Obama, as he often did, went around the table and asked us to offer our views on whether to ask the Egyptian leader to leave office now. There was no disagreement —our entreaties were falling on deaf ears in Cairo, and our hopes for an orderly transition were fading. The president decided to call Mubarak and press him to step down immediately, while he could still shape a transition and avoid greater chaos and violence.

I joined the president and several of his White House aides in the Oval Office for the call. I always admired how any president managed to focus on a phone conversation with a foreign leader with so many aides buzzing around. Donilon, Denis McDonough, and Deputy National Security Advisor Ben Rhodes were huddled in one corner looking over the president's talking points. The president's two senior Middle East advisors, Dennis Ross and Dan Shapiro, took notes furiously against the back of the Oval Office couch, where Chief of Staff Bill Daley was sitting and listening intently. Robert Gibbs, the president's spokesperson, shed his suit jacket and began to pace. Obama was leaning back in his chair, legs crossed, working through his argument.

As I stood off to the side listening, I could piece together Mubarak's patronizing and inflexible response. The Egyptian leader thought Obama was hopelessly naïve—unaware of just how indispensable Mubarak was to order in Egypt. As the call continued, I could see Obama's frustration rising, and I couldn't help thinking of scenes I had witnessed there going back to the Reagan administration. Each of Obama's recent predecessors had been sucked, some more willingly than others, into the morass of a region that remorselessly drained their political capital and consumed their attention.

Obama had entered office determined to change the terms of American involvement in the Middle East. He had no illusions about massive disengagement from a region he knew he couldn't ignore; what he sought was a different kind of engagement, a reversal of the unilateral and overly militarized habits of his predecessor. He would wind down America's troop presence in Iraq, rely on a smaller counterterrorism footprint made up of drones and special operations forces, and place a bigger emphasis on diplomacy to deal with Iran's nuclear program and the Israeli-Palestinian peace process. He would shift more of America's strategic bets to Asia, and a whole range of other pressing global questions, like nuclear nonproliferation and climate change, that had sometimes been neglected or undermined in the decade since 9/11. But now the Arab Spring, the revolutionary drama of which Egypt was only one act, was inexorably tugging him back to the crisis-driven Middle East focus that he had hoped so much to escape.

* * *

THE BRITISH PRIME minister Harold Macmillan may or may not have actually said, in response to a question about what most affects the course of government strategies, "Events, dear boy, events." But it's an apt observation. Statesmen rarely succeed if they don't have a sense of strategy—a set of assumptions about the world they seek to navigate, clear purposes and priorities, means matched to ends, and the discipline required to hold all those pieces together and stay focused. They also, however, have to be endlessly adaptable—quick to adjust to the unexpected, massage the anxieties of allies and partners, maneuver past adversaries, and manage change rather than be paralyzed by it. "Events" can create openings and opportunities; they can just as easily reveal the limits of even the most thoughtful and nuanced strategies. Playing the long game is essential, but it's the short game— coping with stuff that happens unexpectedly—that preoccupies policymakers and often shapes their legacies.

The Middle East is particularly challenging terrain for American strategy. By the time the revolts of the Arab Spring began to erupt, the region had twice as many people as it did when I arrived at my first post in Amman in the early 1980s. Sixty percent of the population was under the age of twenty-five, and it was urbanizing nearly as fast as Asia. Job markets couldn't cope, and youth unemployment ran higher than in any other part of the world. Corruption was endemic. The emerging middle class was frustrated, with economic growth siphoned to elites. Arab political systems were almost uniformly authoritarian, generally repressive and unresponsive to demands for political dignity and better governance. A generational change in leaderships had been under way for more than a decade, but hopes of new directions wilted quickly. Educational systems had little to offer young people eager to compete in a relentless twenty-first-century world, and the deficit in women's rights was robbing societies of half their potential.

The Arab order in early 2011 was still one that had the United States as its principal frame of reference. The Arab street despised most aspects of American policy, whether in Iraq or Palestine or else-where, and its leaders resented the Bush 43 administration's crusades and blunders. They were, however, accustomed to America's central-ity in their world, schizophrenic in their simultaneous resentments and expectations of American influence. They continually exagger-ated our ability to affect events, and we did the same.

We also both underestimated how unsettling a changing Ameri-can role might be. When Obama laid out his broad strategy for the region in an eloquent speech in Cairo in June 2009, the immediate reaction across the Arab world was enthusiastic. He was the anti-Bush—in tone and substance. He promised a "new beginning," and conveyed an understanding of the many ills of the Arab world, and a realization that jobs, security, opportunity, and dignity were the keys to a better order, not democratization through the barrel of a gun. Many Arab leaders, not surprisingly, cherry-picked from the speech—embracing Obama's willingness to reexamine America's role while ignoring his call for them to undergo their own reexamination. His message also inflated expectations in Washington and the region far beyond his ability to deliver. That was certainly true when his early efforts to bridge Israeli-Palestinian differences ran aground on Bibi Netanyahu's artful intransigence, the habitual inclinations of an aging Palestinian leadership, and the lack of interest of most of the Arab states in investing in the issue. It was true when it became clear that there was little appetite and even fewer resources to support political and economic reform more robustly and creatively. And it became even more evident when another element of Obama's Middle East policy came into sharper focus—his intention to reduce our military role and shift America's strategic investments to other parts of the world.

Extricating ourselves from the central security role to which regimes had become accustomed proved far harder than Obama anticipated. Nervous Arab autocrats feared American abandonment nearly as much as the reckless exercise of our power. The new U.S. administration discovered that it was tied to the old regional order in more ways than it had first thought. When the early rumblings of the Arab revolts began, the difficulty of the trade-offs between significant security relationships and aspirations for change—and the sheer unpredictability and erratic course of events—became painfully apparent.

Few people in the Obama or George W. Bush administrations needed to be persuaded of the fragilities of the Arab political and economic order. Obama's Cairo speech made clear his concerns. Clinton was even more pointed in an address she gave in Doha in January 2011, just a dozen days before Tahrir Square erupted, warning that "the region's foundations are sinking into the sand." After 9/11 and the Bush administration's shift from a traditional Republican foreign policy of restraint and containment to unilateralism and preemption, Secretary Rice had spoken bluntly about the weaknesses of autocratic rule, and the risks of confusing authoritarian order with stability. It was the right message; after the Iraq War, however, the Bush administration was the wrong messenger.

Career diplomats in the Middle East had been arguing for decades that stability was not a static phenomenon, and that the United States shouldn't be blind to changes that were inevitable. I had tried to make the same arguments going back to my time as a junior officer in Jordan in the early 1980s. Like many of my colleagues, I continued to make them from the Policy Planning Staff, as an ambassador in the region, and from the Near Eastern Affairs bureau. None of this was particularly new.

What was new, and profoundly challenging, was the speed with which change moved once it began—propelled by advances in technology and social media. On December 17, 2010, Mohamed Bouazizi, a twenty-six-year-old proprietor of a street stall, self-immolated outside a local municipal building in Tunisia, in a desperate final protest against the harassment of local police. Demonstrations and violent clashes followed, spreading rapidly across the country. Within a month, President Zine El Abidine Ben Ali fled, and secular and Islamist oppositionists began to negotiate transitional arrangements. When I visited shortly thereafter, my report to Secretary Clinton was cautiously upbeat: "Tunisia's revolution is still incomplete, and its transition only just begun, but so far Tunisians are handling the challenges before them with more steadiness than most would have imagined before Ben Ali's sudden ouster, and considerable national pride in being the first of the Arabs to set out to reclaim their sense of dignity."[1]

The revolution in Tunisia quickly spread to the biggest and most consequential Arab state of all, Egypt. On January 25, the first crowds began to form in Tahrir Square, calling for extensive reforms and the end of Mubarak's rule. Most of the protestors were young, peaceful, passionate, tech-savvy, and energized by what had happened in Tunisia. The scenes were incredibly powerful, especially for someone like me, who had walked on that square and long admired Egyptians and the stoicism with which they coped with poverty and an overweening state. This all seemed hopeful, a genuine bottom-up movement to bend the arc of history. But events were soon to get a lot more complicated.

* * *

THE FIRST OFFICIAL American reactions to the Tahrir demonstrations were guarded. Egypt had weathered countless political storms over seven millennia, and after thirty years in power Mubarak's rule seemed tattered but durable. The military was the one truly national institution. It was vested in the status quo, and in the large slice of the Egyptian economic pie that it possessed. The United States was similarly vested in that status quo, with $1.3 billion in military aid and a substantial economic assistance program reinforcing Egypt's willingness to keep the peace with Israel, allow the American military access and overflight rights, share information about regional threats, and cooperate (more often than not) diplomatically.

In the initial aftermath of the January 25 protests, Clinton said in a press conference, with more hope than conviction, that "our assessment is that the Egyptian government is stable and is looking for ways to respond to the legitimate needs and interests of the Egyptian people." Vice President Biden said he "would not refer to Mubarak as a dictator."[2] Obama himself, mindful of what the United States had at stake, and of growing agitation among regional leaders desperately hoping that the Arab Spring fever would break in Egypt, shared the instinctive caution of his most senior advisors.

That all changed swiftly over the next week. While the armed forces kept a studied distance, Egyptian police and security forces clamped down hard, beating and arresting hundreds of protestors. After Obama's early calls failed to make a dent in Mubarak's thinking, and after Suleiman's appointment as vice president failed to impress the Tahrir crowds, concerns in the administration grew. On the Sunday talk shows on January 30, Clinton dodged questions about whether Mubarak should resign, but emphasized the need for an "orderly transition," warning of the dangers of chaos in the absence of a careful process.

Her comments masked an increasingly uneasy debate in unending meetings that week in the Situation Room, as some of the president's younger advisors pressed for a more forceful stance. At different times and in different ways, Susan Rice (then ambassador to the United Nations), Ben Rhodes, and Samantha Power (then a senior

NSC staff official) all argued that the United States risked being "on the wrong side of history," and should identify itself much more clearly with the demands of the protestors and insist publicly upon Mubarak's immediate resignation. Biden, Clinton, Gates, and Donilon were more wary, concerned about the consequences of too strong an American push on Mubarak, both in Egypt and in the wider region.[3]

I understood the power of what was unfolding in Tahrir Square, and the injustices and indignities that so energized the protestors. It was clear to me that Mubarak had to go; the question was how to get him to move before events overtook whatever agency he still had left. I was skeptical of the "right side of history" argument, simply because in my own experience in the Middle East, history rarely moved in a straight line. Revolutions were complicated, and most often ended messily, with the best-organized rather than the best-intentioned reaping the immediate gains.

Riding back with Clinton from yet another White House meeting that week, I suggested sending a private envoy to see Mubarak and deliver a firm message from the president. It would be a last effort to persuade him to agree to step down before we would have to call for his departure explicitly and publicly. The emissary needed to be someone Mubarak knew and trusted. I mentioned Frank Wisner, a retired diplomat who had grown close to Mubarak as ambassador in Cairo in the late 1980s. Clinton liked the concept, and recommended it to the president, who agreed. Wisner met with Mubarak in Cairo on Monday, January 31, and conveyed a set of points that mirrored what the president had conveyed in earlier calls. A savvy and vastly experienced diplomat, Wisner found the points prepared by the NSC staff to be painfully precise—like the helpful prompt to "pause for reaction" after the initial passage—but delivered the message faithfully and effectively. He reported that he thought Mubarak would be responsive.

He was not. Mubarak continued to offer too little too late, to take steps that even a week earlier might have had some chance of producing a dignified departure for him, and the more orderly transition for Egypt that we sought. The situation worsened on February 2, when thugs supporting Mubarak rode camels and horses into Tahrir Square, clubbing and beating demonstrators. Appalled, the White House stepped up its rhetoric, pressing the case for Mubarak to begin the transition "now," but stopped just short of calling for his immediate exit.

Wisner inadvertently complicated matters further when he said publicly in a video appearance at the Munich Security Conference on February 5 that he believed it was "critical" that Mubarak stay in office until the fall elections to steer the transition. He was speaking as a private citizen, but by this point his trip to Cairo had become public and it was easy for people to confuse his views with those of the administration. For exactly that reason, we had urged him not to do the Munich appearance, but evidently not strongly enough. The president and Donilon were furious, and Jake Sullivan and I tried to outdo one another's contrition in the immediate aftermath. I wrote to Jake that evening that he should shoot me if I ever suggested another emissary.

The Egyptian president gave another televised speech on February 10, a meandering and embarrassing performance that did nothing to ease the intensifying anger of the protestors. The armed forces, under Defense Minister Mohamed Hussein Tantawi, finally made clear to Mubarak that they would no longer defend him, and that it was time to step down. He resigned on February 11, handed power over to the military, and flew off to his residence in the Sinai resort town of Sharm el-Sheikh. The Mubarak era was over. The scenes of jubilation in Tahrir Square were as remarkable as they were heartening. It was hard not to feel hopeful, and the president had steered U.S. interests through extremely complicated terrain as skillfully as anyone could have. In many respects, however, the challenge for American policy was just beginning.

The Supreme Council of the Armed Forces (SCAF), led by Tantawi, became the interim arbiter of governance, and pledged early elections for a new civilian government. Inevitably, there was a certain amount of well-intentioned flailing around in Washington as we sought to stay in touch with Egyptian officers and officials. At one particularly prolonged Deputies Committee meeting, we set off on a wild exercise in Rolodex diplomacy, with agencies tasked with compiling lists of virtually every Egyptian who had ever been to a U.S. military staff college or on an exchange program. I pointed out that that was what we had an embassy for, but in the characteristically American rush to "do something," a pile of spreadsheets with phone numbers was dutifully compiled and then largely neglected. It was an early indication of the White House's understandable but ultimately self-injurious instinct to micromanage from Washington and underutilize its embassies abroad.

In addition to the challenges of Egypt's transition, we faced an extremely nervous group of regional leaders. Mubarak's overthrow was stunning for them, and many would remain bitter for years about perceived American disloyalty. In a long conversation with me a few months later, King Abdullah of Saudi Arabia was blunt: "You abandoned your best friend. If you had stood firmly with Mubarak right at the beginning, he would still be with us."

My arguments made little difference to Saudi leaders who saw the fires of the Arab Spring burning all around them, with unrest already breaking out in Bahrain and Yemen. The truth was that it was beyond America's power to throw Mubarak under the bus; powered by decades of repression and corruption, the bus was already rolling over him by the time Obama called for transition. I flew quietly to Amman on February 12, the day after Mubarak's resignation, to encourage King Abdullah to stay ahead of the wave of change. It was our most direct conversation in nearly two decades, and he said he was already thinking about steps that he might take to open up Jordan's political and economic systems.

I visited Cairo on February 21–22, the first senior American official to arrive since the revolution. The mood in Tahrir Square was exuberant, with thousands of people still camped out, reveling in a national pride that many had never felt before. Walking along the Nile corniche to the Foreign Ministry, we passed piles of barbed wire and dozens of armored vehicles in front of the partially burned-out state television building. Banks had reopened without a disastrous run on the Egyptian pound, and the economy was sputtering back to life. "The political class," I wrote to Clinton, "is filled with genuine enthusiasts for change, as well as ex post facto revolutionaries, eager to declare their heretofore well-concealed antipathy for the Mubarak regime and claim that they were really with the revolutionaries in Tahrir Square all along."[4]

I cautioned, however, that "expectations are unrealistically high." The military leadership was struggling with transparency, a concept that didn't come naturally. A number of political leaders were worried by the military's rush to hand off to civilian rule. Cramming constitutional revisions and parliamentary and presidential elections into the next year, I predicted, would "benefit only the Muslim Brotherhood and the remnants of the NDP [the old official party]—the only organized parties on the playing field for early Parliamentary elections."[5]

The youth leaders I met, many of whom had orchestrated the sweeping Tahrir Square movement, were equally skeptical of the SCAF and the United States. Their energy and commitment were apparent and admirable, but they were already struggling to translate their success on the street into results at the ballot box. Organizing effective political parties was proving much harder than mobilizing crowds at Tahrir. They were determined to break down the web of privilege and protection that the elite had long enjoyed under Mubarak, but unsure how to get started. Still a little surprised at how quickly their movement had toppled a president, they were—like most revolutionaries in the first flush of victory—starting to squabble among themselves.

Secretary Clinton traveled to Egypt in March, and I returned in

June and then again in January 2012. Several other senior American officials came through as well, doing our best to amplify the hard work of an embassy constrained by security conditions, reduced staffing levels, and the ordered departure of family members. We tried to help bolster economic confidence, but offered more free advice than tangible assistance—limited partly by the reluctance of the SCAF to risk necessary reforms, and partly by budgetary stringency and partisan paralysis in a Washington still working its way out of the 2008 recession. Our message on the political side was also a bit conflicted. On the one hand, we emphasized to the SCAF the dangers of moving to elections too quickly, before giving a chance for new political parties to organize. On the other hand, we worried about the perpetuation of military rule, especially as intermittent violence continued, with the U.S.-supplied Egyptian security forces at center stage. A rapid move to civilian rule seemed attractive from that point of view. In the end, it probably didn't make much difference what we thought, since the SCAF was anxious to make a handoff and get out of the unaccustomed political limelight, and the Egyptian public even more sensitive than before the revolution about foreign encroachment.

President Obama made a speech at the State Department in May 2011, highlighting our support for post-revolutionary transitions in Egypt and Tunisia, as well as outlining longer-term strategy for the region and the Israeli-Palestinian peace process. The tone of his remarks was pitch perfect, making clear our intention to support forces for reform. There was little to offer, however, beyond words. The speech reflected Obama's fidelity to his long-game strategy and the priorities that underpinned it; his sober sense about the generational nature of the unfolding challenge and steep near-term odds facing voices of openness and pluralism; the risk of making the Arab Spring about us, as opposed to about the people in the region; and the harsh reality that the political and fiscal climates at home would in any case prevent the administration from providing anything close to the kind of support transitional regimes needed over the long term.

After my June 2011 trip, I told Clinton and the White House what they already suspected: Further progress toward a successful democratic transition was "certainly not a sure thing now."[6] When I came back to Cairo in early 2012, parliamentary elections had produced a strong showing by the Muslim Brotherhood (MB), which had won nearly half of the seats in the lower house. Combined with another quarter of the seats won by Salafists, the result was a dramatic victory for Islamist parties. The United States had largely avoided interaction with the Brotherhood up to this point, both because of their anti-American ideology and in deference to Mubarak. The Brotherhood reciprocated our reluctance and suspicion, but they had clearly emerged as a political force in Egypt, and I was authorized along with our new ambassador in Cairo, Anne Patterson, to meet with senior MB representatives and test the waters.

Our first encounter was in a nondescript office at the headquarters of the Brotherhood's Freedom and Justice Party, in downtown Cairo. Our host was Mohamed Morsi, the party's secretary-general and nominal head. Short and stocky, with a trim black beard, Morsi was circumspect, as unsure of how to approach a meeting with Americans as we were with him. While he had studied at the University of Southern California decades before, Morsi's English was halting, and he stuck to Arabic in our conversation. I stressed that the United States had no business backing particular parties in Egypt; what we supported was a broader evolution toward democratic institutions, shaped by Egyptians themselves. I emphasized that we hoped to sustain partnership with Egypt, in our mutual self-interest, built around economic progress for Egyptians, regional security, and continued adherence to existing agreements, especially the Egyptian-Israeli peace treaty. Morsi said that was all consistent with the Brotherhood's outlook, but I left our meeting not entirely convinced. It was a bit surreal sitting with Morsi and two of his colleagues, who had probably done a total among them of forty or fifty years in Mubarak-era jails. They had been on their best behavior, but it was hard to tell whether to take self-avowed moderation at face value, or whether it cloaked a more complicated agenda. They were a movement used to life in the shadows, distrustful of outsiders, and not inclined to share power once they obtained it.

My overall impression of Egypt a year after the revolution was decidedly mixed. It was, I told Clinton, "a pretty confused place."[7] The economy was sliding, with the SCAF tarnished and uncertain and the revolutionary youth who dominated Tahrir Square a frustrated and politically disconnected bunch. Meanwhile, some senior civilians in the interim government overseen by the SCAF had decided to burnish their own revolutionary and popular anti-American credentials instead of moving swiftly on reform. Chief among them was Minister of International Development Fayza Abul Naga, a longtime Mubarak supporter who had, I suspected, quickly turned his photo face first against her office wall when he was deposed. She instigated trumped-up cases against a number of American NGOs, eventually resulting in the arrests and detentions of several U.S. citizens, which we labored for months to undo.

Contrary to initial MB promises that they wouldn't run a candidate in the June 2012 presidential elections, the Freedom and Justice Party put forward Morsi as its nominee. Supported in no small part by Qatar, and to a lesser degree Turkey, he won by a narrow margin, revealing a deeply polarized electorate. I visited in early July, soon after his inauguration, and Clinton returned later that month. We urged him to govern inclusively, focus on the economy, and stick to the treaty with Israel. He was careful about the last point, not interfering with the operational channels that the Egyptian military and intelligence services maintained with the Israelis, and working constructively with Clinton to avert a major Israeli clash with Hamas in Gaza in November. Morsi, however, got nowhere on the economy, and was a disaster at inclusive governance. He and the MB had no experience running public-sector institutions, and little interest in sharing the burden with other politicians or technocrats. Late in the fall, he began an effort to further revise the constitution to entrench presidential prerogatives, and in turn the Brotherhood's centrality in Egyptian politics.

By the spring of 2013, tensions were rising rapidly. Street demonstrations intensified, drawing together a flammable mix of disgruntled revolutionary youth and Cairenes frustrated by economic decline and two years of uncertainty. The armed forces, now led by General Abdel Fattah el-Sisi, hung back at first, always anxious to protect their reputation. After massive street protests in late June, however, Sisi decided to act. Morsi was arrested on July 3, and the military again took power. Most of the Egyptian public seemed relieved, eager for order and predictability, the luster of their revolution long worn away.

Sisi moved quickly to crush the Brotherhood, encouraged by Saudi Arabia and the UAE, both of whom poured billions of dollars into stabilizing the Egyptian economy. The military's actions clearly fit the classic definition of a coup, notwithstanding the considerable popular support for Sisi's decision. Under U.S. law, formally designating Sisi's intervention as a coup would have required an automatic cutoff of U.S. security and economic assistance. The president was unhappy with the military's move, which set a complicated precedent in a region still in the throes of revolts of various stripes and guaranteed even greater polarization in Egyptian society and ever greater civilian strife. He was also mindful, however, of the mood of the Egyptian public, our continuing reliance on security partnership with Egypt, and the value of retaining some leverage over Sisi and a postrevolutionary transition that seemed unending.

We spent long hours in the Situation Room trying to thread the needle and avoid cessation of assistance. Lawyers and those of us pretending to be lawyers edited and reedited formulas we thought could finesse the problem. Finally, we split the difference. The White House asserted that no judgment on whether this was a coup or not was required by law, and therefore it was choosing not to choose. Looking back, we should have simply given a straight answer, called the coup a coup, and then worked with Congress to avoid the blunt tool of complete aid suspension. Instead, to make clear his displeasure with the coup that wasn't a coup, and the subsequent steps Sisi took against the Muslim Brotherhood, the president suspended shipment of certain weapons systems, including F-16s and M1A1 tanks, which were never essential to Egypt's main security priority—fighting a growing Islamist insurgency in the Sinai. In the end, we won favor with no one and managed to antagonize just about everyone—besieged Islamists, repressed revolutionaries, our regional friends and partners, and of course the Egyptian military and Congress.

* * *

SECRETARY KERRY ASKED me to return to Egypt and assess the situation, which I did in mid-July, ten days or so after Sisi overthrew Morsi. I found Sisi in a not-so-conciliatory mood. Some in his new interim government, like Vice President Mohamed ElBaradei, the former IAEA head, advocated a focus on economic recovery, renewing the political transition, and leaving the door open to the Brotherhood to reenter politics in the future. In our conversation, Sisi was unmoved by that view, and dismissive of differences within the Brotherhood over how to approach its predicament and whether to try to sustain itself as a political party. He was already enamored of his popular standing and taken by his image as the man on the white horse. Seemingly overnight, his photos appeared on walls all over Cairo. Dressed in uniform, his eyes hidden behind 1970s-era Arab strongman sunglasses, he exuded an air of mystery and command. More trouble was already brewing, with thousands of Brotherhood members and their families camped out at Raba'a Square in central Cairo, demanding Morsi's release and reinstatement. I told Kerry that this was not going to end well.

The secretary sent me back to Cairo again in August to try to dampen tensions. I spent the next eight days working with a European Union counterpart, Bernardino Leon, whose optimism and persistence in trying to find ways to deescalate had an infectious effect on me—but not on Sisi or the Brotherhood leadership. We shuttled back and forth between Sisi and two former MB government ministers who had not yet been arrested and were still in touch with their underground leaders, including the aging MB Supreme Guide. They were, however, unable to talk to either Morsi, who had been moved to a prison in Alexandria, or Khairat el-Shater, the Deputy Supreme Guide and number two in the organization, now in Cairo's notorious Tora Prison. The two former ministers agreed to consider an initial series of confidence-building measures at Raba'a—moving people out of the square, in return for a thinning out of security forces in the area and the opening of a dialogue with the new government. They also sought the release of a senior MB official at Tora, Saad al-Katatni, as a gesture of goodwill, and to create a more authoritative channel for further discussions with Sisi and his subordinates. Sisi was reluctant to agree to any of this, distrustful of the MB and inclined to press his advantage. He seemed slightly more open at the outset on the issue of Katatni, but within a few days had lost interest in that too.

We did manage to persuade the Egyptian authorities to let us visit el-Shater at Tora, along with two visiting Gulf Arab foreign ministers, Abdullah bin Zayed of the UAE and Khalid Attiyah of Qatar. The improbable idea was to try to get el-Shater's support for deescalation.

After a long wait in the lobby of our hotel, surrounded by muscular Egyptian security personnel in suits talking nervously into their headsets, we set off for Tora late one night. It took about forty minutes for our convoy of cars to reach the forbidding century-old prison complex on the southern edge of the city. We arrived well after midnight.

El-Shater was being held in the maximum security, or "Scorpion," block in Tora. Scorpion had about a thousand political prisoners, many of them hardcore MB members, held in about three hundred cold stone cells. Stories of torture and mistreatment were legendary here, and you could feel the grimness of the place as we walked down several dimly lit and foul-smelling corridors toward the warden's office.

The four of us arranged ourselves in front of a desk, behind which sat the unsmiling warden. He offered us tea, and a few minutes later el-Shater was escorted in by two prison guards. Clad in prison pajamas and wearing cheap plastic sandals, he was still an imposing figure—six foot four, solidly built and bearded. He was pale and had a hacking prison cough, but appeared unbowed by his confinement. He shook hands with each of us, sat down, and engaged us for the next two hours, unintimidated by the company, unapologetic about anything the Brotherhood had done, and definitely unhurried—since he clearly had no place else to go.

El-Shater's tone was polite, but there was no mistaking his bitterness as he denounced the UAE for complicity in the coup and the United States for its acquiescence. His gestures grew animated. At one point he accidentally bumped my shoulder. One of the prison guards sprang into action, but backed off quickly when el-Shater smiled broadly and said he was just punctuating his comments, not intending to threaten anyone. Bernardino and I outlined the deescalatory steps we had been discussing with the two MB ex-ministers, and the two Gulf Arab ministers asserted their interest in a nonviolent resolution.

El-Shater listened carefully. He said it was hard for him to comment on the particulars in confinement, cut off from his colleagues and the situation at Raba'a. But he asked practical questions about our proposal, and emphasized his commitment to nonviolence and a serious political dialogue. It just couldn't be a dialogue between "prisoners and jailers." He closed on a hard note, reminding us that neither he nor the Brotherhood were strangers to privation, and would be unyielding in the face of pressure. "I'm sixty-three years old," he said. "I've spent many years in Egyptian jails, and I am ready to spend many more."

As we drove back to the hotel, I told Bernardino that our effort had been worthwhile, but I doubted we'd get any more traction. We briefed our MB interlocutors the next day on the conversation with el-Shater, but they were immobilized by the mounting tensions and the difficulty of getting clear signals from their leadership. Sisi was hardening his stance too, sensing that this was the time to bludgeon the Brotherhood into submission and reassert order for Egyptians tired of more than two years of unrest.

In the end, we only postponed the moment of reckoning. Convinced we had reached a diplomatic dead end, I flew home on August 8. A few days later Egyptian security forces swept into Raba'a Square and the nearby al-Nahda Square, killing nearly one thousand Brotherhood supporters. It was a brutal move, as bloody as it was unnecessary. Sisi had cemented his authority at Egypt's expense, sowing the seeds of an even more violent Islamist movement in the future.

Undoubtedly, we had made our share of tactical mistakes in handling Egypt's transition. We should have pressed harder for a more deliberate transition timetable right after the revolution, giving secular parties more time to organize. We should have pushed more vigorously against Morsi's power grab in late 2012; instead, we misread the depths of the popular groundswell that Sisi seized so quickly and effectively, and were inhibited by fears that we would be accused once again of cutting legitimate Islamist politics off at the knees. A more direct declaration that July 3 was a coup might have sobered the Egyptian military and given us more leverage with other political players.

Even with the passage of time, however, I still suspect that American influence was incapable of fundamentally altering the course of events. Mubarak waited too long to act, and it was beyond our power to save him. Of course, we bore some of the responsibility for his autocratic rule, given the significance of our support over three decades. Of course, we could have done more to encourage him to undertake serious reforms. We never, however, had the capacity to transform him into a modernizer, no matter how hard we might have tried.

Egypt's Arab Spring—like some of the other uprisings in the region—was more of a decapitation than a revolution. It failed to redefine the military's grip on the country, and as a result, it was inevitable that the generals would reassert their authority as soon as their interests were threatened. There was little we could have done to alter the military's calculus or stage-manage the collision between Sisi and the Brotherhood. Nor could we have easily erased the deep sense of betrayal and grievance felt by some of our Gulf Arab partners, as well as the Israelis, all of whom saw our handling of Mubarak's demise and Egypt's transition as further evidence of our "withdrawal" from the region and lack of resolve. Those perceptions, however unfair, still linger and corrode.

* * *

ARAB AUTOCRACIES HAD seemed alike in their surface stability, but in 2011 each revolt was unstable in its own way. They erupted in parallel, each casting its own shadow onto the others. We struggled to draw meaning from one experience that might help decipher and manage the next. It was hard to find consistency amid the jumble of societies and idiosyncratic personalities and frantic—frequently violent—changes.

Most idiosyncratic of all was Qaddafi. He had stuck to his part of our deal on terrorism and the nuclear issue. But he continued to rule with weirdness and repression, convinced that a strong and sometimes brutal hand was essential to hold together a country that a colonizing Italy had invented from a mishmash of loosely connected regions and tribes. He had atomized the Libyan armed forces and security services to protect against coups, and for similar reasons deliberately prevented the emergence of real courts, legislative bodies, or political parties that could challenge his authority. Qaddafi's personal style remained decidedly unhinged. His bizarre ninety-minute speech to the UN General Assembly in the fall of 2009 was hardly an advertisement for his soundness of mind. He rambled and ranted, occasionally consulting scraps of paper that he had scattered on the podium, veering from one crazy comment to another. His interpreter was so frustrated that after seventy-five minutes he shouted, "I just can't take it anymore," slammed down his headphones, and stormed out.

We kept our end of the bargain, however—normalizing relations, removing sanctions, and setting up an embassy in Tripoli. Led by Gene Cretz, the embassy managed to decipher the Qaddafi regime and all its strangeness and interpret its behavior to Washington. For his sins, Gene became one of the early casualties of WikiLeaks when his cables became public. In one especially vivid telegram, he described Qaddafi's "voluptuous Ukrainian nurse," a passage that did not endear him to the Libyan leader.[8] After one of Qaddafi's henchmen told us with chilling candor that "people get killed here for writing things like that," Clinton withdrew Cretz from Tripoli at the end of 2010.

It was not a surprise when Libyans' fractiousness spun up after the breathtaking revolutions on either side of them, first in Tunisia and then in Egypt. It was also not a surprise when Qaddafi reacted with characteristic venom and violence. Soon after Mubarak's resignation next door, emboldened Libyans staged large-scale protests in Tripoli and Benghazi, traditionally a stronghold of anti-Qaddafi and Islamist movements. Intent on restoring fear in his domestic audience, and not particularly concerned about his wider audience, Qaddafi ordered the army to retake Benghazi, a city of seven hundred thousand, and "wipe out the rats and dogs" who resisted. "We will find you in your closets," he declared. "We will have no mercy and no pity."[9]

We tried and failed to dissuade Qaddafi. I telephoned my old negotiating partner, Musa Kusa, now Libya's foreign minister, three times in February. In the first call, he complained that we had stabbed Mubarak in the back and didn't understand the ugliness that was likely to unfold across the region. In our subsequent conversations, I told him that Qaddafi's violence against his own people had to stop. I warned him that it would undo not only what we had worked to achieve over the past decade, but the Qaddafi regime itself. Kusa repeated that we didn't understand the situation or the implacability of his leader. But when I told him again that this would not end well, he sighed heavily and said, "I know." Kusa defected to the United Kingdom one month later.

President Obama was wary of direct American military involvement, but the pressure to act mounted as Qaddafi's forces neared Benghazi. There were significant splits among Obama's advisors, although as is often the case in the retelling of policy debates, I don't remember them to have been quite as sharply defined as later reported. Biden and Gates made clear their reservations, arguing that there was no vital U.S. national interest at stake; that we already had our hands full trying to wind down wars in Iraq and Afghanistan; and that we had no idea where intervention might lead. Others maintained that the United States had a responsibility to protect innocent civilians. Acknowledging that the searing experience of Rwanda weighed on her, Susan Rice was especially outspoken. So was Samantha Power. And Hillary Clinton, in one of those rare moments in which she and Bob Gates diverged, eventually spoke out in favor of U.S. military action. No one dismissed or downplayed the risks.

In the end, Obama told Gates, it was a "51–49" call. A number of factors ultimately tipped the balance in favor of military action. First was the likelihood of a bloodbath, and the risks for the United States, moral as well as political, of not acting to prevent it. Some observers later argued that it might have been possible to negotiate a deal with Qaddafi to avert further violence and begin a political transition. I saw little evidence of that. When I later met Kusa, by then living in exile in Qatar, he said he knew Qaddafi as well as anyone, and believed in the spring of 2011 that the mercurial Libyan leader was living in his own world, determined to fight to the end. This was existential for Qaddafi, not the kind of strategic choice he had made with us a decade before. A meeting between an American delegation

led by NEA assistant secretary Jeff Feltman and Libyan regime representatives in July 2011 went nowhere, and revealed no signs of Qaddafi's willingness to step down or concede anything. I always thought
the alleged readiness to negotiate of Saif al-Islam, Qaddafi's son and
sometime mouthpiece in the West, was vastly overstated. His rhetoric
as the revolution grew was as nasty as his father's, and his capacity for
self-delusion nearly as large.

Second, Obama had to weigh action or inaction in Libya against
the wider backdrop of the Arab Spring. In mid-March 2011, the revolutions in Tunisia and Egypt looked complicated but promising, with
relatively little bloodshed. Unrest was bubbling across the region,
from Syria to Yemen and Bahrain. To watch while Qaddafi put a violent end to the Libyan uprising would send an awful signal, both
about the possibilities for peaceful change and America's seriousness
in encouraging it. Moreover, Qaddafi was the one Arab leader who
united his peers in common antagonism. Nothing brought the region's leaders together like antipathy for the Libyan dictator and his
regime. Over four decades, Qaddafi had tried at one time or another
to sabotage—or assassinate—just about everyone around the Arab
Summit table. They didn't doubt his vengefulness, and the Arab
League called in March for the UN to intervene.

For Obama, Libya was one case where he didn't have to worry
about regional reaction. Several Arab states, including the UAE and
Jordan, had even made clear that they'd join in an air operation in
Libya. With Gulf Arab sensitivity about our "abandonment" of
Mubarak still stinging, this was also an opportunity for us to recover
some of their confidence.

Third, while post-Qaddafi Libya would be uncharted territory, it
appeared to contain the ingredients for a relatively stable transition.
Libya's oil wealth provided a financial cushion, and an incentive for
cooperation. The country's population was small and significant expertise existed in the Libyan diaspora. The leadership of the political

opposition, most of whom had been in exile for some time, seemed responsible.

Fourth, our principal European allies were champing at the bit to act militarily. President Sarkozy was full of bravado about the need to protect Libyan civilians in Benghazi, ideally with the United States and with NATO organizing the mission, but independently if necessary. With Libya just across the Mediterranean, the Europeans had a profound self-interest in getting the post-Qaddafi transition right.

Finally, a UN Security Council resolution authorizing intervention seemed achievable, and would give the operation the international stamp of legality and legitimacy that America's second Iraq war lacked. The Russians and Chinese had already supported one resolution, in late February, condemning Qaddafi's brutality. President Medvedev had indicated to the vice president on March 10 that Russia would likely abstain on a new resolution, and Putin had been unenthused but disinclined to countermand his protégé. The U.S. Congress was also strongly in support of limited military action, with the Senate unanimously backing a March resolution endorsing American participation in a no-fly zone.

The potential downsides were not insignificant. A decade before, we had employed careful diplomacy to pry Qaddafi away from international terrorism and the pursuit of weapons of mass destruction, on the proposition that he could keep his regime if he changed his behavior. Abetting his overthrow now could undo that message for other proliferators. The still-raw wounds of post-Saddam Iraq were also a reminder of everything that could go wrong once authoritarian lids were removed from pots seething with sectarian and tribal troubles. Nevertheless, I thought the odds were weighted toward intervention—narrowly—and saw inaction in the swirling regional circumstances of the spring of 2011 as potentially even more problematic.

With similar reservations, Obama opted for carefully calibrated military action to stop Qaddafi's forces short of Benghazi. In discussions at the White House on the evening of March 15, the president was displeased with the initial recommendations he received, dismissing the notion that a no-fly zone would block Qaddafi's tanks and artillery, the bigger threats to civilians in Benghazi. After his advisors regrouped, Obama approved what was basically a "no-drive" option, under which coalition aircraft could strike at Qaddafi's ground forces, now strung out along the coast road to Benghazi. In only two days, Susan Rice deftly maneuvered a resolution legitimizing the use of force through the Security Council—the first time in its history that the UN had authorized force to forestall an "imminent massacre"—and Obama emphasized publicly that the U.S. role would be limited. The United States would contribute "unique capabilities"— taking out Libyan air defenses, aerial refueling, intelligence support, precision strikes—at the front end of the mission, which would be led by our international partners. There would be no U.S. troops on the ground.

Although he was later pilloried for an unnamed White House official's inartful characterization of the U.S. strategy as "leading from behind," the president's actions looked strikingly successful at first. Benghazi was spared Qaddafi's attack, and his forces were beaten back. Rebel militias regained momentum, and by August had taken Tripoli. Almost inevitably, the civilian protection mission morphed into backing for the rebel ground forces, and Qaddafi's overthrow— precisely what Moscow had feared, and what we had assured them would not be the case. After Tripoli fell, Qaddafi went on the run. He was eventually captured and ignominiously killed in Sirte in October, near where I last met him, at a more hopeful moment, in 2005.

In the immediate aftermath of Qaddafi's downfall, the Libyan operation seemed a classic example of how Obama's "long game" strategy could limit American exposure in the Middle East and prod others to step up. It cost the Pentagon less than a billion dollars, half of what we were spending in Afghanistan every week. Our European and Arab partners carried out 90 percent of the air sorties. The UN sent a political mission into Tripoli to help a transitional government; oil production resumed; and we began to plan a training program for new Libyan security forces as militias demobilized. Chris Stevens, an intrepid Arabist who had been stationed in Tripoli before the revolution and had then taken a freighter into Benghazi during the revolt to lead our diplomacy with the opposition, became our first ambassador to post-Qaddafi Libya in the early summer of 2012.

I visited Chris and his team in Tripoli in July, just after Libya's remarkably smooth first postwar elections. Secular parties had done unexpectedly well, and Islamist groups had not fared nearly as impressively as they had in Egypt or Tunisia. I had grown to respect Chris immensely in his previous posts in the Middle East, where at different times he had been my "control officer," managing my visits to Jerusalem and Damascus, among other places. He had an easygoing professionalism that won over Arabs as well as American colleagues, and by now knew Libya better than anyone else in the Foreign Service, as well as the broader foreign policy bureaucracy.

At the end of a long day of meetings, we decompressed over beer at his modest residence on the makeshift embassy compound. In the wake of the elections, he was cautiously upbeat, recognizing all the troubles on the landscape but confident in his ability to connect with Libyans and play a useful role. He acknowledged that security was a difficult problem and would likely become the country's Achilles' heel. He stressed that he would be careful, not just for his own sake, but for the entire mission. But he knew that there was no such thing as zero risk in our profession. That conversation has haunted me ever since.

On a trip to Jordan in September, I received the kind of call you always dread in the middle of the night. It was the State Department Operations Center, informing me that there had been an attack on American diplomats in Benghazi. There was no further information. A few hours later, a somber senior watch officer told me that Chris Stevens and three of our colleagues had been killed. I was numb and horrified as I learned more of the details. Chris had been on a brief visit to Benghazi, where we kept a small diplomatic outpost—not a formal consulate, but a base from which we could keep in touch with developments in the political center of Libya's east, where the revolution had started. After a day of meetings in town, Chris and his security detail had returned for the night to our tiny compound. Shortly after 9 P.M., a group of Libyan extremists launched a coordinated attack, overwhelming the compound's defenses. Fierce fighting continued until after midnight at a second American compound, run by the CIA, located a mile or so away.

I spent that sleepless night in Amman and continued on to Baghdad in the morning, as scheduled. I cut short my trip there to accompany Chris's remains and those of our other colleagues back to the United States a couple days later. It was the longest plane flight I can remember, sitting in that cold, cavernous C-17 aircraft across from four flag-draped coffins. It was all surreal; I barely recall landing at Andrews Air Force Base, or the terribly sad arrival ceremony at which the president and Secretary Clinton spoke.

It didn't take long for the Benghazi attack to become a political football at home. Legitimate questions about what more we should have done on security were wrapped up in a set of investigations and hearings that were astonishingly cynical, even by the standards of modern Washington. When Secretary Clinton fell and suffered a concussion, and thus was unable to testify before Senate and House committees in December, I stepped in on short notice, along with my friend Tom Nides, the deputy secretary for management and resources.

We spent seven hours before the Senate Foreign Relations Committee and the House Foreign Affairs Committee. There is nothing like a high-profile hearing on a contentious, politically charged issue to focus your mind, or remind you just how brutal Washington politics can be. We did our best to project a calmness that neither of us felt. Nides leaned over before the House hearing began and whispered, "If you screw up, you're on your own, buddy." That broke the tension, and we soldiered on. We tried to be honest about our mistakes, and precise about the steps we were already taking to tighten security, while making clear that there could never be a risk-proof approach to diplomacy. Our colleagues overseas often operated in dangerous places, and that would remain the nature of our profession.

The Benghazi tragedy and the endless political circus around it substantially lessened the administration's appetite for deeper involvement in Libya. Preoccupation with security made it difficult for American, European, and UN personnel to function. Tensions among Libyan militias increased, and disorder mounted. Other Arab states began to support competing proxies, with the Egyptians and Emiratis backing some groups in the east, and the Qataris funneling money and arms to Islamists. ISIS and al-Qaeda affiliates sprung up. The fumbling authorities in Tripoli alternately clamored for and resisted Western help, complaining about lack of support but allergic to systematic advice or the practical requirements of signing memoranda of understanding or following through on their commitments.

Our embassy continued to perform valiantly, when it could operate in-country. On one visit in the spring of 2014, Deborah Jones, our ambassador, managed to corral all of the major rebel militia leaders to meet with me and discuss how they might coexist for the national good. It was a memorable scene, the motley crew of self-professed revolutionary heroes more suspicious of each other than they were of the Americans, with their bodyguards all standing just outside the room, fingers on triggers. We made little headway. I reported to Secretary Kerry that I had never seen Libya "in a more fragile state."[10] President Obama was less diplomatic in his *Atlantic* interview with Jeff Goldberg a couple years later. Libya, he said, had become "a shit show."

The president wasn't far off. Our intervention in 2011 had saved thousands of innocent lives, at relatively modest initial cost to the

United States. Without a strong post-intervention American hand, our neat "long game" coalition stumbled—the incapacity and irresolution of most of the Europeans painfully exposed, most of the Arabs reverting to self-interested form, and rival Libyan factions unified only by their ardent opposition to any meaningful foreign support and engagement. Libya became a violent cautionary tale, whose shadow heavily influenced American policy toward the far more consequential drama unfolding in the Levant—Syria's horrendous civil war.

* * *

HINDSIGHT NEITHER DIMINISHES the continuing pain and cost of Syria's civil war, nor illuminates any easy choices for policymakers. As I write this, more than half a million people have been killed. Thirteen million more, approximately two-thirds of the country's prewar population, have been driven out of their homes, at least half of them flooding across Syria's borders and unsettling political order and local economies in the Middle East and Europe. ISIS sprang out of the sectarian chaos of Syria and a still-wounded Iraq. Outside powers preyed on Syria's divisions, from Iran and Russia to the Gulf Arabs, settling scores and angling for advantage across its battered landscape. The Assad clan has clung to power with unyielding harshness, mowing down peaceful protestors and gassing civilians. Syria remains bloody and broken, its recovery a distant aspiration, its pathologies still threatening its neighborhood.

It is hard not to see Syria's agony as an American policy failure. Many see it as the underreaching analog to the disastrous overreach of the Iraq War a decade before. As someone who served through both, and shared in the mistakes we made, I am not persuaded by the analogy. There were times during Syria's protracted crisis when more decisive American intervention might have made a difference. Like many of my colleagues, I argued for more active support in 2012 for what was then still a relatively moderate, if ragtag, opposition, and for responding militarily to Assad's use of sarin gas in the summer of 2013. Neither step, however, would necessarily have turned the tide.

It was not only the shadow of Libya and its torment that hung over those choices, it was also the far darker shadow of Iraq. In terms of Obama's "long game" calculus, having the discipline to avoid getting sucked into another military entanglement in the Middle East, which would likely only underscore the limits of our influence in a world of predators for whom Syria's battles were existential, was paramount. It took cold-blooded rigor of the sort that Jim Baker and Brent Scowcroft would have admired to resist the clamor for direct military action against Assad, tempting as it was.

Yet again, where we ran into trouble was in our short game. We misaligned ends and means, promising too much, on the one hand— declaring that "Assad must go" and setting "red lines"—and applying tactical tools too grudgingly and incrementally, on the other. If you added up all the measures we eventually took in Syria by the end of 2014, including a more ambitious train and equip program for the opposition, and telescoped them into more decisive steps earlier in the conflict, their cumulative impact might have given us more leverage over Assad, as well as the Russians and Iranians. They wouldn't on their own have produced Assad's downfall, but they might have created a better chance for a negotiated solution. It was in many ways another lesson in the risks of incrementalism.

In the Assad family playbook, conciliation was a fatal weakness, suspiciousness a guiding principle, and brutishness an article of faith. Nevertheless, before 2011, the Obama administration tested with Assad whether some modest improvement in relations might be possible. Special Envoy for Middle East Peace George Mitchell had extensive discussions in Damascus about reviving the Syrian track of the peace process, and I visited Assad twice to gauge his seriousness about clamping down on cross-border support for extremists in Iraq and broader counterterrorism cooperation. After a long one-on-one conversation with him in February 2010, I reported to Secretary

Clinton that it made little sense to get our hopes up about the Syrians. "The safest bet," I said, "is that they will evade and obfuscate; that's generally their default position."[11]

When the Arab Spring began to break in early 2011, Assad showed none of the initial hesitation that, he believed, had unraveled Ben Ali and Mubarak. Their experiences cast their own shadows onto the young Syrian dictator's thinking, which was reinforced by reminders from his hard-edged family and advisors about Hafez al-Assad's rigid rulebook. In Dara'a, near the border with Jordan, a group of school-children spray-painted antiregime slogans on the wall of their building. "It's your turn, Doctor," was their not-so-subtle message to the ophthalmologist turned president in Damascus. They were arrested and tortured, sparking demonstrations. Syrian security forces re-sponded harshly, with two dozen civilians killed on April 9.

As protests mounted across the country, so did the death toll. An armed opposition began to emerge, fragmented but gradually more threatening to the regime. In July, our ambassador in Damascus, Robert Ford, visited Hama, a large city north of Damascus that Hafez al-Assad had leveled thirty years before to suppress Islamist dissent. Hama had become another scene of large, peaceful protests, and the demonstrators showered Ford with flowers. Assad dug in harder, stubbornly resistant to calls for dialogue with dissidents. President Obama had been careful in his rhetoric, but the explosion of violence over the summer and Assad's intransigence finally led him to con-clude publicly that Assad had to go. "For the sake of the Syrian peo-ple," he said, "the time has come for President Assad to step aside."

There was still a widespread sense in the region, and in the ad-ministration, that Assad's demise was only a matter of time. King Abdullah of Saudi Arabia told me that Assad was "finished." King Abdullah of Jordan had a similar view. In Abu Dhabi, Crown Prince Mohamed bin Zayed was more nuanced; he thought Assad was on the ropes, but "could hang on for a long time" if the opposition didn't squeeze hard now. Fred Hof, the State Department's senior advisor on

Syria, said Assad was "a dead man walking." The U.S. intelligence community didn't push back against that assessment.

Following the president's judgment on Assad, the administration went through its own collection of tactical steps. Sanctions were enacted against senior Syrian regime officials; the European Union acted along similar lines; the Arab League spoke out against Assad; and an effort began to obtain UN Security Council authorization for tougher measures. With the bitter experience of the Libya resolutions and Qaddafi's overthrow fresh in their minds, however, neither the Russians nor the Chinese were interested in signing any more blank checks. They repeatedly vetoed even the mildest of resolutions condemning Assad's bombardment of unarmed civilians—undercutting international pressure and proving to Assad he would face no sanction for his war crimes. Their vetoes were callous and destructive, only exacerbating the human tragedy unfolding in Syria.

Despite setbacks at the UN, we engaged intensively with the Russians to try to find a pathway to a negotiated transition. In conversations with Secretary Clinton and me, Sergey Lavrov asserted that Russia was not "wedded" to Assad, but would not push him out, and worried about who or what might come after him. Obama and Putin had a testy exchange on Syria on the margins of a G-20 summit in Mexico in early June 2012. In Geneva at the end of the month, Clinton and Lavrov agreed to a formula brokered by former UN secretary-general Kofi Annan, who was serving as UN envoy on the Syria crisis. According to the Geneva Communiqué, Russia and the United States agreed to press for the formation of a transitional governing body in Syria, "with full executive powers," whose composition would be determined by "mutual consent" of the current Syrian authorities and the opposition. We believed "mutual consent" was effectively a veto for the opposition over Assad's continued authority; the Russians conceded no such thing, and insisted that they weren't going to lean on Assad to begin to transfer power. The communiqué was less an agreement than a neat summary of our differences.

I followed up in Geneva in December and then again in January 2013 with Lakhdar Brahimi, who succeeded a deeply frustrated Annan as UN envoy, and Mikhail Bogdanov, the Russian deputy foreign minister responsible for the Middle East. I had considerable respect for both of them. Brahimi was the UN's most accomplished troubleshooter, a former Algerian foreign minister with a sure feel for the Middle East and a passionate commitment to resolving conflicts. Bogdanov was the best of Russia's impressive cadre of Arabists, with long experience in Syria and an encyclopedic knowledge of its regime and personalities.

In the winter of 2012–13 the Russians were growing nervous about Assad's staying power. He had been steadily losing ground to opposition forces, regime morale was declining, and he was having trouble finding recruits for his military. In our private conversations, Bogdanov was candid about his concerns about Assad, and about the extent to which fighting in Syria was becoming a magnet for Islamic extremists. He was equally concerned about the difficulty of shaping a stable post-Assad leadership, and dubious about the political opposition, which was weakly led and divided. Bogdanov said he saw no signs of significant defections from Assad's inner circle or military and security leadership; Bashar's father had built a system around the notion that insiders would either hang together or hang separately, and that didn't seem to be cracking.

We went round and round with Brahimi about how to translate the Geneva Communiqué into practice, but spun our wheels. We simply could not convince the Russians that we had a plausible theory of the case for the day after Assad, and the Russians were uninterested in offering their own. By the early spring of 2013, the sense of Russian urgency and nervousness evaporated as a substantial influx of Hezbollah fighters from Lebanon and Iranian material support gave Assad a boost and his fortunes began to shift on the battlefield. I doubt the Russians were ever serious about pressuring Assad to leave, and they lacked the leverage to accomplish that unless the Iranians agreed, which was never going to happen.

Our own lack of leverage was a major diplomatic weakness. The argument for doing more in 2012 to bolster the opposition was never, at least in my mind, about victory on the battlefield. It was about trying to demonstrate to Assad and his outside backers that he couldn't win militarily, and that his political options were going to narrow the longer the fighting continued. It was a way to manage the opposition, and to use our provision of training and equipment to help make them a more coherent and responsive force. And it was a way to herd the cats among the other supporters of the opposition—to try to discipline the feuding Gulf Arabs, help ensure that we weren't acting at cross-purposes with one another, and keep their assistance away from the more extreme groups to which some of them were drawn. I hated the then-fashionable term "skin in the game," which always seemed too glib in the face of Syria's ugly realities, but that was essentially what this was about—giving greater weight and credibility to our political strategy.

Most of Obama's senior advisors advocated this approach. At the end of the summer of 2012, Clinton joined David Petraeus, now director of the CIA, and Leon Panetta, who had succeeded Gates the year before as secretary of defense, in a concerted effort to persuade the president to approve a more ambitious train and equip program. Obama was unconvinced. In the subsequent recollections of some of the protagonists, this debate and the pivotal NSC meeting in the Situation Room is portrayed as a kind of "Gunfight at the OK Corral," with the president alone against the passionate and ironclad arguments of his subordinates. I don't remember it in quite the same way.

It was like so many high-level deliberations among smart people about complicated problems—harassed by time pressures, domestic critics, and impatient allies. Clinton and Petraeus did argue carefully for doing more, and like most people in the room that afternoon, I agreed. The president asked penetrating questions, for which none of us had especially compelling answers. Our understanding of the capacity and makeup of the Syrian opposition was in truth quite limited. Predictions of Assad's fragile future were far more educated guesses than scientific conclusions, and no one really knew what it would mean when the Iranians and Russians doubled down in response to any increase in American support for the opposition. With the legendary success of its covert program in Afghanistan in the 1980s as the unspoken predicate, the intelligence community tended to overstate how fast and how effectively it could arm the Syrian rebels. And fears of what had later happened in Afghanistan, with the U.S.-armed mujahedeen morphing into the Taliban and embracing bin Laden, loomed large for Obama. It was not an easy call.

* * *

BY CONTRAST, I thought the choice to respond to Assad's later use of chemical weapons (CW) was more clear-cut. In unscripted public remarks in August 2012, Obama declared that Assad's use of chemical weapons would cross "a red line." Throughout the rest of 2012 and the first half of 2013, we became more and more convinced that Assad was employing sarin gas and other chemical weapons against his own people. He seemed to be testing the edges of our response, with fairly small-scale use gradually growing bolder. I had been asked by the White House twice in the spring and early summer to telephone Syrian foreign minister Walid Muallem, with whom I had dealt for decades, and make clear that we knew what his regime was doing and would not tolerate it. If it continued, there would be consequences. Muallem listened both times and smugly dismissed my claims. "We're not responsible," he said. "Maybe it's your Islamist extremist friends."

Then on August 21, the Syrian military used sarin against civilians in Ghouta, a rebel-controlled suburb of Damascus. More than fourteen hundred people were murdered, many of them children. The intelligence on this attack was solid, and gruesome video footage was shown around the world. Susan Rice, now national security advisor, convened a series of Principals Committee meetings to consider options. The overwhelming consensus of the group was that the issue was not whether to respond militarily, but how. American warships were positioned in the eastern Mediterranean, their cruise missiles well within range of a variety of potential targets—the airfields from which chemical attacks had been launched, suspected CW depots, and Assad's own palace and helicopter fleet. The French were ready to join in a strike. So were the British—at least until a disastrous, ill-prepared vote in Parliament on August 29 denied Prime Minister David Cameron the authority to act militarily.

At the request of the White House, John Kerry appeared in the State Department's Treaty Room on August 30 and made a forceful statement, which I helped craft, and which all but promised military action. Both the secretary and I went home that evening convinced that the president would order a strike over the weekend. I firmly believed, like Kerry, that it was the right call. Assad had not only crossed our red line, but had violated a crucial international norm.

There were obvious downsides. Striking at chemical weapons facilities risked plumes of poisonous materials, and we knew we couldn't locate or destroy all of their stockpiles. Assad might up the ante and lash out even more brutally, pushing us all down a very slippery slope. It seemed to me, however, that we were on firmer ground than proponents of the slippery-slope argument would admit. I sympathized with the president's cynicism about the Washington establishment's tendency to retreat behind the argument that "American credibility is at stake" as the all-purpose justification for the use of force. This was not just about our credibility. Our intelligence was incontestable, and a strong punitive strike in response to CW use would be aimed clearly at defending an international norm and deterring future use. It didn't imply an effort at regime change, or direct intervention in the civil war. It was the best case for using force that we'd have against Assad, and the best near-term window to shape the conflict's trajectory.

Kerry called later that night to tell me that there had been a change in signals. "I can't believe it," he said, "but the president just called to say we're holding." The chain of events had unfolded rapidly. Early on Friday evening, the president had gone for his customary end-of-the-day walk around the South Lawn of the White House with his chief of staff, Denis McDonough. Denis was as good a sounding board as the president could hope for—thoughtful and whip smart. Obama was uneasy about moving forward without congressional authorization; a strike in Syria could carry with it all sorts of unintended consequences, and Congress needed to take some ownership. If we were going to use force, we should do it the right way and break the bad habit of executive overreach (and congressional evasiveness) that had proved so corrosive since 9/11. Cameron's parliamentary fiasco the day before was a reminder of what could go wrong, but the president was determined.

The following day, Obama made a brief public statement indicating that he would seek congressional authorization for a strike against Assad. Prospects for approval were dim. Few Republicans wanted to be helpful to Obama, and many Democrats were uneasy, afflicted by 2003 Iraq War déjà vu. The French felt abandoned. Our Arab partners were appalled, and saw the decision as another sign of American wavering—one more sin in the litany that had begun with "abandoning" Mubarak.

Meanwhile, Jake Sullivan and I went off to Oman in early September to resume secret talks with the Iranians. We made significant headway on the nuclear issue, certainly more than we had expected. Some critics have alleged that it was the secret talks and preserving their potential that caused Obama to hesitate about a strike against Assad, whom the Iranians were fiercely backing. I never once heard the president voice that concern. It always seemed to me that his choices on Syria at this moment had much more to do with the risks of getting mired in another conflict there than the risks of jeopardizing the secret channel with Iran. In fact, Jake and I sent a note to the White House during that early September round in Oman arguing that a strike (which we both favored) would complicate but not blow up the talks. The Iranians were perfectly capable of compartmentalizing our relations, with Foreign Minister Javad Zarif beginning a nuclear negotiation while Quds Force commander Qassem Soleimani did his best to threaten our interests across the Middle East. We ought to be able to compartmentalize too.

Over the medium term, we thought, it would actually help—reminding a variety of audiences, including the Iranians—that there were circumstances in which we would use force to protect our most critical interests in the region. That would be an unsubtle signal of our determination to ensure, by whatever means necessary, that Iran did not develop a nuclear weapon. It would also demonstrate that even if we reached an agreement on the nuclear issue, we would not ease up on other contested areas. That was a message that would help manage some of the inevitable angst from regional friends.

While we were negotiating secretly in Oman, events moved quickly on the Syrian CW issue. The president saw Vladimir Putin, the recently reinstalled Russian president, at the G-20 meeting in St. Petersburg in the first week in September. Putin pitched a vague proposal for a diplomatic resolution of the CW problem, with Assad potentially agreeing to ship his remaining chemical stockpiles out of the country and end his program. It was hard to know how seriously to take the Russians. When Kerry was asked by the press in London on September 9 about what could be done to avoid military action in Syria, he responded offhandedly that the Syrians could turn over all their chemical weapons immediately, but expressed disbelief that they would. Lavrov called him right afterward and insisted that the Russians wanted to work with us on "our initiative." In one of diplomacy's stranger recent turns, Kerry, Lavrov, and their teams hammered out a framework agreement for the removal of Syrian CW, which they announced on September 14 in Geneva. It was a significant step, even though the Syrians concealed some remaining stocks from international inspectors. A diplomatic agreement to remove Assad's declared CW arsenal was in many ways a better outcome than a punitive military strike. The lingering impression, however, was that the Obama administration had blinked at the moment of military decision. It would leave an enduring mark.

Assad was willing to make a show of conceding chemical weapons to his Russian patrons, but his singular determination to stamp out the opposition never wavered. He was convinced that what he had bought for giving up chemical weapons, at least temporarily, was a "get out of jail free" card on future American use of force against him. Faced with significant manpower shortages, he was also able to count on the Iranians to fill the gap, principally by sustaining Hezbollah and other Shia militias.

Secretary Kerry was relentless in his pursuit of diplomatic openings, and logged endless hours on the phone and in meeting rooms with Lavrov. The Russians had neither the leverage nor the inclination to try to show Assad the door, however unseemly a client he might be. Putin's tolerance for unseemliness was high, and he enjoyed the emerging narrative in the Arab world that Russia was a more reliable partner than America. As King Abdullah of Saudi Arabia told me, "The Russians are wrong to back Assad, but at least they stand by their friends." Kerry was equally relentless in arguing in Washington for more support for the opposition, and later for targeted use of force against the Assad regime, to stem the tide of regime advances and bolster America's diplomatic hand. He didn't find much appetite in the White House, where the holes in the argument and the risks of setbacks always outweighed the potential gains.

I was invited to an informal afternoon discussion in the Oval Office between the president and his White House advisors in the summer of 2014, a two-hour session focused mainly on the Syria crisis.

We talked about how moderates were losing strength within the opposition, and Sunni extremists were gaining. This fit Assad's narrative that he was the last person standing between secular order in Syria and Islamic radicals. The Russians, I thought, were unlikely to engage in serious diplomacy, let alone throw their limited weight behind a political transition. I argued at one point that we needed to put "more pieces on the board" to reanimate diplomacy—to create a bigger and more effective train and equip program for the waning moderate opposition groups, and consider some form of "safe zones" in a few places in Syria along the borders of Jordan and Turkey. There the moderate opposition could train, safeguard displaced Syrians, and begin to develop habits of governance that could at least point in the direction of a future transition.

This was not the first time the president had heard these arguments. He listened carefully and didn't dismiss them out of hand, but it was not hard to sense his impatience with recommendations for safe zones, which begged much bigger questions of who exactly would help protect them and at what cost, not to mention the tangled issue of international legal justification.

As 2014 wore on, it was the dramatic and unexpected rise of ISIS, the fall of Mosul, and the grave risk to Iraq's stability that ultimately persuaded the White House to act more boldly. A $500 million Pentagon-led train and equip program was launched for the moderate Syrian opposition, aimed ostensibly at fighting ISIS, not Assad. It proved to be too cumbersome, too little, and too late to have any significant effect on the Syrian civil war. A coalition of Islamist fighters who benefited from some combination of CIA and Gulf Arab support was making notable gains, causing grave concern in Moscow.[12] As a result, in the early fall of 2015, Putin intervened more decisively in Syria, using a relatively modest military deployment to maximum political effect. Russian airstrikes steadied Assad's forces and helped them press their advantage on the ground. The American-led campaign against ISIS, accelerating as I was leaving government at the end of 2014, eventually rolled back the ISIS caliphate in Mosul and Raqaa. Bashar al-Assad remained in Damascus, having regained control of most of Syria's major population centers, refuted predictions of his demise, and devastated his country for generations to come.

* * *

THE COMPLICATED STORIES of Syria, Libya, and Egypt during the Obama administration were only parts of a larger American policy tableau in the Middle East. Obama's broad strategy—his long game—was to gradually break the region's decades-long psychological, military, diplomatic, and political hold on American foreign policy. He knew we couldn't detach ourselves entirely or neglect the festering risks; it was time, however, to shift the balance of tools we employed. For too long, the president thought, we had invested too much in an ill-considered combination of policy instruments, partners, and objectives. It was time to realign and rebalance—use our leverage where we could and solve the issues of biggest consequence to regional stability like Iran's nuclear program or the Arab-Israeli conflict; construct two-way streets where for too long U.S. policy was giving a lot and getting too little in return from its partners and allies; and finally make a significant effort to help the region fill the deficits in education and economic and political modernization on which extremists fed.

It made eminent sense. It just turned out to be much harder to execute than Obama expected. The distant promise of the long game was held hostage by the infinite complexities of the short game, by twists and turns that surprised him, and tactical choices and tradeoffs that frustrated all of us. By the second term, the rhythm of White House principals and deputies meetings, well over half of them focused on the Middle East, made it difficult to see where the rebalance to Asia and other priorities had gone. Some of this, of course, was simply what international politics are all about. Assumptions don't always hold. The unexpected intrudes. Yet precisely because Obama and his closest advisors had such strong convictions about the wisdom of their long game, they were sometimes reluctant to adjust to unforeseen forces and new facts.

It was the Arab Spring that brought all this into sharpest relief. For all their drama and consequence, the Arab revolts during the Obama era were part of a much longer process, an early round in what will be a series of struggles to deal with the ills of a profoundly troubled part of the world. Egypt, Libya, and Syria were not the only societies affected, as Tunisians and Yemenis can attest, and they won't be the last. Theirs were just the most compelling for American policy. With all the inevitable tactical missteps, and things we might have done differently or better, the Obama administration's approach in Egypt was basically sound. We recognized the limits of our power, handled Mubarak's departure about as well as we could have, and preserved a security relationship that—warts and all—still mattered.

We made serious mistakes in Libya. They had less to do, in my view, with our initial decision to act, and more with our failure to plan for and sustain a realistic approach to security after Qaddafi's fall. We helped prevent a massacre, and played a critical role in a tactically successful military intervention. We got our medium-term assumptions wrong, however; we badly overestimated Libya's post-Qaddafi resilience and the staying power of our partners, and underestimated the ferociousness of the counterrevolutionary pushback, including from Egypt and some of our closest Gulf partners.

Syria is most troubling of all. A major American military intervention would not have solved the conflict, and would likely have made it worse for us. The mistake we made between 2012 and 2014 was that we regularly paired maximalist ends with minimalist means. More modest objectives (a much slower pace toward post-Assad governance, for example) and more concentrated means (such as an earlier, more robust train and equip program for the opposition) would have been a more coherent combination. We might have given ourselves more diplomatic leverage, and enhanced the chances for a negotiated transition, if we had acted sooner and stronger—particularly in the late summer of 2012 and over the CW red line a year later. Instead, we did plenty to escalate the conflict and far too little to end it.

Ultimately, Obama could not escape his inheritance in the Middle East. The array of problems facing him was much less susceptible to the application of American power in a world in which there was less of that power to apply. The events of the Arab Spring turned Winter overshadowed in many respects Obama's effort to reset America's role in the region and the world over the long term. His nuclear deal with Iran, however, would reinforce his convictions about the power of diplomacy and America's pivotal leadership role.

9

Iran and the Bomb: The Secret Talks

LATE ONE NIGHT in February 2013, I climbed into an unmarked U.S. government Gulfstream jet parked on the deserted tarmac at Andrews Air Force Base. Secretary Kerry's parting words, delivered with his characteristic optimism and self-assurance, still rang in my head: "We've got the diplomatic opportunity of a lifetime." I felt far more uncertain.

I spent much of that seventeen-hour flight to Oman reviewing briefing books, talking through strategy and tactics with our negotiating team, and trying to come to grips with the task before us. It had been thirty-five years since the United States and Iran had had sustained diplomatic contact. There was baggage on both sides, and massive mutual mistrust. The diplomatic stakes were high, with Iran's nuclear program accelerating and military conflict between us an increasing possibility. The politics in both our capitals were explosive, with little room for diplomatic maneuver. International diplomacy had run aground, its thus far desultory exchanges missing a key ingredient—a direct discussion between the two principal protagonists, the United States and Iran.

For all the anxiety, it was also hard not to feel a sense of possibility. Here was a chance to do what diplomats spend their whole careers trying to do. Here was a chance to apply tough-minded diplomacy, backed up by the economic leverage of sanctions, the political leverage of an international consensus, and the military leverage of the potential use of force. And here was a chance to demonstrate the promise of American diplomacy after a decade of America at war.

* * *

IRAN HUNG OVER much of my career, a country synonymous in American foreign policy terms with troubles, threats, and blunders. Iran seemed a menacing and impenetrable presence, too big and dangerous to ignore, but too intransigent to engage. It was a mine-field for diplomats, and nobody had a good map.

I took the Foreign Service entrance exam in November 1979, a few days after the seizure of our embassy in Tehran and the beginning of a hostage crisis that brought down a president. Iranian-backed terrorists twice bombed our embassy in Beirut, and killed more than two hundred Marines in another attack there. The Iran-Contra scandal nearly brought down a second president.

The sweeping success of Desert Storm in 1991 propelled American influence in the Middle East to its zenith. The Clinton administration worked hard to contain Iran, but also explored in the late 1990s a possible opening with the Khatami government. It never got very far. The post–9/11 landscape offered a similar opportunity, which we never seized. Instead, the U.S.-led overthrow of Iran's bitter historical adversaries in Kabul and Baghdad, and the chaos that ensued, delivered Iran a strategic opening that it was only too pleased to exploit.

In late 2001, the U.S. intelligence community began to track two clandestine nuclear sites in Iran: a uranium enrichment plant at Natanz and a facility in Arak that could eventually produce weapons-grade plutonium. These efforts, undeclared to the IAEA, built on

Iran's overt civilian nuclear energy program, which began during the shah's time—ironically, with the initial support of the United States.

The revelation of the covert sites in the summer of 2002 set off a diplomatic dance that continued for the next several years. The UN Security Council passed resolutions demanding that Iran suspend its enrichment work. Iran instead plowed stubbornly ahead. Given the unwillingness of the Bush administration to engage directly with Iran, our European allies (the United Kingdom, France, and Germany, or the "EU-3") began a negotiation with the Iranians that showed fitful progress, as Tehran sought both to preserve its enrichment program and the long-term possibility of weaponization and at the same time avoid economic sanctions. Russia and China later joined the EU-3, which was eventually rebranded as the P5+1 (the five permanent members of the UN Security Council plus Germany).

This all boosted the market for international diplomatic acronyms, but didn't make much of a dent in Iranian behavior. By the last year of the Bush administration in 2008, despite the imposition of several rounds of UN sanctions against Iran and growing international concern, the Iranians had accumulated half the amount of low-enriched uranium they would need to enrich further and make a single bomb. They were spinning more than four thousand primitive IR-1 centrifuges at Natanz, and were making halting progress toward more sophisticated models.

While the American intelligence community concluded famously in 2007 that the Iranian leadership had suspended its weapons work back in 2003, the fact that they were clearly determined to keep their options open in the face of mounting international pressure was deeply troubling. An unconstrained Iranian nuclear program or a regime clearly bent on a weapons program would add yet another layer of risk and fragility to an already unstable region. Our friends—the Gulf Arab states and, especially, Israel—had to take that threat seriously.

As the Bush administration grappled with the damage done by the Iraq War, some of its senior figures began to recognize that its stubborn insistence on not engaging directly in P5+1 diplomacy with Iran had become counterproductive. An early probe for direct talks in May 2003, orchestrated by the enterprising and well-intentioned Swiss ambassador in Tehran, was never pursued. I was traveling in the region when Tim Guldimann, about to complete his ambassadorial tour in Iran, came to Washington and met with my deputy, Jim Larocco, to present a short paper that he insisted had been drafted in cooperation with Iran's ambassador in Paris, the nephew of Iranian foreign minister Kamal Kharazi. Guldimann said the whole effort had been sanctioned at high levels of the Iranian government. The document itself was intriguing, offering a wildly ambitious dialogue across the whole range of U.S.-Iranian differences. Jim and my other NEA colleagues pressed Guldimann hard on who exactly in Tehran had endorsed the paper, and how explicitly that was conveyed. Guldimann was too vague for Jim's taste. The tangled history of ill-sourced messages and double-dealing cast a shadow on our deliberations.

We conveyed the document and an account of Jim's conversation to Secretary Powell and Deputy Secretary Armitage—noting our doubts that it bore the stamp of the highest level of Iran's leadership, but recommending that we test the proposition and reopen the contacts with Iran that had been suspended a year earlier. Powell and Armitage agreed. But in the heady immediate aftermath of the invasion of Iraq, there was little White House interest in talking to a charter member of the "axis of evil," and a conviction that direct engagement would be a reward for bad behavior. For Vice President Cheney and hardliners in the administration, the calculus was clear: If the Iranians were worried about being next on the American hit parade after Saddam, it wasn't a bad idea to let them stew a little.

Throughout the remaining two years of my time in NEA we continued to make the case for dialogue with Iran. I repeated the argument in my December 2004 transition memo to Secretary Rice. I also added a proposal—which was adopted—to restart a serious program of Persian-language training for a small cadre of American diplomats, and then station them in several posts on Iran's periphery to develop expertise and prepare for an eventual resumption of contacts. The "Iran Watchers" initiative had as its inspiration what we had done more than seven decades before in preparing Russian-language specialists for eventual reopening of diplomatic relations with the Soviet Union.

By the time I returned to Washington from Moscow in the spring of 2008, the mood had begun to shift a little. Chastened by the postwar mess in Iraq, President Bush had replaced Don Rumsfeld with Bob Gates at the Pentagon. The vice president's hawkish views were less dominant, and Rice was pressing on several fronts for more active American diplomacy.

In late May 2008, I sent Secretary Rice a long memo entitled "Regaining the Strategic Initiative on Iran." I began by arguing that "our Iran policy is drifting dangerously between the current muddle of P5+1 diplomacy and more forceful options, with all of their huge downsides." Our unwillingness to engage directly with Tehran was costing us more than the Iranians, and deprived us of valuable leverage. "The regime has constructed a narrative which portrays Iran as the victim of implacable American hostility," I wrote, "increasingly gaining the diplomatic upper hand regionally and globally, with the American administration—not Iran—increasingly the isolated party. Reviving significant pressure against Iran's nuclear program requires us to puncture that narrative."[1]

I had two practical suggestions. First, it was long past time for the United States to join our European, Russian, and Chinese partners at the negotiating table. I had few illusions that the government of Mahmoud Ahmadinejad, let alone the deeply suspicious Supreme Leader, was ready to negotiate seriously. By not engaging, we were giving them an easy out—allowing them to hide behind the pretext that they couldn't really be sure about P5+1 proposals, because the

Americans weren't there to back them up. Our physical presence would put us on the high ground, put the Iranians on the defensive, strengthen solidarity with our negotiating partners, and better position us to pivot to more sanctions if Tehran balked again.

My second idea would revive an initiative that had already been kicked around at lower levels in the administration. I suggested to Rice that we should propose quietly to the Iranians that we staff our interests section in Tehran with a few American diplomats, revising the arrangement that had been in effect since the assault on our embassy in Tehran in 1979, under which the Swiss represented our interests in Iran. We would reciprocate by allowing the Iranians to staff their interests section in Washington, managed by the Pakistani government, with a handful of Iranian diplomats. Like the argument for joining the P5+1 talks, the focus was on tactical advantages. I had little expectation that the Supreme Leader would actually agree to such a proposal. The last thing he wanted to see was a long line of Iranian visa applicants around a U.S. diplomatic facility in Tehran staffed by Americans; for the Ayatollah Khamenei, this would be the ultimate Trojan horse. The proposal, which would inevitably become public, would only further cement our grip on the high ground. I suggested that we pitch the idea to the Iranians through the Russians, who had good high-level channels in Tehran and whose support would be crucial if we had to go back to the UN Security Council for tougher sanctions.

I concluded with a broad argument, echoing the classic containment concept that Rice knew so well as a recovering Sovietologist. In dealing with a profoundly hostile adversary beset by its own serious internal contradictions, I said, "a successful strategy will require calculated risk-taking on our part . . . with the same combination of multiple pressure points, diplomatic coalition-building, wedge-driving among Iran and its uneasy partners, and selected contacts with the regime that animated much of Kennan's concept." Moreover, we should simultaneously explore "creatively subversive ways to accentuate the gap between the regime's deeply conservative instincts and popular Iranian desire for normalization with the rest of the world, including the U.S."[2]

Rice saw the possibilities immediately, and knew that we needed to inject some new American initiative into nuclear diplomacy with Iran. The proximate opportunity in the talks themselves was the presentation by Javier Solana, the de facto European Union foreign minister, of a renewed P5+1 proposal to Iran. The essence of his proposal was a freeze on Iranian nuclear activities, including enrichment, and a reciprocal freeze on new UN Security Council sanctions, which would allow space for negotiations on a comprehensive nuclear deal. Solana conveyed this plan in Tehran in June 2008, and the Iranians pledged to respond at a follow-up meeting in Geneva in July. Rice decided to seek the president's approval for me to attend the Geneva meeting—and to also get his blessing on the interests section idea.

One morning in early July, I rode over with the secretary to one of her regular sessions with President Bush to make our pitch. Now nearing the end of his tenure, he looked a little grayer, but his decency and good humor were undiminished.

"Burnsie," he said with a familiar smile as I walked in behind the secretary, "it's good to have you back in Washington." Vice President Cheney sat in an armchair next to the president, less visibly enthused about my homecoming. I joined Rice on a couch alongside Bush, and she quickly laid out our case. The president asked a couple questions about how the interests section proposal would work, and expressed skepticism about what impact joining the Geneva talks with the Iranians would have on their behavior, but saw the value of trying both. The vice president started to object, arguing that we shouldn't reward the Iranians by appearing at a meeting. Bush cut him off. "Dick," he said with a wave of his hand, "I'm okay with this, and I've made up my mind." A lot had changed since the first term and the run-up to the Iraq War, I thought to myself. Diplomacy had its uses after all.

On July 19 in Geneva, amid massive media attention, I broke the taboo on direct American participation in the nuclear talks. I joined my P5+1 colleagues around an oblong table in a cramped meeting hall in the old city. I had been reminded by the secretary and Steve Hadley to keep my game face on and look appropriately sober while the cameras filmed the opening of the first session. They had also both suggested that it might be best to remain silent during the talks and simply witness the Iranian reply to Solana. The first point made sense. The second did not. If the purpose of joining the talks was to emphasize our seriousness and tag Iran as the diplomatic problem child, the silent treatment would backfire. Looking across the table directly at Saeed Jalili, the head of the Iranian delegation, I made a simple statement. I said that I hoped the Iranians understood the significance of the signal we were sending by joining the talks. We knew what was at stake on the nuclear issue; we were determined to prevent Iran from developing a bomb and to hold it to its international obligations; and we were firmly behind the P5+1 proposal. I emphasized that Iran had a rare opportunity before it; we could only hope that it would take advantage of it.

Jalili took careful notes, and smiled faintly throughout. I got lots of sidelong glances from him and his colleagues, who seemed to find the American presence unnerving. Jalili then embarked on nearly forty minutes of meandering philosophizing about Iran's culture and history, and the constructive role it could play in the region. He could be stupefyingly opaque when he wanted to avoid straight answers, and this was certainly one of those occasions. He mentioned at one point that he still lectured part-time at Tehran University. I didn't envy his students.

Jalili wound up his comments by handing over an Iranian "non-paper." The English version was mistakenly headed "None Paper," which turned out to be an apt description of its substance. Solana and the rest of us looked at it quickly, at which point my French colleague helpfully groaned and muttered, "Bullshit," which caused Jalili to look somewhat startled—and me to lose my game face. Fortunately, the cameras were long gone.

In a quick note to Secretary Rice that evening, I reported that "five and a half hours with the Iranians today were a vivid reminder that we may not have been missing all that much over the years." Nevertheless, our P5+1 colleagues were delighted that the United States was now visible and engaged. The Russians and Chinese seemed particularly impressed. However disappointing the Iranian response, we were back on the high ground.[3]

Neither joining the Geneva meeting nor the interests section initiative produced any substantive breakthroughs as the Bush administration came to an end. I joined Rice for a quiet meeting with Sergey Lavrov in Berlin later in July, and pitched the interests section idea. Lavrov agreed readily that Russia would convey it to Ali Akbar Velayati, the Supreme Leader's foreign policy advisor. But then the war in Georgia intervened, the Russians lost interest in being the messenger, we lost interest in the Russians, and the idea never went any further. We had, however, laid some of the groundwork for Barack Obama's much more active and imaginative approach to the Iranian nuclear dilemma.

* * *

AS HE MADE clear during his campaign for president, Obama sought a mandate to wind down America's wars in the Middle East and to make diplomacy the tool of first resort for protecting American interests. He advocated direct, unconditional engagement with adversaries, embroiling him in an early disagreement with his hard-nosed rival in the Democratic primaries, Hillary Clinton. By the time he took office in January 2009, Iran loomed as the biggest test of both of those propositions—whether diplomacy backed up by economic and military leverage could produce results, and whether direct contacts with our toughest adversaries could pay off.

President Obama found an effective partner for his Iran diplomacy in Clinton. She was instinctively more cautious about engaging the Iranians, and more skeptical about the chances of ever reaching an agreement that would deny Tehran a bomb. She agreed, however, that direct engagement was both the best way to test Iranian seriousness and the best way to invest in the kind of wider international coalition that we'd need to generate more pressure on Iran if it failed those initial tests.

Three days after she was sworn in as secretary of state, I sent Clinton a memo entitled "A New Strategy Toward Iran." I began by trying to encapsulate our fundamental purpose:

> Recognizing that Iran is a significant regional player, our basic goal should be to seek a long-term basis for coexisting with Iranian influence while limiting Iranian excesses, to change Iran's behavior but not its regime. That means, among other things, preventing Iran from achieving nuclear weapons capability; channeling its behavior so that it does not threaten our core interests in a stable, unitary Iraq and an Afghanistan that is not a platform for the export of violent extremism; and gradually reducing Iran's capacity to threaten us and our friends through support for terrorist groups. We should also speak out consistently against human rights abuses in Iran.[4]

I argued for a comprehensive approach. As with China in the early 1970s, it made sense to employ careful and incremental tactics at the outset, but as part of a coherent long-term strategy. "We should set," I said, "an early tone of respect and commitment to direct engagement, however severe our differences." I added the obvious: "Dealing with Iran will require enormous patience, persistence and determination. Deeply conspiratorial and suspicious of American motives, and riven by factions especially eager to undermine one another in the run-up to Iran's Presidential elections in June, the Iranian elite will be prone to false starts and deceit." We shouldn't underestimate the reality that, especially for the Supreme Leader and the hard men around him, animus toward the United States was the core organizing principle for the regime. But, I continued, "we should deal with the Iranian regime as a unitary actor, understanding that the Supreme Leader (not the President) is the highest authority. We have failed consistently in the past when we tried to play off one faction against another."

I also emphasized that we shouldn't lose sight of Iran's vulnerabilities. "Iran is a formidable adversary . . . but it is not ten feet tall. Its economy is badly mismanaged, with rising rates of unemployment and inflation. It is vulnerable to the ongoing sharp decline in oil prices, and to its dependence on refined petroleum products. It has no real friends in the neighborhood, distrusted by the Arabs and the Turks, patronized by the Russians, and suspicious of the Afghans." Finally, I stressed that "we need to be always conscious of the anxieties of our friends, as well as key domestic constituencies, as we proceed with Iran." I warned that our Sunni Arab partners would be nervous that we were abandoning them for a new Persian love interest. The Israelis would be at least as worried, given the undeniable threat that Iran's proxies and nuclear and missile programs posed for them. We'd have a big challenge managing Congress and its widespread aversion to serious engagement with Iran. And, I argued, "we must make sure that the Administration speaks with one voice, and avoids the divisions which beset the last Administration."[5]

Convinced by the argument, Clinton brought discipline and skill to the task. President Obama was eager to begin, and he convened a series of meetings in early 2009 to hammer out a broad strategy, close to the one I had tried to lay out for the secretary. Obama's inheritance on Iran was difficult. When he told the Iranians in his inaugural address on January 20 that "we will extend a hand if you are willing to unclench your fist," Tehran had already stockpiled enough low-enriched uranium for a nuclear weapon. Its missile systems were advancing. And while we had no firm evidence of a revival of Iran's earlier weaponization efforts, we could never be entirely sure.

In March, the president sent a videotaped Nowruz message to the Iranian people and, in a subtle effort to signal his lack of interest in forcing regime change, referred to the government by its formal name—the Islamic Republic. He committed the United States to "engagement that is honest and grounded in mutual respect." The Iranian popular reaction was overwhelmingly positive. The regime, particularly the Supreme Leader, remained skeptical.[6]

In early May, the president sent a long secret letter to the Ayatollah Khamenei. The letter tried to thread a needle—the message needed to be clear, but written in a way that would not cause too much controversy if it was leaked. In the letter, Obama reinforced the broad points in the Nowruz message. He was direct about his unwavering determination to prevent Iran from acquiring a nuclear weapon, and his support for the P5+1 position that Iran was entitled to a peaceful civilian nuclear program. He also made clear that it was not the policy of his administration to pursue regime change, and indicated his readiness for direct dialogue. The Supreme Leader replied a few weeks later, trying to thread a similar needle. His message was rambling, but at least by the standards of revolutionary Iranian rhetoric not especially edgy or sharp. While it offered no explicit reply to the president's offer of direct dialogue, we understood it nevertheless as a serious indication of his willingness to engage. President Obama responded quickly, in a short letter that proposed a discreet bilateral channel for talks, naming me and Puneet Talwar, a senior NSC staffer, as his emissaries.

All this halting momentum, modestly encouraging given the usual tribulations of dealing with Iran, came to an abrupt stop when the Iranian presidential elections in June turned into a bloodbath. The regime's ballot stuffing and repression of a surprisingly potent Green Movement opposition led to violence in the streets, documented by cellphone-wielding Iranian citizens and broadcast around the world in dramatic fashion. The government cracked down with its customary brutality, with paramilitary militias beating demonstrators, thousands arrested, and dozens killed. The White House's public response was initially tepid, less because of concern that it would jeopardize the fledgling effort at talks and more because the message from Green Movement leaders was not to suffocate them with an American embrace and allow the regime to paint them as U.S. stooges. In hindsight, we should have politely ignored those entreaties and been sharper in our public criticism from the start. Such criticism, which we eventually made quite strongly, was not only the right thing to do, it was also a useful reminder to the Iranian regime that we weren't so desperate to get nuclear talks started that we'd turn a blind eye to threatening behavior, whether against Iran's own citizens or our friends in the region.

As the summer of 2009 wore on, we continued to invest systematically in our P5+1 partners. Part of this had to do with an intriguing new idea that had emerged from IAEA director General Mohamed ElBaradei. Near the end of his tenure, ElBaradei still smarted from his frequent clashes with the Bush administration, but was anxious to help the new American administration get off on a more positive footing. The Iranians had sent a formal request to the IAEA in early summer, notifying them that the Tehran Research Reactor (TRR), which produced medical isotopes, had nearly exhausted the supply of 20 percent enriched uranium fuel plates that the Argentines had supplied in the 1990s. The implication seemed clear: Either ElBaradei would produce an alternative supplier, or the Iranians would produce the material themselves—and move closer to weapons-grade enrichment.

ElBaradei had the beginnings of a creative proposal. Why not call the Iranian bluff and supply the fuel plates, which posed no risk of being used for enrichment or weapons purposes? Bob Einhorn, my Baker-era Policy Planning colleague and now a senior advisor on nonproliferation issues at State, and Gary Samore, his counterpart at the NSC staff, took this one very interesting step further. Why not offer to supply the fuel plates for the TRR, but insist in return that the Iranians "pay" with about twelve hundred kilograms of 5 percent enriched uranium, roughly the amount that it would take to produce a batch of 20 percent fuel plates (and roughly the amount for one bomb's worth of material) to replenish the original Argentine shipment? Subtracting it from the then Iranian stockpile of about sixteen hundred kilograms would leave only four hundred kilos, far less than what they would need if they wanted to try to break out toward a weapon. It would take the Iranians a year or so to get back to one bomb's worth of material. That would provide time and space for serious negotiations about both the interim "freeze for freeze" proposal and a comprehensive solution.

Another priority that spring and summer was to strengthen cooperation with Russia on the Iran nuclear problem. The Georgia war in August 2008 had cratered U.S.-Russian relations, and the Obama administration had begun its effort to "reset" the relationship. Cooperation with Russia was the key to making the P5+1 effective. If the Iranians realized that they couldn't separate Moscow and Washington, and that we and the Russians might actually work together on much tougher sanctions, there might be a chance of focusing minds in Tehran. President Obama's conversation with Dmitry Medvedev in London in April 2009 was an excellent start. Secretary Clinton stayed in close touch with Foreign Minister Lavrov, and I had several long, quiet meetings with Deputy Foreign Minister Sergey Ryabkov, my counterpart and Russia's representative in the P5+1 talks. Ryabkov and I discussed the TRR proposal, and began to outline a cooperative arrangement in which Russia might produce the fuel plates for the TRR and take the Iranian low-enriched material in return.

Events came to a head in September 2009. As the annual meeting of the UN General Assembly approached in New York, which would be followed shortly by a G-20 summit in Pittsburgh, U.S., British, and French intelligence uncovered damning evidence of a covert Iranian enrichment site, buried deep inside a mountain near Qom. What made the clandestine site especially alarming was its relatively modest scale; with a capacity of only about three thousand centrifuges, it was much too small to produce enriched uranium fuel for a civilian nuclear power plant, but big enough to produce material for one or two nuclear bombs a year. Apparently nervous that Western governments might be poised to expose them, the Iranians sent a brief, seemingly innocuous note to ElBaradei informing the IAEA (many months after they were obligated to) of vaguely described construction work near Qom, at a site they called Fordow.

ElBaradei walked into a previously scheduled meeting at the Waldorf Astoria hotel in New York with me, Samore, and Einhorn on the evening of September 20. A little jet-lagged, and unaware of what we already knew about Fordow, ElBaradei reached into his pocket and handed us the Iranian notification. As Gary, Bob, and I each took turns looking at it, struggling to seem nonchalant, we quickly realized that it referred to the covert enrichment facility at Qom. We now had a fair amount of leverage with the Iranians, and a powerful argument to use with the Russians. Medvedev was angered by the revelation, partly because the Russians had again been caught off guard, and partly because the Iranians had apparently deceived them too. When President Obama announced the breach we had uncovered a couple days later in Pittsburgh, it deepened the resolve of the P5+1 to push the Iranians hard at the meeting that had already been scheduled in Geneva on October 1, and left Tehran backpedaling.

Led again by Javier Solana, my P5+1 colleagues and I met with Saeed Jalili and the Iranian delegation at a chateau outside Geneva on a sunny day in early October. We spent a desultory three hours in the morning delivering familiar positions across the table. Impatient and concerned that we'd miss the moment, I took advantage of the break for lunch, walked up to Jalili, shook his hand, and said, "I think it would be useful if we sat down and talked." He agreed, having presumably gotten advance permission from Tehran. And so began the highest-level conversation between the United States and Iran since 1979.

We walked over to a small side room and sat down around a polished round table with seats for four. Bob Einhorn joined me, and

Jalili was accompanied by his deputy, Ali Bagheri. Puneet Talwar arrived a few minutes later and sat behind Bob. Jalili was more soft-spoken than in our prior encounter. There were no set pieces this time. This was the first bilateral talk we had ever had with the Iranians on the nuclear issue, and I didn't want to waste it with a long preamble. I was also mindful that Jalili, with or without bombast, remained deeply suspicious of this whole interaction. He was a true believer in the Islamic Revolution, and he had come by his convictions through bitter experience. Wounded fighting the Iraqis in the 1980s, he had lost part of his right leg and walked with a distinct limp. Like many in his generation, he had learned the hard way in the trenches that Iran could trust no one and could only rely on itself.

I laid out carefully the TRR swap concept that ElBaradei had already previewed to the Iranians. Bob added some details, to make sure Jalili and Bagheri understood precisely what we were proposing. Jalili asked a few questions, but seemed to accept the core concept, and to appreciate how Iran would benefit from such a reciprocal arrangement. I also made clear, in a straightforward tone, that the consequences of rejecting the proposal, especially in light of the Qom revelation, were certain to be substantially tougher sanctions. Jalili seemed confident that Tehran would approve. "Our viewpoint," he said, "is positive." After we broke up, I asked Bob to go through the TRR proposal one more time with Jalili's deputy. They produced a paragraph summarizing our understanding, which we agreed that Solana could make public. Our P5+1 partners were supportive, relieved that we finally seemed poised to make some headway.

While hopeful, I told Secretary Clinton on the phone later that afternoon that the chances were probably less than fifty-fifty that the deal would stick in Tehran. Unfortunately, my pessimism proved well founded. A follow-up meeting in Vienna, hosted by the IAEA later in October, collapsed when the Iranians tried to walk back key provisions, particularly the shipment of twelve hundred kilograms of material to Russia. That was the crucial confidence-building step. The irony was that President Ahmadinejad was the biggest booster of the TRR agreement in Tehran, anxious to improve his standing after the disastrous fixed election and show that he could "deliver" the Americans. I assumed that Jalili's positive response in Geneva reflected Ahmadinejad's eagerness, and perhaps also wider regime worries after the Qom revelation that they needed to find a way to ease tensions. The Iranian president's political rivals, some of whom had been involved in the nuclear negotiations before and might otherwise have taken more supportive positions, didn't want Ahmadinejad to get the credit for any breakthrough, however modest. Iranian politics are a brutal contact sport, and the TRR deal was one of its many casualties.

As we had warned Jalili, his rejection of the deal led us to pivot to greater pressure against Iran. Secretary Clinton played a particularly effective role in helping Susan Rice, our ambassador at the United Nations, cajole the members of the Security Council toward a much tougher sanctions resolution, finally passed as UN Security Council Resolution 1929 in early June 2010. The Iranians played their usual critical role in helping us to persuade key members of the council, announcing in February 2010, for example, that they were beginning to enrich to 20 percent, ostensibly for the TRR. Russia's position was crucial; among the permanent, veto-wielding members of the council, we could count on strong support from Britain and France for more substantial sanctions, and China tended on the Iran issue at least to defer to Russia. Frustrated by the Iranians after the Qom disclosures and the failed TRR experiment, and increasingly confident in the possibilities of selective cooperation with the United States as the "reset" evolved, Medvedev eventually came around to support Resolution 1929.

An improvised effort in May by Brazil and Turkey to rescue the TRR proposal and stave off a new round of sanctions was too little, too late. In mid-May, Presidents Luiz Inácio Lula da Silva and Recep Tayyip Erdoğan went to Tehran and announced with great fanfare that they had brokered a breakthrough. The problems with their vaguely worded declaration were manifold: Since the Iranians now had accumulated enough low-enriched uranium for two bombs, exporting half would still leave them with enough for a bomb, if they chose to enrich to weapons-grade; the arrangements for shipping the material out of Iran to be swapped for TRR fuel plates were unclear; and Iran had already started enriching to 20 percent, another new problem. The bigger issue was that we had put enormous effort into getting Russia and China on board for what became UN Security Council Resolution 1929, and it would have been foolish to turn back unless the Iranians had made a spectacular move. This wasn't.

Passage of Resolution 1929, aimed in part at isolating Iran from the international financial system, was an enormous relief. I was at the high school graduation of our younger daughter, Sarah, in Georgetown on the day the vote took place in New York. Much to the consternation of the watch officers at the State Department Operations Center who had been connecting me with calls to P5+1 counterparts and a variety of American colleagues earlier that day, I happily turned my cellphone off for a few hours to enjoy Sarah's moment.

Resolution 1929 provided a platform for additional U.S. sanctions against Iran, as well as significant new EU measures. The U.S. steps, adopted overwhelmingly by Congress two weeks later, were aimed in part at reducing international purchases of Iranian oil, the lifeblood of its crumbling economy. The EU followed in July with a stringent package of its own. Far more than any previous combination of sanctions, these took a serious toll on the Iranian economy. By the end of President Obama's first term, the value of Iran's currency and its oil exports had each declined by 50 percent.

Iranian nuclear advances, however, continued to move at a dangerous pace. By the end of 2012, it had a stockpile of nearly six bombs' worth of 5 percent enriched material, and probably half a bomb's worth of 20 percent material. It was spinning more and more centrifuges at its openly declared site at Natanz, installing centrifuge cascades at Fordow, experimenting with more advanced centrifuges, and continuing work on its heavy water plutonium-producing site at Arak. Its missile systems were increasing in range and sophistication.

The country most alarmed by these developments was Israel. Although appreciative of all the effort that had gone into stepping up sanctions, Prime Minister Netanyahu argued throughout the latter part of Obama's first term that sanctions and diplomacy would be too slow to curb Iran's nuclear ambitions, and that military action would likely be required. His clear preference was to press Obama toward U.S. military action, especially against the deeply embedded enrichment facility at Fordow. Obama was unconvinced by the logic or necessity of force at this stage, and deeply irritated by Netanyahu's heavy-handed attempts to manipulate him in the run-up to the 2012 presidential elections. The Israeli leader's efforts to badger and maneuver Obama into a more belligerent approach had the opposite effect, deepening and accelerating his commitment to finding a way short of war to stop the Iranians.

Even a sweepingly effective attack on the Iranian program, Obama believed, would only set back the Iranians by two or three years. They would undoubtedly regroup, take their program fully underground, and very likely make a decision to weaponize, with wide popular support in the aftermath of a unilateral U.S. or Israeli strike.

Obama and Clinton worked carefully to manage Netanyahu's pressure and demonstrate U.S. determination to ensure by whatever means necessary that Iran would not acquire a nuclear weapon. National Security Advisor Tom Donilon deepened consultations with the Israelis on intelligence, as well as on sanctions and diplomatic strategy. We stepped up the transfer of sophisticated military systems to Israel, and accelerated our own plans for a new, fifteen-ton bomb that could penetrate Fordow. The United States and Israel reportedly jointly developed and deployed a malicious computer worm dubbed Stuxnet to sabotage, at least temporarily, the Iranian program. This campaign helped deflect Netanyahu's push to bomb, but it was clear as President Obama began his second term that the drumbeat would get louder again if we couldn't make diplomacy work. As Hillary Clinton would later describe it, "the table was set" for a renewed diplomatic push, with sanctions eating away at the Iranian economy and a Supreme Leader in Tehran nervous about a repetition of the unrest that had so unsettled his regime in the summer of 2009.[7] What was still missing, however, was a direct channel with the Iranians.

* * *

THE STORY OF how the Omani back channel to Iran emerged seems, like so many things in diplomacy, a lot neater in retrospect than it did at the time. Sultan Qaboos, an engaging ruler of the old Arab school, had navigated complicated currents at home and in the region for more than four decades, and had maintained a good rapport with the Supreme Leader in Tehran. Eager to play the intermediary, and nervous about the dangers of conflict so close to home, Oman sent the new U.S. administration a series of low-key overtures about its readiness to establish a channel to Iran.

The principal messenger for the sultan was Salem Ismaily, a clever, urbane, persistent, and resourceful advisor, who, in the ambiguous way in which Middle East elites often function, moved easily between the worlds of officialdom and private business, and was often used as a trusted fixer and negotiator. Salem was supremely confident of his ability to set up a reliable channel to Tehran, although sometimes murky about who exactly he was dealing with on the Iranian side. Given the checkered history of American-Iranian contacts, we were always skeptical of new initiatives, which often turned out to be over-enthusiastic at best, and duplicitous at worst.

But Salem's steady and upbeat insistence that he could deliver, backed up by long-standing trust in Qaboos, set the Omani overtures apart. What solidified my confidence in Salem and his relationships in Tehran was his role in securing the release of three young American hikers who had strayed into Iran along the border with Iraqi Kurdistan in the summer of 2009. They were arrested and thrown into the dismal confines of Evin Prison in downtown Tehran, where American embassy hostages had been held many years before. The hikers faced deep uncertainty. We tried through a variety of channels to secure their release, with no luck—until Salem got involved. Using his contacts in Tehran and the sultan's reputation and resources, he managed over the next two years to negotiate the release of all three Americans.

In October 2011, shortly after the hikers had returned home, Secretary Clinton met with Qaboos in Muscat, and concluded that the Omani channel was our best bet. President Obama spoke a couple times by phone with the sultan, and was similarly impressed, especially by Qaboos's conviction that he could deliver contacts with Iranians fully authorized by the Supreme Leader. I shared the view that the Omanis offered a promising opening, although I always wondered whether their relative success with the Iranians was a matter of their influence and ingenuity, or perhaps simply that they were a convenient vehicle for the Iranian regime when it decided to unburden itself of problems (like the hikers) or test channels with some plausible deniability. It also always appealed to the Iranians to sow dissension among the Gulf Arabs and use the Omanis to irritate the Saudis.

Even more energetic in his promotion of the Oman channel was Senator John Kerry, chairman of the Senate Foreign Relations Committee. Kerry had long been persuaded that the United States had to come to terms with Iran's nuclear progress and engage directly. Coordinating with Clinton and Donilon, he had a series of meetings and phone calls with the sultan and Ismaily in late 2011 and 2012, which made him a passionate advocate of the Oman channel. He made clear his commitment to exploring a dialogue with the Iranians, and his interest in playing a personal role.

At around the same time, Salem came to us with a new proposal, which he and the sultan were certain bore the approval of the Supreme Leader. He suggested a direct U.S.-Iranian meeting in Muscat, quietly facilitated by the Omanis. He asserted that the Iranians would be prepared to address any issue, but wanted to focus in particular on the nuclear problem. He was uncertain who would lead the Iranian team, but thought it might be Ali Velayati. After some debate in Washington, we decided to suggest a preliminary, preparatory meeting at a lower level. We had been burned so many times in the past few decades that caution seemed wise.

Jake Sullivan, still serving as Secretary Clinton's Policy Planning director, and Puneet Talwar were natural choices to represent the United States at this exploratory session. Puneet had joined me for innumerable P5+1 rounds, and was a key player in the TRR initiative. Jake was Hillary Clinton's closest policy advisor. He had her full confidence, and the president's trust.

In early July, Jake was off on yet another overseas trip with the secretary when I called him and asked if he could break off for a couple days in Oman. He didn't hesitate, and made his way from Paris to Muscat, where, hosted by Salem, he and Puneet spent a long and not particularly encouraging day with a mid-level Iranian delegation. Jake reported that the Iranians had been almost entirely in "receive mode," and seemed intent on securing some kind of substantive down payment for any future talks. They were particularly focused on the thorny issue of their "right" to enrichment—something that the Treaty on the Non-Proliferation of Nuclear Weapons did not explicitly convey, and that their continuing violation of successive IAEA and UNSC resolutions did little to promote. With his usual candor, an unusually effective mix of Minnesota politeness and East Coast hardheadedness, Jake made clear that the issue was what the Iranians would do to satisfy powerful international concerns, not the other way around.

Over the next few months, as the American elections approached in November, both sides regrouped. We made clear, through Salem, that we were ready for further meetings but weren't in any rush. Sanctions pressure was building, and we wanted the Iranian government to feel the pain.

Following President Obama's second inauguration, John Kerry succeeded Hillary Clinton as secretary of state. On the same day his nomination was announced, Kerry asked me to stay on as deputy secretary. I had planned to retire, but I was glad to accept.

It was obvious that Secretary Kerry, like the president, wanted to make Iran negotiations a priority for the second term. Sensing an opening, Salem conveyed renewed interest from the Iranians in meeting again, this time at a higher level, with a deputy foreign minister heading their delegation. We eventually settled on March 1, 2013, in Oman. I would lead the American team, with Jake as my alter ego. He had already become my closest collaborator in the Obama administration—the best of his generation of foreign policy thinkers and practitioners, strategically creative as well as tactically adept. We'd be joined by Puneet and Bob Einhorn; Jim Timbie, whose encyclopedic knowledge of nuclear issues and four-plus decades of negotiating experience made him a quiet national treasure; Richard Nephew, a specialist on sanctions; and Norm Roule, the senior advisor on Iran in our intelligence community.

The president convened several meetings in February to review our approach. In all my three decades in government, this was—along with the bin Laden raid in 2011—the most tightly held effort. The White House Situation Room, usually crowded with cabinet officials and backbenchers, was unusually spare. Only a handful of people in the White House and the State Department knew of the secret talks, and we went to great lengths to preserve their discretion. Meetings on this issue didn't go on our public calendars, or bore innocuous titles; documents related to the talks were kept only on the ultra-secure White House communications systems.

By this point, the president's grasp of the Iranian nuclear issue and his policy sense were both well developed. His expectations were realistic; he knew the odds that the Iranians would be willing or able to accept sharp limitations on their nuclear program were low. He also knew the dangers of being played by Tehran, as had happened too many times before. Yet he was determined to test the proposition, and secure in the investment he and Secretary Clinton had made in the first term on sanctions and international solidarity. "We're as well positioned to negotiate as we've ever been," Obama said in one session in the Situation Room. "We've set this up right. Now we'll see if we can make this work."

President Obama laid out the framework for our effort crisply. First, our direct channel wasn't a substitute for the wider P5+1 channel, but a pragmatic complement. Agreements on the nuclear issue could only come through that broader group, since it was the source of much of the international pressure that was starting to weigh on Tehran.

Second, we would have to keep the bilateral channel secret. The Iranians, facing enormous internal pressures, and filled with suspicion of American motives, warned that any premature disclosure would make it impossible to continue. Secrecy would help prevent opponents in both capitals from smothering the initiative in its crib— but it would carry future costs, feeding stab-in-the-back criticisms from some of our closest partners, particularly the Israelis, Saudis, and Emiratis. We knew that secret talks would be hard to sustain. In the age of omnipresent information technology and never-ending media scrutiny, it was unlikely that we could avoid disclosure for long. Oman was a relatively quiet and off-the-beaten-path place, but it was also a fishbowl in its own way, under the intermittent scrutiny of a variety of intelligence services.

We also knew that transitioning from a direct channel back into multilateral talks would be complicated and awkward. Some of the best foreign diplomats with whom I had ever worked had been or remained part of the P5+1. I didn't much enjoy the idea of keeping our efforts from them. But we would never have gotten as far as we later did, as relatively fast as we did, if we had been trying to negotiate with the Iranians in the glare of international publicity, and solely in the inevitably more cumbersome P5+1 process.

The president stressed a third point. We would focus the back-channel talks on the nuclear issue, which was the most pressing and explosive of our many problems with Iran. It was the concern around which we had united the international community and built such powerful pressure, and the one on which the Iranians seemed prepared to engage. Moreover, our Gulf Arab partners were adamant that we not widen the aperture of the nuclear talks and address Iran's non-nuclear transgressions, unless they were in the room. The purpose of the secret bilateral talks would be to test Iranian seriousness on the nuclear issue, and jump-start the broader P5+1 process.

This was a fairly transactional and unsentimental view of the nuclear negotiations, without any grand illusions of overnight transformations in Iranian behavior or U.S.-Iranian relations. I was a short-term pessimist about the prospect for such changes, given the cold-blooded nature of that regime, its resilience and practiced capacity to repress, and the opportunities before it to meddle in a troubled Arab world. We knew we'd have to embed any progress on the nuclear issue in a wider strategy to push back against threatening Iranian behavior in the region, and preserve leverage and non-nuclear sanctions to draw on.

The president's fourth bit of guidance cut right to the core of the transactional challenge. We would indicate to the Iranians, carefully, that if they were prepared to accept tight, long-term constraints on their nuclear program, with heavily intrusive verification and monitoring arrangements, we would be prepared to explore the possibility of a limited domestic enrichment program as part of a comprehensive agreement. There had been considerable internal back-and-forth on this issue, beneath the president's level, less over whether to play this card than when. I thought it was best to do it at the outset, as a sign of our seriousness and a test of theirs, putting the burden squarely on the Iranians to show that they would accept tough constraints, and make clear in practical terms that they wouldn't be able to break out to a bomb. Tom Donilon was a little uneasy about that tactic. He wanted to see more tangible evidence of Iranian seriousness before playing a card that—however carefully framed the proposition— would be hard to put back in the deck.

The president was convinced that we'd never get an agreement with the Iranians without some limited form of domestic enrichment. They had the knowledge to enrich, and there was no way you could bomb, sanction, or wish that away. Maybe we could have gotten to a zero enrichment outcome a decade earlier, when they were spinning a few dozen centrifuges. That was extremely unlikely to happen in 2013, with the Iranians operating some nineteen thousand centrifuges, and with broad popular support across the country for enrichment as part of a civilian program. The president wanted to cut to the chase in the back-channel talks, and that made sense to me. He approved the caveated formula we suggested, but placed heavy emphasis on the verb "explore." This was not a promise or a guarantee.

Finally, the president reminded all of us that the chances of success were "well under fifty-fifty." We'd keep all our other options open. We'd keep developing the "bunker buster" bomb we'd need to strike Fordow. The Pentagon would "set the theater" and demonstrate through regular deployments and thorough preparations that our military was prepared to act. We'd keep up other efforts to slow and obstruct the Iranian program. And we'd be ready to pivot again from a failed negotiating effort to even stronger sanctions. If direct talks went nowhere, it would be harder to blame the United States, and easier to build more pressure against a recalcitrant Iran.

At the end of our last meeting, the president shook hands with Jake and me and said simply, "Good luck." Obama was staking a lot on this uncertain enterprise, and we were determined to do all we could to make it work.

* * *

WE WOULD SOON get used to long flights to Oman in unmarked planes with blank passenger manifests, but I was too restless on that first trip at the end of February 2013 to sleep, wondering what lay ahead. Salem met us on arrival at a military airfield in Muscat, upbeat as always, and confirmed that the Iranian delegation, led by Deputy Foreign Minister Ali Asghar Khaji, had arrived just before us.

We drove about thirty minutes outside Muscat, to a secluded military officers' club on the Arabian Sea. Its four walls became the boundaries of our little universe for the next few days. Our team spent that first evening reviewing our approach to the start of talks the next morning and hashing out roles and responsibilities. Our expectations were modest, but after many months of internal debate and planning, we were just glad to finally get started.

The next morning was typically hot and humid. I went out on an early-morning stroll, but the sauna-like conditions did little to cure me of my jet lag. Salem, the chief of the royal court, and the head of Omani intelligence greeted both delegations as we walked into the meeting room, which offered a panoramic view of the sea. I shook hands with Khaji and his colleagues, who included Reza Zabib, the chief of the Iranian Foreign Ministry's North America division; Davoud Mohammadnia, from the Ministry of Internal Security, or MOIS; representatives of Iran's atomic energy agency; a capable Iranian interpreter; and what I always assumed were a number of listening devices to record our conversations. We sat on opposite sides of a long table, too weighted down by history to enjoy the view or the moment. The Omanis, clustered around the head of the table, offered a few brief words of welcome and then departed. There was then an awkward pause.

I broke the silence by asking Khaji if he wanted to speak first. In what was an early indication that the Iranians were mostly on a reconnaissance mission, he deferred to me. I then made a brief presentation, along the lines the president had approved in the Situation Room a few days before. I tried to strike a respectful but candid tone. This was an important moment for both of us, a rare chance to talk directly and privately. We had no illusions about how hard this would be. While it was not our purpose to point fingers or lecture, there were profound mutual suspicions, and a long record of Iranian defiance of its international obligations that had provoked widespread concern. There were too many unanswered questions; too many obvious disconnects between the requirements of a realistic civilian nuclear energy program and the pace and lack of transparency of Iran's efforts; and too much disregard for the clear requirements of a series of UN Security Council resolutions. There was a serious and growing risk that Iran's domestic enrichment capacity could be quickly and covertly converted to produce weapons-grade, highly enriched uranium. That concern cut right to the core of what was at stake and the dilemma we faced.

The nuclear issue was not just a dispute between Iran and the United States, but between Iran and the P5+1, and the broader international community. I repeated the president's message in his earlier letters to the Supreme Leader—it was not the policy of the United States to seek regime change in Iran, but we were absolutely determined to ensure that Iran did not acquire a nuclear weapon. Any hope for a diplomatic resolution would require Iran to understand the depth of international concerns and act upon them. I repeated bluntly that failure to take advantage of the uncertain window before us would certainly increase the costs to Iran, and the risk of military conflict.

The key to any diplomatic progress would be Iran's willingness to take concrete, substantial measures to give the rest of us confidence that a peaceful program could not be converted into a weapons program. If Iran were ready to do that, I continued, we would be willing to explore whether and how a domestic enrichment program could be pursued in Iran, as part of a comprehensive settlement of the nuclear issue. That settlement would require many difficult, long-term Iranian commitments, and intense verification and monitoring provisions. Should we eventually reach a satisfactory agreement, the United States would be prepared to call for an end to all United Nations and unilateral sanctions against the Iranian nuclear program. Such a process would likely have to unfold in phases, with early practical steps to build confidence, leading to a comprehensive agreement.

There was enormous skepticism in both our capitals, I concluded. I shared much of that skepticism, but if the Supreme Leader's fatwa against nuclear weapons was serious, then it shouldn't be impossible to find a diplomatic path forward and prove the skeptics wrong. We were certainly prepared to try.

As I went through this presentation, Khaji and his colleagues listened and took copious notes. There were a few cold stares, and some head-shaking, but no interruptions. The Iranians in Oman were a welcome change and stark contrast to the doctrinaire, obstructionist Jalili-led delegation in the P5+1 talks. They were professionals, mostly career diplomats, and it wasn't hard to sense a shift in style and seriousness of engagement.

When I was done, Khaji took the floor. His tone was measured, even when he recited a long and predictable list of grievances about American policy. He spoke sharply about the unfairness of UN Security Council resolutions, the assassinations of Iranian nuclear scientists, and the U.S. public emphasis that "all options are on the table." He objected to American references over the years to the use of "carrots and sticks" against Iran. Raising his voice, he exclaimed, "Iranians are not donkeys!"

Khaji had little of substance to offer, although he stressed that he "wanted to look to the future." The Iranian delegation had clearly taken note of my heavily caveated comment about domestic enrichment, but they were looking for (and probably expecting) more. Khaji asserted that Iran would defend its "right" to the whole nuclear fuel cycle, including enrichment, "at any cost." We went back and forth over this argument, emphasizing our conviction that no such explicit "right" was granted by the NPT. The problem that Iran's defiant behavior had created was simply that there were serious and growing international doubts about whether it wanted only a civilian pro-

gram, or might pursue a military one. The onus was on Iran to dis-
prove those doubts. Constant reassertion of imaginary rights was not
going to get anywhere.

In the first of several one-on-one conversations, Khaji and I sat
privately after the opening plenary meeting. He was approachable
but guarded, and acknowledged that he was encouraged that we were
finally talking to each other directly. He appealed almost plaintively
for acceptance of Iran's right to enrich, implying that it would be hard
to engage without it. At one point he pulled out a bulky file of papers,
which appeared to be Omani notes from alleged conversations with
various Americans, including members of Congress, acknowledging
Iran's right to enrich. I explained that in our political system, members of Congress did not speak for the president. I repeated our position, said I was sure those conversations were taken out of context or
were well-meaning Omani garbles, and stressed that we needed to
focus on what was practical if we were going to get this process off the
ground.

We spent the next couple days covering essentially the same terrain over and over. I took evening walks with Khaji around the officers' club compound, and Jake and my other colleagues had similar
chats with their counterparts. There was a powerful cognitive dissonance at the heart of our discussions at this stage, which never entirely disappeared throughout the secret talks. The Iranians would
maintain, in a tone of wounded pride, that the nuclear problem was
all a big misunderstanding, that they had done nothing wrong, never
had explored steps toward a bomb, and had acted within their international rights. Sanctions were unjust and should be lifted. We responded firmly that the Iranians would never get anywhere in nuclear
negotiations if they didn't realize that they had a gaping credibility
problem—not just with the United States but with the wider international community.

Near the end of our final session on March 3, Jake and I told the
Iranians bluntly that there wasn't much point in continuing the se-

cret talks if they weren't going to think much more seriously about the tangible steps they would need to take. The Iranians were wildly unrealistic in their expectations; they weren't in the same ballpark, or even playing the same sport, as an increasingly determined international community.

Zabib made an impassioned plea as we wrapped up the last meeting. He recounted a trip to New York years before, and a large sign he had encountered at JFK airport on his arrival. Torturing his English syntax a bit, he recalled that it read "Think the Big." "That's what you Americans must do," he said. "Think the big. If you do, everything will become better." I smiled at Jake. Neither of us could think of a succinct way to explain that the issue here was not the elasticity of our thought process, but the seriousness of Iran's commitment. So we simply urged them to think about everything we had discussed over the previous three days in Oman, and to consider the choices that lay before them.

It was an incongruous conclusion to an incongruous first round. We reported back to Washington that we were "miles apart on substance." Khaji was an able diplomat, but not empowered. None of that was unexpected, after so many years of not talking to one another directly. The atmospherics were significantly better than the more sterile P5+1 process had been, with at least the possibility of less polemical and more practical conversations, and maybe more room for creativity. Zabib's plea to "think the big" did not exactly fill us with confidence, but it was at least a start.

We retraced our seventeen-hour journey and arrived back in Washington on March 4, our secret still intact. The next day, with Secretary Kerry out of the country, the president asked to see Jake and me in the Oval Office so we could report directly on our discussions in Oman. The president was sitting in his usual chair in front of the fireplace, having just finished his regular morning intelligence briefing. He listened attentively. We went through our impressions, careful not to oversell what was just a first step on a long road. "I never expected immediate progress," the president said. "This may or may not work. But it's the right thing to do. Let's just hope we can keep it quiet, and keep it going."

* * *

WE HAD LEFT that Omani beach compound still not convinced that our secret initiative had a future. Events over the rest of the spring were not reassuring. The P5+1 met with Jalili and the Iranians in Almaty in early April, but made no headway. We had made clear through Salem Ismaily and the Omanis that we were ready to resume the back-channel talks, but the Iranians were consumed by the run-up to their presidential elections in June. There was no point in running after them; we had no idea who would succeed Ahmadinejad, and it made sense to wait and see.

The unexpected election of Hassan Rouhani in June 2013 created a modest new sense of possibility. A former lead nuclear negotiator and a wily survivor in the unsentimental world of revolutionary Iranian politics, Rouhani saw the toll that international sanctions (as well as Ahmadinejad's erratic populist mismanagement) had taken on the country's economy. He managed to persuade the Supreme Leader that Iran needed to explore a more serious nuclear negotiation and consider some real compromises, or face a resurgence of the internal political unrest that had jarred the regime in the summer of 2009. In hindsight, it was useful to have launched the secret channel while Ahmadinejad was still president and before Rouhani was elected. Had we waited until after the election, it might have appeared to the ever-suspicious Khamenei that we were fixated on Rouhani and neglecting the ultimate decision-maker. It also cost Rouhani far less political capital to push for direct talks with the Americans when the more hawkish Ahmadinejad government had already crossed that Rubicon.

Rouhani had a resourceful partner in his new foreign minister, Javad Zarif, who emerged as the new face of Iranian diplomacy. With a doctorate from the University of Denver, where he (like Condi Rice) had studied under Madeleine Albright's father, Zarif had served for many years as Iran's permanent representative to the United Nations in New York. He was a formidable diplomat. He knew how to navigate his own treacherous political system and squeeze the most out of his instructions—and he knew how to use his talents and sympathetic image, as well as a sometimes frustrating gift for melodrama, to cajole and maneuver the rest of us.

President Obama's short congratulatory message to Rouhani received a rapid and positive reply. Rouhani was inaugurated on August 4, and two days later announced publicly his readiness to resume the P5+1 talks. The Iranians also told the Omanis that they wanted to restart the back-channel process, and Salem came away from conversations in Tehran that summer convinced of newfound seriousness. We agreed to meet again at the beach compound in early September.

In preparation, we took stock of our approach. Our long-term challenge remained the same: to cut off the pathways that the Iranians might use to develop a nuclear weapon. By the time of Rouhani's inauguration, they had accumulated a substantial stockpile of enriched uranium. Meanwhile, they were continuing construction of their heavy water plant at Arak, moving steadily to create a potential plutonium pathway to a bomb. A covert effort remained our biggest concern.

We had substantial negotiating assets. UNSC sanctions, as well as U.S. and EU measures, were having a major impact. Markets for Iran's oil exports were rapidly contracting, and Tehran was starved for hard currency, with over $100 billion in oil revenues frozen and inaccessible in overseas banks.

We were determined to get the most out of that leverage. A two-stage process still made the most sense, given the mistrust between us, and the urgency of freezing their nuclear progress to give us time to try to negotiate a comprehensive deal. We'd seek in an initial phase to stop the advance of the Iranian nuclear program, across all of its fronts, in return for no further nuclear sanctions. In addition, we'd try to roll back key aspects of their program, especially their 20 percent enrichment effort, in return for limited sanctions relief. We'd also seek initially to apply the most intrusive inspection procedures possible, across the entire supply chain, from uranium mines and mills to centrifuge production and storage. That would create a solid precedent for longer-term verification provisions in a comprehensive agreement.

The president convened a session shortly before we returned to Oman to give us our final guidance. Vice President Biden, Secretary Kerry, and Susan Rice, who had recently succeeded Tom Donilon as national security advisor, were there too, along with a tiny circle of officials who knew of the back channel. All the principals by this point knew the details of the nuclear issue and our approach. The president's grasp of arcane technical details was impressive, as was John Kerry's, who was eager to dive in himself at the right time.

As the president concluded the meeting, he motioned Jake and me over as he walked out the door of the Situation Room. "You guys know what needs to get done," he said. "I trust you. So don't screw it up." He smiled slightly, but we couldn't decide whether to feel buoyed by his confidence, anxious about his warning, or some of both. Those are the moments when you'd almost prefer the comfortable straitjacket of fourteen pages of single-spaced instructions.

The Iranian delegation this time was led by two deputy foreign ministers, Majid Takht-Ravanchi and Abbas Araghchi. In Zarif's mold, both had done graduate degrees in the West, Ravanchi at the University of Kansas and Araghchi at the University of Kent in the United Kingdom. Both were tough Iranian patriots, skeptical of doing business with Americans and dogged in arguing their positions. We discovered that they could also be creative problem-solvers. In the hours and hours of conversations that followed, we exhausted the whole range of emotions, searching for practical solutions, occasionally pounding the table or walking out of the room, and sometimes even finding a little bit of humor in our shared predicament. While trust was always in short supply between Iranians and Americans, I developed considerable professional respect for Ravanchi and Araghchi, although I doubted that expressing that publicly would be career-enhancing for either of them.

Ravanchi and Araghchi were professional diplomats, not ideologues, but they were no less committed to Iran, no less proud of the revolution, no less determined to show that they could hold their own in the diplomatic arena. They were often guarded about the difficulties they faced at home, although they would sometimes confide that they had a Supreme Leader who was just waiting to say "I told you so" and prove that the Americans could not be trusted and that Obama was just as bent on regime change as Bush.

From the start, the atmosphere in the September round was much different, and more encouraging, than what we had experienced in March. We conducted the negotiations in English, without translation, which made for much easier and more informal discussions. Ravanchi and Araghchi were comfortable in their interactions with us, always careful to stay within the bounds of their instructions, but uninhibited in going back and forth in more formal plenary sessions or smaller conversations. They agreed that first day that a two-phase approach was best. We talked about the broad outline of a comprehensive deal, but agreed quickly that we'd get stuck if we tried at this early stage to get much beyond general principles. We spent most of our time on what it would take to put together a six-month interim accord. They had thoroughly digested our exchanges with Khaji. While they would regularly come back at the issue of a "right" to enrichment, they understood our position and didn't belabor the point, at least at this stage.

The pattern for our meetings in the back channel soon took shape. We would begin with a five-on-five plenary session, and then break for separate conversations, sometimes one-on-one and often Araghchi and Ravanchi with Jake and me, while our colleagues would get into more detail on the limitations and verification measures we had in mind, and the sanctions relief at the front of the Iranians' mind.

Our biggest challenge was countering Iranian expectations of the magnitude of sanctions relief that we could offer for the interim phase. We believed that the best tool we had for providing limited relief was the frozen oil revenue that was gradually building up in foreign banks, at a rate of roughly $18 billion every six months. Metering out a fraction of those funds would allow us to preserve the overall architecture of sanctions, and keep all the leverage we'd later need for comprehensive talks. Not surprisingly, the Iranians had a vastly different definition of what "limited" relief meant. They insisted stubbornly that all $18 billion should be released in return for their acceptance of six-month limitations on their program. We indicated early on that we could consider no more than about $4 billion.

Another problem was Iranian concern about how much they could count on a commitment by the U.S. administration not to enact new sanctions for six months, given the role of Congress. It was not an unreasonable worry. We explained at length how our system worked, and why we believed an administration commitment would hold up, assuming that Iran limited its program substantially along the lines we were discussing. But the Iranians were never entirely reassured by the formulas we offered, and the truth is that we weren't either, given the uncertain state of American politics. "The best thing we can do," I told Araghchi, "is make a solid agreement, and then live up to it scrupulously." Those words would ring hollow a few years later.

While it was clear after this session that we still had a tough slog ahead of us, we could now see that a first-step understanding was possible. With relatively modest sanctions relief, we could freeze their program, and roll it back in some important respects. Rouhani and Zarif seemed to want to show their own critics at home that they could produce early progress and begin to ease sanctions pressure. We reported all this to the White House and Secretary Kerry, conscious of the value of underpromising and overdelivering. We also stressed the Iranians' concern that we keep this channel secret. In our side conversations, both Ravanchi and Araghchi had worried that premature disclosure would torpedo the talks at home.

We agreed with the Iranians to meet next in New York later in September, when the annual UN General Assembly session would provide good cover for Ravanchi and Araghchi to come with Zarif, as well as Rouhani, who was making his first visit to the UN as Iran's president. We had four rounds of talks over nearly two weeks in New York, and made considerable progress. Jake and I put an initial draft text on the table in our first discussion with Ravanchi and Araghchi on the evening of September 18, in a room at the Waldorf Astoria. We were acutely aware of the danger of negotiating with ourselves as time wore on, but it quickly became apparent that we could much more effectively drive the process by taking the pen. We also realized that the only way we could really be sure that we were making progress was to put notional understandings on paper. Araghchi in particular bristled at our continuing insistence that we couldn't provide more than a small fraction of frozen Iranian oil revenue during the initial six-month period, and at our emphasis on mothballing nuclear infrastructure to reassure us that frozen centrifuges could not simply be reactivated. We kept at it, and over the next week painstakingly removed brackets around contested language and agreed on significant portions of the interim agreement.

As productive as the New York rounds were, they had their moments of minor drama too. Just as the Iranians were walking down the hall to our meeting room at the Waldorf, Jake and I noticed that hanging on the wall across from the room was a large framed photo of the shah visiting the Waldorf in the 1970s. We tried to take it down quickly, but it was firmly attached to the wall. Ravanchi and Araghchi didn't seem to notice as we hurriedly ushered them through the door. The last thing we wanted was to offend our counterparts or inspire a forty-minute recitation about America's support for the ancien régime.

We conducted several more rounds later in the week across town, away from the hustle and bustle of the United Nations meetings, at a hotel on Manhattan's West Side. The Iranian delegation had no trouble moving in and out of the hotel quietly. With its kaleidoscope of humanity, Manhattan was one place where five guys with white shirts buttoned all the way up and no ties could blend in easily.

Our progress in the direct bilateral talks set the stage for Secretary Kerry's first encounter with Zarif, on the margins of a P5+1 ministerial meeting at the UN on September 26. In their thirty-minute tête-à-tête, Kerry and Zarif reviewed the encouraging results of the back channel so far, and agreed that we should keep at it. It was the first half hour of what would be endless hours of face-to-face meetings, texts, and telephone calls between them; their relationship and drive was at the heart of everything that was later achieved.

Meanwhile, Jake was trying to explore the possibility of a meeting between Rouhani and Obama. The initial signals we received from Zarif and the Iranian negotiators were positive, but Rouhani and his political advisors got more concerned about the potential backlash in Tehran the more they considered the idea. Rouhani had already made quite a splash at the UN, sounding decidedly unlike Ahmadinejad as he acknowledged the Holocaust, and working with Zarif in a flurry of meetings and interviews to put a much different face on Iranian diplomacy. Once the Iranians began to press us to agree to preconditions for even a brief pull-aside encounter, invoking the familiar plea for some recognition of a "right" to enrich, it was apparent that the effort to engineer a meeting was not worth it.

Somewhat to our surprise, the Iranians came back to us with a proposal for a phone call between the two presidents on Rouhani's last day in New York. There were no preconditions. The call was connected as Rouhani was in his car on the way to the airport. The brief silence during the connection felt like a lifetime. Not surprisingly, Jake was anxious—about whether he had been given the right number, or whether this was all a setup in which some radio host in Canada would pop up on the line in an elaborate prank. Finally, the call connected. Obama and Rouhani had a cordial fifteen-minute conversation. Obama congratulated Rouhani on his election, and stressed that they now had an historic opportunity to resolve the nuclear issue. Mindful that a variety of foreign intelligence services might be listening, Obama made only an oblique reference to the secret bilateral talks. Rouhani responded in the same constructive tone, closing with a somewhat surreal "Have a nice day" in English. The glimmer of possibility was steadily getting brighter.

We met twice more in October in the familiar confines of the Omani beach club. Sanctions relief remained a source of great irritation to the Iranians. We wouldn't budge from our position of roughly $4 billion in relief over six months, far short of the $18 billion that the Iranians sought. We still had sharp differences over restrictions on the Arak heavy water facility, as well as over the continuing Iranian insistence on language about their "right" to enrich. Trying to anticipate some of the main lines of concern expressed by critics of the P5+1 process, we pressed relatively late in the game for a freeze on new centrifuge production, not just their installation. That set Araghchi off. "What are you going to demand next?" he asked, with an air of deep exasperation.

We talked at length with the Iranians about how best to handle the resumption of P5+1 meetings in Geneva in mid-October, in the middle of our extended back-channel talks that month. We both recognized that we were approaching the point where we would merge the two processes, but we had made surprising strides in the secret bilateral talks, and thought it was worth seeing how far we could get by the end of October. Araghchi suggested that Iran make a general presentation to the P5+1, laying out the broad contours of a two-phase approach, including interim and comprehensive agreements. The Iranians left out the details to which we had tentatively agreed, as well as the areas of continuing disagreement, but it was useful to introduce the framework. By the time we completed an intensive two-day back-channel session on October 26–27, we had a draft text that still had five or six contested passages, but that was beginning to resemble a solid step forward after so many years of tension on the nuclear issue. In a meeting with Sultan Qaboos just before we flew home from Muscat, I again expressed our appreciation for everything he had done to make this channel work. "We're getting close," I assured him.

* * *

THE PRESIDENT WAS pleased with the progress we had made, but intent in his lawyerly way on "buttoning it down tight." We were genuinely surprised that we had come such a long way in such a short time. We were equally surprised that the back channel had stayed secret through eight rounds. We realized that that would not last much longer, with at least two journalists already beginning to put some of the pieces together.

A new P5+1 round under the leadership of EU high representative Cathy Ashton was scheduled to begin on November 7 in Geneva. With Wendy Sherman, my exceptional successor as undersecretary for political affairs and as head of our P5+1 delegation, joining us for the late October back-channel talks in Oman, we had told the Iranians that we would inform our multilateral partners of our direct bilateral meetings before the November session. They were a little nervous, but understood that the time had come. We scheduled another back-channel round on November 5–7 to see if we could remove another bracket or two in the draft text, before turning it over to our P5+1 partners for their consideration as the basis for rapid completion of an interim agreement.

Wendy had the unenviable task of briefing our P5+1 colleagues on the back-channel effort. The debate about when to tell our closest allies about the secret talks had been extensive. I was torn, having spent years as undersecretary working with my P5+1 counterparts, and understanding the very real concerns of the Israelis and our Gulf Arab partners, but also acutely aware of the risks of leaks and premature public disclosures. The White House preferred, in any case, to hold off as long as we could in the fall of 2013, but by the end of October there was no longer any good reason to wait.

Starting with Ashton, who knew as well as anyone that bilateral U.S.-Iran talks were essential, Wendy laid out the quiet effort we had been making, and the main areas of agreement and disagreement with the Iranians. Some of our partners were not entirely surprised. The British government, for example, had excellent contacts in Oman, and was generally aware of our progress. The president had also taken Prime Minister Netanyahu into his confidence at the end of September, in a one-on-one conversation at the White House. Netanyahu was not surprised either, since the Israelis had their own sources in the region, but he was decidedly less understanding than the Brits. He saw our back channel as a betrayal.

On November 5, we met with the Iranians at the Mandarin Hotel in Geneva, on the other side of town from the InterContinental, where the P5+1 session would take place a couple days later. The president and Secretary Kerry told us to make a final push to improve the draft text, which now bore the suitably anodyne title "draft joint working document." We made a little more progress on defining a "pause" on Arak, but still had bracketed language there. We had made quite a bit of headway on specifying the elements of a freeze on enrichment at Natanz and Fordow, and on conversion and dilution of Iran's existing stockpile of 20 percent enriched material. We were close to an understanding on sanctions relief in return, at roughly the $4 billion figure over six months that we had set out at the start of the back-channel talks. We also settled on an unprecedented set of verification and monitoring measures that would serve as a solid foundation for much more detailed arrangements in an eventual comprehensive agreement. The draft text we produced with Ravanchi and Araghchi still had three or four difficult brackets to resolve in its four and a half single-spaced pages.

It was probably inevitable that the handover to the P5+1 would have its awkward moments. Some of our European colleagues were impressed by our progress, but not happy about being kept in the dark. Ashton did a superb job of focusing the group on the opportunity the draft text offered. With Zarif already in Geneva to take charge of the Iranian team, John Kerry flew in on November 8. French foreign minister Laurent Fabius was close on his heels, bringing both considerable Gallic ego, a bit bruised over the back channel, and some solid ideas on how to tighten language, especially on Arak. Sergey Lavrov and the other ministers flew in too.

The next couple of days had lots of drama, some contrived and some reflecting real frustration, emotion, and exhaustion. Pressures were building in Washington for another round of sanctions, and Zarif faced his own share of domestic suspicions and second-guessing. Some of our P5+1 partners were still smarting over the back channel. Ashton and Kerry skillfully defused most of the tensions within the P5+1, and we developed a revised text that the group supported. It built on the back-channel draft, filling in new proposed language in some of the bracketed areas, and adding a few new sentences.

Zarif was not thrilled to see this updated text on November 9. The Iranians knew that the bilateral draft we had been working on for months still had brackets with unresolved differences over language. They also knew that it would have to be reviewed and accepted by the rest of the P5+1, who would undoubtedly want to put their own stamp on it. As Zarif reminded Kerry, he faced a tough audience in Tehran, and any shifts in language, however minor, were troublesome. Like other accomplished diplomats, Zarif was also a gifted thespian, and his head-in-hands expressions of gloom and duplicity unsettled some of the other ministers.

After a long day and night of discussions, the ministers agreed to consult in their capitals and convene another, hopefully final, round of talks in Geneva on November 22. The back channel had still not become public, and we worried that their revelation would complicate completion of an interim agreement. Jake and I arrived back in Geneva on November 20 to help bridge the final gaps with the Iranians. Coordinating closely with Ashton, and joined by Sherman, we met with Araghchi and Ravanchi on the twenty-first. We further narrowed our differences. The Iranians seemed more relaxed about preambular language on enrichment, in which we had carefully separated the words "right" and "enrichment," using the first to refer explicitly to NPT language on the widely acknowledged right of members in good standing to peaceful nuclear energy, and the second in the much more conditional sense of an Iranian demand that might be applied if mutually agreed, long-term limitations on its program were developed. We made some headway on Arak, as Araghchi and Ravanchi grudgingly accepted French edits to more tightly define a cessation of construction activity at the site.

We also pinned down an excellent set of verification measures, including 24/7 surveillance arrangements at Natanz and Fordow, and access to each step along the nuclear supply chain. On sanctions relief, we wound our way toward the formula that Kerry and Zarif eventually agreed upon. Its core was $4.2 billion in unfrozen Iranian oil revenue, metered out in six monthly installments. It had a few additional provisions, notably a relaxation of sanctions on the auto industry, whose main beneficiary was French automaker Renault. Zarif recounted to us with a mischievous glint in his eye that Fabius had spent most of their bilateral sessions in Geneva on this issue, not on Arak and the other questions on which he had been so voluble in public.

Throughout November 22 and 23, John Kerry was his usual relentless self, nudging Zarif toward the finish line, working with Ashton to manage the P5+1, and staying in close touch with the president by secure phone. Jake and I came over to the InterContinental Hotel for the final push, using service elevators and stairwells to get up to the secretary's suite. Our cloak-and-dagger seemed a little silly at this stage, but it had become habitual over the past eight months, and we figured it was worth it if we could keep the back channel under wraps until an interim agreement, now termed the "Joint Plan of Action," could be reached.

We could sense that the Iranians were in a hurry to finish the deal, before their own politics became an even bigger impediment. We didn't think we needed to concede anything further on sanctions, and were confident that we had succeeded in preserving most of our leverage for the much more complex task of negotiating a comprehensive accord. Borrowing a famous Mel Gibson line from the movie *Braveheart*, as he urged his Scottish compatriots to stand firm in the face of charging English cavalry—and with a little of the giddiness that comes from high stakes and little sleep—Jake and I kept repeating to each other "Hold, hold, hold" as the Iranians kept probing for concessions.

By 2 A.M. on November 24, we were nearly there. The ministers were straining one another's patience by this point, and I met with Ravanchi to iron out the last bits of language. Tired and relieved, we quietly congratulated one another. Ashton mobilized all the ministers for a signing ceremony at 4 A.M. Araghchi called me thirty minutes before the ceremony to say that he had "just two or three more changes to make" in the text. The Iranians were never entirely satisfied until they had overreached on nearly every issue and tested every last ounce of flexibility. I laughed politely. "It's a little late for that," I said. "We're done."

The Joint Plan of Action (JPOA) was a modest, temporary, and practical step. Iran froze its nuclear program for an initial six months, and rolled it back in key respects, especially in disposing of its existing stockpile of 20 percent enriched uranium. It accepted intrusive monitoring arrangements. In return it got limited sanctions relief, and a commitment not to increase sanctions for six months.

The JPOA aroused more than a little controversy. Prime Minister Netanyahu said publicly on November 24 that it was "the deal of the century" for Iran. I told Ravanchi that hyperbolic statements like that should help his selling job at home, and he smiled with some satisfaction. Then the congressional critics joined in, predicting that the Iranians would cheat and the whole edifice of sanctions that we had so painstakingly put together over the years would collapse, long before a comprehensive deal could be negotiated. None of that turned out to be true. The JPOA was a solid agreement, in many ways better for us than for the Iranians, who still faced huge economic pressure. It offered us and the Iranians an opportunity to show that we could actually each live up to our sides of a fair bargain, and it gave the president and Secretary Kerry the time and space to negotiate a final agreement.

* * *

NEWS OF OUR back channel broke a few hours after the signing of the JPOA, helping to explain how the P5+1 and Iran had concluded the interim deal so quickly. Spent after this long effort and more than three decades in the Foreign Service, I intended to retire at the end of 2013. I had promised John Kerry when he asked me to remain as deputy secretary that I'd stay on for his first year. In the end, encouraged by him and the president, and admiring them both immensely, I would keep at it for an additional year, until late 2014.

I was especially touched when President Obama invited me to lunch at the White House to reinforce the case for continuing at State. He was an adroit closer. We sat in his small private dining room just off the Oval Office, with tall windows looking out onto the Rose Garden. Over a relaxed conversation, we covered everything from our daughters and the current NBA season to the Iran negotiations and the state of the State Department. "I don't want to play on your Irish Catholic guilt," he said, "but I consider you to be the ultimate professional, and it would mean a lot to me if you would stay for another year." I noted that he was doing a pretty good job on the Irish Catholic guilt part—and that he had had me at the lunch invitation.

With the back channel now history, Jake and I played a supporting and episodic role in the negotiations for a comprehensive nuclear agreement that consumed 2014 and the first half of 2015. In all those hours and days of secret talks, we had built some rapport with Aragh-chi, Ravanchi, and their other colleagues, as well as with Zarif. While the Iranians knew that the road to a comprehensive deal went through the P5+1, it was also clear that what were now overt and frequent U.S.-Iran contacts were the core of the effort. Even the distinctly un-sentimental Iranians could get a little nostalgic sometimes about the seemingly simpler days of the back-channel talks in 2013.

Secretary Kerry threw himself into the comprehensive process, and he and Zarif were its prime movers. Wendy was tireless, and a deft leader of a vastly expanded negotiating team, including Timbie and Roule and terrific experts from Treasury, Energy, and other de-partments. Energy Secretary Ernie Moniz's nuclear expertise and cre-ativity helped to bridge gaps with his Iranian counterpart, Ali Salehi, a fellow MIT alum. I joined our team a few times in the cramped confines of the Palais Coburg hotel in Vienna, where both the slow rhythm of multilateral negotiations and the buffet menu became very familiar. At Kerry's request, I saw Zarif privately a couple times in the second half of 2014. Before marathon talks in Lausanne in the spring of 2015, I met quietly in Geneva with Araghchi and Ravanchi. With congressional impatience and appetite for new sanctions growing, and the Iranians backtracking on key issues, I told them bluntly, "We have come so far, but maybe we should start thinking about a world without an agreement." That helped get their attention.

Kerry's talks with Zarif and Ashton in Lausanne in late March and early April 2015 were the longest continuous negotiation that a secre-tary of state had engaged in since Camp David in 1978. A framework for a Joint Comprehensive Plan of Action (JCPOA) was announced on April 2, and the final deal emerged in July. In return for the grad-ual lifting of sanctions, Iran made a permanent commitment never to develop a nuclear weapon, and accepted substantial, long-term limi-tations on its civilian nuclear program. Ninety-eight percent of Iran's stockpile of enriched material was removed, and so were nearly two-thirds of its centrifuges. The deal also cut off Iran's other potential pathways to a bomb, eliminating the heavy water reactor core at Arak and the capacity to produce weapons-grade plutonium. Extensive verification and monitoring measures were put in place, some of them permanent. For the next decade, at least, Iran's "breakout time"—the time it would theoretically take to enrich enough weapons-grade uranium for a bomb—was extended from the two or three months frozen in the JPOA to at least one year. We had achieved our objective, and we diverted a potential path to war.

* * *

IT WAS HARD to imagine when we embarked on that first secret flight to Oman in early 2013 that diplomacy could resolve the Iranian nuclear issue, at that time the most combustible challenge on the international landscape. The even longer history of grievance and suspicion in America's relations with Iran was another massive obstacle. The politics in Tehran and Washington were corrosive, offering little room for maneuver or incentive for risk-taking. The nuclear problem itself was maddeningly complicated and opaque. There was little reason to think that we could overcome any one of those obstacles, let alone all of them.

Neither the JPOA nor the JCPOA were perfect agreements. In a perfect world, there would be no nuclear enrichment in Iran, and its existing enrichment facilities would have been dismantled. But we don't live in a perfect world, and perfect is rarely on the diplomatic menu. We couldn't neatly erase by military or diplomatic means Iran's basic know-how about enrichment. What we could do was to sharply constrain it over a long duration, monitor it with unprecedented intrusiveness, and prevent its leadership from building a bomb.

For all its trade-offs and imperfections, this was a classic illustration of how diplomacy can work. We set out at the beginning of the Obama administration, building on tentative steps taken at the end of the Bush administration, to test Iranian seriousness directly and invest in a wider coalition, and to build a stronger sanctions program. Our willingness to engage in direct talks and think creatively was a critical ingredient. It put the Iranians on the defensive, removed a pretext for their inaction, and solidified our coalition. When Tehran proved unwilling or incapable, it gave us the opportunity to build substantial economic leverage. Always lurking just over the horizon was the reality of American military power, backing up our determination to ensure that, by one means or another, Iran would not develop a nuclear weapon.

When our leverage had reached a kind of critical mass, we had to use it or risk losing it. Sanctions had so much impact on Iran because they were international, and widely, if often grudgingly, supported. Once Rouhani and Zarif took office and portrayed Iran in a more pragmatic and sympathetic light, it was time to put diplomacy to a rigorous test. Framing the issue as a question of whether Iran could accept sufficiently tough, long-term constraints in return for sanctions lifting and the possibility of limited domestic enrichment was key. There would have been no agreement without sharp constraints and strong monitoring—but there would also have been no agreement if we had insisted on zero enrichment. As Araghchi once put it to us, a civilian nuclear program, including enrichment, was "our source of national pride, our moon shot."

In the first few years after completion of the JCPOA, contrary to the prediction of its opponents that Iran would cheat, the IAEA and the U.S. intelligence community repeatedly affirmed Iranian compliance. Iran's economy did not become a juggernaut as a result of sanctions relief. The agreement deprived the regime of the argument that outside pressure—not chronic mismanagement, corruption, and misallocation of resources—was the source of the grim economic circumstance of most Iranians. Widespread protests in the summer of 2017 demonstrated that the clerical leadership was not sitting comfortably in Tehran. Much as the Supreme Leader feared during the nuclear negotiations, the deal had exposed the regime's vulnerabilities, not erased them.

Meanwhile, Iran continued to export instability across the Middle East, exploiting and accelerating chaos in Syria and Yemen, its forces and proxies locked in a bitter regional competition with Saudi Arabia and other Sunni Arab states. President Obama had always understood that the nuclear agreement would have to be embedded in a wider strategy for reassuring our friends and partners, who were unnerved by the prospect that dialogue with Tehran might someday temper our support for them. The nuclear deal explicitly reserved the option for the United States and its partners to take measures against the Iranian government for non-nuclear transgressions; but it was still tempting for critics to caricature the administration's approach as constraining Iran's nuclear ambitions but enabling its regional troublemaking.

Donald Trump came into office with visceral contempt for the JCPOA, which he called "the worst deal ever." He was dismissive of its practical merits in limiting Iran's nuclear program, and of the whole notion that there was value in the classic diplomacy of building coalitions and hammering out negotiated solutions, with all the give-and-take they required. His was a much more unilateralist impulse, aimed not so much at a better deal with the Iranians as at squeezing them so hard that they'd either capitulate or implode. Despite the entreaties of other P5+1 players, and despite zero evidence of Iranian noncompliance, Trump pulled the United States out of the JCPOA in May 2018.

I was surprised only that he had taken so long to withdraw, given the vehemence of his views. It was nevertheless a dispiriting moment, after years of effort to produce an agreement in which I continued to believe firmly. I wondered what we might have done differently to better insulate the deal. Perhaps we could have pressured the Iranians longer through the interim accord, the JPOA, and extracted more concessions from Tehran—on the duration of certain enrichment restrictions, for example. But the reality was that politics in both the

United States and Iran were tortured and impatient, and it was always a lot harder than it looked from the outside to hold the P5+1 together, especially after serious rifts began to emerge over other problems, like Ukraine or the South China Sea.

We could have done a better job, both before and after the comprehensive nuclear agreement was reached, of confronting the wider challenge of Iran in the Middle East. A willingness to take more risks against the Assad regime after the Syrian civil war began in 2011 would have sent a strong signal to Iran, and cushioned the disquieting effect of the nuclear deal for the Saudis and our other traditional friends. Some of their angst, however, was simply unavoidable. They were deeply worried by the tumult of the Arab Spring, and the prospect of an eventual regional order in which Iran couldn't be denied a place. But we could have done more to show that the nuclear agreement was the start, not the end, of a tough-minded policy toward Iran.

It certainly would have helped shield the JCPOA from Trump's decision to withdraw if we had been able to anchor it better politically at home. It would have been harder to undo as a formal treaty than as an executive agreement. In a deeply polarized Washington, however, the two-thirds affirmative vote in the Senate required for a treaty was virtually impossible. The fact that public opinion polls showed 60 percent of Americans were opposed to withdrawing from the nuclear agreement was not a sturdy enough defense.

Trump's abrogation was another reminder of how much easier it is to tear down diplomacy than to build it. Pulling out of the nuclear deal alienated allies who had joined us in the effort for many years. Reimposition of U.S. sanctions in the face of opposition from partners further damaged a tool of policy already suffering from abuse, driving other countries to lessen reliance on the dollar and the U.S. financial system. It also betrayed an obsession with Iran that exaggerated its strategic weight and undermined larger priorities like rebuilding alliances or managing great power rivals.

Trump's demolition of the Iran deal was a further blow to our own credibility, to international confidence that we could keep our end of a bargain. "Credibility" can be an overused term in Washington, a town sometimes too prone to badger presidents into using force to prop up our currency and influence around the world. But it matters in American diplomacy, especially at a post-primacy moment when our ability to mobilize others around common concerns is becoming more crucial. With its echoes of the muscular unilateralism on the road to the Iraq War in 2003 and the seductive appeal of remaking regional order through American power, the decision to abandon the JCPOA signaled anew a dangerous dismissiveness toward diplomacy. It was exactly the kind of risky, cocky, ill-considered bet that had shredded our influence before, and could easily do so again.

10

Pivotal Power: Restoring America's Tool of First Resort

DEPARTURES COMPEL US to look backward as well as forward. I was doing a little of both as I stood onstage in the State Department's ornate Benjamin Franklin Room at my retirement ceremony in the fall of 2014. It was an extraordinarily generous send-off, which left my ego straining at its moorings. The room was packed with family, friends, colleagues, and diplomatic counterparts. There was a video compilation of congratulatory messages from all the living secretaries of state going back to Henry Kissinger.

President Obama made a surprise appearance and spent time with my family. In his remarks, he reminded the audience of his confinement in Perm as a freshman senator a decade before, of some of our other, more productive adventures in the years that followed, and of the unheralded sacrifice of Lisa and the girls and all Foreign Service families. Vice President Biden was his usual bighearted self, working the room with infectious enthusiasm. Secretary Kerry announced the naming of one of the department's auditoriums in my honor. I was touched by his thoughtfulness—and amused by several

condolence messages that my staff subsequently received from colleagues overseas assuming the worst.

As the ceremony continued and the kind words multiplied, I realized that the sense of detachment I had developed as a military brat,
and refined during all those years on the move from one post and
assignment to another, was fading fast. Lisa and I had taken our oaths
of office in this very room thirty-three years earlier—I had known one
employer, one institution, and one profession ever since. It was hard
to say goodbye, but I was proud of the modest role I played in the
larger drama of American diplomacy.

My mind wandered to an even more elegant, and certainly more
consequential, setting a quarter century before, to that massive hall in
Madrid's royal palace where I had glimpsed the centrality and power
of American diplomacy on full display. It was a memory that seemed
increasingly distant, dulled by the realities of a changing international landscape. America's unipolar moment was, by definition,
temporary. Inevitably, our relative power would diminish as other
players became wealthier, stronger, and more assertive. In the midst
of these dramatic geopolitical shifts, some of which we accelerated
with our own mistakes, we also lost our way in diplomacy. At first
lulled by the experience of post–Cold War dominance and then
shocked by 9/11, we gradually devalued diplomatic tools. All too
often, we overrelied on American hard power to achieve policy aims
and ambitions, hastening the end of American dominance, deepening the desire and capacity of adversaries to upend the American-led
international order, and disillusioning the American public.

As that lovely retirement ceremony and my own career drew to a
close, I could see that the next generation of American diplomats
would have a difficult hand to play. Their challenge, however, became
exponentially more severe two years later with the election of Donald
Trump. During his presidency, our relative influence diminished further and faster, as did our capacity and appetite to lead. Our role

withered, leaving our friends confused, our adversaries emboldened, and the foundations of the international system we built and preserved for seven decades alarmingly fragile.

The administration's profoundly self-destructive shock and awe campaign against professional diplomacy only compounded the challenge. Its early unilateral diplomatic disarmament, born of equal parts ideological contempt and stubborn incompetence, was taking place at precisely the moment when diplomacy mattered more than ever to American interests, in a world where we were no longer the only big kid on the block but still a pivotal power best positioned to lead the world in managing the problems before us.

The window for defining a strategy for a changing international landscape, and America's pivotal role, is slowly closing—but it is by no means shut. That strategy will require a new compact on diplomacy, one that reinvests in diplomacy's core functions and roles, adapts smartly to new challenges and realities, and reinforces the connection between leadership abroad and rejuvenation at home.

* * *

WHOEVER WAS ELECTED president in 2016 would have had to contend with a complicated set of dilemmas rooted in both a rapidly shifting international environment and a disaffected domestic mood. Donald Trump didn't invent them, nor could Hillary Clinton have avoided them. As Americans went to the polls in November 2016, theirs was a world in the midst of historic transformations, which would strain the capacity and imagination of any new administration.

The reemergence of great power rivalry was in some ways a return to a more natural state of international affairs than the bipolar contest of the Cold War or the moment of American dominance that followed. Yet it carried complex risks and trade-offs, for which American statecraft was out of practice. China's ambition to recover its accustomed primacy in Asia had already upended many of our comfortable post–Cold War assumptions about how integration into a U.S.-led order would tame, or at least channel, Chinese aspirations. President Xi Jinping was flexing his muscle not only in Asia but all the way to the gates of Europe and the Middle East. Our traditional allies in Asia, as well as new partners like India, were taking notice and adjusting their strategic calculations—raising regional temperatures and increasing uncertainties.

China's dynamism, and that of the broader Asia-Pacific region, only highlighted further the struggles of Europe—beset by internal political crises and external pressures, including from a resurgent Russia. Putin continued to punch above his weight, exploiting divisions within Europe, settling scores in Ukraine and Syria, and sowing chaos beyond his wildest ambitions in the American elections.

Alongside these great power frictions, crises of regional order continued to bubble, products of both the strengths of local competitors and the weaknesses of failing states. The Middle East remained best in class in dysfunction and fragility. No longer the global energy player it once was, no longer able to sustain its rentier economies, no longer able to camouflage its deficits of opportunity and dignity, much of the Arab world teetered on the edge of more domestic upheavals, with extremists eager to prey on its vulnerabilities. Africa's future carried both promise and peril, with a population likely to double to two billion by the middle of the twenty-first century and unresolved problems of regional conflict, poor governance, and food, water, and health insecurity all looming large. The Americas remained the natural strategic home base for the United States, poised to benefit from the possibilities of a "Pacific Century," but burdened by inequalities and a limited U.S. attention span.

Beyond the unsettled rivalries of states, and the decaying foundations of regional stability, the old postwar order groaned and creaked, its institutions overdue for adaptation. The five permanent members of the UN Security Council were jealous guardians of an outdated system, and the international financial and trade institutions struggled with serious reform. Meanwhile, the transformative effects of climate change were becoming more evident with each passing season. With polar ice caps melting, sea levels rising, and weather patterns swinging wildly, the implications of an environment badly damaged by human behavior grew more dangerous and immediate. The prospect of half the world's population facing significant water shortages was a mere two decades away.

The pace of the revolution in technology made the impact and dislocations of the Industrial Revolution look plodding by comparison. Advances in machine learning, artificial intelligence, and synthetic biology moved at breathtaking speed, outstripping the ability of states and societies to devise ways to maximize their benefits, minimize their downsides, and create workable international rules of the road. More broadly, authoritarian regimes used the apparently decentralizing power of technology to consolidate control of their citizens.

The competition, collisions, and confusion that all these forces produced had been building for some time, and their contours were faintly apparent even in the heady aftermath of the Cold War. In the memo for incoming secretary of state Christopher in January 1993, I highlighted the schizophrenia of the emerging international system, with the globalization of the world economy unfolding alongside the fragmentation of international politics. Power balances and relative positions were bound to be fluid, and often profoundly disorienting. "The resulting chaos," I added, "is enough to almost—almost—make one nostalgic for the familiar discipline and order of the Cold War."[1] A quarter century later, my nostalgia was still under control, but the problem loomed much larger.

The diplomatic profession, like other endangered vocational species during this period of profound disruption, was overwhelmed by existential angst. I witnessed firsthand during the course of my career how the near monopoly on presence, access, insight, and influence that diplomats used to have in foreign capitals and societies was eroding. As a young diplomat in the Middle East in the early 1980s, I wrote "airgrams"—deliberate, long-form analyses that took several days to reach Washington by diplomatic pouch. Senior officials traveled with increasing frequency to foreign capitals, but the unhurried nature of communication kept diplomatic channels in the forefront and diplomats on the front lines, with considerable reach and autonomy.

A decade later, the "CNN effect" during the Gulf War demonstrated the ubiquity of real-time information, and in the years that followed the Internet tore down the remaining barriers to information and direct communication. Heads of state and senior officials across government departments could interact easily and directly, leaving foreign ministries and embassies feeling anachronistic. Non-state actors—heads of massive philanthropic foundations, civil society activists, and corporate CEOs, among many others—wielded increasing international influence, shaping and funding a wide array of policy agendas. WikiLeaks displayed the vulnerabilities of "confidential" reporting, and social media muddied what once seemed like clear channels for shaping public opinion.

Despite considerable efforts by secretaries of state from both parties, we often failed to adapt wisely to this new reality, letting core skills atrophy while falling behind the curve as new policy challenges, players, and tools emerged. Budgets dropped precipitously after the Cold War, with a 50 percent cut in real terms for the State Department and foreign affairs budget between 1985 and 2000. Secretary Baker opened a dozen new embassies in the former Soviet Union without asking Congress for more money, and under Secretary Albright intake into the Foreign Service ground to a halt. More broadly, the steady militarization and centralization of policy turned into a gallop after 9/11, inverting the roles of force and diplomacy, diverting American power down the tragic dead end of the Iraq War, and distorting both strategy and tools.

It is of course true that the chances for successful diplomacy are vastly enhanced by the potential use of force. There is often no better way to focus the minds of difficult customers at the negotiating table than to have those remarkable tools on full display in the background. That was what gave force to Baker's persuasive skills in the run-up to Madrid, and to Kerry's diplomacy with the Iranians. "You have no idea how much it contributes to the general politeness and pleasantness of diplomacy," mused George Kennan, "when you have a little quiet armed force in the background."[2]

Overreliance on military tools, however, leads into policy quicksand. That was the lesson of the battleship *New Jersey* lobbing shells into Lebanon in the early 1980s, unconnected to workable strategy or diplomacy. And it was the lesson, on a far more disastrous scale, twenty years later in Iraq.

The militarization of diplomacy is a trap, which leads to overuse—or premature use—of force, and underemphasis on nonmilitary tools. "If your main tool is a hammer," as Barack Obama liked to say, "then every problem will start to look like a nail." Even Pentagon and military leaders went out of their way to highlight the perils of the imbalance between force and diplomacy. Secretary of Defense Bob Gates regularly reminded Congress that U.S. military band members outnumbered foreign service officers, and one of his successors, Jim Mattis, famously noted that cutting funding for diplomacy would require him "to buy more ammunition."

Gates and Mattis understood that the weight of the military's mission and capabilities can erode a focus on diplomacy, or distort its central tasks. In Iraq and Afghanistan, diplomats found themselves slipping into supporting roles in the military's counterinsurgency strategy, preoccupied with local social engineering and the kind of nation-building activities that were beyond the capacity of Americans to accomplish. It sometimes seemed as if we were trying to replicate the role of the nineteenth-century British Colonial Service, not play the distinctive role of the American Foreign Service. We were being challenged to pour increasingly limited civilian resources into long-term efforts to build governance and economic structures that could only be constructed by Iraqis and Afghans themselves. The more immediate and consequential function of diplomats on the ground was the persistent, head-banging work of persuading senior national leaders to bridge sectarian divides, minimize corruption, and slowly create some sense of equitable political order. In wider terms, it was the job of diplomats to try to build regional support for fragile national governments in conflict zones, and to limit external meddling.

If the militarization of diplomacy was one post–9/11 trap, over-centralization and micromanagement by a swollen NSC staff was another. There was no way that the five dozen or so professionals on the NSC staff of Colin Powell in the late 1980s, or the similarly sized staff of Brent Scowcroft under Bush 41, would suffice in the post–9/11 era. The tempo of counterterrorism activities and the demands of a global economy meant that the White House had to expand its coordinating capacity. But the fivefold growth over a quarter century was a classic case of overreach. The NSC staff continued to attract the most seasoned political appointees and many of the very best career officers from cabinet agencies. Their natural temptation was to take on more operational roles. Their proximity to the Oval Office deepened their sense of mission, and their energy and talent fueled their enthusiasm for not only coordinating but also shaping and executing policy.

The problem was that this made a self-fulfilling prophecy of complaints about lack of initiative and drive from other agencies, particularly State. On the rugged playing fields of Washington bureaucratic politics, State has often found itself elbowed to the sidelines. Assistant secretaries responsible for critical regions would be squeezed out of meetings in the Situation Room, where back benches were filled with NSC staff. With a dwindling sense of being in on the takeoff of policy deliberations or decisions, it was in some ways natural for even fairly senior State personnel to feel disconnected from responsibility for the landing, for policy execution. None of that is an excuse for the failure of the department to show more drive and ingenuity, get out of our own way bureaucratically, streamline our structure, and energize our culture. But overcentralization and overmilitarization made it a lot harder than it needed to be.

In the midst of too many aborted takeoffs and crash landings, as the international arena grew more threatening, and as the blood, treasure, and opportunity costs of America's misadventures grew more obvious, a yawning gap emerged between a Washington establishment deeply committed to American global leadership and a less convinced American public. Making the case for American leadership in an emerging global order was becoming harder by the day.

The Clinton administration faced an early version of this challenge after the Cold War. As we wrote to incoming secretary Christopher, the post–Cold War transition "leaves you and the President with a very tough task. It was relatively easy during the Cold War to justify national security expenditures and build support for sustained American engagement overseas. It is infinitely harder now." By 2016, ritual incantations of terms like "liberal international order" failed to resonate beyond the Beltway "blob," and the disconnect between our easy conceits about American indispensability and a citizenry's doubts that we had our priorities in the right order continued to grow.

The legacy of the first decade of this century, of two massively expensive and debilitating wars and a global financial crisis, reinforced a sense not only of fatigue about foreign entanglements, but also genuine resentment. Much of the American public had a visceral understanding of the widening gaps in wealth and opportunity across our society, and of the failure of successive administrations to address serious infrastructure problems. And much of the public understood instinctively that we had made some poor choices about overseas commitments, at a time when we were probably less exposed to anything resembling an existential foreign danger than at any point in recent decades. Their mistrust and doubts were aggravated by the perceived success of rivals and adversaries on the back of America's sacrifices and missteps. Bureaucratic reforms and legislative fixes wouldn't matter unless this fundamental rift was healed

* * *

THE TRUMP ADMINISTRATION took these inherited challenges, accumulated over three post–Cold War decades, and made them much worse. It diminished American influence on a shifting international landscape, hollowed out American diplomacy, and only deepened the divisions among Americans about our global role.

Like Barack Obama, Donald Trump recognized that America's approach to the world needed to change significantly. Like Obama, Trump focused on the right question: How should the United States reshape its strategy at a moment when the unipolar dominance of the post–Cold War era was passing, and popular support for active American leadership was fraying? Both saw the need for rebalancing security relationships with allies who had long borne too small a share of the burden, and economic relationships with rivals like China, who had enjoyed protectionist trade advantage long after their "developing country" rationale had faded. Both were willing to break with convention in dealing directly with adversaries, and both were innately skeptical of foreign policy orthodoxy. Their answers to the core question of reshaping American strategy, however, were vastly different.

President Obama sought to adapt American leadership and the international order that we had largely shaped and preserved for seven decades. He sought to apply the sense of enlightened self-interest that had animated American foreign policy, at its best, since the days of the Marshall Plan in Europe—a commitment to enlarge the circle of people and countries around the world with a shared stake in rules and institutions that enhanced our security and prosperity. His attitude was grounded in realism about the limits of American influence. Obama's concern for avoiding overreach and commitment to playing the long game in the face of short-game crises could sometimes come across as diffidence. But he had a fundamental optimism about where the arc of history would carry a United

States that carefully cultivated a model of political and economic openness and updated the alliances and partnerships that set us apart from lonelier powers like China and Russia.

There was nothing diffident about President Trump. His aim was not to adapt, but to disrupt. He came into office with a powerful conviction, untethered to history, that the United States had been held hostage by the very order it created; we were Gulliver, and it was past time to break the bonds of the Lilliputians. Alliances were millstones, multilateral arrangements were constraints rather than sources of leverage, and the United Nations and other international bodies were distractions, if not irrelevant.

Instead of the enlightened self-interest that drove Obama and most of post–World War II American foreign policy, the Trump administration took office more focused on the "self" part than the "enlightened." Trump's "America First" sloganeering stirred a nasty brew of belligerent unilateralism, mercantilism, and unreconstructed nationalism. On the international stage, the new administration often used muscular posturing and fact-free assertions to mask a pattern of retreat—abandoning in rapid succession the Paris climate accords, the Trans-Pacific Partnership, the Iranian nuclear agreement, and a slew of other international commitments. Disruption seemed to be its own end, with little apparent thought given to "plan B" or "what comes next." Trump's approach was more than an impulse; it was a distinct and Hobbesian worldview, but far less than anything resembling a strategy. Not surprisingly, adversaries took advantage, allies hedged, and already strained institutions teetered.

The image of possibility and respect for human dignity that attracted so many around the world, despite all our flaws, grew more and more tattered. Many years of representing the United States abroad had taught me that the power of our example mattered more than that of our preaching. Now our example was increasingly one of incivility, division, and dysfunction, and our preaching had less to do with highlighting human rights abuses wherever we saw them and more to do with insulting allies and indulging autocrats.

The Trump administration's hollowing out of the State Department embodied its ideological convictions and temperamental instincts. To be fair, American diplomacy was unsettled before Trump. Decades of unbalanced investment in defense and intelligence had taken its toll. The department's failure to rein in its counterproductive bureaucratic and cultural habits did not help. But the new president's dismissiveness toward professional diplomats, like his wider approach to America's role in the world, took a complicated situation and made it a crisis.

In July 2018, President Trump asserted at a press conference in Finland with President Putin that he was an advocate of "the powerful tradition of American diplomacy," but his behavior bore no resemblance to thoughtful, well-prepared exemplars of that tradition like Jim Baker.[3] Trump's view of diplomacy was narcissistic, not institutional. Dialogue was unconnected to strategy; the president seemed oblivious to the reality that "getting along" with rivals like Putin was not the aim of diplomacy, which was all about advancing tangible interests. And "winging it" in crucial high-level encounters was a prescription for embarrassment—especially when dealing with experienced autocrats like Putin, who rarely winged anything.

For the Trump White House, the Department of State was a realm of "deep state" heresy, of closet Obama and Clinton supporters bent upon resisting the new administration. That was a major, if convenient, misapprehension. If anything, career foreign and civil service officers at State are almost loyal to a fault, eager for the opportunity to deliver for a new administration, and hopeful that their expertise will be valued, if not always heeded. What they got from the White House was an attitude of open hostility, reflecting the distrust of convention and professional expertise that fueled the Trump political phenomenon and energized the new president.

Trump's first secretary of state, Rex Tillerson, just dug the hole deeper. An accomplished former head of Exxon, Tillerson had an insular and imperious style, a CEO's skeptical view of the public sector, and an engineer's linear view of how to remold diplomacy. He embraced the biggest budget cuts in the modern history of the department; launched a terminally flawed "redesign process"; cut himself off from most of the building; drove out many of the most capable senior and mid-level officers; cut intake into the Foreign Service by well over 50 percent; and reversed what were already painfully slow trendlines toward better gender and ethnic diversity. Most pernicious of all was the practice of blacklisting individual officers simply because they had worked on controversial issues in the previous administration, like the Iran nuclear deal.

The savaging of American diplomacy as the Trump administration consolidated its grip was not the first such assault in our history, but it was in many ways the worst. There is never a good time for diplomatic malpractice. This just happened to be a particularly dangerous moment.

* * *

ALEXIS DE TOCQUEVILLE once wrote, "The greatness of America lies not in being more enlightened than any other nation, but rather in her ability to repair her faults."[4] The Trump era poses a test of our capacity for self-repair beyond even Tocqueville's imagination. It would be foolish to underestimate the damage to our standing and influence, and to the prospects for shaping a stable international order for a challenging new age. Nevertheless, our recuperative powers and underlying strengths are still formidable.

No longer the dominant player that we were after the end of the Cold War, no longer able to dictate events as we may sometimes have believed we could, we nevertheless remain the world's pivotal power— able to update international order in a way that reflects new realities but sustains our interests and values. Over the next several decades, assuming we don't keep digging the hole deeper for ourselves, no other nation is in a better position to play that pivotal role, or to navigate the complicated currents of twenty-first-century geopolitics.

Our assets are substantial. We still spend more every year on defense than the next seven countries combined. Our economy, despite risks of overheating and persistent inequalities, remains the biggest, most adaptable, and most innovative in the world. Energy, once a vulnerability, now offers considerable advantages, with technology unlocking vast natural gas resources, and advances in clean and renewable energy accelerating. Demography is another strength. Compared to our peer competitors, our population is younger and more mobile, and if we could stop doing so much practical and moral damage to ourselves on immigration issues we could lock in that strategic edge for generations. Geography sets us apart, with our two liquid assets—the Pacific and Atlantic oceans—insulating us to some extent from the kinds of security threats that expose other major powers. Diplomacy ought to be another advantage. We have more allies and potential partners than any of our peers or rivals, with greater capacity for coalition-building and problem-solving.

Our advantages are not permanent or automatic. To maintain them, we have to do a far better job of husbanding them wisely and applying them with care and purpose. It is a truism that effective foreign policy begins at home, with sustained attention to the domestic foundations of American power. And yet for all the injuries we've inflicted on ourselves in recent years—for all the unforced errors, for all the hollowing out of both diplomacy as a tool of policy and of the American idea as a source of global influence—we still have a window before us in which we can help shape a new and more durable international order before it gets shaped for us.

Fashioning a strategy for America in a post-primacy world is no easy task. The most famous American strategy of the postwar era, Kennan's containment doctrine, went through a number of significant variations during the decades before the end of the Cold War.[5] At its core was a commitment to invest in the resilience of the community of democratic, market-based states that the United States led, and a cold-eyed recognition of the weaknesses that would eventually unravel the Soviet Union and its unwieldy Communist bloc. A balance of military strength, economic vigor, and careful diplomacy helped avoid direct conflict, avert nuclear war, and manage competition in the post-colonial world.

In the post–Cold War era, none of us had the intellectual dexterity to fashion a simple slogan to match Kennan's concept. As we tried to suggest in the January 1993 memo to Christopher, a strategy premised on the "enlargement" of the coalition and ideas that had won the Cold War was enticing, but had inherent limits in a world in which challenges to regional order were bound to emerge, globalization would produce its own contradictions and collisions, and America's temporary dominance would inevitably be contested by the rise of others. As enlargement encountered constraints, and as we compounded them in Iraq in 2003 and in the financial crisis several years later, we struggled to shape a post-primacy alternative.

A successful American strategy beyond Trump will likely have to return to Obama's central propositions about rebalancing our portfolio of global investments and tools, sharpening our attention on managing competition with great power rivals, and using our leverage and our capacity to mobilize other players to address twenty-first-century challenges. That ought to be infused with a bold and unapologetic vision for free people and free and fair markets, with the United States as a more attractive exemplar than it is today.

Asia continues to loom as our first priority, with China's rise the most consequential geopolitical trend of our time. President Trump's unpredictability and detachment have opened the playing field for China, offering an unexpectedly early path to dominance in Asia. That China and its neighbors, as well as the United States, are entangled economically, their future prosperity wrapped up in one another's success, is a brake on conflict, but not a guarantee against it.

The unease among other players across Asia about Chinese hegemony creates a natural opportunity for Washington to knit together relationships with traditional allies like Japan and emerging partners like India. That was the origin of the Bush 43 administration's long-range bet on India, which meant bending the rules on nonproliferation for an even wider strategic gain.

A deeper American focus on Asia makes transatlantic partnership more, not less, significant. It implies a new strategic division of labor with our European allies, where they take on even more responsibility for order on their continent, and do even more to contribute to possibilities for longer-term order in the Middle East, while the United States devotes relatively more resources and attention to Asia. It also demands a sustained effort at a trade and investment partnership that addresses new economic realities, expectations, and imperatives. That argues for a renewed Atlanticism, built on shared interests and values, in a world in which a rising China, a resurgent Russia, and persistent troubles in the Middle East ought to cement a common approach. Our main security challenge now is to consolidate, not expand, NATO—bolstering the sovereignty and political and economic health of Ukraine outside anyone's formal military structures, and deterring Russian aggression. We have a deep interest in encouraging a vibrant, post-Brexit European Union.[6]

A more durable twenty-first-century European security architecture has eluded us in nearly three decades of fitful attempts to engage post–Cold War Russia. That is not likely to change anytime soon—certainly not during Putin's tenure. Ours should be a long-game strategy, not giving in to Putin's aggressive score-settling, but not giving up on the possibility of an eventual mellowing of relations beyond him. Nor can we afford to ignore the need for guardrails in managing an often adversarial relationship—sustaining communication between our militaries and our diplomats, and preserving what we can of a collapsing arms control architecture. Over time, Russia's stake in healthier relations with Europe and America may grow, as a slow-motion collision with China in Central Asia looms. With the return of great power rivalry, we'll have an increasing interest in putting ourselves in the pivotal position, able to manage relationships and build influence in all directions.

Disorder in the Middle East will remain that troubled region's default position for years to come. Pessimists are hardly ever wrong there, and they rarely lack for company or validation. A hard-eyed look at our own interests argues for less intensive engagement. We are no longer directly dependent on Middle East hydrocarbons. Israel is more secure than ever before from existential threats. Iran is a danger, but an opportunistic power, its ambitions bounded in a Sunni-majority region, as well as by simmering domestic discontent and a moribund economy. Despite Russia's resurgence, there is no external adversary to compel our attention, as there was during the Cold War.

As President Obama discovered, however, deleveraging in the Middle East is sometimes destabilizing in its own right. Insecurity in the region is a powerful contagion, and threats regularly metastasize beyond its boundaries. The United States can't afford to neglect its leadership role—while applying a massive dose of humility and rejecting the large-scale military and nation-building efforts of the recent past, which were doomed to failure in a region that has often been a graveyard for military occupiers and social engineering projects by outsiders, however well intentioned. As part of a long-term strategy, we should reassure our traditional Arab partners against the threats they face, whether from Sunni extremist groups or a predatory Iran. But we should insist in return that Sunni Arab leaderships recognize that regional order will ultimately require some modus vivendi with an Iran that will remain a substantial power even if it tempers its revolutionary overreach. We should also insist that they address urgently the profound crisis of governance that was at the heart of the Arab Spring. Genuine friendship with Israel should impel us to push for the two-state solution with Palestinians that is already past its expiration date, but without which Israel's future as a Jewish, democratic state will be in peril.

President Trump's disregard for Africa and Latin America has been foolish, as demography and a variety of uncertainties and possibilities reinforce their strategic significance for the United States. Similarly, his antipathy for multilateral agreements and international institutions will leave his successors with a huge rebuilding task, especially since renovation and adaptation were already long overdue. It was an historic mistake to walk away from the Trans-Pacific Partnership; with a subsequent effort in Europe, we could have anchored two-thirds of the global economy to the same high standards and rules as our own system, helped emerging markets join the club over time, and shaped China's options and incentives for reform. None of that is to suggest that we don't have to do a much better job of insisting on fair, two-way-street provisions in trade agreements, and of cushioning their effects on important sectors of our own economy and labor force. Walking away from imperfect agreements, however, is rarely better than addressing their imperfections over time.

Trump's rejection of the Paris climate accords and spectacular backtracking on our global commitments on migration and refugees were also devastating, deepening mistrust of our motives and reliability. There has been no hint of American leadership on a host of accelerating technology questions, from cyber threats to the impact of rapid advances in artificial intelligence, that are likely to transform geopolitical competition in the twenty-first century in the way that the Industrial Revolution transformed it in the nineteenth and twentieth centuries. In the emerging power configuration, American resources and influence are relatively less substantial than they were a decade ago, and even more damaged as a result of the Trump administration's policies. Nevertheless, in all these areas, the United States has a pivotal role to play, and the quality of its diplomacy will be the key to playing that role well.

* * *

"MY GOD, THIS is the end of diplomacy," sighed Lord Palmerston, Britain's foreign secretary, a century and a half ago when he was handed his first telegram. It was not the first time that diplomacy's demise seemed imminent, and it was not the last. As the second decade of the twenty-first century draws to a close, the notion of American diplomacy as a tool of first resort seems quaint, if not naïve, like pining for the return of the village watchmaker in a smartwatch world.

Selling the practical virtues of diplomacy is a complicated undertaking. For all the debate about "hard power," "soft power," and "smart power" in recent years, diplomacy is most often about quiet power, the largely invisible work of tending alliances, twisting arms, tempering disputes, and making long-term investments in relationships and societies. Diplomacy is punctuated only rarely by grand public breakthroughs. Its benefits are hard to appreciate. Crises averted are less captivating than military victories; the lower costs to consumers that come from trade agreements are less tangible and direct than a closing factory; the preventive care that occupies most diplomats is less compelling than the military's dramatic surgical triumphs. In the new era of disorder before us, however, the quiet power of American diplomacy has never mattered more.[7]

There is no neat alchemy for renewing American diplomacy, but there are at least three imperatives: reinforcing the core roles and qualities that continue to sustain successful diplomacy; adapting diplomatic tradecraft to manage new challenges; and revitalizing a compact with an American public less certain of the purpose and importance of American leadership.

Over the course of my career, we struggled and often failed on all these counts. Lulled into complacency by a seemingly more benign post–Cold War international environment and our unipolar dominance, we let atrophy the essence of diplomacy—the ability to cajole, persuade, browbeat, threaten, and nudge other governments and political leaders in directions consistent with our interests and values. Stunned by the earthquake of 9/11 and its aftershocks, we entered a prolonged period of strategic and operational distraction. Stabilization, counterinsurgency, countering violent extremism, and all the murky concepts that mushroomed in the era of the great inversion proved to be flawed guideposts for the adaptation of American diplomacy. We tended to oversell the merits of diplomats as social workers and undersell the core role of diplomats in hammering out the best relations we could between states, from the like-minded to the nastily adversarial.

Even as funding and State's relative role diminished, we spread our diplomatic wings further and took on issues and missions for which we lacked expertise and the means to make a meaningful difference. We compounded the problem by failing to build the expertise and operational agility that we'd need to confront the increasingly urgent challenges of this century, from the revolution in technology to climate change. That all combined to make it infinitely harder to demonstrate the power and purpose of American diplomacy at its best, precisely at the moment when we needed it most, and at a time when the political foundations at home critical to effective leadership abroad were collapsing.

* * *

THE CORE ROLES and qualities of good diplomats are not fundamentally different today from what they were in earlier eras. George Kennan and George Shultz both described diplomats as "gardeners," painstakingly nurturing plants and partners and possibilities, always alert to the need to prune, weed, and preempt problems. Their prosaic description may not fit well on a recruiting poster, but it still rings true today.

Others have referred to diplomats as conductors or organizers. In music, conductors ensure that all the instruments of an orchestra come together as one. In foreign policy, diplomats similarly harness all the tools of American statecraft—from the soft power of ideas, culture, and public diplomacy, to economic incentives and sanctions, intelligence-gathering and covert action, and military assistance and the threat of force—to achieve policy aims. Diplomats are classic organizers, whether in mobilizing the levers of American influence, shaping international alliances, or bridging divides with adversaries. Jim Baker played all of these roles in helping George H. W. Bush build the Desert Storm coalition, less a gardener than a herder of geopolitical cats. A political animal at heart, he understood instinctively how important it was to "remember your base"—to tend to international alliances, the great force multiplier of U.S. influence.

Effective diplomats also embody many qualities, but at their heart is a crucial trinity: judgment, balance, and discipline. All three demand a nuanced grasp of history and culture, mastery of foreign languages, hard-nosed facility in negotiations, and the capacity to translate American interests in ways that other governments can see as consistent with their own—or at least in ways that drive home the costs of alternative courses.

Judgment is essential to navigating foreign terrain in America's best interest. I have yet to find a better frame for the basic challenge of diplomatic judgment than Reinhold Niebuhr's "serenity prayer": "God grant me the serenity to accept the things I cannot change, the courage to change the things I can, and the wisdom to know the difference." Like any aphorism, Niebuhr's insight can be twisted in lots of different ways. Neoconservatives cited his "courage" to justify the invasion of Iraq in 2003; critics of the war pointed to his "wisdom" as the most compelling argument for restraint. What cannot be overstated, however, is the importance of sound judgment in a world of fallible and flawed humans—weighing ends and means, anticipating the unintended consequences of well-intentioned actions, and measuring the hard reality of limits against the potential of American agency.

When diplomacy succeeds, it is usually because of an appreciation of its limits, rather than a passion for stretching beyond them. Durable agreements are rooted in mutual self-interest, not one-sided imposition of will, and they frequently carry the baggage and imperfections of compromise, the inevitable consequences of the give-and-take of even the most fruitful negotiations. That was the story of the Iran nuclear agreement, and Qaddafi's negotiated abandonment of terrorism and weapons of mass destruction. It was an appreciation of the limits of power that encouraged George H. W. Bush and his team to stop short of overthrowing Saddam in 1991, after the rapid success of Desert Storm in expelling Iraq from Kuwait. Bush, Baker, and Scowcroft were patient practitioners of Hippocratic diplomacy, intent on doing no harm in uncertain circumstances, guided by prudence and judicious use of America's power and tools.

When circumstances offer rare openings for diplomatic agency, diplomats have to be able and willing to make big bets. That was the genesis of the Bush 41 administration's masterful management of German reunification, and of Jim Baker's brilliance in translating military victory in Iraq into a diplomatic triumph in Madrid. American leverage was at its zenith in that period, but it took sound diplomatic judgment to apply it skillfully and seize historic openings.

Professional diplomats have an obligation to offer their honest judgments, however inconvenient. To policymakers and elected officials predisposed to "do things," career diplomats and their broken-record warnings about potential consequences or pitfalls can seem terminally prudent. Americans see themselves as problem-solvers, and the notion that some actions are best avoided can seem almost un-American to political leaders. Ambassadors in the field always face a tension between warning of possible policy failures and recognizing that gloomy analysis is not a policy.

Secretary of State Dean Acheson once complained that senior diplomats tended to be "cautious rather than imaginative."[8] Most of his successors, including the ten I served directly, have harbored similar concerns, some more openly than others. It is true that career officers sometimes seem to take particular relish in telling a new administration why its big new idea is not so big or so new, or why it won't work. It is also true that the increasing roles in foreign policymaking of both the NSC staff and other agencies over successive administrations have tended to bring out the more passive (or passive-aggressive) side of the State Department.

From Joe McCarthy to Donald Trump, American demagogues have doubted the loyalty and relevance of career diplomats, seeking to intimidate and marginalize them. Those are the most extreme circumstances, in which good people are forced out of the Foreign Service or muzzled. In my own career, I never had to face those extremes. I learned from remarkable professionals like Tom Pickering that policy initiative and a willingness to provide candid views were an essential part of being a career diplomat, especially as you became more senior. It never made sense to him, or to many in my generation, simply to serve as a postman for Washington decisions, or to wait for White House choices without first trying to shape them. I always admired the way Secretary Rice encouraged me to continue to provide my warnings of the looming trainwrecks with Putin's Russia and argue alternative policy courses, even though she had her own views, and the White House theirs. Never once did I feel that my two rubles from Moscow were unwelcome or irrelevant.

I have nothing but admiration for colleagues who in recent decades decided that they could no longer serve policies in which they did not believe. More than a dozen Foreign Service professionals resigned over American nonintervention in the Balkans in the early 1990s. Several others left over the Iraq intervention a decade later. Many more have resigned in protest of the Trump administration's assault on American diplomacy and the values that sustain it. Short of resignation, officers are obliged to exercise discipline and avoid public dissent. But they also have a parallel obligation to express their concerns internally and offer their best policy advice, even if the truths they perceive are unpalatable. A State Department in which officers are bludgeoned into timidity, or censor themselves, or are simply ignored, becomes a hollow institution, incapable of the disciplined diplomatic activism that this moment in history demands of the United States.

Balance is an equally important diplomatic trait, for diplomats are constantly called to manage inevitable trade-offs—among tactical choices, between short- and long-term goals, of practical interests and less tangible values. Diplomacy is often unavoidably transactional. It is a mistake, however, to lose sight of the enlightened self-interest that connects immediate choices to strategic possibilities, and embeds short-term interests in wider questions of principle.

The problem of promoting respect for human rights in authoritarian societies, where we also have important security interests, is particularly complicated, and sometimes particularly painful. There is no perfect diplomatic playbook for managing this dilemma. The Trump administration has tended simply to abdicate, reserving its condemnation only for those autocracies with whom we are sharply at odds, like Iran. Much as I am convinced of the flaws of that approach, which just feeds the arguments of Putin and other autocrats that the United States is fundamentally hypocritical and only promotes democracy and human rights to suit its own strategic purposes, our record in other administrations is hardly pristine.

Tone certainly matters. I have yet to meet the foreign leadership, or society, that responds well to being lectured to or patronized by Americans. Nor is ritual invocation of American exceptionalism especially compelling against the backdrop of our current exceptionally unappealing domestic landscape. Yet there is also no substitute for raising human rights concerns directly and plainly. Addressing them is a matter of any state's long-term self-interest, not a favor to the United States or anyone else. Pressing those concerns is also a matter of who we are as Americans, and of our commitment to ideas of political tolerance, pluralism, and respect for diversity that remain a source of enduring strength.

I admired the way Hillary Clinton stepped up in the case of the blind Chinese dissident Chen Guangcheng. She took real risks, for the right reasons. In other cases over the years, however, we often had far less satisfying outcomes. I had countless conversations over the past couple decades with dictators in the Middle East and Central Asia and other hard places, pushing for a specific prisoner to be released, or to consider some general easing of repression. I also had countless conversations with local human rights activists, listening to their concerns and explaining as honestly as I could that we would continue to try to help, but also had interests in military access or counterterrorism cooperation that we couldn't easily jettison. Those were the trade-offs that were hardest to swallow.

Pulling off the myriad balancing acts of diplomacy demands discipline—the self-awareness to be humble and question assumptions. Too often, we've lulled ourselves into diplomatic wishful thinking, an almost willful cluelessness about what's really driving events abroad and the long-term consequences of our actions. After the Gulf War, many of us assumed naïvely that Saddam Hussein's regime would collapse of its own contradictions. However skeptical we may have been about much of the intelligence suggesting that Saddam possessed weapons of mass destruction in the run-up to the 2003 war, it didn't occur to us that the Iraqi dictator would manufacture the illusion that he retained them to ward off external and internal foes. Our failure of imagination obstructed more honest debate about the core rationale for war and our judgments about the risk of alternative courses. The wider tragedy, of course, was stubborn refusal to see clearly the inexorable complexities of the day after.

After the uprising of 2011 in Syria, many assumed mistakenly that the popular momentum that had swept away Ben Ali and Mubarak so quickly was bound to make short work of Assad. Even after the

Syrian president demonstrated his staying power, there was a similarly flawed assumption that Syria's bloodletting could be contained within its borders. Millions of refugees flooding neighboring countries, and eventually Europe, soon exposed the shortsightedness of that proposition. During the same period in Libya, there was too much wishful thinking about the independent capacity and will of our closest European allies, and too little appreciation of how hard it would be to put together any semblance of political order in a society that Qaddafi had stripped bare of modern institutions.

It proved especially hard to imagine the pace of events in Russia after the end of the Cold War. Yeltsin's Russia had shown the limits of American agency, but there was still a presumption that Moscow had little alternative to accepting a subordinate, if grudging, role in Europe. The expansion of NATO membership stayed on autopilot as a matter of U.S. policy, long after its fundamental assumptions should have been reassessed. Commitments originally meant to reflect interests morphed into interests themselves, and the door cracked open to membership for Georgia and Ukraine—the latter a bright red line for any Russian leadership. A Putin regime pumped up by years of high energy prices and wounded pride pushed back hard. And even after Putin's ruthless annexation of Crimea, it proved difficult to imagine that he would stretch his score-settling into a systematic assault on the 2016 American presidential elections.

Clairvoyance is an unattainable quality for any diplomat, but it pays to encourage rigorous questioning of assumptions. Informed by history and experience, diplomats have to be more unconventional in their thinking, and more assertive in testing accepted wisdom. Judgment, balance, and discipline remain the core qualities of diplomatic practice.

* * *

IN TODAY'S WORLD of digital and virtual relationships, there is still no good substitute for old-fashioned human interactions—not in business, romance, or diplomacy. The ability to build personal relationships, bridging what the legendary CBS journalist Edward R. Murrow called the "most critical link in the chain of international communication, the last three feet," remains at the heart of effective diplomacy.

A reaffirmation of the core of American diplomacy, a business of human relationships, is necessary but not sufficient to make it effective for a new and demanding era. We also need to build modern capabilities and skills on top of that traditional foundation. Our efforts at transformation to date have tended to focus on the capillaries of institutional change, rather than the arteries—more on how we look than how we work. That has to change.

We can begin by developing a clearer sense of diplomatic strategy, with a more rigorous operational doctrine.[9] The U.S. military has long embraced the value of systematic case studies and after-action reports. Career diplomats, by contrast, have tended to pride themselves more on their ability to adjust quickly to shifting circumstances than on more systematic attention to lessons learned and long-term thinking. As part of a post-Trump reinvention of diplomacy, there ought to be new emphasis on tradecraft, rediscovering diplomatic history, sharpening negotiation skills, and making the lessons of negotiations like the Dayton Peace Accords or the Iranian nuclear talks accessible to practitioners.

A reinvention of diplomacy would also mean updating American diplomatic priorities, with sharper focus on issues that matter more and more to twenty-first-century foreign policy, particularly technology, economics, energy, and climate. My generation and its predecessor had plenty of specialists in nuclear arms control and conventional energy issues; throw-weights and oil pricing mechanisms were not alien concepts. In my last few years in government, I spent too much time sitting in meetings on the seventh floor of the State Department and in the White House Situation Room with smart, dedicated colleagues, collectively faking it on problems and opportunities flowing from the technology revolution. The department, and the executive branch in general, should be more flexible and creative in order to attract tech talent, including through temporary postings and mid-level entry, just as we did at the dawn of the nuclear age.

The same is true in matters of commerce and economics. In our memo to Warren Christopher a quarter century ago, I wrote that it was already increasingly "hard to separate economic security from national security."[10] It is impossible today. In that paper, we argued that economic diplomacy "has to be a central feature of almost every aspect of our policymaking; nothing will affect our prospects in the world over the rest of this decade more significantly than the skill with which we shape the international economic environment and compete in it."[11] Since George Shultz's tenure, across my whole career as a diplomat, the State Department has been trying fitfully to step up its game on economic statecraft and commercial diplomacy. As an ambassador abroad, I spent a substantial amount of my time promoting American businesses and working to create a level playing field on which they could compete. There is much more that can be done.

Updating our knowledge and skills is a critical factor in molding a new diplomatic doctrine. Applying that doctrine successfully, and building a stronger sense of strategic purpose, also means making State a more dexterous institution. Individual American diplomats overseas can be remarkably innovative and entrepreneurial. As an institution, however, the State Department is rarely accused of being too agile. We have to apply our gardening skills to our own messy plot of ground, and do some serious institutional weeding.

State's personnel system is far too rigid and anachronistic. The evaluation process is wholly incapable of providing honest feedback and incentives for improved performance. Retention, especially of the most promising junior and mid-level officers, is becoming tougher. Promotion is too slow, tours of duty too inflexible, and mechanisms to facilitate careers of families with two working parents insufficient and outdated.

State's internal deliberative process is just as lumbering and conservative, with too many layers of approval and authority. During my last months as deputy secretary, I received a one-page memo on a mundane policy issue—with a page and a half of clearances attached to it. Every imaginable office in the department had reviewed it, and a few that severely strained my imagination. Like a number of my predecessors, I failed in my efforts to streamline the clearance process. The problem was not just the time-consuming nature of the process, but also the tendency to homogenize judgments. If you're the mid-level desk officer responsible for relations with Tunisia, for example, your sense of accountability for the quality of both the prose and the policy recommendations naturally tends to diminish in direct proportion to the number of other layers and officials involved. Responsibility needs to be pushed downward in Washington, and ambassadors in the field need to be empowered to make more decisions locally.

Delayering is long overdue—in Washington and in our embassies. If the right people are put into the right places in a tighter organizational structure, the result can be a more nimble, more responsive institution, better able to make the case for a more central role for diplomacy. And if greater authority is pushed to the field and personnel allocated more strategically to critical posts, State ought to become more quick-footed, and chiefs of mission more adept at directing the work of their interagency country teams. Embassy reporting and analysis will still matter—but less for its volume and more for its distillation of meaning and policy implications from the avalanche of information that flows into the U.S. government.

Smart adaptation to the realities of today's world and policymaking environment will require diplomats to become even more effective at managing physical risk. Diplomacy is a dangerous business. As the walls in the entrance hall of the State Department remind us, with their long lists of names of diplomats who died while serving overseas, physical risks are not new. In the 1970s alone, four U.S. ambassadors were killed at their posts. At the end of the decade, the entire embassy staff in Tehran was taken hostage. Since the Beirut embassy bombings in the early 1980s, and even more so after the East Africa embassy bombings of 1998, American diplomatic facilities have been constructed to strict, often fortresslike specifications. Over the past two decades, the diplomatic security budget increased by roughly 1,000 percent.[12]

Managing physical risk has become progressively more complicated in recent years, as policy choices have put diplomats in greater danger while absence of political courage at home has left them with less backing and support. With many members of Congress alternating between dismissiveness of diplomacy and political scapegoating when attacks occur, the department has inevitably become more risk-averse. As Chris Stevens knew, however, demanding zero security risk can mean zero diplomatic achievements. We have to learn and apply the painful lessons of Benghazi, and take every prudent precaution, but we cannot hole up behind embassy walls and still do our jobs.

* * *

WHAT THIS MOMENT also requires—alongside the refinement of core skills and the adaptation to new realities—is a new domestic compact, a broadly shared sense of American purpose in the world, and of the relationship between disciplined American leadership abroad and middle-class interests at home.

When I was a junior diplomat, George Shultz used to invite outbound U.S. ambassadors into his office for a farewell chat. He would walk over to a large globe near his desk (which many years later I had in my own office as deputy secretary) and ask each ambassador to point to "your country." Invariably, the ambassador would put a finger on the country of her or his assignment. Shultz would then gently move their finger across the globe to the United States—making the not-so-subtle point that diplomats should always remember who they represent and where they come from. Not a bad lesson to reinforce today.

As the 2016 U.S. presidential elections made vivid, the pews in the church of American global leadership have grown deserted. The preaching of the gospel by the foreign policy "blob" continues unabated—often unpersuasive and sometimes a little self-righteous. It's time for some honest stocktaking and a more concerted effort to ensure that American diplomacy is more intimately connected and responsive to the needs and aspirations of the American people.

This is not a novel challenge. One of the most significant, if least noted, passages in Kennan's "Long Telegram" comes at the very end. After elegantly analyzing the sources of Soviet conduct and making the case for containment, Kennan emphasizes in a few dozen words at the conclusion of his fifty-three-hundred-word message that the key to success would be "the point at which domestic and foreign policies meet"—the resilience of our society, and its connection to a disciplined, fundamentally optimistic approach to America's engagement in the world.

The last four administrations have all begun their terms with a similarly sharp focus on "nation-building at home," and a self-conscious determination to be rigorous about overseas commitments. Secretaries of state as different in their backgrounds and styles as Henry Kissinger and Jim Baker had a shared appreciation of the critical value of connecting with the American public, and constantly renewing a workable domestic compact. Kissinger spent much of his last two years as secretary delivering a series of a dozen "heartland" speeches around the country, laying out the case for careful international engagement to safeguard American security and prosperity. Baker understood that politics was as crucial an element of successful diplomacy as geopolitics. Every one of their successors has at one time or another emphasized the tight link between economic security and national security. Our transition memo to the Clinton administration stressed that the new administration would need to "spend considerable time and effort selling the inter-relationship of foreign and domestic policy to the American people. Few people will take that argument for granted any more."[13]

The challenge is that each successive administration often failed to marry its words with deeds, seemingly taking on more and more global responsibility and risks at greater expense and sacrifice for American society, with little obvious, direct benefit. If Martians landed in Washington and discovered that we are nearing our second decade of a military campaign in Afghanistan—despite all the issues elsewhere in the world and all the turbulence at home—they would likely get back on their spacecraft and look for alternative habitat. Most Americans share that sense of disbelief and exasperation about where and how we've invested our blood and treasure in recent decades.

As a result, making the basic argument for diplomacy as a tool of first resort, as a key to realizing the promise of America's pivotal role, will remain an uphill battle. Nevertheless, its main ingredients are straightforward. The starting point is candor and transparency about the purpose and limits of American engagement abroad. It's more effective to level with the American people about the challenges we face and the choices we make than to wrap them in the tattered robe of untempered exceptionalism or fan fears of external threats. Overpromising and underdelivering is the surest way to undermine the case for American diplomacy.

Another ingredient is demonstrating that diplomacy and international influence are aimed as much at facilitating and accelerating domestic renewal as they are at shoring up global order. That does not mean embracing narrow-minded, art-of-the-deal mercantilism. What it does mean is ensuring that the American middle class is positioned as well as possible for success in a hypercompetitive world, that we build open and equitable trading systems, and that we don't shy away from holding to account those who do not play by the rules of the game.

Our challenge is simply to underscore the powerful connection between smart American engagement in the world and our success at home. When the State Department plays a valuable role in nailing down big overseas commercial deals, as we did in a $4 billion Boeing sale in Russia more than a decade ago, it rarely highlights the role of diplomacy in creating thousands of jobs in cities and towns across the United States. There are growing opportunities to work closely with American governors and mayors, many of whom are increasingly active in promoting overseas trade and investment.

A workable domestic compact also depends upon a healthy relationship with Congress. With rare exceptions, members of Congress do not see advocacy for diplomacy as a political asset. The State Department does not have military bases or defense production plants in their states or districts, and includes relatively few constituents among its seventy thousand employees—the majority of whom are in any case foreign nationals working at posts overseas.

Members of Congress are mostly ambivalent about diplomats and diplomacy, although there are still probably a handful who sympathize with the unbridled hostility of Otto Passman, the legendary postwar congressman from Louisiana. "Son," Passman told one of my State Department predecessors a couple generations ago, "I don't smoke and I don't drink. My only pleasure in life is kicking the shit out of the foreign aid program of the United States of America."[14]

I never had the pleasure of dealing with Passman, and most of my encounters with Congress were relatively positive (the Benghazi hearings in 2012–13 were a notable exception, a thoroughly politicized circus aimed less at thoughtful oversight and more at partisan score-settling). As a diplomat, I testified before congressional committees off and on for nearly two decades, never wildly enthusiastic about the experience, but always mindful of its significance.

Like my senior colleagues at State, I also often briefed members informally. While serving as ambassador in Amman following the death of King Hussein, I returned to Washington regularly to lobby for increased financial assistance and support for the bilateral free trade agreement. Those trips always paid important dividends, and I found that ambassadors returning from the field had particular credibility with members of Congress and their staffs. That was particularly true as members traveled abroad less frequently, which was more and more the case in my last decade or so in government, with a few deeply committed exceptions like Senator John McCain.

Compared to the Pentagon and the CIA, however, State was generally far less persistent and systematic in making its case on the Hill. Defense and CIA would deploy significant numbers of personnel to troll the corridors of Congress and seek out opportunities to brief or answer questions. We were more cautious, reactive, and detached at State, and paranoia about missteps led the department to discourage young diplomats from building relationships with congressional staff. Building more effective ties to the Hill is tougher and more labor-intensive now than it was when I entered the Foreign Service, at a time when a relatively small number of senior members, in the congressional leadership and among committee chairs, could command the movement of legislation and budget resources. Power is more diffuse now, just like on the wider international landscape, but that makes congressional outreach all the more important.

A new domestic compact on diplomacy involves reciprocal responsibilities. The State Department and the executive branch have an obligation to follow through on serious reform, streamlining structure, modernizing communications, and finding a rational balance for budgets and roles across the national security community. To make it a two-way street, Congress will need to provide more resources for diplomacy, and offer more flexibility in pooling funds and maximizing their utility. This partnership will only take hold if it's embedded in a wider compact with citizens that restores their faith in the wisdom of American leadership and the significance and utility of diplomacy.

* * *

AS AMERICA ACCELERATED its rise to global power more than a
century ago, Teddy Roosevelt took the stage at the Minnesota State
Fair and drew new attention to an old proverb. "Speak softly and
carry a big stick," he reminded the audience, "and you will go far." His
point was not about belligerence, but balance, as the United States
launched itself into a complicated and competitive world. Roosevelt
saw clearly the interconnected value of force and diplomacy, the need
to invest wisely in both to best serve America's interests. The international successes of the next century would not have surprised him,
nor would he have been surprised when imbalances between force
and diplomacy caused some of our most serious failures.

Of course we ought to ensure that our military's big stick is more
imposing than anyone else's, that our tool of last resort is potent and
durable. But big sticks will only take us so far, and we need urgently
to renovate diplomacy as our tool of first resort. Its importance in a
post-primacy world is only growing, and we isolate only ourselves,
not our rivals, by its deeply misguided disassembly. Calculated neglect has already done permanent damage, and the sooner we reverse
course, the better.

That will be much easier said than done. While there is much that
America's diplomats can do to prove their value and relevance, they
ultimately depend on wise leadership—in the White House and in
Congress—to make the policy and resource decisions and provide the
political backing that will unlock the promise of American diplomacy.

The good news is that there are plenty of reasons to be optimistic
about the potential of American diplomacy. As I hope the pages of
this book have helped to illustrate, it is an honorable profession, filled
with good people and strong purpose. Another of Teddy Roosevelt's
well-known sayings was that "life's greatest good fortune is the chance
to work hard at work worth doing." By that standard, my long experience as an American diplomat was incredibly fortunate. While it may
sometimes not seem so apparent in the age of Trump, the experience
of the next generation of diplomats holds just as much promise. The

image and value of public service is scarred and dented right now, but the diplomatic profession has never mattered more, or been more consequential for our interests at home and abroad.

The rebuilding process will be daunting, but we have a lot going for us—enduring sources of national strength, a pivotal role to play in a competitive world, and no existential threats before us. If we can recover a sense of diplomatic agility out of the muscle-bound national security bureaucracy that we've become in recent years, we can help ensure a new generation of security and prosperity for Americans.

One of the benefits of serving overseas, of a life in diplomacy, is the chance to see your own country through the eyes of others. From that first visit to Egypt at eighteen, to my years at Oxford and postings abroad, to constant travels in senior State Department jobs, I certainly became accustomed to the hostility with which particular American policies are viewed. I knew all too well the resentments that come with our weight in the world and how we have sometimes thrown it around. Through all that mistrust and suspicion, however, I also saw what people expected of us—a sense of possibility, of pragmatism, of recognizing problems and flaws and trying to fix them. That's who we still are—limping from self-inflicted political injury, challenged increasingly in a world of rising powers and shifting currents, but with a resilience that has always set us apart. "You're testing our faith like never before," a longtime European diplomat told me recently, "but I wouldn't bet against you—at least not yet." I wouldn't bet against us either. My faith in our resilience, like my pride in American diplomacy, remains unbounded.

Acknowledgments

My greatest good fortune as a diplomat was the extraordinary company in which I served. While never seeking or getting the credit they deserve, the friends and colleagues who shared this diplomatic journey enriched my life and honored our country with their skill and sacrifice. I could never acknowledge them all in these pages, but I am forever in their debt.

This book was a different kind of journey, but it benefited no less from the thoughtful support of many friends and colleagues.

At the Carnegie Endowment for International Peace, my new professional home, I have been blessed with an exceptional team. Matan Chorev, my chief of staff at the State Department and now at Carnegie, embodies the very best of his generation of foreign policy thinkers and practitioners. Utterly selfless, an elegant writer and editor, and a terrific friend, Matan has been indispensable to this project from its inception. He and Seth Center, a gifted diplomatic historian at the State Department, did a superb job of organizing more than thirty years' worth of memos, cables, and other archival documents and helping me think through how best to structure the book and its arguments.

My treasured friend, Mary Dubose, has put up with me and deftly organized my professional life for nearly three decades, and made sure to keep me focused and on track. Three exceptionally talented James C. Gaither Junior Fellows, Miles Graham, Rachel Mitnick, and Austin Owen, were invaluable research assistants. Kathleen Higgs, Carnegie's library director, could not have been more helpful. Tim Martin, Carnegie's digital director, imagined and built a beautiful website for the book and the digital diplomatic archive. I am especially lucky to have worked closely at Carnegie with two wonderful board chairs, Harvey Fineberg and Penny Pritzker, whose encouragement for this undertaking has been unstinting.

I am deeply grateful to the many indefatigable readers who plowed through all or parts of the draft manuscript. They include: Salman Ahmed, Rich Armitage, Tom Carothers, Derek Chollet, Ryan Crocker, Liz Dibble, Bob Einhorn, Mohamed el-Erian, Jim Fallows, Jeff Feltman, John Lewis Gaddis, Frank Gavin, Jeff Goldberg, Tom Graham, Dan Kurtz-Phelan, Dan Kurtzer, Jim Larocco, Neil MacFarlane, Jef McAllister, Denis McDonough, Aaron Miller, Nader Mousavizadeh, Marwan Muasher, Evan Osnos, Jen Psaki, Philip Remler, Rob Richer, Dennis Ross, Norm Roule, Eugene Rumer, Dan Russell, Karim Sadjadpour, David Satterfield, Jake Sullivan, Ashley Tellis, Dmitri Trenin, Andrew Weiss, and Alice Wells. A presentation of an early draft at Carnegie's "Research in Progress" seminar was particularly useful, and I'm grateful to Milan Vaishnav for the opportunity and to my colleagues for their frank and constructive feedback.

I owe a special debt of gratitude to a first-rate team at the Department of State who made possible the declassification of over one hundred documents and diligently reviewed the manuscript. Behar Godani is a gem, as are her colleagues—Kathy Allegrone, Anne Barbaro, Geoffrey Chapman, Alden Fahy, Paul Hilburn, and Daniel Sanborn. The State Department could not ask for more skilled and committed professionals.

I am also indebted to two remarkable institutions for providing ideal settings for extended periods of writing. Sir John Vickers and the fellows of All Souls College, Oxford, graciously hosted me as a visiting fellow in the autumn of 2017. The Rockefeller Foundation gave me a similar opportunity at its spectacular Bellagio Center in the spring of 2018, where my main challenge was not getting too distracted by the perfect view of Lake Como out my study window.

Andrew Wylie, my literary agent, has been an enthusiastic advocate and marvelous guide, as he has been for so many other lucky authors. I could not have been in better hands than at Random House. Andy Ward is the perfect editor—confident in his craft, and a rigorous and exacting partner. Chayenne Skeete did a wonderful job coordinating the all-star Random House team of Anna Bauer, Debbie Glasserman, Greg Kubie, Beth Pearson, and Katie Tull. Their support meant the world to me, and to the success of this project.

This book, like the rest of my professional life, is built on the bedrock of a loving family. I never had to look any further than my parents for the best role models I could hope to find. With his intellect and integrity, my father epitomized public service. My mother set an impossibly high standard of faith, decency, and compassion. My three brothers have inspired me by their own examples, kept me grounded, and embarrassed me year after year in fantasy football.

Dedicating this work to Lisa barely scratches the surface of what I owe her, and what her love and sacrifice have made possible for me. From that first day in the A-100 entry class almost forty years ago, she has been my best friend and most caring and constructive critic. By far our greatest accomplishments together are our two daughters, Lizzy and Sarah. Now remarkable young adults, they are a source of immense pride and joy. The diplomatic life that unfolds on the pages of this book is full of boldface personalities and dramatic events, but it was family that made it whole.

Appendix

The declassified documents in the pages that follow are a small sample of one diplomat's imperfect efforts to provide ground truths, strategic advice, and—on occasion—disciplined dissent. Nearly one hundred additional cables, memos, and emails from my thirty-three-year career in the Foreign Service are available at burnsbackchannel .com. My hope is that this memoir and archive make vivid the power and purpose of American diplomacy—both in our recent past, and in the era unfolding before us.

Excerpt: Memo to Secretary of State–Designate
Warren Christopher, January 5, 1993, "Parting Thoughts:
U.S. Foreign Policy in the Years Ahead"

In Policy Planning, our task was to look over the horizon and prepare American diplomacy to seize new opportunities and manage emerging challenges. The transition memo excerpted below offered the incoming Clinton administration a strategy for navigating the post–Cold War international landscape.

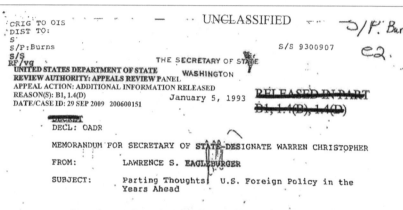

CRIG TO OIS   UNCLASSIFIED   D/P. Burns
DIST TO:
S
S/P:Burns   S/S 9300907   e2.
S/S
RF/vg   THE SECRETARY OF STATE
UNITED STATES DEPARTMENT OF STATE   WASHINGTON
REVIEW AUTHORITY: APPEALS REVIEW PANEL
APPEAL ACTION: ADDITIONAL INFORMATION RELEASED
REASON(S): B1, 1.4(D)
DATE/CASE ID: 29 SEP 2009 200600151   January 5, 1993   RELEASED IN PART
                                         B1, 1.4(B), 1.4(D)

SECRET
DECL: OADR

MEMORANDUM FOR SECRETARY OF STATE-DESIGNATE WARREN CHRISTOPHER

FROM: LAWRENCE S. EAGLEBURGER

SUBJECT: Parting Thoughts: U.S. Foreign Policy in the
                   Years Ahead

     In a few weeks, you will become the first Secretary of State confirmed by the Senate in the post–Cold War era. The world that awaits you is a much different place than the one you and I have known through many years of government service. It is a world in the midst of revolutionary transition, in which you will have both an historic opportunity to shape a new international order and a sobering collection of problems to contend with.

     During your tenure, many achievements are possible: a genuine new partnership with Japan for global economic growth and security; a new trans–Atlantic compact linking us to the European democracies; the gradual incorporation of a reforming Russia and the East Europeans into a stable European system; peaceful reunification of the Korean peninsula; normalization of relations with a reforming Vietnam; the departure of Castro and the peaceful emergence of a free Cuba; expansion of free trade arrangements and consolidation of democratic institutions throughout the Hemisphere; nonracial democracy in South Africa; the invigoration of UN peacekeeping and peacemaking capabilities; and, not least, a whole series of Arab–Israeli peace agreements.

     That's the good news. The bad news is that there are at least as many troubles awaiting you as opportunities. Three immediate problems top the list, in my view: (1) the possible outbreak of a general Balkan war; (2) a breakdown of reform in Russia and a reversion to some form of authoritarian rule; and (3) the continuing threat of deepening global recession and trade wars between regional blocs, fueled by a collapse of the Uruguay Round and domestic political weaknesses throughout the West.

     Other potential troubles include: B1

UNCLASSIFIED

SECRET UNITED STATES DEPARTMENT OF STATE
REVIEW AUTHORITY: CHARLES E LAHIGUERA
CLASSIFICATION: SECRET REASON: 1.4(B), 1.4(D)
DECLASSIFY AFTER: 4 JAN 2018

UNCLASSIFIED

~~SECRET~~

- 2 -

continued trade tensions with the Japanese and perhaps the lingering danger of nuclear war on either the Korean peninsula or in South Asia; a revived threat to Western interests in the Persian Gulf, from either a rearmed Iran or an unrepentant Saddam; or a breakdown in the Middle East peace process.

With the humility born of recent experience, let me offer a few personal thoughts on the post-Cold War world, and then on what I see to be the main policy challenges before you. To flesh out these questions, I am also sending you a more detailed collection of papers prepared by the Policy Planning Staff. I don't necessarily agree with every argument made in them, but they are a useful and provocative way to think about what lies ahead.

The Post-Cold War Setting

My starting point is a simple one. It seems to me that the basic purposes of American foreign policy are still to ensure the physical security and economic prosperity of our people, and to promote our values wherever we can -- at least in part for the common sense reason that democracies are less likely to threaten us and healthy free market economies are more likely to enhance our own economic well-being. As I look at prospects for advancing those core purposes over the next few years, a number of trends and developments in the post-Cold War world strike me as especially critical.

First, the most obvious consequence of the demise of the Soviet Union is that for the first time in fifty years we do not face a global military adversary. It is certainly conceivable that a return to authoritarianism in Russia or an aggressively hostile China could revive such a global threat, but that is not likely in the short term. We retain a vital stake in preventing domination of four key regions -- Europe, East Asia, the Persian Gulf, and Latin America -- by a hostile, non-democratic regional power. But it is hard to see any immediate regional threats of this nature with the end of the Cold War and the defeat of Iraq.

Second, in the absence of a global military threat, the most important global challenge we face is the emergence of an increasingly interdependent and competitive international economy. Creating and sustaining jobs at home depends more and more on exports, which in turn depend upon both renewed growth in the world economy and improved American competitiveness. We

~~SECRET~~

UNCLASSIFIED

432

- 3 -

face stiffer and stiffer competition from our closest allies,
continued obstacles in protected markets in Europe and Asia, as
well as the danger of a collapse of order in the global trading
system. We retain substantial internal strengths -- a massive
domestic market, a flexible work force, high productivity, and
traditions of ingenuity and entrepreneurship -- but our
domestic economic shortcomings undercut our competitiveness.
They devalue U.S. leadership and, perhaps more importantly,
threaten domestic support for strong international engagement.

Third, the broadest systemic challenge that we face is the
deconstruction of the system of states that emerged as a result
of World War II and postwar decolonization, and that was held
in place by the Cold War. Alongside the globalization of the
world economy, the international political system is tilting
schizophrenically toward greater fragmentation. Most
dramatically in the former Soviet empire, but more generally
wherever state boundaries and racial, national, ethnic or
religious identities do not coincide, the old state system is
being transformed or is at least under strain. The resulting
chaos is enough to almost -- almost -- make one nostalgic for
the familiar discipline and order of the Cold War. Our basic
stake is in peaceful processes of change rather than in
clinging blindly to existing maps; but promoting such processes
is going to require great patience and skill, and creative ways
of safeguarding human and minority rights. Chaos in the
international political system is also going to confront us
increasingly with the dilemma of whether to take part in
limited military interventions in situations which do not
directly threaten our vital interests, but which endanger
innocent civilian populations and pull hard on our values and
humanitarian traditions. Somalia is only the first of these
kinds of challenges.

Fourth, as peoples reorganize themselves in the wake of the
Cold War, ideological competition continues. The collapse of
Communism represents an historic triumph for democracy and free
markets, but it has not ended history or brought us to the
brink of ideological uniformity. A great wave of democratic
institution-building is taking place, driven by a surging
post-Communist interest in the political and economic
empowerment of individuals. But democratizing societies that
fail to produce the fruits of economic reform quickly, or fail
to accommodate pressures for ethnic self-expression, may slide
back into other "isms", including nationalism or religious
extremism or some combination of the two. In much of the
world, including parts of it that are very important
strategically for us, Islamic conservatism remains a potent
alternative to democracy as an organizing principle.

Fifth, the proliferation of weapons of mass destruction and
advanced delivery systems is likely to be the central security
challenge of the 1990s. It is entirely possible that as many
as eight or ten new powers, many of them authoritarian and

UNCLASSIFIED

~~SECRET~~

- 4 -

anti-Western, could acquire ballistic missiles equipped with nuclear or biological warheads by the end of the decade. Such a development would dramatically destabilize important parts of the world, and could even threaten the physical security of the United States. Proliferation becomes an even more dangerous phenomenon when it intersects with fragmentation in the international political system, increasing the number of unstable actors with an incentive to acquire weapons of mass destruction.

Sixth, a variety of new transnational threats have appeared, particularly environmental degradation, drugs, and the spread of deadly diseases like AIDS. Such dangers demand collective action rather than purely national responses. They also require an aggressive, new international scientific agenda, in which American leadership will be critical.

Seventh, and perhaps most importantly, you will be tackling all these challenges at a moment in our history when many Americans will be preoccupied with domestic problems, and when budgetary constraints on the conduct of American foreign policy are likely to be tighter than at any point in the last half-century. This leaves you and the President with a very tough task. It was relatively easy during the Cold War to justify national security expenditures and build support for sustained American engagement overseas. It is infinitely harder now. More and more, you will need to link our involvement clearly and directly to American ideals, and particularly to American economic needs. And, more and more, you will need to point clearly to what other governments are doing to bear their fair share of the cost and burden. These tasks will require a radical restructuring of our national security institutions, most of which were designed for the Cold War. And they will require that you and other senior Administration officials -- and especially the President himself -- spend considerable time and effort selling the inter-relationship of foreign and domestic policy to the American people. Few people will take that argument for granted any more.

The Importance of American Leadership and Five Key Policy Tests

Against that backdrop, I am convinced absolutely that American leadership is as important in this period of revolutionary transition in the international system as it was during the Cold War. Our self-interest, especially our economic self-interest, requires it. And for better or worse, peoples and governments still look to us to make sense of the changes swirling around them and show some initiative and purpose. No one else can play that role. The Communist regimes have collapsed or are discredited. The European

~~SECRET~~

~~SECRET~~
- 5 -

Community is consumed with its own problems, and by no means as monolithic in its view of political issues as we once hoped (or feared) it would be. And the Japanese are neither ready nor willing for such a task now. The bottom line is that in this time of uncertainty, the United States has a unique role to play -- as a provider of reassurance and architect of new security arrangements; as an aggressive proponent of economic openness; as an exemplar and advocate of democratic values; and as a builder and leader of coalitions to deal with the problems of a chaotic post-Cold War world.

I have yet to see a term or phrase which captures the essence of America's new role and strategy as neatly as Kennan did with "containment" at the outset of the U.S.-Soviet confrontation. While this may simply reflect my own lack of creativity, I suspect that it may be some time before such a term emerges, perhaps after the contours of what lies beyond this transitional period are clearer. In the meantime, I believe the major challenges you face will fall into five broad, interconnected categories:

- Renewing the adhesion -- the cement -- that held the democratic community together and won the Cold War;

- Promoting long-term expansion of that community to include our former Cold War adversaries, while coping in the meantime with the massive uncertainties and instabilities left in the wake of the collapse of Communism;

- Pressing a new regional agenda in what used to be the "Third World", composed of conflict resolution, nonproliferation, democratic institution-building, and economic growth;

- Competing aggressively in an open international economic system, while protecting the environment;

- Restructuring our national security institutions for the post-Cold War world.

1995 Moscow 883, January 11, 1995,
"Sifting Through the Wreckage: Chechnya and Russia's Future"

Following the collapse of the Soviet Union, violent separatism in the North Caucasus posed an enormous challenge for President Boris Yeltsin: His military's botched attempt to put down the Chechen insurrection during the winter of 1994–95 was emblematic of the "slow crumbling" of the new Russian state. This cable conveyed to Washington the depth of the crisis in Chechnya and its consequences for Russia and U.S. policy.

UNCLASSIFIED U.S. Department of State Case No. MP 2015-07420 Doc No. C06317048 Date: 05/03/2017

SECRET

PTQ3213

RELEASE IN FULL

DECLASSIFIED

-SECRET-   PTQ3213

PAGE 01   MOSCOW 00883 01 OF 04 111657Z
ACTION SS-00

INFO LOG-00, QASY-00 ADS-00   /000W
----------------9ABC4B 111657Z /38
O 111652Z JAN 95
FM AMEMBASSY MOSCOW
TO SECSTATE WASHDC IMMEDIATE 9782
MOSCOW POLITICAL COLLECTIVE
INFO AMEMBASSY TALLINN
AMEMBASSY VILNIUS
AMEMBASSY RIGA
CIS COLLECTIVE

-S E C R E T- SECTION 01 OF 04 MOSCOW 000883

EXDIS   DECAPTIONED

E.O.12356: DECL:OADR
TAGS: PREL, RS
SUBJECT: SIFTING THROUGH THE WRECKAGE: CHECHNYA AND RUSSIA'S FUTURE

1. SECRET- ENTIRE TEXT.

SUMMARY AND INTRODUCTION

---

2. THE CHECHEN CRISIS IS FAR FROM OVER, BUT IT HAS
SECRET-

SECRET

PAGE 02   MOSCOW 00883 01 OF 04 111657Z
ALREADY LAID BARE THE WEAKNESS OF THE RUSSIAN STATE
AND THE TRAGIC FLAWS OF ITS FIRST DEMOCRATICALLY-
ELECTED PRESIDENT. YELTSIN'S BLUNDERS, BORN IN LARGE
PART OF AN INCREASINGLY INSULAR STYLE OF DECISION
MAKING, HAVE RAISED A NUMBER OF FUNDAMENTAL QUESTIONS.
WHAT ARE THE CONSEQUENCES OF THE CHECHEN DEBACLE FOR
RUSSIA? IS YELTSIN IN CONTROL? WHAT IS HIS FUTURE?

Declassification Authority: Geoffrey W. Chapman, OCA, Senior Reviewer,
A/GIS/IPS

UNCLASSIFIED U.S. Department of State Case No. MP 2015-07420 Doc No. C06317048 Date: 05/03/2017

SECRET

WHAT IS THE FUTURE OF REFORM? WHAT ROLE WILL THE
MILITARY PLAY IN RUSSIAN POLITICS? IS A BREAK UP OF
THE RUSSIAN FEDERATION LIKELY? HOW WILL RUSSIAN
FOREIGN POLICY BE AFFECTED? WHAT ARE THE IMPLICATIONS
FOR U.S. POLICY?

3. NOT SURPRISINGLY, THERE ARE NO NEAT ANSWERS TO ANY
OF THESE QUESTIONS. LIKE MOSCOW IN MID-WINTER, THE
RUSSIAN POLITICAL LANDSCAPE TODAY IS MOST ACCURATELY
PORTRAYED IN VARYING SHADES OF GRAY, NOT BLACKS OR
WHITES. NEVERTHELESS, WHAT FOLLOWS IS AN ATTEMPT TO
PROVIDE SOME VERY PRELIMINARY ANSWERS, OR AT LEAST TO
BETTER FRAME THE QUESTIONS. PARAS 17-23 OFFER SOME
BROAD GUIDELINES FOR US. POLICY. END SUMMARY AND
INTRODUCTION.

THE EMPEROR HAS NO CLOTHES
----

4. THE CHECHEN CRISIS HAS LAID BARE THE WEAKNESS OF
THE RUSSIAN STATE AND THE TRAGIC FLAWS OF ITS FIRST
DEMOCRATICALLY-ELECTED PRESIDENT. MOST RUSSIANS HAVE
BEEN SHOCKED BY THE ABYSMAL PERFORMANCE OF THEIR
                    SECRET

SECRET

PAGE 03   MOSCOW 00883 01 OF 04 111657Z
MILITARY, A KEY SYMBOL OF STATE POWER AND ONE OF THE
FEW REMAINING NATIONAL INSTITUTIONS TO HAVE ENJOYED
WIDESPREAD RESPECT. THE MILITARY MACHINE THAT ONCE
BOASTED IT COULD REACH THE ENGLISH CHANNEL IN FORTY-
EIGHT HOURS HAS BEEN UNABLE TO SUBDUE "BANDIT
FORMATIONS" IN A TINY REPUBLIC WITHIN RUSSIA IN OVER A
MONTH. THIS INEPTITUDE -- PROBABLY EVEN MORE THAN THE
LOSS OF CIVILIAN LIVES WHICH HAS SO EXERCISED MOSCOW'S
LIBERAL INTELLIGENTSIA -- HAS LED RUSSIANS, AND
ESPECIALLY ELITES, TO QUESTION BORIS YELTSIN'S
COMPETENCE TO GOVERN.

5. WHAT RUSSIANS ARE WITNESSING IN CHECHNYA IS THE
FURTHER SLOW CRUMBLING OF THEIR STATE. DECAY AND
GOVERNMENTAL INADEQUACY ARE EQUALLY, IF LESS
GRAPHICALLY, APPARENT ELSEWHERE -- IN PUBLIC HEALTH,
THE ENVIRONMENT, ECONOMIC INFRASTRUCTURE, PUBLIC
MORALITY, AND PUBLIC SAFETY AND ORDER. THE POPULAR
MOOD SEEMS AS DOWNBEAT AS MOSCOW'S MID-WINTER GLOOM;
RECENT POLLS SUGGEST THAT OVER TWO-THIRDS OF VOTERS
THINK THE COUNTRY IS GOING IN THE WRONG DIRECTION.

6. WHERE DID YELTSIN GO WRONG? HIS EFFORTS OVER THE
PAST YEAR BROUGHT A PERIOD OF RELATIVE STABILITY
WELCOMED BY MOST RUSSIANS, WHO WERE EXHAUSTED BY THE
TUMULTUOUS CHANGES OF RECENT YEARS. BUT YELTSIN MADE
LITTLE HEADWAY IN USING THAT COMPARATIVE POLITICAL
CALM TO CONSOLIDATE STATE, AND PARTICULARLY
DEMOCRATIC, INSTITUTIONS. INSTEAD, HE DREW BACK EVEN
FURTHER FROM THE TIME-CONSUMING AND MESSY PROCESS OF
FORGING A CONSENSUS AMONG DISPARATE POLITICAL FORCES.
SECRET

SECRET

PAGE 04   MOSCOW 00883 01 OF 04 111657Z
HE HAS RELIED INCREASINGLY ON A SMALL, NARROWING
CIRCLE OF ADVISORS WHOSE DISTINGUISHING FEATURE IS
THEIR POLITICAL DEPENDENCE ON YELTSIN HIMSELF.

7. SOME OF THOSE IN THIS INNER CIRCLE -- FIRST
PRESIDENTIAL ASSISTANT ILYUSHIN, SECURITY COUNCIL
SECRETARY LOBOV, AND FIRST BODYGUARD KORZHAKOV COME
IMMEDIATELY TO MIND -- HAVE NEVER BEEN NOTED FOR THEIR
REFORMIST INSTINCTS. OTHERS MAY HAVE MORE LIBERAL
INCLINATIONS, BUT IN WHAT SEEMS THE PREVAILING
SYCOPHANTIC ATMOSPHERE OF KREMLIN COURT POLITICS IT IS
HARD TO KNOW WHETHER THE PRESIDENT IS OFTEN TOLD WHAT
HE DOESN'T WANT TO HEAR. WHILE IT IS IMPOSSIBLE TO BE
CERTAIN, A NUMBER OF OUR CONTACTS HAVE TOLD US
RECENTLY THAT YELTSIN HAS ACCESS TO A VARIETY OF
SOURCES OF INFORMATION (AN OBSERVATION THAT KREMLIN
IRE WITH MEDIA COVERAGE OF CHECHNYA TENDS TO
REINFORCE), BUT TENDS TO RELY ON INACCURATE AND SELF-
SERVING ACCOUNTS FED HIM BY THE POWER MINISTRIES AND

SECRET

NNNNPTQ3214

SECRET   PTQ3214

PAGE 01   MOSCOW 00883 02 OF 04 111657Z
ACTION SS-00

INFO LOG-00 OASY-00 ADS-00   /000W
------------------9ABC5B 111657Z /38
O 111652Z JAN 95
FM AMEMBASSY MOSCOW
TO SECSTATE WASHDC IMMEDIATE 9783
MOSCOW POLITICAL COLLECTIVE
INFO AMEMBASSY TALLINN
AMEMBASSY VILNIUS
AMEMBASSY RIGA
CIS COLLECTIVE

S E C R E T SECTION 02 OF 04 MOSCOW 000883

EXDIS

E.O.12356: DECL:OADR
TAGS: PREL, RS
SUBJECT: SIFTING THROUGH THE WRECKAGE: CHECHNYA AND
RUSSIA'S FUTURE

THE INTELLIGENCE SERVICES. IT IS ALSO IMPOSSIBLE TO
BE CERTAIN TO WHAT EXTENT YELTSIN IS MANIPULATED BY
THOSE AROUND HIM; WHAT SEEMS CLEAR IS THAT THE CLOSED
DECISION MAKING SYSTEM WHICH HE HAS OPTED FOR OFFERS
FEW BRAKES ON BAD ADVICE OR BAD INSTINCTS.

8. THE CHECHEN DISASTER IS IN SOME WAYS A LOGICAL
SECRET

SECRET

PAGE 02   MOSCOW 00883 02 OF 04 111657Z
OUTGROWTH OF THIS INSULAR STYLE. STEP BY STEP OVER
RECENT MONTHS, YELTSIN AND HIS ADVISORS HAVE BLUNDERED
FURTHER INTO A QUAGMIRE, WITH BAD POLICY CHOICES
BEGETTING WORSE ONES. THE TRAGIC IRONY IS THAT THE

SAME MULISH STUBBORNNESS THAT PRODUCED YELTSIN'S
GREATEST TRIUMPHS MAY NOW PROVE TO BE HIS UNDOING.

9. YELTSIN'S MISMANAGEMENT OF THE CHECHEN CRISIS,
COUPLED WITH HIS INCREASINGLY DISTANT LEADERSHIP STYLE
AND THE CONTINUING PAIN OF ECONOMIC TRANSITION, HAS
LED TO A COLLAPSE OF HIS POPULAR SUPPORT. IN A RECENT
NATIONWIDE POLL, ONLY 18 PERCENT OF RUSSIANS EXPRESSED
CONFIDENCE IN HIS LEADERSHIP -- AND THAT WAS BEFORE
THE ASSAULT ON GROZNYY WAS LAUNCHED. MORE IMPORTANT,
THE CHECHEN FIASCO HAS RESULTED IN A PROFOUND LOSS OF
RESPECT FOR YELTSIN AMONG KEY POLITICAL ELITES --
INCLUDING THE MILITARY, SECURITY FORCES, AND THE
MEDIA. HE CAN NO LONGER UNIFY THE COUNTRY AS HE ONCE
DID IN THE WAKE OF THE FAILED AUGUST 1991 PUTSCH. TO
RESTORE HIS SAGGING FORTUNES, HE IS RESORTING TO MORE
NATIONALISTIC RHETORIC AND POLICIES. INDEED, MANY OF
HIS CRITICS -- BOTH RADICAL REFORMERS AND HARDLINE
OPPONENTS -- ARE ARGUING THAT HE HAS ALREADY STARTED
DOWN THE PATH OF AN AUTHORITARIAN RESTORATION.

THE FUTURE OF REFORM
----

10. WHILE IT WOULD BE A MISTAKE TO DISCOUNT THIS
POSSIBILITY, THE CURRENT SITUATION DOES NOT LEND
                    SECRET

                    SECRET

PAGE 03   MOSCOW 00883 02 OF 04 111657Z
ITSELF TO NEAT CONCLUSIONS, EITHER ABOUT YELTSIN'S
FUTURE OR THE FATE OF POLITICAL AND ECONOMIC REFORMS.
LIKE MOSCOW IN MID-WINTER, THE RUSSIAN POLITICAL
LANDSCAPE TODAY IS MOST ACCURATELY PORTRAYED IN SHADES
OF GRAY, NOT BLACKS OR WHITES. WHILE IT IS NOW TOO
LATE FOR YELTSIN TO RECOVER THE HEROIC DEMOCRATIC
MANTLE HE ONCE WORE, IT IS STILL NOT TOO LATE
(ASSUMING NO CATASTROPHIC DETERIORATION OF HIS HEALTH)
FOR HIM TO MAINTAIN ENOUGH OF HIS AUTHORITY TO LIMP
ALONG TO THE SCHEDULED PARLIAMENTARY ELECTIONS AT THE
END OF THIS YEAR AND PRESIDENTIAL ELECTIONS IN JUNE
1996, AVOIDING AN EXTRA-CONSTITUTIONAL UPHEAVAL. HE
STILL APPEARS TO RETAIN SUPPORT AMONG POLITICAL ELITES
IN RUSSIA'S REGIONS, WHERE THE CHECHEN CRISIS HAS SO
FAR NOT HAD THE RESONANCE THAT IT HAS HAD IN THE
CAPITAL. BLUNDERING IN CHECHNYA HAS SEVERELY TESTED
MILITARY DISCIPLINE, BUT IT DOES NOT YET APPEAR TO BE
AT THE BREAKING POINT.

SECRET

11. THAT ASSUMES THAT YELTSIN "TAKES" GROZNYY SHORTLY
AND KEEPS THE VIOLENCE THAT WILL INEVITABLY CONTINUE
IN CHECHNYA AT A MORE MANAGEABLE AND LESS VISIBLE
LEVEL. IT ALSO ASSUMES THAT HE CHANNELS DISCONTENT
WITHIN THE MILITARY BY PLEDGING REAL REFORM AND MORE
RESOURCES FOR THE MILITARY, AND SHAKES UP THE SENIOR
LEADERSHIP -- WHICH IS A QUESTION NOT JUST OF FIRING
GRACHEV BUT OF FINDING THE RIGHT PERSON TO REPLACE
HIM. THE RESULT WILL NOT BE PRETTY, BUT IT WOULD BE
ENOUGH TO SUSTAIN YELTSIN IN POWER UNTIL THE END OF
HIS PRESIDENTIAL TERM, AND IN THE PROCESS BUY MORE
TIME FOR RUSSIA'S HALTING EXPERIMENT WITH POLITICAL
                    SECRET

SECRET

PAGE 04   MOSCOW 00883 02 OF 04 111657Z
PLURALISM.

12. IT IS IMPORTANT TO KEEP IN MIND THAT THE CHECHEN
TRAGEDY HAS THUS FAR DEMONSTRATED THE RESILIENCE OF AT
LEAST SOME OF THE POLITICAL CHANGES OF RECENT YEARS.
PUBLIC INDIGNATION OVER CHECHNYA HAS BEEN FUELED BY
THE RUSSIAN MEDIA'S INDEPENDENT, VIGOROUS, AND
CRITICAL REPORTING, REINFORCED BY WESTERN MEDIA
BROADCASTS, TO WHICH RUSSIANS HAVE REGULAR AND
UNIMPEDED ACCESS. THE FAILURE TO CRACK DOWN ON THE
MEDIA MAY BE ONLY FURTHER EVIDENCE OF THE STATE'S
WEAKNESS, BUT IT COULD ALSO MEAN THAT RESPECT FOR
PLURALISM IS TAKING ROOT.

13. ANY EFFORT TO RESTORE AUTHORITARIAN RULE IN
RUSSIA WOULD ALSO BE TEMPERED BY CONTINUING DEVOLUTION
OF POWER AND AUTHORITY TO RUSSIA'S REGIONS. AGAINST
THE BACKGROUND OF THE CENTRAL GOVERNMENT'S DECLINE,
REGIONAL ELITES ARE CONSOLIDATING POWER LOCALLY. MOST

SECRET

SECRET

NNNNPTQ3216

SECRET   PTQ3216

PAGE 01   MOSCOW 00883 03 OF 04 111658Z
ACTION SS-00

INFO LOG-00 OASY-00 ADS-00   /000W
------------------9ABC6D 111658Z /38
O 111652Z JAN 95
FM AMEMBASSY MOSCOW
TO SECSTATE WASHDC IMMEDIATE 9784
MOSCOW POLITICAL COLLECTIVE
INFO AMEMBASSY TALLINN
AMEMBASSY VILNIUS
AMEMBASSY RIGA
CIS COLLECTIVE

S E C R E T SECTION 03 OF 04 MOSCOW 000883

EXDIS

E.O.12356: DECL:OADR
TAGS: PREL, RS
SUBJECT: SIFTING THROUGH THE WRECKAGE: CHECHNYA AND
RUSSIA'S FUTURE

ENJOY THEIR NEWFOUND PREROGATIVES AND WILL BE LOATHE
TO CEDE THEM BACK TO MOSCOW UNDER ANY CONDITIONS.
THIS IS A HEALTHY DEVELOPMENT, FROM OUR PERSPECTIVE,
AS LONG AS IT DOES NOT PROCEED TO THE POINT WHERE IT
THREATENS RUSSIA'S UNITY. IF IT DOES, THAT IS MORE
LIKELY TO BE THE RESULT OF DECAY AND DISARRAY IN
MOSCOW THAN OF ANY REGIONAL URGE TO SEPARATISM, WHICH
SECRET

SECRET

PAGE 02   MOSCOW 00883 03 OF 04 111658Z
REMAINS GENERALLY WEAK.

SECRET

14. EVEN IN THE BEST SCENARIO, HOWEVER, RUSSIA'S
POLITICAL EVOLUTION WILL REMAIN A LONG, UNEVEN, AND
VOLATILE PROCESS. UNDER YELTSIN AND HIS SUCCESSORS,
THERE IS LIKELY TO BE A CONSTANT, INTENSE
PREOCCUPATION WITH RESTORING EFFECTIVE STATE POWER AND
RECOVERING RUSSIAN NATIONAL PRIDE, NOW FURTHER
TARNISHED BY THE SELF-INFLICTED WOUND OF CHECHNYA.
THAT WILL MEAN A CONSTANT RISK FOR THE FORESEEABLE
FUTURE THAT RUSSIA'S EXPERIMENT WITH POLITICAL
PLURALISM WILL BE UNDERMINED OR OVERTURNED BY A MORE
FUNDAMENTAL DESIRE TO ENSURE ORDER IN SOCIETY. MUCH
WILL OF COURSE DEPEND ON THE ECONOMY; IF THE 1995
BUDGET FALLS APART AS A RESULT OF CHECHNYA
EXPENDITURES AND BROADER INDISCIPLINE, AND THUS
INFLATION CONTINUES TO RISE, THE POLITICAL
CONSEQUENCES COULD BE SEVERE.

MASKING RUSSIA'S WEAKNESS IN FOREIGN POLICY

15. IN FOREIGN POLICY TERMS, MILITARY INTERVENTION IN
CHECHNYA HAS BEEN A DISASTER FOR RUSSIA -- ISOLATING
IT INTERNATIONALLY, EXPOSING ITS WEAKNESS TO OTHER
FORMER SOVIET STATES OVER WHICH IT SEEKS INFLUENCE AS
WELL AS TO ATTENTIVE REGIONAL POWERS LIKE IRAN, CHINA,
AND TURKEY, AND PLAYING INTO THE HANDS OF FORMER
WARSAW PACT STATES WHO WILL SEEK TO ACCELERATE THE
PROCESS OF NATO EXPANSION. RUSSIANS ACROSS THE
SECRET

SECRET

PAGE 03   MOSCOW 00883 03 OF 04 111658Z
POLITICAL SPECTRUM ALREADY FEEL AN ACUTE SENSE THAT
THE WEST IS TAKING ADVANTAGE OF RUSSIA'S WEAKNESS, AND
THAT IS LIKELY TO BECOME MORE RATHER THAN LESS
PRONOUNCED AS A RESULT OF THE DEEPLY EMBARRASSING
EXPERIENCE IN CHECHNYA. IN A CHAOTIC DOMESTIC
POLITICAL SETTING, ASSERTIVE POLICIES ABROAD REMAIN
ONE OF THE FEW THEMES WHICH UNITE RUSSIANS.

16. ARMED WITH A VERY WEAK HAND, AND INCREASINGLY
ESTRANGED FROM RADICAL REFORMERS AND DEPENDENT ON
YELTSIN HIMSELF, ANDREY KOZYREV WILL CONTINUE TO
SEARCH FOR TACTICAL OPPORTUNITIES TO ASSERT RUSSIA'S
GREAT POWER STATUS, WITH AN EYE TO FORM (A SEAT AT THE
TABLE OF THE "POLITICAL G-8") AS MUCH AS SUBSTANCE.
RUSSIAN DIPLOMACY IS LIKELY TO REMAIN PRIMARILY
FOCUSED ON THE NEAR ABROAD AND EUROPEAN SECURITY. ON

UNCLASSIFIED U.S. Department of State Case No. MP-2015-07420 Doc No. C06317048 Date: 05/03/2017

SECRET

THE FORMER, THE GOVERNMENT OF RUSSIA WILL AIM AT A
MINIMUM TO PREVENT "OUTSIDE POWERS" FROM GAINING
INFLUENCE AT RUSSIAN EXPENSE, MINDFUL OF GROWING
ECONOMIC CONSTRAINTS ON RUSSIAN AMBITIONS. ON THE
LATTER, DRIVEN BY A FEAR OF EXCLUSION AND A PROFOUND
SENSE OF STRATEGIC WEAKNESS, KOZYREV WILL SEEK TO BUY
TIME ON NATO EXPANSION AND STRETCH OUT THE PROCESS FOR
AS LONG AS POSSIBLE.

COPING WITH UNCERTAINTY: U.S.-RUSSIAN RELATIONS IN
THE MONTHS AHEAD

---

17. AGAINST THE BACKDROP OF MOUNTING DISARRAY IN
        SECRET

            SECRET

PAGE 04   MOSCOW 00883 03 OF 04 111658Z
RUSSIA AND CONTINUING RUSSIAN ASSERTIVENESS IN FOREIGN
POLICY, MANAGING THE U.S.-RUSSIAN RELATIONSHIP WILL BE
MORE DIFFICULT, MORE FRUSTRATING, AND LESS PREDICTABLE
THAN AT ANY TIME SINCE THE FALL OF THE SOVIET UNION.
GIVEN THE INCREASINGLY CLOSED AND UNSTABLE STYLE OF
THE CURRENT LEADERSHIP, AND THE ABSENCE OF REAL
INSTITUTIONS TO ABSORB POLITICAL PRESSURES, SUDDEN
TURNS ARE INEVITABLE, AND WE WILL NEED TO LEARN TO
XPECT THE UNEXPECTED. OUR INFLUENCE OVER EVENTS IN
RUSSIA WILL REMAIN MARGINAL, AND OUR RANGE OF POLICY
CHOICES WILL OFTEN BE UNSATISFYING. NEVERTHELESS,
SEVERAL KEY POINTS ARE WORTH BEARING IN MIND AS WE
FRAME OUR POLICY.

18. FIRST, WE NEED TO KEEP A SENSE OF PERSPECTIVE.
RUSSIA IS EMBARKED UPON A LONG-TERM, REVOLUTIONARY
PROCESS OF RE-DEFINITION, WHOSE ULTIMATE OUTCOME WILL
REMAIN UNCERTAIN FOR YEARS TO COME. RUSSIA'S
AUTHORITARIAN TRADITIONS WEIGH HEAVILY ON THIS

UNCLASSIFIED U.S. Department of State Case No. SECRET-07420 Doc No. C06317048 Date: 05/03/2017

SECRET

NNNNPTQ3217

SECRET   PTQ3217

PAGE 01   MOSCOW 00883 04 OF 04 111658Z
ACTION SS-00

INFO LOG-00 OASY-00 ADS-00   /000W
------------------9ABC78 111658Z /38
O 111652Z JAN 95
FM AMEMBASSY MOSCOW
TO SECSTATE WASHDC IMMEDIATE 9785
MOSCOW POLITICAL COLLECTIVE
INFO AMEMBASSY TALLINN
AMEMBASSY VILNIUS
AMEMBASSY RIGA
CIS COLLECTIVE

S E C R E T SECTION 04 OF 04 MOSCOW 000883

EXDIS

E.O.12356: DECL:OADR
TAGS: PREL, RS
SUBJECT: SIFTING THROUGH THE WRECKAGE: CHECHNYA AND
RUSSIA'S FUTURE

PROCESS, BUT THERE ARE ALSO UNMISTAKABLE SIGNS THAT
POLITICAL PLURALISM (THE INDEPENDENCE OF THE MEDIA IN
THE CHECHEN CRISIS, FOR EXAMPLE) AND ECONOMIC REFORM
(THE EMERGENCE OF A DYNAMIC PRIVATE SECTOR) ARE AT
LEAST BEGINNING TO TAKE ROOT. THOSE SYSTEMIC CHANGES
WERE NOT PRODUCED BY A SINGLE POLITICAL PERSONALITY,
NOR ARE THEY LIKELY TO BE EASILY ERASED.
SECRET

SECRET

UNCLASSIFIED U.S. Department of State Case No. ~~M R 2015~~-07420 Doc No. C06317048 Date: 05/03/2017

PAGE 02   MOSCOW 00883 04 OF 04 111658Z

19. SECOND, WE MUST CONTINUE TO EMPHASIZE OUR SUPPORT FOR SUSTAINABLE REFORM POLICIES, NOT PARTICULAR PERSONALITIES. WE REMAIN IN CONTACT WITH A BROAD RANGE OF RUSSIAN LEADERS, AND WE WILL CONTINUE TO CAST A WIDE NET. THAT DOES NOT MEAN THAT WE SHOULD RUSH TO DISTANCE OURSELVES FROM YELTSIN. YELTSIN AS CATALYST FOR REFORM HAS BEEN SEVERELY WOUNDED, MOST LIKELY FATALLY SO; BUT HE IS STILL THE ELECTED PRESIDENT OF RUSSIA. THE BROADER POINT IS THAT WE SHOULD AVOID THE TEMPTATION TO OVER IDENTIFY WITH, OR OVERREACT TO, ANY PARTICULAR POLITICAL FIGURE.

20. THIRD, FAR FROM ABANDONING HOPE IN POLITICAL REFORM IN RUSSIA, WE SHOULD REDOUBLE OUR EFFORTS IN THOSE AREAS IN WHICH POTENTIAL COUNTERBALANCES TO AUTHORITARIAN TRENDS ARE MOST LIKELY TO EMERGE. ACTIVE SUPPORT FOR AN INDEPENDENT MEDIA IS ONE CLEAR EXAMPLE. SO ARE STEPS – ESPECIALLY THE CREATIVE USE OF EXCHANGE VISITS -- TO BOLSTER THE LEGISLATIVE AND JUDICIAL BRANCHES OF GOVERNMENT AT ALL LEVELS, AND TO CULTIVATE REGIONAL ELITES WHO MAY INCREASINGLY HOLD THE KEY TO THE RUSSIAN POLITICAL BALANCE. A FOCUSED MILITARY-TO-MILITARY CONTACT PROGRAM IS ANOTHER VALUABLE TOOL.

21. FOURTH, WE NEED TO RECOGNIZE THAT ASSERTIVENESS AND NATIONALIST THEMES WILL CONTINUE TO FIGURE HEAVILY IN RUSSIAN FOREIGN POLICY, BUT THAT DOES NOT NECESSARILY MEAN THAT COLLISIONS WITH CORE U.S. INTERESTS ARE UNAVOIDABLE. YELTSIN'S RECENT POLICIES,
                    SECRET

                    SECRET

PAGE 03   MOSCOW 00883 04 OF 04 111658Z
STRONG NATIONALIST RHETORIC NOTWITHSTANDING, HAVE BEEN BROADLY CONSISTENT WITH OUR GOALS IN KEY AREAS LIKE UKRAINE – BY FAR OUR GREATEST CONCERN IN THE NEAR ABROAD. AND WHATEVER THE INTENTIONS OF YELTSIN'S SUCCESSORS, RUSSIAN MILITARY AND ECONOMIC CAPABILITIES WILL LIKELY BE SHARPLY CONSTRAINED FOR YEARS TO COME.

22. FINALLY, AND PERHAPS MOST IMPORTANTLY, WE NEED TO PRIORITIZE BETTER AMONG THE MANY CONCERNS ON OUR AGENDA WITH THE RUSSIANS. TWO YEARS AGO, WE COULD PRETTY MUCH HAVE IT OUR WAY ON A WHOLE RANGE OF ISSUES, SO LONG AS WE PAID SOME MINIMAL DEFERENCE TO RUSSIAN SENSIBILITIES. THAT IS NO LONGER THE CASE.

UNCLASSIFIED U.S. Department of State Case No. ~~M R 2015~~-07420 Doc No. C06317048 Date: 05/03/2017

SECRET

WE CAN'T SUCCEED IF WE DEFINE ALL OUR CONCERNS AS HIGH
PRIORITY; AND WE CAN'T INSIST ON MAKING EVERY PROBLEM
A TEST OF THE RELATIONSHIP.

23. STEADINESS AND CONSISTENCY OF PURPOSE WILL BE
HARD TO MAINTAIN AMIDST DEEPENING DOMESTIC PRESSURES
IN BOTH RUSSIA AND THE UNITED STATES. THERE ARE
DANGERS ON BOTH SIDES OF CONTRIBUTING TO SELF-
FULFILLING PROPHECIES; RUSSIANS IN PARTICULAR HAVE
TENDED SINCE NOVEMBER 8 TO SEE GREATER FRICTIONS WITH
THE U.S. AS INEVITABLE, AND HAVE PROBABLY BEEN MORE
PRONE TO TAKE RISKS IN RELATIONS WITH US AS A RESULT.
THERE ARE ROUGH WATERS AHEAD, FOR RUSSIA AND FOR U.S.
POLICY, BUT WE NEED TO TRY AS BEST WE CAN TO KEEP OUR
COURSE PLOTTED ON LONG-TERM POSSIBILITIES FOR CHANGE
IN RUSSIA WHICH REMAIN PROFOUNDLY IN OUR INTEREST.
PICKERING

        SECRET

                SECRET

PAGE 04   MOSCOW 00883 04 OF 04 111658Z

1999 Amman 1059, February 7, 1999,
"King Hussein's Legacy and Jordan's Future"

The death of King Hussein—the Middle East's longest-serving ruler—was a traumatic event for Jordan and a pivotal moment for the country's relationship with the United States. This cable outlined the challenges facing King Abdullah II as he took the throne, and it argued for doing everything we could to support a critical partner during a time of tumultuous transition.

DECLASSIFIED

~~CONFIDENTIAL~~ PTO8362

RELEASE IN PART
1.4(D)

PAGE 01   AMMAN 01059 01 OF 02 071239Z
ACTION NODS-00

INFO LOG-00 CCOE-00 SAS-00   /000W
------------------A006D8 071239Z /38
O 071242Z FEB 99
FM AMEMBASSY AMMAN
TO SECSTATE WASHDC IMMEDIATE 1223

~~CONFIDENTIAL~~ SECTION 01 OF 02 AMMAN 001059

NODIS   DECAPTIONED
FOR THE PRESIDENT AND SECRETARY ALBRIGHT FROM AMBASSADOR

E.O. 12958: DECL: 2/7/19
TAGS: PREL, JO
SUBJECT: KING HUSSEIN'S LEGACY AND JORDAN'S FUTURE

CLASSIFIED BY AMBASSADOR WILLIAM J. BURNS FOR REASON 1.5 (B) AND (D)

1. (C) MR. PRESIDENT: JOHN FOSTER DULLES REPORTEDLY SAID SOME FORTY-FIVE YEARS AGO THAT KING HUSSEIN WAS "AN IMPRESSIVE YOUNG FELLOW. IT'S A SHAME NEITHER HE NOR HIS COUNTRY WILL LAST VERY LONG." HUSSEIN PROVED FAR MORE RESOURCEFUL THAN DULLES AND MANY OTHERS COULD IMAGINE. HE TOOK AN IMPOVERISHED, BARELY LITERATE SOCIETY AND TURNED IT INTO A RELATIVELY STABLE, MODERN STATE. IN A REGION HARDLY NOTED FOR SUCH TRAITS, HUSSEIN BUILT A COUNTRY WITH A REPUTATION FOR TOLERANCE AND OPENNESS, AND A COMMITMENT TO LIVING IN PEACE WITH ITS NEIGHBORS. WHILE HE MADE HIS SHARE OF MISTAKES ALONG THE WAY, HE TOUCHED US ALL DEEPLY WITH HIS COURAGE AND
~~CONFIDENTIAL~~

PAGE 02   AMMAN 01059 01 OF 02 071239Z
DECENCY -- NEVER MORE SO THAN IN HIS LAST HEROIC BATTLE WITH THE CANCER THAT KILLED HIM.

THE CHALLENGES AHEAD

2. (C) KING HUSSEIN LEAVES BEHIND A JORDAN INFINITELY BETTER OFF THAN WHAT HE INHERITED NEARLY HALF A CENTURY AGO, BUT STILL BURDENED WITH ENORMOUS CHALLENGES. CHIEF AMONG THEM IS AN ECONOMY IN DEEP TROUBLE. IF YOU WERE TO ASK MOST JORDANIANS IF THEY WERE BETTER OFF NOW THAN WHEN YOU LAST VISITED JORDAN FOUR YEARS AGO, THE ANSWER WOULD BE A RESOUNDING "NO." UNEMPLOYMENT IS TWENTY-FIVE PERCENT AND RISING; STANDARDS OF LIVING ARE FALLING; AND THE GAP BETWEEN THE CONSPICUOUSLY-CONSUMING ELITE OF WEST AMMAN AND THE REST OF THE COUNTRY IS GROWING. ECONOMIC WEAKNESS EXPOSES JORDAN TO REGIONAL PREDATORS, LIKE SYRIA AND IRAQ, AND MAKES IT MUCH HARDER TO DEAL WITH STRUCTURAL CHALLENGES LIKE BROADENING POLITICAL PARTICIPATION AND INTEGRATING JORDANIANS OF PALESTINIAN ORIGIN INTO

Declassification Authority: Geoffrey W. Chapman, OCA, Senior Reviewer, A/GIS/IPS

A POLITICAL SYSTEM FROM WHICH THEY HAVE BEEN LARGELY EXCLUDED FOR DECADES.

3. (C) HOW JORDAN RESPONDS TO ALL THOSE CHALLENGES MATTERS TO US FOR SOME VERY PRACTICAL, UNSENTIMENTAL REASONS. WITHOUT A STABLE PARTNER ON THE EAST BANK OF THE JORDAN RIVER, THE PALESTINIAN-ISRAELI PEACE PROCESS WOULD BECOME MUCH MORE PROBLEMATIC. WITHOUT JORDAN'S SUPPORT, OUR STRATEGY IN IRAQ WOULD BECOME HARD TO SUSTAIN. IF WE DIDN'T HAVE A FRIENDLY STATE AT THE POLITICAL AND GEOGRAPHICAL CENTER OF THE REGION, WE'D HAVE TO TRY TO INVENT ONE. FOR ALL THOSE REASONS, WE HAVE A POWERFUL STAKE IN HELPING THE JORDANIANS NAVIGATE THROUGH WHAT IS BOUND TO BE THE MOST TRAUMATIC
CONFIDENTIAL

PAGE 03   AMMAN 01059 01 OF 02 071239Z
PERIOD IN THEIR HISTORY, AS THEY COPE WITH THE LOSS OF THE ONLY LEADER MOST OF THEM HAVE EVER KNOWN.

A TIME OF TESTING FOR ABDULLAH

4. (C) IT'S HARD TO IMAGINE A MUCH MORE INTIMIDATING SET OF CIRCUMSTANCES FOR A NEW HEAD OF STATE THAN THOSE FACING KING ABDULLAH. IN THE LAST TWO WEEKS, HE HAS GONE FROM SPECIAL FORCES COMMANDER TO CROWN PRINCE TO REGENT TO KING, SUCCEEDING ONE OF THE LAST TRULY LEGENDARY FIGURES ON THE WORLD STAGE. BUT ABDULLAH HASN'T BUCKLED UNDER THE PRESSURE YET, AND I DON'T THINK HE WILL. HE STILL HAS A LOT TO LEARN ABOUT NON-MILITARY ISSUES; HOWEVER, HE HAS THE SAME RESTLESS ENERGY AND TOUCH WITH PEOPLE THAT HUSSEIN ALWAYS HAD, AND HIS LOYALTY TO HIS FATHER AND TO JORDAN IS INTENSE. (AT ONE POINT IN THE 1980'S, WHEN HUSSEIN WAS FACING ONE OF HIS PERIODIC ROUNDS OF ASSASSINATION THREATS, ABDULLAH SLEPT OUTSIDE HIS FATHER'S BEDROOM DOOR WITH A PISTOL FOR NIGHT AFTER NIGHT.)

5. (C)

1.4(

HASSAN IS NOT HAVING AN EASY TIME ADJUSTING TO BEING DUMPED AFTER THIRTY-FOUR YEARS AS CROWN PRINCE, BUT HE HAS BEHAVED WITH DIGNITY AND IS READY TO TRY TO PLAY A CONSTRUCTIVE ROLE. ABDULLAH'S WIFE, RANIA, IS A PARTICULAR SOURCE OF STRENGTH AND COMMON SENSE. HER PALESTINIAN ORIGIN MAKES HER A NATURAL POLITICAL ASSET; EVEN MORE IMPORTANT HAS BEEN HER LEVELLING INFLUENCE ON ABDULLAH AND THE REST OF THE ROYAL FAMILY OVER THE PAST TWO DRAMATIC WEEKS. SHE HAS ALREADY
CONFIDENTIAL

PAGE 04   AMMAN 01059 01 OF 02 071239Z
ENCOURAGED ABDULLAH TO REACH OUT AND BROADEN HIS CIRCLE OF ADVISERS, WHICH FITS BOTH HIS NATURAL INCLUSIVE BENT AND HIS NEED TO SHOW THAT HE IS MORE THAN JUST A MILITARY MAN.

OUR ROLE

6. (C) AS ABDULLAH COPES WITH A DIFFICULT TRANSITION, WE WILL NEED
TO TRY TO SUPPLY A STEADINESS AND SENSE OF PERSPECTIVE THAT THE
JORDANIANS MAY BE AT LEAST TEMPORARILY INCAPABLE OF PROVIDING
THEMSELVES. IT IS WORTH KEEPING IN MIND SEVERAL GENERAL POINTS:

-- FIRST, OUR SUPPORT WILL BE AT LEAST AS IMPORTANT SIX MONTHS OR
A YEAR DOWN THE ROAD AS IT IS NOW. JORDANIANS ARE LIKELY TO RALLY
AROUND ABDULLAH IN THE SHORT RUN, AND OUR EFFORTS AND THOSE OF
OTHERS TO STABILIZE THE DINAR AND SHORE UP JORDAN HAVE BEEN VERY
TIMELY. BUT THE REAL CHALLENGE TO ABDULLAH COULD COME SOME MONTHS

CONFIDENTIAL

CONFIDENTIAL   PTQ1033

PAGE 01   AMMAN 01059 02 OF 02 071239Z
ACTION NODS-00

INFO LOG-00 CCOE-00 SAS-00   /000W
-----------------A006DD 071239Z /38
O 071242Z FEB 99
FM AMEMBASSY AMMAN
TO SECSTATE WASHDC IMMEDIATE 1224

C O N F I D E N T I A L SECTION 02 OF 02 AMMAN 001059

NODIS
FOR THE PRESIDENT AND SECRETARY ALBRIGHT FROM AMBASSADOR

E.O. 12958: DECL: 2/7/19
TAGS: PREL, JO
SUBJECT: KING HUSSEIN'S LEGACY AND JORDAN'S FUTURE

AHEAD, IF THE ECONOMY REMAINS STUCK IN THE MUD AND THE REGIONAL
PICTURE FAILS TO IMPROVE. OUR COMBINED ECONOMIC AND MILITARY
ASSISTANCE PROGRAM, WHICH INCLUDING SUPPLEMENTAL REQUESTS SHOULD
TOTAL $1 BILLION OVER THE NEXT THREE YEARS, PROVIDES AN EXCELLENT
BASIS FOR PROVIDING STRONG SUPPORT.

-- SECOND, WE WILL NEED TO BE CAREFUL NOT TO OVERLOAD THE CIRCUITS
WITH ABDULLAH, ESPECIALLY AT FIRST. HE IS GENUINELY COMMITTED TO
THE MAIN POLICY LINES LAID DOWN BY HIS FATHER, BUT WILL NEED A
LITTLE TIME TO FIND HIS FOOTING. WE SHOULD ALSO AVOID FEEDING ANY
PERCEPTION THAT WE ARE TRYING TO TAKE ADVANTAGE OF THE TRANSITION
TO BEND JORDANIAN POLICY IN OUR DIRECTION.

1.4(D

-- THIRD, THE TRANSITION IN JORDAN IS JUST THE FIRST IN A SERIES
OF SUCCESSIONS LIKELY TO OCCUR IN A REGION DOMINATED FOR DECADES BY

THE SAME LEADERS. CIRCUMSTANCES IN EACH SOCIETY WILL DIFFER --
WHETHER IT'S SYRIA OR SAUDI ARABIA OR THE PALESTINIAN AUTHORITY OR
ANY OF THE DOZEN MIDDLE EASTERN STATES FACING A LONG-AWAITED
TRANSITION. WHILE NO ONE SHOULD EXAGGERATE JORDAN'S ROLE AS A
TREND-SETTER, A SUCCESSFUL TRANSITION IN JORDAN WOULD AT LEAST
OFFER A POSITIVE EXAMPLE AND SUSTAIN THE KIND OF FRIENDLY, MODERATE
REGIME THAT BEST SERVES OUR INTERESTS. MOREOVER, GIVEN ABDULLAH'S
TIES TO THE YOUNGER GENERATION OF GULF LEADERS, HELPING HIM FIND
HIS FOOTING IN JORDAN MAY HELP INDIRECTLY TO CEMENT RELATIONS AMONG
STATES WHICH WILL BE IMPORTANT TO US FOR YEARS TO COME.

A FINAL NOTE
----

7. (C) IT'S HARD TO LOOK AHEAD WITHOUT REFLECTING ON THE
EXTRAORDINARY LIFE OF KING HUSSEIN. EVEN IN HIS FINAL DAYS, HE
SHOWED THE SAME STUBBORN COURAGE THAT HE HAD ALWAYS DISPLAYED. HIS
DOCTORS EXPECTED HIM TO DIE VERY SHORTLY AFTER HE RETURNED TO
JORDAN, UNCONSCIOUS AND WITH VITAL ORGANS SHUTTING DOWN, BUT HE
HUNG ON FOR SEVERAL MORE DAYS. IT WAS ALMOST AS IF, CONSCIOUS OR
UNCONSCIOUS, THE KING WAS DETERMINED TO SHOW THAT ONLY HE -- NOT
CNN OR ANXIOUS FOREIGN AUDIENCES OR MEDICAL EXPERTS OR ANYONE ELSE
-- WOULD DECIDE WHEN HE WOULD MAKE HIS EXIT. IN HIS OWN PROUD WAY,
HE HELD CENTER STAGE RIGHT UNTIL THE END.
            CONFIDENTIAL

        PAGE 03   AMMAN 01059 02 OF 02 071239Z

8. (C) HUSSEIN LIVED A LIFE THAT ALWAYS RAN AGAINST THE ODDS. JOHN
FOSTER DULLES WAS JUST THE FIRST IN A LONG LINE OF PEOPLE TO
UNDERESTIMATE HIM, AND TO UNDERESTIMATE JORDAN. IT'S WORTH
REMEMBERING THAT AS JORDANIANS, AND ALL OF US, CONTEMPLATE A FUTURE
WITHOUT HUSSEIN. HIS SUCCESSOR AND THE JORDANIAN PEOPLE FACE
DAUNTING CHALLENGES, AND STEEP ODDS, BUT THEY HAVE THE CAPACITY TO
COPE WITH THEM. IT IS VERY MUCH IN OUR INTEREST, AND IT IS A VERY
FITTING TRIBUTE TO HUSSEIN, TO DO ALL WE CAN TO HELP THEM. BURNS

        CONFIDENTIAL

<< END OF DOCUMENT >>

2000 Amman 6760, December 5, 2000,
"Peace Process: Relaunching American Diplomacy"

From my perspective as the American ambassador in Amman, the collapse of the Camp David peace talks and the outbreak of the second Palestinian Intifada were ominous signs for Jordan and the broader Middle East. In a highly unusual move, I joined our ambassador to Egypt, Dan Kurtzer, in authoring a joint cable that shared our thoughts from the region on U.S. policy and made the case for the Clinton administration to articulate its own parameters for a peace deal.

C06323473lED U.S. Department of State Case No. MP-2015-07420 Doc No. C06323473 Date: 06/27/2017

DECLASSIFIED

RELEASE IN PART
1.4(B),1.4(D)

~~SECRET~~   PTQ1973

PAGE 01   AMMAN 06760 01 OF 03 051617Z
ACTION NODS-00

INFO LOG-00 CCOE-00 SAS-00   /000W
------------------A7C5A0 051617Z /38
O 051609Z DEC 00
FM AMEMBASSY AMMAN
TO SECSTATE WASHDC IMMEDIATE 7539
INFO AMEMBASSY CAIRO IMMEDIATE
AMEMBASSY TEL AVIV IMMEDIATE
AMCONSUL JERUSALEM IMMEDIATE
AMEMBASSY DAMASCUS IMMEDIATE
AMEMBASSY BEIRUT IMMEDIATE
AMEMBASSY RIYADH IMMEDIATE
WHITEHOUSE WASHDC IMMEDIATE

~~SECRET~~ SECTION 01 OF 03 AMMAN 006760

NODIS SIERRA   DECAPTIONED

DEPARTMENT FOR THE SECRETARY, A/S WALKER AND
SMEC/ROSS; WHITE HOUSE FOR NSA BERGER, RIEDEL AND
MALLEY

FROM AMBASSADOR KURTZER AND AMBASSADOR BURNS

E.O. 12958: DECL: 12/5/20
TAGS: PREL, EG, JO, XF
SUBJECT: PEACE PROCESS: RELAUNCHING AMERICAN
DIPLOMACY
~~SECRET~~

PAGE 02   AMMAN 06760 01 OF 03 051617Z

REFS: (A) CAIRO 7716 (B) CAIRO 7946

CLASSIFIED BY AMBASSADOR DAN KURTZER AND AMBASSADOR
BILL BURNS FOR REASON 1.5 (B,D)

1. (S) AS SEEN FROM CAIRO AND AMMAN, U.S. POLICY IN
THE PEACE PROCESS AND OUR OVERALL POSTURE IN THE
REGION ARE STILL HEADING IN EXACTLY THE WRONG
DIRECTION. WITH OUR INTERESTS UNDER INCREASING
SCRUTINY AND ATTACK, WE ARE ACTING PASSIVELY,
REACTIVELY AND DEFENSIVELY. THERE IS NO GUARANTEE
THAT A BOLDER, MORE ACTIVIST AMERICAN APPROACH WILL
STOP THE HEMORRHAGING -- BUT IT SEEMS CLEAR TO US THAT
THINGS COULD GET A LOT WORSE UNLESS WE REGAIN THE
INITIATIVE.

2. (S) OUR STAKE IN REVERSING THE DRIFT TOWARD MORE
VIOLENCE, REBUILDING AMERICAN CREDIBILITY, REFOCUSING
ATTENTION ON THE POSSIBILITIES OF A POLITICAL PROCESS,

Declassification Authority: Geoffrey W. Chapman, OCA, Senior Reviewer,
A/GIS/IPS

UNCLASSIFIED U.S. Department of State Case No. MP-2015-07420 Doc No. C06323473 Date: 06/27/2017

AND GETTING AS FAR AS WE CAN OVER THE NEXT SEVEN WEEKS
TOWARD A FRAMEWORK AGREEMENT IS SELF-EVIDENT. WHAT IS
LESS OBVIOUS IS HOW TO GET FROM HERE TO THERE. ONE
OPTION IS TO FOLLOW BARAK'S LEAD. THAT MAY SERVE WHAT
HE SEES TO BE HIS TACTICAL INTERESTS AT THIS POINT,
BUT IT'S HARD TO SEE HOW IT SERVES OURS.

1.4(

AMMAN 06760 01 OF 03 051617Z
A SECOND OPTION IS TO SEE IF WE CAN EXTRACT
FROM THE PALESTINIANS A CLEARER SENSE OF HOW FAR
THEY'RE PREPARED TO GO RIGHT NOW, AND THEN USE THAT TO
CRAFT AN APPROACH TO BARAK. BUT IT'S UNLIKELY THAT
ARAFAT WILL LEVEL WITH US AT THIS POINT; AND WHILE
RECENT EGYPTIAN AND JORDANIAN EFFORTS WITH THE
PALESTINIANS HAVE BEEN HELPFUL, IT'S NOT AT ALL CLEAR
THAT THEY WILL PRODUCE A WORKABLE STARTING POINT.

3. (S) THAT LEAVES IT TO US TO LAY OUT THE HARD TRUTHS
-- FOR ALL PARTIES -- THAT MUST UNDERPIN ANY ENDURING
POLITICAL SOLUTION. AS WE HAVE TRIED TO EMPHASIZE IN
REFTELS, THAT WILL REQUIRE THE POLITICAL WILL TO STAND
UP FOR WHAT WE HAVE FOUGHT SO HARD FOR OVER THE PAST
EIGHT YEARS, AND A READINESS TO DECLARE THE
INDEPENDENCE OF OUR POLICY.

4. (S) THE CRITICAL ELEMENTS OF AN EFFECTIVE AMERICAN
APPROACH INCLUDE THE FOLLOWING:

-- ARTICULATE A "CLINTON VISION" FOR THE PEACE
PROCESS: WE HAVE A UNIQUE BUT WASTING OPPORTUNITY TO
TAKE ADVANTAGE OF A REMARKABLE ASSET: THE PERSONAL
REPUTATION AND DEMONSTRATED COMMITMENT OF PRESIDENT
CLINTON. HE HAS BUILT UP SUBSTANTIAL PERSONAL CREDIT
WITH THE PARTIES OVER THE YEARS, AND NOW IS THE TIME
TO USE IT. HE CAN SKETCH A VISION OF WHAT HE BELIEVES
A COMPREHENSIVE PEACE WILL REQUIRE OF ALL PARTIES --
PALESTINIANS, ISRAELIS, AND ARAB STATES ALIKE. HE
WILL HAVE TO BE WILLING TO SAY THINGS TO EACH PARTY
THAT THEY WILL NOT WANT TO HEAR, BUT THAT IS THE
                    SECRET

PAGE 04   AMMAN 06760 01 OF 03 051617Z
DEFINITION OF A BALANCED AND CREDIBLE APPROACH (OUR
IDEAS FOR SUCH A U.S. PACKAGE ARE CONTAINED IN REF A).

1.4(

-- MAKE PUBLIC THE RESULTS OF CAMP DAVID II: THE
EGYPTIANS, JORDANIANS, AND MANY OTHERS IN THE REGION

BELIEVE THAT PRESIDENT CLINTON MADE ENORMOUS PROGRESS
WHEN HE BROUGHT THE PARTIES TOGETHER AT CAMP DAVID.
THEY BELIEVE THESE RESULTS SHOULD BE MEMORIALIZED AND
PURSUED VIGOROUSLY IN SUBSEQUENT NEGOTIATIONS. PART
OF LAYING OUT OUR VISION SHOULD BE TO MAKE SURE THAT
WE DO NOT LOSE WHAT WE HAD IN HAND IN CAMP DAVID.
THIS CAN BE DONE IN AN OP ED PIECE OR ARTICLE IN A
JOURNAL.

-- EMPOWER THE FACT-FINDING COMMISSION: WE OUGHT TO

SECRET

SECRET   PTQ1976

PAGE 01   AMMAN 06760 02 OF 03 051617Z
ACTION NODS-00

INFO LOG-00 CCOE-00 SAS-00   /000W
------------------A7C5B0 051617Z /38
O 051609Z DEC 00
FM AMEMBASSY AMMAN
TO SECSTATE WASHDC IMMEDIATE 7540
INFO AMEMBASSY CAIRO IMMEDIATE
AMEMBASSY TEL AVIV IMMEDIATE
AMCONSUL JERUSALEM IMMEDIATE
AMEMBASSY DAMASCUS IMMEDIATE
AMEMBASSY BEIRUT IMMEDIATE
AMEMBASSY RIYADH IMMEDIATE
WHITEHOUSE WASHDC IMMEDIATE

S E C R E T SECTION 02 OF 03 AMMAN 006760

NODIS SIERRA

DEPARTMENT FOR THE SECRETARY, A/S WALKER AND
SMEC/ROSS; WHITE HOUSE FOR NSA BERGER, RIEDEL AND
MALLEY

FROM AMBASSADOR KURTZER AND AMBASSADOR BURNS

E.O. 12958: DECL: 12/5/20
TAGS: PREL, EG, JO, XF
SUBJECT: PEACE PROCESS: RELAUNCHING AMERICAN
DIPLOMACY
            SECRET

PAGE 02   AMMAN 06760 02 OF 03 051617Z

AVOID GETTING AMERICAN FINGERPRINTS ALL OVER THE FACT-
FINDING COMMISSION, AND AVOID GETTING CAUGHT IN THE
TRAP OF PRE-NEGOTIATING ALL OF ITS PROCEDURES WITH THE
ISRAELIS AND PALESTINIANS. WE HAVE NO ILLUSIONS ABOUT
THE SUBSTANTIVE VALUE OF THIS EXERCISE, BUT IF THE
COMMISSION'S FIRST TRIP IS PERFUNCTORY AND MAKES IT
LOOK AS IF WE'RE SIMPLY CHECKING A BOX, IT WILL HURT

OUR INTERESTS CONSIDERABLY THROUGHOUT THE REGION.

-- SHAPE AN "INTERNATIONAL OBSERVER PRESENCE" TO OUR
LIKING: WE DON'T UNDERSTAND WHY WE AND ISRAEL HAVE
TAKEN SUCH A DIM VIEW OF PROPOSALS FOR AN
INTERNATIONAL PRESENCE IN THE TERRITORIES. WHILE SOME
PALESTINIAN PROPOSALS MAKE LITTLE SENSE, THE GENERAL
IDEA OF INTERPOSING INTERNATIONAL OBSERVERS SEEMS WELL
WORTH EXAMINING. IF SHAPED CAREFULLY, IT COULD EVEN
BECOME A CATALYST FOR SUSTAINED IMPLEMENTATION OF THE
SHARM EL-SHEIKH UNDERSTANDINGS, IN WHICH BOTH SIDES
HAVE A STAKE. IF WE'RE NOT GOING TO BE ABLE TO MAKE
THIS ISSUE GO AWAY, WHY FIGHT THE PROBLEM ? WHY NOT
TRY TO TAKE THE LEAD IN MOLDING SUCH AN INTERNATIONAL
PRESENCE?

-- KEEP THE SUPPLEMENTAL ASSISTANCE PACKAGE INTACT OR

1.4(D

SECRET

PAGE 03   AMMAN 06760 02 OF 03 051617Z

1.4(D)

-- SEEK URGENT CONGRESSIONAL APPROVAL OF THE JORDAN
FTA, IF POSSIBLE ALONGSIDE THE SUPPLEMENTAL PACKAGE:
THIS WOULD BE A BIG BOOST FOR ABDULLAH, AT A TIME WHEN
LITTLE ELSE IS GOING RIGHT FOR JORDAN. WE SHOULD ALSO
RESPOND TO MUBARAKQS SPECIFIC REQUEST TO THE PRESIDENT
TO START TALKS NOW WITH EGYPT ON A FTA.

-- TALK PEACE NOT WAR: HAVING DEVOTED MORE THAN TWO
DECADES TO ACTIVE PEACEMAKING IN THIS REGION, WE MUST
NOT YIELD TO CRITICS OR TO THOSE WHO EXULT IN THE
PROBLEMS WHICH THE OSLO PROCESS IS CONFRONTING. IT IS
ENTIRELY SENSIBLE TO WARN REGIONAL PARTIES PRIVATELY
AGAINST THE DANGERS OF ESCALATION AND REGIONAL
CONFLICT, BUT WE HAVE TO BE CAREFUL NOT TO RAISE FEARS
OF WAR IN OUR PUBLIC STATEMENTS. ON THE CONTRARY, WE
OUGHT TO BE ON A PUBLIC RELATIONS BLITZ, BOTH AT HOME
AND ABROAD, ON WHY IT IS ESSENTIAL TO KEEP GOING IN
THE SEARCH FOR COMPREHENSIVE PEACE, AND HOW MUCH
GROUND WAS COVERED IN THE CAMP DAVID SUMMIT LAST
SUMMER.

C06323473 ED U.S. Department of State Case No. MP-2015-07420 Doc No. C06323473 Date: 06/27/2017

SECRET

PAGE 04   AMMAN 06760 02 OF 03 051617Z
-- ENGAGE, ENGAGE, ENGAGE: WE DO NOT SPEND ENOUGH
TIME JUST TALKING TO OUR FRIENDS IN THE REGION.
ESPECIALLY NOW, WHEN OUR INTERESTS ARE INCREASINGLY
THREATENED IN THIS REGION, WE NEED TO HAVE SENIOR
DIPLOMATS OUT HERE AS MUCH AS POSSIBLE. (EARLY
RESCHEDULING OF UNDERSECRETARY PICKERING'S TRIP TO
SEVERAL ARAB CAPITALS WOULD BE VERY USEFUL.) OUR
WILLINGNESS TO ENGAGE AND LISTEN IN WHAT WILL
ADMITTEDLY BE A VERY TOUGH DIALOGUE WILL BE AN
IMPORTANT ELEMENT IN RECONSTRUCTING OUR STRATEGIC
RELATIONSHIPS THROUGHOUT THIS REGION.

5. (S) AS WE HAVE EMPHASIZED BEFORE, WE KNOW THERE ARE
REAL RISKS IN THE APPROACH WE HAVE OUTLINED, AND NO
GUARANTEES THAT IT WILL PRODUCE ANY FORMAL AGREEMENTS
(LET ALONE A FAPS) WITHIN THE NEXT SEVEN WEEKS. BUT
WE ARE ALSO CONVINCED THAT THE COSTS AND RISKS OF
INACTION ARE MUCH GREATER. PRESIDENT CLINTON HAS MADE

SECRET

SECRET   PTQ1978

PAGE 01   AMMAN 06760 03 OF 03 051617Z
ACTION NODS-00

INFO LOG-00 CCOE-00 SAS-00   /000W
              --------------------A7C5B5 051617Z /38
O 051609Z DEC 00
FM AMEMBASSY AMMAN
TO SECSTATE WASHDC IMMEDIATE 7541
INFO AMEMBASSY CAIRO IMMEDIATE
AMEMBASSY TEL AVIV IMMEDIATE
AMCONSUL JERUSALEM IMMEDIATE
AMEMBASSY DAMASCUS IMMEDIATE
AMEMBASSY BEIRUT IMMEDIATE
AMEMBASSY RIYADH IMMEDIATE
WHITEHOUSE WASHDC IMMEDIATE

S E C R E T SECTION 03 OF 03 AMMAN 006760

NODIS SIERRA

DEPARTMENT FOR THE SECRETARY, A/S WALKER AND
SMEC/ROSS; WHITE HOUSE FOR NSA BERGER, RIEDEL AND
MALLEY

FROM AMBASSADOR KURTZER AND AMBASSADOR BURNS

E.O. 12958: DECL: 12/5/20
TAGS: PREL, EG, JO, XF
SUBJECT: PEACE PROCESS: RELAUNCHING AMERICAN

UNCLASSIFIED U.S. Department of State Case No. MP-2015-07420 Doc No. C06323473 Date: 06/27/2017

C06323473¹ED U.S. Department of State Case No. MP-2015-07420 Doc No. C06323473 Date: 06/27/2017

DIPLOMACY
      SECRET

PAGE 02   AMMAN 06760 03 OF 03 051617Z

ENORMOUS CONTRIBUTIONS TO PEACE IN THIS TROUBLED
REGION OVER THE PAST EIGHT YEARS. WE SHOULDN'T LET
THEM WASTE AWAY WITHOUT A FIGHT.

BURNS

      SECRET

<< END OF DOCUMENT >>

Email to Secretary of State Condoleezza Rice,
February 8, 2008, "Russia Strategy"

As the George W. Bush administration reached the end of its second term, looming policy "trainwrecks" threatened to push U.S.-Russia relations to a new post–Cold War nadir. In this email to Secretary Rice from Moscow, I made plain the risks of a collision and tried to offer my best advice on how to avoid a collapse in bilateral ties.

C06394587ED U.S. Department of State Case No. MP-2015-07420 Doc No. C06394587 Date: 09/15/2017

REVIEW AUTHORITY: Paul Hilburn, Senior Reviewer   RELEASE IN FULL

From: Burns, William J (AMB-Moscow) (Moscow)
Sent: Friday, February 08, 2008 9:22 AM
To: Beecroft, Robert S
Cc: S_SpecialAssistants; Negroponte, John D; Burns, Nicholas R; Fried, Daniel
Subject: Russia Strategy

SECRET

February 8, 2008

Madam Secretary,

I know you are wrestling with a number of very difficult issues involving my ever-congenial hosts, ranging from Kosovo to Bucharest to the next 2x2 meeting. Following are some personal thoughts on what's at stake with the Russians, what's driving them, and what may be possible over the next few months. I still think it's possible to make a big, strategic play with Putin in the Kremlin; it will get harder after he leaves in May, because Medvedev will be too weak initially to make bold choices, and Putin won't want to be seen to be making them for him. By that point, moreover, the Russian inclination will be simply to wait for the next Administration.

1. The next couple months will be among the most consequential in recent U.S.-Russian relations. We face three potential trainwrecks: Kosovo, MAP for Ukraine/Georgia, and missile defense. We've got a high-priority problem with Iran that (post-NIE) will be extremely hard to address without the Russians. We've got a chance to do something enduring with the Russians on nuclear cooperation, with a 123 agreement almost signed and more to be done on GNEP and counter-proliferation. And we've got an opportunity to get off on a better foot with a reconfigured Russian leadership after

1

Medvedev's likely election, and to help get the Russians across the finish line into WTO this year, which is among the most practical things we can do to promote the long-term prospects for political and economic modernization in this proud, prickly, complicated society.

2. My view is that we can only manage one of those three trainwrecks without doing real damage to a relationship we don't have the luxury of ignoring. From my admittedly parochial perspective here, it's hard to see how we could get the key Europeans to support us on all three at the same time. I'd opt for plowing ahead resolutely on Kosovo; deferring MAP for Ukraine or Georgia until a stronger foundation is laid; and going to Putin directly while he's still in the Presidency to try and cut a deal on missile defense, as part of a broader security framework.

3. I fully understand how difficult a decision to hold off on MAP will be. But it's equally hard to overstate the strategic consequences of a premature MAP offer, especially to Ukraine. Ukrainian entry into NATO is the brightest of all redlines for the Russian elite (not just Putin). In my more than two and a half years of conversations with key Russian players, from knuckle-draggers in the dark recesses of the Kremlin to Putin's sharpest liberal critics, I have yet to find anyone who views Ukraine in NATO as anything other than a direct challenge to Russian interests. At this stage, a MAP offer would be seen not as a technical step along a long road toward membership, but as throwing down the strategic gauntlet. Today's Russia will respond. Russian-Ukrainian relations will go into a deep freeze, with Moscow likely to contemplate economic measures ranging from an immediate increase in gas prices to world market levels, to a clampdown on Ukrainian workers coming to Russia. It will create fertile soil for Russian meddling in Crimea and eastern Ukraine. There'd be much chest-thumping about repositioning military assets closer to the Ukrainian border, and threats of nuclear retargeting. The NATO-Russia Council would go on life support, or expire altogether. On Georgia, the combination of Kosovo independence and a MAP offer would likely lead to recognition of Abkhazia, however counterproductive that might be to Russia's own long-term interests in the Caucasus. The prospects of subsequent Russian-Georgian armed conflict would be high.

4. If, in the end, MAP offers are made to Ukraine and Georgia, you can probably stop reading here. I can conceive of no grand package that would allow the Russians to swallow this pill quietly. If we opt to defer MAP, while making clear that it is coming eventually, we have a chance to explore a strategically ambitious package with Russia, which could help anchor our relationship and some of our most significant global interests for some time to come. I do not mean to suggest that Putin and company would view a deferral of MAP as a great strategic concession and leap enthusiastically to greater moderation on other questions; they are not an especially sentimental bunch. But the way would at least be clear to probe for accommodations that would suit our most vital needs, and to find a way to agree to disagree on Kosovo without huge collateral damage.

5. I'd see two parts to a bold package of understandings to pursue with Putin. The first would be a security framework, and the second would be a renewed commitment to economic cooperation. The first would be a lasting contribution from both Presidents to a safer world and a reflection of the unique capabilities – and unique responsibilities – that the United States and Russia continue to have in the nuclear field. The second would be, over the medium and longer-term, the most effective means of advancing the President's freedom agenda, and a way to help lock Russia into global economic organizations and rule of law. That won't change the reality that Russia is a deeply authoritarian and overcentralized state today, whose dismal record on human rights and political freedoms deserves our criticism. But it will reinforce over time the instincts for private property and market-driven opportunity, and the vastly increased connections that young Russians have to the rest of the world through foreign travel and the Internet, that are slowly but unmistakably transforming this society.

6. A security framework might include several ingredients. Completion of a 123 agreement, progress on GNEP, and a common diplomatic approach on DPRK and Iran (following a third UNSCR) would be the starting point. A second component would revolve upon how we manage our own remaining nuclear arsenals. That means meeting Bratislava commitments on Nunn-Lugar upgrades by the end of 2008, and a Russian commitment to sustain them. It also means seeking an agreement in principle on post-START, involving a legally-binding text whose level of detail and shape would fall somewhere between the Moscow Treaty and START-I. (We might also consider support for Putin's global INF treaty, however slim the chances for success.) A third feature could be a reinvigoration of counterterrorism cooperation, including the new Global Initiative against Nuclear Terrorism, and greater Russian contributions in Afghanistan. And fourth, and most challenging, would be missile defense.

7. I don't know if Putin can be persuaded at this stage to do a deal on regional missile defense cooperation that would allow us to move ahead on Polish and Czech deployments. But it's still worth a try, if only as a way to show the Allies that we've exhausted every avenue. To make a dent in Putin's thinking, and overcome the objections that he's likely to hear from a deeply skeptical Russian bureaucracy, you and Secretary Gates would probably have to convey to Putin directly a revised U.S. paper, indicating a willingness to make a maximum effort to reach an understanding with the Russians before formalizing agreements with the Poles and Czechs (it wouldn't work to announce a deal during the Tusk visit to

Washington on March 10 and then try to reach an accommodation with Putin). We'd also have to go further in indicating a readiness to link operationalization of sites to concrete evidence of long-range missile capability (via flight testing), and in finding a formula for continuous mutual presence at each other's sites.

8. An economic basket would include a hard push on WTO, built around Kudrin's visit to Washington in April. It would also feature the launching of a new government to government economic dialogue in the spring, led by Reuben Jeffery and his Russian counterpart, and possible visits to Russia by Secretary Paulson and Secretary Gutierrez (with a renewed business to business dialogue emerging from the latter). The possible appointment of a new, high-level energy envoy for Eurasia could be another opportunity (especially if it was someone like Don Evans, whom the Russians know and trust).

9. Tactically, it would be essential to roll all this out as a really significant strategic play, conveyed at least in broad terms from the President to Putin. A piecemeal approach won't succeed. A first step might be a call to Putin from the President in the second half of February, maybe after the Africa trip but well before the March 2 Russian Presidential election. Then there could be a 2x2 meeting in Moscow, shortly after the election, to allow a detailed, direct engagement with Putin, Medvedev and others. To focus Putin's interest, the President might keep open the possibility of a brief stop in Moscow after Bucharest, if/if sufficient progress had been made. While the odds of success would be long, it's at least conceivable that the two Presidents could ultimately point to a security framework, including a missile defense understanding; a coordinated approach on Iran, following passage of a third UNSCR and the Majles elections; agreement to disagree on Kosovo; and significant movement on WTO. All that would protect our core interests, play to Putin's sense of legacy, and get relations with Medvedev off to a promising start. At worst, we'd have built up capital with the Allies for making such an effort, which we'd no doubt have to drawn on to manage the fallout from Kosovo and missile defense.

10. I fully recognize that all this is much, much easier said than done. But even partial success would help cushion some of the trainwrecks that lie ahead, and help create an atmosphere in which eventual decisions on MAP might go down easier.

Best regards,

Bill Burns

Memo to Secretary of State Condoleezza Rice, May 27, 2008, "Regaining the Strategic Initiative on Iran"

In 2008, the Iranian nuclear program was accelerating and American diplomatic efforts were stalling. In this memo to Secretary Rice, I laid out a new approach for strengthening U.S. leverage on the nuclear issue and advocated joining the negotiations between Europe, Russia, China, and Iran.

UNCLASSIFIED U.S. Department of State Case No. ~~SECRET~~ P of 120 Doc No. C06419958 Date: 09/21/2017

UNDER SECRETARY OF STATE
FOR POLITICAL AFFAIRS
WASHINGTON

RELEASE IN FULL

Copy

May 27, 2008

~~SECRET/Eyes Only~~
DECL: 5/27/2018

NOTE FOR THE SECRETARY

Seen by

NOV 2 1 2008

FROM: P – Bill Burns

P

SUBJECT: Regaining the Strategic Initiative on Iran

Madam Secretary,

1. Our Iran policy is drifting dangerously between the current muddle of P5+1 diplomacy and more forceful options, with all of their huge downsides. Following are some preliminary thoughts on how we might use the remaining months of this Administration to regain the strategic initiative, revive leverage over Iran, and frame a sustainable, long-term approach to the Iranian challenge on which the next Administration might build.

<u>The Iranian Challenge</u>

2. The Iranian regime today is simultaneously cocky and insecure. Awash in $130/barrel oil, Tehran is defiantly continuing to enrich uranium, and pugnaciously pressing its hand in Lebanon and Iraq. But oil revenues can only partially compensate for Ahmadinejad's economic incompetence and 30% inflation, aggravated by financial sanctions. Iran has no natural regional allies, and remains suspicious that erstwhile partners like Syria ultimately have higher priorities (like the Golan). Having possibly overplayed its hand in Basra, the Iranian regime has been reminded that Iraqi nationalism can trump Shia bonds. And the regime is still beset by fundamental contradictions, caught between its own retrogressive traditionalism and popular pressures for modernization.

~~SECRET~~
Classified by: P, Bill Burns
E.O. 12958 Reasons: 1.4(b) and (d)

RELEASE AUTHORITY: Paul Hilburn, Senior Reviewer

~~SECRET~~
-2-

3. The basic dilemma we face is that the most dangerous dimension of Iranian behavior -- its nuclear program -- is both broadly popular in Iran as a symbol of national modernization and self-assertiveness, and likely to outpace the internal contradictions which will eventually cause either the implosion of the current regime or the mellowing of its behavior. This is a race that we, and the rest of the international community, are still losing.

4. Part of the problem is also that the Iranian regime has been largely successful in camouflaging its vulnerabilities. That is not just a product of $130/barrel oil, although that certainly doesn't hurt. The regime has constructed a narrative which portrays Iran as the victim of implacable American hostility, increasingly gaining the diplomatic upper hand regionally and globally, with the American administration -- not Iran -- increasingly the isolated party.

5. Reviving significant pressure against Iran's nuclear program requires us to puncture that narrative. That means calculating every step we take not only with a view toward the immediate impact on the regime, but also toward the international, regional and domestic Iranian audiences that are so critical to Tehran's inflated self-confidence. A successful strategy will require calculated risk-taking on our part, applying pressure at as many points as we can, while simultaneously exploring creatively subversive ways to accentuate the gap between the regime's deeply conservative instincts and popular Iranian desire for normalization with the rest of the world, including the U.S.

Elements of a New, Long-Term Strategy

6. I can think of no safer prediction today than that Iran will not agree to suspension of enrichment and reprocessing in response to the P5+1's refreshed incentives package. We have neither enough sticks nor enough carrots in play right now to fundamentally alter Iran's calculus. Anticipating that the current P5+1 process is going to run out of steam during the summer, we ought to craft a bolder and more systematic approach that might help us rebuild momentum through the rest of the year.

7. Tempting as each might seem, I'd be very careful at this stage about the two bookend options before us, either the use of force against Iranian nuclear sites to set back their program, or a unilateral, unconditional offer of direct, bilateral

~~SECRET~~

-3-

dialogue on all subjects. I'm deeply opposed to the first, which would in any case only make sense as a genuine last resort; the truth today is that we are nowhere near exhausting all our other possibilities. The second is intriguing, and may have made sense in 2003, when our leverage was significantly greater, but leaping to that conclusion under current circumstances could only feed Iranian hubris.

8. Conceptually, our renewed approach ought to borrow from classic containment theory, based on Kennan's original notion of how you deal with a profoundly hostile adversary beset by its own serious, and ultimately fatal, internal contradictions. Iran is not the Soviet Union, and it does not pose an existential threat to us (although it could to Israel). But our overall strategy should employ the same combination of multiple pressure points, diplomatic coalition-building, wedge-driving among Iran and its uneasy partners, and selected contacts with the regime that animated much of Kennan's concept.

9. **First,** we should shore up international pressure against Iran's nuclear ambitions. The Iranians hate UNSC resolutions not so much because of the practical impact of sanctions, but because of their political symbolism in underscoring Iran's isolation. A fourth sanctions resolution in early fall, with as much teeth as we can put in it, really does have diplomatic value. (Even talking about sanctions against refined petroleum products and gasoline would have an impact on Tehran.) Another resolution would provide cover for other, more biting, financial sanctions outside the formal bounds of UNSC actions.

10. **Second,** we should continue to look vigorously at ways we can unilaterally (and in partnership with other key players) disrupt the nuclear program and squeeze Iran's financial system. There is still more room for tougher enforcement of existing sanctions, and creative application in areas like insurance coverage that would slowly undermine the Iranian economy.

11. **Third,** we should be more active in disrupting Iran's regional position. Direct Iraqi expressions of discontent with Iranian meddling are quite effective. Kinetic responses in Iraq to Qods Force and Special Group threats, without public fanfare, is a language the Iranian regime understands. More broadly, we can pursue tighter cooperation with the GCC+3, perhaps including discussion of security assurances

-4-

against Iran -- even as we keep the door open for Iran's participation in regional security dialogue. On Afghanistan, we should also push back hard when Iranian behavior crosses coalition interests, but consider revived dialogue on practical issues like counter-narcotics, perhaps on the margins of an UNGA 6+2 meeting.

-- Deepening consultations with Turkey on Iran also helps get Tehran's attention, even if the Turks are reluctant to actually do much; the Iranian regime seems far more wary about Turkey, a big Moslem society whose modernization in the last three decades dwarfs their own feeble economic accomplishments, than it does about the Gulf Arabs, about whom the Iranians love to be dismissive and patronizing.

-- Syria's flirtation with peace talks with Israel, via the Turks, also presents an opportunity. The Iranians don't trust the Syrians, but depend on them heavily to sustain their connection to Hizballah and influence in Lebanon. Any contacts that we have with the Syrians in the current environment will help unnerve the Iranians, and that is not a bad thing.

12. **Fourth**, we should consider how we might use carefully-structured contacts with Iran to turn the tables on Tehran diplomatically, put them back on their heels tactically, and exploit the disconnect between the regime's need to paint the U.S. as the enemy at the gates and the Iranian population's thirst for access to American society and the rest of the world. Such contacts should include Parliamentary exchanges, more sports and cultural visits, and more innovative broadcasting and outreach, including use of Farsi-speaking U.S. officials on Iranian programs.

-- More ambitiously, I'd strongly recommend a well-orchestrated proposal to set up a U.S. visa office or interests section in Tehran. There are a number of variants, the simplest of which would involve sending 3 or 4 American diplomats to work under our current protecting power (for which the Iranians would no doubt insist on reciprocity in Washington). The default position of the Iranian regime will be to reject such an offer, but we can make it very awkward for them to do so, especially if we package it with 1000 scholarships for Iranian students and a willingness to talk directly with Iranian officials about how to set up an office.

-5-

-- We might combine a visa office proposal with a parallel offer to have the American political director (me) join our P5+1 colleagues in a second round of talks in Tehran, if /if the Iranians agree to the "freeze for freeze" idea that Solana will explore with them as a limited duration step to facilitate pre-negotiations. (The Iranians would have to cap their nuclear program for six weeks, and we would agree not to pursue new sanctions during that period -- which we probably couldn't do anyway.) We would not change our stance on Ministerial-level participation; that would still depend on Iranian suspension.

Plan of Action

13. All of this is, of course, much easier said than done. The trick would be to implement the visa office idea and limited direct contacts in a way that significantly enhances our diplomatic leverage, and gets us something in return -- if not from the Iranians, then in terms of better cooperation from the P5+1 and wedge-driving between the regime and the Iranian people. Like Ronald Reagan and George Shultz in opening the U.S.-PLO dialogue in late 1988, we would also be breaking a taboo in a way that would strengthen the hand of the next Administration.

14. There are a number of options for introducing the ideas of a visa office and limited participation in P5+1 talks. On the visa office, you could use a trusted private intermediary, perhaps via the Iranian PermRep in New York. You could use the British. Or you could use the Russians -- which probably carries both the biggest risks and the biggest payoff.

-- What I would suggest is that you meet privately with Lavrov and try to trade the visa office and limited P5+1 participation offers for Russian agreement -- if the Iranians turn us down -- to a fourth resolution, with as much teeth as we can get, and an informal commitment to continue to slow-roll implementation of past missile contracts. Buying the Russians into this approach is key to sustaining international consensus through the end of the year.

SECRET
-6-

-- If the Russians agreed, we could use them to convey our offers. On the visa office or interests section, we'd also insist that the Iranians designate someone with whom we could follow up directly, and who we could be confident represented the Supreme Leader. It's possible that that channel could be used for other subjects in the future, but the initial conversation would be about the visa office.

15. We'd still retain the cards that matter most to Tehran, including security guarantees and limited enrichment programs. There are strong arguments against playing those now. We need to rebuild leverage first, and regain the initiative. But by launching the limited steps that I've suggested here, we'd have a chance to upset Iranian calculations, and set in motion a workable, long-term strategy -- whether the Iranians accepted our offer or not. That would be a valuable contribution to the next Administration, and to American interests for years to come.

SECRET

Email to Secretary of State Hillary Clinton, February 22, 2011, "Note for the Secretary from Bill Burns: Cairo, February 21-22"

Written less than two weeks after the ouster of President Hosni Mubarak, this dispatch from Cairo tried to capture both the exuberant mood in Egypt's streets as well as the depth of the challenges facing the country's new leadership. Throughout my tenure as undersecretary and deputy secretary, I frequently sent such first-person notes to capture my impressions and offer recommendations.

RELEASE IN FULL

From: Doyle, Robert F
To: Macmanus, Joseph E; S_SpecialAssistants; Sullivan, Jacob J
Cc: Steinberg, James B; Feltman, Jeffrey D; Wells, Alice G; "mspence@osc.eop.sgov.gov"; Nides, Thomas R
Subject: Note for the Secretary from Bill Burns: Cairo, February 21-22
Date: Tuesday, February 22, 2011 4:21:28 PM

SECRET

February 22, 2011
Cairo

Madam Secretary,

Amidst the bloody chaos next door and continued tumult elsewhere in the region, Egypt's ten day old transition is taking on more and more significance. My impression after two very full days of meetings in Cairo is that Egyptians are pointed in a positive direction, with no shortage of potential political and economic pitfalls ahead. The mood here remains generally optimistic. The Supreme Council of the Armed Forces has so far managed its unaccustomed role with more finesse than most would have suspected. Soldiers are still being treated like celebrities, with mothers perching their kids on the sides of tanks for souvenir photos. Walking along the corniche yesterday to the MFA, we went past piles of barbed wire and dozens of armored vehicles in front of the State TV building, with demonstrators, families and sidewalk vendors combining to create the street party atmosphere of this still incomplete revolution. Banks have reopened without disaster, and the fundamentals of the economy are not in bad shape. Youth leaders are deeply proud of the historic role that they've played. The political class is filled with genuine enthusiasts for change, as well as ex post facto revolutionaries, eager to declare their heretofore well-concealed antipathy for the Mubarak regime and claim that they were really with the revolutionaries in Tahrir Square all along. There is a powerful sense that what has happened is irreversible, and a feeling of new possibility and promise. That's the good news.

The not-so-good news is that expectations are unrealistically high. The military leadership is struggling with transparency, a concept which doesn't come naturally. Their evident determination to hand off to civilian rule in six months is raising doubts on the part of both youth leaders and political figures like Amr Mousa and Mohamed el-Baradei, both of whom worry that trying to cram Constitutional revisions, Parliamentary and Presidential elections into the next half year will benefit only the Muslim Brotherhood and the remnants of the NDP – the only organized parties on the playing field for early Parliamentary elections. The business community is spooked both by political uncertainty and what appear to be an open-ended series of prosecutions against ex-Ministers and the business elite that prospered under Mubarak. The current government, reshuffled this evening to add a few more opposition leaders, is weak and increasingly criticized by youth activists. The emergency law is still in place, and state security has not gone away. None of this should be all that surprising less than two weeks after the end of the Mubarak era, but it would be a mistake to underestimate the challenges that lie ahead.

RELEASE AUTHORITY: Paul Hilburn, Senior Reviewer

UNCLASSIFIED U.S. Department of State Case No. MP-2015-07420 Doc No. C06420058 Date: 09/21/2017

I found Field Marshal Tantawi self-assured and more engaging than I remember him in our previous meetings. He will never be accused of being voluble, but he clearly is proud of the role that he and the senior military leadership are playing, and of the trust with which they are regarded today by most Egyptians. Always risk averse in the past, and a stubborn defender of the military's business empire against economic reform, Tantawi nevertheless appeared determined to carry out a crisp political transition. He was very appreciative of the President's letter, and stressed his firm commitment to strong U.S.-Egyptian relations. Margaret Scobey and I praised the military's role, and emphasized the wider significance of Egypt's transition for a region in the midst of its own profound set of transitions. I pressed for more openness and inclusiveness, urging, for example, that the SCAF ensure that the committee preparing draft constitutional amendments go on television and get around the country in the weeks ahead to explain their efforts, and solicit public and expert reaction. I also raised the value of asking the UN to quietly send technical electoral experts to Cairo to help navigate the very complicated terrain of preparing for both Parliamentary and Presidential elections. I probed him on the wisdom of trying to do Parliamentary elections in only a few months, before Presidential elections, noting the difficulty of organizing new parties and ensuring a level playing field. He was unmoved on that issue, but agreed on the importance of engaging with people more broadly on the proposed constitutional amendments (which may be ready as early as this weekend), and kept the door open on a potential role for UN technical experts. (I subsequently followed up with U/SYG Lyn Pascoe, who confirmed that he will be coming to Cairo next week with a team of experts.) Tantawi also asked in general terms for short-term economic help, citing in particular the collapse of tourism revenue. He said he would appreciate our continuing informal advice on the transition, indicating that he had seen the paper we had sent him on other transition experiences, and found the Indonesia example to be especially relevant.

PM Shafiq came off as well-intentioned but uncertain of his role. He complained openly of his lack of connection to the SCAF, noting that he continued to argue for putting Presidential elections first and preparing more carefully for Parliamentary elections. He was clearly preoccupied with the Cabinet reshuffle, although he engaged in a useful conversation with David Lipton on the need to address both short-term economic recovery problems and medium-term modernization. In a separate conversation, the Minister of Finance offered a sensible overview of Egypt's economic challenges, arguing for debt relief from the U.S. as part of an effort to provide "fiscal space" during the crucial first few months of the political transition, and stressing his interest in creating private sector jobs and encouraging small and medium sized enterprises.

FM Aboul Gheit was less argumentative than usual, although he argued vehemently against EU and Australian ideas about "Friends of Democratic Egypt" or donors conferences, maintaining that "Egypt is not Pakistan or Somalia." He and the Minister of International Cooperation laid out their case for writing off the roughly $350 million in bilateral debt payments that Egypt owes the U.S. this year, and also urged an increase in bilateral ESF. David pointed out that debt relief is very complicated, and might undercut Egypt's message to investors that its economy is fundamentally sound. We explained the reprogramming of $150 million in ESF for immediate job creation and other potential short-term economic programs. We also made clear our intent to support a range of civil society groups, registered as well as non-registered. Aboul Gheit pushed back, not surprisingly, but we were equally insistent, and his resistance was a little half-hearted. (I doubt that this is the last word on this issue. Although it did not come up in the Tantawi meeting, Aboul Gheit indicated that the SCAF is also very sensitive about any change in the pattern of democracy assistance.) We also spent some time discussing the mess in Libya and changes elsewhere in the region. Aboul Gheit was matter of fact in his conclusion that "Qadhafi's days are numbered, and that's good."

We also saw Amr Mousa, who was pretty upbeat about the transition so far and clearly intent on becoming a Presidential candidate. His interest in his role at the Arab League is obviously fading fast, and he made only a passing reference to our UNSC veto. Mohamed el-Baradei was sharply critical of the SCAF's lack of transparency and rushed timetable, but he expressed his determination to work with youth leaders to create a new political party and compete in Parliamentary elections. He was a little coy about his own potential Presidential candidacy. We met with several groups of political party leaders, human rights activists and civil society figures, as well as U.S.-based NGO's. All stressed familiar concerns about the pace of the transition and the need to prepare more carefully and transparently. Perhaps the most interesting of our conversations was with several youth leaders, who had driven events in Tahrir Square and remained intent upon achieving sweeping political change. They were adamant about replacing the Shafiq government, and generally impatient and suspicious of the agenda of the SCAF. They may overestimate their ability to keep filling Tahrir Square in the short-run, to keep up pressure on the current leadership, but there's no mistaking their commitment and energy.

I'll talk later tonight to Cathy Ashton, with whom I am overlapping in Cairo, and will have some further ideas for you on how we might work with the EU, the UN and all the various Egyptian players to continue to urge careful preparation for elections. On economic issues, David will be developing his own thoughts, but we agree that Egypt has two main economic challenges. The first is to maintain financial stability in the face of uncertainty around the political transition. Economic disruptions during the period of protest, as well as wage and subsidy demands in the wake of Mubarak's departure, are significant problems. We will want to help Egypt avoid financial instability, which would likely take the form of inflation and currency depreciation, in order to create an environment of economic calm in which political dialogue can take place. Our help can include bilateral support from the U.S. and EU, loans from the IFIs, and possibly financial support from Egypt's regional partners.

In the longer term, Egypt's most pressing need is economic modernization. Economic growth needs to be restored, but in a way that provides opportunity to the young, the unemployed and those who have not been part of the formal economy. We and other donors can provide assistance aimed at building human capital, promoting the private sector, and strengthening credit programs to broaden access to finance. But aid alone is not sufficient. Egypt's economy grew rapidly in the past decade, with several years of seven percent growth, attracting more than ten billion dollars per year in foreign investment. Too much of the fruits of that growth went to the privileged and the connected, who obtained special protections and advantages from the government. That created widespread resentment. The challenge ahead is to restore growth while breaking down the web of privilege and protection. Egypt will need a program for economic modernization, elimination of the many controls that restrict private entrepreneurship, and an opening up to trade and competition. We and the Europeans should explore how we can support such a program, including by offering enhanced market access, either by expanding existing programs such as Qualified Industrial Zones, or, over time, pursuing new and improved trade agreements.

I also had a chance to do a townhall meeting with American and Egyptian embassy employees, and conveyed your appreciation. They are an extraordinary group, very well-led by Margaret.

All in all, Egypt's transition, for all its obvious challenges, offers remarkable opportunities. Getting it right matters enormously at this moment of sweeping changes across the region.

I fly to tomorrow morning to Tunis, where another tricky transition is already underway.

Best regards,

Bill

Sensitivity: Sensitive
Classification: SECRET//NOFORN
Classified by: bill burns, u/s, p, state
Reason: 1.4(d)
Declassify On: 2036/02/22

Bibliography

Abdullah II, King of Jordan. *Our Last Best Chance: The Pursuit of Peace in a Time of Peril*. New York: Viking, 2011.

Albright, Madeleine. *Madam Secretary: A Memoir*. New York: Miramax, 2003.

Allison, Graham T. *Destined for War: Can America and China Escape Thucydides's Trap?* Boston: Houghton Mifflin Harcourt, 2017.

Art, Robert. *A Grand Strategy for America*. Ithaca, N.Y.: Cornell University Press, 2013.

Bacevich, Andrew. *American Empire: The Realities and Consequences of U.S. Diplomacy*. Cambridge, Mass.: Harvard University Press, 2002.

Baker, James A., with Thomas M. DeFrank. *The Politics of Diplomacy: Revolution, War, and Peace, 1989–1992*. New York: G. P. Putnam's Sons, 1995.

Baker, Peter, and Susan Glasser. *Kremlin Rising: Vladimir Putin's Russia and the End of Revolution*. New York: Scribner, 2005.

Beschloss, Michael, and Strobe Talbott. *At the Highest Levels: The Inside Story of the End of the Cold War*. Boston: Little, Brown, 1993.

Bohlen, Charles. *Witness to History: 1929–1969*. New York: W. W. Norton, 1973.

Brands, Hal. *Making the Unipolar Moment: U.S. Foreign Policy and the Rise of the Post–Cold War Order*. Ithaca, N.Y.: Cornell University Press, 2016.

Brooks, Stephen, and William Wohlforth. *America Abroad: The United States' Global Role in the 21st Century*. New York: Oxford University Press, 2016.

Brzezinski, Zbigniew. *Second Chance: Three Presidents and the Crisis of American Superpower.* New York: Basic Books, 2008.

——. *The Grand Chessboard: American Primacy and Its Geostrategic Imperatives.* 2nd ed. New York: Basic Books, 2016.

Bull, Hedley. *The Anarchical Society: A Study of Order in World Politics.* 4th ed. New York: Columbia University Press, 2012.

Bush, George H. W., and Brent Scowcroft. *A World Transformed.* New York: Random House, 1998.

Campbell, Kurt. *The Pivot: The Future of American Statecraft in Asia.* New York: Twelve, 2016.

Chandrasekaran, Rajiv. *Imperial Life in the Emerald City: Inside Iraq's Green Zone.* New York: Knopf, 2006.

Chollet, Derek. *The Long Game: How Obama Defied Washington and Redefined America's Role in the World.* New York: PublicAffairs, 2016.

Chollet, Derek, and Ben Fishman. "Who Lost Libya?" Response to Alan Kuperman. *Foreign Affairs,* May/June 2015.

Christopher, Warren. *In the Stream of History: Shaping Foreign Policy for a New Era.* Stanford, Calif.: Stanford University Press, 1998.

Clinton, Hillary. "Leading Through Civilian Power." *Foreign Affairs,* November/December 2010.

——. *Hard Choices.* New York: Simon & Schuster, 2014.

Cohen, Eliot. *The Big Stick: The Limits of Soft Power and the Necessity of Military Force.* New York: Basic Books, 2017.

Coll, Steve. "The Back Channel." *New Yorker,* March 2, 2009.

——. *Directorate S: The C.I.A. and America's Secret Wars in Afghanistan and Pakistan.* New York: Penguin Press, 2018.

Colton, Timothy J. *Yeltsin: A Life.* New York: Basic Books, 2008.

DeYoung, Karen. *Soldier: The Life of Colin Powell.* New York: Vintage, 2007.

Engel, Jeffrey A. *When the World Seemed New: George H. W. Bush and the End of the Cold War.* New York: Houghton Mifflin Harcourt, 2017.

Feith, Douglas J. *War and Decision: Inside the Pentagon at the Dawn of the War on Terrorism.* New York: HarperCollins, 2008.

Freedman, Lawrence. *A Choice of Enemies: America Confronts the Middle East.* New York: PublicAffairs, 2008.

Freeman, Chas. W., Jr. *Arts of Power: Statecraft and Diplomacy.* Washington, D.C.: United States Institute of Peace Press, 1997.

——. *The Diplomat's Dictionary.* Washington, D.C.: United States Institute of Peace Press, 1997.

Friedman, Thomas. "Foreign Affairs; A Dangerous Peace." *New York Times,* January 12, 1999.

Fukuyama, Francis. *America at the Crossroads: Democracy, Power, and the Neoconservative Legacy.* New Haven, Conn.: Yale University Press, 2007.

Gaddis, John Lewis. *The Cold War: A New History.* New York: Penguin Press, 2005.

——. *Strategies of Containment: A Critical Appraisal of American National Security Policy During the Cold War.* New York: Oxford University Press, 2005.

——. *George F. Kennan: An American Life.* New York: Penguin Press, 2011.

Gall, Carlotta, and Thomas De Waal. *Chechnya: Calamity in the Caucasus.* New York: New York University Press, 1998.

Gates, Robert. *Duty.* New York: Knopf, 2014.

Gellman, Barton. *Contending with Kennan: Toward a Philosophy of American Power.* New York: Praeger, 1984.

Ghattas, Kim. *The Secretary: A Journey with Hillary Clinton from Beirut to the Heart of American Power.* London: Picador, 2014.

Goldberg, Jeffrey. "The Obama Doctrine." *Atlantic,* April 2016.

Green, Michael. *By More Than Providence: Grand Strategy and American Power in the Asia Pacific Since 1783.* New York: Columbia University Press, 2017.

Haass, Richard. *Foreign Policy Begins at Home: The Case for Putting America's House in Order.* New York: Basic Books, 2013.

——. *A World in Disarray: American Foreign Policy and the Crisis of the Old Order.* New York: Penguin Press, 2017.

Hill, Fiona, and Clifford Gaddy. *Mr. Putin: Operative in the Kremlin.* Washington, D.C.: Brookings Institution Press, 2013.

Hoffman, David E. *The Oligarchs: Wealth and Power in the New Russia.* New York: PublicAffairs, 2002.

Hoffmann, Stanley. *Chaos and Violence: What Globalization, Failed States, and Terrorism Mean for U.S. Foreign Policy.* Lanham, Md.: Rowman & Littlefield, 2006.

Holbrooke, Richard. *To End a War.* New York: Random House, 1998.

Ikenberry, G. John. *Liberal Leviathan: The Origins, Crisis, and Transformation of the American World Order.* Princeton, N.J.: Princeton University Press, 2011.

Jentleson, Bruce W., and Christopher A. Whytock. "Who 'Won' Libya? The Force Diplomacy Debate and Its Implications for Theory and Policy." *International Security* 30, no. 3 (2006): 47–86.

Jervis, Robert. *American Foreign Policy in a New Era.* Abingdon, UK: Routledge, 2005.

Kagan, Robert. *Dangerous Nation: America's Foreign Policy from Its Earliest Days to the Dawn of the Twentieth Century.* New York: Knopf, 2006.

——. *The Jungle Grows Back: America and Our Imperiled World.* New York: Knopf, 2018.

Kaplan, Robert. *The Revenge of Geography: What the Map Tells Us About*

Coming Conflicts and the Battle Against Fate. New York: Random House, 2012.

——. *The Return of Marco Polo's World: War, Strategy, and American Interests in the Twenty-First Century*. New York: Random House, 2018.

Kennan, George. *Memoirs, 1925–1950*. Boston: Atlantic–Little, Brown, 1967.

——. *Memoirs, 1950–1963*. Boston: Atlantic–Little, Brown, 1972.

Kerry, John. *Every Day Is Extra*. New York: Simon & Schuster, 2018.

Kessler, Glenn. *The Confidante: Condoleezza Rice and the Creation of the Bush Legacy*. New York: St. Martin's, 2007.

Kirkpatrick, David. *Into the Hands of the Soldiers: Freedom and Chaos in Egypt and the Middle East*. New York: Viking, 2018.

Kissinger, Henry. *Diplomacy*. New York: Simon & Schuster, 1994.

——. *World Order*. New York: Penguin Press, 2014.

Leigh, David, and Luke Harding. *WikiLeaks: Inside Julian Assange's War on Secrecy*. London: Guardian Books, 2011.

Lieven, Anatol, and John Hulsman. *Ethical Realism: A Vision for America's Role in the World*. New York: Pantheon, 2006.

Lippman, Thomas. *Madeleine Albright and the New American Diplomacy*. New York: Basic Books, 2000.

Lynch, Marc. *The New Arab Wars: Uprisings and Anarchy in the Middle East*. New York: PublicAffairs, 2016.

Matlock, Jack. *Reagan and Gorbachev: How the Cold War Ended*. New York: Random House, 2004.

McDougall, Walter A. *Promised Land, Crusader State: The American Encounter with the World Since 1776*. Boston: Houghton Mifflin, 1997.

McFaul, Michael. *From Cold War to Hot Peace: An Ambassador in Putin's Russia*. New York: Houghton Mifflin Harcourt, 2018.

Mead, Walter Russell. *Special Providence: American Foreign Policy and How It Changed the World*. New York: Routledge, 2002.

Menon, Shivshankar. *Choices: Inside the Making of India's Foreign Policy*. Washington, D.C.: Brookings Institution Press, 2016.

Miller, Aaron David. *The Much Too Promised Land: America's Elusive Search for Arab-Israeli Peace*. New York: Bantam, 2008.

Morgan, Dan. *Merchants of Grain: The Power and Profits of the Five Giant Companies at the Center of the World's Food Supply*. New York: Viking, 1979.

Muasher, Marwan. *The Arab Center: The Promise of Moderation*. New Haven, Conn.: Yale University Press, 2009.

——. *The Second Arab Awakening: And the Battle for Pluralism*. New Haven, Conn.: Yale University Press, 2014.

Norris, John. "How to Balance Safety and Openness for America's Diplomats." *Atlantic*, November 4, 2013.

Obama, Barack. *The Audacity of Hope: Thoughts on Reclaiming the American Dream.* New York: Crown, 2006.

O'Hanlon, Michael E. *Beyond NATO: A New Security Architecture for Eastern Europe.* Washington, D.C.: Brookings Institution Press, 2017.

Ostrovsky, Arkady. *The Invention of Russia: From Gorbachev's Freedom to Putin's War.* New York: Viking, 2015.

Packer, George. *The Assassins' Gate: America in Iraq.* New York: Farrar, Straus & Giroux, 2005.

Parsi, Trita. *Losing an Enemy: Obama, Iran, and the Triumph of Diplomacy.* New Haven, Conn.: Yale University Press, 2017.

Pickering, Thomas. Oral History Interview. Association for Diplomatic Studies and Training, April 18, 2003.

Pope, Lawrence. *The Demilitarization of American Diplomacy: Two Cheers for Striped Pants.* Basingstoke, UK: Palgrave Macmillan, 2014.

Powell, Colin L. *My American Journey.* New York: Random House, 1995.

———. *It Worked for Me: In Life and Leadership.* New York: Harper, 2012.

Rhodes, Ben. *The World As It Is: A Memoir of the Obama White House.* New York: Random House, 2018.

Rice, Condoleezza. *No Higher Honor: A Memoir of My Years in Washington.* New York: Crown, 2011.

Ross, Dennis. *The Missing Peace: The Inside Story of the Fight for Middle East Peace.* New York: Farrar, Straus & Giroux, 2004.

Sakwa, Richard. *Chechnya: From Past to Future.* London: Anthem Press, 2005.

Sanger, David E. *The Inheritance: The World Obama Confronts and the Challenges to American Power.* New York: Harmony Books, 2009.

———. *Confront and Conceal: Obama's Secret Wars and Surprising Use of American Power.* New York: Crown, 2012.

Sargent, Daniel J. *A Superpower Transformed: The Remaking of American Foreign Relations in the 1970s.* New York: Oxford University Press, 2015.

Sestanovich, Stephen. *Maximalist: America in the World from Truman to Obama.* New York: Knopf, 2014.

Sherman, Wendy. *Not for the Faint of Heart: Lessons in Courage, Power, and Persistence.* New York: PublicAffairs, 2018.

Shevtsova, Lilia. *Yeltsin's Russia: Myths and Reality.* Washington, D.C.: Carnegie Endowment for International Peace, 1999.

———. *Putin's Russia.* Washington, D.C.: Carnegie Endowment for International Peace, 2005.

Shifrinson, Joshua R. "Deal or No Deal? The End of the Cold War and the U.S. Offer to Limit NATO Expansion." *International Security* 40, no. 4 (2016): 7–44.

Shultz, George P. *Turmoil and Triumph: My Years as Secretary of State.* New York: Scribner's, 1993.

Slaughter, Anne-Marie. *A New World Order*. Princeton, N.J.: Princeton University Press, 2009.

Smith, Charles. *Palestine and the Arab-Israeli Conflict*. New York: St. Martin's, 1992.

Stent, Angela E. *The Limits of Partnership: U.S.-Russian Relations in the Twenty-First Century*. Princeton, N.J.: Princeton University Press, 2014.

Talbott, Strobe. *The Russia Hand: A Memoir of Presidential Diplomacy*. New York: Random House, 2002.

Taubman, William. *Gorbachev: His Life and Times*. New York: Simon & Schuster, 2017.

Telhami, Shibley. *The World Through Arab Eyes: Arab Public Opinion and the Reshaping of the Middle East*. New York: Basic Books, 2013.

Wehrey, Frederic. *The Burning Shores: Inside the Battle for the New Libya*. New York: Farrar, Straus & Giroux, 2018.

Woodward, Bob. *Plan of Attack: The Definitive Account of the Decision to Invade Iraq*. New York: Simon & Schuster, 2004.

———. *Obama's Wars*. New York: Simon & Schuster, 2010.

Worth, Robert Forsyth. *A Rage for Order: The Middle East in Turmoil, from Tahrir Square to ISIS*. New York: Farrar, Straus & Giroux, 2016.

Wright, Thomas. *All Measures Short of War: The Contest for the Twenty-First Century and the Future of American Power*. New Haven, Conn.: Yale University Press, 2017.

Zakaria, Fareed. *The Post-American World: Release 2.0*. New York: W. W. Norton, 2012.

Zeleny, Jeff. "A Foreign Classroom for a Junior Senator." *Chicago Tribune*, September 23, 2005.

Zelikow, Philip, and Condoleezza Rice. *Germany Unified and Europe Transformed: A Study in Statecraft*. Cambridge, Mass.: Harvard University Press, 1995.

Notes

PROLOGUE

1. Memo to Secretary of State–Designate Christopher, January 5, 1993, "Parting Thoughts: U.S. Foreign Policy in the Years Ahead."
2. Henry Kissinger, *Diplomacy* (New York: Simon & Schuster, 1994), 836.

CHAPTER 1: APPRENTICESHIP: THE EDUCATION OF A DIPLOMAT

1. 1984 Amman 6594, July 16, 1984, "The Changing Face of Jordanian Politics."

CHAPTER 2: THE BAKER YEARS: SHAPING ORDER

1. George Kennan, *Memoirs, 1925–1950* (Boston: Atlantic–Little, Brown, 1967), 326–27.
2. Thomas Friedman, "Washington at Work; In Quest of a Post–Cold War Plan," *New York Times*, November 17, 1989.
3. Quoted in Michael Beschloss and Strobe Talbott, *At the Highest Levels: The Inside Story of the End of the Cold War* (Boston: Little, Brown, 1993), 25.
4. George H. W. Bush and Brent Scowcroft, *A World Transformed* (New York: Random House, 1998), 12.
5. Memo to Deputy Secretary Eagleburger, April 10, 1990, "Deepening U.S.–East European Relations."
6. Quoted in John Lewis Gaddis, *The Cold War: A New History* (New York: Penguin Press, 2005), 248.

7. David Hoffman, "U.S. Envoy Conciliatory to Saddam," *Washington Post*, July 12, 1991.

8. Memo to Under Secretary Kimmitt, August 4, 1990, "Kuwait: The First Post–Cold War Crisis."

9. Memo to Kimmitt, August 20, 1990, "Containing Saddam: Diplomatic Options."

10. 1990 Riyadh 2457, November 20, 1990, "Reflections on Post-Crisis Security Arrangements in the Persian Gulf."

11. Memo to Secretary Baker, April 30, 1992, "Foreign Policy in the Second Bush Administration: An Overview."

12. Memo to Secretary of State–Designate Christopher, January 5, 1993, "Parting Thoughts: U.S. Foreign Policy in the Years Ahead."

Chapter 3: Yeltsin's Russia: The Limits of Agency

1. 1994 Moscow 35565, December 9, 1994, "Russia on the Eve of the Vice President's Visit."

2. William Jefferson Clinton, "Remarks to the American Society of Newspaper Editors," Annapolis, Maryland, April 1, 1993.

3. Strobe Talbott, *The Russia Hand: A Memoir of Presidential Diplomacy* (New York: Random House, 2002), 5.

4. 1994 Moscow 27483, September 22, 1994, "Yeltsin and Russia on the Eve of the Summit."

5. Tom De Waal, "Chechnya: The Breaking Point," in *Chechnya: From Past to Future*, ed. Richard Sakwa (London: Anthem Press, 2005), 187.

6. 1995 Moscow 883, January 11, 1995, "Sifting Through the Wreckage: Chechnya and Russia's Future."

7. Interview with Secretary Christopher, *MacNeil/Lehrer NewsHour*, PBS, November 13, 1994.

8. Thomas Pickering, Oral History Interview, Association for Diplomatic Studies and Training, April 18, 2003.

9. 1995 Moscow 5788, February 22, 1995, "Yeltsin and Russia Totter On."

10. 1995 Moscow 19971, June 26, 1995, "Coping with Uncertainty: Russia on the Eve of the Vice President's Visit."

11. 1995 Moscow 6176, February 24, 1995, "Ambassador's Meeting on Chechnya with Disaster Relief Expert."

12. 1995 Moscow 19896, June 26, 1995, "Ingush and Chechen Views on the Fred Cuny Case."

13. Ibid.

14. 1995 Moscow 26910, August 23, 1995, "Cuny Case."

15. 1995 Moscow 19971.

16. Richard Holbrooke, *To End a War* (New York: Random House, 1998), 117.

17. 1995 Moscow 32066, October 5, 1995, "Thoughts on the Eve of the VP's Meeting."
18. Memo of Conversation Between Presidents Clinton and Yeltsin, May 10, 1995, National Security Council and NSC Records Management System, "Declassified Documents Concerning Russian President Boris Yeltsin," Clinton Digital Library.
19. 1994 Moscow 35186, December 6, 1994, "Russia and NATO."
20. 1995 Moscow 32066.

CHAPTER 4: JORDAN'S MOMENT OF TRANSITION:
THE POWER OF PARTNERSHIP

1. 1999 Amman 615, January 26, 1999, "A Poignant Farewell."
2. Jeremy Konyndyk, "Clinton and Helms Nearly Ruined State. Tillerson Wants to Finish the Job," *Politico*, May 4, 2017.
3. 1999 Amman 1059, February 7, 1999, "King Hussein's Legacy and Jordan's Future."
4. "Jordan's Hussein Says His Cancer Is Curable," CNN, July 28, 1998.
5. Hourani letter to author, April 1984.
6. Dana Priest, "CIA Taps Richer for Operations Post," *Washington Post*, November 30, 2004.
7. 1998 Amman 9928, November 5, 1998, "Your Visit to Jordan."
8. 1998 Amman 9517, October 20, 1998, "Staying Ahead of Events in Jordan."
9. 1999 Amman 1059.
10. 1999 Amman 3867, May 10, 1999, "A Young Man in a Hurry."
11. 2000 Amman 698, February 8, 2000, "Keeping a Sense of Perspective About King Abdullah's First Year."
12. 2000 Amman 1909, April 12, 2000, "Political Drift in Jordan."
13. 1999 Amman 1588, February 26, 1999, "Jordan in Transition."
14. 2000 Amman 5743, October 15, 2000, "The Tragedy Across the River and Jordan's Uncertain Future."
15. Ibid.
16. 2000 Amman 6760, December 5, 2000, "Peace Process: Relaunching American Diplomacy."
17. 2001 Amman 336, January 22, 2001, "Abdullah Faces a Troubled New Year."
18. 2001 Amman 1658, April 2, 2001, "King Abdullah's Visit to Washington."

CHAPTER 5: AGE OF TERROR:
THE INVERSION OF FORCE AND DIPLOMACY

1. "CIA Beirut Station Chief Is Among the Dead," *Washington Post*, December 25, 1988.

2. Email to Secretary Powell, March 24, 2004, "Note from Bill Burns: Libya, March 23."
3. "Remarks to the Senate Foreign Relations Committee," April 17, 2001.
4. Memo to Powell, February 15, 2002, "Moving to Tenet Implementation."
5. Paper for Powell from Bureau of Near Eastern Affairs and the Policy Planning Staff, August 30, 2001, "Strategies for Preserving U.S. Political Capital in the Middle East."
6. 2002 Riyadh 06674, October 21, 2002, "Talks in Egypt and Jordan."
7. Memo to Deputy Secretary Armitage, November 19, 2001, "Deputies Committee Meeting on Iraq."
8. Interview with Richard Armitage, "Bush's War," *Frontline*, PBS, December 18, 2007.
9. 2003 Amman 00467, January 22, 2003, "Meetings in Bahrain and UAE, January 21–22."
10. Memo to Powell, February 14, 2002, "Regional Concerns Regarding Regime Change in Iraq."
11. Email to Powell, April 1, 2002, "Next Steps on Middle East."
12. Memo to Powell, July 29, 2002, "Iraq: The Perfect Storm."
13. Email to Powell, August 16, 2002, "Iraq and the President's UNGA Speech."
14. Memo to Powell, January 16, 2003, "Today's Iraq PC."
15. Memo to Powell, July 22, 2002, "Role of the External Iraqi Opposition."
16. Email to Powell, July 11, 2003, "Rethinking Our Iraq Strategy."
17. Email to Powell, March 22, 2003, "Middle East: Update, 3/22 (1500)."
18. Ibid.
19. Memo to Powell, June 11, 2002, "Principals Meeting on Middle East."
20. Email to Powell, June 13, 2002, "Rice Meeting with Israelis, June 13."
21. Ibid.
22. Memo to Powell, June 25, 2002, "President's Speech: Short-Term Follow-Up."
23. Quoted in Aaron David Miller, *The Much Too Promised Land: America's Elusive Search for Arab-Israeli Peace* (New York: Bantam, 2008), 352.
24. Quoted in Charles Smith, *Palestine and the Arab-Israeli Conflict* (New York: St. Martin's, 1992), 513.
25. Memo to Powell, March 11, 2003, "Read-Out of Libya Meetings."
26. Email to Powell, February 6, 2004, "Libya Talks, February 6."
27. Memo to Secretary of State–Designate Rice, December 6, 2004, "Policy Paper for the Bureau of Near Eastern Affairs."

Chapter 6: Putin's Disruptions: Managing Great Power Trainwrecks

1. Memo for the Record, October 22, 2006, "A Birthday Dinner with Putin's Politburo."

2. 2006 Moscow 6759, June 26, 2006, "Your Visit to Moscow."

3. Ibid.

4. 2006 Moscow 1925, February 28, 2006, "Lavrov's Visit and Strategic Engagement with Russia."

5. 2008 Moscow 886, April 1, 2008, "Your Visit to Sochi."

6. Email to Secretary Rice, April 11, 2006, "Note for the Secretary from Bill Burns."

7. 2006 Moscow 6759.

8. 2006 Moscow 1925.

9. 2006 Moscow 11939, October 25, 2006, "Your Visit to Moscow."

10. Ibid.

11. Angela E. Stent, *The Limits of Partnership: U.S.-Russian Relations in the Twenty-First Century* (Princeton, N.J.: Princeton University Press, 2014), 147.

12. Email to Rice, February 16, 2007, "Thoughts on Munich and Russian Government Reshuffle."

13. Email to Rice, January 31, 2007, "Thoughts on Lavrov Visit."

14. Ibid.

15. Ibid.

16. Email to Rice, February 16, 2007.

17. 2007 Moscow 2776, June 11, 2007, "June 9–10 Conversations with Putin and His Senior Advisors."

18. 2007 Moscow 2588, June 1, 2007, "Your Meeting with Putin at G-8."

19. Email to Rice, February 8, 2008, "Russia Strategy."

20. Stent, *The Limits of Partnership*, 167.

21. 2008 Moscow 886.

22. Ibid.

CHAPTER 7: OBAMA'S LONG GAME: BETS, PIVOTS, AND RESETS IN A POST-PRIMACY WORLD

1. In 1982, Walter J. Stoessel, Jr., became the first active foreign service officer appointed deputy secretary of state. Lawrence Eagleburger (1989–92) and John Negroponte (2007–9) were both retired from the Foreign Service when they were appointed deputy secretary by George H. W. Bush and George W. Bush respectively.

2. Memo to Secretary Rice, August 27, 2008, "Indian Civil Nuclear Initiative."

3. Memo to Secretary Clinton, March 20, 2009, "A New Partnership with India."

4. The best account of the back-channel talks is Steve Coll, "The Back Channel," *New Yorker*, March 2, 2009. The Pakistan discussions are also addressed in Memo to Clinton, June 12, 2009, "Seizing the Moment with India."

5. Hillary Clinton, *Hard Choices* (New York: Simon & Schuster, 2014), 83–100.
6. Contemporaneous personal notes.
7. Memo to Clinton, February 13, 2009, "February 11–12 Meetings in Moscow."
8. Ibid.
9. Email to Clinton, September 7, 2009, "Note for the Secretary: Missile Defense."
10. Memo to Clinton, December 5, 2011, "Monday Update."
11. Michael McFaul, *From Cold War to Hot Peace: An American Ambassador in Putin's Russia* (New York: Houghton Mifflin Harcourt, 2018), 254.

CHAPTER 8: THE ARAB SPRING: WHEN THE SHORT GAME INTERCEDES

1. Email to Secretary Clinton, February 23, 2011, "Note for the Secretary from Bill Burns: Tunis, February 23."
2. Hillary Clinton, "Remarks with Spanish Foreign Minister Trinidad Jimenez," January 25, 2011, and Joe Biden, *PBS NewsHour*, January 27, 2011.
3. Robert Gates, *Duty* (New York: Knopf, 2014), 504.
4. Email to Clinton, February 22, 2011, "Note for the Secretary from Bill Burns: Cairo, February 21–22."
5. Ibid.
6. Email to Clinton, June 30, 2011, "Note for the Secretary from Bill Burns: Tunis and Cairo, June 27–30."
7. Email to Clinton, January 12, 2012, "Note for the Secretary from Bill Burns: Egypt, January 10–12."
8. "WikiLeaks Cables Reveal Personal Details on World Leaders," *Washington Post*, November 28, 2010.
9. Muammar al-Qaddafi, radio address, March 17, 2011.
10. Email to Secretary Kerry, April 25, 2014, "Tripoli, April 23–24."
11. Email to Clinton, February 17, 2010, "Note for the Secretary from Bill Burns: Meetings in Damascus, February 17."
12. Ernesto Londono and Greg Miller, "CIA Begins Weapons Delivery to Syrian Rebels," *Washington Post*, September 11, 2013.

CHAPTER 9: IRAN AND THE BOMB: THE SECRET TALKS

1. Memo to Secretary Rice, May 27, 2008, "Regaining the Strategic Initiative on Iran."
2. Ibid.
3. Memo to Rice, July 19, 2008, "Meeting with Iranians, July 19."

4. Memo to Secretary Clinton, January 24, 2009, "A New Strategy Toward Iran."

5. Ibid.

6. "A Nowruz Message from President Obama," March 19, 2009.

7. Philip Rucker, "Hillary Clinton Defends Her 'Hard Choices' at State Department," *Washington Post*, May 14, 2014.

CHAPTER 10: PIVOTAL POWER: RESTORING AMERICA'S TOOL OF FIRST RESORT

1. Memo to Secretary of State–Designate Christopher, January 5, 1993, "Parting Thoughts: U.S. Foreign Policy in the Years Ahead."

2. From a 1946 lecture at the National War College, quoted in Barton Gellman, *Contending with Kennan: Toward a Philosophy of American Power* (New York: Praeger, 1984), 126–27.

3. "Remarks by President Trump and President Putin of the Russia Federation in Joint Press Conference," Helsinki, Finland, July 16, 2018.

4. Alexis de Tocqueville, *Democracy in America*, volume 1, chapter XIII (1835).

5. John Lewis Gaddis, *Strategies of Containment: A Critical Appraisal of American National Security Policy During the Cold War* (New York: Oxford University Press, 2005).

6. Michael E. O'Hanlon, *Beyond NATO: A New Security Architecture for Eastern Europe* (Washington, D.C.: Brookings Institution Press, 2017).

7. James Goldgeier and Elizabeth N. Saunders, "Good Foreign Policy Is Invisible," ForeignAffairs.com, February 28, 2017.

8. Charles W. Freeman, Jr., *The Diplomat's Dictionary* (Washington, D.C.: Institute of Peace Press, 1997), 84.

9. Charles Freeman, Lecture Series at Watson Institute of International and Public Affairs, Brown University, 2017–18.

10. Memo to Christopher, January 5, 1993.

11. Ibid.

12. John Norris, "How to Balance Safety and Openness for America's Diplomats," *Atlantic*, November 4, 2013.

13. Memo to Christopher, January 5, 1993.

14. Quoted in Dan Morgan, *Merchants of Grain: The Power and Profits of the Five Giant Companies at the Center of the World's Food Supply* (New York: Viking, 1979), 301.

Index

Abbas, Mahmoud, 188–89, 190, 196
Abdullah of Jordan, 24, 28, 112, 123, 124,
    128–45, 151, 154, 166, 181, 184, 197,
    248, 303, 447; Aqaba Roadmap
    summit, 188–89; Bush 43 and, 184,
    187; H. Clinton and, 247; Saddam
    and, 136–37; Syria and, 324
Abdullah of Saudi Arabia, 155–56, 303,
    324, 332; Qaddafi plot and, 194
Abkhazia, 201, 221, 230, 233, 274
Abramovich, Roman, 217
Abrams, Elliott, 188, 189
Acheson, Dean, 48, 409
Afghanistan, 123, 158, 171, 269, 279,
    328, 394–95; Obama and, 261,
    273; Russia in, 22, 49, 159; U.S.-
    Russia cooperation, 276, 279, 282;
    U.S. war in, 160, 164, 195, 291, 315,
    318, 338, 419
Africa, 10, 391, 405
African Union, 269
Ahmadinejad, Mahmoud, 341, 353, 368,
    374
Ahtisaari, Martti, 230
Albright, Madeleine, 115–16, 117, 120,
    127, 129, 177, 369
Alexeyeva, Lyudmila, 216

Algeria, 154
Al Jazeera, 166
al-Qaeda, 12, 27, 121, 123, 157–58, 164,
    178, 208
Amanpour, Christiane, 128
Anarchical Society, The (Bull), 20
Annan, Kofi, 325, 326
Anti-Ballistic Missile (ABM) Treaty, 231
Arab Human Development Reports, 150
Arab-Israeli peace talks, 30, 31, 34, 40,
    49, 66–75. *See also* Camp David
    Accords; Israeli-Palestinian peace
    talks
Arab League, 284, 316, 325
Arab Spring, 8, 135, 284, 287, 293–96,
    299–318, 324–25, 335, 386, 404.
    See also Assad, Bashar al; Mubarak,
    Hosni; Qaddafi, Muammar al-
Arafat, Suha, 247–48
Arafat, Yasser, 31, 40, 66, 67, 73, 128,
    130, 139, 154, 155, 178–90, 196;
    Camp David talks, 141–42; Iranian
    arms and, 180; Sharon and, 150,
    153
Araghchi, Abbas, 370–73, 375, 377, 379,
    380, 382, 384
Armenia, 77

Armitage, Rich, 145, 152, 157, 164, 165, 167, 171, 175, 195, 203, 340
Ashrawi, Hanan, 70, 71, 73
Ashton, Cathy, 376–80, 382
Asia: Burns travels to, 270–72, 279; Obama and, 265–72; U.S. allies in, 391; as U.S. priority, 402–3. *See also* China; *specific countries*
Assad, Bashar al-, 140–41, 151, 154–55, 158, 160, 322, 323, 334, 412–13; agreement on chemical weapons, 323, 328–29, 331; Arab Spring and, 324–25; Burns meets with, 323–24; Iranian and Hezbollah support, 326, 328, 330, 332; political transition and, 323–31; Russia and, 325–28, 332, 333
Assad, Hafez al-, 31, 44, 61, 67, 70–73, 75, 119, 130, 133, 139, 324, 326
Attiyah, Khalid, 310
Aung San Suu Kyi, 270–71
Aushev, Ruslan, 101
Australia, 269, 270
Aziz, Tariq, 31–32, 57, 62–64

Bagheri, Ali, 352
Bahrain, 133, 151, 155, 160, 316
Baker, Howard, 36
Baker, James, 8, 9, 43–44, 47, 70, 78, 141, 244, 246, 323, 399, 418; Aziz and, 57, 62–64; Burns and, 60, 61–62, 70, 74, 77–78; five principles for the Soviet breakup, 77; German reunification, 54–56, 61, 107; Gulf War and, 60–64, 65, 408, 409; Iraq policy, 57; Madrid Peace Conference, 3, 394, 409; Middle East peace and, 66–75; Policy Planning Staff and, 48, 49; post–Gulf War trips, 69, 71–73; press and, 62; Russian coup attempt and, 76; as secretary of state, 3, 8, 43–81, 115, 248; Shevardnadze and, 50–55, 58; Soviets and Gulf War, 58, 62; Soviet Union's dissolution and, 43–44, 49–56, 76–78; staff for, 46–47, 70; Yemen and, 62
Balkan conflict, 5, 78, 115, 229, 410
Baltic states, 52–53, 230
Barak, Ehud, 139, 141–42, 150

Barzani, Masoud, 177
Basayev, Shamil, 99
Basma, princess of Jordan, 128
Battikhi, Samieh, 125, 133
Begin, Menachem, 141
Ben Ali, Zine El Abidine, 154, 299, 324, 412
Benedicto, Lincoln, 25, 26
Benghazi, Libya, 284, 314, 317, 318, 319–201, 417, 420
Berdimuhamedov, Garbanguly, 279
Berezovsky, Boris, 207
Bessmertnykh, Aleksandr, 43, 44
Biden, Joe, 251, 254, 278, 284, 290, 300, 301, 315, 370, 388
bin Laden, Osama, 253–56, 328, 359
Blair, Tony, 130, 163, 194
Bogdanov, Mikhail, 326
Bohlen, Chip, 85, 203
Bosnian War, 78, 92, 100, 105–6; Dayton Agreement, 107, 414; Holbrooke and, 106–7; Srebrenica massacre, 106
Bouteflika, Abdelaziz, 154
Bradley, Bill, 106
Brahimi, Lakhdar, 326
Brazil, 353–54
Bremer, Jerry, 175–76, 178
Brownfield, Bill, 48
Bulgakov, Mikhail, 204
Bulgaria, 53
Bull, Hedley, 20, 21
Bundy, McGeorge, 34
Burma, 270–71
Burns, Bob, 17–18
Burns, Jack, 17–18
Burns, Lizzy and Sarah, 84, 105, 117, 204, 205, 243, 354, 388
Burns, Mark, 17–18
Burns, Nick, 258
Burns, Peggy, 17
Burns, William F., 17, 116
Burns, William J., 17–20, 22, 29; assistant secretary of state for NEA, 8, 39, 145–46, 152–99, 301, 340–41; enters the Foreign Service, 22–23; fall of the Berlin Wall and, 53; heads transition from Christopher to Albright, 115–16, 392; Iran nuclear deal and, 330–31, 337–84; Iraq

War and, 165, 173, 175–78, 196–99, 203; Jordan as first diplomatic post, 15–17, 23–28, 113, 296, 298; killing of bin Laden and, 253–56; Marshall Scholarship at Oxford, 19–21, 275, 423; at NSC's Near East and South Asia Directorate, 33–42; 9/11 and, 157–60, 256; Obama years, overview of, 291–92, 335–36; as principal deputy, Policy Planning Staff, 42, 43–81, 298, 349; promoting American business, 415; retirement, 388–90; as special assistant to Deputy Secretary Whitehead, 32–33; as staff assistant, NEA, 29–33; as State Department deputy secretary, 251, 256–92, 295, 299, 301–83, 416, 417; as State Department executive secretary, 110, 113–14; as State Department undersecretary for political affairs, 241, 249–56; Ukraine diplomatic efforts, 289–91; as U.S. ambassador, Jordan, 8, 112–45, 298–99, 420–21; as U.S. ambassador, Russia, 8, 200–242; as U.S. minister-counselor, Russia, 84, 85–110

Bush, George H. W. (Bush 41), 4, 39, 130, 244, 292, 409; Arafat and, 41; Baker as chief of staff, 78; Baker as secretary of state, 3, 8, 9, 43–81, 115, 248; bilateral nuclear testing agreements and, 52; cabinet and staff for, 45; Central America and, 49; Congressional address, post–Gulf War, 69; diplomacy and, 8, 45, 246, 292; foreign policy, 9, 43–81; German reunification and, 44, 61; Gulf War and, 44, 45, 56–65, 68, 408, 409; Helsinki summit, 53–54; Madrid Peace Conference, 3; Malta summit, 53–54; Saddam's assassination attempt, 136; Soviet Union's dissolution and, 43–44, 49–56, 76–78; Syria and, 44

Bush, George W. (Bush 43): Abdullah and, 184, 187; ABM Treaty and, 231; Bucharest summit, 239; Burns and, 343; Iran's covert nuclear sites and, 338–40, 341, 343; Iraq War and regime change, 156–57, 161–68, 173–78, 179, 190, 195, 197, 371; Israeli-Palestinian conflict and, 178–90; Libya, Qaddafi, and, 190–95; Middle East policy and, 145, 297, 298; missile defense strategy, 227, 231–34, 236, 238; national security team, 151; NATO expansion and, 230–31; post-9/11 militarization of policy, 161; Powell as secretary of state, 145, 151–52, 156, 159–60, 162, 164–76, 178–82, 186–88, 195, 198, 203, 340; Putin and, 208–9, 213, 220, 235, 236, 239–40, 290; Rice as secretary of state, 195, 200–204; Rice's *Foreign Affairs* article in 2000 and, 151–52; Roadmap initiative, 187–89; Rose Garden Middle East Peace speech, 184–86; Russian policy, 200–242, 292; second inaugural address and freedom agenda, 209; State of the Union speech, 165; U.S.-India partnership, 257–61, 403

Cambodia, 270
Cameron, David, 329, 330
Campbell, Kurt, 265–66, 267, 269
Camp David Accords, 141, 382
Carlucci, Frank C., 36, 38
Carpendale, Andrew, 49, 76, 78
Carter, Jimmy, 21, 34, 114, 130, 141–42
Carty, Lisa, 22–24, 29, 63, 84–85, 105, 157, 248, 256, 388, 389; in Jordan, 112, 113, 117, 120, 124; in Russia, 85–90, 204, 217, 244, 245
Central America, 41, 49
Chalabi, Ahmed, 138, 164, 170, 171, 174, 175, 176, 198
Charles, prince of England, 130
Chechnya, 94–96, 99, 216, 217, 223; Beslan massacre, 208–9; Burns and, 84; Cuny case, 99–103; first war, 82–84, 96–103; Grozny destruction, 82, 83, 96–97; OMON massacre, 83; second war, 84, 99, 206
Cheney, Dick, 45, 50, 60, 78, 151, 185, 195, 230, 340, 341, 343; Iraq War and, 156, 161, 163, 166–67, 171–72, 180–81

Chen Guangcheng, 265–68, 412

Chernomyrdin, Viktor, 93–94, 99

China, 4, 5, 6, 98, 209, 245, 256; Bush 41 and, 49; Chen affair, 265–68, 412; Deng Xiaoping's reforms, 22; diplomacy of, 269–70; as global power, 268, 271, 402–3; Gulf War and, 62; Iran nuclear weapons and, 339, 353, 354; Kissinger and, 34; Korean Peninsula and, 271; Obama and, 261, 265–72, 276, 292; Paris climate agreement and, 272; South China Sea claims, 270, 386; Syria and, 325; Trump and, 397, 402, 405; U.S.-China dialogues, 266, 267, 271–72; U.S. in Libya and, 317; U.S. relations with, 5, 8, 265–72, 291, 390–91

Chirac, Jacques, 130

Chollet, Derek, 49

Christopher, Warren, 5, 81, 98, 106, 114–16, 392; transition memo to, 402, 415, 418–19, 430–34; as secretary of state, 5, 81, 98, 106, 114–16, 396

climate change, 5, 12, 272, 296, 392; Paris climate agreement, 272, 398, 405

Clinton, Bill, 80, 98, 190, 227, 247, 282; Bosnian War and, 105–6; Albright as secretary of state, 115–17, 120, 127, 129, 177; Camp David talks and Clinton Parameters, 141–42, 144, 451; Christopher as secretary of state, 5, 81, 98, 106, 114–16, 396; Cuny case and, 101; ILA and, 137–38; Iran and, 338; Iraqi sanctions, 138; Jordan and, 118, 120, 126, 128, 130–32; Libyan secret talks, 191; Moscow visit, 104–5; NATO expansion and, 107–11; Operation Desert Fox, 136; Palestinian reform and, 179; Russian policy, 90, 91, 93–94, 98, 104, 109; transition memo to Christopher, 4–5, 81, 396, 402, 415, 418–19, 430–34; Wye River Memorandum, 126; Yeltsin and, 93, 103–5, 108–9

Clinton, Hillary, 247, 250, 268, 390; Asia and, 269, 270; Assad, Syria,
and, 323–25, 327–28; Benghazi attack and, 320; bin Laden's killing and, 253–55; Burns and, 247–50, 254–56, 261–62, 265–68, 274–75, 280–82, 286, 299, 304, 306, 307, 323–24, 352; China and Chen affair, 265–68, 412; Egypt's Arab Spring, Mubarak, and, 294, 300–301, 304–7; European allies and, 272–73; Suha Arafat and, 247–48; Gates and, 251; India and, 261–62, 269; Iran diplomacy and, 345–46; Iran nuclear deal and, 352, 353, 356, 357, 360; Iraq War vote, 247; Lavrov and Russian "reset," 275; leadership of, 268; Libya and, 314, 315; Moscow trip, 281–82; Putin's animus against, 286; Russia and, 274–75, 288; as secretary of state, 245, 247–88; START agreement and, 281

Cohen, Bill, 127

Cold War, 6, 21 48, 396; containment doctrine, 401–2; ending, 3, 4, 43, 55, 58; post–Cold War order, 79–80, 393, 406–7

Collins, Jim, 25

Cretz, Gene, 314

Crimea, 233, 290, 413

Crocker, Ryan, 146, 160, 165, 171

Cuba, 52, 62, 115

Cui Tiankai, 267–68

Cuny, Fred, 84, 99–103

Czech Republic, 53, 109, 230; U.S. missile sites and, 231, 233, 234, 275, 280

Dai Bingguo, 269–70

Daley, Bill, 121–22, 295

Dayton Agreement, 107, 414

Deng Xiaoping, 22, 268

Desert Shield, 60

Desert Storm, 64–65, 78, 79, 119, 159, 162, 409; American stature in Middle East and, 6, 338; U.S.-led coalition, 62–63, 67, 133, 137, 173–74, 408, 409

diplomacy, 10–12; adaptability and, 296, 406, 416–17; Bull's description, 20; challenges, 213; "clientitis," 134;

CNN effect, 393; complexities, U.S.-Russia relations, 242; credibility and, 387; future of U.S., 389–90, 402–23; importance today, 406; inversion of force and, 149, 245, 253, 295, 389, 393, 394, 407; Iran nuclear deal and, 330–84; Israeli withdrawal from Lebanon and, 30–31; Kissinger's description, 10; limits of, 292; new domestic compact for, 12, 406, 417–21; Obama's reshaping of, 397–98; Palmerston on, 406; physical risk and, 416–17; post–Cold War, 79–80, 393, 406–7; post-9/11, 117, 158–59, 168, 172, 179, 190, 407; roles and qualities of good diplomats, 10, 12, 407–13; secret talks with Libya, 190–95; showing up, Central Asia and, 279; technology and new realities, 393; tending the garden, 30; as tool of first resort, 406, 419; Trump and, 9, 12, 13, 397–99; updating and reinventing, 413–21. *See also* U.S. State Department; *specific countries; specific crises*
Djerejian, Ed, 25
Donilon, Tom, 251, 255, 263, 267, 269, 294, 295, 301, 302, 357, 361–62, 370
Duberstein, Ken, 36
Dudayev, Dzhokhar, 84, 95–96, 100
Dulles, John Foster, 118, 129

Eagleburger, Lawrence, 46, 64, 78, 81
East Asia Summit, 269
Egypt, 20, 151, 319; Arab Spring and, 284, 293–96, 299–313, 314, 335; Burns's summer in, 18–19; Burns visits, post-revolution, 303–6; Bush 43 meeting with foreign minister, 186–87; Camp David Accords, 21, 293; Eilts as U.S. ambassador, 18, 19; mood of, 153; Mubarak deposed, 293–95, 299–304, 306, 312, 313; Muslim Brotherhood and Morsi, 304, 306–10, 311, 312, 313; Obama's Cairo speech, 297, 298; post-Qaddafi Libya and, 321; Saudi Arabia, the UAE, and, 308; Sisi takeover, 308–10, 312–13; as U.S. ally, Gulf War, 60–61; U.S. Middle East policy and, 293; U.S. aid to, 300
Eilts, Conrad, 18–19
Eilts, Hermann F., 18–19
Einhorn, Bob, 48–49, 349, 351–52, 359
ElBaradei, Mohamed, 309, 349, 351, 352
Erdoğan, Recep Tayyip, 353–54
Europe/European Union (EU), 3, 7, 209, 391; Bush 43's Roadmap initiative and, 187; Eastern Europe, post–Cold War, 33; Egypt revolt and, 309–10; EU-3/P5+1 Iran nuclear negotiations, 339–45, 348–50, 354, 358, 360, 361, 364–69, 374–79, 381, 382, 386; future of U.S. and, 403; Iran sanctions and, 354; Libya intervention and, 317; Poland, Hungary, and Soviet breakup, 51, 53; Russia, Ukraine, and, 288; Syrian intervention and, 329, 330; Syrian refugees in, 322, 413; Syrian sanctions and, 325

Fabius, Laurent, 378, 379
Fahd of Saudi Arabia, 57, 60
Faisal of Jordan, 137
Fayyad, Salam, 183, 188
Feith, Doug, 161, 165, 187
Feltman, Jeff, 316
Ford, Gerald, 130
Ford, Robert, 324
France: Iran nuclear deal and, 378, 379; Minsk agreement, 291; NATO expansion and, 230, 238, 241; Obama and, 272–73; Russia-Georgia conflict and, 241; Syrian intervention, 329, 330
Friedman, Tom, 49, 62
Fukuyama, Frank, 48, 54, 55

G-7 and G-8, 93, 99, 131, 133, 215, 218, 228, 235, 256, 287
G-20, 262, 275, 288, 325, 331, 350
Gaidar, Yegor, 90
Gannon, Matthew, 148
Gardiner, Colonel, 124

Garner, Jay, 175
Gates, Bob, 50, 394; secretary of defense, Bush 43, 220–21, 224, 232, 234–35, 341; secretary of defense, Obama, 251, 254–55, 280, 301, 315, 327
Gates Foundation, 11
Genscher, Hans-Dietrich, 55, 61
Georgia, 111, 201, 212, 221–22, 225; attack on Tskhinvali, South Ossetia, 241; breakaway republics in, 201, 221; NATO membership and, 230, 233, 239–40, 241, 413; Rose Revolution, 209, 221, 222, 229, 278; Russian aggression in, 273, 274, 278, 285, 345, 350
Germany: as ally, Gulf War, 61; Burns and family in, 84–85; fall of the Berlin Wall, 53; G-8 summit, 235; Helsinki Act, 54; Minsk agreement, 291; NATO and, 54, 55, 230, 238, 241; Obama and, 272–73; reunification, 3, 44, 54–56, 61, 76, 77, 107; UN Security Council and, 263
Gibbs, Robert, 295
Glaspie, April, 57–58
globalization, 4, 6–7, 12, 392, 396
Global War on Terrorism, 208
Goldberg, Jeff, 321
Gorbachev, Mikhail, 3, 6, 44, 50–53, 55, 56, 67, 90, 216; Helsinki summit, 61; Malta summit, 53–54; putsch against, 76; resignation, 77; Sinatra Doctrine, 51
Gore, Al, 91, 93–94, 98, 101
Grachev, Pavel, 96
Graham, Tom, 48
Grozny, Chechnya, 82, 83, 96–97, 100, 102
Guldimann, Tim, 340
Gulf War, 44, 45, 56–65, 119, 133, 338; restraint of Bush 41 and ending of, 65, 409; UN resolution and, 62, 63, 64, 65. See also Desert Shield; Desert Storm
Gusinsky, Aleksandr, 89

Hadley, Steve, 220, 232, 258, 259, 344
Hagel, Chuck, 244

Haig, Alexander, 22
Hamad, Amir, 155
Hamas, 130, 190, 307
Hamzeh, prince of Jordan, 123
Hannah, John, 49, 76
Hariri, Rafik, 154, 196
Hassan of Jordan, 121–29, 133
Helms, Jesse, 116, 117
Hezbollah, 35, 326, 332
Hof, Fred, 324–25
Hoffman, David, 62
Holbrooke, Richard, 106–7
Hourani, Albert, 24, 124
Hu Jintao, 269
Hungary, 51, 109, 230
Hun Sen, 270
Husseini, Feisal, 69–70, 71, 73
Hussein of Jordan, 24, 27, 28, 31, 40, 57, 67, 112–13, 118–23, 126–31, 247, 420; Burns and, 112, 120, 128; B. Clinton and, 120, 126, 128; Dulles on, 118; Madrid Peace Conference and, 72; successor, 121–29; Wye River Memorandum, 126, 128, 139
Hussein, Saddam, 3, 15, 30, 31, 57, 61, 67, 119, 412; Bush ultimatum to, 63; governance of Iraq and, 56–57; Gulf War and, 44, 45, 64–65; invasion of Kuwait, 56, 57–58; Iran-Iraq War and, 30, 37; missile fired at the USS *Stark*, 38; plot to assassinate Bush 41, 136; radical nationalism of, 65–66; regional concerns about, 156; repression by, 72; sons of, 137; toppling, 162, 163–65, 173, 174, 190, 196; UN Resolution 1441 and, 172; U.S. policy and, 30, 57–59, 156; U.S. regime change goal and, 135–38, 156–57, 161, 163, 164, 167–69, 171–72, 179, 190, 195; WMD and, 135–36, 152, 162, 165–66, 169, 172, 173, 197, 412

Ikenberry, John, 48
India, 8, 209, 245, 391, 403; back-channel talks; Bharatiya Janata Party, 264; Burns and Modi, 264–65; Bush 43 and, 257–61; Obama and, 256–57, 261–65, 291,

292; Pakistan and, 262–63; UN Security Council and, 263–64

Indonesia, 270

Indyk, Martin, 191, 192

International Atomic Energy Agency (IAEA), 259–60, 309; Iran and, 338, 349, 351, 352, 358, 384

Iran, 34, 58, 65, 98, 269; American hostage crisis, 21, 338, 357, 417; denounces 9/11, 158; election of Khatami, 151; Iraq War and, 169, 177, 196, 197; Israeli seizure of arms shipment, 180; Middle East instability and, 385; nuclear weapons and, 212, 245, 273, 276, 280, 295, 334, 338–39, 350–51, 354–55, 362, 364, 369–70, 377; Obama's diplomacy, 273, 295, 345–48; presidential elections and Green Movement, 348–49; Qaboos and secret talks, 155; release of American hikers, 356–57; Russia and, 227, 232–34, 275–78, 282; sanctions on, 220, 339, 342, 343, 350, 353, 354, 364–65, 372, 379, 384, 386; Stuxnet and, 355; Syria and, 322, 326, 332; U.S. missile defense and, 231, 233, 275, 276, 277, 280; U.S. policy and, 8, 65, 160, 165, 291, 361. *See also* Iran nuclear deal

Iran-Contra affair, 8, 35–36, 338

Iranian Revolution, 22, 37, 159

Iran-Iraq War, 24, 30, 31, 37, 49, 56; Iraq fires on the USS *Stark*, 38; UN-brokered cease-fire, 39; U.S. reflagging of Kuwaiti ships, 37–38; USS *Samuel B. Roberts* strikes Iranian mine, 39; USS *Vincennes* shoots Iranian airliner, 39

Iran nuclear deal (JPOA and JCPOA), 330–31, 337–85, 414; Burns and Jalili, 351–52, 353; Burns and Omani back channel, 330–31, 337–38, 356–77, 383; Burns and Ryabkov, 350; Talwar and, 348; France and, 378, 379; Obama-Rouhani conversation, 374–75; P5+1 and, 339–45, 348–52, 354, 358, 360, 361, 364–69, 374–79,

381, 382, 386; Qom and, 350–53; Russia and, 350, 352, 353, 378; as triumph of diplomacy, 383–84, 414; TRR proposal and, 349–50, 352, 353–54, 358; Trump and, 385, 386–87, 398

Iraq: Anbar Province, 16; Burns in, 15–17, 319; Fallujah, 16; Jordan and, 119, 135, 136–38; Kurds and, 72, 135, 163; Kuwaiti invasion and Gulf War, 45, 56–65, 119, 159; ISIS in, 322; Murphy and Aziz, 31–32; 9/11 and, 165; Oil for Food Program, 138; Operation Desert Fox, 136; post-Saddam planning, 171, 174; smart sanctions on, 138, 156, 159, 160, 170; U.S. regime change goal, 135–38, 156–57, 161, 163, 164, 167–69, 171–72, 179, 190, 195

Iraqi National Congress, 164

Iraq Liberation Act (ILA), 137–38, 164

Iraq War, 6, 173–78, 298, 315, 408; Abu Ghraib and, 178, 197; Blackwater contractors killed, 177–78; Burns's evaluation of, 196–99, 203; Bush's televised speech on, 173; Coalition Provisional Authority, 175–76, 178; failure of diplomacy and, 394; fall of Mosul, 333; "Future of Iraq" project, 171; inversion of force and diplomacy and, 149, 393, 394; Iran's gains from, 338; Kurds and, 177; misguided U.S. decisions, 174, 175–76, 197–200; Obama and, 244, 295; opponents, 166; "The Perfect Storm" memo and, 168–69; proponents, 161–65, 167, 168, 171–72; Putin's view of, 209; State Department advice on, 162, 163, 165–72; U.S. Congress vote on, 172, 247; WMD and, 165–66, 172, 173

ISIS, 321, 322, 333–34

Ismaily, Salem, 356–59, 363, 368, 369

Israel, 404; Baker and, 66–75; Burns's trip to, 153; Camp David Accords, 21, 293; Hamas and, 307; Iran nuclear threat and, 339, 355; Iraqi Scud missile strikes in, 64; Jenin refugee camp incident, 183–84; Jordan and, 119, 123, 130, 135;

Israel (*cont'd*):
    Lebanon and, 30–31, 154; nuclear
    weapons and, 257; Obama and, 297,
    334; Operation Defensive Shield,
    181–84; Palestinian conflict, Bush
    43 years, 178–90; PLO terrorism
    in, 66, 153, 181, 182, 183; Sharon's
    election, 150; Syria and, 69, 73, 75,
    139–41, 155; U.S. relations with, 64,
    67, 141, 404; West Bank and Gaza,
    40, 49, 66, 67, 139, 189; Wye River
    Memorandum, 126, 139
Israeli-Palestinian peace talks, 30, 40,
    66–75, 160–61, 188–89, 295, 305;
    Bush 43's Roadmap, 187–89;
    Clinton Parameters, 141–42, 144,
    178, 451; Madrid Peace Conference,
    3–4, 6, 13, 70, 72–75, 389, 394,
    409; Oslo Accords, 75, 119, 139,
    182; two-state solution, 139–40,
    144, 149, 180, 181, 185, 187, 404–5
Ivanov, Igor, 201
Ivanov, Sergey, 201, 202, 213, 214, 227,
    228

Jalili, Saeed, 344, 351, 353, 365, 368
Japan, 49, 79, 263, 269, 403
Johnson, Lyndon B., 61, 114
Jones, Deborah, 321
Jones, Jim, 251, 277
Jordan, 112–46; Abdullah's leadership,
    132–46; Aqaba, 248–49; Arab-
    Israeli peace talks and, 40; Burns
    as U.S. ambassador, 8, 112–45,
    298–99, 420–21; Burns's first
    diplomatic post, 15–17, 23–28, 113,
    298; Bush 43 and, 186–87; GID
    and, 119, 125, 133; B. Clinton and,
    118, 120, 126, 128, 130–32; Hassan
    and, 121–29, 133; Howeitat tribe,
    26; Hussein's leadership, 118–22;
    Iraq and, 119, 135, 136–38; Israel
    and, 123, 130, 135; Madrid Peace
    Conference and, 71, 72; Palestinians
    and, 27, 118, 135, 139–40; problems
    in, 118–19; Qualifying Industrial
    Zones program, 132; refugee camps
    in, 122; refusal to join Desert Storm
    coalition, 67, 133, 137; risks for
    diplomats in, 27, 120–21; Syria

and, 119, 133, 140–41; terrorism
    in, 120–21; U.S. embassy, Amman,
    15, 24–25, 27, 120; U.S. Libyan
    intervention and, 316; Zarqa, 27

Kaabneh, Abdul Hafez Marei, 126
Kabariti, Abdul Karim, 126–27, 133
Kadyrov, Ramzan, 217
Kansteiner, Walter, 49
Kappes, Steve, 194
Karimov, Islam, 77–78, 279
Kasparov, Garry, 216
Katatni, Saad al-, 310
Kazakhstan, 95, 279
Kemerovo, Siberia, 88–89
Kennan, George, 47–48, 78, 85, 109, 111,
    203, 204, 394, 401, 418
Kennedy, John F., 34
Kennedy, Pat, 115, 116
Kerik, Bernie, 177
Kerry, John, 247, 248; Burns and,
    248–49, 289, 309–10, 321, 381,
    388; climate change and, 272; Iran
    nuclear deal and, 357, 359, 370,
    372–74, 377–79, 381, 382, 394; Iraq
    War vote, 247; as secretary of state,
    245–49, 264, 272, 288–89, 309,
    359, 367; Syria and, 288, 328–30,
    332; U.S.-India partnership and,
    264; U.S.-Russia relations and, 288
Khaji, Ali Asghar, 363, 365–66, 367
Khalaf, Rima, 125
Khamenei, Ayatollah, 342, 348, 356,
    357, 365, 368, 371, 384–85
Kharazi, Kamal, 340
Khatami, Mohammad, 151, 338
Khatib, Abdul-Ilah al-, 125
Khodorkovsky, Mikhail, 207, 235
Khomeini, Ayatollah, 58
Kim Jong-un, 271
Kimmitt, Bob, 46–47
Kislovodsk, Russia, 43
Kissinger, Henry, 10, 25, 34, 46, 48, 175,
    268, 388, 418
Klebnikov, Paul, 223
Kohl, Helmut, 55, 61
Korzhakov, Aleksandr, 89
Kosovo, 229–30, 232, 233, 234, 236,
    237
Kozyrev, Andrey, 98, 108

Kurtzer, Dan, 41, 48, 70, 74, 143, 451
Kusa, Musa, 160, 192, 193, 194, 314–15
Kuwait, 37, 56, 60, 133, 145, 155; Iraqi invasion of, 57–58, 64–65; post–Gulf War, 69

Lake, Tony, 107
Larocco, Jim, 145–46, 157, 340
Latin America, 256, 405
Lavrov, Sergey, 201, 205, 214, 237, 238, 274, 281, 350; diplomacy and Syrian conflict, 325, 328–29, 332; Iran nuclear negotiations and, 345, 378
Lawrence, T. E., 248
Lebanon, 24; American hostages in, 35; battleship *New Jersey* shelling of, 394; bombing of U.S. embassy, 26, 338, 417; bombing of U.S. Marine barracks, 26, 338; Hariri assassination, 196; Hezbollah in Iraq, 326, 330, 332; Israel and, 30–31, 154; Satterfield as ambassador, 146; Syria and, 154, 196
Leon, Bernardino, 310–12
Libya: al-Qaeda in, 321; Arab Spring and, 284, 314–18, 335; Benghazi and, 284, 314, 317, 318, 319–20, 417; Burns and Kusa, 160, 314–15; Burns's reports to Kerry, 321; Lockerbie bombing and terrorism, 39–40, 148, 160, 190, 191, 193, 194; post-Qaddafi, 316–17, 319, 321–22, 335, 413; Qaddafi and, 147–49, 313–18; sanctions on, 33, 191, 195, 314; U.S. embassy, Tripoli, 314, 321; U.S. diplomacy and, 149, 158, 190–95, 314; U.S. intervention, 314–18, 321–23, 335
Litvinenko, Aleksandr, 223
Lugar, Dick, 243–45
Lula da Silva, Luiz Inácio, 353–54
Luzhkov, Yuri, 240

Macmillan, Harold, 296
Madrid Peace Conference, 3–4, 6, 13, 70, 72–75, 389, 394, 409
Mamedov, Georgiy, 93
Marshall, George, 47–48

Marshall Plan, 48, 397
Maruf, Taha Mohieddin, 130
Maskhadov, Aslan, 96, 102
Mattis, Jim, 394
McCain, John, 248, 421
McDonough, Denis, 251–52, 295, 330
McFarlane, Bud, 35
McFaul, Mike, 273–74, 277, 279, 283, 286–87
McRaven, Bill, 254, 255, 256
Medvedev, Dmitry, 201, 214, 227–28, 229, 232, 234, 236, 240, 278, 279; Biden and Burns visit and, 284; H. Clinton and Burns visit and, 281; Iran nuclear deal and, 353; Obama and, 269, 273, 275–77, 280, 281, 287, 350; U.S. intervention in Libya and, 317; U.S. visit, 282–83
Menon, Shivshankar, 262–63, 264
Merkel, Angela, 239, 273
Meshal, Khaled, 130, 190
Middle East, 5, 6, 329; autocratic governance in, 296–97, 298, 313, 404, 411; Burns's recommendations, post-9/11, 159; Burns's trips to, 69, 153–57, 181–84, 188–89; Burns's view of Egypt's Mubarak and the Arab Spring, 301–3, 335; Bush 43's policies and, 187–89, 297; H. Clinton's Doha address, 298; dysfunction and economic problems, 150–51; educational systems in, 297; Gulf War and U.S. influence in, 6, 63–65, 338; instability of, 298, 385, 391, 404; Iran as threat in, 339, 347; Islamists in, 5, 59; Israeli-Palestinian dispute and, 24, 178–90; new generation of leaders, 150–51, 297; Obama's strategy, 334, 335, 404; Policy Planning Staff's position on Saddam's aggression, 58–59; post-Qaddafi Libya and, 321; Qaddafi disliked in, 316; radical nationalism, 65–66; regional development bank proposed, 65; Russia as partner in, 332; Sunni and Shia competition, 169, 174, 176, 177, 197, 198, 244, 333; Syrian civil war and Gulf Arabs, 322; Syrian refugees and,

Middle East (*cont'd*):
322; U.S. drone strikes and, 252, 253, 295; U.S. partners in, 339, 359, 360, 361, 386, 404; U.S. policy and, 56–57, 65, 67, 156, 159–63, 178, 196, 246, 285, 293, 295–99, 334–35, 345, 404; U.S. seen as abandoning Mubarak, 303, 313, 314, 316, 330; U.S. seen as wavering on Syria, 330; women's rights in, 297. *See also specific countries*
Miles, Dick, 88
Miller, Aaron, 48, 67, 70, 74, 180
Mills, Cheryl, 265
missile defense strategy: Bush 41 and, 52; Bush 43 and, 227, 231, 232–34, 236, 238; Obama and, 267, 275–80; phased adaptive approach, 280; Russian concerns, 231, 275, 276–77, 278
Mitchell, George, 323
Modi, Narendra, 264–65
Mohammadnia, Davoud, 363
Mohammed VI of Morocco, 154
Moniz, Ernie, 382
Morocco, 151, 154
Morsi, Mohamed, 306–10, 312
Muallem, Walid, 328
Muasher, Marwan, 187
Mubarak, Hosni, 57, 60–61, 67, 69, 72, 130, 142, 151, 153–54, 163, 166, 412; Arab Spring and overthrow of, 293–95, 299–304, 306, 312, 313, 314, 324; Obama and, 295, 300, 301–2, 335; Sharm el-Sheikh summit, 188
Mulford, David, 259
Muna, princess of Jordan, 124
Munich Security Conference, 302
Murphy, Dick, 29–32, 40–41, 146
Murrow, Edward R., 414
Musharraf, Pervez, 263
Muslim Brotherhood, 304, 306, 308–113

Naga, Fayza Abul, 307
Nagy, Imre, 51
NATO: Bosnian War and, 106; Bucharest summit, 236, 239; expansion, 55–56, 91, 92, 98, 105, 107–11, 208, 225, 230, 413; future

of, 403; intervention in Libya and, 317; Partnership for Peace, 108; Russian agreement with, 109; unified Germany and, 54, 55; Membership Action Plan, 221, 230, 232–34, 236–40
Nazarbayev, Nursultan, 279
Negroponte, John, 37–38, 178
Nemtsov, Boris, 216
neoconservatives, 161, 196, 221, 408
Nephew, Richard, 359
Netanyahu, Benjamin, 66, 128, 130, 139, 297, 355, 377
Nicaragua, 35, 52
Nidal, Abu, 192
Nides, Tom, 320–21
Niebuhr, Reinhold, 408
9/11 terrorist attack, 8, 157–61, 256; diplomacy post–9/11, 117, 158–59, 165, 168, 172, 179, 190, 395, 407; Putin support for the U.S. and, 208, 277
Nixon, Richard, 268; NSC and, 34
Noor, queen of Jordan, 112–13, 123, 126
North, Oliver, 35
North Caucasus, 94–95, 99–103
North Korea, 212, 231, 234, 257, 271; sanctions on, 220; Six Party Talks, 271
Nuclear Suppliers Group, 258, 259–60
Nunn, Sam, 243–44
Nunn-Lugar program, 78

Oakley, Bob, 36, 37–38, 39
Obama, Barack, 243–92, 394, 397, 402; Afghanistan War and, 273; Arab Spring and, 284, 287, 293–96, 299–318, 335; Burns and, 8, 243–45, 333, 362, 367–68, 381; Burns's overview of, 291–92, 335–36; Bush 41 model and, 246, 292; Cairo speech, 297, 298; China visit, 276; climate change and, 296; H. Clinton as secretary of state, 245, 247–88; Deputies Committee, 251–52; diplomacy as first tool, 345; domestic concerns, 276; drones and special operations, 253, 295; Egypt and Mubarak, 293–96, 299–313, 335; European allies and, 272–73,

317, 318–19; Iran, secret message to the Ayatollah, 348; Iran, videotaped Nowruz message, 347–48; Iran nuclear deal and, 337–84; Iraq War and, 244, 295, 323; Kerry as secretary of state, 245–49, 264, 272, 288–89, 309, 359, 367; killing of bin Laden, 253–56, 359; leadership of, 250–53; "leading from behind," 318; Libyan intervention, 315–18, 321–23; Medvedev and, 269, 274, 275–77, 282–83; Middle East and, 246, 295–99, 334–35, 345, 404; missile defense strategy, 267, 275–80; in Moscow, 243–45; national security advisors, 251, 252, 269; nuclear nonproliferation and, 296; Pakistan and, 261–63; Putin and, 244, 277–79, 288, 290, 325; regime change and, 285, 330, 348, 364, 371; short- vs. long-game strategy, 245, 293, 296, 305, 318–19, 322, 323, 334, 335, 397–98; Syria policy, 252–53, 322–36; TPP and, 269; U.S.-China relations, 261, 265–72, 291, 292; U.S.-India partnership, 256, 261–65, 269, 291, 292; U.S.-Russia reset, 242, 246, 273–84, 288, 291–92, 350, 353

Obeidi, Abdelati, 192
Oman, 155, 330, 331, 356–77, 383
Organization for Security and Co-operation in Europe, 102, 108
Oslo Accords, 75, 119, 139, 182

Pakistan, 10, 39, 253–54, 257, 276; back-channel talks; Obama and, 261, 262–63; A. Q. Khan network, 192
Palestinians and Palestine Liberation Organization (PLO), 31, 40, 49; Baker and peace talks, 66–75; Bush 43's Roadmap initiative, 187–89; Israeli conflict, Bush 43 years, 178–90; Jordan and, 135, 139–40; non-PLO leaders, 69–70, 71; Obama and, 297, 334; refugee camps, 113, 183–84; Second Intifada, 138, 150, 159, 178–79; Sharon protests, 142; terrorism by, 33, 66, 153, 181, 182, 183; UNRWA

and, 183; U.S. dialogue with, 66; West Bank and Gaza conflict, 49, 66, 73, 139, 179–80, 189; Wye River Memorandum, 126, 139. *See also* Arafat, Yasser; Israeli-Palestinian peace talks
Palmerston, Lord, 406
Panama Canal Treaty, 21
Panetta, Leon, 253, 255, 327
Pankin, Boris, 73, 74
Passman, Otto, 420
Patterson, Anne, 306
Pearce, David, 168
Peres, Shimon, 31
Perry, Bill, 107
Petraeus, David, 327–28
Pickering, Tom, 60, 86–90, 97, 98, 99–101, 104, 410
Poindexter, John, 34–35
Poland, 51, 109, 230; U.S. missile sites and, 231, 233, 234, 275, 280
Politkovskaya, Anna, 223
Powell, Colin, 152, 159–60, 162, 395; Bosnian War and, 78; Burns and, 39, 42, 145, 152, 155, 159–60, 166, 172–73, 174, 175, 176, 180–82, 185, 188, 195, 198, 203, 204, 340; as Bush 41's chairman of Joint Chiefs of Staff, 45, 78; Iran nuclear weapons and, 340; Iraq War and, 164, 166–70, 172, 175; Israeli-Palestinian conflict and, 160–61, 180–82, 185; 9/11 and, 157, 159–60; NSC and, 36–37, 251, 252, 395; Operation Desert Shield and, 60; "The Perfect Storm" memo and, 169; Reagan and, 38, 41; as secretary of state, 145, 151–52, 156, 159–60, 162, 164–76, 178–82, 186–88, 195, 198, 203, 251, 340; smart sanctions and Iraq, 156, 159, 170; UN speech, 172–73
Power, Samantha, 300–301, 315
Pritzker, Penny, 264
Putin, Vladimir, 6, 8, 206–42, 270, 273, 413; Arab Spring and, 284–85; as Arab world partner, 332; Beslan massacre and, 208–9; Biden and Burns visit, 284–85; Bucharest summit, 239, 241; Burns and,

Putin, Vladimir (*cont'd*):
    200–202, 213, 228–29, 236–38,
    277–83; Bush 43 and, 208, 213,
    220, 235, 236, 239–40, 277–78,
    290; character and personality,
    206–7, 224, 237, 239, 278, 281–82;
    Chechen conflict, 84, 99, 208; H.
    Clinton and Burns visit, 281–82;
    concept of sovereign democracy, 215;
    corruption and excess, 223; Crimea
    and, 290, 413; disinformation and,
    117; "dizziness from success" and,
    225; election meddling by, 242,
    391, 413; Eurasian Economic Union
    and, 288, 289; Gates and, 223–24,
    234; Georgia, Ukraine, and,
    221–22, 236–38, 240, 241, 278,
    285, 288–90, 386, 391; Kosovo and,
    229–30; Medvedev and, 234, 240,
    276, 278, 282, 284–85; Munich
    Security Conference and, 223–24;
    NATO expansion and, 230–32,
    237–38, 240; Novo Ogaryovo
    dacha, 236, 277, 281; Obama and,
    277–83, 288, 290, 325; opponents
    and critics, 216, 223; personal
    animus for H. Clinton, 286;
    relations with the U.S., 158, 208–10,
    213, 218, 219, 224, 226–29, 231–32,
    235–38, 277–83; return to power,
    285–86, 287, 331; Rice meets with,
    200–202; Saakashvili and, 221,
    230, 240, 241; successor for, 213,
    222, 225–29; Syria and, 331–32,
    333; troubles in Russia and, 226;
    Trump and, 399–400; U.S. Libyan
    intervention and, 317; U.S. long-
    game strategy, 403; U.S. missile
    defense concerns, 231, 232, 278;
    U.S.-Russian reset and, 278–79,
    288, 291–92; wildlife conservation,
    281–82

Qaboos of Oman, 155, 356, 357, 376
Qaddafi, Muammar al-, 33, 40, 130,
    147–49, 158, 313–14; Arab Spring
    and U.S. intervention, 284, 313–18,
    335; Burns and, 147–49; death
    of, 285, 318; difficulties with,
    194–95; negotiated abandonment

of terrorism and WMD, 190–95,
    219–20, 313, 317, 409
Qaddafi, Saif al-Islam, 194, 316
Qatar, 155, 298, 307, 310, 315, 321

Rabin, Yitzhak, 75
Rania of Jordan, 112, 124, 146, 247
Raphel, Arnie, 39
Rashid of Jordan, 126
Ravanchi, Majid Takht-, 370, 371, 373,
    377, 379, 380–81, 382
Rawabdeh, Abdul Raouf, 133
Reagan, Ronald, 191, 295; Baker and,
    46–47; foreign policy legacy, 41;
    Gorbachev and the Soviet Union,
    50; Haig as secretary of state, 22;
    Iran-Contra affair, 8, 35–36; Iran-
    Iraq War and, 37–38; Lebanon
    and, 33–34; NSC and, 34; PLO,
    Arafat and, 41, 66; Rumsfeld and,
    26; Shultz as secretary of state, 29,
    30, 40–41; terrorist attacks during
    term, 33, 39–40
Remler, Philip, 101–2
Rhodes, Ben, 295, 300
Rice, Condoleezza, 151–52, 169, 171, 185,
    186, 251, 369; Bucharest summit,
    239; Burns and, 200–204, 207, 211,
    218, 224, 225, 232–34, 241, 260,
    345, 410; Burns's messages about
    Putin and Russia, 224, 225, 232–34,
    239–40; Burns's posting to Moscow
    and, 203–4; Burns's transition
    note to, 195–96, 340; India nuclear
    agreement and, 258–59, 260;
    Moscow visit, 235; P5+1 nuclear
    negotiations and, 343, 345; Putin
    and, 200–202, 211, 220, 221, 410;
    as secretary of state, 195, 200–260
Rice, Susan, 251, 263, 300, 315, 318,
    329, 269, 353, 370
Richer, Rob, 127
Romania, 53
Rood, John, 259, 260–61
Roosevelt, Franklin Delano, 215
Roosevelt, Theodore, 422
Ross, Dennis, 33, 36, 39, 46; Baker
    and, 45–78; Bosnian War paper,
    78; on German reunification, 55;
    on Middle East peace, 67; Obama

and, 295; as Policy Planning Staff director, 46–49, 53, 78; on Saddam Hussein, 57, 58; Soviet Union's dissolution and, 76

Rouhani, Hassan, 368, 369, 372, 373, 384

Roule, Norm, 359, 382

Rumsfeld, Donald, 26, 151, 161, 164, 167, 173, 175, 185, 197, 220, 341

Rusk, Dean, 269

Russia (former Soviet Union), 245, 269; Afghanistan War and, 22, 49, 159; American primacy and, 4; Arab Spring and, 284; Arab states and, 6; Balkan diplomacy and, 92; Bosnian War and, 106; Burns and Biden visit, 284–85; Burns and H. Clinton visit, 281–82; Burns and Holbrooke visit, 106–7; Burns and Obama in, 243–45, 276–78; Burns and Soviet Union's dissolution, 76–78; Burns as U.S. ambassador, 8, 200–242; Burns as U.S. minister-counselor, 85–110; Burns's cables from, 91–92, 107–8, 207, 209–11, 221, 223, 239–40; Burns delivers Obama-Clinton letters, 273–75; Burns's evaluation of, 286; Burns's North Caucasus travels, 94–95, 99–103; Burns's "Russia Strategy" email, 457–59; Burns's trips to, 217, 281–82, 286–87; Bush 41 and, 43–44, 49–56, 61, 76–78; Bush 43 and, 187, 200–242, 292; Chechen conflict, 82–84, 96–103, 435–46; B. Clinton and, 5, 104–5; coup attempt in, 76; Crimea annexation, 290, 413; dissolution of the Soviet Union, 4, 5, 33, 43–45, 49–56, 76–78, 413; economy of, 90–91, 207, 225; election meddling in U.S. and Europe, 229, 242, 286, 391, 413; FSB, 102–3; G-8 and, 93, 99, 215, 218, 228, 235, 287; Georgia and, 241, 273, 274, 276, 285, 345, 350; Gore-Chernomyrdin Commission, 93–94; Gulf War and, 62; Iran and, 227, 232–34, 275, 278, 280, 282, 339, 350, 352–54; Iran-Iraq War and, 37, 38; Iran nuclear deal and, 345, 378; Iraq War and, 209; Jackson-Vanik Amendment and, 212, 218, 238, 287; joint statement denouncing Iraq's Kuwaiti invasion, 58; Kissinger and, 34; Madrid Peace Conference and, 69, 70; Magnitsky Act, 288; McFaul as U.S. ambassador, 286–87; media in, 97; MGIMO, 215; middle class and, 285–86; Moscow, 89–90; Moscow Metro, 215; murder of journalists, 223; murder of Nemtsov, 216; NATO expansion concerns, 55–56, 91, 92, 105, 107–8, 111, 208, 221, 225, 230, 232, 236, 413; Near Abroad, 91; NGOs restricted in, 222; nuclear cooperation and, 211–12, 219–20, 234; Nunn-Lugar program, 78, 243; Obama and U.S. "reset," 242, 246, 273–81, 283–84, 288, 291–92, 350, 353; Pickering as U.S. ambassador, 86–90, 97–101, 104; Qaddafi's enriched uranium sent to, 219–20; Rice visits, 235; Snowden, 288; Spaso House, 204–5, 214, 243, 244; spy scandal, 283; START agreement, 52, 234, 274, 276, 280–81, 282; surveillance of U.S. ambassador, 204–5; Syria and, 67, 284, 322, 325–27, 333, 391; technology sector, 282–83; U.S. and ABM Treaty, 231; U.S. consulates and staff in, 87, 205; U.S. embassy, Moscow, 85, 205; U.S. exchange programs with, 212, 220; U.S. intervention in Libya and, 317; U.S. investment and Boeing deal, 219, 420; U.S. Middle East policy and, 67; U.S. missile defense and, 231, 275, 276–77, 278, 280; U.S. relations with, 8, 82–111, 160, 200–242, 273–83, 325, 350, 403–4; U.S. senators visiting, 243–45; U.S. sports diplomacy, 205; U.S. trade with, 212, 218–19, 234, 238; Winter Olympics, Sochi, 238, 289; WTO and, 201, 212, 218, 232, 234, 236, 283, 287, 291. *See also* Gorbachev, Mikhail; Putin, Vladimir; Yeltsin, Boris

Rwanda, 315
Ryabkov, Sergey, 350

Saakashvili, Mikheil, 201, 202, 221, 230,
    240, 241, 242
Sadat, Anwar, 19, 141–43
Sadr, Muqtada al-, 177
Saleh, Ali Abdullah, 62, 155
Salehi, Ali, 382
Samore, Gary, 349, 351
Sarkozy, Nicolas, 239, 241, 317
Sarvath, princess of Jordan, 126
Satterfield, David, 29, 146
Saudi Arabia, 56, 65, 67, 133; Burns
    visits, 155–56; Bush 43 meeting
    with foreign minister, 186–87;
    Grand Mosque attack, Mecca, 159;
    Iran and, 385, 386; Jordan and,
    119; Madrid Peace Conference and,
    72–73; Operation Desert Shield
    and, 60; Sisi in Egypt and, 308; as
    U.S. ally, 60; U.S. policy and, 59
Schwarzkopf, Norman, 60
Scowcroft, Brent, 45, 46, 50–51, 60, 78,
    246, 323, 395, 409
Serbia, 78, 106
Serdyukov, Anatoliy, 235
Shalgham, Abdel Rahman, 192
Shamir, Yitzhak, 31, 40, 64, 66, 67, 69,
    70, 72–73, 75
Shapiro, Dan, 295
Sharaa, Farouk al-, 75, 141
Sharon, Ariel, 138, 142, 150, 154, 155,
    178, 179, 181, 182, 185–86, 188–90;
    Arafat and, 150, 153
Shater, Khairat el-, 310–12
Sheikh, Sharm el-, 142
Sherman, Wendy, 376–77, 379
Shevardnadze, Eduard, 50–53, 55, 58
Shultz, George, 29, 30, 32, 36, 40–41,
    115, 116, 415, 417
Singh, Manmohan, 257, 259, 261, 262,
    264
Sisi, Abdel Fattah el-, 308–10, 312–13
Snowden, Edward, 288
Sochi, Russia, 217, 236, 238, 239–40,
    289; Winter Olympics, 238, 289
Solana, Javier, 343, 344, 351
Soleimani, Qassem, 331
Solzhenitsyn, Aleksandr, 216

Soros, George, 100
South Korea, 269
South Ossetia, 201–2, 221, 230, 241,
    274
Spellings, Margaret, 220
Stalin, Josef, 95
Steinberg, Jim, 256
Stevens, Chris, 319–20, 417
Strategic Arms Reduction Treaty
    (START), 52, 234, 274, 276,
    280–81, 282
Stratford, Dick, 259
Suleiman, Omar, 294
Sullivan, Jake, 265, 267, 290–91, 302,
    381–82; Iran nuclear deal and, 358,
    362, 366–67, 371, 373–75, 379–80
Surkov, Vladislav, 214–15, 222, 227, 287
Syria, 30–31, 158, 160, 316, 412–13; Arab
    Spring and, 324, 335; assessment of
    U.S. policy, 322, 323, 327, 335–36;
    Baker and, 44, 61; Burns's views on,
    322–23, 326, 328, 329, 332–33,
    335–36; chemical weapons, 323,
    328–29, 331, 336; civil war,
    322–34; Hama, 324; Iran and, 385;
    Islamic extremists in, 326; Israel
    and, 69, 73, 75, 139–41; Jordan and,
    119, 133, 140–41; Lebanon and, 154,
    196; Obama and, 252–53, 322–34;
    Obama's "red line" and, 328,
    329–30, 332, 336; refugee camps,
    113; Russia and, 67, 225, 284, 288,
    331–32, 391; sanctions on, 325;
    U.S. ambassadors to, 146, 324; U.S.
    involvement in, 323, 333, 386

Tajikistan, 279
Talabani, Jalal, 177
Talbott, Strobe, 93, 106–7, 110, 117
Taliban, 158, 160, 161, 164, 208, 328
Talwar, Puneet, 348, 352, 358
Tantawi, Mohamed Hussein, 302–3
Tarawneh, Fayez, 125
Tenet, George, 127, 151, 153
terrorism: attack on the *Achille Lauro*,
    33; attack on Jordanian hotel and
    tourist sites, 121; attack on U.S.
    embassy, Beirut, 26, 338; attacks
    on U.S. embassies, East Africa,
    121, 123; Beslan massacre, 208–9;

bombing of U.S. Marine barracks, Beirut, 26, 338; Lockerbie airliner bombing, 39–40, 148, 160, 190, 191, 193, 194; 9/11 terrorist attack, 157–60; PLO and, 41, 178, 181, 183; Qaddafi abandonment of, 190–95; Qaddafi's attack on a West Berlin disco, 33; U.S. policy of no concessions, 35

Thatcher, Margaret, 21

Tillerson, Rex, 400

Timbie, Jim, 359, 382

Tocqueville, Alexis de, 400

Tower, John, 36

Trans-Pacific Partnership (TPP), 269, 398, 403, 405

Treaty on the Non-Proliferation of Nuclear Weapons (NPT), 257

Trump, Donald, 7, 8, 389–90, 397–99; China and, 402, 405; foreign policy, 9, 12, 13, 398, 405, 411; Iran nuclear deal and, 385, 386–87; Paris climate agreement and, 398, 405; Putin and, 399; State Department and, 399–400, 410

Tunisia, 71, 154, 284, 299, 305, 314, 316, 319, 335

Turkey, 60, 71–72, 98, 176, 307, 353–54

Turkmenistan, 279

Tutwiler, Margaret, 46–47, 62, 70, 74

Ukraine, 111, 212, 225, 386, 403; EU and, 288–89; Minsk agreement, 291; NATO membership and, 230, 232, 237–38, 240, 413; Orange Revolution, 201, 209, 222, 229, 278; Putin and, 222, 238, 240, 285, 288–90, 391; Russia and Crimea, 289–90; U.S. diplomacy and, 290–91

United Arab Emirates (UAE), 133, 156, 166, 308, 311, 316, 321, 324

United Kingdom: Brexit, 7; Burns as Marshall Scholar at Oxford, 19–21, 275, 423; Obama administration and, 272–73; secret diplomatic talks with Libya, 191, 192, 194; Syrian intervention and, 329

United Nations: actions against Saddam's Kuwait invasion, 60; Arafat and, 41; brokered cease-fire of Iran-Iraq War, 39; Bush's Roadmap initiative and, 187; Gulf War resolution, 61, 62, 63, 64, 65; Iran sanctions, 339, 342, 343, 353, 364–65; Iran's covert nuclear sites and, 339; Iraq sanctions, 160; Libya intervention and, 317, 318, 319; Libya sanctions, 191, 195; Madrid Peace Conference and, 72, 73; Oil for Food Program, 138; Powell's speech about Saddam and WMD, 172–73; Qaddafi speech, 313–14; Russia supports sanctions against Iran and North Korea, 220; Security Council, 391–92; Security Council Resolution 242, 40, 72; Security Council Resolution 1441, 172; Security Council Resolution 1929, 280, 353, 354; Security Council resolution on Libyan revolt, 284; Syrian civil war, Assad, and, 325–26, 329; Trump and, 398; UNSCOM and Iraq's weapons, 135–36; U.S.-Russian cooperation on Iran, 282

United Nations Relief and Works Agency for Palestine Refugees (UNRWA), 183

United States: assets and advantages of, 401; backlash against globalization, 7; democracy, free markets, and liberal order, 4, 402; economy, 4, 6, 11, 401; global leadership, 4, 7, 9, 11, 13, 17, 45, 67, 80, 161, 242, 245, 387, 389, 391, 396, 402, 409; military-intelligence complex, domination of, 245, 253, 295, 389, 393, 394, 399; multilateralism, 80; political polarization, 7, 281; post–Cold War order, shaping of, 8, 58, 65, 79–81, 92, 109, 110, 116, 117, 161, 219, 227, 242, 245, 292, 389, 391, 396, 397, 402, 406, 430, 457; public's priorities vs. Washington's, 7, 396, 406, 417–21; reassertion of American hegemony, 161; strategy for a post-primacy world, 387, 401–2, 422. *See also specific presidents*

U.S. Arms Control and Disarmament
    Agency, 17
U.S. Congress: Benghazi hearings,
    320–21, 420; Bush 41's address
    post–Gulf War, 69; Chechnya,
    Russia, and, 98; diplomats and,
    420–21; foreign affairs budget
    cut, 116, 117; Hyde Act, 258;
    intervention in Libya and, 317;
    intervention in Syria and, 330;
    Iranian sanctions and, 372; Iraq
    Liberation Act, 137–38, 164; Iraq
    War vote, 172, 247; Jackson-Vanik
    Amendment, 212, 218, 287; King
    Abdullah and, 133; Magnitsky Act,
    288; START agreement and, 281
U.S. National Security Council (NSC):
    Burns assigned to, 33–42; Chen
    affair and, 267; development of,
    34; foreign policy and, 410; Iran-
    Contra affair and, 35–36; Near
    East and South Asia directorate,
    33, 36, 39; Obama presidency
    and, 250, 251, 252, 267, 273;
    Poindexter as national security
    advisor, 34–35; Powell's Policy
    Review Group meetings, 36, 37;
    Reagan administration and, 33–35;
    recommendations, Arab Spring and
    Mubarak, 301; Russia expert and,
    273; size of and staffing, 252, 395;
    Soviet Union, Gorbachev, and, 51;
    Tower Commission Report and,
    36; White House Situation Room
    briefings, 38–39
U.S. State Department: American
    business abroad and, 212, 219,
    420; American diplomacy and
    power at peak, 3; Arms Control
    and Disarmament Agency and,
    116; budget cuts, 393, 400, 407;
    Burns as ambassador to Jordan,
    112–45; Burns as ambassador
    to Russia, 8, 200–242; Burns as
    deputy secretary, 251, 256, 271;
    Burns as Executive Secretariat
    head, 113–14; Burns as executive
    secretary, 110; Burns as minister-
    counselor, 84–110; Burns assigned
    to Baker's staff, 43–81; Burns

assigned to Jordan, 23–28; Burns
    as undersecretary for political
    affairs, 241, 249, 251; Burns enters
    the Foreign Service, 22–23; Burns
    moves to the NSC from, 33; Burns
    returns to, 42; cautious mindset
    of the Foreign Service, 54–55;
    Congress and, 420–21; country
    teams, 87; "deep state" and, 399;
    deputy secretaries, 46; diplomacy's
    importance and, 7; diplomatic
    mandate of, 23; embassy, Baghdad,
    175, 178; embassy, Beijing, 266;
    embassy, Moscow, 85, 205; Foreign
    Service, 22–24; homosexuality and,
    22; international cooperation and,
    10–11; "Iran Watchers" initiative,
    341; mentoring in, 86; 9/11 and,
    157–60; Obama and, 250, 303;
    Operations Center, 113–14, 319,
    354; Powell's modernization of, 152;
    press corps, 62; Russian consulates
    and staff, 205; Trump and, 7,
    8, 9, 12, 13, 399, 410; updating
    recommendations, post-Trump,
    413–21; U.S. citizens overseas
    and, 11, 25; U.S. Information
    Agency and, 116–17; visas for
    foreign students and tourists, 11;
    Washington headquarters, 30. *See
    also specific secretaries of state*
U.S. State Department, Bureau of
    Intelligence and Research, 165
U.S. State Department, Bureau of
    Near Eastern Affairs (NEA), 29,
    165; Burns at, 8, 29–33, 145–46,
    152–99, 299, 301; Burns on the
    road, 153–57; Burns's transition
    note and conversation, 195–96;
    Feltman in Libya and, 316; "Future
    of Iraq" project, 171; Iraq War
    recommendations, 168–72, 174,
    197; Israeli-Palestinian conflict
    and, 179–90; as the "Mother
    Bureau," 29; Murphy heads,
    29–32; 9/11 and, 157; "The Perfect
    Storm" memo, 168–69; post-9/11
    recommendations, 161–62, 163,
    166; Roadmap initiative, 187–89;
    size and staffing, 152–53

U.S. State Department, Policy Planning Staff, 46, 47–49, 114, 349; Baker's use of, 48, 49; Burns at, 42–81, 298, 349; Burns-Ross talking points for Aziz meeting, 63; German reunification and, 54, 55, 76, 77; Middle East policy and, 298–99; paper on Arab states and post–Gulf War, 65; paper on Bosnian War, 78; paper on Soviet breakup, 75–77; Ross at, 46–49, 78; Soviet Union, Gorbachev, and, 51; staff members, 48–49; strategy for post–Cold War order, 79–80; transition memo to Christopher, 4–5, 81, 396, 402, 415, 418–19, 430–34
Uzbekistan, 77–78, 279

Vance, Cyrus, 114
Velayati, Ali Akbar, 345, 358
Vieira de Mello, Sérgio, 176
Vietnam, 270
Viets, Dick, 25
Vladivostok, Russia, 89
Volgograd, Russia, 217

Wang, Bob, 266, 267
Warsaw Pact, 92, 98, 107, 108, 109
Weinberger, Caspar, 36, 38
Weisglass, Dov, 185–86, 187, 189
Whitehead, John, 32–33
WikiLeaks, 314, 393
Wilson, Joe, 165–66

Wisner, Frank, 301–2
Wolfowitz, Paul, 161, 164, 169
Woodward, Bob, 169
World Trade Organization (WTO), 132, 201, 212, 218, 232, 234, 236, 283, 287, 291

Xi Jinping, 391

Yanayev, Gennady, 76
Yang Jiechi, 270
Yanukovich, Viktor, 285, 288–89
Yeltsin, Boris, 8, 51, 76, 77, 86–109, 206, 224, 413; Chechen conflict, 83–84, 94, 96–103, 435; B. Clinton and, 90, 91, 93–94, 103–5, 108–9; Cuny disappearance and, 101; health issues and drinking of, 91, 96, 109, 130; Hussein's funeral and, 130–31; NATO expansion and, 230
Yemen, 62, 155, 316, 335, 385
Yugoslavia, 78, 92

Zabib, Reza, 363, 367
Zarif, Javad, 331, 368–69, 370, 372, 374, 378, 379, 382, 384
Zarqawi, Abu Musab al-, 27, 178
Zayed, Abdullah bin, 310, 324
Zayed, Mohammed bin, 166
Zayed, Sheikh, 156
Zhang Yesui, 271
Zhirinovsky, Vladimir, 91
Zinni, Tony, 160–61, 180
Zoellick, Bob, 46, 47, 55

ABOUT THE AUTHOR

WILLIAM J. BURNS is president of the Carnegie Endowment for International Peace. He retired from the U.S. Foreign Service in 2014 after a thirty-three-year diplomatic career. He holds the highest rank in the Foreign Service, career ambassador, and is only the second serving career diplomat in history to become deputy secretary of state. Prior to his tenure as deputy secretary, Ambassador Burns served from 2008 to 2011 as undersecretary for political affairs. He was ambassador to Russia from 2005 to 2008, assistant secretary of state for near eastern affairs from 2001 to 2005, and ambassador to Jordan from 1998 to 2001. Ambassador Burns earned a bachelor's degree in history from La Salle University and master's and doctoral degrees in international relations from Oxford University, where he studied as a Marshall Scholar. He and his wife, Lisa, have two daughters.

burnsbackchannel.com

In Peace
and
War

AMERICAN MARITIME HISTORY PROJECT INC. 1600-2000

HISTORY INFORMS THE FUTURE

In Peace and War

A History of the U.S. Merchant Marine Academy at Kings Point

Jeffrey L. Cruikshank
and Chloë G. Kline

BICENTENNIAL
1807
WILEY
2007
BICENTENNIAL

John Wiley & Sons, Inc.

Copyright © 2008 by the American Maritime History Project, Inc. All rights reserved

Published by John Wiley & Sons, Inc., Hoboken, New Jersey
Published simultaneously in Canada

Wiley Bicentennial Logo: Richard J. Pacifico

Design and composition by Navta Associates, Inc.

Library of Congress Cataloging-in-Publication Data:

Cruikshank, Jeffrey L.
    In peace and war : a history of the U.S. Merchant Marine Academy at Kings Point / Jeffrey L. Cruikshank and Chlöe G. Kline.
        p. cm
    Includes bibliographical references and index.
    ISBN 978-0-470-13601-0 (cloth)
    1. United States Merchant Marine Academy—History. I. Kline, Chlöe G. II. Title. III. Title: History of the U.S. Merchant Marine Academy at Kings Point.
    VK525.U6C65 2007
    387.5071'173—dc22

                                                                2007006473

Printed in the United States of America

10   9   8   7   6   5   4   3   2   1

From struggle . . . comes strength

The Merchant Marine Song

Heave ho!
My lads, heave ho!

It's a long, long way to go,
It's a long, long pull with our hatches full,
Braving the wind,
Braving the sea,
Fighting the treacherous foe.

Heave ho!
My lads, heave ho!

Let the sea roll high or low,
We can cross any ocean, sail any river, give us the goods and
    we will deliver,
Damn the submarine!
We're the men of the Merchant Marine!

Contents

The American Maritime History Project   ix

Foreword by Vice Admiral Joseph D. Stewart, USMS   xiii

Acknowledgments   xvii

1   A Norfolk Interlude: Serving the Maritime Industry, 2003   1

2   Planting the Seeds   29

3   Conceived in Peace: 1937–1941   51

4   Embodied in War: 1940–1945   79

5   Making Peacetime Headway: 1945–1950   125

6   Weathering New Storms: 1950–1960   151

7   Building on the Foundations: 1955–1970   179

8   Widening the Scope: 1970–1980   211

9   The Guns Return: 1970–1980   245

10   Safe Harbor: 1980–1987   283

11   Broadening the Mission: 1987–1992   319

12   Reinventing the Academy: 1993–1999   355

13   Renewal, Tragedy, and Commitment: 2000–2004   387

14   Scenes from an Education: 2003–2006   413

Appendix A	Maritime Administrators	445
Appendix B	Superintendents, USMMA	446
Appendix C	Academic Deans, USMMA	447
Appendix D	Commandants/Regimental Officers, USMMA	448
Appendix E	Hall of Distinguished Graduates	449
Appendix F	Cadets and Graduates Killed in World War II	452
Appendix G	Number of Graduates by Year and by Nation, State, and Territory (1938–2006)	458
Appendix H	Names of Academy Buildings and Locations	460
Appendix I	Academy Training Ships	463
Appendix J	Oral Histories	465
Appendix K	Alumni Business Leadership Rankings	468
Appendix L	List of Contributors to the American Maritime History Project for the History of the U.S. Merchant Marine Academy	469
Notes		471
Bibliography		501
Photo Credits		504
Index		505

The American Maritime History Project

The American Maritime History Project, founded in 1996, seeks to record, preserve, and communicate the four-hundred-year story of America's rich seafaring history.

Ryan, George J.
President, Lake Carriers Associa-
    tion (Ret)

Seiberlich, Carl J. (deceased)
Rear Admiral, USN (Ret)
Maritime and Intermodal
    Consultant

Sherman, Fred S.
Managing Partner, Management &
    Transportation Associates
Maritime Consultant

Yocum, James H.
Investment Adviser
Former Chair, USMMA Alumni
    Association

History Adviser
Roland, Dr. Alex
Professor and Former Chair,
    History Department
Duke University

Advisory Committee
Ackerman, James H. Esq.
    (deceased)
Law Office, J. H. Ackerman
Maritime Attorney

Aron, Peter A.
President, J. Aron Charitable
    Foundation

Billy, Dr. George B.
    (Secretary)
Librarian, USMMA

Braynard, Frank O.
Maritime Historian, Author,
    Lecturer
Curator Emeritus, American Mer-
    chant Marine Museum

Brickman, Dr. Jane P.
Professor and Head of Humanities,
    USMMA

Cushing, Dr. Charles R.
President, C. R. Cushing & Co.
Naval Architect

Femenia, Jose
Professor and Head of Engineer-
    ing, USMMA
President, SNAME (1999–2000)
Marine Engineer

Forster, Donald W.
Chairman, Power Technology
    Marine Engineer

Hayden, Reginald M. Jr., Esq.
Hayden & Milliken, PA
Maritime Attorney
Former Chair, USMMA Alumni
    Association

Hightower, John
President, Mariners' Museum

Kelly, Edward V.
Vice President, American Maritime
    Officers

Kiefer, Robert H.
George G. Sharp, Inc. (Ret)
Marine Engineer

Kurz, Adolph B. (deceased)
Keystone Shipping Co.

Maitland, Guy E. C., Esq.
Managing Partner, International
 Registries

Markoe, Dr. Karen E.
Chair, Department of Humanities,
 Maritime College
State University of New York

Maxtone-Graham, John
Maritime Historian, Author,
 Lecturer

McCready, Lauren S.
Rear Admiral, USMS (Ret)
Professor and Head of Engineer-
 ing, USMMA

Moore, Captain Arthur R.
Maritime Historian, Author

Palmer, Dr. Janet F. (Ret)
Former Registrar, USMMA

Renick, Captain Charles M.
President Emeritus
American Merchant Marine
 Museum

Searle, George R.
Past National President
American Merchant Marine
 Veterans
(World War II)

Shirley, James T. Jr., Esq.
Haight Gardner Holland & Knight
Maritime Attorney
Former Chair, USMMA Alumni
 Association

Starer, Brian D., Esq.
Haight Gardner Holland & Knight
Maritime Attorney

Stewart, Joseph D.
Vice Admiral, USMS
Superintendent, USMMA

Wallischeck, Commander Eric Y.
Waterfront Director, USMS
Yocum Sailing Center, USMMA

Wilcox, Thomas
Director, Maine Maritime Museum

Foreword

I am pleased to provide these introductory comments for *In Peace and War*, a new and comprehensive history of the institution at which I am honored to serve.

I'd like to offer observations in three categories: where this unusual volume comes from, its principal lessons—at least as I see them—and the relevance those lessons might have for our future as a school and a nation.

First, the origins of this book: over the past five years or so, an independent foundation called the American Maritime History Project (AMHP) has launched a series of projects aimed at documenting and illuminating a generally misunderstood industry, the United States merchant marine. The chair and driving force behind that foundation is an alumnus of this Academy, Eliot H. Lumbard, Esq., a member of the class of '45, a mariner, public servant, criminal justice reformer, and valued counselor. Eliot seeks no recognition for himself, and he has struggled to keep his name out of any prominent place in this volume. The fact that these particular words are appearing in print means that he has lost that struggle—an unusual occurrence for a man as energetic and determined as we all know Eliot to be. But it is a war he deserves to lose. Thank you, Eliot.

Eliot and his distinguished colleagues on the AMHP board of directors first commissioned a survey of the domestic maritime industry, dating back to the colonial era and continuing up to the present. That book project was tentatively titled *The Way of the Ship: A Maritime History of the United States, 1600–2000*. As it progressed, it became clear that the story of this Academy needed to be treated separately and in a different way. That realization led to the commissioning of this book.

I think that decision says a great deal about both the AMHP and its leadership. There was already in existence at that time a history of Kings Point (as this school is affectionately known to its graduates and other friends). That book, written by C. Bradford Mitchell and titled *We'll Deliver*, was published in 1977. It covers the school's founding in the late 1930s through the "permanency" campaign of the early 1950s, and it remains an indispensable resource for scholars interested in that period. But the AMHP wanted more. They wanted to know how Kings Point fit into the longer and larger maritime tradition that is their principal interest. They also wanted to have documented the half-century or so of Academy history not covered by Mitchell's book—from the mid-1950s to the present—and implicitly, to get on the record a number of firsthand witnesses to the story of this Academy and the industry it has served so well.

We are fortunate that they established this last priority. Already, at least one of the hundred-or-so voices recorded for this project has been stilled. I personally am grateful that the collective wisdom of those voices—about this Academy, about the maritime industry, and about life's larger challenges and priorities—has been captured, and that it will be available through our own Bland Library to future generations of researchers.

The AMHP also made the all-important decision to hire two Boston-based writers, Jeffrey L. Cruikshank and Chloë G. Kline, to research and write this book. For the better part of three years, Jeff and Chloë haunted our archives, patiently picked our brains, attended Academy events, conducted research in libraries and other repositories around the nation, and even sailed with our cadets on merchant vessels in two oceans.

They did a great job, and I will mostly let their work speak for itself. But I do want to make a few observations of my own about the lessons contained in the following pages.

First and most important, this school produces a much-needed "product": highly skilled mariners, licensed by the U.S. Coast Guard to operate merchant vessels. We were given this charge in peacetime, way back in the 1930s, by a federal government deeply alarmed by the *Morro Castle* disaster and other maritime tragedies. But we really learned how to deliver upon it in the dark months following America's entry into World War II. (This is one reason why the title of this history—"in peace and war," borrowed from the inscription on the flag of the U.S. Maritime Service—is so appropriate.) Our product has changed in subsequent decades, reflecting a changing nation and a changing industry. But although the mission of Kings Point has broadened over those decades, it has not drifted—not an inch.

A second lesson is that the industry that consumes our product, the U.S. maritime industry, broadly defined, poses special challenges. Changing technologies, changing political contexts, a changing regulatory environment, and especially changing economics have forced us to reinvent our curriculum on a regular basis. In the following pages you will read about the transition from steam to diesel power, experiments with nuclear-powered merchant ships, containerization, environmentalism, terrorism and port security, and a host of other forces that prompted change in the outside world. You will also read how Kings Point embraced and responded to those changes, usually despite limited resources.

This introduces a related lesson: since our founding, we have benefited greatly from our flexibility, optimism, and opportunism. Always the most underfunded of the five federal academies, Kings Point nevertheless has consistently found ways to move forward. That can-do attitude has encouraged people in and out of government to bring us special challenges. Perhaps the most dramatic of these was the directive from our parent organization, the U.S. Maritime Administration, or MARAD, to incorporate female cadets into this community in the mid-1970s. The other federal academies watched with great interest (and maybe even some skepticism) as we ran our experiment—and then arrived to take notes when it became obvious that our experiment would succeed.

But we also learn well from other places. When something gets broken at Kings Point, we fix it based on what we can learn at Annapolis, West Point, the Coast Guard and Air Force academies, the state maritime schools, and other leading institutions. In my own tenure, for example, we have worked hard to upgrade our regimental experience. Commandants Art Athens and Bob Allee borrowed pages from the other federal academies and then came up with a blueprint for a revised operation that is unique to Kings Point.

That's the good news. But a paradoxical and sobering lesson also emerges from the following pages. Despite our past successes, we can't take Kings Point for granted. As recently as the mid-1990s, a group of budget cutters in Washington proposed to close down this school. (Failing that, they proposed to implement a tuition system, which surely would have meant the back-door death of Kings Point, as it would mean the death of any of the other federal academies.) I am sure that these budget cutters were well intentioned, but I know from personal experience that they were fundamentally misinformed. As a former Marine, I know that when this nation sets out to project power overseas in a sustained way, it needs ships—and, by extension, it needs the mariners to sail them. At the risk of greatly oversimplifying the logistical challenge, there is simply no other way to get enough beans and bullets from here to there.

What should we do with this new history of Kings Point? Well, first, we should read it. It's a great story, well told. Anyone interested in learning why things are the way they are—at this Academy, in maritime education, in higher education, and in the maritime industry—will benefit from reading *In Peace and War*.

Second, we should consider and debate the policy implications that grow out of this history. Internally, how do we retain our intensely practical form of education, leading to a deck or engineering license, and still provide a broad-gauge undergraduate experience? How do we balance the competing demands of our four pillars—academics, Sea Year, the Regiment, and physical activity—in a way that challenges our students most productively?

Externally, how do we as a maritime nation develop a longer memory, so that we will never again forget the importance of ships and mariners to our economic welfare? In recent years, and especially in the wake of the terrorist attacks of September 11, 2001, national security has emerged as the most compelling issue of our time. How do we ensure that our sailors, ships, shores, ports, and waterways are woven into the warp and woof of every discussion of national security?

There are no easy answers. But I hope that this book, and the others soon to follow from the American Maritime History Project, will illuminate and enliven this all-important debate.

—Vice Admiral Joseph D. Stewart
United States Maritime Service,
Superintendent, U.S. Merchant Marine Academy
Maritime Administration

Acknowledgments

The authors would like to thank the many people who made this book possible. Our interview list is elsewhere; thanks to those hundred-plus individuals who shared their recollections.

At the Academy, Joe Stewart, Warren Mazek, and Bob Safarik served as principal contacts, door-openers, and interpreters of Kings Point from the vantage point of Wiley Hall. Charlie Renick, John Jochmans, and Marty Skrocki provided historical context and documents. George Sandberg, Arthur Donovan, Jose Femenia, David Van Oss, Eric Wallischeck, and Thad Gaebelein provided helpful faculty viewpoints as well as enthusiasm for the project. Two commandants in a row, Art Athens and Bob Allee, helped introduce us to the Regiment. Gene McCormick and Pete Rackett helped us with alumni-related issues, gave personal perspectives, and provided endless amounts of contact information.

George Billy and his wonderful library staff get a paragraph of their own. Thanks to all of you. Maybe we also can put Luis Bejarano, retired Kings Point librarian, who shared many key documents with us, in this distinguished group.

Away from the campus, Paul Krinsky, Tom Matteson, and Tom King, the retired superintendents, sat for interviews, looked at drafts, and provided extensive commentaries. Lauren McCready reviewed the entire manuscript, with special attention paid to the founding era.

Many alumni and alumnae, older and younger, helped. Warren Leback (who would have made a first-rate editor) scrutinized every successive draft. Jim Shirley provided very helpful guidance, as did Carl Seiberlich, Milt Nottingham, Fred Sherman, and the late Dave O'Neil.

We owe special thanks to CSX Lines for allowing us to catch a ride from Long Beach to Honolulu, and to Maersk Sealand for taking us from Newark to Norfolk.

Many, many midshipmen sat for conversations, formal and informal. Special thanks are owed to Joe Baran and Logan Bennett, whose footsteps we dogged aboard ship.

And finally, thanks to Eliot Lumbard, ably assisted by Tony Romano, whose single-mindedness made the American Maritime History Project—and this book—possible.

1

A Norfolk Interlude
Serving the Maritime Industry: 2003

On a surprisingly balmy day in late October 2003, the MV *Maersk Carolina* makes her way into port in Norfolk, Virginia.

The *Carolina* is 958 feet long and is rated to carry 50,698 tons (gross). She was built in Ulsan, South Korea, by Hyundai Heavy Industries Company, for Denmark's Maersk Sealand, and was launched on November 8, 1997. Originally christened the *Grete Maersk*, sailing under the Danish flag, she has recently been renamed and reflagged as a U.S. vessel. Maersk participates in the U.S. government's Maritime Security Program, which provides $2.1 million per year in operational subsidies to each of the forty-seven vessels in the program, designed to ensure that a fleet of U.S.–flagged commercial vessels will be available to the United States in times of national emergency.[1] As a result, the *Carolina* now flies the U.S. flag, and is manned by a twenty-one-member American crew.

The huge ship—the length of three football fields, plus a few end zones—has a capacity of 4,300 "20-foot-equivalent units (TEUs)." This means that, with some careful space planning, she can carry roughly 2,000 containers that are 40 feet long, 8 feet wide, and 8½-feet high. Each container can hold up to 50 tons of "general cargo"—everything from textiles from India to floor tiles from the Mediterranean to frozen seafood. When the *Carolina* gets up to full speed, it can take half a mile of water to effect an emergency stop, going from full ahead to full astern. So she creeps, rather than cruises, into Norfolk.

The MV *Maersk Carolina* receives a timely nudge from a tugboat as she makes her way out of Port Elizabeth, New Jersey.

For most of the last few miles of her trip, she is piloted by a local harbor pilot, who has come aboard in the outer harbor to help guarantee a safe arrival at the Maersk docks. Two tugs stand at the ready as the *Carolina* nears those docks. On the bridge with the harbor pilot is Captain David E. Bell, making his tenth visit to Norfolk as master of the *Carolina*. Although the pilot is doing the hands-on "conning" in this final approach to the pier in his harbor, which he knows intimately– ordering slight adjustments in course and engine speed, communicating with the tugs by radio, and so on–the *Carolina* remains Bell's legal responsibility. So, in an unobtrusive, collegial sort of way, not hovering, occasionally making an observation about the proceedings, Bell monitors the pilot's every decision, ready to step in when necessary.

David Bell is a graduate of the United States Merchant Marine Academy at Kings Point, New York, class of '72. Bell grew up in Gamboa, a small town in the Canal Zone in Panama, where his father worked as a policeman. Throughout his childhood, he watched great ships of all stripes and colors inch their way through the canal. Bell originally aimed to join the navy, but after thinking hard about opportunities for service as a Kings Point graduate, and the relative salary of the navy versus the merchant marine, he began leaning toward the latter. On his second try, he was admitted to Kings Point.

His Sea Year—a critical component of the Kings Point education, which deploys Academy cadets on merchant vessels for the equivalent of a full academic year—put him on a sequence of four cargo ships and a tanker that took him to Japan, Korea, Okinawa, Guam, Hawaii, the U.S. West Coast, the east and west coasts of South America, Vietnam, and the Philippines.

Bell graduated into a tough shipping economy. The Vietnam War, which had stimulated an already booming maritime industry for the better part of a decade, was winding down. Bell wound up piloting a 65-foot fishing boat based in St. Petersburg, Florida, taking tourists out on day trips. He next worked briefly for Ingram Ocean Systems, which ran two integrated tug/barges, but left Ingram to fulfill his navy obligation.

This was not an unusual track. In return for their government-sponsored education and training, Kings Point graduates are expected to sail on their licenses on a merchant ship at least four months every year for a period of five years and complete two weeks of naval reserve duty each year, or serve active duty in the navy for five years. Alternatively, they can pursue shoreside maritime employment if that employment is approved by the U.S. Maritime Administration (MARAD), the agency that supervises Kings Point.

After his navy hitch, Bell took a job running a dinner-restaurant ship, which paid a decent wage but offered few long-term prospects. All the while, Bell yearned to get out on the deep water again. His chance came in January 1974, when he shipped out as third mate on the SS *Columbia*, a United States Steel ship that ran semifinished steel products from the East Coast to the West Coast through the Panama Canal. He upgraded to a second mate's license in June 1976, and then moved over to the tanker trade, where he spent the next twenty years carrying crude oil and occasionally a load of grain. He quickly earned his chief mate's license and upgraded to master in 1978. But the industry was still suffering, and it wasn't until February 14, 1984, that he took command of his first ship: the *Rover*, a tanker operated by the Stamford, Connecticut–based OMI Corporation, which was part of the navy's Near Term Preposition Group on the Indian Ocean island of Diego Garcia. As he recalls, "There's nothing like going on your own ship for the first time, and you're the captain. There's nobody to call when you've got a problem. You're the guy they're calling. It was a little old rustbucket of a ship, for sure. But for me, it felt like the Starship *Enterprise*."[2]

Eventually, Bell and OMI parted company. When Bell heard that Maersk was reflagging four ships as part of the new Maritime Security Program, he sent in his résumé. He sailed as chief mate on the *Maersk Texas* for one trip, then as master for five years, and, in January 2003, took over as master of the *Carolina*–or, more accurately, as one of two masters of the *Carolina*. Like most deep-water merchant ships, the *Carolina* has two alternating crews; when one is on duty, the other is ashore. Each crew makes two round trips, for a total of ninety-eight days at sea, and then gets an equal amount of time off as the alternate crew takes over the *Carolina*.

Sailing a container ship, says Bell, is mostly routine. Once you've visited a port three or four times, there are no more surprises. Out on the high seas, you point the ship in the right direction, keep a watchful eye out for traffic, and carefully monitor the state of your crew and your ship. If you're lucky, nothing much happens.

On January 3, 2003, the alternate master of the *Carolina* got unlucky. On that day, his ship was on a six-day run from the Mediterranean to Halifax, laden with goods ranging from oranges to cotton, when it ran into a fierce North Atlantic winter storm on the southern tip of the Grand Banks, off Newfoundland. The *Carolina* took a vicious beating, the likes of which only those who have traversed the North Atlantic in winter can imagine. It lost something like 130 containers over the side and sustained heavy damage to its superstructure. Many of the remaining containers tumbled out of their orderly stacks, collapsing upon and crushing one another. When the *Carolina* limped into Halifax, onlookers were stunned at the destruction on deck. "She must have been hit by one hell of a wave," said one.[3]

Inevitably, the captain of the *Carolina* came in for criticism. "But in fact," Bell says soberly of his counterpart, "he probably *saved* this ship, and its crew. No loss of life, and only one or two people injured."

Also on the bridge of the *Carolina*, as she makes her careful way into Norfolk's inner harbor, is Third Mate John Logan Bennett, who graduated from Kings Point only a few months earlier, as a member of the class of 2003.

By the time the *Carolina* is ready to close in on its appointed pier, yet another player has entered the picture. This is the docking pilot, who takes responsibility for the very last leg of the ship's journey. Bennett stands at the ship's throttle, awaiting the docking pilot's commands. Captain Bell and the harbor pilot maintain a casual vigilance in the background.

"Dead slow ahead," the docking pilot says, looking intently out the window at the slowly closing gap between ship and pier.

"Dead slow ahead," repeats Bennett, adjusting the ship's throttle, which causes a bell to sound both on the bridge and far below deck in the engine room.

And a few minutes later: "Full stop."

"Full stop," repeats Bennett.

Aided by the bow and the stern thrusters, the tugs are now doing most of the work, pushing on the starboard bow and stern, nudging the sixty-thousand-ton ship's port side against the dock. There is an almost imperceptible impact—a tiny shudder that ripples across the giant ship—and the bridge signals "FWE" (finished with engine) to the engine room. This leg of the trip has ended without incident.

Logan Bennett—he rarely uses his given name—grew up in Charlotte, North Carolina. He played linebacker for a powerhouse football team in Charlotte, and planned to attend a large, football-oriented school. But his high school coach strongly encouraged him to apply to the Merchant Marine Academy. "If you work hard there," he remembers his coach saying, "you'll be set for life." He had no particular yen to see the world; in fact, he had never been on an airplane before making a visit to Kings Point in his senior year of high school. Nor was there any maritime tradition in his family. (His father was an electrician, and his mother a data-entry clerk.) But he liked what he saw and decided to enroll.

After surviving the regimentation of his plebe year, he went to sea for his Sea Year on the MV *Sealand Integrity*, an Atlantic-class vessel (ACV) containership. En route from England to Algeciras, Spain, a fire broke out on deck. Bennett loaned his knife (standard gear for Academy cadets on Sea Year journeys) to a crew member who was

The MV *Jeppesen Maersk* approaches the MV *Maersk Carolina* while the *Carolina* is in transit between New Jersey and Norfolk, October 2003.

frantically trying to cut loose a burning tarpaulin. After retrieving his knife, Bennett manned a hose until the fire was safely out.

The *Integrity* later made stops in Germany, Italy, and Malta, in addition to Spain. It was a lot of world to see for a kid from Charlotte who had never been south of Daytona or west of Atlanta. He recalls that he was desperately homesick on his first trip across the Atlantic, on a ship with eighteen other men from all walks of life—except, perhaps, his own—but he decided to tough it out and see what would come next.

Football fell by the wayside, in part because Bennett decided he was a step too slow to play competitively, and in part because he was getting too small. (He lost thirty-five pounds under the Academy's demanding physical regimen.) He took academics very seriously, enrolling in the rigorous Ship's Officer program, which prepares cadets to sit for the deck license and also allows them to qualify as a Qualified Member of the Engineering Department (QMED). Depending on which scoring system is subscribed to, he graduated either number one or number two in his class at the Academy.

Maersk came interviewing at Kings Point, liked what they saw in Bennett, and offered him a third mate's berth—the standard starting point for a freshly minted Academy "deck" graduate. He went aboard the *Carolina* in the late summer and began his first forty-nine-day run, which took him from Newark to Norfolk into Charleston, across the Atlantic through the Straits of Gibraltar, and into the Mediterranean. From there, the ship traveled on to Gioia Tauro, a major Italian container trans-shipment port, through the Suez Canal in Egypt; down through the Red Sea to Jeddah, Saudi Arabia, and Salalah, Oman; then to Jawaharlal Nehru, India; and returned by way of Algeciras, Spain. "And from Algeciras," he concludes in his recitation of the ship's itinerary, "we go to Halifax, and then back to Newark."

While at sea, a third mate's life consists mainly of four-hour bridge watches, day and night. As third mate, Bennett's duties included the morning and evening eight to twelve watches. While in port, the third mate follows a hectic six-hours-on, six-hours-off schedule, in what amounts to a frantic group effort to unload and reload the ship. The days of the "girl in every port" are long over, Bennett says; there simply isn't time enough in ports today. Now, while docking, the third mate mans the throttle, makes sure that the quartermaster on the rudder control correctly executes steering commands, records times and positions, notes changes in the bridge's complement, and generally makes himself useful. Useful is an understatement in Bennett's case: Captain David Bell notes that he has seldom, if ever, been so impressed with a third mate.[4]

His most challenging moment so far, as a third mate? Bennett thinks for a minute and then responds. "Being in the Mediterranean, having the con [control of the ship's direction], going twenty-two knots, and having thirty little fishing boats all around you radioing to please turn left and not run over their nets. That's when I might call Captain Bell in his quarters and ask if he might possibly come up to the bridge and stand by."[5]

Several miles to the west, Port Captain Jessica S. Mowrey is monitoring the *Carolina*'s arrival in port. A 1997 graduate of the Academy, Mowrey is Maersk's "designated person ashore" (DPA) for the *Carolina* and her three sister ships: the *Georgia*, the *Missouri*, and the *Virginia*. As the DPA, Mowrey needs to be constantly aware of where her vessels are, and where they will be next. Should any problems arise,

A view from the MV *Maersk Carolina* as she prepares to dock in the port of Norfolk.

Mowrey—the primary on-shore liaison for the ships' captains—tends to be the first to hear about it.

On most days, Mowrey arrives around eight a.m. at Maersk's Norfolk headquarters in a one-story, brick-clad building that helps to anchor a nondescript suburban office park. The floor plan is mostly open. Rows of gray filing cabinets separate the Commercial Operations Division, where Mowrey sits, from the commercial engineers. The first thing she does is to go through e-mail and voice messages to check on the four vessels under her care. Often, these messages will define the course of her day by surfacing the on-board issues that Mowrey has to make her own. These can range from the commonplace (a captain needs more time in a port), to the unusual and potentially dangerous (a ship is heading directly toward some serious weather), to pretty much everything in between. When the more serious problems arise, Mowrey may find herself called in at any time of the day or night. "It can be a twenty-four-hour job,"[6] she says.

On this day, in addition to the *Carolina*'s entry into port, the captain of another vessel has called in to report a lost ten-ton anchor. Mowrey has been trading a flurry of e-mails with the captain and crew all morning, trying to figure out just how and why this happened. She is also trying to track down a new anchor of the correct weight and size (a fifty-thousand-dollar investment, even without the requisite shot of chain) and conclude how long it will take to get it installed on the ship. In the meantime, Mowrey has to work with the captain to figure out what the impacts of a lost anchor will be; for example, the ship may need additional tug escorts (at a cost of up to a thousand dollars each) in the next several ports that it will visit.

Mowrey is now in her third year of employment with Maersk Line. Upon graduating, she chose to go on active duty with the U.S. Marine Corps, in which she served for three and a half years. When her rotation was up, she started looking for jobs using the Kings Point online Alumni Job Opportunity Bulletin and came across an engineering opening at Maersk. Though the job wasn't even in her department—she was a "deckie" rather than an engine major—she decided to call the company and ask what was available. Soon after that, she found herself working in the personnel department, and several months later she made the transition to operations.

As Maersk's youngest port captain, Mowrey is still unsure of where her career path will lead. For the most part, she loves her job. Though she thinks that she would have enjoyed going to sea, she also appreciates having a "regular" lifestyle and enjoying the comforts of home. The size of her company, she points out, is a "huge advantage," because it affords her lots of different paths to choose from as she continues in her career. In the near term, she plans to interview for admission into a Maersk management program, and she believes that she is a strong candidate for a position.

"And after that," she says, "we'll see what comes next."

The executive offices at the Maersk Line's Norfolk headquarters are across the building and down the hall from Mowrey's desk. One of these offices, well appointed, but not opulent, is occupied by Stephen Carmel, Kings Point, '79, who today is a senior vice president with Maersk. Carmel, who sailed for more than ten years after graduating, came ashore in 1990 as a port captain with U.S. Marine Management, at the time a wholly owned subsidiary of Maersk.

Carmel grew up in a steel-mill town in rural Pennsylvania. Chafing at the confines of small-town life, he chose Kings Point because it would allow him to see the world, and also because it was a free college education. His primary goal upon graduating was to command a ship as soon as possible. He chose to join the Military Sealift Command (MSC), because this would allow him longer stints at sea and thus a faster advancement on his license. After spending five years with MSC and earning his master's license, Carmel moved to a position with Maritime Overseas. He sailed with them for five years, first as chief mate and then as master. He then came ashore with U.S. Marine Management, in a position similar to the one Jessica Mowrey now holds down the hall and across the way.

In 1997, U.S. Marine Management merged with Maersk Line. Since that time, Carmel has been responsible for all operating activities in Maersk's American-flag maritime division. He spends part of his time overseeing the daily routines of running a fleet of twenty-six container ships, and the rest of his day on new business development.

Today, he notes, company operations are running smoothly. (The exception is the anchor incident, but Carmel knows that Jessica Mowrey is bird-dogging that issue.) So Carmel begins his workday by meeting with a team of engineers he has assembled to investigate a parametric rolling incident that has been affecting some of Maersk's large container ships. This phenomenon involves a large roll angle generated in head/stern sea conditions with long-crested waves, which causes unpredictable and violent rolling. Parametric rolling has been experienced on ships for centuries, but its effect on modern containership designs has been unexpectedly significant.

The stakes are high, as the *Carolina*'s near disaster off Newfoundland amply illustrated: 130 containers lost and many more destroyed. Carmel's team is working with weather experts and naval architects to understand exactly what happened in that episode, and to adapt operating procedures to prevent similar losses in the future.

In addition, Carmel has budgeted some time today to concentrate on a forward-looking strategic concept for an Afloat Forward Staging Base for the Department of Defense. This is a project that Carmel has been working on since the Afghanistan conflict, when Maersk was approached by the military and asked to design a new type of "sea base," a vessel on which to base its special forces. Carmel, working with a team at Maersk, has developed a plan to transform one of its S-class carriers—among the largest and fastest container ships in the world—into a helicopter carrier for assault troops. Carmel hopes to see a contract with the government in place within the next year. This would represent a lightning-fast pace in the world of government procurement, Carmel acknowledges. He readily admits, too, that there's a lot of conceptual development yet to be done on the project.

The outsourcing of military functions to private operators has become much more common in the post–September 11, 2001, world. The conflicts in Afghanistan and Iraq, for example, drew heavily on the services of private ship operators, and not surprisingly, there is a lot of industry interest in this area. In fact, Carmel has been asked to present the Afloat Forward Staging Base concept in the following week at an expeditionary warfare conference in Panama City, Florida.

Of course, commercial maritime interface with the military is not new. It dates back at least to the days of the Phoenician traders, who from time to time outfitted their galleys with sails and rams at the behest of the military. The efforts of the Military Sealift Command are only the latest in this long tradition.

"But demand is continuing to rise," Carmel concludes. "As a result, both the MSC and private operators are being called upon to help the military come up with a new model for modern warfare."

Across town, at Camp Pendleton near Virginia Beach, another Kings Point graduate is similarly focused on the commercial/military interface. But Andrew M. Kallgren, Kings Point, '89, is eyeing the challenge through the lens of the Military Sealift Command itself.

Kallgren grew up in Stamford, Connecticut, and chose the Merchant Marine Academy mainly as a result of his love for competitive sailing (of which there is a great deal at Kings Point). Like Steve Carmel, Kallgren lined up a job with Military Sealift Command months before graduating. Unlike Carmel, however, this choice wasn't simply about a speedy ascent to the helm. Rather, on the advice of one of his mentors at Kings Point, Kallgren was placing a bet on the direction of his industry's future.

Kallgren became concerned about the health of the maritime industry early on in his time at the Academy. In fact, he still recalls the shock of hearing a professor at Kings Point give the entering plebes a particularly dismal forecast. "My first year," he explains, "I was in one of the introductory courses, probably marine science, and there was an old captain teaching the course. He looked out across my class of twenty-five or thirty, and he told us quite frankly that he would be surprised if *any* of us were able to sail on our licenses when we graduated, or make a career in the merchant marine, and that we were going down the wrong path. It was kind of disappointing at the time!"[7]

But the maritime industry is famously cyclical, and by the time Kallgren graduated in 1989, the old captain's prediction had proven wrong: there were once again maritime jobs to be had. Kallgren, however, had gotten a vicarious look at the hard times, and still believed that Military Sealift Command represented the best bet for steady maritime employment.

Kallgren sailed with the MSC for the next nine years: first on a "roll on, roll off" (RO/RO) ship, the USNS *Mercury*, which carried ammunition and military equipment all over the world, and subsequently on a cable ship, the USNS *Neptune*, pulling up and extracting data from government cables that had been laid on the ocean floor. Later in his MSC experience, Kallgren witnessed a symbolic milestone for the military while serving on the USNS *Kilauea*. That ship, he explains, was one of the first ammunition vessels that the navy converted to civilian operation. It was an experiment in outsourcing that proved to be a remarkable success. The civilian crew was tasked with everything that the navy crew had done, including some classified tasks, and was able to do it with a fraction of the manpower and cost. In addition, the navy found that a civilian crew offered them more continuity and reduced their training responsibilities. The crew members were somewhat older, better trained, and further along in their careers. Unlike the navy crew, they weren't frequently rotated ashore to new positions. These were professional seamen, and they ran a professional ship.

Today, this model is being extended to ever-higher levels within the navy. In fact, the USS *Coronado*, one of the navy's command ships, recently sailed under a mixed civilian/military crew. This was the first time, Kallgren explains, that a civilian crew was entrusted with the care of a three-star admiral, who was directing war-fighting from the vessel, and the experiment was carefully scrutinized by military and private-sector observers alike.

Kallgren married and came ashore in 1998, taking a post with MSC's training division. Soon after, he was transferred to personnel and put in charge of placement for the deck positions on MSC ships, and then promoted to head of all marine placement for MSC ships. In this capacity, Kallgren has experienced firsthand the growing need for civilian support of the military. In fact, he admits, he often finds himself scrambling to meet this need.

On this particular fall day, for example, he's trying to man the USNS *Supply*, which is gearing up for deployment. *Supply* is one of the navy's larger auxiliary ships, and one of the first of its class to be transferred to MSC operation. As such, there's a lot of pressure on Kallgren to get it up to full capability as soon as possible. There are also more subtle pressures. "As far as I can tell," he explains, "a lot of navy personnel aren't too happy that we're getting this ship. The fleet commanders want to challenge the ship. They want to make sure it has the same capability it had before, at least as far as the logistics elements. Can it run so many rigs at one time, and flight quarters simultaneously? Can it keep up the pace, as far as fuel, ammunition, food for supplying the carrier battle group? It's a very conspicuous challenge."[8]

The *Supply* has a crew complement of 177 civilians, but on this particular day there are only about 140 on board. In other words, Kallgren is down about 30 bodies from a full crew. And just to complicate things, many of the crew members who are on board, Kallgren admits, are "pretty green." These are not ideal circumstances under which to be conspicuous.

Today, he's using carrots, sticks, and all the other tools at his disposal to solve the *Supply*'s staffing shortfall. Several recruiters in his department are combing the United States (and also looking abroad) to find mariners with the necessary skills who might be interested in signing on. Meanwhile, Kallgren is reviewing the minimum staffing needs of several other ships under his control, to see if he can get away with pulling people from other assignments to work on the *Supply*. Compounding his challenge is the fact that the *Supply* is a gas turbine–powered ship. This narrows the engineer pool dramatically, since most U.S. mariners today are trained to operate diesel ships.

Kallgren is also what's known as the proposing official for disciplinary matters concerning MSC personnel afloat. As such, on any given morning, he's likely to find one or two cases on his desk that require his attention. These range from minor alcohol infractions to more serious charges.

Today, for example, he's faced with an unusual situation. One of his captains has contacted the office to report an apparently unbalanced crew member, who in the course of performing routine navigational chores has dramatically misplotted the position of the ship. (The vessel was operating off the coast of California; the crew member somehow came up with a position somewhere off the Philippines, and it appears to have been something other than an honest mistake.) After some discussion, Kallgren works out an arrangement whereby the ship will detour to a nearby port and drop the sailor off for psychiatric evaluation.

One of the most difficult parts of Kallgren's job is coordinating time for MSC personnel to take training courses ashore. MSC uses navy schools for refresher and upgrading courses, but often the MSC manning complement is so tight that crew members can't be spared to take on-shore training courses. Traditionally, the navy has dealt with this problem by carrying larger crews with redundant skill sets, thereby freeing up individuals for on-shore rotations. It's a staffing luxury that, for better or worse, is not available to MSC personnel, and Kallgren has to squeeze in training time when and wherever possible.

He confidently expects the number of mariners employed by MSC to rise dramatically over the next several years: from roughly four-thousand to more than six thousand personnel. "Am I confident that those higher numbers will significantly ease the manning situation?" he asks rhetorically. "Well, not if demand continues to grow apace."

Not that scheduling navy training is easy, of course. Across town, at the Center for Naval Engineering on the Norfolk Naval Base, Lieutenant Commander John C. Hazlett, Kings Point, '96, shakes his head and smiles a little ruefully as he describes his current task: revising and coordinating the training needs of the thirty-three thousand enlisted engineering sailors in the Navy.

Unmanageable? Impossible? Well, *yes*, at least under current circumstances. Throughout its history, the navy has struggled against long odds to make sure that its sailors have the correct training for the jobs they are asked to do. Yes, the redundancy pointed to by Kallgren helps somewhat. At the same time, however, the rapid rotations that characterize service in the navy today greatly complicate the training challenge. In theory, sailors have been sent to different schools to learn specific tasks before being assigned to certain jobs. In practice, sailors were often overtrained in one area, even while they lacked crucial skills in others. Or they didn't get a chance to practice their new skills soon enough, which in some cases meant a round of refresher training.

These realities have led in turn to a navy tradition of extensive on-board training. This approach assures that the sailors have job-specific skills, but it also tends to be highly inefficient. If every task that is being performed is also being taught, the ship must carry well over its necessary complement. On-board training also contributes to the seeming overpopulation of navy ship bridges: both students and teachers are at work.

In response, Hazlett and his group are engaged in a truly radical experiment. They are attempting to design a computer model that will help deliver training to the individual sailor—where it's needed, when it's needed—and eliminate costly redundancies.

Hazlett, who graduated from Kings Point in 1996, was always interested in a career on the water, though his first goal was Annapolis, rather than Kings Point. Growing up in Lorain, Ohio, a small town just west of Cleveland on Lake Erie, Hazlett surveyed the huge ore freighters that plied the Great Lakes, day in and day out, during the seasons when the lakes were navigable. Some days he dreamed of sailing these great freighters; other days he leaned toward active duty in the navy. He applied to Annapolis during his last year of high school but was not admitted, and instead attended community college for a year. Then he heard about Kings Point from a recent graduate who had attended his high school. He applied, was accepted, and decided to attend, still aiming for a navy career after graduation.

During his Sea Year, however, his perspective shifted. Hazlett was surprised by how much he enjoyed the merchant marine, and decided to sail on his license for a while after graduating. In the summer of 1996, therefore, he took a job with the Andrie Shipping Company, hauling asphalt on tugboat-propelled barges on the Great Lakes. He had realized his childhood ambition, but it was not all he had hoped for (he gently describes the asphalt business as a "less than desirable climate"), and he moved back to New York to take a first mate's position with New York Fast Ferry, a high-speed commuter ferry operating between Staten Island and midtown Manhattan. This company folded in 1997, and Hazlett found himself again looking for employment.

At this point, his career took yet another interesting turn. He heard about an opening in the continuing education program at Kings Point, and decided to apply. Christopher J. McMahon, Kings Point, '77, had been hired in 1994 as director of the Academy's Global Maritime and Transportation School (GMATS). As part of an effort to reinvent that program, McMahon hired Hazlett in 1998 to head up the nautical science and marine transportation department. Hazlett describes what happened next to the larger program as a "meteoric rise"; under McMahon's leadership, GMATS went from a staff of seven people (and cash on hand of about three hundred dollars) to a highly profitable program with a staff of more than thirty people by December 2002. In part this was due to revised training regulations promulgated by the International Maritime Organization, a UN offshoot, which mandated new or refresher courses for a large number of merchant seamen. But it also reflected the entrepreneurial spirit of the program's leaders.[9]

In 2002, Hazlett left GMATS to take up his current job at the navy's Center for Naval Engineering, after he had worked in curriculum development at Kings Point. Hazlett is primarily tasked with working on the navy's Five Vector System, a new interactive computer model that will eventually track the certifications and qualifications of every navy sailor. The ultimate goal is to give sailors the ability to "detail" themselves—that is, to give them the opportunity to pick their own assignments by showing them what positions are available that match their qualifications, and/or what training they will need to complete to qualify for specific positions. To this end, Hazlett's group is capturing every single task that a naval engineer completes, and classifying these by skill level. (Similar teams, meanwhile, are also working on the Five Vector project for deck and other divisions.)

The end result will be a system that will allow sailors to be more proactive in defining their own careers. It will also provide the navy with significant savings—no small concern in a time of smaller defense budgets and larger defense responsibilities. The navy will no longer be training sailors in the same skills multiple times. Skill retention is expected to be greater, as sailors learn skills that they will actually be using in their next position. Although only three rates are currently functional, Hazlett expects the system to be fully operational in two years.

"In the meantime," he says, "we have our work cut out for us."

.   .   .

One sailor who might have benefited from the Five Vector model is Sharon Thorpe McIlnay, a member of the Kings Point class of '99. McIlnay grew up in Huntington, a small town in central Pennsylvania located not far from Penn State University. She had little experience on the water as a child, but in choosing to attend Kings Point she continued a long tradition of seafaring in her family; among others, her grandfather was a Dutch merchant mariner (and later a member of the U.S. Navy), and her uncle sailed in the navy. Partly because of these family ties, McIlnay chose to go active duty in the navy after graduating from Kings Point with an engineering degree.

McIlnay's logical first step in the navy would have been to attend the navy's Surface Warfare Officer School (SWOS). But because of Kings Point's relatively late mid-June graduation date, SWOS had already filled its spring class, and McIlnay had to wait for the November class. In the meantime, she was detailed to the Military Sealift Command as a damage-control instructor with the Afloat Training Team. In this capacity, McIlnay taught firefighting, antiterrorism, and chemical, biological, and radiological defense courses onboard MSC ships. She then completed the SWOS program, as well as an advanced gas turbine school and a communications officer school. After finishing up this third round of training, she got her first seagoing assignment: a tour of duty aboard the destroyer USS *Stump* as an auxiliaries officer, supervising all of the engineering equipment not associated with main propulsion, including potable water, steering gear, hydraulics, sewage, and steam.

McIlnay became engaged in 2002, after several years aboard the *Stump*. She says today that she would have liked to remain on active duty, but she and her fiancé encountered difficulties when consulting with navy officials about possible colocation. The navy assignment officers could guarantee only that they would try to station the two in the same place every other tour. The prospect of eighteen-month tours apart—or, in the worst case, more than that—held little appeal for the young couple, and McIlnay decided to leave the navy.

McIlnay sailed briefly with the National Oceanic and Atmospheric Administration (NOAA). She then landed a shoreside position as a potable-water applications engineer with Newport News Shipbuilding, a subsidiary of Northrup Grumman, in Newport News, Virginia. The job was an instant fit, thanks to McIlnay's experience with potable water on the *Stump*.

In one sense, water is the mortal enemy of a ship. At the same time, it is a ship's lifeblood. Water not only keeps mariners clean, healthy, and hydrated, it also plays a vital role in the basic operating systems of most ships. As a result of her time on the *Stump*, McIlnay understood better than most the importance of a reliable potable water system aboard ship.

> I have a real appreciation for water usage on board. Basically, the dis-tilling plants are designed to meet the criteria of thirty gallons of water per person, per day. If you waste any of that water, or lose any of that water, there's no buffer built in. There's no way to recover it. There were too many nights on the *Stump* when I had to get up and go walk the fresh-water system to find out where the leak was, because we were losing too much water. And sometimes it's not as simple as a leak! Sometimes people are just using way too much water. It's no fun; you want to choke them, actually, because they're not the ones getting up in the middle of the night walking the system. I would like to avoid that for future sailors.[10]

Today, McIlnay is working on the potable water systems for two new navy aircraft carriers, the Nimitz-class *George H. W. Bush* and an even newer vessel, a yet-to-be-named CVN21–class carrier. McIlnay's primary task is preparing the specifications for the equipment that the vessels will need. She passes these specs on to the designers she works with; they then figure out how to run the pipes and integrate the potable water system equipment into the ship's multiple operating sys-tems. These designs are passed on to the naval architects, who inte-grate them into the overall ship design, taking into account weight, center of gravity, and other considerations.

The *George H. W. Bush* is the tenth Nimitz-class aircraft carrier, scheduled for completion in 2008. As such, its design is almost com-plete—in fact, some component parts are in the prefabrication stage—so McIlnay is mainly adapting new technologies into an existing carrier "package." The CVN21 class, by contrast, is still in the concept stage. It will be a substantially different design, and therefore gives McIlnay opportunities to work on early-stage conceptual design.

McIlnay stresses that she enjoys her work, continues to learn new and interesting things at Newport News, and is pleased to be able to put the engineering skills that she learned at the Academy to good use. At the same time, she admits, she finds her thoughts drifting seaward.

She and her fiancé are planning a move to Bremerton, Washington, in the near future–he's being transferred to the carrier USS *Carl Vincent*–and she's starting to look for merchant marine opportunities in that area.

"I really enjoy being at sea," she explains. "If my fiancé is going to be on deployment, I might as well look for a ship."[11]

Kings Point graduates are not found only on or near the water. In the center of Norfolk's compact financial district, the admiralty law firm of Davey & Brogan, named in part for partner and Kings Point graduate Patrick Brogan, '79, makes its home in a formidable nineteenth-century three-story stone building that also houses the city's venerable Virginia Club, a formerly all-male eating club that not so long ago admitted its first female members. Across the street, appropriately enough, is the Norfolk World Trade Center and Customs House.

Patrick Brogan grew up in McLean, Virginia, and credits his sea-faring ways to his mother's side of the family. Her father sailed on merchant ships in World War I, and her brother attended the Pennsylvania State Nautical School (which closed its doors in 1947), and later became a rear admiral in the naval reserve. Brogan spent a year at Virginia Tech, but–as one of twelve children–eventually found the tuition bills prohibitive. With encouragement from a high school classmate who had chosen to attend Kings Point, he started over at Kings Point.

Brogan began as a dual-degree candidate (majoring in both engineering and deck-related studies), but eventually narrowed his focus to engineering alone. Soon after he graduated, he joined the Marine Engineers Beneficial Association (MEBA, a tradition-rich maritime union, founded in 1875) as a third assistant engineer. The first time he walked into the union hall in Norfolk, he recalls, there were two jobs on the board that he could have taken: a permanent position on a tanker that was sailing an East Coast route, or a temporary job on a break-bulk ship heading to the Mediterranean and North Africa.

He opted for break-bulk, and adventure. (Break-bulk is the way most cargo was shipped before the advent of containerization–that is, on pallets, in bags or crates, or loose in tanks. Break-bulk ships spend more time in ports due to greatly extended loading and unloading times, and their sailors tend to see more of the shoreside world.)

Brogan sailed with MEBA for the next three years, but by the end of this time, shipping jobs were becoming scarce, and he decided to change direction. He took the LSATs, did well, and was admitted to law school at William and Mary in Williamsburg, Virginia. Over the next three years, he took every admiralty law course that the school offered.

Brogan had already fulfilled his obligation to serve for six years in the naval reserve. After graduating from law school, however, he decided to accept an offer from the navy's Judge Advocate General Corps (JAG) instead of an offer from a private admiralty law firm in Norfolk. Brogan worked first as a JAG litigator, defending navy personnel, and then as a staff judge advocate. In the latter position, he worked on a legal advisory team to the commander in chief of the Atlantic Fleet, offering counsel on day-to-day regulation issues, and also overseeing investigations into collisions and other accidents.

In 1990, Brogan took a phone call from Phil Davey, a Norfolk acquaintance who had decided to launch his own admiralty law firm. Davey was familiar with Brogan's reputation and credentials, and asked him to join him in starting the new firm. The offer came at a propitious time, and Brogan decided to accept.

The firm has grown steadily since then. Currently, it serves as port representative to six of the thirteen international protection and indemnity clubs (simply put, mutual insurance companies that insure many international vessels), and these relationships guarantee the firm a steady stream of work. (Because of the large amounts of capital involved, no ships sail without marine insurance coverage.) In addition, Davey & Brogan does a good deal of tugboat work (some of the most collision-prone vessels, simply because of the nature of their work), and also represents terminal operators and other shore-based litigants.

For the most part, Brogan loves his work—which, as he explains, is a good thing. "Admiralty law," Brogan says, "is a specialty that you shouldn't undertake unless it's in your blood and it's something you like to do. It's not as lucrative as the high-profile areas of the law. We do it because we like it. We do it because we grew up on the water."[12]

Like his colleagues, Brogan works on several cases simultaneously. This morning, he's preparing to take a deposition from an expert witness in a case in Baltimore. The case involves a tug that was involved in a collision just outside the Chesapeake & Delaware Canal, the man-made waterway that connects the Delaware River with the Chesapeake Bay and the Port of Baltimore. One ship, it seems, was traveling south from the canal to the bay when it ran into a two-mile stretch of heavy fog. Visibility suddenly fell to no more than 150 feet. The southbound ship, sailing more or less blind, barely missed the tugboat that Brogan is now representing but collided with the barge that Brogan's tug was towing, and then hit another tugboat behind it. The claimant's witness will be attempting to prove that Brogan's tug was at fault; Brogan will be trying to find the holes in his argument. Meanwhile, he will also be putting time into another case in the eastern district of Virginia, for which settlement talks are already under way.

The number of containers passing through the Hampton Roads/Norfolk/Virginia Beach area has risen by as much as 15 percent a year in the last several years. Unlike other maritime-related professions in the region, though, maritime attorneys are not necessarily reaping the benefits of this growth. This is partly because individual vessel capacity has risen along with container traffic, so Norfolk isn't necessarily seeing more ships enter its harbor. Technology continues to improve as well, improving safety conditions and reducing collision-related incidents.

But Brogan doesn't foresee a significant reduction in his caseload, either. "As long as there are ships in Norfolk," he says, "there will be disagreements and accidents. And as long as that's true, there will be a need for admiralty lawyers."

A steady rise in container traffic does mean more business for some parts of the maritime industry in the Norfolk area. One of those areas is the terminal side of the business: the companies that get the containers to and from the docks.

For instance: Virginia International Terminals, a port complex that consists of three different ports in the Norfolk area and one inland truck/rail terminal in Front Royal, has been enjoying a steady rise in demand for its services. Vance C. Griffin, Kings Point, '84, is currently serving as operations supervisor at Portsmouth Marine Terminal, one of those three ports. He estimates that the number of containers processed through his terminal has risen by as much as several hundred *per day* over the past year.

Griffin grew up in New Bern, North Carolina, and first heard about Kings Point through a friend who had attended the Academy and couldn't say enough good things about the experience. Griffin knew very little about the maritime industry, but he was interested in a military career and liked the option of pursuing active duty after graduation. His Kings Point experience confirmed this preference and added a new dimension: Griffin now hoped to use his knowledge of shipping in the military. After graduating in 1984, he joined the army and reported to Fort Eustis, a Transportation Corps bastion in Newport News, to complete basic training. He followed this up with a second course in equipment maintenance, and then joined the 368th Transportation Company, a stevedoring and longshoremen operation. (Simply put, stevedores supervise cargo-handling tasks on the docks, loading and unloading ships and containers, and in some cases, maintaining and repairing containers. Longshoremen work the cargo under the supervision of the stevedores.) Thanks to his Kings Point experience, which had included a port-operations internship, Griffin found the stevedoring environment a familiar one.

Four years into his army service, however, Griffin felt he needed to reevaluate his career path. He was still enjoying his work and had been put on the army's promotion list, but now he had a wife and child to support. He heard of an opening at Virginia International Terminals (VIT), sent a resume in, and was offered the position. Two months later, he reported for work at VIT.

Griffin moved around among VIT's three local marine terminals, working for a year at the Newport News Terminal, and for another four years overseeing rail operations at the Norfolk Terminal. Then, in 1993, he was promoted to operations supervisor at the Portsmouth Terminal, on the Portsmouth side of the Midtown Tunnel that connects Norfolk and Portsmouth.

From his office in a well-groomed commercial building, which on this October day is in the midst of a noisy renovation, Griffin oversees the daily operations of his terminal. VIT's personnel don't do any stevedoring themselves. Instead, Griffin (and his counterparts at the other two marine terminals) works closely with several local stevedoring companies—for example, leasing equipment to them and providing them with operators for specialized equipment owned by VIT. Griffin also oversees the daily traffic of trucks in and out of the terminal, the "stuffing" and "stripping" (loading and emptying) of containers at the Portsmouth Marine Terminal warehouses, and the coordination of heavy lifts (that is, of any equipment too large or too heavy to be loaded into containers, and needing special gear and handling).

On this October day, Griffin is overseeing a series of heavy lifts of large transformers, each weighing between 287,000 and 398,000 pounds. With his orange hard hat and vest at the ready, he talks on the phone with representatives of the two railroads who will be receiving the transformers later in the day. He has already been down to the terminal this morning, coordinating with the three heavy-lift crane vendors who are working the vessel that has brought in the transformers, and most likely he will make his way down to the docks again before the day is out. The most important part of his job, he explains, is keeping in constant communication with the many players:

"There's a lot of communication involved. A large part of my job is keeping things coordinated and ensuring that we provide the best service. That's what we're here for. We don't sell a product, a widget, or an automobile. We sell service. That's what we want to do the best. We want our customers to conclude that it's the best quality service that they could possibly get anywhere, across the East Coast ports. And I think we do a pretty good job at that."[13]

Another crucial element of Griffin's job is keeping his container yard organized, up-to-date, and flowing. Portsmouth is one of the smaller terminals in the area—two hundred acres, in contrast to Norfolk's eight hundred-plus—and this means that the Portsmouth operators need to use their every available inch efficiently. They also need to make sure that every piece of machinery can be relied upon. If just one component in the complex logistical chain goes down, Griffin explains, backups and turnaround time will increase rapidly—and he'll have a good view out his office window of a long line of unhappy truckers.

One final wrinkle in the job is that it's impossible to plan precisely for the week ahead—or even the next day. He is continually adjusting and readjusting, making sure that whatever container traffic comes his way is moved along as quickly and efficiently as possible.

"So, no," he admits, "I almost never know exactly what's coming at us. On the other hand, I've been around long enough to be able to make a pretty good guess."

At the other end of the Midtown Tunnel, and at the end of an industrial cul-de-sac, is the one-story brick building that serves as home to Cooper/T. Smith Stevedoring, one of the largest stevedoring companies in the Norfolk area. And in one of the corner offices of this building sits the company's senior vice president, Patrick C. Hall, a member of the Kings Point class of '71.

Hall, who grew up in southeast Nebraska, dreamed of becoming a fighter pilot. That dream seemed within his grasp when he was recruited to play football at the Naval Academy. As it turned out, however, Annapolis had too many linebackers that year and asked Hall to go to a naval prep school—and play football—for one year, and then reapply. Though he was almost certain to be admitted after that year if all went well, Hall began wondering what would happen if he were injured on the football field. Would he lose his spot, and his shot at flying?

So Hall turned down prep school and instead attended Rockhurst College in Kansas City for one year. During that year, he applied to the Merchant Marine Academy, was accepted, and enrolled. By this time Hall had quite a bad case of wanderlust, which his subsequent Sea Year experiences at Kings Point only began to satisfy. And, he told himself, he would *still* have the option of appling to flight school after graduating.

But he was destined for disappointment, at least in the short term. Toward the end of his Kings Point years, he took the navy flight physical and failed the eye exam. Frustrated, he toyed briefly with the idea of enrolling in the Marine Corps, but finally decided that because he had enjoyed what he had seen of the civilian maritime world, he would choose to sail, and enrolled in the naval reserve.

He graduated from Kings Point at a difficult time for the commercial industry—in 1971, the year of his graduation, the Masters, Mates, and Pilots (MMP) union temporarily closed its books to new members, and he considered himself lucky to land a job working as a superintendent trainee for McGrath Stevedoring on the Brooklyn waterfront. Only months after his arrival, though, the International Longshoremen's Association (ILA) called a strike over stalled contract negotiations.

The strike turned out to be long and disastrous. No cargo was moved except by management acting as longshoremen; and it wasn't unusual for a ship to sit in port for three weeks to a month, waiting for its turn to unload. As a member of management, Hall himself worked the ships for more than two months, loading and unloading ships. When asked today to reflect on that time, he chuckles. "When I explain to people what I do," he says, "they generally say, 'Oh, you mean like *On the Waterfront.*' And you know, when I first got to those docks in Brooklyn, it was a lot like that."[14]

From Brooklyn, Hall moved on to a brief stint in Norfolk, and then to Houston as a ship superintendent. Houston at that time was booming, and Hall found himself working fifteen-hour days, seven days a week. After sustaining this grueling schedule for as long as he could, he decided to go back to sea, landing a position as a chief mate/relief captain on a Zapata Petroleum supply boat, plying the harbor of Sfax, Tunisia.

In late 1973, Hall found himself back ashore and looking for work near Hampton Roads. His wife had chosen the area as a place for the family to settle down. Hall began working the phones in search for a shoreside job, a task made more difficult by the recession that was then taking hold across the U.S. economy. Finally, at ten p.m. on New Year's Eve, he got an interview with Nacirema, a stevedoring company, and was offered a position stuffing containers for the navy. After only two weeks, the company called on him for another task.

> I got a phone call from the vice president, a Captain Chambers, who had sailed in World War II. He called me in, and said, "I understand from your background you know something about rubber." I said, "Well, I worked some rubber in Brooklyn." He said, "Good. We've got a new account coming in. It's Central Gulf Line. They've got this new concept called LASH ships—Lighter Aboard Ship. The first ship is due the day after tomorrow. I want you down there to work it." I had no idea what he was talking about.
>
> We went to work in late January of '74, and the first ship had fifteen thousand tons of baled and crated rubber on it, and nobody had the slightest idea what to do with it. Over the next two years, we managed to set up a system, and work it through, and it became very, very efficient.[15]

Hall's success in the unlikely realm of bulk rubber earned him a position as operations manager at Portsmouth Marine Terminal, where he worked for almost a year. Then, in 1976, Nacirema lost the Central Gulf account, and a new company called Cooper Stevedoring came into Norfolk to take over the account. They knew they needed some expertise on the ground in Norfolk, and in June 1976, David Cooper called up Hall and offered him a job running Cooper Stevedoring's Norfolk operations.

Hall, then just twenty-eight years old, accepted the position. He soon found out that the job description included not just Norfolk, but all of the company's East Coast operations. In the ensuing years, Hall helped Cooper Stevedoring (and later Cooper/T. Smith, after the company's 1983 merger with T. Smith & Sons) expand into Baltimore, Wilmington, Moorhead City, Charleston, Savannah, Jacksonville, and Brunswick.

Today, as senior vice president, Hall keeps a watchful eye on daily operations, helping his staffers figure out how many longshoremen to hire for the next day's work, or how to unload noncontainerized cargo in and around a series of rain delays. (Plywood doesn't like to get rained on.) At the same time, he also worries about new strategic directions for the company. For example, he is currently developing far-ranging concepts aimed at relieving the growing logjams in the maritime industry, as major ports on both the east and west coasts get increasingly crowded. Meanwhile, highway transportation is also feeling the squeeze, especially on the East Coast's Interstate 95, and more particularly in the Northeast Corridor. One project that Hall is working on—about which he'll say a little, but not a whole lot—involves moving construction debris by barge from the overcrowded Northeast through an intercoastal shipping corridor to landfills in the Southeast.

"So that's what my job tends to look like," Hall concludes. "I keep one eye on daily operations, and another eye on what I hope turns out to be the horizon."

The ten individuals profiled in the preceding pages share several important traits. First, they are all graduates of the United States Merchant Marine Academy at Kings Point, New York, the subject of this history.

Second, they work in (or, in the case of the crew of the *Maersk Carolina*, sail large ships into) the Hampton Roads area of Virginia, which includes Norfolk, Newport News, Portsmouth, Virginia Beach, and Hampton Roads proper.

Third, they have chosen to make their careers in or around the maritime industry, broadly defined.

These ten individuals, chosen from among the roughly three hundred Kings Point graduates working in the Norfolk area—of whom something like two-thirds work on, near, or around the water—

illustrate the wide range of maritime careers (military and commercial) for which Kings Point prepares its graduates.

Our illustration, however, only begins to show the true reach of the Merchant Marine Academy, as embodied by its graduates. More than 95 percent of the goods shipped into the United States arrive on ships bigger and smaller than the *Maersk Carolina*, through ports bigger and smaller than Norfolk. The *Carolina* is one of 237 (and rising) privately owned U.S. vessels of a thousand gross tons or more.[16] (The government owns another 179, and U.S. ownership of foreign-flagged vessels expands the definition of the merchant fleet enormously.) Norfolk, for its part, is only one of twenty-one U.S. ports that process more than 100,000 TEUs over the course of a year. (Norfolk itself processed 1,093,000 TEUs in 2003.[17])

The presence of a large navy base in Norfolk, and the presence of so many Kings Pointers in the navy, somewhat swells the ranks of Academy graduates in the Hampton Roads area. But Kings Pointers can be found in the maritime infrastructure of all major U.S. ports, across the U.S. fleet, and in all branches of the armed forces. In a sense, therefore, our ten subjects stand in for literally thousands of other Kings Pointers, in ports around the country and on ships around the world, whose stories of their place in the maritime infrastructure are equally compelling.

In this way Kings Point has a daily and profound effect on the maritime, and by extension, on the national economy. Water transportation is the lowest-cost form of transportation, and it is vital to national economic health. But like the industry it serves, Kings Point has struggled against great odds. It has reinvented itself many times. It has worked hard to maintain the support of a public that sometimes forgets the "fourth arm of defense," and sometimes overlooks the fact that almost all of what America imports and exports travels by ship.

This is the saga of the U.S. Merchant Marine Academy at Kings Point. Founded as the U.S. Merchant Marine Cadet Corps in the late 1930s, the Academy has since trained more than twenty thousand mariners, and provided more commissioned officers for the naval reserve program than any institution other than the naval academy.

It is a story that could begin at one of any number of junctures in history. We will begin with a young maritime nation struggling to escape from the influence of an older and far more powerful maritime nation.

2

Planting the Seeds

The story of the Academy begins before the birth of the nation. The first settlers from England were both profoundly influenced by, and dependent upon, the sea. Ships had brought them to this strange new land, and ships became lifelines for the young society. Especially in the rocky northern regions, which proved ill-suited to agriculture, the ocean was the most reliable source of food and income.

Shipbuilding immediately became a major focus of the young nation; the first American built seagoing vessel, the pinnace *Virginia*, built to carry settlers from the Popham Colony (near present-day Bath, Maine) back to their native England, appeared in 1607,[1] thirteen years before the Pilgrims established the first permanent settlement in Massachusetts. Northern shipyards multiplied quickly, and even the agrarian South supported some shipyards by the early 1700s. By 1724, British shipbuilders felt so threatened by the growing American shipbuilding industry–now supplying roughly half of the mother country's seagoing vessels–that they tried unsuccessfully to limit the import of American-built ships to England.[2]

The merchant ships built by the young colonies proved crucial in the struggle for independence from Great Britain. The infant Continental Navy took a severe beating in the Revolutionary War; out of an already tiny fleet of thirty ships in 1776, barely nine remained in service five years later. In that same year, however, 449 American merchant vessels plied the seas, carrying 6,735 guns, and they provided a

crucial supplement to the navy. These were privateers—privately
owned merchantmen, fitted out both to ship goods and to fight when
necessary. They transported goods and ammunition, carried envoys to
and from Europe, and between 1775 and 1783 destroyed three times as
many British ships as did the hard-pressed Continental Navy.[3]

By the end of the century, French privateers were turning the
tables on American merchant ships in what became known as the
Quasi-War, a very real (though undeclared) conflict in which French
vessels terrorized the East Coast of the United States, seizing 330 U.S.
merchant vessels in 1797 alone. The navy in effect no longer existed by
this time, and had to be re-created by the first secretary of the navy,
Benjamin Stoddert, an experienced operator of merchant ships. Stoddert oversaw the launching of six new navy frigates (originally authorized by Congress in 1794 in response to the Barbary Pirates' threat in
the Mediterranean)—all commanded by former merchant mariners—
and moved quickly to arm merchant ships. These actions made the
waters of the East Coast much less profitable for the French privateers,
and the conflict gradually subsided by the end of 1800.[4]

Maritime trade continued to be a crucial industry for the young
republic. Indeed, England's failure to respect the shipping rights of the
United States helped spark the War of 1812.[5] Privateers played an
even more significant role in this new war with England. At the outbreak of the conflict, there were more than forty thousand American
merchant seamen, eight times more deep-sea sailors than could be
found in the ranks of the navy. Privateers captured 1,300 British ships
(as compared to 254 captured by the navy),[6] effectively shutting down
the British shipping industry, which had dominated most of the Western Hemisphere, and scoring a smashing economic victory over that
formidable maritime nation.

In 1818, the Black Ball Line was established as the first scheduled
packet service between New York and Liverpool, ushering in a new
era of prosperity for American shipowners; the decades following,
from 1830 through 1860, would become known as the golden age of
U.S. shipping. This was the heyday of the celebrated clipper ships, and
builders in the United States competed to create better-designed vessels of ever greater speed, beauty, and size. As Kings Point–affiliated
maritime historians Arthur Donovan and Andrew Gibson detail, over
this thirty-year period, clipper ships doubled in size and tonnage, with
speeds up to fifteen knots (just over seventeen miles per hour).[7] Briefly,

world trade was dominated by these graceful triumphs of craft and design, sailed with great skill and resourcefulness.

After midcentury, though, the U.S. merchant marine began a slow decline. American shipowners continued to rely on their wooden sailing ships, even as their British competitors were looking to the future by investing in the iron-screw steamer. Another dent in the U.S. maritime industry resulted from a growing preference among American shipowners for less expensive foreign labor. In addition, in the late 1850s, the industry was hampered by legislative cutbacks introduced by the Southern congressional leadership, including the termination of subsidies for U.S. flag vessels that carried the U.S. mail. As this crucial support dried up, shipbuilding slowed, particularly in the experimental area of iron-hulled ships and steam propulsion.

The Civil War posed further difficulties for the industry. In the early years of the conflict, the North rushed to convert its merchant vessels into armed cruisers, and, along with newly constructed naval steamships, these ships proved highly effective in blockading Southern ports. More than half of the ships that participated in the blockade, as well as 80 percent of the officers, came directly from the merchant fleet, and the Union victory was due in part to the contribution of the merchant marine.[8]

But this maritime victory came at a high price. During the war, Confederate raiders destroyed more than 110,000 tons of Northern-owned shipping. These losses, as well as larger economic forces such as escalating marine insurance rates, forced many Northern shipowners to sell out to foreign investors. In 1860, American shipowners sold 17,000 tons of shipping to foreign concerns, and in 1865, this figure jumped to 133,832 tons. When losses inflicted by Confederate raiders were added to this trend, the toll was staggering. From a prewar high of nearly 2.5 million tons in 1861, the U.S. merchant fleet had declined to a little more than half that size by the end of the war, and was carrying only 32.2 percent of the nation's foreign trade.[9]

A Training Program Is Born

The end of the Civil War brought what maritime historian Winthrop Marvin termed an "ominously small recovery."[10] Already, the cyclical nature of the merchant marine—a cycle fueled by economic expansions and contractions, government policies, and the rhythms of war—was becoming a source of concern to policymakers. By the late 1860s and into the 1870s, the continued decline of the merchant fleet, the lack of professionalism sometimes exhibited by its officers, and the gradual shift to foreign crews and vessels over the course of a half-century prompted a national debate over U.S. maritime policy. A House committee created in 1868 under the leadership of Congressman John Lynch (R-Maine) was charged with investigating the causes of the decline, and with finding ways to increase tonnage and regain a position as an important player in world maritime activities.[11] This committee was heavily influenced by the shipbuilding industry, however, and recommended no changes to existing laws.

The national debate was also influenced by an 1865 disaster on the Mississippi River, in which the large riverboat SS *Sultana*'s steam boiler exploded midjourney, destroying the vessel and killing more than fifteen hundred on board. Many of the victims were Union soldiers or prisoners of war returning to Illinois from combat at Vicksburg. This episode, widely blamed on the incompetence of the engineering crew, led to increased scrutiny of merchant mariner officer standards and licensing, and eventually to legislation in 1871 and 1872, signed by President Ulysses Grant, which required licenses and set standards for operators of steamship boilers. Concern for improved boiler operation also led to the establishment, three years later, of the first ship engineers' union, the Marine Engineers Beneficial Association (MEBA), which still functions today.

An 1874 act of Congress—intended "to encourage the establishment of public marine schools"—was the next tentative step in the direction of a federal approach to developing merchant marine officers. In a very modest way, it pointed toward a more modern and effective merchant marine. The act authorized the secretary of the navy to "furnish . . . a suitable vessel of the Navy, with all her apparel, charts, books, and instruments of navigation . . . to be used for the benefit of any nautical school . . . at each or any of the ports of New York, Boston, Philadelphia, Baltimore, Norfolk, and San Francisco."

The disrepute into which the merchant service had fallen can be inferred from the last sentence of the act: "*No person shall be sentenced to, or received at, such schools as punishment or commutation of punishment for crime.*"[12] Congress, in other words, felt compelled to state explicitly that merchant marine schools were not to be used as an alternative to prisons, workhouses, or reform schools.

These ships were offered not to the states but to the leading ports of the country, and the act authorized no expenditures beyond the maintenance of the vessels. This was a form of industry assistance, rather than a formal federal training program. If the ports named could get organized to take advantage of the provisions of the act—and also, presumably, to put some money on the table—the federal government was willing to do its part to help promote commerce.

Only the Port of New York did so, at least for the time being. It established the New York Nautical School on the sloop of war USS *St. Mary* in the summer of 1874. This fully operational vessel soon became the leading source of trained junior officers for the nation—although admittedly there was little competition for this title—and set a precedent on which other port-based programs, and later, elements of a new federal program, would be modeled.

It was a full fifteen years before another port followed New York's lead. In 1889, Philadelphia established a school on the USS *Saratoga*, based on the Delaware River. In 1891, Boston became the third port to offer a program, aboard the USS *Enterprise*. In contrast to the New York school, these two newer institutions explicitly cast themselves as state schools, rather than port schools, from the outset. This soon proved to be a wise course of action. In 1911, Congress authorized payments of up to twenty-five thousand dollars in matching subsidy grants to the state schools—an incentive that prompted New York (in 1915) to become a state school to take advantage of the new grants.

But there was a problem. As a general rule, these three schools favored citizens of their respective states. (It appears that there were some regional exceptions to this rule.) Lawmakers saw an obvious inequity in expending federal tax dollars on schools that were open only to a small percentage of the national population, and which were concentrated in one region of the country. In 1891, therefore, Congress complemented this approach by passing the Ocean Mail Act, sponsored by Maine senator William P. Frye, and enacted as the Postal Aid Law. As well as providing general operating subsidies for steamship companies operating U.S. flag vessels, this act initiated a new method of "on the job" training for would-be merchant mariners. The program required that all ships built with federal subsidy under the Postal Aid Law carry one American cadet under the age of twenty-one for every thousand tons gross register, "to be educated in the duties of seamanship."

The program was notable for its durability, if nothing else. For the next fifty years, this was the best alternative to coming "up the hawsepipe," the mariner's term for starting on the bottom rung as an ordinary seaman on deck or a wiper in the engine room, and slowly working one's way up through the shipboard ranks. And on the face of it, the Ocean Mail Act should have provided a major boost to officer training, both in terms of scale and quality. As it turned out, though, there were three major flaws in the fledgling program. First, there were no clear criteria for cadet selection, which often led to unqualified or uninterested young men being selected for a cadet's position. Second, although the act called for "reasonable pay" for the cadets, who ranked as petty officers, the pay was almost never reasonable from the cadets' point of view. Last, and most important, there were no standards governing the shipboard experience. By and large, the cadets were assigned menial tasks and treated as unskilled labor. Few "mail cadets" actually learned navigation, seamanship, or engineering, and fewer still prepared themselves to earn merchant marine officers' licenses.

A Merchant Marine Unprepared for War

Because of these flaws, the Ocean Mail Act was largely ineffectual in its training objectives. Its subsidy program turned out to be a failure, as well. In part because of the inadequacies of this act, foreign vessels made steady gains in shipping U.S. goods throughout the 1890s and the early twentieth century. "The millions now paid to foreigners for carrying American passengers and products across the sea," declared President Grover Cleveland in his 1894 address to Congress, "should be turned into American hands."[13] This assertion could hardly be argued with; yet no one (including Cleveland) could articulate a clear maritime policy.

The merchant marine also received vocal support from Theodore Roosevelt, assistant secretary of the navy in the next administration, then vice president, and president from 1901 to 1908. At the time of his appointment by McKinley to the assistant secretary post, Roosevelt was a budding politician, and had written a well-received naval history of the War of 1812.[14] Roosevelt was also a staunch supporter of naval strategist Admiral Alfred Thayer Mahan, who preached the doctrine of command of the sea, both to "drive the enemy's flag from it" and to "close the highways by which commerce moves to and from the enemy's shores."[15]

Mahan, who argued that the United States needed not only a powerful navy but also port facilities and coaling stations around the world, had a huge impact on the young Theodore Roosevelt. When Roosevelt became president after President McKinley's assassination, he worked to greatly strengthen the navy; by 1907, the Atlantic battle fleet was, according to Secretary of the Navy Victor Metcalf, "the most powerful fleet of battle ships under one command in any navy."[16] Even Roosevelt was unable to implement all aspects of Mahan's theories. Supplies and logistics for the Great White Fleet, for example, were provided by foreign flag vessels chartered by the navy.

Theodore Roosevelt deserves credit for his tireless advocacy on behalf of the merchant marine. As he declared in his 1905 message to Congress, "To the spread of our trade in peace and the defense of our flag in war a great and prosperous merchant marine is indispensable. We should have ships of our own and seamen of our own to convey our goods to neutral markets, and in case of need to reinforce our battle line."[17]

As has so often been the case with the merchant marine, the politicians' pronouncements exceeded their actions. True, the U.S. coastal fleet was continuing to flourish: by 1910, the coastal fleet totaled almost 6.7 million tons—roughly ten times the size of the foreign fleet.[18] The opening of the Panama Canal in 1914 also increased the emphasis on both coastal and intercoastal shipping. But on the eve of World War I, the U.S. international merchant fleet remained almost nonexistent. Foreign ships transported more than 90 percent of U.S. imports and exports.

As the foreign shipping situation worsened with the outbreak of World War I, it became clear that the government would have to step in. President Woodrow Wilson, one of the most maritime-minded presidents of the modern era, exhorted Congress to take action. Without a merchant marine, Wilson argued, "our independence is provincial, and it is independence on land only and within our borders."[19]

Belatedly, the politicians realized that a lack of international shipping capacity could hurt the United States even in the case of conflicts that didn't involve the nation directly. Critical materials such as bauxite ore, used in the production of aluminum, and not produced domestically, couldn't be brought in, and U.S. products couldn't be gotten out. Wilson was painfully aware, for example, of the plight of the cotton farmers in the South (most of whom, like Wilson, were Democrats). Following the outbreak of war in 1914, many of the British and

French vessels that had served the cotton trade were called to war, and shipping rates (including vital marine insurance rates) for cotton soared a staggering 1,000 percent.[20] According to maritime industry historians Andrew Gibson and Arthur Donovan, the effects of this disruption in shipping were far-reaching, affecting the nation's transportation infrastructure as well as farming and industry: "Goods piled up on docks, railroad cars could not be unloaded, trains sat idle on the tracks, cars were not available to carry products from farms, mines and factories—in short, much of the nation's transportation system and the economy it served came to a halt."[21]

In response, Congress passed and President Woodrow Wilson signed two major pieces of legislation: the Seaman's Act of 1915 and the Shipping Act of 1916. The Seaman's Act was the product of a twenty-year crusade by Andrew Furuseth, head of the International Seamen's Union, and focused mainly on the appalling conditions often endured by sailors. The act eliminated imprisonment as a punishment for desertion, improved safety and living conditions at sea, and reversed centuries of discrimination, including the Supreme Court's notorious 1897 *Arago* decision, which ruled that sailors (and Native Americans) were not covered by the Thirteenth Amendment, and thus were subject to involuntary servitude.[22]

The Shipping Act of September 1916 was equally revolutionary, creating for the first time a federal entity dedicated to the advancement and protection of the merchant marine: the United States Shipping Board. Explicitly, the Shipping Board was supposed to promote the development of the merchant marine and to regulate foreign and domestic shipping. Along these lines, the board instituted regulated competition, allowing shipping companies to meet and share economic data, and effectively exempting them from antitrust laws. The board would protect the nation and its merchant marine from outside interference to "free American shippers from the dictation of foreign owners who, on orders from belligerent governments, were directing what goods a ship could and could not carry."[23]

In addition, the Shipping Board was specifically charged with making sure that the United States had a sufficient number of merchant ships for transport in case the nation was drawn into war. To advance this cause, the board required all militarily useful ships to encourage their officers to be naval reservists. This policy soon proved its effectiveness: Eighteen months after this measure was enacted, when the United States was drawn into World War I, these ships were called to active duty, and augmented the navy with 538 additional vessels, though no more than 378 were in use at any one time.[24]

At first, like its predecessor the Ocean Mail Act, the Shipping Act enjoyed little success in encouraging shipbuilding in the United States, due primarily to ineffective government leadership. Though the government allocated vast resources to both the Shipping Board and its subsidiary, the Emergency Fleet Corporation (EFC), established to oversee wartime shipbuilding, no new vessels built with government funds were launched until 1918. Finally, in July 1917, Edward N. Hurley was appointed chairman of the Shipping Board and president of the EFC, and the Shipping Board sprang into action, ordering the building of more than fourteen hundred *merchant ships*,[25] an astounding and unprecedented federal commitment to shipbuilding, which would ultimately cost the nation almost three billion dollars.[26]

As an additional measure, the Shipping Board seized and took title to all vessels belonging to belligerent nations in U.S. ports, and all ships under U.S. construction for foreign nations, as well as all U.S. oceangoing steel vessels over 2,500 tons.[27] These vessels were a crucial stopgap, allowing the United States to ship 911,047 troops with the necessary food and military supplies to France (the British merchant fleet moved another million), and also to overcome the German submarine threat by force of numbers.[28]

Then, suddenly, the seemingly endless European war ended before even a quarter of the ships that had already been ordered were completed. (None of the new ships authorized by the board were launched in 1917,[29] and only 470 were launched before the armistice of 1918.[30]) Under intense pressure from the shipbuilders, most of this unprecedented construction was continued, leading to a huge postwar surge in merchant ships controlled by the United States.

But what of the men to sail these ships? The Shipping Board also instituted training programs for officers, creating six-week free officer training schools for any physically fit men under the age of fifty-six who had served at least two years at sea. The results were mixed, at best; of the sixty-three hundred graduated before Armistice Day, only half had received licenses. Quality, too, was suspect. In many quarters, the merchant fleet was known derisively as the "Hooligan Navy."[31]

The federal cadet program, meanwhile, had sunk into almost complete ineffectiveness, with only a few companies still holding Postal

Aid contracts. The state schools had fared somewhat better, enjoying a brief revival during the war (and helped by the 1919 reopening of the Pennsylvania state nautical school after a six-year hiatus), but the problem of producing well-trained and professional officers was ever-present, and would continue to grow throughout the next decade as ships continued to become larger and more complex.

Lessons Slowly Learned

By 1920, the United States was again a major shipping power, with its flag fleet ten times larger than it had been only six years earlier. For the first time since 1863, half of the goods entering U.S. ports were trans-ported in U.S. flag vessels. Soon, though, it became painfully clear that too many vessels had been built for the U.S. merchant marine to absorb, and that many of the government-constructed ships would have to be sold. The postwar disposition of almost fourteen hundred ships was slow, difficult, and expensive. Ships that had cost more than two hundred dollars per ton to build were sold off for as little as five dollars a ton.[32] A glut had been created, devastating ship prices world-wide. Many operators didn't buy the vessels even at these bargain prices, and the government enacted a program to assign ships to "man-aging operators," a highly costly venture.[33]

This fueled the frustrations of Republicans in Congress, who were generally not supportive of the government's involvement in ship-building. The Merchant Marine Act of 1920–often called the Jones Act, after Republican senator Wesley Jones of Washington, the bill's primary sponsor–was a direct response to the perceived excesses of the Emergency Fleet Corporation. The legislation returned shipping firmly to the realm of private ownership, and though it legislated pref-erential treatment for domestic shipping, it virtually ignored the realm of foreign trade.

The disposal of the huge oversupply of government-constructed ships provided a rich ground for critics of the Harding administration. After all, Harding–according to Albert Lasker, the man he appointed to head the U.S. Shipping Board–had proclaimed that the merchant marine was the issue that "interested him the most in becoming presi-dent."[34] Within months of assuming power, though, the Harding administration was selling off or scrapping its fleet at an enormous loss.

But there was at least one silver lining: The great ship selloff, combined with the lingering perception that the nation had been caught unprepared for World War I, persuaded a small group of far-sighted Americans to begin a systematic lobbying effort in support of a merchant marine that would stay strong outside the cycles of mobilization and demobilization.

In 1925, Congress, influenced by the British view of their merchant marine (or Merchant Navy, as the British referred to it) as one arm of national defense, established the Merchant Marine Reserve as a component of the naval reserve. Once again, it was only half a measure, at best; almost no funds were appropriated for the program, and no specific training program was mandated. About fifteen hundred merchant marine officers joined the new reserve, only to find that it was a shell of a service.

Clearly, this was inadequate, and in 1928 Congress attempted yet again to improve the state of maritime affairs with the Jones-White Merchant Marine Act, again sponsored by Senator Wesley Jones. Through this act, Congress was once again seeking to serve two related ends: to upgrade and expand the U.S. fleet by awarding construction loans, and to increase American-flag services on designated foreign trade routes through mail contract subsidies.

The Jones-White Act, later known as the Merchant Marine Act of 1928, repealed the cadet training provisions mandated by the 1891 law, replacing them with similar measures under the supervision of the postmaster general. Again, the number of cadets, the method of their selection, their payment, and their training were left to the discretion of the individual shipping companies. With conditions at sea still difficult, and with monthly salaries of between twenty-five and forty-five dollars, the opportunity had little appeal.

Moreover, the lack of clear standards and guidelines for instruction meant that productive learning experiences were the rare exception. As Thomas Woodward, one of the first members of the soon-to-be-created Maritime Commission, later reported of this period, "A survey among the larger steamship companies and data procured from various sources convinced the Commission that the Cadet system . . . has been prostituted in the interest of special privilege insofar as a method for training merchant officers was concerned." In many cases, he added, politicians used their influence to procure berths for young men "during vacation periods, to give them a taste of the sea."[35]

If the goal of the Jones-White Act was to get young mariners educated and licensed, then the legislation was an abject failure. (Jones himself later tried to distance himself from the act, and its failure ultimately contributed to his senatorial defeat in 1932.)[36] A 1938 study, based on reports from thirteen subsidized lines operating under the 1928 act, showed that of a total of 1,987 cadets who completed training voyages between 1932 and 1937, only 100 received their officer licenses.[37]

Among policy makers, though, the Jones-White Act did spark widespread discussions about training, and several differing factions began to weigh in. The problems inherent in the training program were generally understood and accepted; consensus as to the *solutions* to these problems, though, was harder to achieve. Ernest Lee Jahncke, assistant secretary of the navy from 1929 to 1933, suggested that the Naval Academy increase its complement of midshipmen, and then allow a certain number of students to resign upon graduation and take positions in the merchant marine. Proposals were also floated to improve and expand the state schools.

And, for the first time, voices began to be heard in favor of a new federal academy, one that would be open to all Americans, equal in stature to West Point, Annapolis, and the Coast Guard Academy in New London, and devoted exclusively to training deck and engineering officers for the U.S. merchant marine.

An Advocate Emerges

The strongest of those voices belonged to a young mariner named Richard R. McNulty. A 1919 graduate of the Massachusetts Nautical School, McNulty was technical assistant to the director of the division of research of the U.S. Shipping Board. McNulty had experience both at sea and ashore; having served as a third and a second officer with the American Line after graduation, he then accepted a position in 1920 as a nautical scientist in the Hydrographic Office of the Navy Department.[38] During this time, he also received a bachelor's degree from Georgetown's School of Foreign Service. McNulty then returned to industry as the shoreside assistant to the marine superintendent of the C. D. Mallory Transport Lines. By the time he was hired by the U.S. Shipping Board, therefore, McNulty had accumulated a wide range of experiences in and around the U.S. shipping industry.

At the U.S. Shipping Board, McNulty steadily increased his base of knowledge, completing extensive research on shipping management, the merchant marine naval reserve systems of the United States and other countries, and—most important for his future career—the processes whereby other nations developed their merchant marine officers.

This became an area of intense thought and study, even an obsession, for McNulty. Between 1929 and 1934, he published articles in the *Marine Journal*, the *Naval Institute Proceedings*, and the *Nautical Gazette*, in which he articulated his views on the best ways to train officers for the merchant marine. McNulty clearly saw his crusade as an uphill battle, in which he was fighting a lack of interest among the general public and shipowners as well as entrenched union opposition. In a 1930 *Nautical Gazette* article, McNulty compared his efforts to "the famed story of the bull dashing out his brains after a feverish attempt to make an exit in a four-foot wall."[39]

McNulty's early suggestions for a national academy were extremely detailed and not always calculated to make friends. In the same 1930 article, McNulty recommended establishing the school at the Coast Guard Academy in New London (and transferring all of the Coast Guard cadets to the Naval Academy), abolishing the state schoolships, and maintaining the national academy through appropriations from the navy and commerce departments.[40]

His underlying arguments in favor of a maritime academy, however, gradually began to win support, pushed along by periodic disasters at sea. Four years later, in an article written shortly after the 1934 *Morro Castle* disaster, described below, McNulty soberly reminded his readers of the importance of the issue: "To again forget the value of trained men is unthinkable. *Something will be done*."[41]

McNulty was a strong advocate for training that would raise the professional character and competence of the merchant officer. He believed that the rewards of the training should not be limited to command at sea, but should also prepare the officer candidate to enter executive and administrative positions in shipping offices, government departments, and the foreign service. McNulty also advocated a well-organized merchant marine naval reserve program, and periods of naval training similar to those offered British seamen by the British Royal Naval Reserve.

Finally—and most important for our story—he advocated the establishment of a shore-based federal merchant marine academy that would serve young men from all across the nation. This new academy, McNulty declared, should provide its graduates with an education comparable to that enjoyed by the graduates of West Point and Annapolis.

The idea of shore-based merchant marine schools was relatively novel. The "schoolship" model still predominated—as, for example, the New York State Maritime Academy, which was based on two ships, the 5,500-ton USS *Empire State*, and a demasted classroom schooner, the *Annex*, both docked at the Brooklyn Navy Yard. Retired Kings Point engineering professor Harrison O. Travis, a 1937 gradu-ate of the New York State School, recalls an education that was com-pletely centered around the two ships; the cadets ate, slept, and studied on the *Empire State*, and took two cruises each year on this vessel. On the *Annex*, the cadets took machine shop, learned knot-tying, and became acquainted with general shipboard equipment. Virtually the only non-shipboard element of the training was a morning run around the Navy Yard to keep the cadets in shape.[42]

But McNulty's novel idea of shore-based maritime education was beginning to gain momentum on the state level. The California State School, for example, established a shore campus at Tiburon, near San Francisco, in 1929. At the same time, the New York State School, under the direction of retired navy captain James Harvey Tomb, undertook what turned out to be a painfully slow, decade-long process of building a shore-based facility at Fort Schuyler in the Bronx. In arguing for a shore-based school, Tomb wrote of the state maritime schools that "the equipment . . . has always been crude and antiquated. There is serious lack of instructors, of lab equipment, and of American textbooks. The handicap from lack of modern facilities is pathetic."[43]

McNulty, ever the opportunist, sought to merge this trend with his own ideas. In a September 1931 *Nautical Gazette* article, for example, he explored the possibility of converting one of these state institutions into the federal academy—a solution that was politically unfeasible and never seriously pursued.

McNulty's views received support from the Third National Confer-ence on the Merchant Marine, held in 1930. The conference created a Committee on the Training of Officer Personnel chaired by Admiral Hutchinson Cone, a member of the U.S. Shipping Board. The Cone Committee, as it came to be known, circulated questionnaires to more than eight thousand leaders in commerce, shipping, labor, education, and government. They received more than sixty-five hundred replies, which seemed to indicate a strong consensus in favor of what the survey had described as a "National Merchant Marine Academy Shore Station."

McNulty also received support from the New York State School's superintendent. Captain Tomb was the preeminent figure in cadet training at this time, and his willingness to lend his name to the cause of a federal academy was remarkable. His peers at the Massachusetts and Pennsylvania schoolships were less supportive, perhaps fearing that a federal academy would threaten their existence. These fears were fully justified; in the questionnaire mentioned above, almost three-quarters of those responding favored the abolishment of the state system of training should a federal academy be established.

Captain James Harvey Tomb, the first superintendent of the Merchant Marine Academy, seated at his desk in Wiley Hall, September 11, 1942.

Tomb was the first superintendent on the state level to argue persuasively that the training of merchant marine officers was a federal, and not solely a state, function.[44] In a 1932 article in the *U.S. Naval Institute Proceedings*, Tomb called upon the federal government to develop a clear policy: "With the modern development of our merchant marine it is now imperative for the federal government to outline its policy for the education of merchant marine officers."[45]

Tomb envisioned two possible solutions, both involving government aid: "Two courses are open: a) the government to enter the educational field and to establish national merchant marine academies, b) the government to continue its past policy in considering education for private careers as a state function and to encourage education in the merchant marine profession by gift of suitable land."[46] In large part due to his strong, steady, and somewhat unlikely advocacy for a federal academy, his was one of the first names to be suggested for the superintendency of that new academy, if and when such an institution got off the ground.[47]

A Tragedy Brings Progress

Although McNulty's cogent articles had an impact on policy makers, the early 1930s were not a propitious time to act on his recommendations. In part due to the calamitous effects of the Depression, the merchant marine was again suffering setbacks. This had an immediate and profound impact on the state schools, which each year generated a small new crop of licensed officers, most of whom were unable to find employment as officers. Not surprisingly, the leaders of these institutions made a strong case that even more merchant marine officers—such as those who would be minted by a new federal academy, for example—were completely unnecessary. The maritime unions, too, weighed in against any more additions to the labor pool.

Then, disaster struck, a tragedy that shook an industry and paved the way for the founding of the modern American merchant marine. On September 8, 1934, the SS *Morro Castle*—a four-year-old fast turbo-electric Ward Line passenger liner running between New York and Havana, Cuba, and built under the provisions of the 1928 Act—caught fire and burned off the coast of New Jersey. According to a subsequent investigation, the crew negligently permitted a small fire to rage out of control. Then, adding shame to their ineptitude, they commandeered most of the seats in the lifeboats. A total of 134 people died, including 91 of the 318 passengers. (Also killed were federal mail cadets William Hillstrand and Alexander Ross.) The incompetence of the crew was clearly to blame for many of the deaths. But rumors also abounded that the fire was set deliberately to provide an infusion of insurance money to the financially troubled Ward Line and its parent company, Atlantic, Gulf, & West Indies Steamship Lines[48]—rumors fueled in part by the long criminal record of the ship's radio operator.

Only four months later, a second passenger liner owned by the Ward Line, the SS *Mohawk*, collided with the Norwegian freighter SS *Talisman* and also sank off the coast of New Jersey. Again, lives were lost, and again, crew incompetence and dangerous conditions aboard ship were alleged. (This time, however, the captain and all but one of the ship's officers went down with the vessel.) In an era in which ships were still the only option for transoceanic travel and international trade, the public was deeply concerned about maritime safety. The twin disasters soon led to enormous public pressure to tighten ship safety and construction standards on the federal level, and inevitably raised again the question of officer training.

At the same time, the industry was under siege from yet another direction. In February 1933, Alabama senator Hugo Black, subsequently a Supreme Court justice, headed a congressional investigation of fraud in the maritime industry, specifically regarding abuse of U.S. ocean mail contracts and subsidies. The testimony from these investigations, which ran for more than a year, filled nine volumes and provided damning evidence of rampant corruption and ineptitude. The Black Committee eventually turned its findings over to the Post Office Department, and its final report was delivered to Congress in March 1935.

Accompanying the report was a statement from President Franklin Delano Roosevelt, a former assistant secretary of the navy and lifelong sailor, and certainly the staunchest advocate among modern U.S. presidents of a strong U.S. merchant marine. Roosevelt's message cited a number of reasons why Congress should adopt direct, "honest" subsidies to support the shipping industry:

> To me there are three reasons for answering this question in the affirmative. The first is that in time of peace, subsidies granted by other nations, shipping combines, and other restrictive or rebating methods may well be used to the detriment of American shippers. Second, in the event of a major war in which the United States is not involved, our commerce, in the absence of an adequate merchant marine, might find itself crippled because of its inability to secure bottoms. Third, in the event of a war in which the United States itself might be engaged, American-flag ships are obviously needed not only for naval auxiliaries, but also for the maintenance of reasonable and necessary commercial intercourse with other nations. We should remember the lessons learned in the last war.[49]

Roosevelt was convinced that the American public would accept such subsidies—and conversely, that it was important to get away from the disguised subsidies of the past, which failed to provide the industry with the support it needed. Though Senator Black himself was in favor of outright government ownership of merchant marine vessels, in the end Roosevelt's reasoning won the day.[50]

The Black Committee's report included no specific recommendations on training. But a separate report, prepared by the Interdepartmental

Committee on Shipping Policy, and submitted at the same time as the Black report, recommended the establishment of a national merchant marine academy.[51] Many minds were converging on the same solution.

A Modern Merchant Marine

Congress—finally spurred to action by disaster, scandal, and an activist president—undertook a far-ranging reform of the shipping industry. On April 15, 1935, Democratic representative Schuyler Otis Bland of Virginia, chairman of the House Merchant Marine and Fisheries Committee, and Republican senator Royal S. Copeland of New York, then the chairman of the Senate Committee on Commerce, introduced bills into the House and the Senate dismantling the postal subsidy system and creating a revamped system of direct construction and operating subsidies.

The act, which originally contained no provisions for a federal academy, proposed to continue the practice of requiring subsidized ships to carry federal cadets. The wording was remarkably similar to earlier legislation: "every vessel operating under a contract in force under this part . . . shall be required to carry two cadets . . . compensated by the contractor in the amount of not less than $30 per month . . . and shall be afforded every opportunity to serve an apprenticeship in, and be instructed concerning, the navigation and operation of the vessel."[52]

But the act was soon adjusted. The U.S. Shipping Board, under the guidance of director J. C. Peacock, submitted a proposed amendment to the legislation, authorizing the establishment of a merchant marine academy.

> The Secretary of Commerce, with the approval of the President, is hereby authorized and directed to establish a Merchant Marine Academy for the training of citizens of the U.S. as officers for service on vessels documented under the laws of the U.S. . . . The educational program of the cadets required in Section 512(a) shall be under the supervision of the Merchant Marine Academy.[53]

This amendment was included verbatim in the final draft of the Merchant Marine Act of 1936. It was passed by Congress and signed into law by President Roosevelt on June 29, 1936.

Both Peacock's amendment and the preamble to the act, in which the need for "trained and efficient" merchant marine personnel was acknowledged, seemed to commit the government to implementing a modern training program. This proved easier to legislate than to achieve.

While the shipping industry apparently had few objections to the still largely undefined plan, maritime labor registered its strong opposition. The objections, voiced among others by Andrew Furuseth (the still-powerful but increasingly erratic president of the International Seamen's Union), centered on organized labor's assertion that the only acceptable training for merchant marine personnel was experience at sea. In a 1930 letter to the editor of the *Nautical Gazette*, for example, Furuseth railed against schoolships, claiming that they had "never accomplished anything of note, except to teach young men the advisability of keeping away from the sea." No man, he asserted, ever became a seaman "except by actual experience at sea."[54]

According to union leaders, allowing youths to skip this essential training would destroy the time-honored up-the-hawsepipe system and weaken the caliber of merchant marine officers. The unions favored instead an academy that would offer further training for those who already had received licenses. Lines were being drawn in the sand.

Our story necessarily focuses on the subject of officer training for the merchant marine. It is worth noting, though, that training was only a small piece of the Merchant Marine Act of 1936, a sprawling, ambitious piece of legislation that subsequently became the foundation for the modern maritime industry. The law was flawed, as even the first Maritime Commission chairman, Joseph P. Kennedy, freely admitted; but it was also transformational in its impact.[55]

One of its most important effects was the creation of the U.S. Maritime Commission, an organization that soon exhibited the type of vision and leadership that had been so lacking at the U.S. Shipping Board. An interim commission, chaired by Rear Admiral Henry W. Wiley, was created to begin planning for the Maritime Commission.

Another figure important in the history of cadet training entered the scene at this point: Telfair Knight, a political appointee and former businessman and real estate executive from Florida. Knight was appointed secretary to the commission, and eventually worked with Wiley to establish the Merchant Marine Cadet Corps.

Ten months later, on April 15, 1937, a permanent five-man commission was confirmed, led by financier and former Securities and Exchange

Rear Admiral Telfair Knight, secretary to the first Maritime Commission and later commandant of the U.S. Merchant Marine Cadet Corps. (Photographed in May 1951.)

Commission head Joseph P. Kennedy. Kennedy, better remembered today as the father of President John F. Kennedy, not only knew President Roosevelt but also had some relevant experience, having served during World War I as an assistant general manager in the Bethlehem Steel Company's Fore River shipyards in Quincy, Massachusetts.[56] The other members of the commission were Retired Navy Rear Admiral Emory S. Land, Thomas Woodward, Retired Navy Rear Admiral Wiley, and Edward Moran Jr. (of New York tugboat fame).

The duo of Kennedy and Land proved surprisingly effective. One of the secrets to their success was the ready access that the two enjoyed to the president. Land later recalled that he and Kennedy generally met with Roosevelt once a week, often on Wednesday mornings. The semiparalyzed Roosevelt, who preferred not to put on his leg braces early in the morning, received the two shipping leaders in his bedroom, and conversed with them over breakfast as he sat upright in bed. As Land later put it, "When Joe Kennedy came out of that meeting, everybody knew his orders were coming right from the President."[57] Land's statement underplays his own relationship to Roosevelt; by the time Land retired from the navy in 1937, the two had known each other and been "closely associated" for many years in the Navy Department, dating back to World War I.[58]

Kennedy himself was not particularly involved with the training concerns of the maritime industry; as the specter of war in Europe again raised its head, his primary interests were union relations and shipbuilding, both of which he knew to be critical to the strength of the merchant marine. As it turned out, his tenure at the Maritime Commission was brief. (He resigned some ten months later, in February 1938, to become ambassador to the Court of St. James's, United Kingdom.) His leadership and connections had unquestionably

strengthened the fledgling commission and helped put it on the right
path. But Kennedy himself noted
upon his departure that the work had
only just begun. In his letter of resignation, he admitted that "the shipping problem is far from solved, and
that it is going to take some exceedingly strenuous measures on the part
of the U.S. to preserve a fleet of anything like the present proportions in
either foreign or domestic trade."[59]

As is often the case in bureaucracies, the real action was taking place
several levels down from the Joe
Kennedys and Emory Lands. In particular, the training questions were
being addressed by the Division of
Personnel, initially staffed by two senior officers, Daniel S. Ring and Philip

Rear Admiral Emory S. Land, a
member of the first Maritime
Commission.

King. Commissioner Wiley, according to Sam Schell, assistant director
of the division of transportation (and later executive officer of the War
Shipping Administration), felt somewhat insecure about his commercial shipping expertise, and made his interest in this area known by
continually expressing his interest in "handling men."[60] The commission soon named Wiley Commissioner in Charge of Training.

With Knight as his assistant, Wiley steered his division into the
complex realm of cadet training. As they undertook this task, they
turned with increasing frequency to another commission employee for
advice. Soon, Wiley realized he couldn't function without this unique
resource. Richard R. McNulty–researcher, author, and longtime agita-
tor for national maritime officer training–was hired by Wiley in
August 1937. Although initially assigned to the Division of Research as
a senior operating cost analyst, he eventually transferred to the Personnel Department, where he could devote himself full-time to the challenge of officer training.

There, he took up the work that would eventually earn him a singular nickname from a grateful merchant marine community: Father
of the Academy.

3

Conceived in Peace

1937–1941

If this history were a play, the curtain for act II would rise upon a bustling office scene in downtown Washington. A prominent wall calendar tells us that this is a day in mid-December 1941, only a few days after the calamity of Pearl Harbor.

Office workers in uniform and the prominent portrait of Franklin Delano Roosevelt on the wall tell us that this is some sort of government office, and from the clutter and bustle and noise level, we can infer that it is the epicenter of some sort of important activity.

In the foreground, we see a rather short, serious-looking man hunched over a desk, busily scribbling notes on a manuscript. The thick volumes piled up on his desk appear to be law books, but his desk (like the others around the office) is adorned with nautical bric-a-brac. A young woman is sorting through a stack of reports at another desk, evidently searching for a particular piece of paper. Over by the door to the hallway, another man is signing for a telegram that has just been delivered by a Western Union messenger. He scans the contents of the message quickly, registers surprise on his face, and then stops to read it more carefully.

In an adjoining office, a debonair-looking man is speaking on the phone, apparently to a U.S. senator. He jabs the air with his forefinger to make a point. "Yes, Senator," we hear him say. "But we think there's another way of looking at this." A pause. "Well, yes, Senator. But surely this is both an economic issue *and* a national defense issue."

In the outer office, another phone rings. The young woman answers it brightly. "Cadet Training Program, Mrs. Bozeman speaking. May I help you?"

She pauses, listening, then calls over to the seated man. "Captain McNulty," she says, "it's Lauren McCready. He says he's had no luck in Newport News, and would like to know where he should head next. He's heard of another possibility up the coast."

Before McNulty can respond, the man holding the telegram speaks up. "Excuse me, Captain," he says, now grinning broadly, waving the buff-colored sheet, "but you might want to see this first." He strides quickly over to McNulty's desk and hands him the telegram.

McNulty reads it aloud: "Purchase price of one hundred thousand dollars approved. Carmody to arrange six-month lease pending congressional approval. Reply appreciated ASAP."

He nods. A smile flits across his face, creating unaccustomed wrinkles. "Well, well, Kirk. I wasn't sure we'd ever live to see this day."

Then he looks back across to the other side of the office. "Mrs. Bozeman," he says to the young woman, who is still waiting patiently with her hand over the telephone's mouthpiece, "tell young McCready to turn around and head back here as soon as possible. Tell him we've got our campus."

Getting Off the Ground

Some version of that small drama was played out in the Commerce Building offices of the Maritime Commission in Washington, D.C., at the very end of 1941. As it turned out, this was one of the scenes that immediately preceded the construction of the United States Merchant Marine Academy at Kings Point, New York.

But four years earlier, in the fall of 1937, this climactic moment was a very long way off indeed. Congress had authorized a training program with the act of 1936, but no one knew exactly what this meant. Even those within the newly formed Maritime Commission were puzzled. For the time being, and for the foreseeable future, the Academy existed mainly in the mind of Richard R. McNulty.

In 1937, the Maritime Commission was primarily concerned with a move to terminate the existing mail contracts and negotiating in their place a new Operating Differential Subsidy Program. The training jurisdiction of the Maritime Commission was still confined to subsidized

Rear Admiral (then Captain) Richard R. McNulty, supervisor of cadet training, photographed on a training cruise to South America in 1939. McNulty would come to be known as the Father of the Academy.

vessels, and the program was continuing to function more or less as it had before the 1936 act. True, the Personnel Division, under Philip King and Daniel Ring, had established minimum training requirements for the cadets selected for the program. But selection itself was still the responsibility of the operators, and the shipboard training of most cadets remained haphazard and inadequate at best.

Increasingly, both from within and outside of the government, there were calls for a complete overhaul of the system. The families of cadets then in the system were among the most vocal in demanding improvements. For example, in a November 1937 letter to W. C. Peet Jr., secretary of the Maritime Commission, Randolph Branch wrote to complain about his son's treatment as a cadet on board a U.S. Lines vessel. Then—perhaps in hopes of sniffing out a better training experience for his son—he switched gears. "I have seen in the papers that Mr. Kennedy has recommended a nautical school of some sort," Branch wrote at the end of his letter. "May I ask whether this is to be a school for sailors or potential merchant officers?"[1]

Another spur to action was Senate Resolution 96, passed in March 1937. This nonbinding vote urged the Maritime Commission to prepare, "with the cooperation of the Secretary of the Treasury, the Secretary of the Navy, and the Secretary of Commerce, tentative plans for the establishment of an Academy for the training of licensed personnel for the Merchant Marine of the United States."[2] Based on this resolution, it is clear that at least some people in Congress felt that a new federal academy was the only solution to the seemingly intractable merchant marine training problem.

For the time being, though, the majority of the commission's members believed that their first training priority was the existing sea-based training program. And here, at least, some limited progress was being made. The commission had appointed Admiral Henry W. Wiley as commissioner of training, and Telfair Knight—the debonair gentleman in the inner office in our dramatization above—became Wiley's second in command. The commission also had undertaken a serious and comprehensive study of the existing program, and had begun contemplating alternative approaches, including the one suggested by the Senate resolution.

Admiral Wiley, in a memo written two months after the Senate action, outlined a cautious response. "The Commission is in favor of establishing a national Merchant Marine Academy," he wrote, "and is prepared to make a study of this subject, but feels that the time is not ripe for such an institution as the training of unlicensed personnel appears to the Commission to be more pressing."[3]

This was the public face of a major internal disagreement that, in the commission's early years, hobbled its efforts to implement a new officer training program. Richard McNulty, writing decades later about that formative period, recalled that both of the top two designated advocates for maritime training—Wiley and Knight—had strong reservations about establishing an academy.[4] Wiley remained more interested in unlicensed training, and Knight, according to McNulty, feared that pushing a federal academy would antagonize representatives from states with existing nautical schools, some of whom were important allies of the new commission.

Consensus in favor of a national academy—and the telegram announcing where it would be born—were still a long way off.

Embracing, and Not Embracing, a Sister Service

One pressing question concerned which branch of the government should administer merchant marine officer training, for both initial licensing and license upgrading. Few thought that the Maritime Commission itself would supervise a training program; most signs seemed to point to either naval or Coast Guard supervision. In a memo dated March 15, 1937, Rear Admiral R. R. Waesche, Commandant of the U.S. Coast Guard, articulated the traditional military standpoint that a single federal agency should have responsibility for the training of merchant marine personnel. Not surprisingly, he concluded that the Coast Guard was the agency best suited for this duty.[5] The commission duly passed on this suggestion to the Division of Personnel, but the issue continued to spark disagreement and controversy for the next several years.

The issue surfaced again at an April 1, 1937, meeting. The Maritime Commission was presented with a House proposal to create a commission to "study and make a report on the establishment of a Merchant Marine school at New London, Connecticut."[6] The location suggests that this proposal was weighted heavily toward Coast Guard jurisdiction. The proposed commission to study the possibility was slated to include eight members—one senator, one representative, one member of the Coast Guard, one member of the navy, one representative of marine workers, and three members of the public.

The Maritime Commission responded by pointing out to the House that, while its members had no particular objection to the proposal, they *did* feel that it would be appropriate for them to have a seat at the table. The proposal slid quietly under the waves.[7]

Suggestions for supervision of the training program were coming from all sides, but the commission did not rush to embrace any of them. Commissioner Kennedy asked the chair of the Senate Committee on Commerce to delay any legislation in order to give the group more time to study the possibilities. "The Commission realizes the extreme importance . . . of an adequate supply of well-trained licensed officers," Kennedy wrote. "At this time, however, we are not in a position to say whether there is a shortage of licensed officers or whether such a shortage is imminent."[8]

While Kennedy's caution was understandable—a complete overhaul of the program was likely to have far-reaching implications for both industry and national defense—the commission's hesitancy was making outside supervision of training ever more likely. Coast Guard supervision was a very real possibility, due in large part to the efforts of Admiral Wiley (and the fact that the Coast Guard had experience in training large numbers of seamen). During three separate commission meetings in June and July 1937, the commission considered but declined to act on a draft bill presented by Wiley that called for the training of merchant marine personnel under the supervision of the Coast Guard. Wiley finally withdrew the memo on July 21, pending action by the full commission.[9]

Wiley continued to focus his energy and attention on unlicensed training rather than officer training.[10] From both his statements and actions, it is clear that he would have been quite content to hand off the problem of officer training to another organization. He presented yet another version of this plan on October 14, and again his proposal involved Coast Guard supervision of a training program—this time, a one-year course consisting of three months on shore, six on a training ship, and a final three aboard a Coast Guard cutter.

Consideration of this measure was again postponed, but Coast Guard control of training received another indirect plug on September 20, 1937, when Chairman Joe Kennedy gave the keynote speech at the Coast Guard Academy's commencement ceremonies. Kennedy drew a parallel between the kind of training needed by the merchant marine and that offered by the Coast Guard Academy. And while he did not openly endorse Coast Guard supervision of merchant marine training, he came very close. "We in the Maritime Commission feel that our merchant marine needs the kind of leadership developed in your training here," Kennedy proclaimed. "We must have discipline aboard our merchant ships—not the iron discipline of military force, but the discipline required by the necessity of efficient operation."[11]

In October 1937, Wiley made a gesture toward reclaiming some control over the officer training program for the Maritime Commission. He presented the commission with a memo arguing that jurisdiction over maritime personnel matters should rest exclusively with the commission, including appointment and control of the U.S. Shipping Commissioners. (Traditionally, Shipping Commissioners were responsible for the protection of sailors' rights in port; the post was established in 1872 to fight shanghaiing of seamen by shipping companies.) He further suggested that the supervision of apprentices for the sea service should be included in the duties of the Shipping Commissioners. This plan would put the

Maritime Commission in charge of sea apprenticeship, but only indirectly—and it would put those apprentices in the hands of shore-based individuals (the Shipping Commissioners) who were both independent and manifestly unprepared to supervise them in any meaningful way.

Perhaps recognizing the difficulties inherent in this plan, Wiley also made it clear that these suggestions were intended to supplement the training program that he had previously presented to the commission, in which he argued for Coast Guard supervision of the program.[12]

In this same meeting, the divided opinions that precluded a quick resolution to the training question surfaced once again. The commission engaged in a long discussion about the advisability of forwarding Wiley's recommendations to Congress. Kennedy was hesitant to endorse the recommendations because of potential union opposition. He didn't think it was a good idea to spend any money on the program, he explained, until Congress fully understood the situation, including the fact that the unions would probably fight giving jobs to training school graduates. Several East Coast unions, he pointed out, had recently passed resolutions to this end.[13] Kennedy didn't distinguish between union opposition to licensed and unlicensed training, but many of the union arguments against federal training focused on the training of licensed officers.

Admiral Land, a Naval Academy graduate and a staunch believer in officer training—his support eventually proved invaluable to the Merchant Marine Academy—countered that despite job uncertainty, the course of training would be of immense value to the graduates, and could in no way be considered a bad investment. In executive session, the commission voted to work out the details without making a financial outlay, and then to recommend that the program be adopted immediately.[14]

The Cadet Corps Is Born

Even as supervision remained uncertain, the cadet training program began to take on a life of its own. On March 7, 1938, the commission issued General Order 23, giving the Maritime Commission the authority for the first time to designate the men who would be eligible for cadet training. This was to be accomplished through an "eligible list," to be drawn up by the Maritime Commission, and from which operators would select cadets. Though participants in previous maritime training programs had been unofficially known as cadets, General Order 23 formally established the rating of "cadet"–a traditional international commercial maritime title–for the first time. A cadet was defined as a young man on the eligible list who was in training (or was to be trained) for a license as a third mate or third assistant engineer. The rating of cadet officers was also established for cadets who were graduates of the state nautical schools, the U.S. Naval Academy, or the U.S. Coast Guard Academy. The plan was described in the *New York Times* as part of a unified training program under the Merchant Marine Act of 1936.[15]

As Kennedy had foreseen in October, the unions objected to officer training quickly and loudly. The United Licensed Officers Association protested, writing that "more licensed officers are now unemployed than at any previous time in twenty years," and fretted that government intervention would simply make a bad situation worse.[16] The National Organization of Masters, Mates and Pilots attacked the state schools, saying that their graduates rarely stayed at sea. The union depicted men trained before the mast–that is, its own membership–as "inured to hardship . . . superior officers, and better marine timber despite an occasional lapse in culture or a split infinitive."[17]

On May 26, Admiral Land weighed in to the contrary, stating that in his opinion, the unions were overreacting. The Maritime Commission was simply improving on a program that already existed, he argued. He reassured C. F. May of the Masters, Mates, and Pilots of America (MMP) that the system would not necessarily increase the number of licensed officers: "I seriously doubt whether there will be more cadets assigned than have heretofore been carried under that designation."[18]

The Maritime Commission continued to fine-tune General Order 23, and several changes were enacted almost immediately. On March 24, on the recommendation of a review committee made up of Telfair Knight, Commander W. N. Derby of the U.S. Coast Guard, and H. H. Robson of the United Fruit Company, the cadets were divided into two groups: deck cadets and engine cadets. Both groups were required to be high school graduates. In addition, the engine cadets also had to have either two years of shipyard or manufacturing experience, or had to have completed a vocational high school or technical college course.

A group of ninety-nine cadets was absorbed into the system under

General Order 23, issued as noted above on March 7, 1938, and this group became the nucleus of what was slowly becoming known as the Cadet Corps. New cadets were also appointed in the weeks following, on recommendations from their senators.[19] But when word of the new system began to spread, the response was both gratifying and alarming. More than 10,000 requests for information and 3,275 completed applications were received from would-be cadets. With only 300 openings in the foreseeable future, it was clear that the system would have to be modified to reduce the number of eligible men.

On January 1, 1939, General Order 23 gave way to General Order 28, which included several significant changes. First, and most important, eligibility would now be determined by a process of national competitive examination. A young man interested in the Cadet Corps would have to receive a passing mark in the examination that was either the highest in the congressional district in which he took the exam, or equal to the lowest of the high marks across the nation. In other words, prospective cadets were competing first against men in their home district, and second against the high scores of men from other districts. Those cadets who were on the eligible list from General Order 23, but who had not yet been assigned to ships, were required to take the examination to reestablish their eligibility.

Second, at the request of Captains Robert Henderson (a member of the Board of Governors of the California State Nautical School) and J. H. Tomb (New York State Nautical School Superintendent), the upper-end age limit for cadets was raised from twenty-three to twenty-five. Tomb pointed out that many of the cadets entering his school were twenty-one or twenty-two, which meant that under General Order 23, they would be too old to qualify as an officer of the Cadet Corps upon their graduation.

Plans under consideration at this point included one to two years of sea training, a year of intensive shore training, and then another one to two years of sea training. The shore training would reflect the specialties of the cadets. Deck cadets were to be taught electricity, radio, gyroscope, and navigation; maritime law, economics, and commercial practices; and ship sanitation. Engine cadets were to be taught advanced mathematics, applied thermodynamics, applied physics, and basic electricity, and the use of the lathe and all related tools. The plans also called for annual examinations and mandatory license examinations at the end of the course of study.[20]

The United States Maritime Service Is Born

All of this represented progress, of course, but Congress wanted the Maritime Commission to move more quickly. After all, Congress had authorized a training program with the act of 1936, and as far as the legislators could see, nothing much had happened. This unhappiness came to a head in June 1938 with the passage of an amendment to the Merchant Marine Act of 1936.

The Bland Amendment was named for its sponsor, Virginia congressman Schuyler Otis Bland, who was emerging as a forceful advocate of merchant marine officer training. It called for a comprehensive training plan to be put in front of Congress by the Maritime Commission no later than January 1939. Evidently, Bland and others believed in the power of a deadline, and they created a tight one for the commission.

The Bland Amendment stipulated one other crucial change: the creation of a United States Maritime Service, a uniformed, military-style government organization to oversee the training of licensed and unlicensed merchant marine personnel. This was a practical compromise to one of the conflicts that had been preventing swifter action. The commission needed to train thousands of young men, and this meant a substantial infrastructure. Logically, the military would have been the place to turn, but the amendment specified that the new U.S. Maritime Service was to be administered by the Coast Guard, possibly due to union objections to military oversight. This provision was logical enough under the circumstances, and certainly in keeping with the direction originally laid out by the Maritime Commission, but it led to several confusing episodes during the next several years as various authorities tried to figure out exactly who was responsible for which aspects of merchant marine training. Ultimately, the new U.S. Maritime Service was placed in the Maritime Commission as a stand-alone service, and so it continues to this day.

Another significant change came with the enactment of the Naval Reserve Act of 1938, passed by Congress on June 25. This expanded the qualifications for naval reserve status from the act of 1925 to include men in training on public vessels of the United States. The navy accordingly created a new cadet category for merchant marine trainees, and the state nautical schools began enlisting students as of

November 10. At this point, the federal cadets were not commissioned in the naval reserve, probably because they were not able to receive the required training in naval science while on merchant vessels.[21]

Building a Curriculum

Throughout 1938, under mounting pressure from Congress, the Division of Maritime Personnel continued to examine and reexamine the existing training system. The commission also built up its in-house expertise. The first recruit was Francis Shallus Kirk, in October 1938, as assistant supervisor of cadet training. The second hire—arguably long overdue—was Richard R. McNulty, who transferred in from the Division of Research in mid-December 1938. (The Division of Research continued to support training efforts; McNulty would later praise Director Alfred H. Haag as having exerted more effort than any other government official to force both the public and Congress to come to grips with an inadequate merchant marine.[22]) McNulty's new title was supervisor of cadet training, and he was now third in command of training after Wiley and Knight. In February 1939, the Division of Training was formally established, with Knight as director and McNulty as assistant director. Toward the end of February, Mrs. Willard Bozeman, McNulty's secretary from the Division of Research, joined the division as Francis Kirk's assistant.

Commander F. Shallus Kirk, USMS, assistant supervisor of cadet training, photographed in 1951.

Cadet training was divided into three units: the administrative unit, the educational ("ed") unit, and the nautical schools unit. Most of the activity for the next year took place within the Ed unit, as McNulty, Kirk, and other new hires—notably a recent engineering graduate of New York University named Lauren McCready —worked to design a curriculum for both shore and sea-based training.

Devising a suitable curriculum represented a major challenge, in part because cadet training was now envisioned as a mix of on-the-job training and correspondence school. For their "book learning," the cadets would have to depend on a flow of pamphlets, manuals, and other materials from Washington. With this challenge in mind, the commission sought the help of the most qualified experts in the land. Captain Felix Reisenberg, master mariner, was consulted on seamanship; George C. Manning, a lecturer at MIT, on naval architecture; Roy Chamberlain, master mariner and Harvard Law graduate, on the law of the sea; senior surgeon Car Michel, on shipboard first aid and hygiene; and many others.[23]

Other figures not yet of legendary status also contributed. Lauren McCready, for example, recalled an incident that took place early in his Washington tenure. McNulty walked up to McCready's desk and barked a question: "Do you know spherical trigonometry?"

"No, sir, I don't." McCready had studied engineering at NYU, but had never run across this critical underpinning of celestial navigation.

"Well, *learn* it," said McNulty, "and write a manual."

McCready bought a beach ball, translated trigonometry—which he did understand—to *spherical* trigonometry, and wrote the manual.

In these varied ways, generally under McNulty's watchful eye, the commission began preparing its own pamphlets and course of instruction for the cadets. The effort promised to be expensive. In a July 1938 memo, L. V. Kielhorn of the Coast Guard Institute estimated that the commission's total cost for pamphlets on seamanship, naval architecture, law of the sea, first aid and ship hygiene, navigation, and marine engineering would run around $55,000.[24]

Obviously, a global floating correspondence school, which is more or less what McNulty was envisioning,

Vice Admiral (then Lieutenant Commander) Lauren S. McCready, an engineering professor at the Academy, in his office on January 7, 1943.

couldn't simply consist of a one-way flow of information from Washington outward. There would need to be a system of quizzes, remote grading, and feedback. Specifically on this subject, Kielhorn's memo noted that the commission had decided that the Coast Guard Institute, an educational unit (ed unit) of the Coast Guard specializing in correspondence courses, would receive cadet exam papers from the commission, grade them, and then return them to the commission.

Notably, the Coast Guard would not carry on any direct correspondence with the cadets, or maintain any student records. In other words, even as the commission sought to draw upon Coast Guard resources, it was taking steps to limit the role and influence of that sister service.

A Long-Awaited Report

Meanwhile, the January 1939 deadline loomed for the report to Congress called for by the Bland Amendment.

McNulty had labored over this report behind the scenes while still in the Research Division—"in my spare time, weekends, etc.," as he wrote to one correspondent—with a particular focus on a course of study.[25] His summaries on foreign merchant marine training were scrutinized and debated within the ed unit. Telfair Knight referred to this process in a letter to Alfred Haag (at this point still McNulty's boss) on October 24, 1938. "I have seen a very thorough memo prepared by Mr. McNulty on this subject of training required by other maritime nations," he wrote. "I would like to request that [Admiral Wiley] be furnished officially with a copy of McNulty's memo . . . with any other recommendations or suggestions which the Division of Research may have to offer."[26]

McNulty's efforts intensified as the congressional deadline approached, and as he moved from description to prescription. In early December, he solicited reactions to his Outline of Courses for Cadets from Captain James H. Tomb, superintendent at Fort Schuyler, who had paid a visit to McNulty in his Washington office a week earlier. "Would be grateful for any criticism you may care to offer," McNulty wrote.[27]

A week later—and two days before he officially moved over from the Research Division—McNulty forwarded to Telfair Knight a copy of a letter he had received from Yale mechanical and marine engineering professor H. L. Seward, who responded favorably to McNulty's thirty-two-page mimeographed Cadet Training. "I found it interesting, rather good, and comprehensive for the purpose intended," Seward wrote. McNulty informed Knight that Seward had "submitted some excellent suggestions," which might be included in the final draft of the report. And, McNulty reported, still more authorities were expected to weigh in. "I expect comment from Massachusetts and California schools," he wrote in closing, "and some ship operating friends within the next week."[28]

The commission's *Report to Congress on the Training of Merchant Marine Personnel*, submitted on January 1, 1939, began by listing seven arguments in favor of a thorough training system for the U.S. merchant marine. Because they represent the first modern, official justification for federal involvement in merchant marine training, and because many are still debated today, they warrant a full restating here:

1. New ships with their complicated equipment and modern design require skilled seamen and engineers.

2. Money expended in training will be saved in large part by reduction in repair and maintenance expenditures through more efficient personnel.

3. Seamen of ability will also make for more effective shore personnel which it is desirable to recruit from shipboard.

4. Safety at sea for passengers and cargo is substantially increased through employment of well-trained men.

5. It will improve seamen's opportunities for advancement.

6. It will strengthen our merchant marine in competition with foreign-flag ships.

7. It will provide men of increasing skill for national defense should an emergency arise.[29]

These opening arguments introduced two main sections. The first was an encyclopedic report on the qualifications and training of merchant officers and unlicensed personnel of foreign nations. Japan, Holland, Germany, Great Britain, Italy, Norway, Sweden, Denmark, and France appeared in these pages; these write-ups grew entirely out of research done by McNulty in previous years. The reasons for comparison were clear: an earlier report had concluded that while American merchant officers were the best paid in the world, they ranked near the bottom in measurements of competence. (The Japanese, who were paid 33 percent of American wages, came in at the top in terms of competence.[30]) The 1939 report was especially complimentary of the Japanese national training system, with its two main academies at Tokyo and Kobe. Both Japanese schools offered a remarkably comprehensive course of training over a five-and-a-half-year period, of which at least one year was spent at sea. According to the report, moreover, close to 90 percent of the graduates of these schools *remained* at sea.

The second main section of the report summarized all the existing entities that played a role in the training of merchant marine personnel, including the state nautical schools, the Merchant Marine Naval Reserve, the Naval Reserve Officers Training Corps, the "cadet system on Government operated and subsidized vessels" (not yet officially referred to as the Cadet Corps), the U.S. Maritime Service, the U.S. Maritime Service training system, the Coast Guard Institute, vocational high schools, and other schools and agencies. While the report was generally positive regarding the work of these individual organizations, the picture that emerged was one of an uncoordinated and inefficient patchwork.

The Maritime Commission concluded its report by asking Congress for help in strengthening the cadet system. Specifically, the commissioners asked for the authority to arrange extension and correspondence courses for cadets on ship; to print, publish, and purchase textbooks, equipment, and supplies; to pay necessary supervisory expenses; and to use the facilities of the Coast Guard Institute (at commission expense). This, again, was a more limited role for the Coast Guard than either Waesche or Wiley had originally envisioned.

Notably, the commission stopped well short of recommending a federal academy. In fact, it even stated that "the State nautical schools and our own cadet training system may obviate the necessity for the establishment of a federal academy for merchant officers." Rather than recommending an academy, the commission proposed to study the question further.

This represented a victory for the pragmatists within the Maritime Commission. McNulty claimed years later that he was absolutely in favor of recommending a federal academy at this juncture (the end of 1938, the beginning of 1939) and that he argued passionately for including that recommendation in the report to Congress. His arguments, he recalled, were vetoed by higher-ups, notably Telfair Knight.[31]

Tension was beginning to build between these two men. Knight, an ex-movie executive and skilled political operative, focused on the political landscape in Washington, and made decisions based in large part on his assessment of the art of the possible. McNulty, by contrast, was an idealist—even a zealot—who was determined to realize his vision of a federal merchant marine training academy. More and more often, the pragmatist and the visionary found themselves on opposite sides of the fence.

A South American Field Trip

McNulty remained undiscouraged, and Knight, to his credit, continued to give McNulty his rein. The best evidence for this was a remarkable trip that McNulty took in the spring of 1939.

The expedition was probably McNulty's idea, but it needed approval at the highest levels of government. Admiral Land asked Secretary of State Cordell Hull to help open doors for McNulty across Central and South America, in a complicated itinerary that included visits and vessel changes in Cuba, Panama, Colombia, and Ecuador. Hull assured Land that the full resources of the U.S. government would be made available to McNulty on his travels.

Land also pulled strings in the Canal Zone, writing to the governor of the Panama Canal and asking if he could "arrange for Mr. McNulty to transit the canal in some British vessels carrying cadet-apprentices. It is his desire to observe the British cadet training system after which ours has been patterned." Again, the necessary approvals were forthcoming.[32]

McNulty left New York City on April 20, 1939, aboard the SS *Mexico*, a New York & Cuba Mail S. S. Company freighter bound for Havana with two cadets aboard. He renewed an old acquaintance with the ship's first officer—whom he knew from Massachusetts Nautical School days—stood watches, and quizzed the two cadets on their shipboard training. In a letter to Telfair Knight, he recorded his initial impressions:

> The day after sailing I spent about bridge and decks with deck officers and Cadet Meacham. This young man was sea sick, but never the less kept working. We sent him to flying bridge to work and get air. He felt better in afternoon.
>
> After Captain's inspection I went below to observe Engineer

Cadet Stein. Found this lad stripped to waist working with First Assistant Clifford on repairs to generator. . . . The engineering cadet is making first trip to sea. He has spent two years at Akron University–in engineering. Did not get sea sick. Is keenly interested in learning marine engineering.[33]

The *Mexico* arrived in Havana on April 25. The next day, McNulty rented a car to make a seventy-mile trip to the Cuban naval academy at Mariel. He was received with great ceremony by the director general of the school, and–from a balcony–reviewed the Cuban merchant marine corps as it executed infantry drills "with the precision of West Pointers," as McNulty put it. He was surprised to learn that the academy trained more cadets for the Cuban merchant marine than for the Cuban navy and marine corps combined.

McNulty next joined the American President Lines' SS *President Polk*, bound for Panama. His four days aboard the *Polk* gave him the opportunity to engage the ship's unnamed "bos'un" in an extensive dialogue about the relations among the Maritime Commission, the unions, the cadets, and the ship operators. His next letter to Knight illustrates the murky waters that the Maritime Commission had to navigate:

> I was informed by Bos'un that members of S.U.P. [Sailors' Union of the Pacific] can not forget the part played by "company" cadets during strikes of '34 and later years. It is contended that cadets were utilized as, and assisted in the recruiting of, strike breakers. Further, the operators used them as cheap labor during normal times. As a result, the crew do not feel that they should assist cadets with practical instruction. Nor should cadets be allowed to work at crew jobs, because this would minimize amount of overtime pay which crew could earn. . . . I pointed out to Bos'un that Commission has specifically stated in its Cadet regulations that cadets must not be utilized to displace a regular member of crew. And, we do not approve of any overtime for Cadets.
>
> We have started in right direction by restricting appointments to deserving young men–after exams–and carefully checking operators re use as cheap labor. No trouble is anticipated with operators if we show them we are sincere. However, with S.U.P. members it will take time to change bitterness. But it can be done. It simply is not natural for a real sailor man to refuse assistance to willing and able young men.[34]

McNulty transited the Panama Canal aboard the British tramp freighter SS *Tacoma City*. This gave him the opportunity to see firsthand the process and products of the British cadet-training system, which had served as a model for the emerging U.S. system. Although McNulty found the British cooperative, he wasn't particularly impressed with either the quality of the British cadets or the training they received:

> The cadets (apprentice deck officers) aboard *Tacoma City* do not compare with the American boys I have observed to date. Our boys make a better appearance, and most certainly are better educated. . . . These boys do much dirty work and apparently get little time to tackle books.
>
> Courses for British cadets are similar to ours. We differ in that lectures and quizzes are mailed from Britain by technical colleges every six weeks and apprentices are obligated to return same. We could do the same if we had a larger staff.[35]

On his passage to Guayaquil, Ecuador, aboard the U.S. passenger ship MS *Santa Barbara*, McNulty was very pleased with the progress that was being made by the three cadets aboard. He quizzed them on their "book learning," to which they were devoting an average of four hours a day. He was gratified to learn that one of the engine cadets had passed a difficult test: He had been given five solid bars and told to turn out five five-eighths-inch bolts on a lathe. "He did it very efficiently," McNulty enthused. "All five were within a few thousandths of perfect." A deck cadet was "a favorite of all officers," and had "all of his uniforms and books."[36]

Guayaquil fully lived up to its reputation as a dangerous and pestilential port. Ten minutes after McNulty checked into his hotel, an Ecuadoran army plane crashed into the apartment building across the street, killing twenty people and injuring many others. Shortly thereafter, McNulty came down with a raging fever that required a brief hospitalization on his return trip through the Panama Canal.

This return trip also gave McNulty the chance to watch Japanese cadets in action. He boarded the Japanese MV *Santos Maru* of the O.S.K. Line, talked with the *Santos Maru*'s Captain Aso, and observed two cadets—one deck, one engine—at work. McNulty knew that the Japanese training system was the most rigorous in the world, and in a subsequent letter, he pointedly reminded Telfair Knight of the advantages of "that famous Tokio [sic] Merchant Marine School. Five and one half years course (three years at school, one year in sail, one half year in Navy Yard, and one year as cadet on a commercial vessel)."[37]

In his last letter to Knight, McNulty expressed the hope that the commission would find his reports from the field useful. Characteristically, McNulty knew where he stood on that question, and expressed his opinion in no uncertain terms. "Much has been learned on this voyage," he concluded. "It was a damned good idea."

While McNulty was exploring cadet training in South and Central America, Congress was considering the recommendations of the January 1939 report that McNulty had principally authored. Early in August, it accepted those recommendations, incorporating them into the 1939 Amendments to the Merchant Marine Act of 1936. With this action, congress officially sanctioned the concept of a training program at sea—which, as we have seen, was already well under way.

Upon receiving this approval, McNulty started work on a plan for the "Expansion of Cadet Training," which almost certainly would comprise some kind of shore-based training. For the time being, however, there was neither congressional approval nor funding for such training, and the commission therefore focused on fine-tuning its ship-based cadet system.

Rough Seas

The first national competitive cadet entrance examination, prepared by the American Council of Education, was administered on April 17, 1939. The exam included questions on both cultural and mathematical subjects: English grammar, English literature, American history, algebra, plane geometry, and physics. (The subsequent four examinations, administered amid heightened concerns about national defense, omitted the cultural subjects.) A total of 450 young men sat for the exam, and 166 passed, thus becoming the first names on the Maritime Commission's eligible list, published on June 15, 1939.[38]

At this point, now a year into the program, there were 266 cadet officers and cadets at sea under the supervision of the Maritime Commission. The cadets were supervised by a triumvirate of the ships' masters (now responsible for the training of the cadets under their command), three district supervisors (who served as liaisons with the cadets in the ports of New Orleans, New York, and San Francisco, and forwarded their written work to the educational unit in Washington), and finally, McNulty himself.[39]

The indefatigable McNulty insisted on getting firsthand knowledge of the training conditions of the cadets. He made regular visits to the three district offices, as well as to the state schools. He also made annual inspection visits to vessels with cadets on board. After one such visit, in March and April 1940, McNulty wrote a memo reporting some progress in cadet training and the attitude of the ships' officers toward the cadets. But he also continued to argue for increased shore training.[40]

When Telfair Knight presented this memo to Wiley, he amended McNulty's recommendations. "Mr. McNulty realizes, as do I," wrote Knight, "that some of these recommendations are not practicable for adoption at the present time." He added that both he and McNulty felt that the Maritime Commission should "chart a course" toward a federal academy. In fact, he was again papering over a significant difference of opinion between himself and his impatient subordinate.

On another inspection visit in 1941, McNulty met for the first time Captain Giles C. Stedman, the urbane and personable master of the new passenger liner SS *America*—at that time, the largest merchant ship ever built in the United States, and the flagship of U.S. Lines.[41] Stedman's training programs for the cadets aboard his ships over the previous twenty years had impressed McNulty, and had influenced McNulty's own thinking about shipboard training. Stedman would later become McNulty's choice to succeed Captain Tomb as the Academy's second superintendent.

McNulty's thirst for firsthand knowledge reflected his innate curiosity, but it also reflected the serious challenges faced by his Cadet Corps. Especially on the West Coast, the maritime unions were still hostile to the training program, and union members on board vessels with cadets often did their best to make the experience as uncomfortable and unrewarding as possible. District representatives often sent in bleak reports to the ed unit. "Cadets on the SS *President Hayes* were not permitted to use the lathe," read one. "Cadets on the SS *President Polk* were only given cleaning work," read another, "because the crew refused to work at any task in which cadets participated."[42]

There were even isolated incidents of cadets being assaulted by union members. On October 16, 1940, for example, Cadet James

Lippard was attacked by two crew members on the SS *Lara*.[43] One of the two attackers had his license suspended for twenty days; the other received no punishment.

Ship operators, too, were known to abuse cadets. McNulty became practiced at writing polite but firm letters to shipping company executives, reminding them of regulations concerning cadet overtime, polishing and cleaning, mail sorting, and book study, and asking them to inform their ships' masters of the same. "No cadet officer or cadet shall work in excess of eight hours a day, except when necessary to save the vessel," reads a typical McNulty letter from this period. "Polishing and cleaning must not be given to cadet officers . . . paper work for cadets must not exceed an average of six hours per week."[44]

In addition, the logistics of matching up cadets with ships were proving challenging. Though vessels were required to carry a certain number of cadets based on the ships' tonnage, many sailed without cadets because the commission had failed to fill these vacancies. In an internal report, McNulty informed Knight that in a six-week period in September and October 1939, twelve vessels had sailed without cadets due to the district supervisors' inability to put bodies on the docks in time.[45]

And as the months went by, safety became an increasing consideration. In the early stages of the European hostilities, the Maritime Commission began trying to avoid placing cadets on trans-Atlantic routes, where the German U-boat threat was increasingly a factor. Although cadet officers continued to be assigned to these routes, no one was eager to put the commission's young charges in harm's way.

Troubles and Transitions

As suggested above, the district offices in New York, New Orleans, and San Francisco were finding it increasingly difficult to carry out their assigned tasks. Port inspector-instructors were hired in August and September 1939 for each of the three stations, both to supervise the shipboard work of the cadets through in-port vessel visits and to supervise the cadets while they were between vessels. Clearly, this argued for the creation of some sort of receiving station for cadets. The problem was initially solved by arranging "independent study programs"–offering preparatory studies under the auspices of the Maritime Commission– at the state nautical schools in New York and California (or in the case of New Orleans, at the Naval Air Station in Biloxi, Mississippi). This was of necessity a temporary solution; regulations published by the Maritime Commission in October 1939 defined a four-year training course, of which the third was to be spent on shore. The Maritime Commission could piggyback on the state facilities while it was serving only a small number of cadets awaiting their ship assignments, but by 1941, when shore training was supposed to begin in earnest, a permanent solution would have to be found.

The New York district initially had the easiest time of it, using facilities at the recently completed Fort Schuyler facilities of the New York State School. Philip C. Mahady, the New York port inspector-instructor, negotiated a deal with Superintendent Tomb which allowed the Maritime Commission to rent space at Fort Schuyler, and Edward A. Lane Jr., a recent Fort Schuyler graduate, was appointed cadet officer-instructor for the federal cadets, a post he held until called to naval duty in the fall of 1940.

During the annual cruise of Fort Schuyler's schoolship, SS *Empire State*, in the spring of 1940, Arthur G. Morrill—assistant supervisor of cadet training for practical instruction—arranged a relocation of the New York contingent of the federal Cadet Corps to the privately operated Admiral Billard Academy in New London, Connecticut. But this proved to be only a brief displacement, with the unit soon returning to Fort Schuyler, where it would remain until the move to Kings Point in January 1942.

During this time, a subtle transition occurred within the New York unit. As it grew both in numbers and cohesiveness, it shifted from being simply a receiving station to a de facto cadet training school. In part, this was due to the newly acquired naval reserve status of the cadets, who, starting on October 5, 1940, were officially enrolled as cadets in the Merchant Marine Reserve. The naval science course mandated by the navy was the first significant shore-based course, and led naturally to an expansion of the introductory shore training that cadets had been receiving while awaiting assignment on ships. Former U.S. Lines master John F. "Jackie" Wilson, who had replaced Lane during the Admiral Billard sojourn, soon was teaching six subjects to the cadets. More instructors were added to the ranks as the shore year of training for the 1939 cadets approached. In the spring of 1941, Hugh A. Andrews, Peder Gald, Charles W. Ferris, and Einar Mangodt joined Wilson at Fort Schuyler.

This growth constituted both good news and bad news. As the New York contingent of the Cadet Corps grew stronger, the situation at Fort Schuyler became increasingly untenable. With its regular complement of New York State School students, a separate and fast-growing navy ensign indoctrination school, and the now-growing numbers of federal merchant marine cadets and instructors, Fort Schuyler had far surpassed its reasonable occupancy limits. In October 1941, therefore, the search for a new home began in earnest.

Meanwhile, the other two district offices were experiencing even greater difficulties. The San Francisco office was the first of the three to get its receiving station up and running—in the fall of 1939—but this success was short-lived. Port Inspector-Instructor Harold V. Nerney (a 1925 Massachusetts Schoolship graduate) arranged for temporary housing for the program aboard the California Nautical School's training ship, the SS *California State*. But he failed to find replacement housing for the cadets during the California school's training cruise that began in January 1940, and the station was forced to close for four months. The station then reopened aboard the *California State*, only to have to move again after another six-month stay. At that point, the cadets moved into naval barracks on the SS *Delta King*, and several months later onto her sister ship, the SS *Delta Queen*.

Like its counterpart in New York, the San Francisco District Office was outgrowing its on-again, off-again accommodations. As a result, it relocated once again, this time to the Hunter Liggett Naval Barracks on San Francisco's Treasure Island in late November 1941, where it would remain until a more permanent arrangement could be made at nearby San Mateo in 1942.

The New Orleans District Office—lacking either state schools or naval barracks to offer temporary sanctuary—experienced an even more troubled infancy. The station opened in the spring of 1940 at the Coast Guard Air Station in Biloxi, Mississippi. This arrangement lasted until November, when the Coast Guard needed its space back. After several anxious months, the cadets moved to the commandant's house at the Algiers Navy Yard in February 1941. Again, this solution proved temporary; by November 1941, the Navy had found a use for this space, and Allen C. Hoffman—the fourth port inspector-instructor in the Gulf District's short history—again faced a crisis. With a naval and military build-up occurring in an area of limited accommodations,

Hoffman was unable to find any acceptable quarters. If the commission wanted space in New Orleans, the frustrated Hoffman told Washington, it would have to purchase it.

McNulty rushed down to the gulf, and with his help, several acceptable properties were found. At this point, however, the commission was authorized to purchase only ships, not land, so McNulty bought a 120-foot houseboat, the *North Star*, and then leased a piece of land along the east bank of the Bayou St. John near Lake Pontchartrain, where a group of cadet school buildings would be built. Classes were scheduled to begin on October 24, and the shore school was due to be completed by January 2, 1942.

Even before these building plans got under way, however, a chance meeting caused by bad weather led the school to its ultimate site in the small town of Pass Christian, Mississippi. During a training cruise on the *North Star*, a storm drove Lieutenant Commander S. A. Jennings and Commander A. E. Champeau into Pass Christian's Bay St. Louis, where they moored at the Inn by the Sea. The men looked covetously at the three spacious buildings—large enough to provide space for several hundred cadets—as well as at the forty-acre parcel of land on which the buildings were situated. Upon making inquiries, they were thrilled to learn that the owners wanted to sell the hotel. When the owners offered the property to the men for reasonable terms, and threw in a one-hundred-foot yacht for good measure, the offer seemed too good to refuse.

McNulty received the necessary authorizations from the commission, and on August 29, 1942, bought the property for $145,000.[46] In at least one sense, Pass Christian seemed an especially appropriate choice. In 1812, five American gunships engaged in a battle there with British admiral Alexander Cochrane. Although the American ships were defeated, they inflicted heavy damage on the British fleet.

The San Francisco district soon found a home as well, and at much less expense. In the wake of the Pearl Harbor attack, San Mateo County authorities offered the Maritime Commission twenty acres of land on the rocky Coyote Point outcropping of San Mateo Point— south of San Francisco, but on the bay—and in January 1942, this offer was gratefully accepted. The commission then purchased an additional nineteen adjoining acres and commissioned architect Gardiner Dailey to draw up plans for the school. Construction was begun in

A Saturday-morning regimental review and inspection at the U.S. Merchant Marine Cadet Basic School in Pass Christian, Mississippi, photographed on November 20, 1942.

Architect Gardiner Dailey's buildings on the San Mateo basic school campus blend into a grove of eucalyptus trees.

June, and completed in only fifty-one days.[47] The result was a stunning campus that seamlessly blended contemporary-looking buildings into a dramatic landscape dotted with towering eucalyptus trees. It later earned recognition as one of five outstanding examples of American architecture from the Museum of Modern Art in New York.

The siting of the Pass Christian shore station was facilitated by the threat of war, and the creation of the San Mateo station was accelerated by the reality of war. By this time, of course, national security was of paramount importance, and temporary wartime training installations were springing up all across the country. Suddenly, after years of futile effort, it was becoming easier for the Maritime Commission to bend the rules, and to find the funds to support a service that was now recognized belatedly as a crucial element in the national defense.

The East Coast Finds Its Home

The same context applied to the efforts to find a campus for the New York school, which was beginning to be viewed as the centerpiece of the training program. As in New Orleans and San Francisco, the search for facilities acquired a new urgency under the clouds of war. In the fall of 1941, therefore, the ed unit sent out several men to scout the East Coast.

McNulty, as usual, was an active participant. In September, his team made what he thought was a very promising find in South Dartmouth, Massachusetts. This was the Hetty Green estate, then occupied by her son, Colonel Green, on three hundred acres near the port of New Bedford which were surrounded by water on two sides. The buildings would accommodate three hundred cadets immediately. The size and location of the estate greatly appealed to McNulty, but the Green heirs tripled their asking price during the negotiations (from $200,000 to $600,000), and the Maritime Commission reluctantly moved on. Locations at Groton and Mystic, on the Connecticut coast, were also considered. Spherical trigonometrist, engineer, and jack-of-all-trades Lauren McCready spent several weeks scouring the area between Newport News and Baltimore.

Then, in early December, the late Walter P. Chrysler's estate came on the market, 12 acres in the northwest corner of the village of Kings Point in the town of Great Neck, on Long Island's Gold Coast, and the

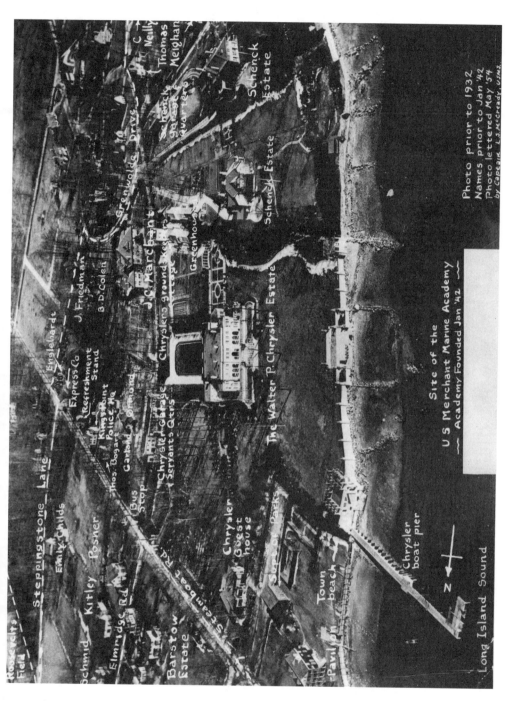

An aerial shot of the site of the U.S. Merchant Marine Academy campus taken prior to 1932. Building and street names written in by Vice Admiral Lauren McCready.

model for the fictional East Egg in F. Scott Fitzgerald's *The Great Gatsby*. The original asking price was $175,000, but the auto magnate's heirs were willing to do their part for the war effort and lowered their asking price to $100,000.

As in San Mateo, the war prompted a speedy resolution of the deal. On December 7, 1941, Japanese bombs fell on Pearl Harbor, and the United States was at war. On December 8, the commission's executive director, Sam Schell, recommended purchase of the Chrysler estate. Within days, Knight and Commissioner John Carmody negotiated a purchase agreement that included an initial six-month lease, thus giving the Maritime Commission time to secure formal congressional approval of the purchase.

The Cadet Corps now had three homes—one on each coast—and none too soon. Within months, surpassing anyone's expectations, enrollment in the corps would increase fivefold.

4

Embodied in War
1940–1945

The last week of January 1942 was a frigid one, even by the standards of coastal Long Island deep in midwinter. On the afternoon of January 24, the temperature failed to make its way out of the teens. The wind off Long Island Sound was relentless. If one could pick one's moving day, this would not be it.

The uniformed men standing on the old wooden pier of the former Chrysler estate, on the end of Steamboat Road in the village of Kings Point, New York, tried not to shiver as they looked southwestward, scanning the sound for signs of an arriving boat. They had been hard at work all that morning, as well as night and day for the better part of the three previous days. In some ways, this sudden lull in activity—the enforced idleness, the waiting in the cold—was harder on the men than the frenetic work they had suspended.

The activity had been centered on a large white mansion on a knoll above the sound, constructed in 1916 by New York merchant Henri Bendel. The palatial three-story residence was later purchased by auto baron Walter D. Chrysler; during his residence there, Chrysler had enjoyed looking across the sound to admire the gleaming Art Deco spire atop the midtown Manhattan office building that bore his name.

The men had been lugging boxes and supplies into every corner of every room, scrubbing, scraping, and shining. The work required to convert the residence into the beating heart of a new federal maritime academy seemed endless, with one improvisation after another. The dark-paneled dining room transformed itself into a mess hall as planks on sawhorses replaced carved-oak tables and rough benches supplanted Walter Chrysler's ornate dining room set. An officer's mess sprang up in the butler's pantry. All of the upstairs rooms in the residence, and many of the spaces in the garages—of which there were three, all heated—were strewn with mattresses, interspersed with the occasional bed. Preliminary attempts had been made to transform the billiard room and the playroom into makeshift classrooms.

Now, only a few days after the initial contingent of officers and enlisted men had arrived on the campus to begin the frenetic transformation, the first cadets were leaving behind their borrowed quarters just across the sound at the New York State Merchant Marine Academy's Fort Schuyler. Appropriately, the young mariners were rowing across the sound in large wooden rowboats called monomoys, with the Cadet Corps' commanding officer John F. "Jackie" Wilson at a steering oar, to take up residence and continue their studies at their institution's new home. (Among those in this first contingent of students was engineering cadet Maurice Gross, who later would spend more than three decades as a professor in the engineering department.) The members of the informal welcoming committee stood shoreside, stamping their feet against the cold, waiting for the event that later became known, somewhat irreverently, as "Wilson's Landing." Finally, a cheer went up. The boat had been sighted.

Beyond the initial cheering, salutes, and handshakes as the cadets disembarked at Kings Point on that frigid afternoon, there was little time wasted on ceremony. Already the culture of the institution had been reshaped by war: pragmatic, focused, and goal-oriented. First and foremost, officers and cadets were determined to get the academy operational, and as soon as possible. In short order, the arriving cadets joined work teams and began helping with the various tasks already under way. Some went to a nearby greenhouse, recently emptied, to help construct double-decker beds. Others headed for the kitchen to help with the evening meal. Still others pitched in on the continuing task of transforming Walter Chrysler's former showplace into a functioning component of a war machine.

Seen in that light, no task was unimportant, nor was there a moment to lose.

Cadets descend the main staircase in the old Chrysler house soon after arriving at the Academy in January 1942. Cadet quarters, the mess hall, and classrooms were all located in the Chrysler mansion in the first months at the Academy.

Man Proposes, War Disposes

In early 1942, the German army controlled most of continental Europe. British merchant shipping had been decimated by the German U-boat force. Japan had taken Thailand, Guam, Wake, and the Northern Gilbert Islands, and was advancing in the Philippines. On February 15, the British naval base at Singapore fell, and suddenly the United States was in the middle of a war that the Allies seemed to be losing.

The American entry into the war, little more than a month earlier, had profoundly changed the nature and ambition of the Cadet Corps. As of January 6, 1942, all members of the Cadet Corps holding commissions in the naval reserve were ordered to active duty.[1] (Almost all were quickly assigned back to the Maritime Commission to continue their training.) And every cadet engaged in sea training was, by definition, squarely *in* the war zone. The nation had watched anxiously as the British merchant fleet was devastated by German submarines; now cadets of the fledgling corps were facing this same threat, even before they left the corps to sit for their licenses.

The war also affected the administration of the Cadet Corps. While wartime pressures facilitated the purchase of land and buildings for shore-based training stations, those same pressures also disrupted the Maritime Commission's carefully laid plans for the length and the course of study. Now, urgently, the nation needed merchant seamen—even including those who hadn't completed the training that had been contemplated for them in peacetime. Cadets who had begun their third-year shore training in September 1941, for example, were immediately sent off to sit for their license examinations, and from there they went directly to merchant ships.

The first priority for McNulty and the Maritime Commission before Pearl Harbor had been the *quality* of the education the cadets would receive. Now, unexpectedly, *quantity* emerged as a more pressing need. In his first wartime State of the Union address, delivered on January 6, 1942, President Roosevelt called for a nearly eightfold increase in the production of merchant ships, from 1.1 million deadweight tons in 1941 to 8 million deadweight tons in 1942. The production goal for the following year would double, Roosevelt promised, to an astounding 16 million deadweight tons.

Along with this dramatic increase in ships, of course, would come a need for trained officers and seamen. The Maritime Commission was charting new ground, uncertain as to how many ex-seamen, especially retirees, would give up their lives ashore to return to the wartime merchant marine. The commission decided that it should attempt to train enough men to supply the total number needed. To hit the target, fifteen hundred officers would have to be minted by the state academies, and six thousand by the Cadet Corps—an astounding and unlikely total.

Applicant requirements, formerly designed to constrict the funnel, now relaxed dramatically. The six-hundred-cadet statutory limit established in peacetime was suspended. The fifth national competitive exam, administered in December 1941, was never graded, and emergency regulations passed on January 8 waived the exam altogether as a requirement for future applicants. To get mariners through the pipeline as quickly as possible, the new regulations outlined a greatly reduced twenty-two-month course of study. Cadets would receive payment of sixty-five dollars a month, along with room, board, and transportation expenses, but would be expected to buy their own uniforms and textbooks.

Finally, the federal schools also received their first official names. The federal academy at Kings Point and the cadet schools at San Mateo and Pass Christian became, respectively, the U.S. Maritime Commission Academies of the Atlantic, Pacific, and Gulf Coasts. Together, the three campuses constituted the facilities of the U.S. Merchant Marine Cadet Corps.

The federal government now viewed these new facilities as critically important to the war effort, in part because the state schools could not begin to accommodate the fast-growing need for officer candidates. Those schools were training vastly increased numbers of students—for example, New York's Fort Schuyler, already bursting at its seams, saw an increase in its allocation of federal cadets from eighty to five hundred—but these numbers could not meet the new need. The Chrysler estate would have to be greatly expanded and pressed into service immediately. In view of these dire circumstances, as described urgently in communications from Telfair Knight, Congress approved both the purchase of the estate for $100,000 and the expenditure of another $825,000 for the necessary alterations and additions to the campus. This sum comprised the costs of new buildings, equipment, and temporary wooden buildings supplied by the federal government to accommodate the corps' expanded ranks.

The project's preliminary phases proceeded with amazing speed. On January 13 and 14, two representatives of the architectural firm Alfred Hopkins and Associates met with the Maritime Commission to show preliminary sketches for an expanded campus.[2] The site plan was completed by the two architects within days—a remarkable accomplishment, made even more impressive by the fact that the campus plan remains fundamentally unchanged to this day. As soon as the site plan was finished, the contractors, Vermilya-Brown Company, completed a cost study—also within days. Congress approved the proposed expenditures on January 20, and the first group of maritime service officers and enlisted men arrived at the academy on January 21. Contracts with Vermilya-Brown were let on February 28.

Among the first to set foot on the new campus was the Maritime Commission's training aide Lieutenant Lauren McCready, who most recently had been teaching the use of the slide rule to federal cadets at Fort Schuyler. Commanding Officer Wilson asked McCready to help make the new facility ready for the cadets, and so, recalls McCready, he got into his new '41 Ford on January 21, drove over the Whitestone Bridge (the Throgs Neck Bridge had yet to be constructed), made his way eastward to Great Neck and down Steamboat Road to Kings Point, and parked his car under the mansion's impressive porte cochere. Along with a Coast Guard CPO named Davidson, Lieutenant Max Marshall, and others, McCready defined and set in motion the thousand things that needed to be accomplished to get the embryonic Academy's doors opened almost overnight.

Among the greatest difficulties in those early days was the near-complete lack of teaching tools and equipment. Again, improvisation carried the day. McCready recalls an opportunity that arose in the furnace room of the Chrysler residence: "Luckily for us, they had a big industrial boiler, not an ordinary residential boiler. A big, cast iron monster, probably eight feet by seven feet. It had an oil burner, pressure gauges, try-cocks, water-gauge glasses, siphons, stop valves, safety valves, and so on. I was able to use that system to teach the cadets everything they needed to know about boilers. Primitive? Perhaps. But that boiler probably saved the lives of many men."

Cadets hard at work in the Chrysler greenhouse, converted into the Academy shop in early 1942. In the foreground, a cadet works on a Sebastian lathe.

The machine shop, a central resource in the training of future ships' engineers, was even more primitive. For the first several weeks of the new Academy's existence, the shop consisted of a bucket of tools that went wherever it was needed.

This birthing process can kindly be described as chaotic. Almost with their bare hands, McCready and his equally young colleagues built an Academy from the ground up. They improvised, made do, went without, and plotted ways to respond to the day's most urgent need. And even as they were putting out fires, they were also trying to create the systems and procedures that would some day get them out of the firefighting business.

Necessity was the mother of the Academy. It shaped the Academy's character, and that character—inventive, tough, resilient, practical-minded, self-confident, and even a little cocky—would characterize the institution for many years to come.

A Campus Rises

When McCready first arrived at the former Chrysler residence on that January afternoon, the twelve-acre estate consisted of the 1916 main residence, three garages (with apartments above them), a house that had belonged to the estate superintendent, a greenhouse, an outdoor pool with two bathhouses, a boathouse, and the pier. Over the next several months, the government also purchased several adjoining properties: movie mogul Joseph Schenck's estate, consisting of two large residences and a garage abutting the eastern side of the Chrysler estate; the Marchant house, just across 3rd Street before Greenwolde Drive; the Posner and Schmidt residences at the corner of Steamboat and Elmridge; the Bogart house, on Steamboat Road; the Merrill House, north of Steamboat Road; the Meighan House, home of a former star of silent movies; and Randall Hall, home of a motion picture executive. By October 1943, the campus had grown to forty-six acres, with fifty-three permanent buildings.

Here again the Academy got a boost from the national crisis. When the federal government approached local homeowners with a reasonable offer, all agreed to sell their properties in the interests of national defense. (The specter of eminent domain may also have been a factor.) Not that they were *happy* about the situation. Lauren McCready, who had the uncomfortable job of evaluating many of

these houses as potential Academy buildings, later recalled the awk-
wardness of entering these residences on McNulty's orders:

> I would show up on people's doorsteps with three or four cadets.
> The owners would open the door, and I would say, "Beg your par-
> don, ma'am. I'm Lieutenant McCready. May I measure your
> home?" There was nearly always an audible gulp, but they would let
> us in. We'd make up a little booklet of plans, and later McNulty, in
> Washington, would mark up all the available spaces: "storage, stor-
> age, classroom," etc.
>
> The worst one was Louis Posner's house. Mrs. Posner let us in, and
> was perfectly charming . . . but when we got up to her sewingroom, with
> her newly installed skylight, she just started crying. That was tough.[3]

The transformation of the estate presented difficult logistical challenges. Most important, of course, the enlarged property had to be rendered immediately useful as an academy. At the same time, it had to

An aerial photograph of the U.S. Merchant Marine Academy campus taken in the
1940s, showing the extensive buildings acquired in the early 1940s.

be altered with an eye toward the future, in ways that would permit the Cadet Corps to continue to grow and evolve. Long-term needs could not get in the way of short-term requirements, but neither could the reverse be true. Figuring out these trade-offs was far from a simple exercise, especially because the officers responsible for overseeing the physical redevelopment process were also creating a new shore-based curriculum essentially from scratch.

One clever solution involved the use of temporary facilities. The Maritime Commission requisitioned twelve forest-green wooden buildings left over from the New Deal's Civilian Conservation Corps (CCC) days. Partially disassembled and trucked over from the Adirondack State Park in New York and from Fort Dix, New Jersey, these structures were intended to serve a variety of purposes until more permanent solutions could be devised. Six would serve as barracks for the cadets, three would serve as classrooms and labs, and the remaining three would be refitted as a drill hall, barracks, a new mess hall, and a staff barracks. The structures were named after famous sailing vessels: *Argonaut, Bonita, Corsair, Defiance, Eclipse, Fearless, Greyhound, Hornet, Intrepid, Juniper, Kathay,* and *Lightfoot.* Delivered on February 18, they required fourteen weeks to install and equip for their new purposes. The first nine were located on what is now Barney Square, to the left of the Chrysler building as one approached it from the main gate.

Carl Seiberlich—a cadet in this chaotic period, and later the first Academy graduate to make flag rank in the navy—reflects back on a strange coincidence growing out of those temporary barracks:

> The first two weeks I was at Kings Point, I worked at nailing together the CCC barracks. I moved into the one that had "Hornet" painted on it. The one next door was called "Intrepid."
>
> If somebody had said to me then, "Hey, kid—you're going to make captain aboard the *Intrepid* twenty years from now, and twenty-six years from now, you're going to command the *Hornet,* and pick up astronauts returning from the moon," I would have said, "You're crazy." But that's what happened.[4]

Meanwhile, the existing buildings were pressed into service. One of the former Chrysler garages housed Seamanship, the Schenck theater and Marchant house became classrooms, the Marchant garage doubled as an armory, the greenhouses evolved into the washrooms, and most other buildings (including the Schenck house and garage, the Bogart house, and the Schmidt house) were pressed into service as barracks. Sick bay was first laid out on the second floor of the former Chrysler garage on a stormy night in March 1942, and stocked mainly with aspirin tablets and a set of surgical instruments.[5] It was soon relocated to the Posner residence, while the Merrill house became the Athletic Headquarters.

But throwing up temporary buildings and retrofitting existing mansions and their outbuildings represented only a partial solution. The new academy also needed new buildings. And so, on June 11, a week and a half after installation of the CCC structures was completed, the contractors began pouring concrete for the foundations of Palmer Hall, the first in what was to be a cluster of six new barracks.

Then, suddenly, construction stopped.

A Coast Guard Coup

Throughout the spring of 1942, the government was struggling, with mounting desperation, to deal with the German threat to merchant shipping. Off the eastern coast of the United States, German U-boats taking part in Operation *Paukenschlag* (Drumbeat) were sinking U.S. merchant vessels at the catastrophic rate of two a day. The U-boat fleet

CCC huts offered temporary living and working facilities during the construction process.

Tools were checked out of the tool shop at the Academy daily. Here cadet-midshipmen line up to receive their tools.

sank 125 Allied ships in May 1942 alone (totaling more than 584,000 gross tons), and another 131 ships in June.[6]

In retrospect, it seems clear that the navy, under Admiral Ernest J. King, dragged its feet in adopting some simple measures that could have reduced the number of these sinkings, including organizing ships into protected convoys, shore blackouts, and the use of the Civil Air Patrol to force down the U-boats in the sea lanes.[7] In the absence of these defensive measures, more ships were needed. On February 7, 1942, President Roosevelt signed an executive order creating the War Shipping Administration (WSA) to oversee the operation, purchase, charter, insurance, repair, maintenance, and requisition of new and existing ships. (Ship*building* was left under the control of the Maritime Commission.) These were duties that had previously belonged to the Maritime Commission, but wartime exigencies necessitated the transfer. Admiral Emory S. Land, chairman of the Maritime Commission following Joseph Kennedy's departure, also became administrator of the WSA, assuring the close cooperation of the two organizations. Land's dual role, and as well as his "direct personal contact"[8] with Roosevelt, made him a highly effective czar of all U.S. maritime activity and personnel.

Two weeks later, a similar executive order signed by the president transferred all federal maritime training responsibilities to the Coast Guard. (This indirectly placed training under the control of the navy; on November 1, 1941, Roosevelt's Executive Order 8929 had transferred the Coast Guard to navy department control.) This appeared to be merely another adjustment that would allow the Maritime Commission to focus purely on shipping. In addition, it seems to have been part of an effort to consolidate merchant marine jurisdiction under one organization; on February 28 of the same year, the Bureau of Marine Inspection and Navigation (which oversaw ship inspection, marine safety, and personnel licensing) was also transferred to the Coast Guard. But the speed and secrecy with which the training transfer was accomplished—and Land's strong objections to the plan—suggest behind-the-scenes maneuvering by the Coast Guard.

On March 2, Land wrote a memo to the director of the budget, formally requesting that the transfer of training functions be immediately deleted. Other government officials seem to have more or less ignored the offensive executive order. Although the Division of Training had been officially abolished, Knight, McNulty, and the rest of the office continued to function as before, and refused to relocate to Coast Guard headquarters.

At first, the new management structure created few ill effects, and the Academy even received additional appropriations. In March 1942, the Maritime Commission transferred $3 million to the Coast Guard to construct a school that could accommodate 2,400 cadets in wartime and 1,200 in peacetime. Another $3 million was added the following month.

Then, in April, the Coast Guard made an abrupt about-face, halting all construction at Kings Point, evidently on the grounds that the Academy was only a temporary wartime installation and should not be benefiting from these kinds of long-term physical investments. Admiral Waesche said as much during an inspection visit to Kings Point, when he commented to an assistant that the Academy was not permanent, and would come down after the war.[9] If Waesche was right—if the new Academy was only a temporary wartime resource— then it was indeed subject to regulations that forbade the use of permanent construction techniques and materials, including steel and concrete, in the creation of war-related facilities.

Needless to say, this interpretation was completely at odds with the ed unit's concept of the Academy, and the Washington-based educators refused to accept their fate without a fight. According to McNulty, the Washington crew, in desperation, went straight to the top. According to one account, Admiral Land phoned President Roosevelt directly, explaining the situation and pleading for his help. Immediately following this conversation, Admiral Waesche received a phone call of his own. "Get the hell out of Kings Point," Roosevelt reportedly barked, "and stay out!"[10]

In his diary, Joe Kennedy recounted a similar story. During an April 1942 meeting, Roosevelt told Kennedy that he had been disturbed by reports from Land that the navy was taking over the merchant fleet, and had called Admiral Ernest King to register his displeasure. According to Kennedy, King quickly backtracked when confronted, claiming that he'd simply been making a study of the matter, and had no plans to take over the merchant marine.[11]

In either case, the Coast Guard lost no time in exiting Kings Point. In mid-July, a new executive order shifted control of merchant marine training to the Division of Training of the War Shipping Administration, headed by Captain Edward Macauley (who had replaced the now retired Admiral Wiley), with Knight as director and McNulty as assistant director. The bureaucracy then addressed the issue of permanency: construction at Kings Point was authorized on a "semi-permanent" basis. This chiefly meant that the building material would be locally quarried beige Oyster Bay sandstone, rather than marble or granite, thus skirting both wartime restrictions and heavy transport costs.[12]

The resolution of this interservice skirmish led to one more permanent legacy: a new name. During the Coast Guard's regime, a sign had been erected on the front gate of the Kings Point property that read, "The United States Coast Guard Merchant Marine Academy." When the Coast Guard left, a new sign was put up in its place. The Academy became, simply, the "United States Merchant Marine Academy." At the same time, the Academy was coming to be known by the nickname that would soon become interchangeable with its official name: Kings Point.

Work Resumes

By late summer, the building program was back on track. According to the August 1942 edition of *Polaris*, a student-run publication that became enormously successful, the construction project was "on full steam ahead." The CCC buildings, then being used as barracks, class-rooms, and the kitchen, would be replaced by twelve permanent build-ings, seven of which would be barracks, accommodating two thousand cadets and the administrative staff. The Engineering, Naval Science, and Academic Buildings were then being built on the north side of the administrative building. "The most outstanding building," *Polaris* reported, "will be the Engineering Building. Diesel and steam labs, and a machine shop, will occupy the wings." There was also some dis-cussion about installing a complete engine room from a Liberty ship, for training engineering students in as close to a real-life environment as possible, but the scarcity of engines put this plan on hold.

The first of the new residence halls, Palmer Hall, was named for Nathaniel P. Palmer, sealer and captain of the ship *Hero*, and claimed by the U.S. government as the discoverer of Antarctica in 1820. It was com-pleted in the late fall. The building had four "decks," or floors, each with room for approximately seventy-five cadets, bunked four to a room. The rooms averaged 16 by 16, with two double-tiered metal bunk beds, one shared wooden desk (of which each cadet had a corner), four wooden chairs, four built-in lockers, and two washstands. (These were not the most luxurious of accommodations, but they were far better than what many cadets would later experience at sea.) There were two bathrooms on each floor, with six showerheads in an all-tile shower.

In March 1943, Kings Point celebrated another milestone with the completion of Delano Hall, the new mess building. Delano was osten-sibly named for Amasa Delano, the acclaimed maritime author, but the name doubled as a subtle tribute to President (and Academy patron) Franklin Delano Roosevelt. Delano boasted a capacity of twelve hundred cadets, and included a state-of-the-art public address system for announcements. Its galleys included roasting ovens, deep fryers, gas ranges, electric ranges, steam kettles, vegetable steamers, cook tables, ice boxes, prep tables, and a dishwashing unit. *Polaris* hailed it as being "as modern as science can make it."[13] The last CCC hut was taken down soon after Delano was opened; slowly, the Acad-emy's campus was taking form.

As the formal September 30, 1943, dedication day approached, more new buildings opened their doors. These included Furuseth Hall, where the "preliminaries" were housed, Bowditch Hall, Fulton Hall, Samuels Hall, O'Hara Hall, Murphy Barracks, Cleveland Bar-racks, Jones Barracks, Barry Barracks, and Rogers Barracks. Most of these names, honoring famous figures from maritime history, were bestowed by Richard McNulty with the help of his wife, Sue. (See Appendix H.) It was Sue McNulty who suggested that one of the buildings should bear the name of a famous female mariner, and she nominated the intrepid Mary Patten, whose name graces today's Patten Clinic, for the honor. Mrs. McNulty also came up with the school's motto: *Acta Non Verba* ("deeds, not words"). The three-word phrase captured the practical orientation and spirit of the new Academy and its leaders, and helped define the institution in the years to follow.

A Wartime Curriculum Is Forged

Even as the buildings rose, the rapidly growing ranks of instructors at Kings Point were busy shaping a curriculum. The training program had relatively simple goals in these war years, mainly due to the limited amount of time allotted to the course of study. This was set initially at twenty-two months, but in December 1942, the urgent need for ships' officers caused yet another compression of the curriculum. The War Shipping Administration's General Order 24 limited the fourth class (i.e., "first year") basic instruction period to twelve weeks at San Mateo, Pass Christian, or Kings Point. This would be followed by a minimum of six months as third classmen on merchant vessels, and then thirty-six weeks of second and first class instruction at Kings Point. In other words, the entire course of study now shrank from twenty-two to eighteen months, with all advanced training being conducted at Kings Point.

The schools voiced little objection to these changes, of course, driven as they were by necessity. The instructors at the "basic schools" (as San Mateo and Pass Christian were coming to be known) and the Academy adjusted their curriculum to the new time constraints. Groups of deck and engine cadets who had completed the program now graduated and shipped out every two weeks, license and navy ensign commission in hand, to take their places in the growing world conflict.

Obviously, though, these time constraints meant that the Academy had to carefully consider the priorities that it was establishing for these war-bound cadets. According to a *Polaris* article by Lieutenant Junior Grade Wendell C. Allen, head of the educational measurement program of the ed unit, deck cadets needed to master navigation and the handling of ships, cargo, and men. Engine cadets needed to become

sound machinists and practical electricians, skilled in the operation
and maintenance of shipboard power plants, and, like their deck counterparts, experts in the handling of men.[14]

Engineering, seamanship, and navigation therefore were the Academy's top priorities in the early months of 1942. Naval science joined
this list after August 1942, when all federal cadets were officially
named midshipmen in the U.S. Naval Reserve. Naval science courses
were required for cadets to obtain commissions in the USNR upon
graduation.

Teaching at this time was accomplished mainly through a lecture-
demonstration method, with liberal use of visual aids and laboratory
work. Instructors were given detailed lesson plans, prepared by officers
in the educational unit in Washington, showing the precise content of
each lesson. This assured standardization of instruction, crucial in light
of the high turnover of personnel dictated by the war.

Visual signaling training for all cadets soon emerged as another
priority; in an era of mandatory radio silence, flags, blinking lights,
and semaphore were the primary means of communication while in
convoy, and when entering or leaving port. (In fact, visual signaling
was the first class held at the Academy—on January 28, 1942, only four

Cadet-midshipmen at the Academy receive lifeboat training in monomoy boats.

days after Wilson's Landing–with seamanship not beginning until two days later.) According to *Polaris*, two masts with yards and halyards were set up on the main lawn, so that cadets could visualize two ships signaling to each other using international code flags.[15]

Signaling instruction repeatedly proved its worth. In June 1940, cadet William O'Reilly's frantic signaling from the SS *Washington* narrowly averted the sinking of this large passenger vessel, carrying more than seventeen hundred refugees, by a hostile submarine off the coast of Spain. A 1943 story in *Polaris*–purposely vague, to avoid giving away any secrets to the enemy–recounts another cadet's experience in putting his training to good use.

> When entering a strange, foreign port, Cadet Carlos A. Freeman on board the SS _____ noticed the shore station flashing a series of "K's" on the blinker. He thought for a moment and recalled his visual signaling instruction that he received at the Academy–a series of "K's" on the blinker means, "You should stop your vessel instantly."

Cadets attend a visual signaling class at the Academy in 1942.

Immediately, he informed the officer on watch who instantly rang full speed astern. The vessel which was proceeding at sixteen knots quickly lost speed but not fast enough. Still making headway at the speed of five knots, the ship ran aground.

Luckily, the damage was slight. Due to the watchfulness of Cadet Freeman, disaster was averted, and the precious cargo reached its destination.[16]

Engineering classes started up shortly after signaling instruction, but here the lack of equipment proved a difficult hurdle. The Academy relied heavily on the resourcefulness of the people who led the various departments, and nowhere was this more the case than in engineering. Lauren McCready had been named head of engineering in February 1942, and his skills at procuring much-needed equipment soon became legendary at the Academy. McCready became a familiar face at the Navy Yard's Annex at Bush Terminal in Brooklyn, where he scrounged for surplus or outmoded equipment. In fact, until funds started to roll in during the late spring, the machine shop was entirely equipped with castoffs. On one notable expedition, McCready obtained the emergency diesel generator engines that had been removed from the great French luxury liner SS *Normandie* before she burned and capsized at her New York pier in February 1942.

The engineering curriculum, too, was largely borrowed. McCready based the Academy's engineering curriculum in large part on that of his alma mater, New York University. Other department heads, including Harry Crow of the Naval Science Department and Delwyn Hyatt of the Seamanship and Navigation Department, similarly shaped the curricullums of their respective departments.

Cadets also made numerous field trips in these early years, in part to compensate for areas in which the Academy lacked expertise or equipment. In August and September 1942, for example, groups of cadets visited Brooklyn's Sperry Gyroscope Plant to observe the production of gyroscope compasses, the Hayden Planetarium in the Museum of Natural History, and General Electric's Service Shop on West 13th Street in lower Manhattan. At this last facility, under the tutelage of Captain McCready, cadets saw armatures being rewound, insulated, and baked; witnessed the dynamic balancing of turbines; and learned about special heat treatments.

Over time, these trips paid unexpected dividends, as the Academy made friends and covertly assessed talent in industry. Charles Hubert was one such dividend: employed at the GE Service Shop, he proved himself a very strong teacher, and soon was recruited to teach electrical engineering at the Academy.

In September 1942, another change occurred—although unheralded at the time—that had an enormous impact on the Academy in subsequent years. Up until this time, study on ships was essentially a continuation of the prewar "correspondence school" approach—that is, a sequence of pamphlet-based lessons and quizzes. Now, this method was replaced by the "Sea Project," which *Polaris* described as "another step towards making this Academy the Annapolis of the Merchant Marine."

The Sea Project was formulated along practical lines, with an emphasis on actual experience. The projects—a series of weekly exercises created by instructors on the Academy faculty—were specific to deck and engine specialties. A typical exercise in the engine Sea Project involved preparing a diagrammatic sketch of the fuel cycle, from double bottoms to boilers. The deck Sea Projects included problems such as: "Explain by word and sketch how you would rig a bos'n chair. Indicate size, type, and length of rope used." [17] Cumulatively, these exercises, which were graded at the Academy after the cadet returned to shore, would familiarize the cadets with every key system on their ship.

From the start, these projects defined a learning experience that was broader than the particular assignments at hand. True, a cadet could probably diagram the fuel cycle on his own, but he could do so more accurately and efficiently if he could persuade the ship's chief engineer to help him with the project. This process of working with, and seeking help from, an expert was itself a valuable exercise; the arrogant, self-important, or inattentive cadet wouldn't get very far with an overworked ship's officer.

Moving a critical piece of the learning experience offshore created new kinds of risks and difficulties. Cadets on merchant ships faced the same dangers as officers and seamen. Increasingly, they were bombed, strafed, torpedoed, and sometimes even sunk. It was hard to concentrate on a Sea Project after an air raid. Even when a cadet survived a sinking, his Sea Project did not. In many cases, the cadet got a new ship and started over.

The Sea Project also underscored the headaches of administering an educational program that sent its students directly into a global conflict. Simply keeping track of where all the cadets *were* at any given point in time was a Herculean task. Many cadets changed vessels multiple times—not only due to sinkings and other disasters, but also due to health issues, bureaucratic snafus, missed connections, and changes in plans. Even in the best of circumstances, the supervision of cadets in foreign ports was hit-or-miss. As a result, some cadets remained stuck at sea for many months, or even years, hoping to encounter someone with the authority to give them orders to return to the Academy. One cadet from San Mateo, Douglass C. North (a future Nobel Laureate in economics), was twice promoted on his ship in the Pacific and never actually made it to the Academy for his advanced training.

Gunnery training, added in early 1943, was a nod to the unusual circumstances facing cadets during their sea training. Warrant Officer Horton H. Spurr, the drillmaster, was in charge of the training, which he proclaimed was "equal, or superior, to that given to men in some branches of the armed forces." The south side of O'Hara Hall was converted into an ordnance row, with large gun-loading machines, dummy

Commander John F. "Jackie" Wilson interviews two cadet-midshipmen who have just returned from sea duty to undergo advanced training at the Academy.

mines, torpedoes, and paravanes. Cadets were given instruction in sidearms, the 20-millimeter Bofors AA gun, the 50-caliber Browning, and the 30-caliber Lewis machine gun. In addition, two 5-inch guns on the campus were used for instruction purposes, and one-pounders were used on the TV *William Webb* in live ammunition instruction on Long Island Sound. Once a cadet fired a one-pounder, according to Spurr, "his gun shyness [left] him."[18] Cadets were also bused to a Navy live firing range on Long Island's south shore at Long Beach, where they shot 20-millimeter guns seaward at aircraft-towed targets.

A Dangerous "Campus"

World War II was fought, in part, on and around the merchant ships that served as the extended classrooms of the young Academy. In the

Cadets at Kings Point, Pass Christian, and San Mateo all received regular gunnery training. Here, Pass Christian cadet-midshipmen practice at the U.S. Navy Firing Range in Shell Beach, Louisiana, in January 1945, before their assignment to sea duty.

two weeks immediately following Pearl Harbor, cadets Roger T. Wayland and Donald J. Stephenson watched in horror as Japanese planes made daily runs over Manila Harbor, dropping tons of high explosives on their ship and the other U.S. vessels in the harbor. One of these ships was badly damaged, and its crew was captured. Among them was Cadet William V. Mitchell, who would survive more than three years as a prisoner of war in the Philippines.

For a short time, Academy cadets escaped the ultimate sacrifice. Throughout the winter of 1941–1942, cadets and administrators held their breath, hoping somehow to avoid the inevitable. But on March 20, 1942, the dreaded news finally arrived.[19] Cadet Howard P. Conway Jr. had been lost on the SS *Liberator*, a Lykes Brothers ship that was torpedoed while traveling alone off the east coast of the United States. The mess hall at the Pass Christian campus was later named in his honor.

Kings Point was (and continues to be) the only federal academy to put its students in harm's way, and, as it learned on that March day in 1942, it did so at a price. Between 1942 and 1945, 142 Kings Point cadets were lost in action and countless others survived sinkings all around the world, from the icy waters off Murmansk to the remote ports of Sicily, and from the Gulf of Mexico to the ports of Indonesia. There is no exact count, but something like 650 ships sank with cadets on board.

The Academy also lost members of its rapidly growing alumni body. Sixty-eight graduates of the Academy and the Cadet Corps died in World War II, both as members of the merchant marine and as officers in the navy. George W. Alther, a 1940 cadet officer graduate from Melrose, Massachusetts, died in 1943 while serving as second mate on the SS *Timothy Pickering*. His heroism was later honored with the Merchant Marine Distinguished Service Medal, but his sacrifice was by no means unique. Academy graduates served as engineers and officers on naval destroyers, chief mates and engineers on Liberty ships, and even airline pilots ferrying bombers to the war zone. And like their younger colleagues, many gave their lives in the line of duty.

Even those cadets who survived the war rarely made it through without at least one close shave. Often, cadets underwent long and arduous ordeals before returning to the Kings Point campus to complete their training. The following four stories,[20] by no means atypical of the cadet experience in wartime, highlight the daily perils of having the high seas serve as one's campus during World War II.

The torpedo struck the SS *Potlatch*, a twenty-two-year-old Weyerhauser Steamship Company vessel, on its port quarter near the engine room just before four p.m. on June 27, 1942. Like many ships, she was attacked at the changing of the watch. The blast was so powerful that crew members at first thought that two torpedoes had struck the ship simultaneously.

The *Potlatch* was then approximately 650 miles east of the Virgin Islands, traveling alone en route from New York to Suez, Egypt, via Trinidad. She carried some seventy-five hundred tons of army supplies and a deck cargo of trucks and tanks, as well as a thirty-nine-man crew and sixteen naval armed guards.

Two of those crew members were Kings Point cadets, Michael J. Carbotti and Nathan J. Kaplan. Carbotti, asleep in his cabin when the torpedo struck, leaped out of bed to pull his clothes on as the ship started to list to port. On deck, chaos reigned. The first lifeboat launched by the crew was sucked into a gaping hole in the ship's side and capsized. The crew launched the second boat successfully, along with four life rafts. The *Potlatch* sank within five minutes. Miraculously, only six men had died in the explosion or went down with the ship.

The German submarine U-153 surfaced after the attack. It collected spare tires floating on the surface, then pulled up alongside the rafts to interrogate the survivors. After giving the crew directions to the nearest land—directions that later turned out to be false—the submarine departed.

Thus began an incredible odyssey. The forty-nine survivors were distributed among the one boat and four life rafts, the rafts were secured by lines to the boat, and the small flotilla set off on a desperate mission of survival, sailing north by northwest. Ship's Master John J. Lapoint, with no instruments, steered by the stars.

It was a nightmarish journey, demarcated by disasters. On the sixteenth day, they ran out of food. On the seventeenth day, the sharks that had been circling the flotilla attacked, savaging the arm of a man who was rinsing a cup in the water. (After suffering for the next seven days, the shark's victim died.) On the eighteenth day, the survivors ran out of water. A crew member died of exposure, a stark reminder of the fate that most likely awaited all of them.

On day 28, desperate for water, the crew spotted a deserted island. Landing the boat amid the reefs and crashing surf proved difficult and dangerous, in large part because they were so weak. Once ashore, they built a fire and sent out parties in search of food and water. Finally, animal tracks led them to a spring, and the most desperate part of their struggle was over.

After a day and a half of recuperation, the forty-seven survivors climbed back into their lifeboats and once again made sail. After thirty-six hours, they spotted another island, which—lacking even the resources of the first—could be used only as a stopping point. The next morning, they again sailed north by northwest until they arrived at a large island blessedly dotted with houses and farms.

Rowing up onto the beach, they were welcomed warmly by the locals, who offered them food and American cigarettes. One islander who owned a small schooner offered to take them to an even larger island, where ships occasionally called. The *Potlatch*'s crew readily accepted. On their first night at sea, a white signal light emerged from the darkness, blinking out a message: *You are rescued.* Within a half hour, they were aboard a palatial diesel-powered yacht skippered by American heiress Betty Carstairs, who fed them sandwiches and coffee.

The next day, they were in the Bahamian capital of Nassau. There they were the honored guests of Wallis Simpson, the duchess of Windsor. She found places for them in hospitals and hotels, fed them six-course dinners, and was photographed with them. To the blushing Kaplan she presented a beautiful pair of gaily colored pajamas. "As anxious as we were to get back to the States," Carbotti later commented, "we had to admit she was showing us a swell time."

They reached U.S. soil thirty-nine days after being torpedoed. Army transport planes flew the survivors to Miami, where they boarded trains and ships for home.

Late in the afternoon of November 2, 1942, the MS *Sawokla*, an American Export Lines ship, was transiting the Indian Ocean, en route from Ceylon (now Sri Lanka) to Cape Town, South Africa. The *Sawokla* had just unloaded war supplies in Calcutta, and was carrying jute, coarse canvas bales, and about 850 tons of diesel fuel back to America. There were fifty-nine people aboard: forty-one crew, thirteen naval armed guards, and five passengers. Third mate Stanley Willner, a past Cadet Corps cadet officer now on his first voyage as a ship's officer, craned his neck as he stood watch on the bridge, scanning the rough seas.

Just below the horizon, just out of his line of sight, the German naval surface raider SS *Michel* lurked in the dark waters. For more than five hours the raider had been stalking the *Sawokla*, keeping its smoke-stack in its sights.

Just after 9:35 p.m., Willner gasped in amazement as the outlines of a ship took shape in the darkness ahead of him. He immediately rang the captain's quarters, but within minutes the *Michel* had loosed her first torpedo. The captain was blown overboard by the force of the impact and lost. For the next seven minutes, the *Michel*'s guns relentlessly bombarded the *Sawokla*, which sustained several waterline hits as well as a direct torpedo hit below the smokestack. By 9:49, the ship was listing heavily to starboard, and in only seven more minutes she disappeared beneath the choppy seas. Later that night, Willner, semiconscious and badly injured, was pulled from the floating wreckage by the crew of the *Michel*.

Willner and thirty-nine other survivors had escaped the inferno of the *Sawokla*, but their ordeal had just begun. They spent the next three years as prisoners of war. The ensuing two months on the *Michel* would be the only time during their ordeal when they received reason-able treatment, including decent food and—in Willner's case—critically needed medical care. In February 1943, Willner and his fellow mer-chant marine prisoners, including his good friend and second mate on the *Sawokla*, Dennis Roland, were handed over by the Germans to the Japanese at a base in Jakarta, Indonesia, and taken to Singapore to begin a long and arduous march to Changi Peninsula, the central receiving station for all prisoners of war in this area.

The next two years were a devastating mix of brutally hard work, rampant disease, appalling living conditions, and insufficient and often putrid food. Willner was put to work with "H-Force," a group of largely British, Australian, and New Zealand POWs assigned to forced labor on the Burma-Siam railway along the infamous River Kwai. It was a deadly assignment: some 30 percent of the thirty-three hundred men in H-Force died. Willner was initially one of the lucky few; his job was to ride the elephants used to pull tree stumps out of the ground. This appeared to be a plum assignment, giving him a respite from bru-tal manual labor, but the animals' rough hairs tore Willner's bare legs to shreds. After several weeks, a fellow POW who was a doctor advised him to change his assignment before he bled to death, so it was back to the trenches. Willner's years in H-Force were an experience he would never forget, or forgive.

Willner's release in 1945 following Japan's surrender brought both relief and shock. After three years of being surrounded by filth and disease, he found himself unable to sleep in the bed offered to him on his first night of freedom, and slept instead on the hard concrete floor next to the bed. As he began to recover, Willner realized that fellow former prisoners of war who were members of the armed forces were being treated very well—given clean uniforms, free food, and many other benefits. Willner and his fellow merchant mariners, by contrast, were ignored by the authorities, and had to turn to the United Seamen's Service for money, food, and help in getting back home.

This injustice made a profound impression on Willner. Along with Dennis Roland, he worked for decades to earn veteran's status through litigation for merchant seamen in World War II. The effort finally bore fruit in 1988, despite opposition by some veterans groups, including the VFW, more than four decades after his ordeal.[21]

The Liberty ship SS *Timothy Pickering*, an American President Line vessel, lay at anchor at Avola, Sicily, in the second week of July 1943. She had just completed a voyage from Alexandria, Egypt, arriving in the second wave of an invasion force trying to carve out a Sicilian beachhead. Her crew complement included forty-three merchant mariners, twenty-three naval armed guard, and one hundred British troops. Among the crew was a young cadet-midshipman named Chris Brennan, a native of Springfield, Massachusetts, who was fresh from his basic training at Kings Point and ready to take on the world.

The ship was anchored some seven hundred yards offshore, next to a sheer rock bluff that rose high into the sky above them. The *Pickering*'s cargo was a mariner's nightmare: hundreds of tons of TNT and high-octane gasoline. Gingerly, the crew unloaded crates and drums over the side of the ship onto the decks of waiting supply barges.

It was 10:40 in the morning. Suddenly, over the top of the cliff, a lone German Stuka dive-bomber, with its engine cut to avoid detection, swooped down and dropped its bomb. The bomb struck forward of number-four hold, penetrated the deck, and exploded in the engine room and number-four deep tank.

Brennan was below decks, sipping coffee in the mess room, when his ship blew up. The force of the explosion was astounding: the sound of the blast was heard on ships as far as fifty miles out to sea. According to nearby observers, the *Pickering* seemed to dissolve into thin air. As flaming debris rained out in all directions, two other nearby ships were set afire.

Miraculously, Brennan was still alive. Knocked unconscious by being thrown against a bulkhead, he came to a few seconds later, to find that his ship had been transformed into a blazing inferno. The situation looked hopeless.

Crawling on his hands and knees out of the mess hall into the flaming passageway, he discovered that the force of the explosion had driven the engine up through the main deck into the galley. Unable to see through the dense smoke, he felt his way inch by inch down the passageway. Suddenly, he found himself swimming. The explosion had neatly sliced the ship in two between the midships' house and the number four hold, and the aft half of the ship had sunk within seconds.

Brennan was out of the frying pan and into the fire—literally. Burning gasoline had transformed the surface of the water into a sheet of flame. Burned, wounded by shrapnel, and in shock, he swam through the burning waters toward a nearby British landing barge. There he again lost consciousness.

Transferred from the barge to a ship to a shoreside army hospital, Brennan awoke to learn that only nineteen men had survived the disaster. Among those who perished were the three other cadets aboard: William L. Lyman, Warren P. Marks, and Lawrence D. McLaughlin, all from New Jersey. In a small way, these mariners had been avenged when a 20-mm gun crew—which included a cadet-midshipman on a nearby U.S. merchant vessel—had brought down the attacking Stuka as it leveled off after its attack on the *Pickering*.

On a sunny June day in 1943, nineteen-year-old cadet-midshipman James J. Hewitt boarded the MV *Halma*, a Danish-built freighter, flying the U.S. flag but carrying an expatriate crew, that was leaving the United States in a North Atlantic convoy. Hewitt had just finished his twelve weeks of basic training in the Cadet Corps and was embarking on his first journey with the merchant marine. He was ready, he felt, for whatever would come his way, but under his breath, of course, he was praying for a routine trip.

His prayers went unanswered. On their second day out, Hewitt's ship got separated from the convoy in a dense fog, and Hewitt realized that his training was about to be put to the test. This was no drill on Long Island Sound, no abstract scenario discussed in navigation class. This was twenty-foot seas, limited visibility, and enemy ships lurking nearby.

At 5:20 a.m. that same day, three torpedoes crossed the bow of Hewitt's vessel. The Norwegian skipper tried to outrun the sub, but at noon, a torpedo blasted through the port side of the number three hold. The explosion threw Hewitt against a steam valve, knocking him unconscious. But the cold Atlantic waters rushing into the ship revived him, and he was able to board a lifeboat with fifty-four others. They were picked up by a fishing boat and taken to Halifax, Nova Scotia. Hewitt had survived his first test.

After a brief respite at home in Plainfield, New Jersey, Hewitt returned to New York for reassignment, this time aboard a Liberty ship. His vessel again sailed in convoy, bound for North Africa through the Mediterranean. This time, Hewitt's luck held on the voyage, if just barely. Two ships in the column ahead of his ship and the one directly behind it were sunk, but Hewitt's ship made it safely to port in Cape Bon, Tunisia.

After only a few days of being tied up there, however, the ship was attacked by German dive-bombers and torpedo planes. While manning one of the 20-mm guns during a strafing attack, Hewitt received shrapnel wounds that required medical attention upon his return home.

In January 1944, Hewitt returned to sea. His new vessel made it to the west coast of Italy in time to take part in the U.S. landing at Anzio on January 22. Over a harrowing several days, Hewitt watched the surrounding merchant vessels being picked off one by one during day after day of intense aerial bombing. His own ship seemed strangely invulnerable as German bombers made seventy-nine unsuccessful air sorties trying to sink her.

During one afternoon of bombing and strafing attacks, Hewitt was again manning a 20-mm gun when two bombs fell within five feet of the vessel. The ship's deck plating and sides were sprung, but her crew persevered, and gunners on the ship were able to shoot down a twin-engine bomber. The plane reeled and crashed into the side of the ship, spewing shrapnel in every direction. Some of it found Hewitt, who crumpled in the gun tub with metal shards in his head and spine. He and others who had been wounded were carried ashore to an army field hospital on the Anzio beachhead. The fight raged on, but by the end of the day, the ship had undergone such relentless pounding that the captain decided to ground her to save her cargo and hull.

Hewitt no doubt breathed a sigh of relief to find himself in a hospital ashore; but his respite was short-lived. Soon after his arrival there, German planes bombed the hospital, burying Hewitt beneath debris, where he remained for several hours before he was pulled from the wreckage. Hewitt was transferred to a hospital in Naples, and his ship was refloated and towed to Taranto for repairs.

After a brief period of recuperation, Hewitt returned to board his vessel when she was ready to sail for the United States. Their route wound through the Mediterranean, where the ship was subjected to daily attacks by planes and submarines. This time, however, she escaped damage and made it safely home to the States.

Cadet-midshipman Hewitt's eventful Sea Year was finally over. After three months of hospitalization and rest, he returned to the Academy in September 1944 to finish his officer training. At a ceremony in Wiley Hall, Hewitt was awarded the Merchant Marine Mariner's Medal by Captain P. C. Mahady, commandant of cadets, in recognition of his conduct during his terrifying month on the Anzio beachhead.

The Collective Struggle

Those on board merchant ships in World War II, even when sailing as part of a convoy, often saw their entire world compressed into the fight for the survival of a single ship, or even one individual. Meanwhile, however, the larger war continued, with each side struggling for control of the vital shipping routes.

In this war, the American merchant marine was better prepared than in World War I. In part due to the farsighted provisions of the Merchant Marine Act of 1936, the industry had begun to steadily ramp up ship production in the late 1930s. When the war began, shipbuilding was able to expand promptly to meet the need, and both 1943 and 1944 were record-breaking years for ship production (1,849 and 1,786 respectively).[22] Henry J. Kaiser, an industrialist who was new to the maritime industry, was instrumental in the enormous output of Liberty ships in 1941–1942. In all, 2,710 Liberty ships—

each designed to carry the equivalent of three hundred railroad box cars—were built as part of the emergency cargo effort. The first, the SS *Patrick Henry*, was completed by Bethlehem Steel's Sparrow Point yard in September 1941, and more than a hundred more followed in the next year. Construction time for these ships was sharply reduced, due in part to the switch from riveting to welding, and also to new techniques of modular construction and prefabrication. In one well-publicized stunt, the Kaiser yards built a Liberty ship in only five days—discouraging news for the Axis that was counting on disrupting transatlantic shipping and starving Britain into surrender.[23]

These ships manned and supplied the great war machine in Europe and the Pacific. Although they carried troops, ammunition, fuel, and other critical materials to the front, they were only lightly armed, and they quickly became attractive targets for enemy forces. One of the most dangerous routes, early in the war, was along the Atlantic Coast. Again, this vulnerability was primarily due to the unwillingness of U.S. Navy admiral Ernest J. King to adopt basic precautions, including the protection of coastal convoys and East Coast blackouts. (King preferred to reserve his fleet for anticipated sea battles with the German Navy.) While transatlantic convoys in early 1942 were escorted by the U.S. Navy as far as the mid-Atlantic (where the Royal Navy took over), coastal and Gulf merchant shipping was basically on its own, with tragic consequences.

In the first six months of 1942, before effective convoy systems had been put into place, nearly four hundred Allied ships were lost in the North Atlantic, U.S. coastal waters, and the Caribbean.[24] For a time, more U.S. ships were being sunk than were being built—though the situation never approached that endured by the British, who suffered net tonnage losses in both 1942 and 1943.[25] In all, 1942 was the deadliest year of the war for the American merchant marine, with a total of 373 vessels destroyed—156 of them between May and July alone.[26]

In the fall of 1942, trouble intensified in the Mediterranean and also along the northern coasts of Europe. In the latter category was the dreaded Murmansk run, aimed at supplying Russia, and described as "a savage arctic gauntlet . . . of German U-boats, heavy cruisers, scout planes, torpedo bombers, dive-bombers, and icebergs."[27]

Raymond Holubowicz was one among many who survived

This navy photo shows an unidentified U.S. convoy steaming across the Atlantic during World War II.

enemy action on the way to Murmansk. A cadet who hailed from Cudahy, Wisconsin, Holubowicz ran into trouble on his first trip eastbound out of New York. His vessel, SS *Syros*, part of convoy PQ 16, was sunk by a German submarine at 73.57N, 17.30E, in late 1942. His engine counterpart, Cadet John Brewster, was killed by the explosion. Holubowicz was rescued after half an hour in the ice-cold waters, and joined the westward-bound SS *Hybert*, convoy PQ 13, only to be sunk again by "friendly" mines off the coast of Iceland. Rescued a second time, Holubowicz headed back to Murmansk on the Liberty ship SS *J. L. M. Curry*, with convoy PQ 18, and helped to discharge cargo from this vessel while under enemy air attack. On the trip home, Holubowicz encountered another foe, never forgotten even in time of war: Mother Nature. His ship ran into a gale and broke into three pieces. Rescued once more, this time by a British vessel, Holubowicz finally made it back to Kings Point a year after first shipping out.[28]

The Pacific war was also gaining in intensity in the summer of 1942. Engine Cadet William H. Thomas was one of many who had close shaves in these waters. While on board the SS *Edgar Allen Poe*, Thomas was awakened one night in November by horrific explosions; a Japanese torpedo had torn through the engine room, killing the first assistant engineer and a fireman, and injuring a twenty-five-year-old oiler. Thomas's heroic response, in which he descended into the inferno of the engine room to rescue the injured oiler, later earned him the Maritime Commission's Distinguished Service Medal, the third so granted.

The first cadet to receive this award posthumously was Engine Cadet Edwin O'Hara, one of the enduring heroic figures of Academy lore. O'Hara served on the Liberty ship SS *Stephen Hopkins*. On September 27, 1942, the *Stephen Hopkins* came under attack by a pair of German surface raiders while sailing alone from Cape Town to Paramaribo, Dutch Guyana, to load a cargo of bauxite for delivery to the United States. Captain Paul Buck decided to fight, rather than surrender his ship, and a terrific battle ensued. After the ship's armed guard officer Ensign Kenneth Willett, and his armed guard gun crew were critically injured while firing on the German raider *Stier*, the nineteen-year-old O'Hara rushed to Willett's battle station and single-handedly took over the stern 4-inch gun. Only five shells had escaped the explosion that had injured Willett, and O'Hara single-handedly

Cadet-Midshipman Edwin O'Hara at the U.S. Merchant Marine Cadet Basic School at Pass Christian, prior to his sea training.

fired them all—an amazing feat—into the German blockade runner *Tannenfels*. The *Stier* was set afire and sunk in the confrontation, marking the only instance in which a U.S. merchant ship sank a foreign naval surface vessel. After he fired the last shell, O'Hara was caught by a direct hit and died at his station. The Academy's athletic building was named in O'Hara's honor in March 1943, and O'Hara was posthumously awarded the Distinguished Service Medal by President Roosevelt.

The following year, 1943, was still a bloody one for the merchant marine, with 204 U.S. merchant ships sunk or damaged.[29] Convoys were being protected on the long-distance runs, and long-overdue precautions, including escorted coastal convoys, were finally easing the situation in U.S. waters, but losses in other parts of the world continued to mount. In part because more cadets had shipped out (there were now more than thirty-six hundred cadets on merchant ships),[30] cadet casualties continued to rise. In March alone, twenty cadets were killed in action. Half of these fatalities occurred on March 10, 1943, when ten cadets were killed on three separate ships, two in the North Atlantic and one in the Caribbean. The corps' worst loss on a single ship during the war came on January 9, 1943, when five cadets were killed on the SS *Louise Lykes*, torpedoed by a German submarine in the North Atlantic while en route to Belfast with war supplies. All seventy-four of her crew perished.[31]

Another tragedy occurred on December 2, 1943, when 105 German airplanes launched a devastating attack on the important fuel and ammunition port of Bari, Italy, which served the huge U.S. air base at Foggia. The German aircraft scored a direct hit on the SS *John Harvey*, loaded with ammunition and weapons, including one hundred tons of lethal mustard gas.[32] The explosion set off a chain reaction; two other vessels loaded with ammunition moored alongside the *John Harvey* also exploded. The grisly toll for the day included more than seventeen ships, one thousand Allied seamen, and cadets Richard B. Glauche, Alvin H. Justis, and Marvin H. Brodie of the *John Harvey*; James A. Hope and Jay F. Litton of the SS *John L. Motley*; and Francis B. Tone of the SS *Samuel J. Tilden*.[33] Academy graduate Fulton Edison Yewell Jr., second mate on the *John L. Motley*, was also killed during the action.

One cadet who survived the attack later spoke of a dread that would not subside: "All the bombs seemed to be dropping again within you. You were so shaky that even the slightest sound shocked you. And you felt that particular anxious feeling of a man who is not in control of himself, and knows it."[34] This feeling of apprehension was not unusual, and it was not limited to cadets at sea. By 1942, the Kings Point campus was receiving a constant stream of cadets returning from their ships to complete advanced training. In the mess hall, on the waterfront, and within cadet formations, the air was rife with hair-raising tales of enemy attacks, shipboard heroics, and lifeboat ordeals. The stories were resonant for preliminaries and experienced students alike, for all cadets at Kings Point knew that they would soon be headed back into the fray.

In the early months of 1943, the outcome of the war hung in the balance. The maritime losses were so extreme that many doubted the

United States or Great Britain could continue to fight much longer. In the first twenty days of March, for example, German U-boats sank seventy-two Allied cargo vessels,[35] setting a pace that, if sustained, would strangle the Allied supply line. In May and June 1943, however, the tide slowly began to turn as the Allies finally began to hold their own at sea. In 1944, 130 merchant ships were lost, a little over one-third the losses sustained two years earlier.[36] Meanwhile, U.S. shipyards in that year delivered 1,786 ships.[37]

The middle of the year saw a crucial milestone: the amphibious landing on France's Normandy Beach on D-Day, June 6, 1944. The D-Day landing was one of the greatest undertakings in maritime history, involving twenty-seven hundred Allied merchant ships. Here too, cadets played a role. One nineteen-year-old midshipman, Charles Fowler, took control of a tank landing craft when his commanding officer was killed by enemy fire. Under intense bombardment, and despite the fact that his steering gear had been destroyed, Fowler ran his craft onto the beach, unloaded his tanks, and then got a bulldozer to push his ship back into the water. Using the engines to steer his damaged vessel, Fowler brought her safely back to England.[38]

After Germany's surrender in May 1945, the Allies concentrated their efforts on the Pacific theater. Losses in this area were statistically lower than in other regions of combat—less than 10 percent of merchant ship losses occurred in the Pacific[39]—but those who sailed in the Pacific saw some of the war's most horrific fighting. The last Academy cadet known to have lost his life in the war died in the Pacific on April 6, 1945, when the SS *Hobbs Victory*, laden with ammunition, exploded when hit by kamikazes at the harbor of Kerama Retto, near Okinawa. Deck Cadet Alexander Harris died in the engagement.

Slowly, the end of the conflict was approaching—and so was the time when cadets at sea would be able to put down their arms, sleep without fear of midnight torpedoes, and resume their studies in peace.

A Dedication and a Superintendent

The formal dedication of the United States Merchant Marine Academy at Kings Point, New York, took place on September 30, 1943.

Little more than a year and a half had passed since cadets first had set foot on its grounds, but the Academy had undergone a complete transformation. The former Chrysler mansion, now the administration building, had been renamed in honor of Admiral Wiley, who died in May 1943 at the age of seventy-three. Six new barracks, a mess hall, and several academic buildings had been erected, and the plant was now fully self-sustaining, with its own heating system (with two Liberty ship boilers also used for engine instruction), fire department, and water supply.

The dedication ceremony was held in O'Hara Hall, in front of the Regiment and two thousand guests; and a nationwide radio hookup allowed several million more listeners across the country to listen in. The ceremony began with a message from President Roosevelt from Washington, D.C., read to the assembled visitors by Sam Schell, executive officer of the War Shipping Administration. Roosevelt's words were both complimentary and inspiring. One phrase in particular became both a touchstone and a point of affirmation for the young Academy: "This Academy serves the Merchant Marine as West Point serves the Army and Annapolis serves the Navy."[40]

The Regiment in formation on Dedication Day, September 30, 1943.

Commissioner Macauley followed Schell. Macauley used the occasion to present the Merchant Marine's Distinguished Service Medal to Cadet-Midshipman Frederick Zito. Zito had risked his own life to save that of a ship's fireman who, in the process of abandoning their torpedoed ship, had become entangled in the rope of a cargo net and was hanging upside down off the side of the ship. The young cadet climbed up the boat falls from his lifeboat, extricated the fireman, and both fell into the sea, from which they were rescued. "For your quick thinking and coolness under action and your valor shown on this occasion," Macauley read, "you are hereby commended."[41]

Commissioner Telfair Knight also spoke, paying tribute to McNulty, whom he called the "guiding genius" of the Academy, and a "capable engineer" who had created the campus and the Academy. McNulty himself was not in attendance. Intensely shy, and disliking ceremony of any sort, he had arranged to be in California at the time of the dedication. By coincidence, he was there with another ed unit personality who would play a major role in the Academy, and with whom he would later cross swords: Gordon McLintock.

Following Knight's speech, Macauley officially presented Captain James Harvey Tomb with the command of the Academy. This presentation was only a formality; Tomb had been superintendent of the Academy since April 11. McNulty had identified Tomb as his choice for superintendent well before this date, but there was some delay while Tomb detached himself from Fort Schuyler, where he had been superintendent for fifteen years.

Following the ceremony, the crowds moved to Kendrick Field (later renamed Tomb Field), where a formal review of the 2,500 cadets, divided into 3 battalions and 18 companies, was held on the grounds. Captain Giles Stedman, commandant of cadets, presented the Regiment before approximately 8,900 guests. More than 76 busloads of people had been ferried in from the Great Neck train station, and another 1,200 cars were parked on the grounds of the Academy.[42]

Tomb was both an unlikely and an obvious choice as first superintendent of the Academy. An 1899 Annapolis graduate, he first saw action in the Boxer Rebellion and the Philippine uprising. He began World War I as an ordnance inspector but finally took command of a ship—the USS *Aroostook*—and earned the Distinguished Service Medal for his role in the Northern Barrage mine-laying operations.

Dedication Day also included a regatta of monomoy races on Long Island Sound.

Tomb seemed assured of a brilliant naval career until tragedy struck at Honda Point, the northern entrance of the Santa Barbara channel, in 1923.[43] On September 8, the navy's Destroyer Squadron Eleven was making its way down from San Francisco. Poor visibility and an error in dead reckoning on the part of Captain Edward H. Watson, the squadron's commander, whom all were to follow, were fatal; seven destroyers and twenty-three lives were lost on the rocky shores of Honda Point that evening. Though Tomb himself was not directly responsible for the disaster, the episode effectively wrecked the naval careers of every officer who survived.

Derailed and detoured, Tomb nevertheless found a way to distinguish himself in the field of maritime education. In 1927, he assumed command of the New York State Nautical School (which in 1929 changed its name to the New York State Merchant Marine Academy). He was primarily responsible for securing Fort Schuyler, an abandoned army post in the Bronx at the junction of the East River and Long Island Sound, and turning it into a shore-based maritime school. Building the new campus, which was completed in 1938, was an epic struggle that lasted the better part of a decade, involving multiple jurisdictions and some of the most powerful politicians and massive egos in New York State history. (Governor Franklin D. Roosevelt was one; State Parks Commissioner Robert Moses was another.) Only Tomb's personal perseverance enabled the state school to secure the Fort Schuyler site, and then complete the necessary changes to make the site functional.

Arguably, the physical task of building a school was even harder at Fort Schuyler than at Kings Point. According to the terms of the school's lease from the War Department, which controlled the site, Tomb was forbidden from making *any* alterations to historic Fort Schuyler, or the property upon which it sat. This was clearly untenable. At one point, the school desperately needed to open a hole in one of the fort's exterior walls to create an access road for emergency and service vehicles. Coolly, Tomb ordered his crew to place sufficient dynamite at the base of the offending wall, and then blew a substantial hole in it. After the fact, he received a stern letter from Roosevelt—by this time, *President* Roosevelt—ordering him to refrain from blowing up any more of the historic property. "It was a ticklish situation," Tomb later recalled in a laconic third-person write-up, "but the Superintendent took full responsibility."[44]

At both maritime academies, Tomb appears to have been a universally loved figure—a dignified but warm man who was, by all accounts, a superb officer and leader. Even while serving as the superintendent of a state academy, he had been an ardent advocate for a federal academy, and his stature as an authority in maritime education lent the infant Academy at Kings Point some much needed credibility.

Tomb retired only a month or so after the formal dedication of the school. Although his tenure at the Academy was brief, his attachment to the school remained strong. In an interview with *Polaris* a year after his departure, he was prompted to talk about what he was doing in retirement. "Oh, it doesn't matter what I'm doing," he replied. "It's the Academy that counts. That Academy is my heart's blood."[45]

The Second Superintendent

Tomb was succeeded by another larger-than-life figure: the dashing and debonair Captain Giles C. Stedman, who had gained national celebrity for saving dozens of lives at sea and commanding great merchant vessels. Like Tomb, Stedman lent his enormous personal credibility to the young Academy, and also earned it some welcome headlines.

Stedman began his sea career in 1917 in the navy–to which he would return briefly in World War II–but found his true calling in the merchant marine. As he told a reporter many years later:

> In 1917, before crossing [the ocean] on the [USS] *Ossippee*, I visited the Brooklyn Navy Yard with a shipmate by the name of Tom Brophy. . . . At one of the docks lay an interned four-funnel German liner of about 18,000 tons. It was a spectacle for young eyes. Neither of us were yet voters. We stopped and took an eyeful. After five silent

The dashing and celebrated Captain Giles Stedman, the second superintendent of the U.S. Merchant Marine Academy, on the bridge of a ship.

> moments pregnant with emotion, Brophy turned to me and with much deliberation said, "Boy, when a fellow gets to be captain of a ship like that, he sure has picked himself a man's sized job." I can tell you frankly that nothing I had ever heard from human lips had such a stimulating effect on my ambitions as Tom Brophy's comment that day, seventeen years ago in the Brooklyn Navy Yard. Then and there he planted irrevocably in my mind the idea of a man-sized job. I owe it to Brophy that my feet are now on a quarterdeck.[46]

In 1922, Stedman accepted a position with United States Lines. Three years later, while serving as chief officer on the SS *President Harding*, he was the hero of a daring sea rescue in the Atlantic, personally piloting a small lifeboat through high seas to save the imperiled crew of an Italian vessel. The American media seized upon the story of the young mariner–first lauding his skill and stamina, and then praising the grace with which he handled his newfound fame.[47] Stedman, still in his twenties, ducked out of a ticker-tape parade from the Battery piers to city hall, telling one of his crew that it was "a little too much" for him.[48]

By 1931, he had worked his way up to Master, commanding the

SS *American Merchant*, a combination passenger and cargo vessel owned by U.S. Lines. Then, in 1933, in an implausible turn of events, Stedman masterminded a dramatic Atlantic ocean rescue of yet another foundering merchant ship. The British *Evening World* called it the "most courageous [rescue] ever carried out on the high seas."[49] And once again, he won plaudits for his modesty. Accepting an award in New York's City Hall, Stedman characteristically deflected attention from himself: "I fully realize that in accepting this medal of valor, I do so not as an individual, not as one person, but as the representative of the officers and crew of the *American Merchant*."[50]

In 1940, Stedman became the first commanding officer of the SS *America*, flagship of U.S. Lines, and the nation's largest passenger vessel, built with construction subsidies provided by the 1936 act. To a degree that is hard to render a half century after the demise of the great transatlantic ocean liners, Stedman was an authentic celebrity, hobnobbing on and off his ship with the rich and powerful. New York gossip columnist John McClain labeled him the "Clark Gable of the seas." The passenger list on one of his runs included Ignace Jan Paderewski, Herbert Hoover, Joe Kennedy, Cordell Hull, Charlie Chaplin, Douglas Fairbanks, Bernard Baruch, three U.S. senators (Glass, Borah, and Johnson), Henry Ford, and J. P. Morgan, among others.[51] Late in 1938, to the dismay of ranks of young socialites, he took himself off the eligible-bachelor lists by marrying Florence L. Schick, the wealthy widow of razor blade magnate Jacob Schick.

Although a darling of high society, Stedman was anything but superficial. In fact, he was an intelligent and thoughtful officer, who among other things took very seriously his training obligations under the terms of the federal program in the 1930s. It may have been his careful attention to the education of the cadets in his charge that first brought him to the attention of Richard McNulty. In an interview with *Marine Progress* in 1941, Stedman used his own career as an illustration of the need for officer training, in part to keep qualified people at sea:

> Early in 1922, I was included in a group of young officers who placed the new *President Harding* in commission. Within a few years, four of these five officers had left the service. Of the four, two became lawyers, one an aeronautical engineer, and one a judge in Boston. *I alone remained at sea.* These men had the stuff that good officers are made of—they are the kind we want to hold on to. We need

better conditions aboard ship. And we need advanced training for officers.[52]

Stedman was slotted to serve as the Academy's first superintendent; a letter to the Navy Bureau of Navigation from Admiral Land on January 24, 1942, requested Stedman's transfer to the position of superintendent of the Academy. The navy replied, politely but firmly, that Stedman would not be free for at least two months, and possibly more. In the meantime, Tomb was recruited as the first superintendent. In May 1942, Stedman accepted a position at the Academy as commandant of cadets, in which role he oversaw the formal review on Kendrick Field at the 1943 dedication of the school. When Tomb departed on October 16, Stedman took over as superintendent.

At the Academy, as at sea, Stedman was known as a stickler for discipline. In that spirit, he strengthened the school's embryonic regimental system considerably during his watch. The regimental system had been operational since August 1942, when the administration appointed a staff of cadet officers and petty officers "to mold the Corps into an efficient and well-organized unit."[53]

On December 16, 1942, with Stedman's active encouragement, this system was expanded and formalized. At that time the corps was divided into two battalions of four companies each, although in accordance with naval regulations, the plan was to increase this to three battalions of six companies each, once the corps had reached its full strength. Midshipman George Agee was named as the first regimental commander. A system of demerits for misconduct was also put in place at this time, and cadets were assigned to watch stations around the twenty-four-hour clock.

The regimental system gave the cadets much-needed structure in an environment that was still largely unformed. It offered them leadership training—confidence in their ability to influence their own lives, and the lives of others—that for many would prove invaluable in the dangerous places they were soon to visit. And finally, it instilled a sense of tradition in the Academy, and in time became a defining element of the institution.

Putting the Pillars in Place

By its September 30, 1943, dedication day, the United States Merchant Marine Academy at Kings Point—only a year and a half old—had emerged as a clear focal point for merchant marine officer training. True, the state academies had increased in size, and a new state academy had opened in Castine, Maine, in 1941. But their overall complement of cadets remained far smaller than that of the federal academy. The Cadet Corps' Gulf and Pacific schools had begun growing into their new facilities, but, as noted above, they were now explicitly cast as "preliminary" or "basic" schools, training fourth-class cadets in elementary seamanship, navigation, and engineering to prepare them for their first six months at sea.

While the state academies and the federal academy have been rivals at various times in their history, they were first and foremost *collaborators* during the national emergency of World War II. The Academy benefited greatly from good relations with its sister academies, who, after all, had been there first, and whose graduates helped create the federal academy. (Richard McNulty, a graduate of Massachusetts Maritime, was the most important, but there were many others.) And the Academy was able to help—and help itself—when a sister academy fell on hard times. When the Pennsylvania state academy closed in 1947, for example, Kings Point welcomed all Pennsylvania cadets who wanted to transfer, and also received a major infusion of faculty talent.

Our story has a necessarily narrow focus. It is worth noting, in passing, that the U.S. Maritime Service in the early days of the war established a wide range of maritime training schools, including officer's schools at Fort Trumbull in New London, Connecticut, and Alameda, California, offering licensing-exam preparation for seamen with at least fourteen months' experience; radio schools on Gallups Island in Boston Harbor and Hoffman's Island in New York Harbor; unlicensed seamen's schools at Brooklyn's Sheepshead Bay (with up to fifteen thousand in attendance) and St. Petersburg, Florida; and a wide variety of specialist schools, upgrading schools, and correspondence schools.

But these schools were viewed from the outset as temporary wartime installations. The Academy at Kings Point was different. The fact that it took physical form during the war obscured the fact that before the war, Congress had created a *permanent* institution. The Academy's rivals and detractors, especially after the war, downplayed this fact of prewar history.

The job of the Academy's supporters, therefore, was to put the pillars in place that would help the institution do its vital wartime work—and also to survive when the national emergency receded.

The most tangible of these, of course, was the magnificent new campus at Kings Point. The cadets who had experienced the school's previous homes—at the now defunct Admiral Billard Academy in New London, where the school was located from May to September 1940, and later at Fort Schuyler—knew how lucky they were. "When temporary quarters seem crowded and schedules seem erratic," as one *Polaris* editorial writer put it, "remember that the Academy has been relocated three times since the beginning of 1939, and each move was for the better."[54]

Another pillar was naval reserve status. On August 8, 1942, the chief of naval personnel announced that all federal cadets would be appointed midshipmen in the naval reserve. From this point on, the cadets were formally called "cadet-midshipmen." This status, leading to naval commissioning, came to be considered one of the three crucial components to a Kings Point education, along with the bachelor of science degree, first granted to the class of 1947, and, of course, the United States Coast Guard license as a merchant marine officer.

Yet another pillar was the Sea Project, forerunner to the Sea Year. In one sense, the Sea Project was simply a logical extension of the "floating correspondence school" strategy that the Maritime Commission had employed in the prewar era, before a campus became available. But the Sea Project was also different in that it was consciously conceived as an integral part of a larger educational program—a six-month immersion in the practical applications of the "book learning" that had preceded it, and would follow it. Along with the Regiment, it also was one of several devices fostered by the Academy to help cadets embrace self-discipline and take responsibility for their own education.

The regimental system was another key pillar. It helped impose order on an institution that might otherwise have verged on the chaotic. "When rules and regulations conflict somewhat with individual freedoms," *Polaris*'s editorial writers advised, "remember that the personnel of the Cadet Corps now number in the hundreds; it merely takes a little thought to realize that only by common-sense restrictions can order be maintained and ultimate aims in training be achieved."[55] But the Regiment also provided leadership (and "followership") opportunities, and helped prepare the cadets for the combat situations that all would anticipate, and some would soon encounter.

Not inconsequentially, the Regiment generated many hours of "volunteer" labor for the benefit of the Academy. At first, the Academy's leaders had intended to emulate West Point's system of "disciplinary walking," that is, marching off demerits, but soon hit upon a different scheme. "Only because there was such a large amount of small jobs to be accomplished," *Polaris* reported wryly, "were the cadets allowed to work instead of walk."[56] A typical job for a physical training period might involve clearing the future Roosevelt Field of "trees, poison ivy, and prickers."[57]

The cadets, too, did their part to strengthen the institution. Even with pressing wartime concerns, they found the time to organize the successful newspaper, *Polaris*, which began publishing in August 1942 with a circulation of nine hundred and grew to ten times that circulation by the following year. *Polaris* quickly emerged as the most reliable picture of what was going on at Kings Point; equally important, it established itself as a means whereby cadets returning from sea could impart some of their hard-won wisdom to their juniors. "Sleep with

First Lady Eleanor Roosevelt tours the Academy grounds on May 6, 1944, in Vice Admiral Lauren McCready's 1941 Ford.

your cabin door open," returning cadets would write, "because a torpedo strike can jam your door shut. Never sleep on the hatch covers, because you risk getting blown overboard. Wear clothing at all times when in dangerous waters. Have a lifebelt and a flashlight handy. Know where your boots are."[58]

Two cadets, Roland Fiore and Richard Reddy, wrote the school's alma mater. Others organized student clubs, such as the Tin Fishermen (known in later years as the Tin Fish Club), an organization restricted to those cadets who had survived sinkings at sea due to enemy action and returned to Kings Point. By the fall of 1943, 147 cadets on campus had qualified for membership in the Tin Fishermen. (Membership in this club eventually exceeded four hundred cadets.) "The first activity of this new society," *Polaris* reported, "was when they took part in a coast-to-coast broadcast over the Blue Network on October 12. Several members of the club spoke of their experiences."[59] These efforts were good for the cadets, and they were also good for Kings Point.

More pillars remained to be put in place. For the moment, however, the Academy was well born, and had reason to be optimistic about the next phase of its evolution.

5

Making Peacetime Headway
1945–1950

It was a perfect day for a football game: crisp and clear, with only a few stray breezes off Long Island Sound. And finally, following the Japanese surrender on August 14, 1945, the world was at peace.

The date was September 29, 1945: the eve of the second anniversary of the dedication of the United States Merchant Marine Academy at Kings Point. As Superintendent Giles Stedman surveyed the crowd massing on Kendrick Field, he had many reasons to feel pride, satisfaction, and excitement.

That morning, the Academy had kicked off its first ever Alumni Day. Many of the several hundred alumni in attendance had obtained special leaves, either from their merchant marine employers or from the navy, so that they could participate in the daylong schedule of events. In his remarks at the opening ceremony—addressed to the cadets, but written with the Academy's distinguished guests in mind—Stedman praised the alumni for their achievements during the war, in which most in the Regiment assembled that morning had fully expected to be involved.

"Their outstanding ability and devotion to duty during the war," Stedman said of the alumni, "not only has brought honor and glory to themselves, but it has also enhanced the fame and dignity of the Academy far and wide, wherever men of the sea congregate. As the years go by and their numbers increase, they will do much to insure a merchant marine and a maritime policy benefiting the stature of this nation as a leading world power. Their very presence here today lends solidarity to this institution."[1]

After Stedman's remarks, the first president of the newly formed alumni association, Lieutenant Andor E. Utheim, '42, talked about the Academy's growing alumni ranks in which the current midshipmen would soon find themselves. "You, the gentlemen of the Regiment," he said, "today will have the eyes of the alumni upon you. Many of them are masters of their vessels, many are chief engineers, and many are naval officers. They will see themselves in you, not as masters in command of a vessel, but as Kings Pointers. Today they will relive with you their undergraduate days, days that are only a few years past. Tomorrow they will again be the officers manning our merchant marine and naval vessels, where you will soon take your place among them."[2]

The morning featured stirring oratory in abundance, but included subdued moments as well. At morning colors, as the Regiment lined the oval in front of Wiley Hall, Lieutenant Commander Irving S. Pollard, the Academy's chaplain, offered a prayer to the memory of the cadet-midshipmen whose lives had been lost in the war. The regimental commander, Guyland L. Centner, placed a wreath from the newly formed alumni association on the War Memorial—a stone sarcophagus just to the east of the Amphitrite Fountain, and under continuous guard. A bugle sounded a melancholy taps.

Throughout the morning, alumni and midshipmen alike paused to pay tribute to their fallen comrades. Many tossed coins into the fountain, which was doubling as a collection vessel for the permanent memorial that the Academy hoped to erect in the coming year. For the time being, however, the sarcophagus and a frieze in Delano Hall picturing a midshipman manning a 50-caliber machine gun, and bearing the names of the cadets lost in action, would honor the memory of the war dead.[3] The frieze was soon covered with a large painting of the SS *America*, amidst fears that the growing list of cadets lost in action would harm the morale of the Regiment. Also, there were derogatory remarks at the artist's conception of fighting a German U-boat with a 50-caliber machine gun.

And now, as the blue-and-gray Kings Point Mariners took the field to face the Rensselaer Polytechnic Institute team in their first-ever intercollegiate competition, Stedman had reason to feel some personal satisfaction. It was his own exertions that had brought intercollegiate football to Kings Point, partly because he thought it would be good for his school, and partly because he liked nothing better than a good

An early Mariners football game on the Academy's Kendrick Field.

game. "He has a love of athletics," the *New York Times* had reported a decade earlier, back in his days as a ship's master, "that takes him up to one of the baseball parks as soon as his ship reaches port, or to the hockey games during the winter season."[4]

In the previous spring, with Stedman's strong support, Kings Point varsity teams had begun competing in baseball, wrestling, basketball, and tennis.[5] Now football's time had come, and Stedman and his fellow Mariners fans soon had something to celebrate. Bob "Stormy" Pfohl, the Mariners' right halfback, picked off an errant pass in the Mariners' end zone and ran it back 101 yards for a touchdown. The crowd erupted–and this was only the beginning of a good day for the team, and for legendary coach Earl Brown. The inspired Mariners beat Rensselaer 26 to 19, getting the Kings Point football tradition off to a proud start.

That September day also marked the beginning of other Kings Point traditions, most important among them a tradition of alumni support of and loyalty to the Academy. In the years to come, and sooner than anyone could have predicted, this support literally would mean the difference between life and death for the institution.

From the Clouds of War

The U.S. merchant marine emerged from World War II as a major sea power. In 1939, the United States had controlled only 14 percent of the world's ships; by 1945, that figure had risen to 54 percent, or 5,529 of the total 10,175 ships on the oceans.[6] The Maritime Commission was close to achieving its goal of having U.S. flagships carrying 50 percent of the country's imports and exports.

The merchant marine had helped to ensure the nation's security and secure the peace, but it had paid a heavy price. Of the roughly 6,000 merchant ships that sailed under the U.S. flag, 624 were sunk by enemy action and 130 more were damaged.[7] In addition, of the approximately 250,000 merchant mariners, almost 7,000 were killed, or 2.73 percent of their ranks. Only the marines suffered a higher percentage of losses, with 2.9 percent killed in action. (The navy's war dead, by comparison, were 1.49 percent of the total force, with .88 percent of those killed in action.[8]) And yet, once again, the contributions of the merchant marine went largely unrecognized. Returning G.I.s were greeted with ticker tape parades and the G.I. Bill—which gave them the financial wherewithal to go to college, and otherwise pick up civilian life where they had left it off—but the returning merchant mariners received no such welcome or privileges.

The Maritime Commission was deluged with letters from the parents of cadets, as well as from cadets themselves, complaining of the injustice of cadets not receiving the benefit of the G.I. Bill. Roosevelt would most likely have agreed to help the merchant mariners, including the cadets; indeed, a handwritten note by FDR on a 1943 letter from Robert Patterson, the acting secretary of war, confirms that Roosevelt believed that the War Department should consider "officers and members of the crews of ships of the Merchant Marine as members of the armed forces." And when signing the G.I. Bill, Roosevelt commented, "I trust Congress will soon provide similar opportunities to members of the merchant marine who have risked their lives time and time again during the war for the welfare of their country."[9] Admiral Land even worked with Samuel Rosenman, Roosevelt's counsel and speechwriter, on legislation to give merchant seamen the same benefits as veterans of the Armed Services.[10] But Roosevelt's successor, Harry Truman, was disinclined to extend these benefits to merchant mariners (as were many veterans' groups), and this inequity was not rectified until 1988.

Despite the apparent strengths of the industry, its postwar circumstances bore an eerie and ominous similarity to those following World War I. Again, the United States had a significant surplus of vessels. Even after scrapping damaged and obsolete ships, assigning some ships to the naval reserve, and selling off others to foreign operators, the United States had thirty million tons of excess shipping. New trends in shipping and transportation, moreover, were starting to impact maritime shipping. Land-based trucking transportation systems, for example, were slowly increasing—although this would not have a major impact until the onset of the Eisenhower Interstate Highway System in the 1950s—and commercial airline transportation was already proving cost- and time-effective for passengers and compact freight shipments.

By the end of 1945, Pan American Airlines had completed plans to create a fleet of passenger airliners, each with a seating capacity of 236. As *Polaris* pointed out, a single airplane flying to Europe would be able to carry two-thirds of the capacity of an eleven-thousand-ton liner, and get there in nine hours rather than seven days. The war had "proved the safety and superiority of air travel." Change was literally in the air.[11]

It was also on the waves. U.S. operators were switching in ever increasing numbers to foreign flags, especially Liberian and Panamanian registry, which permitted ship operators to avoid the United States' higher labor costs and relatively strict maritime regulations, as enforced by the Coast Guard. In addition, union jurisdictional conflicts and wildcat strikes continued to plague the industry, creating service unpredictability and souring the public on the reliability of the U.S. maritime industry in general.

In this uncertain environment, the Maritime Commission's Training Division would have to act quickly to secure public support—and government funding—for the federal merchant marine academy. Yes, the prewar legislation that led to Kings Point stated clearly that this was a permanent institution. But history was not necessarily on the Academy's side. In the past, both the public and the government had been quick to withdraw their support from the merchant marine when it was no longer needed to respond to a crisis of national defense. Would it happen again?

Repositioning

In December 1941, the Training Division had acted with speed and audacity to align itself with the war-related needs of the country—shortening programs, adapting courses, and pushing thousands of mariners through the educational pipeline at ever greater speeds. But with

Knight and McNulty at the helm, the division had never lost sight of its original vision for the Academy as a permanent, four-year institution. Now that vision would be challenged. The Academy would have to define an identity and mission distinct from support for the war effort. It would need to achieve understanding and acceptance in both public and governmental opinion as it sought to readapt to the peacetime environment.

The ultimate goal was to become an academically accredited, degree-granting institution. Without this status—which would put the Academy on an equal footing with the other federal academies, as well as other colleges and universities—the institution at Kings Point had little hope of permanent governmental support.

To achieve accreditation and permanency, the Academy would have to succeed at several things concurrently. First, and most important, the school's curriculum would have to be adjusted in terms of both its length and content. Second, the Academy would need to establish, clarify, and strengthen its identity. This comprised activities that ranged from a clear statement of the school's mission to the development of intercollegiate athletics and the strengthening of the Regiment. All of these elements, it was hoped, would also strengthen the support of another vital resource already mentioned—the alumni.

Some of this work was well under way. The first official statement

The Regiment assembled for morning colors before Wiley Hall, on May 30, 1945.

of the Academy's mission, for example, was published in June of 1943, in *Polaris*. Though announced by McNulty, it was prepared by Lieutenant Commander Delwyn Hyatt, the head of the Seamanship and Navigation Department. It read as follows:

> To attract to the U.S. Merchant Marine a high type of young American with a definite ambition to become an officer in the Service: to impart to him the necessary academic background, and the fundamentals of a practical nautical education essential to a successful career at sea; to develop in him a high sense of honor, uprightness, and loyalty; to instill in him a pride in his profession, and a determination to uphold the traditions of the Merchant Marine; and, by effective teaching, training, and guidance, to send him forth to his calling with a deep respect and affection for the U.S. Merchant Marine Cadet Corps and its Academy.[12]

Judging from the lack of explicit references to wartime and national defense, this mission statement was conceived with the Academy's postwar activities in mind. The statement proved extremely durable, remaining essentially unchanged for the next quarter-century.

As the intensity of the war ebbed slightly in the early months of 1944, the Training Division set in motion several initiatives aimed at ensuring the long-term survival of the Academy. One of the most significant of these initiatives came in May, with the establishment of a Congressional Board of Visitors. Public Law 301, approved by Congress on May 11, 1944, provided for a board "similar to that provided for the U.S. Coast Guard Academy," comprised of the chairman of the Senate Commerce Committee, the chairman of the House Committee on Merchant Marine and Fisheries, three senators designated by the Senate Commerce chair, and five representatives designated by the House Merchant Marine and Fisheries chair.[13] The first Board of Visitors included its chairman, Schuyler Otis Bland, the Virginia congressman who had sponsored the Merchant Marine Act of 1936 and had emerged as a staunch advocate for the Academy, and New York representative Eugene Keogh, who later proved to be an important ally during the Academy's campaign for accreditation.

The first Board of Visitors convened at the Academy on September 29, 1944. This inaugural visit was weighted heavily toward the ceremonial; the board spent many hours touring the Academy, listening to the Academy orchestra play selections from *Show Boat*, and enjoying cocktail receptions and a dinner hosted by Superintendent Stedman. On the more substantive side, Stedman delivered a lengthy address in which he described in detail the curriculum, buildings and grounds, and administration of the Academy. Members were also given the results of a 1943 government survey on maritime training, and Admiral Land sent Chairman Bland a memo recounting the legislative history of the Academy.

The recommendations of the board were few in number but sweeping in scope. First, and most important, the board members recognized the "necessity of maintaining a permanent Merchant Marine Academy." They also recommended careful expansion of the campus, a full four-year curriculum, an admissions system based on geographic quotas, and increased publicity. Finally, they urged the Academy to keep up with modern developments in the maritime industry, noting in particular Britain's recent decision to place revolutionary new radar equipment on all of its merchant vessels.[14]

In this and future years, the congressional visiting committee served as an important sounding board for the Academy, and also— informally—as its strongest advocate in the halls of Congress. Some issues emerged as perennial concerns, and so the Board of Visitors addressed those issues every year. In its 1945 report, for example, the board reiterated its major conclusion from the previous year: "To dispel any misunderstanding . . . [the Board] desires to strongly emphasize the fact that the U.S. Merchant Marine Cadet Corps was created prior to the war pursuant to the provisions of the Merchant Marine Act of 1936 . . . and that its site at Kings Point, NY, was acquired for the purpose of constructing a permanent Merchant Marine Academy."[15]

Individual members of the board also picked up on issues of particular interest to them, and to their friends at Kings Point. Eugene Keogh, for example, sponsored two bills in 1946, the first authorizing the Academy to build a chapel and library, and the second permitting the Academy to grant the Bachelor of Science degree after it received its academic accreditation. Although these were only modest steps, they too helped lay the foundations for both accreditation and permanency.

Extending the Curriculum

The Academy's proposed four-year curriculum was approved by Admiral Land and the War Shipping Administration on September 17,

1945. By this point, the new curriculum had been in the planning stages for some time, and the WSA's goal was to have it implemented by the summer of 1946.[16]

The move was a prerequisite to eventual accreditation, and therefore couldn't come too soon. But the large complement of students who had been admitted on a biweekly schedule during the previous three years made for an extremely complex transition. The initial steps toward a longer course of studies had been taken in the last eighteen months of the war, when the need for new officers eased somewhat and the curriculum could be extended to two years. On October 1, 1945, less than two months after the cessation of hostilities, the course of study was again extended–this time, to three years, of which six months would be spent at one of the basic schools, six months on a merchant vessel, and twenty-four months at Kings Point. College mathematics, physics, English, history, and Spanish were added to the curriculum at this time, significantly broadening the Academy's offerings.

At this point, classes were still on a monthly rotation, allowing cadets returning from their Sea Year to begin their Academy training within weeks of arrival. The administration aimed to shift to a quarterly system as soon as student logistics permitted.

In May 1946, the final transition to a four-year curriculum began. The most immediate and noticeable change was a shift to semiannual admissions, instead of biweekly. For the first time, the composition of the student body at the Academy remained relatively constant throughout the year. Second classmen reporting before May 1, 1945, became the first group to graduate from the four-year program. These cadets were split into sections depending on their date of arrival, and their course of study was thus determined by how many classes they had already completed at the Academy. The most recent arrivals completed fewer classes to graduate, but all cadets completed minimum requirements. Courses in marine insurance, commercial law, maritime law, international law, human relations, Portuguese, and French were added to the curriculum.

These language courses complemented the modest humanities curriculum that was already in place, largely through the efforts of Charles Ferris. In the wartime years, Ferris, recalled by a colleague as a "peppery little fellow," had implemented a freshman composition program, and created a course called United States and World History, largely borrowed from a similar course at MIT.[17] The result was the Department of History and Languages. Like his counterpart Lauren McCready on the engineering side, Ferris remained at Kings Point until 1976, and put an indelible stamp on what evolved into the Department of Humanities.[18]

Another significant postwar change was the return to the annual competitive entrance examination, abandoned since the exam given the morning before the attack on Pearl Harbor. At the same time, the administration instituted a quota system based on the populations of the forty-eight states, and 630 of the 750 cadets were admitted based on these quotas. Outside of this quota system, the remaining 120 appointments were allocated to unlicensed seamen who had a minimum of six months of service aboard a ship or in the Maritime Service and who had received a passing grade on the exam. This provision was a gesture toward union leaders, who objected to the Academy in part because they claimed it disadvantaged young men trained only on ships.

Meanwhile, the Academy's complement of students (and staff) was gradually reduced from its wartime highs. On July 1, 1945, the total complement of cadets numbered 4,391,[19] already a significant reduction from totals of well over 7,000 cadets in 1944. This was cut further by capping the number of annual appointments at 750 cadets, and numbers were reduced further in subsequent years.

In planning for a four-year curriculum, the Training Division encountered a dilemma that would continue to bedevil the Academy in all future curriculum-design efforts: lack of time. The crux of the issue was that the Academy offered a full practical engineering curriculum, along with humanities and other courses as required for accreditation, in a total of three years instead of four. The Sea Year, although one of the Academy's most important and beneficial learning experiences, caused extreme compression in the time available for shore-based education. The challenge was such that some even suggested adding a year onto the Academy's program. As an Academy adviser commented to the Board of Visitors in 1946, "The [Superintendent] is giving a four year technical course in three years. If you want my honest opinion, I would [suggest] that you give him four years' time, plus one year at sea. Then you would do a most outstanding job."[20] This plan was never seriously pursued, and the curricular compression caused by the Sea Year remained a stumbling block throughout the accreditation process.

Extending the Foundations: Athletics and the Library

Superintendent Stedman was both a sports fan and a fitness fanatic. During his years as a U.S. Lines captain, he enthusiastically recommended exercise to all passengers on his vessels, and he frequently sponsored "deck tennis" competitions, using either an eight- or a twelve-pound medicine ball. "If you're not used to it," Stedman told a reporter, "the exertion is apt to keep you in bed the next day."[21]

In the early years of the war, of course, cadets at Kings Point focused on more practical forms of physical training: four hours a week devoted primarily to upper body strength, monomoy rowing, swimming, and abandon-ship drills. Intramural athletic contests, including tennis, handball, softball, track, boxing, wrestling, volleyball, fencing, basketball, and gymnastics, were held after class hours, often pitting company against company and battalion against battalion. And although the Academy could boast the presence of top instructors, such as Greg Rice, a specialist in stamina development and a world champion distance runner, athletic competition with the outside world remained a dream.

In the spring of 1945, with the war winding down, Stedman initiated a program of varsity athletics. As noted, the Academy fielded intercollegiate teams in wrestling, basketball, tennis, and baseball—and to the delight of everyone involved, both the wrestling and basketball squads enjoyed undefeated seasons. Stedman also began work on a new athletic field to better accommodate the teams. Five more intercollegiate teams were fielded in the fall of 1945, including cross-country, swimming, sailing, boxing, and, at long last, football.

Very quickly, athletics became more than just an outlet for the cadets and a means to help them keep physically fit. Intercollegiate athletics were also emerging as an ever more significant factor in school choice, and thus were vital to the Academy's competitiveness in the student market. As Stedman noted in his address on Alumni Day: "One of the last steps in placing Kings Point on equal footing with other outstanding educational institutions is the culmination of our athletic program by participation in intercollegiate varsity competition."[22] Athletics, considered part of a well-rounded educational program, also were emphasized by accreditation boards. If Kings Point wanted to play in the big leagues, it would have to offer a credible program of varsity sports.

Equally important to the impending accreditation campaign was the state of the Academy's library. The second Board of Visitors report highlighted an acceptable library as an immediate and obvious need of the Academy.

The first iteration of the Academy's library, back in the hectic early days of 1942, was nothing more ambitious than a selection of recreational reading collected from Great Neck families by Lieutenant Horton H. Spurr, a drill and gunnery instructor, and a local tennis and golf instructor, Alexander Bannwart. The two scavengers collected two carloads of books, which they tucked into various corners of the Chrysler and Schenk mansions for use by the cadets.

In 1943, one of the school's first chaplains, the Reverend Irving Pollard, was appointed the first librarian of the Academy, and space for the library was reserved on the first deck of the nautical science building, Bowditch Hall. Almost from the start, this space was recognized as insufficient for an adequate reference library. A full twenty-five years elapsed, however, before the library got the space it needed.

But the Academy's library took a large step forward in 1946, with the hiring of the energetic and highly qualified Luis Bejarano as the school's first full-time librarian. Bejarano combined an advanced degree in library science from Columbia University with four years' service in the navy. Over time, he oversaw a complete reorganization of the existing materials, and developed an acquisition program that added important reference materials and student handbooks to the holdings. By the end of his tenure, the library's collection had grown to some thirty thousand volumes.

Bejarano developed a clear vision of the library's needs, partly through visits to the libraries of other institutions, and partly through a careful analysis of the Academy's programs. Based on that vision, he demanded—and got—special treatment for his library. As he recalled:

> I started buying books like crazy. We convinced the administration that one room in Bowditch was not going to be enough for the library—that we needed the whole first floor, and possibly the second floor—and that we needed a staff of about five to start with, and more later on.
>
> They were shocked. They thought the librarian would get a little cubbyhole, and hand out books when a cadet wanted one. So I had to educate everybody there.[23]

Bejarano's calls for additional staff, more space, and bigger acquisitions budgets might have gone unheeded, given the multiple demands on the Academy's limited resources. But like the athletic program, he had powerful external allies: first the school's advisory boards, and later its accrediting committees. These outside authorities greatly strengthened Bejarano's hand, and—with the notable exception of physical space—advanced the library's cause.

Going for Accreditation

With encouragement from Eugene Keogh, Congress in 1946 officially conferred upon the Academy the right to grant the bachelor of science degree—provided, however, that the school first gained accreditation from the Association of American Universities. In preparation for the accreditation process, the Academy's academic departments performed some self-evaluations in 1946 and also sought the advice of the Congressional Board of Visitors.

But accreditation proved a long and rocky process. One complicating factor was a serious lack of financial support from Congress. In 1946, Telfair Knight submitted to Congress a $30 million Maritime Commission budget, which comprised both cadet training and personnel training by the Maritime Service. The Bureau of the Budget reduced that figure to $9 million, substantially less even than the prewar 1940 budget of $12 million. Knight, stunned, estimated that the Maritime Commission would be unable to function with less than $20 million.

These kinds of budgetary constraints eventually forced the closure of the basic schools at San Mateo and Pass Christian, and greatly complicated the Academy's struggle for accreditation. There simply wasn't enough money to do everything that needed to be done. The other service academies, meanwhile, seemed well taken care of, and this offended those with responsibility for Kings Point. In a 1947 memo to a functionary in the House Office Building, McNulty noted that the government's investment in West Point equaled almost $200 million, or $102,000 per cadet, approximately twelve times the amount invested per cadet at the Merchant Marine Academy.[24]

Feeling the need for more expertise, the administration retained an outside consultant, Joseph Kochka, to help in the accreditation process. Kochka was a graduate of the first class of the Georgetown School of

Foreign Service, and a World War I veteran celebrated for his harrowing stories of wartime experiences in the forests of the Argonne. The administration initially hired him as a consultant in 1946 while he was on leave from an advisory position with the Washington, D.C., public schools. In 1947, Kochka retired from that school system after twenty-six years and volunteered his services to the Academy. His recommendations ultimately proved instrumental in defining the course that the Academy would set.

One of Kochka's first tasks was to assist the academic departments with their self-studies, and to collaborate with department heads to formulate a philosophy of education for the Academy. This effort produced a thoughtful document that stressed the Academy's focus on developing well-rounded cadets who would be citizen leaders as well as officers, and who would be qualified for positions on shore as well as at sea.

Proposed Philosophy of Education of the USMMA:

The United States Merchant Marine Cadet Corps has been established to prepare carefully selected American citizens for careers of nautical leadership, which is so necessary for the development of foreign and domestic commerce and the national defense of the United States. The education of Cadet-Midshipmen is directed primarily toward attainment of professional excellence as officers of the United States Merchant Marine, and with further emphasis upon their qualifications as officers of the United States Naval Reserve. Beyond the attainment of technical excellence, the Cadet-Midshipmen are further familiarized with the fundamentals of the marine industry so that they may advance beyond service at sea into responsible shore-side positions requiring executive and administrative ability. The Academy recognizes society's need for effective, responsible citizenship. Through close group living within the Regiment, through courses studied, and through extra-curricular activities, practical experience and training are provided to this end. The constant aim is to graduate men with nautical competence, and with a general education, men who are well-fitted to cope with the moral, social and spiritual challenges which confront them today, and who are eager to continue their development through life. The entire resources of the Cadet Corps and its Academy are marshaled for the high purpose of administering a program of theoretical and practical courses, including undergraduate service at sea, which provide the finest possible education for these essential young men, with the full expectation that their services as loyal officers of high caliber will reward the nation with talented marine leadership afloat and ashore.[25]

Again, the Academy was effectively distancing itself from its very recent role as a narrowly focused training school. Instead, it was fostering its identity as a general education institution, which prepared young men for careers throughout the industry and, by extension, for life in general.

Kochka was cautiously optimistic about the Academy's eventual accreditation, but he also was realistic about its weaknesses. As he pointed out in congressional hearings in 1946, an institution aspiring to accreditation must possess several qualifications. One was high technical competence—already a strength of the Academy—and a rich general education program, which was still very much a work in progress. But another key qualification, the ability of its graduates to do successful work on a postgraduate level, Kochka saw as a major stumbling block. He guessed in 1946 that this might take an additional two years to achieve.[26]

Other obstacles loomed ahead. One, as mentioned, was the library. Another was the qualifications of the Academy's faculty. To meet its wartime requirements, the school had hired people, including many engineers, who possessed extensive practical experience. Not surprisingly, few of these practically oriented individuals held advanced academic degrees. Now the rules were changing. Stated simply, an accrediting institution was likely to look askance at a faculty that included almost no PhDs and relatively few master's degrees.

From Stedman to McNulty

In the midst of this sustained introspection, the Academy experienced a changing of the guard in the superintendent's office.

In late 1945, Giles Stedman, now a rear admiral in the navy, decided to return to U.S. Lines, in part because the company was offering him the opportunity to establish a new office in the Philippines. Before he left, though, he tendered an offer to one of his favorites—a proposition that, if accepted, would have had long-term effects on the Academy's engineering department. Stedman called the young Lauren McCready into his office and, without much in the way of preliminaries, made his offer. "Mac," he said, "I have a matter to discuss with you. I'm moving out and taking over [U.S. Lines in] the Philippines, and I'd like you to come with me."

McCready was taken aback. A proposal from Stedman, perhaps the nation's most respected ship's master in the prewar era, was not something to be turned down lightly, and McCready liked and respected Stedman as a person. At the same time, McCready already felt a strong affection for the Academy. Reluctantly, he told his superintendent that although he admired greatly Stedman's command and loved working for him, his own place was at the Academy.

The departure of its dashing and popular leader was a blow to the Academy. A *Polaris* article described the cadets' response to Stedman's announcement of his retirement, read during mess hall, as a "conspiracy of silence," as cadets contemplated the loss of a "valued friend."[27]

Continuity of vision was assured with the selection of Stedman's successor: the Academy's "father" and supervisor of the Cadet Corps, Richard R. McNulty. But the transition held some challenges. McNulty, who had been promoted to commodore only a year earlier, was profoundly uncomfortable in the spotlight, and later recalled that

Vice Admiral Richard R. McNulty, the third superintendent of the Academy, speaks at his change of command ceremony on April 1, 1946.

he needed much "pushing" to make the move from Washington to Kings Point. At the urging of both Stedman and Telfair Knight, as well as many of his other friends, McNulty finally agreed to assume the position–provided that he didn't have to make any speeches! He stuck to this resolution during his tenure, skipping most ceremonial occasions in favor of frequent trips on the TV *Kings Pointer* and visits to foreign nations to study their merchant marine training systems. "Anything," he would later reminisce, "to avoid pomp and circumstance."[28]

An Initial Rejection

Finally, in 1947, the Academy felt prepared for its first outside academic evaluation. Dean Fernandus Payne, chairman of the Department of Zoology at the Indiana University and a member of the Association of American Universities (AAU)–the body specifically authorized by Congress to extend accreditation to USMMA–completed an unofficial survey of the Academy. As Joseph Kochka had anticipated, he gave the school mixed reviews. The AAU Committee subsequently declined a preliminary application for approval of the Academy's program, citing the lack of preparation of Academy students for graduate study.

Preparing students for graduate work, of course, was not a primary goal of the Academy, or of the other federal academies, which were fully accredited. Perceiving an inequity, the Academy pressed the AAU Committee for details. The committee's chairman, Dean Henry Bent, gave an indirect response. He stated that the relative youth of the Academy was a matter of great concern, and there were doubts as to its ability to attract and retain faculty members.

He also offered an unusual suggestion: that the Academy abandon its quest for accreditation altogether. Both Bent and the University of Indiana's Dean Payne had concluded that the Academy would suffer if it conformed to the fairly rigid standards of college accreditation. They believed that accreditation as a technical school was more appropriate for the Academy, and suggested that the Training Division work on changing the relevant legislation, allowing the Academy to grant a degree without AAU accreditation.[29]

This first rejection constituted a major blow to the Academy and its administration, who had set their sights on full accreditation. But Knight and McNulty, well accustomed to rethinking their game plans, were not to be deterred. Ignoring the recommendation of Bent and Payne, they continued to pursue accreditation.

Upon the recommendation of the Congressional Board of Visitors, another board was established to help the Academy upgrade its curriculum: the Academic Advisory Board (AAB). The suggestion to create this body first came up at the May 1946 Congressional Board meeting, and was met with general approval. At the 1947 meeting, the Congressional Board recommended that Congress give the Maritime Commission authority to appoint an Academic Advisory Board, and in August, the House of Representatives passed a bill to this effect. The first meeting of the Academic Advisory Board (known thereafter, informally, as the Advisory Board) took place eight months later.

Like the Congressional Board of Visitors, this first Advisory Board surveyed the Academy and generally approved of what it saw. But because the board consisted of educational experts, including Dean Payne, its recommendations were more detailed and practical.[30]

First and foremost, the Advisory Board emphasized the importance of the library as an integral part of the teaching and research program. They recommended increasing budget allocations, the hiring of additional staff, and improving the effectiveness of the library. Two-thirds of the library's holdings had yet to be catalogued, they pointed out, and this was unacceptable.

Second, the Advisory Board recommended strengthening the faculty. "There is some evidence of weakness with respect to background preparation," the board concluded, "and in numbers in relation to current teaching load and enrollment." The board called attention to several obstacles to the recruitment, training, and retention of competent faculty, including the lack of stable financial support, inadequate tenure and retirement provisions, limited opportunity for faculty growth, minimal research activities, and no plan for faculty promotion beyond the rank of senior lieutenant, with corresponding salary increases. This last was deemed to be a serious omission, which constituted "a failure to recognize the importance and dignity of the teacher."

In addition, the Advisory Board took aim at some of the administrative procedures of the Academy and the Maritime Commission. Specifically, the board recommended lengthening the minimum tenure of the Superintendent to four years, creating the post of academic dean, and establishing a faculty Educational Policy Committee to foster educational continuity and provide continued study and examination of the educational program.

The Advisory Board's final recommendation echoed the unwelcome advice of the earlier visitors from the Association of American Universities. The board recommended that the Academy seek congressional authorization to grant the Bachelor of Science degree *without* accreditation. Like the AAU, the Advisory Board concluded that the Academy would be hurt more than it would be helped if it were forced to conform to the constraints of accreditation. "The quality of instruction offered at the Academy should be of the best," the board wrote, "but the program offered should be judged solely in terms of the Academy's objectives. It should not be modified in a way inconsistent with these objectives in order to meet the requirements of any accrediting association."

This recommendation, although forcefully made, once again was not heeded. Accreditation was a clear objective of both the Training Division and the Academy administration, and they were not to be swayed.

But several other Advisory Board recommendations were pursued with alacrity. The position of academic dean, for example, was created almost immediately, and Captain William Randall, USMS, previously a dean at the University of Georgia, was appointed to the post on September 15, 1948. In addition, according to an internal memo written by McNulty in late April 1948, the Academy and the Training Division were taking steps to implement other AAB suggestions, including developing a plan for faculty promotion, hiring additional library staff and making additional appropriations for the library, and investigating the creation of a faculty educational policy committee.

Perhaps the most interesting aspect of this period is the emergence of the Academy's strong sense of self. Ignoring identical recommendations from two boards that had far more experience in things educational than the Kings Pointers, McNulty, Knight, and their colleagues persisted in their quest for accreditation.

A Coup d'État

In the spring of 1948, after only two years, Rear Admiral Richard McNulty's term as Superintendent came to an abrupt and ugly end. Simply put, he was pushed out of office by the combined maneuvering of two Training Division officials in Washington: Telfair Knight and Gordon McLintock. It stands as a particularly sad episode in the Academy's history.

By all accounts, McNulty was far more effective as a visionary, propagandist, gadfly, intellectual innovator, and advocate than he was as a superintendent. He lacked much interest in either political or social maneuvering. He was shy, and a mediocre public speaker who preferred to duck ceremonies whenever possible. (As noted earlier, he did not attend the dedication of the Kings Point campus for which he was primarily responsible.) He lacked the ability to cultivate important allies—for the Academy, and for himself. Proclaimed by many to be the "father of the Academy" (and so anointed by the assistant secretary of commerce decades later), he was ill equipped to protect himself from the maneuvering of his foes in Washington.

These included Telfair Knight, who, as a political strategist of the highest order, evidently could no longer tolerate McNulty's weaknesses in this realm. Nobody knew better than Knight what McNulty's contribution had been. In fact, on numerous occasions, Knight had credited McNulty as the guiding force behind the Academy. He had also, according to McNulty, encouraged McNulty to accept the post of superintendent two years earlier. Now, things had changed. The written record is sketchy, and none of the principals are still alive, but it appears that Knight concluded that the Academy needed a stronger leader, someone who could build support for the Academy in the halls of power.

Two years to the day from when his term began, therefore, McNulty was called back to Washington. He had been kicked upstairs to the position of supervisor of the Cadet Corps. He was replaced at Kings Point by a Scotsman of gallant maritime heritage, Gordon McLintock.

McNulty was devastated by the forced change in command. Though he remained in Washington for another two years as supervisor of the Cadet Corps, his mental and physical health declined. His first strategy was to outlast Knight in the Washington office, but on September 30, 1950, he finally threw in the towel. With his wife, Sue, McNulty drove to southern California, where he spent two years recuperating on a ranch.

In 1953, he returned to the maritime industry, taking a survey of the maritime courses being offered by the Shipping Department of the Georgetown School of Foreign Service. Following the submission of his report in June 1953, Georgetown created a Department of International Transportation, with McNulty as its head. He retired from this position in 1969, becoming professor emeritus and serving in a consulting capacity for two years.

McNulty's Academy experience remained a bitter memory. For many years—in fact, throughout the twenty-two-year superintendency of Gordon McLintock, he refused to set foot on the Kings Point campus. His unhappiness was somewhat assuaged in 1976, when, thanks to the efforts of the Alumni Association, he was formally named "Father of the Academy" by Assistant Secretary of Commerce Robert Blackwell. By the time of his death on November 1, 1980, he had finally achieved some peace of mind about the Academy, and was able to celebrate his enormous contributions to it.

A Hurdle Cleared

By the time Gordon McLintock was installed as the Academy's fourth superintendent in April 1948, the Academy was far down the road toward being accredited, though the formal process continued to drag on for another year and a half. Although accreditation came on McLintock's watch, McNulty and his predecessor Stedman deserve the credit for the accomplishment.

By early 1948, the AAU had discontinued its accreditation activities, so the evaluation had to be completed by a new accrediting body, the Middle States Association (MSA). The MSA sent the Academy an exhaustive questionnaire in 1948. It requested information on the purpose of the Academy, curriculum vitae for every faculty member, self-evaluations by each of the departments, a complete curriculum listing, and course descriptions. The Academy's response, completed in January 1949, ran more than three hundred pages and represented an enormous effort on the part of the faculty.

The departmental evaluations, in particular, reflected the results of the long campaign for accreditation. Each stated a clearly articulated vision and showed a growing sense of that department's role within the larger institution. The departments also demonstrated a growing awareness of their own shortcomings and needs. For example, many cited the need for a lighter instructor load. Some mentioned the need for increased resources in terms of equipment, teaching aids, a stronger library, and—of course—money.

The Academy's response to the questionnaire also included a

cogent summary of the needs served by the institution. The school's leaders argued persuasively that ocean shipping and foreign trade (both imports and exports) were essential to the national economy, and were greatly advanced by the officers trained at the Academy. Highly skilled merchant marine personnel also assured operating safety and economies, and thus preservation of the funds invested in the shipping industry by the taxpayers. National defense concerns, recently the most powerful argument in favor of the Academy's existence, were mentioned only in passing.

The Middle States Association conducted its official visit to the Academy in March 1949. This coincided with the second meeting of the Academic Advisory Board—which, by the way, now believed that the Academy was fully up to any reasonable standards of accreditation.

The board continued to have many ideas about how to improve the Academy. One of these deserves particular note, as it is indicative of a structural tension between the Academy's faculty and administrators—a tension that was destined to increase over time. The board advocated an increased faculty role in the planning and implementation of the educational program. While the board specified that this did not entail a weakening of the administration, it argued that "an effort should be made to secure for the Academy all the rich benefits that come to an educational institution from full participation of the faculty in the formulation and operation of the academic program."[31]

Already, the faculty played an increased role in the Academy's direction. The number and influence of faculty committees, although still far less than at other colleges, grew steadily. At the same time, though, the military and training traditions of the war era continued to exert their powerful influences. In fundamental ways, the Academy was not like other schools, and the faculty had to carve out its role in a very particular context. This tug-of-war between faculty and administration would intensify in the next decade.

In a report finalized in November 1949, the MSA unanimously agreed to grant the Academy its long-coveted accredited status. (In the interim, Congress had removed the last barrier by changing the wording of the law to allow accreditation by any accrediting institution.) The word came too late to affect the December 1949 graduation ceremony, so the first bachelor of science degrees were granted by the Academy in June 1950. Degrees were awarded first to the class of December 1947, and then to the subsequent graduating classes.

The MSA's report contained suggestions for improvements, but declared that the program of the institution was in accordance with its announced objectives, and explicitly rejected a narrowly vocational mission for the school. This illustrates the MSA's particular stance on accreditation. While the AAU had prescribed narrowly defined qualifications for accreditation—for example, adequately preparing its students for graduate study—the MSA inclined toward letting schools adopt a more individualistic stance. The MSA looked primarily at two criteria: first, whether the school was accomplishing its mission, however that was defined; and second, whether in so doing, they included enough broad subject matter to approximate a liberal arts education. In the case of the Academy, the answer to both questions was clearly "yes."

The MSA did, however, note that because of the peculiar circumstances of the Academy, educational compromises had been made, which represented a continuing challenge to the institution: "Applying rigid academic standards, the curriculum is somewhat thin for a strictly liberal arts course on the one hand, or a strictly engineering course on the other. Perhaps the fairest description would be that the Academy offers a very liberal science and engineering major in the liberal arts!"[32]

The battle had been hard fought, and well won. The United States Merchant Marine Academy was now fully accredited, on an equal footing with its sister institutions, and ready to fight its next battle.

Hurricanes and Harbingers

In a sense, that battle was already under way, and the Academy was losing. Financial constraints threatened to cripple the school, even as it was beginning to prevail in its accreditation campaign.

In June 1947, the Maritime Commission was forced to close the San Mateo campus, transferring all cadets to Kings Point. This influx of fourth-class cadets sparked new traditions in the regimental lifestyle, including indoctrination of the plebe class. Future superintendent Paul Krinsky, who had begun his preliminary training at San Mateo in February 1947, was among those who were transferred to Kings Point that June. In a 1960 article for *Polaris*, Krinsky recalled the indoctrination by upperclassmen as somewhat severe, and remembered that "we were constantly made aware of our lowly social and intellectual status." With the benefit of hindsight, however, he admits that the period of hazing was relatively brief and not overly demoralizing. Most of the upperclassmen had been in the war, and were more interested in finishing up their Kings Point career and moving on than in harassing the newcomers.[33]

Pass Christian, the Training Division's Gulf Coast basic school, was initially spared closure. Mother Nature, though, had other plans. On the afternoon of September 16, 1947—coincidentally the fourth anniversary of the formal opening and dedication of the Pass Christian campus—cadets and staff received word that a major hurricane was bearing down on them. All anniversary celebrations were canceled. Cadets rushed to nail down windows, board up doorways, and carry equipment from the low-lying O'Brien Building—out on the pier—to Reisenberg Hall and higher ground.

After a long, sweltering, and gusty night, the storm's full fury broke. In the next thirty minutes, the water level in the bay rose four feet. By noon, it had risen to within a foot of the ceiling of the first deck. The windows gave way. The O'Brien Building broke in the middle, lifted slightly, and floated away, with only its red roof showing above the raging water. The battalion, huddled on the second deck of Reisenberg, was told to prepare for the worst. If the building collapsed, all hands were to swim for the grove of pine trees on the south side of the base.

Finally, at two p.m., the waters began to recede, flowing out of the doors and windows in what one observer called "great whirlpools of eddying current."[34] Chairs, mattresses, and notebooks floated out to sea with the water. Reisenberg was in a state of near collapse, and it was clear that the cadets had to be moved. By nine a.m. the next morning, they were aboard trains on their way to Kings Point, where they would join their San Mateo colleagues. The Pass Christian campus reopened briefly, but it never fully recovered, and on March 27, 1950, it was closed permanently.

Among the transplants to Kings Point in that fateful year of 1947 were fifty Filipino students: the first beneficiaries of the State Department's Philippine Rehabilitation Act of 1946, which provided for the appointment of fifty Filipino cadets per year at the U.S. Merchant Marine Academy. Under Public Law 701, there were also ten cadets from South American countries, including Cuba, Chile, Brazil, Colombia, Peru, Argentina, Panama, Uruguay, Paraguay, and Venezuela. These forays into training relationships with foreign

A contingent of cadet-midshipmen from Pass Christian march in the Red Cross Day Parade at Bay St. Louis, Mississippi, on March 22, 1943.

countries and educational institutions gave the Academy some much needed credibility, and allowed the school a small role in the implementation of federal foreign policy.

The publicity didn't hurt, either. The Academy had not received much public notice since its inception in 1941. These international education efforts were newsworthy, however, and the media and the public took note.

The cruise of the TV *Kings Pointer* down the coast of South America in the winter of 1946–1947 administered another dose of helpful publicity to the Academy. This voyage came as part of a limited experiment with large-tonnage training vessels at the Academy. Unlike the case of the state maritime academies, residential training at USMMA had always been primarily land based, relying on industry ships to provide cadets with practical experience out on the water. In the postwar era, however, the school had its pick of surplus ships, and in the summer of 1946 the school accepted the four-hundred-foot turbo electric ship *Devosa*, which had been used as a troop transport vessel in the war. On August 1, 1946, the *Devosa* was rechristened as the training vessel

Kings Pointer, the first in a long line of ships so named, and in December, one hundred first classmen and the entire third class set sail on the three-month South American training cruise.[35]

But this would be the only extended training cruise undertaken by the Academy, as fiscal woes and the shortcomings of the vessel combined to make further voyages impractical. The vessel was also too large to be comfortably moored at the Academy, and it was decided that cadets would receive more useful training aboard working merchant ships. And, it must be noted, the training cruise had earned far more media attention in South America than in the United States, and it was in the United States that the looming battles for funding and permanency would be fought.

6

Weathering New Storms
1950–1960

On April 1, 1948, George Gordon McLintock began a twenty-two-year term as fourth superintendent of the Academy, a tenure unparalleled for its length, productivity, and turbulence. McLintock served longer than any other superintendent of a federal academy; the only man who approached his record was Brigadier General Sylvanus Thayer, superintendent of West Point from 1817 to 1833.[1]

McLintock was controversial in his own day, and his complex legacy has been interpreted and reinterpreted in the decades since he was nudged off the stage in 1970. His detractors have found much to criticize in his record. His arrival, as discussed in the previous chapter, was clouded by backstage maneuvering and deceptions. His long tenure at the Academy was marred by episodes in which his actions indisputably harmed the image and stature of the school. His faculty chafed under his iron rule. And by the end of his tenure, the Academy's cadets—traditionally respectful of authority—were in near-open revolt against his administration.

At the same time, McLintock's formidable political abilities and well-cultivated connections saved the Academy in one of its moments of gravest peril. McLintock rallied congressional and public support for the Academy when that support was most desperately needed, and thus kept the Academy alive. McLintock apparently relied heavily on his relationship with Louisiana representative (and House majority leader) Hale Boggs Sr.–the two shared an office in the Maritime Commission in Washington in the early 1940s[2]–to bolster the Academy's position in Washington. In addition, like Giles Stedman, McLintock enjoyed moving in the highest circles of society. His galas for the wealthy Gold Coast socialites of Long Island's fabled North Shore lent new visibility and prestige to the school. Among them were CBS magnate William S. Paley and diplomat and philanthropist Jock Whitney, who employed McLintock's father. As a leader in the campaign for a new North Shore hospital, McLintock won friends among the most powerful politicians in New York, including Nassau County Republican boss J.

An official portrait of Vice Admiral Gordon McLintock, the fourth superintendent of the Academy.

Russell Sprague; Representative Leonard W. Hall of Nassau County, Republican National Committee chairman; and Republican senator Irving Ives. Sprague, a member of the Republican National Committee, was one of the key architects behind Eisenhower's successful bid for the presidency in 1952, and (along with Hall) subsequently played a behind-the-scenes role in getting Eisenhower to think fondly of the Academy.

McLintock also proved highly adept at luring guests from Washington up to the Academy, which sometimes suffered from low visibility in the nation's capital. Two hundred congressmen visited the Academy in April 1950, and another one hundred in May of the following year. In December 1952, Mrs. Dwight D. Eisenhower, soon to be first lady of the United States, toured the campus, escorted by a proud Admiral McLintock.

As long-time colleague Lauren McCready later noted, McLintock was "nimble of mind, and creative of circumstance."[3] These skills served the Academy well when, in 1953, Maritime Administrator Louis Rothschild began a clandestine attempt to shut the school down. They also served McLintock himself well when his own job was threatened in the late fifties and early sixties. McLintock rescued first the Academy, and then himself.

Skilled as he was at cultivating outside support, McLintock proved far less successful at winning friends and building support within the Academy. His formative leadership years were spent at sea on British and U.S. vessels, where the master's word was law. As it turned out, this tradition had only minimal relevance to the Academy, which was still very much controlled by government functionaries in Washington. In addition, the Academy had made the momentous decision in the later years of World War II to effect a fundamental transition, from the *training* universe to the *education* universe. As the Academy became less like a ship and more like a college, McLintock found it hard to adjust to changing circumstances. McLintock himself had never earned a bachelor's degree, and although he received an honorary degree from Hofstra University, he was arguably underqualified for his position once the Academy became an accredited institution of higher education.

But McLintock continued in his authoritarian—some said dictatorial—ways. As a result, he regularly came into conflict with faculty and students. The problem intensified as McLintock's tenure lengthened and he became more personally identified with the Academy. If people ventured to criticize some aspect of the Academy with which McLintock had become so personally identified—even constructive criticism—the superintendent inevitably heard them criticizing *him*. Issues that elsewhere would have been the grounds for a healthy debate were perceived as insubordination, or worse.

The Making of a Superintendent

According to both his detractors and his supporters, Gordon McLintock had a forceful personality and a regal bearing to go with it, traits that infuriated some and captivated others, and reflected his unusual background.

He hailed from a long line of British seafarers and shipbuilders. His paternal grandfather ran a shipyard, and his maternal grandfather owned a fleet of Mediterranean sailing vessels. His father William had achieved near-legendary status in British sailing circles for his remarkable exploits as acting chief engineer on the SS *Titania*. While crossing the South Atlantic in 1900, the *Titania*'s tailshaft fractured, losing her propeller and immobilizing the ship in midocean. Somehow, William

McLintock succeeded in replacing the shaft and the spare propeller while *still at sea*–a difficult enough task even in a well-equipped ship-yard, and one that had never before been successfully accomplished in midocean.[4]

Gordon McLintock first went to sea at age fifteen, after graduating third in his class from Sevenoaks preparatory school in England. As he later wrote:

> My family had been connected with shipping on the maternal side since 1594 and on the paternal side since 1715. I knew from child-hood the fascination of a father who brought home "man-eating tur-tles," or a monkey, or a case of Jaffa oranges, or twenty pairs of kid gloves for my mother, or a tube of ostrich feathers for my sister. I heard uncles talking of Hong Kong and Java, and of kangaroos in Australia. These places were as familiar to them as their home towns, and I longed to be like them, at home in all the world.[5]

He was indentured as a cadet on the SS *Wentworth* in the British Merchant Navy, and in later years, he was sought after for his color-ful tales of those years at sea–voyages on which he studied by oil lamps in South African ports, went hungry on a voyage from New York to Australia, and was awarded a large bar of yellow soap for shoveling coal all night. From these tales emerged hints of a willful, self-contained character. While serving as chief officer, on one voyage, his vessel encountered severe weather and was in danger of founder-ing. The master of the ship ordered him to jettison several thousand barrels of gasoline–an order that McLintock declined to carry out. After the storm abated, the master was much relieved that his precious cargo was still on board, and ignored McLintock's selective following of his orders.

At the end of World War I, McLintock's father accepted a position as a marine superintendent in the Port of New York, and the family relocated to the United States. Gordon McLintock first secured employment in the United States in 1920 as a quartermaster on the SS *Lewis Luckenback*, which at the time was the largest cargo vessel in the world. He continued to sail in the merchant marine throughout the 1920s, and earned his master's license in 1926, though he may never have sailed on this license. In 1930, he moved to the Bureau of Marine Inspection and Navigation, the U.S. maritime vessel licensing and inspection service that performed many of the marine safety duties that today are performed by the Coast Guard. He worked in Marine Inspection for twelve years before being transferred to active duty in the newly created Maritime Service as a chief inspection officer of the training organization. There, he first came across Richard McNulty and Telfair Knight, as well as coworker Hale Boggs. In 1946, he became a special assistant to Knight.

From there, with both Knight and McLintock plotting to achieve the same end—having McLintock replace McNulty—it was only a short step to the Academy.

Comparing Stomachs: Kings Point as the Stepchild

In the fall of 1953, five years into Gordon McLintock's superintendency, the Academy was still struggling to get on an even keel.

In some ways, life at Kings Point had begun to stabilize. The curriculum had been reduced to a realistic 240 course hours, and the daily schedule of the cadets had been streamlined to allow for extra study and even some leisure time. A final transition to annual rather than semiannual admissions was under consideration, and the admissions process had been relocated from Washington to the Academy. A language lab had been set up, and the institution had begun to offer some counseling to the cadets. The school, in other words, was beginning to look more like a traditional educational institution.

Financially, though, the Academy was losing ground, and its competitive position was threatened. The Academy still lived year-to-year and hand-to-mouth, subject to the whims of the annual congressional budget cycle. In the 1953 fiscal year budget, for example, Congress eliminated the $65 monthly stipend paid to the cadets, a cash infusion that many cadets counted on for the purchase of textbooks, uniforms, and sundries. The monthly paycheck—a reasonably generous sum, in 1953 dollars—had been an important recruiting tool, and its sudden termination placed the Academy at a disadvantage vis-à-vis the other federal service academies, whose cadets continued to receive similar stipends.

The cut didn't come as a total surprise; because of budget shortfalls in the early 1950s, such a move had been under consideration for several years. As early as 1950, the general manager of the Maritime Administration (a successor agency to the Maritime Commission, created by Reorganization Plan No. 21, effective May 24, 1950) was asked to estimate the savings that might result if cadets were given uniforms and textbooks instead of the sixty-five-dollar allowance.[6] Shortly thereafter, incoming cadets were notified by letter that they would not be receiving the anticipated stipend. Following a public outcry and a congressional intervention, funds were found to restore the stipend. Not so in 1953.

The Academy's 1953 budget, as authorized by Congress, raised many other concerns at Kings Point. In a report to the Academic Advisory Board, McLintock noted that Congress had allocated only $2,053,640 of the requested $2,750,000. This shortfall continued an alarming three-year trend of decreasing budgets, which necessitated both smaller enrollments and program cutbacks. "The members of Congress will be sorry to learn," McLintock wrote in his 1953 report to the Congressional Board of Visitors, "that to save fuel, we had to close the Cadet-Midshipman Activities House, the center of all the cadets' extra-curricular activities such as the Camera Club, Latin-American Club, Debating Club, Radio Club, and *Hear This*, the cadet newspaper. We have also had to close, to save fuel, the Museum Ship [*Emery Rice*]."[7]

The board reacted to these cuts with indignation. Especially offensive to the congressional overseers was the blatant inequity between the treatment of cadets at the Academy and those at the other federal service academies. "We wish to enter on the record in the strongest terms," they noted in their 1953 report, "that there should be no differences in existence among the several academies with respect to the monthly allowances granted students in training."[8]

To underscore its point, the board cited a specific injustice: unequal food rations. The board emphasized that it was "distressed to learn that even in the matter of allowances for food rations, the Kings Pointer is not on a parity with his brothers in training at other federal academies. The board is unable to accept the strange philosophy that an eighteen-year-old stomach at Kings Point requires less food than an eighteen-year-old stomach at West Point."

There could be no other interpretation: Congress did not consider the Merchant Marine Academy to be equal in stature to the other federal academies.

A Sneak Attack

Underfunding and an implicit lack of respect at the congressional level were bad enough. But these dangers paled in comparison to the threat posed by an assault from the very branch of government charged with protecting and promoting the Academy: the Maritime Administration. The attack was all the more devastating for being unexpected.

Newsday, the Long Island–based daily, broke the story first. On November 17, 1953, the paper breathlessly told of "an undercover plot to sink the Merchant Marine Academy at Kings Point and leave its 890 cadets foundering in a turbulent political sea."[9]

According to the *Newsday* account, the treasurer of the Academy's alumni association had given the paper a copy of a letter from Maritime Administrator Louis Rothschild to Goodwin Knight, acting governor of California, inviting him to a meeting in Washington with administrators of the state maritime academies to discuss the possible closure of Kings Point. No representatives from either the Office of Maritime Training or Kings Point were invited to the meeting. Citing a surfeit of merchant marine officers, and noting that the Department of Commerce had to make deep cuts in its budget, Rothschild confessed that he was considering asking the state schools to assume full responsibility for maritime officer training.

McLintock, who told *Newsday* that he had "no official warning of the move," may or may not have been surprised by the contents of the letter. (There is some evidence, as explained below, that he may have had *unofficial* warning from Rothschild.) But he must have felt betrayed by the roundabout way he learned of Rothschild's intentions. Up to this point, Rothschild had been publicly supportive of the Academy. In fact, less than a month earlier, McLintock sent the Maritime Administrator a letter thanking him for his "personal intervention" to allow repairs to copings and gutters at the Academy. "May I say that we are vigilant of the trust you repose in us all," he concluded, "and that we preach and practice the personal economy of the public fund."[10]

Rothschild was a largely unqualified political appointee of the new Eisenhower administration. A graduate of Yale University and a civic and mercantile leader in his hometown of Kansas City, Missouri, Rothschild had no previous maritime experience. In a larger context of demobilization and government "downsizing," he had come under intense pressure to cut his budget. As he saw it, shutting down all federal maritime training institutions had to be considered, including not only Kings Point but also the seamen's training stations at Alameda, California, and Sheepshead Bay, New York. "We have two alternatives," he explained to critics in Congress. "We can either withdraw federal support from the state academies, which would force them to

cut down in size, or we can work . . . to consolidate the state and federal academies. . . . Either Kings Point will absorb the state academies,
or the state academies will absorb Kings Point." [11]

Two things seem abundantly clear, in retrospect. First, Rothschild
had already made his decision and decided that the state schools
should absorb Kings Point. Second, he had very little understanding of
the Academy he was surreptitiously proposing to dismantle.

The Academy's Friends Respond

To Rothschild's discomfort, he soon gained that understanding. First
came an outpouring of congressional support for the Academy. Two
Long Island congressmen, Steve Derounian and Frank Becker—both
Republicans—led the initial charge. Immediately after the first article in
Newsday appeared, the two legislators dispatched a stinging telegram to
Rothschild (simultaneously released to the press), which accused the
maritime administrator of "flouting the will of Congress" through the
"scuttling of a national maritime training policy strengthened and supported by repeated enactments over the last ten years." They protested
vigorously against "lodging a national responsibility in the care of others." [12]

This telegram, quoted frequently in the press over the next several
weeks, marked only the beginning of an energetic campaign to save
Kings Point. The campaign had many fathers, including national
Alumni Association president James Murphy, '44, and the New York
chapter's Melvin Tublin, '49, and treasurer Frank Sinnott, '50. Sinnott's father had been the Democratic county clerk for Brooklyn, and
Sinnott himself "grew up on the knee of [Congressman Eugene]
Keogh." [13] Keogh himself played a pivotal role by bringing the issue
"across the aisle" to the Democratic side of the house.

But perhaps most important in this key struggle was the Washington, D.C., chapter, led by Milt Nottingham, '44, and Joseph Baker, '47.
Joe Baker was then a building-supply salesman based in Washington,
D.C., and he soon came to appreciate Nottingham's calm hand. "Milt
was a master mariner," Baker noted, "and had been to sea, and was
sort of the granddaddy to all of us. He was older, and served as a
steadying factor. At that point, I was wearing bright ties and loud
sports coats, and Milt was Mr. Conservative. He kept us from going
wild, and messing things up. A marvelous, marvelous man." [14]

But bright ties notwithstanding, Baker understood something about the political game. His father had been extremely close to Alexander Wiley, a Republican senator from Wisconsin who had served on the Kings Point Congressional Board of Visitors, and who had arranged for Baker's appointment to the Academy. "I can't tell you how close they were," said Baker. "Wiley used to come visit us at our house on the beach, for example." So Baker had ready access to Wiley, and was comfortable dropping in on his father's old friend at the Senate Office Building. Through the New York Kings Pointers, Baker was also introduced to Representative Derounian, whom he recalls as a key ally. "Steve Derounian was *the* man," Baker explained. "I mean, his office became our office. He gave us a file drawer in one of his file cabinets, and told his staff that we could go in any time we wanted. It was just beyond belief, the way he opened up to us."[15]

Baker, Nottingham, and several others drafted a bill to make the Academy a permanent institution, and therefore immune to budget cuts or the whims of a particular administrator. Senator Wiley had his legislative assistant rewrite the bill in legalese, and suggested that Baker contact William K. Van Pelt, a Republican colleague from Wisconsin, to do the same on the House side. (The legislation that grew out of these parallel efforts ultimately became known as the Wiley-Van Pelt Bill.) Wiley also opened doors among his Senate colleagues so that Baker could make his pitch, and generate interest in the cause. "He called Hubert Humphrey on the phone, for example," Baker recalled, "and said, 'I'm going to send a friend of mine over there to see you.'"

Meanwhile, the National Association and the New York chapter took the fight to the national stage. Alumni chapters were organized across the country by national secretary John W. Tiernan, '43, later chairman of the national alumni body, and numerous friends of the Academy were rallied to the cause. The mail-in campaign that resulted was unprecedented in the maritime industry.

Between November 21 and 25, Rothschild received letters of protest from nine U.S. senators, many of them senior, and eight members of the House of Representatives. It must have been a sobering experience to get wrist-slaps from leaders as politically and geographically diverse as Maine's Margaret Chase Smith, Wisconsin's Joe McCarthy, and Louisiana's Russell Long.[16]

Meanwhile, a second torrent of letters and telegrams, numbering in the hundreds and all supportive of the Academy, poured into Rothschild's office from private citizens, citizen's groups, and Kings Point alumni. The Alumni Association effort was reinforced by the Association of Parents and Friends of Kings Point (APF), an ad hoc organization led by John Scherger, a Hempstead, Long Island, resident whose son was at Kings Point and would graduate in the class of 1956. Scherger was recruited to the cause by his friend and congressman, Leonard Hall (R), who knew of the Academy's troubles in Congress and urged Scherger to mobilize the parents of Academy cadets.[17]

As chief clerk in charge, Nassau County Supreme Court, Scherger was well acquainted with both the local and Washington political scenes. With behind-the-scenes help from Luis Bejarano, the Academy librarian, Scherger established the APF as a lobbying organization for Kings Point. As government employees, Academy faculty members were barred from lobbying, but Bejarano's discreet involvement in the campaign proved to be critically important.

The maritime industry rallied to the cause as well, with the ship operator States Marine Corporation being among the most vocal of the early protesters. Later, during related congressional hearings in March 1954, the three major U.S. steamship trade associations—the American Merchant Marine Institute, the Association of American Shipowners, and the Pacific American Steamship Association—also came forward to testify in support of the Academy.

Except for his first statement in *Newsday*, McLintock maintained a public silence, probably due to his personal respect for the chain of command. But a June 1954 letter from McLintock to Rothschild suggests strongly that the superintendent's silence also was imposed from above. In that letter, McLintock asked for permission to accept an invitation to address the Association of Mayors of Nassau County. "You will recall," McLintock wrote his superior, "that last October you gave me an acute case of laryngitis! I am somewhat fearful of it becoming chronic, and wonder if you would be inclined to lift the ban." He went on to promise Rothschild that he would deliver a "non-controversial, non policy talk on the Academy, and or the Merchant Marine."[18]

There is no evidence that McLintock took outright steps to fight his boss. On the other hand, based on McLintock's skillful political maneuverings at almost every juncture, it is inconceivable that he was *not* involved in fighting his boss's decision. According to local legend, McLintock invited Rothschild to visit the Academy soon after he began his attempts to shut the Academy down. Rothschild, the story goes, was impressed by what he was seeing—so much so, in fact, that in the middle of the tour, he turned to one of his aides and demanded angrily, "Is this the place you asked me to close?"[19]

Permanence from the Jaws of Defeat

Thanks in large part to the outpouring of public support for Kings Point, Administrator Rothschild began to back away from his position. In January 1954, he agreed to fund the Academy through the 1955 fiscal year.

But his actions had reopened old wounds. By suggesting that the state schools should assume all officer-training responsibility, he had pitted the state academies against the federal academy. To be fair, it is possible that one or more of the state academies encouraged, or even precipitated, Rothschild's moves. (A letter from an alumnus of the California State Academy to Rothschild, for example, refers to earlier meetings with Rothschild, and hints at an alliance of long standing between the Maritime administrator and the state academies.[20]) But Rothschild had a responsibility to keep the bigger picture in mind, a responsibility that he abdicated by siding with the state academies even before the public debate was joined.

In March, a House subcommittee of the Merchant Marine and Fisheries Committee, headed by Representative Van Pelt, began an investigation of merchant marine training. A central point of debate emerged quickly: should Kings Point be put on an equal footing with the other federal academies? A Senate subcommittee of the Interstate and Foreign Commerce Committee held hearings on the same issue in June 1954.

At this juncture, the Academy's Congressional Board of Visitors emerged as an effective advocate. In a report to both houses of Congress, the board recommended that Congress introduce legislation to make the Academy a permanent institution. Included in the report was a statement from the Academic Advisory Board dealing with the thorny issue of state versus federal responsibility for maritime officer training. That board found "clear and unequivocal evidence" in the Merchant Marine Act of 1936 that such training was the responsibility of the federal government. It went on to state that this responsibility "must be assumed and discharged at the Federal level. The common defense is a Federal responsibility, and the officers participating in that defense must owe their allegiance to the Federal unity." It also pointed out that Kings Point was the only facility with the capacity to expand quickly in response to a national emergency.[21]

The June 1954 Senate hearings also delved into the financial side of the debate, which (as it turned out) had been distorted by personnel within the Maritime Administration to Kings Point's disadvantage. One core issue was whether it cost more to educate officers at the federal academy than at the state academies. Although answering such a question necessarily involved judgment—in other words, deciding exactly how to compare apples to apples—some members of the Maritime Administration were inclined to stack the deck against Kings Point.

For example, in a January 5, 1954, memo to Rothschild from Acting Deputy Maritime Administrator Thomas Stakem Jr., Stakem stated that the annual cost per cadet at Kings Point was $2,976, with the equivalent amount for New York's Fort Schuyler being $2,339. Stakem noted that he obtained these figures from Admiral Hollie J. Tiedemann, who had replaced Vice Admiral Telfair Knight as commandant of the Maritime Service upon the latter's retirement in 1952. In the memo, Tiedemann also noted that Academy cadets actually cost the government nothing during their Sea Year, but Stakem rejected this reasoning. "I did not want to include in the attached memo," Stakem added, "Admiral Tiedemann's thought that a truer average cost per cadet for Kings Point Academy was $2,232, which is arrived at by taking ¾ of the actual 1953 costs of $2,976. I do not agree with his reasoning in this regard."[22] By the time these figures were forwarded to Representatives Derounian and Becker later in the month, all reference to the Sea Year had been expunged, and the higher number for Kings Point had been endorsed by the Maritime Administration.

Luckily for the Academy, the Senate hearings developed a different set of cost assessments for Kings Point and the state academies. Kings Point, concluded the Senate investigators, cost the government $2,374 per cadet per year, and the state schools cost $2,377.[23] In other words, cost, cited by the Maritime Administration as a rationale for shutting down Kings Point, was not an issue.

The House subcommittee did not take long to reach its conclusions. On June 3, 1954, chairman Van Pelt introduced H.R. 9434, which stipulated that the secretary of commerce "shall maintain a Merchant Marine Academy at Kings Point, New York, for the instruction and preparation for service in the Merchant Marine of selected persons as officers thereof," and that the graduates of that school should be required to serve in the naval reserve. The bill also contained provisions to improve the Academy's appointment program, place the Academy on parity with the other service academies, and restore cadet-midshipman pay.[24] The Committee on Merchant Marine and Fisheries approved the bill the following month, but removed the clause making naval reserve status mandatory, stating instead that graduates "may be required to belong to the Naval Reserve," a change apparently made at the request of the Department of the Navy.

With this amendment, the bill passed the House on July 30, 1954, with little debate, and the Academy's supporters anticipated smooth sailing in the Senate. This confidence was misplaced. The corresponding Senate bill, S. 3610, sponsored by Wiley of Wisconsin, Herbert Lehman (D) of New York, and Irving Ives (R), also of New York, did not reach the full Senate floor until August 28–very late in the session. When Congress adjourned three days later, the Senate still had not taken any action on the bill.

It was only the first of several frustrating setbacks. In response, the Alumni Association intensified the letter-writing campaign to Congress and local media outlets. The House bill was reintroduced by Van Pelt in January 1955, and was passed unanimously by the House on May 17. Kings Point also received a boost on March 21, when Californian Clarence Morse replaced Rothschild as Maritime administrator. In August 1955, Morse delivered a graduation address at Kings Point that forcefully affirmed the role of the Academy in future Maritime Administration policy.

Once again, however, the Senate was slow to act. Members requested a comprehensive study of current maritime officer training, including an estimate of the future demand for maritime officers, a request that led to the vote on the Academy's future being rescheduled for January 1956. Senator Warren G. Magnuson, Democrat from Washington, chaired the subcommittee that undertook the requested study.

Throughout the fall of 1955 and the early winter of 1955–1956, it appeared that the Academy's prospects were growing brighter–that Magnuson's study would be favorable, and that the legislation would be approved. Ultimately, this optimism proved well founded. The report submitted by Magnuson's subcommittee recommended that the federal government continue support to both Kings Point *and* the state academies. On February 7, 1956, the Senate unanimously passed H.R. 6043 without amendment.

The momentous vote was oddly anticlimactic. After two years of subterfuge, public and private debate, lobbying, and logrolling, the final passage of the bill took less than a minute. Only fifteen senators were on the floor. Two of the bill's most stalwart supporters, New York senators Ives and Lehman, were not even in the Senate chamber when it took place.[25] On February 20, 1956, President Eisenhower signed the permanency bill into law, securing the Academy's position as the fifth federal service academy.[26] The pen Eisenhower used to sign the bill was given to Joe Baker, the "most important cog in the permanency fight."[27] At long last, permanency had been won.

On the day Eisenhower signed the bill, Clarence Morse sent Superintendent McLintock a telegram authorizing him to grant his cadets a special twenty-four-hour liberty in celebration of the school's hard-won victory. A photograph from that day suggests that Kings Pointers fully understood the significance of that victory. It shows the Regiment standing in Barney Square, hats raised above their heads, cheering vigorously.[28] For the moment, at least, their academy was no longer in danger.

A New Power Emerges

The long fight for permanency effected a change that few could have understood at the time—a change with both good and bad implications. The mobilization of the school's alumni base proved critical to the institution's survival. The national chapter of the Alumni Association was now a political force to be reckoned with; though based in New York City, the organization enjoyed ready access to the maritime administrator and members of Congress. And many alumni, now almost two decades out of the school, were also moving into positions of prominence and influence. Along with their representatives in Congress and their trade associations, they brought pressure to bear effectively in ways that helped carry the day.

The emergence of new power bases caused some discomfort for Gordon McLintock. Better than most, he knew the power of influence. He did not welcome the prospect that others—either on his faculty, or among his alumni—might presume to wield influence in the name of Kings Point. On the other hand, he was well aware that the Academy would often need outside advocates in Washington.

Perhaps because of this need (or perhaps because he wanted to keep a closer eye on the alumni), McLintock, at the suggestion of Dean Guy Trump, invited the national organization to move its head-quarters to the Academy. The move proved beneficial for the young association, which was far from financially stable. With able assistance from Captain Victor E. Tyson, '43, the Academy liaison, the Alumni Association instituted annual dues and lifetime membership dues, and began to build a solid financial foundation.

Tyson, a popular and skillful nautical science professor, was a behind-the-scenes presence in the Alumni Association (and elsewhere at the Academy) for decades, and his interventions were often credited with giving Academy organizations a new lease on life. When the Academy yearbook, *Midships*, found itself in a deep financial hole, Tyson was called in to reorganize the publication, and *Midships* was soon turning a profit. When the Alumni Association began running a surplus, it was Tyson who stepped in and arranged to buy then-

Captain Victor E. Tyson, a powerful behind the scenes presence at the Academy during McLintock's superintendency.

valuable AT&T shares with the extra funds. And it was Tyson's work that laid the groundwork in the decades to come for the Alumni Association to begin soliciting and accepting donations from the growing alumni base.

Fighting within the Ranks

Even as the Academy presented a united front during its campaign for permanency, a bitter internal struggle over the status of the faculty at the Academy had been sparked.

Since passage of the Bland Amendment in 1938, faculty and staff at the Academy, as well as employees of the Maritime Administration, had been members of the U.S. Maritime Service. In the spring of 1954, however, Administrator Rothschild completed a reevaluation of all Academy personnel according to the 1949 Classification Act, a civil service function, rather than the 1936 Merchant Marine Act. As a subset of this group, faculty members were asked to write their own job descriptions and were evaluated by the Maritime Administration's chief of Classification and Wage Administration of the Personnel Office.[29]

As a result of the reevaluation, 44 members of the Academy staff were raised in rank and salary, 101 remained in place, and 128—including 9 faculty members—were downgraded one or more ranks.[30] This was troubling, especially to the 128 who were downgraded. Additional red flags were raised when it became apparent that the reevaluation was a precursor to a planned conversion of *all* maritime service personnel to civil service status. This move, which effectively would give Academy faculty civilian rather than quasi-military status (and incidentally save the Maritime Administration roughly fifty thousand dollars a year), brought immediate and angry reactions from the faculty.

"Conversion," as it came to be known, was far from a new idea. As early as 1947, Joseph Kochka, the Academy's farsighted educational adviser who contributed so much to the accreditation campaign, had raised the issue in a meeting with the Congressional Board of Visitors. He pointed out that, unlike their counterparts at most other colleges, professors and instructors at the Academy lacked both tenure, the traditional guarantor of academic freedom, and retirement benefits. At the same time, unlike many of their peers in government, they lacked civil service protection. Kochka saw this as a serious dilemma for the

Academy and its faculty, and others agreed.[31] In 1952, in a preliminary move, the attorney general ruled that the Academy's administrative employees were civilian employees of the United States for the purposes of the Civil Service Retirement Act.[32]

But when the issue resurfaced after the reevaluation in 1954 and a full conversion to civil service was proposed, the faculty balked. To some extent, this reflected their sense of loyalty to the Maritime Service, and their clear preference for a connection with the military tradition. More immediately, they objected to the demotions resulting from the realignment.

The firestorm was touched off by two faculty members, Lieutenants James Walsh and Mariano Maya, who had been demoted as a result of the preconversion reevaluation. Walsh and Maya sought advice from the American Association of University Professors (AAUP)—which, because of the Academy's recent accreditation, now had standing to involve itself with faculty rights at Kings Point.[33] The AAUP, following standard practice for tenure-violation complaints, wrote to McLintock and asked for his side of the story; McLintock dutifully forwarded the letter to Washington for an official reply.[34]

This did not sit well with the AAUP, which sent McLintock another letter, again stating that the AAUP needed his version of the story before it could proceed. "It is the custom of this association," the association noted somewhat sharply, "to address inquiries to the responsible administrative heads of accredited institutions of higher education whenever we receive apparently serious complaints alleging violations of the generally accepted principles of academic freedom and tenure."[35]

Martin A. Mason, dean of the George Washington University School of Engineering and a longtime and highly respected member of the Academic Advisory Board, seconded that opinion. He wrote his own complaint to Rothschild, stating that McLintock should have "accepted without delay his responsibility to state his position and the reasons therefore."[36]

In fact, when considered in terms of both job security and overall financial benefits, conversion to civil service status was a reasonably good deal for the faculty. Certainly the Maritime Administration took this view, and expected to complete the conversion by July 1. But when the faculty met on June 8, 1955, to discuss conversion, its members were unanimous in their opposition.

At this point, the comptroller general was asked to rule on the treatment of faculty members' accumulated leave and "position in grade" in the Maritime Service. His decision threw up another road-block to civil service conversion: he ruled that, in the event that con-version took place, accumulated leave owed to the individuals involved would have to be paid in a lump sum. The cost was estimated to be roughly $250,000, a figure that was simply not available to the resource-starved Maritime Administration.[37]

Conversion went on hold. In the ensuing two years, many attempts were made to resolve the issue through legislation, rather than administrative action. Significantly, both McLintock and aca-demic dean Dr. Guy Trump went on record in support of the proposed legislation.[38] Though it was unclear whether this was done at the Mar-itime Administration's request or of their own volition, their willing-ness to go against the faculty's position further strained relationships between the faculty and the administration.

Why did the faculty continue to object so vociferously to the pro-posed change? A letter written in 1958 by six department heads—L. E. Bejarano, J. M. Dittrick, C. W. Ferris, Peder Gald, Lane Kendall, J. W. Liebertz, and Lauren McCready—sheds some light on the faculty posi-tion. Because the school was an arm of the national defense structure (the professors argued), uniformed, military status was necessary to maintain and teach military discipline, leadership, and preparedness. The six signatories argued that civil service status was "an anomalous arrangement that would be utterly alien to the organic unity of philos-ophy and purposes of this institution, one that would replace 'heroic encounter between teacher and student' with bureaucratic stultifica-tion and despair."[39]

Another significant argument against conversion can be found near the end of the letter: pay cuts. "The proposed conversion would cut the take-home pay of each officer of the Academy from $1,000 to $600," the manifesto stated, "which would result in the loss of many of the Academy's best men." Curiously, they added that arbitrary demo-tions during the past several years had "affected the morale and secu-rity of [the] teaching staff," without recognizing that conversion to civil service status would improve this situation.

The fight over faculty status continued for several more years. Legislation mandating civil service status for the Academy's faculty was not passed until late in 1961, effective January 1, 1962. Among other things, the legislation affected the faculty dress code. Up to that point, most faculty and (male) staff members had worn the maritime service uniform with pride—but this was about to change. As a congressional committee explained:

> The view has been expressed that the wearing of the uniform was necessary as an element in the system of discipline at the Academy. However, this practice does not prevail at the Naval Academy nor at a number of military schools throughout the country and it is the view of the committee that while uniforms should be worn by those members of the staff concerned with cadet discipline, the wearing of the uniforms by instructors solely concerned with the educational aspect of the institution is not a necessary requirement for the proper functioning of the institution.[40]

Uniforms were only the most visible part of the conversion process, which remained a sore point with certain faculty members for years afterward. And although McLintock had little influence in decisions regarding conversion, the drawn-out drama contributed to a growing rift between the superintendent and his faculty, as well as between McLintock and members of his advisory board.

In a paradoxical way, McLintock's autocratic leadership style also hurt him throughout this controversy. At a juncture when a strong leader might have been expected to deliver, on behalf of his faculty, McLintock proved unwilling or unable to do so.

A Challenge to Academic Tradition

Meanwhile, the faculty and administration were becoming embroiled in an increasingly bitter dispute about faculty rights in relation to the proposed civil service conversion. A faculty steering committee proposed resolutions opposing the conversion in early 1958, and that committee was promptly disbanded by the Maritime Administration the same spring.

In response, the faculty established the Faculty Committee on Personnel Matters (FCPM), intended to improve communication between faculty and administration. In July, this committee requested from the Maritime Administration (now coming to be known by the nickname "MARAD," which we will use henceforth) a definition of what constituted "improper political activity" with regard to opposition to MARAD-sponsored legislation. The inquiry went unanswered. The committee prepared a report comparing the civil service conversion bill with a Maritime Service conversion bill; according to Bejarano, that report was suppressed.[41]

In May 1959, McLintock abolished the FCPM. Discontent grew, fueled by a lack of faculty meetings, restrictions on promotions, and the absence of a clear policy on research and sabbaticals. Morale was deteriorating, and word of that decline was leaking out around the edges of the school.[42]

Finally, in the fall of 1959, the federal government decided to intervene. On November 14, Representative Herbert Bonner, chair of the Merchant Marine and Fisheries Committee, announced that he was appointing a subcommittee to investigate "any morale problems that may prove to exist" at Kings Point. Democratic representative Herbert Zelenko of New York, whom Bonner designated as the chair of that subcommittee, stated that the committee was going to "bring to the attention of Congress the problems of Kings Point,"[43] and in so doing, help determine whether the teaching staff should be civilian or military. Zelenko had served on the 1959 Congressional Board of Visitors, which had included some unflinching criticism of the Academy's administration in its report, and he was well acquainted with the Academy.[44]

Testimony from those hearings, held in New York in the first week of December, was unpublished, but media accounts of the sessions were peppered with dramatic revelations.[45] Some of the most startling testimony came from the Academy's chaplain, John McKenna, who testified (among other things) that the Regiment had no respect for McLintock.[46] McLintock, called to testify, objected strenuously to the charge. He asserted that he had not only the respect, but also the *affection* of the cadets. Under questioning, however, McLintock admitted that his estimation of his standing among the cadets came largely from the regimental commander and his adjutant—in other words, the two cadets most likely to be his supporters.[47]

The testimony generated at those hearings was damaging enough to the Academy's reputation, but what followed was far worse. On December 16, 1959, a *Newsday* reporter, Arnold Brophy, visited the Academy and lunched with a number of senior faculty members.[48] Academy librarian Luis Bejarano, one of the officers at the table that day, was later accused of inviting Brophy to the Academy so that he could deliver a disparaging statement about McLintock to the media.

Bejarano maintains, however, that Brophy called *him*, and intimated that if the librarian would not agree to meet with him, Brophy would show up on campus and start talking to cadets about the hearings.[49] Government investigators later confirmed the first point, testifying that Brophy had been sent to Kings Point by his editor, and did not come at Bejarano's invitation.[50]

Bejarano had been in open conflict with McLintock for some time, mainly about the funds appropriated for the library, and he had testi-fied to this effect at the December hearings. But Bejarano had a gift for public relations. He had worked tirelessly with John Scherger during the permanency campaign, and helped win that most important prize for the Academy. For those reasons, it seems unlikely that he would have met with Brophy in hopes of damaging the Academy's image.

In any case, Brophy met Bejarano for lunch at the officers' club. Other officers were with them around the tables, including Charles Ferris, Charles Hubert, Lawrence Jarrett, Lane Kendall, Lauren McCready, Leland Pearson, and Walter Von Gronau. The discussion lasted about forty-five minutes. Many of the faculty members voiced their dissatisfaction with McLintock, *without* agreeing to be quoted to that effect.

The plot soon thickened. After lunch, Brophy paid a visit to McLintock, and apparently employed some old reporter's tricks. According to a memo written by McLintock, Brophy claimed that:

> He had in his possession a statement from approximately 10 faculty members calling for the resignation of Admiral McLintock. Brophy then read the statement. He said that these men had asked him to have his newspaper print this statement. He added that these men believed that they represented 90 percent of the faculty. He also stated that these men ranged from the ranks of captain down. When queried on this point, he read the following list: two captains, three commanders, four lieutenant commanders, three lieutenants, one lieutenant (jg)—thus correcting his initial guess of ten to an accurate figure of thirteen. When it was obvious that the two captains were easily identified, Mr. Brophy said that in fairness to these two men he would read the rest of the names. He then consulted a list in his pocket and read the remaining names.[51]

McLintock, furious, wrote to Maritime Administrator Clarence Morse that same afternoon and demanded that all thirteen faculty members be removed. He also included the alleged faculty statement, which began, "The Superintendent does not have our respect as an administrator or educator. . . . We feel that Admiral McLintock has been using his position for personal advantages and prestige and in so doing has ignored the problems of the Academy and has failed to provide effective leadership which we need. He has lowered morale of the faculty and of the cadets so the most effective job cannot be done."[52]

Morse ordered an immediate investigation of the situation. On December 29, Acting Maritime Administrator Walter Ford recommended the dismissal of Bejarano and the reprimand of six other officers: Ferris, Hubert, Kendall, McCready, Pearson, and Von Gronau. All of those reprimanded had served multiple years at the Academy.[53] Many of them, including Bejarano, had been members of the FCPM and had testified before the Zelenko committee. None was granted a hearing or the right to appeal.

Bejarano—upon whom McLintock's wrath had fallen most heavily—appealed to the Maritime Administration's personnel officer, and later to the courts under the Veterans Preference Act (protecting the employment rights of veterans), and still later to the Civil Service Commission Board of Appeals, but all to no avail. Finally removed from the Academy on March 4, 1960, he was never to return to the Academy's employ, although, as we will see, he continued to play a key role in the Academy's history. Though New York papers, including the *New York Times* and Long Island's *Newsday*, loudly condemned the action, McLintock would not be swayed.

In August 1960, another faculty member fell victim to McLintock's disfavor. Chaplain John T. McKenna, whose December testimony had been widely reported, was recalled from Kings Point by the chief of navy chaplains and reassigned without warning. In a subsequent hearing run by Representative Zelenko, it emerged that McLintock had kept a secret file on McKenna, conducted discussions with his subordinates on the possibility of ousting him, and kept from McKenna the fact that complaints were being lodged against him. Testimony from the proceedings illustrate McLintock's strong bias against McKenna:

> Zelenko: Here complaints are being made by fellow officers and you ask them to put allegations in writing. Is there any Government procedure that you know of in such a situation, where fellow officers

complain about another one of their colleagues, in order to protect the rights of a party who is being complained against?

McLintock: He is a very strange contentious man.

Zelenko: I asked you something, nothing to do with him. I am asking you a general question. What is the procedure when one officer complains about another one, if you know of any such procedure?

McLintock: The procedure is to prefer charges if the complaint is serious enough.

Zelenko: And before you prefer charges, is it proper to inform the officer that complaints are being made against him?

McLintock: Yes.

Zelenko: Did you do it?

McLintock: No.

Zelenko: You violated the procedure, did you not?

McLintock: He is a Chaplain.

Zelenko: Did you violate procedure or did you follow it?

McLintock: I did not follow the procedure.

Zelenko: You mean because he is a Chaplain you would not tell him that somebody was complaining against him, that you had told those people to put these complaints in writing?

McLintock: Because he was Chaplain McKenna.[54]

McLintock's arbitrary approach to the exercise of power came through loud and clear, but under the existing organizational structure, little could be done to rein him in. Zelenko's subsequent recommendations were pointed, including a complete reorganization of the Academy staff, and term limits and written educational qualifications for the superintendent. But none of these proposed reforms was acted upon.

McLintock had now been superintendent for twelve years—more than four times as long as any other Kings Point superintendent—and had no intention of leaving. Nor did he give any indication that he intended to change the way he dealt with his faculty. He was the ship's master, whose word was law; he needed no consultation and brooked no disagreement.

A Pillar Is Removed

Another continuing outside stress on the institution in this era resulted from upheavals in the naval reserve status of the Academy graduates in the 1950s and 1960s. In 1952, the Armed Forces Reserve Act abolished the merchant marine reserve, thus depriving both Academy and state maritime academy cadets of the highly prized status of midshipmen. Along with the bachelor's degree and the Coast Guard license, reserve midshipman status was considered to be one of the three major benefits of an Academy education, and the removal of this benefit promised to hurt the Academy's appeal to applicants—all the more so because it also meant that cadets were now eligible for the military draft.

The effects of this change were not immediately evident; in fact, there is some evidence that the same practice of appointing Academy cadets to the merchant marine reserve continued for more than a year, even though the Reserve had ceased to exist. Finally, on July 12, 1954, the chief of naval personnel sent a pertinent "Recruiting Service Note" to all naval recruiting officers. "The Judge Advocate General," the chief noted, "has indicated that there has been no legal authority for the appointment of Merchant Marine midshipmen since 1 January 1953, when the Armed Forces Reserve Act became effective, and therefore, they have no legal status in the Naval Reserve."[55]

The memo specified policy changes resulting from the ruling. As a substitute for the program, cadets appointed after the effective date would "upon their request" be enlisted in the naval reserve as officer candidates, in which position they would be required to complete two years of active duty after graduation, and receive a commission as ensign, naval reserve. The optional reserve status, and the active-duty component that this now encompassed, represented a significant change from prior practice. Prospective candidates entering the federal and state academies in the fall of 1954, moreover, would have to serve on active duty for three years. (A navy regulation, however, did allow merchant marine officers who had served more than six months on active duty in the navy to request an early discharge to serve in the merchant marine.[56])

Attempts in 1955 by MARAD to pass legislation reinstating the status of midshipmen in the naval reserve proved unsuccessful. The measure passed the Senate but it stalled in the House, and, although the Association of Parents and Friends of Kings Point rallied to this cause, as they had to permanency, the measure failed.

In this instance, the Congressional Board of Visitors was less active than it had been on the permanency issue. In a 1956 report, John Scherger noted that the board didn't lend its support to the bill until after the House Armed Services Committee had concluded its meetings. In any case, the friends of the Academy this time were fighting a losing battle. Merchant marine naval reserve status for midshipmen at Kings Point was not reestablished until 1964–and then only briefly. At the end of 1965, the merchant marine reserve program was again abolished–ultimately to be replaced by a naval reserve commission, reinstituted for the class of '68. But the turmoil and uncertainty concerning naval commissions in this period undercut a key rationale for the Academy's existence and hurt its competitive position.

Increased Demand, Reduced Supply

In the meantime, by an accident of historical timing, graduates were again serving in the nation's defense. On May 1, 1950, in connection with the Korean conflict, the navy offered one year's active duty to half of the 1950 graduating class.[57] In 1951, more than 1,100 Kings Point graduates were on active duty in the U.S. Navy as reserve officers, and approximately 350 more were accepted into the regular components of the armed forces.[58] In addition, graduates in the merchant marine were contributing to the flow of soldiers and supplies to the Korean peninsula.

In 1949, the Military Sea Transportation Service (or MSTS, later called the Military Sealift Command) was established under the auspices of the navy, and it became the single managing arm for the Department of Defense's ocean transportation needs, providing combat logistics support. Graduates were well represented in this service, and in both the Korean and Vietnam wars, the MSTS transported enormous numbers of soldiers and countless tons of supplies.

For example, during the Korean conflict, commercial vessels, frequently staffed by Academy graduates, played an important role: more than 85 percent of all the cargo shipped to Korea was carried on U.S. commercial vessels.[59] In the Vietnam War, commercial and MSTS ships transported more than 95 percent of the supplies needed for that conflict.

In short, the young mariners being produced by the Academy were vitally needed in both conflicts. In 1952, in fact, graduations were accelerated by a month to meet the nation's need for officers. (Similarly, in 1966, the August graduation ceremony was moved to early June, and in 1967 it was moved forward an additional six months to January in order to meet the need for merchant marine officers in the

Vietnam conflict.) It was deeply ironic—as Kings Point historian Brad Mitchell pointed out in *We'll Deliver*—that 1952 was also the first year that plebe enrollment at Kings Point dropped below three hundred, due to budgetary constraints. The Academy was required by the government to graduate its students ahead of schedule to meet a pressing national defense need. At the same time, by cutting the Academy's budget, Congress was reducing the future supply of those officers.

A Waiting Game

Congressman Herbert Zelenko, McLintock's legislative tormentor, was not the only person to whom the idea of limiting the superintendent's reign had occurred. MARAD, which had placed McLintock in power in 1948, was finding him more than they wanted to handle.

The first open suggestion to displace McLintock came from then undersecretary of transportation, Clarence D. Martin Jr., in June 1961. Maritime Administrator Thomas Stakem greeted this suggestion with little enthusiasm, guessing that McLintock would opt for retirement on his own in the near future. "As you are aware," Stakem wrote to another government official, "McLintock has been Superintendent for over thirteen years as opposed to the two- or three-year superintendent's terms at other Federal Academies. Too, he will reach his sixtieth birthday in February 1963 and have completed over thirty years federal service and will be eligible for full retirement annuity. It is my belief that he will seek retirement at the end of Kings Point Academic Year in September 1963." [60]

The next Maritime administrator, Donald Alexander, was less sanguine, but he mentioned to Secretary of Commerce Luther Hodges that he was looking for a replacement for the durable superintendent at Kings Point. In a letter dated August 28, 1962, Hodges replied that he was pleased that Alexander was proceeding along these lines. He also referred to the conclusions of a recent Academic Advisory Board report, which had recommended that the Academy's next superintendent should have an outstanding background in maritime matters and administration.

But every attempt to remove McLintock proved unsuccessful. (Melvin Tublin, '49, later recalled that hearing Washington alumni representative Milton Nottingham, '44, announce that a Maritime administrator was planning to replace McLintock was in effect a prediction of the administrator's own resignation.[61]) To some extent, this was a case of MARAD's own work coming back to haunt it. On January 1, 1962, the conversion process described earlier came to Wiley Hall: Gordon McLintock was transferred from his former maritime service status to a civil service position, at the rank of GS-15. Under the rigid guidelines of civil service—which mandated dismissal "for cause" only—it was now impossible to remove McLintock from his position without extensive written documentation justifying such an action. Ultimately, McLintock would outlast several more Maritime administrators, remaining in his post as superintendent of the Academy until 1970.

Gordon McLintock grew larger than life, and his story refuses to fit comfortably within the confines of a single chapter. In the preceding pages, we have focused on the key events and trends in McLintock's tenure which involved external constituencies, either primarily (e.g., permanency) or as a result of internal disputes going public. But McLintock's twenty-two-year tenure also comprised many important changes in the life of the Academy itself—including curricular changes, new buildings on campus, and changing student roles—and these are the subject of our next chapter.

7

Building on the Foundations

1955–1970

The Academy had won an important battle in 1949 with the awarding of academic accreditation. Among other things, the decision by the Middle States Association of Colleges and Secondary Schools (MSA) removed the last barrier that stood in the way of Kings Point awarding degrees to its graduates—a congressionally imposed condition that the Academy's leaders were determined to meet.

But accreditation was far from a onetime challenge. The Middle States Association, while generous in its praise for what the Academy had accomplished in a relatively short time, had also spotlighted several areas in which improvement was necessary, including faculty status, the curriculum, and the excessive workload of both faculty and students.

Accreditation typically is reviewed at ten-year intervals. In theory, therefore, the Academy had time to address these areas of weakness. But intermittent political upheavals, funding crises, and conflicts between the faculty and administration hindered progress on some of these issues. And, as its closest advisers had warned all along, there were difficulties inherent in trying to make Kings Point "more like a college." The Academy's close ties to a fast-changing industry, its distinctive curriculum and Sea Year, its inadequate budget and physical plant, its subordinate relationship to a sometimes unpredictable agency in Washington, and its obligations to serve the national defense, all helped complicate the reaccreditation of Kings Point.

Even as the Academy was attempting to leap the hurdle of reaccreditation, it was venturing into new arenas and making new friends. At the urging of the federal government, Kings Point faculty ranged far afield, helping mariners in other countries create their own merchant marine academies. The Academy also accepted the challenge of training crews for the world's first nuclear-powered merchant vessel.

In the middle of most of these debates, dramas, and advances, of course, stood the unique figure of Gordon McLintock. As aide Richard O'Leary recalls, "He loved that institution with every fiber of his being. In fact, he thought he owned it. You know, he was there for so long that in some ways he had an unrealistic idea of what he was, and what his relationship was to the people down in Washington, whom he basically detested. He wanted it to be an autonomous place, and to be able to do anything he pleased. On the other hand, he saved the place probably three or four times."[1]

McLintock literally rebuilt the Academy to his liking: securing funding for a chapel and building the library that the accreditation teams said was absolutely necessary. He championed the dual-license program, and reordered the Academy's curriculum to accommodate this elite program. But even as McLintock built and innovated, he made enemies, including the "people down in Washington." Ultimately, he was compelled to leave the Academy he had so transformed.

A Debate and a Deferral

In 1950, the McLintock administration decided to award retroactively the recently sanctioned USMMA degree to early graduates of the school. The Academic Advisory Board—always the Academy's most attentive overseer, and sometimes its fiercest critic—harshly scolded the administration for this action, which the board felt would compromise the Academy's reputation as a legitimate educational institution and possibly even endanger its accreditation.

True, the awarding of retroactive degrees was specifically authorized by the congressional act that gave the Academy degree-granting status, pending accreditation, but in the opinion of the board, Academy administrators interpreted this power much too broadly. The board noted (in its 1951 report) that 565 of the 2,608 retroactive degrees awarded were given to applicants whose only qualification was a master's or chief engineer's license. "The degree has been awarded on this basis," scolded the board, "to men whose maritime training took place before the Academy was established at Kings Point, and who never received an educational training in any way comparable to that . . . which forms the basis for the accrediting of the Academy by the Middle States Association."[2]

The board went on to remind the Academy that, having accepted accreditation, it now had responsibilities that it could not ignore:

> The Academy is now no longer merely a service institution. It has, on its own initiative, sought and secured admission as a qualified member of the recognized family of academic institutions of the United States. As a consequence, it is expected to uphold, protect, and defend the academic standards of our country with an interest and sincerity of purpose paralleling that with which it meets its concurrent obligations as a national service academy.[3]

In its 1953 report, the board continued to prod the Academy to improve and refine its methods of education. The report's language was optimistic, and, by the standards of academic committees, occasionally even poetic: "One may say the rough form of the educational process at Kings Point has been hewn; now there may be started the continuing refinement of detail which will ensure academic and professional sufficiency."[4] But there were cautionary notes as well. It was not too soon, the board pointed out, to start retooling those aspects of the academic program that the Middle States Association was certain to scrutinize when it returned to Kings Point during reaccreditation.

And finally, there were notes of admonition:

> Out of sincere devotion to the Academy and loyal anxiety to help it achieve a respected place among other accredited, degree-giving institutions, we have tried to bring our varied academic experiences and our joint judgment to bear upon the Academy's academic problems. It is heartening to find that many of these suggestions have been acted upon. It is frankly disheartening to find others—and among them certain vital matters—seemingly ignored.[5]

What did the Academic Advisory Board feel was being ignored? The board highlighted several issues. First, it felt that general education still was being shortchanged at the Academy in favor of practical subjects. Close cooperation between faculty and administration was the exception rather than the rule. The library was woefully inadequate.

Finally, promotion, salary increases, and tenure, as well as a broad respect for scholarship and research, were needed to strengthen the academic environment.[6]

Despite the appointment in March 1955 of Dr. Guy Trump, the Academy's first civilian dean, many of these issues were not addressed effectively until the 1960s. Though a faculty curriculum committee had been active in the early 1950s, it had fallen victim to faculty/administration tensions in the second half of the decade, and thus the curriculum as a whole remained largely unexamined. As the date for the reaccreditation visit by the MSA approached, it became abundantly clear that the Academy was unprepared to undergo a rigorous academic inspection.

Bowing to the inevitable, McLintock wrote a letter in May 1958 to F. Taylor Jones, executive secretary of the Commission on Institutions of Higher Learning of the MSA, requesting a three-year deferral of the Academy's reevaluation. He based the request on two grounds. The first was the civil service conversion legislation, already submitted to Congress but not yet acted upon, which left the entire faculty in an unsatisfactory state of limbo. Second, McLintock stated, the Academy had begun a study, at the recommendation of the Advisory Board, of the adequacy of the course content at the Academy, "particularly in view of the technological developments which are rapidly taking place in the maritime industry."[7] McLintock estimated that this project, involving the creation of a special advisory committee and a questionnaire that would be sent to all graduates and their employers, would take at least two years to accomplish.

In response to this request, the MSA agreed to defer the process until the fall of 1962. Because accrediting boards don't generally grant deferrals unless the institution in question is considered to be in good standing, this was at least a limited vote of confidence in the Academy. But all parties knew that much work remained to be done.

In the Trenches

Some of this work, aimed at improving the experience of the cadets, was already under way. The first of these was the splitting of the Sea Year from a full year at sea to two half-years, during both the second and third class years. This was done partly to stem attrition; the uninterrupted year at sea, as well as the transition from this unregimented lifestyle back to the disciplined and heavily academic life of the Academy, had proved too difficult for many students. The split also was effected partly to improve athletic competition at the Academy. By allowing students involved in a fall sport to take their Sea Year during spring semesters, and vice versa, the Academy could strengthen its athletic teams and broaden the Academy's appeal to prospective applicants.

This, apparently, was an experiment designed by McLintock, who in the summer of 1957 recommended the change, which at first applied only to athletes, primarily to "improve the Academy's athletic progress."[8] A 1961 Curriculum Advisory Committee recommended extending this split Sea Year to all cadets.

The Academy also made an effort to adjust the Sea Year program to better fit into the rest of the training program, and at the same time to crack down on delinquent sea projects. In 1957, third-class-year counselor Lieutenant Lee Pearson was appointed to keep in close contact with all the cadets at sea, and also to keep track of the status of sea projects. The content of those projects also changed: the much unloved math assignments were eliminated, and the Rules of the Road assignment was completely revised and updated. Two years later, these changes seemed to be producing results: the student newspaper *Hear This* noted that the quality of the sea projects had improved steadily since the reforms went into effect.[9]

Like the first round of Sea Year reforms, an admissions policy adjustment in 1962–precipitated by a conflict between McLintock and a new Maritime administrator, Donald Alexander–was also aimed in part at protecting the Academy's athletic programs. From 1958 onward, it had been accepted practice for McLintock to send a list of "superintendent's appointments" to the Maritime administrator for approval. These lists generally consisted of "scholastically eligible" athletes who had been recruited by Harry Wright, the football coach, but who had not been admitted to the Academy through the standard examination and appointment system. In June 1962, however, Alexander refused to approve these appointments, saying that he considered them illegal.[10] Making the situation particularly awkward was the fact that Wright, assuming that past practice would be repeated, had already made commitments to the young men on the list. Many had already turned down other schools in anticipation of attending the Academy. Clearly, the administration was on the hook to find a solution.

After some wrangling, MARAD and the Academy hit upon a

compromise made possible by some semantic finessing. MARAD's chief counsel examined athlete selection at West Point, the Naval Academy, and the Air Force Academy, and found that each used a system whereby "secretarial" or "presidential" appointments were used to admit students from the country at large, with no reference to the competitive exams. Although Kings Point had a different legislative history, its charter, too, allowed for secretarial appointments, with no other stipulation than that the candidates be qualified for admission. So, in addition to the full quota of 314 students admitted in 1962 on the basis of the competitive exam, 26 young men specifically recruited and appointed as "secretarial appointments" were also allowed to enroll. While a total of 340 students would strain Kings Point's facilities, experience suggested that administrators could anticipate something like two dozen dropouts within the first week or ten days, which would bring the head count back down to a more manageable size.

A New Lease on Life

The questionnaire promised by McLintock in his deferral request to the MSA was sent out in the fall of 1959 to all graduates of the Academy's four-year course then serving on merchant ships, as well as to the port captains and port engineers of all major steamship companies. Briefly stated, the survey sought to determine courses that were most helpful to graduates (as well as least helpful), and to solicit suggestions on additional material that should be covered by the Academy curriculum.

The response from both graduates and steamship company executives was overwhelmingly positive. The assistant to the marine superintendent of the United Fruit Company sent a typical response, calling the Academy "unparalleled in education and training for the Merchant Marine," and adding that "graduates in our employ have been consistently excellent officers, requiring only that extra touch that comes with practical experience alone." Both deck and engine graduates were similarly laudatory, stating that the Academy's academic program was excellent, and approving the balance that had been struck between professional and cultural subjects.

At the same time, the Academy set up a special advisory committee and a faculty committee to examine the curriculum. Again, reports were favorable. The committee's chairman, President Jess Harrison Davis of the Stevens Institute of Technology, reported that "the present curriculum is well designed and provides a satisfactory vehicle for meeting the mission of the Academy; namely, the training of officers for the U.S. Merchant Marine, and the development, through this training, of professional, educated men."[11] The committee did offer several suggestions for improvements, including extending the then-experimental split Sea Year to all students; giving additional time to personnel relations, gas turbines, instrumentation, and electronics; and offering refresher courses for merchant marine officers.

By 1962, academics at Kings Point appeared to be stronger than ever before. The academic side of the shop was now headed by Dr. Arthur Sanford Limouze, who had arrived in 1961 from the New York State Maritime College to take over as academic dean, a position that had been vacant for two years. The Advisory Board reported that there was a general consensus that the Academy was on the right course. The changes recommended by the outside curriculum committee had been adopted; an approved faculty salary scale (established by Dean Limouze) had been put into effect; new and up-to-date equipment had been ordered for the Academy; the academic performance of the students was solid; and maintenance and repairs to the physical plant were proceeding satisfactorily. The Academic Advisory Board specifically mentioned the good impression created by the performance of the cadets at a formal regimental review.[12]

In short, the Academy finally seemed positioned for smooth sailing. Once again, however, a sudden storm arose. The July 1963 report of the MSA's accreditation team, based on their visit to Kings Point in November 1962, granted only conditional accreditation.

The MSA wasn't satisfied with the curriculum self-study already conducted by the Academy, and asked for a more comprehensive study. Reading between the lines, the underlying issue once again was the balance between vocational and general education. The MSA suggested convening a committee, populated by representatives from industry, the Coast Guard, and the faculty, to determine the minimum vocational subjects needed to meet licensing requirements, and to enable graduates to perform shipboard duties. The MSA further recommended that, based on the findings of this committee, the Academy's faculty should figure out how to offer adequate vocational training while placing the least demands on the cadets' time.[13]

Next, the MSA recommended that a second group of faculty members and distinguished representatives of other degree-granting

institutions should define the minimum general education requirements needed to justify the awarding of a bachelor's degree. The
results of these two studies, the MSA explained, could then be used to
strengthen the curriculum, and "remove any questions regarding suit-
ability of the program as the basis for a degree."[14] The MSA scheduled
a follow-up visit for 1965, at which point it would determine the Academy's progress and make a final decision on reaccreditation.

This report required urgent action, and McLintock and his faculty
moved swiftly. Immediately after the release of the MSA's findings,
McLintock asked six members of the Coast Guard and industry—
including a port captain, a retired commodore, and a commander and
a captain from the Coast Guard—to serve on the first committee specified by the MSA. Four distinguished academics, including Dr. Levering
Tyson, former president of the MSA; Dr. Harold W. Dodds, president
emeritus of Princeton; Dr. Henry M. Wriston, president emeritus of
Brown; and Dr. William T. Alexander, president of the Webb Institute
of Naval Architecture, agreed to form the second committee. Both
groups would be aided, as appropriate, by Academy faculty.

Because of the MSA's tight framing of the issue, the results of the
committees' work conformed closely to MSA concerns. The industry-
oriented committee recommended a reduction in the instructional
hours allocated to vocational subjects, and endorsed measures
designed to expand math and science course offerings. Academy faculty, meanwhile, also came up with a proposal for a revised curriculum
that would include increased exposure to the humanities. The members of the second committee, consisting of outside-world academics,
approved this proposal, which they believed compared favorably to
many liberal arts colleges.

In June 1964, the two committees met together and approved the
changes, and the Academy agreed to implement the new curriculum in
1964. With these changes in place, MSA inspection committee members were unanimous in approving the program for reaccreditation in
1965. Once again, the battle had been won, but only through sustained hard work by the Academy's faculty and supportive outsiders.

Exporting the Academy

The impact of the Cold War was felt in a variety of ways across the
U.S. educational establishment. Fears about Sputnik and an alleged

"missile gap" led to enormous investments in science and technology, which trickled and rippled down through all levels of the academy. Meanwhile, U.S. graduate and professional schools were strongly encouraged by the federal government to work with their counterparts overseas, both to make friends for the United States and to erect a further bulwark against communism.

The Academy took part in this movement, although resource constraints limited the school to relatively modest efforts. Beginning in the late 1950s, Academy faculty members were sent to Indonesia and Turkey to help those countries establish their own merchant marine academies.[15]

In 1958, for example, the International Cooperation Administration (ICA) of the U.S. State Department picked Professor Raymond Eisenberg to head a program to help the Republic of Indonesia set up an effective merchant marine academy. Eisenberg took with him Professor C. L. Sauerbier as acting faculty head, Commander Sidney O. Carlson as acting head of the Engineering Department, and Lieutenant Commander John H. LaDage as acting head of the Nautical Science Department. These three, along with their families, set up residence near Djakarta, Indonesia, where, according to *Hear This*, "each family is learning to speak the language so that friendly relations may more easily be realized."[16] In the following year, three more instructors were nominated to join the effort: Lieutenant Commander Myron Thomas and Professor Michael Bishansky taught steam engineering, and Professor Edward Law taught diesel propulsion.

This first program proved such a success that a similar program in Turkey was initiated in 1960. "I guess I did a decent enough job," recalled Eisenberg, "that when the State Department got a similar request from the Turkish government, they asked for my services again."[17] So Eisenberg again represented Kings Point, this time as an adviser to the Turkish Nautical College at Istanbul.

The ICA also arranged for the Academy to provide training at Kings Point for foreign officers. The first two groups included five licensed officers from Indonesia and five from Turkey, all of whom pursued a six-month course of study. And in the fall of 1961, a group of seven Indonesian cadets was admitted for a two-year training program at Kings Point, to prepare them to assume positions of leadership in the Indonesian merchant marine.[18]

Other groups conducted less formal but still concentrated studies of how Kings Point did its work. In the 1960s, for example, the Academy received visits from representatives of the National Maritime Development Institute, Taipei; students from the Spanish Naval Academy at El Ferrol; and naval officers from Thailand, Korea, Turkey, Brazil, Vietnam, the Philippines, and Ethiopia.

Collectively, these efforts to share what the Academy had already learned about the education of merchant marine officers—efforts made both at Kings Point and on foreign shores—earned goodwill for the school and built its reputation in maritime-minded nations around the world.

Atoms for Peace: The Academy Enters the Nuclear Age

One substantial innovation in the Academy's curriculum focused on nuclear physics and engineering. This development indirectly reflected the nation's growing fascination with all things nuclear—and, more directly, also reflected the impetus of an Eisenhower administration program called Atoms for Peace. This ambitious program is best known for having spawned the commercial nuclear power industry in the United States and in allied nations abroad. But its impact also extended to the maritime field, nurturing the development of nuclear propulsion systems for merchant vessels. These systems came to a short-lived fruition in the NS (Nuclear Ship) *Savannah*.

The project was undertaken by the Atomic Energy Commission (AEC), established by Congress in 1946 to manage the country's atomic energy resources and explorations. By 1949, with the Soviet development of an atomic bomb, the arms race was in full swing, and the AEC was devoting much of its resources to keeping the United States in the race.

In at least one realm, the nuclear propulsion of warships, the United States held a commanding lead. As Atoms for Peace began to moderate the warlike face of atomic fission, the AEC suggested (in late 1954) putting these advanced propulsion technologies to work in a merchant ship. The concept met with an immediate endorsement from President Eisenhower, who apparently suggested that the commission try to launch a nuclear ship within three months.[19]

This was a fantasy; building a nuclear-powered merchant ship and training a crew to sail her would require years, not months. But Eisenhower was determined. At his request, the AEC completed a feasibility study in the spring of 1955. The report estimated a daunting price tag

Midshipman James Havasy of the U.S. Merchant Marine Academy stands at the bow of the NS *Savannah* on January 6, 1966, before boarding the ship to begin his Sea Year assignment.

of $31 million for the ship, with thirty months of work required simply to retrofit a standard cargo ship with the same type of reactor used by navy warships.[20] The navy's Admiral Hyman Rickover strongly resisted the program because it threatened to divert some of his own nuclear resources, and partly because he didn't believe that a commercial crew could be properly trained to man a nuclear vessel, and he feared negative repercussions for his own program if the merchant crew failed.[21] Nevertheless, Eisenhower approved the plans, pointedly directing that Rickover have no involvement whatsoever, and urged full speed ahead.

On July 30, 1956, Congress passed Public Law 848, which authorized the Commerce Department, MARAD, and the AEC to build and operate a nuclear-powered merchant ship, "capable of providing shipping services on routes essential for maintaining the flow of foreign commerce of the United States."[22] The name of the ship, NS *Savannah*, was suggested by Major General Henry Benton Saylor–apparently on the advice of maritime historian Frank Braynard–as a tribute to the American SS *Savannah*, the first ship to cross the Atlantic under a combination of steam and sail, back in 1819.

The AEC had originally conceived of the *Savannah* as more of a showcase than a functioning commercial vessel. But the law, as passed, called for a fully operational ship, and by 1957, MARAD and the AEC were pursuing a functional commercial prototype. To this end, they decided to have their reactor unit custom-built, rather than retrofitting a navy unit to fit a merchant ship. The engineering firm of Babcock & Wilcox won this contract, and was also retained to train the crews needed to operate the new vessel. The naval architecture firm George C. Sharp, Inc., won the design contract for the *Savannah*. And, following a clearly defined bidding process, the government selected States Marine Lines from among seven shipping companies interested in operating the *Savannah*.

Training the *Savannah*'s Crew

Everyone involved understood that the *Savannah*'s crew would be one of the vessel's most essential safety systems. (In fact, crew training for the ship had been specifically authorized by Public Law 848.) The training needs for the engineering officers in particular would be extensive; engineering crews aboard the *Savannah* would need special instruction in the operation and maintenance of nuclear power plants as well as a basic theory of reactor technology. The *Savannah*'s deck officers, while requiring a less detailed understanding of nuclear science, would still need a general knowledge of reactor operation and familiarity with nuclear terminology. And because deck officers bore primary responsibility for personnel–on ship and ashore–they would also need training in radiological hazards and health physics.

Two Kings Point faculty members, professors Steve Gregurech and Maurice Gross, were inspired by the concept and were among the first to receive nuclear training for the *Savannah* project, starting with a six-month course at Union College. This was followed by a full year of cooperative study at the Oak Ridge School of Reactor Technology. After they had completed this training, MARAD loaned them to the *Savannah* project on a full-time basis to serve as instructors for the first ship crew-training program, which began its selection of engineering officers in September 1958.

Industry interest in the program was intense. For the sixteen available engineering slots, States Marine received more than two hundred applications. The applicants were selected after rigorous screening, which included written tests administered by the Educational Testing Service as well as personal interviews with Babcock & Wilcox, MARAD, and States Marine officials.

On September 29, 1958, a total of sixteen officers—along with twenty other students from steamship companies, maritime educational institutions (including Academy professor Moses "Mo" Hirschkowitz), and the Coast Guard—embarked upon a fifteen-month course of training. A second group began training on April 15, 1959, to provide replacements for members of the first group, should that become necessary. All members of this second group already had science or engineering degrees from accredited schools, so the academic-studies portion of their training was reduced.

In Mo Hirschkowitz's case, he recalls, he and his supervisor, Lauren McCready, more or less willed Hirschkowitz into the training program: "I couldn't get official approval. I was waiting at the Academy, and no word came. So I just picked up my family and went, with no official word that I should go. But also with no official word that I shouldn't go. I just couldn't get an opinion from Washington, and time was running out. McCready backed me up on that one. From my perspective, he was the powerhouse behind it. He was the one who had to convince Washington."[23]

The training took place in Virginia, at Lynchburg College, which supplied space for classrooms, labs, and the *Savannah* simulator—a full-scale operating model of the main control console of the ship, then under construction. Maurice Gross, a member of the Kings Point engineering faculty, served as director of the training program. The academic phase, which encompassed formal classroom instruction, seminars, lab work, and experiments, lasted for thirty-one weeks. After this time, students were assigned to thirty weeks of field training at various reactors throughout the country. On May 4, 1959, six deck officers joined the training program at Lynchburg for a shorter course of study involving thirteen weeks of academic work, followed by field training including radiological health courses, cruises on naval nuclear subs, and a course at the Naval Damage Control School.

While the Lynchburg physical facilities were adequate for the training program's purposes, and while the proximity to Babcock & Wilcox's nearby headquarters had been helpful to the young program, the college itself had little expertise in nuclear science. At Kings Point, however, the relatively new nuclear program had been making great strides, and in recognition of this fact, MARAD announced in 1960 that future crew training would take place at Kings Point.[24]

The Academy's expertise in nuclear science had been growing since 1954, when the head of the Department of Mathematics and Science, Professor C. D. Ingersoll, initiated a course in atomic and nuclear physics. In the fall of 1959, similar electives in nuclear physics were being offered to interested cadets, and Mo Hirschkowitz, recently returned from the first *Savannah* crew training, was drawing up plans for a nuclear lab. The November issue of *Hear This* announced the conversion of part of Furuseth Hall to a Nuclear Science and Engineering Center.[25]

Commander C. W. Sandberg, assistant head of the Department of Engineering, discusses the control of the NS *Savannah*'s primary system with a group of *Savannah* trainees in March 1964.

By this time, several additional instructors—including McCready, assistant head of engineering Clifford W. Sandberg, and Dr. Albert Swertka, a nuclear physics teacher in the Department of Mathematics and Science—had received special training. Gross and Swertka took the lead in setting up a yearlong program for training *Savannah* crew members, in which Gross taught nuclear engineering and Swertka taught nuclear physics. (Representatives from MEBA, the union that was expected to control the engineering positions on the *Savannah*, also worked with the Academy to design the program.) With a few exceptions, every engineer who was licensed to operate the *Savannah* passed through this program. In October 1960, the Academy added a subcritical reactor to its growing nuclear lab, supplementing its existing inventory of Geiger-Muller counters, Wilson cloud chambers, Van de Graaf generators, scintillation counters, and other relatively exotic equipment.

MARAD's decision to shift crew training to the Academy further strengthened the Kings Point program, in part through the transfer of the enormously useful *Savannah* simulator from Lynchburg to Kings Point. The cost of the crew-training transfer from Virginia to New York totaled something under $125,000,[26] which, given the quickly rising costs of the program as a whole, was a relatively small amount. By

A nuclear training course at the USMMA in the mid-1960s.

May 1963, for example, States Marine had already paid out $464,000 for training expenses, and the government had shouldered another $699,000.[27] Meanwhile, the Academy was racking up its own set of bills, including $50,000 to convert Furuseth Hall and $35,000 to complete the Nuclear Engineering Laboratory.[28]

The symbolic payoff of all this investment came on April 24, 1962. That was the day when the Academy's subcritical reactor, using fuel supplied by the AEC, was first put into service for training purposes. Subcritical simply meant that the reactor could not achieve critical mass, and therefore was a reasonably safe teaching technology. Mo Hirschkowitz explains the uses to which the reactor was put:

> You could get a neutron flux pattern to show the core characteristics. You could irradiate a sample, and activate it, and use that as a source of neutrons. But you have to have the nuclear physics to understand what you're doing. For example: you're dealing with instruments. Well, the problem with instrumentation is, do you believe the instruments? How do you establish your confidence in what you're measuring? That's why you have to have the theory. There are a lot of things you've got to recognize.
>
> Our program was *practical*. We were *plant operators*. I used to take nuclear programs at MIT in the summertime. These were special courses, run by people in the industry, and this particular professor was running it. He said, "I want Kings Pointers to come and take their graduate studies with me." I said, "Well, I'm proud of our students, but why would you pick a Kings Pointer?" He said, "When I get a graduate student, if he's a mathematician, all he wants to do is math. Physicist, all he wants to do is physics. The Kings Pointer makes it *work*."[29]

In the midst of this progress, however, dark clouds were gathering for the *Savannah*. Jurisdictional union disputes were growing increasingly contentious between the Marine Engineers' Beneficial Association (MEBA) and the International Organization of Masters, Mates and Pilots (MMP), as well as separate disagreements between both unions and States Marine Lines. On May 13, 1963, after several rounds of negotiations and work stoppages, the government dismissed all of the ship's engineers (all members of MEBA), and also terminated its contract with States Marine Lines.[30] The selection and training process would have to start again from scratch.

Though this transition moved relatively swiftly, with American Export Isbrandtsen Lines chosen within weeks to take over the operation of the ship, the government had become wary of more crippling conflicts among the unions, and between the unions and the shipping companies. In the summer of 1963, therefore, it decided to train a backup crew to provide emergency coverage for the *Savannah*. The backup crew included several Kings Point faculty members, Pasquale Nazzaro and future superintendent Paul Krinsky being among the deck officers. It gained sufficient experience and confidence to take the *Savannah* out on a sea trial on April 21, 1964. The unions chose not to perceive this "shadow crew" as a threat, although they clearly held back from embracing the concept. One member of the Brotherhood of Marine Officers (BMO) who accompanied the crew on its sea trial said that the experience was "uneasy . . . for everyone involved," and that the backup crew was "greatly relieved" when it was over.[31] Another member called it "highly improbable" that the backup crew could take the vessel out on a real voyage,[32] though Krinsky noted that the backup crew did, in fact, take the ship out on a weekend trip.[33]

Yet another Kings Point faculty member accompanied the *Savannah* on its second cruise, to Europe, which took place in the fall of 1964. Lauren McCready joined the *Savannah* as a seaman and trainee in Philadelphia, and he sailed with the ship to Naples, Lisbon, Barcelona, and Greece, among other ports of call. In Italy, the ship's master, McCready, and the rest of the crew were invited to a papal audience with Pope Paul VI at St. Peter's. To this day McCready recalls the gleaming marble and red velvet at the Vatican and treasures the silver papal key ring he was given at the end of the audience.

As it turned out, this European trip represented the highwater mark of the *Savannah* project. Over the next several years the program slowly collapsed, falling victim to a combination of unfavorable economics, shifting perceptions of nuclear power, ongoing labor disputes, and national politics. Simply put, nuclear propulsion could not be made economically viable on merchant ships unless it was adopted widely, allowing the industry to achieve economies of scale. But unless oil prices rose to unprecedented heights, thereby making nuclear power cost competitive, no shipping company would even consider converting to nuclear, with its potential liabilities and growing public-relations problems.

Despite these larger-world setbacks, the Kings Point nuclear

Midshipman Michael Nichols, '67, explains the control console of the NS *Savannah* to his classmate Midshipman James Havasy, '67. Both midshipmen were assigned to the *Savannah* as part of their Sea Year.

program continued to grow in scale and scope. In 1967, for example, the Academy completed a high-precision water chemistry lab. Longer term, the case can be made that the *Savannah* program, although in some ways a self-limiting experiment, served as a valuable experience in unexpected ways. The Academy produced ten to twelve graduates of the program each year, who were able to use their skills both in the navy and in the commercial nuclear power industry. A market opportunity had opened up, and the Academy's faculty had moved to exploit that opportunity. In future decades, as the Academy contemplated ventures in the field of continuing education, the memory of the *Savannah* program engendered both caution and confidence.

Responding to the Container Revolution

The second major change in the curriculum in the 1960s was inspired by yet another revolution in the shipping industry—this time a more durable and far-reaching revolution. This radical transition, moreover, took place not in top-secret laboratories but on the docks and roadways of the United States.

One day in the 1940s, after sitting in the cab of one his trucks in the Port of Newark and waiting for port stevedores to come unload the vehicle–a wait that sometimes lasted hours–trucker Malcolm McLean began dreaming of a more efficient system of cargo loading. Why, wondered McLean, couldn't they simply pick up the back of his trailer truck and stick it on the ship, thereby replacing multiple ship cargoes (and reducing manual labor) with one self-contained unit?

Replacing break-bulk cargo handling, which had dominated ship-ping since ships were invented, was an idea that would revolutionize the industry. It was also ahead of its time. It was 1956 before the first converted tanker, McLean's SS *Ideal X*, made an experimental trip from Newark to Houston, carrying fifty-eight 35-foot containers on deck.[34] And though this trip was deemed a success, another decade passed before the container revolution really took hold and the first transatlantic containership service was operative.[35]

But when it *did* take hold, it did so with a vengeance. The funda-mental rules of shipping were rewritten.[36] The container revolution resulted in dramatically shorter port time for merchant vessels, better-protected cargo (and thus reduced loss from both weather and theft), and it sparked the modern trend of declining employment in port and other cargo-handling facilities. An equally profound impact on the industry–and by extension, on the Academy curriculum–was caused by the construction of a new generation of modern ships to carry out the container revolution. The first dedicated containerships, built in 1957, could carry 226 containers (more than six times as many as the *Ideal X*).[37] During the 1970s and 1980s, containerships continued to grow in size and capacity; by the late 1980s, a new containership could carry as many as 3,000 twenty-foot equivalent (TEU) containers.[38]

The ships were also becoming increasingly automated, cutting the need for crew to operate the ship almost in half. The winter 1965 issue of *Polaris* cited four companies that were leaders in shipboard automa-tion: Gulf and South American, MooreMcCormack, U.S. Lines, and Lykes.[39] The article cited the engine controls of U.S. Lines' *American Racer* as a case in point: "All major and minor functions are centralized at the control console–can be monitored by a single engineer. Data loggers provide a continuous stream of temperatures, pressures, and conditions in all vital areas, further reducing the tasks of watch personnel. Bridge control console provides instantaneous speed and

The SS *Matsonia* arriving at a terminal in Honolulu. The *Matsonia* is an early Ro/Ro (Roll On/Roll Off) trailership, owned by Matson Lines.

directional control of the engine."[40] Watch-standing, above and below decks, would never be the same.

The Dual-License Program

Reading these tea leaves, one could easily conclude that this new generation of ships would require fewer officers with multiple skill sets. With this in mind, the Academy in the mid-1960s began crafting a dual-license major, a program that would prepare cadets for both deck and engine licensing that became known as the dualie program.

Mo Hirschkowitz, who was deeply involved in the *Savannah* experience, adds a complementary perspective: "McCready and I started the dual-license program, which I see as an outgrowth of the *Savannah*. When we had the *Savannah*, there were so many technical problems that the deck people had to cope with, because there was no ship that was inspected as much as the *Savannah*. Every port you entered had hundreds of questions. So they had to learn engineering, as well as deck."[41]

In September 1965, a total of twenty-eight hand-picked cadets began a pilot program designed to test the feasibility of dual training. Although other factors were considered in the screening process, these cadets generally represented the top 10 percent of the entering class as measured by high school grades and by their performance on the entrance exam.[42] Based on the success of this pilot program, a new curriculum was designed, calling for a total of 3,010 class hours for the duals (as opposed to 2,890 for engineers and 2,750 for deck candidates). The Sea Year was also adjusted for these cadets, who spent six months as an engineering cadet and six months as a deck cadet. In part because the dual program was academically demanding, it continued to attract gifted and highly motivated students.

Superintendent McLintock, a staunch supporter of the dual concept, was extremely proud of his elite new program. In a 1967 article in the *Long Island Daily Commercial Review*, McLintock was quoted as saying that the "eyes of the maritime countries of the world are focused on the Academy" because of the program, which he believed would create the "omni-competent" officer.[43]

The dual-licensing program was founded on the assumption that over time, the lines between the deck and engine departments would blur, and that omnicompetent officers would rule the waves. This assumption gradually proved to be unfounded. In real life, Kings Point graduates who held both licenses almost always wound up specializing at any one time in either deck or engine—and in their professional lives rarely called attention to the fact that they held two licenses. But the dual program survived as an elite "program within a program," and employers often looked to hire dual graduates simply because they were known to be an elite—smart, disciplined, and accomplished.

Life at Ground Level

When describing a superintendency as event-filled as Gordon McLintock's, it is easy to lose the flavor and pace of day-to-day life. In and around the battles for accreditation, the international ventures, the curricular changes, and major changes in the physical landscape, the life of the Kings Point community went on much as it always had. Faculty taught, students learned and graduated, and administrators found ways to make ends meet. Of necessity, our text focuses on the exceptional, but life at the Academy in the 1950s and 1960s, as everywhere, was overwhelmingly dominated by the *routine*.

In this section, we look briefly at the routine. These stories, too, tend to revolve around the central figure of McLintock, reminding us, paradoxically, that he was both a commanding presence and simply another member of a human community.

In the 1950s, Clifford W. Sandberg served as assistant head of the Engineering Department, second in command to department head Lauren "Mac" McCready. Beginning in the spring of 1951, Sandberg began keeping a journal, which included (among others) the following observations:

6/19/51

An announcement [regarding a four-year extension of McLintock's superintendency] is reported to us to have been made at the noon mess before the Regiment. Mac [McCready] looked so glum when he told me this. . . . I myself can't see why in the world McLintock would leave the Academy . . . there is too much of interest here . . . just the other evening, he had dinner with Nelson Rockefeller and Charles Lindbergh over at [U.N. Ambassador] Garreau's residence outside the gate.

6/20/51

Just about 2 in the afternoon of a very beautiful day with the temp someplace in the 80s. Everything is a nice rich green and the silence is suddenly broken by the odd rhythm of a single drum . . . I look out my window toward the Oval and there I see the graduates practicing their marching and lining up for the exercises tomorrow. The public works truck and the blue dungareed white-hatted public works men are milling about, shoving chairs in place and getting the speaker's platform in shape . . . the platform is out from under the porte-cochere for the first time, and now the distinguished guests will get baked under the sun just like the graduates and the faculty.

[The following entry, same date, was typewritten on the back cover of the Annual Athletics Award Night Dinner:]

Attended this dinner and seated near me at the Faculty Table was Mac, Chaplain Harpole, and Lou Bejarano the Librarian. After half-hour after the dinner began, the Admiral appeared in gleaming whites. Later Bejarano described it, "And there we were, sitting at the end of the day . . . tired . . . even the Cadets were somewhat rumpled . . . when suddenly appeared this apparition from Heaven . . . he looked like he had a spotlight on him."

6/21/51

Graduation Day . . . for the Class of June 1951 . . . intermittent sprinklings of rain but it looks as though the ceremonies will be held outdoors again.

Everyone is in whites (the officers, that is), and we mill around the groups of Cadets and parents returning smartly-given salutes . . . look closely at the girl friends and conclude that we are really beginning to get old . . . no definite mood among the members of the faculty, except the usual range of opinions that accompany the wearing of whites . . . some like it, and some don't.[44]

A second perspective comes from Richard O'Leary, a 1950s graduate of Maine Maritime, who, after making hundreds of crossings of the North Atlantic on the SS *United States*, signed on in 1962 as special aide to the superintendent. He recalls his unique indoctrination into the ways of the Academy:

My first day was in August. McLintock went to the opening of the lower level of the George Washington Bridge that day, so he wasn't there much in the afternoon.

The next day he came back, and he said, "I have a plan." There were two offices there, with two secretaries in between. He said, "I'm going to move you in to my office for a month. I'm going to put you on one side of me. I'll be close to the door, and mail will go through me first. And your desk will be right beside mine." This was in Chrysler's bedroom, there at the Academy. "And after that month," he continued, "I'm going to move the desk to the other side, and the mail, and the phone calls, and all are going to go to you first. And then I'm going to move you into the other office."

I was stunned by that, but we proceeded down that road. And people would come in—the dean, and various department heads, and Congressmen—and they'd see me sitting there and think, you know, "What in hell is this?" They'd kind of look at me as if expecting me to get up and go out. And he told me, "You don't go out for anyone. You just stay here."

So this went on for a month, and then he literally moved the desk to the other side. It was supposed to end in a month. And it went on for like two and a half months. And he used to love to tell me stories, read things to me, and tell me about all the difficulties, and troubles, and who the people were that in his view were bad, and who was good. And I had a wonderful time, very frankly. He really had a great sense of humor.

At the end of two months, or maybe two and a half months, he said, "Okay, I hate to do this, but I'm going to move your desk out to the other office."[45]

After three and a half years as McLintock's aide, O'Leary became commandant of midshipmen. He was assigned the job because the Regiment was in a state of relative disarray, and McLintock wanted someone he could trust in this sensitive position. O'Leary's immediate predecessor had been fired because the students had staged a boycott of Delano Hall's food, protesting against its alleged poor quality, on the same day that Supreme Court Justice William O. Douglas dined at McLintock's house. They had then called in the newspapers to tell the story: *students go hungry while bigwigs feast.* McLintock wanted no repeat performances.

O'Leary soon decided that the problem was larger than the Regiment. As he saw it, a number of factors, external and internal, were combining to undermine morale. He therefore sought ways to strike a balance between discipline—which he saw as absolutely critical—with fun, sometimes using the famously starchy McLintock as a foil.

For example, during football season, the cadets had a tradition of wearing the silliest hats they could find to lunch on the day before the big game. As they filed into Delano at 11:45 one Friday, wearing a bizarre assortment of headgear, O'Leary rushed over to McLintock's office in Wiley. There he persuaded the superintendent to don the tricorn hat that McLintock had received as a guest of honor at the New York premiere of *Mutiny on the Bounty*, and then hustled McLintock into the Delano galley, off the mess hall. O'Leary picks up the story:

> So I stashed him in the galley, and I said, "I'll give you a signal, and then you come out with that hat on."
>
> So I went in there, and they're all sitting there with their hats on, all happy before the football game the next day. I went up to the microphone, and said, "I'm sorry to have to tell you this. This is my fault, not yours, since I allowed you to wear optional headgear. But the superintendent is very, very upset about it, and he's come here to speak to you about it." And I gave him the signal, and he

came flying out with that three-cornered hat on, and the place just absolutely *exploded*, because it was such a contrast to how they viewed him.[46]

Early in his tenure as commandant, O'Leary visited the other four service academies in search of ways to improve the Regiment at Kings Point. At West Point, he learned that the plebes were kept entirely separate from the Regiment for their first several months at that academy, and they were not brought into the mainstream of regimental life until they were officially "accepted" by the upperclassmen. O'Leary implemented a similar system at Kings Point, where it persists to this day. Acceptance Day, held in September (and distinct from the formal recognition of the plebe class which occurs each spring), has emerged as a highlight of the academic year.

Reflecting the tenor of the turbulent 1960s, disciplinary problems continued on O'Leary's watch.[47] One incident in March 1967, in which a student was dismissed for organizing a mass movement of cadets to throw the regimental commander and regimental executive officer into Long Island Sound, evolved into a much-publicized court case involving academic due process. The student appealed his dismissal from the Academy through the federal court system in New York—an appeal that ultimately proved successful.[48]

O'Leary left Kings Point unexpectedly in the summer of 1968. He therefore missed the Regiment's ultimate act of rebellion against an increasingly autocratic superintendent.

Building the Academy's Chapel

One of Gordon McLintock's most visible accomplishments was a significant expansion and improvement of the Kings Point campus. The creation of the nuclear science laboratory and the conversion of Furuseth Hall have already been mentioned; in addition, a major renovation of Fulton Hall, the engineering building, took place in the early sixties, and many labs were updated and improved. Repairs to Land Hall were completed in 1962, and the waterfront was renovated in 1963.

Without a doubt, though, McLintock's most important additions to the physical landscape were Mariner's Chapel, completed in 1961, and the library, completed in 1969.

In one sense, it is amazing that it took so long for Kings Point to

An undated photo of the Academy's chapel, one of Superintendent McLintock's pet projects.

get a chapel and a library. Every year since 1945, the Congressional Board of Visitors had described these two facilities as "immediate needs" of the Academy. Congress authorized their construction in 1948, as part of the same bill that created the Academic Advisory Board. A second bill that same year authorized the Academy to accept private funds to assist in the construction of the buildings. This speaks to the central problem: there was simply no money available for new construction, especially in the lean years of the 1950s.

McLintock decided to tackle the chapel first. In the 1949 report to the Congressional Board of Visitors, he wrote that "an active program for the solicitation of funds for the Chapel is under way," and added that a nationwide committee of prominent individuals would soon be appointed to help with the fund-raising.[49]

But private donations came slowly. Admiral Richard McNulty,

McLintock's disaffected predecessor, was named national secretary of the committee down in Washington. By November 1950, Telfair Knight had to report to the acting chief of maritime operations that only $78,234 of the $500,000 goal had been raised by the committee. Knight stated bluntly that he didn't think much more money would be forthcoming unless "forceful action" was taken.[50]

In 1951, after another unproductive year had gone by, the Academy hired a professional fund-raising consultancy to help with the project. McNulty had left MARAD by this time, and was replaced as national secretary of the campaign by McLintock himself. General John M. Franklin, president of U.S. Lines, agreed to head the National Committee. Within a year, the campaign was more than halfway completed. Donated funds had reached $263,000, more than $27,000 of which, McLintock pointed out proudly, had been raised at the Academy. The largest individual contribution was $15,000 received from Academy neighbor Alfred P. Sloan; the smallest, 25 cents, was sent in by a twelve-year-old boy in California who saw a televised interview with McLintock.[51] Much of the success of this phase of the fund-raising effort was later credited to McLintock's wife, Wynne, who was a favorite both on campus and among Long Island's well-heeled social elite. Wynne frequently took over the Academy gymnasium to hold large bridge/whist parties to raise funds for the chapel (one such event raised $3,500), and also hosted formal balls at the Waldorf-Astoria.[52] Wynne left another lasting legacy at Kings Point in the writing of the "Cadet's Prayer," which is still recited today.[53]

The flow of donations again slowed in the mid-1950s, with 1955 seeing an inflow of only $6,000. But renewed efforts by the McLintocks in the later 1950s paid off, and by 1959 (thanks in part to a timely $100,000 contribution from the

Wynne McLintock, wife of Superintendent Gordon McLintock, was a well-loved figure at the Academy.

government to cover the interior furnishings) adequate funds were finally in hand to begin construction. But costs continued to climb—the final cost of the chapel totaled roughly $680,000—so fund-raising continued throughout the construction phase.

Groundbreaking for the chapel took place in the fall of 1959, and the building—designed by Eggers and Higgins, also designers of the National Gallery of Art in Washington—was expected to be completed by May 1960, in time for the first-class cadets to graduate from the chapel. Problems with the clay subsoil, however, necessitated additional foundation supports, leading to delays. Almost a year behind schedule—and, arguably, almost two decades overdue—the chapel was dedicated on May 1, 1961.

On that early spring day, the five-hundred-seat interfaith chapel glowed with golden light from Long Island Sound. The interior had been furnished through the special congressional appropriation, on a motion by Representative Keogh, and the new pews gleamed white, with freshly varnished mahogany trim. The interfaith altar contained an automatic turntable mechanism to allow rotation between the Catholic, Protestant, and Jewish altars. In the cupola, 102 feet above sea level, a 1,200-candlepower light served as a beacon for vessels plying the upper East River and Long Island Sound, and was added as a navigation aid on government charts. John F. Kennedy, the recently inaugurated president, sent greetings to the assembled dignitaries: "Our nation has ever sought divine guidance in its hours of thanksgiving and its moments of peril. On the high seas, between heaven and the deep, men of all faiths feel a sense of brotherhood with the infinite. May this Chapel ever inspire those who pause here to dedicate themselves to the service of their fellow men."[54]

Every detail of the interior reflected the specific purpose of the chapel. The imposing wooden lectern was a gift from the Maritime Board of Great Britain, and the reading platform was from the deck of the British Merchant Navy training ship the HMS *Conway*. The Catholic tabernacle portrayed a nautical motif, and the menorah on the Jewish altar had a dolphin base.[55] The chapel also paid tribute to the dead; a large book in a pedestal case near the front altar reminded the reader to "Tell America," and contained the names of every U.S. merchant mariner killed in the First and Second World Wars.[56] To this day, a page in the volume is turned each morning by the midshipman officer of the day.

Another Victory, and a Gaffe

Despite the repeated assertions by the Congressional Board of Visitors and the Academic Advisory Board about the necessity of an adequate library at Kings Point, it took even longer to break ground on a library building. Not until April 1967, almost a quarter-century after the founding of the campus, was the student newspaper finally able to report that the new library facility was finally "on the way up."[57]

This welcome news followed years of debate about the best way to solve the library challenge. In 1960, the Academy made plans to purchase the neighboring Barstow Estate to house a new library and officers' quarters. Later that same year, however, the Maritime Administration decided that it didn't have the necessary funds to complete the purchase, and the plan was put on hold. The estate was purchased by the Alumni Association's Alumni Fund almost fifteen years later, but by then, other plans had been suggested for the library.

The next library plan suggested the conversion of Wiley Hall, the former Chrysler mansion, which had housed the administrative offices of the Academy since its founding. A structural study of the building was completed in May 1961, and concluded that although the floors would need reinforcement, it was possible to convert Wiley to a library while retaining some administrative offices in the building. But the appeal of this solution was entirely financial, and when it looked like additional funds might become available in 1962, the conversion plan was abandoned.

The promised funds did not materialize until 1964, when Congress finally authorized $750,000 for construction of a new library for Kings Point. (An additional $250,000 for furnishings was promised once construction was under way.) The library—like the chapel, designed by the architectural firm of Eggers and Higgins—was conceived as a three-story structure (counting its basement) to be erected between Fulton and Bowditch, and providing space for more than a hundred thousand volumes and three hundred occupants. And like the chapel, the library experienced cost overruns; by the time McLintock's shovel turned over the first sod on the site, the estimated cost of the project had risen to $787,100. Unlike the chapel, however, the new library, a Modernist concrete structure, represented an aesthetic departure for the Academy. *Hear This* described the new building as "completely contemporary, inside and out."[58]

The completion of the library should have represented a personal triumph for McLintock and librarian Everett H. Northrop. Instead, largely as a result of McLintock's autocratic impulses, it sparked an unnecessary power struggle with Washington. McLintock had decided that his new building should be named after Richard Henry Dana Jr., author of the classic *Two Years Before the Mast: A Personal Narrative of Life at Sea*. Without pausing to run the idea by his superiors in Washington, McLintock had Dana's name carved in the concrete lintel above the library's main entrance.

MARAD, meanwhile, had its own idea about whom the new library should honor: Schuyler Otis Bland, chairman of the House Merchant Marine and Fisheries Committee during the founding years of the Academy, and longtime friend and supporter in Congress of both MARAD and the Academy. (Bland had also helped secure government funds for the library.) When MARAD forwarded its decision to McLintock, he pointed out that he had already carved Dana's name in the building. Maritime Administrator Andrew Gibson, incensed by McLintock's high-handed ways, ordered him to *keep carving*.[59] The names of noted maritime authors Jack London and Herman Melville were then carved into the concrete lintel to conceal McLintock's gaffe, and a brass plaque by the front entrance proclaimed the building Bland Library.

A Legend Departs

Inevitably, Gordon McLintock became an anachronism. As his twenty-two-year superintendency stretched on, details of the Academy community began to escape his notice and his grasp.

Meanwhile, the world was changing, too, and McLintock proved ill equipped to deal with the new landscape. The 1960s were a decade of protest and turmoil on college campuses throughout the United States (notably at nearby Columbia University, where protests attracted local and national media attention), with students defying authority, demanding more control over their lives, and, increasingly, an end to U.S. involvement in the Vietnam War. The Academy was not immune to these trends. The cadets wanted more freedom, more openness, and more privileges, but McLintock either didn't hear these grumblings or chose not to respond to them.

The departure of Commandant Richard O'Leary in 1968 forced McLintock back into the fray. Once again, the Regiment got restive. In December of that year, McLintock wrote the midshipmen a letter, asking them to assist him in strengthening communication on campus, and to bring into the open any grievances contributing to "a disquiet-ing undercurrent of discontent and unhappiness within the Regi-ment."[60] What McLintock expected in response to this overture was unclear, but it was almost certainly not what he received.

A month later, in January 1969, the Regiment submitted a unan-imous and extraordinary eighty-page document, dubbed the White Paper, that recounted in great detail numerous and specific complaints of the Regiment against the system under which they lived, and also against the administration. The document's introduction set a com-bative tone: "To a man, the Regiment is dissatisfied with the system-ized absurdity under which we live. The medieval logic with which each of us is treated cannot be allowed to continue; the continued existence of the present atmosphere at this institution can, in fact, lead only to a more widespread dissent with a patently intolerable situation."[61]

But the White Paper also displayed the desire to offer *constructive* criticism; the cadets specifically stated in the introduction that, rather than a litany of complaints, their missive represented "a sincere attempt on the part of the men who live under this System to define its myriad defects and to delineate some means of correcting them."[62]

The cadets argued that their needs had been subordinated to those of the administration. Specific complaints addressed an allegedly excessive course load, deficiencies in the regimental system, an ineffec-tive class system, a lack of respect for the views of the midshipmen concerning the Academy's facilities, a lack of transparency concerning the disbursement of the fees paid by the cadets, and the limited role and powers of the Midshipman Council. More mundane complaints also were discussed in detail. For example, the Regiment objected to one of McLintock's favorite dress requirements: the paper collar. These collars—stiff, hot, and uncomfortable—had long since gone out of fashion, but McLintock required their use because he felt they gave the Regiment a sharper appearance.

These complaints must be viewed in the larger context of student unrest, the worst of which was yet to come. But the manifesto must have been a stunning blow to McLintock, who thought himself a skilled ship's master, in close touch with his crew. According to Paul Krinsky, who had become assistant dean in 1965, it was doubly hard because McLintock was by this time thoroughly identified with the

Academy, at least in his own mind: "The Academy became Gordon McLintock, and vice versa."[63]

McLintock's response to the cadets' complaints was immediate, and surprisingly conciliatory. He agreed to install student representatives on all committees studying matters concerning midshipmen. In fact, he acquiesced to many of the demands made by the midshipmen, and he agreed to establish committees to study other complaints. Though he did not directly address the heavy course load, the cadets won major concessions related to their other complaints.[64] Paper collars, still sacrosanct, were not mentioned.

Maybe this small rebellion was the last straw for MARAD. Maybe this new evidence that the superintendent's grasp was slipping, combined with the embarrassment of the library squabble, added on to the many battles of previous years, finally persuaded MARAD to act. Maybe the fact that McLintock's beloved wife Wynne was ailing made him less inclined to continue his long struggle to retain power. "He really didn't mind leaving at that point," says longtime colleague Lauren McCready. "He told me, 'You know, Mac, I should have left long ago, because without Wynne there helping me, it's all hollow.'"[65]

In the spring of 1970, Maritime Administrator Andrew Gibson approached McLintock with a deal: in return for a third star as vice admiral, McLintock would retire and leave the Academy. McLintock agreed, and after graduation in June 1970, his long-anticipated departure became a reality.

By all accounts, he left behind an imprint that few others could claim or hope to match.

8

Widening the Scope
1970–1980

Under the warm midmorning sun on June 20, 1970, the Regiment of the United States Merchant Marine Academy stood at parade rest in Barney Square, most eyes fixed on the spectacle before them. They wore dress whites, from their shoes up to their caps, and stood almost motionless. The occasional movement of a white hat or a white-clad body, though, reinforced the impression of a vast sea of white—a sea that was calm now, but might not always be so calm.

Before them, close to the enormous flagpole that dominated the center of the campus, stood a much smaller group: the Academy's commanding officers. And their eyes, in turn, were fixed on the imposing figure of newly commissioned Vice Admiral George Gordon McLintock, addressing the Regiment for the last time as superintendent of the Academy. McLintock's twenty-two-year reign was coming to a close, and a new era was beginning.

Admiral McLintock concluded his brief remarks, read his orders, and cleared his throat. Then, in the crisp tones of his English-accented voice—his command voice—he addressed his assistant superintendent, Victor E. Tyson, '43. "Captain Tyson," he intoned, "haul down my flag." On this cue, an honor guard rendered a fifteen-gun salute.[1] The officers standing before the Regiment saluted, and upon the sounding of the last gun, slowly lowered the admiral's flag from above Wiley Hall. The blue flag with the three stars, denoting McLintock's vice

211

admiral's rank, continued to snap in the breeze during its final descent, as if reluctant to relinquish its position of authority.

As McLintock's flag was being folded, Captain Tyson stepped forward to the microphone and introduced a somewhat less imposing man standing to the right of Admiral McLintock: Rear Admiral Arthur B. Engel.

Engel was a 1938 graduate of the Coast Guard Academy, who had worked his way up through the ranks to become superintendent of that sister academy in New London. He also had been the head of the Department of Applied Science and Engineering in New London for four years, and later commanded the Coast Guard Yard at

An official portrait of Rear Admiral Arthur B. Engel, the fifth superintendent of the USMMA.

Curtis Bay, Maryland. Now he was to succeed McLintock, and thus become the first person ever to head two federal service academies.

Later, word would circulate that he had not been Maritime Administrator Andrew Gibson's first choice for the Academy post. (The preferred candidate had taken another position at the last moment, forcing Gibson to resort to his backup candidate.) But for the moment, Engel's qualifications for his new job seemed unassailable, and on this beautiful day, at the turn of the season from spring to summer, anything seemed possible.

The Academy community had more concrete reasons for optimism as well. Many in the Regiment and the alumni population had grown disillusioned with McLintock; now, their hopes for positive change had been rekindled by an article the previous week in *Newsday*, which noted that Engel voluntarily had instituted at the Coast Guard Academy many of the same reforms and privileges demanded by the Merchant Marine Academy's midshipmen in their 1969 White Paper.[2] Faculty members, too, were intrigued; they had taken comfort from Engel's comments in the same article about the need to increase the number of electives at the Academy.

Admiral Engel stepped forward to the microphone, and read his orders. Then he executed a right face while McLintock turned 90 degrees to the left, so that the two men wound up facing the Regiment. Admiral Engel raised his hand in a stiff salute and proclaimed, "I relieve you, sir."

"I stand relieved," McLintock replied.

Engel turned back to the microphone. Now it was his turn to address the assistant superintendent: "Captain Tyson, break out my flag."

At these words, Tyson turned to the regimental commander and asked him to order the Regiment to present arms. The honor guard then executed a thirteen-gun salute. Upon the report of the first gun, Admiral Engel's flag began its ascent up the Wiley Hall flagpole. Engel, who had been holding McLintock's flag, now turned to the retiring admiral and handed it to him. Then he turned to the Regiment and spoke briefly on the theme of a new day.

It *was* a new day, in a new season, and in a new decade. The Regiment, as noted, was ready to welcome new leadership. The faculty was eager for better communication, more input, and a leader who would strengthen the Academy academically. Engel, for his part, had enjoyed his tenure at the Coast Guard Academy. He looked forward to enjoying the same kind of success at this new Academy.

A Confrontation and Its Aftermath

The aura of order and calm on that June morning was deceptive. In truth, Engel was taking over a school that very recently had been plunged into turmoil. The backdrop, as on so many other college campuses across the country, was the Vietnam War, which was sparking disagreement and dissension even at normally conservative Kings Point. Events came to a head in May 1970, after a group of Ohio National Guardsmen opened fire on student protesters at Kent State University and killed four of them. Across the nation, students stalked out of classrooms, boycotted final exams, and demonstrated against the government's actions.

At the Academy, students were preparing to march in the Armed Forces Day Parade, scheduled for May 16 in New York City. Admiral McLintock believed strongly that his school should be represented in the parade—and, of course, he liked few things better than a day of military pomp and pageantry.

To those students at the Academy who were strongly opposed to the Vietnam War, this seemed an insult to the memory of the students who had died at Kent State. The dissident group met in the week before the parade, drew up, and signed a defiant petition. "It is our intent," read the petition, "not to march in the Armed Forces Day Parade as a symbol of support for a military action we deplore. It is our patriotic duty as Americans and midshipmen in the U.S. Naval Reserve to display and dramatize our opposition to the war and the recent expansion into Cambodia."[3]

This action was a direct challenge, and most Academy administrators—up to and including the formidable Admiral McLintock—took it as such. (One exception, according to the student newspaper, was Assistant Dean Paul Krinsky, who "showed some understanding of the cause."[4]) After consulting with Maritime Administrator Gibson,[5] McLintock presented the petitioners with three choices: "*Remove your name from the petition, submit your resignation from the Academy, or anticipate dismissal on May 19.*" And, McLintock added pointedly, "*be fully prepared to represent your Academy in the Armed Forces Day Parade.*"

At the regimental review marking the silver anniversary of the Academy, September 30, 1968, Acting Maritime Administrator James Gulick presents the Vietnam Service Ribbon to Midshipman Michael J. Ehrmann, Superintendent McLintock stands to the right.

The protest imploded. All but one of the students backed down immediately, thereby avoiding dismissal, and the Regiment paraded down the streets of Manhattan without incident. But the superintendent's swift and decisive action failed to defuse the highly emotional issue. The next development in this unhappy episode came from an unexpected quarter when a vigilante group decided to take matters into its own hands. One evening in the week following the parade, several of the midshipmen who had signed the petition were sent forged notices instructing them to report to the gatehouse. Upon their arrival, they were seized by masked midshipmen, and their heads were shoved into mailbags. Though some were able to escape, several others were taken to the boathouse, where they were allegedly struck, and later had their heads shaved.

The original actions of the petitioners had caused some discord in the Regiment. The actions of the vigilantes, however, sparked a furious response from the rest of the student body, a fury exacerbated by allegations that certain faculty members knew who the perpetrators were and were shielding them.

Faced with an unprecedented uproar, as well as clear evidence of violations of civil rights, Academy administrators saw no choice but to bring the FBI onto campus—a singular event in Academy history. Eventually, the members of the vigilante group were punished (with twenty-five demerits and, for implicated members of the first class, exclusion from graduation ceremonies), and the Academy began to settle back into its accustomed routines. But it was a strange and sad ending to Gordon McLintock's long tenure as superintendent, and an inauspicious prelude to the Engel era.

Under the Microscope

Engel, of course, was aware of this backdrop, and, as his comments to *Newsday* indicate, he also knew that changes were needed in the intellectual life at the Academy. One of his first actions as superintendent, therefore, was to recruit outside expertise to help him understand the institution that he now led. Arthur Thompson, dean of Boston University's Department of Engineering, was retained by MARAD in 1971 to conduct a comprehensive study of the Academy.

Thompson studied the curriculum, academic departments, faculty, administration, and culture of the Academy. His report, completed in

July 1971, provided a comprehensive picture of the Academy's strengths and struggles. One of the first subjects of his report was the Academy's mission statement, which between 1970 and 1971 changed in several small but significant ways. A comparison of the two statements—especially in their first, second, and fourth goals—makes the point:

Mission, 1970–71 catalogue

To attract a high type of young American with a definite ambition to become an officer in the U.S. Merchant Marine;

To impart to him the necessary academic background and the fundamentals of a practical nautical education essential to a successful career at sea;

To develop in him a high sense of honor, uprightness, and loyalty;

To instill in him a pride in his profession, and a determination to uphold the traditions of the Merchant Marine; and

By effective teaching, training, and guidance, to send him forth to his calling with a deep respect and affection for the USMMA and its Regiment of Midshipmen.

Mission, 1971–72 catalogue

To graduate an outstanding young American with a definite ambition to serve as a leader in the U.S. Maritime industry;

To impart to him the necessary academic background and the fundamentals of a nautical and military education essential to a successful maritime career;

To develop in him a high sense of honor, uprightness, and loyalty;

To instill in him a pride in his profession, and a determination to uphold the traditions of our Maritime heritage; and

By effective teaching, training, and guidance, to send him forth to his calling with a deep respect and affection for the USMMA and its corps.[6]

The subtle changes in wording addressed the decades-old tension between professional training and a broad-gauge education, and they clearly pushed in the direction of a broader focus. Officer training, for thirty years the primary focus of the Academy, no longer even appeared directly in the mission statement. The "Merchant Marine," moreover, had been supplanted by the "maritime industry."

Midshipmen get some valuable experience at sea on the bridge of the TV *Kings Pointer* in November 1974.

This shift had been in the making for some time, and Dean Thompson had nothing but praise for it. He recommended that "the new statement of mission should be on the desk of every faculty member so that what he does individually, and what he does collectively, as a faculty, may bring early realization of these goals."[7]

Although he was an academic without any military background, Thompson commented on the regimental system and its effect on intellectual life at the Academy. Drawing on interviews with the Command Board and the Midshipman Council–a student elected board established in 1965 to enable student input on matters of policy, but with little practical impact–Thompson lamented what he saw as a culture of "anti-intellectualism" among the students:

> It's very interesting, and most reassuring, that the students want learning. They so fiercely want to be proud–intellectually proud–of Kings Point. I spoke with the Command Board and the Midshipman Council separately. Though they had different perceptions on some issues, on one they were quite together–they wanted to be proud of their learning, their faculty–some they are proud of, some not. But basically they admitted to an anti-intellectual climate.

"If it's not due tomorrow, it's not due."

"If it can't be ponied, it can't be done."

"A student who takes his studies seriously is a curve-breaker, or a pimp."[8]

Thompson suggested several possible explanations for this counterproductive climate, including the regimental organization, the students' heavy course load, the faculty's heavy teaching load, the traditions of keeping the faculty in uniform and using them as counselors, and–predictably–the balance between vocational training and academics. On each of these points, the report offered recommendations to counter the alleged anti-intellectualism, including lowering the credit load for students; allowing one semester each year free from teaching for the faculty; putting faculty in civilian clothing; hiring a full-time director of counseling for the school; and placing increasing emphasis on the school as an institution of higher learning as well as a vocational school.

Thompson also advocated a better integration of the academic and regimental worlds within the Academy. His comments reflect what he perceived to be a deep divide between the two areas:

> What I observe at the regimental-academic interface is that the functions are quite bifurcated. I had two meals with the students, I saw no faculty there. I'm told they rarely come. One faculty member told me that the flagpole divides the campus–academics on one side, the Regiment on the other. The day divides also–after 3 or 4 p.m., it's predominately regimental. I note that no regimental officer sits with the Academic Board, that no faculty member sits with regimental officers on their committees.[9]

Thompson stopped short of either condemning the regimental system or endorsing it in its then-current incarnation. He stressed that he could see no reason why a regimental system per se should impair the learning environment, and suggested that regimentation could very well enhance learning. The problem, he asserted, was that the two "sides of the campus" were not working together to create the best possible learning experience. His prescription: ensure that each discipline understands and complements what the other is doing. Mutual appreciation and coordination, he concluded, would lead to a far more effective realization of the Academy's mission.

Expanding the Scope

On the academic side, the Thompson Report recommended exploring two thorny academic areas for the Academy—accreditation of the engineering program and the establishment of academic majors. These were two very distinct directions. To those with an understanding of realities at the Academy, they may have appeared mutually exclusive. How could the school enhance its engineering offerings sufficiently to earn program accreditation, and at the same time broaden its general education base enough to offer academic majors beyond the traditional "deck" and "engine" specializations? And how could the already overworked students at the Academy be asked to take on *more* academic responsibilities?

The report didn't attempt to offer a simple solution for this dilemma and, as noted above, it acknowledged that the student workload was already heavy. But Thompson expressed the firm conviction that the Academy had to deliver on its double-pronged responsibility—professional education *and* academic education. He added, pointedly, that the U.S. Air Force Academy, the Naval Academy, and the Naval Postgraduate School all had accredited engineering programs. Why couldn't the Merchant Marine Academy succeed in this realm, just like its sister academies?

Engineering accreditation, as Thompson saw it, would not be a huge stretch for Kings Point. Quantitatively, the Academy's program, which required 212 quarter credits, already was close to Engineers' Council for Professional Development (ECPD) requirements for accreditation. With the addition of some upper-level courses in the senior year, including engineering design, analysis, and synthesis,[10] and with some attention to the flow of the curriculum throughout the four years, the Academy could achieve engineering accreditation with relative ease.

Academic majors would pose a far greater challenge. As Thompson pointed out, however, the Academy had already taken the first crucial steps toward the establishment of elective programs. Engineering electives had been offered at the Academy since the first foray into nuclear engineering in the late 1950s; in the 1960s, midshipman interest in general electives had grown, and courses were offered in management, accounting, psychology, and the humanities. But these courses could only be taken as an overload—that is, on top of the already full course of study required for the deck or engine major. The midshipmen objected vociferously to this state of affairs, and in response, Dean Janus Poppe established an electives committee in 1969, with midshipman representation. The committee recommended that space be made in the schedule for electives, and in 1970, the curriculum committee responded by reducing the number of quarter hours required for graduation. This action freed up twenty-one quarter hours of electives for deck midshipmen, and eighteen quarter hours for engine midshipmen.[11]

Thompson suggested expanding this program, and allowing it to lead naturally to majors beyond the "license" departments. "Granted," Thompson wrote, "it is implicit in the training of the student at Kings Point that he should be prepared for the Coast Guard exam." But, he continued, "if licensing were the single objective of Kings Point, the students are overtrained, the baccalaureate unnecessary."[12]

In these assertions, Thompson was alluding to the decades-old debate about the real purpose of the Academy: If this is only a vocational school, the Academy should do less. But if this is a school with an intellectual agenda, it must continue to broaden its offerings.

Academic Minors Come to Kings Point

Even as Thompson was preparing his 1971 report, the elective program at the Academy was expanding. At that point, the school offered sequential elective programs in oceanography, nuclear engineering, engineering science, math for science and technology, math for management, chemistry, management, transportation administration, English and comparative literature, and history and civilization.[13] By 1973, the course catalog listed ninety-eight electives.

The newfound breadth of instruction produced at least one casualty: the decades-old tradition of cadets marching to all their classes together. As Walter Gunn, a 1959 graduate who returned to the Academy as assistant academic dean in 1972, remarked upon this small but symbolic change, "One side-effect of the elective courses is that marching to class, for all but underclassmen, is now an impossibility, since the number of combinations of required courses and the ninety-eight electives is enough to boggle one's mind, much less allow stable sections like the ones with which you used to 'hup' around."[14]

The sequential electives program was upgraded to a formal minors program in the 1972–1973 school year. That first year, thirty midshipmen graduated with a minor; by the following year, this

Four students, soon to become plebes, gather at the front gate of the Academy in 1970.

number had doubled. In 1975, the number reached an even hundred, where it would stay for the next several years. The most popular minors were management, nuclear engineering, small vessel operations, marine machinery design, and law.

Computer science also emerged as a significant part of the curriculum during this decade. Professor Walter McDonald had introduced computers to the Engineering Department in 1968, arranging for time-sharing services from General Electric, and organizing informal after-hours computer classes for interested faculty and students.[15] In 1972, Gunn noted that computer science had been integrated into the curriculum for the fourth class year. "The Office of Computer Science," reported Gunn proudly, "now sports a 1004 computer and eight tele-types tied into a time-sharing computer facility by direct telephone lines."[16] Elective courses involving computers were also introduced; in February 1979, the Department of Maritime Law and Economics, in cooperation with Marine Management Systems, offered a new experi-mental course called Marine Management Planning, aimed at teaching the "methodology of applying modern computer techniques and pro-grams to the solution of managerial problems in the maritime industry."[17]

One group of students couldn't take advantage of the minor pro-gram—or even of individual electives. With an estimated 20 percent overload in coursework,[18] the cadets aiming for dual certification in engine and deck (the so-called "dualies") barely had time to fit in the required courses, much less make room for optional classes. The dual program was adjusted in the early seventies to reduce this workload, but its heavy required course load still precluded any extra elective courses. For this reason, Thompson in his report questioned the pro-gram, and this criticism, among others, continued to dog the dual pro-gram in subsequent years.

The Faculty Matures

Thompson's examination of the Academy faculty spotlighted the insti-tution's ongoing commitment to self-improvement. The era of the old "sea dogs," hired during wartime to teach specific practical skills, was gradually coming to a close. By 1970, more than half of the faculty held master's degrees, and more than one-fifth held doctorates. An additional nineteen faculty members, noted Thompson, were then pursuing their doctoral degrees.

This upgrading had been in process for years. Engineering profes-sor Maurice Gross, for example, received a master's degree in mechan-ical engineering in 1955, after years of taking night courses at New York University. And in 1962, electrical engineering faculty head Charles Hubert was given six months' leave to pursue graduate studies in elec-trical engineering at the Polytechnic Institute of Brooklyn. This, as Hubert recalls, was the origin of the Academy's sabbatical program:

> That's when they finally got around to granting sabbaticals. Now, the
> way that came about was, I wrote a letter to [engineering department

head] Lauren McCready to tell him that I would like to do some further study in the electrical field. I went to night school, but going to night school, it's hard to accomplish much. It's very slow. So they gave me six months off to go back to school, which was very interesting. You know, you hear all the complaints that faculty have about the administration—and I've had plenty of complaints, also—but the administration does at times do some good things.[19]

Lauren McCready, too, got the benefit of additional education. He remembers making a weekly trek with colleague Moses Hirschkowitz to the same Polytechnic Institute, as both pursued doctorates in the history of science. Though this PhD program folded before they were able to earn their degrees, both men received additional master's degrees.

As Hirschkowitz recalls this interlude, their return to school was undertaken partly to satisfy Washington, which was clamoring for more advanced degrees among the Kings Point faculty. But for Hirschkowitz, a member of the curriculum committee, the PhD program also provided him and McCready with an opportunity to think about science from a nonengineering standpoint. This was a crucial ability, Hirschkowitz believed, given that one of the Academy's key challenges was figuring out how to sell its program to nonengineers.[20] In this group, Hirschkowitz explains, were not only students but the nonengineering faculty:

> One time, for example, the members of the curriculum committee were going to cut out some of the time allocated to a very important course in engineering. One of the fellows on that committee was a wrestling coach, whose name was Clem [Stralka]. And Clem said, "Why do you have to know that?" And I said, "Clem, when you teach your students a certain way to grip an arm, our course will tell you why that works."[21]

Another side benefit to the weekly excursions to Brooklyn, recalls Hirschkowitz, was the opportunity to sit in a car with Lauren McCready for two hours—an hour going into Brooklyn, and an hour coming back—discussing and solving the problems of the universe. Hirschkowitz later claimed that he learned as much from these conversations as he did from the degree program.

Thompson praised the Academy for its commitment to increasing the percentage of its faculty holding advanced degrees, and he also pushed for a continuing upgrading, especially as the school moved toward academic majors, engineering accreditation, and graduate programs. His report highlighted an interesting opportunity that had its roots in the Academy's massive wartime expansion. Nearly half of the Academy's faculty, Thompson noted, had been at the institution more than twenty years. Many were now approaching retirement, and a large number of replacement faculty members would have to be recruited more or less simultaneously. Thompson urged the administration to use this historical accident to the institution's advantage, continuing to upgrade the faculty, and placing increasing emphasis on the PhD as a requirement for entering faculty.

Paul Krinsky, who had been appointed assistant dean in 1965 and was promoted to acting dean in 1972 and academic dean in 1973, took this responsibility seriously. Over the next decade, Krinsky had the opportunity to bring in three new department heads: Gerald P. Francis in engineering, Lawrence Ferrari in math and science, and Clark Reynolds in humanities. As Krinsky explains it, these three "pedigreed" scholars (all with PhDs) helped the Academy make the transition to a more academic culture:

> You know, my own academic background had been at Kings Point. I had tried to keep abreast. I had attended conferences, and things like that. But these three, all of whom came from academe, opened a window on this new world. They had a completely different vision of how the academic process worked.
>
> That helped us to, number one, modernize some of the academic procedures. It led indirectly to more faculty involvement in the governance process. It also lent support to the notion that your faculty should be credentialed–highly credentialed.
>
> So for the first time, we had some support at the department level for hiring new people with the proper credentials, and to be a little harder on promotion criteria, and retention criteria. Tenure is not an easy thing to deal with. But when it came to promotions, you could sweat people a little bit, and make them produce a little bit more. All of that changed the faculty culture, and those three people–Francis, Ferrari, and Reynolds–were key to this. I learned a tremendous amount from them.
>
> Two of them in particular, Clark Reynolds and Jerry Francis,

took on the Academy culture. Not in the sense of a confrontation. They melded in. They fit in. They developed a real affection for the way the place worked, without being co-opted by our history and traditions. And in this particular period, that was very important.[22]

As Krinsky points out, recruiting agents of change to serve as department heads was a way to overcome tradition and break the mold. Kings Point department heads traditionally had been tough on the promotions side; now, the institution was signaling, they were going to be equally tough on the recruitment side. And although none of these three change agents stayed long at the Academy, their impact was felt for many years afterward.

Wrestling with a Research Center

Another manifestation of the Academy's increasing emphasis on academics was the National Maritime Research Center (NMRC), a program initiated and supported by Andrew Gibson and Marvin Pitkin, respectively, the Maritime administrator and MARAD'S director of research. The seeds for this venture were planted in July 1969, when Gibson and Pitkin organized an industrywide conference at Woods Hole, Massachusetts. The conference—which took place, coincidentally, during the week of Neil Armstrong's July 20 walk on the moon—included workshops and panels on a wide range of industry topics. One of these topics was the role of Kings Point in the modern era, so the Academy's administration and faculty were well represented at Woods Hole.

The real action took place at the clambake at the end of the conference. As Lauren McCready later recalled:

> Gibson arrives [at the clambake]. He was a graduate of the old *Nantucket*—a tough man, and smart. So he drags me aside, and that was the closest thing to a kick in the pants I was ever given. He grabs me, and says, "Listen, you guys at Kings Point—wake up! Understand? You're asleep down there. You're doing nothing."
>
> I muttered something in response. Then he said, "Look, I'll give you some money. You team up with Webb Institute, and start some research." And he gave us about $90,000. So the command at the clambake was, "*Do* something. Wake up and start research." To which I said, "Yes, sir."[23]

McCready submitted a list of projects that the NMRC would undertake—a list that Pitkin approved in its entirety—and waited for further developments. At this point, though, the process began to bog down. Gibson had no authority to hire incremental bodies for the new research program, so to staff it, he had to shift around existing billets within MARAD. One very logical place to find such slots, of course, was the Academy itself. But Gibson's suggestion to shift six existing Academy billets to the new NMRC, according to McCready, raised hackles, particularly with Superintendent Engel. "We had an Academy affair at the club one afternoon," McCready explained. "Here I am drifting through the open door, and here's Engel, and he puts his fingers right in my face, like that. He says, 'You're not getting those six billets!' Just like that. Well, that was very rude and unmannerly. But eventually, the climax was that I *did* get the six."[24]

But another problem soon surfaced, and this lay in the Kings Point faculty itself. McCready found himself energized by the challenge that Gibson had thrown down before him, seeing research as a "lofty pursuit," but many of his colleagues responded differently. "The first shock," he recalls, "was that they didn't care." So even as he was fighting for his billets, McCready also was fighting to get people interested.

Gibson had settled on McCready because the longtime head of the engineering department was charismatic and persuasive, as well as intellectually curious. If anybody could motivate the Kings Point faculty to venture in new directions, it was McCready. And in short order, McCready assembled a formidable team, including Acting Assistant Dean Harold Katz, Assistant Head of Engineering Clifford Sandberg, Engineering Professor Stanley Wheatley (who later succeeded McCready as head of the NMRC), and Engineering Professor H. O. Travis. McCready himself eventually left the Engineering Department to concentrate full time on the research center.

A second and related program began in January 1972, this time aimed at involving the school's most capable students in research. The top twelve students in the first class were invited to participate in the Kings Point Scholar Program, and four cadets accepted the invitation. These four completed research reports on the "problems and potentials of importing large volumes of Liquefied Natural Gas into the U.S,"[25] and were granted twelve credits for their work.

But the crown jewel of the NMRC was the Computer Aided Operations Research Facility (CAORF), completed in 1976. Built by the Sperry Piedmont Company and housed in a specially constructed wing of Samuels Hall, CAORF was a state-of-the-art marine simulator. Simply put, the simulator consisted of a ship's bridge and a curved screen, with computer-driven projectors above the bridge projecting a scene onto the screen. If someone on the bridge turned the wheel to the right, the scene shifted to the left. Beginning as a relatively limited visual arc, the CAORF simulator ultimately expanded to a 240-degree view, with full-color imagery of multiple ports and waterways programmed into the system. In an enthusiastic review in a 1976 edition of the alumni-oriented *Kings Pointer*, John Manning, '59, reported:

> Bridge equipment can be changed easily to meet the requirements of a given experiment. There is a gyro pilot control panel and helm unit which, via the control computer, drives the indicators of rudder angle, heading, and rate of turn. There are true motion and relative motion radars, a variety of communications systems, and throttle control either from the bridge or via telegraph to the "engine room."[26]

The CAORF simulator provided a safe and cost-effective way to study issues like shiphandling and navigation, bridge equipment design, and harbor design. It was originally conceived as a research tool. In subsequent years, however, Academy faculty members found ways to put the simulator to work as a very effective bridge management teaching tool. By so doing, they guaranteed that the simulator would continue to receive infusions of money for periodic upgrade.

This makes an important point about innovation—at Kings Point, and also farther afield. In retrospect, the NMRC must be judged a noble failure in that it never attained the stature hoped for by Gibson, McCready, and its other dedicated promoters. "We didn't have the horsepower," explained Paul Krinsky. "We were ill-equipped to do this as a faculty." And, over time, as Krinsky further explained, the NMRC became increasingly disassociated from the Kings Point mainstream:

> See, they had a big research and development group in MARAD. And the R&D group at Kings Point was not part of Kings Point; it was part of MARAD. I believe that some of them came over from the NS *Savannah* project.
>
>   In any case, this all operated as a separate entity, with the Academy being the landlord. They were entrepreneurs, in addition to being

engineers, and whatever. Their vision was, "Hey, we're going to take this thing, and we're going to the *moon* with it." But this was another source of great friction between them and us, because in fact, we never really did play a role with it. We provided paper clips, and janitorial services, and were always being blamed for not helping—but they were always seeking out tasks that we couldn't possibly help with.

On the other hand, the offspring of the NMRC enjoyed unanticipated successes on the local level. In the late 1970s, for example, CAORF helped the Academy meet new and more stringent training regulations put in place by the Coast Guard (which in turn was implementing the requirements of the international maritime governing body, the UN-related Intergovernmental Maritime Consultative Organization, or IMCO). As it turned out, training midshipmen on the CAORF simulator allowed the Academy to meet increased requirements for sea experience, without actually increasing the amount of time that midshipmen spent at sea. Although Andrew Gibson's vision of a world-class maritime research facility at Kings Point was not realized, other benefits accrued to the Academy and justified the investments that he and others had made in that vision.

Diversity Comes to the Academy

A central characteristic of the Merchant Marine Academy, one that it shares with the other four federal academies, is that it is ultimately a creature of the federal government. The story of the NMRC makes this point: an activist administrator in Washington got an idea, and exerted a direct and substantial influence over the school's research program. In other cases, Washington's influence has been brought to bear as part of larger societal trends. And whereas a private college tends to experience that influence gradually and incrementally, Kings Point occasionally experiences it overnight, and in full force.

One example came in the 1970s, with the increased admission of minorities. This was largely an outgrowth of governmental policy in the late 1960s. In an attempt to encourage all colleges and universities to increase minority student representation, the federal government threatened to withhold funding for those schools unwilling to end discrimination in their admissions processes. It also began encouraging schools to engage in what came to be called affirmative action in recruiting and admitting students.

Unlike some of the schools that the government was trying to influence, the Academy had never had a policy of excluding minorities. The first African American graduate, Joseph Banks Williams, graduated from the Academy in 1944, and later served in Kings County as a justice of the New York State Supreme Court. During his Sea Year, Williams sailed on the Liberty Ship SS *Booker T. Washington*, under the command of Captain Hugh Mulzac, the first black captain of an American merchant marine ship. (Williams later established a scholarship fund at the Academy in honor of Captain Mulzac.) But in truth, Williams was one of a minuscule number of black students who attended the Academy; by 1968, the Academy had graduated only thirteen black students.

One of these was Joe Scroggins, a 1963 graduate. On balance, he says, his experience at Kings Point was a positive one. "I would say my experiences at the Academy were good, for the most part," he recalled. "I went there determined to get an education, above all else, and I never ran into any racial problems, or anything like that."[27]

On the other hand, he admits, there were things that the Academy didn't do particularly well, because it had so little experience in dealing with minority students, and because there were so *few* of them:

A 1963 Academy graduate, Commander Joe Scroggins Jr., returned to the Academy in 1968 as assistant dean in charge of minority recruiting.

On my first day, I looked around, and there were three minority plebes there: me and two others. We were all in different companies, and scattered out. I'm not sure if the Academy knew we were black before we got there. They may have. But before they started recruiting, this type of thing happened. There were always students who just for some reason or another got into the system. I mean, this is the way it had been—they had always had one or two. So there were a few black upperclassmen, and we would go seek them out, and find out where things were in town.

There were some problems that I don't think the administration really thought about very much. Things like getting a proper haircut, because, you know, hair is *different*. And of course, the upperclassmen would go outside to get their hair cut. So that meant they never used [Academy] monies that were allotted for their haircuts, because they had to go outside.

Another problem I experienced when I was a cadet had to do with dating. At that time, there were no women at the Academy. So when they sponsored dances, they would invite women over from the local girls' school, and they were all white women. They never made an effort to bring in minority women, to give the minority students the option to date.

After graduating, Scroggins shipped out of New York on a third mate's license and began working his way up through the ranks with Grace Lines, American Export Lines, and U.S. Lines. Scroggins was fully anticipating spending the next twenty years of his life at sea, winning his master's license and eventually retiring. After returning from a particularly arduous six-month tour to Vietnam in 1968, however, Scroggins was feeling some career anxieties. It was then that he received an unexpected phone call from Andrew Gibson, then assistant secretary of commerce. Gibson had an interesting proposition for Scroggins: a job at the Merchant Marine Academy, conducting a nationwide recruitment program for racial minority students.

The offer held great appeal for the young black mariner. He had long been troubled by what he termed a "revolving door policy," whereby, for a variety of reasons, colleges admitted underqualified African American students and then expelled them when they were unable to succeed. He saw a chance to break this cycle and do some good. In addition, the war-weary seaman admitted after some soul-searching, the timing was good. So Scroggins returned to the Academy in 1968 as assistant dean in charge of minority recruiting, with the specific goal of increasing minority applications.

Working mainly with results from the standardized achievement tests, Scroggins identified likely targets for admission to the Academy and sent out mass mailings across the country. He followed up with personal visits, encouraging strong candidates to apply, reassuring those who were wary of attending a federal academy, and lobbying members of Congress to nominate his candidates. His hard work paid off to a remarkable degree: in July 1969, the Academy welcomed twenty-two black students, more than in the previous twenty-seven years combined.

Meanwhile, he worked to improve the life of black students at Kings Point. He sent the Academy barbers out to learn how to cut African American hair. He made sure that African American women were invited to the Kings Point dances. He ordered subscriptions to magazines aimed at black audiences. Finally, he encouraged the black community in Great Neck to welcome the new students into their homes. Scroggins wanted to ensure, he recalls, that "nobody was sitting in their room on Thanksgiving."[28] He also acted as an informal counselor to this first generation of black students, many of whom had never lived in a predominantly white environment.

The number of minority students increased substantially in the 1970s under a recruitment program led by Academy graduate Joe Scroggins Jr.

In September 1972, with strong encouragement from staffers at MARAD, Scroggins left the Academy to pursue a degree at the Harvard Business School. He resumed his maritime career after graduating from Harvard, and in 1994 was appointed by President Bill Clinton to serve as a commissioner on the Federal Maritime Commission (a regulatory body), the first African American to receive such an appointment. He was replaced at the Academy by Commander Emanuel Jenkins, who continued in this position until being appointed director of admissions in 1975. The program continued to be an institutional priority under Jenkins's leadership; in 1972, for example, he made a total of 5,800 minority contacts.

Jenkins and his successor, Lieutenant Commander Bruce Grigsby, who joined the office in 1975, also initiated an important new recruitment tool: the Kings Point Information Representatives Program. This involved alumni visits to high schools in their home areas, at which they talked up Kings Point and answered questions about the Academy. Of the seventy-six volunteers who participated in 1975, twenty were black graduates who agreed to pay special attention to the recruitment of minority candidates.

Throughout much of this period, moreover, efforts to increase diversity at the school were also aided by the industry itself, which was seeing significant increases in opportunities for minority candidates in the early 1970s. Between 1968 and 1975, for example, minority employment in the shipbuilding industry increased from 17.7 percent to 28.2 percent, with the largest gains in the white-collar job arena—from 3.5 percent to 10.8 percent.[29] For those minorities who might still be wondering if the maritime world welcomed blacks, these appeared to be promising signs.

Leading the Way

The arrival of women at Kings Point was an even clearer example of the federal government imposing a historic change on the Academy on relatively short notice—and, in the process, opening doors for young women.

In 1972, a new federal civil rights law containing a section known as Title IX went into effect. Although Title IX in recent years has become synonymous with athletic opportunities for women, the statute had far greater scope, prohibiting discrimination on the basis of gender by any educational institution receiving federal money. Many traditionally male bastions began dragging their feet to prevent—or at the very least, delay—the arrival of women. These foot-draggers included the other four federal academies, even though the armed forces they served had long included women in their ranks.

At Kings Point, as elsewhere, feelings were strongly mixed. The maritime industry almost defined the term "male bastion," and some wondered aloud if it made sense to train women to work aboard ships. Others doubted that women would be up to the rigors of regimental life, life at sea, or of an engineering-oriented curriculum. Still others simply wanted to preserve the Academy's all-male tradition.

For better or worse, the Academy didn't get to choose. In the fall of 1973, Acting Dean Paul Krinsky got a phone call from Maritime Administrator Robert Blackwell. Blackwell, Krinsky recalls, simply laid down the law:

> This was a command decision by Bob Blackwell. I got a call one day, and he told me, "Well, we're going to take women in this year." That was it. I mean, the stroke of the pen. He said, "You're going to do this." So we just ground into action, and we did it. Of course, Admiral Engel was the guy who had to get everybody together, and that required the participation and cooperation of everyone.
>
> There was a great deal of resistance. It surprised me. I never realized personally that this would be considered an invasion of what had previously been a male preserve, which was supposed to be left untouched. Midshipmen were very, very antagonistic toward it.[30]

So—amidst some shock—Kings Point went first among the five federal service academies.[31] In the fall of 1973, an ad hoc administrative team started trying to address a host of new issues as they prepared for the arrival of women in the summer of 1974. Krinsky focused on academic issues; Assistant Superintendent Vic Tyson and Commandant Ed Knutsen took responsibility for figuring out how to integrate women into the Academy culture.[32]

First and foremost, Krinsky and his colleagues worried about where to house these new plebes. Initially, discussions focused on a separate barracks for women. It was later agreed—wisely, according to Krinsky—to integrate the female cadets into the existing dorms. "I always said, somewhat facetiously," Krinsky later explained, "that we realized that you couldn't build a strong enough wall to keep the males out, or the women in."[33]

The decision reflected a larger policy, mostly implicit, that governed the integration of women into the Kings Point community. It was generally agreed that in order to meet the Academy's own standards—and not incidentally, to limit rumblings among the male population at the school—the requirements for the women had to be as close as possible to the standards for men. Academically, the program was identical. Modifications in the physical education requirements, intended to accommodate differences in upper-body strength, initially caused a stir; women were exempted from wrestling and boxing, taking classes in Ping-Pong instead. The women objected vociferously, and in subsequent years, Ping-Pong was abandoned in favor of classes in self-defense and fencing.[34]

Some dilemmas, happily, had been foreshadowed by the minority experience at Kings Point, so analogous solutions were at hand. A barber had to be taught to cut women's hair. Additional items had to be stocked in the ship's store. And ultimately, these young women were going to need someone on the staff who could counsel them as they broached the all-male bastion of the Academy.

While these kinds of quiet progress were being made at Kings Point, the four other federal service academies continued their active resistance to the admission of women. But it was a lost cause. In July 1974, a subcommittee of the House Armed Services Committee held hearings on a bill admitting women to the service academies. And in October 1975, Public Law 94–106, admitting women to the federal service academies, passed by a margin of 303–96, and President Gerald Ford signed the measure into law. Not surprisingly, the military academies, which now had unmistakable marching orders, turned to the only similar institution that had any relevant experience: Kings Point.

Charles Renick, director of alumni affairs at the time, describes the scene soon after the verdict was passed down from Washington. "The first thing the General up at West Point did," Renick explained, "was helicopter down here. I remember he landed down by the swimming pool with all his aides, the commandants that deal with the students, and so forth. He said, 'Tell me everything. Every detail, every problem.' So they all looked at us for a while. The biggest problems were in dress, and that apparently caused real furors."[35]

Kings Point, it should be noted, had its own difficulties coming up with an appropriate uniform for the women. According to Engel's aide, Ken Force, Engel originally had decreed that the women wear military skirts that fell below the knee. The skirts initially selected, however, were tight below the knee. As a result, the first regimental review that included women was universally judged a disaster. (One observer went so far as to say that the women looked like "walking penguins."[36]) In addition, the administration had apparently assumed that the Academy tailors would simply be able to adjust the men's uniforms to women's bodies. Not so, recalls Frances Yates, a member of the first class of women:

> They weren't really ready to outfit us in the way they should have. Basically they thought they could take the men's uniform and just tailor it to our bodies. But the tailor shop at the Academy was just used to outfitting men, so when the tailor either balked, or couldn't tailor the uniforms, they had to take us off the campus to get it done.
>
> When you're a plebe candidate, you're not supposed to leave the campus at all. And the guys in the class thought this was a perk. You know, "Here the girls get to go on a field trip to the uniform shop." Of course, it wasn't just going there and coming back. We'd have to stop at McDonald's or something! It made for some tension: they thought these were little perks that we were getting away with.[37]

Not until these problems were solved were the women able to successfully march in step.

Sea Years and Scandals

Amid great anticipation, the first fifteen women arrived at the Academy in July 1974 to begin their indoctrination. Though their rooms contained full-length mirrors and drying rods over the sinks, their accommodations otherwise weren't much different from those of their male counterparts. At first, doors separated the male and female living quarters in the two company areas in which women were housed, but in the face of objections from both male and female cadets, these were removed almost immediately.[38] And aside from a truly intense level of media scrutiny (including reporters hovering at the gates of the Academy), indoctrination proceeded that summer much as it had the summer before, although an occasional short bob could be seen in the sea of buzz cuts. Frances Yates recalls that the media attention was one of the most difficult aspects of her first days at Kings Point:

> The Academy tried to keep us contained, because the media was there, and it was such a new thing for them. They were trying to spotlight us all, I guess, which of course led to problems down the road. You would have thought that there were fifteen people in the class of 1978, instead of the 360 that walked through the door that day. There were a lot of hard feelings about that, in the four years that I was there, but it's one of those situations. You have young people in a very difficult situation that they've never confronted before.[39]

Captain Mary Bachand McWilliams, a Great Neck schoolteacher and a member of the U.S. Coast Guard Reserve, was hired as an adviser to the women's program from 1974 to 1976. McWilliams met

The first group of women students arrive at the Academy in 1974 and prepare for indoc.

the first women plebes in the fall of 1974, and in a 1977 article in the *Kings Pointer*, she shared her assessment of that first class:

> I was immediately impressed with their pluck, good humor, and, most importantly, dedication to survival in a seemingly alien milieu. But, to my way of thinking, they appeared to lack full comprehension of the monumental breakthrough their admission to the Academy represented. Here was a truly unique group—not only the first to be admitted to any Federal academy, but also to become the first females to be licensed as officers in the merchant marine—and they seemed blasé! Even at that time it was virtually certain that the admission policies at the military, naval, and air force academies would be changed. But when women would graduate from the other schools, they'd embark on careers in service components which had had female members for 30 years. These Kings Pointers would, upon graduation, be sailing into a previously all-male preserve![40]

According to the people who lived through it, the success of the integration of the first group of women into the Academy owed much to the extraordinary caliber of those fifteen young women who chose to be the Academy's pioneers. Ten of the fifteen remained at the end of that difficult first year, in many cases having braved a sea of implicit (and sometimes explicit) disapproval. Now they faced their next challenge: Sea Year.

McWilliams details some of the steps the Academy took to ensure a productive educational experience for its pioneering female cadets:

> Advance planning and close liaison with the shipping companies resulted in their being assigned with the minimum of difficulty. Tankers were avoided, and, where possible, the women's assignments were paired with midshipmen from the second class. It was gratifying to learn of the generally favorable evaluations of the performance of women in these assignments, particularly since this was to be a totally new experience for them, [and] it also might have been a downright traumatic experience for the masters of some of those vessels!
>
> An interesting change in attitude concerning sailing as a career should be mentioned here—some who'd earlier expressed some doubts about jobs at sea have become veritable "old salts" as a result of having had two sessions of training. Several have indicated that they intend to seek jobs sailing after graduation.[41]

Women plebes join their male counterparts in formation during indoc in 1974.

Meredith Neizer, '78, in an article that appeared in *Newsday* after her return from her Sea Year, reflected favorably on her experience. "It was great," Neizer recalled. "I felt like a tossed salad in the beginning. It took me a while to get my sea legs. I was scared to death in the beginning, too. I was worried about getting a hard time from the men. But it didn't happen. Everything was beautiful. Absolutely fantastic."[42]

Third Mate Thomas Bontemps, also interviewed for the article, added that Neizer was not exactly what the crew had expected from a female midshipman. "The stories we had heard were that the girls were all foul-mouthed Russian shotputters," he said, not mincing words. "But she was nice, nothing like that. She wasn't trying to push her way around and get special treatment. We more or less tried to make it easy for her."[43]

In their public comments, McWilliams, Neizer, and others took care to create a positive image of the female cadets' experiences at sea. But the women from Kings Point *did* experience occasional difficulties during their Sea Years. Frances Yates, who had a generally positive experience during her Sea Year, recalled that on her second ship, the captain summoned her soon after boarding and told her to contact the Academy training representative because he didn't want her on the ship. (She declined.)[44] And at times, these difficulties even included sexual harassment. Simply put, some male mariners considered the female cadets fair game. In response, Charles Renick remembers, the Academy established a system for the women to use if they encountered trouble during their voyages:

> They had a code. If a young woman was really getting put upon, it wouldn't be politic for her to ask if they could send a radio message saying, "Help; the captain is trying to get me to sleep with him!" So she had been instructed to say something like, "I'm having trouble with my sea project," or something like that, with a code word included. And that meant that at the very next port, they would be prepared to yank her off.[45]

Meanwhile, back at Kings Point, other kinds of challenges cropped up. In 1977, a highly publicized incident, involving a male and female cadet found in bed together in the woman's room, hit the local papers. (One New York tabloid treated it as page-one, banner-headline news.) Because the woman was a plebe, and because she refused to identify her partner (who had left her room by the time the commanding officer arrived), the woman was expelled from the Academy. The young man, meanwhile, was not punished, although his identity was known. This apparent double standard led, in turn, to a media circus and public outcry, and the woman was eventually reinstated by MARAD.[46]

Newspapers often focus on the strange, the thrilling, and the titillating. An experiment as bold and risky as the coeducation of Kings Point—and by extension, the merchant marine—was bound to provide grist for this kind of mill. Perhaps what is most remarkable about this difficult period of transition, in the mid- to late 1970s, is how *little* went wrong, and how well both the female and male cadets of Kings Point performed under pressure.

A New Accreditation Debate

Concurrent with this revolution in the composition of the student body was a major change on the academic side of the house. This second revolution was sparked in 1977, and was led by an unlikely constituency: the Academy's alumni.

Of course, the graduates of Kings Point had never shied away from defending Kings Point. The Alumni Association played a critical role during the fight for permanency in the 1950s, and in the mid-1970s, it mounted a concerted effort to fight the Ford administration's move to impose tuition. And although the association had supported specific facets of the Kings Point experience, including athletics, clubs, facilities, and loans for needy cadets, the alumni had generally steered clear of trying to influence the Academy's academic program.

In the second half of the 1970s, though, this changed. A group of alumni became concerned that the Academy was ignoring a critical responsibility—accreditation of its engineering program—and that this was hurting both the Academy's reputation and the employment prospects of its graduates.

Like undergraduate programs in general, undergraduate engineering programs nationwide are subject to review by a professional accreditation board, which holds these programs to standards of depth, breadth, and rigor. Arthur Thompson's 1971 report had recommended accreditation by the ECPD, and had included an in-depth analysis of what the Academy would have to do to meet the ECPD requirements. Over the years, individual alumni had pushed the Academy to seek accreditation, but successive administrations had hesitated. Finally, concluding that gentle prodding wasn't going to work, alumnus David O'Neil, '61, decided to up the ante.

O'Neil was an experienced sailor and marine engineer who had started his own business, Seaworthy Systems, in 1973. He had applied for membership in the Institute of Marine Engineers in the early 1970s while working at Pratt & Whitney and was rejected because his degree was not a certified ECPD degree. The Hartford, Connecticut, Alumni Association chapter, which O'Neil was working to revitalize, was heavily weighted toward engineers, many of whom had suffered similar frustrations at one point or another because they lacked an accredited degree. They were more than willing to lend their names to a petition asking the Academy to revisit the issue. O'Neil forwarded the petition to Superintendent Engel.

Engel did not take kindly to O'Neil's initiative, viewing it as rank interference in the school's internal affairs. O'Neil later recalled running into Engel at an Academy function and getting an earful for his trouble:

> Engel put on a little show. He chewed out the engineering faculty head first of all, just to get me shaking in my boots. And then he stuck his finger in my chest, and basically said I could buy football helmets, and shoulder pads, and keep my nose out of academics. "It's none of your business. We run it here. You guys, alumni, have got nothing to do with it."
>
> And I said, "Well, we have a disagreement then, sir," and some other few words. But I wasn't going to back down.[47]

Sometime in the fall of 1977 O'Neil joined forces with Ron Hickman, '49, a Bechtel engineer who had been agitating within the Texas alumni chapter for engineering accreditation. Together, they prepared a questionnaire for Academy engineering graduates from the classes of 1955, 1965, and 1970, seeking a clearer picture of the scope of the problem. Of the 541 questionnaires mailed, 143 were returned. Of those responding, about a quarter said that their careers had been hindered by the lack of an accredited engineering degree—not as compelling a percentage as O'Neil and Hickman had anticipated. On the other hand, their cause was bolstered by another response on the questionnaire, in which 98 percent of those responding stated that they believed that ECPD accreditation was consistent with the mission of the Academy.

Hickman, perhaps suspecting that the administration would be more easily influenced by its peers than by the school's graduates, also included statements from several rival institutions that offered accredited programs. The response from the Coast Guard Academy, Art Engel's old turf, verged on a taunt: "If an institution is to proclaim that it does have engineering as an undergraduate curriculum, then it certainly should measure up to those things which can be perceived to be national standards. The only adequate national standard relative to this is ECPD." And the nearby New York State Maritime College added that accreditation was "validation of the professional substance of our registered curriculum and is a concise indicator to prospective employers, ashore and afloat, and to grad schools, of the stature of the degree."[48]

Gradually, the campaign gained momentum. In 1978, the Engineering Department designed an elective program in marine engineering systems to meet ECPD accreditation standards. The program consisted of the standard marine engineering curriculum, but also included an additional six courses: differential equations, stress analysis, analysis and design, basic ship design, thermal systems analysis, and automatic control systems. The department also set in motion the ECPD application process for this program, hoping to achieve accreditation by 1982.

Retooling: The Diesel Engineering Program

Another curricular shift during this period came as a direct response to industry trends. In the late 1970s, the maritime industry was trying to adjust—quickly—to a commitment made by the American government to convert the U.S. flag fleet from steam turbine to diesel. At that time, almost 85 percent of U.S. ships were driven by steam turbine. This was almost the exact reverse of the rest of the maritime world, in which roughly 85 percent of ships were run on diesel power, a more efficient and cheaper system, and the U.S. government had decided that American ships needed to get in step with international trends.

But changes in ship design meant changes in the personnel who would run the new ships. Specifically, the industry needed engineers qualified to run and maintain diesels. While this meant training the next generation of engineers in diesel theory and practice, political realities argued in favor of retooling at least some of the existing steam engineers. Faced with this complex challenge, Maritime Administrator Bob Blackwell turned to the Academy—and once again, the challenge fell into the lap of Academic Dean Paul Krinsky. As Krinsky later recalled, "They needed a quick fix to upgrade engineers. That was the challenge that Bob Blackwell threw our way. This was 1978, roughly. [Engineering department head] Jerry Francis had been aboard about a year. And they came to us, and they said, 'Can you do this?' We said, 'Of *course* we can do this.' I'm not sure we had any idea *how* we would do it, but Jerry was real bright."[49]

The Academy's response included both curricular and infrastructural components. Professors George D. Kingsley and M. David Burghart designed the Marine Diesel Engineering Modernization Program for the midshipmen. Meanwhile, with MARAD's eager assistance, the Academy upgraded spaces and purchased (or received gifts of) the necessary engines and related equipment. Before the end of 1978, according to a report to the school's Advisory Board, the Academy's expanded diesel arsenal included:

> A Colt-Pielstick PC-2 training engine complete with turbo-charger, pumps, tools, auxiliary training aids, etc.; a Sulzer RND-M training engine, complete with pumps, piping, tools, auxiliary training aids, engine and bridge consoles, associated control systems, etc.; and a Sulzer 3AL25/30 running engine. In addition, the modifications include a new clean diesel lab which has been established to house special training aids, engine room and bridge console units, interfacing control systems, and a dedicated instructional area.[50]

Although much of this investment was aimed at educating midshipmen, it also was designed to help the Academy take its first steps into a new realm: the development of a continuing education program in marine diesel engineering. USMMA instructors (including Kingsley and Burghart, who wrote most of the texts used for the course) teamed up with factory representatives to teach an intensive four-week program to help experienced steam engineers make the transition to diesel. This team-teaching format proved very popular, and the program soon enjoyed the benefit of good word-of-mouth among the ranks of experienced engineers.

Even more helpful, the Coast Guard approved the four-week course as equivalent to six weeks of sailing time. With this all-important imprimatur, the success of the new endeavor was guaranteed. The first five runs of the new diesel course sold out almost immediately, and enrollments in the program remained steady over the next decade. And, as in the case of the *Savannah* program, when the time came for the Academy to consider a more extensive continuing-education program, marine diesel engineering served as a useful precedent.

Trouble at the Helm

Even as the Academy was registering the clear successes detailed in this chapter, trouble was again brewing in the office of the superintendent. Arthur Engel, whose tenure at the Academy had prompted high hopes in most quarters, was proving a bad fit.

In many ways, Engel brought the trouble on himself. He had enjoyed a successful Coast Guard career, and he had led that service's academy with energy and skill. But he evidently found it difficult to leave the Coast Guard behind—even though, as we will see in the next chapter, the Coast Guard had already left *him* behind. Equally troubling, Engel had no ties into the maritime industry that his new Academy was supposed to serve, and showed no particular interest in forging such ties.

Engel was also a victim of circumstance. The maritime industry suffered a sharp decline in the mid-1970s, and jobs were scarce. Kings Point graduates found themselves temporarily excluded from the powerful maritime officers' unions, and, unable to secure permanent positions, some vented their frustrations on their alma mater and the man who headed it. Once again, moreover, Kings Point was put in play by actions of the federal government, which initiated a campaign in 1976 to charge tuition at the Academy.

9

The Guns Return

1970–1980

On paper, Arthur Engel had all the right qualifications to be a great superintendent. He looked the part and had played the part, having successfully piloted the Coast Guard Academy. But Engel, it turned out, was fundamentally out of touch with the maritime industry, with Kings Point, and even with his beloved Coast Guard.

His choice of uniform makes the point. Engel refused to don the uniform of the U.S. Maritime Service during his time at Kings Point. He continued to wear the dark blue uniform that he had worn while superintendent of the Coast Guard Academy, even though this particular uniform had been retired by the Coast Guard itself in favor of a lighter shade of blue.

This might have been dismissed as only a trivial offense, except that Engel placed great stock in this kind of symbolism. He personally dictated the design of the first (impractical) uniform worn by the female cadets. And, as Kent Flick, '75, recalled, Engel's interest in the dress code extended to the level of work clothes:

> He got up in front of the whole school one day, and said, "We're no longer going to have blue jeans as part of our work uniform, because hippies wear blue jeans, and hippies smoke pot. So that's why we're not going to wear blue jeans anymore."
>
> I mean, people couldn't believe he said that. So the leaders of the student body, the president of the class, and all that, go up there, and

245

they're appealing to him. You know: "What is this? The navy wears blue jeans. This is ridiculous!"

Ultimately, he made us switch to these blue polyester coveralls. Actually, he wanted white coveralls, like the Coast Guard, but somebody pointed out to him that, no, the Coast Guard doesn't wear those anymore. He didn't know that. So they finally settled on blue.[1]

In some cases, Engel seemed to go out of his way to show disrespect for Academy symbolism. Ken Force, Engel's aide for many years, recalls that when the much-beloved eagle that had long perched on the flagpole near Barney Square fell from its lofty post—felled by a rusted-out retaining pin[2]—Engel refused to have the popular mascot fixed and repositioned on the pole. The eagle wasn't sufficiently "military," Engel claimed, and told Force to throw it away.[3] Unbeknownst to his superior, Force stashed the eagle away in a storage room to await the arrival of a more eagle-friendly superintendent. In September 1980, only a month into the tenure of Engel's successor, Admiral Thomas King, the eagle was "repainted, regilded, and returned to its commanding post."

The following morning, Force later recalled, there were two broken eggs at the base of the flagpole, the lighthearted response of the Regiment to an emblem re-enthroned.

Commander Kenneth R. Force was hired as the Academy's director of music in 1970, and he organized a series of enormously popular "Tattoos" in the 1970s.

Over the course of his decade-long tenure, Engel's relations with both the alumni and the Regiment declined steadily. In the company of alumni, he often made the serious gaffe of instructing them in the Coast Guard tradition. To the students, he seemed erratic and out of touch. In 1976, the Regiment organized a formal "protest review," an event unprecedented in the history of the Academy. Engel, who didn't lack for courage, went out and "trooped the line," even as the public-address system blared out the Regiment's low opinion of him.[4]

Another famous incident of unrest, and one that achieved national attention, occurred during a graduation exercise late in Engel's tenure. As families, friends, and dignitaries gathered to watch the class of 1978 receive diplomas, a single-engine plane buzzed lazily over the field, towing a long banner with a clearly visible message: SAVE KINGS POINT. FIRE ENGEL. The plane, it later turned out, had been hired by a disaffected group of alumni and current midshipmen.

The MARAD Wars

Engel antagonized yet another key constituency: his superiors in Washington. Judy Chadwick was, at the time, a highly placed administrator at MARAD who later married her former boss, Maritime Administrator Andrew Gibson. She recalls Gibson's frustrations with Engel, exacerbated by the fact that Gibson himself had selected Engel. "That was a selection," Chadwick explained, "which Andy later admitted was the wrong decision. I can remember him saying to Engel something like, 'You don't understand. I'm trying to build a cathedral here, and you can't even see above the ground floor!'"[5]

Gibson left MARAD in 1972 to become assistant secretary of commerce for maritime affairs (and subsequently for domestic and international business), and therefore only had to wrestle with Engel for two years. But his successor, Robert Blackwell, battled with Engel for a full eight years, a struggle reminiscent of MARAD's attempts in the 1960s to oust Gordon McLintock. As had been the case with McLintock, however, the superintendent's civil service status protected him from removal except in cases of clear misconduct, which created an uphill battle for Blackwell.

The situation began to heat up in mid-decade. According to people familiar with the circumstances of Engel's hiring, when he accepted the post in 1970, he made a gentleman's agreement to leave his post

after four (or at the most, five) years.[6] During a pivotal meeting with
Blackwell in May 1975, however, Engel revealed that he had changed
his mind about leaving, and so set in motion a chain of events that
would leave reputations damaged on both sides of the controversy.

The only surviving firsthand account of this pivotal meeting
comes from a grievance report that Engel filed almost two years later,
in February 1977:

> About the first week in May 1975, I visited Mr. Blackwell in his office
> in Washington, at his request, to discuss my tenure with him. Dur-
> ing the discussion he asked me my age. I replied "61," as I had just
> become 61, on May 1, 1975. This particularly remained in my mem-
> ory as it made me feel he was objecting to me as being too old for the
> job. Our discussion at this meeting involved Mr. Blackwell's telling
> me I had been appointed by the Assistant Secretary, Andrew E. Gib-
> son, Mr. Blackwell's predecessor, and that as manager, he felt he
> should have his own man as Superintendent of the Merchant Marine
> Academy. I replied, that I had tenure and would not resign. He said
> he would have to study his rights—implying to me he would seek
> some means of removing me.[7]

Blackwell did not take any immediate action, perhaps due to a letter Engel sent to him in early July 1975, in which Engel stated that he
was planning to retire at the end of June 1976.[8] But June 1976 came
and went, and Engel made no moves toward the door. On July 19,
1976, therefore, Blackwell wrote Engel a letter detailing a long list of
complaints against him, and notifying him that he proposed to remove
him "no earlier than thirty calendar days from the date you receive this
notice."[9]

The first charge was that Engel had used government "funds,
property, personnel, or other resources for purposes not authorized by
law." Specifically, he was charged with using a USMMA work force to
trim hedges, rake leaves, and patrol the grounds of the Alumni Association's Lundy estate. (The circumstances surrounding the acquisition
of this property are described later in this chapter.) Second, Blackwell
accused Engel of insubordination for failing to enforce a "Buy American" mandate in procuring materials for Melville Hall, and for submit-
ting a request for funds to the Department of Commerce, thereby
bypassing MARAD. (Blackwell further observed that the misuse of
personnel detailed in the first charge could also be considered insubor-

dination.) Finally, Blackwell accused Engel of failing to hire a minority recruiter, even though MARAD had allocated a slot for that position.[10]

In retrospect, the charges seem trumped up, a heavy-handed attempt to embarrass or intimidate Engel into resigning. If so, the strategy backfired. Engel's response, dated August 5, 1976, was comprehensive and well documented. He included affidavits from groundskeepers, patrol leaders, and members of his administration, all supporting his contention that he was both following normal operating procedures and acting in the best interests of the Academy. For example, he demonstrated that he had organized an evening patrol of the Lundy estate after the mansion had been broken into, in the knowledge that the estate, then owned by the Alumni Association, was eventually going to be donated to the Academy, and that the school therefore had a vested interest in the property. When ordered to stop this patrol, he pointed out, he had done so immediately, and had asked the Kings Point village police to take over.[11]

His rebuttal of the charges relating to the minority recruitment position was equally forceful. Engel pointed out that the position had been vacant for only four months, and then only because MARAD refused to adjust the grade of the position (GS 12) so that the Academy's first choice could be employed.

Clearly, Engel had few admirers, either on or off the campus. But just as clearly, he had not engaged in any dereliction of duty that would justify his removal. His full-bore response to MARAD effectively ended Blackwell's first attempt to oust him. In late September 1976, Engel received a letter from Blackwell informing him that while it appeared that the charges did not constitute cause for removal, Blackwell still looked forward to a circumstance that would let him pick the Academy's leader.[12]

An event that occurred in late August, however, raised more serious concerns about Engel's conduct as superintendent, and brought on a second attempt to remove him from his position. In this incident, a female employee of MARAD who was in the process of being transferred to the Academy payroll was clandestinely investigated by the Academy for alleged unprofessional conduct. Assistant Superintendent Leonard Nichols later explained that he was primarily concerned about the woman's alleged actions on campus, which supposedly included drinking beer with an athletic team on the athletic fields, but the investigation eventually extended to contacting people off campus in an apparent attempt to catch the woman in an affair with another employee of the Academy. When they came to light, these activities prompted a furious communiqué from Blackwell to Engel:

> The authority of your office does not extend into arbitrarily delving into an Academy employee's private life. The personal views of any management official concerning an employee's personal life style does not give that official a right to personally investigate or direct or permit subordinates to investigate an employee's home life or personal affairs. The recent unwarranted invasion of an employee's privacy is untenable. Whether you personally directed or encouraged, or merely condoned the egregious actions of your subordinates in this matter is immaterial. I hold you personally responsible for their behavior.[13]

Again, in the final analysis, the incident did not warrant Engel's removal from office. His administration, including Len Nichols, supported Engel's claims that he had known nothing of the affair. When Nichols personally wrote a letter of apology to the employee in question in September, the incident seemed closed.[14]

But Blackwell continued to try to compel Engel to resign, now resorting to less direct methods. In mid-December, Engel received a letter informing him that he was temporarily reassigned to MARAD's Washington offices. Blackwell had tasked Engel with writing a report on the role of the federal government in the training of merchant marine personnel, a topic that had generated "much public discussion and controversy" in recent months,[15] and therefore supposedly needed a high-level study. But it was distasteful make-work, pure and simple, designed to precipitate Engel's surrender. "They were sure he would never take an assignment in Washington," said Ken Force, "and go through all that aggravation."

Blackwell wrote to Engel that he anticipated the assignment would last around six months, and that he would make the necessary arrangements to replace Engel during his absence. The letter made no reference to the incidents of the previous summer, but the media were quick to make that connection. "The Superintendent," said *Newsday*, "has been reassigned after receiving a confidential reprimand over a recent incident in which academy officials investigated an employee's sex life."[16]

One thing that MARAD should have learned about Arthur Engel, by this point, was that he relished a good fight. He accepted his orders—since to do otherwise would have constituted insubordination, and grounds for dismissal—and appeared in Washington on the designated day. Meanwhile, he launched formal grievance proceedings against Blackwell.

A Welcome Relief

To fill the seat temporarily vacated by Engel, MARAD tapped Captain Thomas A. King, '42, then MARAD's eastern region director. King was the first Kings Point graduate to occupy the superintendent's office, and he was immediately embraced by both the Regiment and the Kings Point alumni population.

Everything about King's training and experience was reassuring. He was a member of the first group of federal cadets who had been selected (in 1941) by means of a competitive exam. Reporting to Fort Schuyler in February 1941, he completed four weeks of basic training and boarded the SS *Mormacswan* as a deck cadet for his sea training. After six months at sea, during which his vessel made an unescorted voyage into the dangerous waters of West Africa, King was recalled to the newly established federal academy at Kings Point. In July 1942, after completing the wartime course of study, King received his license and was hired by U.S. Lines. He sailed throughout the war and, thanks in part to the desperate shortage of experienced mariners, worked his way up the ranks and earned a master's license in the astoundingly short interval of three years.

King continued sailing with U.S. Lines until 1949, when he took a leave of absence to work for the Economic Cooperation Administration in Korea. In June 1950, he was evacuated when hostilities broke out with North Korea. In 1951, MARAD asked King to participate in the creation of the National Shipping Authority to activate mothballed World War II–vintage vessels for service in Korea. Then, in 1958, King was offered the position of MARAD's Gulf Coast regional director. Eight years later, he was transferred to New York City to perform the same duties in the Atlantic region.

By the time he was asked to fill in at the Academy, therefore, King had extensive experience and contacts, both in the industry and with MARAD. He understood and was liked and trusted by both ship operators and the bureaucrats in Washington.

Interviewed by the student newspaper near the end of his first, brief tenure at the Academy, King reflected on the challenges he faced taking over from the temporarily departed Engel:

> I felt there were some problems, and I'd heard that it would be desirable to improve morale, but I can't say that I came on campus and looked around and was so wise that I could see exactly what was wrong or what had to be done. Generally, I felt that there was a need to communicate and to make the Superintendent visible and to be willing to talk to people, not only the Regiment, but all through the organization, and I've tried to do that.[17]

Simple steps, but welcome ones. King's willingness to listen to people, and to be a visible presence on the campus, were viewed by many as a major step in the right direction—so much so that when, after three months, King announced during a lunch with the Regiment that Admiral Engel had completed his report and was being reassigned to the Academy, the news was greeted with loud boos from the cadets. The Regiment then rose as a body and gave King a standing ovation for his brief performance as superintendent of their Academy.[18]

The Problem, and the Solution

The report that Engel produced during his three-month stint in Washington was never released to the public. Blackwell later informed Engel that the report was "so inadequate that its publication would prove embarrassing . . . under no circumstances can it be released."[19]

As with many documents that are suppressed, legends grew up around the Engel report. Some had it that the report recommended closing the Academy, while others alleged that it advocated abolishing MARAD itself. In fact, a reading of the document reveals that Engel had no harsh words for either institution. The organization that came in for the most criticism from Engel was the navy (for not doing enough to promote merchant marine training and the merchant marine reserve). And Blackwell's claims of the report's overall inadequacy seem exaggerated, to say the least. Many of Engel's findings were reasonable and well argued, and some—including a recommendation to establish a clearly defined service commitment for Academy graduates, as described below—subsequently were implemented.[20]

Engel's other recommendations included creating a committee

with government, union, and industry representation to establish a
MARAD–led system for the training of unlicensed personnel; creating
a similar committee to establish a MARAD plan for refresher and
upgrade training; clearly identifying and making public all government subsidy funds used for training; performing a study comparing
the cost effectiveness of the Academy and the Calhoon MEBA school
for license upgrading (Engel believed such a study would reflect favorably on the Academy); and preparing a plan to cover a shortage in
maritime personnel predicted by a recent MARAD study.[21]

The most controversial suggestion in the report involved the naval
auxiliary function of the merchant marine, which Engel believed had
to be clarified at the national level. The report stated that the attitude
displayed by the navy precluded the success of a merchant marine
naval reserve, or of the integration of Academy graduates into the
existing naval reserve. If the navy couldn't be convinced to mend its
ways, Engel argued, then the federal government should reinstitute a
U.S. maritime service as the training arm of MARAD, and create a
maritime service naval reserve, which would be supervised by the
Coast Guard.

In any case, the report was buried, and Engel returned to Kings
Point as an increasingly unpopular figure. Though he hinted to *Hear
This* that he was planning to retire soon, he continued to delay his
departure. This may have been the result of his reluctance to give up
the salary and benefits of his superintendent's post, or it may have been
fueled by an understandable desire to outlast his longtime nemesis,
Blackwell. Meanwhile, however, regimental discipline was eroding to
an alarming extent. In March 1979, an editorial cartoon in *Hear This*
portrayed Wiley Hall with two black balls raised on the flagpole instead
of a flag. The caption, playing on a section of the maritime Rules of the
Road, read, "A vessel not under command shall exhibit two balls or
similar shapes in a vertical line where they can best be seen."[22]

As long as Engel retained his civil service status, however, it was
impossible for MARAD to remove him. As Andrew Gibson had discovered a decade earlier with Gordon McLintock, MARAD had to
sweeten the deal. In 1979, therefore, Samuel B. Nemirow, Blackwell's
successor as Maritime administrator, invited Engel to join an elite management corps, the Senior Executive Service, created by the Civil Service Reform Act of 1978.[23] It was separate from the Civil Service
General Schedule classifications, offering higher salaries and more

flexible benefits. On the other hand, members of this new service served at the discretion of their superiors, which meant that they could be forcibly retired on three months' notice.

Engel accepted MARAD's invitation to join the Senior Executive Service in June 1979. It is unclear whether Engel understood the implications of accepting the new classification. Dean Paul Krinsky, who along with another senior colleague was asked to sign the same agreement, feels that Engel knew that this agreement would lead to his dismissal, and only signed it because he finally was ready to depart. Ken Force, Engel's aide, believes differently; he recalls being summoned to the admiral's office by Engel's secretary, who was afraid that Engel had "signed something he shouldn't have":

> I was sitting down in my office in the band room, and the phone rang, and it was Betty Danson, the Admiral's secretary. And of course at that point, the Admiral had been here ten years, and it was really an atomic war between him and MARAD. And she said, "Ken, I think the Admiral signed something he shouldn't have signed." I said, "What's that?" She said, "This merit pay thing." I said, "What?!" And I flew up there as fast as I could across the campus.
>
> Engel looked at me and said, "Oh, no problem. I'm going to get more money," he said, "more benefits." And Edna, his wife, had taken it and dropped it in the mailbox. I knew that was going to be the kiss of death.[24]

Over at 26 Federal Plaza in Manhattan, at MARAD's eastern regional office, Tom King had received a similar offer from MARAD. As King saw it, the opportunity to accumulate up to several months of leave, and take the equivalent in a lump sum at the end of one's government service, outweighed the loss of civil service protection. King signed the form, and thereby joined the Senior Executive Service. In his case, nothing much changed.

But when Art Engel called King asking for advice as to whether he should sign on the dotted line, King had mixed feelings:

> Art called me, and as always, we were on friendly terms. He said, "So, Tom, what do you think of this?" I said, "Well, Art, I've done it." He said, "Well, do you think I should?" And I said, "Art, I think you should read the document. If you sign it, you give up your right

of tenure, such as it is, and you're exposed to the whim of the administrator." I just didn't want him to sign the document and then be surprised. Well, he signed the document. And Art's acceptance of the Senior Executive Service arrived on Nemirow's desk, and Nemirow fired him the next day.[25]

Engel's formal dismissal came in September, after the requisite three months of service had elapsed. *Newsday*, reporting on the dismissal, quoted Representative Lester Wolff of Kensington, Long Island, as saying that Engel had received "shabby treatment."[26] But the views of the majority may have been summed up by a third-year midshipman, interviewed for the same article: "He's not a force here. We need some new blood."[27] Engel was replaced temporarily by Deputy Superintendent Howard Casey, while MARAD began a search for his successor.

Turf Wars in the Industry

The distractions caused by the troubled relationship between Engel and MARAD could not have come at a worse time. Throughout the 1970s, Kings Point once again came under pressure from a variety of outside interests. The first of these forays was mounted by the unions who represented deck and engineer officers in the maritime industry, and their opposition to Kings Point constituted a serious threat to the Academy.

The unions' position was less the result of malice, and more a response to a sharp decline in the maritime industry. The late 1960s had been a time of relative optimism for the industry and the Academy, thanks in large part to expanding shipborne commerce resulting from the Vietnam War. Early in the course of that conflict, Secretary of Defense Robert McNamara expressed his belief that the still-limited war effort could be supplied mainly through airlift. But as the conflict expanded, it became painfully obvious that air transport would be inadequate, and in 1965, fifty ships operated by merchant mariners were activated from the National Defense Reserve Fleet through a General Agency Agreement (GAA).[28] The purpose of this reactivation was clear: to help carry the nearly eight hundred thousand tons of supplies, including fuel, ammunition, and equipment, that were needed every month at the height of the war.

Those ships were not alone, of course. Over the next five years, forty U.S. companies operated 172 ships carrying a total of about 8.9 million tons of cargo to Vietnam. But at its peak, the Reserve Fleet accounted for about eight thousand seagoing positions[29] and carried about 25 percent of the materials needed to fight the war.[30]

By 1969, however, the reserve fleet was no longer needed, thanks in large part to more efficient operations on the ground in Vietnam. In the spring of 1970, MARAD announced that the last scheduled GAA ship, the SS *Santa Clara Victory*, had left Sunny Point, North Carolina, for Thailand.[31] And although the shipping boom was now over, the merchant marine had again come to the aid of the nation—and also to the attention of influential politicians.

One of these was Richard M. Nixon, who in 1967 and 1968 was campaigning in the 1968 presidential election. One of his campaign speeches, "Restoring the U.S. to the Role of a First-Rate Maritime Power," contained a comprehensive plan to improve the maritime industry, and it also invoked the Cold War through frequent references to the Soviet Union's vast expansion of *its* state-owned merchant marine.

As maritime historians Arthur Donovan and Andrew Gibson point out, Nixon's campaign commitments to help the maritime industry were unusual enough, but his determination to deliver on these promises *after* he was elected was even more surprising.[32] Nixon's maritime policies took the form of the Merchant Marine Act of 1970, the first major piece of legislation aimed at improving the merchant marine since the act of 1936. The act of 1970, as presented by Nixon to Congress, proposed a two-pronged approach. First, it provided for an aggressive program of shipbuilding: some thirty new ships a year for the next ten years. Second, to encourage efficiency, Nixon's bill proposed to lower the construction subsidies from 50 percent to 35 percent over a several-year period. Finally, the bill also included operating subsidies for bulk carriers, a major innovation.

Congress held hearings on the Merchant Marine Act through much of 1970, and the bill became law in October. According to Gibson and Donovan, the law "stimulated the largest peacetime private shipbuilding program in U.S. history."[33] Over the next five years, more than a billion dollars was expended on capital improvements to shipyards. And while the industry produced an average of only twelve ships per year, well below the anticipated thirty, the new ships were so large that the industry still met its projected yearly tonnage estimates.

In the long run, however, the results of the 1970 act were disappointing. Gibson and Donovan point to one overriding reason: existing maritime policies still contained restrictions that made U.S. international shipping an overly expensive option. In a fiercely competitive international shipping environment, U.S. shipbuilders simply couldn't increase their efficiency to the point where they could compete financially.[34]

The situation took a dramatic turn for the worse in 1973 with the Arab-Israeli War and the resulting oil embargo. Tankers all over the world were laid up as oil prices surged and international demand dropped, and the U.S. building program was among the hardest hit. Subsidies soon jumped back up to 50 percent; nevertheless, the shipbuilding industry shifted to much less expensive shipyards in Japan, Korea, and Taiwan.[35] Jobs in shipyards and on merchant vessels disappeared at an astonishing rate. In short order, the United States was carrying only 5 percent of its own trade. Meanwhile, the Soviet Union was carrying more than 50 percent of its trade in state-owned ships.[36]

The MEBA Wars

Kings Point graduates were suffering along with the rest of their industry. To make a bad situation worse, the unions were reacting to the shortage of jobs by closing their books to new members—and specifically to Kings Pointers.[37]

The economic situation had been deteriorating for several years. In 1970, members of the International Union of Masters, Mates and Pilots (MMP), faced with a ratio of 2.5 men for every job, voted to limit their membership to 1.5 times the number of jobs.[38] The new rule took effect by the time the class of 1971 graduated, and it had an immediate effect on employment prospects. These prospects only worsened over the next two years; by graduation 1973, only 45 percent of graduates were pursuing jobs at sea. Another 40 percent had found shoreside jobs, and 10 percent were on active duty with the armed forces.

Soon after the MMP's action, the primary engineer's union, the Marine Engineers' Beneficial Association (MEBA), followed the MMP's lead and closed its books to Kings Point graduates. MEBA justified its actions by citing the shortage of jobs at sea. That was true enough. At the same time, however, a long and troubled history by this point was coming to bear on the MEBA/Kings Point relationship, and those troubles were soon to come to a head.

The story dates back to a curious episode in the late 1950s, when the Academy and MEBA began looking for a way to collaborate in the realm of license upgrades for MEBA engineers. On the face of it, the proposal made sense. The Academy had extra capacity in terms of physical plant, and its faculty knew how to teach engineering; MEBA, for its part, needed to come up with a more systematic approach to aid its members by securing upgrade training for licensed engineers above the third assistant level. Discussions between Superintendent Gordon McLintock and MEBA president Jesse Calhoon resulted in a tentative agreement in the 1958–1959 time period. At the last possible minute, however—with MEBA representatives in a conference room on the Kings Point campus waiting to ink an agreement that had already been approved by the MEBA board—the Academy backed out.

The reasons are unclear. The simplest explanation would be that, not for the first or last time, Gordon McLintock got out ahead of MARAD and found himself reined back in. But one administrator on the periphery of these discussions recalls concerns at the Academy about the prospect of housing a group of older, experienced mariners on campus in the very midst of the Regiment. McLintock, the proponent of demerits and the much-despised paper collar, demanded regimental *discipline*; a contingent of worldly-wise engineers (some of them married) living in the barracks would almost certainly undermine that discipline.

Of course, if any word of these concerns made its way back to MEBA, it certainly would have been deeply offensive to the union. Reflecting back on this episode almost a half century later, Jesse Calhoon says that he and MEBA harbored no hard feelings toward the Academy. (He recalls that McLintock blamed the last-minute unraveling on MARAD, which seemed credible to MEBA.) After failing to cut a similar deal at Texas Maritime, Calhoon persuaded his union to buy a rundown hotel in Baltimore for $1.5 million as the headquarters for MEBA's training efforts. A half decade later, in 1966, MEBA sold the rehabilitated facility for $8.5 million and used the profits to help bankroll a brand-new facility in Easton, on Maryland's eastern shore. This new union school eventually was named Calhoon College, in honor of MEBA's longtime guiding light.[39]

Others remember this history very differently. Longtime Academy administrator Charlie Renick, for example, asserts that Calhoon was "livid" at the rejection, and vowed publicly to shut down the Academy. Calhoon, says Renick, began telling audiences that "the closest Academy graduates get to the sea is the anchor at the end of the football field." This was sensitive ground, striking directly at the rationale for the Academy's existence. Partly in response to the perceived MEBA attack, the Academy undertook a survey of all its alumni, asking (among other things) how many were still in the industry. After twenty years, the study revealed, something like half of all Kings Pointers were still working jobs related to the maritime field.

Armed with the results of this survey, Renick went to visit Calhoon at MEBA's well-appointed offices on Lower Broadway in New York. Calhoon made small talk and was thoroughly cordial. He listened to Renick's commentary and, according to Renick, brushed it aside: "I made our case. Calhoon said, 'Yes, yes; I know all about that. The point is, we're going to close you.' In other words, the numbers didn't matter. They were going to do whatever it took to shut us down. And then, friendly as can be, he took me to the Whitehall Club for lunch."[40]

At least one more episode comes to bear on the Academy/MEBA relationship. As noted earlier, MEBA and Kings Point worked together in the early sixties on the officer-training program for the NS *Savannah*. (Presumably, Calhoon and his union colleagues had decided to bury the hatchet long enough to collaborate for this important purpose.) But once again the deal fell through. When the U.S. government changed prime contractors in the spring of 1963, MEBA was displaced. Although the Academy had no control over these higher-level machinations, it certainly galled MEBA to see a replacement union set up camp at Kings Point and draw upon background work that MEBA itself had done. And still more irritations, unfortunately, were to come.

After MMP and MEBA closed their books to Academy graduates in 1971, careers at sea seemed out of reach for many Kings Pointers. In 1975, only 48 percent of graduates obtained sea-going berths–and none of these were on union ships.[41] Congress turned a blind eye to the union maneuvering that led to these dire circumstances, and instead responded to the shortage of job opportunities by proposing a bill, H.R. 10413, to restrict the entering class sizes at Kings Point and the state maritime academies.

Milt Nottingham, '44, the Kings Point Alumni Association representative in Washington, protested. Testifying in front of the House
Merchant Marine and Fisheries Committee, he said that the school
would be unable to continue operations if enrollments were reduced.
He also stressed that the refusal of MEBA and MMP to admit
nonunion graduates "made it impossible for the federal and state graduates to obtain seagoing berths on union ships."[42] At the end of the
day, however, the committee declined to open this political can of
worms.

Where the politicians feared to tread, however, the media eagerly
waded in. In the fall of 1976, CBS's *60 Minutes* produced a segment on
the "political financing activities of MEBA."[43] Like many segments on
this weekly news program, the piece was a morality play, with the
unions cast as the heavy and the Academy playing the good guy. (It is
worth noting that Don Hewitt, who produced the show for CBS, was
a Kings Point prelim in the early 1940s and sailed to England as a
cadet.) The host, Dan Rather, commented at length on MEBA's campaign contributions to influential politicians, and on Calhoon's personal vendetta against the Academy:

> One of [Calhoon's] enemies is the United States Merchant Marine
> Academy at Kings Point, New York. Since World War II, the Acad-
> emy has been graduating merchant marine engineers and deck offi-
> cers. It's a four-year course similar to Annapolis or West Point,
> totally funded by federal tax money at about $14 million a year. And
> you'd think it would be a prime source for engineers on seagoing
> vessels.[44]

After Superintendent Engel declined to participate, Rather interviewed Academy official Charles Renick. He stated on the air that
MEBA had closed its rolls to Kings Point grads, effectively denying
them jobs in the deep-water fleet. Rather then interpreted this fact for
his viewers:

> You see, Calhoon has vowed he'd like to shut down the USMMA,
> plus end federal support to six state schools that train marine engi-
> neers. Calhoon says these people aren't properly trained, plus, there
> just aren't enough jobs to go around.
>   Calhoon's critics point out that if he's successful in shutting
> down the federally sponsored schools, there's one school left to train

engineers, the Calhoon-MEBA School of Marine Engineering in Baltimore, a school that, for some reason, has found seagoing jobs for its grads in the past seven years.

Calhoon's school is paid for by shipping companies and the American taxpayers. Through a complicated agreement, ship owners pay about four million a year into a fund for Calhoon's school. But half these ships are under federal subsidy, so the owners get a refund.

And what is the upshot of that? Well, the American taxpayer is paying for the education of cadets at the USMMA, whose grads can't get jobs on ocean-going vessels, and the taxpayer is also paying a good part of the tab for Calhoon's students, who do get the jobs.[45]

Also interviewed for the segment was Milt Nottingham, the Academy's longtime advocate in Washington. Nottingham appeared over the strong objections of Captain Warren Leback, '43, head of the Alumni Association and future Maritime administrator, who worried about the effect the show might have on relations with the maritime unions. Nottingham felt strongly, however, that the potential benefit of exposing the Academy to millions of viewers—and of exposing union influence on Congress—far outweighed any potential fallout with the unions.[46] His testimony on the show provided concrete examples of the extent of that influence:

> Rather: Nottingham says that when he appears before a congressional committee, he can expect maybe four members present, two of them paying attention. The number present when Calhoon appears at the same hearing?
>
> Nottingham: Perhaps as many as three times that number. Somewhere in the neighborhood of ten or twelve members would be the least, I would think.
>
> Rather: And how many of those are listening?
>
> Nottingham: I would say that Calhoon generally commands their full attention.[47]

The show, which aired on October 3, rippled across the media. Within a week, the *Washington Post* was editorializing in opposition to Calhoon's "vendetta" against the school.[48] Unexpectedly, the unions' heavy-handed tactics (at least as depicted by *60 Minutes*) had cast the Academy in a sympathetic light, a David doing battle with the Goliath of organized labor.

For his part, Jesse Calhoon interpreted the *60 Minutes* segment as a personal attack, which he ascribed to members of the Kings Point alumni community rather than the Academy itself. Recalling the episode many years later, he chuckles at what he still considers a tactical mistake on the part of his detractors:

> They included a sentence in that show that I would have paid them $50,000 to include, and they stuck it in there for free. It was something like, "Nobody can get anything done with MARAD unless they first clear it with Jesse Calhoon." Well, that was the best goddamn ad I ever got in my life.
>
> Two weeks after that show aired, the head of a Texas tugboat company walked into my office. "I surrender!" were the first two words out of his mouth. Turns out he had seen the show, made the rounds of MARAD, the White House, Congress, and so on, and had decided that nothing *did* happen without my blessing. Well, true or not, that's a real good thing to have your customers think about you.[49]

Meanwhile, the dramatic nationwide coverage sparked by *60 Minutes* and its aftermath galvanized the Kings Point alumni body. Later the same month, the Alumni Association's Project ACTA was born: a signal event in the history of the Academy.

ACTA (the Latin word for "deeds," borrowed from the Academy's *Acta Non Verba* motto) was founded "to support and strengthen the mission of Kings Point, to keep the USMMA open and functioning, to end hiring practices that discriminate against USMMA grads, to broaden the mission, and to strengthen the American merchant marine."[50] Organized under the auspices of the Alumni Association's policy committee by concerned alumni, ACTA immediately recruited strong and politically savvy leaders, including past Alumni Association presidents Milt Nottingham, James Yocum, Joseph Mahoney, and Warren Leback. These leaders, in turn, hired an old friend of the Academy to coordinate the project: former Academy librarian Luis Bejarano.

Bejarano's actions on behalf of the permanency campaign—and his heated battles with Gordon McLintock—have been described previously. After being dismissed from the Academy, Bejarano accepted a job at neighboring Hofstra University, where he served as vice president of development for more than fifteen years. Throughout that

Midshipman William Smith, president of the class of 1974, receives the USMMA Aumni Association Award from graduate James Yocum, '47, during the 1974 awards convocation.

period, he maintained close ties with many at the Academy, as well as with the leadership of the Alumni Association. In light of those ties, as well as his previous experience in organizing support for the Academy, he was a natural fit with ACTA.

By December 1976, Bejarano had set in motion a well-organized campaign of letter writing, personal visits, and phone calls to congressmen in Washington. Bejarano personally addressed thirty-six groups in three months, including alumni chapters of the USMMA and Fort Schuyler, Navy League councils, American Legion posts, Rotary clubs, and Lions clubs.[51] The Alumni Association also began publishing a monthly newsletter, *ACTA/News*, to keep alumni up to date and suggest courses of action for alumni to take, both on the local and national level.

The broad outreach campaign coordinated by ACTA brought a swift and powerful response in Washington.[52] John Tower, a senator from Texas, wrote to ACTA that he was "appalled at the blatant exercise of power" on the part of Calhoon's union. Senator Harrison Williams of New Jersey responded by saying that he didn't believe that Congress would consider reducing support for the Academy, and that "we should be expanding the job opportunities available to those who have chosen a career in our nation's merchant marine, rather than arbitrarily reducing them." Representative Marjorie Holt of Maryland added that it seemed "totally incomprehensible at a time when we recognize the need to strengthen and expand our merchant fleet that we would consider closing such a vital component of our merchant operations. May I assure you that I will oppose any efforts during the 95th Congress to curtail Kings Point's operation."

Meanwhile, however, trouble was brewing on a second front. And although the battle was not of the Academy's making, the school and its allies found that they had to respond to this new threat.

The Specter of Tuition

While the Nixon administration had been extremely supportive of the maritime industry, and by extension, Kings Point, the Ford administration that commenced with Nixon's resignation turned out to be less friendly. In February 1977, friends of the Academy were shocked to see that President Ford's national budget for 1978 proposed severe budget cuts for Kings Point. (As it turned out, this proposal was Ford's last budget; after the fall 1976 elections, it became President-elect Carter's budget.) According to this proposed budget, the reduction in funding would be made up for by charging tuition and room-and-board fees to Academy midshipmen.

At this particular moment, the Academy's administration was in disarray. Engel had just arrived in Washington to begin working on his report, and his temporary replacement, Tom King, was still feeling his way. As a result, there was little coordinated reaction to this proposal from within the Academy. Fortunately for the school, the Alumni Association's Project ACTA was prepared to take on another battle for the Academy.

The stakes were enormous. If the Carter administration enacted Ford's proposal, that action very likely would sound a death knell for Kings Point. As the only service academy forced to charge tuition, Kings Point would be at a severe disadvantage relative both to its sister academies and to private colleges with substantial scholarship funds. (One way to explore this question is to turn it around and ask another: how many cadets would enroll at *any* of the federal academies without the enormous incentive of a free education?) As Maritime Administrator Blackwell testified before an ad hoc Select Committee on Maritime Education, chaired by Representative Gerry Studds of Massachusetts, the initiative very likely would transform Kings Point from a national resource to a regional school.[53] Warren Leback, president of the Alumni Association, called the proposal "unprecedented and shortsighted," and warned that it would "threaten one of the world's foremost institutions in maritime education."[54]

In this fight, unlike some before and after, Kings Point found that it had a wide array of allies. The state academies, for example, also stood to be hard hit by the Ford proposal, and joined forces with Kings Point to protest the implementation of tuition. The military also objected to the move, calling it "discriminatory," and arguing that it might "set a precedent which would spread to other federal academies," and thereby "affect recruitment."[55]

ACTA also worked another issue behind the scenes, focusing on ensuring the impartiality of a federal study of maritime officer education that had been commissioned by Congress in August 1976. The chairs of the House Merchant Marine and Fisheries Committee and the Senate Commerce Committee, Representative Leonor K. Sullivan and Senator Warren G. Magnuson, had asked the General Accounting Office to "investigate whether the federal government should continue to fund Kings Point and provide financial support for the several state maritime academies."[56]

That work had begun in the summer of 1976. By 1977, rumors were flying that the report would prove unfavorable to the state academies. Journalist Robert J. Wagman, in a syndicated story printed in several newspapers, reported that a preliminary draft of the report was "rigged from the start in order to make it certain that the probers have concluded that the most effective way the U.S. can train merchant marine officers is through union schools."[57]

Again, ACTA organized letters of protest to Congress and the GAO and, through interventions of members of Congress and other government officials, succeeded in obtaining substantial revisions to the study. When the report was published in June, ACTA praised it as "much fairer," adding that many earlier objectionable statements had been removed, and lauding the fact that the report now documented its sources and acknowledged differences of opinion.[58]

The GAO report found that "federal involvement in merchant marine officer education is justified if the graduates of the academies are needed and find employment as licensed officers in the merchant marine."[59] To some extent, of course, this was a loaded statement, given the oversupply of officers and the fact that—through no fault of their own—many graduates were unable to find employment. The report did note, however, that a large percentage of merchant marine officers, the World War II generation, would be retiring in the next ten to fifteen years, and that the officer corps would then consist of a larger number of graduates.[60] It also noted that the naval training offered at the USMMA provided an advantage over the union schools. In sum, the report constituted only a lukewarm endorsement of Kings Point and the state academies, but without the intervention of Project ACTA, it could have been extremely damaging indeed.

Meanwhile, ACTA was not only fighting that particular battle to at least a draw; it was also winning a larger war by winning the support of Jimmy Carter. A graduate of the Naval Academy, President Carter had expressed his support for the Academy during his campaign. In a September 1976 letter to Engel, Carter wrote, "I favor an effective American flag fleet backed by a force of skilled and highly-trained seamen and officers trained in both industry and government-run schools. I do not favor, nor am I considering, the phase-out or de-emphasis of the Merchant Marine Academy. I believe the Merchant Marine Academy should continue to play a strong role in supporting our merchant marine."[61]

After he took office, Carter delivered on his promise. He disregarded Ford's budget proposals and increased appropriations to the Academy to assure a continued government subsidy of tuition.

The unions, too, backed down. In March 1977, even before the release of the GAO report, Bud Lamy, vice president of the Atlantic Coast division of MEBA, told a group of Kings Pointers that MEBA had "never barred any graduate from employment simply because he was an Academy graduate."[62] He also told the group that the union rule requiring 365 days at sea (a rule that had greatly handicapped USMMA and state school graduates in favor of union school and "hawsepipe" candidates) had been stricken from the books, effective 1976. MEBA was now open to all Academy graduates—or at least, all of those willing to pay the $2,500 initiation fee and membership dues. Those who joined would then ship out on group three status for two hundred days, after which time they would step up to the higher-seniority group two. (Lamy did not point out, however, that union-school candidates still had a distinct advantage; because their sea experience while at school was completed under union contract, union graduates were admitted directly into group two.)

The loosening of union rules coincided with an easing of the over-supply in manpower in the maritime industry. By 1979, for example, the Great Lakes shipping companies were actually facing a shortage of qualified officers, and Academy personnel urged graduates to consider job opportunities on the Lakes. And figures for the 1979 graduating class showed the largest percentage in years pursuing opportunities at sea: 91 percent of the class accepted sailing positions with unions and with shipping companies.

On the federal level, one inequity remained. Unlike the other service academies, midshipmen at the Academy still received no payment for their service while in training. This disparity reflected a second fact, which represented a continuing liability for the Academy. Unlike the graduates of the other federal academies, Kings Point graduates still had no legal obligation to serve in the merchant marine or the armed services after graduation. The Merchant Marine Reserve program, abolished in 1965, had been replaced by the Naval Reserve Commission, requiring graduates who wished to retain the commission to complete a certain amount of sailing time on their licenses.[63]

The Reserve Commission was an attractive option in the late 1960s, not least because it offered a draft exemption. But after the repeal of the draft in 1973, the motivation to pursue a commission in the naval reserve declined. At the same time, the number of available industry positions was dropping precipitously. Without an obligation to serve in the armed services or the maritime industry, Academy graduates would be less and less likely to sail on their licenses—and the Academy would continue to be vulnerable to political attack.

The Service Obligation: The Next Front

The Academy's supporters soon addressed this vulnerability. In late June 1977, soon after the release of the GAO study, Luis Bejarano and Project ACTA representative W. McNab Miller III spent a week in

Washington working with Milt Nottingham. Their collective goal: to draft legislation for a mandatory merchant marine service obligation, with the blessing of MARAD.[64]

The bill, as finally drafted, proposed service for Academy graduates in the American merchant marine or in the maritime industry for a minimum of five years following graduation. The wording took into account the broadened mission that the Academy was now embracing, effectively equating jobs in the maritime industry with service as an officer of the merchant marine. In the event that a graduate failed to fulfill this obligation, the secretary of the navy would have the authority to order that graduate into active duty for whatever portion of the time was not served.

No action was taken on this proposed legislation for several years, though the House Ad Hoc Select Subcommittee on Maritime Training, headed by Congressman Gerry Studds, did study it. In January 1979, however, Congressman Les AuCoin was appointed the new chair of the subcommittee, replacing Studds. Soon after his appointment, AuCoin introduced HR 5451, which came to be known as the Merchant Marine Training and Education Act of 1980. The act, which cleared the Senate on September 30, 1980, and was quickly signed into law by President Carter, incorporated elements of the 1936 act, as well as the 1956 act establishing the USMMA as a permanent institution.

In addition, the act set forth guidelines for obligatory service requirements for graduates of the USMMA and the state academies. These included completing the course of instruction; fulfilling the requirements for a merchant marine officer's license; maintaining that license for at least six years following graduation; application for midshipman status in the U.S. Naval Reserve upon admittance to the Academy,[65] and application for a commission in the naval reserve or other armed services reserve after graduation, with six years of service if accepted; and serving five years as a merchant marine officer, an employee of a maritime-related industry, or an officer on active duty in the armed forces (three years for state maritime graduates).[66]

In conjunction with the passage of the bill, Secretary of the Navy W. Graham Clayton Jr. reestablished a merchant marine reserve program within the naval reserve.[67] The program would train midshipmen to operate U.S. flag merchant vessels in close coordination with naval vessels in times of national emergency. It also specified that merchant marine officers would not be called to active duty in a national emergency, but instead would continue to serve on merchant ships in their licensed capacity. This was the first time since 1965 that the navy had offered a merchant marine reserve program, and it was instituted at the Academy as a requirement starting in 1980 (that is, applying to the class of 1984).

The reserve offered two options: sailing aboard a U.S. flag vessel as a licensed deck or engine officer for at least four months every two years for a period of six years, and completing two weeks of active duty navy training each year for six years; or, serving on full-time active duty in the navy or other service for three years, and then sailing as a licensed deck or engine officer aboard a U.S. flag vessel for four months every two years, and completing two weeks of active duty navy training each year until completion of the obligation.[68]

A Slanted "Inquiry"

As if to underscore the importance of the obligatory service bill, a series of highly critical articles appeared in the *Philadelphia Inquirer* in 1979, blasting the USMMA as a waste of taxpayers' money. The articles, which were written by journalist Beth Gillin Pombeiro, were nationally syndicated and appeared over the course of a week, and were heavily slanted against the Academy. They retold old crises, and recited dusty complaints against Kings Point.

"Tax Millions Spent on a Toy for Shippers." "Loopholes as Big as the U.S." "A War Baby Thriving in Peace." "Going to Sea: A Moral Duty Easily Ignored." These headlines alone revealed the bias of the series. Beneath the headlines, Pombeiro attacked the Academy's alumni, Regiment, admissions policies, record on minority recruitment and hiring, and faculty policies. Judging from the occasional insider's insight that showed up in the stories, it appeared that Pombeiro was being fed information—perhaps by a well-placed current or former employee of the Academy—but this suspicion was never confirmed.[69]

Many of the allegations were presented out of context, and some of them, including Pombeiro's assertion that the Academy was created as a temporary wartime installation, were simply untrue. But some of the statements regarding obligatory service contained enough truth to cause headaches for the Academy's administration:

"Taxpayers are now spending $42,000 for each academy student's four-year education—more than the cost at Harvard or Princeton or the University of Pennsylvania. Yet recipients of this free college education are not legally obliged to pursue careers as officers on American ships; many of them do it but briefly, some not at all."[70]

It was a case of selective truth-telling. Pombeiro neglected to mention that the cost of a Kings Point education was several times lower than that of an education at the other federal service academies, or that the tuition charged by the likes of Harvard was far less than the true cost of an Ivy League education. She underplayed the fact that many Kings Point graduates *couldn't* pursue jobs at sea because they had been closed out by the unions. And finally, she made no reference to the legislation then pending in Congress to require obligatory service.

In a letter to the *Philadelphia Inquirer*, reprinted in the *Kings Pointer*, an angry Assistant Secretary of Commerce for Maritime Affairs and Maritime Administrator Samuel B. Nemirow refuted Pombeiro's assertions, calling her articles a "vicious and heavily slanted attack on the USMMA."[71] The fact remained, however, that the *Inquirer* had devoted six front-page articles and more than a thousand column-inches to the attack, and those stories had been picked up by many other newspapers. The damage had been done, and the school and its supporters would spend a long time repairing that damage.

Stepping Up: The Alumni Association

Among the most important of those supporters were the school's graduates. Gradually, as noted in previous chapters, Kings Pointers were becoming more influential, wealthier, and more politically active. Increasingly, the growing Alumni Association took on important legislative and lobbying tasks in Washington. They spearheaded the campaign to accredit the engineering curriculum. And not least important, efforts by the Alumni Association led to the purchase of the Academy's first new property since the hectic wartime acquisitions.

The property in question was the neighboring Barstow estate, originally the property of the first mayor of Kings Point, William S. Barstow. A friend of Thomas Edison (and an apprentice at Edison Machine Works, a predecessor company to General Electric), Barstow had built up a considerable fortune through patents and investments. The government began efforts as early as 1960 to buy the property, but these initial attempts were derailed by the Bureau of the Budget.

When the government failed to make a competitive offer, the estate was purchased by Frederick W. I. Lundy, a local restaurant owner.

The Academy, already short of elbow room, seemed to have lost a rare opportunity to expand. But when Superintendent Engel came on board in 1970, he asked the Alumni Association to make a new effort to acquire the property. Herman Brickman, a resident of Kings Point and a business associate of Lundy, helped broker an agreement with Lundy, and in 1974 the negotiators announced that they had struck a remarkable deal. The Alumni Association's Kings Point Fund would purchase the estate for $500,000, below market value, and in addition, Lundy would donate the mansion's furnishings, valued at $400,000, to the fund. The fund would give the estate to the government for use by the Academy, but before this could be done, the $400,000 mortgage would have to be paid off.

In the meantime, there was much to be done. The summer 1979 issue of *Kings Pointer* recounted some of the changes that had to be made and the difficulties encountered:

> The grounds of the estate, which were pretty much a jungle when the property was acquired, have been reclaimed to their former elegant beauty; three sets of quarters were renovated and rented to members of the Academy staff; and the big four-stall garage was turned over to the Midshipmen's Automotive Interest Club. The main floor of the beautiful mansion, which was the site of homecoming class reunion parties in 1976 and '77, is now the home of the Academy's new maritime museum, and the ten bedrooms on the second and third floor are being used to billet students of the diesel school.
>
> For those at the Academy who have worked on the day-to-day problems of the estate, it has been a very personal project. We have had to deal with break-ins, worry about freeze-ups in zero weather, battle floods when storm drains became plugged, attend Village meetings, deal with complaints of the neighbors, and learn to live with the Academy's "ghosts." There was the thrill of discovering, tucked away in a cupboard, a collection of early "home recordings" containing the voices of such notables as Madame Curie, the Prince of Wales, President von Hindenburg, and Thomas Edison, and there was the frustration of seeing the mansion's magnificent crystal chandeliers, mirrors, and carved walls being sold at auction.[72]

The fledgling Merchant Marine Museum turned out to be a primary beneficiary of the new purchase. The museum, which had been housed on the TV *Emery Rice* during the last few years of that vessel's working life, had been in search of a permanent home since the late 1940s. Charles Renick, who championed the museum's cause in the early 1970s, at one point secured an offer from Maritime Administrator Gibson to use a back wing in Samuels Hall, but the CAORF simulator took priority and the museum was again homeless. When Renick heard about the new acquisition (and learned that there were no specific plans for its use), he quickly jumped in to secure the space for the museum. In 1979, the newly reorganized American Merchant Marine Museum moved into its new quarters, and Dr. Mel Jackson, who had just retired as maritime curator at the Smithsonian, was named the curator. Jackson, considered the dean of American maritime curators, laid out the museum and set its course.[73]

The Kings Point Fund paid off the mortgage on the Lundy estate in 1979 through the sale of two of its twelve-meter America's Cup yachts, *Courageous* and *Independence*. On March 23, officers of the Alumni Association presented the deed to the property to Secretary of Commerce Juanita Kreps, in Washington, D.C. Kreps thanked the association for its loyalty and patriotism in making the gift, which would benefit many generations of future Kings Pointers as well as visitors to the American Merchant Marine Museum.

Campus Contributions

Arthur Engel, controversial as he was, deserves credit for improving the physical plant and infrastructure of the Kings Point campus. Even as budgets were tightening in the 1970s, Engel proved skilled at squeezing money from Washington for renovations and additions to the campus. Ken Force considers Engel's ability to do this—especially while engaged in almost constant skirmishes with MARAD—nothing short of miraculous:

> I think he knew the ways to go into government, from his experiences at the Coast Guard Academy. He had gotten that whole gym complex up there, and the renovations of barracks. He was good at that area, and for some reason, he knew the ins and outs of where stuff was funded. So he was able to pull all that off, which was a miracle.

Nothing would have happened without him. That's for darn sure. He got more money in here than anybody else did. . . . We've got magnificent tennis courts here that you never would have seen if he didn't play tennis.[74]

In 1971, Engel developed a five-year plan for modernizing the campus. Much of the planning was overseen by Engel's able assistant superintendent, the ubiquitous Vic Tyson. A principal thrust of Tyson's modernization effort was life/safety code-compliance upgrades in the dormitories, which had remained almost completely untouched since the Academy's founding three decades earlier. In addition, the most pressing quality-of-life issues were addressed: new flooring and carpet were installed, rooms were painted, the overhead lighting in passageways was changed to "bright modern fluorescent fixtures," and new furniture was purchased.[75]

In addition, Engel tackled Samuels Hall, installing ventilators, lighting fixtures, suspended ceilings, and, as related earlier, the CAORF facility. Athletics also benefited from Engel's and Tyson's efforts (Tyson was also chair of the Athletic Board); in addition to waterfront renovations, a wrestling room, and tennis and squash courts, Engel added a wing to O'Hara Hall with an Olympic-size swimming pool, diving pool, and locker room and equipment areas. Engel also championed a one-story steel grandstand on Tomb Field with restrooms, enclosed concession stands, and locker areas for home and visiting teams. And, at long last, with the upgrading of Roosevelt Field, the Academy had its own baseball diamond and soccer field.[76]

On the Waterfront

Thanks in part to Engel's infrastructural improvements, athletics at the Academy improved steadily during the 1970s. Some of the most remarkable changes took place on the waterfront. Ever since the first midshipmen had organized the Windjammers Sailing Club, racing the heavy monomoy boats on Long Island Sound during the war years, waterfront activities had been popular at Kings Point. This first generation of sailors was limited to competing against sailing clubs from local colleges and academies, but by 1945, the Academy boasted a varsity sailing team, and by 1948, the Mariners were competing in–and winning–local regattas, including the Metropolitan Championship and the Middle Atlantic Associate Member Championship. In 1954, the Mariners placed fourth in the National Intercollegiate Sailing Championships, the only team in the Nationals representing a federal academy.

But the waterfront program lagged behind what might have been expected of an institution preparing students for careers at sea. McLintock admitted as much in his 1962 statement to the Advisory Board: "Kings Point has always maintained an enviable record in small boat sailing. . . . However, it was embarrassing when foreign merchant navy training establishments invited USMMA to participate in overseas races and we had to advise that the Academy did not have a seagoing yacht."[77] Kings Point could hold its own with the dinghies, but it couldn't compete in regattas.

This began to change in 1958, when the Academy asked the Naval Academy to lend it a yawl for use in the Bermuda Yacht Race of that year. Even though the loaner had sprung a leak on the way down to Bermuda, the crew turned in a "creditable performance,"[78] and with the help of well-placed friends, the Academy decided to try to acquire its own yacht. Soon after this, the *Minot's Light*, a fifty-eight-foot ketch, was donated to the Academy by a Mr. Warden of Philadelphia.

David O'Neil, a plebe who arrived at the Academy in 1957, remembers being recruited to the sailing team, mainly because of his previous sailing experience:

> I remember [Lieutenant Commander Bob May] at a lifeboat class the first week I was there. "How many of you guys have rowed before? Anybody sailed before?" Two hands go up. "Anybody sailed on a boat over thirty feet before?" One hand is up—mine. "Forty feet?" One hand. "Seventy feet?" He said, "What's the name of the boat you were on, Mister?" I could tell he probably thought I was lying. I said, "I was on the *Cotton Blossom.*" "*Cotton Blossom*! You sailed that?" He said, "You in the owners' parties?" And I said, "No, Sir, I worked on deck." "I want to see you after." So anyway, I became one of the gang.
>
> And he said, "Well, we're getting this yacht, *Minot's Light.*" He was careful enough. I remember he quizzed me, "What's this? What's this?" And of course they were very basic things. I breezed through. And he says, "You know, you've got more experience here than anybody in this whole place, and you're only a plebe." So he

says, "I want you to join the sailing team." So for my first week I was glowing, because the big boats weren't there, and this fifty-eight-foot ketch was coming. It was a boat I'd heard of before—a big boat—and we're going to Bermuda. So anyway, I was one of these guys that thought I had landed in the right place at the right time.[79]

In 1959, the Academy was also given *Salmagal*, a fifty-four-foot yawl donated by Arthur B. Homer, president of Bethlehem Steel, and *Icefire*, a forty-five-foot yawl donated by Jacob Isbrandtsen. As a result, the Academy now had the boats with which to compete, but still lacked facilities and funds for maintenance. Much of the necessary maintenance work was done by the sailing team itself, on nearby City Island. The cadets improvised—begging, borrowing, and sometimes even making spare parts themselves. At times, O'Neil recalls, these efforts were misinterpreted:

What they didn't realize was how much work it was. We got very few pleasure-sailing hours. It was all work. But we were thought of as deal-pullers—you know, guys who didn't have to march in the reviews because they got out Saturday morning. We got to go out on the boats with a box lunch, and we disappeared. Well, it wasn't that way. We were working our asses off.

So then Captain ["Bud"] Travis came in as regimental officer, and he was hell on wheels. And I guess he was looking over who's logging in and out, who's getting out of things, you know. And he sees that this O'Neil takes guys over to City Island. So he snuck around the boatyard, found the boat. And, of course, we hear a ladder rattling against the hull as he's coming up. He calls out, "Alright, nobody move! Listen up! I'm going to run down the roll. Say 'here' when I call your name!" And of course, everybody's there—sweating up a storm, and dirty as hell. So he said, "Okay, carry on. As you were."

By Monday he was feeling guilty. He called me down to his office and he said, "You guys do this every weekend?" I said, "Yes, sir." "Well, what do you do that for?" I said, "We don't have any money to maintain the boats. We *are* the maintenance crew. And besides that, we're doing the S-boats in the basement, and we're doing this, and we're doing that. And if we're going to represent the school in sailing, this is the way it's got to be done." He said, "I had no idea. I thought it was just a boondoggle."[80]

The waterfront facilities also required considerable work. Renovations for the shoreline and piers were urged, among others, by Lieutenant W. P. Chaisson Jr., an adviser to the sailing team in the early 1960s, who pointedly noted in *Polaris* that Kings Point's waterfront lagged well behind those of the other federal academies. The proposal endorsed by Chaisson included floating piers, a 425-foot bulkhead, installation of a jumbo boom and winch, an observation platform on the top of the boatshed at the end of Crowninshield Pier, and a new two-story building with two floating launching ramps.[81] The renovations were approved by the administration in 1963 and implemented soon thereafter.

These upgrades to the facilities set the stage for the next important development: the hiring of Captain Arthur "Joe" Prosser. Prosser, a former Canadian commando and skipper of sixteen ships of war, served as commanding officer of the HMCS *Oriole*, the Canadian Navy's primary sail training vessel. He signed on at the Academy in

The Academy's Sailing Master, Captain C. A. "Joe" Prosser (center), with Emil "Bus" Mosbacher, skipper of the twelve-meter yacht *Weatherly*, winner of the 1962 America's Cup, and Douglas Mercer, '57 (right), whose father, Henry D. Mercer, chairman of the board of States Marine Lines, donated the yacht to the Academy.

1965 as sailing master and soon dramatically transformed the Kings Point waterfront program. Prosser increased participation by organizing a training regime in which more experienced midshipmen served as sailing instructors for the new recruits, and in 1973, the *Kings Pointer* proudly proclaimed that over the prior twelve months, the midshipmen had logged in excess of forty thousand hours in the water on small craft.

In the fall of 1978, led by first classman Alex Smigelski, Kings Point ranked first among North American college sailing teams. Smigelski was named College Sailor of the Year at the end of that

The Kings Point sailing vessel *Nina* wins the Mayor's Cup and the New York Bay Schooner Race in October 1967.

season (the first of many Kings Pointers to receive that honor), after piloting the Kings Point dinghy team to a victory in the North American Intercollegiate Dinghy Championship. In recognition of these feats, Smigelski subsequently received the Academy's coveted Admiral Stedman Athletic Award, presented annually to the senior who demonstrates the highest level of achievement, sportsmanship, and general excellence in athletics.[82]

The Band Plays On

Another extracurricular activity was gaining in popularity and stature in the 1970s. This was the Academy's marching band.

In 1971, the Academy band consisted of twenty-eight instruments, twenty-five of which dated back to World War II. Participation in the band was haphazard, and its musical output was lackluster at best. Not surprisingly, the band received little internal or external recognition. Two short years later, the Kings Point band appeared on national television in the halftime parade at the Cotton Bowl, and presented a stirring rendition of "Heave Ho" at the inauguration of President Richard Nixon.

What brought about this striking change? Gerard Riordan, '50, reporting on this transformation in the 1973 *Kings Pointer*, pointed to several factors, including the creation of a special company for the band, with separate quarters, and the solicitation of private and federal funds for new instruments.

But the major agent of change, Riordan noted, was a thirty-two-year-old professional musician with "an infectious enthusiasm" for military bands and music, Lieutenant Commander Kenneth R. Force.[83] A graduate of the Manhattan School of Music, Force was hired away from New York's Port Chester High School in 1970 as the Academy's director of music. When he arrived, he recalls, the Academy band was "so bad it was not to be believed."[84] Force knew he had an extended task of rehabilitation ahead of him. In the meantime, though, one problem demanded an immediate fix. That problem, he explained, was "The Admiral's March," the tune played to honor the superintendent at all formal reviews:

> I watched my first review, and they were out there, and the next thing I know, these kids go into "The Admiral's March," honoring

the superintendent. Now, there's a big high note in there that goes "dum ba dum ba dum," and on that high note, everybody *absolutely couldn't make it*. I watched all these officers, and this obviously went on every time they did a review, because all the officers grabbed their hands into a fist when this note came, and closed their eyes and ears. So I said, "This is my first repair job."

At that time, we did reviews every Saturday here. My first review was the following week. I said to the band, "This is what you do. When you play "The Admiral's March," play it *three times faster than normal*." And to the two kids who played the cymbals, I said, "When we get to that goddamned high note, you hit those cymbals *as hard as you goddamned can*. I don't want to hear anything else. Hit the cymbals!"

So we get out there. And sure enough, they play it triple time, they hit the cymbals loud, and it's over almost before it begins. So the band goes marching down the street, and I'm feeling very good about myself.

Force returned to his office convinced that he had dodged a large bullet. No sooner had he sat down at his desk, though, than the phone rang. It was Engel's secretary, Betty Danson. "You'd better come and see the admiral," Force recalled her saying. "In fact, he'd like to see you right now." Having an inkling as to what might be on Engel's mind, Force envisioned his newfound career coming to a sudden end:

So I go up there, scared out of my mind. And he says, "Good job today, Lieutenant Force. Very good. Very good. But could you tell me about 'The Admiral's March?'"

So I said, "Well, sir, when John Philip Sousa was the head of navy bands at Great Lake in World War I, he said that "The Admiral's March" should go much faster, to depict the brightness of an admiral." Engel thought a second. He looked, he said, "Is that true? Really?" I said, "Yes. And that's why we played that fast, sir. We're playing the authentic Sousa tempo." He said, "Well, thank you for telling me." So of course we continued playing that way. Every week we played it as fast as we could, and got to that high note, and got *out* of there as fast as we could.

About a year later, the Admiral invited down the U.S. Coast Guard band. These are all professional musicians, and a Commander Broadwell, also a pro, was the band director.

Broadwell walks in, sort of a dour guy. And he looks at me, and he says, "You're the band director?" I said, "Yeah." He said, "You son of a bitch. You're the one who got me in trouble about 'The Admiral's March!'" Apparently Admiral Engel had called the Coast Guard Academy and told the new superintendent that the Coast Guard band was playing "The Admiral's March" wrong– that it should go much faster, to depict the brightness of an admiral. So from then on, the Coast Guard band had to play it much faster.[85]

In addition to inventing new tempos and uses for the cymbal, Force also introduced another tradition to the Academy: the *tattoo*. A corruption of the Danish term for "turning off the beer taps," a tattoo is a military production involving music and pageantry, which evolved over the centuries from an evening drum call summoning the troops to quarters. When Force brought the tattoo to Kings Point, it was the first such performance by a U.S. band in two hundred years. The tattoo became enormously successful over the next several years, bringing in sellout crowds from Great Neck and beyond. Force built enormous sets, including (for one memorable event) a nine-hundred-pound steel ship model that hung from the ceiling of O'Hara Hall, while the band paraded below, accompanied by bagpipes (courtesy of the Nassau County Police Band), an organ grinder and a monkey, a camel, and two elephants bearing signs that read, SAIL MERCHANT MARINE.

The Father of the Academy Acknowledged

The long-delayed formal recognition of Admiral Richard R. McNulty, the moving force behind the founding of Kings Point, finally came in 1976, again thanks to efforts by the Alumni Association.

Throughout the long McLintock era, McNulty had received little recognition from the Academy for his role in the Academy's founding. The Academy administration building, the old Chrysler mansion, bore the name of Admiral Wiley, first head of the Maritime Commission's Division of Training, even though Wiley at times worked *against* the founding of a shore-based school for officer training. The student center, appropriately enough, had been named in honor of Admiral Emory S. Land, who worked closely with Joseph Kennedy and

Franklin Delano Roosevelt to make the Cadet Corps a reality. Captain Tomb, the first superintendent, was recognized through the renaming of the Academy's parade ground and playing field (originally Kendrick Field), in his honor. Even Admiral Vickery—in charge of shipbuilding in the founding era, but a relatively minor player in the realm of training—was commemorated by the Academy gatehouse. Richard R. McNulty, however, had vanished almost without a trace.

McNulty did not know this firsthand. Early in McLintock's reign, he had vowed never to return until a Kings Pointer took the helm of the Academy. Throughout the 1950s, 1960s, and the first half of the 1970s, McNulty remained bitter about the events that had led to his departure from the Academy. Although his subsequent career at Georgetown had been quite successful, his rejection by the school that he had created continued to rankle. By 1974, McNulty was living in a nursing home in Rockport, Massachusetts. His wife had died in 1969, leaving him, in his own words, "lacking interest in living."[86] He was twice admitted to Bethesda Naval Hospital, where he was diagnosed as suffering from malnutrition.

He obviously kept track of his beloved Academy—in a 1974 interview, for example, he mentioned at least three times that Kings Point was the highest academically ranked military academy in the country[87]—but he felt that the Academy had lost track of him. A faithful few did continue to correspond with the admiral, however, including Lauren McCready, Charlie Renick, and Milt Nottingham, and after McLintock's departure, these friends and others began a campaign to recognize McNulty for his accomplishments at the Academy.

On March 17, 1976, this recognition finally came to pass. McNulty was formally designated the Father of the Academy, and advanced to the rank of vice admiral, USMS, by Assistant Secretary of Commerce Robert Blackwell. Blackwell personally presented McNulty with a plaque commemorating his "farsighted leadership in designing and developing the federal program for the training of officers for the American merchant marine and particularly, for establishing the U.S. Merchant Marine Academy."[88] In light of McNulty's failing health, the ceremony was held in Beverly, Massachusetts, at the home of Alumni Association president Joseph Mahoney.

McNulty would not live to see a second recognition bestowed upon him by the Academy. On November 1, 1980, a year after his death, the recently acquired Lundy estate was renamed the McNulty Campus in his honor. The admiral's sister, Mrs. E. Crowley, represented the family at the ceremony on October 17, 1981, unveiling a sign bearing McNulty's name.[89] At long last, the Academy that McNulty had created bore witness to his contributions.

10

Safe Harbor
1980–1987

On October 16, 1981, the evening before the Academy's annual homecoming celebration, the officers' club at the Academy was filled to capacity. Academy graduates, many in suits, others in uniform, pressed in around crowded tables, greeting old friends and making new ones.

It was a relaxed and jovial group, and the good feelings its members exhibited that evening reflected larger trends. For the first time in years, the Academy that they loved was enjoying a measure of relative peace and stability.

The early 1980s offered a welcome respite from the turmoil of the late 1960s and the 1970s. In many corners of the campus, people were catching their breath, mending bridges, and looking to the future. Relations with the industry, with the unions, and with the U.S. Maritime Administration were finding an even keel. The traditions of the Academy, some of which had seemed to take a backseat during much of Admiral Engel's tenure, were reemerging as touchstones for both the faculty and midshipmen.

This rediscovered sense of cohesion extended to the Academy's alumni, and it partially explains why this particular group had assembled that October night in the officers' club. The Alumni Association's Awards Committee had spent months selecting outstanding members of the Kings Point community to honor for their contributions both to the Academy and to the industry, and tonight would

Rear Admiral Thomas King
became the Academy's sixth
superintendent in July 1980.

see the conferring of those awards. On a signal from Pete Rackett, cochair of the Awards Committee and master of ceremonies, the Academy's Colorguard and Fanfare Trumpet Detachment, led by Captain Ken Force, marched crisply into position and presented the colors, bringing the assembled group to attention.

The two spotlight awards both honored the Academy's past and looked to its future. The Academy's new superintendent, Rear Admiral Thomas King, was honored as Alumnus of the Year. The award recognized King "not only for attaining the prestigious office directing his alma mater, but also for the high regard he has earned among maritime industry, labor, and graduates of the Academy, young and old." King, Rackett proclaimed, was "the embodiment of the Academy's mission."[1]

Looking back to the past, Rear Admiral Lauren McCready, who four decades earlier had used a beach ball to puzzle his way through the Academy's manual on spherical trigonometry, and who since that time had instructed countless Kings Point midshipmen, was given honorary alumnus status. Rackett paid tribute to McCready's many achievements and his central role in the Academy's development. "Few graduates," Rackett observed, "have not been touched by his accomplishments."[2]

Fifteen graduates also received awards for outstanding professional achievement. The diversity of those award winners underscored the range of industries and institutions in which Academy graduates had distinguished themselves. They included, among others, navy captain William Fahey, chief of the Operations Branch of the Joint Chiefs of Staff; David O'Neil, owner and president of Seaworthy Systems, one of the largest marine engineering consultancy firms in the United States; James Clark, vice president and general manager of Sea Land Systems' Gulf Atlantic Division; Anthony Fiorelli, president and CEO of General Defense Corporation, the leading supplier of tank ammunition to the U.S. Army; Michael Schneider, head of the undersea surveillance branch on the staff of the chief of naval operations; and Alan Loesberg, a senior partner of one of New York's most successful admiralty law firms.

One final award given out that night captured both the changing face and the long-standing traditions of the Academy. Julianne Ahlgren, '80, was honored for "tremendous courage and dedication to her ship and her shipmates." As second assistant engineer on the Military Sealift Command oiler *Taluga*, she was badly injured in an engine-room explosion while on watch. Despite burns that covered almost 80 percent of her body, Ahlgren refused any aid for herself until she had cleared the fireroom and alerted the chief engineer to the emergency.

Ahlgren, a member of the third graduating class to include women, demonstrated by her example that the Academy's most recent graduates both understood and honored its proudest traditions.

Returning to the Helm

After a long and difficult decade, Admiral Engel's tenure had finally ended, and the Academy needed new leadership. In the fall of 1979, with Engel off the Academy stage, Deputy Superintendent Howard F. Casey stepped in as acting superintendent, giving MARAD time to conduct a search for an appropriate successor to Engel. Casey, a Silver Star recipient in World War II, had been assistant Maritime administrator in the mid-1970s. A gifted mathematician, he was well liked at MARAD and the Academy, and was generally considered a strong candidate for the superintendent's position. But the Alumni Association was pushing strongly for a Kings Pointer to be appointed the next superintendent, and submitted four names for MARAD's consideration: Captains Thomas King, '42, and Thomas Patterson, '44, both out of MARAD; Rear Admiral Carl Seiberlich, '43, the first Kings Pointer ever to make flag rank in the navy; and Coast Guard vice admiral Robert Scarborough, '44, who achieved the same distinction in the Coast Guard.[3]

Given their recent experience with Engel—and for those with long memories, with McLintock before him—MARAD officials were determined to find the right man. High on their list of qualifications for the next superintendent, presumably, was a demonstrated aptitude for *peacemaking*. Both MARAD and the Academy needed someone who could rebuild the bridges between those two institutions, between the Academy and the industry, and between the Academy's administration and the Regiment.

MARAD's short list of candidates for superintendent included three of the names suggested by the alumni: Tom King, who had led the Academy for four months during Engel's Washington assignment, Tom Patterson, and Carl Seiberlich. Patterson, a longtime captain in the U.S. Navy and later a rear admiral in the maritime service, was initially interested in the post, but after several months had passed without any apparent change in Engel's status, Patterson asked to be taken out of consideration because he felt the uncertain time frame was hindering his effectiveness as MARAD's West Coast regional director. (Several years later, Patterson was asked by Maritime Administrator Harold Shear to become the deputy superintendent at Kings Point, a post Patterson filled skillfully for three years before electing to retire.) Seiberlich removed himself from the pool as well; as the first commander of the navy's personnel department, he had committed himself to a complicated organizational project, and was unable to leave his post.

Thus King quickly emerged as the chosen candidate, and Seiberlich (who had been supportive of both King and Patterson) facilitated MARAD's selection by helping King obtain a commission in the naval reserve. As Seiberlich recalled:

> I was a great promoter of Tom King once it became clear he was the consensus candidate. But he didn't have a commission in the merchant marine reserve, and I was then commander of the navy personnel command. So I went to see the secretary of the navy, and explained to him that we needed Tom King, with his experience, and we needed to get him commissioned.
>
> I got his commission put together as a captain in the merchant marine reserve. And then I hand-carried it over to the Congress, and we put it as a rider on a bill, and we got him commissioned as a captain in the merchant marine reserve and the naval reserve in five days—a process that normally takes months.
>
> Normally they only send the list over once a year, and they put it all on one bill. But I felt Tom King was the right man, and therefore, if I had to take extraordinary strides to get him commissioned in the merchant marine reserve, I was going to get it done. And that's what we were able to do.[4]

With the help of Seiberlich and other influential figures, King was selected on July 13, 1980, as the sixth superintendent of the Academy, and the first Kings Pointer to hold the office. He was commissioned as rear admiral in the maritime service the following day.

King fit MARAD's bill in every way. Unlike Engel, who had shown little interest in the maritime industry, King was steeped in industry practice and blessed with extensive contacts. Though he had graduated from the Academy too early to receive a degree, he was a valued member—even an informal leader—of the Kings Point alumni community. A longtime MARAD insider, he could be counted on to work with the bureaucracy instead of against it; and during his tenure at MARAD, King had proven himself to be a peacemaker, working to repair the breaches that inevitably occured in the course of doing business.

King's style of leadership invites comparison with that of Ronald Reagan, then only months away from being elected president of the United States. King, like Reagan, was a highly effective communicator. He was both admired and trusted by those he commanded. He established a well-defined agenda for his administration—a short list of priorities—and he was not swayed from pursuing those goals. In areas outside of his specific focus, he didn't hesitate to delegate responsibility to those with greater expertise, including his dean, Paul Krinsky, '50. But he also had a deep understanding of the institution that he directed, and was fully prepared to act, based on that understanding.

Welcomed to the Throne

Though there were probably no midshipmen left at Kings Point who remembered King from his brief 1977 stint as superintendent, his appointment was greeted very favorably by the Regiment. Speaking to the *Kings Pointer*, Regimental Commander Midshipman Robert Schatzman of Spring Lake, New Jersey, called the move "a real morale booster. We think the world of King, and we believe he's concerned about us, and will listen to our ideas and suggestions."[5]

In the same article, King reminisced about his own experiences as a cadet at Kings Point:

> I can recall marching in Great Neck's Memorial Day Parade, and being royally chewed out by Horton Spurr for looking less than

sharp. Of course, my section had just returned from sea, and our marching was a bit rusty. In fact, it was horrible.

And then there was a calisthenics drill at Kings Point nearly forty years ago. This also took place right after sea duty, and we were being put through a really rigorous exercise program. I was out of breath, huffing and puffing, and I thought, "It's all over now. I'll never make it." Fortunately, I did make it, but now, every time I walk past that spot, I think, "That's where I almost expired."[6]

King's words served to remind both midshipmen and alumni that he had strong credentials as a Kings Pointer. Many older readers of the alumni magazine could recall their own encounters with Horton Spurr, and their own near-death experiences with calisthenics.

As suggested above, King was also extremely well liked among the Academy's alumni. Part of this affection grew out of his prior role as acting superintendent; probably the larger part grew out of his close ties to the industry. As Charles Renick recalled:

> King came to us as somebody everyone in the industry knew. During the Korean War he made a name for himself, and then he was Maritime administrative director at New Orleans, for the southern region. Then they moved him up to New York.
>
> At that time, those directorships were big jobs and came with big offices. In New York, the director's offices occupied a whole floor in the Federal Building, and they had responsibility for all the subsidies for all the shipping companies in New York, Boston, and the whole East Coast down to Philadelphia and Baltimore.
>
> All of that came under King's authority. So he knew everyone, and everyone knew him. And he was a very likable fellow, a hale-and-hearty guy whom everybody liked.[7]

The alumni publication immediately came out in support of King's appointment. James Yocum, '47, president of the Alumni Association, noted that he and his colleagues in the association had "worked long and hard for this moment."[8]

The faculty and administration, too, generally approved of King's appointment, deeming him an honest and loyal leader. Captain Robert Safarik, '61, whom King recruited as his assistant commandant in 1983, remembered King as, "competent, serious, a mentor, a very sincere person. You knew that if you did your job, you'd stay out of trouble, because he was a straight arrow. He really was. If you did it by the book, and did a good job, he'd be extremely loyal to you. And that cut both ways, of course. If he'd told me to walk off the pier, I'd have walked off the pier."[9]

After years of erratic and imperious leadership, the Kings Point community finally had a leader they could trust and respect.

Setting Goals

Almost from his first day on the job, King began working to put out the local fires, to build bridges between the Academy and MARAD, and to find ways that the school could better serve industry needs. A 1980 article in the student newspaper, reporting on King's goals as incoming superintendent, reflects many of these priorities: ending "the uncertainty and instability" at Kings Point; improving "the morale and pride of the Regiment;" and keeping the maritime industry better informed about the Academy.[10]

King later explained that when he took the reins, the institution had become alienated from its natural allies: the Maritime Administration and the industry. He "tried to change that," he recalled:

> I tried to become part of the team, so to speak, to get greater support from our national headquarters, both financially, and politically. . . .
> I hoped that I would be able to reorient the institution to make it more identified with the maritime industry. I felt that the organization needed some loosening up, and some reorientation. I also felt that there was a great deal more potential here than was being realized, and that the Academy had the capability to do many things.[11]

What emerges from these and similar comments made by King is a focus on the *future*. What could the Academy do better in the future? What new assignments could it take on? But King knew well that before it could step into its future, the Academy had to shore up its most important relationships. Paul Krinsky, King's dean and later his deputy superintendent, recalls that King had the capacity to draw on tradition to move forward:

> Tom effectively smoothed relations between the Academy and the Maritime Administration. That was number one. Number two, he worked closely with the alumni, and had their respect. Number

three, Tom was part of the industry in New York City. He belonged
to every committee, every board—*everything*—and was closely identified with that.

And so all of these things which we did not have before—identity, friendship, and respect from the Maritime Administration, the
alumni, and the industry—we now had, and you had to ask yourself:
how did we survive *without* that? Suddenly Tom King comes in, and
he brings all that together—a man of the old school, also receptive to
new things.[12]

Like his nearly coterminous counterpart in the White House, King
took office with a reservoir of goodwill, and he deepened that reservoir
over time. And for Tom King, as for Ronald Reagan, external circumstances soon tested the depth of that goodwill and fully taxed his leadership skills. The bridges that he built, and the institutions he
strengthened, proved vital to the Academy as the maritime industry
suffered wrenching reversals in the early 1980s.

Changing Seas in Washington

Nine months after King assumed the reins at Kings Point, Ronald Reagan was sworn in as the fortieth president of the United States, and for
the ninth consecutive time, the U.S. Merchant Marine Academy band,
led by director Ken Force, participated in the inaugural parade.

Friends of the Academy cautiously embraced the new administration. During his presidential campaign, Reagan had pledged his strong
support for the maritime industry. As many observers saw it, the need
for such support was dire. By 1980, U.S. ships were carrying less than
5 percent of the nation's foreign commerce—in other words, a state of
decline that hadn't been seen since before World War I.[13] In a speech
to maritime industry executives in 1980, candidate Reagan promised to

- Provide a unified direction for all government programs affecting
  maritime interest of the United States
- Ensure that the vital shipbuilding mobilization base is preserved
- Improve utilization of military resources by increasing commer-
  cial participation in support functions
- Recognize the challenges created by cargo policies of other nations

- Restore the cost competitiveness of U.S. flag operators in the international marketplace
- Revitalize the domestic water transportation system
- Reduce the severe regulatory environment that inhibits American competitiveness.[14]

That was the good news. But to the perceptive observer, there were warning flags flying on inauguration day. The Republicans had won their resounding victory in the November 1980 elections, capturing both the White House and the Senate, in part by running against government. As it turned out, Reagan's inauguration ushered in a new era of so-called supply-side economics, which assumed that deep tax cuts would prompt an economic boom—and, not incidentally, force significant reductions in the scale and scope of government.

But for the maritime industry, "smaller government" generally translated into reduced subsidies and fewer protective regulations, which in turn translated into even more decline. So far from helping an already struggling maritime industry, the economic policies of the Reagan administration would deal the industry a body blow.

The gap between Reagan's maritime promises and policies can be attributed, in part, to Reagan's longtime domestic economic adviser, Martin Anderson, who was appointed assistant to the president for policy development upon Reagan's election. Anderson, according to maritime historians Andrew Gibson and Arthur Donovan, "categorically opposed all government subsidies to industry."[15] Meanwhile, Anderson's wife, Annelise, was appointed to the Office of Management and Budget (OMB), and was given oversight of the Maritime Commission. Within months, her office had released what Gibson and Donovan later described as a "poorly researched document attacking the national security argument for supporting the U.S. flag merchant marine."[16]

This document marked the beginning of what appeared to be a systematic weakening of the Maritime Administration. In August 1981, OMB transferred MARAD from the Department of Commerce to the Department of Transportation. Coincident with this departmental shuffle, OMB stripped the Maritime administrator of the title of assistant secretary for maritime affairs, and shifted all policy-related responsibilities to the secretary of transportation. This action, according to most observers, greatly diluted MARAD's influence on maritime policy.[17] It also complicated budgeting: perhaps through an oversight, appropriations for MARAD remained in the control of the Senate Appropriations Subcommittee that controlled the budgets for the departments of State, Justice, and Commerce but not Transportation, where MARAD now resided. As Vice Admiral Albert Herberger, Maritime administrator in the mid-1990s, later recalled, this meant that MARAD was stuck in bureaucratic budget limbo:

> The budget was terrible. We were getting zeroed out on the budget. We couldn't get any incremental changes. They weren't even covering the government-sanctioned pay raises. So a pay raise would come in, and we'd have to eat it out of our operating funds.
>
> And that was because MARAD had shifted from the Department of Commerce. Our appropriations stayed in State, Justice, Commerce—so there we were, with the Federal Maritime Commission, Small Business Administration, and so on. The Appropriations Committee had no interest in us. And every year, there was a crisis at one or the other—State, Justice, or Commerce—where they were decrementing all the other budgets 10 percent, 15 percent, to throw in resources to build more prisons, or go after the drug problem, or whatever. So we were just there, with nobody sponsoring us. We could no longer go to the secretary of transportation because we weren't in his budget.[18]

A stark example of the effects of this transition on the maritime industry arose nine months later, in May 1982, when Secretary of Transportation Drew Lewis announced that the administration would not be seeking funds for shipbuilding subsidies for 1982 or 1983. Lewis called the move temporary (which it wasn't), and added that there was an important loophole for shipowners. He cited the 1981 Reconciliation Act, in which Congress stipulated that shipowners—one of two groups who would be hurt the most by the abolition of shipbuilding subsidies—for one year would be allowed to buy foreign-built ships that would be eligible for operating differential subsidies.[19] Shipyards, the other potential victims of the policy shift, were actually in pretty good shape. By this time, the administration had announced its plans for a six-hundred-ship navy, and it appeared that shipyards would be busy for the foreseeable future building this huge fleet.

Less than a month after announcing the suspension of subsidies, Lewis sounded a very different note in a commencement speech at

Kings Point. He referred to a "new maritime policy" which would "halt and reverse our maritime decline." Those listening closely, however, heard Lewis say that this policy would not be implemented through "massive federal outlays," but through a reliance on the "inherent strengths and resources of the private sector."[20] Again, the Anderson policy against subsidizing private industry prevailed, and the maritime industry suffered. By December 1984, Lloyd's List was reporting that 60.4 million tons deadweight shipping were laid up at piers around the world.[21]

But the impact of the Reagan policy was felt at Kings Point well before 1984. A *New York Times* article published in June 1982 cited the graduating students' frustrations with a weakening job market: "Unlike seniors from past classes who had no trouble lining up maritime careers, the class of '82 has not had an abundance of job offers. A check last week found that half of . . . 256 [graduates] had not found maritime work."[22] In 1969, the article continued, 94 percent of graduates had found jobs at sea within three months of graduation. In 1979, the corresponding figure was 95.6 percent. In 1981, it had dropped to 74 percent, and the outlook for 1982 was even bleaker.

Rather than addressing the root causes of the weakening job market, the Department of Transportation responded by reducing the Academy's entering class size. The classes entering in 1983 and 1984 were cut by 10 percent. Over the next three years, additional cuts were made; by 1987, the class had been cut by approximately 25 percent. From an entering class of 354 in 1982, the Academy's incoming pipeline had shrunk to 266 in 1987.[23]

As jobs at sea continued to dwindle, the Academy once again faced difficult questions about its relevance. Traditionally, the Academy's supporters had relied on two central arguments for its continued existence. These were summarized in the school's mission statement: supplying officers for the maritime industry (i.e., an economic rationale), and supplying trained officers for the naval reserve (i.e., a defense-related rationale). The collapsing job market called the economic rationale into question, and—with forces within the government now questioning the importance of the merchant marine to national defense—the defense rationale also was coming under attack. Budget-cutters could argue that there was no longer any compelling reason to underwrite the Academy.

And that, apparently, is what they did. At some point in the first two years of the Reagan administration, OMB apparently circulated a memo calling for the closure of the Academy.[24]

The recommendations in this memo were not pursued by OMB, in part because of a Department of Transportation study performed at OMB's request in June 1983. This study found that the Academy was a "valid and major institution of maritime training" that produced high-quality graduates.[25] The report also provided welcome ammunition to Academy supporters. It pointed out, for example, that even though decreasing enrollment at the Academy necessarily would raise annual per-student costs from $52,000 to $71,000, the Academy still would enjoy much lower total costs-per-student than any of the other four federal service academies.

But other forces were at work on behalf of the Academy as well. Inside the school, Superintendent King was working hard to rally the industry behind his institution, in large part by changing the way the Academy related to that industry. Outside the school, meanwhile, the Academy's increasingly influential alumni population stood up to defend their alma mater.

Fixing the System

One of the primary barriers to better industry connections encountered by King upon his arrival was the composition of his faculty. By the 1980s, most members of the original wartime faculty had retired, and many among the new generation of professors, although they brought academic credentials important to the Academy's accreditation, had little experience in the maritime industry. One of King's first priorities, therefore, was to weed out faculty members who were unable or unwilling to gear their teaching toward the maritime industry. As he later recalled:

> I saw that many of the faculty here who had replaced the original faculty—which was very much maritime-oriented—were people who were journeymen educators. They would have a job here, and they would have a job at Queens College at night, and so forth. They really had no identification with the industry.
>
> I remember one economics professor who had his students studying how public housing in New York City was financed. I said to him, "Well, that would seem to be a suitable approach for a

regular institution. But financing the American merchant marine is one of the major problems of this industry. You have the government Title XI mortgage insurance. You have all sorts of incentives, and problems to overcome, in financing a fleet of ships."

I said, "People just don't plunk down the full cost of a ship. It's financed. You have the operating subsidy, you have the construction subsidy, you have limitations there. If you want to do an economic study, why don't you study the American merchant marine? Why are you studying public housing?"

And he said, "Well, I don't know anything *about* the American merchant marine." So here he was walking around in a uniform, and yet knew nothing about the American merchant marine, and didn't have any interest in it. And I thought, "How far has this *gone* within the faculty?"[26]

King resolved to address this problem. Among other concrete actions, he made it clear that he was willing to veto appointments to tenure if he felt the candidate was not sufficiently in tune with the maritime industry.

But in his efforts to increase industry experience among faculty members, King faced one major limiting factor: the faculty's lack of diversity. In 1980, the USMMA faculty consisted of seventy-seven people. Of this number, none were women; none were black, Hispanic, or Native American; and only one was Asian. Though women and blacks were well represented on the staff (at 44 percent, combined), they were concentrated in the lower grades of service.[27]

Both King's administration and MARAD were determined to take steps to improve this situation. A plan developed in 1980 called for actions that would increase the number of minority applicants for both faculty and staff positions, with the concrete goal of hiring six minority faculty members by the end of fiscal year 1980—an ambitious target for a small faculty. It was especially ambitious in light of King's goal to build a faculty that was in touch with the maritime industry.

To hit this target, the Academy worked on many fronts. These included, for example, contacting potential female and minority candidates in universities with marine science and technology programs comparable to the Academy's; advertising in periodicals aimed at minorities, and using professional minority recruitment organizations; establishing part-time positions to accommodate "qualified candidates who are not now available for full time employment, but will be in the future"; and establishing an Equal Opportunity Recruitment File to keep track of applications of female and minority candidates.[28]

Changing a faculty, particularly in the tenured ranks, is a painfully slow process, especially if the institution is not in a position to expand its ranks. But the first steps toward effecting that change are recognizing the need to change, and putting a plan in place to get there. Early in King's superintendency, the Academy took these first two steps.

The Challenge of Continuing Education

In another effort to strengthen its ties to the maritime industry, the Academy developed a new focus on continuing education. The idea of offering specialized training to working mariners at Kings Point was not new, of course; the NS *Savannah* program had enjoyed notable success at the Academy in the 1960s, offering specialized nuclear engineering training to merchant marine engineering officers.

Hoping to build on this success, the Maritime Administration as early as 1962 developed a proposal for postgraduate or "refresher" training of merchant marine officers at the Academy. The proposal envisioned a four-week course, offered approximately eight times per year, and tailored to deck or engineering officers. The deck course would have included instruction in "electronic aids to navigation, stability and trim, meteorology, ship behavior, and damage control,"[29] while the engineering course would have included "electricity, air conditioning, turbines, boilers, automatic controls, and auxiliary equipment."

For whatever reason, these courses were never offered. In 1964, however, the Civil Service Commission sponsored an executive seminar center at the Academy, offering career upgrading courses for government employees in GS-14 and GS-15 positions. The full curriculum offered ten two-week courses on a wide range of subjects, including the administration of public policy, the intersection of social needs and federal programs, and national defense–related topics.[30] These programs had little relevance to maritime affairs, and didn't particularly play to the Academy's strengths. Nevertheless, the executive seminars helped get Kings Point onto the radar screen of many in Washington, and they continued to enjoy success well into the 1980s.

As the *Savannah* program wound down in the 1970s, maritime-related continuing education at the Academy slowed too, and seemed in danger of disappearing altogether. New industry trends in the late seventies, however, brought about a revival. As related previously, Academy faculty developed a new undergraduate diesel engineering course, and at the same time established an intensive four-week upgrading course for working engineers. The course, which was significantly subsidized by MARAD, was directed by engineering professor Captain Robert Madden, '59. Over a period of several years, hundreds of marine engineers were trained at Kings Point to crew the new diesel vessels then under construction.

In 1978, the diesel upgrading courses were formalized as the Continuing Education program at the Academy, and engineering professor Commander Stanley G. Christensen was named the program's director. The courses offered included fundamentals of marine diesel systems, diesel propulsion systems for marine engineers, repair techniques for slow speed diesel engines, and diesel ship operation and control for chief mates and masters.

In 1979, Charles Renick, writing in the *Kings Pointer*, reported another new development in continuing education at the Academy. Renick noted that Kings Point, through the auspices of the Alumni Association–sponsored U.S. Maritime Resource Center (MRC), was increasingly being called upon to host industry meetings and symposia. In February 1979, for example, the Academy hosted a seminar titled Diesel Ship Propulsion in the United States, cosponsored by the Institute of Marine Engineers and the U.S. Maritime Research Center. Another industry seminar, Oil Imports and Transportation to the United States, was scheduled for May, and cosponsored by Burmah Oil.[31] And in June, two dozen ships' masters attended a one-week seminar, The Master's Liability Today, at which Academy faculty and guest lecturers discussed "potential legal problems faced by master mariners."[32]

The Maritime Resource Center was headed by Admiral Carl Seiberlich, '43, and Alumni Association president Charles R. Cushing, '56. The goal—in the spirit of the National Maritime Resource Center of the early 1970s—was to make the Academy a "focal point for maritime research and affairs."[33] Over the course of the next several years, the number and scope of the MRC seminars continued to increase. Although still relatively small-scale, they again put Kings Point in the minds of decision makers in industry and government. The MRC also laid the foundation for the modern program of continuing education at the Academy.

In addition to the seminar program, course-based continuing education was also flourishing under Superintendent King. In a 1982 article in the *Journal of Commerce*, King stressed the increasingly important role that he believed continuing education would play in the maritime industry.

> Each and every step forward into the era of automated controls, each advance in the systems approach to navigation, collision avoidance, on-board computers which perform trim and stability calculations, and such tanker techniques as oil washing and tank inerting–all of these innovations bring with them implicit responsibilities for both maintenance and training.
>
> In the future, refresher training must be accepted as a requirement for licensed shipboard personnel. No longer will it be advisable or responsible for a mariner to secure his senior license and then simply renew it time and again for twenty to thirty years. "Back to school" will be the mariner's future way of life if he is to avoid becoming the unseaworthy seaman.[34]

With King's strong support, the continuing education program at Kings Point expanded into new fields, as suggested by industry trends. In 1985, for example, in addition to the diesel engineering courses, the Academy offered a one-week course in improving the fuel efficiency of steam power plants, and another program in the analysis of shipboard vibration.[35]

Continuing education took another step forward in 1985 with the establishment of the Master Mariners Readiness Course, created and taught by navy captain Herman Fritzke, '48. This weeklong course, fully funded by MARAD, targeted senior civilian masters and deck mates who might be called upon to command merchant ships during a national emergency, as well as port captains and fleet operating managers. The course served as a complement to the Ready Reserve Fleet concept, which had been introduced in the early 1980s to deal with strategic sealift emergencies, and focused on the crucial interface between the maritime industry and the navy.

A 1985 description of the course in the Academy's annual report noted that "operating merchant ships under enemy threat is significantly different from operating in peacetime." It pointed out that most merchant marine officers were "unfamiliar with the functions of the National Shipping Authority that governs the employment and use of merchant ships in a national emergency; few have had training in performing those tasks that are required when under naval control."[36] The Master Mariners Readiness Program, according to the Academy, offered efficient training in the "practical and crucial aspects of shipboard tasks during a period of national emergency leading to mobilization."

The Academy's continuing education program grew incrementally through the 1960s, 1970s, and early 1980s. Slowly but surely, it gained credibility, stature, and momentum. But even this limited success created new challenges. Simply put, the program was only loosely organized. When it first began to generate a surplus, for example, there was no mechanism in place to deal with this welcome cash infusion. Initially, and awkwardly, the surplus was funneled through the Melville Hall Officers' Club—a temporary solution, at best. To develop into a stable, self-supporting, and opportunistic entity, the continuing education program would have to become far more businesslike.

Modernizing the Curriculum

As noted earlier, Tom King felt comfortable delegating important tasks to able subordinates. One of those tasks, early in his tenure, was the challenge of updating the curriculum. The subordinate to whom he entrusted this task was Academic Dean Paul Krinsky.

Krinsky came to the task well qualified. As academic dean under Admiral Engel, he had already steered the Academy through several important advances in the curriculum. One of these, an initiative begun in the mid-1970s, was the design of an elective program in marine engineering systems that would meet the Engineers' Council for Professional Development accreditation standards. By the time King took office, this accreditation process was well under way, aided in part by sympathetic outsiders. (Dr. Irene Peden is a case in point. A member of the Academy's Advisory Board and a professor of electrical engineering and associate dean at the University of Washington in Seattle, Peden helped analyze the program and suggest areas for improvement.) The new curriculum offered greater depth in mathematics, and a significant engineering design component. In 1982, soon after a new engineering department head, Captain Edward Wiggins, took office, the new governing body—the Accrediting Board for Engineering and Technology (ABET)—approved the new program.

In another important advance, Krinsky began laying the groundwork in the mid-1980s to incorporate computers into the curriculum
far more extensively. The 1984 academic plan laid out a five-part road
map to increased computer use:

- Study the feasibility of incorporating increased computer usage
  into various courses in the engineering curriculum.

- Look closely at use of microcomputers in physics and chemical
  teaching in the 1980s. Investigate the possibility of a micro-
  processor lab, experiments done with the aid of microprocessors,
  interfacing of microprocessors, and using a microcomputer to
  help students learn graphics.

- Explore the desirability/necessity of requiring all entering students to bring a "personal computer."

- Increase the use of computers in all relevant disciplines of the
  Marine Transportation Dept. Revise course content in appropriate disciplines of the dept to take advantage of the latest in computer tech and applications in those courses which can be
  enhanced by such techniques.

- Develop a faculty awareness and comfort with computers as used
  ashore in the industry and on-board ship. Through specific training increase facility at a predetermined level, through structured
  exercises and requirements. Through industry contacts determine the levels of competence that seem to be appropriate in different areas, and seek to achieve such levels.[37]

The third component listed above, requiring all students to bring
or acquire a personal computer upon enrollment at Kings Point, was
implemented in 1988. One of the first such requirements in the nation,
it seemed appropriate to Krinsky and his colleagues for a school with
a heavy focus on engineering.

Meanwhile, other areas of the Academy's academic program were
making advances on their own, even without strong pushes from the
administration. The Computer Aided Operations Research Facility
(CAORF) simulator, for example, was emerging as an indispensable
facet of midshipman training. The immediate impetus for this development was the need to meet new, stricter sea-time requirements established by the Intergovernmental Maritime Consultative Organization

(IMCO), but the benefits of the simulator as a training aid quickly became apparent. As the *Journal of Commerce* commented approvingly, "Where can a merchant marine officer trainee face the hair-raising situation of commanding a vessel dead in the water and about to collide with two other ships? It happens every day on the ship's bridge simulator at the US Merchant Marine Academy."[38]

The class of 1982 was the first to experience a thirty-hour bridge simulation course. Superintendent King proudly called this a "quantum training step forward."[39] In little more than a decade, the simulator had traveled a long way from its roots as a tool for an isolated outpost of MARAD researchers.

Nautical Science Meets Business

Strong institutions scrutinize and hold themselves to high standards. King's administration, as noted, ushered in a period of relative calm and stability. This enhanced the institution's self-confidence, which in turn opened the door to some much-needed self-evaluation.

In this period, for example, the Nautical Science Department posed some tough questions about its own "deck" degree, and, after some tugging and pulling, came up with some interesting answers. Through these efforts, the department added academic depth to its core offerings, and concurrently succeeded in adapting those offerings to the changing needs of the maritime industry.

Dean Paul Krinsky describes this maturation of the deck degree as the Academy's last large step in the transition from a training program to a collegiate degree. Engineering, of course, had recently completed the transition from purely practical training to a more rigorous education, and the accreditation of the marine engineering systems program in 1982 served as formal validation of this transition. But the change came harder and more slowly on the deck side of the shop.

As explained in previous chapters, engineering at the Academy was based from the outset on engineering programs at traditional schools. Tightening up the marine engineering program, therefore, had largely involved giving students increased exposure to the theoretical sciences that were crucial to the practice of engineering. The nautical science program had always lacked an equivalent unifying academic core; as a result, modernizing the nautical science program was rarely so straightforward. Dean Krinsky, a deckie himself, saw this problem clearly:

Nautical science, in its purest form, was just that. It was knots and splices, navigation, and cargo handling. Then electronics came in, and so forth. But it was essentially a body of knowledge that had to do with driving a ship. And so in some ways, it was an inferior academic curriculum, fleshed out with more of the humanities, perhaps, and more business courses.

The business courses were always in there. It was called Ship's Business when I went to school. You learned about the documents that were needed to clear and arrive a ship, and so forth; manifests, and things of that nature. But the department didn't have that conventional, recognizable body of knowledge that you would find in other academic environments.[40]

The first step, as Krinsky and his change-minded colleagues saw it, was to build up the "conventional" knowledge surrounding the nautical science degree. The Academy had started down this road in the 1950s and 1960s, when it had offered to deck midshipmen increased instruction in business and in the humanities. But as of 1980, these classes were located in the Maritime Law and Economics Department, rather than in the Nautical Science Department. This led to some fragmentation, and prevented the capturing of some obvious synergies between the disciplines.

The first voice to raise the possibility of merging the Maritime Law and Nautical Science departments belonged to Lee Pearson, acting head of the Nautical Science Department.[41] His successor, Captain W. T. McMullen, embraced the idea, and worked with Paul Krinsky and Maritime Law and Economics Department head Larry Jarrett to achieve the consolidation. McMullen, in a 1980 memo to Krinsky, cited faculty support for a merger, and articulated the basic rationale for the move. "Philosophically," the memo read, "it is anomalous to retain the present divided structure when both departments have a direct, vital, and related interest in the Deck midshipmen. Their interests are not disparate."[42]

The idea generated opposition. Jarrett, for one, was initially less than enthusiastic. He agreed to further study of the proposal, however, and in time came to support the move. His support proved crucial. "He was the last remaining senior department head," Krinsky explained, "and he was one of my mentors. He had been Acting Dean before [Janus] Poppe."[43] In other words, his opinion carried great weight. Gradually, Krinsky brought Jarrett around to a new way of looking at things, and in March 1982, Krinsky, McMullen, and Jarrett agreed in principle to the merger.

Many details remained to be fleshed out. Later the same month, a faculty committee, comprised of three representatives from each department, was formed to study the matter. Nautical science professors Commander Robert Meurn, '58, Captain A. G. Fialcowitz, and Lieutenant Commander J. E. Hall were tapped to join the committee, along with Commanders H. Katz, R. Hershey, and H. A. Allen from the Department of Maritime Law and Economics. In their early meetings, the group formulated some basic principles. For example: the new department would offer a core curriculum to all deck midshipmen, with courses in both nautical science and maritime business administration. In addition, midshipmen would have the option of taking an elective concentration in one of the two areas. Within three months, the committee had developed a comprehensive core and elective curriculum for the new department.[44]

A knottier issue, and one that McMullen had foreseen in his 1981 memo, was leadership of the new department. The committee recommended a single department head and two division chiefs, one for each of the component areas of nautical science and maritime business administration. In June 1983, McMullen was named head of the new department, while Commander Robert Meurn was named chief of the Division of Nautical Science, and Captain Harold Katz was named chief of the Division of Maritime Business Administration. Jarrett, whose support had been crucial to the smooth transition, agreed to step down, and was named distinguished professor of law and associate dean for special projects.

As an addendum to the change, Krinsky also redesignated the Shipboard Training Office as the Department of Shipboard Training. The shift gave the Sea Year curriculum equal weight with the other departments, and thereby formally recognized the importance of the Sea Year to the Academy degree. Both changes were approved by Maritime Administrator Harold Shear in late March 1983, and took effect July 1.

Krinsky later admitted that he had some hesitation, and even misgivings, regarding the departmental merger:

> I have no pride of authorship in this, really. I, like others, have many times along the way said, "Maybe this was a mistake. Maybe we ought to just fragment the whole thing again."

But I felt then, and I still feel now, that the idea of turning out a deck officer who understands the whole concept of transportation and logistics, in the new mode of the marine transportation business, is as sound a thesis as turning out a marine engineer who knows how to operate a ship, but understands how to design the engines, and what makes them work, and understands the scientific background of it. That's what makes the Kings Point curriculum a little bit different.[45]

The road after the merger still presented bumps. One point of irritation was that humanities classes were moved into Samuels Hall, which had recently been renovated for use by nautical science classes, with specially designed equipment lockers and other features. "Instead of teaching how Herman Melville might have used the equipment," commented one faculty member, "they were teaching Herman Melville."[46] The fact that the terminal degrees in the two divisions were different also required careful attention from the administration. A PhD was required for tenure in maritime business, whereas an unlimited master's license (with sailing time on that license) was required in nautical science.

Most observers agreed that, despite these challenges, the merged department prepared graduates to function more effectively in a fast-changing and difficult maritime climate. Closer to home, the change also paved the way for a continued modernization of the deck curriculum.

Restoring "Honor" to the Honor Code

The turmoil of the 1970s, by most accounts, had damaged the morale of the Regiment. Taking advantage of the new tone of calm and civility, the Academy's administration worked to rebuild that morale. A key step in that direction was the restructuring of the honor code.

The Academy had first adopted an honor code in 1957. This first code was imposed upon the midshipmen without their input, and—not surprisingly—attitudes toward it were mixed. Within three years of its implementation, the matter was put to a vote by the Regiment. In April 1960, more than 75 percent of the student body voted to retain some kind of honor code. Over the next several months, however, as the Cadet Honor Board held multiple meetings regarding possible revisions to the code, the process bogged down and stalled. Ultimately, the board proved unable to come to a consensus. In 1961, therefore, the negotiations were placed in the hands of an honor committee, composed of members of all of the classes. This ad hoc committee worked with the Regiment and the faculty to establish an honor system that was both rigorous and workable. This system continued in effect for more than twenty years, with mostly positive results.

Like its sister academies, however, Kings Point was not immune to honor code infractions, nor to dereliction of duty on the part of the board that regulated the code. One troubling case arose in the early 1980s, when a student who was accused of cheating, and was believed to be guilty by the faculty, was absolved by the Midshipman Honor Board. The faculty was outraged, and this sequence of events persuaded Superintendent King to suspend the code, pending a reevaluation of the whole honor system. King then set up a committee to conduct that reevaluation.

One of the faculty members who served on that committee was Captain Christopher McMahon, a 1977 graduate who had returned to the Academy in 1984 as a navigation instructor. The main problem with the code as it had operated in the 1960s, McMahon recalls, was that it had no effective oversight. With the input of members of the Regiment, the committee worked to update this structure. "What we did," McMahon explained, "is we came up with a tiered approach where the midshipmen essentially maintained control, but there was oversight. The classes that were here in 1984 and 1985 were very instrumental in building this new honor program."[47] Essentially, the committee decided to add a new entity to the chain of responsibility, creating the Honor Review Board to oversee the Midshipman Honor Board. The Honor Review Board, composed of commissioned officers, was given the prerogative to remand any case back to the Midshipman Honor Board with suggestions for further study. The Honor Review Board could then pass on the Midshipman Honor Board's findings to the superintendent with one of three recommendations: to approve without changes, to approve with changes, or not to approve.[48]

The committee also considered the controversial "no tolerance" clause that served as a centerpiece of the honor codes at sister institutions. Both the West Point and Air Force Academy codes stated that a cadet "will not lie, cheat, or steal, nor tolerate those who do." Although this was hard to argue with in principle–why would someone "tolerate" misbehavior in others?–it led directly to difficult choices. If Cadet A knew that Cadet B had violated the code, then Cadet A was obligated to turn Cadet B in to the authorities or be considered as guilty as Cadet B. Many in the Kings Point administration felt that this simply wasn't true (Cadet B was clearly more guilty than Cadet A) and that it placed an undue burden on cadets.

Admiral King concurred, believing that changes to the code were necessary, especially in light of changes in the larger society:

> I think the honor code has a cyclical aspect. I think it reflects what's happening in the society at large. Given that fact, can you take these young people from society, and bring them in here, and expect them to automatically adhere to a code that is probably not being observed in much of society, in terms of the basic principles involved? I think that it runs in cycles. But given that basic fact, we tried to instill the honor code, and support the honor code.[49]

The Academy had been lucky, according to King, that it had not suffered the kinds of scandals that had come to light at other federal institutions–notably West Point in 1951 and 1976, and the Air Force Academy in 1965, 1967, and 1984.[50] The revisions to the code aimed to remove the element of luck, and replace it with discipline.[51]

A Period of Transition

As superintendent, Tom King focused on the big picture. When he worried about regimental morale, he tended to focus on the morale of the Regiment *as a whole*. Particular subsets of the Regiment, for example, the female cadets, did not receive any special attention from Admiral King.

Although the female cadets were regarded with a gender-blind eye by King's administration, which was how most of these young women preferred it, most of the time, their presence at the Academy still raised hackles among traditionalists. As a result, female midshipmen sometimes had to deal with insensitivity, ignorance, and even abuse. The growing conservatism of the broader society in the Reagan years, during which liberal shibboleths like diversity and affirmative action began to come under fire, exacerbated the situation.

Part of the problem stemmed from the simple fact that the women were a highly visible minority. They couldn't *help* but stand out. A female midshipman summed up this dilemma in the student newspaper in 1978: "Unfortunately, being a visible minority makes it impossible to blend into the woodwork like so many of the white majority have done so skillfully. One is also subjected to extraordinary preferential treatment (commonly known as preferential punishment to the Kings Point women), as one can immediately be identified in a crowd of midshipmen."[52]

Even the male cadets acknowledged that their female counterparts sometimes suffered from "preferential punishment." In a 1983 interview with the *El Paso Times*, Midshipman Willie Solis commented that life at the Academy could be particularly tough on the women. "Maybe because they're girls," Solis observed, "they might catch more guff. They don't have to take boxing class, but they get yelled at just the same as guys. They're always crying."[53]

Occasionally, the administration took steps to improve the lot of women on campus. But this often served mainly to annoy the male students, who saw female classmates getting special privileges, which in turn led to the women being further isolated.

Jane Brickman, a humanities professor who was tapped to run the new women's advisory program in 1983, recalls the bitterness that arose among the male midshipmen when she arranged for a series of special lunch meetings for the women students:

> The thing that had the most impact, but also got the men so rattled, was our special lunch meetings. We would have them in Land Hall, and I'd get a nice lunch made for the women. Sometimes we'd just talk. Sometimes we would have a guest speaker. In certain years we had Christmas parties, and we invited the men. But the men would say, "Oh, they're bitch sessions." Or, "They're getting special privileges."
>
> At first, the women were able to shrug these things off. But as the climate became more conservative, more and more of the women were more intimidated by these comments.
>
> We did learn, because at first I was calling meetings at 3:15 on Wednesday afternoon, which was a time of day when they had no classes. But what I was doing was getting the women out of regimental responsibilities. I soon mended my ways, and looked for other times.

> I would get a policewoman in once a year, who would talk about sexual harassment, and rape, and what to do about those kinds of things. Sometimes we'd have people talking about eating disorders. Sometimes we would do "dress for success," and makeovers. And then other times, we would just invite people from the Marine Transportation Department or Engineering in to talk.[54]

The women's advisory program was discontinued in 1994, when the faculty and administration concluded that there was no longer a compelling need for it. In retrospect, the program can be seen as a transitional device, a way to help female cadets who happened to be at the Academy in the difficult early years of coeducation, when many constituencies—students, faculty, administrators, and alumni—were getting used to the strange idea of women at Kings Point. Yes, singling women out for special attention created unanticipated difficulties for those women, but the absence of such efforts could have led to greater difficulties.

It is worth noting that the first women faculty members, hired in the King administration, also hit bumps in the road. Brickman, who was initially brought on as an adjunct faculty member in 1981, recalls being greeted by wolf whistles the first time she set foot in an Academy classroom:

> I hadn't been told anything about the Academy. I came from a liberal arts tradition, and I had taught before. But, you know, I walked into class—it was an all-male class—and they *whistled*. Now, that had never happened to me before.
>
> Also, they were supposed to stand up. No one told me, but they were supposed to stand up and come to attention. When I walked in, some were standing up, some were sitting down. I was so overwhelmed by this experience, because I was a new teacher there, and I didn't know what to expect.[55]

A lack of effective faculty orientation and mentoring was partly to blame. Brickman, who in 1994 became head of the Department of Humanities, found ways to thrive in the Academy environment. Many of her female peers were not as resourceful. According to Brickman, several other women who worked at the Academy in the early 1980s felt ostracized by their male peers, and soon left the Academy.

But Brickman's was not an isolated success story. Another female

The Academy's eighth superintendent, Rear Admiral
Thomas Matteson, presents an award to humanities
professor Jane Brickman, who ran the first Women's
Advisory program in the early 1980s.

faculty member who flourished at the Academy in this transitional
period was Susan Petersen Lubow. Hired in 1979 as a temporary physical education instructor and shortly thereafter as the coach of the
men's swimming team, Petersen Lubow, then an instructor at a Long
Island high school, remembers telling her interviewers at the Academy
not to give her the job if they were simply filling a female quota. "I figured I'd never get hired after saying that," she recalls. "But I did."

Petersen Lubow soon demonstrated the energy that has character-
ized her work at the Academy ever since. She helped revamp the
school's lifesaving program. She learned fencing at her own expense so
that she could teach it to female cadets in their phys ed classes. (In the
mideighties, she persuaded the athletic director to let her dump the
fencing program—which the female cadets hated—in favor of aerobics
classes, which she later expanded to include men.) She played a
key role in getting men's lacrosse, men's water polo, and women's

swimming teams started. (Shortly thereafter, Leslie Custer, '85, won a national title in the two-hundred-yard backstroke.) She also resurrected and coached the dormant cheerleader squad.

Especially in the first half of the 1980s, Petersen Lubow encountered various kinds of subtle discrimination—and not-so-subtle opposition. "There were a couple of people here," she recalls, "who were doing everything they could to block me from getting tenure." Her difficulties were exacerbated by the revolving-door pattern that had emerged for athletic directors: "My first ten years here, we had four different ADs [athletic directors]." As a result, there was no one in the hierarchy for a young phys ed instructor to go to for guidance.

She solved that problem in typical fashion: by becoming athletic director herself. First offered the job on a temporary basis for four months in 1989, she soon won the job on a permanent basis and continued to move forward. Money proved a critical challenge. She inherited an appropriated budget for physical education classes of approximately $18,000, intended to cover equipment, professional service contracts, repairs, and so on. This was down from the mid-eighties appropriations high watermark of $36,000, due to Academy-wide budget cuts.

Her "NAFI" budget—that is, "nonappropriated funds instrumentality" money, principally derived from alumni donations—was similarly starved, at a grand total of around $400,000 to cover all varsity athletics and competitive club sports. The result of the money shortfalls could be hair-raising. For example, six weeks before the start of basketball season early in her tenure as athletic director, she learned that one of the basketball backboards in O'Hara Hall was broken beyond repair—at full extension, it was one inch below regulation height—and that replacing it would cost $20,000. "This $20,000 is nowhere in my budgets," Petersen Lubow recalled, "either government-appropriated or NAFI. But if I don't fix the backboard, I may not have a basketball season. So I found an alum who was willing to loan me the $20,000 through the NAFI account. In the end, after we'd started paying him back, he decided to donate most of the money anonymously."[56]

Bob Lavinia, '70, subsequently worked with several other alumni to help Petersen Lubow revitalize the dormant Blue and Gray Club, which had been organized years earlier to facilitate alumni donations to athletics. (Other key players in this effort included Tom Hughes, '80; Russ McVay, '64; John Mandel, '64; and Pete Rackett, '61.) With the help of these and other alumni leaders, Petersen Lubow gradually increased her nonappropriated funds budget from around $400,000 to nearly $2 million.

The principal reason why both budgets (government-appropriated and NAFI) had to grow was that her department continued to take on new responsibilities, including an expanded life-saving program, now renamed the Aquatic Survival program, CPR training, and water safety requirements related to the International Standards of Training, Certification, and Watchkeeping (STCW). The Department of Physical Education and Athletics took complete responsibility for competitive club sports, and later for the Academy's intramural program. Most recently, the department has assumed responsibility for helping cadets meet the navy's physical fitness requirements.

Meanwhile, the athletics menu has continued to expand to the point where today, twenty-five varsity sports (men's and women's combined) are offered at the Academy, including four at the waterfront. The most recent arrival: women's basketball, implemented in 2000. "We needed that to fulfill our NCAA sponsorship requirements," Petersen Lubow explained, "and also for competitive reasons. We needed to be competitive within our conference, and also in the larger market for talented female students. Out of something like 420 comparable Division III schools in the United States, 418 had women's basketball, and we didn't."

Pete Rackett, vice president of the USMMA Alumni Foundation and a longtime friend of athletics at the Academy, seconds this opinion:

> We realized that there were a large number of women whom we were trying to recruit who were playing basketball. They wouldn't even *look* at us, because we didn't even have the sport here. The fact is, Athletics makes a lot of first approaches to people who come to the school, whether or not they end up participating in sports.[57]

After a quarter century of efforts by female faculty members like Jane Brickman and Susan Petersen Lubow, women have become full-fledged members of the Academy community, shaping not only its intellectual offerings and its physical fabric, but its very composition. And in that period of transition, the "gender quotient" of issues has gradually become less important. As in the larger society, women and men have become members of equal standing in the community.

In the end, of course, the measure of the Academy is the success of its graduates, and this is the brightest part of the picture of women at Kings Point. In September 1980, Julie Berke, the wife of Herman Berke, '44, president of the Point Shipping Corporation in New York City, offered a $10,000 prize to the first female deck graduate from Kings Point to earn an unlimited master's license, and an equal amount to the first female engineering grad to earn an unlimited chief engineer's license. In the running were twenty-two women. Twenty-three had graduated in the first two years, and all but one—a woman who had gone to Harvard to pursue a degree in business administration—were then sailing on their licenses.

One of those competing for the prize was Della Anholt, a 1978 graduate who by the early 1980s was working as a tugboat captain (and also as a third mate on cargo ships). A June 1983 article in *Cosmopolitan* detailed some of the trials—and triumphs—of Anholt's job:

> Occasionally, Anholt does run into resentment from sailors who never went to school but instead "came up the hawsepipe"—a sea expression for starting at the bottom and climbing up the lower ranks. This, added to the fact that Anholt is 28 and attractive, has caused a clash or two. "Once I was on a ship overseeing the off-loading of oil and had several men working under me," she recalls. "An officer said to me, 'Wait till the captain sees you, there's going to be trouble.' When I asked why he told me, 'Well, you have three strikes against you. He sneers at anybody from the Academy; he worked his way up; and he doesn't like women—especially good looking women.'
>
> "In the end, though, it came out all right. I did my job and performed really well, and the next morning the captain walked over to me and said, 'You know, I was watching you out there, and I've changed my mind. You women are all right.'"[58]

Anholt's experience was not atypical. Most members of the first generation of women graduates of Kings Point experienced similar kinds of sexism and skepticism; most were able to overcome these obstacles and achieve professional success.

The winners of the Julie Berke Award, Nancy Wagner, '78, and Jeanne Kraus, '79, epitomize this success. Wagner, a 1978 graduate who is now a San Francisco Bay pilot, was the daughter of a Kings

Pointer and the granddaughter of a shipbuilder. Wagner sailed on Exxon tankers after graduation and received the Berke Award in 1985 after attaining her master's license.[59] Kraus, who made her career with Exxon, won the prize on the engineering side. But although these two women enjoyed the fastest ascent to the top licenses, they were by no means unique in their success. Other female graduates were making their mark, including, for example, Teresa Olsen Preston, '78, who also sailed with Exxon. After receiving her chief mate's license in 1985, Preston sailed on the *Exxon Baltimore*, a 52,000-DWT black oil/asphalt carrier in the Gulf/East trades. She later proudly counted herself the first mother among the group of early female Academy graduates to receive her unlimited master's license.

Women also performed well in the larger maritime business community. Kathy Metcalf, another '78 graduate, sailed for Sun Oil as a third mate after graduation, and later became health and safety coordinator for Sun Oil's marine department. Meredith Neizer, '78, received an MBA from Stanford University after graduating from Kings Point, served as a White House Fellow (1986–1987), and later became project supervisor with the Port Authority of New York and New Jersey. Frances Yates, '78, sailed for Texaco and later became a product trader for Amerada Hess in Manhattan.[60]

The success of these women did much to improve the morale of the female midshipmen at the Academy. Amy D. Shames, '88, in an article in the *Kings Pointer* in 1988, underscored the importance of the early women graduates as role models:

> Thanks to our pioneering predecessors, the idea of "women at sea" is becoming less foreign. While there have been a few instances of harassment at sea, these are isolated incidents and in no way reflect the usual atmosphere or attitudes of shipboard life. . . . The original eight are living testimony to our abilities. They are successful Captains, Chief Engineers, Pilots, Businesswomen, wives and mothers. They are our role models. We are filled with admiration for them, and we congratulate them on their unique achievements.[61]

In this period of transition—society's, as well as the Academy's—women at Kings Point struggled to fit in, and earn the respect of their classmates. They continued to display the tenacity and courage of their predecessors, both at the Academy and in industry. They continued to break down barriers and chart new courses.

Life at Ground Level

As the Academy administration waged campaigns to improve relations with the industry, upgrade the Academy's curriculum, and make the campus more welcoming to more kinds of people, life within the Regiment continued more or less on its steady course. A defining feature of any small, intense, and focused institution is a relative detachment from the rest of the world, and the Academy proved this rule. For most Kings Pointers, their universe while in residence at the Academy was effectively bounded by the Regiment, athletics, and academics.

But most students, even while immersed in regimental life, also held in mind the prize that they were working toward. Willie Solis, interviewed in the *El Paso Times* in 1983, remarked that when he first arrived at Kings Point, the Academy seemed less like a college and more like a prison. "No TV," he reported. "No radio. They didn't even let us drink sodas. It was only milk and water with your meals."[62]

Academy plebes stand at attention during indoc in 1986.

And the plebe-year restrictions only began with mealtimes: "Walk six inches from the walls. No walking on the grass. Square your corners. Underwear on the left side of the wardrobe, black socks squarely in the middle. Salute your superiors." First-year cadets or plebes became accustomed to constant discipline. Solis recalled becoming so disoriented with the rapid-fire questions aimed at him by his superior officers during indoctrination that at one point, when asked his name, he replied, "Sir, El Paso, Texas, *sir*."

Like many students, however, Solis found that this discipline was more than balanced by the freedom and exploration associated with his time at sea. During his Sea Year, Solis visited Hawaii, Guam, Panama, Malaysia, Indonesia, Japan, Hong Kong, Taiwan, Korea, Morocco, Egypt, Turkey, and Italy. And, as he pointed out to the *El Paso Times*, the Academy offered more options than any of the other federal academies after graduation. Naval Academy graduates were tied into naval service, Coast Guard grads to the Coast Guard, but the education provided by the Academy left open a myriad of career choices, both at sea and on shore.

As suggested above, the broader world was also gradually making its way into the Academy, although most often on the institution's own terms. The Academy had educated foreign visitors in the past, including officers and cadets from Turkey and Indonesia in the 1960s, cadets from the Philippines in the 1950s and 1970s, and Libyan students under the auspices of a two-year training program funded by oil companies through the State Department between 1959 and 1961. Hoping to raise the level of foreign participation in the early 1970s, the Academy had also requested legislation in 1973 to permit a small number of foreign students to attend the Academy yearly, a privilege enjoyed by the other federal service academies, but this legislation was not enacted.[63]

Progress came with the passage of the Maritime Education and Training Act of 1980, which allowed the Academy—with the approval of the secretary of state—to admit up to thirty students at any given time from nations outside of the Western Hemisphere. (The sponsoring nations would reimburse the United States for the cost of educating the students, thus leaving the Academy's budget and the enrollment of U.S. citizens unaffected.) These students would be admitted to the full four-year Kings Point program, and those who completed the Academy's course of study would be granted the bachelor of science degree.

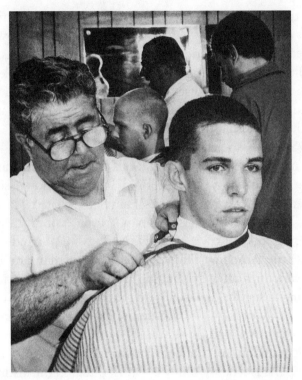

A plebe gazes warily at his new look during indoc,
1986.

In addition, Kings Point in the early 1980s also admitted increased
numbers of students from Panama. This, too, represented the expansion of a long tradition. The Maritime Administration's General Order
97, which was the implementation order covering Academy operations
after the passage of the Merchant Marine Act of 1936, provided scholarships for "up to 12 Latin American cadets at any one time, not more
than 2 from each of the Latin American Republics." In the late 1940s
and early 1950s, these quotas were consistently filled, and small numbers of Panamanian students were among them.[64]

When Congress passed the Maritime Training and Education Act
in 1980, the Panama Canal Commission was studying the need for
training Panamanians to prepare for the transition of the canal to Panamanian control in 2000. When completed, the Panama Canal Treaty
included provisions for the training of Panamanian mariners at Kings
Point. The Academy was well known to canal administrators through

the large number of graduates who had found work in the Canal Zone, especially as pilots, including Captain Justin Bonanno, '43. Bonanno, who was later referred to by Paul Krinsky as the "mainspring of the operation,"[65] worked as a liaison between the Canal Commission and Academy admissions officer Emanuel Jenkins.[66]

Together, Captains Bonanno and Jenkins identified likely candidates, and worked with the Panamanian government to process their applications. It was largely thanks to their efforts that the Academy welcomed its first two students from Panama, Juan C. Cazorla and Juan B. Chung, to the class of 1982. In subsequent years, the Panamanian contingent remained a small but vital part of the Kings Point community.

Blue Skies and Well-Wishers

Thomas King retired from his post as superintendent in June 1987. He had presided over a difficult era for the industry, in which the U.S. fleet shrank substantially, and seagoing berths for Kings Pointers shrank proportionately. But the Academy had survived the industry's woes, and graduates were fulfilling their service obligation through shoreside jobs and the armed services.

On the day of King's departure, June 17, the Academy overflowed with friends, alumni, and the Regiment, gathered to thank King for his service to the Kings Point community and to wish him well in the future. In his departing comments, King paid tribute to that community, which had both given him the foundation and the capstone of his career: "The classic sea voyage of a trading ship commences with departure from a home port, then makes numerous ports of call before concluding with a safe landfall and return to that home port. My career has figuratively tracked that classic voyage. This academy . . . is the home port for my maritime career voyage. That voyage started and will soon end in this safe harbor. I would have had it no other way."[67]

But King was nowhere near the end of his voyages on behalf of Kings Point. In September 1987, he took over as executive director of the Alumni Association's foundation, and also agreed to head the Kings Point Challenge, a new capital campaign. In this role, King oversaw the growth and development of the Alumni Association's fundraising efforts.

In keeping with Academy tradition, King's successor was sworn in at the same ceremony. The Academy's seventh superintendent was Paul Krinsky, '50, who had been promoted to deputy superintendent and rear admiral in May 1985.

The second alumnus to fill the post of superintendent, Krinsky was the first to make his way up through the Academy's faculty and administrative ranks. He had been a professor, director of admissions, and assistant academic dean under Admiral Engel, and academic dean and deputy superintendent under Admiral King. As a result, Krinsky knew the institution forward and backward—the faculty, the Regiment, the staff, and the facilities. His appointment ensured continuity between the two administrations, but it also opened the door to a new era.

11

Broadening the Mission
1987–1992

On a bright fall day in 1987, as trumpets blared a celebratory fanfare, hundreds of red, white, and blue balloons sailed into the blue sky above the Academy's Fitch Building, between Bland Library and Samuels Hall.

At that moment, the Fitch Building was getting a new name, the Babson Center, and a new tenant, the Alumni Association. The name paid tribute to the generosity of a son-and-mother team, James and Ethel Babson, who had been contributing to Kings Point for more than thirty years. James L. Babson was a 1944 graduate of the Academy and president of Babson Brothers, a Skokie, Illinois–based company that manufactured and distributed milking and milk-separating machines; his mother, Ethel, had recently passed away at the age of 104.[1]

Jean Babson, Jim's wife, cut the ceremonial blue and gray ribbons in front of the building's spruced-up front entrance, which led into the Academy's new alumni center. A long round of applause accompanied the balloons and the fanfare.

Both newly minted superintendent Paul Krinsky and Alumni Association president Charles R. Cushing, '56, paid tribute to the Babsons, whose generosity had done more than simply sustain Academy programs over the years. That tradition of generosity, Cushing explained, was literally the inspiration for and the beginning of the Alumni Association's fund-raising efforts. Cushing told the story of the

Jean Babson, wife of alumnus James L. Babson, a 1944 graduate of the Academy, cuts the ribbon opening the Alumni Association's offices in the newly renamed Babson Center in 1987; Charles Cushing stands next to the Babsons.

moment when, thirty years earlier, Jim Babson had approached then Lieutenant Commander Victor E. Tyson, Academy liaison to the Alumni Association, and asked him if there was anything the Academy especially needed.

Tyson, who had never met Babson and wasn't quite sure where the question was leading, looked him up and down and said, "Well, we sure could use some typewriters."

Babson nodded, and asked, "And how much will one of those run you?" Tyson replied, "About fifty dollars."

He watched as Babson took out his checkbook. He continued to watch as Babson carefully scribed a five and a zero, and then another zero, and amazingly, *another* zero onto the check. *Five thousand dollars!*

The crowd laughed appreciatively. Then Tyson himself got up and added a coda to the story. At that early stage, the Alumni Association had never received a donation. And so, as Tyson recalled, Babson had made the check out to Tyson himself. When Superintendent McLintock got wind of this unorthodox financing conduit—Babson to Tyson to the Academy—he pinned back his executive officer's ears.

Building dedications invite hyperbole, but this was no hyperbole. Babson's donation, way back in the late 1950s, led directly to the establishment of the Kings Point Fund.[2] At first, there were fears that the fund-raising entity might mar the legendary collegiality of the alumni body, and thus the fund was made a subsidiary of the Alumni Association. Twenty years later, in 1981, the name was changed to the USMMA Foundation.

At around this same time, the association also began to consider the future of donations to the Academy. The large wartime classes had been succeeded by much smaller postwar classes, and organizers anticipated a point in the future when annual contributions might not close the Academy's chronic operating deficits. Federal budgets were shrinking. Meanwhile, as Frank Sinnott noted in the Spring 1981 *Kings Pointer*, the Academy needed *more* support for things like:

> present and future major investments in academic areas: lab equipment in engineering and nautical science, the library, more sophisticated training aids, and on-campus symposia. Expanded public relations and recruiting programs are needed to inform the public of the Academy's vital role in training and education within the maritime industry. The physical plant, now almost forty years old, is suffering in some areas from fiscal restraint.[3]

Clearly, a long-term solution was needed, and from this need was born, in 1986, the Kings Point Challenge. The challenge was an endowment-like fund, the inspiration of Cushing (alumni president 1986 to 1989) and Melvin Tublin, '49 (alumni president 1957 to 1961). With the active encouragement of Cushing, Tublin created a charitable foundation and wrote the first check, for one thousand dollars, to the new fund. The "challenge" in the campaign's title was to raise five million dollars in endowment and to prepare the next generation of Kings Pointers for their vital role as backers of the Academy.[4]

Another person honoring the Babsons that day was Tom King, recently retired from the role of superintendent and already tackling his next challenge. King had been asked to become executive director of the three alumni organizations: the association, the USMMA

IN PEACE AND WAR

Foundation, and the Kings Point Challenge. Under the leadership of National Chair Kenneth DeGhetto, '43, the challenge was off to a strong start by the time King took the reins. In the spring of 1987, King noted that $1.25 million had already been pledged to the Challenge through 1986, with almost 30 percent of this in hand.[5] All parties to the venture, however, knew that there was still a long way to go to reach the final goal of a five-million-dollar endowment.

The first step, they agreed, was changing the way Kings Pointers thought about the Academy's fiscal circumstances, and about their own role in maintaining the school's vitality. Giving had been generally considered a goodwill gesture among graduates rather than a responsibility, but if alumni were to remain proud of their alma mater, this had to change. Yes, the Academy was funded primarily by the federal government and didn't rely on the support of its graduates for its survival. But annual federal support was always linked to the fiscal health of the national government, and even in the best of times many of the Academy's academic programs were underfunded. In addition, federal funds didn't support many programs that were of primary importance to both midshipmen and graduates, such as athletics, the band, sailing, and other clubs and activities.

With DeGhetto's efforts, and with the well-known and respected King in the executive director's chair, Kings Pointers gradually began to shift their outlook and provide strong and steady financial support for the Academy. Edward J. Harsche, '62, who accompanied DeGhetto on many fund-raising trips, emphasizes that this shift was critically important to the Academy's long-term fiscal health. "Kings Point," Harsche explained, "realized that the retreat of the government was going to make things come up short at the Academy. The ability of the alumni to band together and start funding things the government wouldn't has been essential; and it's something that Kings Point now does better than any of the other federal academies."[6]

One alumnus who responded positively was James H. Ackerman, '44.[7] A ship's master, admiralty lawyer in the firm of Ackerman, Ling, Russell & Mikrovich, vice chair of the USMMA Foundation, and a founding member of the Los Angeles/Long Beach alumni chapter, Ackerman's contributions to the Academy were so significant that in 1988 Superintendent Krinsky issued a directive that the auditorium in Bowditch Hall be known "now and forever as the Ackerman Auditorium, in recognition of Jim Ackerman's professional and philanthropic interests and achievements."[8] The anchor at Vickery Gate, as well as the maritime library in the Yocum Sailing Center, also were named in Ackerman's honor.

A peril inherent in this increased fund-raising, of course, was a possible reduction of congressional support. If the Academy could tap private dollars, Congress might well ask why the nation's taxpayers should underwrite Kings Point.

At this early stage in the development of private support for the Academy, alumni leading the effort simply took it on faith that Congress would not punish the institution for showing initiative, and for closing gaps that the government had failed to fill. Their faith, as it turned out, was rewarded. On more than one occasion, congressional leaders stressed that they were impressed by the high level of commitment shown by Kings Pointers toward their alma mater. Far from cutting government support as the school's endowment began to grow, the government gradually increased its allocations for the Academy.

But the Academy got very little that it didn't ask for, and didn't get a lot of what it *did* ask for.

Taking the Helm

The Academy's seventh superintendent, Paul Krinsky, '50, entered office in the fall of 1987 with an ambitious agenda. Many of his initiatives were extensions of the King administration's policies, which he had helped shape, but now the pace and scope of change increased significantly.

This was not unexpected. Unlike any superintendent since Richard McNulty, Krinsky had been involved with the inner workings of the Academy for years before taking the top job. He needed no time to assess a new environment or cultivate faculty support. Krinsky's initiatives ranged from the visionary to the more mundane, from long-term strategic planning to housing reassignments. While the overall pace of change sometimes proved difficult for the small Academy community to accommodate, most of these changes ultimately benefited the school.

One of the most important successes on Krinsky's watch was the signing of a faculty contract. This issue had been festering for more than twenty years by the time Krinsky took the helm. The faculty had first formed a union, led by faculty members Kenneth Lazara and Donald Paquette, in 1965, under the auspices of the United Federation of College Teachers (UFCT). Superintendent McLintock recognized the union in October 1966, and after a year and a half of negotiations, both sides agreed to a contract. The contract covered all but one issue: whether the salaries of USMMA faculty were negotiable. Because the parties were unable to reach agreement, the issue was referred to the Federal Labor Relations Authority. When the authority ruled in favor of the union, the Engel administration refused to negotiate, and summarily terminated the contract on December 31, 1973.[9]

The union reacted even before this action formally took effect, filing claims in December 1973 alleging "dilatory tactics in salary negotiations,"[10] and in February 1974 objecting to the contract cancellation. The administration was not found guilty in either case, but the dispute continued to rankle. Over the next fifteen

The Academy's seventh superintendent, Rear Admiral Paul L. Krinsky, '50, was the first superintendent to make his way up through the Academy's administrative ranks.

years, disputes continued over unfair labor practices, creating a sometimes acrimonious atmosphere. (One participant later recalled that when a negotiator on one side said, "Good morning," the response from the other side was likely to be, "What do you mean by *that*?") Additional complaints were filed in 1974 regarding salary practices, and in 1976 regarding alleged "unilateral [management] actions which changed past policies . . . without consulting, conferring, or negotiating" with union representatives.[11] The 1976 document also highlighted a failure to notify union representatives of these changes, as well as a uniform policy that was allegedly in violation of the Merchant Marine Act of 1936. These complaints were withdrawn several months later because the union felt that they would not get a fair hearing from the U.S. Department of Labor.[12]

In addition, the union filed complaints in 1978 relating to a letter printed in the *Chronicle of Higher Education* written by Humanities Department head Captain Clark Reynolds, expressing "certain negative views concerning unions."[13] And yet another grievance filing was threatened in February 1984, for the administration's failure to provide the union with documents relating to faculty salaries.[14]

These differences stemmed at least in part from the fact that the negotiating teams were operating in uncharted territory: the intersection of civil service and higher education. Professor Howard Beim, union president from 1978 to 1982, vice president from 1982 to 1984, and frequent member of the negotiating team well into the 1990s, explains, "In effect, we were rewriting the civil service code as it applied to faculty at the Merchant Marine Academy. Every aspect of it had to be determined. And there were many questions of negotiability along the way. One of the big issues was accountability. That is, the faculty would see themselves as college teachers who happened to be working for the federal government. Whereas management would see us as federal employees who happened to be college teachers. That different view led to incredible conflict."[15]

In September 1984, after eleven years of discord, Paul Krinsky, then academic dean, replaced John E. Lewis, assistant superintendent for administration, as the chief negotiator for the administration. Union leadership had changed not long before this, with President Kenneth Lazara being replaced by Commander Theodore Haendel. In addition, the union shifted its affiliation from the UFCT to the American Federation of Government Employees (AFGE), and thereby gained access to professional negotiator Joseph Fallon.

Relations between management and labor soon began to improve. In 1988, the union and administration reached an agreement on the ground rules for negotiations. And in 1989, the Academy and the union finally inked their first formal agreement in more than fifteen years. The contract covered everything from faculty salaries to professional development to disciplinary and adverse actions. It also outlined a new system of arbitration to deal with the inevitable disagreements between the administration and its employees.[16]

Gradually, an unhappiness that had lingered for the better part of two decades began to be replaced by a spirit of mutual respect and cooperation.

Saber-Toothed Tigers and New Realities

One of the quiet but more critical innovations to occur on Krinsky's watch was a new emphasis on strategic planning.

Krinsky had long pondered the means and ends of the institution to which he had dedicated his professional life. Although he is remembered today as an agent of change, he was at heart a traditionalist, quick to defend the Academy's traditions and slow to embrace radical change. He recalls a heated debate he had with English professor Ralph Brady back in the 1960s:

> At a curriculum meeting one day, Brady told a story about saber-toothed tigers. There was a culture, he said, that depended entirely upon hunting saber-toothed tigers. And then, when the saber-toothed tiger became extinct, this poor society had no place to go. They became extinct, too. Brady said, in so many words, "If you're simply training deck officers and engineering officers for the merchant marine, you're training people to hunt saber-toothed tigers. This is changing faster than you are. You have to change."
>
> I resisted that at first. I came from the vocational-school background. I felt that if you took the knots and splices out of the deck officer, and the grease and steam out of the engineering officer, this institution would vanish in a puff of smoke.[17]

Twenty years later, as superintendent, Krinsky was faced with a fast-changing industry, in which shipboard job opportunities for Academy graduates were rapidly declining. To his credit, Krinsky was willing to scrutinize the traditions and the mission of the institution in light of these changed circumstances.

Other voices, too, were beginning to weigh in on the mission. What was timeless? What was amenable to adjustment, in light of changing circumstances? Krinsky, who had been doing some hard thinking of his own, took concrete action in 1986 by retaining Henry Kozlowski as a strategic consultant and professor of marine transportation. He asked Kozlowski and the newly hired academic dean, Dr. Warren Mazek, to evaluate the mission and goals of the Academy in the context of a rapidly declining U.S. maritime industry.

The two made a formidable pair. Kozlowski was a former strategic planner and senior vice president for American Presidential Lines, and he knew the industry intimately. Mazek had a master's in economics from Indiana University and a PhD in economics from the University of Pittsburgh. He had been a professor at Florida State University for almost twenty years—and dean of the College of Arts and Sciences for thirteen of those years—when he was hired to succeed Krinsky as academic dean. Apart from a few years as an economic consultant to a maritime firm, Mazek had little experience in the maritime industry, but his academic credentials were unassailable. Together, Kozlowski and Mazek set out to develop a list of the important questions facing the Academy, both as an academic institution and as an industry feeder.

The duo's first initiative involved a systematic polling of industry leaders. For four months, they conducted hourlong interviews with more than forty "leaders of the industry, military, and political and commercial organizations,"[18] and received frank assessments of the "future of the maritime industry, likely trends in shipboard and onshore organization, skills required of graduates, the proper role of the Academy in the future, and the quality of [Academy] graduates."[19] Those interviewed included industry leaders such as Bruce Seaton, president of American President Lines, and Frank Iarossi, president of Exxon Shipping; military experts such as former chief of naval personnel, Admiral James L. Holloway, and General Alfred Hansen of the Joint Chiefs of Staff; government representatives, including Maritime Administrator John Gaughan; and prominent alumni, such as Charles Cushing, Captain Warren Leback, Eugene McCormick, Milton Nottingham, David O'Neil, Jack Ring, Vice Admiral Robert Scarborough, Rear Admiral Carl Seiberlich, and Fred Sherman.

One point of consensus that emerged from those discussions was that one of the traditional justifications for an American merchant marine—support for U.S. international trade—was becoming less compelling. Although most interviewees agreed that an American merchant marine would continue to exist in some form for the foreseeable future, they observed that the industry was experiencing a steady decline in the number of companies and U.S. flag commercial vessels. Smaller crews would man larger and more efficient ships, and these crews would become more involved in ship management.

In addition, there was a consensus that shipboard jobs would no longer be "life-long career objectives."[20] Merchant marine officers had to be better prepared for shoreside management positions. Officers therefore needed a more complete understanding of their industry, including its economics, management, and regulation.

The interviewees also questioned the extent to which the merchant marine would be involved in future military emergencies—the second oft-cited justification for the U.S. merchant marine and its Academy.

On the one hand, recognition seemed to be growing that manning difficulties would likely occur in the Ready Reserve Force and on other support ships that might be called up in case of a national emergency. But military representatives seemed unwilling to support a merchant marine reserve program, so this appeared to be a weak reed to lean upon.

On a more positive note, Mazek and Kozlowski noted, the chief logistics officer of the Joint Chiefs of Staff had perceived "an urgent military need for officer logisticians," and had "identified the USMMA as a potential provider of comprehensive logistics training in broader transportation systems concepts."[21]

The interviews did not specifically focus on changes to the Academy's mission or curriculum. But based on what they heard, the strategic planners at the Academy were able to establish guidelines for future initiatives. Dean Mazek, writing in the *Kings Pointer*, summarized those guidelines:

> First, there is a strong feeling that the Academy needs to significantly strengthen basic business education, especially in economics, emerging management models and practices (such as participatory management), finance, marketing, and labor relations.
>
> Second, it is clear that shipboard organization is changing. Crews are likely to be smaller. While the US might not adopt the Japanese model whereby in 1988 all maritime grads will be dual trained watch-standers, there is the belief that cross-training will become more essential. Changes are coming, but their precise nature is unclear: in the meantime, the Academy must make its curriculum more flexible so that emerging shipboard requirements can be met quickly and effectively.
>
> Third, not only must our students be more knowledgeable about general business practices, but the Academy needs to introduce training and education in transportation logistics, including intermodalism. This was strongly emphasized by both industry and military leaders.
>
> Fourth, the Academy does not escape the widespread national criticism of higher education in general that communication skills of grads are poor.
>
> Fifth, we received great encouragement to vigorously expand in continuing education programs.[22]

Committees were formed in the fall of 1987 to study these issues. Additional committees were also formed to look into Academy admissions, a possible change from a quarter to a trimester schedule, and leadership and the Regiment. Changes resulting from these evaluations, summarized in the following pages, were implemented over the following half decade, creating an "intense and busy" schedule for the faculty. Isolated grumblings could occasionally be heard about the pace of change, but, as Mazek noted pointedly in a 1987 article, "if the Academy is to continue to be the premier institution of maritime training and education, it can be no other way."[23]

A New Mission Statement

The first noticeable change resulting from the strategic planning sessions came in the Academy's mission statement. The new statement was recast as a brief articulation of the institution's mission, followed by seven goals. This change reflected a trend toward shorter and more compelling statements of institutional purpose, and had the incidental benefit of requiring less frequent revision. Certainly, the Academy's planners achieved both clarity and impact:

> Mission: To serve the economic and security interests of the U.S. by providing our merchant marine and armed forces with highly-qualified officers and providing maritime-related activities with well-educated professionals and leaders.

The Academy's revised goals were stated as follows:

> Goals: To graduate licensed officers of the highest quality to serve aboard ships of the Merchant Marine and to serve as officers in the armed forces, and to become a primary source of leadership for the maritime industry.
>
> To establish and maintain faculty, staff, and support facilities to provide educational and training programs of the highest quality to meet the needs of the maritime industry and commercial and military transportation systems.
>
> To develop well-educated, skilled officers, who are self-disciplined, ethical, responsible, and articulate and possess a sense of loyalty to the United States of America and the principles for which it stands.
>
> To maintain interaction with the maritime industry and the

military and to monitor emerging trends and prepare for future needs and contingencies.

To attract highly qualified and motivated young men and women from all states, consistent with its role as a federal academy, to pursue careers in maritime-related fields.

To offer quality continuing education programs, which respond to the evolving needs of the maritime industry and military.

To maintain and enhance the Academy's national and international reputation as a prime institution of maritime training and learning.[24]

The commitment in the mission statement to provide the nation's armed forces with "highly qualified officers" was not new, but previous Academy mission statements had referred only to commissioned officers in the naval reserve. Previous mission statements had referred specifically to "United States flag merchant vessels"; now, reflecting industry realities, that limitation was dropped. Earlier mission statements had contemplated a stint at sea for the Academy's graduates, after which they would come ashore to serve in the maritime industry; now, Academy graduates might aim for industry leadership without extended sea duty.

Notably, this new mission statement was the first in the Academy's history to mention "continuing education," reflecting the increasing importance of that activity. And finally, the second and last goals, focusing on assembling the resources to offer "programs of the highest quality" and on the school's national and international reputation, indicated an emerging institutional awareness about its proper place in the world. Aspiring to "be the best" entailed new responsibilities.

This broader mission statement received a stamp of approval from an outside consultant, Dr. John R. Hook, chair of the Business and Economics Department at Mount Saint Mary's College, who completed a report on the Academy in March 1988. On the subject of the expanded mission, Hook wrote:

> You have already identified for yourself the problem of too few jobs in the maritime industry, and the need to search for expanded mission. . . . I think this issue can be dealt with through good orientation and an emphasis on the positive features of an Academy education: low cost, quality curriculum, and training for leadership (anywhere). I do see the mission problem as important, but mainly due to its

potential impact on external support (possible even ultimately institutional survival). I also see positive signs in the way you are moving—to emphasize logistics, for example.[25]

Superintendent Krinsky, who in his previous post as deputy superintendent had jump-started the strategic planning process, ultimately declared himself pleased with the result:

> The changes to the mission answered the dilemma of the continued contraction of the industry, giving the Academy and its graduates some much-needed maneuverability. The trick was to keep all of those other technical things in the program, and make sure that that was going to be the best possible program going—and also bring in new things, and improve, and grow, and expand.[26]

And so, some twenty years after Krinsky and his colleagues had first argued about saber-toothed tigers, the Academy committed itself to striking out in new directions. Two new courses of study, one of which went into the design phase even before the strategic planning process was complete, underscored the point.

Intermodalism and Change

In key areas of the curriculum, the administration chose not to await the completion of the research by the strategic planning subcommittees. Logistics emerged from the interview process as such a clear and immediate priority that the Academy introduced logistics courses in the fall of 1987, only months after the first draft of the strategic plan was completed, and implemented an expanded logistics program the following year.[27]

A critical piece of logistics was the newly emerging field of intermodalism: transport from point A to point B using more than one mode of transportation. As Dr. Bernard Abrahamsson, head of the Marine Transportation Department, explained, intermodalism was to the 1980s what containerization was to the 1960s: "an old and simple concept, with new and complex implementations."[28] The "new" part of intermodalism was the emerging capability, using containers, to provide point-A-to-point-B service under *a single bill of transport*. This called for much greater cooperation between the modes, and a new concept of shipping as an extension of the production process. This, in turn, meant new areas of expertise were necessary for those entering the maritime industry, including high-tech information management systems, such as Electronic Data Information, and in-transit visibility systems, such as container bar-coding.

One of the first priorities for the new program in transportation management and logistics was to find a leader. Paul Krinsky recalls the search and its resolution:

> We tried to recruit a department head who would have the ability to literally combine the seagoing and the logistics shoreside transportation modes together. It turned out to be a very difficult job. The interesting part of it is that the first gentleman we had—Bernard Abrahamsson—looked like he was tailor-made for the job.
>
> Abrahamsson had been trained as a seafarer in Stockholm, Sweden. He had served at sea for a good number of years, and ended up working on Israeli ships. He came to this country, left the seagoing profession, earned a PhD in economics, and taught at various business schools. He had all of those things going for him: a PhD in economics, business education background, and experience as a ship's officer. So we hired him.[29]

Abrahamsson was instrumental in designing the full logistics program, first offered in the fall of 1988. In addition to its traditional nautical science foundation, the program included eleven core business courses for deck majors: accounting, microeconomics, macroeconomics, business law, management processes, marketing, finance, maritime law and insurance, and a three-course sequence in logistics. A series of electives (also open to marine engineering majors) was planned, including logistical decision making, chartering, admiralty law, port management, marine insurance, and labor relations.

Abrahamsson encountered opposition, primarily from those within his own department who didn't welcome these changes. But he enjoyed the resolute backing of Dean Warren Mazek, who was determined to see the changes through to completion. Abrahamsson and Mazek also received support from some unexpected quarters. Principal among these was General Alfred Hansen, who had recently left the Joint Chiefs of Staff to head up the Air Force Logistics Command. In an article in the *Kings Pointer*, Superintendent Krinsky praised Hansen's contributions, which included the assignment of army and air force officers to Kings Point to augment faculty expertise in this area.[30] Hansen, Krinsky wrote, helped the Academy greatly by widening the lens of the intermodal curriculum to include military applications.

Another original strategic-planning interviewee, Rear Admiral Carl Seiberlich, '43, was also instrumental in fostering the Academy's intermodal and logistics degree. Seiberlich knew the subject well: as director of military programs at American President Lines, he helped create that company's intermodal system, and was a strong believer in both the commercial and military applications of intermodalism. (He was later APL's coordinator for Desert Shield/Desert Storm.) Seiberlich recalled that there was initially some resistance to the concept at the Academy:

> I felt very, very strongly that the graduates here really had to understand the intermodal system end to end, because that's where you make your profit. Everybody in the intermodal system has their roots in some mode, and they have their strength in that mode. But they also have to understand the connectivity of these modes, not only in the physical movement of the cargo, but in the information, and the supporting business practices. I worked at this for about five years. I appeared before the strategic planning boards, and talked to the superintendents, and all that kind of stuff. Dean Mazek did a lot to make this happen, even though there were those on the faculty who really wanted to keep the status quo.[31]

Abrahamsson himself did not stay at the Academy long enough to savor the success of the program he had helped design and implement. By all accounts a skilled strategic thinker and able curriculum designer, Abrahamsson's expertise lay more in social science than in nautical science. And, even with the strong backing of Mazek, he lacked the stamina to impose major changes on the relatively traditional department he headed. As Paul Krinsky recalled, "He was a nice man. Turns out he was too nice. He was the first head of the new department. And it was suffering growing pains, and Bernard got batted around the ears for a few years. He finally said it was time for him to move on."[32]

Abrahamsson's departure was a setback to the cause, but not a mortal blow. The reason was simple: Dr. Richard Stewart, '73, took up the cause of intermodalism and logistics where Abrahamsson left off. After graduating from Kings Point, Stewart had sailed on Gulf Oil tankers, earning his master's license in 1977. After a two-year stint with Inter-Ocean Transport, serving as chief mate on the UST *Pacific*, the largest ship ever built in the United States, Stewart sailed first as chief mate and then as master for several Texas-based shippers. In 1986, he came ashore as the fleet manager of three Texas-class bulk vessels and four Falcon-class tankers.

Stewart also kept one foot in academia, earning his master's degree while ashore between 1975 and 1982, with a specialty in the environmental management of transportation systems. (His thesis examined the feasibility of setting up a hovercraft system on Lake Michigan.) One day in 1987, while attending a Kings Point alumni meeting in Houston, Stewart ran into friend and mentor Don Brown, '49, who asked if he had ever considered going into teaching. As Stewart recalls, "That conversation grew out of the fact that I had, for some time, been a strong proponent of cadets. I'd bring them into the office, as well as on the ships, and loved working with them, and teaching them. I said, 'No, I haven't thought about that, Don.' He showed me an ad in one of the journals for a job at Kings Point. I applied for it, and got it. And took about a $30,000 pay cut, as I recall."[33]

Stewart taught for the first two quarters of 1988, then, by prior arrangement, went back to sea. When Bernard Abrahamsson left Kings Point, Warren Mazek persuaded Stewart to come back to the Academy ahead of schedule as the interim chair of the Division of Marine Transportation. During his tenure at Kings Point, Stewart earned a PhD from Rensselaer Polytechnic Institute's Lalley School of Management. He also involved himself not only in the refinement of the logistics and intermodalism curriculum, as described subsequently, but also in the Mazek/Kozlowski strategic planning efforts, and in the initial planning for a new initiative: the Ship's Officer program.

Inventing the Ship's Officer Program

This second new program to grow out of the strategic planning process was partly inspired by a Japanese manning plan that had been implemented in the 1980s, whereby all officers below the rank of captain and chief engineer served in dual-purpose watchstanding roles. To some in the industry, this looked like the wave of the future. The Coast Guard, meanwhile, was also considering creating a new watchstanding license, on the theory that more advanced technology would allow centralized monitoring of all ship controls, and thus require officers with a broad understanding of both disciplines.

One motivation for exploring the ship's officer concept, as Richard Stewart recalls, was to strengthen the deck program, both for the sake of that program and for the sake of its graduates. "I was of the belief, as were other members of the [Nautical Science] department, that with the changes in technology, plus the advent of STCW, that deck officers should have more advanced education in engineering—no ifs, ands, or buts about it. And out of that conviction developed the Ship's Officer program."[34]

But another vision of the Ship's Officer program was as a replacement for the dual program.[35] The biggest difference between the two programs—and it was a significant one—was that the Ship's Officer program as it was then conceived would not prepare graduates for both a deck and an engine license. Instead, graduates would prepare themselves to take the deck license exam but would also have a strong foundation in engineering, including the basic operations of the ship's power plant, auxiliaries, and automatic controls. Because of this, fewer credits would be required to complete the ship's officer degree than had been required for the dual degree, and midshipmen in the program would have time to take more elective courses.

Since 1969, almost four hundred Kings Pointers had completed the dual program, thus entering the workforce with two licenses. Few, however, actually spent a significant amount of time sailing on both licenses, and few had encountered circumstances in which both licenses were called upon in the same position. In fact, most dualies thought of themselves as engineers first and deckies second. (Two notable exceptions to this rule were honored at the Academy's 2002 homecoming celebration. Carol Curtiss, '80, and John Becker, '82, each achieved—and sailed upon—licenses as both chief engineer and master, making them two of only four mariners known to have accomplished this feat at that time.) Though the dual program had been a reasonable guess in 1965 regarding future trends in the industry, the industry had never embraced the concept and had made few efforts in the intervening years to accommodate these exceptionally skilled individuals.[36] For these reasons, and because of the academic rigor of the dual program, enrollments declined steadily in the 1980s. Only seventeen plebes from the class of 1987 selected the dual program, and those who chose it generally cited the sheer challenge of the program rather than the career opportunities it held forth.[37]

From the faculty's point of view, moreover, there were additional problems with the dual program. Dual students were receiving a weaker nautical science curriculum as a result of all the engineering courses that had to be squeezed into their schedule. They had to take the third assistant engineer's licensing exam in the third quarter of their first class year, in other words, before they had finished some of the courses intended to prepare them for that exam. Dual students were only able to log 150 days of sea time in their deck cadet capacity. And finally, dual students couldn't take elective courses because of their daunting course load.

All of these appeared to be reasonable arguments for replacing the dual program with the ship's officer program. When push came to shove, however, the Academy did not push. The dual program enjoyed great prestige among alumni and influential industry leaders, and many of these constituents objected vociferously to its proposed discontinuance. The program therefore took its place alongside the dual program in 1989 instead of replacing it.

In addition to the nautical science curriculum—that is, the standard deck curriculum—ship's officer majors were required to take fourteen engineering courses, including engineering graphics, marine engineering, engineering shop, engineering science, naval architecture, auxiliary steam plant operations, ship systems operations, diesel engine operations, electrical engineering, and computer usage.[38] Because of time restrictions, however, ship's officer majors took fewer courses in transportation and logistics.[39] The result, according to the Academy's 1990–1991 catalog, was a graduate who was:

> fully capable to serve aboard ship as third mate, but [with] sufficient familiarity with marine engineering to be able to converse meaningfully with engineering personnel, read blueprints, specifications and repair requisitions, have elementary skills in diagnosing conditions displayed by monitoring equipment, be familiar with tools, repair machinery, and testing equipment, be capable of elementary troubleshooting of the ship's bridge controls, and have a basic understanding of the maintenance requirements of deck, propulsion, and auxiliary equipment.[40]

The program was first offered on a pilot basis in 1989 to fifty students in the class of 1993 and was an immediate success. Though the Coast Guard ultimately decided not to sanction the watchstanding license that had been widely anticipated, it did acknowledge the new program by allowing ship's officer graduates to sit for the Qualified Member of the Engineering Department (QMED) exam—the highest unlicensed position in the engine room—as well as the third mate's license. The ship's officer program thus became the first new license program to be approved by the U.S. Coast Guard since the Academy's own dual license program, approved several decades earlier.

Rethinking the Regiment

The strategic plan also looked at matters beyond the curricular. In particular, it examined one of the most distinctive characteristics of the Academy: the Regiment.

The regimental system posed a particular dilemma for the planners. It appeared to be in need of change—and yet, for a variety of reasons, it was difficult to change.

To many alumni, the Regiment remained the single most compelling memory of their days at Kings Point. Many believed strongly that regimental life had taught them both personal discipline and leadership, and they attributed their subsequent career success to those qualities. Almost all subscribed to the notion that in times of crisis, a strict adherence to military discipline could mean the difference between life and death for those aboard a merchant ship. Any proposal to substantially change the role of the Regiment, therefore, would be sure to run into strong resistance from the alumni.

Another reason why changing the Regiment was difficult was that the Regiment was a moving target, both in terms of its means and its ends. In fact, generations of students at the Academy over five decades had experienced not one regiment, but a wide variety of regiments, reflecting changing times, rules, attitudes, superintendents, commandants, and students.

Yet another conundrum facing the planners was that most people appreciated regimental life more in hindsight than in real time. For most people, looking back on a highly structured environment tends to be more gratifying than actually living through it. The Academy found itself in the difficult position of prescribing strong medicine whose beneficial effects often were not appreciated before several decades had passed.

Almost from its inception, cadets had grumbled about the strictures of the Regiment, and had sometimes worried aloud about its relevance. Most of the time, this grumbling stayed at a relatively low level. Sometimes, though, the grumbling rose above the level of background noise and demanded attention from the Academy's leaders.

The planners in the late 1980s realized that they were in one of those periods of relative discontent. As always, the causes for the discontent remained murky but probably included, for example, some of the personalities involved at that time; the ongoing shift of the Academy toward a more "military" posture, in the context of the Reagan-era 1980s defense buildup; and a general disillusionment among the midshipmen about their job prospects in a sharply declining shipping industry. A 1987 article in *Hear This*, the student newspaper, touches on several of these points, and expresses a more generalized discontent:

> There used to be a time when C.O.'s [company officers] were people to whom a midshipman could go for help and advice in the Regimental system. . . . Communication was possible and helpful. The Regiment had an extremely positive feeling within its ranks. Many traditions were observed; class structure was recognized willingly.
>
> During the last few years (3), a new type of C.O. has descended onto the KP campus, [who has] changed the attitude of the midshipmen from one of pride and interest in Academy affairs to one of frustration, distrust, and complete disunity . . .
>
> The Academy is at a present state where certain Midshipmen Officers are using their newly acquired power to "weed out" less fortunate classmates. This unfortunate change in attitude can be linked to the change in the Academy's mission from one of solely Merchant Service to one inclusive of military service.
>
> Last year the class of '86 clashed heavily with the Commandant's staff when the "screws were tightened." Complete havoc resulted within the Regiment, and a long list of unfortunate incidents resulted. Similar incidents are appearing throughout the Academy this year, in the Regiment's own "underground" war with the Commandant's staff. As in any war, though, nobody is winning.[41]

What was going on here? By the mid-1980s, as the Subcommittee on Leadership and Student Life noted in a 1990 planning report, there was "considerable confusion and hostility towards the Regimental Program" among Academy midshipmen. Students were told that the regimental lifestyle was preparing them for careers as officers in the maritime industry, and yet their experience during Sea Year was almost invariably the opposite of "regimented." According to the subcommittee, this inconsistency created "confusion and disgruntlement" toward the system, and eventually, by extension, toward the Academy.[42]

Faculty member Chris McMahon, '77, who joined the Academy's Department of Marine Transportation in January 1984, elaborated on this theme:

> This is a unique school, in the sense that it's a military school, but for 25 percent of your four years here, you're out in the real world. And you're not just in the real world in, say, New York. You're around the world overseas, on a commercial ship where you don't wear a uniform, and there's no semblance of regimental discipline.
>
> This is a challenge for Kings Point. You go through plebe year, and you learn "yes sir," and "no sir," how to shine your shoes, how to march. Then you go out to sea, and you meet some of the most colorful people in any society, anywhere. And you yourself are no longer subject to shining your shoes, and cutting your hair, and doing all the things that you have to do in the Regiment. There's a whole different social order on a ship. There's a whole different rank structure. There's a whole different way of doing your job.[43]

The Academy's planners continued to credit the regimental system with instilling values in the midshipmen, including "integrity, honor, responsibility, self-discipline, concern for your people, high standards of personal appearance, and high standards of conduct."[44] And certainly, regimental life was essential preparation for subsequent service in the armed forces, toward which increasing numbers of midshipmen were aiming. The planners therefore were not inclined to jettison the Regiment simply because students were grumbling, or because the regimental system didn't appear to mesh with shipboard realities in the later 1980s. At the same time, though, they concluded that the gap between regimental expectations at the Academy and the reality of life on board merchant ships had grown too large for many midshipmen to bridge.

As a result, the committee recommended shifting the rationale for the regimental system: away from merchant marine officer preparation and more explicitly in the direction of leadership training. The regimental lifestyle, the committee observed, called for many sacrifices on the part of the midshipmen. Students were subjected to extremely strict discipline, restricted freedoms, and a class system that allowed some hazing of plebes. But these students would accept these sacrifices more willingly, the committee further reasoned, if they could be given a compelling rationale for the experience. If the regimental system could be shown to make students more effective leaders later in life, it could more easily gain their support.

To further rebuild student support for the regimental system, the committee also recommended that midshipmen regulations be stream-lined and simplified, with substantial input from the midshipmen themselves. It recommended a loosening of the class rates system, specifically as it related to the "no fraternization" clause. This particular set of restrictions, which limited even basic conversation between juniors and their superiors, was deemed to be both counterproductive and difficult to enforce.

But the sharpened focus on leadership as the main rationale for the Regiment in turn created a new challenge: creating additional opportunities for exercising that leadership. The aforementioned Hook report of 1988 had first highlighted this problem. Hook noted that, as then organized, the regimental system allowed only 45 percent of the first class to assume leadership positions—certainly discouraging the 35 percent of the class who applied for these posts and were turned down, and possibly discouraging many among the remaining 20 percent who never applied at all.

Hook had suggested modifying the structure of the Regiment—from companies of one hundred midshipmen to companies of fifty, and from two shifts a year to three—to give more cadets the chance to hone their leadership skills. These recommendations dovetailed with those of U.S. Army colonel Howard Prince, head of West Point's Department of Psychology and Behavioral Sciences, who helped Commandant Robert Safarik with a concurrent study of the regimental system. In the fall of 1988, therefore, the Regiment was reorganized into ten companies (and no battalions) to create more leadership opportunities.[45]

The Regiment would continue to evolve, of course. But by voting firmly in favor of the continuation of regimental life at Kings Point—albeit with some modifications and reorientation—the school's leaders had reaffirmed one of the pillars that made the Academy a distinctive educational environment. And as several of the state maritime academies moved to loosen their regimental systems in subsequent years, Kings Point became all the more distinctive.

Refining Continuing Education

The strategic planning process also affirmed the important role that continuing education played at Kings Point.

On one level, this affirmation simply acknowledged an established fact. The school's Continuing Education program had been steadily gaining ground, both in terms of scale and visibility. By 1987, it was fully self-supporting and even generating some surplus funds. It was clear, though, that some elements of the program still needed to be formalized. One of the first priorities of the Subcommittee on Continuing Education—which included Captains Douglas Hard, '62, Harold Katz, Robert Madden, '59, and Perry Walter as well as Commander Anton Shurpik and Lieutenant Commander John Nunnenkamp, '74—was to develop a mission statement for continuing education at the Academy. They agreed upon the following formulation: "To offer quality programs significant to the Maritime community, including commercial, non-commercial, and military, enabling them to improve their everyday operating efficiency, respond to world events, and advance rapidly with new technology."[46]

The statement was notable in part for its inclusiveness, asserting that the Academy's continuing education mandate comprised commercial shipping, military transportation, and noncommercial boating. Again, this reflected an established reality: in response to industry demand, Kings Point was already serving a diverse mix of constituencies.

In the late 1980s, for example, a group of New York City tug companies approached the Academy with a specific request. In recent years, most of these companies had experienced one or more significant oil spills that had proven costly both in terms of money and public relations. Could the Academy devise a program to train the crews manning the tug companies' oil barges, and thereby minimize this unwanted exposure?

In response, the continuing education program, under the leadership of new director Perry Walter, designed an intensive one-week course, which drew almost entirely on existing Kings Point faculty members. (Participating professors received additional compensation for their efforts.) The course, fully funded by the tug companies, was an immediate success, and over the course of several years, it trained several hundred tug and tanker employees.

Although the Academy had previously hosted seminars paid for
by private companies under the auspices of the alumni-sponsored U.S.
Maritime Resource Center, this was the first instance of a continuing
education course being directly funded by private-sector money, and it
prompted some changes in the program's financial structure. In the
past, such funds had been channeled through the Melville Hall Officers Club's NAFI (nonappropriated funds instrumentality).[47] As the
influx of private-sector dollars increased, however, this mechanism
became unworkable.

Eventually, Walter and the Academy designed a solution whereby
the continuing education program was incorporated as a private company under the auspices of the Alumni Association. Because the U.S.
Maritime Resource Center had already played a useful role in hosting
industry seminars at the Academy (and was practiced at accepting
private-sector dollars), it was decided to use that structure as a financial frame for the Continuing Education program.

The program continued to expand under its new format in the
early 1990s. Responding to sealift lessons learned in the Gulf War, the
Master Mariners Readiness program was expanded to two weeks in
1991, and renamed the National Sealift Training Program. And in
response to the 1990 federal Oil Pollution Act—itself a response to the
landmark *Exxon Valdez* Alaskan environmental disaster, mandating
double-hulled tankers, better officer training, and increased safety
training—the Maritime Resource Center developed a series of safety-
related courses. These had multiple benefits. First, and most important, they increased safety at sea. But they also made the Academy's
continuing education programs even more relevant and visible to the
maritime community. By the early 1990s, the Maritime Resource
Center was generating more than one million dollars annually in
tuition from its wide range of program offerings.

Despite this growing volume, the program was not yet generating
significant surpluses. The main reason for this was that Superintendent Krinsky believed that continuing education at Kings Point ought
to be run on a break-even basis—in effect, as a service to the industry—
and his approach set the tone in this transitional period. But others at
the Academy were beginning to ask if the school couldn't take a more
entrepreneurial stance. Couldn't Kings Point tap its facilities and the
expertise of its faculty, create new revenue streams, and begin to help
address the institution's chronic financial woes?

Off the Radar

A noticeable gap in the strategic planning mandate defined by Superintendent Krinsky and Dean Mazek in this period was the physical infrastructure at Kings Point. Although Krinsky continued the dormitory renovations begun on King's watch, updating the campus never became a major focus of his administration. In part, this resulted from an admitted reluctance on Krinsky's part to engage in budget fights in Washington. For most of Krinsky's tenure, the budget remained constant at the Academy: enough to cover existing programs, but with no additional funds to catch up on deferred maintenance, or to make necessary investments for the future. The only exception to this came in 1992, when Krinsky, at the strong urging of the Academy's Advisory Board and members of his administration, met with Secretary of Transportation Sam Skinner in Washington to make an urgent request for funds to complete much-needed capital improvements. Though the federal budget was already complete by the time Krinsky made his pitch, Skinner managed to steer an additional $5 million, the proceeds from a planned sale of several aged surplus Ready Reserve Force ships, toward the Academy, to meet its most pressing capital needs.

In general, however, the campus—buildings and equipment—was in a state of slow decline. There was marked deterioration of the living facilities, and even some visible decline in the academic buildings, which had been remodeled in the 1970s. This was an ominous pattern, since almost all of the Academy's buildings had been built at once, and were therefore obsolescing on the same schedule. When the bill finally came due, it would be a large one.

One exception to this gradual slide into obsolescence came at the waterfront. A study of the Cressy Building in 1987 found that the waterfront center was in "imminent danger of collapse."[48] In a textbook case of unintended consequences, the building's woeful state may have been influenced by the presence of its younger, uphill neighbor, the Mariners' Chapel. According to some studies, the chapel, constructed in 1961, was prompting a slow landslide down the hill toward Long Island Sound and, in the process, disturbing the foundations of the Cressy Building.[49]

Despite the dire findings of this study, it was no sure thing that the Academy could find a way to respond to this looming crisis. Captain Joe Prosser, the salty tattooed mariner who had supervised the sailing teams for more than two decades, had been pushing for a dedicated sailing facility for many years. Despite his popularity with students and alumni, however, he had never been able to win support for the idea.

Prosser died in April 1986, and his departure seemed a serious blow to the chances for an updated facility. But there were new winds blowing on the waterfront. The department was restructured after Prosser's death, with the creation of the Department of Waterfront Activities now responsible for varsity and recreational sailing, boating, and crew facility operations and maintenance, and operational oversight of the TV *Kings Pointer*. Lieutenant Commander Gary Gehring was hired as the master of the *Kings Pointer* and the assistant director of waterfront activities. And several months later, Krinsky asked faculty member Chris McMahon, a 1977 graduate with his chief master's license and who had gone back to school at American University for an advanced degree in business, to become director of the waterfront program. McMahon, a close friend of Prosser's, had already decided to leave academia and head back to sea, but out of loyalty to both Prosser and the program, he agreed to take the job.

Almost immediately, McMahon started pushing Krinsky to find the money for a new sailing center. With Krinsky's focus elsewhere, however, this proved an uphill battle. After several years, McMahon was able to sell Krinsky on the concept of a prefabricated structure that could house all of the waterfront facilities.

McMahon enlisted alumnus Eric Wallischeck, '83, a dual graduate then working in the Alumni Association's Development Office, to help him sketch out preliminary plans for the new center. And as the two began playing with architectural concepts, they realized that the prefab concept was simply inadequate for the type of program Kings Point deserved. With Wallischeck's fund-raising experience in the backs of their minds, the two began to shift their concept from a modest government-funded facility to a larger, more ambitious project that would be partially funded by alumni donations. Their primary goal, according to Wallischeck, was not necessarily a beautiful structure that would ornament the campus and its striking setting—that would be out of reach, financially—but rather, a large and flexible structure that would accommodate the Academy's growing waterfront programs. Substantial early gifts, especially from Jim Yocum, '47, and Jim Babson, '44, provided crucial impetus for the project.

McMahon, who had started this ball rolling, left the Academy in 1990 to enroll in a theological seminary in Berkeley, California. (As he later explained, he needed to "take a time out, and go look at the meaning of life."[50]) Wallischeck was hired in 1991 to replace him as sailing master and to oversee the construction of the building he had so casually sketched out three years earlier. Wallischeck, then only thirty years old, recalls that he was looking at two big challenges at once. The first was to grow into a job that required leadership, self-confidence, and initiative, and the second was to bring in a large and complicated building. "I was handed a contract," Wallischeck recalled, "and told to bring the building to fruition. And that was certainly a challenge. Dealing with the contractors, and the construction process, and setbacks, and all of these kinds of things. We broke ground in '93, and it was going to be a year to build, and it took two years. So that was a bit frustrating."

The project encountered numerous setbacks and delays. For example, at one point, the contractor's teams began driving piles into the floor of the bay to shore up the foundation of the new building. Almost immediately, the operators of the CAORF simulator, just across the street, protested vigorously; this kind of a pounding, they insisted, could wreck CAORF's fragile computers. In the end, the contractor had to auger holes into the muck for *each individual pile*, adding three months to the project time line. The final costs of the project skyrocketed, from $1.6 million to $2.1 million, giving Wallischeck more than one sleepless night.

But there was good news to celebrate, especially when the project came to a close. More than $1.5 million of the final building costs had been raised from private donations (a full $1 million of this from James Yocum), demonstrating once again that the Academy's alumni and other friends could be relied upon to support a compelling cause. And against what looked like formidable odds, the Academy wound up with the Yocum Sailing Center, a state-of-the-art, fully functional building—what Wallischeck proudly calls a "first-class facility for a first-class operation."[51]

Back to the Drafting Table

Krinsky's first strategic planning initiative proved so useful to the Academy that the administration undertook a second round of planning in

1992–1993. Although the process did address some mistakes made in the first round (for example, because some faculty had felt left out of the interview process in that previous round, Krinsky, Mazek, and Kozlowski decided this time to bring industry leaders to campus), it grew directly out of and largely emulated the earlier initiative.

But this second round of planning also reflected dramatic changes in the external environment. These included the continued expansion of container traffic and intermodal transportation, the stunning and abrupt end of the Cold War, structural changes in the industry and continued decline in shipboard employment, the increasing demand for U.S. military sealift capacity (as evidenced by military needs during the 1990 Gulf War), and possible repercussions of the Oil Pollution Act of 1990.

Guided by these external factors, and also influenced by the input of industry leaders, the revived Strategic Planning Committee formulated six "propositions" that would guide future developments in the Academy's curriculum and programs.[52] The first was that maritime education and training would continue to constitute the core of the Academy's program, and intermodal connections would receive greater emphasis. This affirmed the traditional water transportation mission of the Academy, but also recognized the new global industry that was forming around intermodal transportation.

Second, the committee decided that obtaining the U.S. Coast Guard officer's license would continue to be a graduation requirement for all Kings Pointers. In the wake of the Gulf War, this was a timely reminder that Academy-trained licensed officers constituted a valuable—even vital—national resource in times of mobilization. In a related vein, the committee also affirmed the continued priority given to regimental and leadership training, and the requirement that all students be midshipmen in the U.S. Merchant Marine Reserve-U.S. Naval Reserve, and qualify for a commission.

In addition, the committee reaffirmed the importance of the Strategic Transportation Alliance with the U.S. armed forces. This carried forward the initiative begun by General Alfred Hansen after the previous round of strategic planning, in which the Academy developed an integrated civil-military transportation and logistics program, principally through the leadership of officers from each military service.

Finally, reflecting the increasing national (and even worldwide) emphasis on maritime safety, the committee proposed emphasizing education and training in support of maritime safety and environmental protection. This emphasis would manifest itself both in the undergraduate curriculum and in the continuing education program.

One of the most significant long-term changes resulting from this second round of strategic planning was the development of an engineering management major. The program, as proposed by the Department of Engineering, added six courses in management to the marine engineering major, substantially expanding the shoreside options open to engine majors. This program was implemented in 1998 under the name Shipyard and Marine Engineering Management (the name was later reversed, to Marine Engineering and Shipyard Management); by that point, it included more than twelve targeted business and management courses.

The 1993 plan also called for external initiatives and "input-output" initiatives, aimed at improving both the raw material (candidates) and products (graduates) of the Academy. Among the external goals cited were strengthening contributions to the national defense and sealift capacity; creating greater integration within the U.S. Department of Transportation, including the Coast Guard; expanding continuing education programs; creating a maritime and intermodal transportation center; and expanding the Academy's international maritime community role.

Central to the input-output initiatives were improvements to the school's admissions department. In the view of the Strategic Planning Committee, this was likely to involve a rigorous recruiting program, appropriate publicity, and academic policies and procedures designed to support retention. One of the first priorities was to update the school's "viewbook," a printed portrait of the institution, aimed at potential applicants and their parents, which was a basic recruiting tool for most undergraduate schools. To this end, in 1991 Superintendent Krinsky asked Martin Skrocki, the Academy's public information officer, to revise the viewbook and other publications. Skrocki hired an outside design firm to work on the redesign, and the influence of the viewbook that resulted can still be seen in current publications.

Next, Krinsky hired Captain James Skinner to head the Admissions Department and streamline the recruitment system. Skinner recalls a clear consensus when he arrived in December 1992 that the system was in trouble. "Admiral Krinsky knew there were things wrong in admissions," Skinner explained, "in part because he had been in admissions at one time. And even though he was only going to be here six months after I was hired, he wanted to take action. He didn't want to leave the ship with a serious list, taking on water, and have that be part of his legacy."[53] Skinner had been director of admissions at Norwich University in Vermont and Mass Maritime Academy before accepting the Academy post, and he called upon these experiences to begin developing a professional and productive recruitment process.

Skinner also streamlined key aspects of the acceptance process. Before his arrival, for example, there was no set date for the stringent medical exam that students were required to pass in order to attend the Academy. In far too many cases, prospective cadets who had received letters of acceptance would wait to take their physicals until almost literally the day before they were supposed to arrive at the Academy. Not surprisingly, some flunked. Skinner recalled the chaos that resulted:

> My predecessors would line up cars of alternates down the road leading up to the front gate of the Academy. And as students didn't look like they were going to appear that [matriculation] day because they didn't get medically qualified the night before, the admissions officers would go down the roadway and hand letters of appointment to students waiting in cars with their parents.
>
> In my first month here, I said, "Okay, *that's* not the way it's going to happen any longer. From now on, everyone will be medically qualified by June 1, and I'm going to tell them on January 30, 'You must get going on this *right now.*' We pushed it and pushed it. And from that point forward, we had a very good idea of who was coming and who wasn't.[54]

These and other changes had the hoped-for effect. Although Skinner's new team, with its new approaches, experienced some initial dips in applications (for reasons that will be discussed subsequently), the changes had a positive impact on the quality of applicants to the Academy, and also on the number of those who accepted appointments.

A Proving Ground

Effective strategic planning doesn't take place in a vacuum. *Context* is critical as an institution sets out to redefine its ends and means.

In the period between the first and second strategic planning efforts conducted by the Krinsky administration, the national defense context changed dramatically. Among many other changes, the merchant marine was once again on the radar screens of military and congressional planners in Washington as an essential component of military sealift. Once again, however, it had required a national emergency to bring about this shift. And once again, as they had done many times before, Kings Point administrators sought to seize the moment, and cement the place of the Academy into the nation's defense constellation.

The crisis, of course, was the 1990 Gulf War, the first full-blown conflict involving U.S. forces since Vietnam. The war involved transporting huge amounts of material and large numbers of people over great distances to a remote and generally inhospitable theater of conflict. By all accounts, the merchant marine performed admirably in supporting and supplying this new type of warfare.

At the same time, however, the merchant marine was taxed to the limit. There were barely enough ships, and nowhere near enough qualified American mariners. The Gulf War made it clear that the steady weakening of the maritime industry had left the nation's military sealift system in jeopardy. Warning bells had been tolling for years about the decline of the merchant marine. Only a few years earlier, in fact, the 1987 Commission on Merchant Marine and Defense had cited the insufficiency of the nation's sealift capabilities in times of national emergency. But it required a highly visible ride out to the cliff edge, with American lives hanging in the balance, to underscore the urgency of these concerns.

Some background is needed to understand this brush with disaster, which resulted both from the declining merchant marine workforce and from a new strategy of warfare that had been embraced by the U.S. military. The thaw in relations between the United States and the U.S.S.R. in the late 1980s brought about a reevaluation of the resources needed for national security. The U.S. defense establishment shifted from a policy of containment to one of power projection. Rather than maintaining regional bases in strategic locations to contain a rival superpower, the Pentagon planners embraced a strategy that involved "small, flexible, and rapidly transportable forces capable of responding to a regional crisis anywhere national interests are threatened."[55]

This necessitated a transition from a strategy that relied primarily on airlift (with materials already prepositioned near potential areas of conflict) to one that also relied on sealift, in both the initial (or "surge") and sustainment phases of conflict. To meet this need, supply and logistics for the armed forces were placed under the command of a new entity, the United States Transportation Command (TRANSCOM).

TRANSCOM, established in 1987 as a successor to the Joint Deployment Agency and based near St. Louis, Missouri, was only the latest attempt to coordinate the vast supply of resources needed for successful military maneuvers, an issue that had been generating friction since the end of World War II. Because the U.S. armed forces employed a heavily segmented approach to conflict—with minimal cooperation between separate military entities—cooperation and coordination, even in the vital arena of sealift supply, remained difficult. In fact, until the passage of the Goldwater-Nichols Department of Defense Reorganization Act in 1986, consolidation of military transportation functions was *illegal*.[56] This had created problems during the ill-fated Iranian hostage rescue attempt in 1980 as well as during the U.S. invasion of Grenada three years later. In both cases, as one researcher later noted, "inter-service rivalry hindered military effectiveness."[57]

TRANSCOM oversaw three component groups: the air force's Military Airlift Command (MAC), the navy's Military Sealift Command, and the Army's Military Traffic Management Command. On paper, the structure looked sensible, but it contained two serious flaws. First, TRANSCOM's commander wielded little authority except during wartime; in times of peace, the component groups controlled their respective transportation modes. Desert Storm soon illustrated the problems inherent in this approach, and in 1992, the charter was rewritten to give more continuous control to the TRANSCOM commander.

The other flaw in the system was even more bureaucratic. TRANSCOM and most of its component parts resided within the Department of Defense budget (DOD). The DOD had already demonstrated many times over that it was far more willing to invest in airlift than in sealift. In 1990, the president of the Shipbuilders Council of America, John Stocker, noted that although 95 percent of military cargo would be carried by sea, the DOD spent only 5 percent of its supply budget on sealift, with 95 percent going to airlift.[58] This imbalance clearly handicapped the Military Sealift Command and several of its component parts: the Afloat Prepositioning Force, the National Defense Reserve Fleet (NDRF), and the Naval Inactive Fleet (a subset of the NDRF).

Congress didn't do much better by sealift capability. When MARAD, responsible for buying and maintaining ships in the Ready Reserve Force (the other subset of the NDRF), requested $239 million for the fleet in 1990, Congress cut this amount by more than 60 percent, to $89 million.[59]

An even greater dilemma for the nation's sealift command lay in finding crews. Although the government had acquired ninety-eight ships for the Ready Reserve Force between 1984 and 1990, it was unable to man even half of these ships. There was no reserve system comparable to the National Guard, and thus there was no guaranteed supply of mariners.

The activation of the Ready Reserve Force in the context of Desert Storm in 1990 created an immediate need for more than three thousand technically competent mariners.[60] The Maritime Administration sent out urgent appeals to mariners both at sea and on shore. Perversely, though, those working mariners who were willing to leave their jobs to join the war effort had no automatic right to reemployment; therefore, many declined to volunteer. MARAD found itself reduced to begging the maritime unions to call members out of retirement, and to cancel all earned leave. In response to MARAD's urgent pleas, the Academy contacted more than seventy-five hundred of its alumni, going as far back as the class of 1955, and in some cases, even farther.[61] (According to anecdotal reports, some members of classes dating back to the 1940s were contacted.) Several members of the Academy staff, including the commandant of midshipmen, were released to active duty service,[62] and more than 152 midshipmen served on vessels supporting the war.[63]

Even these desperate measures weren't enough. The United States proved unable to man enough ships to satisfy the initial demand for sealift in the first crucial months of the war.

Another problem emerged in the operation of the ships. The average Ready Reserve Force ship was thirty years old, and more than 70 percent had steam propulsion systems—but most mariners trained since the late 1970s were diesel operators, with little or no experience with steam systems.

All in all, it was a sobering picture. In light of all of these facts, the Desert Shield/Desert Storm operations in 1990 represented something of a logistical miracle. Ships involved in the sealift effort carried more than three million short tons of cargo, and more than twenty-seven hundred passengers.[64]

The miracle was qualified somewhat, however, by the time frame involved. The U.S. and coalition forces had more than seven months during which to stockpile the necessary supplies and forces in the theater. Under less favorable circumstances, according to historians Arthur Donovan and Andrew Gibson, the "inadequacies of America's sealift capability would have been disastrous."[65] In the first three months of the buildup, moreover, forty-seven of the seventy-three ships used to position supplies and forces for the U.S. invasion were foreign-flagged. As historian and Marine Corps major L. A. Mercado points out, had the hostilities begun earlier, few of these foreign-flag lines would have jeopardized their ships and crews to supply the U.S. forces.[66]

In the final analysis, the merchant marine came through heroically in Desert Shield/Desert Storm, shoring up an operation that might otherwise have been a disaster. Kings Point played a small but crucial role in this larger drama. General Colin Powell, chairman of the Joint Chiefs of Staff, paid tribute to the Academy's role in his commencement speech at the Academy in June 1992:

> The founding spirit of *Acta Non Verba* lives on. In August of 1990, Saddam Hussein invaded Kuwait, and our friends and allies in the Middle East turned to the United States for help. We turned to you, and you answered our call. Kings Pointers, when called to service, indeed lived up to the motto, "Deeds Not Words."
>
> Sealift was the workhorse of our deployment and our sustainment operations. Ninety-five percent of all equipment and supplies reached the Persian Gulf by ship. . . . The entire Kings Point family joined in that massive effort. Some even came out of retirement to return to the sea, including Captain Robert Wilson, who sailed as second mate on a Navy sealift ship at the age of eighty-two!
>
> Many of you served during Desert Shield and Desert Storm as part of your sea training. We are very proud of you.[67]

Once again the midshipmen and graduates of Kings Point had more than pulled their weight in the nation's conflict. And once again,

Chairman of the Joint Chiefs of Staff (and later secretary of state) Colin Powell delivered the commencement address at the Academy in 1992.

politicians and military leaders had emerged from a conflict with a clear understanding of the need to build up the merchant marine as arm of the national defense structure. "From a national security perspective," Vice Admiral Paul Butcher, deputy commander of TRANSCOM, told Congress in 1990, "We need to revitalize our U.S. maritime industry."[68]

Butcher's words served as a timely reminder, prompted by a very close call. But it remained to be seen if that message would prove durable—and if it had been heard by the Clinton-Gore team, which was rapidly gaining momentum in its quest to replace George H. W. Bush in the White House in 1992.

12

Reinventing the
Academy
1993–1999

Another Engel?

The question wasn't publicly voiced, but it was on the minds of many in the Kings Point community in the early months of 1993, when Maritime Administrator Captain Warren Leback, '44, announced that Rear Admiral Thomas Matteson would succeed Paul Krinsky as eighth superintendent of the Academy.

Rear Admiral Thomas T. Matterson became the Academy's eighth superintendent in June 1993

Matteson arrived at the Academy fresh from heading up the Coast Guard Academy, thereby becoming the second former Coast Guard Academy superintendent to head Kings Point. This similarity alone was enough to raise some hackles. But many among the Kings Point alumni community were doubly aggrieved. Transportation Secretary Andrew Card, who had attended Kings Point in the late 1960s and received an honorary degree from the institution in 2001 (when he was chief of staff to President George W. Bush), had ignored their suggestions for superintendent, and had selected the one candidate on the short list who wasn't a Kings Point graduate.

Maritime Administrator Warren Leback, '44, later recalled that the objections that greeted Matteson's appointment had little to do with Matteson himself. In fact, those who knew him well, and had served under him, had nothing but praise for Matteson's leadership ability.

Andrew Card, secretary of transportation and chief of staff under President George H. W. Bush, attended the USMMA in the 1960s. Here he receives an honorary degree from Dean Warren Mazek.

I encountered some resistance from some of the alumni when we appointed Matteson. They said, "Wait a moment! We got another Coast Guard admiral. Remember Engel?" But I replied, "Wait, you're being unfair to the man." Plus, that happened twenty years ago, or close to it.

Before we made some of the decisions I went around to both the ranking enlisted personnel in the Coast Guard, and the officers that were not flag rank, and several in the Regiment up at the Coast Guard Academy, and I posed them a question. I didn't ask about his character, and everything else. I asked, "Would you serve under Admiral Matteson again?" And they said, "Yes, with no problems."[1]

These responses convinced Leback, and he threw his support behind Matteson. His support was well deserved; Matteson was a strong and qualified candidate and became an effective and well-liked superintendent.

A 1957 Coast Guard Academy graduate, Matteson had assumed command of that institution in June 1989. Before that, he had headed the Office of Personnel and Training in Washington, D.C. He had also served at sea on the Coast Guard cutter *Castle Rock*, and had completed flight training at naval air stations in Pensacola and Corpus Christi. Though not an academic, he held a master's degree in management science from the Naval Postgraduate School at Monterey, California, and had graduated from the Air War College at Maxwell Air Force Base in Alabama. Although Matteson had had some exposure to the commercial maritime industry while serving in a Coast Guard position in New Orleans, he had no direct working experience in the industry. But unlike Arthur Engel, his predecessor twice removed, Matteson proved ready to engage with and learn from that industry.

Matteson was aware of the Engel legacy coming into the Academy, and aware that the alumni had favored the appointment of one of their own as superintendent. He was doubly impressed, therefore, when members of the Kings Point Alumni Association rallied to his side the minute his appointment was announced and pledged to do all they could to help him get up to speed:

> After I was selected, I got a call from the president of the Alumni Association, Jack Ring. And he said, "Admiral, I'd like to visit you." I said, "Sure. That would be great, Jack." "I'll be up tomorrow," he said. "We'll go to dinner at the Lighthouse Inn in New London."

And he came up with a legal pad, which I still have somewhere, of a list of things, and he said, "This is what you need to do." Now, I mean, this was after they had pushed so hard for their candidate.

Jack left that meeting that night, and he said, "Here's your schedule." And for three, possibly four Saturdays that I was off and available, I took the train from New London down to New York and went to Don Yearwood's office, who was running a shipping company at the time. And Kings Pointers in the New York area that were involved in various aspects of the maritime industry such as shipbuilding, unions, ship operations, et cetera, would come in and lecture me for two or three hours about what was going on in the industry, and so on. Was I well prepared? No. But was I aware of my surroundings? Was I aware of many of the things the alumni thought were critical? Absolutely.[2]

Matteson met the alumni more than half way. In the long run, he proved to be more in the mold of Thomas King and Paul Krinsky: a "people person" who related well to the Academy's key outside constituencies. He worked effectively with the alumni as well as the Kings Point faculty. His insider experience in Washington, moreover, helped him navigate yet another rocky episode in the Academy's relationship with Washington.

Under Fire

Matteson had enjoyed a smooth tenure at the Coast Guard Academy, and he and his wife were already acquainted with the Kings Point culture through their experience in New London. It was partly this awareness, in fact, that had led him to apply for and accept the Academy post:

> Dottie and I very much enjoyed our four years at the Coast Guard Academy, and we had been down to Kings Point more than once. We played football against them and so on, and we knew Paul and Audrey [Krinsky] well. And I had other irons in the fire, but I said, you know, "I just don't want to stop doing this. These kids are a lifeblood to me, and to Dottie too." We just loved what we were doing, and I said, "You know, we can keep doing this."[3]

Almost immediately, however, the situation at Kings Point became utterly unlike anything Matteson had faced in New London. The first intimation of trouble was an alarm bell—a *loud* alarm bell—that Matteson heard in July 1993. This was only a month after Matteson's swearing-in ceremony, and he was making his first official visit to MARAD's headquarters at D and Seventh streets in Washington. Vice Admiral Albert Herberger had been named as the Clinton administration's choice for Maritime administrator, but he was still awaiting confirmation.

As Matteson made his rounds, a high-ranking MARAD official pulled him aside. "Now, I don't want you to be *concerned* about this," Matteson recalled the official saying, "but Vice President Gore has circulated a report recommending that the Academy be closed."[4]

The report she referred to was a draft of Vice President Albert Gore's National Performance Review (NPR), the result of six months of intensive study of alleged inefficiencies and redundancies in the federal government. As Matteson soon discovered, the stated goal of the review was a more entrepreneurial government, a government that "works better and costs less," that would guarantee citizens more effective, efficient, and responsive service.[5]

The first three steps in the process, as detailed by the report, would be to eliminate unneeded programs ("the obsolete, the duplicative, and those that serve special, not national interests"); collect more money (through increased user fees where applicable, and by collecting unpaid debts); and reengineer government activities to incorporate more sophisticated computer systems and telecommunications capabilities.[6]

By September 1994, according to an NPR status report,

- $46.9 billion of NPR's $108 billion in proposed savings are already enacted.
- $16 billion in savings is pending before Congress.
- Federal employment has dropped 89,500 positions.
- $695 million in savings results from ending federal subsidies for wool and mohair.
- The Defense Department's overhaul of its travel process will save $1 billion over five years.
- The Federal Communication Commission's auctions of new radio frequencies are raising millions.
- Government's use of a Visa card for small purchases is saving $50 million this year.[7]

Ending federal subsidies for mohair, most agreed, made sense. Inevitably, though, some undeserving targets got swept up in the NPR's broad net. The government's opinions on what constituted "unneeded programs" sometimes proved poorly researched and short-sighted. The maritime industry seems a perfect example: once again, the government was forgetting the lessons of a recent war, and proposing policies that would cripple the industry. The report, according to maritime historians Arthur Donovan and Andrew Gibson, recommended repeal of "just about every law or regulation that had provided subsidies and protection for the past fifty years,"[8] including the Jones Act and other cabotage laws, and the cargo preference laws. It also recommended cutting off all federal grants to the state maritime academies, and the closing of the National Oceanic and Atmospheric Administration officer training facility at the Fort Eustis army base.

In its original form, the report also called for the closure of the Merchant Marine Academy. None of the members of the NPR team had visited the Academy or spoken to Academy personnel. The recommendations, it seems, were based on earlier studies, perhaps including the previously mentioned Office of Management and Budget memo, attributed to Annelise Anderson, which called for the closure of the Academy.[9]

This was the state of things in the summer of 1993, as Admiral Tom Matteson took the helm at the Academy. The Academy was once more under fire, and at the greatest risk of outright closure in forty years.

Stepping Up

In one sense, Matteson walked into the boxing ring with his hands tied behind his back. He could—and did—work to bolster morale at the Academy and maintain a high profile in Washington. But the Academy needed funds to organize its defense, and as a government employee, he couldn't legally solicit any monetary aid from alumni or other leaders in the maritime industry. His options, as he later recalled, were strictly limited. "You can't legally go seek funds from alumni," Matteson explained. "A president of a university will go out and twist arms, and so on, and so forth. You can't do that. You can't even use a government phone line, legitimately, to say, 'You know, I need some money for a lobby. Can you help us out?'"[10]

Once again, as in previous crises, the Academy's alumni stepped forward. Project ACTA, first created to combat similar congressional efforts in the 1970s, swung back into gear to mobilize the Kings Point alumni base. Fred Sherman, '55, resigned his position as head of the Alumni Association to take responsibility for Project ACTA. His first notion, he recalled, was to work the crisis through MARAD:

> Our initial strategy was to say, "Okay, we're going to work with you, MARAD, and support your efforts to support Kings Point." But everybody that we went to said, "If you take that tack, you'll get killed, because MARAD has a terrible relationship with Capitol Hill. You can't throw rocks at MARAD, but you've got to disassociate yourself from your sponsoring agency." Which is a fine line to walk, but that's what we ultimately did.[11]

This meant that Sherman and his colleagues had to rile up the Academy alumni population once again. This time, even more than in prior rounds, the result was something like dropping a lit match onto kindling: alumni (and other industry leaders) were so outraged by the proposed recommendations that there was an immediate and powerful outcry. The flood tide of personal visits that ensued, as well as an outpouring of letters and phone calls, did much to shore up the Academy's case in Washington.

Meanwhile, the alumni body also was flexing its muscle behind the scenes. Former superintendent Tom King—who had left his leadership post with the Alumni Association and was then serving as a member of the board of ATTRANSCO, a privately owned tanker company—was contacted one afternoon by a member of the Alumni Association. The alumni wanted King to reach out to an old friend and fellow member of the Kings Point class of 1942.

That classmate was Lane Kirkland, '42, national president of the AFL-CIO and a monumental figure in the landscape of American organized labor, and by extension the Democratic Party. The labor movement had been instrumental in Bill Clinton's successful run for the presidency, and Kirkland had ready access to the new president. King was happy to oblige:

> I called Lane's office in Washington, and Lane was in Europe. I spoke to his secretary, whom I knew, and the answer was that Lane is down on the Riviera at such and such a number, and he's attending a garden party. So I just called that number, and I got the lady

Lane Kirkland, '42, national president of the AFL-CIO (bottom left), stands next to
Superintendent Matteson (bottom right) during the 1997 commencement ceremonies
at the Academy. Like many of his fellow alumni, Kirkland had strong proprietary
feelings about Kings Point. Alumnus Charles Raymond (center right) is also pictured.

there, who was an American. And she said, "Yes, Lane is out in the
garden having cocktails." So I said, "Would he please break away for
a phone call? Tell him that Tom King is calling." So Lane, bless his
heart, he broke away from the cocktail party, and came in.

I told him what was going on. And he said, "All right, I'll tell you
what you do. Write a letter to the White House saying what you
want to say for my signature, and give it to such-and-such a person,
and I will deal with him, and he has my authority to put my signature on it."

So I called Milt Nottingham and told him what we wanted. And
Milt, who is very good at writing, said he'd do it.[12]

Nottingham wrote the letter and delivered it to Kirkland's office,
and from there it made its way to Vice President Gore's desk. Events
moved quickly, and—from the Academy's point of view—in the right
direction. Shortly thereafter, when Kirkland showed up at the White
House to receive the Presidential Medal of Freedom, the highest civilian award given by the federal government, he was pulled aside by
Gore. "Lane," Gore reportedly said, "I want you to know that I've
taken care of your alma mater."[13]

The final version of the 1993 Gore report, published in early September, had indeed been adjusted. Instead of outright closure, it recommended a 50 percent cut in government spending on the Academy and the imposition of tuition charges to cover the resulting gap.

Not to be overlooked in this dramatic episode is the role of Milt Nottingham, who once again stepped in at a critical juncture. By this time, Nottingham was in his fourth decade of service to the Academy, having organized the Washington chapter of the Kings Point alumni in 1951, and having played a role in almost every critical episode in the relationship between Kings Point and the federal government in the ensuing forty years. Along with other prominent Washington-area Kings Pointers, for example, Nottingham helped found (in 1984) the Governmental Affairs Committee, which helped look after the Academy's interests on Capitol Hill.

Nottingham also played an important informal role, according to his longtime friend Vice Admiral Robert H. Scarborough, USCG, '44, serving two generations of Kings Point cadets as Uncle Milt, and opening his Spring Valley home (known to cadets as Chez Nottingham) to midshipmen who found themselves in need of a temporary Washington-area billet. "For a half-century, he has been the focal point for the Academy, and its students, in Washington," said Scarborough.[14]

Round Two

Any celebrations at the Academy resulting from the reprieve offered by the September report were short-lived. Although the Academy had dodged an outright execution, applications for admission started to decline almost immediately, in response both to the lingering effects of the Gore report and the threat of tuition. It soon became clear that the tuition plan, if implemented, would simply kill the Academy by inches. By November, applications were down 25 percent from the previous year.[15] The fight to save the Academy had only just begun.

Vice Admiral Al Herberger, '55, who assumed the post of Maritime administrator on September 14, 1993, only days after the amended NPR report was published, went into this fracas under full sail. In addition to jawboning bureaucrats at the Office of Management and Budget and the National Economic Council, Herberger also spent a lot of time working with members of the military, trying to convince Defense officials to acknowledge that they needed a healthy merchant marine. Surprisingly, given the recent experience of the Gulf War, this proved an uphill battle. As he recalled: "I was trying to get Defense to own up to the fact that they need [the maritime industry]. We could get individual military officers saying, "Yes, we need it," but we could not get a statement out of a senior official. Every time we got close to it, they would back away with the fear that whatever came about as a result, they'd have to pay for. And since they weren't willing to do that, that justified saying whatever they needed to say in order to keep away from that."[16]

At the same time, Herberger tried to create an alliance among the various factions of the maritime industry. This proved almost as difficult as winning the support of the military; for the better part of a century, shipowners, shipbuilders, and mariners had been locked in a death spiral, unable or unwilling to cooperate even on issues of vital common concern. Nevertheless, Herberger persisted, and ultimately was able to extort some semblance of unity among this fractious group.

Herberger was also able to elicit some support for the Academy's cause from the state maritime schools. The relationship between the federal academy and the state schools had deteriorated in recent years. It had been further damaged by the well-publicized remarks of a retired naval flag officer with a history of animosity toward Kings Point, who asserted that the state schools could provide the nation with merchant marine officers without the help of the Academy. Herberger, obviously, disagreed with this assessment. He also felt strongly that the whole group—not just Kings Point—was under fire, and that squabbling among the maritime academies could amount to a form of group suicide. Again he tried to create some common ground:

> I started an annual meeting of all the academies. The state academies did this already, but they met alone, and Kings Point wasn't included. So I said, "If I'm going to the meeting of the academies, all the superintendents and presidents are coming at the same time."
>
> First meeting we had was at Texas A&M. And the retired navy rear admiral started in on all of this budget stuff. And I said, "Stop!" I said, "Look, this whole area doesn't get the kind of funding it should—Kings Point, the state academies—and it's not going to do us any good to be fighting amongst ourselves, and trying to outgun each other. We need to come together, find the common ground, and

Maritime Administrator vice admiral Albert Herberger, a 1955 graduate of the Academy, speaks at the Academy in May 1994.

go for more total budget." I said, "That's the way I'm going to approach it. I'm not going to sit here at these meetings and just have this thing nitpicked to death."

It worked. And then every year that I was there, we had the annual meeting, and we got away from the individual friction between the schools, and collectively came together.[17]

Of course, Herberger also had to demonstrate to the state academies that he wasn't simply showing favoritism toward his own alma mater. When he fought the budget wars in Washington, he made sure that the state academies benefited, as well as Kings Point. For example, he played a key role in getting two of the state-based training ships, the *Empire State* and the *Bay State*, into the Ready Reserve Force, netting about two million dollars in federal funds per year for each ship.

Project ACTA's effort was also continuing, with intense letter writing campaigns, visits, and phone calls to congressmen. Fred Sherman, '55, once again began coordinating an "education process"[18] for the general public and members of Congress. In a March 1994 appearance before the House Committee on Merchant Marine and Fisheries, he instructed the assembled representatives on the consequences of charging tuition at the Academy, the inconsistencies in the National Performance Review's recommendation, the value of Kings Point graduates, the leadership role played by Kings Point graduates, the changing maritime industry, and the low federal costs of a Kings Point education. Meanwhile, ACTA also won the support of various influential groups for its "No Tuition" movement, including the AFL-CIO Council, the Maritime Trades Department of the AFL-CIO, the American Legion, and the Maritime Law Association of the United States.[19]

Sherman, working even further behind the scenes, persuaded the other federal academies that they should make common cause with Kings Point. This, he recalled, was no simple task: "They blew us off initially until we said, 'Have your lawyers let us know where in the law it says they can't charge tuition at Annapolis.' And they could not find it. And that's when they decided, 'Hey, well, maybe we will at least not *oppose* putting this into the defense authorization bill.' They became quiet allies."[20]

All of these efforts, in the foreground and the background, paid off in April 1994. At that point, a bill was introduced into the Senate that prohibited charging tuition at any of the service academies. The National Defense Authorization Act of 1995 explicitly reinforced this prohibition against tuition.

Permanency Reaffirmed

To all appearances, the alumni and other friends of Kings Point had successfully navigated the Academy out of danger. Kings Point was no longer slated for closure, and the specter of tuition charges seemed to have been permanently vanquished.

The somewhat battle-weary Kings Point alumni, however, remained on high alert. For one thing, traditional bases of power were shifting in Washington. The House Merchant Marine and Fisheries Committee–the maritime industry's staunchest ally in Congress for many decades–fell in 1994 to the powerful sword of House Speaker Newt Gingrich, as a result of hearings of the Joint Committee on the Organization of Congress. (Ultimately, Merchant Marine and Fisheries was the only major committee casualty of the so-called Gingrich Revolution.) At the same time, the Academy's direct parental organization, MARAD, commanded ever less power and respect. Finally, the

Department of Transportation could not always be counted on as a strong ally of the Academy.

This last point was underscored in the spring of 1995, when the inspector general of the Department of Transportation, Mary Schiavo, authored a report calling yet again for the closure of the Academy. Based on a financial analysis and a comparison with the state maritime academies, the report stated that:

> MARAD continues to operate the USMMA when state academies offer comparable education at a lower cost. We estimate that the Federal Government could save between $15 to $26 million annually if responsibility for educating approximately 960 students presently enrolled at the USMMA is transferred to the MARAD-supported state academies. Further, MARAD needs to strengthen controls over assuring USMMA and state academy students and graduates meet their obligations incurred in exchange for Federal assistance.[21]

The first finding, that the Academy should be closed, was immediately disputed by Secretary of Transportation Federico Peña. In his response, Peña wrote that the analysis fell short in a number of areas, and did not "evaluate the benefits derived from the USMMA's continued operation, nor . . . provide an in-depth and comprehensive analysis of all factors relating to any savings that might result from its recommended actions. As a result, the draft report does not provide a rationale sufficient for this Administration to reconsider its policy regarding the USMMA."[22]

MARAD's Herberger was equally dismissive of the central finding, writing that the report "failed to make a case" for the closing of the Academy: "No attempt was made to explain the purpose of the Academy, its historical context, or the evolution of its academic programs. . . . The USMMA is the undisputed leader in maritime education worldwide, and . . . the excellence of the Academy program legitimizes our leadership in international bodies like the International Maritime Organization of the U.N."[23]

Notably, both Herberger and Peña acknowledged that service obligations for the graduates of both the Academy and the state maritime academies needed active enforcement. Herberger's memo went a step further, outlining specific plans to meet this goal.

These prompt and strongly worded responses effectively silenced the inspector general. In a June 1995 memo, Schiavo described the recommendation to close the Academy as "closed."[24] The much-buffeted Kings Point alumni, however, did not let down their guard. Project ACTA, now a permanent lobbying organization, continued to work behind the scenes to create support for legislation that would reaffirm the Academy's permanency as a federal institution.[25]

In hopes of becoming more proactive and less reactive, Project ACTA also initiated (in the spring of 1995) a project called Vision 2000. A steering committee headed by alumnus Dave O'Neil, '61, was formed to "identify those issues critical to the future of the Academy."[26] With the help of a nationally recognized consulting firm, as well as O'Neil's friend and classmate Donald Forster, '61, the committee mailed out questionnaires to more than sixteen thousand alumni, friends, and faculty of the Academy and consulted with top industry leaders. Subcommittees of Vision 2000 examined the Academy's funding; its communications with government, industry, and the public; its curriculum; and a range of other issues.

The recommendations resulting from Vision 2000 were "evolutionary rather than revolutionary"[27] and generally meshed well with the school's own perceptions of its needs. Vision 2000 served as an important guide in both the Academy's 1995 accreditation process and the planning guidance of the subsequent administration headed by Rear Admiral Joseph D. Stewart. An Alumni Association report written in April 2000, moreover, credited Vision 2000 with helping the school achieve important goals, including a stronger emphasis on logistics and intermodal transportation.

Upgrading the Old, and Launching the New

Though the battles in Washington occupied much of the attention of the Academy's administration in the mid-1990s, upgrading the educational experience at Kings Point remained a primary challenge. Superintendent Matteson did his best to maintain morale among the Regiment—a trying task, in those difficult months when it appeared as if the Academy might be going under!—and also to continue Krinsky's emphasis on the curriculum.

One of Matteson's highest priorities was to strengthen the Regiment. This priority reflected his sense that the Kings Point community wanted this kind of recommitment to the regimental system. The Regiment was widely believed to have "softened" somewhat under

Krinsky's academically oriented tenure, and many alumni and midshipmen hoped that Matteson would correct this trend. But an institutional recommitment to the Regiment also reflected Matteson's own strong belief in that system. As he explained:

> The Regiment creates people who are disciplined, and who learn through being required to do a certain number of things in a certain amount of limited time.
>
> Time is always limited. There's never enough time. Kings Pointers learn how to prioritize. They learn how to discipline themselves, and how to discipline their thinking. And that comes in part from a regimental system that requires you to do other things besides go to class, and eat, and sleep. And when you get out into the service, or out into the industry, you're prepared.
>
> And by the way, we're not producing civilians only here. We're producing people who are expected to be able to assume the mantle of a commissioned officer in any of the services. And we shouldn't forget the fact that Kings Point is the only academy in which you can accept a commission in any one of the services. Every year, when you go to graduation, somebody's got every color uniform on. They go, and they succeed in those services.
>
> Would they do that without a regimental system? I don't know. Are they better prepared, with the benefit of a regimental system? Absolutely, yes. They are better prepared.[28]

Some at Kings Point worried that Matteson might go overboard in his evident zeal to tighten up the regimental system. (History suggested that abrupt lurches in the direction of heavy-handed discipline from the top tended to backfire, fomenting discord among the Regiment.) But these fears turned out to be groundless. While his administration did place more emphasis on the Regiment, Matteson was also respectful of the Regiment's powers of self-discipline and refrained from top-down manipulation of the system: "When I came in, they expected all of these instantaneous changes, [and that] the ax was going to come down. The Regiment was scared to death that I was going to take away all their privileges, and it was going to be worse than West Point. Well, it wasn't!"[29]

On the academic side, Matteson had the benefit of Krinsky's prior investments in strategic planning, and he continued to push to fruition many of the initiatives launched by Krinsky. Thanks to extensive

The Regiment stands at review in 1994.

groundwork that had already been laid, for example, the Academy during Matteson's tenure launched two new majors: logistics and intermodal transportation, and marine engineering and shipyard management. Each of these significant initiatives deserves some attention.

On Krinsky's watch, as noted, the faculty had developed an expanded intermodal and logistics program that formed a major part of both the ship's officer and the marine transportation degree. But the Academy had yet to implement a full-fledged degree program in this area. In Matteson's opinion, this placed Academy graduates at a disadvantage in an increasingly intermodal transportation environment:

> Remember that by 1993, we were already dealing with a seamless transportation system. Cargo might be moving by water, air, barge, and rail—all with the same company, and one bill of lading.
>
> The breakbulk stuff was over. I mean, you weren't putting stuff on the dock, and then putting it in somebody else's truck. It was a new way of thinking. And executives in the industry had to think at one speed when they were talking about a ship, and another speed when they were talking about an airplane, and they had to be prepared to

deal with two different unions, and so on, and so forth. But we were not putting out graduates who were prepared to think that way.

So I was very concerned about the academic curriculum. I didn't think that we were where we should be, logistically. In terms of providing a product to the industry, we were four or five years behind where we should have been, with a logistics major. We needed a logistics major very badly, and I started on that immediately.[30]

Interim head of the Division of Marine Transportation, Richard D. Stewart, '73, strongly agreed with this assessment. He also knew that logisticians in the early 1990s were in huge demand, and that the Academy would have a hard time recruiting a "star": there was a limited tradition of academic research at the Academy, teaching loads were heavy, the institution was on an eleven-month schedule, and the Academy wasn't an accredited business school (as were many schools with strong logistics departments). Stewart convinced Matteson that the Academy would have to offer an unusually high starting salary to a prospective hire, as well as competitive research funding.

With these recruiting tools in hand, Stewart was able to make an inspired hire in Jon S. Helmick, a young research assistant professor of logistics on the faculty of the University of Miami School of Business. Helmick, a protégé of Nicholas Glaskowsky, a leading figure in the field, arrived at the Academy in 1995 and worked with the department to build a practical, hands-on logistics program. Helmick interviewed key figures in the military and commercial logistics and transportation field and also conducted extensive needs assessments with industry associations to uncover industry priorities. He also focused on retaining the maritime core competencies that were central to the Academy; the resulting program was one of the few in the nation to explicitly combine logistics and intermodalism.

With Matteson lending his support, the full major was implemented in 1998 and has since become one of the most popular majors at the Academy. In its first year alone, sixty-five of one hundred deck graduates were logistics and intermodal majors.[31]

The new degree grew directly out of ongoing changes in the industry. Intermodalism was becoming the bedrock of all transportation systems, and containers were becoming the bedrock of intermodalism. Intermodalism was also the foundation of a government program introduced in 1997 called the Voluntary Intermodal Sealift Agreement, which legislated a new degree of cooperation between MARAD, the Department of Defense, and commercial shipping companies to meet military sealift surge and sustainment requirements. These companies formed part of a container-based intermodal chain designed to ensure the seamless delivery of goods in times of emergency. Commercial companies that agreed to provide these crisis-related services would have priority when peacetime Department of Defense contracts were being awarded, thus creating closer working relationships between government and the transportation sector in times of both peace and war.

Engineering Meets Business

Under Matteson's leadership, the Academy also moved forward with a third engineering degree: marine engineering and shipyard management.

Proposals for an engineering management program had been floated several times already, principally by Professor Douglas Brown, acting department head of engineering in the mid-1990s, and Professor Boris Butman. Brown and Butman had invested significant time and energy in the design of the proposed engineering-management program, which was similar to an engineering program offered at West Point, although not modeled directly on it. But the program had failed to gain the active support of the administration.

Then, in 1995, an energetic new player arrived on the scene from across the Sound. Jose Femenia came to the Academy as the new head of engineering from the New York Maritime Academy at Fort Schuyler, where he had been teaching since 1964 and had headed the engineering department since 1974. In the mid-1980s, Fort Schuyler, which had become increasingly academically oriented during the early years of Femenia's tenure there, had begun to experience a reversal of this trend, moving back toward a more practical program. Femenia, strongly inclined toward the more academic orientation, began to think about relocating to a more congenial context. Although at first reluctant to consider Kings Point, the traditional archrival of Fort Schuyler, he began thinking about the many good friends he already had on the Kings Point faculty, largely as a result of professional contacts. In 1995, he decided to make the move.

Soon after arriving at the Academy, Femenia took a look at the engineering-management program proposal and liked what he saw. In his opinion, the program's lack of momentum had more to do with its name than its content:

> We were sitting around one day, and Boris [Butman] was bemoaning the fact that this wasn't getting anywhere. I've known Boris since about 1980, and we had talked at a lot of meetings and so forth. I knew where he was coming from. Boris asked if I could help: "Could you talk to the dean? Could you talk to Admiral Matteson?"
>
> And I said, "Boris, in my opinion, the reason the program isn't getting anywhere is the title, and the focus. You guys want an 'engineering management' program. We are the Merchant Marine Academy. Let's just retitle the thing. Let's call it shipyard management. Instead of talking about engineering management, refer to courses as shipyard management, shipyard production. Just change the modifier to 'shipyard.'"
>
> That's basically what he did. And all of a sudden, this was terrific. This was the greatest thing since candy. It flew right through, including right through the Maritime Administration.[32]

The resulting program (first called Shipyard Management and Marine Engineering, and a year later—at the request of the midshipmen—changed to Marine Engineering and Shipyard Management) was launched in 1995. It combined the traditional engineering degree with preparation for a wide range of professional shipyard positions, including ship systems and marine equipment design, management of ship construction and repair, research, operations, and marketing. Its focus, according to Femenia, is unique: "We're the only institution in the nation that offers an undergraduate program focused at shipbuilding, and not focused at naval architecture, and ship design. Everybody tells us that we as a nation aren't too smart in building ships, and that's why the rest of the world is beating us hands down. So this is a program that hopefully will help rectify that, in time."[33]

Femenia made another important contribution to his department soon after his arrival by reinvigorating the engineering electives. His latitude in making these changes resulted in part from the Academy's conversion to a trimester system (see Shifting the Calendar), a change that spurred significant curricular reorganization across the board. When he arrived, Femenia recalled, midshipmen in the marine engineering program were permitted to select six free electives from among any of the electives offered by the Academy. To the newly installed department head, this seemed like a little too much latitude. An engineering major could conceivably take no engineering electives, and yet graduate with the same degree as an engineering major who took all engineering electives. Femenia tightened up the process, reducing the number of free electives to two.

He also took advantage of the change from the quarter system to the semester system, modifying the Marine Engineering Systems program to allow for five minor tracks. As part of this system, ten students must be interested in a track for it to be offered in a given year. For example, in 2002, the minor elective series offerings included aeronautics, environmental engineering, electrical engineering, naval architecture, nuclear engineering, and mechanical systems. This system, which essentially makes students vote with their feet, puts a great deal of weight on what Femenia refers to as "barracks wisdom":

> Barracks wisdom dominates. If you get a strong class leader—and by "class leader" I'm not necessarily talking about a regimental leader; I'm talking about somebody whom kids *follow*—if you get a strong class leader who says, "I'm going into naval architecture," a lot of kids follow him. Okay? Whereas if you get a strong class leader who says, "Naval architecture stinks," nobody takes it. In other words, a class leader has tremendous, tremendous impact on how classes respond.
>
> I know that very well, and I watch it very carefully. You can hear the rumbles and get a sense of what's going on. So I know, for example, that offshore engineering's going to go next year, because they're talking about it. And on the other hand, if there's only one kid who wants Aeronautical, I say, "Hey, you want aeronautical? I can't guarantee it. But I can tell you what to do. Lobby for it. Go talk with your classmates."[34]

Clearly, the revised system occasionally means a student isn't able to get his or her first choice of an engineering minor. On the other hand, it has fostered the emergence of a broader and more meaningful engineering curriculum. And—not incidentally—it puts faculty in the position of competing for students, which is a strong incentive to keep courses lively and current.

The Death of the Dualie

The dual-license program—which had been scrutinized in the 1987 strategic planning initiative, called into serious question, but ultimately left unchanged—was suspended by Matteson starting with the class of 2003. In part, this was due to growing curricular pressure caused by ever increasing International Maritime Organization (IMO) regulations. And in part, it was due to Matteson's own hard-nosed assessment of the long-term value of the dual program.

In 1995, the IMO approved a sweeping amendment to its Standards for Training, Certification, and Watch Keeping (STCW) regulations. Among other things, the new standards called for increased training time at sea. Although the new rules would not be fully enforced until 2002, they quickly had a major impact on institutions of maritime training around the world. In the Academy's case, the STCW requirements had to be superimposed upon an already burdensome workload.

In the case of the dual program, they proved unattainable. Because the "dualies" needed additional sea time both as engine *and* deck cadets, the increased sea time added up to an incremental *180 days* of sea time for dual majors. In response, the Academy proposed an increased reliance on the CAORF simulator, and the Coast Guard agreed to cut the number of additional sea days by two-thirds (that is, to 60, rather than 180). But this would still have necessitated an additional year of training for the dual majors, and—Dean Warren Mazek later remembered—the administration decided that no feasible compromise was in sight and ended negotiations with the Coast Guard.

Although the Academy made a good-faith effort to defend the dual program, some at Kings Point had doubts about its value even before the IMO's and Coast Guard's actions. Superintendent Matteson, for example, perceived a basic unfairness in a situation in which the scheduling needs of the dualies were dictating the schedule for the entire Regiment. As he explained:

> There were something like 950, 960, or 970 students at Kings Point, and something like 30 or 40 of them were dictating the academic schedule. Why? Because the dualies were the ones who didn't have electives.

So we had to find a way to work this class, this class, this class, and that class in for the benefit of the dualies, and everything else had to revolve around them. It was a scheduling nightmare—an absolute *nightmare*. And guess what? It was an even bigger nightmare when a dualie failed a course.[35]

Marine Transportation Department head George Sandberg agreed with this assessment. He also had some reservations about the quality of the deck officer that the dual program was producing, from his observations as an instructor on the CAORF simulator:

On the simulator, the dual sections would come together as a group, and they were terrible. They couldn't navigate, they had casualties, they ran aground, they'd have collisions. And I looked into that, and realized that the dual students hardly took any navigation. They took one course, and excuse my language, the faculty here referred to it as "the bastard course," because it included cargo, seamanship, and navigation all in one course.

The dual sections just weren't getting the material. Would they pass license? Yes. Why? Because they were as smart as they were. These were the high achievers. They could study on their own and pass licenses. But they were not, in my estimation, on a par with the straight deck officers the Academy was producing. And we needed to graduate the same level of deck officers. We couldn't have two different levels of deck officers—those who had taken all these courses, and those that hadn't.[36]

Sandberg brought his concerns to the attention of department head Richard Stewart, and the two worked to rectify the situation. By the time Sandberg became department head in 1995, dualies were taking the same deck courses as the straight deck majors. But this refusal to cut corners meant that the program became more and more unwieldy, and the number of students who couldn't complete the program continued to rise. According to Sandberg, it became clear that the program was not feasible in the Academy's four-year calendar.

Matteson faced a great deal of opposition when he proposed to suspend the dual program. Much of this negative reaction came from alumni, some of whom felt that the "elite" dual program—rigorous and demanding—reflected well on their alma mater. In fact, Matteson agreed with this assessment, as far as it went, but he had become convinced that the program called for too many compromises on the part of the Academy, and that non-dualies were paying too high a price to sustain it. And just as important, as Matteson saw it, the program created a product of only limited value to its industry:

> Look: we produce a *product*. We should be producing a product that makes the users of that product say, "This is what I need." The users of the product are the individuals and the companies in the maritime industry, and I never met any of them who said they needed a dualie. Not one. Sure, there were companies that would say, "I'll look for a dualie." But they didn't hire a dualie because a dualie was a dualie. They hired a dualie because they know how much the dualie had to go through to get what he or she got. Not because of the education that they got, but because of the effort that they had to expend.
>
> I was faced with a program that many of the alumni took a great deal of pride in, particularly if they were dualies. They were saying, "You know, this is the plum. This is the only academy where you can do this." Yeah, that's absolutely true. But what good is it?
>
> So I was opposed to it, and I eliminated it as a specific degree option. Dean Mazek and I finally agreed that, "If you come to the Academy with sufficient college credits to allow you to take two majors, fine. But we're not going to start you out fourth class year in a curriculum that has two majors."[37]

Technically speaking, the dual curriculum is still on the books at the Academy, available to those students with sufficient credits from prior college experience. But in practice, it lives on mainly in memory. Students who want exposure to both the deck and engine sides of the shop can select the Ship's Officer program. And so, despite occasional heartfelt pleas from alumni, there are no current plans to revive the dual program.

Shifting the Calendar

Another task that fell to Matteson was the difficult and unpopular job of shifting from a quarter-based to a trimester-based academic calendar. This, too, proved a thorny issue, essentially pitting the drawbacks of the Academy's frenetic pace against the difficulties of making the transition to a trimester system.

The issue was first raised in the early 1980s by a faculty forum committee chaired by Professor Arch Davies. That committee proposed making the switch, but because of pending International Maritime Organization changes and the complicated engineering-program accreditation process, the change was never made.

The issue resurfaced during Paul Krinsky's strategic planning process in 1987. A subcommittee of the Strategic Planning Committee took up the subject and cited immediate benefits for the Academy upon conversion: alleviating the hectic pace of instruction, reducing instructional and administrative overhead, and enjoying the pedagogical advantages inherent in longer courses.

The report also noted a major disadvantage to the shift: its effect on the Sea Year, which had split into two equal halves of two semesters each. The trimester schedule would necessitate an unequal division of the time spent at sea—a shorter, one-trimester time period and a longer, two-trimester time period. This would create constraints on the assignments of students to the splits based on their majors. For example, if the Academy continued to offer the Marine Engineering Systems program only twice a year, students in one of the three Sea-Year splits would not be able to take the course, and those who needed the course would be limited in their choice of Sea-Year splits. This in turn could conflict with additional athletic constraints created by trying to keep athletes on campus during the semester of their primary sports seasons.

These difficulties were not insurmountable in and of themselves. But when compounded by the general reluctance of the faculty (and then Superintendent Krinsky) to embrace such a major shift, this 1989–1990 effort to move to the trimester system died a quiet death.

Another plan that emerged in the early 1990s offered an alternative concept in which there would be two longer trimesters (roughly equivalent to the semesters followed by many universities and college systems) and a shorter summer trimester. The concept was that all subjects would be taught in the fall and spring semesters, but only the professional subjects would be taught during the summer session. This plan, however, faced strong objections. The faculty union opposed the new scheme, citing concerns that it would reduce the teaching load (and thus the salary) of faculty members in the academic departments.

By the time Superintendent Matteson arrived on the scene, the issue was dormant. Matteson, though, was strongly in favor of the shift. He was influenced, he explained, by his family's own personal experience:

> I have a daughter who graduated from a university that had the quarter system, based on ten-week academic quarters. I watched her, and I was convinced in my mind as a father that it was "take, pass, and forget," and that was life. The building-block process that an educational system *should* be just wasn't occurring. Yes, there were prerequisites, and so on, but you didn't *remember* much of anything.
>
> So I got to the Academy, and I was preloaded; I really was. I saw the same thing. It was so clear. We would sit down at student boards, and midshipmen would say, "I passed it. It doesn't make any difference." And I talked to them, and we'd be discussing differential equations, or something else, and I'd say, "Well, what about so-and-so? What about this course, or that course?" "Well, I passed those courses." I'd say, "That's not the *point*. Remember you did this, this, and this?
>
> "Well, yeah," the student would say back, "but I don't remember that."[38]

Matteson insisted that the faculty take up the matter once more. He found a strong ally in Dean Warren Mazek, who had previous experience of a calender shift from his tenure at Florida State University. Another ally was the recently recruited engineering head, Professor Jose Femenia. Femenia, who had been accustomed to a semester-based system at Fort Schuyler, found himself in agreement with Matteson's and Mazek's assessment of the pedagogical problems inherent in the quarter system.

With most senior members of the administration now in favor of the shift, the stage was set for change. Another impetus came in 1995, when three subcommittees of the Middle States Association review team strongly suggested that the faculty reexamine the conversion recommendations.

At this point, Admiral Matteson established a committee, chaired by Dr. Charles Weber, assistant head of the Department of Math and Science and a member of the Academy faculty since 1972, to examine several alternative calendar plans. Mazek examined the conclusions of this committee and recommended to Matteson that the committee do further work on a trimester proposal, including creating tentative course schedules for the various majors.

At first, the difficulties of fitting four quarters' worth of work into three semesters seemed insurmountable. Jose Femenia later recalled scratching his head over the amount of coursework that had to be fit into each semester:

> The dean wanted a week between semesters, and we had the Christmas lead period, and the commandant wanted four weeks in June and July for indoctrination, and cleaning up the barracks, and all that stuff. So I sat down with a yellow pad and a bunch of sharp pencils. I said, "All right. I have fifty-two weeks. I subtract one week between semesters, I subtract this for the commandant," and so on. I ended up with like forty-two weeks.
>
> I said, "Okay, how can I do it in forty-two weeks?" Well, it didn't work. That was using fifteen-week semesters. Fourteen weeks of teaching, and one week of exam. That's forty-five weeks, and I had only forty-two, or whatever. So I said, "What do I do *now*?" So I played. I played with moving the academic year around. I just couldn't get it to work.
>
> Then it came to me. I said, "Oh, *man*, God didn't say that a class session has to be fifty minutes!" So I said, "Okay, I can do it with thirteen weeks of teaching, and one week of exam. That's forty-two weeks. That's perfect." So I said, "All right, now what's the difference? The difference is I lose one week. Well, if I take fifty minutes, and ratio it by fourteen over thirteen, it comes out to fifty-four minutes." So I rounded it up to sixty minutes.[39]

This notion of sixty-minute classes solved the first major difficulty, but the flow of courses for entering students in each major still had to be determined by the Engineering and Marine Transportation departments. In addition, a transition curriculum had to be designed for courses that had started on the quarter system but would finish on the trimester system. This enormously complicated task was undertaken by Weber, who designed a master plan for courses and majors and wrote drafts of the transition trimester curriculums for each academic major.

One of the largest challenges that both Weber and the departments encountered was the repackaging of courses. Because the Academy had to move from eighty courses to fifty, some courses would have to be combined in order to avoid eliminating subject material. As Weber explained:

In some cases, you can put things together pretty simply. Physics I and II were put together into physics I. Physics III and IV were put together into physics II, with a little bit of dropping. So that worked pretty well. But in other cases it was not as smooth.

We had two courses under the quarter system called differential equations I and calculus IV. These had to be combined under the new system into engineering math I. This is a sort of generic name, but it really covers two topics that are quite different. We weren't terribly happy about that, and we still aren't really happy about that. But remember, we're trying to take eighty courses and make fifty courses out of them, so there's no way it's going to fit perfectly.[40]

According to Mazek, Weber's meticulous contributions were of immeasurable value to the process.

We had to make some cuts. There had to be give and take. And that was the beginning of a negotiation process. This is where Charlie was absolutely magnificent. Charlie developed the schedules, the curriculum matrix, term by term for all the majors. Then we got these two Sea-Year splits. So you double the number of curricula you have to design, because half were at sea, and half were here. Charlie worked like a dog on that. He did really good work.[41]

These efforts later earned Weber a Bronze Medal Award from the Maritime Administration,[42] but more important from an institutional point of view, the resulting system met with the approval of the administration as well as most of the faculty.

The final hurdle involved winning the support of the faculty union. Initially, as in the late 1980s, the union expressed concern that a revised schedule might reduce teaching loads, and thus salary and benefits. After considerable negotiations among Matteson, Mazek, and Academy personnel director Tom Goodwin and the faculty union, all parties agreed on a redefinition of the faculty workload, and the union withdrew its opposition to the trimester conversion.

As Femenia pointed out, the curriculum emerged the stronger for these adjustments. "I now brag to people that I have an engineering program that involves twelve academic semesters, " he explained. "I have a program that most people would drool at. I've got three semesters of intensive co-oping focused at their major, and nine academic semesters. No other school around has *that*."[43]

In addition, the shift compelled all faculty members to reevaluate their own courses and refresh their teaching plans. For Superintendent Matteson, this particular outcome had been one of his unspoken goals for the process from day one:

> I'm not afraid to say that I had an ulterior motive. More than one or two members of the Kings Point faculty hadn't changed their planning, or their classes, in all the time they had been there. They taught the same thing, the same way, year after year after year. And I knew that if we went to the trimester, they couldn't do that any more. They would have to sit down and go through their textbooks and redo the course. They might teach it the same way time after time after that, but at least *once* they would have to do that.[44]

Much of the actual work of conversion came on the watch of the superintendent who succeeded Matteson in 1998: Rear Admiral Joseph Stewart. Matteson acknowledges that he took some criticism for this outcome. On balance, he argued, it wasn't necessarily a bad thing:

> One of the criticisms that I heard was, "You did all this, and then you dropped it in Joe Stewart's lap." The work was really the year and a half that we took with the study, making the changes, setting up the charts, going through all the things that had to be done. In some ways, it was probably better that a new guy came in, at that point, because he was handed a plan in which he had no pride of authorship.
>
> And Joe could tweak it to his liking. He wasn't sitting up nights, saying to himself, "Gee, I remember when we did this. If I change it now, people are going to get all upset." That didn't bother him, because he just didn't know about it. So I think in some ways, my leaving was probably a good thing for the trimester.[45]

By most accounts, the transition to the trimester plan proved difficult to pull off, especially for those students caught in the middle of their Sea Years. (It was a little bit like exchanging currencies in which the denominations didn't quite match up.) But according to many of those same accounts, the conversion has been a positive step for the Academy. It has delivered the promised benefit of an improved teaching environment, if not a more reasonable pace. ("I don't think the more reasonable pace ever materialized," commented Commandant Bob Allee.)[46] And perhaps, as Tom Matteson hoped, it is creating a more *cumulative* educational experience, in which students retain more of what they've learned, and build more effectively upon those foundations.

A Crisis, and a Turning Point

One of Maritime Administrator Herberger's priorities in 1993, as he began fighting to save the Academy from extinction at the hands of the National Performance Review, was to reinforce the perception of the Academy as an institution of national significance. One way to do this, he decided, was to upgrade the Academy's Continuing Education program. Others shared his commitment to such an upgrade: retooling the program had also been identified as a priority in the Academy's 1992–1993 strategic planning initiative.

As noted earlier, the Maritime Resource Center, under the direction of Perry Walter, had been offering advanced training to mariners from around the country for more than ten years. But by 1993, continuing education at Kings Point was at a crossroads. The industry's conversion from steam to diesel had largely been accomplished, causing enrollments in the diesel program to plummet. The training program set up in the late 1980s for New York City tug-company tankermen also was in decline. And the surge of enrollments in the early 1990s caused by mariners taking safety-training courses mandated by the Oil Pollution Act of 1990 had subsided precipitously.

Suddenly, this limited menu of continuing education programs couldn't bring in even enough tuition to sustain the infrastructure that had been built up around them. By 1993, the program was "screaming in the red," according to one observer. Many staff members, seeing the handwriting on the wall, were departing for more stable positions elsewhere. Walter, who had overseen the previous round of growth, was overburdened by his extensive duties as head of the Department of Professional Development and Shipboard Training and resigned his position in continuing education at the end of 1993.

Mostly for reasons of bureaucratic convenience, continuing education still fell under the supervision of the Alumni Association. This structure worked fine as long as the Maritime Resource Center was thriving. Now it was heading for the rocks, no one was at the helm, and no one in the Alumni Association felt qualified to plot a new course. Arthur Erb, '43, acting director of the Alumni Association–

replacing Fred Sherman, then working full-time for Project ACTA–
surveyed a set of bleak scenarios.

Erb considered the short list of people qualified to take on this difficult job at such a critical junction. At the top of Erb's list was Chris
McMahon, the iconoclastic and entrepreneurial former faculty member who had left the Academy's Waterfront Department in 1990 to
pursue a degree in ministry. Erb placed a call to McMahon, who made
it clear that he wasn't interested–either in the position, or in a return
to the Academy. But during a subsequent visit to Kings Point to see
some old friends, McMahon ran into Erb at the Academy gate, and
the two talked for several hours about the situation. Finally, McMahon
succumbed to Erb's increasingly urgent appeals and declared his willingness to return to Kings Point.

Admiral Matteson then weighed in. Perhaps worried about the
viability of the overall program, he suggested that McMahon be
appointed acting director of continuing education. McMahon balked.
"I said, 'I won't take the job as acting director. You need to give us
enough time. You need to have a director. So it's either going to be me,
or you get your own person. And if it's not me, no hard feelings. I
don't need to be here. I've got plenty of other places to go.' So they
said, 'No, no; we'll make you the director.'"[47]

There was little time to waste on negotiations; firefighting was the
order of the day. McMahon grabbed for the hoses. In the summer of
1994, shortly after McMahon's formal installation as director, the program was renamed the USMMA School of Continuing Education.
Concurrently, it moved out from under the Alumni Association's
umbrella and went under the Academy's direct control. The limited
assets of the Maritime Resource Center were transferred to the new
program, which was established as a new "non-appropriated funds
instrumentality," or NAFI.[48] (Much of the groundwork for this conversion had been accomplished by Perry Walter, who had designed,
though not implemented, a business model based on the graduate
school of the Department of Agriculture.) The next steps were to
establish a board of directors and revamp the staff. McMahon cut
costs significantly, mainly by releasing several staff members who were
no longer necessary to the scaled-back program. He then rehired
Commander John Hanus, '88, who had been an instructor under Walter and knew that program well. Hanus joined as associate director.

Despite drastic cost reductions, the program remained on

extremely shaky ground. In October 1994, as McMahon later recalled ruefully, the Continuing Education program had a grand total of $300 in its checking account.[49] To meet its next payroll, the program had to borrow $20,000 from assets that had been reserved to cover the Maritime Resource Center's ongoing outside seminar program. The only reason the center was willing to float the loan was that continuing education could demonstrate that it had enough receivables in its pipeline to cover the amount. But a closer shave would be hard to imagine.

Slowly–*painfully* slowly, from McMahon's perspective–continuing education began to gain momentum. Jump-starting the program, he recalled, mainly involved peppering the industry with proposals for new courses, finding takers, and filling as many seats as possible:

> We just started canvassing the industry and force-feeding as many courses as we could to just get started. And finally, somewhere in '95, it started to take off. We hired our first new employee in January 1995–our first program manager. And then we continued to grow, so that we're now training around thirty-five hundred students per year, primarily in one- and two-week programs. We now have about thirty people on the staff, and financially the program is very successful.[50]

Over the next several years, the program made steady gains in both participants and income. In 1999, reflecting the broadening scope of the program, it was renamed the Global Maritime and Transportation School (GMATS) and restructured into three divisions of study mirroring the Academy's own focus: Nautical Science, Marine Engineering, and Transportation Management and Logistics.[51] By the year 2000, the program offered more than three hundred subjects to more than thirty-five hundred students per year. By so doing, it not only made an important contribution to the industry but also reinforced the Academy's status as a significant national resource–the outcome that MARAD Administrator Herberger had envisioned some seven years earlier.

Looking Forward

If Tom Matteson expected a quiet, end-of-career posting when he arrived at Kings Point in 1993, he was surely disappointed.

Barely installed in office, he found he had to fight off two mortal threats to the Academy. Vice Admiral Albert Herberger, Maritime administrator during Matteson's tenure, recalled that Matteson brought the right skills to the job:

> Matteson was absolutely the right guy to be there during the National Performance Review episode. Because he came from four years at the Coast Guard Academy, Matteson was right up to speed on how to handle the day-to-day morale, and problems that come up with the faculty, staff, and the students. On how sensitive they would be to the kind of news that was coming out of Washington, and answer the questions. He was great. There was none of that old Coast Guard indifference to the maritime industry that had gone on when they were first in charge in the 1940s. None of that came out. He was a great superintendent.[52]

Once these two threats were resolved, Matteson also had to tackle a series of tough curricular challenges, kill off a popular program, respond effectively to pressure from MARAD to build a vibrant continuing education program, and wade into the thankless task of changing the academic calendar.

Not surprisingly, five event-filled years at Kings Point proved to be plenty for Tom and Dottie Matteson. In 1999, they took their deferred retirement.

Once again, Kings Point needed new leadership—and once again, the challenges were urgent.

13

Renewal, Tragedy, and Commitment

2000–2004

One of the Academy's ongoing challenges, both during and after the permanency crisis of the early 1990s, was funding. On both the capital and operational side, Kings Point was running on fumes.

Meanwhile, the Regiment was once again demanding attention. Changing times brought new kinds of students to the Academy, and a changing outside-world context argued for new kinds of leadership training at Kings Point. In a particularly tragic way, moreover, the outside world intruded on the regimented, orderly Academy community, testing the mettle of both its students and its administrative and faculty leaders.

And finally, the Kings Point alumni population played an ever-more important role in the life of the Academy, helping to resolve challenges that had been plaguing the institution for many years.

Budgeting 101: The Challenge for Kings Point

The funding issue was not new for the Academy, of course, which had been expected to do more with less for most of its existence. But as the campus continued to age, as appropriations remained flat, and as inflation continued at its modest but corrosive pace, the situation at Kings Point was becoming increasingly precarious.

It was this situation that had prompted Superintendent Krinsky and members of the Alumni Association to pay their unprecedented visit to Transportation Secretary Samuel Skinner in late 1991, resulting in a onetime windfall of $5 million from the sale of several Ready Reserve Fleet ships. (The Academy at that time also received a bump-up of $1.85 million in its base budget to begin addressing the challenges of deferred maintenance.[1]) But while these funds were badly needed, the Academy was given only five months to encumber the entire $5 million—an anomaly of the federal budget process—and the rush to identify projects and solicit proposals led to as many frustrations as solutions. In the wake of this cash infusion, moreover, appropriations increases from Congress remained minimal for the rest of the decade.

And Kings Point as well as its parent organization, MARAD, failed to object to this treatment. The Academy had dodged two bullets in the mid-1990s, mainly through the intervention of its alumni. No one was particularly inclined to draw new fire by making demands for significantly more resources.

But by any measure, those resources were badly needed. Because the Academy is not an especially complicated entity in financial terms, it is easy to spot the effects of chronic underfunding. To do so, one simply has to review the school's major revenue and expense lines.

On the *income* side, almost all of the Academy's funds come directly from government appropriations. While the Academy operates NAFIs to finance activities not directly related to the school's mission—for example, continuing education (GMATS), the financing of varsity athletics and waterfront activities, Melville Hall, and the operation of the Ship's Store—these relatively small enterprises are run more or less on a break-even basis and therefore contribute only very small sums to the school's operating budget.

In addition, the school receives supplementary funds each year from the Alumni Association. These contributions come in the form of income from the endowment funds controlled by the association, and from additional grants in kind or cash aimed at specific purposes. In most cases, these grants are not used to support recurring expenses, such as salaries, and therefore don't augment the school's core operating budget. Depending on the performance of the endowment and the scope of the annual grants, the Academy receives several million dollars each year from the Alumni Association.

As for *expenditures*, the Academy lists five major cost categories. First are midshipmen costs, which includes funds for midshipmen's uniforms, textbooks, instructional equipment, at-sea training, food service contracts, supplies, equipment, medical and dental expenses, library books, and physical education/fitness. Unlike the other service academies, Kings Point does not give its midshipmen a salary while they are students (though they receive salaries from their respective shipping company while at sea); the largest share of the salaries paid to students at other federal academies, however, goes toward uniforms and books, which the Academy provides to its students free of charge.[2]

The second major cost category is the basket of expenses associated with the instructional program, comprising faculty salaries and all funds needed to support the educational infrastructure. (Included in this latter category, for example, are funds to support the Academy's training vessel, the TV *Kings Pointer*.) Third is the Academy's Maintenance, Repair, and Operating Requirement, which supports the repair and operation of the Academy's buildings and grounds. The fourth area is Program, Direction, and Administration. This includes salary and support costs for the executive, regimental, and administrative staffs, including the superintendent's office, the external affairs office, the admissions office, the chaplain program, the waterfront program, and the commandant's office.

Finally, the Academy invests—or sometimes, only *tries* to invest—in its infrastructure. The Capital Expenditure Program provides resources to "sequentially renovate or construct buildings and facilities that have been deemed to be the most critical."[3] The program is based on the

A view of the TV *Kings Pointer* and Long Island Sound from the back of Wiley Hall. The World War II Memorial is in the foreground.

Academywide Facilities Master Plan, commissioned by MARAD in the late 1990s, and to which this narrative will return shortly.

Not surprisingly, it was this last line that was starved most painfully as Academy budgets remained flat in the 1990s. For a campus that mostly had been constructed sixty years earlier within a two-year period, and was therefore obsolescing in lockstep, the growing mountain of deferred maintenance posed a very serious dilemma indeed.

If congressional interest in Kings Point can be inferred from appropriations levels, then it is fair to say that, with one exception, Congress remained largely indifferent to Kings Point throughout the 1990s. The exception came in 1991–1992, when the Kings Point alumni's Governmental Affairs Committee, headed by Vice Admiral Robert H. Scarborough, secured a significant increase in operating funds. But over the subsequent seven years, appropriations remained largely flat.[4] Raises mandated by the federal government's Office of Personnel Management for the most part went unfunded; vacated positions therefore went unfilled as the salaries associated with those positions were redistributed to pay for increases in wages and benefits. And in some cases, moreover, operating funds were transferred to wage and benefit lines to cover existing positions.

Throughout the 1980s and 1990s, in other words, Kings Point received more or less level funding in absolute dollars. Since this was a period of controlled but measurable inflation, the result was what Project ACTA called "real dollar cuts."[5] The Academy's leaders began to worry not just about protecting the integrity of the academic pro-

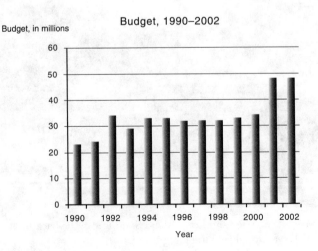

Budget, in millions   Budget, 1990–2002

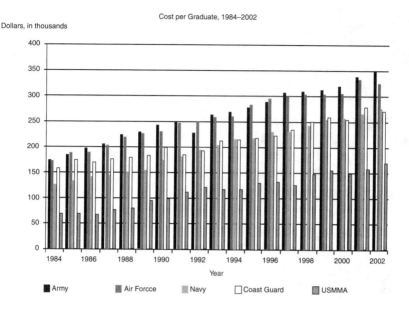

Cost per Graduate, 1984–2002

Dollars, in thousands

Year

■ Army   ■ Air Forcce   ■ Navy   □ Coast Guard   ▨ USMMA

gram, but also about basic health and safety issues. The 2000 ACTA report, for example, cited a water pipe rupture that had caused extensive damage to rare books in the library, and a lack of potable water in some Academy buildings.

Particularly frustrating, from the point of view of the Academy's advocates, was the fact that Kings Point continued to be a far more cost-effective educational venture than its sister federal academies. In 1995, continuing a decades-long pattern, the Academy had a four-year cost-per-graduate of $129,000 compared to $218,000 at the Naval Academy, $219,000 at the Coast Guard Academy, $277,000 at West Point, and $283,000 at the Air Force Academy.[6]

So the story was not complicated, and the need was clear. Throughout the 1990s, people pointed to the obvious: Kings Point needed and deserved higher funding levels. Nevertheless, the Academy's budget woes didn't begin to ease until the arrival of a new decade—and a new leader.

Defining the Priority

This was the picture inherited by the Academy's current superintendent, Vice Admiral Joseph D. Stewart, USMS, when he was appointed to head Kings Point in August 1998.

Superintendent Joseph D. Stewart, the ninth superintendent of the Academy.

A 1964 graduate of the Naval Academy, Stewart had long been interested in education. Growing up in a small town near Annapolis, he was profoundly influenced by the teachers and coaches at his small local high school, and resolved to himself that he would one day find a way to become an educator, coach, and mentor.

He reached that goal by a round-about route. Following his training at the Naval Academy, Stewart enjoyed a distinguished career in the Marine Corps. He worked for many years coordinating logistics support for the Marine Corps with the U.S. Transportation Command.[7] Along the way, he earned master's degrees in operations research and management from the Naval Postgraduate School and Salve Regina College. During his Marine Corps service, Stewart also taught mathematics and was the assistant lacrosse coach at the Naval Academy.

Stewart's entire exposure to Kings Point through 1997 had been a quick visit in June 1995 to attend commencement exercises. Milt Nottingham, '44, the Academy's longtime advocate in Washington, knew Stewart through a family connection. Nottingham arranged to have him represent the Marine Corps at the ceremony, which involved swearing in the Kings Point graduates who were accepting commissions in the corps.

As he was planning his scheduled retirement from the marines, Stewart began scanning the want ads in the *Chronicle of Higher Education*, where one day he came across the announcement of the superintendent's position at Kings Point. He applied for the job, considering it a long shot at best. He was surprised at what happened next:

> One Saturday morning I was working in my office in Marine Corps headquarters, and Riaz Latifullah, who ran the [Washington D.C.] Project ACTA office called me up and told me he'd like to help me prepare for my interview. And so he came over and I thought,

"Wow, you know, this is really pretty nice. Why are these guys helping me?"

Obviously, they got a list of all the applicants and decided what direction they wanted to go in. That's my take on it, anyway. It was really pretty helpful, because it was actually the only time I've ever had to go for a job interview.[8]

Stewart evidently did well before the screening panel, which included his predecessor, Tom Matteson, Dean Warren Mazek, and several MARAD representatives, and he was offered the job. He arrived at the Academy in July 1998 as a rear admiral, exchanging his two stars in the Marine Corps for two in the U.S. Maritime Service.

Almost immediately, he established himself as a visible presence on the campus. Obviously a people person, he mingled easily with the Regiment. He began looking for allies among the faculty and administration, but he wasn't in any hurry, he recalls, to assert his authority:

Everybody kept saying to me, "What's your *vision*? What are you going to try to accomplish?" At the risk of sounding like an idiot, I kept saying, "I don't have a clue. I've got to look around a little bit."

But quite honestly, I got used to that situation in the Marine Corps, because every two or three years you got transferred somewhere, and you walked into some job that you didn't understand, and you just had to kind of put your feet on the ground, figure it out, and do the best you could. Plus, I wasn't worried about getting promoted. I figured if something bad happened and they didn't like me, and I got fired or something, the world wouldn't come to an end, because I had already finished one career.

So I was really doing this for the adventure, and to try to make a contribution to the world in some way.[9]

As it turned out, Stewart's vision of education had to take a backseat to his sense of responsibility to the young people in his charge. Simply put, the Kings Point infrastructure had deteriorated to such an extent that Stewart felt he first had to exert his leadership skills toward a specific, prosaic, and urgent end: *fixing the buildings.*

Defining the Need

The marines, Joe Stewart recalled, always felt as if they didn't get their fair share of the Department of Defense budget. But in all his years in the Marine Corps he had "never seen a base or a barracks that was in as bad shape, physically, as Kings Point."[10]

Stewart put some time into figuring out why the Academy's infrastructure was so deficient. One answer, of course, was the lack of funds: at that point, the Academy received roughly a million dollars a year for maintenance and repairs. Nothing remotely capital-intensive could be undertaken on that budget.

But other problems popped up as well. Stewart had gained experience with capital and operating budgets during his days as a Marine Corps logistician, and he was surprised to find that the Academy's finances weren't the exclusive concern of a single individual. Assistant Superintendent John Jochmans was the de facto chief financial officer, but he wore many other hats as well. Going up the ladder to MARAD, Stewart was again surprised to discover that the parent organization had a similar structural problem. Both parent and child had been starved for money for so long, it seemed, that neither saw the point of committing a full-time body to budgeting and finance.

But in Stewart's mind, this was a vicious circle: you couldn't get the money if you couldn't make the case that you needed it, and that you would use it wisely once you got it. Not sure he had the authority to create a position he wanted to call director of resource management, based on a model at West Point, he asked MARAD for permission. When MARAD's first reaction was negative, Stewart stepped sideways. He found an ally elsewhere at MARAD and went ahead and created the post anyway. The subsequent screening process yielded an internal candidate, Jim Amoroso, who took over the Academy's finances and began attending the school's operating-group meetings. Stewart saw the change as both substantive and symbolic:

> I mean, it wasn't a revolutionary act or anything. But I thought it at least put everybody on notice, including the people in Washington whom we dealt with, that we thought that budgeting, and financial planning, and taking care of your resources was *important*. And so Amoroso started coming to the staff meetings, and became an important part of our management team. The point was that, unlike John Jochmans, Amoroso didn't have a whole ton of other jobs. He had *one* job.

But this was only the first skirmish in Stewart's larger campaign. He began drawing upon the Academy's nascent financial capabilities to come up with a new and realistic operating budget. Through the helpful intervention of recently appointed MARAD administrator Clyde Hart, he secured an offsite audience with Secretary of Transportation Rodney Slater. Slater was an Arkansas lawyer who had been in charge of the Arkansas state highway system and a friend and political appointee of President Clinton. Slater was sympathetic but knew almost nothing about the maritime industry or the federal academies, including Kings Point. "We more or less started from scratch," said Stewart.

Meanwhile, Stewart began pushing for a solution to the school's crumbling infrastructure. From his Marine Corps days, he understood that major capital projects need to be guided by master plans. There was no such plan for the Kings Point campus, and Stewart knew that realistically, he couldn't move forward without one. Despite tight resources throughout the system, therefore, he secured an allocation of $400,000 from MARAD, and commissioned a campus master plan. Assistant Superintendent John Jochmans took the lead on the facilities master plan. He worked with a contracted master-planning firm to produce a thick binder that described everything that the campus needed to "bring the Academy into the twenty-first century," including infrastructure improvements, new buildings, updates to comply with the Americans with Disabilities Act, and deferred maintenance.[11]

In the master planning process, Stewart and Jochmans acquired a new ally in Deputy Maritime Administrator Bonnie M. Green, whom Clyde Hart had designated as his liaison with Kings Point. Green had served on the board of St. Mary's College in Maryland, her alma mater, since 1993. The college had been through a major renovation and construction project, and Green was a firm believer in the importance of planning. Green also understood the importance of *realism* in any such capital plan. When the initial cost estimates for fixing the campus came in at between $180 and $240 million, Green put her foot down. The number, she said, shouldn't exceed $125 million over ten years.

With the benefit of hindsight, imposing an artificially low ceiling may have been a tactical error. But the participants in the process, even those, like Joe Stewart, who sometimes bridled under Green's supervision, credit her with making the planning process work. "She picked that plan up off the floor at MARAD," recalled one person close to the process, "where it wasn't given a lot of respect, and put her name on it, and beat it into shape. And she deserves a lot of credit for that."[12]

But a plan is only as strong as its allies. Since the dismantling of the House Committee on the Merchant Marine and Fisheries in the Gingrich Revolution, Kings Point and MARAD had had few powerful allies in Congress. Where would Stewart and his newfound MARAD allies go to find $125 million?

Making New Friends

The planning proceeded intensely throughout 1999 and into 2000. In this same time period, of course, the Academy's other activities continued apace. Over at the Babson Center, for example, the USMMA Foundation's director of individual giving, Mary-lou Jorgensen, was focusing on getting the Academy's new superintendent out in front of alumni around the country. Stewart was already proving himself to be a strong salesman for the school. So Jorgensen put him on a plane with alumni leaders Ken DeGhetto, '44, and Ed Harsche, '62, and the trio went out in search of new friends for the Academy.

The plane she put them on belonged to Ed Harsche, who had worked in the maritime industry for a decade before deciding to go into the homebuilding business in Pennsylvania's Pocono Mountains. Over the next twenty years, his company built some five hundred homes, established itself as a licensed mortgage banker in thirty-eight states (with offices in twenty-six states), and also set up an abstract company that arranged closings. "All doing pretty well today," he says in a matter-of-fact tone.[13]

As he prospered professionally, Harsche felt an increasing tug to help out his alma mater. "It was time to give something back," he recalls. He became a member of the board of the Kings Point Foundation and, in the late 1990s, the foundation's chairman.

One city in which Harsche's plane touched down in 1999 was Clearwater, on Florida's west coast. There, Jorgensen had tapped a local politician and entrepreneur, Gerald S. Rehm, '48, to host an intimate luncheon in the small city of Largo, just south of Clearwater. The point of the meeting, Jorgensen told Rehm, was to let a couple of prominent Central Floridians hear the new superintendent's plans for the school.

Like Ed Harsche, Jerry Rehm had led a colorful life since his graduation from Kings Point. He sailed for Waterman Steamship for two years, then came ashore as a manufacturing planner for Sperry Gyro-

scope, which transferred him to Clearwater. Rehm and his family settled in the then sleepy surroundings of Dunedin, Florida, a town of
seven thousand people in 1959 when Rehm arrived there. Three years
later, upon the death of a city commissioner, Rehm was appointed to
the city council. Taking a shine to local politics, Rehm ran for mayor
in 1964, won, and served three terms. Mayor Rehm led a drive to
rezone and master-plan the entire community, and he also spearheaded a campaign to turn a group of undeveloped islands off the
coast of Dunedin into a state park; today, six-hundred-acre Caladesi
Island is considered a gem of the Florida park system. Hard to do if
you are "sailing the oceans blue."

Through these experiences and others, Rehm became a committed
planner. He also became a real estate broker, and in 1965 the business
manager of the foundation set up by drugstore mogul Jack Eckerd.
Eckerd's unsuccessful runs for governor and the U.S. Senate rekindled
Rehm's own political ambitions, and in 1980 he won a seat in the
Florida Senate, where he served for the better part of a decade. Three
years later, the Kings Point Alumni Association honored him with its
Professional Achievement Award, in part because he had succeeded in
politics, where few Kings Pointers tended to venture.

Rehm did not rest on his laurels. In 1984, he acquired the Florida
Candy Factory, a bankrupt Clearwater enterprise that had been mak-
ing its trademark Angel Mint since 1919 but had fallen on hard times.
Rehm bought the candy company from the bank, put the company's
former owner on his payroll, and turned the struggling firm around.
Today, Angel Mint is sold all over the United States.

Mary-lou Jorgensen knew this history and saw Jerry Rehm as a
logical host for her 1999 luncheon gathering in the Clearwater area. At
that lunch, Rehm met both Joe Stewart and Ed Harsche for the first
time. Rehm was impressed by both of them. "I should do something
for Kings Point," Rehm recalled thinking to himself after talking with
Harsche and hearing Stewart's low-key pitch.

The following year, Jorgensen asked Rehm to host a second Clearwater lunch. He agreed, and in the early weeks of 2000 Stewart
brought along his nearly completed master plan, as well as his Superintendent's Planning Guide. Rehm recalled:

> As I heard this plan out, I realized it was the first time there had ever
> been a real *plan* for the Academy—one that looked at every aspect of

the capital needs of the place, including an analysis of each building, how many square feet of space needing which kind of renovation, and so on.

And I'm looking around the table and seeing Ed Harsche and Ken DeGhetto, who are giving and giving and giving to the Academy. And once again, I said to myself, "Self, get up off your butt and do something for Kings Point."

Rehm already knew what he could do for Kings Point. He didn't have $125 million in his bank account, but he knew someone who worked someplace who did.

Finding Money, Building Bridges

Back in 1960, Rehm had served on an academy advisory board to Florida congressman William C. Cramer. The board's job was to recommend young people for appointments to the federal military academies. Also on that board was a young staff member who was shortly to become a state senator from St. Petersburg named C. W. "Bill"

Congressman C. W. "Bill" Young (R–FL), an important advocate for the USMMA in Congress, crosses Barney Square with Superintendent Stewart.

Young. In that context, Rehm and Young became what Rehm calls "project buddies." When State Senator Young moved on to Congress in 1970, representing Florida's Tenth Congressional District, he and Rehm stayed in close touch. By 2000, Young was the senior member of the Florida congressional delegation and the chairman of the enormously powerful House Appropriations Committee.

Beginning in February 2000, at a Lincoln's Day dinner, Rehm spoke to Young of his rekindled interest in the United States Merchant Marine Academy: "I told him, 'Prior to this superintendent, I couldn't have come and asked you for help. We didn't have the leadership, and we didn't have the plan. Now we do. I want to bring the superintendent in, and have him go through the plan with you.' After about forty-five minutes of this, poor Bill threw up his hands and said, 'Okay! Okay! I'll meet with him.'"

The meeting took place on March 21, 2000, at Young's Washington office. Representing Kings Point were Jerry Rehm, Ed Harsche, and Joe Stewart. Stewart delivered the presentation, and, according to Harsche, made a highly favorable impression on Young. "Jerry and I helped," he said. "But it was Joe Stewart's ability to tell Congressman Young the Academy's story that made the difference. It was him, and his personality, that did it."

Rehm added that Young had a consistent record of strong support for national security throughout his political career. "He's a patriot," Rehm explained. "What Joe Stewart basically did was to show him how Kings Point fits into the bigger picture. And if you're interested in the security of America like Bill Young is, you get the point." That Young was also hearing from an articulate two-star general who had done his homework—several pounds' worth—clearly didn't hurt the cause. As further background, Rehm provided Young with financial data prepared by Project ACTA.[14]

The cause was strong, and the timing was propitious; although budgets had already been drawn up for the next fiscal year, the so-called mark-up phase of the budget process was just beginning. Over the next few months, Young's staffers went looking for thirteen million dollars that they could shift in the direction of Kings Point. The hunt proved successful, and the first thirteen-million-dollar installment was built into the Academy's fiscal 2001 budget. This incremental money had to be spent within nine months, and the ability of Joe Stewart's team to do so effectively gave Stewart "complete credibility," as Rehm later recalled.

Significantly, Young's office found a way to make subsequent appropriations multiyear, meaning that the Academy would not be under pressure to encumber the funds under undue time pressures—a mistake that had been made in the past.

Meanwhile, two parallel stories were unfolding. The first involved efforts to bring the Senate along with the House. According to Jim Shirley, '65, then national chairman of the Alumni Association, Vic Mavar, '44, a personal friend of Senate majority leader Trent Lott, took the lead in this critical area.

The second story involved the Academy's parent organization, MARAD. For several years in the later 1990s, as budgets at MARAD and Kings Point became tighter and tighter, relationships between the two became strained. Jerry Rehm told Congressman Young that in his opinion, the Kings Point budget couldn't be dealt with in isolation—in other words, that the larger Maritime Administration budget needed to be addressed. On July 25, 2001, Young met with former administrators Al Herberger and John Graykowski and pledged to find ways to help address MARAD's perennial budget shortfalls.[15]

On August 6, 2001, Bill Young took a tour of Kings Point, the campus that he had pledged to help but had never seen in person. Joe Stewart and Ed Harsche hosted the delegation from Washington, which included Young's wife, Beverly, who was known to be a strong advocate for military personnel in her own right. As Harsche recalled:

> They flew into LaGuardia and came over on a Coast Guard boat. They spent the whole day with us. Joe and I did all the explaining, and showed where the needs were, and just how poor some of the situations were.
>
> It happened to be one of the hottest days of the year. Everyone was sweating terribly in those barracks—us, the cadets, everybody. And I'm pretty sure that the reason that the dorms are getting air conditioning is that Beverly Young took her husband aside and told him that the midshipmen's living conditions were absolutely intolerable.

And that, said Joe Stewart, was the whole point of the multipronged, multiyear effort. He didn't step into the job at Kings Point looking to launch a $130 million building project, but that was the direction, he explained, in which his sense of leadership took him:

Leadership is taking care of the people who are in your charge. It just seemed to me that here we had a school—a great school—but we weren't taking care of our students. So that had to be the first priority: to try to do better at that. I mean, I'm *still* embarrassed to go into the barracks and see how some of these kids are living right now. It's just not up to federal academy standards. But thanks to people like Congressman Young, and Ed Harsche, and Jerry Rehm, it will be.

On September 27, 2001, the Kings Point Alumni Association honored Jerry Rehm as its Kings Pointer of the Year. In a letter to Joe Stewart, Bill Young praised Rehm as an example of the kind of leader that Kings Point produces.[16] For its part, the Academy honored Bill Young's contribution by preparing a citation that reads:

> Congressman Young has been a member of Congress from Florida from 1970 to the present. As chairman of the House Appropriations Committee of the 106th Congress, he provided for the accepting by Congress of Rear Admiral Joseph Stewart's Academy Master Plan for updating facilities of the Academy to meet the challenges of the 21st century. Congressman Young's 30 years of commitment to national security is manifested by his actions, as Chairman of Appropriations, to provide the capital funding required to implement the Superintendent's Master Plan for the Academy.

The citation accompanies the picture of Young that hangs in the vestibule of Bland Library next to that of Schuyler Otis Bland—arguably the best congressional friend of Kings Point before Young arrived on the scene. For each of the past several years, largely through Young's efforts, an additional thirteen million dollars has been allocated toward the physical transformation of Kings Point.

Joe Stewart admits that some members of the Academy community—students, faculty, staff, and alumni alike—were at first frustrated by the slow pace of visible changes. "It's not like you can just call up a contractor and he comes by the following Monday," Stewart says wryly. "You have to do your homework. And we use our facilities pretty intensively, and there's only so much disruption this campus can take at one time."

But a visitor touring the Academy in the early years of the twenty-first century will see signs of an unprecedented physical-plant renaissance. Work crews swarm over dormitories that are being rehabilitated for the first time in decades. The signs of progress begin at the very entrance to the campus, where a rehabilitated and expanded Vickery Gate, funded by a combination of government and alumni dollars, houses an upgraded admissions office and literally presents a new face of the Academy to the outside world. The Dean and Barbara White Family Foundation, established by Dean White, '45, and his wife, Barbara, helped make the new facility possible by offering a "double challenge grant" (i.e., contributing $1.6 million to match $800,000 in donations from other USMMA alumni and friends). The new White Center was subsequently named in their honor.[17]

These signs of progress not only reflect the (partial) resolution of longstanding financial challenges to Kings Point, but also a deeper involvement in the school's affairs on the part of its alumni popula-

Secretary of Transportation Norman Mineta with Superintendent Stewart at a regimental review on May 1, 2001.

tion and a maturing of its Alumni Association. In Washington, the Alumni Association's Governmental Affairs Committee, founded in 1985, with its political arm, Project ACTA, played an instrumental role in the expanded funding efforts described above. "In addition," wrote James T. Shirley, who served as national chairman from 2000 through 2003, "we also increased our local chapter activities to get a better foothold at the grassroots level, enabling better communications on a regular basis with congressmen in as many districts as possible."[18] A new alumni capital campaign, five times larger than any previous campaign undertaken on behalf of the Academy, also got under way in 2003. A new Industry Affairs Committee was created, headed by alumnus and former Maritime Administrator Albert J. Herberger, which has helped forge new ties between the Academy and the maritime industry as well as among the various components of that industry.

Meanwhile, the USMMA Parents' Association, although not formally connected with the Alumni Foundation (as the association was renamed in 2002), has worked closely with that group to bring pressure to bear on congressional delegations from all over the country when issues important to Kings Point have surfaced on Capitol Hill. The Parents' Association is administered out of Kings Point but extends to chapters in forty-five states, the U.S. Virgin Islands, and the Republic of Panama. In addition to its lobbying efforts, it continues to play its original role: to serve as both an effective recruitment tool and an informal support network for Academy families. As member and Kings Point author Mary Jane Fuschetto noted:

> We have supplied hundreds of supportive activities for midshipmen, such as pizza parties, cards and care packages for finals, Christmas Balls, All-Academy dinners, graduation gifts, and host families for those "mids" without a place to go on holidays. We sponsor All-Academy Days, and hand out information at college fairs. . . . Parent clubs have hosted USMMA athletic teams as they competed in distant states, providing meals and festivities in their honor. We have also increased the amount of news articles about USMMA in local papers, and provided much positive public-relations information about USMMA free of charge to our communities.[19]

First lady and future senator, Hillary Rodham Clinton addresses the Regiment during her campaign for senator, at the 2000 commencement ceremonies.

Local associations also sponsor meetings and social events for the families of current midshipmen, and encourage participation by candidates and their parents, thereby making the Academy accessible and approachable to candidates and their families.

Terrorism and Tragedy

On the morning of September 11, 2001, two hijacked commercial passenger airplanes were flown into the twin towers of the World Trade Center in New York's downtown financial district.

Admiralty attorney Jim Shirley, a member of the Kings Point class of '65 and the national chairman of the USMMA Alumni Association, was working in his law office at Holland & Knight, across the street at 195 Broadway. He had planned to have breakfast with incoming Alumni Association president Gene McCormick where they had breakfasted several times previously—at Windows on the World, on the 107th floor of the Trade Center—but for reasons Shirley can't remember, he and McCormick opted instead for bagels in a conference room at Shirley's office on the 24th floor. When the impact came,

Shirley at first thought New York was having an earthquake; but looking out the west-facing windows of the law firm, he could see the terrible truth. When firefighters began evacuating buildings adjacent to
the World Trade Center as a precaution, Shirley and McCormick
descended twenty-four flights of stairs to street level and started walking east down Maiden Lane, away from the World Trade Center site.

At that point, Shirley recalled, he had no idea that the towers
might fall. When he heard a "roar coming down from the sky," he
guessed that yet another plane was being crash-landed, perhaps on
Broadway. Then he looked behind him and saw a terrifying sight: a
roiling cloud of debris coming down Maiden Lane behind them, filling
the street to the very tops of the buildings on either side, like a wall of
water bursting out of a dam. Along with everyone else on the street,
Shirley and McCormick took off running but soon were overtaken by
a blinding, noxious cloud that turned day to night, and had to rely on
memory and instinct until they reached the East River.

Like people around the world, members of the Kings Point community watched horrifying television images of the towers burning
and eventually collapsing. But the ones at the Academy had special
connections to the tragedy. First, many of the school's distinguished
graduates, including Jim Shirley, worked in the immediate vicinity of
the World Trade Center. And second, the clouds of smoke and dust
rising from the site of the towers were clearly visible across Long
Island Sound at Kings Point. In every way, this was a disaster on the
Academy's doorstep.

At approximately eleven a.m., the New York City Fire Department's Marine Division made an urgent request for help from Kings
Point. Thus began a nine-day operation that included Academy midshipmen, faculty, and staff in both rescue and recovery operations,
which eventually won widespread praise for Kings Point.

But the immediate challenge was to move people to and away from
the site of the disaster. Commander Eric Wallischeck, director of
Waterfront Activities, established a command center in the Yocum Sailing Center. Nine Academy vessels, ranging in length from twenty-five
to sixty-five feet, were immediately pressed into service. (After the first
day, operations were scaled back to four boats.) Wallischeck and his
colleagues established a communications link to the Fire Department's
Marine Division 6, operating out of the Brooklyn Navy Yard. Taking
direction from Marine Division personnel, as well as from the Coast

Guard's on-the-scene commander, Academy vessels worked around the clock to ferry firefighters and rescue personnel based in Brooklyn, Staten Island, and New Jersey to and from ground zero. It was initially anticipated that, going in the opposite direction, the boats would assist in the evacuation of victims who had been injured either in the initial attack or in the subsequent collapse of the towers. (In fact, the Academy at one point was slated as a Nassau County staging site for a mass evacuation, when estimates of casualties ranged as high as the tens of thousands.) As events unfolded, however, there were few injuries beyond those killed in the attacks.[20]

In addition to providing water transport, Academy midshipmen and staff who were also trained as EMTs provided basic medical treatment and first-responder services to injured firefighters and other emergency personnel. They also helped set up triage and morgue facilities at ground zero and elsewhere.

A subsequent citation from the secretary of transportation detailed some of the accomplishments of the Kings Point community in response to the disaster:

> Over the course of nine days, USMMA assets moved in excess of 1,500 firefighters, EMTs, police officers, and other rescue personnel; and, moved several tons of food, water, rescue supplies, and materials from locations in Brooklyn and New Jersey to the landing area. . . .
> Over 150 USMMA personnel participated in the operation, over the course of 200 hours, with 263 individual afloat tours of duty, and several hundred vessel movements. No USMMA personnel were injured and operational readiness exceeded 98 percent. USMMA's service was invaluable to the men and women of the New York City Fire Department, and all those affected by the tragedy. By their outstanding courage, resourcefulness, and commitment of service over self, the members of the United States Merchant Marine Academy participating in Operation Guarding Liberty reflected great credit upon themselves, and have upheld the highest traditions of the Department of Transportation.[21]

Congressman Bill Young, who had first visited the campus he was helping to rejuvenate only five weeks before the attacks, wrote a letter to Joe Stewart expressing his gratitude to the Kings Point community for its swift and effective response: "It is in times such as these that the best in our nation and the American people shines through. It is also a time when we understand the need to have the best educated and trained merchant mariners to be ready to respond on a moment's notice to our national security and commerce needs at sea. On behalf of my colleagues in Congress, I say thank you to you, your midshipmen, and staff for answering this critical call."[22]

According to a letter to the Kings Point alumni community from Jim Shirley, there were surprisingly few Academy graduates killed in the disaster.[23] The two known victims, Bob Colin, '74, and Gilbert Granados, '75, were in the South Tower when it was struck. But as Shirley somberly noted, many friends, acquaintances, and coworkers of Kings Point alumni were among the victims that day, some presumably lost in the act of saving others.

On September 5, 2003, the new Coast Guard station at Kings Point, built on the grounds of the Academy in 2001, was renamed in honor of Lieutenant Commander Gilbert Granados, who at the time

Midshipmen gather for morning colors in front of Wiley Hall.

of his death at the World Trade Center was a retired officer in the Coast Guard reserve.

The Regiment and Leadership

The World Trade Center rescue and recovery operation involved twenty-two first class midshipmen, twenty-nine second class midshipmen, twenty-one third class midshipmen, and eighteen plebes. They acquitted themselves admirably under difficult and stressful conditions. "On Wednesday amid the chaos," wrote one New York firefighter to Superintendent Stewart, "I noticed cadets from Kings Point in their coveralls and caps walking and surveying the area. They looked and acted top notch."[24]

Had Stewart not been thinking about the state of the Regiment, the World Trade Center episode surely would have focused him upon that issue. As he was well aware, several of the state maritime academies had been backing away from the regimental experience in recent years. And although attrition at Kings Point was lower than in previous eras, several dozen young people still left the Academy in any given year, some of whom cited the regimented Kings Point lifestyle as the reason. So, Stewart asked himself, was the Regiment still relevant?

He decided that the answer was assuredly yes:

> First, they are in the United States Naval Reserve, so they clearly have that reason for being military. It's like being in an NROTC unit, where you do need some military training in order to be able to do that.
>
> But in addition, and more important, I think the leadership training that you get out of this experience is really exceptional. I think that having this regimental system, and having it be somewhat military, really gives you that laboratory for a leadership experience. And to me, one of the great things about this Academy is that we don't have a great big staff. I think one of our strengths is we don't have a deep bench in terms of staffing, so the midshipmen end up doing a great deal here. Obviously, the Commandant plays an active role. But there's an awful lot that those midshipmen do that they wouldn't get the authority to do at one of the other federal academies.[25]

Even as he was looking for ways to solve the Academy's pressing infrastructure problems, therefore, Stewart also began looking for ways to reinforce the Regiment as a "laboratory for leadership experience." As part of that priority, he initiated a search for a commandant who would share his perspective.

The individual he ultimately settled upon–Captain Arthur Athens–was, like Stewart himself, a Naval Academy graduate (class of '78), a marine, and a lacrosse player. After sixteen years of active duty, Athens had left the corps to head a nonprofit organization called Officers' Christian Fellowship (OCF), which engages in outreach to the U.S. military and helps individuals integrate their faith and profession. After accomplishing his goals at OCF, Athens went in search of his next challenge, and came upon the commandant's position at Kings Point. "I did speak to Admiral Stewart when I came up here for the interview," Athens recalls, "but he just talked a bit about what was going on at the Academy. It really was just a friendly conversation more than a grilling at that point." He took up his new post in January 2000.

Stewart continued his relatively hands-off posture toward the Regiment, telling Athens in so many words that it was the commandant's job to define his role. Athens, accustomed to having ample running room, responded positively. He set two short-term goals: to bring the regimental leadership together as a team and to reestablish the respect from the departments of the Academy toward the commandant's department. Athens, by all accounts, had inherited a good team from his predecessor; now the goal as Athens defined it was to get them pulling together more effectively toward the endpoint of leadership.

One member of that team was Thad Gaebelein, who was a part-time company officer and part-time member of the History Department. He soon recognized in Art Athens a kindred spirit. According to Gaebelein, "Athens immediately began asking the questions that I had been asking: How exactly do we want to run this regiment? What are the overarching theories of leadership that lie behind it? Why do we do what we do, and how can we do it better?"[26]

Shortly after his arrival at Kings Point in May 2000, Athens organized a four-day retreat at Long Island's Port Jefferson for his company officers and led a sustained discussion aimed at answering those key questions. Based on that discussion, and many that followed, Athens and his colleagues settled upon four regimental values that would serve as their building blocks: integrity, respect, courage, and service. Then they started thinking through the ways that these values might be embodied in the day-to-day life of the Regiment. Central to that process, Gaebelein recalls, was the decision to move from an authoritarian model of leadership–"drive them up the hill," to an inspirational model: "lure them up the hill" by inspiring them with a new style of leadership.

Not surprisingly, this same debate was then going on at the other federal academies. West Point's General Dave Palmer, superintendent of that school from 1986 through 1991, had initiated a similar debate during his tenure, which had led West Point away from a relatively authoritarian, hazing-oriented regiment. And as Athens well knew, his own alma mater was wrestling with similar issues:

> I know the commandant down at the Naval Academy pretty well, and we've talked a lot, both philosophically and practically. They would say that the Regiment is a direct preparation to be a naval officer. I mean, you're going to be on board ship, and you're going to have to keep your room neat, you're going to have to keep your hair cut. And in their case, the potential of direct combat drives them to say, "This kind of system makes sense."
>
> The question mark that all the academies have faced is, you know, "How hard?" How miserable do you really make it for the cadets? I think all the academies have moved in the direction of saying that it cannot be as draconian as it once was, but that structure is still a good thing.[27]

Athens also wrestled with the fact that, unlike the service academies, Kings Point was not necessarily preparing its graduates for a military career. Cadets looking forward to an *industry* experience didn't necessarily embrace the regimental experience on the face of it, in the way a West Pointer would. The Sea Year experience, too, created interesting dynamics, as had been noted in previous assessments of the Regiment. "Many, many of the things that they're required to do here are certainly not required out there," says Athens of the Sea Year. "I mean, the hair, the belt buckles, all those parts that come with the military aspect–they are not a part of Sea Year at all."

But each time Athens found his faith in the regimental system wavering, he would run into someone in industry who would rush to reassure him of its importance. One reassurance involved Marshall Carter, the chairman and CEO of Boston's State Street Bank between 1992 and 2000. What was Carter looking for in potential hires?

Carter, a former marine, said he looked for people who could figure out what's most important in a complex situation, and people who understood (as Athens recalls it) "plain old basic small-unit leadership." Carter, for one, believed that a well-designed regimental system imparted exactly those skills.

So the challenge, as both Joe Stewart and Art Athens had anticipated, was to create more opportunities to learn leadership, and particularly small-group leadership. It was not a new lesson—in fact, prior reviews of the Kings Points regimental system had reached more or less the same conclusion—but it came at a time when the Academy had to choose whether to strengthen the Regiment or allow it to slowly wither away.

Art Athens left Kings Point to take a teaching position at Annapolis in 2003, and left many of the questions about exactly *how* to strengthen the Regiment to his successor. Once again, Joe Stewart had a clear sense of what kind of leader he was looking for, and this time, the answer was found on his own waterfront, in the person of Captain Robert Allee, '68.

Senator John McCain (R-AZ) addresses the Regiment during commencement exercises on June 18, 2007.

History in Real Time

For the Academy, the early years of the twenty-first century have been a period of taking stock, reinvestment, and innovation.

Physical reinvestment is visible, noisy, and disruptive—and therefore easy to see and eventually celebrate. But less obvious investments are not necessarily less important. Investments in the Regiment, and in the leadership program that lies behind regimental life, also make the bridge from the past to the future.

Such investments are necessarily partial steps. The Academy's financial woes, for example, are far from resolved. But its administrators, alumni, supporters in Congress, and other friends can point with pride at their ability to jointly define and solve budget shortfalls that previously had seemed intractable. Similarly, school administrators can point to progress in a realm—the teaching of leadership—where progress mostly comes in inches.

Much of the credit for that progress belongs to Joe Stewart. With his institution now working off its backlog of repairs and renovations, and with somewhat improved prospects on the operational side, Stewart can focus more attention on the educational side of the shop. He has recently begun a strategic planning initiative intended to build on the initiatives of his predecessors. Among the many subjects the planners are now considering is the addition of deck and engine graduate programs to the Academy's offerings (now authorized by Congress), a step that is long overdue in the eyes of many, but difficult to accomplish without some overlap with other institutions and a deeper involvement in port and shipboard security.

Perhaps most important, Stewart has demonstrated to the Academy community that it has the unparalleled asset of strong leadership. This assessment seems to be shared in other quarters. In June 2003, he was promoted to vice admiral by Maritime Administrator captain William Schubert, '74, who cited Stewart's "outstanding performance, dedication to mission, and inspirational leadership."[28] Stewart thereby became the first Superintendent of Kings Point to serve in that capacity as a three-star admiral.

And, as the final chapter will detail, leadership has become an increasingly important part of the Kings Point experience and the Kings Point product.

14

Scenes from an Education

2003–2006

In the engine control room of the CSX *Consumer*, Cadet-midshipman Joe Baran, '05, bends over a chest-high tabletop and scrutinizes a large book of engineering drawings. The *Consumer* is a CSX Lines container ship (owned today by Horizon Lines) headed from Oakland to Honolulu via Long Beach. Chief Engineer Tom Dutton stands off to his right, close enough to give Baran guidance if he asks for it, but not so close that he'll distract or intimidate the younger man.

On this warm morning in February 2003, Baran and Dutton are grateful for the room's air-conditioning, a surprising amenity for a steamship of this vintage. But when SeaLand built this ship more than a quarter century ago, in 1974, it spared no expense to protect its then state-of-the-art automation system. The heart of that system was—and still is—a pair of card-driven computers, 30 feet long by 8 feet high.

The room is also surprisingly quiet, allowing Baran to leave his bright-red, ear-protecting headphones perched on top of his head. In the left rear pocket of his overalls is a grimy yellow flashlight; in his right rear pocket is a pair of work gloves.

Baran is attempting to trace out one of the ship's systems, using one of two copies of the ship's original blueprints, which Dutton has dug out of storage for him. It was a complicated system to begin with, made more complicated by the many changes that have occurred over the past quarter century, none of which show up on these "as-built" drawings. Baran's tracing is a small piece of one of the eight written Sea Year

413

projects, which he must complete while on board the ship, and which will be graded upon his return to the Academy. These projects are in addition to the hours of work he puts in daily for the ship's officers.

"This part doesn't make sense," Baran mutters at one point, puzzling over a schematic, tapping at the offending section with his forefinger.

"Keep at it," Dutton says with a friendly grin. "It's *gotta* make sense. Otherwise the ship doesn't work."

This is Baran's second ship this year, and his fourth in two years. His first this year was a diesel containership out of Port Elizabeth, New Jersey, and bound for the Mediterranean. When he heard a few weeks back that he'd be going aboard another containership, he expected to more or less be able to find his way around. He was in for a surprise. The *Consumer* was a venerable old steam-powered vessel, with lots of unexpected elements, including the split-deck house and other strange design features. But the biggest surprises were in the engine room.

"When I went on my first ship this year," Baran explains, "I could just walk in the engine room, and it would be more or less familiar. But when I got on here, it was just totally different—I've never seen anything like this before. For one thing, it's really *crowded*."

Baran is a second classman (i.e., in his third year) at Kings Point. He grew up in Poughkeepsie, New York, along the Hudson, although he never felt any particular tug from that ancient river. In fact, aside from some sailing at summer camp, he had never been out on the water, or even thought much about getting out on it. As he finished up his Catholic high school education, he went looking for a place where he could get an engineering education. He applied to the Coast Guard Academy, West Point, Norwich Academy, and Kings Point, all schools with good engineering programs. The Kings Point track coach got in touch with his counterpart at Baran's high school, Baran visited the Academy, and he decided to apply.

He completed his first year, his plebe year, and then faced a choice: ship out in July, or stay another trimester and go to sea at the end of October. Baran chose the latter, mainly to be able to run cross-country in the fall.

Tom Dutton is one of two chief engineers who divide up the chief's job on the *Consumer*: two months on, two months off. A 1963 graduate of the New York State Maritime Academy at Fort Schuyler, Dutton sailed briefly, saved up enough money to buy his first

A view of containers stacked on the MV *Charlotte Maersk*, as seen from the CSX *Consumer*.

Corvette, worked in Chevrolet's testing and development labs for a few years, and then raced professionally on the Can-Am circuit for ten years. In the late 1970s he went back to sea.

Cadets are regularly assigned to the *Consumer*. "Mainly," Dutton said, "from Kings Point. Sometimes from Texas, and sometimes from Mass Maritime." He and the rest of his crew give their young visitors as much help as they ask for and no more. As Dutton elaborates:

> When they ask guys questions, the guys go out of their way to help them. The permanent second's real good, for example. He'll take them under his wing and try to show them stuff if they show interest, you know. But if they don't show interest, then he doesn't. None of the guys take it on themselves to be a teacher. They expect it to come from the cadet: what he or she wants to learn, they'll show him or her. And they're all good at that. I always try to have the cadets

stand all the watches, because all the watches do different things. So in the course of the time that they're out here, they'll stand watch twelve to four, four to eight, and eight to twelve. The four to eight blows tubes, tests the boilers with chemicals, and all that. The twelve to four takes care of all the oil–transferring lube oils, purifying lube oils, and all that stuff. And the eight to twelve takes care of all the water-distilling systems that make our water. So he gets to see all that, too. And plus he gets to chat with the guys. He's down there, and there's time where they can sit and talk, and that kind of stuff. That's part of the education, too.[1]

Dutton estimates that he spends about eight hours a month, or for him, the equivalent of a short day, answering questions for cadets. "We always help them," he says, "whatever they ask for."

Up on the bridge of the *Consumer*, Chief Mate Kent Flick, a 1975 graduate of Kings Point, finishes laying out the *Consumer*'s course from Long Beach to Honolulu. He's not going through the motions, exactly–he's far too deliberate for that–but on the other hand, he's charted this course and made this run literally scores of times. And once the local pilot gets you out of the somewhat tricky Long Beach harbor, you more or less point the ship toward Honolulu, and stay on one heading for four days: 248 degrees, full ahead.

Leaving the chart spread out on the table in the chartroom just behind the bridge, Flick now takes one more look at his cargo manifest, a listing of the on board cargo. The *Consumer* and a sister ship run continuously from the West Coast to Hawaii, a so-called scheduled liner service, maintaining an eclectic pipeline of goods ranging from rental cars to toilet paper. "We stop running," Flick says, "and Hawaii runs out of toilet paper in a week." During the West Coast lockout in late 2002, the *Consumer* and her sister ship were specifically exempted from that labor dispute, and the Hawaiian pipeline stayed open.

As much as Tom Dutton, Kent Flick is in love with this old ship, of which he's been the chief mate since 1993. In that role, Flick oversees the distribution of cargo weight. It's his job to be sure that the ship's stability is "tender" but not *too* tender. "Tender is when you've got a nice, easy, long roll," he explains. "And if you're too tender, you come over here"–he leans way over to his right–"and you kind of stay over here for a while, and you start wondering, 'Are we going to fall over, or are we coming back?'"

But the *Consumer*'s design makes this job easier. It has several unusual features, including a transverse set of ballast tanks to prevent listing and an elaborate antiroll system of flume tanks. These are strategically positioned tanks of water that, by means of a call to the engine room, Flick can trim up to partially counteract the ship's roll. This ship can carry up to eight hundred containers (sixteen hundred TEUs), depending on their size. (Newer, larger containerships can carry four thousand.) Each stack of four containers can weigh up to ninety tons. Without ballast tanks and flume tanks, and without careful positioning of the cargo, the *Consumer* would be at risk of rolling like a bathtub on the waves.

Like Joe Baran, Kent Flick, who graduated from high school in Indiana back in the early seventies, had no particular notion of going to sea. As a senior in high school, he went to a seminar where all five federal academies—Army, Air Force, Navy, Coast Guard, and Merchant Marine—made presentations. A neighbor had a son two years ahead of him in school, who was then midway through his schooling at Kings Point. "So of course," Flick recalls, smiling wryly, "they gave him time off to come and talk to me. And he told me a pack of lies, you know, 'Oh, it's like a country club. Lots of women around. Come and go as you please. Parties all the time. Wear your hair the way you want.' Turned out to be not exactly that way."

Early in his plebe year at Kings Point, Flick was given the standard choice of specializing in deck or engine. Instead, he chose the dual program, a grueling regimen comprising many more course credits and leading to licenses as both a third mate and a third assistant engineer. Only a small percentage of highly qualified cadets were allowed—or chose—to elect the dual program; a smaller percentage, including Flick, actually graduated with both licenses.

For his Sea Year, actually spread over two school years, he shipped out as both a deck cadet and an engine cadet each year: first on a ninety-day trip to Hong Kong on the engine side, then as a deckie on a voyage to North Europe, then as an engine cadet to West Africa, and then on the deck of a barge to North Europe again.

Graduating in June 1975, a bad year for the maritime industry, Flick couldn't find a deep-sea berth. He finally accepted a nonunion job moving a supply boat from the Gulf of Mexico to Alaska. "So I delivered it," he recalls. "And we got up there, and the company realized that in the Gulf of Alaska, they had to have licensed officers on board at all times. So they kept us on but at Texas wages, which meant that of course we were the lowest-paid people in all of Alaska."

Over the next few years, Flick alternated between jobs at sea and earning an MBA at Kent State University. Like Dutton, he bought himself a Corvette. ("Or maybe two," Flick admits.) By now a firm believer in maritime unions, he haunted the union halls, trying to find work in a still-tight shipping economy. One day in 1977, he landed a six-month job out of the New York union hall because none of the other mariners in the hall that day were willing to fly on an airplane to get to the job. "It wasn't just that they didn't want to fly," he recalls, "but also they didn't really want to go to sea. They were called 'professional night mates,' meaning that they were shore-based and stood night watches in port. They just didn't go to sea much. I suppose they had to now and then, but they skirted the rules as much as they could."

Flick wanted to go to sea, and still does. Today, a quarter century later, he is the chief mate on the *Consumer* and is waiting for a captain's berth. A Kings Point classmate is the master of the *Trader*, another ship in the CSX fleet. (The master of the *Consumer*, Captain Fred Cook, is a graduate of Maine Maritime.) "So you bump into a few my age who are still at sea," he says, "but most of them are hanging it up, especially those who aren't masters yet. Which hopefully I'm at the door of."

Flick's younger brother Kerry also graduated from Kings Point, class of '81, six years behind him. His son Kenny, finishing up his junior year in high school back home, is now thinking about college, and about Kings Point.

Does Flick want his son to go to the Academy?

"Yes," Flick replies. "I hope he does."

Four Pillars

In two different generations, and in two very different industry contexts, Joe Baran and Kent Flick each experienced the Academy's Sea Year, in which cadets spend the better part of a year learning the industry from within. They are taught on U.S. flag ships by U.S. merchant marine officers, many of them Kings Point graduates. Sea Year is a learning experience that distinguishes Kings Point from every other institution of higher learning in the United States—and for that matter, probably the world.

But Sea Year is only one of four vital ingredients in the Academy's educational experience. Superintendent Joseph Stewart refers to these four ingredients—Sea Year, academics, the Regiment, and athletics—as the "four pillars" of the Academy education. The pillars are tightly interrelated. With the obvious exception of Sea Year, which happens all around the world on its own schedule, they exert their influence more or less concurrently, 24/7. They compete for the cadets' time, physical energy, and brain space. Collectively, they add up to more than a full load, forcing cadets to set priorities and manage their time effectively.

Stewart came up with the four pillars notion by a somewhat roundabout route. On the eve of an important football game he ran into his football coach, who was in a foul mood. The reason? A number of his star players were on restriction as a result of minor regimental infractions. According to Academy rules in effect at the time,

Seven members of the Rosenberg family graduated from Kings Point, including the five brothers pictured here: Allen Rosenberg, '45 (center), and clockwise from upper left, Cy Rosenberg-Roberts, '50, Jack Rosenberg, '55, Barry Rosenberg, '63, and Alexander Rosenberg, '69.

students on restriction for disciplinary reasons couldn't participate in interscholastic athletics.

The superintendent, a Naval Academy graduate, began thinking about this rule. As a Division III school, Stewart reasoned, the Academy didn't make money on its teams. (In fact, football at the Academy is subsidized, along with all other sports.) So if the football team wasn't a cash cow, why did the school offer a football program? Obviously, there were industry considerations; students tend to choose schools that offer strong athletic programs. Alumni, too, had to be considered. Academy alumni come out strong for their teams, especially a football game against archrival Coast Guard on a beautiful fall day, and some alumni are rumored to give more generously to their school when things go well on the playing fields. But all these reasons still didn't add up to an adequate justification for a sports program.

Stewart found himself thinking about the words on his high school diploma, which hangs in a prominent location in the admiral's quarters, where he sees it every day. "He has satisfied the requirements as to conduct, character, and scholarship," reads the diploma in part. These words helped answer the question that Stewart had been pondering. As he recalls:

> I realized that the only reason we have athletics is because it's part of the *education*. We believe that there's more to an education than what goes on in the classroom. So I decided that we should send a signal that we were looking for a well-balanced graduate who was getting a *real* education, not just a nose-in-a-book-type education. And that's when I started talking about the four pillars, and when we changed some of the rules regarding discipline.
>
> I'm sure a lot of the faculty still don't agree with me. But I truly believe in the four pillars. I believe the academics are critical, the Regiment is critical, the Sea Year is critical, and physical activity– broadly defined–is also critical. You wouldn't tell a kid he couldn't go to class if he was in some sort of disciplinary trouble. Why deny him or her access to another part of his or her education?[22]

The interrelationship among several of the four pillars manifested itself to Stewart in an unexpected way in the fall of 2003. By tradition, before each football game, the Regiment marched across the campus to Tomb Field in a gesture of unity with each other and with the team. Cadets took their places in the stands and cheered their team on. But when halftime arrived, also by tradition, cadets were allowed to leave. At a particular game in the fall of 2003, they did so in numbers large enough to offend the football team, parents of players, and visiting alumni.

This struck Stewart as disrespectful. At his regular Monday staff meeting two days later, he told Commandant Bob Allee to inform the Regiment that henceforth, cadets would be expected to stay for the entire game. No one present at the meeting objected, as Stewart recalls, but the story the following day was different: "The midshipmen probably found out about it on Tuesday and started voicing their displeasure. Some of them went to see the commandant, and some of them came up here. They were really emotional about it. And one of the reasons was, as I remember, that exam week started the following Monday. They said that they needed to be able to study, that they were going to flunk their exams and so on."

Stewart and Allee held their ground and kept sending the same messages: Support your classmates. Operate as a team.

The following Saturday, at the Western Connecticut game, Stewart watched with pride as the Regiment marched onto Tomb Field in precise formation. He was less pleased, however, when he realized that everyone in the Regiment was carrying a briefcase. It was, he realized, a silent but eloquent protest against his edict.

The superintendent, picking his battles, chose not to intervene at that moment. A few nights later, however, as dinner was being cleared in Delano Hall, he took the floor. Some in the Regiment must have suspected that they were in for it; if so, they were right. Stewart gazed around the now-hushed hall, first left, then right, catching pairs of eyes as he went. Then, planting his fists on his hips, elbows flared out wide, looking every inch the Marine Corps general he was before arriving at the Academy, Stewart made it perfectly clear to the assembled cadets that he was *not amused* by the silent demonstration. *Totally unsat*, he called their performance.

He said that he expected no similar shenanigans at the upcoming Coast Guard game in New London. In fact, he said, he expected *no hijinks at all*. (The intense rivalry between Coast Guard and Kings Point had led to some excesses in the past.) Cadets would attend the game, they would cheer on their team, and they would return to Kings Point. *Period.*

"And that's about what happened," Stewart concludes in his quiet drawl. "In fact, up in New London, they were great. Just great."

It is interesting to note that despite his annoyance, Stewart made no effort to root out the ringleaders of the Briefcase Demonstration. "Yes," he admits, "it ticked me off. But at the same time, it *did* take some ingenuity to come up with that, and some leadership to orchestrate it throughout this whole place. The problem was, this was not leadership in the right direction. As I made very, very clear to them."

It's also interesting to note that if the cadets are to be taken at their word, and there is no reason to doubt them, they meant no disrespect to their teammates in leaving games early. Given the rare luxury of a few free hours, most wanted to put that time into studying for their upcoming exams.

Once again, academics, the Regiment, and athletics were competing for the cadets' time. (And time was so scarce in large part because the shipboard education of Sea Year, the fourth pillar, requires the school to deliver four years of schooling in just over three on-campus years.) In response, the cadets made a set of choices that arguably hurt team unity, and in response to their response, the superintendent took steps to

Cadets throw their caps into the air in a traditional celebratory gesture at the 2005 commencement.

defend that unity. Throughout, the subtext was about leadership, which, Joe Stewart will tell you, involves not only good time management but also a certain amount of putting yourself in the other guy's shoes.

And, of course, a willingness to draw the line every now and then.

"Indoc": Where the Regiment Takes Root

To comprehend the spirit and vision of a Kings Point education, one needs to understand the Regiment of midshipmen, the largely self-policing organization through which student life at the Academy is tightly controlled. And understanding of the Regiment begins with a look at indoc: the indoctrination period that takes place before the formal beginning of plebe year, during which entering students learn about the military discipline that governs most aspects of life at the Academy.

All five federal academies have some form of indoc, which serves the same purposes as basic training in the armed forces: toughening you up, teaching you to be an effective part of a team, and beginning a reorientation of the most basic ways that you look at the world. Indoc is demanding, and it is calculated to put stress on the candidates. The point of this stress, according to Commandant Robert Allee, '68, is not to "drive anyone out . . . but it *does* make any candidate who isn't sure if he or she wants to be here think hard about whether or not he or she should continue."[3]

The other federal academies devote as much as six weeks to indoc; at Kings Point it lasts an intensive two weeks. In these two weeks, the plebes are steered through all the paperwork and administrative steps needed to get them integrated into the system; introduced to the daily routine of the Academy; taught how to wear and care for the uniform; given physical capability tests; instructed in physical training, swimming, basic boat handling, and water survival; introduced to marching and drill practice; and instructed in the history, traditions, rules, and regulations of the Academy.

This means that almost every day of indoc at Kings Point is likely to be an intense one.[4] And the first day for many plebes is the most intense of all.

It begins, typically, on a warm morning in July, officially at seven a.m., although some impatient plebes standing on the sidewalk outside O'Hara Hall actually get in the door before then. But most arrive between eight and ten o'clock. Some pose for a photo with their parents outside Vickery Gate, in front of the new sign (paid for by the school's alumni) that flashes WELCOME ABOARD! in bright electronic letters.

The parents then walk their young charges to the line that has formed alongside O'Hara. They cluster there a little aimlessly while the line inches forward, with younger brothers and sisters gaping at this strange new environment. Academy personnel in dress whites gently encourage parents to take a guided tour of the campus or visit the museum across the street. Most decline; they want to spend these last few minutes with their son or daughter. Already a few of the moms have tears on their cheeks.

On the faces of their sons and daughters, meanwhile, registers a mix of excitement, bewilderment, and apprehension. Standing there on the sidewalk, carrying duffel bags that contain all the worldly possessions that they have brought along from previous lives, they know that a symbolic moment of separation is coming. As they step inside the west end of O'Hara, most search out their parents in the crowd and give them a cheerful wave—in a real sense, the last wave of childhood.

They step from the bright sunlight into a relatively gloomy hallway. Their first stop, in mid-hallway, allows for a gross check of height, weight, and body fat. This is conducted by midshipmen who go about their business with cool professionalism. (To the incoming students, these upperclassmen, thoroughly disciplined, in khaki uniforms from the caps on their heads down to their shiny black shoes, look like ancient mariners; in fact, they are only a year or two older than the new arrivals.) The incoming plebes have been advised to arrive in good physical condition. Here is their first moment of truth at the United States Merchant Marine Academy: if they appear to be out of shape, they will be directed to the medical team for a full-dress physical. At that juncture, if they are deemed to be grossly overweight, they can be bounced immediately.

The midshipmen working the scales, tapes, and calipers also examine the length of the plebe's hair. If they conclude that the plebe is too shaggy by Academy standards, they write an "H" in water-soluble magic marker on the back of the plebe's left hand. Most plebes, male and female, have arrived at Kings Point with what they considered a short haircut. Many now sporting H's on their hands are in for a surprise.

Stepping inside the cavernous main space of O'Hara, which ordinarily is a venue for basketball and other sporting events, today looks like it might be hosting a high school science fair with its succession of large tables demarcated by largely hand-lettered signs. The first of these tables belongs to admissions. Here, plebes have their documents checked, receive their name tags, and otherwise make themselves known to the Academy. The inevitable late enrollee gets special handling as necessary.

Next comes the financial aid table. Students at the Academy get reimbursed for expenses for their initial trip to the school, for travel expenses related to Sea Year, and for their final trip home, hopefully at the end of four years. They can expect to pay something like $10,000 in fees over those four years, including $5,000 in the first year, of which $2,200 is for the required personal computer. Other than these fees and incidentals, the Kings Point education is free, although cadets agree in writing to serve their country and keep their licenses active for a specific amount of time after graduation.[5]

The commandant's table is next, where a team of administrators sets up records as necessary and otherwise helps work the new recruits into the system. Unless plebes have a relative who has attended Kings Point or one of the other federal academies, they most likely have only a vague idea of what a commandant is. Most likely, they have no clue about how central a role that person will play in their lives over the next four years. As one Academy official tells a visitor: "The commandant *owns* these kids once they're here."

Next in line is the Department of Naval Science table. On Acceptance Day, several months from now, the plebes who have made it through indoc and their first month and a half of school—which will be most of them—will be accepted into the Naval Reserve, Inactive Service. As at the other federal academies, they will raise their right hands and take a solemn oath to defend the United States and its Constitution against all enemies, domestic or foreign. (At Kings Point, however, the students remain civilians by virtue of their inactive service status, and are therefore not subject to the Uniform Code of Military Justice.) Their obligation to serve either in the naval reserve, on active duty, or in a maritime-related position begins on the first day of their third year of schooling. Before that, as at the other federal academies, a cadet can leave the school without penalty, and no obligation to reimburse the government for the education provided up to that point. Beginning on the first day of that third year, they are committed.

This relationship with the navy is a central reason why the Regiment exists at Kings Point. The Academy certifies to the navy that a graduating Kings Pointer is qualified to serve in the navy and become an officer. Part of being qualified for navy service is the internalization of military discipline, both from the perspective of being first a follower and then a leader, and this is serious business. At the appropriate time, the navy will scrutinize the record of each midshipman—not only the academic record, but the record of personal conduct in and out of the Regiment—to determine if that young man or woman is fit for naval service. Life within the Regiment, both as a leader and a follower, helps make him or her fit.

One more factor sets Kings Point apart from the other federal academies. At the end of four years, a graduate can continue on in the naval reserve, or can request an active duty commission in any of the branches of the military: army, air force, navy, marines, or Coast Guard, or the National Oceanic and Atmospheric Administration. The various services value Kings Pointers and engage in a friendly competition for them. All the services maintain one or more full-time representatives on campus who teach specific courses, such as naval science, taught by the navy reps, or run activities for interested cadets ("What's life like in today's army?"). The exception to the rule is the Marine Corps, whose rep is attached to the commandant's staff, and whose influence will be very much in evidence on this first day of indoctrination.

Next is the health services desk, where, inevitably, there are more forms to fill out. If a plebe has arrived with medications, the health-services team impounds the medication, checks it out, and (usually) gives it back at the end of day. In the rare event that a medication is deemed to be "noncommissionable," a frank discussion ensues. Is the incoming student willing and able to function without this medication? Is there another way to address the underlying medical condition? If not, he or she will most likely make a quick departure from Kings Point.

The band table, the next stop on the serpentine tour through O'Hara, is the only station that engages in unabashed marketing. Two extremely personable young men sit at the table, jumping up to greet each passing plebe with a smile and a handshake. Behind them stands a large folding exhibit panel featuring color-glossy action shots of the Academy's marching band in full regalia. The list of incoming students includes a certain number of plebes who have been trained in music and have indicated a willingness to play in the band, but the list is always too short, and these recruiters need to find additional talent. Truth be told, no particular talent, or even a musical background, is needed. (It is at least a minor miracle that within weeks the new recruits will be folded into the band, which, of course, will have just lost a number of its sophomore members to Sea Year, and the repopulated band will be cranking out ambitious tunes while marching in sharp formations.) "If they're enthusiastic," says one of the two recruiters, "hey, that's all we need."

Today, the recruiters need to score some successes but not *too* many successes. The band lives together as one of the Regiment's five companies, and the band's barracks can't accommodate more than fifty plebes overall. So they buttonhole all students who pass by, sounding them out regarding their interest in the band. Most decline, usually saying that they plan to do sports instead. The most resolute of these are quickly sent on to the next table. But when someone appears to be on the fence, the marketers swing into gear: "Oh, you can play sports, too! Don't worry, we'll take good care of you! On my first day, I said 'no way' to band, but got talked into it—the best thing that ever happened to me!"

When plebes agrees, the recruiters write a big B in a water-based orange marker on the back of their right hand and send them off to the next table.

Captain Ken Force, leader of the band since 1970, shows up to encourage and eavesdrop on his "salesmen." To a colleague who happens to be standing nearby, he talks enthusiastically about how the new visitor center at the Roosevelt Presidential Library at Hyde Park, New York, has taken sixty copies of the band's latest CD on consignment. The reason? The CD includes a tune called "The Fala March." Evidently, FDR aficionados snap up all sorts of things that include the name of Roosevelt's dog Fala, and this bodes well for the Academy band's CD sales. "Plus, of course," says Force, with his characteristic enthusiasm, "it's *some great music!*"

The last station the incoming students encounter before leaving O'Hara consists of the regimental tables. In contrast to the band area, this is a bare-bones station. Here students are instructed to leave their personal gear, which will be delivered later to their quarters by company officers, and they learn which company they've been assigned to. Male students have been randomly distributed across the four nonband companies; female students have separately been distributed randomly. (If a plebe has come away from the last table with a B on his or her hand, the midshipmen at the regimental table note that change on their master list.) Every plebe is given a small pad and pen for note-taking, as well as a copy of *Bearings*: a tiny soft-cover book full of Academy and maritime-related facts that they will be expected to memorize in the coming months.

Then, in groups of a half dozen or so, they are led down a flight of stairs and back out into the sunlight, this time on the east end of O'Hara, away from the eyes of their family members on the other side of the building.

Here things change dramatically. Here they encounter their first drill instructors, upperclassmen who have volunteered to come back early from their summer vacations to give the incoming plebe candidates their first taste of "followership," seen at the Academy as the first step on the path to leadership. The drill instructor is also known by tradition as a "pusher" in the sense of one who pushes you in a desired direction. Pushers are not necessarily polite. In fact, they tend to get right up in your face and make loud demands of you. These demands are a central part of the indoctrination and training experience that will continue all year, but they are at their most intense in the first months of a plebe candidate's experience, leading up to the Acceptance of the candidates as plebes, and members of the Regiment, in September.

Here's what one cadet later recalled of the indoc experience, reconstructing the monologue he delivered as a drill instructor. The somewhat disoriented plebe emerges from the shadows of O'Hara into the bright sunlight and hears something like the following, delivered in a very loud "command" voice:

> Stand on an X and face me. Good morning. My name is Midshipman Lieutenant Hembree, first class. I am your regimental drill and ceremonies officer. I am going to teach you the position of attention, five basic responses, and how to properly sound off.
>
> Look at me now. Your heels are together and your toes are separated at a forty-five-degree angle. Make a fist as if you were holding a roll of quarters. Your thumbs are on the seams of your trousers. Your arms hang naturally. Stand up straight. Your chest is out. Your shoulders are back. Your chin is in. Your eyes are straight ahead and your mouth is shut. Slightly bend at the knees so that you do not pass out. This does not mean squatting. Just do not lock your knees. You are now in the position of attention. This means you are not looking at me. Your eyes are straight ahead.

The five basic responses. The five basic responses are "Sir, yes sir," "Sir, no sir," "Sir, no excuse, sir," "Sir, I will find out, sir," and "Sir, aye-aye, sir." Repeat after me. "Sir, yes sir" [candidates repeat], "Sir no sir" [candidates repeat], "Sir, no excuse, sir" [candidates repeat], "Sir, I will find out sir" [candidates repeat], "Sir, aye-aye sir" [candidates repeat].

Other than the five basic responses, you will sound off before you speak. To sound off, say, "Sir, candidate last name, company, sir." Sound off now. [Candidates sound off.]

From this point forward, use only what I have taught you: the position of attention, the five basic responses, and sounding off. A word of advice, candidates: *pick up the intensity*. Give it your all and you will do just fine. Welcome to Kings Point.[6]

Often the drill instructors work in pairs, standing on either side of the small knot of plebes, shouting questions at high volume. Let's imagine that Midshipman Lieutenant Hembree has a female counterpart working with him today. As the dazed plebes are still processing what he's told them, she steps forward and, picking names off of random name tags, begins peppering individual plebes with questions, testing them on what they've just learned. (Now, confusingly, the correct answers are bracketed by "ma'am," as in "Ma'am, yes ma'am!") She teaches them to "square" corners—"Left heel, right toe, *Turn*. Do it again! Better!" She instructs them how to hold their *Bearings* book out at arm's length in front of them, and she warns them that they'd better start memorizing its contents, for which they will be held responsible. Meanwhile, Midshipman Lieutenant Hembree swoops in and aims the occasional question at a plebe: "Did you understand that, Jones?" "Sir, yes sir!" (Woe to the plebe who answers Hembree with "Ma'am, yes ma'am.")

Much of what follows, over the next hour or so, is a blur. With drill instructors nipping at their heels like border collies, yelling at them if they fail to square, the plebes are literally run through a series of stations in adjacent buildings, sometimes encountering impromptu signs with exhortations on them:

WALK FASTER!

DON'T LOOK AROUND!

ARE YOU READY?

YOU'D BETTER BE!

One rite of passage takes place at the barbershop, where plebes learn that an "H" on the hand stands for "haircut." Three chairs along one wall service the male students; another two on an adjacent wall service the women (and the occasional male overflow). The students in the chairs look at themselves in the mirror apprehensively as Gino Pellicone and his colleagues mass-produce two-minute haircuts, buzz-cuts for the men and approximately shoulder-length cuts for the women.

Next stop: Ship's Store, where students pick up their initial issues of gear, including uniforms, cargo shorts, shirts, socks, foul-weather gear, sweats, shoe trees for their dress shoes, and a hard-bound book (*Service Etiquette*, intended to help impart military decorum to the students). They stand in line with unwieldy piles of clothes stacked up to their chins, waiting to get their supplies rung up and stuffed into large brown-paper shopping bags. Although the cashier rings up totals for each plebe, these totals are for inventory-control purposes; the students are not charged for this initial outfitting.

That's the good news. The bad news is that the students, still being pushed along by energetic drill instructors, now have to run down hallways toting heavy paper bags on their left hips. They burst out the last door into the sunlight, this time into Barney Square, clutching their supplies in one hand and—following the instructions of the drill instructors who herded them out the door—holding up fingers to indicate the number of their assigned company: one, two, three, or four. Yet another set of drill instructors yells them toward a line that corresponds to their company, often running alongside a student and barking orders.

On this day, a plebe standing in the Company Four line drops her bag in response to a shouted command. The bag splits, distributing her supplies on the blacktop around her feet. Almost simultaneously, another plebe overshoots his target and actually runs into the Company Two sign, knocking it over.

Drill instructors, feigning outrage, close in for corrective action. Both plebes, surveying the wreckage, assume that they're done for.

But neither is correct, of course. This is all part of indoc.

The parents and other family members, meanwhile, have been struggling to catch a glimpse of their offspring as they run from one building to the next. But the Academy has set up a perimeter, marked off by ropes and gently policed by polite midshipmen in full dress, that the parents are unable to penetrate. After watching their child disappear into O'Hara, they move northward along the perimeter to the opening between Barry and Jones Halls and Bowditch Hall, where—if they are sharp-eyed—they can get a distant glimpse of plebes lining up by company (and the occasional brown-paper shopping bag splitting open).

Finally, they are offered something they can sink their teeth into: a parents' meeting in Ackerman Auditorium featuring welcoming comments by Superintendent Stewart, Dean Warren Mazek, and the Commandant, Bob Allee. At this meeting, Allee does most of the heavy lifting. He is both tough and reassuring. "As a former superintendent used to say," he comments, "'they're *mine* now.' But don't worry; we'll take real good care of them."

In a soothing voice, he explains that the plebes can't call home until a week from Sunday. They won't have e-mail access until they get their computers at the end of indoc, seventeen days away. "They'll write you then, immediately," he deadpans, "right after they communicate with their boyfriends or girlfriends." The Academy will post daily indoc updates and pictures on the Web, so parents can participate vicariously in that way. Feel free to send goodies during indoc, he says, but be aware that they'll be sharing those goodies with all forty kids on their decks. This is part of the team focus of indoc, he explains. So either send a *lot*—brownies for forty—or wait until after indoc.

A few parents ask questions and get answers from the appropriate Academy official. But the parents have been told that at the end of this session they'll have a last chance to see their children, so most are impatient to get back outside. On a cue from the commandant, they leave Ackerman and head for Barney Square, walking at a fast clip, some even trotting, worried that they might miss something.

A few more minutes go by as the last parents arrive at Barney Square. Then they see several groups of women and men marching crisply from the barracks and converging upon the blacktop of Barney Square, in front of Delano Hall. The marchers are wearing blue USMMA caps, light blue shirts, dark blue shorts, white socks, and brand-new matching running shoes. To their collective astonishment, the parents realize that these young men and women—now standing at attention facing the steps of Delano Hall, with their backs to the onlookers—are *their kids*.

Admiral Stewart takes the microphone and asks the regimental commander to let the assembled plebes stand at ease. (When that order is issued, the sea of blue relaxes slightly.) Stewart then takes a few minutes to thank retiring admissions director Jim Skinner, and presents him with an award from the Maritime Administration for distinguished service to the Academy. On Jim Skinner's watch, Stewart notes, combined SAT scores increased to an average of 1,250, putting the Academy on an even footing with some of the nation's most prestigious schools.

After weeks of limited contact during indoc, Marla Vignocchi is reunited with her son, Anthony, during Parents Weekend in 2000. Many parents notice a marked change in their children following indoc; typically, there are exclamations and perhaps a few tears as parents see their sons and daughters transformed into young men and women.

This commentary provides Stewart with a segue to his main purpose today, which is welcoming the incoming students. "With Jim Skinner's help," he says, "we looked at almost seven thousand kids, and out of them, we picked two hundred eighty-six—you. As far as I'm concerned, you're the best kids in the United States. We're going to make you mariners, and we're going to make you leaders. We want *every one of you* to make it. And every one of you is capable of making it, or you wouldn't be here.

"There are two things to think about," he goes on, "even as these guys and gals may be yelling at you a little bit in the next week or two. The first is *commitment*. Your desire to succeed will get you through here. But you have to demonstrate a commitment to yourself, and to each other.

"The second," he continues, "is *teamwork*. You wouldn't have come here if you weren't looking for a challenge. Well, you've found it. We'll give it to you. But you'll find that in almost everything you do here—except for test-taking, of course—you'll do better if you pull together and help each other out. You'll soon find out that we have what we call unit runs, which means that the entire unit runs together. We start together, and we finish together. Why? Because we have to learn to think and act *as a unit.*"

As he speaks, the cadets stand almost motionless. Parents on the periphery of Barney Square move along the edge of the crowd, trying to spot the son or daughter who is now submerged in the ranks of several hundred identical-looking plebes, and—if successful—looking for a good camera angle.

An alumnus, class of '44, stands as still and as straight as the cadets. His granddaughter is in those blue-on-blue ranks, and he doesn't much care where; he is full to bursting with pride.

Here and there a father can be seen smiling, shaking his head, marveling at the transformation that already has been wrought behind that mysterious perimeter.

Here and there a mother can be seen wiping tears off her cheeks. Most likely she understands that a bridge has been crossed, and a transition has begun. Her child, delivered up only a few hours earlier, won't be coming home again. Into that child's place will step a grown man or woman.

Indoc is *hard*. Students are pushed to their physical limits and get barely enough sleep. They learn to do things, like marching in tight formations, that seem foreign—even pointless. They have come to Kings Point to study marine engineering, or how to pilot a thousand-foot freighter; instead, they are first asked to learn the school's alma mater and study its history. They are badgered by tough-sounding men and women who expect their questions to be answered precisely and their orders to be executed properly. A sloppy performance, either physical or mental, is likely to elicit a quick corrective action: "Drop and give me fifty."

As noted, the Merchant Marine Academy has two weeks to accomplish what the other federal academies accomplish in six. At some of those sister institutions, there is little or no shouting in the first week; the experience focuses more on team-building, group bonding, and so on. For plebes at those academies, of course, the shouting still comes; it just comes later.

There's a second advantage enjoyed by regimental leaders at, say, West Point, an advantage that carries beyond indoc through the whole undergraduate experience. At West Point, plebes naturally take their regiment seriously. They understand regimental life is the path to subsequent career success. They also understand that the drill instructor who is pushing them today may be their lieutenant several years down the road and on the other side of the world—or, possibly, vice versa. It's a long-term relationship, something like the ties within a family: you're stuck with me, and I'm stuck with you. In the army, everyone has his or her clear role to play—leader or follower—and regimental life at West Point is the preamble to army life.

All of this is less true at Kings Point. Yes, life aboard a merchant vessel involves a strict hierarchy, and in crisis situations orders issued must be followed *instantly* and *correctly*. As noted, regimental training is a necessary prerequisite to service in the naval reserve, where many Kings Pointers meet their service obligation. (Outside of the navy itself, Kings Point historically has been the largest single provider of officers to the naval reserve.) But at Kings Point, by and large, students are training to go into a private-sector job after graduation, afloat or ashore, even though they will perform military service of one sort or another—active duty or reserve—along the way. Most are *not* planning to be career military officers (although in fact a sizable minority of each class, 25 percent in recent years, does wind up spending at least a first career in the military).

Not surprisingly, therefore, some students put minimal effort into regimental life during their time at Kings Point. They don't seek out leadership positions, and instead, they attempt to "fly below the radar" of the Regiment.

Many graduates, however, will tell you that this is a mistake. Looking back on their time at the Academy, they'll tell you either that they are glad they put extra energy into regimental life, or that they wish they had put more time into it while at Kings Point. They'll volunteer that in a fundamental way the Regiment is just like the other three pillars of the school. Just like academics, athletics, and Sea Year—in fact, just like most things in life—you get back out of it what you put into it.

Sitting for the License

In addition to Admiral Stewart's four pillars, the Academy is distinguished by the three credentials it offers: the undergraduate bachelor of science degree, the commission in the naval reserve, and the merchant mariner's license. In most cases, it is the prospect of earning these credentials that lures students to Kings Point in the first place. These credentials, taken together, position the Academy's graduates for success in an amazing variety of contexts.

Kings Point earned the right to award a bachelor's degree only after years of struggle. The right to confer an accredited engineering degree grew out of a second sustained struggle, also described in previous chapters. Over the decades, the reserve commission has been removed and returned and has shifted from the merchant marine reserve to the naval reserve.

The one credential shared by every single graduate of Kings Point over the school's sixty-plus-year history has been the license conferred on the graduating student by the United States Coast Guard. Actually, that construction gets it slightly backward; more accurately stated, students can't graduate from Kings Point without earning their license. Increasingly, this distinguishes the Academy from state maritime schools, which no longer impose this requirement on their students. But students at Kings Point are educated through the generosity of federal taxpayers. Without exception, the expectation is that they will earn their licenses and then pay back the investment that their country has made in them—and the way they earn that license is to sit for the license exam.

When Bess and Margaret Truman visited Kings Point on March 3, 1946, they passed by the Amphitrite Fountain, an elegant holdover from the days when the estate belonged to Walter Chrysler. Margaret Truman paused and tossed a few coins to the goddess in the center of the fountain for good luck.[7] Unless she was so informed, the president's daughter wouldn't have known that she was only one of a long string of young people, before and after her, who sought good fortune from the goddess Amphitrite.

Just after lunch on a sunny Tuesday in June almost sixty years later, two engine midshipmen pause alongside the Amphitrite Fountain. Carefully shifting their books from one hip to the other, each reaches into a pocket of his khaki uniform, pulls out a coin, and throws it into the fountain without commentary.

Then one of the two midshipmen spots a coin sitting on the concrete lip of the fountain. "Wow!" he exclaims, leaning over carefully to pick it up. "That guy isn't going to have any luck today!"

He tosses this additional coin into the fountain, as well. "Now I've got that guy's luck," he says, only half joking, "*and* my luck."

The two midshipmen, along with the rest of the members of the graduating class, have just begun the four days of testing that will determine whether they will graduate and become qualified to serve as officers in the merchant marine. The experience more or less defines the phrase "high-stakes test." After four years of schooling, it all comes down to this: seven modules, and they have to pass all seven. Deckies have to get at least a 90 percent on the rules-of-the-road module, demonstrating that they know who does what under what circumstances out on the water, an 80 percent on terrestrial and celestial navigation, and at least a 70 percent on the other two modules. Engineers have to get at least a 70 percent on everything.

If they fail up to two of the seven modules this week, they can take those modules again at Kings Point during the following week. If they fail three or more modules this first time out, however, they will have to make arrangements to take the entire exam again on their own time—but this time at the Coast Guard's regional exam center in Lower Manhattan. Until they pass, they can't graduate.

After paying their respects to the goddess Amphitrite, the two midshipmen continue on their way toward O'Hara Hall, where the testing is taking place. On their way, they compare notes on the morning session, which ran from 8:20 to 10:30. Both midshipmen had been through the license seminar offered by Commander Ray Gardner, a member of

Deck and engineering midshipmen from the class of 2006 sit for a module of their licensing exam in O'Hara Hall. Engineering students are on the left of the hall, deck students on the right. Every Kings Point alumnus has experienced this license test set-up.

the faculty, as well as the class of '79, aimed at helping students prep for the exam; both had called up numerous sample questions from the National Maritime Center Web site as part of their preparation. Nevertheless, the morning session had been grueling. "You could have cut the tension in there with a knife," says one cadet. His classmate agrees. Both were up until three a.m. last night, and they are running on adrenaline.

Ray Gardner has made a deal with the senior class. If they achieve a 90 percent first-time pass rate or better, he will shave his head. It is unlikely that he'll have to do so; 90 percent would be a spectacular performance. Even mid-80s would be very solid.

Now the students have reassembled outside O'Hara for the Tuesday afternoon testing session, which starts at one o'clock. Approximately two hundred midshipmen mill around outside O'Hara, chatting loudly, occasionally laughing. Given the undertone of excitement and nervousness, they might be mistaken for a group of undergraduates waiting for admission to a sporting event or a rock concert—except, of course, that these students are all dressed in identical khaki uniforms and are all carrying the tools of examination. A closer look would reveal a few more distinguishing features among this group of undergraduates. No one is overweight, for example. No one is slouching. No one sports a (visible) tattoo.

The group includes two dozen women. They are easier to spot from slightly above because their caps are split along the top and spread down the middle, accommodating their slightly larger hairdos, whereas the male caps come to a peak, front to back. Here and there, one sees an African American or Asian American face in the crowd. In the past, it was somewhat easier for Kings Point to attract qualified minority students with the promise of a free education. Today, some universities are offering minority students a free ride through the master's level, or even through a doctoral program, changing the context within which Kings Point must find, woo, and win qualified minorities.

Finally, the door opens, and the midshipmen begin climbing the stairs into O'Hara. As they pass through the door, they remove their caps and tuck them into their belts. A few cross themselves reflexively, seeking help from a higher authority. They are well aware that the worst is yet to come, including the motors module tomorrow and the electrical module on Thursday afternoon. The engineers still have to get through "generals," also rumored to be a bear.

Just as it was almost four years earlier, when these midshipmen first arrived at Kings Point for indoctrination, O'Hara is once again filled with tables. This time, though, it's one table per student, with the engineers sitting to the left of the center aisle and the deckies sitting on the right. Today, something like seventy would-be engineers are sitting themselves down, and just over one hundred would-be deckies. The bantering that died outside has not resumed. By the time U.S. Coast Guard examining official Cathy Galante steps forward to address them, the huge hall is nearly pin-drop silent.

"Okay, people," she begins, "please fan out your Bowditches and clear the memory on your calculators." Around the room, large volumes are picked up and fanned out to demonstrate that there are no crib sheets hidden in them. Normally, the Coast Guard supplies copies of the *American Practical Navigator* to people sitting for a license exam, but the group at Kings Point is so large that the midshipmen are requested to bring their own.

As the midshipmen are complying with this order, Galante walks from table to table, checking IDs to confirm that people are who they say they are, and also making sure that there are no unauthorized materials on the work surfaces. Some midshipmen take off their class rings and put them on the table in front of them; others put framed pictures of their mothers or girlfriends in front of them for inspiration; still others put religious artifacts in a prominent place on their table. Within reason, Galante allows for inspiration.

When the last Bowditch has hit the desk and the last calculator memory has been cleared, Galante speaks once again. "I know you were all nervous this morning," she says. "Some of you may still be. But please just follow my instructions and concentrate on doing your best, and you'll be fine. First, print your last name, first name, Social Security number, and the first five digits of the module code found on the front of your test booklet."

She goes on to review the same rules that she laid down in the morning session. "If you have a problem of a general nature," she says, "raise your hand and one of us will come to your table." At the front of the hall with her are a half-dozen blue-suited Coast Guard officials. Although Kings Point faculty are welcome to stand at the front of the hall and lend moral support to their students, only Coast Guard personnel are permitted to walk the floor. "If you have a problem with the wording or premise of a specific question," Galante continues, "you have the right to dispute that question, but you must answer it today to the best of your ability."

This is not a theoretical scenario. In a recent round of testing, one question in the rules-of-the-road module made reference to a situation of "low visibility." But in the published version of the rules of the road, as codified by the Coast Guard, there's no mention of low visibility; it's either "restricted visibility" or "clear visibility." A cadet protested use of the word "low," and that protest was upheld.

Galante is a civilian based at the Coast Guard's regional exam center in New York City. An educator by training, she was working as an executive assistant at the Coast Guard station on Governor's Island in the early 1990s when the post of Maritime school administrator became vacant. Since that time, she has administered license exams at both Kings Point and the State University of New York Maritime College (Fort Schuyler) in the Bronx. She administered the dualie exam at Kings Point until that program was discontinued, and recently began running the exams for the Ship's Officer program, which requires deckies to take an additional half-dozen exams to earn endorsements (but not a license) on the engine side.

Galante also works with Kings Point to provide appropriate Coast Guard credentials at the beginning and end of a Kings Point education. Before a cadet can go to sea during Sea Year, for example, he or she has to receive formal documentation from the Coast Guard. As a result of tightened security, this now involves an initial round of fingerprinting during indoc, requiring a midsummer trip by Galante to Kings Point, and a second round of fingerprinting when midshipmen reach their senior year.

Upon her cue, the midshipmen walk up to the folding tables at the front of the hall, pick up the relevant packet of questions—deck or engine—and some scratch paper, and head back to their individual tables.

Not too far into the testing session, hands begin to go up among the deckies. Galante goes from one table to the next, quietly conferring with each cadet who has raised a hand. The problem is the same in all cases: the photocopying is too light, making it hard for the midshipmen to read some of the test questions. Galante, obviously not happy about this unusual snafu, confers with her colleagues at the front of the room. They dig through the remaining tests and find replacement booklets to help the midshipmen decipher the illegible questions.

Over the course of the following few days, Galante says—based on more than a decade of administering these tests—the Kings Pointers will gradually calm down and the tension level in the room will decline. This is in part because they will have become accustomed to test taking, and in part because, by the end of the week, they'll be mentally and physically exhausted.

They will not have long to await the verdict. The modules will be graded almost in real time by the Coast Guard team that is stationed for the week at Kings Point. The results will be turned over to the chairman of the Marine Transportation and Engineering departments—and subsequently to the dean and superintendent—and then posted on Friday afternoon outside the deck and engine departmental offices.

And then will come one of Kings Point's most hallowed rituals. Students who have passed every module are entitled to ring the ship's bell outside Wiley Hall, signifying their formal admission to the brotherhood (and increasingly, the sisterhood) of merchant mariners. This is a moment of exhalation and triumph for the midshipmen, a rite of passage that marks their accomplishments and signals the beginning of the next stage of their lives.

Ray Gardner, however, will not be shaving his head. The graduating class will post a pass percentage rate in the high 80s—an extremely good performance, but not good enough to compel the professor to reach for his razor.

Looking to the Future

The American merchant marine is an industry that frustrates even its biggest supporters and puzzles even its most expert interpreters.

More than almost any other industry, it is both vital and invisible. More than 95 percent of all the goods that enter the United States do so in the hold or on the deck of a ship, but few Americans know that. In fact, the sheer growth of the maritime industry, especially in the wake of containerization, has led to the growth of massive new port facilities far away from the public view. The residents of New York City used to live with a thriving seaport at their southern and western doorsteps; now, most of that activity takes place in relatively remote Port Elizabeth, New Jersey. (Even if you went looking for Port Elizabeth and found it, you couldn't get in: recent security concerns have made these facilities inaccessible to unauthorized visitors.) The same could be said of Boston, San Francisco, Los Angeles, and other port cities. Shipping has gone out of sight and out of mind.

In ever increasing numbers, moreover, the ships that enter American ports no longer fly the U.S. flag. Many Americans have a vague understanding that their merchant marine is in steep decline, and by many important measures, they are right. At the beginning of 2003, for example, more than 30 percent of the world's ocean-trading merchant tonnage was owned by Greek and Japanese shipping lines. U.S. companies have reinforced and even exaggerated this sense of decline by shifting overwhelmingly to foreign-flag vessels, mostly in an effort to sidestep financially burdensome U.S. litigation, environmental and labor liability exposures, and other regulations.

At the same time, however, U.S. companies still own a sizable 74.1 million deadweight tons of merchant shipping, mostly sailing under foreign flag registry. This places the United States fifth overall, behind Greece, Japan, Norway, and China.[8]

As recently as the "reinventing government" effort of the 1990s, detractors of Kings Point looked at the evidence of decline in the U.S. merchant marine—although not the countervailing evidence—and asked an obvious question: Why spend federal money on an institution that trains its graduates for an industry that is in decline? Is this a case of protecting the last buggy-whip manufacturer?

In October 2000, the *Journal of Commerce* summed up the dilemma:

> Kings Point has always played a role that is difficult to explain to the layman. Unlike West Point or the Naval, Coast Guard, and Air Force Academies, Kings Point does not feed a specific service; all Kings Pointers graduate as commissioned officers, though less than 20 percent go on active duty in one of the services. Kings Point's chief mission is to train young men and women for careers in the U.S. merchant marine, but that is an institution whose rationale for national and economic security is perennially debated and whose future is hardly secure.[9]

As the institution moves forward in the twenty-first century, this issue will most likely continue to be hotly debated. These are ultimately questions for legislators and industry leaders to answer, with input from the public. Recent events in the Middle East and elsewhere suggest, however, that it is in the interests of this country to maintain a strong flag fleet, both to act as a reliable support for the nation's military endeavors and to protect against possible terrorist attacks by sea.

The Academy, of course, has asked itself these same hard questions—in part to be able to respond to questions from others, and, as we have seen, as a necessary part of strategic planning. Time and again, Academy administrators have returned to two historically rooted justifications for the Academy.

The first is support of U.S. military endeavors. By early May 2005, MARAD had activated eighty-five Ready Reserve Fleet ships, moving almost 25 percent of the equipment needed to support the U.S. armed forces operation in Iraq.[10] Once again, commercial ships were called upon to carry essential fuel, ammunition, and equipment to a theater of war (and once again, Academy cadets were aboard those ships). This not only frees navy personnel for other duties, it turns out to be surprisingly cost-effective.

The second justification for the Academy's existence is economic: to provide leaders of the civilian maritime industry, as well as of other related transportation industries and services. Yes, the U.S. flag deep-sea industry has declined dramatically in recent decades. But this is not the case for inland shipping—for example, on the great rivers and lakes of this continent—and the concept of short-sea shipping to alleviate road congestion (as on Interstate 95 on the East Coast) is also gaining a lot of currency in the industry. It is also not the case for the Military Sealift Command, which is increasingly operating navy-owned ships with smaller civilian crews (incidentally saving the country significant expense). Finally, the U.S. maritime industry infrastructure ashore serves all ships arriving in U.S. ports, and has grown along with foreign trade.

Even the deep-water jobs are far from a hopeless case. Recent studies have predicted an impending worldwide shortage of thirty-five thousand officers.[11] Some of those positions, surely, will be filled by U.S.–trained officers, even if they are not on U.S.–flagged ships. The Academy has been contacted by operators of specialized fleets, for example, LNG tankers, who are very interested in ensuring a supply of skilled officers into the indefinite future.

In addition, in an era of increasing risk of attacks on American soil, government and industry leaders are stressing the importance of safer and more transparent systems of transportation for goods onto U.S. soil. A recent article in the newsletter of the Institute of South East Asian studies comments, "Historically, shipping has played a pivotal role in world trade. Yet for all its global significance, the shipping industry is vast, poorly regulated, frequently beyond the reach of the law, and often secretive in its operations. Despite a raft of new maritime-based anti-terror legislation, the world's oceans and the shipping industry remain an attractive domain for terrorist operations."[12]

How do these global concerns come to bear on a relatively small school in the north shore of Long Island? In the 2004 edition of *The Best 350 Schools and Colleges*, published by the Princeton Review, Kings Point was ranked as one of the nation's best colleges. (The rankings were based on student surveys involving more than 106,000 students at the 351 colleges included in the publication.) The editors described the institution as enjoying "excellent leadership training," with "small classes," and "dedicated professors."[13]

The Academy also showed up on two of the publication's "top twenty" lists. Kings Point came in fourth in student/community relations, as ranked by the students. This measurement may be interpreted as a proxy for the traits instilled by the regimented lifestyle at the Academy. Drug use at the Academy among the student body is estimated by students to be very low. Neighbors of the Academy rarely encounter misbehaving cadets. Residents of Kings Point and Great Neck attend football games, exercise on the Academy's track, and join the faculty for lunch in Melville Hall on Wednesdays during the school year. When they do so, they are likely to be greeted by cadets with a respectful "Good morning, ma'am," or "Good morning, sir." Most often, these cadets are seen in uniform.

Kings Point also came in an impressive tenth-in-the-nation on the top twenty list when students were asked the question, "Are your instructors good teachers?" Off the record, some faculty members admit to being pleasantly surprised by this ranking. (It is not always easy to know what that polite and respectful cadet is *actually* thinking about your lecturing skills.) One reason for this high ranking may be that most teachers have actually *lived* the subjects that they teach. Another is that the typical professor at Kings Point has made a conscious commitment to the art of teaching, as opposed to being in the forefront of research. As engineering department head Jose Femenia explains:

> The Academy's faculty is truly connected with the goals of the academic programs. Within the two professional departments, the majorities of the faculty members are either mariners, or practitioners in their disciplines, and thus . . . the faculty has the ability to

connect theory with practice and refer to real examples relating to the majors being studied.

Another distinguishing characteristic is that they are first and foremost teachers . . . faculty members who do research at the Academy do it as a secondary, collateral professional responsibility to enhance the knowledge base for the industry and profession, not as their primary responsibility to the institution.[14]

In recent decades, the Academy also has been receiving national recognition for its success in training leaders. Over a recent fifteen-year period, for example, Kings Point achieved high standing on all three Standard and Poor's business leadership lists (1985, 1990, and 1996), which ranked 550 educational institutions in the United States by the number of leading business executives they produced in proportion to their average number of graduates. The Academy ranked between tenth to eighteenth, putting it in the company of institutions like Yale, Princeton, Harvard, MIT, Williams, and Dartmouth, among others. (See Appendix K.) Simply put, these are astounding results for a school of Kings Point's size and focus.

Kings Point sets out to produce "competent, well-educated, professional officers and leaders of quality, integrity, and high ethical standards" for the maritime industry, and it succeeds in that mission.[15]

Along the way, it seems, it also produces leaders for the nation.

President George W. Bush addresses the Regiment during the 2006 commencement ceremonies. This was the first visit by a sitting president to the USMMA.

APPENDIX A

Maritime Administrators

September 26, 1936–April 15, 1937*	Admiral Henry A. Wiley, USN
April 16, 1937–February 17, 1938*	Joseph P. Kennedy
February 18, 1938–January 15, 1946*	Admiral Emory S. Land, USN
June 3, 1946–April 16, 1949*	William W. Smith
June 6, 1949–May 23, 1950*	Philip B. Fleming
August 8, 1950–October 1, 1952	E. L. Cochrane
October 2, 1952–June 30, 1953	Albert W. Gatov
July 1, 1953–February 25, 1955	Louis S. Rothschild
March 16, 1955–May 1, 1960	Clarence G. Morse
July 1, 1960–February 22, 1961	Ralph E. Wilson
February 23, 1961–October 8, 1961	Thomas E. Stakem
October 9, 1961–October 31, 1963	Donald W. Alexander
March 2, 1964–June 30, 1966	Nicholas Johnson
March 25, 1969–July 6, 1972	Captain Andrew E. Gibson
July 7, 1972–April 9, 1979	Robert J. Blackwell
July 19, 1979–July 31, 1981	Samuel B. Nemirow
October 19, 1981–May 31, 1985	Harold E. Shear
November 26, 1985–March 26, 1989	John A. Gaughan
October 11, 1989–January 20, 1993	Captain Warren G. Leback '44
September 14, 1993–June 30, 1997	Vice Admiral Albert J. Herberger '55, USN
August 6, 1998–January 2000	Clyde Hart, Esquire
December 6, 2001–February 12, 2005	Captain William G. Schubert '74
September 6, 2006–present	Sean T. Connaughton, Esquire, '83

---

*Title of office is Chairman of the Maritime Commission

APPENDIX B

Superintendents, USMMA

April 11, 1942–October 16, 1943	Captain James Harvey Tomb (USN)
October 16, 1943–April 1, 1946	Rear Admiral Giles C. Stedman (USN)
April 1, 1946–April 1, 1948	Rear Admiral Richard R. McNulty (USMS)
April 1, 1948–June 15, 1970	Rear Admiral George Gordon McLintock (USMS)
June 15, 1970–September 30, 1979	Rear Admiral Arthur B. Engel (USCG)
September 30, 1979–July 13, 1980	Howard F. Casey (acting)
July 13, 1980–July 1987	Rear Admiral Thomas A. King '42 (USMS)
July 1987–July 1993	Rear Admiral Paul L. Krinsky '50 (USMS)
July 1993–July 31, 1998	Rear Admiral Thomas T. Matteson (USMS)
July 31, 1998–present	Vice Admiral Joseph D. Stewart (USMS)

APPENDIX C

Academic Deans, USMMA

1948–1949	Commander Francis S. Kirk, USMS
	(chief, Academic and Research Division)
1949–1951	Captain William M. Randall, USMS
1952–1955	Captain Peder Gald, USMS
1956–1959	Dr. Guy W. Trump
1960–1961	Commander John J. O'Hearne, USMS (assistant dean)
1962–1965	Dr. Arthur Sanford Limouze, Capt. USMS
1965–1966	Captain Lawrence Jarett, Esq., USMS (acting)
1967–1972	Captain Janus Poppe, USMS
1973–1984	Captain Paul L. Krinsky, USMS
1985–1986	Captain W. T. McMullen, USMS (acting)
1986–2007	Dr. Warren F. Mazek
2007–	Dr. Shashi Kumar

APPENDIX D

Commandants/Regimental Officers, USMMA

May 19, 1942–December 20 1943	Captain Giles C. Stedman
December 20, 1943–1945	Captain Phillip C. Mahady
1944*	Lieutenant R. E. Salman
1945*	Commander John F. Wilson
1945*	Commander F. A. Litchfield
1946–1961*	Commander R. H. O'Connell
1962–1965*	Commander H. O. Travis
1965–1966*	Captain Victor E. Tyson '43
1966–1968*	Commander Richard D. O'Leary
1968–1969*	Captain Robert Wall
1969–1970*	Captain Edward Knutsen (acting)
1970–1977	Captain Edward Knutsen
1977–1981	Captain Robert T. Madden '59
1981–1984	Captain John J. Jochmans '66
1985–1989	Captain Robert L. Safarik '61
1989–1998	Captain Donald J. Ferguson
1998–2002	Captain Robert Larsen '72 (acting)
2002–2003	Captain Arthur J. Athens
2004–present	Captain Robert Allee '68

---

* Title of office is Regimental Officer

APPENDIX E

Hall of Distinguished Graduates

The Hall of Distinguished Graduates, located in Vickery Gate, was established in 1994 to recognize and honor graduates whose outstanding careers will be immortalized to establish proud traditions and inspire graduates to carry on the heritage of Kings Point.

The list below is in order of induction.

Joseph B. Williams '44
October 14, 1994
First African American graduate, New York State Supreme Court judge

J. Lane Kirkland '42
September 25, 1995
President, AFL-CIO

Romulo M. Espaldon '50
October 13, 1995
Philippine ambassador to Saudi Arabia and Yemen

Kenneth A. DeGhetto '43
September 28, 1996
Chairman of the board of Foster Wheeler Corporation and Association/chairman of alumni endowment fund, the Kings Point Challenge

Rear Admiral Carl J. Seiberlich, USN (retired) '43
September 28, 1996
Distinguished merchant marine and navy careers, first Kings Pointer to attain flag rank

Vice Admiral Robert H. Scarborough, USCG (retired) '44
October 17, 1997
First three-star admiral, deputy commandant of U.S. Coast Guard

449

Captain Warren G. Leback '44
October 17, 1997
Steamship company president and Maritime administrator

Captain Leo V. Berger '43
October 9, 1998
Formed the Apex Marine Corporation, eventually consisting of twenty-two vessels

Capt. J. W. Clark '40
October 9, 1998
Distinguished career in the maritime industry, both as master mariner and shipping
    company executive

Elliot M. See Jr. '49 (posthumously)
October 1, 1999
First Academy astronaut. Participated in flight training for Manned Space
    Center in 1962; chosen in 1965 as command pilot for Gemini 9 mission.
    Tragically, on February 28, 1966, he was killed in a plane crash prior to sched-
    uled space flight

Rear Admiral Thomas A. King, USMS (retired) '42
October 1, 1999
First alumni superintendent. Provided tireless and lifelong work on behalf of the
    maritime industry and the USMMA

Dr. Douglass C. North '43
October 1, 1999
Received the Nobel Prize in Economics in 1993. In 1996 was elected a
    Fellow of the British Academy and installed as the Olin T. Spencer Professor in
    Arts and Sciences, Washington University, St. Louis

James H. Ackerman, Esquire, '44
October 6, 2000
Distinguished admiralty lawyer and philanthropist (Ackerman Auditorium)

Vice Admiral Albert J. Herberger, USN (retired) '55
October 6, 2000
Maritime administrator and first Academy USN three-star admiral

John T. Diebold '46
February 20, 2003
Father of automation and business consultant

John "Jack" Brooks '44
February 20, 2003
Real estate investor, part owner of NFL Oakland Raiders, and philanthropist
    (Brooks Stadium)

Sidney A. Thompson '52
February 20, 2003
Distinguished educator, superintendent Los Angeles (CA) School District

James H. Yocum '47
February 19, 2004
Philanthropist (Yocum Sailing Center)

James A. Babson '44
February 19, 2004
Hotel/real estate owner and philanthropist (Babson Center)

Erik F. Johnsen '45
February 17, 2005
Chairman and director of International Shipholding Corporation

Adrian Zaccaria '66
February 17, 2005
President and chief operating officer of the Bechtel Group

Anthony J. Fiorelli '51
February 16, 2006
Outstanding careers in pioneering naval nuclear power, managing a highly success-
    ful defense systems company, and as a technical adviser to Wall Street financial
    institutions; also successfully directed a $45 million alumni fund-raising
    campaign

Petro Kulynych '43
February 16, 2006
Fifty-year career with Lowe's Companies, ultimately becoming its managing
    director and chairman of the board

David A. O'Neil '61 (posthumous)
February 8, 2007
Author, inventor, and entrepreneur with a long list of awards and recognitions to
    his name

APPENDIX F

Cadets and Graduates Killed in World War II

Name of Cadet	Name of Ship	Date	Deck/ Engine	Location
Lewis, Richard E.	*Azalea City*	2/20/42	D	North Atlantic
See, Robert J.	*Azalea City*	2/20/42	E	North Atlantic
Conway, Howard P., Jr.	*Liberator*	3/19/42	E	U.S. East Coast
Holbrook, Richard H.	*Bienville*	4/6/42	E	Indian Ocean/Red Sea
Magee, James J.	*Edward B. Dudley*	4/11/42	D	North Atlantic
Brandler, Carl A.	*Munger T. Ball*	5/4/42	E	Gulf of Mexico
Bruaw, Glenn R.	*Heredia*	5/9/42	D	Gulf of Mexico
Ebel, Irwin S.	*Heredia*	5/9/42	E	Gulf of Mexico
Brewster, John P.	*Syros*	5/26/42	E	Murmansk
Chunosoff, Peter N.	*Alcoa Pilgrim*	5/28/42	D	Caribbean
McCauliffe, Kenneth	*Tela*	6/8/42	E	Caribbean
Kern, Otto E., Jr.	*Richard Henry Lee*	7/5/42	E	Murmansk
Foote, Calvin S.	*Pan Atlantic*	7/6/42	D	North Atlantic
Cathey, Vincent G.	*Robert E. Lee*	7/30/42	E	Gulf of Mexico
DiCicco, Joseph C.	*American Leader*	9/10/42	E	South Atlantic
Tyne, Gordon A.	*American Leader*	9/10/42	D	South Atlantic
Amborski, Norbert	*Stone Street*	9/13/42	D	North Atlantic
Bole, Robert J., III	*Wichita*	9/19/42	D	Caribbean
Klien, Chester E.	*Wichita*	9/19/42	E	Caribbean
Wright, Donald S.	*Cornelia P. Spencer*	9/21/42	D	Indian Ocean/Red Sea
Bergeson, Burton B.	*John Winthrop*	9/24/42	D	North Atlantic
Palmer, Robert V.	*West Chetac*	9/24/42	E	Caribbean
Sturges, Jonathan F.	*John Winthrop*	9/24/42	E	North Atlantic
Chamberlain, Arthur R.	*Stephen Hopkins*	9/27/42	D	South Atlantic
O'Hara, Edwin J.	*Stephen Hopkins*	9/27/42	E	South Atlantic
Nauman, Robert S.	*Firethorn*	10/7/42	E	Indian/Red Sea
Rovella, Louis J.	*Firethorn*	10/7/42	D	Indian/Red Sea

Name of Cadet	Name of Ship	Date	Deck/ Engine	Location
Schuster, Samuel	*Examelia*	10/9/42	D	South Atlantic
Spilman, Bernard W.	*Examelia*	10/9/42	E	South Atlantic
Alexander, Joseph P.	*Angelina*	10/17/42	D	North Atlantic
Krusko, Joseph W.	*Angelina*	10/17/42	E	North Atlantic
Everhart, Robert R.	*William Clark*	11/4/42	D	North Atlantic
Garritsen, Herman G.	*William Clark*	11/4/42	E	North Atlantic
Smith, Peter J.	*William Clark*	11/4/42	E	North Atlantic
Farrell, Richard P.	*Nathaniel Hawthorne*	11/7/42	D	Caribbean
Frohn, David H.	*Francis Drake*	11/7/42	D	unknown
Guilford, George E.	*La Salle*	11/7/42	E	Indian Ocean/Red Sea
Pennington, Fred	*La Salle*	11/7/42	D	Indian Ocean/Red Sea
Weis, William R., Jr.	*Nathaniel Hawthorne*	11/7/42	D	Caribbean
Ginnelly, William B.	*Scapa Flow*	11/14/42	E	South Atlantic
Egenthal, Meyer	*Sawokla*	11/29/42	E	Indian Ocean/Red Sea
O'Hara, William V.	*Sawokla*	11/29/42	D	Indian Ocean/Red Sea
Branigan, Philip G.	*James McKay*	12/7/42	D	North Atlantic
Erhlich, Leonard L.	*James McKay*	12/7/42	E	North Atlantic
Hetrick, Walter C., Jr.	*James McKay*	12/7/42	E	North Atlantic
McKelvey, John	*James McKay*	12/7/42	D	North Atlantic
Giovinco, Joseph	*Coamo*	12/9/42	D	Caribbean
Levett, Henry A.	*Coamo*	12/9/42	D	Caribbean
Viridakis, George	LOST IN TRAINING	12/12/42		
Ackerlind, Edward J.	*Maiden Creek I*	12/31/42	E	U.S. East Coast
Carriere, Warren B.	*Maiden Creek I*	12/31/42	D	U.S. East Coast
Charlton, Denniston, Jr.	*Arthur Middleton*	1/1/43	D	Mediterranean/Black Sea
Gafford, Ben P.	*Arthur Middleton*	1/1/43	E	Mediterranean/Black Sea
Limehouse, Albert M.	LOST IN TRAINING	1/5/43		
Chrobak, Michael M.	*Louise Lykes*	1/9/43	E	Northeast Atlantic
Gassner, Charles C.	*Louise Lykes*	1/9/43	D	Northeast Atlantic
Miller, Allen G., Jr.	*Louise Lykes*	1/9/43	D	Northeast Atlantic
Vancure, Robert C.	*Louise Lykes*	1/9/43	E	Northeast Atlantic
Walters, Eugene W.	*Louise Lykes*	1/9/43	D	Northeast Atlantic
Corrigan, Vincent J.	*Charles C. Pinckney*	1/27/43	E	Mid-Atlantic
Lamac, Robert L.	*Charles C. Pinckney*	1/27/43	D	Mid-Atlantic
Hammershoy, Jay A.	*Henry R. Mallory*	2/2/43	E	North Atlantic
Holland, Richard E.	*Henry R. Mallory*	2/2/43	D	North Atlantic
Race, George R.	*Henry R. Mallory*	2/2/43	E	North Atlantic
Linde, William R.	*Jeremiah Van Rennselaer*	2/2/43	E	North Atlantic
Gavin, Edward J.	*Dorchester*	2/3/43	E	North Atlantic
Tyler, Samuel T.	*Dorchester*	2/3/43	D	North Atlantic
Pitzely, David H.	*West Portal*	2/5/43	D	North Atlantic
Province, James H.	*West Portal*	2/5/43	E	North Atlantic
Quayle, Harry, Jr.	*Daniel H. Lownsdale*	2/18/43	D	Mediterranean/Black Sea

Name of Cadet	Name of Ship	Deck/ Date	Engine	Location
Hollander, Maxwell	*Rosario*	2/21/43	D	Northeast Atlantic
Burlison, Harry M.	*Jonathan Sturges*	2/23/43	D	North Atlantic
Kohlmeyer, Ralph J.	*Jonathan Sturges*	2/23/43	E	North Atlantic
Lietz, Grover P.	*Jonathan Sturges*	2/23/43	E	North Atlantic
Wilson, William C.	*Jonathan Sturges*	2/23/43	D	North Atlantic
Gordon, John R.	*Nathaniel Greene*	2/24/43	E	Mediterranean/Black Sea
Miller, George C., Jr.	*Wade Hampton*	2/28/43	D	North Atlantic
Bourell, Randall P.	*Meriwether Lewis*	3/2/43	D	North Atlantic
Clarke, Alan R.	*Meriwether Lewis*	3/2/43	D	North Atlantic
Maher, Daniel J.	*Meriwether Lewis*	3/2/43	E	North Atlantic
McCann, Francis T.	*Meriwether Lewis*	3/2/43	E	North Atlantic
Cordua, James S.	*William C. Gorgas*	3/10/43	D	North Atlantic
Hanzik, Edwin	*William C. Gorgas*	3/10/43	D	North Atlantic
Moon, James O.	*William C. Gorgas*	3/10/43	E	North Atlantic
Wiggin, Edwin P.	*William C. Gorgas*	3/10/43	D	North Atlantic
Gradus, Arthur J.	*Richard Bland*	3/10/43	D	Murmansk
Tamplin, Charles W.	*Richard Bland*	3/10/43	D	Murmansk
Buck, Michael Jr.	*James Sprunt*	3/10/43	E	Caribbean
McGrath, Howard T.	*James Sprunt*	3/10/43	E	Caribbean
Rowley, James R.	*James Sprunt*	3/10/43	D	Caribbean
Tucek, John P.	*James Sprunt*	3/10/43	D	Caribbean
Byrd, Lee T.	*Harry Luckenbach*	3/17/43	D	North Atlantic
Meyer, Walter J.	*Harry Luckenbach*	3/17/43	E	North Atlantic
Miller, Francis R.	*Harry Luckenbach*	3/17/43	E	North Atlantic
Parker, William H.	*Harry Luckenbach*	3/17/43	D	North Atlantic
Lambert, John R.	*James Oglethorpe*	3/17/43	D	North Atlantic
Record, Richard	*James Oglethorpe*	3/17/43	E	North Atlantic
Kellegrew, Thomas	*John Drayton*	4/21/43	E	Indian Ocean/Red Sea
Stadstad, Jack N.	*John Drayton*	4/21/43	E	Indian Ocean/Red Sea
Connors, Aubrey G.	*Robert Gray*	4/21/43	D	North Atlantic
Siviglia, Stephen	*Robert Gray*	4/23/43	E	North Atlantic
Talbot, John O.	*John Morgan*	6/1/43	E	U.S. East Coast
Wilkinson, Benjamin H.	*John Morgan*	6/1/43	D	U.S. East Coast
Bogardus, Henry J., Jr.	*William King*	6/6/43	E	Indian Ocean/Red Sea
Carter, John M.	*Esso Gettysburg*	6/10/43	E	U.S. East Coast
Landron, Joseph J., Jr.	*Esso Gettysburg*	6/10/43	E	U.S. East Coast
Miller, Alphonse I.	*Esso Gettysburg*	6/10/43	D	U.S. East Coast
Green, William H., Jr.	*Samuel Heintzelman*	7/1/43	E	Indian Ocean/Red Sea
Stewart, John N.	*Samuel Heintzelman*	7/1/43	D	Indian Ocean/Red Sea
Watson, John H.	*Peter Minuit*	7/8/43	D	Bermuda
McCall, George D.	*Robert Bacon*	7/13/43	D	Indian Ocean/Red Sea
Lyman, William L., Jr.	*Timothy Pickering*	7/14/43	D	Mediterranean/Black Sea
Marks, Warren P.	*Timothy Pickering*	7/14/43	E	Mediterranean/Black Sea

Name of Cadet	Name of Ship	Date	Deck/ Engine	Location
McLaughlin, Lawrence D.	*Timothy Pickering*	7/14/43	E	Mediterranean/Black Sea
McCann, William E.	*Thomas Paine*	8/4/43	E	Unknown
Derick, Robert J.	*J. Pinckney Henderson*	8/19/43	E	North Atlantic
Prickett, Roscoe J., Jr.	*J. Pinckney Henderson*	8/19/43	D	North Atlantic
Pancratz, George E.	*Bushrod Washington*	9/14/43	D	Mediterranean/Black Sea
Sempell, William S.	*Bushrod Washington*	9/14/43	E	Mediterranean/Black Sea
Atchison, Alan A., Jr.	*Theodore Dwight Weld*	9/20/43	D	North Atlantic
Netcott, Roland E.	LOST IN TRAINING	9/26/43		
Biemel, Peter J.	*Salmon P. Chase*	11/1/43	E	Mediterranean/Black Sea
Brodie, Marvin W.	*John Harvey*	12/2/43	E	Mediterranean/Black Sea
Glauche, Richard B.	*John Harvey*	12/2/43	D	Mediterranean/Black Sea
Justis, Alvin H., Jr.	*John Harvey*	12/2/43	E	Mediterranean/Black Sea
Hope, James A.	*John L. Motley*	12/2/43	D	Mediterranean/Black Sea
Howard, Edward D.	*John L. Motley*	12/2/43	D	Mediterranean/Black Sea
Litton, Jay F.	*John L. Motley*	12/2/43	E	Mediterranean/Black Sea
Tone, Francis B.	*Samuel J. Tilden*	12/2/43	E	Mediterranean/Black Sea
Driscoll, Joseph L.	*Robert Erskine*	1/6/44	D	Mediterranean/Black Sea
Nolan, Ronald C.	*Wildwood*	1/10/44	D	Atlantic
Rosenbloom, J. R.	*Charles Henderson*	1/19/44	D	U.S. East Coast
Zapletal, Edwin S.	*Paul Hamilton*	4/20/44	D	Mediterranean/Black Sea
Schultz, Bernard	*Cape Ugat*	7/18/44	D	Unknown
Lawrence, Leroy P.	*Jacksonville*	8/30/44	D	Northeast Atlantic
Gerstacker, Charles F.	LOST IN TRAINING	10/4/44		
Carey, Thomas B., Jr.	LOST IN TRAINING	11/2/44		
Kennedy, Donald A.	*Lee S. Overman*	12/12/44	E	North Atlantic
Kannitzer, Donald J.	*John Burke*	12/28/44	D	Philippines
Du Chene, Roy, Jr.	LOST IN TRAINING	1/30/45		
Harris, Alexander W.	*Hobbs Victory*	4/6/45	D	Okinawa
Artist, John W.	*Saint Mihiel*	4/9/45	D	North Atlantic
Polcari, Dante L.	*Saint Mihiel*	4/9/45	D	North Atlantic

A total of 142 cadets were killed.

Name	Navy/Merchant Marine	Ship	Date	Deck/ Engine
Victorino, Richard L.	Navy	Unknown		D
Berwick, Thorndike J.		Unknown	1941	E
Farr, William Maxwell		Unknown	1941	D
Wilkie, Richard Bryce	Navy	Unknown	6/21/41	D
Bialek, Carl	Navy		11/2/41	E
Walter, Robert S., Jr.	Merchant Marine	*General Richard Arnold* (USAT)	1/8/42	D
Jones, Oliver Meeker	Merchant Marine	*Independence Hall*	3/7/42	D
Blair, Charles Emil	Merchant Marine	*William C. McTarnahan*	5/16/42	D

Name	Navy/Merchant Marine	Ship	Date	Deck/Engine
Maciorowski, Ceslaus Adam	Merchant Marine	*Wichita*	9/19/42	E
Herndon, James Dale	Merchant Marine	*LaSalle*	11/7/42	E
Scharpf, Theodore	Merchant Marine	*Charles C. Pinckney*	11/23/42	E
Doell, Charles Henry	Merchant Marine	*Caddo*	11/23/42	D
Harris, Henry Edward, Jr.	Merchant Marine	*James McKay*	12/7/42	E
Baumann, Frederick William	Merchant Marine	*Louise Lykes*	1/9/43	E
Wolfe, Harry Arthur Jr.	Merchant Marine	*Louise Lykes*	1/9/43	D
Edwards, David Lincoln	Merchant Marine	*Jonathan Sturges*	2/23/43	D
Rivera, Rafael Ramirez	Merchant Marine	*William C. Gorgas*	3/10/43	D
Kernan, Le Roy William	Merchant Marine	*Harry Luckenbach*	3/17/43	D
Alther, George Walter, Jr.	Merchant Marine	*Timothy Pickering*	7/14/43	D
McNabb, Henry Duke	Navy	Unkown	9/11/43	D
Allen, Drew	Merchant Marine	Unkown	9/19/43	E
Waters, Kenneth Alvah	Merchant Marine	SS *Exhibitor*	9/21/43	D
Yewell, Fulton Edison, Jr.	Merchant Marine	*John L. Motley*	12/2/43	D
Greene, Paul	Merchant Marine	Unknown–American President Lines	12/5/43	E
Trzebuchowski, Thaddeus T.	Merchant Marine	*Suffolk*	12/11/43	D
Allen, Robert Walker	Navy	Unknown	1/11/44	E
Zech, Walter William	Merchant Marine	China National Aviation Corporation	3/7/44	D
Tynan, Donald Joseph	Merchant Marine	*Pan Pennsylvania*	4/16/44	E
Secunda, William John	Merchant Marine	*John Straub*	4/19/44	E
Whitehead, Frederick D., Jr.	Navy	Unknown	4/20/44	E
Roach, Floyd Walter	Merchant Marine	*Jean Nicolet*	7/2/44	E
Rutan, George Morris	Merchant Marine	*Jean Nicolet*	7/2/44	D
Kannberg, Walter Frederick	Merchant Marine	*Quinault Victory*	7/17/44	E
Lyons, Gordon Wallace	Merchant Marine	*John Barry*	8/28/44	D
Wentworth, Robie Knowles	Merchant Marine	*Jacksonville*	8/30/44	E
Lee, Walter Hay	Merchant Marine	*American Leader*	9/18/44	D
Simmons, Robert C.	Navy	849 Bomber Squadron	9/27/44	E
Lemerise, Edward	Navy	Unknown	10/10/44	E
Grant, Harry	Merchant Marine	*Francis G. Newlands*	10/31/44	D
O'Neill, William John, Jr.	Navy	Unknown	11/1/44	E
Strom, Lloyd Stanley	Navy	Unknown	11/10/44	E
Hendy, James Morley	Merchant Marine	*Gilbert Stuart*	12/44	D
Hogue, Charles Wayman	Navy	Unknown	12/11/44	E
Lawrence, Joseph R., Jr.	Navy	Unknown	12/12/44	D
Anido, Alfredo Ignatius	Navy	Unknown	12/18/44	E
Stauffacher, Edwin Ray, Jr.	Merchant Marine	*John Clayton*	1/1/45	D

Name	Navy/Merchant Marine	Ship	Date	Deck/ Engine
Chue, Peter Chung Ying	Merchant Marine	*Lewis L. Dyche*	1/4/45	E
Forsyth, Arthur Churchill	Merchant Marine	*Zebulon Pike*	1/15/45	D
Sherman, Edward Stanley	Merchant Marine	*Zebulon Pike*	1/15/45	D
Graziano, Antonio Vito	Navy	Unknown	2/1/45	E
Dengler, Clarence Bert, Jr.	Merchant Marine	*Spring Hill*	2/5/45	
Stevens, Niles Kendall	Merchant Marine	SS *George H. William*	2/23/45	D
Schaffer, Isidore	Merchant Marine	*Thomas Donaldson*	3/20/45	E
Herstam, Gordon Alan	Navy	USS *Goodhue*	4/2/45	D
Treseder, Keith William	Merchant Marine	*Logan Victory*	4/6/45	D
Anderson, Richard Pershing	Navy	USS *Bush*	4/6/45	E
Maloney, James LeRoy	Merchant Marine	*Saint Mihiel*	4/9/45	E
Grieshaber, George P.	Navy	USS *Kidd*	4/11/45	E
Anderson, Herbert Evald	Merchant Marine	*Cyrus McCormick*	4/18/45	E
Teague, Semon Leroy	Navy	USS *Terror*	5/1/45	E
Dell'Aquila, Alfredo	Navy	USS *Jamestown*	5/5/45	E
Bartlett, Howard Spencer	Navy	USS *Bunker Hill*	5/11/45	D
Jones, Thomas George	Merchant Marine	*William B. Allison*	5/24/45	E
Nemitz, Ralph Henry	Merchant Marine	USMS *Staff*	6/10/45	
Callesen, Floyd Kenneth	Navy	USS *Kalk*	6/13/45	E
Heidt, Theodore Albert	Merchant Marine	SS *Link Splice*	11/4/45	D
Lorenz, Robert	Navy	Unknown	1/4/46	D
Kostal, Michael Frank, Jr.	Navy	Unknown	1/17/46	E

A total of 68 graduates were killed.

APPENDIX G

Number of Graduates by Year and by Nation, State, and Territory (1938–2006)

Information compiled and provided by the Registrar's Office, USMMA.

Number of Graduates by Year, 1938–2006

Year	No. of Graduates	Year	No. of Graduates	Year	No. of Graduates
1938	10	1963	191	1988	217
1939	136	1964	191	1989	172
1940	184	1965	219	1990	199
1941	119	1966	196	1991	169
1942	378	1967	200	1992	159
1943	1,164	1968	178	1993	202
1944	3,857	1969	213	1994	220
1945	1,496	1970	181	1995	219
1946	778	1971	212	1996	190
1947	471	1972	212	1997	218
1948	298	1973	196	1998	182
1949	216	1974	182	1999	180
1950	352	1975	202	2000	217
1951	306	1976	230	2001	199
1952	225	1977	226	2002	176
1953	271	1978	244	2003	198
1954	159	1979	253	2004	180
1955	163	1980	244	2005	218
1956	163	1981	269	2006	202
1957	231	1982	256		
1958	163	1983	237	Total	21,099
1959	225	1984	236		
1960	160	1985	231		
1961	206	1986	240		
1962	191	1987	219		

Number of Graduates by Nation, State, and Territory, 1938–2006

Location	No. of Graduates	Location	No. of Graduates
Alabama	131	South Carolina	121
Alaska	29	South Dakota	35
Arizona	100	Tennessee	104
Arkansas	56	Texas	559
California	1,999	Utah	51
Colorado	201	Vermont	60
Connecticut	653	Virginia	574
Delaware	100	Washington	394
District of Columbia	154	West Virginia	45
Florida	628	Wisconsin	293
Georgia	229	Wyoming	17
Hawaii	103		
Idaho	66	Bermuda	1
Illinois	675	Brazil	1
Indiana	193	Canada	4
Iowa	128	Chile	2
Kansas	110	Colombia	4
Kentucky	77	Costa Rica	4
Louisiana	270	Cuba	1
Maine	145	Ecuador	2
Maryland	552	El Salvador	1
Massachusetts	973	England	2
Michigan	467	Greece	1
Minnesota	264	Guam	2
Mississippi	121	Haiti	1
Missouri	278	Honduras	1
Montana	70	Jamaica	2
Nebraska	101	Mexico	2
Nevada	50	Palau	2
New Hampshire	103	Panama (including Canal Zone)	132
New Jersey	1,591	Paraguay	1
New Mexico	59	Peru	2
New York	4,809	Philippines	93
North Carolina	244	Puerto Rico	25
North Dakota	31	Russia	7
Ohio	727	Trinidad	1
Oklahoma	91	Virgin Islands	5
Oregon	163		
Pennsylvania	1,624	Total	21,099
Rhode Island	152		

APPENDIX H

Names of Academy Buildings and Locations

Barney Square   The Academy's parade deck, named for Joshua Barney, a U.S. Navy officer in the Revolutionary War, and a merchant ship captain by age fifteen.

Barry Hall   Barracks named in honor of Commodore John Barry, first commodore of the U.S. Navy, and former merchant ship master.

Bland Library   Named in honor of Congressman Schuyler Otis Bland (D), representative from Virginia and member of the House Merchant Marine and Fisheries Committee from 1922 until 1950.

Bowditch Hall   Named for American Nathaniel Bowditch (1773–1838), sailor, mathematician, extraordinary navigator, and author of the classic *Practical Navigator* (first edition 1801). Home to the Department of Marine Transportation and Ackerman Auditorium.

Brooks Field House and Stadium   Named in honor of John "Jack" Brooks '44, an engineer, lawyer, real estate developer, and recipient of the Alumni Association's Distinguished Service Award in 1999.

Cleveland Hall   Barracks named after Captain Richard J. Cleveland (1773–1860), astute trader and skilled seaman.

Crowninshield Pier   Houses launches, monomoys, and sailboats used for instruction. Named for Captain Jacob Crowninshield (1770–1808).

Delano Hall   Dining hall named for maritime author and seafarer Captain Amasa Delano (1763–1823), an ancestor of Sara Delano, mother of President Franklin Delano Roosevelt.

Eldridge Pool   A recreational and instructional pool named for Captain Asa Eldridge, a master of clipper ships in the midnineteenth century.

Fitch Building   Headquarters of the Alumni Association (in the Babson Center), this building was named after John Fitch (1732–1798), a self-educated inventor who made significant advancements in the development of steamboats.

Fulton Hall   Named for inventor Robert Fulton (1765–1815), inventor of the first practical steamboat, the *Clermont*. Home to the Department of Engineering and the Department of Mathematics and Science.

Furuseth Hall   Administration building and home to the Department of Naval Science, named in honor of Andrew Furuseth, a Norwegian-born sailor who was

460

instrumental in establishing the Sailor's Union of the Pacific, and was a strong advocate to Congress for seamen's rights.

Gibbs Hall   Named for William F. and Frederick Gibbs, founders of the naval architecture firm Gibbs & Cox. An addition to Fulton Hall, the building houses laboratories and classrooms.

Hague Basin   The area between Mallory and Crowninshield piers, Hague Basin is named for Robert T. Hague, the late director of Standard Oil Company, and a member of the Maritime Commission.

Jones Hall   Barracks named for Commodore John Paul Jones, father of the American Navy and merchant ship master.

Land Hall   Student center named in honor of Admiral Emory S. Land, USN, chairman of the Maritime Commission and the War Shipping Administration, and the "czar" of the merchant marine during World War II.

Mallory Pier   Pier used to tie up the *Kings Pointer* and lifeboat davits used for nautical science instruction.

Melville Hall   Officer's Club, named for Herman Melville (1819–1891), author of *Moby-Dick*.

Murphy Hall   Barracks named for shipmaster James Murphy (1850–1912), who made the voyage from San Francisco to Le Havre in 111 days on the four-masted bark *Shenandoah*.

O'Hara Hall   Named in honor of cadet-midshipman Edwin J. O'Hara, recipient of the Distinguished Service Medal, who was killed at his battle station on September 27, 1942, aboard the Liberty Ship SS *Stephen Hopkins* in WWII. The building houses the Department of Physical Education and Athletics.

Palmer Hall   Barracks named for famed mariner Nathaniel Palmer (1799–1877), discoverer of Antarctica, yachtsman, and ship designer.

Patten Clinic   Medical and dental facilities, named for Mary Patten, who at age nineteen commanded and navigated the clipper ship *Neptune's Car* around Cape Horn to San Francisco in 1856 when her husband (captain of the ship) took ill and the mate was placed in irons for incompetence.

Prosser Building   Named for Captain Joe Prosser, first sailing master and director of Waterfront Activities.

Rogers Hall   Barracks named for Captain Moses Rogers (1799–1821), who commanded the SS *Savannah* on the first transatlantic voyage (1819) by a ship alternating between steam and sail.

Roosevelt Field   Athletic field named for Presidents Theodore and Franklin Delano Roosevelt, both strong supporters of a vital U.S. merchant marine.

Samuels Hall   Named in honor of Samuel Samuels, greatest of the American transatlantic packet commanders. Samuels is best known for his service as master of the *Dreadnought*; in 1859, this ship under Samuels recorded the fastest transatlantic sailing passage ever recorded, making the trip from New York to Liverpool in thirteen days and eight hours. The building houses the Computer Aided Operational Research Facility, the Department of Humanities, and Continuing Education.

Tomb Field   Athletic field named in honor of Captain James Harvey Tomb, USN, first superintendent of the Academy. Location of regimental reviews.

Vickery Gate   Named for Vice Admiral Howard Vickery, USN, deputy administrator for ship construction and vice chairman of the U.S. Maritime Commission in World War II. The Vickery Gate Building was recently modernized to become a new admissions center, thanks to a grant from the Dean and Barbara White Family Foundation.

Wiley Hall   Formerly the home of Walter P. Chrysler, this administration building now bears the name of Admiral Henry A. Wiley, USN, a member of the Maritime Commission and the commissioner in charge of personnel training for the Maritime Commission when the Cadet Corps was established.

Yocum Sailing Center   Sailing, power squadron, crew, and boat servicing center named in honor of alumnus James H. Yokum, '47, and his family.

The Liberty Ship. The *John W. Brown* in convoy off the East Coast, April 1944. (From the original by John Stobart, oil on canvas: 24" × 38".) In the painting, the destroyer has raised the signal flags SC, meaning "sub sighted", and all vessels have started making defensive smoke.

The U.S. Merchant Marine Academy band marches in the rain in the parade at the January 20, 2001, inauguration of President George W. Bush.

First Officer Ben Lyons (USMMA class of 2000) in the charthouse with Captain Christopher Rynd, master of the new RMS *Queen Mary 2*. Lyons is believed to be the first American officer hired by the Cunard Line.

Astronaut Mark Edward Kelly graduated with the highest honors from the U.S. Merchant Marine Acadmemy in 1986, and had a long distinguished career as a navy test pilot. He went into space as the pilot for STS-108 *Endeavour* in 2001 and returned to space as the pilot of STS-121 *Discovery* in 2006.

APPENDIX I

Academy Training Ships

TV *Robert Waterman*, 1941

Purchased by the Maritime Commission in 1941 for the Pass Christian school. A 120-foot houseboat yacht, originally called *North Star*

TV *William Webb*, 1941

Donated to Academy in 1941 as the *Nenemoosh*, and rechristened in 1942. A 125-foot diesel-powered yacht

TV *Robert Forbes*, 1941

Donated to the Academy in 1941 as the *Sealove*. A 65-foot gasoline-driven auxiliary schooner

TV *Felix Reisenberg*, 1942

Given to the Academy in 1942 as the *Rhine*. A diesel auxiliary schooner

TV *Emery Rice*, 1942

A 200-foot bark-rigged auxiliary iron steamer. Built for the Navy in 1876, originally called *Ranger*. In 1909, loaned to the Massachusetts Nautical School, where she was rechristened the *Nantucket* in 1918. Rescued for Kings Point and renamed the *Emery Rice* by direction of R. R. McNulty, one of her alumni. Designated a Museum Ship in 1944 after sustaining serious damage in the hurricane of September 1944

TV *McAllister*, 1944

Acquired by the Academy from the Coast Guard in 1944 as the *Walter Q. Gresham*. A 205-foot cutter built in the late 1890s to serve as a federal patrol boat on the Great Lakes

TV *Thomas H. Sumner*, 1944

A 82-foot former fishing purse seiner built in 1940. Acquired from the navy as the *Santa Rosa*

TV *Kings Pointer*, 1946

Formerly *Devosa*, a 427-foot twin-funneled turboelectric Navy attack cargo ship. Rechristened the *Kings Pointer* on August 1, 1946, and completed one international training cruise to Caribbean ports and Rio de Janeiro. Retired February 21, 1947

TV *Vema*, 1947

Three-masted schooner yacht, previously known as *Hussar*. Kept at the Academy until 1950

TV *Ensign Herstam*, TV *Ensign Strom*, and TV *Ensign Whitehead*, 1946

Acquired by the Cadet Corps in November 1946 for use as naval science training vessels. Named in honor of the first three Kings Point graduates killed in action

TV *Kings Pointer*, 1954

Lent to the Academy under the name *Wanderer* by the Sperry Corporation in 1954. Sperry then donated the 111-foot electronics research vessel in 1962 and it was renamed as the second TV *Kings Pointer*

TV *Kings Pointer*, 1972

Christened the *Undaunted*, a tugboat built in 1943 and turned over from the navy to Kings Point in 1972 for training. In 1983, it was certified as a training vessel and used to supplement the Academy's sea training program

TV *Mazurka*, 1981

A 116-foot ketch-rigged, diesel-propelled motor sailer. Acquired in 1981 as a training vessel for the 4th class

TV *Kings Pointer*, 1992

Originally commissioned as the USNS *Contender*, this 224-foot vessel was transferred to Kings Point in October 1992, following a distinguished eight-year career with the navy's Military Sealift Command engaged in ocean surveillance for Soviet submarines

APPENDIX J

Oral Histories

The authors would like to thank the following people for speaking with us–in some cases, more than once–about their experiences at Kings Point and in the merchant marine. Their voices lend legitimacy and life to this manuscript, and we appreciate their contributions.

Name	Date(s) Interviewed
Allee, Captain Robert G., '68	April 27, 2004
Athens, Captain Arthur J.	December 17, 2002
Baker, Joseph, '47	October 13, 2004
Baran, Joseph, '04	February 22, 2003
Beim, Dr. Howard	April 26, 2004
Bejarano, Luis E.	October 10, 2002
Bennett, John Logan, '03	July 11, 2002; October 22, 2003
Brickman, Dr. Jane	December 4, 2002
Brogan, Patrick M., Esq., '79	March 10, 2004
Calhoon, Jesse	August 19, 2004
Carmel, Captain Steven, '79	March 11, 2004
Cook, Captain Fred	February 23, 2003
Cushing, Dr. Charles, '56	August 25, 2004
Davies, Archibald	October 25, 2004
DeGhetto, Kenneth, '43	February 12, 2004
Donovan, Dr. Arthur	February 25, 2003
Dutton, Thomas	February 17, 2003
Eisenberg, Ray	November 5, 2002
Femenia, Jose	December 4, 2002
Flick, Kent, '75	February 17, 2003
Force, Captain Kenneth R.	December 18, 2002
Gaebelein, Thad	October 12, 2004
Galante, Caterina	July 30, 2004
Gibson, Judith Chadwick	August 7, 2003
Giddings, Thomas	October 25, 2004
Griffin, Vance, '84	March 9, 2004
Gross, Maurice, '42	September 19, 2003

Name	Date(s) Interviewed
Hall, Patrick C., '71	March 10, 2004
Hard, Captain Douglas M., '62	October 30, 2003
Harsche, Edward, '62	August 31, 2004
Hazlett, John, '96	March 9, 2004
Helmick, Dr. Jon S.	October 12, 2004
Herberger, Vice Admiral Albert J., '55	October 3, 2003
Hirschkowitz, Moses	November 6, 2002
Hodgson, Commander Thomas	January 11, 2005
Hubert, Charles	December 17, 2002
Jeffries, Jena, '04	May 14, 2004
Jochmans, Captain John J., '66	January 1, 2004
Kallgren, Andrew, '89	March 10, 2004
King, Rear Admiral Thomas A., '42	May 23, 2003
Kingsley, Theodore, '45	April 18, 2003
Krinsky, Rear Admiral Paul L., '50	January 8, 2003
Leback, Captain Warren, '44	February 12, 2004
Lubow, Susan Petersen	January 13, 2004
Lumbard, Eliot H., '45	September 28, 2005
Matteson, Rear Admiral Thomas T.	July 16, 2003
Mazek, Dr. Warren F.	October 4, 2003; April 27, 2004
McCormick, Eugene, Jr., '64	January 26, 2004
McCready, Rear Admiral Lauren S.	November 15, 2002
McLean, Walter, '47	July 26, 2004
McMahon, Rear Admiral Christopher	March 25, 2003
McNeal, David, '04	May 14, 2004
McWilliams, Captain Mary Bachand	July 8, 2004
Meurn, Captain Robert, '58	December 18, 2002
Meyers, Audrey, '04	May 14, 2004
Moore, Michael, '04	May 14, 2004
Mowrey, Jessica, '97	February 26, 2004
Muller, Gerhardt	October 3, 2003
Mund, Commander David	May 13, 2004
Nottingham, Milton, Jr., '43	October 2, 2003
O'Leary, Richard	April 3, 2003
O'Neil, David A., '61	April 11, 2003
Palmer, Dr. Janet	December 18, 2002
Patterson, Rear Admiral Thomas, '44	August 17, 2004
Rackett, Peter, '61	January 13, 2004; June 1, 2004
Rehm, Gerald, '48	August 31, 2004
Renick, Captain Charles M., '47	November 5, 2002

Name	Date(s) Interviewed
Safarik, Captain Robert L., '61	October 24, 2002
Sandberg, Captain George	December 18, 2002; January 27, 2004
Schubert, Captain William, '74	October 2, 2003
Scroggins, Joe, Jr., '63	July 16, 2003
Segert, Rebecca, '04	May 14, 2004
Seiberlich, Rear Admiral Carl J., '43	October 3, 2003; August 13, 2004
Sherman, Fred, '55	January 23, 2004
Shirley, James T., Jr., Esq., '65	October 31, 2003
Skinner, Captain James M.	November 11, 2003
Skrocki, Martin	June 12, 2003
Stewart, Vice Admiral Joseph	October 3, 2002; June 8, 2004
Stewart, Dr. Richard D., '73	October 22, 2004
Thorpe, Sharon, '97	March 9, 2004
Travis, Harrison	November 20, 2002
Tublin, Melvin, Esq., '49	August 25, 2004
Van Oss, Captain David, '68	May 13, 2004
Wallischek, Commander Eric, '83	September 19, 2003
Weber, Dr. Charles	April 27, 2004
Wichert, William	December 17, 2002
Yates, Captain Frances, '78	November 11, 2003

APPENDIX K

Alumni Business Leadership Rankings

1996 Ranking of American Business Leadership

Based on Standard and Poor's "Executive/College Survey" and studies conducted by Virginia Military Institute's Office of Institutional Research in 1985, 1990, and 1996 (no other years were studied).

		Prior Ranking	
		1990	1985
1.	Yale	1	1
2.	Princeton	3	2
3.	Dartmouth	4	4
4.	Harvard	5	3
5.	Williams	6	5
6.	MIT	8	7
7.	Washington & Lee	7	8
8.	Cornell	9	10
9.	University of Pennsylvania	11	12
10.	Davidson	16	22
11.	Stevens Institute of Technology	14	20
12.	Colgate	19	29
13.	Lafayette	27	31
14.	Bowdoin	17	21
15.	Virginia Military Institute	20	23
16.	Lehigh	25	26
17.	Webb Institute	15	19
18.	U.S. Merchant Marine Academy	10	16
19.	Columbia	12	11
20.	Rensselaer Polytechnic Institute	31	38
21.	Brown University	26	27
22.	Illinois Institute of Technology	13	15
23.	Amherst	22	6
24.	North Carolina State University	–	41
25.	New York University	18	18

APPENDIX L

List of Contributors to the American Maritime History Project for the History of the U.S. Merchant Marine Academy

$1,000 and Above

James H. Ackerman and Evalyn M. Bauer Foundation
William P. Bowes
Kenneth A. DeGhetto
John R. Graham
Eugene W. and Gloria Landy Family Foundation
Harry W. Marshall
Daniel E. Meehan
Ellsworth L. Peterson
Gerald S. Rehm
Rear Admiral Carl J. Seiberlich
Superintendent's Campaign for Excellence (Baker Media Endowment)
USMMA Alumni Association, Port of New York Chapter
Dean and Barbara White Family Foundation
James H. Yocum

Up to $1,000

Burnie Acuff
George D. Benjamin
George J. Billy
Michael E. Blecher
Eugene C. Bonacci
Chris and Bruce Bowen, President, USMMA Parents' Organization
Lawrence J. Bowles, Esq.

William J. Bradford Jr.
Jane and John Brickman
Robert G. Bruechert
John A. C. Cartner
Brian E. Cassidy
Dean R. Colver
Dr. B. G. Davis
David R. Dellwo
Edward M. Donaher
Arthur L. Donovan
Fred L. Ebers
Ralph W. Emch
Joseph M. Farrell
Anthony J. Fiorelli Jr.
Hamilton C. Fish Jr.
Mason L. Flint
James J. Gallagher
Michael F. Gallagher
Thomas W. Harrelson
Victor W. Henningsen Jr.
George C. Hogan
Gordon James III
Captain John J. Jochmans
Richard M. Kanaszyc
Robert H. Kiefer
Stephen Kramer
Paul L. Krinsky
J. Smith Lanier II
Captain Warren G. Leback
Robert Lindmark
Joseph W. Liotta

Eugene F. McCormick
Captain Christopher J. McMahon
Mark M. Miller
Milton G. Nottingham Jr.
Mukund Patel
Robert Pollock
Donald F. Ponischil
Donald T. Quinn
Peter J. Rackett
John Francis Ring
C. L. Roberts
Richard Roche
George J. Ryan
Robert H. Scarborough
Robert F. Shelby
Fred S. Sherman
James T. Shirley Jr.
Captain James M. Skinner
Robert W. Solinski
Vice Admiral Joseph D. Stewart
Phillip Strauss
Theodore H. Teplow

Phillip M. Torf
Melvin J. Tublin, Esq.
USMMA Alumni Association, Jacksonville Chapter
USMMA Alumni Association, Long Beach Chapter
USMMA Alumni Association, Long Island Chapter
USMMA Alumni Association, Northern New Jersey Chapter
USMMA Alumni Association, San Francisco Chapter
USMMA Alumni Association, South Central Pennsylvania Chapter
Gerard Voege
Brandt E. Wagner
Francis M. Wagner
Commander Eric York Wallischek
Howard T. Whipple
George C. Wortley
Donald R. Yearwood

Notes

Research Sources
In addition to the oral histories of Academy and industry figures listed in Appendix I and the numerous published volumes included in the bibliography, this history relies on primary source research undertaken at the Academy, the National Archives, and private libraries. The following is a partial list of resources consulted during the writing of this volume.

U.S. Merchant Marine Academy Sources
Academy Archives, Bland Library

Records of the Congressional Board of Visitors and Academic Advisory Board
    Reports on the Academy
    Personal collections
    Student publications
    Polaris
    Hear This
    Alumni publications
    Kings Pointer

USMMA Public Information Office
    Academy press releases and official records

Collection of Martin Skrocki, including correspondence, news articles, and documents

American Merchant Marine Museum

Collection of Captain Charles Renick, including "after action" reports

Outside Sources
National Archives I, Washington, D.C.

National Archives II, College Park, Maryland

Records of the Maritime Commission

War Shipping Administration records, minutes of meetings

Maritime Administration records up to 1950
Maritime Administration archives

Correspondence files, post-1950
Library of Congress
Admiral Land papers
Franklin D. Roosevelt Presidential Library

Roosevelt's records and correspondence
Kennedy Library

Joseph Kennedy papers

Peabody Essex Museum, Salem, Massachusetts

Maine Maritime Academy Archives and Library

1. A Norfolk Interlude: Serving the Maritime Industry: 2003

1. American Maritime Officers, "Maersk Line replacing four MSP ships," American Maritime Officer Web site, www.amo-union.org/Newspaper/Morgue/10-2002/Sections/News/maersk.htm. See also American Maritime Officers, "Maersk begins re-flagging of four containerships for MSP," www.amo-union.org/Newspaper/Morgue/11-2002/Sections/News/maersk.htm.

   The Maritime Security Act of 2003 authorizes the creation of a new Maritime Security Program for FY 2006 through FY 2015, which will ensure operational subsidies to an additional sixty U.S. flag ships in foreign commerce.

2. David Bell, interview by the authors, January 8, 2004.
3. "Halifax Hash," a Web page on the Maersk *Carolina* disaster posted by the law offices of Countryman and McDaniel, www.cargolaw.com/2003nightmare_halifax_hash.html (accessed 5/25/04).
4. Bell, interview.
5. John Logan Bennett, interview by the authors, October 22, 2003.
6. Jessica Mowrey, interview by the authors, February 26, 2004.
7. Andrew Kallgren, interview by the authors, March 10, 2004.
8. Ibid.
9. Christopher McMahon was subsequently promoted to rear admiral and served as transportation attaché in Iraq after the second Gulf War. He is now deputy superintendent of Kings Point.
10. Sharon Thorpe McIlnay, interview by the authors, March 9, 2004.
11. Ibid.
12. Patrick Brogan, interview by the authors, March 10, 2004.
13. Vance Griffin, interview by the authors, March 9, 2004.
14. Patrick Hall, interview by the authors, March 10, 2004.
15. Ibid.

16. U.S. Maritime Administration, "U.S. Flag Merchant Fleet, 2003–1946," U.S. Maritime Administration Web site, www.marad.gov/Marad_Statistics/US-FLAG-HISTORY.pdf.

17. U.S. Maritime Administration, "U.S. Waterborne Foreign Trade, Containerized Cargo," U.S. Maritime Administration Web site, www.marad.gov/Marad_Statistics/Container-03.htm.

2. Planting the Seeds

1. Andrew Gibson and Arthur Donovan, *The Abandoned Ocean: A History of United States Maritime Policy* (Columbia: University of South Carolina Press, 2000), 12.

2. Winthrop Marvin, *The American Merchant Marine: Its History and Romance from 1620 to 1902* (New York: Charles Scribner's Sons, 1902), 8.

3. Ibid., 12–13.

4. Stanley Elkins and Eric McKitrick, *The Age of Federalism: The Early American Republic, 1788–1800* (New York: Oxford University Press, 1993), 643–647.

5. Gibson and Donovan, *The Abandoned Ocean*, 36. As the authors point out, "Free trade and sailors' rights" became a slogan for those in favor of the war.

6. Marvin, *The American Merchant Marine*, 128.

7. Gibson and Donovan, *The Abandoned Ocean*, 43.

8. Marvin, *The American Merchant Marine*, 339.

9. Gibson and Donovan, *The Abandoned Ocean*, 69. By the end of the war, the U.S. offshore fleet was only 1,387,756 tons.

10. Marvin, *The American Merchant Marine*, 343.

11. Gibson and Donovan, *The Abandoned Ocean*, 73.

12. 1874 Act of Congress; our thanks to George Searle for bringing this to our attention.

13. Grover Cleveland's *Second Annual Message*, presented in written form to Congress, December 3, 1894.

14. Theodore Roosevelt, *The Naval War of 1812* (New York: Modern Library, 1999). First published 1882. It's worth noting Roosevelt's contention that the U.S. success in this war was due in large part to the effectiveness of merchant sailors, who had been forced to defend themselves in the decade leading up to the war of 1812.

15. Quoted in Alex Roland's chapter in the *American Maritime History Project*, draft no. 1, October 10, 2002, 15.

16. See Edward J. Renehan Jr., "TR and the Navy," Theodore Roosevelt Association, www.theodoreroosevelt.org/life/TrandNavy.htm.

17. Theodore Roosevelt, "Fifth Annual Address to Congress," December 5, 1905, The American Presidency Project Web site, www.presidency.ucsb.edu.

18. Gibson and Donovan, *The Abandoned Ocean*, 87.

19. Wallace West, *Down to the Sea in Ships: The Story of the U.S. Merchant Marine* (New York: Noble and Noble, 1947), 44.

20. Admiral Carl Seiberlich, interview by David Sicilia, February 2, 2000.

21. Gibson and Donovan, *The Abandoned Ocean*, 104.

22. Rene De La Pedraja, *A Historical Dictionary of the U.S. Merchant Marine and Shipping*

Industry (Westport, CT: Greenwood Press, 1994), 56. Pedraja points out that the court's reasoning was condescending in the extreme: "Seamen are treated by Congress . . . as deficient in that full and intelligent responsibility for their acts which is accredited to ordinary adults, and as needing the protection of the law in the same sense in which minors and wards are entitled to the protection of their parents and guardians."

23. Allan Nevins, *Sail On: The Story of the American Merchant Marine* (New York: United States Lines Company, 1946), 65.

24. Seiberlich, interview. See also Paul G. Halpern's *A Naval History of World War I* (Annapolis, MD: Naval Institute Press, 1994), 436.

25. De La Pedraja, *The Rise and Decline of U.S. Merchant Shipping in the Twentieth Century* (New York: Twayne Publishers, 1992), 58.

26. Gibson and Donovan, *The Abandoned Ocean*, 113.

27. De La Pedraja, *The Rise and Decline of U.S. Merchant Shipping*, 57.

28. Roland's chapter in the *American Maritime History Project*, draft no. 1, 24.

29. Robert Greenhalgh Albion and Jennie Barnes Pope, *Sea Lanes in Wartime: The American Experience, 1775–1945* (Hamden, CT: Archon Books, 1968), 332–333.

30. De La Pedraja, *The Rise and Decline of U.S. Merchant Shipping*, 59.

31. C. Bradford Mitchell, *We'll Deliver* (Kings Point, NY: USMMA Alumni Association, 1977), 12.

32. Albion and Pope, *Sea Lanes in Wartime*, 332–333.

33. De La Pedraja, *The Rise and Decline of U.S. Merchant Shipping*, 60.

34. John Gunther, *Taken at the Flood* (New York: Harper & Brothers, 1960), 128. See also Albert Lasker's *Oral History* from the Columbia University Oral History Research Office, www.columbia.edu/cu/lweb/indiv/oral/interviews.html.

35. Insert on training for a speech by Thomas Woodward, 1937, Records of the Maritime Commission, National Archives.

36. De La Pedraja, *A Historical Dictionary*, 285.

37. F. Shallus Kirk, memo to Philip King, November 7, 1938, Records of the Maritime Commission, National Archives.

38. For a comprehensive history of the American Line, see William Henry Flayhart III, *The American Line: Pioneers of American Travel* (New York: W. W. Norton, 2001).

39. Richard R. McNulty, "A Plan for Federal Merchant Marine Training," *Nautical Gazette*, May 24, 1930.

40. Ibid.

41. McNulty, "Trained Personnel for Subsidized Lines," *Nautical Gazette*, November 24, 1934.

42. Harrison Travis, interview by the authors, November 20, 2002.

43. Captain J. H. Tomb, "The Education of Merchant Marine Officers," U.S. Naval Institute Proceedings, v. 58, no. 9, 1932.

44. Tomb made his case in a 1935 statement to Congress.

45. Tomb, "The Education of Merchant Marine Officers."

46. Ibid.

47. One of the earliest mentions of Tomb's name in connection with the position of superintendent is a letter from William J. Rague of the American Scantic Line to a

member of the London Maritime Commission, National Archives, January 1938.

48. Roland's chapter in the *American Maritime History Project*, draft no. 1, 49.

49. Everett Northrup, "The Origins and Establishment of the U.S. Merchant Marine," master's thesis, Colgate University, June 1951, 17. See also President Franklin D. Roosevelt, "Message to Congress," March 4, 1935, www.usmm.org/.

50. Gibson and Donovan, *The Abandoned Ocean*, 135.

51. Mitchell, *We'll Deliver*, 18.

52. Merchant Marine Act of 1936, 36.

53. U.S. Congress, *To Develop a Merchant Marine*, National Archives.

54. Andrew Furuseth, "Schoolship Training Inadequate for Efficient Merchant Marine Personnel," *Nautical Gazette*, April 5, 1930.

55. In an article in *Business Week*, April 10, 1937, Kennedy called the Merchant Marine Act a "lousy law."

56. Kennedy's detractors pointed out that as an alleged former rumrunner during Prohibition, Kennedy had more than a passing acquaintance with ships.

57. Seiberlich, interview.

58. Emory Scott Land, *Winning the War with Ships* (New York: Robert M. McBride, 1958), 5. Roosevelt's and Land's association dates to World War I, when Land worked in the navy's Bureau of Construction and Roosevelt was assistant secretary of the navy.

59. Letter from Joseph P. Kennedy to President Roosevelt, February 21, 1938, National Archives.

60. Undated note from Schell to McNulty. "Wiley asked me to speak to Kennedy re Wiley taking over training, because he knew men and could do that, but knew no details of shipping generally," collection of Charles Renick.

3. Conceived in Force: 1937–1941

1. Randolph Branch to W. C. Peet, November 17, 1937, Records of the Maritime Commission, National Archives.

2. This chapter deals mainly with the training implications of the Merchant Marine Act of 1936, but it is worth noting that the act also spurred a major U.S. shipbuilding program in the late 1930s. These additional ships also spurred the need for more trained seamen to operate them.

3. Admiral Henry A. Wiley, memo to Joseph Kennedy, May 12, 1937, Records of the Maritime Commission, National Archives.

4. See, for example, McNulty to Milton Nottingham, April 4, 1974, Collection of Milton Nottingham.

5. "Minutes of the Maritime Commission," March 31, 1937, Records of the Maritime Commission, National Archives.

6. Two years later, a "Ninety-day wonder" wartime officer training school was established at Fort Trumbull, offering a three-month course to prepare qualified merchant seamen for deck or engineer license examinations. Several key figures in the Academy's history, including Lauren McCready and Philip C. Mahady, the port instructor for the New York district and later assistant superintendent at the Academy, were recruited away from Fort Trumbull.

7. "Minutes of the Maritime Commission," April 1, 1937, Records of the Maritime Commission, National Archives.

8. Kennedy to Honorable Royal S. Copeland, June 7, 1937, Records of the Maritime Commission, National Archives.

9. "Minutes of the Maritime Commission," July 21, 1937, Records of the Maritime Commission, National Archives.

10. This is reiterated in a memo of May 12, 1937.

11. Kennedy speech at the Coast Guard Academy graduation ceremony, September 20, 1937, Records of the Maritime Commission, National Archives. He also noted the close relationship between the two services and concluded by stating that he was sure he could count on the help of the Coast Guard.

12. It is interesting to note that as late as May 1938, Wiley was still asserting that the Coast Guard was the right agency to supervise training. Memo on training, May 18, 1938, Records of the Maritime Commission, National Archives.

13. "Minutes of the Maritime Commission," October 28, 1937, Records of the Maritime Commission, National Archives.

14. Kennedy, Wiley, Land, and Woodward voted in favor; only Commissioner Moran voted against this measure. Records of the Maritime Commission, October 28, 1937, National Archives.

15. *New York Times*, March 9, 1938, 45. Quoted in Everett Northrup, *The Origins and Establishment of the U.S. Merchant Marine*, master's thesis, Colgate University, June 1951, 32.

16. Northrup, *Origins and Establishment*, 32.

17. Ibid., 33.

18. Emory Land to C. F. May of the Masters, Mates, and Pilots of America, May 26, 1938, Records of the Maritime Commission, Division of Personnel Correspondence, National Archives.

19. Stanley Willner, one of the first Kings Point graduates affected by the U.S. entry into World War II, was also one of the first new appointments to the Cadet Corps, nominated by Senator Harry Byrd (D-Va.).

20. *Report to Congress on the Training of Merchant Marine Personnel*, 1939, 29, Library of Congress.

21. Northrup, *Origins and Establishment*, 36.

22. Richard McNulty, introduction to *Report and Recommendations on Ocean Shipping and Air Transportation Courses* (Georgetown School of Foreign Service, 1954).

23. Director of the Division of Maritime Personnel, memo to the Maritime Commission regarding extension courses for cadets, October 26, 1938, Records of the Maritime Commission, National Archives.

24. L. V. Kielhorn to Philip King, July 14, 1938, Records of the Maritime Commission, National Archives.

25. McNulty to Captain J. H. Tomb, Fort Schuyler, December 8, 1938, McNulty papers, folder 11, Bland Library Archives.

26. Telfair Knight, memo to Mr. Haag, October 24, 1938, Records of the Maritime Commission, National Archives.

27. McNulty to Tomb, December 8, 1938.

28. McNulty to Telfair Knight, forwarding a letter to McNulty from Yale Mechanical and Marine Engineering Professor H. L. Seward, December 14, 1938, McNulty papers, folder 11, Bland Library Archives.
29. *Report to Congress on Training of Merchant Marine Personnel*, 1939, 2, Library of Congress.
30. From an earlier report on merchant marine training, no author noted (though very likely by McNulty), December 1, 1937, Records of the Maritime Commission, National Archives.
31. McNulty to Nottingham, April 4, 1974.
32. Admiral Land to Brigadier General Clarence S. Ridley, governor of the Panama Canal, April 17, 1939, McNulty papers, folder 5, Bland Library Archives.
33. McNulty to Knight, April 25, 1939, McNulty papers, folder 5, Bland Library Archives.
34. McNulty to Knight, May 1, 1939, McNulty papers, folder 5, Bland Library Archives. McNulty's assertion that time would win over union members did seem to hold true; in a second series of inspection visits in 1940, he found tensions to have lessened considerably.
35. McNulty, letter at sea to Knight, May 5, 1939, McNulty papers, folder 5, Bland Library Archives.
36. McNulty to Knight, May 8, 1939, McNulty papers, folder 5, Bland Library Archives.
37. McNulty to Knight, May 19, 1939, McNulty papers, folder 5, Bland Library Archives.
38. C. Bradford Mitchell, *We'll Deliver* (Kings Point: USMMA Alumni Association, 1977), 25.
39. According to one well-placed observer, the decision to open district offices on all three coasts was driven as much by political considerations as by educational imperatives. Another observer points out, though, that the nation's still-inadequate transportation system necessitated at least three stations.
40. McNulty, memo to Commissioner Wiley, "Cadet Officer and Cadet Training Aboard American, British, and Japanese Vessels," June 7, 1939, McNulty papers, folder 4, Bland Library Archives.
41. After Pearl Harbor, the *America* was renamed the USS *West Point*, and was taken into the navy as a fast troop transport.
42. Special Reports on the SS *President Polk* and SS *President Hayes*, on visits by Mr. Corriveau and S. H. Elliot, Correspondence Files of the Division of Personnel, Maritime Commission, National Archives (no date).
43. Director, Division of Training, "Report on Cadet James J. Lippard Assault at Sea," May 14, 1941, Correspondence Files of the Division of Personnel, Maritime Commission, National Archives.
44. McNulty to American Export Lines, June 22, 1939, Correspondence Files of the Division of Personnel, Maritime Commission, National Archives.
45. Supervisor of Cadet Training, memo to Director of Cadet Training, October 25, 1939, Correspondence Files of the Division of Personnel, Maritime Commission, National Archives.

46. Leo B. Guelpa, *The U.S. Merchant Marine Cadet Corps: Its Establishment and Development* (Kings Point: U.S.M.M.C.C. Educational Unit, 1944).

47. C. Bradford Mitchell, *We'll Deliver* (Kings Point: USMMA Alumni Association, 1977), 176.

4. Embodied in War: 1940–1945

1. Everett Northrup, *The Origins and Establishment of the U.S. Merchant Marine*, master's thesis, Colgate University, June 1951, 80.

2. These two architects later created their own firm—La Pierre, Litchfield, and Partners—which was hired by the Academy in the 1960s to modernize the Engineering Department facilities.

3. Lauren McCready, interview by David A. O'Neil, '61, July 21, 1999.

4. Carl Seiberlich, interview by the authors, August 13, 2004.

5. "Patten Hospital Now in New Location," *Polaris*, October 1942.

6. Michael Gannon, *Black May* (New York: HarperCollins, 1998), xix. See also *Operation Drumbeat*, by Michael Gannon.

7. According to Bruce Felknor, Dwight D. Eisenhower wrote in his journal in early 1942, "One thing that might help win the war is to get someone to shoot King." Felknor, *The U.S. Merchant Marine at War, 1775–1945* (Annapolis, MD: Naval Institute Press, 1998), 222.

8. Emory S. Land, *Winning the War with Ships* (New York: Robert M. McBride, 1958).

9. C. Bradford Mitchell, *We'll Deliver* (Kings Point: USMMA Alumni Association, 1977), 53.

10. Undated note from McNulty to Brad Mitchell, Collection of Charles Renick. While McNulty believed this to be accurate, Telfair Knight and others believed that it was actually Macauley who placed the all-important call to Roosevelt.

11. Amanda Smith (ed.), *Hostage to Fortune: The Letters of Joseph P. Kennedy* (New York: Viking, 2001), 546. The quote is from an April 10, 1942, diary entry by Joseph P. Kennedy.

12. It also forever excluded Kings Point from the "ivy league." Because ivy would crack and damage the relatively soft sandstone, a directive was handed down from on high: no ivy.

13. "Cadets Dine in Spacious Delano Hall," *Polaris*, March 1943.

14. "Deck and Engine," *Polaris*, September 1942.

15. "Signalling Courses Give Cadets Insight of Semaphore Uses," *Polaris*, December 1942.

16. "Signalling Instruction Averts Damage to Ship," *Polaris*, January 1943.

17. "Sea Projects Will Replace Quizzes," *Polaris*, September 1942.

18. "Kings Point Cadets Learn to Handle Guns Competently," *Polaris*, February 1943.

19. Though the news of Conway's death was the first to arrive at the Academy, two Academy cadets had died in action during the previous month. The SS *Azalea City*, a freighter carrying a load of flaxseed from Argentina to Philadelphia by way of Trinidad, was torpedoed by the German U-432 about 125 miles

east-southeast of Ocean City, Maryland. Two cadets—Richard Lewis and Robert See—were among the crew of thirty-eight who perished. The facts concerning the sinking of the *Azalea City* (and the deaths of the cadets she carried) would not be known until after the war.

20. With the exception of the Stanley Willner story, these stories have been gleaned from *Polaris* and from *A Careless Word . . . A Needless Sinking*, by Arthur R. Moore. Moore's book was used to fill in many of the blanks created by wartime censorship (or self-censorship) of *Polaris*. Willner's story is based on *Death's Railway: A Merchant Mariner on the River Kwai*, by Gerald Reminick (Palo Alto, CA: Glencannon Press, 2002). For additional stories of cadets at sea during World War II, see also Mitchell's *We'll Deliver*.

21. The lawsuit, brought by Willner, Dennis Roland and others, was Schumacher, Willner, et al. v. Aldridge, 665 F. Supp. 41 (D.D.C. 1987.)

22. Frederic C. Lane, *Ships for Victory: A History of Shipbuilding Under the U.S. Maritime Commission in World War II* (Baltimore: Johns Hopkins University Press, 2001), 8.

23. Andrew Gibson and Arthur Donovan, *The Abandoned Ocean: A History of United States Maritime Policy* (Columbia: University of South Carolina Press, 2000), 166. Standard construction times were closer to two weeks. See also Lane, *Ships for Victory*.

24. Gannon, *Black May*, xxiii.

25. Alex Roland's chapter in the *American Maritime History Project*, draft no. 1, 60.

26. James E. Valle, "U.S. Merchant Marine Casualties," in *To Die Gallantly: The Battle of the Atlantic*, Timothy J. Runyan and Jan M. Copes, eds. (Boulder, CO: Westview Press, 1994), 271.

27. Bruce Felknor, *The U.S. Merchant Marine at War, 1775–1945* (Annapolis, MD: Naval Institute Press, 1998), 248.

28 "Russian Medal Pinned on Alumnus," *Polaris*, August 1944. Holubowicz was given the Russian Medal for Distinction in Action two years after his ordeal. Also from Thomas A. King, "Merchant Marine Cadet Corps," in *To Die Gallantly: The Battle of the Atlantic*, Timothy J. Bunyan and Jan M. Copes, eds. (Boulder, CO: Westview Press, 1994), 280.

29. Valle, "U.S. Merchant Marine Casualties," 283.

30. Mitchell, *We'll Deliver*, 129.

31. These figures are from Arthur R. Moore, '44, *A Careless Word . . . A Needless Sinking* (Kings Point: American Merchant Marine Museum, 1985).

32. The Allies stockpiled this and other chemical agents for use in retaliation against the potential Axis use of these weapons. Unlike World War I, neither side launched chemical attacks.

33. Glenn B. Infield, *Disaster at Bari* (New York: Macmillan, 1971), 143.

34. "Bombs over Bari," *Polaris*, May 1944.

35. Gannon, *Black May*, xix.

36. Valle: "U.S. Merchant Marine Casualties," 263.

37. Lane, *Ships for Victory*, 8.

38. Cadet-midshipman Leon Mirell, "Marine News," *Polaris*, October 1944.

39. Valle, "U.S. Merchant Marine Casualties," 263.

40. Cadet-Midshipman John K. Kilbride, "Thousands Witness Dedication," *Polaris*, November 1943.
41. "A Cadet Hero," *Polaris*, June 1943.
42. Kilbride, "Thousands Witness Dedication," *Polaris*, November 1943.
43. See chapter 3.
44. From a twelve-page typescript dated August 24, 1943, by James H. Tomb, titled "The Saga of Fort Schuyler," Academy Archives, Bland Library. Reprinted in the March 2004 issue of *Fort Schuyler Mariner*.
45. Cadet-Midshipman Raymond Weil, "An Interview with Captain Tomb," *Polaris*, October 1944.
46. *New York Sun*, January 1, 1934. This and other Stedman-related news clips are from scrapbooks contained in Giles Stedman's sea chest in the Bland Library archive.
47. *New York Times*, October 29, 1925.
48. *New York World*, October 30, 1925.
49. *Evening World*, January 21, 1933.
50. "Disasters (on other ships) Put Capt. Stedman in the Limelight," *New York Times*, January 27, 1933.
51. *San Francisco Chronicle*, February 28, 1939.
52. *Marine Progress*, October 1940.
53. "Cadets Appointed to Command Corps," *Polaris*, August 1942.
54. Editorial, *Polaris*, September 15, 1942.
55. Ibid.
56. "Walking Off Demerits," *Polaris*, September 15, 1942.
57. Personal reminiscence of Eliot Lumbard.
58. "Cadets in Action on the High Seas," *Polaris*, August 1942.
59. "Tin Fishermen Organized," *Polaris*, November 1943.

5. Making Peacetime Headway: 1945–1950

1. R. K. MacLeod and I. Suder, "Our First Alumni Day," *Polaris*, November 1945.
2. Ibid.
3. The permanent memorial was donated by Bethlehem Steel in the fall of 1946 and continues to sit at the Academy on the rise from the Long Island Sound before Wiley Hall. The frieze is rumored to be still in place, behind the mural of the SS *America* in Delano Hall.
4. "Disasters (on Other Ships) Put Capt. Stedman in the Limelight," *New York Times*, January 27, 1933.
5. *Superintendent's Report to the Congressional Board of Visitors*, June 8, 1945, Academy Archives, Bland Library.
6. Alex Roland's chapter in the *American Maritime History Project*, draft no. 1, p. 77.
7. James E. Valle, "U.S. Merchant Marine Casualties," in *To Die Gallantly: The Battle of the Atlantic*, Timothy J. Runyan and Jan M. Copes, eds. (Boulder, CO: Westview Press, 1994), 260–261.
8. Bruce Felknor, *The U.S. Merchant Marine at War, 1775–1945* (Annapolis, MD: Naval Institute Press, 1998), 331.

9. From the U.S. Merchant Marine Web site, www.usmm.org.

10. Emory S. Land, *Winning the War with Ships* (New York: Robert McBride, 1958), 216.

11. Cadet-Midshipman Eldon Nyhart, "Air Versus Sea Power," *Polaris*, December 1945.

12. "Cadets' Mission," *Polaris*, June 1943.

13. From a House joint resolution presented in hearings before the House Committee on the Merchant Marine and Fisheries, 78th Congress.

14. *Report of the Board of Visitors to the U.S. Merchant Marine Academy*, September 30, 1944, Academy Archives, Bland Library.

15. *Report of the Congressional Board of Visitors to the U.S. Merchant Marine Academy*, June 8, 1945, Academy Archives, Bland Library.

16. Cadet-Midshipman Mitchell Gordon, "Four Year Course for Kings Point," *Polaris*, November 1945.

17. Thomas Giddings, interview by the authors, October 25, 2004.

18. Archibald Davies, interview by the authors, October 25, 2004.

19. C. Bradford Mitchell, *We'll Deliver* (Kings Point: USMMA Alumni Association, 1977), 129.

20. From accreditation consultant Joseph Kochka's comments in the transcript of the Board of Visitors meeting, May 1946, Academy Archives, Bland Library.

21. From a 1936 edition of the *New York American* in Giles Stedman's scrapbooks, no month included.

22. MacLeod and Suder, "Our First Alumni Day," November 1945.

23. Luis Bejarano, interview by the authors, October 10, 2002.

24. Richard McNulty, memo to the Honorable Willis Bradley, February 1947, Academy Archives, Bland Library.

25. Superintendent's *Report to the Academic Advisory Board*, 1948, Academy Archives, Bland Library.

26. *Congressional Board of Visitors Meeting*, May 1946, Academy Archives, Bland Library.

27. Cadet-Midshipman I. Suder, "Admiral Stedman Retires as Superintendent," *Polaris*, April 1946.

28. From a handwritten note by Richard McNulty titled "Notes on Superintendency," in response to the manuscript of *We'll Deliver*, collection of Charles Renick.

29. Henry E. Bent, secretary of the Association of American Universities, to Richard McNulty, December 8, 1947. Also, Executive Officer Nerney, confidential memo to McNulty, regarding his impressions of the visit of Dean Fernandus Payne, October 16, 1947, Academy Archives, Bland Library.

30. *Report of the Academic Advisory Board to the U.S. Merchant Marine Academy*, March 18, 1948, Academy Archives, Bland Library.

31. *Second Annual Report of the Academic Advisory Board to the USMMA*, March 11, 1949, Academy Archives, Bland Library.

32. Commission on Institutions of Higher Education of the Middle States Association of Colleges and Secondary Schools, *Report of the Inspection of the USMMA*, Academy Archives, Bland Library.

33. Rear Admiral Paul Krinsky, interview by the authors, January 8, 2003.
34. Cadet-Midshipman Roger Beeken, "Hurricane Lashes Pass Christian," *Polaris*, October 1947.
35. Mitchell, *We'll Deliver*, 158–160.

6. Weathering New Storms: 1950–1960

1. Academy press release on McLintock's retirement, 1970.
2. This fact surfaced in several personal recollections and was confirmed in interviews with Fred Sherman (January 23, 2004) and Eugene McCormick (January 26, 2004). Sherman also recalled that McLintock's backyard bordered that of another powerful Washington figure—possibly Gerald Ford, then a Republican representative to Congress from Michigan.
3. Rear Admiral Lauren McCready, interview by David O'Neil, July 21, 1999.
4. From an Academy biographical sketch of McLintock, Academy Archives, Bland Library, supported by the reminiscences of Admiral Lauren McCready in conversations with the authors.
5. Gordon McLintock, *Your Future in the Merchant Marine* (New York: Richards Rosen Press, 1968), 16.
6. Charles Marshall, general manager of the Maritime Commission, to William Duvall, executive secretary of the Subcommittee on Independent Appropriations, House of Representatives, April 14, 1950, Maritime Administration Archives.
7. *Superintendent's Report to the Congressional Board of Visitors*, 1953, Academy Archives, Bland Library.
8. Ibid.
9. "Bare Hush-Hush Plot to Sink Kings Point in June," *Newsday*, November 17, 1953.
10. Letter from George Gordon McLintock to Louis Rothschild, Maritime Administrator, October 24, 1953, General Correspondence File of the Maritime Administration, File TS1.
11. "Lawmakers Rip Proposal to Scuttle Kings Point," *Newsday*, November 18, 1953.
12. Ibid.
13. Melvin Tublin, interview by the authors, August 25, 2004.
14. Joseph Baker, interview by the authors, October 13, 2004.
15. Ibid.
16. Letters from the General Correspondence File of the Maritime Administration, file TS1.
17. Jack Scherger to Robert Angevine, July 30, 2001. Forwarded to the authors by Robert Angevine.
18. George Gordon McLintock to Louis Rothschild, Maritime administrator, June 30, 1954, General Correspondence File of the Maritime Administration.
19. McCready, interview.
20. R. D. Sweeney, California attorney, to Louis Rothschild, January 16, 1954, General Correspondence File of the Maritime Administration.

21. *Seventh Annual Report of the Academic Advisory Board to the USMMA*, Academy Archives, Bland Library.

22. Acting deputy Maritime administrator, memo to Maritime administrator regarding yearly cost per cadet at Kings Point and Fort Schuyler, January 5, 1954, General Correspondence File of the Maritime Administration.

23. U.S. Congress, Hearing before the Subcommittee of the Committee on Appropriations, U.S. Senate, 83rd Cong., 1st sess., on House Resolution 4974, May/June 1954.

24. John Scherger, Association of Parents and Friends of Kings Point to Friends, June 17, 1954, Academy Archives, Bland Library. The proposal to restore cadet pay was quietly shelved.

25. "Kings Point Wins Permanency Fight," *Newsday*, February 8, 1956.

26. Though the Merchant Marine Academy was founded more than ten years before the Air Force Academy, the latter was authorized by Congress in the Act of April 1, 1954, chap. 127, 68 Statute 47, and formally dedicated on July 10, 1955, thus earning its status as the fourth federal academy established by law.

27. Melvin Tublin, interview by the authors, August 25, 2004. Baker later gave the pen to the Academy.

28. C. Bradford Mitchell, *We'll Deliver* (Kings Point: USMMA Alumni Association, 1977), 243.

29. James Peter Walsh, "Faculty Personnel Administration at the United States Merchant Marine Academy: The College Teacher in Federal Service" (doctoral dissertation, School of Education, University of Southern California, June 1961), 159. It should be noted that Walsh was a party in this conflict as one of the nine faculty members demoted by the reevaluation.

30. These numbers are from the Walsh dissertation. The 1956 report of the superintendent to the Ninth Academic Advisory Board includes smaller numbers: 36 promotions and 109 demotions, including 9 faculty members.

31. Excerpts from the transcripts of the first meeting of the 1947 Congressional Board of Visitors, May 12, 1947, Academy Archives, Bland Library.

32. Acting Attorney General Philip B. Perlman to President Truman, February 24, 1952, in Walsh, "Faculty Personnel Administration," appendix C.

33. Walsh, "Faculty Personnel Administration," 183.

34. George Gordon McLintock to Clarence Rothschild, Maritime administrator, November 22, 1954, Maritime Administration Archives.

35. George Pope Shannon to McLintock, December 9, 1954, Maritime Administration Archives.

36. Dean Martin Mason to Clarence Rothschild, Maritime administrator, December 13, 1954, Maritime Administration Archives.

37. *Report of the Superintendent to the Ninth Academic Advisory Board*, March 27, 1956, Academy Archives, Bland Library.

38. Walsh, "Faculty Personnel Administration," quoting from the 1958 *Report of the Superintendent to the Academic Advisory Board*, 274.

39. Lauren McCready, Lane Kendall, C. W. Ferris, Peder Gald, J. M. Dittrick, L. E.

Bejarano, and J. W. Leibertz to Edward Reynolds, chair of the USMMA Advisory Board, March 19, 1958, Academy Archives, Bland Library.

40. Donald Paquette, retired faculty member, to Warren Mazek, June 8, 2004, forwarded to the authors by Mazek.

41. Walsh, "Faculty Personnel Administration," 369.

42. See also the Clifford Sandberg journal entries quoted in chapter 7.

43. Walsh, "Faculty Personnel Administration," 372.

44. *Report of the Sixteenth Congressional Board of Visitors to the USMMA*, Kings Point, November 19, 1959, Academy Archives, Bland Library. The report included the statement, "This Board is alarmingly concerned that in the main, the recommendations [of previous boards] have been ignored."

45. Walsh, "Faculty Personnel Administration," 380. Walsh quotes articles in the *New York Times*, *Newsday*, and the *Daily News*.

46. Walsh, "Faculty Personnel Administration," 380.

47. Ibid., 268. Also cited in *Newsday*, December 16, 1959.

48. Ibid., 380, confirmed by interviews with Luis Bejarano and Lauren McCready.

49. Ibid., 383.

50. Ibid., 383, referring to transcript of Civil Service Commission Hearing, Sect. 14, June 16, 1960.

51. Ibid., 387.

52. Ibid., 388.

53. Ibid., 393.

54. Report of Representative Herbert Zelenko, chairman of the Subcommittee on Kings Point Academy, of the hearing held on September 24, 1960, at the Maritime Administration offices at 45 Broadway, New York City; Academy Archives, Bland Library. Although McKenna appears to have been persecuted by McLintock, cadets from that era tend to confirm that McKenna was, in McLintock's words, a "contentious man" who was a good priest but not a strong advocate of the cadets.

55. Chief of Naval Personnel, note to all Navy Recruiting Officers, Navy Recruiting Service, July 12, 1954, Maritime Administration Archives, 125–154.

56. Our thanks to George Ryan for bringing this fact to our attention.

57. Penrose Lucas Albright, *Briefing Paper for Rear Admiral G. H. Miller Concerning the History of the Merchant Marine Reserve of the U.S. Navy, April 28, 1972*.

58. *Report of the Superintendent to the Congressional Board of Visitors*, 1951, Academy Archives, Bland Library.

59. Salvatore Mercogliano, "Korea: The First Shot," U.S. Merchant Marine Web site, usmm.org/msts/korea.html.

60. Maritime Administrator Thomas Stakem to the Undersecretary for Transportation, June 15, 1961, Maritime Administration Archives.

61. Tublin, interview.

7. Building on the Foundations: 1955–1970

1. Richard O'Leary, interview by the authors, April 3, 2003.

2. *Fourth Annual Report of the Academic Advisory Board to the USMMA*, April 14, 1951, Academy Archives, Bland Library.

3. Ibid.
4. *Sixth Annual Report of the Academic Advisory Board to the USMMA*, June 6, 1953, Academy Archives, Bland Library.
5. Ibid.
6. Ibid.
7. Superintendent McLintock to F. Taylor Jones, executive secretary of the Commission on Institutions of Higher Learning, Middle States Association, May 21, 1958, attachment to the Superintendent's Statement to the Advisory Board, 1962, Academy Archives, Bland Library.
8. *Budget Officer to the Special Assistant to the Maritime Administrator*, July 15, 1957, referring to a July 10, 1957, memo from Admiral McLintock to the Budget Officer, Academy Archives, Bland Library.
9. "Sea Year Crack Down," *Hear This*, October 1959.
10. General Counsel, memo to the Maritime Administrator, regarding secretary of commerce appointments, July 26, 1962, Maritime Administration Archives, Washington, D.C.
11. *Superintendent's Statement to the Academic Advisory Board*, 1962, Academy Archives, Bland Library.
12. *Report of the Advisory Board*, June 8, 1962, Academy Archives, Bland Library.
13. *Report of Reaffirmation of Accreditation of the USMMA*, June 25, 1965, Academy Archives, Bland Library.
14. Ibid.
15. *Superintendent's Report to the Advisory Board*, 1960, Academy Archives, Bland Library. See also *Hear This*, November 1959, March 1960, October 1960, January 1961, June 1961.
16. "Three More Kings Pointers to Indonesia," *Hear This*, November 1959.
17. Raymond Eisenberg, interview by the authors, November 5, 2002.
18. *Superintendent's Statement to the Advisory Board*, 1962, Academy Archives, Bland Library.
19. "Automation and Globalization," *American Maritime History Project*, draft no. 1, 20.
20. Ibid., 21.
21. Ibid., 20.
22. David Keuchle, *The Story of the* "Savannah": *An Episode in Maritime Labor-Management Relations* (Cambridge, MA: Harvard University Press, 1971), 13.
23. Moses Hirschkowitz, interview by the authors, November 6, 2002.
24. Another advantage to Kings Point was the proximity to the nuclear facilities at the national lab at Brookhaven.
25. "Cadets Being Trained for Atomic Ships," *Hear This*, November, 1959.
26. Maritime Administrator Donald Alexander to the Superintendent of the USMMA, memo, November 9, 1961, Maritime Administration Archives.
27. Keuchle, *The Story of the* "Savannah," 30.
28. Superintendent's Statement to the Advisory Board, 1962.
29. Hirschkowitz, interview.
30. Keuchle, *The Story of the* "Savannah," 193.
31. Krinsky notes in a September 18, 2004, letter to the authors that Stan Wheatley,

'48, who had trained with States Marine and was a future director of the National Maritime Research Center, went along on this sea trial to oversee engineering operations and ensure safe operations.

32. Keuchle, *The Story of the* "Savannah", 233.
33. Paul Krinsky, interview by the authors, January 8, 2003.
34. Gerhardt Muller, *Intermodal Freight Transportation*, 4th ed. (Washington, D.C.: Eno Transportation Foundation, 1999), 25.
35. Ibid., 28. Sea-Land started a transatlantic containership operation between Newark and Rotterdam, Bremerhaven, and Grangemouth in 1966.
36. To a large extent, the rules were rewritten by Malcolm McLean's staff, including his designers—especially his chief naval architect, Charles R. Cushing, '56.
37. Muller, *Intermodal Freight Transportation*, 25.
38. Ibid., 31.
39. None of these lines, it is worth noting, was in business four decades later.
40. Brian Hope, '65, "The Industry Reacts to Automation," *Polaris*, Winter 1965.
41. Hirschkowitz, interview.
42. "Dual Program Forges Ahead, Anticipates Needs of Shipping," *Hear This*, April 30, 1968.
43. "Asia fray forces earlier marine school graduation," *Long Island Daily Commercial Review*, January 13, 1967.
44. Excerpt from the personal diary of Commander Clifford W. Sandberg, Academy Archives, Bland Library.
45. O'Leary, interview.
46. Ibid.
47. Commandant Robert Allee, '68, in an e-mail to the authors dated November 3, 2004, points out that the escalation of the Vietnam War and the corresponding rush to educate and graduate Kings Pointers added to tensions in this period, and it constituted a "huge disruption to Academy routine."
48. "Wasson Case Proceedings," *Hear This*, June 24, 1968. The successful appeal of this case postdated this article. *Wasson v. Trowbridge*, 382 F.2d 807, 2d Cir. 1967.
49. *Superintendent's Report to the Sixth Congressional Board of Visitors*, May 6–7, 1949, Academy Archives, Bland Library.
50. Telfair Knight, acting chief of Maritime operations, to the Maritime administrator, memo regarding the chapel, November 9, 1950, Academy Archives, Bland Library.
51. *The McLintocks and the Mariner's Chapel*, 1986, collection of Martin Skrocki.
52. Ibid.
53. The "Cadet's Prayer" includes the first verse of the "Navy Hymn, Eternal Father," written in 1860 by William Whiting. The second verse, written by Wynne McLintock, is:

> Lord, stand beside the men who sail
> Our merchant ships in storm and gale
> In peace and war their watch they keep
> On every sea, on thy vast deep.
> Be with them Lord, by night and day,
> For Merchant Mariners we pray.

54. "Services Mark Sixth Anniversary of Mariners' Chapel," *Hear This*, May 1967

55. Ibid.

56. A recent addition to the chapel is a roped-off pew, symbolically reserved for the 142 cadets lost during World War II. Similarly, at formal Academy dinners in Delano Hall, a table is set next to the podium for the 142 lost cadets.

57. "Library Dream Comes True," *Hear This*, April 1967.

58. Ibid.

59. Judy Chadwick Gibson, interview by the authors, August 7, 2003.

60. Superintendent to the Regiment of Midshipmen, memo, December 12, 1968, Academy Archives, Bland Library.

61. *Recommendations of the Corps of Midshipmen to the Superintendent of the Academy*, January 1969, 6, Academy Archives, Bland Library.

62. Ibid., 7.

63. Krinsky, interview.

64. "Admiral Replies to Recommendations," *Hear This*, February 17, 1969.

65. Lauren McCready, interview by David O'Neil, July 21, 1999.

8. Widening the Scope: 1970–1980

1. According to Coast Guard Vice Admiral Robert H. Scarborough, this fifteen-gun salute honoring a vice admiral (McLintock) would have been followed by a thirteen-gun salute honoring a rear admiral (Engel). Our thanks to Admiral Scarborough (the first Academy graduate to make flag rank in the Coast Guard) for his attention to this detail, among many others.

2. Ed Hershey, "Kings Point Help to Coast Guard Aide," *Newsday*, June 10, 1970, files of Martin Skrocki.

3. "Armed Forces Day Draws Dissent," *Hear This*, June 12, 1970.

4. Ibid.

5. Judith Gibson, interview by the authors, August 7, 2003.

6. Thompson, Arthur T., *Thompson Report*, July 15, 1971. Academy Archives, Bland Library.

7. Ibid.

8. Ibid.

9. Ibid.

10. Ibid.

11. "A look at electives," *Hear This*, April 27, 1977.

12. Thompson report.

13. Ibid.

14. Walter Gunn, PhD, "Return to Kings Point," *Kings Pointer*, Fall 1972.

15. We are grateful to Professor Charles Hubert for bringing this fact to our attention.

16. Gunn, "Return to Kings Point."

17. "New Elective," *Hear This*, February 2, 1979.

18. Gunn, "Return to Kings Point."

19. Charles Hubert, interview by the authors, December 17, 2002.

20. Moses Hirschkowitz, interview by the authors, November 6, 2002.

21. Clem Stralka was also football coach for many years, and was well liked by his players.
22. Paul Krinsky, interview by the authors, January 8, 2003.
23. Lauren McCready, interview by David O'Neil, July 21, 1999.
24. Ibid.
25. Dr. Howard Beim, "Evolution of the Kings Point Scholar Program," *Kings Pointer*, Summer 1976.
26. John Manning, "CAORF," *Kings Pointer*, Summer 1976.
27. Joe Scroggins, interview by the authors, July 16, 2003.
28. Ibid.
29. Martin Skrocki, "A Minority Report from Kings Point," *Kings Pointer*, Spring 1976.
30. Krinsky, interview. John Jochmans adds that the mothers of the male midshipmen tended to strenuously oppose coeducation.
31. The California Maritime Academy enrolled five women in 1972, marking the first time women were enrolled in a U.S. academy. Three of these women, and a transfer student at Maine Maritime Academy who was admitted in 1974, graduated in 1976.
32. Krinsky to the authors, September 18, 2004.
33. Krinsky, interview.
34. Captain Mary Bachand, "Women at Kings Point," *Kings Pointer*, Summer 1977.
35. Charles Renick, interview by the authors, November 5, 2002.
36. Kenneth Force, interview by the authors, December 18, 2002.
37. Frances Yates, interview by the authors, November 11, 2003.
38. Bachand, "Women at Kings Point."
39. Yates, interview.
40. Bachand, "Women at Kings Point."
41. Ibid.
42. "Maiden Voyages," *Kings Pointer*, Winter 1975–1976. Reprinted from *Newsday*, August 15, 1975. Neizer went on to become a White House fellow and later vice president for Office Operations of Martin-Brower, Canada.
43. Ibid.
44. Yates, interview.
45. Renick, interview.
46. Ibid.
47. David O'Neil, interview by the authors, April 11, 2003.
48. "Academy Recommended to Obtain Engineer's Council for Professional Development Accreditation," *Kings Pointer*, Fall 1977.
49. Krinsky, interview.
50. *Status Report on the Department of Engineering*, for the 1978 Advisory Board meeting, Academy Archives, Bland Library.

9. The Guns Return: 1970–1980
1. Kent Flick, interview by the authors, February 17, 2003.
2. Captain Charles Renick, "Home Port," *Kings Pointer*, Fall 1980.

3. Kenneth Force, interview by the authors, December 18, 2002.

4. Force, interview.

5. Judy Chadwick Gibson, interview by the authors, August 7, 2003.

6. Thomas King, interview by the authors, May 23, 2003. According to King, the initial agreement with Gibson was for a five-year tour of duty. Also supported by Charles Renick, interview by the authors, February 25, 2003.

7. Arthur B. Engel, memo to secretary of Commerce for Maritime Affairs, February 14, 1988. Contains excerpts from Engel's *Informal Grievance*, January 11, 1977, collection of Martin Skrocki.

8. Arthur Engel to Robert Blackwell, July 3, 1975, collection of Martin Skrocki.

9. Engel to Blackwell, July 19, 1975, Skrocki collection.

10. Ibid.

11. Ibid., August 5, 1975.

12. Blackwell to Engel, September 21, 1976, Skrocki collection.

13. Ibid., September 7, 1976.

14. Len Nichols to Lynn Burrowbridge, September 22, 1976, Skrocki collection.

15. Blackwell to Engel, memo, December 8, 1976, Skrocki collection.

16. Brian Donovan, "Kings Point Chief Reassigned," *Newsday*, January 18, 1977.

17. Sean Kearney and Bob Burlando, "Captain King Speaks His Mind," *Hear This*, April 27, 1977.

18. Brian Donovan, "Kings Point Superintendent Returns," *Newsday*, April 22, 1977.

19. Blackwell to Engel, memo, May 6, 1977, Skrocki collection.

20. Engel, *The Proper Role of the Federal Government in Training Merchant Marine Personnel*, 1977, Academy Archives, Bland Library.

21. Engel, *The Proper Role of the Federal Government*.

22. "Letters to the Editor," *Hear This*, March 16, 1979.

23. United States Office of Personnel Management Web site, www.opm.gov/ses (accessed September 5, 2003).

24. Force, interview.

25. Thomas King, interview by the authors, May 23, 2003.

26. Richard Firstman and Adrian Peracchio, "Engel, Kings Point Chief, Fired," *Newsday*, September 11, 1979.

27. "Engel, Kings Point Chief, Fired," *Kings Pointer*, Spring 1977.

28. Andrew Gibson and Arthur Donovan, *The Abandoned Ocean: A History of United States Maritime Policy* (Columbia: University of South Carolina Press, 2000), 180.

29. "Conclusion of GAA Program," *On Course, Newsletter of the Maritime Administration*, March/April 1970.

30. Maritime Administrator Andrew Gibson to Eastern Region Director Thomas King, March 30, 1970, Skrocki collection.

31. "Conclusion of GAA Program."

32. Gibson and Donovan, *The Abandoned Ocean*, 198.

33. Ibid., 201.

34. Ibid., 202.

35. Ibid., 203.

36. Thomas Harrelson, '66, "Economic War at Sea," *Kings Pointer*, Summer 1976.

37. This section focuses on the Marine Engineers' Beneficial Association (MEBA), one of three maritime unions that appear episodically in our text. The other two are the Masters, Mates and Pilots (MMP) and the American Maritime Officers (AMO). MEBA was established in 1875, aimed at supporting proper enforcement of the Steamboat Act of 1871, which mandated engineering safety standards for steam-powered vessels. MMP, founded in 1880, grew directly out of the SS *Seawanhaka* tragedy, in which thirty-five passengers burned to death in New York Harbor, and placed its emphasis on deck skills such as navigation and ship handling. The AMO was chartered in 1949 as the Brotherhood of Marine Engineers (BME), an affiliate of the Seafarers International Union of North America (itself an AFL affiliate). In 1957, the BME merged with several MEBA locals, and in 1960 became District 2 MEBA, an autonomous union within a restructured MEBA. The AMO was established as the deck officers' division of District 2, and in 1994 it became a freestanding union.
38. "Union Votes to Close Books; Move Concerns All Midshipmen," *Hear This*, March 25, 1970.
39. Jesse Calhoon, interview by the authors, August 19, 2004.
40. Charles Renick, interview by the authors, August 23, 2004.
41. "Bill Would Restrict Entering Class Size," *Kings Pointer*, Winter 1976–1977.
42. Ibid.
43. "Project ACTA," *ACTA/News*, December 1976.
44. "CBS Looks at Kings Point," *Kings Pointer*, Winter 1976–1977.
45. Ibid.
46. Milton Nottingham, interview by the authors, October 2, 2003.
47. "CBS Looks at Kings Point."
48. "Project ACTA."
49. Calhoon, interview.
50. "Alumni Launch Project ACTA," *Kings Pointer*, Winter 1976–1977.
51. "Speaking Up for ACTA," *ACTA/News*, February 1977.
52. The responses following are from "Project ACTA Mailbag," *ACTA/News*, February 1977.
53. "Latest on Tuition Proposal," *ACTA/News*, May 1977.
54. "Kings Point Alumni Lead Protest of Tuition Proposal," *ACTA/News*, February 1977.
55. "Latest on Tuition Proposal," *ACTA/News*, May 1977.
56. "Academy Facing Federal Study," *Kings Pointer*, Summer 1976.
57. "GAO Report," *ACTA/News*, May 1977.
58. "The GAO Report–Finally! Revisions Are Much Fairer," *ACTA/News*, July 1977.
59. *Report of the Comptroller of the United States: The Federal Role in Merchant Marine Officer Education*, June 15, 1977.
60. Ibid.
61. "What Jimmy Carter Says," *ACTA/News*, December 1976.
62. "MEBA Flying Peace Flag?" *Hear This*, March 25, 1977.
63. Penrose Lucas Albright, *Briefing Paper for Rear Admiral G. H. Miller Concerning the History of the Merchant Marine Reserve of the U.S. Navy*, April 28, 1972.

64. The service obligation's history is confusing, complicated by the fact that it was for many years an obligation of honor rather than statute. Intermittently as well, it appears that cadets signed written agreements to serve. Commandant Robert Allee, for example, recalled (in an November 3, 2004, e-mail to the authors) that when he graduated in 1968, he signed such an agreement and reported to the Navy annually for three years as to what he was doing to fulfill his obligation.

65. The Merchant Marine Naval Reserve had been reestablished in 1978, after a twenty-six-year hiatus, thanks in part to the strong support of Admiral Carl Seiberlich.

66. Milt Nottingham, "Legislative Report," *Kings Pointer*, Fall 1980.

67. Maritime Education and Training Act of 1980, H.R. 5451, Public Law 96-453.

68. Tom Kirk, "'84 Obligation," *Hear This,* October 10, 1980.

69. Renick, interview.

70. Beth Gillin Pombeiro, "Tax Millions Spent on a Toy for Shippers," a series, *Philadelphia Inquirer*, August 19, 1979.

71. "President's Report," *Kings Pointer*, Fall 1979.

72. "Alumni Association Gifts Estate to Academy," *Kings Pointer*, Summer 1979.

73. Charles Renick, "Home Port," *Kings Pointer*, Summer 1979. See also Renick's letter dated October 28, 2004, to the authors.

74. Force, interview.

75. Thanks to John Jochmans for clarifying project priorities.

76. Richard Firstman and Adrian Peracchio, "1976–77: A Capital Period for Capital Projects," *Newsday*, September 11, 1979.

77. *Superintendent's Statement to the Advisory Board*, 1962, Academy Archives, Bland Library.

78. *Superintendent's Statement*, 1962.

79. David O'Neil, interview by the authors, April 11, 2003.

80. Ibid.

81. "Facelifting for Kings Point Waterfront," *Polaris*, Spring 1963.

82. "Mariner Sports," *Kings Pointer*, Fall 1979.

83. Gerard Riordan, "Seventh Company, Sound Off!," *Kings Pointer*, Spring 1973.

84. Force, interview.

85. Ibid.

86. John Christie, "Rear Admiral McNulty: Established Country's Merchant Marine Academy," *Gloucester Daily Times,* June 24, 1974.

87. Ibid.

88. "Blackwell Names 'Father' of the Federal Academy," Academy Press Release, March 17, 1976.

89. Ray Eisenberg, "The McNulty Memorial," The *Lookout*, a publication of the Seaman's Church Institute of New York, November 1981.

10. Safe Harbor: 1980–1987

1. Pete Rackett, "Fanfare, Memories, and Deeds," *Kings Pointer*, Winter 1981.

2. Ibid.

3. Scarborough, in a conversation with the authors, commented that he had no

knowledge that his name was being put forward at this time, and that he couldn't have accepted the job if it had been offered to him. A few years later, he was offered the post of executive director of the Kings Point Alumni Association, and he declined that position.

4. Carl Seiberlich, interview by the authors, October 3, 2003.

5. "A Kings Pointer Takes Command," *Kings Pointer*, Fall 1980.

6. Ibid.

7. Charles Renick, interview by the authors, November 5, 2002.

8. "A Kings Pointer Takes Command."

9. Robert Safarik, interview by the authors, October 24, 2002.

10. "Graduate in Command," *Hear This*, October 19, 1980.

11. Thomas King, interview by the authors, May 23, 2003.

12. Paul Krinsky, interview by the authors, January 8, 2003.

13. Andrew Gibson and Arthur Donovan, *The Abandoned Ocean: A History of United States Maritime Policy* (Columbia: University of South Carolina Press, 2000), 207.

14. Ibid., 255–256.

15. Ibid., 256.

16. Ibid.

17. Coast Guard Admiral Robert H. Scarborough, '44, however, disagrees with this interpretation. In a conversation with the authors, he pointed out that in the Department of Transportation setting, the modal administrators actually outrank the assistant secretaries, and that therefore MARAD's influence was not diluted as the result of this particular administrative change.

18. Albert Herberger, interview by the authors, October 3, 2003.

19. *The Abandoned Ocean*, 257.

20. Stephen Labaton, "Merchant Marine Promised a Boost," *Newsday*, June 22, 1982.

21. "Decline in Idle Merchant Fleet Slowing Down," *Lloyd's List*, December 13, 1984.

22. "For Young Mariners, a Job Quest in Troubled Seas," *New York Times*, June 22, 1982.

23. Charles Renick, "Home Port," *Kings Pointer*, Spring 1987.

24. The authors have not succeeded in tracking down this much-discussed memo. Its purported author, Annelise Anderson, doesn't remember writing such a memo, although she recalls the debates that might have generated it.

25. *Annual Report of the Advisory Board to the USMMA*, January 11, 1985, from the minutes of the Advisory Board, June 1, 1983, Academy Archives, Bland Library.

26. Thomas King, interview by the authors, May 23, 2003.

27. *Affirmative Action Program Plan, FY 1980*, USMMA Archives.

28. Ibid.

29. *Tentative Proposal for Postgraduate or Refresher Training of Merchant Marine Officers at U.S. Merchant Marine Academy*, July 11, 1962, Maritime Administration Archives, general file.

30. *Superintendent's Statement to the Academic Advisory Board, 1964*, Academy Archives, Bland Library.

31. Charles Renick, "Home Port," *Kings Pointer*, Summer 1979.

32. Ibid., Fall 1979.

33. Charles Cushing, interview by the authors, August 25, 2004.

34. Thomas King, "Ship Officer Retraining Needs Stressed as Operation Technology Advances," *Journal of Commerce*, May 17, 1982.

35. *Annual Report of the U.S. Merchant Marine Academy, '85–'86 Academic Year*, Academy Archives, Bland Library.

36. Ibid.

37. *Draft of the 1984 Academic Plan*, February 1984, Bland Library, USMMA Archives.

38. "Kings Point Students Train on British Ship Simulator," *Journal of Commerce*, December 24, 1984.

39. Rear Admiral Thomas King, "Notes from the Superintendent's Log," *Kings Pointer*, Winter 1981.

40. Krinsky, interview.

41. Ibid.

42. Captain W. T. McMullen, memo to Captain Paul Krinsky regarding the merger of the departments of Maritime Law and Economics and Nautical Science, March 30, 1981, files of Dean Warren Mazek.

43. Krinsky, interview.

44. *Interim Report on Marine Transportation Department*, June 1982, Mazek files.

45. Ibid.

46. Richard Stewart, interview by the authors, October 22, 2004.

47. Chris McMahon, interview by the authors, March 25, 2003.

48. *1986 Report of the Advisory Board*, meeting report of the Advisory Board from January 11, 1985, U.S. Department of Transportation, Maritime Administration archives.

49. King, interview.

50. George DeWan, "Failing Grade for Cheaters Breaking the Honor Code," *Newsday*, May 12, 1994.

51. Changes to the honor code are ongoing. A recent Honor Board chairman who completed a revision to the code was Aaron Seesan, a 2003 graduate of the Academy who joined the army. In a tragic footnote to this story, the authors learned as the book was going to press that Seesan had been killed on active duty in Iraq in May 2005.

52. Meredith Neizer, "No More Tears," *Hear This*, May 5, 1978.

53. "El Pasoan in the Merchant Marine: No TV, No Sodas, Lots of Saluting," *El Paso Times*, July 6, 1983.

54. Jane Brickman, interview by the authors, December 4, 2002.

55. Ibid.

56. Susan Petersen Lubow, interview by the authors, January 13, 2004.

57. Pete Rackett, interview by the authors, June 1, 2004.

58. Mary Jo Kaplan, "Women in Nontraditional Jobs," *Cosmopolitan*, June 1983.

59. At this writing, Wagner is a bar pilot helping ships traverse San Francisco's Golden Gate.

60. Helen Stein, "The First Women Grads–Ten Years Later: From the Bow to the Bridge," *Kings Pointer*, Summer 1988.

61. Ibid.
62. "El Pasoan in the Merchant Marine."
63. *Minutes of the Congressional Board of Visitors*, May 11, 1979, Bland Library, Academy Archives.
64. The authors would like to thank Paul Krinsky for documenting this history in his September 18, 2004, letter to us.
65. "Face to Face: Rear Admiral Paul Krinsky," *Kings Pointer*, Fall 1987.
66. Commander Eric Wallischek adds that a number of entering midshipmen were sons and daughters of "Zonians," residents of the Canal Zone, including Bill Conley, valedictorian of the class of '93.
67. Martin Skrocki, "As Admiral King Retires," *Kings Pointer*, Fall 1987.

11. Broadening the Mission: 1987–1992

1. Babson died in July 2004, as the manuscript for this book was being completed.
2. Because the Alumni Association had no way to cash the check, the Academy formed a trust, with Melvin Tublin as chair and Tyson as one of the trustees. This trust later incorporated and became the Kings Point Alumni Fund, then the Kings Point Fund, and eventually the Kings Point Foundation.
3. Frank Sinnott, "USMMA Foundation," *Kings Pointer*, Spring 1981.
4. Ken DeGhetto, '43, "The Kings Point Challenge Campaign," 1986, Academy Archives, Bland Library.
5. Rear Admiral Thomas King, "Notes from the Superintendent's Log," *Kings Pointer*, Spring 1987.
6. Edward Harsche, interview by the authors, August 31, 2004.
7. Ackerman also died in July 2004, underscoring the passing of the Academy torch from one generation to the next.
8. Mary-lou Jorgensen, "Ackerman Honored at Ribbon Cutting," *Kings Pointer*, Summer 1988.
9. We're grateful to Dean Warren Mazek for sharing with us relevant files on faculty union negotiations.
10. "Bargaining History–UFCT," undated, unsigned memo to Madeline Kaufman, Personnel Office, USMMA, from the files of Dean Warren Mazek.
11. Kenneth Lazara, chairman of USMMA chapter of United Federation of College Teachers, to Admiral Engel, April 5, 1976, from the Mazek files.
12. Lazara to Gerard Gumphertz, deputy area administrator, U.S. Department of Labor, November 5, 1976, from the Mazek files.
13. U.S. Department of Labor, "Complaint Against Agency," March 16, 1978 , filed by USMMA Chapter, UFCT Local 1460, from the Mazek files.
14. Lazara, president, AFGE Local 3732, to Thomas King, superintendent, USMMA, February 2, 1984, from the Mazek files.
15. Howard Beim, interview by the authors, April 27, 2004.
16. The negotiations were so difficult that both sides have been reluctant to reopen them, and the 1989 contract is still in effect today.
17. Paul Krinsky, interview by the authors, January 8, 2003.
18. "Strategic Plan for the U.S. Merchant Marine Academy," draft, June

1987, in Strategic Planning, vol. 1, June 1990, Academy Archives, Bland Library.

19. Mazek, "The Academic View," *Kings Pointer*, Fall 1987.

20. "Strategic Planning Project: Summary of Interviews," April 21, 1987, in *Strategic Planning*, vol. 1, June 1990, Academy Archives, Bland Library.

21. Ibid.

22. Mazek, "The Academic View."

23. Ibid.

24. *Strategic Plan for the U.S. Merchant Marine Academy*, June 1987.

25. John R. Hook, *Hook Report*, March 22, 1988, Academy Archives, Bland Library.

26. Krinsky, interview.

27. Mazek, "The Academic View." Note that a logistics and intermodal major was not added until 1998.

28. Bernard Abrahamsson, "Intermodalism," *Kings Pointer*, Summer 1988.

29. Krinsky, interview.

30. "Face to Face: Rear Admiral Paul Krinsky," *Kings Pointer*, Fall 1987.

31. Carl Seiberlich, interview by the authors, October 3, 2003.

32. Krinsky, interview.

33. Richard Stewart, interview by the authors, October 22, 2004.

34. Ibid.

35. Strategic Planning Group, Warren Mazek, chairman, to Rear Admiral Paul Krinsky, superintendent, USMMA, September 15, 1988, in *Strategic Planning*, vol. 2, June 1990, Academy Archives, Bland Library.

36. It should be noted, however, that the industry snapped up dualies to work in nondual roles on the assumption that anyone who survived the rigorous dual curriculum had to be both bright and extremely hardworking.

37. William T. McMullen, memo to Distribution, August 4, 1987, Academy Archives, Bland Library.

38. Rear Admiral Paul Krinsky, superintendent, USMMA, to Captain J. A. Sanial, U.S. Coast Guard, May 9, 1990, in *Strategic Planning*, vol. 2, June 1990, Academy Archives, Bland Library.

39. U.S. Merchant Marine Academy, catalog, 1990–1991, Academy Archives.

40. Ibid.

41. "A Word from the Moral Minority," *Hear This*, April 1987.

42. "A Rationale Statement for the Regimental Program," in *Strategic Planning*, vol. 1, June 1990, Academy Archives, Bland Library.

43. Chris McMahon, interview by the authors, March 25, 2003.

44. "A Rationale Statement."

45. Charles Renick, "Home Port," *Kings Pointer*, Fall 1988.

46. "Report of the Sub-Committee on the USMMA Continuing Education Program," in *Strategic Planning*, vol. 1, June 1990, Academy Archives, Bland Library.

47. See also discussion of NAFIs in chapter 11.

48. Commander Eric Wallischek, interview by the authors, September 19, 2003.

49. The landslide theory is held by many to be myth, but the Cressy Building was without doubt in need of replacement.

50. McMahon, interview.

51. Wallischek, interview.
52. *Strategic Plan: Toward the 21st Century*, U.S. Merchant Marine Academy, Kings Point, NY, March 1993, Academy Archives, Bland Library.
53. James Skinner, interview by the authors, November 11, 2003.
54. Ibid.
55. Major L. A. Mercado Jr., "The Structure of the U.S. Strategic Military System: Is It Adequate and Cost Effective?" Global Security Web site, www.global security.org.
56. "United States Transportation Command: A Short History," USTRANSCOM Web site, www.transcom.mil.
57. Michael P. Noonan and Mark R. Lewis, "Form, Function, and U.S. Defense Transformation," November 8, 2002, Foreign Policy Research Institute Web site, www.fpri.org.
58. Mercado, "The Structure of the U.S. Strategic Military System."
59. Major M. L. Hayes, "The Achilles Heel of Our National Strategy: Sealift," 1992, Global Security Web site, www.globalsecurity.org.
60. Ibid.
61. Ibid.
62. Ibid.
63. General Colin L. Powell, commencement address, June 15, 1992, Academy Archives, Bland Library.
64. Major R. W. Ingles, "U.S. Merchant Marine: Reviving a National Asset," 1992, Global Security Web site, www.globalsecurity.org.
65. Andrew Gibson and Arthur Donovan, *The Abandoned Ocean: A History of United States Maritime Policy* (Columbia: University of South Carolina Press, 2000), 250.
66. Mercado, "The Structure of the U.S. Strategic Military System."
67. Powell, commencement address.
68. Hayes, "The Achilles Heel of Our National Strategy."

12. Reinventing the Academy: 1993–1999

1. Warren Leback, interview by the authors, February 12, 2004.
2. Thomas Matteson, interview by the authors, July 16, 2003.
3. Ibid.
4. Ibid.
5. Vice President Al Gore, *From Red Tape to Results* (Washington, D.C.: Government Printing Office, 1993), preface.
6. Ibid., introduction.
7. Gore, "Creating a Government That Works Better and Costs Less: Status Report of the *National Performance Review*," September 1994.
8. Andrew Gibson and Arthur Donovan, *The Abandoned Ocean: A History of United States Maritime Policy* (Columbia: University of South Carolina Press, 2000), 283.
9. The staff director and one of the principal authors of the *National Performance Review* was Elaine Kamarck, a policy analyst for the Clinton administration. Kamarck declined to comment on the report for this book.

10. Matteson, interview.
11. Fred Sherman, interview by the authors, January 23, 2004.
12. Thomas King, interview by the authors, May 23, 2003.
13. Ibid.
14. Vice Admiral Robert H. Scarborough, telephone conversation with the authors, October 2004.
15. Fred Sherman, president of Project ACTA, statement before the Committee on Merchant Marine and Fisheries, Subcommittee on Merchant Marine, U.S. House of Representatives, March 9, 1994.
16. Admiral Albert Herberger, interview by David Sicilia, February 21, 2000.
17. Admiral Albert Herberger, interview by the authors, October 3, 2003.
18. Sherman, statement.
19. Ibid.
20. Sherman, interview.
21. Office of Inspector General, *Audit Report, Merchant Marine Training Incentives*, MARAD, June 19, 1995, collection of Warren Mazek.
22. Secretary of Transportation, memo to Mary Schiavo, inspector general, responding to draft report on the audit of Merchant Marine Training Incentives, May 26, 1995, collection of Warren Mazek.
23. Maritime Administrator Albert Herberger, memo to Mary Schiavo, inspector general, responding to draft report on the audit, April 12, 1995, Mazek collection.
24. Schiavo, memo to secretary of transportation, June 19, 1995, Mazek collection.
25. Organization of the American Maritime History Project, which eventually led to the publication of the volume, was inspired by this closure fight as well as the need for public understanding of the maritime industry to gain public support.
26. Don Forster, '61, "Vision 2000 Report," USMMAA Board of Directors Meeting, Norfolk, Virginia, April 28–29, 2000, collection of Warren Mazek.
27. Ibid.
28. Matteson, interview.
29. Ibid.
30. Ibid.
31. "Congressman Addresses Merchant Marine Graduates," Academy press release, June 17, 2002.
32. Jose Femenia, interview by the authors, December 4, 2002.
33. Ibid.
34. Ibid.
35. Matteson, interview.
36. George Sandberg, interview by the authors, January 27, 2004.
37. Matteson, interview.
38. Ibid.
39. Jose Femenia, interview by the authors, December 4, 2002.
40. Charles Weber, interview by the authors, April 27, 2004.
41. Warren Mazek, interview by the authors, April 27, 2004.
42. "Manhasset Resident Receives Federal Award," Academy press release, July 16, 1999.

43. Femenia, interview.
44. Matteson, interview.
45. Ibid.
46. Robert Allee, e-mail to the authors, November 3, 2004.
47. Chris McMahon, interview by the authors, March 25, 2003.
48. As explained in previous chapters, NAFIs permit government organizations to take in and expend money outside of the regular congressional appropriations process. NAFIs are governed by a complex set of regulations, but generally operate along the lines of a revolving fund.
49. McMahon, interview.
50. Ibid.
51. A good name that keeps future options open is a strong starting point. "GMATS" was coined by Dean Warren Mazek in a meeting with Chris McMahon and his staff.
52. Herberger, authors' interview.

13. Renewal, Tragedy, and Commitment: 2000–2004

1. John Jochmans, undated note to the authors.
2. It is also worth noting that the salaries paid to cadets at the other service academies are paid not by those academies but by the Department of Defense, a circumstance that complicates apples-to-apples comparisons with Kings Point.
3. USMMA Department of Resource Management, Budget Briefing, May 2003.
4. "Payroll vs. Other Costs, 1990–2002," chart, USMMA Office of Resource Management.
5. James Sanborn, '59, *Project ACTA Chairman's Report*, October 5, 6, 2000, Academy Archives, Bland Library.
6. "Cost per Graduate, 1984–2002," chart, USMMA Office of Resource Management.
7. Rear Admiral Carl Seiberlich worked with Stewart in the development of the Marine Corps' logistics system. "Not a lot of people know it," said Seiberlich, "but he's the guy that basically invented that system."
8. Admiral Joseph Stewart, interview by the authors, October 3, 2003.
9. Ibid.
10. Ibid., August 24, 2004. Unless otherwise attributed, all Stewart quotes in this chapter are derived from this interview.
11. John Jochmans, interview by the authors, January 12, 2004.
12. G. S. "Jerry" Rehm, interview by the authors, August 30, 2004. All subsequent Rehm quotes in this chapter are derived from this interview.
13. Ed Harsche, interview by the authors, August 31, 2004. All subsequent Harsche quotes in this chapter are derived from this interview.
14. Jerry Rehm, letter to Bill Young, March 10, 2000, provided by Rehm to the authors.
15. Ibid., August 22, 2001.
16. Bill Young, letter to Joe Stewart, September 27, 2001.
17. See "$1.6 million Matching Grant for Vickery Gate," *Kings Pointer*, Winter 2002–03.

18. James T. Shirley Jr., letter to the authors, November 8, 2004.

19. Mary Jane Fuschetto, letter to the American Maritime History Project, September 13, 2004. Fuschetto is the author of *Kings Point: Acta non Verba* (Minneapolis: Diversified Graphics, 2003).

20. Commander Eric Wallischek, memo, "Participation by USMMA personnel in World Trade Center Relief Efforts," to Superintendent Joseph Stewart, October 1, 2001.

21. From a copy of the citation provided to the authors by Commander Eric Wallischek.

22. Young, letter to Stewart.

23. Jim Shirley, "Chairman's message," *Kings Pointer*, Winter 2001–2002, C2.

24. Gerard P. Gavin, firefighter 1st grade, FDNY, letter to Joe Stewart, reprinted in the *Kings Pointer*, Winter 2001–2002, C2.

25. Stewart, interview, October 3, 2002.

26. Thad Gaebelein, interview by the authors, October 12, 2004.

27. Arthur Athens, interview by the authors, December 17, 2002.

28. "Merchant Marine Academy Superintendent Receives Promotion," Academy press release, June 4, 2003. Ed Harsche notes that the recognition was not only a well-deserved honor for Joe Stewart but also bodes well for the Academy's future, in that future candidates for the Kings Point superintendency will see the post as a prestigious one, with opportunity for career advancement.

14. Scenes from an Education: 2003–2004

1. Tom Dutton, interview by the authors, February 17, 2003.

2. Admiral Joseph Stewart, interview by the authors, June 8, 2004.

3. Robert Allee, e-mail to Jeffrey L. Cruikshank, August 27, 2004.

4. Indoc is a little different every year, depending on the inclinations of the superintendent and commandant, the nature of the incoming class, and the skill and dedication of the drill instructors. The following account brings together observations and experiences from several different recent years.

5. Graduates of Kings Point have an obligation to serve in the naval reserve for six years and also to keep their licenses active for six years. Because the Coast Guard requires license renewals on a five-year basis, this effectively amounts to a ten-year obligation.

6. Kyle L. Hembree, 1st class, 2004, provided to the authors by Eliot Lumbard.

7. "Section 1-H-1, 1-H-2 Aided in Academy's Development," *Polaris*, December 1942.

8. "Merchant fleets," *Economist*, November 20, 2003.

9. Peter Tirschwell, "An Important Job," *Journal of Commerce Week*, October 23–29, 2000.

10. Press release, May 13, 2005, from the Web site of the U.S. Department of Transportation Maritime Administration, www.marad.dot.gov/Offices/Ship/PRESS_NDRF_RRF_2qtr05.pdf.

11. Captain Robert Kitching, quoting from "Marine Training, Present and Future," the Baltic and International Maritime Council, www.dieselduck.net.

12. Michael Richardson, "Growing Vulnerability of Seaports from Terror Attacks," *Viewpoints*, March 5, 2004.
13. "KP Faculty Ranked Top Ten in Nation by Princeton Review," *Hear This*, September 2003.
14. "What Faculty Members Are Saying about the Rankings," *Hear This*, September 2003.
15. *USMMA Strategic Plan, 1993*, Academy Archives, Bland Library.

Bibliography

_____. *Report of the Comptroller of the United States: The Federal Role in Merchant Marine Officer Education,* June 15, 1977.

Albion, Robert Greenhalgh, and Jennie Barnes Pope. *Sea Lanes in Wartime: The American Experience, 1775–1945* (Hamden, CT: Archon Books, 1968).

Albright, Penrose Lucas, "Briefing Paper for Rear Admiral G. H. Miller Concerning the History of the Merchant Marine Reserve of the U.S. Navy," April 28, 1972.

Amborski, Leonard E. *The Last Voyage: Maritime Heroes of World War II* (Williamsville, NY: Ambor Press, 2001).

Benedetto, William R., *Sailing into the Abyss: The Incredible Odyssey of the SS Badger State* (New York: Kensington Publishing, 2005).

Brodie, Laura Fairchild. *Breaking Out: VMI and the Coming of Women* (New York: Vintage Books, 2001).

Bucheim, Lothar G. *U-Boat War* (New York: Bantam Books, 1979).

Bunker, John. *Heroes in Dungarees: The Story of the American Merchant Marine in World War II* (Annapolis, MD: Naval Institute Press, 1995).

Carse, Robert. *The Long Haul: The United States Merchant Service in World War II* (New York: Norton, 1965).

Clark, Captain John W. *SSS* (Kings Point: American Merchant Marine Museum, 2000).

Elkins, Stanley, and Eric McKitrick. *The Age of Federalism: The Early American Republic, 1788–1800* (New York: Oxford University Press, 1993).

Elphik, Peter. *Liberty: The Ships That Won the War* (Annapolis, MD: Naval Institute Press, 2001).

Engel, Arthur B. *The Proper Role of the Federal Government in Training Merchant Marine Personnel,* 1977.

Felknor, Bruce. *The U.S. Merchant Marine at War, 1775–1945* (Annapolis, MD: Naval Institute Press, 1998).

Flayhart, William Henry III. *The American Line: Pioneers of American Travel* (New York: Norton, 2000).

Furuseth, Andrew. "Schoolship Training Inadequate for Efficient Merchant Marine Personnel," *Nautical Gazette,* April 5, 1930.

Fuschetto, Mary Jane. *Kings Point: Acta non Verba* (Minneapolis: Diversified Graphics, 2003).

Gannon, Michael, *Black May* (New York: HarperCollins, 1998).

——. *Operation Drumbeat* (New York: HarperPerennial, 1991).

Gibson, Andrew, and Arthur Donovan. *The Abandoned Ocean: A History of United States Maritime Policy* (Columbia: University of South Carolina Press, 2000).

Guelpa, Leo B. *The U.S. Merchant Marine Cadet Corps—Its Establishment and Development* (USMMCC Educational Unit, 1944).

Gunther, John. *Taken at the Flood* (New York: Harper & Brothers, 1960).

Halpern, Paul G. *A Naval History of World War I* (Annapolis, MD: Naval Institute Press, 1994).

Infield, Glenn B. *Disaster at Bari* (New York: MacMillan, 1971).

Keuchle, David. *The Story of the "Savannah": An Episode in Maritime Labor-Management Relations* (Cambridge, MA: Harvard University Press, 1971).

Land, Emory Scott. *Winning the War with Ships* (New York: Robert M. McBride, 1958).

Lane, Frederic C. *Ships for Victory: A History of Shipbuilding Under the U.S. Maritime Commission in World War II* (Baltimore: Johns Hopkins University Press, 2001).

Marvin, Winthrop. *The American Merchant Marine: Its History and Romance from 1620 to 1902* (New York: Charles Scribner's Sons, 1902).

McNulty, Richard R. "A Plan for Federal Merchant Marine Training," *Nautical Gazette,* May 24, 1930.

——."Trained Personnel for Subsidized Lines," *Nautical Gazette,* November 24, 1934.

Meurn, Robert J. *Watchstanding Guide for the Merchant Mariner* (Centreville, MD: Cornell Maritime Press, 1990).

Mitchell, C. Bradford. *We'll Deliver* (Kings Point: USMMA Alumni Association, 1977).

Monsarrat, Nicholas. *Cruel Sea* (New York: Knopf Publishing Group, 1951).

Moore, Captain Arthur R. *A Careless Word . . . A Needless Sinking* (Kings Point: American Merchant Marine Museum, 1985).

Muller, Gerhardt. *Intermodal Freight Transportation,* 4th ed. (Washington, D.C.: Eno Transportation Foundation, 1999).

Northrup, Everett. "The Origins and Establishment of the U.S. Merchant Marine." Master's thesis, Colgate University, Hamilton, NY, June 1951.

Pedraja, Rene De La. *A Historical Dictionary of the U.S. Merchant Marine and Shipping Industry* (Westport, CT: Greenwood Press, 1994).

——. *The Rise and Decline of U.S. Merchant Shipping in the Twentieth Century* (New York: Twayne Publishers, 1992).

Reminick, Gerald. *Death's Railway: A Merchant Mariner on the River Kwai* (Palo Alto, CA: Glencannon Press, 2002).

——. *Nightmare in Bari: The World War II Liberty Ship Poison Gas Disaster and Coverup* (Palo Alto, CA: Glencannon Press, 2001).

———. *Patriots and Heroes: True Stories of the U.S. Merchant Marine in World War II* (Palo Alto, CA: Glencannon Press, 2000).

———. *Patriots and Heroes: True Stories of the U.S. Merchant Marine in World War II,* vol. 2 (Palo Alto, CA: Glencannon Press, 2004).

Roosevelt, Theodore. *The Naval War of 1812* (New York: Modern Library, 1999).

Smith, Kevin. *Conflict over Convoys. Anglo-American Logistics Diplomacy in the Second World War* (Cambridge, MA: Cambridge University Press, 1996).

Tomb, Captain J. H. "The Education of Merchant Marine Officers," *U.S. Naval Institute Proceedings,* vol. 58, no. 9, September 1932.

Valle, James E. "U.S. Merchant Marine Casualties," in *To Die Gallantly: The Battle of the Atlantic* Timothy J. Runyan and Jan M. Copes, eds. (Boulder, CO: Westview Press, 1994).

Walsh, James Peter. "Faculty Personnel Administration at the United States Merchant Marine Academy: The College Teacher in Federal Service." Doctoral dissertation, School of Education, University of Southern California, June 1961.

West, Wallace. *Down to the Sea in Ships: The Story of the U.S. Merchant Marine* (New York: Noble and Noble, 1947).

Photo Credits

Index

Page numbers in italics refer to illustrations or photos.

Abrahamsson, Bernard, 331, 332, 333, 334
Academic Advisory Board (AAB), 142–43, 146, 156, 167, 176, 180–82, 185, 204, 207, 243, 274, 343
academic calendar, 373–74, 377–83
academic majors, 219–20
academic minors, 220–22
Acceptance Day, Kings Point, 203
accreditation
  alumni and, 130, 240–41
  bachelor's degree and, 179, 180, 181
  curriculum and, 130, 133, 134, 142, 145, 179, 185–86
  engineering and, 219, 240–42, 270, 301
  faculty qualifications and, 139, 142, 146, 185, 186
  first evaluation and rejection in, 141–42, 143
  granting of, 145–47, 179
  library and, 136, 137, 139, 142, 145
  preparations for, 130, 132, 133, 135, 136, 137–39
  review and reaccreditation of, 179, 185–86, 368, 379
Accrediting Board for Engineering and Technology (ABET), 299
Ackerman, James H., 322–23

ACTA. See Project ACTA administrative unit in training, 61
Admiral Billard Academy, New London, Connecticut, 72, 121
admiralty law, 19, 20–21
admissions, 53, 133, 155
  acceptance process and, 348
  athletes and, 183–84
  class size restrictions and, 260–61, 293, 294
  diversity and, 228–29
  examination for eligibility and, 59, 69, 82, 134
  quota system in, 134
  strategic planning and, 329, 347–48
  World War II and, 82–83
Advisory Board, 142–43, 146, 156, 167, 176, 180–82, 185, 204, 207, 243, 274, 343
Afghanistan conflict, 10, 11
Afloat Forward Staging Base, 10–11
African Americans, 229–32, 229, 231
Agee, George, 119
Ahlgren, Julianne, 285
aircraft carriers, 18
Air Force Academy, 184, 219, 305, 306, 391
Alexander, Donald, 176, 183–84
Alexander, William T., 186
Allee, Robert, xv, 382, 411, 421, 431

Allen, Wendell C., 93–94
alma mater, Kings Point, 123
Alther, George W., 100
alumni (Alumni Association), 145,
　　163, 164, 165–66, 207, 248, 249,
　　270–72, 280, 297, 337
　accreditation and, 130, 240–41, 270
　awards from, *263*, 283–85, 397
　Congress and, 263–64, 363,
　　365–66, 368, 403
　continuing education and, 383, 384
　Engel and, 212, 247
　funding and, 271, 272, 387–88
　fund-raising by, 317, 319–23
　King and, 287, 288, 321–22
　Matteson and, 357–58, 361–63
　permanency and, 366–68
　recruitment by, 232
　support of the Academy by, 127,
　　159, 263–64, 402–3
　survey of, 260
　See also graduates of Kings Point
Alumni Day, 125–26
Alumni Fund, 207
America, 70, 118, 126
American Association of University
　　Professors (AAUP), 167
American Council of Education, 69
American Export Isbrandtsen Lines,
　　195
American Federation of Government
　　Employees (AFGE), 325
American Maritime History Project
　　(AMHP), xiii–xiv
American Merchant, 118
American Merchant Marine Institute,
　　160
American Merchant Marine Museum,
　　272
American Racer, 197–98
Amoroso, Jim, 394
Amphitrite Fountain, 435
Anderson, Annelise, 291, 360
Anderson, Martin, 291
Andrews, Hugh A., 72

Anholt, Della, 312
Annex, 42
apprentices, 56–57
Arab-Israeli War, 257
Arago decision, 36
Armed Forces Reserve Act, 173–74
Association of American Universities
　　(AAU), 137, 141, 143, 145, 147
Association of Parents and Friends of
　　Kings Point (APF), 160, 174
Athens, Arthur, xv, 409–11
athletics, Kings Point, 88, 130, 135,
　　183–84, 240, 249, 309–11, 419
　football, 126–27, *127*, 202, 358,
　　420–23
　sailing, 273–78, *276*, *277*, 344–45
Atomic Energy Commission (AEC),
　　188–90, 194
Atoms for Peace, 188

Babson, James L., 319, 320–21, *320*,
　　344
Babson, Jean, 319, *320*
bachelor's degree, 132, 143, 146, 174,
　　179, 180–81, 434–35
Baker, Joseph, 158–59
band, Kings Point, *246*, 278–80,
　　426–27
Bannwart, Alexander, 136
Baran, Joe, 413–14
Barbary pirates, 30
barracks and dormitories, 92, 233–34,
　　235, 273, 343
Barstow, William S., 270
Bearings (book), 428
Bejarano, Luis, 136–37, 160, 168,
　　170–71, 172, 200, 262–63, 267–68
Bell, David E., 2–5, 7
Bennett, John Logan, 5–7
Bent, Henry, 141
Berke, Julie, 312
Bishansky, Michael, 187
Black, Hugo, 45
Black Ball Line, 30
Black Committee, 45–46

Blackwell, Robert, 145, 233, 242, 247–51, 265, 281

Bland, Schuyler Otis, 46, 60, 131, 132, 208

Bland Amendment, Merchant Marine Act of 1936, 60, 63, 166

Bland Library, Kings Point
Academic Advisory Board on, 181
accreditation and, 136, 137, 139, 142, 145
Bejarano at, 136–37
building of, 207–8
funding for, 132, 207, 208
McLintock and, 180, 203, 207–8, 210

Board of Visitors, 159, 174–75, 204
accreditation and, 137, 142
curriculum and, 134, 142
establishment of, 131
first, 131–32
funding and, 156
library and, 136, 207
permanency and, 161–62

Boggs, Hale, Sr., 152, 155

Bonner, Herbert, 170

Bontemps, Thomas, 238, 239

Bozeman, Mrs. Willard, 61

Brady, Ralph, 326

Branch, Randolph, 53–54

Braynard, Frank, 190

Brennan, Chris, 104–5

Brickman, Jane, 307–8, 309, 311

Brogan, Patrick, 19–21

Brophy, Arnold, 170–71

Brotherhood of Marine Officers (BMO), 195

Brown, Earl, 127

Bureau of Marine Inspection and Navigation, 90

Bush, George W., 356, 444

business administration program, 302, 303

Butcher, Paul, 353

cadets, general
mail cadets, under Postal Aid Law, 33–34, 37–38, 44, 46
Merchant Marine Act of 1928 (Jones-White Act) and, 39–40
state-supported schools and, 32, 33, 38, 40, 42, 43, 44, 58, 60, 65, 70

cadets-midshipmen, Kings Point, 221
academic experience of, 182–83, 184
age limit for, 59
anti-intellectualism among, 217–18
barracks for, 92, 233–34, 235
course load of, 209, 210
daily life of, 155, 199–203, 231, 273, 314–17, 314, 316, 407
disciplinary problems and, 202, 203, 215, 246, 247
diversity and, 228–32, 229, 231, 295
eligible list and, 57–59, 69
formal establishment of rating of, 58
haircuts for, 416, 430
as midshipmen, 94
naval reserve status of, 94, 121, 163, 173–75, 425–26
parents of, 53–54, 160, 403–4, 424, 430–31, 432
protests by, 213–15, 421–22
research programs and, 226
service obligation and, 3, 20, 163, 267–69, 367, 425–26
stipends for, 82–83, 155–56
supervision of, 69–70
training conditions for, 53–54, 70–71
uniforms and dress code of, 83, 209, 234–35, 389
Vietnam War and, 213–15, 214
World War II and, 97–98, 99–107, 108–11
See also regimental system

"Cadet's Prayer," 205

calendar, 373–74, 377–83

Calhoon, Jesse, 258–59, 260–61, 262, 264

California State Nautical School, 42,
    59, 71, 73, 161
Carbotti, Michael J., 101–2
Card, Andrew, 356, *356*
Carlson, Sidney O., 187
Carmel, Stephen, 9–11
Carolina (Maersk Carolina), 1–2, *2*, 4–5,
    6, 7–8, *8*, 10–11, 27
Carter, Jimmy, 264–65, 269
Carter, Marshall, 410–11
Casey, Howard F., 255, 285
CBS, 260–62
Centner, Guyland L., 126
Chadwick, Judy, 247
Chaisson, W. P., 276
Chamberlain, Roy, 62
Champeau, A. E., 74
chapel. *See* Mariner's Chapel
Chrysler, Walter P., 76–78, 79, 80, *81*
Civilian Conservation Corps (CCC)
    huts, 87, *88*, 92
Civil Service Commission, 172, 296
civil service status, faculty conversion
    to, 166–69, 177, 182
Civil War, 31
Clayton, W. Graham, 268
Cleveland, Grover, 34
Clinton, Bill, 232, 359, 361, 395
Clinton, Hillary Rodham, *404*
clipper ships, 30–31
clubs, Kings Point, 123, 240
Coast Guard, 55–56, 57, 60, 63, 65,
    72–73, 315, 347, 357, 405–6, 421
    Engel and, 244, 245, 246, 247,
        279–80
    Kings Point and, 185–86, 228, 243
    licensing and, 220, 334, 336, 337,
        346, 436
    maritime regulations and, 129
    nuclear-powered ships and, 191
    training regulations of, 228, 375
    World War II and, 90–91
Coast Guard Academy, 41, 56, 58,
    131, 212, 241, 245, 280, 358, 391
Coast Guard Institute, 62, 63, 65

Coast Guard Reserve, 236
Cold War, 186–87, 256, 346
Command Board, 217
commencement exercises, *404*, *411*,
    421, *444*
Commerce Department, 157, 189,
    248, 291
commission, Naval Reserve, 175, 267,
    346
Commission on Merchant Marine
    and Defense, 349
Computer Aided Operations
    Research Facility (CAORF),
    226–28, 272, 300–301, 345, 375,
    376
computer model of training, 15, 16
computer science, 221–22, 300
Cone, Hutchinson, 42
Cone Committee, 42–43
Congress
    female cadets and, 234
    Kings Point accreditation and, 146
    Kings Point advocacy by, 132, 152,
        159, 170–71
    Kings Point alumni and, 263–64,
        363, 365–66, 368, 403
    Kings Point as a permanent school
        and, 120, 159, 161–64, 366
    Kings Point class sizes and, 260–61
    Kings Point construction and, 83,
        132, 204, 206, 207
    Kings Point degrees and, 179, 180
    Kings Point funding from, 132, 137,
        151–52, 155–56, 161, 264–66,
        323, 364–65, 390, 396
    maritime policy and, 32, 45
    Merchant Marine Act of 1920
        (Jones Act) and, 38
    Merchant Marine Act of 1928
        (Jones-White Act) and, 39–40
    Merchant Marine Act of 1936 and,
        46–47, 52, 58, 60, 132, 161
    Merchant Marine Reserve and, 39
    merchant marine schools and,
        32–33

Congress (*continued*)
  Maritime Commission report on training to, 60, 63–66, 69
  national maritime academy and, 54, 57, 60, 61
  naval reserve status and, 60–61, 174–75
  officer training and, 33–34, 265–66
  World War I and, 36–37, 38
Consumer, 413–18
container ships, 196–98, *198*, 346, *415*
Continental Navy, 29–30
continuing education, 296–99, 330, 341–42, 383
conversion to civil service status, 166–69, 177, 182
convoys, 108–9, *109*
Conway, Howard P., 100
Cooper/T. Smith Stevedoring, 23, 25–26
Copeland, Royal S., 46
Coronado, 12
Crow, Harry, 96
curriculum, 155
  academic majors and, 219–20
  academic minors and, 220–22
  accreditation and, 130, 133, 134, 142, 145, 179, 185–86
  Advisory Board and, 142–43
  areas of study in, 93–96, *94*, *95*, 98–99, *99*
  elective program in, 219, 220
  extending to four years, 132–34
  faculty examination of, 184–85
  general education requirement in, 181, 186
  initial shaping of, 93–99
  King and, 299–301
  Matteson and, 370–72
  questionnaire to graduates about quality of, 182, 184
  trimesters and, 373–74, 377–83
  See also specific programs
Cushing, Charles R., 297, 319–20, *320*, 321, 327

Dailey, Gardiner, 74, *75*
Dana, Richard Henry, Jr., 208
Davey, Phil, 20
Davey & Brogan, 19, 20–21
deck cadets, 58, 59, 68, 93, 184, 198–99, 219, 222, 296, 301, 302, 312, 436
DeGhetto, Kenneth, 322, 396, 398
Delano, Amasa, 92
Department of Commerce, 157, 189, 248, 291
Department of Defense (DOD), 10–11, 175, 350, 359, 372
Department of Transportation, 291–92, 293, 294, 347, 367
Derounian, Steve, 158, 159
Desert Storm, 351, 352
designated person ashore (DPA), 7–9
diesel engineering program, 242–43, 297
district offices, Merchant Marine Cadet Corps. *See* New Orleans District Office; New York District Office; San Francisco District Office
diversity, 228–32, *229*, *231*, 295
Dodds, Harold W., 186
Donovan, Arthur, 30, 36, 256, 257, 291, 352, 360
dormitories and barracks, 92, 233–34, 235, 273, 343
dress code, 83, 209, 234–35, 245–46
drill instructors, 428–30
dual-license program, 198–99, 222, 335, 375–77, 417
Dutton, Tom, 413–16

Educational Policy Committee, Kings Point, 142–43
educational ("ed") unit in training, 61
Eggers and Higgins, 206, 207
Ehrmann, Michael J., *214*
Eisenberg, Raymond, 187
Eisenhower, Dwight D., 152, 164, 188, 189

Eisenhower, Mrs. Dwight D., *152*
elective program, 219, 220
eligible list, 57–59, 69
Emergency Fleet Corporation (EFC), 37, 38
Emery Rice, 156, 272
Empire State, 42, 72, 365
employment of graduates
  Depression and, 44
  dual-licensing program and, 199, 377
  engineering accreditation and, 240, 241–42
  female cadets and, 312–13
  merchant marine and, 257, 260, 266, 267, 293, 327
  minorities in shipbuilding and, 232
  profiles of graduates and examples of, 1–27
  unions and, 57, 257–61, 266–67
Engel, Arthur B.
  accreditation of engineering program and, 241
  Coast Guard and, 244, 245, 246, 247
  departure of, 254–55
  report on federal role in training and, 250, 252–53
  as superintendent, 212–13, *212*, 243–44, 245–47, 252, 264, 266, 271, 272–73, 279–80, 283, 318
  U.S. Maritime Administration (MARAD) and, 247–51, 253–54
engine cadets, 58, 59, 68, 93–94, 184, 198–99, 219, 222
engineering
  accreditation of program of, 219, 240–42, 270, 301
  cadet training and, 58, 94, 96, 134
  diesel, 242–43, 297
  graduates working in, 9, 13, 16, 17, 19
  jobs in, 240, 241–42
  nuclear, 188–90, 192–94, *193*, 195–96

  shipyard management and, 347, 372–74
engineering management program, 347
Engineers' Council for Professional Development (ECPD), 219, 240–42, 299
Enterprise, 33
Erb, Arthur, 383–84
examinations
  eligibility, 59, 69, 82, 134
  licensing, 59, 434–40, *436*

faculty, Kings Point, 160
  Academic Advisory Board on, 181, 185
  academic deans and, 142, 143
  accreditation and qualifications of, 139, 142, 146, 185, 186
  advanced degrees held by, 222–25
  civil service status and, 166–69, 182
  computer usage and, 300
  curriculum examination by, 184–85
  diversity and, 295–96
  dual-license program and, 335–36
  Engel and, 212, 213
  female, 295–96, 308–10
  foreign academies and, 187
  King and, 288–89, 294–96
  McLintock and, 167, 168, 169–73
  research programs and, 226
  Thompson Report on, 222, 223–24
  union for, 323–25, 378, 381
Faculty Committee on Personnel Matters (FCPM), 169–70
female cadets, xv, 285
  barracks for, 233–34, 235
  Engel and, 248–50
  first class of, 235–39, *236*, *238*
  initial reactions to, 233
  legislation mandating, 232–33
  preparations for, 233–35
  Sea Year and, 237–39
  success of, as graduates, 312–13
  treatment of, 238–39, 306–8
  uniforms for, 234–35, 245–46

female faculty members, 295–96, 308–10

Femenia, Jose, 372–74, 379–80, 381, 443–44

Ferris, Charles W., 72, 133–34, 168, 171, 172

field trips, 96–97

Fiore, Roland, 123

Fitzgerald, F. Scott, 78

Flick, Kent, 245–46, 416–18

football, 126–27, *127*, 202, 358, 420–23

Force, Kenneth R., 235, 246, *246*, 250, 254, 272–73, 278–80, 284, 290

Ford, Gerald, 234, 240, 264, 265

Ford, Walter, 172

foreign officers, training of, 187–88, 315

Forster, Donald, 368

Fowler, Charles, 112

Francis, Gerald P., 224, 242

Franklin, John M., 205

Freeman, Carlos A., 95–96

Frye, William P., 33

funding of Kings Point, 387
  alumni and, 271, 272
  chapel construction and congressional, 132, 137, 155–56, 264–66, 364–65, 390, 396
  construction at Kings Point and, 83, 132, 204–6, 207, 208
  continuing education and, 342
  district office campuses and, 75, 78
  faculty conversion to civil service and, 166, 168
  fund-raising and, 317, 319–23, 399–402
  research at Kings Point and, 225–27

Furuseth, Andrew, 36, 47

Fuschetto, Mary Jane, 403

Gaebelein, Thad, 409, 410

Galante, Cathy, 438–40

Gald, Peder, 72, 168

Gardner, Ray, 436–37

George H. W. Bush, 18

Georgetown School of Foreign Service, 144–45

G.I. Bill, 128

Gibson, Andrew, 30, 36, 208, 210, 212, 214, 225–28, 230, 247, 256, 257, 291, 352, 360

Gingrich, Newt, 366

Global Maritime and Transportation School (GMATS), 16, 385, 388

Gore, Al, 359, 362, 363

Government Affairs Committee, 363, 403

graduates of Kings Point
  active duty requirements of, 3, 17, 20
  career choices for, 315
  jobs for, 244, 257, 260, 266, 293, 326
  profiles of, and examples of jobs held by, 1–27
  questionnaire on courses sent to, 182, 184
  as superintendent at Kings Point, 251, 285, 287–88, 318
  See also alumni

Graduation Day, 201

Granados, Gilbert, 407–8

Great Britain
  Merchant Navy of, 39, 154, 206
  Revolutionary War and, 29–30
  training system of, 41, 68
  U.S. shipbuilding industry and, 29, 30, 31
  War of 1812 and, 30
  World War II and, 81, 82, 108, 112

Green, Bonnie M., 395–96

Gregurech, Steve, 190

Griffin, Vance C., 21–23

Grigsby, Bruce, 232

Gross, Maurice, 80, 190, 191, 193, 222

Gulf War, 342, 346, 349, 364

Gunn, Walter, 220, 221–22

gunnery training, 98–99, *99*

Haag, Alfred H., 61, 63
haircuts, *416*, 430
Hall, Leonard W., 152
Hall, Patrick C., 24–26
Halma, 105–7
Hansen, Alfred, 327, 332, 346
Harding, Warren G., 38
Harrison, Jess, 184–85
Havasy, James, *189*, *196*
Hazlett, John C., 14–16
Hear This (cadet newspaper), 156, 183, 187, 192, 207, 253, 338
heavy lifts, 22–23
Henderson, Robert, 59
Herberger, Albert, 292, 359, 363–65, *365*, 367, 383–85, 386, 400, 403
Hewitt, James J., 105–7
Hickman, Ron, 241
Hirschkowitz, Moses ("Mo"), 191, 194, 198, 223
Hodges, Luther, 176
Hoffman, Allen C., 73–74
Holubowicz, Raymond, 108–9
honor code, 304–6
Hook, John R., 330–31, 340
Hubert, Charles, 97, 171, 172, 222–23
Hull, Cordell, 66
Humphrey, Hubert, 159
Hurley, Edward N., 37
Hyatt, Delwyn, 96, 131

independent study programs, 71–72
indoc (indoctrination period), 423–30
Indonesia, 187, 315
Information Representatives Program, 232
Ingersoll, C. D., 192
Intergovernmental Maritime Consultative Organization (IMCO), 228, 300–301
intermodalism, 331, 332–34, 346, 368, 370–72

International Longshoremen's Association (ILA), 24
International Maritime Organization (IMO), 16, 375, 378
International Seamen's Union, 36, 47
International Union of Masters, Mates, and Pilots (MMP), 24, 58, 194, 259–60
involuntary servitude, 36
Iraq conflict, 11
Ives, Irving, 152, 163, 164

Jackson, Mel, 272
Jahncke, Ernest Lee, 40
Japan, 64–65, 68–69, 81
Jarrett, Lawrence, 171, 302–3
Jenkins, Emanuel, 232, 317
Jennings, S. A., 74
Jones, F. Taylor, 182
Jones, Wesley, 38, 39, 40
Jones Act, 38, 360
Jones-White Merchant Marine Act, 39–40
Jorgensen, Mary-lou, 396, 397
Judge Advocate General Corps (JAG), 20

Kaiser, Henry J., 107, 108
Kallgren, Andrew M., 11–14
Kaplan, Nathan J., 101–2
Kendall, Lane, 168, 171, 172
Kennedy, John F., 205
Kennedy, Joseph P., 47, 48–49, 53, 55, 56, 57, 58, 89, 91
Kent State University, 213, 214
Keogh, Eugene, 131, 132, 158, 206
Kielhorn, L. V., 62, 63
King, Ernest J., 89, 91, 108
King, Philip, 49, 53
King, Thomas
  alumni organizations and, 321–22, 361–62
  background of, 251
  curriculum and, 299–301
  faculty changes and, 294–96

King, Thomas (*continued*)
  goals and, 289–90
  leadership style of, 287
  retirement and, 254–55, 317
  as superintendent, 284, *284*, 285,
    286–90, 294, 298, 305, 306, 308,
    318
  as temporary superintendent, 246,
    251–52, 264
Kings Point Challenge, 317, 322
Kings Pointer (magazine), 227, 237, 270,
  271, 278, 287, 313, 321, 328, 332,
  344
Kings Pointer (training vessel), 149–50,
  217, 389, *389*
Kings Point Foundation, 396
Kings Point Fund, 271, 272, 321
Kirk, Francis Shallus, 61, *61*
Kirkland, Lane, 361–62, *362*
Knight, Telfair, 47, *48*, 54, 58, 71
  Kings Point and, 78, 83, 90, 91, 114,
    130, 137, 141, 141–42, 143, 144,
    155, 162, 205
  McNulty's South American field trip
    and, 66–67, 69
  report to Congress and, 63, 64
  support for a national academy and,
    65–66, 69, 70
Kochka, Joseph, 137–39, 141,
  166–67
Korean War, 175, 251
Kozlowski, Henry, 326–28, 346
Kraus, Jeanne, 312, 313
Krinsky, Paul, 147–48, 195, 214, 242,
  254, 317, 333, 358
  curriculum changes and, 299–304,
    332
  first female cadets and, 233–34
  funding and, 387–88
  King and, 289–90, 299–301
  on McLintock, 209–10
  research programs and, 227–28
  strategic planning and, 325–29,
    331, 342, 343, 346, 369–70,
    378

as superintendent, 318, 319, 322,
  323–31, *324*, 344, 369
upgrading of faculty by, 224–25
Knutsen, Ed, 233

LaDage, John H., 187
Lamy, Bud, 266, 267
Land, Emory S., 48, *49*, 57, 58, 66,
  89, 90, 91, 119, 128, 132, 280
Lane, Edward A., Jr., 72
Law, Edward, 187
law program, 19, 20–21, 302–3
Lazara, Kenneth, 323, 325
leadership, 339–40, 408–11, 412
Leback, Warren, 261, 262, 265, 327,
  355, 356–57
Lehman, Herbert, 163, 164
Lewis, Drew, 292–93
Liberty Ships, 106, 107–8, 109, 110,
  229
library. *See* Bland Library
licensing
  accreditation and, 185
  annual examinations for, 59
  Coast Guard and, 220, 334, 336,
    337, 346
  debate over professional standards
    and, after the Civil War, 32
  definition of cadet and, 58
  dual-license program in, 198–99,
    335
  female cadets and, 312
  Kings Point graduates and, 121, 174
  mandatory examinations at the end
    of course of study and, 59
  service obligation and, 269
  sitting for the license, 434–40, *436*
  World War II and, 82
lifeboat training, *94*
Limouze, Arthur Sanford, 185
logistics program, 331, 332–34, 368,
  370
longshoremen, 22
Lumbard, Eliot H., xiii
Lundy estate, 248, 249

McCain, John, *411*
Macauley, Edward, 91, 114
McCormick, Eugene, 327, 404–5
McCready, Lauren S., 61, 62, *62,*
    122, 200, 281, 284
  dual-license program and, 198
  faculty issues and, 168, 171, 172,
    223
  Kings Point construction and,
    76–78, 83–84, 85–86
  McLintock and, 152, 210
  nuclear-powered ships and, 191,
    193, 195
  research programs and, 225–26, 27
  Stedman's departure and, 139–40
  teaching by, 96, 134
McDonald, Walter, 221
machine shop, Kings Point, *84,* 85
McIlnay, Sharon Thorpe, 17–19
McKenna, John T., 170, 172–73
McKinley, William, 34, 35
McLintock, Gordon, 114
  accreditation and, 145, 182, 186
  autocratic leadership style of, 153,
    169, 173, 208, 213–14
  background of, 153–55
  chapel and, 180, 203, 205
  departure of, 208–10, 211–12, 213
  dual-licensing program and, 199
  faculty and, 167, 168, 169–73
  funding and, 156, 321
  library and, 180, 203, 207–8, 210
  Maritime Administration (MARAD)
    and, 157, 160–61, 176–77, 208,
    210, 258
  morale issues and, 170–71
  politics and, 151–52, 208
  power bases and, 164–65
  Sea Year split and, 183
  special aide O'Leary's perspective
    on, 201–3
  as superintendent, 144, 145,
    151–53, *152,* 164, 176–77, 180,
    200, 274, 323–24
  unions and, 258, 323–24

McLintock, Wynne, 205, *205,* 210
McMahon, Christopher J., 16, 305,
    339, 344–45, 384, 385
McNulty, Richard R., 49, *53*
  accreditation and, 141–42, 143
  background of, 40–41
  chapel construction and, 204–5
  Coast Guard supervision and, 90,
    91
  curriculum for training and, 61,
    62–63, 63–64
  as Father of the Academy, 140, 144,
    145, 281
  formal recognition of, 280–82
  Georgetown School of Foreign Ser-
    vice and, 144–45
  Kings Point administration and, 91,
    93, 114, 118, 130, 131, 137
  McLintock and, 144, 155
  national academy promoted by,
    41–43, 44, 49, 52, 54, 65–66, 70
  report to Congress and, 63, 65–66,
    69
  ship-based training observed by,
    66–69
  shore-based training supported by,
    69, 70, 74
  South American field trip of, 66–69
  as superintendent, 140–41, *140,*
    143–44
  training conditions for cadets and,
    70, 71
McNulty, Sue, 93, 144
McNulty Campus, 282
McWilliams, Mary Bachand, 236–27
Maersk Carolina, 1–2, *2,* 4–5, *6,* 7–8, *8,*
    10–11, 27
Magnuson, Warren G., 163, 265
Mahady, Philip C., 72, 107
Mahan, Alfred Thayer, 34–35
Mahoney, Joseph, 262, 281
mail cadets, 33–34, 37–38, 44
majors, academic, 219–20
Mangodt, Einar, 72
Manning, George C., 62

Manning, John, 227
MARAD. *See* U.S. Maritime Administration
marching band, Kings Point, *246*, 278–80, 426–27
marine engineering and shipyard management, 347, 372–74
Marine Engineers' Beneficial Association (MEBA), 19–20, 32, 193, 194, 257–62, 266–67
Mariner's Chapel, Kings Point
  building of, 203–6, *204*, 343
  funding for, 132, 204–6
  McLintock and, 180, 203, 205
Maritime Education and Training Act, 315, 316
maritime industry
  container ships and, 196–98, *198*
  decline in, 244, 255
  diesel power and, 242
  Engel as superintendent and, 245
  jobs in, 244, 257, 260, 266, 267, 313, 327
  Kings Point mission and, 216–17, 289, 326–27, 329–30
  national defense and, 353
  nuclear-powered ships and, 188–96
  outsourcing of military functions to, 11, 12
  Reagan policies and, 290–91
  service obligation in, 267–69
  support for Kings Point in, 160
  Vietnam War and, 255–56
  See also shipbuilding
maritime law, 19, 20–21, 302–3
Maritime Security Program, 1, 4
Maritime Service, 60, 65, 120, 155, 162, 166, 167, 168
Marshall, Max, 84
Martin, Clarence D., Jr., 176
Marvin, Winthrop, 31
Mason, Martin A., 167
Master Mariners Readiness Course, 298–99, 342

master plan, Kings Point, 395–96, 401
Masters, Mates, and Pilots (MMP) union, 24, 58, 194, 259–60
Matsonia, 198
Matteson, Thomas
  alumni and, 357–58, 361–63
  background of, 356–57
  curriculum and, 370–72, 384
  dual-licensing program and, 375–77
  Gore's threatened closing of Kings Point and, 359–60, 363
  Regiment and, 368–69
  retirement of, 386
  as superintendent, *309*, 355, *355*, 356–60, *362*, 368–69, 370–72, 375–83, 385–86, 393
  trimesters and, 378–83
Maya, Mariano, 167
Mazek, Warren, 326–29, 332, 334, 343, 346, 377, 379, 381, 393, 431
merchant marine
  Civil War and, 31
  clipper ships and, 30–31
  congressional support for, 32–33
  decline of, 441
  Franklin D. Roosevelt and, 45
  Gulf War and, 349
  jobs in, 257, 266, 327
  Kings Point mission and, 216–17, 329
  as a major sea power, 127–29
  naval auxiliary function of, 253
  privateers and, 30
  Revolutionary War and, 29–30
  service obligation and, 267–69
  Theodore Roosevelt and, 35
  surplus of vessels in, 37, 38–39, 128–29
  United States Shipping Board regulation of, 36–37
  Wilson's support for, 35–36
  World War I and, 37, 38–39, 128
  World War II and, 107–11, 128

Merchant Marine Acts
  of 1920 (Jones Act), 38, 360
  of 1928 (Jones-White Act), 39–40
  of 1936, 46–47, 52, 58, 60, 107, 132,
    161, 166, 316, 324
  of 1936, Bland Amendment, 60, 63,
    166
  of 1936, 1939 Amendments to, 69
  of 1970, 256–57
Merchant Marine Museum, 272
Merchant Marine Reserve, 72, 267,
  268–69, 346
merchant marine schools
  establishment of, 32–33
  state support of, 32, 33, 38, 40, 42,
    43, 44, 58, 60, 65, 70
Merchant Marine Training and
  Education Act, 269
Metcalf, Victor, 35
Middle States Association (MSA),
  145–47, 179–80, 181, 182, 185–86,
  379
Midshipman Council, 209, 217
Midshipman. See cadet-midshipmen
Midships (yearbook), 165
Military Sealift Command (MSC), 10,
  11–14, 17, 175, 350, 351, 442
Military Sea Transportation Service
  (MSTS), 175
Miller, W. McNab, III, 267–68
Mineta, Norman, 402
minorities at Kings Point
  as cadets, 228–32, 437
  as faculty, 295–96
minors, academic, 220–22
mission statement, Kings Point,
  130–31, 216–17, 293, 326–27,
  329–31
Mitchell, C. Bradford, xiv, 176
Mitchell, William V., 100
monomoy boats, 80, 94, 273
Moran, Edward, Jr., 48
Morrill, Arthur G., 72
Morro Castle, xiv, 41, 44
Morse, Clarence, 163, 164, 171–72

motto, Kings Point, 93
Mowrey, Jessica S., 7–9, 10
Mulzac, Hugh, 229
Museum Ship, Kings Point, 156

Nacirema, 25
national defense, 76, 146, 291, 293,
  327, 349, 353, 366
National Defense Reserve Fleet
  (NDRF), 255–56, 350
National Maritime Research Center
  (NMRC), 225–28
National Performance Review (NPR),
  359–60, 383
National Sealift Training Program,
  342
National Shipping Authority, 298
Nautical Gazette, 41, 42, 47
nautical science, 301–4, 332, 335
Naval Academy, 40, 41, 58, 184, 219,
  266, 274, 315, 391
Naval Postgraduate School, 219
naval reserve
  cadets and, 121, 173–75, 425–26
  commission in, 175, 267, 346
  Congressional legislation on qualifi-
    cations for, 60–61
  graduates and duty requirement for,
    3, 20, 163
  merchant marine reserve in, 268–69
  United States Shipping Board policy
    on, 36–37
  World War II and cadets in, 81–82,
    94
naval science, 94, 96
navigation, in Kings Point curriculum,
  94, 96
navy
  aircraft carriers in, 18
  Center for Naval Engineering of,
    14, 16
  Engel's report on training and,
    252
  graduates and active duty require-
    ment for, 3, 17, 20, 27

navy (*continued*)
  Judge Advocate General Corps
    (JAG) of, 20
  Korean War and cadets in, 175
  outsourcing of military functions by,
    12
  in Revolutionary War, 29–30
  Surface Warfare Officer School
    (SWOS) of, 17
  Theodore Roosevelt and, 35
  training for sailors in, 14–16
  in World War II, 89, 128
Navy Department, 48, 90, 163
Nazzaro, Pasquale, 195
Neizer, Meredith, 238, 239, 313
Nemirow, Samuel B., 253–55, 270
New Orleans District Office, 70, 71,
  72, 73–74, 120
  Pass Christian, Mississippi, campus
    of, 74, *75*, 76, 93, *99*, 100, 137,
    148, *149*
Newsday, 157, 160, 170–71, 172, 212,
  215, 238, 250, 255
New York District Office, 70, 71,
  72–73, 76
New York Maritime Academy, 42
New York State Maritime College,
  241–42
New York State Merchant Marine
  Academy (New York State Nauti-
  cal School), 33, 42, 43, 59, 71
  Fort Schuyler campus of, 72, 80, 83,
    115–16
New York Times, 58, 172, 293
Nichols, Leonard, 248–50
Nichols, Michael, *196*
Nixon, Richard M., 256
Northrop, Everett H., 208
Nottingham, Milton, 158, 159, 176,
  260, 261, 262, 268, 281, 327, 362,
  363, 392
nuclear physics and engineering,
  188–90, 192–94, *193*, 195–96

Ocean Mail Act, 33–34

Office of Management and Budget
  (OMB), 291, 294, 360, 363
officer training
  federal study of, 265–66
  Kings Point mission and, 216, 293,
    329, 330
  McNulty's promotion of, 40–43, 44,
    49, 52, 54
  Maritime Commission and,
    52–54
  Merchant Marine Reserve and,
    39
  Merchant Marine Act of 1928
    (Jones-White Act) and, 39–40
  Merchant Marine Act of 1936 and
    federal academy for, 46–47, 52, 58,
    60, 132, 161
  merchant marine schools for, 32–33,
    38
  national academy for, 40, 41–43,
    45–46, 54
  Postal Aid Law and, 34, 37–38
  schoolship sea-based model of, 42,
    43, 53, 54
  shore-based academy concept in,
    41–42
  state-supported schools for, 32, 33,
    38, 40, 42, 43, 44, 58, 60, 65,
    70
  World War I and, 37
  World War II and need for, 82,
    83
O'Hara, Edwin, 110, *110*
Oil Pollution Act of 1990, 342, 346,
  383
O'Leary, Richard, 180, 201–3, 208
O'Neil, David, 240–41, 274–75, 284,
  327, 368
O'Reilly, William, 95
outsourcing, 11, 12

packet service, 30
Palmer, Nathaniel P., 88
Panama, 316–17
Panama Canal, 35, 68, 316

parents of cadet-midshipmen, 53–54, 160, 403–4, 424, 430–31, *432*

Pass Christian, Mississippi, campus, U.S. Maritime Commission Academy, 74, *75*, 76, 93, *99*, 100, 137, 148, *149*

Patten, Mary, 93

Patterson, Robert, 128

Patterson, Thomas, 285, 286

Paul VI, pope, 195

Payne, Fernandus, 141, 142

Peacock, J. C., 46, 47

Pearson, Leland ("Lee"), 171, 172, 183, 302

Peet, W. C., Jr., 53

Peña, Federico, 367

permanency of Kings Point, 120, 130, 132, 159, 161–64, 366–68

Petersen Lubow, Susan, 309–11

Pfohl, Bob ("Stormy"), 127

Philadelphia Inquirer, 269–70

Philippines, 81, 100, 148, 188, 315

philosophy of education, 138–39

pirates, 30

Pitkin, Marvin, 225, 226

plebes, 423–33. *See also* cadets

Polaris (cadet publication), 91–92, 93–94, 95–96, 97, 116, 121, 122–23, 129, 131, 140, 147, 197, 276

politics
  McLintock and, 151–52, 208
  unions and, 260–62

Pollard, Irving S., 126

Pombeiro, Beth Gillin, 269–70

Poppe, Janus, 220, 302

Postal Aid Law, 33–34, 46

Potlatch, 101–2

Powell, Colin, 352, *353*

prisoners of war, 100, 103–4

privateers, 30

Project ACTA, 262–64, 267–68, 361, 365, 368, 390–91, 399

Prosser, Arthur ("Joe"), 276–77, *276*, 343–44

Qualified Member of the Engineering Department (QMED), 6, 336–37

Rackett, Pete, 284, 310, 311

radiological hazards and health physics, 190–92

Randall, William, 143

Raymond, Charles, *362*

Ready Reserve Force, 298, 328, 343, 351, 365, 388, 427, 442

Reagan, Ronald, 287, 290–91, 293, 306

Reconciliation Act, 292

recruitment programs
  for cadets, 230–31, 232, 248, 347
  for faculty, 295–96

Reddy, Richard, 123

regimental system (Regiment), Kings Point, 119, 130, *130*, *370*
  academic world integrated with, 218
  Engel and, 212, 247, 252
  honor code and, 304–6
  indoc (indoctrination period) and, 423–24, 427–30
  as a key pillar, 121–22, 419, 421–23
  leadership and, 339–40, 408–11
  morale of, 202–3, 208–9, 304, 360, 368–69
  Stewart and, 393, 408–9, 411
  strategic planning under Krinsky and, 337–39
  Thompson Report on, 218
  White Paper of, 209, 212

Rehm, Gerald S., 396–99, 400, 401

Renick, Charles, 234, 239, 256, 260–61, 272, 281, 288, 297

Report to Congress on the Training of Merchant Marine Personnel, 64–66, 69

Revolutionary War, 29–30

Reynolds, Clark, 224, 324

Rickover, Hyman, 189

Ring, Daniel S., 49, 53

riverboats, 32

Roland, Dennis, 103, 104

Roosevelt, Eleanor, *122*

Roosevelt, Franklin Delano, 45, 46,
    48, 82, 89, 91, 92, 113, 116, 128
Roosevelt, Theodore, 34, 35
Rosenberg family, *419*
Rosenman, Samuel, 128
Rothschild, Louis, 152, 157–58,
    159–61, 162, 163, 166, 167

Safarik, Robert, 288–89, 340
safety, 44–45, 64, 71, 190, 346–47
sailing, 273–78, *276, 277*, 344–45
Sailors' Union of the Pacific (SUP),
    67
Sandberg, Clifford W., *192*, 193,
    200–201, 226
Sandberg, George, 376
San Francisco District Office, 70, 71,
    73, 74, 120
    San Mateo Point campus of, 74–76,
        75, 93, 137, 147
Sauerbier, C. L., 187
Savannah, 188–96, *189, 192, 193, 196*,
    198, 227, 260, 296
Scarborough, Robert H., 285, 286,
    327, 363, 390
Schell, Sam, 49, 78, 113
Schenck, Joseph, 85, 87
Scherger, John, 160, 171, 174–75
Schiavo, Mary, 367–68
Scholar Program, 226
schoolship sea-based training. *See*
    ship-based training
Scroggins, Joe, Jr., 229–32, *229, 231*
sea base, 10–11
Sealand Integrity, 5–6
Seaman's Act, 36
sea training. *See* ship-based training
Sea Project, 97–98, 121
Sea Year, 121, 134, 162, 179, 338, 410
    curriculum changes and, 303
    dual-license program and, 199
    examples of, 3, 5, 15, 24, *196*, 315,
        413–18
    female cadets and, 237–39
    as a key pillar, 121, 418, 419

splitting into two half years, 182–83,
    185
trimesters and, 378, 382
World War II and, 105–7
Seiberlich, Carl, 87, 285, 286, 287,
    297, 327, 333
Senior Executive Service, 253–55
Seward, H. L., 63–64
Shames, Amy D., 313
Shear, Harold, 286, 303
Sherman, Fred, 327, 361, 365–66
ship-based training, *217*
    congressional support for, 69
    curriculum and, 133, 375
    district offices and, 71
    female cadets and, 237
    McNulty's observation of, 66–69,
        70, 71
    matching cadets to ships for, 71
    schoolship sea-based model of, 42,
        43, 53, 54, 61
    Sea Project and, 97–98
    simulators and, 227, 300–301, 375
    supervision of cadets in, 69–70
    training conditions for cadets in,
        70–71
    unions and, 267
    World War II and cadets in, 71,
        81–82, 99–107
shipboard training program, Kings
    Point, 303–4
shipbuilding
    British competition in, 29, 30, 31
    Civil War and, 31
    clipper ships and, 30–31
    in colonial period, 29
    employment of minorities in, 232
    Shipping Act of 1916 and, 37
    subsidies for, 256–57, 292
    World War I and, 37, 38–39
    World War II and, 89, 107–8
Shipping Act of 1916, 36, 37
Ship's Officer program, 6, 334–37
Shirley, James T., 400, 403, 404–5,
    407

shore-based training
  McNulty's support for, 69, 70
  as preferred mode of training,
    41–42, 61
  training course requirements for, 72
  World War II and, 82
simulators, 227, 300–301, 375
Sinnott, Frank, 158, 321
60 Minutes (television show), 260–62
Skinner, James, 347–48, 432
Skinner, Samuel, 343, 387–88
Slater, Rodney, 395
Sloan, Alfred P., 205
Smigelski, Alex, 277–78
Smith, William, *263*
Solis, Willie, 307, 314, 315
Sprague, J. Russell, 152
Spurr, Horton H., 98, 99, 136,
    287–88
Stakem, Thomas, Jr., 162, 176
State Department, 187, 315
state nautical schools
  funding of, 157–58, 161, 162, 265,
    364–65
  schoolship training and, 42, 43
  service obligation and, 269, 367
  shore-based training and, 32, 33, 38,
    40, 42, 43, 44, 58, 60, 65, 70,
    71–72
  support for Kings Point by, 265,
    364–65
  World War II and, 82, 83
States Marine Lines, 160, 190, 191,
    194, *276*
steamships, 31, 32, 33, 34
Stedman, Giles C., *117*
  athletics and, 135
  background of, 117–19
  departure of, 139–40
  McNulty and, 70, 141
  as superintendent, 116–17, 119,
    125–27, 132, 135
stevedores, 22, 23, 24, 25
Stewart, Joseph D.
  background of, 392–93

four pillars and, 418–23
fund-raising and, 399, 400–401
Kings Point infrastructure and,
    393–96, 401–2
plebes and, 431–33
Regiment and, 393, 408–9, 411
as superintendent, 368, 382, 391,
    392, 393–96, *398*, 399, 400–401,
    402, 408–9, 411, 412
Stewart, Richard D., 333–34, 334–35,
    371, 376
Stoddert, Benjamin, 30
strategic planning, 325–29, 331, 337,
    341, 343, 346–47, 369–70, 378
Strategic Transportation Alliance, 346
Studds, Gerry, 265, 269
student clubs, Kings Point, 123, 240
student protests, 208, 209, 213–15,
    247
students. *See* cadets
Sullivan, Leonor K., 265
Supreme Court, 36
Surface Warfare Officer School
    (SWOS), 17
Swertka, Albert, 193

tattoos, *246*, 280
third mates, 7
Thirteenth Amendment, 36
Thomas, Myron, 187
Thomas, William H., 109–10
Thompson, Arthur, 215–20, 222,
    223–24, 240
Tiedemann, Hollie J., 162
Tiernan, John W., 159
Timothy Pickering, 100, 104–5
Tomb, James Henry, 42, 43, *43*, 59,
    63, 70, 72, 114–16, 119, 281
tool shop, Kings Point, *89*
training
  British system for, 41, 68
  Center for Naval Engineering, Nor-
    folk Naval Base, and, 14, 16
  Coast Guard regulations and, 228,
    241

training (*continued*)
  computer model of, 15, 16
  congressional support for, 33
  curriculum created for, 61–63
  demand for better conditions for
    cadets in, 53–54
  federal government role in, 250,
    252–53
  foreign officers and, 187–88, 315
  independent study programs in,
    71–72
  Japanese system for, 64–65, 68–69
  length of study in, 82–83, 93
  McNulty's promotion of, 40–43, 44,
    49, 52, 54
  Maritime Commission and, 52–53,
    55–57
  Maritime Commission report on,
    60, 63–66, 69
  Merchant Marine Act of 1928
    (Jones-White Act) and, 39–40
  Merchant Marine Act of 1936 and
    federal academy for, 46–47, 52, 58,
    60, 132, 161
  Merchant Marine Reserve and, 39
  merchant marine schools for, 32–33
  need for, after graduation, 13–14
  Postal Aid Law and, 33–34, 37–38
  Savannah's crew and, 190–96, *192,
    193, 196*
  schoolship. *See* ship-based training
  selection of cadets for, 53
  shore-based. *See* shore-based training
  state-supported schools for, 32, 33,
    38, 40, 42, 43, 44, 58, 60, 65, 70
  support for a national academy for,
    40, 41–43, 45–46, 54
  unions and, 57, 70–71
  U.S. Maritime Service oversight of,
    60, 65
  World War II and, 82–83, 120
transportation management and logistics program, 332–34
Travis, Harrison O., 42, 226
trimesters, 373–74, 377–83

Truman, Harry, 128
Trump, Guy, 165, 168, 182
Tublin, Melvin, 158, 176, 321
tuition proposal, 240, 264, 265,
  366
Turkey, 187, 188, 315
Tyson, Victor E., 165–66, *165*, 211,
  212, 213, 233, 273, 320–21

uniforms
  of cadets, 83, 209, 234–35, 245–46,
    389
  of Engel as superintendent, 245
  of faculty, 169
unions, 19, 24, 36, 47, 60, 67 129,
  255–56, 283, 351
  faculty and, 323–25, 378, 381
  jobs for graduates and, 57, 257–61,
    266–67
  national academy proposal and, 57,
    58, 70–71
  nuclear-powered ships and, 193,
    194–95
United Federation of College Teachers (UFCT), 323–24
U.S. Lines, 70, 72, 118, 139–40, 197,
  230, 251
U.S. Marine Resource Center
  (MRC), 297–98, 342, 383, 384
U.S. Maritime Administration
  (MARAD)
  athletics at Kings Point and, 183–84
  continuing education and, 296, 298,
    385
  Desert Storm and, 351
  diversity and, 295
  Engel and, 212, 247–51, 253–54
  female cadets and, xv, 239
  intermodalism and, 372
  Kings Point administration and,
    157–61, 215, 289
  Kings Point faculty and, 166, 168,
    169, 232, 381
  Kings Point funding and, 155–56,
    243, 298, 388, 390, 400

Kings Point infrastructure and, 394, 395

Kings Point permanency and, 366, 367

McLintock and, 157, 160–61, 176–77, 208, 210, 258

Matteson and, 359, 386

naval reserve status of cadets and, 174

Reagan administration and, 291–92

Savannah nuclear-powered ship and, 189–90, 191, 192

selection of a superintendent and, 285, 286, 287

training and, 253

U.S. Maritime Commission, 291

congressional mandate for report on training from, 60, 63–66, 69

creation of, 47–48

curriculum for training and, 61–63

disagreement about office training program and, 52–54

eligible list and, 57–59, 69

Kings Point creation and setup and, 76, 83

national academy and, 70

national examination and, 59, 69

shore-based training and, 72

state nautical schools and, 71–72

supervision of training and, 52–53, 55–57, 60, 69–70

U.S. Maritime Service in, 60

World War II and, 81

U.S. Maritime Service, 60, 65, 120, 155, 162, 166, 167, 168, 245

U.S. Merchant Marine Cadet Corps, 27, 65

creation of, 47, 59

eligible list and, 57–59

national examination and, 59

union opposition to, 70–71

World War II and, 81–83, 99–107

USMMA Foundation, 321–22, 396

U.S. Naval Reserve (USNR), 94, 268, 346. *See also* naval reserve

United States Shipping Board, 36–37, 38, 40–41, 42, 46, 47

U.S. Shipping Commissioners, 56–57

United States Transportation Command (TRANSCOM), 350

Utheim, Andor E., 126

Van Pelt, William K., 159, 161

veterans' benefits for cadets, 104, 128

veterans groups, 104, 128

Vietnam War, 3, 175–76, 208, 213, *214*, 255–56

Vignocchi, Anthony and Marla, *432*

Virginia International Terminals (VIT), 21, 22–23

Vision 2000, 368

visual signaling training, 94–96, *95*

vocational high schools, 58, 65

Voluntary Intermodal Sealift Agreement, 371–72

Von Gronau, Walter, 171, 172

Waesche, R. R., 55, 65, 90, 91

Wagman, Robert J., 265

Wagner, Nancy, 312–13

Wallischeck, Eric, 344, 345, 405

Walsh, James, 167

Walter, Perry, 341, 342, 383, 384

Ward Line, 44

War Department, 116, 128

War of 1812, 30

War Shipping Administration (WSA), 89, 91, 93, 113, 132–33

Wayland, Roger T., 100

Weber, Charles, 379, 380–81

We'll Deliver (Mitchell), xiv, 176

West Point, 42, 122, 137, 151, 184, 203, 234, 305, 306, 340, 410, 433–34

White, Dean, 402

White Paper of the Regiment, 209, 212

Wiley, Alexander, 159, 163

Wiley, Henry W., 47, 48, 49, 54, 56–57, 61, 65, 91, 113, 280

Wiley Commission in Charge of
    Training, 49
Wiley-Van Pelt Bill, 159
Willett, Kenneth, 110
Williams, Joseph Banks, 229
Willner, Stanley, 102–4
Wilson, John F. ("Jackie"), 72, 80, 83,
    98
Wilson, Woodrow, 35–36
Wolff, Lester, 255
women. *See* female cadets
Woodward, Thomas, 39, 48
World Trade Center tragedy, 404–8
World War I, 35–36, 37, 39

World War II, xiv, 48, 71, 76, 78,
    81–83, 99–11, 128
World War II Memorial, *389*
Wright, Harry, 183
Wriston, Henry M., 186

Yates, Frances, 235, 236, 239, 313
Yocum, James, 262, *263*, 288, 344,
    345
Young, C. W. ("Bill"), 398–400, *398*,
    400, 401, 406–7

Zelenko, Herbert, 170, 172–73, 176
Zito, Frederick, 114

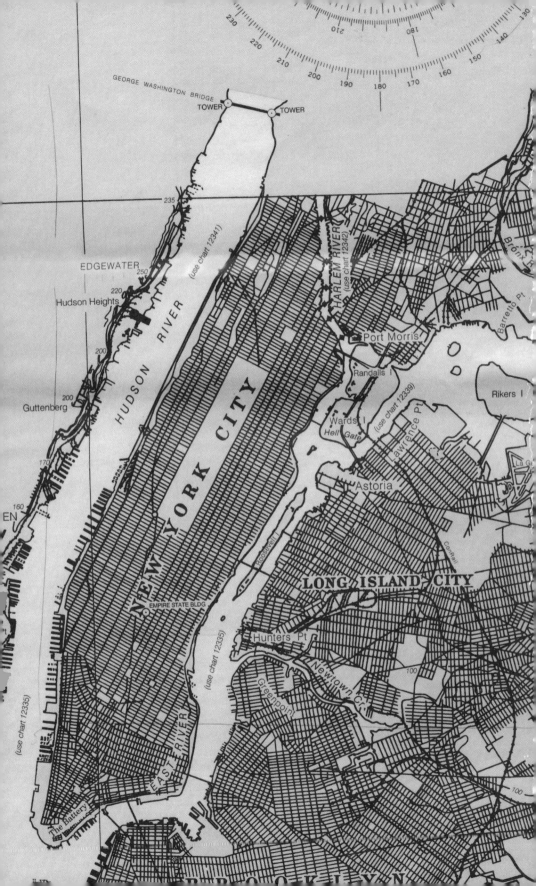